CANADIAN DEMOCRACY

Seventh Edition

CANADIAN DEMOCRACY

Stephen Brooks

OXFORD
UNIVERSITY PRESS

Oxford University Press is a department of the University of Oxford.
It furthers the University's objective of excellence in research, scholarship,
and education by publishing worldwide. Oxford is a registered trade mark of
Oxford University Press in the UK and in certain other countries.

Published in Canada by
Oxford University Press
8 Sampson Mews, Suite 204,
Don Mills, Ontario M3C 0H5 Canada

www.oupcanada.com

First Edition published in 1993
Second Edition published in 1996
Third edition published in 2000
Fourth edition published in 2004
Fifth edition published in 2007
Sixth edition published in 2009

Library and Archives Canada Cataloguing in Publication

Brooks, Stephen, 1956–
Canadian democracy / Stephen Brooks. — 7th ed.

Includes bibliographical references and index.
ISBN 978-0-19-544155-0

1. Canada—Politics and government—Textbooks. I. Title.

JL65.B76 2011 320.971 C2011-905405-1

This book is printed on permanent (acid-free) paper ♾
which contains a minimum of 10% post-consumer waste.

Printed and bound in the United States of America

1 2 3 4 — 15 14 13 12

Brief Contents

Contents

PART III The Structures of Governance 127

PART IV Participation in Politics 293

TODAY
IS VOTING
DAY

PART V Contemporary Issues in Canadian Political Life 401

QUÉBEC
Nous avons le droit d'être différents

Women are Persons...
Les femmes sont des personnes...

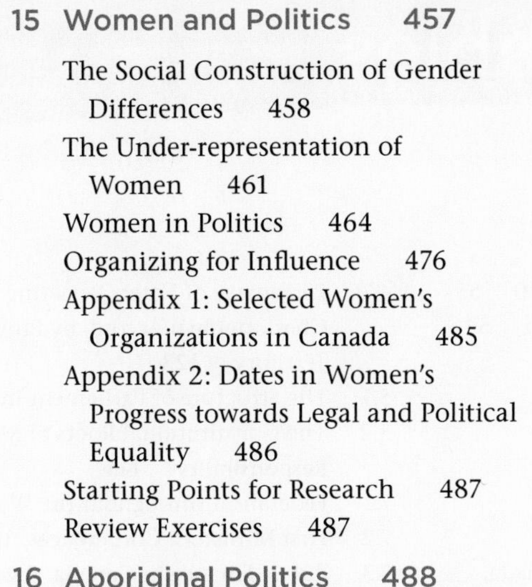

Figures and Tables

Figures

Tables

Boxes

Politics in Focus

Governing Realities

Media Spotlight

Preface

What is democracy? And what is the state of democracy in Canada today? The title of this book—*Canadian Democracy*—is not a judgement or a conclusion. It is, rather, a focus. Over the previous six editions of this textbook, as in the present edition, I have tried to structure my treatment of the key components of Canada's political system around such themes as equality, freedoms, rights, and access. This approach is neither an uncritical celebration of Canadian politics nor a lopsided condemnation of its shortcomings and failures. In using the complex and contested concept of democracy as my touchstone I hope to encourage readers to think about Canadian government and politics in ways that will enable them to assess fairly and realistically the performance of Canada's political system.

Amid the first barrage of pre-election attack ads, Canada's federal politicians returned to Ottawa after the holidays in early 2011 for their first partisan salvos in the House of Commons in the new year. Pundits predicted a spring election or, at the latest, an election in the fall. But then, the focus of public attention and the media, and the focus on democracy, shifted to the Arab world, most significantly Egypt and Libya, as popular uprisings aiming for freer and more democratic societies toppled and struggled to topple non-democratic regimes. In a country such as Canada, which has been proudly (and increasingly) multicultural for the past 40 years—and outward-looking for much longer than that—such a shift in attention to the political world beyond our borders is not surprising. A similar shift happened when Canadians—or some Canadians!—last went to the polls for a federal election.

On 14 October 2008, a smaller percentage of eligible Canadians voted than in any previous federal election in the history of the country. The reasons for this were not entirely clear. There was no shortage of issues dividing the political parties, including Canada's military commitment in Afghanistan, the controversial carbon tax proposed by the opposition Liberal Party, and an economy that was following the United States into what many predicted would be a deep recession. Although voter turnout in Canada had been declining for decades, the indifference of so many voters in 2008 appeared puzzling. Perhaps, like people throughout the world, they were paying more attention to the historic election campaign taking place at the same time in the United States, which resulted in the election of that country's first black president. Matched up against Barack Obama, Sarah Palin, and other charismatic and 'can-you-believe-this!' characters on the American political scene, it may be that Stephen Harper, Stéphane Dion, and company seemed uninteresting to Canadians.

But they recovered their interest several weeks after the re-election of the Conservatives when Stephen Harper's minority government appeared to be on the verge of being toppled by a united opposition and replaced by a coalition of the Liberals and the NDP, supported by the Bloc Québécois. Like Lazarus, Liberal leader Stéphane Dion showed promise of rising from the dead and becoming Prime Minister, despite having presided over his party's loss of 27 seats and having announced his imminent resignation. Constitutionalists and pundits were in a lather. Some called it an attempted coup d'état by the opposition parties. Others said that the replacement of a minority government by the proposed coalition, without the need for a new election, was constitutional. Public opinion was divided. Demonstrations, for and against the proposed coalition, took place in a number of cities. In the end the Governor General, Michaëlle Jean, was freed from having to make what would have been a very difficult and hugely controversial decision by granting the Conservative government's request to *prorogue* Parliament. Thus did Canadians discover a word that few of them knew existed before the constitutional kerfuffle of late 2008.

The 2011 election produced rather dramatic changes in the representation of the parties in the House of Commons. The governing Conservatives won the majority that had eluded them in previous elections. But the big news involved the opposition parties. The Liberal Party suffered its worst defeat since Confederation, falling to third place in the Commons. The NDP surged into second place, largely on the strength of the party's newfound popularity in Quebec. And the Bloc Québécois was reduced to a mere four seats, even its leader Gilles Duceppe going down to defeat. An election is, however, only a moment in time. It remains to be seen whether the startling and, when the election was called, unpredicted results of the 2011 campaign presage enduring changes for the Canadian political map.

That map is today recognizably the same as it was a generation ago, but many of the borderlines, roads, and place names have changed. What has not changed, however, is the fact that all of the central issues in Canadian political life raise questions of fairness, freedom, representation, justice, and dignity. These are values that we associate with democracy. We may not agree on the concrete meaning of these values or on the balance among them that best satisfies our ideal of democracy. But hardly anyone would disagree that whether what is at stake is the location of a landfill or revisions to the Constitution, these values and trade-offs are fundamental to democratic politics.

Canadian Democracy is organized into five parts. The first chapter, Part One, examines some basic concepts in the study of politics and government, including the central concept of democracy. Some readers will have been introduced to this material in a previous course, such as the Introduction to Politics course that is the necessary stepping stone to further political science courses at many universities. I have attempted to address these foundational concepts in ways that link them very directly to Canadian politics, so that even those students who already have taken a sort of 'Political Science 101' course can gain something useful from what might otherwise be familiar territory.

Part Two, Chapters 2–4, focuses on the broad societal context of Canadian politics. Chapter 2 looks at the ideological roots of Canadian political institutions and controversies, highlighting in particular the similarities and differences between the political values and beliefs of Canadians and Americans. Chapter 3 surveys some of the politically significant social and economic characteristics of Canadian society. In Chapter 4, the nature and political impact of regionalism is examined. Part Three, Chapters 5–9, turns to the structures of governance. Here we examine the Constitution (Chapter 5), rights and freedoms (Chapter 6), federalism (Chapter 7), the machinery of parliamentary government in Canada (Chapter 8) and the development of the administrative state and major features of the federal bureaucracy (Chapter 9). Part Four considers the main vehicles for individual and group participation in politics: Chapter 10 discusses the origins and contemporary character of Canada's political parties, their role in politics, and the nature and consequences of our electoral system, party finances, and voting; Chapter 11 looks at the characteristics and influence of interest groups; Chapter 12 examines the crucial place occupied by the mass media in modern democracies and the particular features of the media's role in Canadian politics.

Part Five, Chapters 13–17, focuses on five important issues in modern Canadian politics—language, multiculturalism and diversity, women and politics, the status and treatment of Native Canadians, and Canada's role in the world—that illustrate well the complex interplay of values in democratic politics. Other issues are certainly deserving of attention and instructors may wish to supplement this material with an issue-oriented reader such as Campbell, Howlett, and Pal's *The Real Worlds of Canadian Politics* (fourth edition, 2004) or a policy-oriented text like C. Lydia Miljan's *Public Policy in Canada* (fifth edition, 2008).

Highlights of the Seventh Edition

This seventh edition of *Canadian Democracy* includes many significant changes from previous editions, including:

- ***New and updated content and new chapters.*** As in every edition, this seventh provides the latest data, research, and court rulings that come to bear on many aspects of Canadian politics and society. Every chapter has been updated, in some cases quite extensively. Many of the tables and figures are new and those that are carried over from the last edition have been brought up to date. Some specific changes to note:
    - ✔ Chapter 2, 'Political Culture', includes new data from the 2005–6 round of the World Values Survey and other surveys of public attitudes.
    - ✔ Chapter 6, 'Rights and Freedoms', includes discussion of several new court rulings.
    - ✔ Chapter 9, 'The Administrative State', is a new addition to the book. It includes an examination of the modernization of the Canadian state from Confederation to the present day.
    - ✔ Chapter 10, 'Parties and Elections', includes extensive analysis of the 2011 federal election.
    - ✔ Chapter 14 is an expanded analysis of diversity and multiculturalism policy that includes a comparison of the Canadian experience to that in several other pluralist democracies and an examination of the economic integration of immigrants in Canada.
    - ✔ Chapter 15, a new chapter, is now devoted exclusively to 'Women and Politics', a topic that has been significantly expanded from the previous edition.
    - ✔ Chapter 17 on Canada in the World includes significant new material on the Canada–United States relationship.

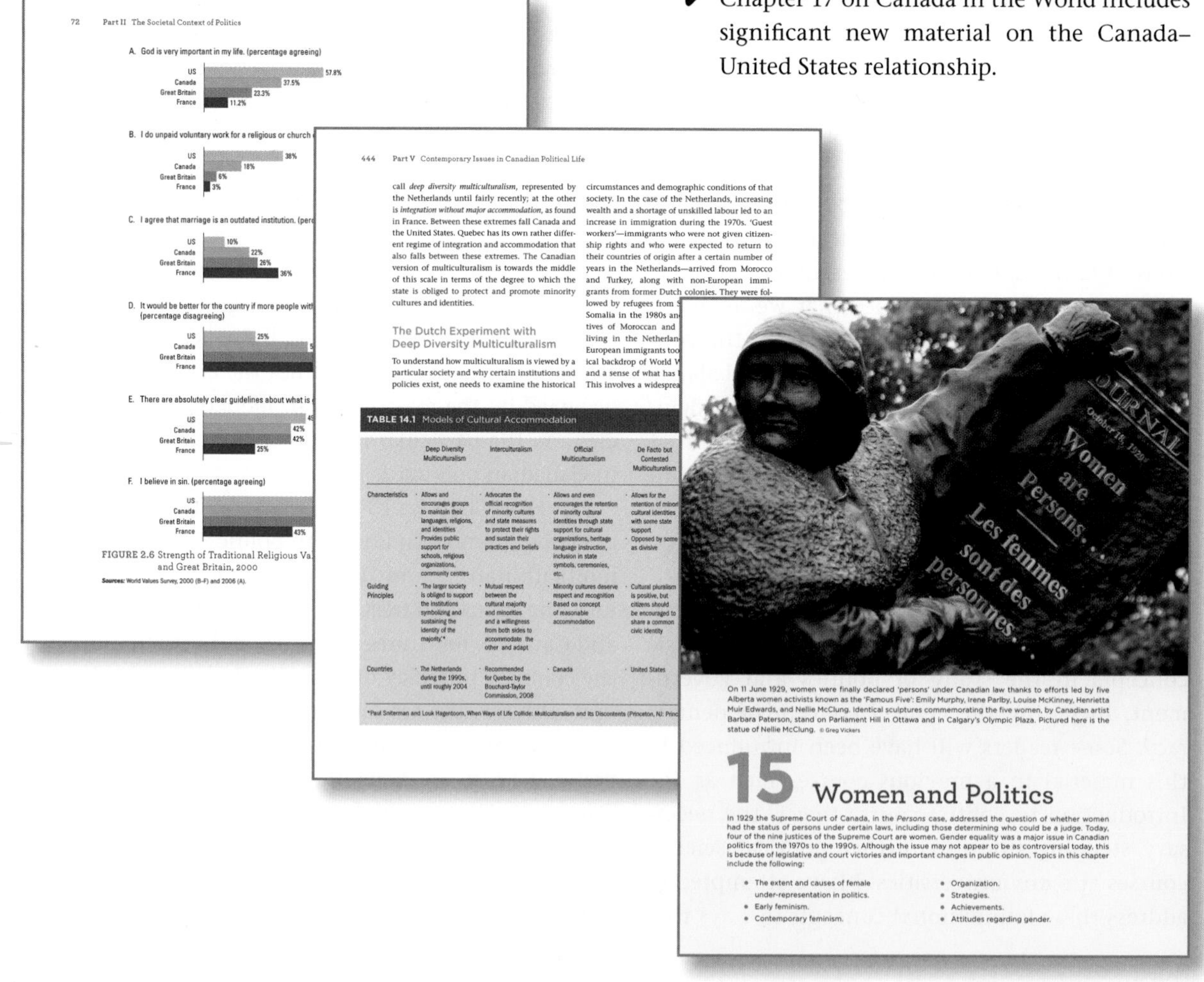

444 Part V Contemporary Issues in Canadian Political Life

call *deep diversity multiculturalism*, represented by the Netherlands until fairly recently; at the other is *integration without major accommodation*, as found in France. Between these extremes fall Canada and the United States. Quebec has its own rather different regime of integration and accommodation that also falls between these extremes. The Canadian version of multiculturalism is towards the middle of this scale in terms of the degree to which the state is obliged to protect and promote minority cultures and identities.

The Dutch Experiment with Deep Diversity Multiculturalism

To understand how multiculturalism is viewed by a particular society and why certain institutions and policies exist, one needs to examine the historical circumstances and demographic conditions of that society. In the case of the Netherlands, increasing wealth and a shortage of unskilled labour led to an increase in immigration during the 1970s. 'Guest workers'—immigrants who were not given citizenship rights and who were expected to return to their countries of origin after a certain number of years in the Netherlands—arrived from Morocco and Turkey, along with non-European immigrants from former Dutch colonies. They were followed by refugees from

TABLE 14.1 Models of Cultural Accommodation

On 11 June 1929, women were finally declared 'persons' under Canadian law thanks to efforts led by five Alberta women activists known as the 'Famous Five': Emily Murphy, Irene Parlby, Louise McKinney, Henrietta Muir Edwards, and Nellie McClung. Identical sculptures commemorating the five women, by Canadian artist Barbara Paterson, stand on Parliament Hill in Ottawa and in Calgary's Olympic Plaza. Pictured here is the statue of Nellie McClung. © Greg Vickers

15 Women and Politics

In 1929 the Supreme Court of Canada, in the *Persons* case, addressed the question of whether women had the status of persons under certain laws, including those determining who could be a judge. Today, four of the nine justices of the Supreme Court are women. Gender equality was a major issue in Canadian politics from the 1970s to the 1990s. Although the issue may not appear to be as controversial today, this is because of legislative and court victories and important changes in public opinion. Topics in this chapter include the following:

- The extent and causes of female under-representation in politics.
- Early feminism.
- Contemporary feminism.
- Organization.
- Strategies.
- Achievements.
- Attitudes regarding gender.

- ***Completely revised photo and political cartoon program.*** An extensive new selection of both contemporary and historic photos as well as insightful and thought-provoking editorial cartoons from renowned artists such as Roy Peterson and Len Norris bring a visual dimension to the discussion of Canadian politics.

- ***Revamped feature boxes.*** With themes that have been refined from the sixth edition and new content highlighting current—and relevant—issues, the following series of features show politics at work.
  - ✔ *Politics in Focus* boxes bring to the fore issues, events, and happenings worth a second look and critical thought.
  - ✔ *Governing Realities* boxes focus on examples of government at work and concepts related to the institutions and processes of government.
  - ✔ *Media Spotlight* boxes highlight key media pieces and editorials and examine the media's role in politics.

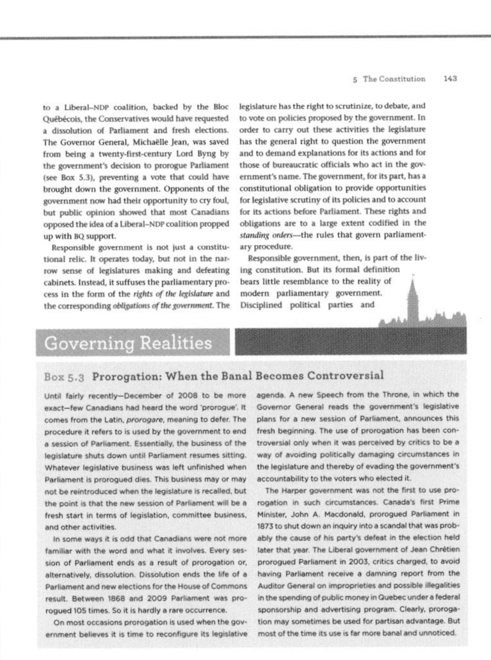

5 The Constitution 143

to a Liberal–NDP coalition, backed by the Bloc Québécois, the Conservatives would have requested a dissolution of Parliament and fresh elections. The Governor General, Michaëlle Jean, was saved from being a twenty-first-century Lord Byng by the government's decision to prorogue Parliament (see Box 5.3), preventing a vote that could have brought down the government. Opponents of the government now had their opportunity to cry foul, but public opinion showed that most Canadians opposed the idea of a Liberal–NDP coalition propped up with BQ support.

Responsible government is not just a constitutional relic. It operates today, but not in the narrow sense of legislatures making and defeating cabinets. Instead, it suffuses the parliamentary process in the form of the *rights of the legislature* and the corresponding *obligations of the government*. The legislature has the right to scrutinize, to debate, and to vote on policies proposed by the government. In order to carry out these activities the legislature has the general right to question the government and to demand explanations for its actions and for those of bureaucratic officials who act in the government's name. The government, for its part, has a constitutional obligation to provide opportunities for legislative scrutiny of its policies and to account for its actions before Parliament. These rights and obligations are to a large extent codified in the *standing orders*—the rules that govern parliamentary procedure.

Responsible government, then, is part of the living constitution. But its formal definition bears little resemblance to the reality of modern parliamentary government. Disciplined political parties and

Governing Realities

Box 5.3 **Prorogation: When the Banal Becomes Controversial**

Until fairly recently—December of 2008 to be more exact—few Canadians had heard the word 'prorogue'. It comes from the Latin, *prorogare*, meaning to defer. The procedure it refers to is used by the government to end a session of Parliament. Essentially, the business of the legislature shuts down until Parliament resumes sitting. Whatever legislative business was left unfinished when Parliament is prorogued dies. This business may or may not be reintroduced when the legislature is recalled, but the point is that the new session of Parliament will be a fresh start in terms of legislation, committee business, and other activities.

In some ways it is odd that Canadians were not more familiar with the word and what it involves. Every session of Parliament ends as a result of prorogation or, alternatively, dissolution. Dissolution ends the life of a Parliament and new elections for the House of Commons result. Between 1868 and 2009 Parliament was prorogued 105 times. So it is hardly a rare occurrence.

On most occasions prorogation is used when the government believes it is time to reconfigure its legislative agenda. A new Speech from the Throne, in which the Governor General reads the government's legislative plans for a new session of Parliament, announces this fresh beginning. The use of prorogation has been controversial only when it was perceived by critics to be a way of avoiding politically damaging circumstances in the legislature and thereby of evading the government's accountability to the voters who elected it.

The Harper government was not the first to use prorogation in such circumstances. Canada's first Prime Minister, John A. Macdonald, prorogued Parliament in 1873 to shut down an inquiry into a scandal that was probably the cause of his party's defeat in the election held later that year. The Liberal government of Jean Chrétien prorogued Parliament in 2003, critics charged, to avoid having Parliament receive a damning report from the Auditor General on improprieties and possible illegalities in the spending of public money in Quebec under a federal sponsorship and advertising program. Clearly, prorogation may sometimes be used for partisan advantage. But most of the time its use is far more banal and unnoticed.

Politics in Focus

Box 17.5 Alberta's Oil Sands and Canada–US Relations

John Podesta served as President Bill Clinton's chief of staff and was a member of the National Security Council under Clinton. These days he is head of the Center for American Progress, a liberal think-tank whose star has shone brighter since the 2008 election of President Barack Obama. Podesta doesn't speak for the current administration, but he certainly represents the views of many within the Democratic Party. So when he was invited to give the keynote address at 'Greening the Oil Sands', a conference held in Washington in June 2010, at which industry and government heavyweights from both sides of the border were in attendance, people listened. And among those listening most attentively were Canada's ambassador to the United States, Gary Doer, and business executives with a stake in the continuation and growth of Alberta's oil exports to the United States.

extraction from tar sands is polluting, destructive, expensive, and energy intensive. These things are facts. I think suggesting this process can come close to approximating being 'greened' is largely misleading, or far too optimistic, or perhaps both. It stands alongside clean coal and error-free deepwater drilling as more PR than reality. . . .

Instead of pursuing energy sources that [are environmentally destructive and that contribute to global warming], the United States and Canada should join in partnership to put in place clean energy policies that will help us harness sources of energy that will never run out and can't risk catastrophe. As President Obama said in Ottawa last year, as two of the wealthiest countries, we can and must be leaders. Energy security is now inter-

Media Spotlight

Box 12.4 Technology, Cognition, and How We Perceive the World

The year 2010 may be remembered as a watershed in the technology of communications. The social networking site Facebook recorded 500 million users. Apple launched its iPad, combining several functions in a medium that is something between a laptop and a cell phone. Twitter, which began in 2008 as a social network, acquired features of a news medium, a transition that may have dated from the Iranian elections of 2009 when Twitter was used by protestors to communicate news about their opposition to the fraud perpetrated by the regime.

The Pew Internet and American Life Project reported

- Old and new media are tied together. New media still have a limited capacity to generate content and rely on traditional media sources for reporting capacity.
- Reportorial journalism—what newspapers and other traditional news outlets do—is shrinking, but commentary and discussion in the media—what cable, radio, social media, blogs, and websites do—is growing.
- 'Technology is shifting power to newsmakers, and the newest way is through their ability to control the initial accounts of events.' The

- ***Updated supporting features.*** As in the previous edition, this one includes *review exercises* at the end of each chapter. These are not conventional questions as appear in many textbooks, but are hands-on exercises requiring students to apply what they have learned and to use practical research skills. Many of these exercises are geared to the media, particularly newspapers, television, and the Internet. The review exercises have been brought up to date, with many of them being new to this edition.
  - ✔ *Starting points for research*, also located at the end of each chapter, provide annotated lists of suggested readings that serve as a jumping-off point for students looking to do further research for assignments and papers.
  - ✔ *Glossary of key terms* at the end of *Canadian Democracy* provides students with a one-stop shopping centre for concepts that are, in many cases, unfamiliar and perhaps a bit specialized for most laypersons. These terms are important to an understanding of the material covered in this book. Some instructors may also find the Glossary useful for testing purposes.

292 Part III The Structures of Governance

Starting Points for Research

Christopher Dunn, ed., *The Handbook of Canadian Public Administration* (Toronto: Oxford University Press, 2002). Virtually all key aspects of the structures and processes of Canadian public administration are covered in this fine collection, with contributions from some of the foremost students of Canadian bureaucracy and policy-making.

David Good, *The Politics of Public Management: The HRDC Audit of Grants and Contributions* (Toronto: University of Toronto Press, 2003). Written by a former assistant deputy minister, this is an award-winning insider's account of the complex circumstances leading to what was believed, at the time, to be an enormous scandal involving lack of accountability in spending by Human Resources and Development Canada.

David Good, *The Politics of Public Money* (Toronto: University of Toronto Press, 2007). A worthy successor to the spenders and guardians analysis found in Donald Savoie's 1990 book, *The Politics of Public Spending in Canada*.

David Johnson, *Thinking Government: Public Sector Management in Canada* (Toronto: University of Toronto Press, 2006). An excellent textbook on public administration in Canada.

Donald Savoie, *Breaking the Bargain: Public Servants, Ministers and Parliament* (Toronto: University of Toronto Press, 2003). Arguably Canada's foremost scholar of bureaucracy and governance explores, in his own words, 'the territory between elected and permanent government officials—a kind of no man's land'.

Review Exercises

1. Visit the government of Canada website <www.gc.ca>. Click on 'About Government'. Now click on 'Government of Canada Institutions' (listed alphabetically). Choose a government institution and click on its website. Find the following information for the institution you have chosen:
   (a) number of employees
   (b) budget
   (c) cabinet minister responsible for the department/agency/Crown corporation
   (d) major programs or functions.
2. Most Canadians believe that public-sector organizations are less efficient than those in the private sector. How would you set about measuring efficiency in private and public organizations? Put together a list of the criteria you would use and how straightforward or difficult each would be to measure. How have you defined 'efficiency'? Are there other qualities that should be taken into account in assessing the performance of public and private organizations? What might they be and can they be measured?
3. Do unelected officials have too much discretion? Can you think of instances where you have encountered public-sector bureaucrats whose decision(s) seemed to have been based on their personal judgement rather than simply and entirely on rules. Can anything be done about such cases? Should anything be done?

- ***Robust ancillary suite.*** The student and instructor companion websites for *Canadian Democracy* are found at www.oupcanada.com/Brooks7e. Comprehensive tools and resources include:
  - ✔ *Student Study Guide* offering short-answer format study questions; self-testing quizzes; glossary; annotated list of relevant websites; suggestions for books, articles, and media resources highlighting political issues in Canada.
  - ✔ *Get Involved* section for students featuring a history of Canadian political parties; interviews and letters from leaders of Canada's major political parties; biographies of political science graduates who have put their degrees to work in exciting careers; links to websites of interest, including The Democracy Project, Elections Canada, The Canadian State: Documents & Dialogue, Democracy Watch, etc.
  - ✔ *Podcasts* providing mini-lectures that hone in on the issues of the day. An extremely popular addition to *Canadian Democracy*'s ancillary lineup in the sixth edition, the selection of podcasts is expanded for this seventh edition.
  - ✔ *Links featuring* audio and visual footage from the CBC archives along with event summaries related to the main themes in each chapter.
  - ✔ *Links pointing to* television ads from the Conservative, Liberal, and NDP 2011 election campaigns.
  - ✔ *Test Generator, Instructor's Manual, and PowerPoint presentations* for instructors, offering a comprehensive array of teaching supports.

COMPANION WEBSITE

Stephen Brooks

Canadian Democracy: An Introduction, Seventh Edition
ISBN 13: 9780195441550

Inspection copy request

Ordering information

Contact & Comments

About the Book

In this fully revised seventh edition, Stephen Brooks continues to explore the characteristics and controversies associated with Canadian politics, covering the basic elements and structures of government (federalism, the machinery of government, the administrative state). He also addresses the social and economic contexts of the country's politics as well as individuals' and institutions' participation in the system and current issues and challenges in the political arena. Highlights of this revised edition include: a new chapter on the administrative state; a new chapter on women in politics; comprehensive updates throughout to bring readers the latest data, research, and analysis of current events; a newly designed interior and a significantly expanded art program; and more and better-integrated ancillaries to enhance both professors' instruction and students' learning.

Instructor Resources

You need a password to access these resources. Please contact your local Sales and Editorial Representative for more information.

Student Resources

- ***'Conversations on Canadian Politics' DVD.*** Available to users of the text, this DVD features interviews—several new for this edition—with experts on various core concepts introduced in the text.

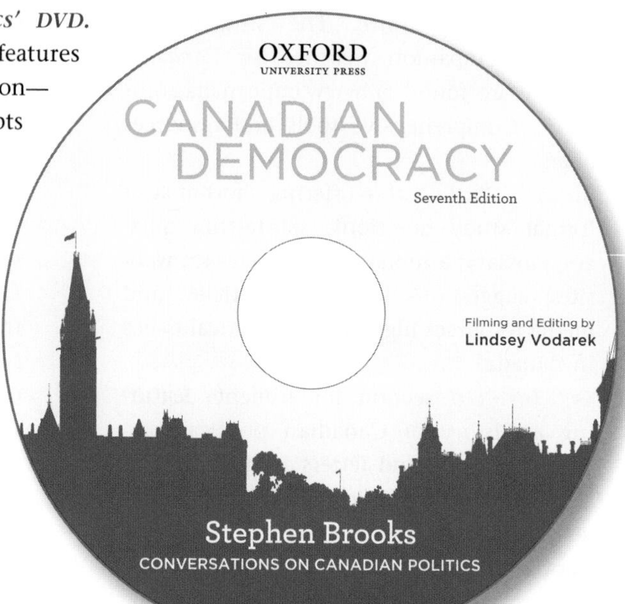

Acknowledgements

Over the years I have been privileged to work with truly exceptional people at Oxford University Press, including Phyllis Wilson, Euan White, Katherine Skene, and Jodi Lewchuk. The reviewers for this edition—Cheryl Collier, University of Windsor; Holly Gibbs, University of Toronto Scarborough; Neil Hibbert, University of Saskatchewan; Wolfgang Koerner, University of Ottawa; J.P. Lewis, University of Guelph; David G. MacDonald, University of the Fraser Valley; and Jonathan Malloy, Carleton University—as well as anonymous reviewers for all seven editions provided thoughtful comments and suggestions that I sometimes followed, and perhaps should have more often. Paul Nesbitt-Larking of Huron University College has offered helpful suggestions over the years. My colleague Lydia Miljan of the University of Windsor generously produced the voting behaviour figures in Chapter 10. Richard Tallman's meticulous editing and advice on points of style and substance have transformed the manuscript for each edition of this book into a much better product. It is always a pleasure to work with him.

I am, as well, deeply indebted to Roy Peterson, award-winning cartoonist of the *Vancouver Sun*. A selection of his political cartoons, as well as those of other Canadian political cartoonists, is sprinkled throughout this book. I think instructors and students will agree that they add both insight and humour to an understanding of Canadian political life.

The Institut du monde anglophone at the Sorbonne provided me with an ideal setting to work on revisions to the previous edition of *Canadian Democracy*. Although I cannot say that working on the revisions for the current edition in my study in Windsor was as inspiring as my office around the corner from the Jardin du Luxembourg, there were certainly fewer distractions. This edition is dedicated to my late father-in-law, Ralph Nelson (1927–2008), a political philosopher who thought that the study of Canada was worthy of the effort.

Stephen Brooks

Windsor, Ontario, and Dearborn, Michigan

Part I
Introduction

We all have an idea of what politics involves. But the term *political science* may be less familiar and, in some ways, more puzzling. The problem arises from the word 'science'. Science evokes images of laboratories, ideas of measurement, and the domain of hard facts on which depend the construction of bridges that do not collapse and medications that cure rather than kill us. The study and understanding of politics, as is true of all forms of human behaviour and organization, would seem to lack the hard edge and to rely on techniques quite different from those characteristic of physics and genetic biology. Can there be such a thing as political science?

The answer is, 'within limits'. 'Political science' expresses the aspiration among those who study politics to do so in an objective way, attempting to understand why things are the way they are, and therefore how they may be changed, rather than how they ought to be. Political science rests on a bedrock of empirical analysis—analysis that seeks to formulate laws about the world of politics and government based on verifiable observation and, in some cases, experimentation—and not on the ideological leanings and personal preferences of the person doing the observing and explaining. But whereas genes may be spliced and the weight-bearing capacity of a bridge may be tested through a computer simulation, political scientists generally have to make do with observing behaviour and the functioning of institutions in less controlled circumstances. How they undertake their analysis of politics and the certitude of their observations may not look very much like the activities and results of those in the natural and applied sciences, but the aspiration to produce objective, empirical knowledge is the same.

Those who study Canadian politics and government rely on the same concepts and analytical methods that are used by those who wish to understand these subjects in France, China, Egypt, or any other society. Power, authority, identity, participation, bureaucracy, integration, stability, and equality are just some of the core concepts relevant to an understanding of politics in any country. In this first section of *Canadian Democracy* we will examine some of the concepts that are crucial to an understanding of politics and government in Canada. This will provide the basis for the subsequent chapters that focus on particular features of Canadian political life.

The Parliament Peace Tower seen through the front gate in Ottawa, Ontario, the nation's capital. Parliament Hill is an area of Crown land on the southern bank of the Ottawa River with a Gothic revival suite of parliament buildings that serves as the home of the Parliament of Canada. © Alamy/Francis Vachon

1 An Introduction to Political Life

To understand politics and government, one requires a tool kit consisting of the fundamental concepts and terms that are useful in analyzing political life. This chapter aims to equip the reader with these tools by examining the following topics:

- What is politics?
- Power.
- State and government.
- Democracy.
- Consent and legitimacy.
- Political identities.
- Political fault lines: old and new.
- Who gets heard and why?

If you want a job that earns you the trust and respect of your fellow citizens, then become a firefighter, nurse, doctor, or pilot. Do not become a politician. In fact, you would fare just about as well in the eyes of your fellow Canadians selling used cars as you would as a politician. This, at least, is the conclusion that emerges from a 2009 *Reader's Digest* poll conducted by the survey research firm Harris/Decima. Politicians came in thirty-ninth of the 41 professions that were ranked according to the trust that Canadians place in them, barely edging out car salespeople and telemarketers.[1] Politicians and their craft have what advertising people would call an image problem.

This image of politicians as untrustworthy, and of their calling as low and dishonest, is not entirely fair. There is no hard evidence that politicians are more likely to be dishonest or have low morals than those in other occupations. Indeed, many if not most people who run for and are elected to public office are motivated by a desire to serve and to improve the lives of those they represent. And popular perceptions notwithstanding, many politicians make significant financial and personal sacrifices by holding public office.

But Canadians do not trust them. To understand why, we need to think about the nature of the politician's craft in societies where not everyone shares the same opinions or has identical interests, and where the political system is such that the votes of about 40 per cent or more of those who bother to cast their ballots will be needed in order for a political party to win a federal election. In these circumstances, politicians and political parties—or at least those serious about winning elections—need to appeal to a range of interests and values. Once elected, they must do the same, balancing competing demands and points of view. On top of this, they may find that their ability to do certain things that may be popular or that they believe to be the right things to do, regardless of public opinion, is limited by circumstances beyond their control. The promises that they made cannot be kept, or perhaps not quite in the form they were made or according to the timetable that was expected. And perhaps they knew or suspected this all along, saying things and making promises with what some might characterize as reckless disregard for their truth or prospects of achievement.

Most Canadians do not follow politics very closely. Surveys show that younger voters tend to be the least interested in politics and less likely to participate than middle-aged and older citizens. A contributing factor to Canadians' political apathy is their lack of trust in their politicians.

It is the messy activity of politics—including the compromises, the occasional evasiveness, the failure to deliver on promises made, and the resulting sense that those elected to public office do not faithfully represent those who put them there—that leads to cynicism about politicians and political parties. Canadians, however, are not alone in their negativity. In fact, in no established democracy do a majority of people say that they have a great deal or quite a lot of confidence in political parties.[2]

A healthy dose of cynicism about politics is probably a good thing, at least if it is cynicism fuelled by knowledge. Cynicism based on ignorance or coupled to apathy, however, can make no such claim. Whether you are a hardened cynic or an enthusiastic fan when it comes to Canadian politics—in fact, if you are like most Canadians your age, you probably do not follow politics very closely and therefore do not feel strongly one way or the other—no judgement about how well the political system works and in whose interests should be uninformed. This book aims to give you that information and the analytical tools needed to evaluate the processes and outcomes of Canadian politics. The conclusions that you draw and the judgements you arrive at are, of course, up to you. Whatever your conclusions, they should not include the belief that politics does not matter in your life and that your thoughts and actions are somehow without political significance. The Polish poet and 1996 Nobel Prize laureate, Wislawa Szymborska, has this to say about such ideas:

> All affairs, day and night,
> yours, ours, theirs,
> are political affairs.
>
> Like it or not,
> your genes have a political past,
> your skin a political cast,
> your eyes a political aspect.
>
> What you say has a resonance;
> what you are silent about is telling.
> Either way, it's political.[3]

What Is Politics?

Politics arises from the fact of scarcity. In the real world it is not possible for all of us to satisfy all of our desires to the fullest extent. Limits on the stock of those things that people desire—wealth, privacy, clean air and water, social recognition—ensure that conflicts will take place between rival claimants. These conflicts explain why politics comes about. But politics is about more than the fact of conflict. It is also about how rival claims are settled. What distinguishes politics from the conflicts, struggles, and rivalries that take place in such settings as the family, the workplace, and the economic marketplace, and in social organizations like churches and labour unions, is the *public nature* of political disputes and the use of public authority—embodied in the state—to deal with them. **Politics**, then, is the activity by which rival claims are settled by public authorities. The boundaries of what is considered to be political are located where the state's authority reaches. Political philosophers sometimes call this the public realm. Beyond this line is the private realm, where the state's authority does not extend.

As Box 1.1 shows, this definition does not have the field all to itself. All of these contending definitions agree that politics is about the exercise of **power**. They disagree, however, about what power relations count as political ones. Foucault, Marx, and the feminist movement define politics in ways that would include the relations between bosses and workers in a corporation, between parents and children in a family, between teachers and students in schools, and between spiritual shepherd and flock in a church. And in a sense they are right. In the words of American political scientist Charles Merriam, 'obviously there is governance everywhere—government in heaven; government in hell; government and law among outlaws; government in prison.'[4] Locke and Easton both offer a more limited definition of politics, one that goes back to Aristotle's conception of the Greek *polis*. They argue that what is distinctive about politics is the association of this activity with a system of settling disputes that is both public and binding on the whole community. At the centre of this system is the state, or government, as those raised in the Anglo-American tradition are more likely to call it.

These definitions disagree in another important way. **Marxism**, postmodernism (Foucault), and feminism associate politics with a pervasive pattern of oppression. Politics is, for them, fundamentally about how inequalities are generated and reinforced through the power relations that exist between classes/gender groups at all levels of society.

Does it matter, in the end, how we define politics? Or is this mainly a harmless diversion for academic hair-splitters? We would argue that there is a very practical reason for rejecting those definitions of politics that confer on all power relations, wherever they may be located and however limited they may be, the title 'political'. If politics is viewed as being everywhere and in all social interactions, we lose the ability to see the boundary that separates the public and private realms. This boundary may not be very distinct, but it is crucial for understanding the politics of any society. Moreover, the existence of such a boundary is necessary in order to protect the freedoms that most of us believe to be important features of a democratic society. Political conflict is largely about where exactly this boundary between public and private should be drawn, what should be considered a proper matter for public life and decisions by the state, and what should remain private matters. We can agree that power relations are ubiquitous without going the next step to claim that politics, therefore, has no bounds.

Not everyone agrees. Political scientist Jill Vickers echoes many of her feminist colleagues when she argues that the public realm/private realm distinction is fundamentally sexist. It is based, she maintains, on a tradition of political thinking that accepted as natural the domination of the public realm by males and the limitation of woman to the private sphere. When women were finally admitted to the public realm it was on identical terms with men, a formal equality that failed to recognize the substantive inequalities in the typical life conditions of males and females.

But whatever sexist biases may have been embedded in the public-versus-private distinction in traditional Western political thought, is it not the case that its contemporary importance lies in the value that it assigns to individual freedom? This, too, says Vickers, is fundamentally sexist. 'The concept of *freedom*', she writes, 'has become an almost totally masculinized idea in Western political thought, meaning *freedom from* constraints—an autonomy in which no dependence on another is required or recognized.'[5] According to Vickers, this is a value with little appeal to most women, who have as their goal 'interdependence among equals' rather than the freedom to act without constraint.

But there is, perhaps, another reason for adopting the more limited definition of politics that we have put forward. Only those power relations that take

Politics in Focus

Box 1.1 Some Important Definitions of Politics and Power

'[A] political system can be designated as those interactions through which values are authoritatively allocated for a society.'

David Easton, *A Systems Analysis of Political Life*

'Political power, then, I take to be a right of making laws with penalties of death and, consequently, all less penalties for the regulating and preserving of property, and of employing the force of the community in the execution of such laws and in the defense of the commonwealth from foreign injury; and all this only for the public good.'

John Locke, *The Second Treatise of Government*

'Political power, properly so called, is merely the organized power of one class for oppressing another.'

Karl Marx and Friedrich Engels, *The Communist Manifesto*

'Basically power is less a confrontation between two adversaries or the linking of one to the other than a question of government. This word must be allowed the very broad meaning which it had in the sixteenth century. 'Government' did not refer only to political structures or to the management of states; rather it designated the way in which the conduct of individuals or of groups might be directed: the government of children, of souls, of communities, of families, of the sick. It did not cover only the legitimately constituted forms of political or economic subjection, but also modes of action . . . which were destined to act upon the possibilities of action of other people. To govern, in this sense, is to structure the possible field of action of others.'

Michel Foucault, *The Subject and Power*

'The personal is political.'

Slogan of the feminist movement

place in the public realm can legitimately be associated with the use of force in its most naked, punitive forms. Compulsion, punishment, and violence do of course take place in all sorts of social settings. It is clear, however, that only the public authorities—those who wield the power of the state—have the legitimate right to back up their decisions with the full power of society. All other power relations are more limited than this. The reason for this difference is that the state is the only institution that can reasonably claim to speak and act on behalf of the entire community, and its unique function is to ensure the conditions for some degree of social order. This social order is a necessary condition for all other social activities, for without it there is no peaceful basis for reconciling conflicts in society.

Power

Power is the ability to influence what happens. It is found in all sorts of settings, not simply political ones. When Microsoft uses its dominant market position in computer operating systems to compel PC manufacturers to integrate its Internet browser into their computers, that is power. When the Vatican issues an official proclamation on same-sex marriage or the ordination of women, elements within the Roman Catholic Church respond. The Vatican has power within the community of Roman Catholics. When a person is persuaded to give up his wallet at gunpoint, his attacker has power. Parents who are able to compel their children's obedience through the threat or fact of punishment, or through persuasive arguments, have power. A television network whose programs shape the issues that viewers are thinking about has power. And when a peaceful demonstration of citizens outside the headquarters of a corporation, or in front of the legislature, changes the behaviour of the targeted institution, that, too, is power. In each of these cases one party affects the behaviour of another, although the reasons for compliance differ.

Social scientists like to unpack the concept of power, breaking it down into species that are distinguished from one another according to the reason why the compliant party obeys. Compliance may result from the threat or use of force (**coercion**); from the ability of A to convince B that a particular action is reasonable or otherwise in B's best interests (**influence**); or from the recognition on the part of the compliant party that the person or organization issuing a command has the right to do so and should be obeyed (**authority**). Politics involves all of these faces of power—coercion, influence, and authority—at various times and in different circumstances. Democratic politics relies primarily on the two non-coercive species of power. But coercion is used, and no democracy is without its system of courts, police, and prisons.

How far coercion and democracy are compatible, however, is an open question. This is illustrated by a famous and timeless exchange between former Prime Minister Pierre Trudeau and CBC journalist Tim Ralfe in October 1970,[6] a few days after the Liberal government had suspended civil liberties by invoking the War Measures Act at the time of the FLQ Crisis in Quebec.

Ralfe: 'Sir, what is it with all these men with guns around here?'

Trudeau: 'Haven't you noticed?'

Ralfe: 'Yes, I've noticed them. I wondered why you people decided to have them.'

Trudeau: 'What's your worry?'

Ralfe: 'I'm not worried, but you seem to be.'

Trudeau: 'If you're not worried, I'm not worried.'

Ralfe: 'I'm worried about living in a town that's full of people with guns running around.'

Trudeau: 'Why? Have they done anything to you? Have they pushed you around or anything? . . . [T]here are a lot of bleeding hearts around who just don't like to see people with helmets and guns. All I can say is, go on and bleed, but it is more important to keep law and order in the society than to be worried about weak-kneed people. . . . I think the society must take every means at

> its disposal to defend itself against the emergence of a parallel power which defies the elected power in this country, and I think that goes to any distance.'

Is Trudeau right? It is one of the great ironies of democracy that, unlike other political systems, it requires that dissenting points of view and opposition to those in power be respected. Arresting people suspected of terrorist acts is, most would agree, necessary to protect democratic government. At some point, however, the protection of law and order may exact a high cost in terms of personal freedoms. In a democracy, those in power must justify their use of coercion as being necessary to maintain such values as freedom, equality, justice, and the rule of law. Inevitably, however, people will disagree over the meaning and relative importance of these values, and over how much coercion, in what circumstances, is acceptable. Whether the issue is the War Measures Act in 1970 or the measures taken to combat terrorism since 11 September 2001, the eternal trade-off is the same.

The practical difficulties that can arise in an *open society*—a society in which individuals are free to speak their minds, associate with whom they wish, and move freely about without having to notify

Police stand guard along a three-metre-high security fence circling the meeting site for G20 Summit leaders in Toronto in June 2010. Security measures, including a five-tier screening process, required accreditation for residents living inside the zone, and temporary extension of police powers, were criticized by some as an unnecessary infringement on personal freedoms during the gathering of world leaders to discuss the stability of the global economy.

or justify their movements to the public authorities—was brought home to Canadians, and even more so to Americans, after the terrorist attacks on the World Trade Center and the Pentagon of 9/11. Access to public buildings became more restricted, border crossings became more time-consuming and stressful, airport security was tightened, and measures were taken to curb the rights of immigrants. Some of these changes proved to be temporary, but many—such as the new air travel security tax that all Canadian travellers have been required to pay since 2002 and the Anti-Terrorism Act, which came into effect in December 2001—have been enduring. But the most lasting and significant impact of 9/11 on Canadian politics has been the reflection and debate it has generated regarding the appropriate balance between individual rights and national security in a democratic society. Some believe that Canadian co-operation with the United States in the creation and maintenance of what officialdom calls a 'common security perimeter' is necessary to protect the open society from enemies who would take advantage of the freedoms it affords to spread terror. Others see such a policy as being democracy's own 'Iron Curtain', and thus a flagrant violation of the principles that the open society is supposed to embody and uphold.

State and Government

The existence of the state is, we argued earlier, a necessary condition for the existence of politics. But what is the 'state'? To this point we have used the terms 'state' and 'government' as though they meant the same thing. This failure to make a distinction between them is often harmless, but it can lead to serious confusion. For example, to argue that the government is corrupt or wasteful, or that its policies are undesirable, does not necessarily call into question the state's legitimacy. It does, however, challenge the authority of the particular people who control the levers of the governmental system. In an established democracy, political activity is far more likely to be directed at influencing and changing the government than at reforming the state.

Canadian political scientist Leo Panitch provides this definition of the **state**:

> [The state is] a broad concept that includes government as the seat of legitimate authority in a territory but also includes bureaucracy, judiciary, the Armed Forces and internal police, structures of legislative assemblies and administration, public corporations, regulatory boards, and ideological apparatuses such as the education establishment and publicly owned media. The distinguishing characteristic of the state is its monopoly over the use of force in a given territory.[7]

Defined this way, the state has three main characteristics. First, it involves territorial boundaries. States have borders, beyond which their legal authority is either nil or strictly limited. Second, the state consists of a complex set of institutions that wield public authority. The courts, the police, and the educational system are outposts of the state's authority no less than are the elected legislature and the bureaucracy. Third, the state is defined in terms of power, what Weber (see Box 1.2) called its 'monopoly of the legitimate use of physical force in the enforcement of its order'. For what purposes and in whose interests this power is exercised are important questions.

Some definitions of the state offer answers to these questions. The Marxist definition in Box 1.2 characterizes the state as an instrument of class oppression. Marx argued that the end of class conflict would sound the death knell for the state. It would 'wither away', no longer having any function to perform. Contemporary Marxists, except for a few diehards, no longer predict the state's demise. Feminists view the state as a patriarchal institution, reinforcing and perpetuating the social superiority of men over women. Many political scientists, and probably most economists, would argue that the state is responsive to any group with enough political clout to persuade policy-makers that it is in their interest to meet the group's demands for public actions on private wants.

An adequate explanation of the state must ask on whose behalf and in whose interests the state's

Politics in Focus

Box 1.2 Alternative Definitions of the State

'The executive of the modern State is but a committee for managing the common affairs of the whole bourgeoisie.'

Marx and Engels, *The Communist Manifesto*

'The state is that fiction by which everyone seeks to live at the expense of everyone else.'

French economist Frédéric Bastiat, *circa* 1840

'L'État, c'est moi.' [I am the state.]

Louis XIV of France

'[The state is that institution which] successfully upholds a claim to the monopoly of the legitimate use of physical force in the enforcement of its order . . . within a given territorial area.'

Max Weber, *The Theory of Social and Economic Organization*

'All state-based political systems are patriarchal—that is, in no country in the world are women equal participants in the institutions of the state or equal beneficiaries in its distribution of power or in the norms and values sanctioned in law and enforced by those institutions.'

Jill Vickers, *Reinventing Political Science*

authority is exercised. Contemporary political science offers four main answers to these questions: **pluralism**, **class analysis**, **feminism**, and **postmodernism**.

Pluralism. Those who see politics as being fundamentally a competition between different interests are likely to conclude that the state responds chiefly to the demands of those groups that are best organized, have superior financial resources, can credibly claim to speak on behalf of large numbers of voters or segments of the population that are influential for other reasons, and are successful in associating their special interests with the general interests of society. The pluralist model assumes various forms, some of which are society-centred. The *society-centred* variants emphasize the impact of groups in society on the state, while *state-centred* variants place greater emphasis on the ability of public officials to act on their own preferences and according to their own interests, rather than merely responding to the demands of voters and interest groups. Pluralist models of the state do not assume that the competition among groups takes place on a level playing field. On the contrary, many of those who work within this perspective argue that business interests occupy a privileged position within this competition. Many pluralist thinkers argue that those who shape our perception of the world, especially those in the media, tend to lean in a particular ideological direction that favours certain interpretations, values, and interests over others.

Class analysis. Beginning with Karl Marx, class analysis has always seen the state in capitalist societies as an instrument through which the small minorities who control most of a society's wealth maintain their social and economic dominance. Precisely how this is done has been the subject of enormous debate, but the state's complicity in perpetuating inequalities rooted in the economic system is an article of faith shared by all variants of class analysis. Few of those who analyze politics from a class analysis perspective today would deny that the demands and interests of subordinate classes influence state decision-makers. But this influence, they argue, is sharply limited by the state's vulnerability to a decline in business confidence, the control that the dominant class has over the mass media and popular culture, and a lack of class consciousness among even the least privileged groups in society that stems from the widespread acceptance—what Marx called 'false consciousness'—of capitalist and individualistic values as normal and inevitable.

Feminism. Feminists view the state as an inherently patriarchal institution. This means that the state, its structures, and its laws all serve to institutionalize male dominance. Increasing the representation of women in elected legislatures, the bureaucracy, and the courts, and creating governmental bodies and programs that recognize women as a group with interests and needs that are not identical to those of men can attenuate this male dominance. However, most of feminist political theory still insists that a state-centred political system will be patriarchal. 'A feminist state that is a structure of authority,' says R.W. Connell, 'a means by which some persons rule over others, is self-contradictory.'[8] It is the hierarchical nature of authority embodied in the state that makes it fundamentally patriarchal. Like Karl Marx's famous prediction that the state would 'wither away' once classes were abolished, many feminists argue that if gender discrimination were to be eliminated the state, *as we know it*, would disappear.

Postmodernism. Postmodernism views the state as an essentially oppressive and even repressive institution. But unlike class analysis and feminism, postmodernism is much more eclectic in the forms of oppression that it associates with the state and public authority. That oppression may be targeted at groups based on their race, gender, ethnicity, sexual preference, or some other trait that places them outside the dominant group in control of the levers of state power and whose values and identity are reflected in the institutions, language, and mores of the society. Postmodernism views the state as a repressive institution in that the structures, laws, and activities that constitute the state repress the expression of some values at the same time as they legitimize and nurture others. Those who embrace this approach comprise what is sometimes called the New Left. The Old Left wished to see the overthrow of the capitalist state and its transformation into the vehicle whereby those without property, money, and status would be able to reform society. Postmodernism is more dubious about the revolutionary visions associated with class analysis and the Old Left, believing that the problem of the state is not simply its relationship to economic power but to forms of oppression and repression more generally. This leads some postmodernists, such as the French philosopher Jean Baudrillard, to despair of the possibility of achieving justice and democracy through the state. Others, such as Richard Rorty, are more optimistic.

A distinction can be made between the state and government. **Government** is a term more usefully reserved for those who have been elected to power. It is more personal than the state, being associated with a particular group of people and, usually, with political parties. In democratic political systems governments are chosen and removed through elections. These elections—the rules and procedures by which governments are formed—are part of the state system. And like the rest of the state, they are much less likely to generate political controversy and to undergo change than are the government and its policies.

Underlying this distinction between state and government is an important practical difference in how each compels the obedience of citizens, corporations, and associations that fall within its jurisdiction. The willingness of individuals and groups to obey the decisions of government—decisions they may vigorously disagree with, and a government they may not have voted for—is based on their view that the state's authority is legitimate. By **legitimacy** we mean that the rules and institutions that comprise the state, and which determine how governments are chosen, are accepted by most people as being reasonable. The legitimacy of the state is, therefore, based on the *consent* of those who are governed. It does not depend on an ever-present fear of the penalties that follow from disobeying the law. It rests instead on what is usually an implicit acceptance of the rules of the political game. If the state's authority, and ultimately the ability of governments to govern, depended on a sort of constant referendum of the popular will, politics would be a brittle enterprise. In reality, this popular consent is not something that people regularly (if ever!) reflect on or consciously avow (the 'Pledge of Allegiance' recited by American schoolchildren has no counterpart in most democracies, and certainly not in Canada).

Perhaps the best way to understand the importance of the state/government distinction in a democracy is to imagine what would happen if a government's ability to pass and implement laws depended on its popularity. Assume for a moment that a government's 'approval rating' sinks to 20 per cent, according to public opinion polls, and that particular actions of the government are opposed by a clear majority of citizens. Should people simply choose to disobey the law and treat this unpopular government as one that has lost its right to govern? And if polls showed that the leader of another political party was clearly preferred by most voters, would this leader have a better moral claim to govern than the discredited leader of the government?

This is a scenario for chaos and anarchy. Democracy requires some measure of stability and respect for rules, including those rules that determine who has the right to govern and how and when that right ends. A particular government or prime minister may be deeply unpopular, but people continue to obey the law and refrain from storming the legislature (although they may organize protests and even throw some tomatoes) because of their implicit acceptance of the state's legitimacy. Government popularity and state legitimacy are not the same.

Government may be upheld by consent or by force. In fact, it is usually upheld by both. When anti-abortion protestors defy court injunctions against demonstrating near an abortion clinic and are arrested and charged for this act of civil disobedience, they are challenging the authority of the state. When Quebec nationalists demand political independence for their province they are registering their belief that the existing boundaries of the Canadian state, and its authority in Quebec society, are not legitimate. And when striking unions ignore back-to-work legislation, and in doing so run the risk of being fined or their leaders being imprisoned, this also goes beyond disagreement with government policy to challenge the legitimacy of the state. The state's authority is sometimes questioned by individuals or by organized interests. When this happens, the public authorities may resort to force in order to crush civil disobedience and maintain their ability to govern.

The question of when citizens may be justified in resisting the law, through either passive disobedience of public authority or violence, is an old one. Two of the world's greatest democracies, the United States and France, trace their modern origins to bloody revolutions undertaken in defence of principles that the revolutionaries believed warranted violence against the state. Some, such as the American writer and libertarian thinker Henry David Thoreau, India's Mahatma Gandhi, and the black civil rights

In a 1992 Gallup Poll, then Prime Minister Brian Mulroney earned an approval rating of just 11 per cent, making him one of the most unpopular Canadian leaders since the inception of opinion polling. His government's introduction of the Goods and Services Tax, a recession, and the failure of the Meech Lake Accord contributed to the decline in his popularity during his second term in office. It was through the processes of the state that Canadians made their dissent known: in the 1993 federal election, the Progressive Conservatives were reduced from 151 seats to a mere 2 in the House of Commons, losing their official party status.

leader Martin Luther King Jr, developed a philosophy of non-violent civil disobedience that has been influential across the world. Others, like some of the leaders of the American student movement of the 1960s, the French students whose actions paralyzed public authority in Paris and brought about the fall of the de Gaulle presidency in 1968, and Malcolm X, whose slogan 'By any means necessary' encapsulates a philosophy of justifiable resistance to unjust treatment, have acted on the premise that violent opposition to the law and those who enforce it is consistent with democracy when it targets oppression and injustice.

The debate over civil disobedience—when it is justified and what forms it may take in a democracy—has resurfaced in recent years, principally around issues associated with globalization and income inequality. Since what the media dubbed the 'Battle in Seattle' in 1999, when the meetings of the World Trade Organization were disrupted by thousands of protestors and scenes of violent confrontations with the police were broadcast live around the world, organized protest has become a standard and expected part of any meeting of policy-makers from the world's wealthiest countries. This led the Liberal government of Jean Chrétien to schedule the 2002 meeting of the G8, the world's eight largest capitalist democracies, in the isolated resort community of Kananaskis, Alberta, from which protestors could be kept at a distance. The experience of street tactics used at anti-globalization protests in Seattle, Genoa, Quebec City, Rostock, and elsewhere has produced, somewhat ironically, a service industry that specializes in providing activist groups with advice and training on confrontations with the police, effective use of the media, and, more generally, strategies and tactics for influence through civil disobedience. Training for Change (www.trainingforchange.org) and the Ruckus Society (www.ruckus.org) are examples of such organizations.

It is, of course, perfectly lawful to provide information that one intends will disrupt the status quo. But what about advice or action that involves breaking the law? Here are three examples of actions that, strictly speaking, appear to involve violations of the law. Do you think that any or all of them can be justified in a democracy?

- On 15 December 2007, an organization called Les Enfants de Don Quichotte, led by the French homeless advocate, Augustin Legrand, set up dozens of tents for the homeless along the Right Bank of the Seine, within steps of Paris's Notre Dame Cathedral. They did not have a permit to do so and the police quickly intervened and dismantled the tents.
- On 10 May 2010, about 100 people linked arms to stop traffic in front of the Federal Plaza in lower Manhattan as a gesture of protest against what they believed to be an unjust immigration law passed by the Arizona legislature that targets people of Mexican heritage for deportation if they do not immediately produce documentation proving their legal status in the US. Thirty-five of the Manhattan protestors, including a Catholic bishop, some city councillors, and several activists, were arrested when they rejected repeated calls by the New York City police to disperse. Similar acts of civil disobedience, some involving protestors chaining themselves together, occurred in Los Angeles, Seattle, in front of the White House, and elsewhere, all triggered by the Arizona law.
- In late April of 2008 about 100 Aboriginal protestors blockaded a stretch of Highway 6 near Caledonia, a community southwest of Toronto. They did so in support of another Native blockade in Deseronto, near Belleville, Ontario, where the provincial police had removed the roadblock erected by protestors. The protestors at Caledonia began occupying a housing development in 2006, claiming that the land rightfully belonged to them, and proceeded to block the town's main road for roughly three months after the police entered the site they occupied. The issue was similar in Deseronto, with Natives claiming that development was taking place on land they rightfully owned.

Although public opinion in these cases and others like them was divided, there is no shortage of Canadians or of citizens in other countries who believe that such resistance is a justifiable reaction to a history of oppression and a political system and justice system believed by some to be heavily biased against the interests of those who have been marginalized. The oppression and violence that the state may inflict on members of the society, the argument goes, warrant self-defence on the part of victims of this oppression and violence.

Government that relies primarily on threats and violence to maintain its rule is generally unstable. Even the most repressive political authorities usually come to realize that popular consent is a firmer basis on which to govern. In some societies the popular consent that legitimizes political rule may appear to emerge more or less spontaneously from the unco-ordinated activities of the media, the schools, the family, governments: from the various social institutions that influence the values and beliefs of citizens. In other societies, the state's legitimacy is deliberately and assiduously cultivated through the organs of official propaganda. The calculated fostering of consent is a characteristic feature of totalitarian rule. **Totalitarianism** is a system of government that suppresses all dissent in the name of some supreme goal. This goal may be tied to the destiny of the 'race', as it was in Nazi Germany, or to 'class struggle', as it was in the Soviet Union under Stalin. Distinctions between the state, government, and society lose all meaning—indeed, they are considered to be subversive—under totalitarianism.

The active mobilization of society by the state, the deliberate manipulation of public attitudes, and the ruthless suppression of dissent by the public authorities are not features that most of us associate with democracy. The way in which legitimacy is generated in political democracies is more subtle than under totalitarian rule, depending primarily on social institutions that are not part of the state system. This gives legitimacy the appearance of being based on the free choice of individuals, an appearance that some argue is an illusion. Marxist critics use the term **cultural hegemony** to signify the ability of society's dominant class to get its values and beliefs accepted as the conventional wisdom in society at large.

Harold Laski, one of the most prominent leftist intellectuals of the twentieth century, argued that American citizens were essentially duped into believing that their society provided equality of opportunity and protection for individual rights. They were sold, he argued, a false bill of goods about 'rugged individualism'—the capacity and desirability of each person relying on his or her own resources to get ahead in life—when, in fact, the complex and interconnected character of modern life rendered obsolete and even absurd a value system suited to a frontier society. The mass media, owned by private capital, the mainstream churches, beholden in various ways to the dominant class, and an educational system, which was penetrated by capitalist values and dependent on bequests and grants from the corporate elite to maintain such temples of learning as Harvard, Yale, Princeton, and Stanford, all were complicit in maintaining the cultural hegemony of the dominant capitalist class. American social critic Noam Chomsky takes this same position in arguing that the privately owned mass media reinforce and perpetuate inequalities in wealth and power by presenting 'facts', images, and interpretations that either justify or gloss over these inequalities.[9] Feminists make a similar case, arguing that sexist attitudes of male superiority are pervasive in social institutions—from the bedroom to the boardroom—so that the legitimacy of patriarchal power relations is reinforced on a daily basis. For both Marxists and feminists, government by 'popular consent' is a sham that conceals the fundamentally undemocratic character of society and politics.

This may strike you as, at a minimum, an exaggeration of the disconnect that may be created between the reality of people's lives and their beliefs about how the world works and what possibilities exist for them. Or perhaps you find the cultural hegemony argument to be plausible. Either way, it directs our attention to something that is quite important in all societies. This is the role played by the various agents of learning. Families, schools, the mass media, governments, and organizations and groups, formal and informal, contribute to the information, ideas, and sentiments that we have about the world around us. Indeed, in many respects the system through which information, ideas, and interpretations are generated and disseminated deserves to be considered the cornerstone of democracy. If our ideas are manipulated, based on falsehoods, and at odds with important aspects of the reality in which we live, no constitution, elections, or grand speeches can turn this sow's ear into a silk purse.

Democracy

'Democracy is like pornography', says classical historian and political commentator Victor Davis Hanson, 'we know it when we see it.'[10] But as is also true of pornography, what one person may believe to be unredeemed smut, another may think is art. And yet a third may say that it is all a matter of personal judgement anyway, no one's standard being, a priori, superior to anyone else's. At the same time, however, Hanson's observation seems commonsensical. Most of us would agree that a country in which free elections are held is almost certainly more democratic than one where they are not. And where we see egregious and persistent violations of human rights or a serious lack of accountability on the part of those who govern, we are likely to be skeptical about claims that such a country is democratic.

But that does not stop leaders in political systems as different as those of Canada, the United States, the Democratic People's Republic of Korea, the People's Republic of China, and the Islamic Republic of Iran from all claiming to be democracies. Democracy is a label to which regimes throughout the world try to lay claim. Obviously they cannot all be democratic without our understanding of this concept being diluted to the point that it becomes meaningless.

In a book published at the height of the Cold War, Canadian political philosopher C.B. Macpherson argued that there are in fact three different types of democracy in the modern world.[11] Only one of these, *liberal* democracy, is characterized by competition between political parties. What Macpherson calls the *developmental* and *communist* versions of democracy do not have competitive elections, and probably would not be considered democratic by most Canadians. But they both claim to attach greater importance to the social and economic equality of individuals than does liberal democracy, in addition to recognizing the formal political equality of citizens. If democracy is about equality, Macpherson argues, the developmental and communist versions are at least as democratic as the liberal version that we in the capitalist world automatically assume to be the genuine article.

If we accept Macpherson's argument that there are three types of democracy, not one, each with a legitimate claim to the title, the world looks like a very democratic place. Leaving aside personal and military dictatorships, and the odd monarchy like Saudi Arabia and the Sultanate of Brunei, most of what is left would seem to qualify. While common sense suggests that democracy is not as widespread as this, Macpherson is challenging us to reflect on what makes politics and society democratic or not. Is democracy a system of government? Or does democracy connote a type of society? Was Canada 'democratic' before the female half of the population received the vote? Do the persistence of poverty and the clear evidence of large inequalities in the economic condition and social status of different groups in Canada oblige us to qualify our description of Canadian society as 'democratic'?

About the only thing that everyone can agree on is that democracy is based on equality. Agreement breaks down over how much equality, in what spheres of life, is necessary for a society to qualify as democratic. Majority rule, government by popular consent, one person–one vote, and competitive elections are the political institutions usually associated with democratic government. But it has long been recognized that the operation of democratic political institutions can result in oppressive government. If, for example, a majority of Quebecers agree that legislative restrictions on the language rights of non-francophones are needed to preserve the French character of Quebec, is this democratic? In order to safeguard the rights and freedoms of individuals and minorities against what Alexis de Tocqueville called 'democratic despotism', constitutional limits on the power of the state over its citizens may be set or the political status of particular social groups may be entrenched in the formal rules and informal procedures of politics. For example, the Canadian Constitution entrenches the coequal official status of the French and English languages at the national level, and the operation of federalism and the Canadian electoral system reinforce the political power of this country's French-speaking minority, 90 per cent of whom live in Quebec.

Perhaps even more important than constitutional guarantees and political practices are the social and cultural values of a society. Tocqueville argued that the best protection against the **tyranny of the majority** is the existence of multiple group identities in society. When individuals perceive themselves as being members of particular social groups—whether a religious denomination, an ethnic or language group, a regional community, or whatever the group identity happens to be—in addition to sharing with everyone else a common citizenship, the likelihood of the democratic state being turned to oppressive ends is reduced. After all, everyone has a personal interest in the tolerance of social diversity because the rights and status of their own group depend on this.

NO GAS MASKS, ROCKS OR SLINGSHOTS NEEDED. (SOME ASSEMBLY REQUIRED.)

Democracies have police forces, courts, and jails. But unlike other forms of government, they do not depend primarily on coercion and violence and they give citizens an opportunity to choose who will govern them.

Some twentieth-century writers argued that cultural values represented the main bulwark against the tyranny of the majority. Democratic government, they have suggested, depends on popular tolerance of diversity. In *The Civic Culture*, American political scientists Gabriel Almond and Sidney Verba make the argument that democratic government is sustained by cultural attitudes.[12] According to this political culture approach, the determination of how democratic a society is must be based on an examination of the politically relevant attitudes and beliefs of the population. This, and not the mere fact of apparently democratic political institutions, is argued to be the true test of democracy and the key to sustaining it.

The civic culture thesis has enjoyed a renaissance in recent years through work on what is called **social capital**. This refers to norms of interpersonal trust, a sense of civic duty, and a belief that one's involvement in politics and in the life of the community matters. Where levels of social trust are low, public authorities must invest more in institutions and policies that rely on repression and force to maintain social order. Social capital is argued to have an economic value, but the main argument made for policies, practices, and institutions that promote social capital is that citizens will be happier and their control over their own lives will be greater (see Box 1.3).

Not everyone would agree. Socialists argue that a society in which a large number of people are preoccupied with the problem of feeding and housing themselves decently cannot be described as democratic. This preoccupation effectively excludes the poor from full participation in political life, and in this way socio-economic inequality translates into political inequality. The formal equality of citizens

Politics in Focus

Box 1.3 Robert Putnam Brings the Gospel of Social Capital to Tampa Bay

In 2005 a civic organization by the name of Creative Tampa Bay (www.creativetampabay.com) invited the well-known Harvard social capital scholar Robert Putnam to give a talk on how to generate social capital and the benefits that follow. Putnam's talk launched this organization's 'Social Capital Project'. It identified the following non-economic benefits for communities in which the attributes of social capital are plentiful:

- People will tend to be healthier, due in part to denser friendship networks.
- There will be less crime because people are more likely to know their neighbours.
- Students will perform better and have higher scores on standardized tests when parents are more involved in community affairs.
- Government will work better when more people get involved in civic life.
- Tolerance of diversity will be greater.

Are these rather impressive claims true? The jury is still out. But the amount of research on and interest in social capital is enormous. Those interested in finding out more about this topic may start by visiting the websites of Harvard's Saguaro Seminar on Civic Engagement in America (www.hks.harvard.edu/saguaro/primer.htm) and the Social Capital Gateway (www.socialcapitalgateway.org).

that democratic government confers, and even the fact that most people subscribe to democratic values, does not alter the fundamental fact that social inequalities produce inequalities in political power. Some critics go even further in dismissing the democratic claims of capitalist societies (see Box 1.4). They argue that inequality results from the simple fact that a very small proportion of the population—the capitalist class—controls the vast majority of the means of economic production and distribution. This inequality in property ownership, Marxists have long argued, far outweighs the importance of 'one person–one vote' and competitive elections in determining the real political influence of different classes in society.

Inequalities between bosses and workers, between parents and children, between men and women, between ethnic or language communities—the list could go on—are often claimed to undermine the democratic character of societies whose formal political institutions are based on the equality of citizens. Indeed, if we use any of the all-inclusive definitions of politics examined earlier in this chapter it is impossible to resist the logic of this argument. Inequalities confront us wherever we turn, and true democracy seems to be terribly elusive. Even if we define politics more narrowly to include only those activities that focus on the state, it is obvious that a small portion of all citizens actually dominates public life. This is true even in the most egalitarian societies. For most of us, participation in politics takes the form of short bursts of attention and going to the polls at election time. Is it reasonable to speak of democratic government when the levers of state power are in the hands of an elite?

The short answer is, 'It depends on what we expect from democracy.' If we expect that all citizens should have the opportunity to participate in the law-making process, we are bound to be disappointed. With some historical exceptions like the Greek *polis* and the township democracies of seventeenth- and eighteenth-century America, examples of direct government of the citizens by the citizens are scarce. Direct democracy survives in some isolated pockets like the couple of Swiss cantons where the *Landsgemeinde*—outdoor gatherings of citizens that take place each spring to vote on important public questions—still exist. Modern technology has, however, created the possibility of direct democracy from people's living rooms in all advanced industrial societies. Everyone who has watched an episode of *American Idol* or its Canadian spinoff knows how this brave new world of participatory democracy could work. Whether over telephone lines or by clicking the mouse of your computer, there is no physical or technological reason why this method of popular choice could not be adapted to political decision-making. There may, however, be other reasons for rejecting what modern technology makes possible.

Perhaps the most commonly advanced reason for rejecting direct democracy via the Internet and for being skeptical about the value of public opinion polls is that many citizens are poorly informed about important public issues much of the time, and it occasionally happens that most citizens are grossly uninformed or misinformed about public issues. What sense does it make to ask citizens what the government's policy should be on a matter about which the majority of people know either little or nothing, and where what they think they know may be factually incorrect?

Thomas Jefferson provided a famous answer to this question. 'Every government degenerates when trusted to the rulers of the people alone. The people themselves therefore are [democracy's] only safe depositories.'[13] Members of the public, Jefferson acknowledged, are often poorly informed or wrong

Governing Realities

Box 1.4 Is Canada a Democracy?

In 1999, Survival International, a non-governmental organization that advocates on behalf of tribal peoples throughout the world, published a study by Colin Samson,[14] a professor of sociology at the University of Essex in the United Kingdom. It compared Canada's treatment of the Innu, who traditionally lived on the tundra of the Labrador Peninsula, to China's treatment of Tibet. Here is some of what the study said:

> [Canada] occupies the land of a previously independent people. The purpose? Both to integrate a 'backward' population into the dominant society, and to control a strategic area and the resources it contains.
>
> In comparing China's occupation of Tibet with Canada's treatment of the Innu, it should be stated clearly that the situation in the two countries is very different. China has imprisoned, tortured and killed thousands of Tibetans in its 49-year occupation; there is intense military repression and control; and any talk of Tibetan independence guarantees a long spell in prison at the very least. In contrast, Canada is not shooting or torturing the Innu; and although the police presence in Innu communities is sometimes oppressive, it is on nothing like the same scale as that of China. Furthermore, Canada has an independent judiciary and democratic institutions.
>
> And yet . . . the long-term plan is similar for both countries: namely, the eventual absorption of a troublesome 'minority' into the larger population, thus opening up valuable land and resources for exploitation. And the Innu, like the Tibetans, are dying. They do not need to be shot—they are killing themselves, at a rate unsurpassed anywhere in the world. The Canadian government bears responsibility for this outrage but does nothing to avoid it—indeed, its actions are calculated to bring about exactly these conditions.

What do you think? Is it fair to compare Canada's treatment of the Innu to China's well-known and often condemned repression of Tibetans? Is the generally unquestioned assumption that Canada is one of the most democratic countries in the world cast in doubt by the claims this study makes?

in their opinions on public matters. But the democratic solution to the problem of an ill-informed public is not to exclude it from the determination of public affairs; rather, it is to educate public opinion. Jefferson placed great stress on the role of the press and public education in producing an informed citizenry.

We often hear that the information explosion generated by satellite communication, television, and the Internet has made us the best-informed generation of all time. But as Neil Postman observes, this conceit fails to address why most people are unable to explain even the most basic elements of issues that have received saturation coverage in the media. This ignorance does not prevent pollsters from asking people for their opinion on matters that they may barely understand and clearly deprives the results of polls of any meaning other than the signals they send to politicians looking for waves to ride. Postman blames modern education and especially the media for this ignorance. Television, the defining medium of the last half-century, is singled out for particular blame.

> What is happening here is that television is altering the meaning of 'being informed' by creating a species of information that might properly be called *disinformation*. . . . Disinformation does not mean false information. It means misleading information—misplaced, irrelevant, fragmented or superficial information—information that creates the illusion of knowing something but which in fact leads one away from knowing. . . . [W]hen news is packaged as entertainment, that is the inevitable result.[15]

The pillars that Jefferson counted on to support democratic government have rotted, according to Postman. The irony is that this has happened in an age when more information from more corners of the world is available to the average person than ever before.

All modern democracies are **representative democracies**. Government is carried out by elected legislatures that represent the people. Citizens delegate law-making authority to their representatives, holding them responsible for their actions through periodic elections. Representative democracies sometimes include decision-making processes that provide opportunities for greater and more frequent citizen participation than simply voting every few years. *Plebiscites* and *referendums*—direct votes of citizens on important public questions—frequently held elections, choosing judges and some administrative officials through election, and formal procedures for removing an elected official before the end of his or her term, as through voter petitions and 'recall' elections, are democratic institutions that appear to allow for widespread citizen participation in public affairs.

This appearance may be deceiving. In countries like the United States and Switzerland, where referendums are a normal part of the political process, voter turnout is usually very low. Partly because of this, and partly because vested interests are quick to spend money on advertising and mobilizing their supporters, critics charge that referendums may produce outcomes that are far from democratic. Indeed, one of the most common accusations levelled at referendums is that they are too easily used as tools of conservative political interests. But this is not always true. A study of the 1998 United States elections found that there were 235 referendums at the state level, about one-quarter of which were initiated by citizen petitions. Many of these referendums had little or nothing to do with political ideology, but others, on issues such as drug liberalization, the environment, affirmative action, animal rights, and abortion, did. In contests with a clear ideological dimension, liberals won more often than they lost.[16]

Respect for rights and freedoms is generally considered a distinguishing feature of democratic government. Which rights and freedoms warrant protection, and in what circumstances they may legitimately be limited by government, are matters of dispute. Libertarians, many economists, and conservative philosophers argue that government that levies heavy taxes on citizens is undemocratic. Their reasoning is that individual choice is reduced when government, representing the collectivity, decides how a large share of people's income will be spent. Others argue that the same levels of taxation actually promote freedom by paying for policies that give less advantaged groups opportunities that they would not have in a 'free' market. Even a value as central to democracy as freedom of speech is sometimes argued to have undemocratic side effects. For example, some believe that any person or organization should have the right to spend money on advertising a particular political point of view during an election campaign. Others argue that unlimited freedom of speech in these circumstances is undemocratic, because some individuals and groups are better endowed than others and, therefore, the points of view of the affluent will receive the greatest exposure.

Rights and freedoms are believed by most of us to be important in democracies, but everyone except extreme libertarians believes that protecting these rights or freedoms can sometimes produce undemocratic outcomes. No surefire test can tell us when democracy is promoted or impaired by protecting a right or freedom. Indeed, this is one of the greatest sources of conflict in modern democracy, sometimes portrayed as a struggle between the competing pulls of individualism (the private realm) and collectivism (the public realm). A private realm that is beyond the legitimate reach of the state is a necessary part of what is sometimes called a free society. Where this realm does not exist—where the individual's right to be protected from the state is obliterated by the state's right to impose its will on the individual—democracy does not exist. Individual freedoms and group rights must enjoy some respect and protection if a society's politics is to be judged democratic.

So how democratic is Canada? According to the Freedom House's World Democracy Audit (www.worldaudit.org), Canada is one of the most democratic countries in the world. But it is not the most democratic country, trailing slightly behind some of the Scandinavian and Northern European democracies. In arriving at its ranking of countries, Freedom House **operationalizes** the concept of democracy, defining it in ways that can be measured so that scores can be assigned to each country. This methodology has the advantage of making explicit the criteria used in determining whether a country is more or less democratic. The criteria used in the Freedom House survey of the world's political systems combine measures of political rights, civil liberties, press freedom, public corruption, and the rule of law in arriving at a country's democracy ranking (see Box 1.5).

A country may have free elections, a constitution that protects rights and freedoms, and a media system that permits the expression of diverse points of view and criticism of the powerful. But if individuals and organizations are able to buy special treatment, or nepotism is rampant, or the law applies to different people in different ways, depending on who they are and who they know, this will undermine a society's claim to be democratic. Corruption, including bribery and special treatment based on friendship and family connections, can be found in any political system. In a democracy, however, such behaviour is considered to be unlawful or at least unethical, depending on how egregiously it violates the rule of law. The **rule of law** may truly be said to be the foundation of democratic government, on which all else rests. 'It means', said Eugene Forsey (1904–91), one of Canada's foremost constitutionalists of the twentieth century, 'that everyone is subject to the law; that no one, no matter how important or powerful, is above the law.'[17] The rule of law means that no public official has the legitimate right to exercise any powers other than those assigned to his or her office by the law. And if someone in a position of public trust attempts to go beyond the authority that the law permits? Then it is up to the courts to check that abuse of power. An independent judiciary is, therefore, a necessary feature of democratic governance.

This is all fine theory. But consider the following two cases. The first asks what sorts of inequalities, in what circumstances, may undermine democratic values and processes. The second highlights the always present tension between majoritarianism and competing visions of democracy.

Who Gets Heard, and Why?

Access to political decision-makers and the ability to influence public opinion are not equally distributed in society. If the president of the Royal Bank of Canada places a telephone call to the federal

Minister of Finance, this call will be returned. Your call or mine probably will not (try it!). For as long as elections have taken place in Canada, individuals and organizations have made financial contributions to political parties and their candidates. For the relatively modest sum of $1,100 per year, you can join the Liberal Party's Laurier Club. Among other things, this buys an invitation to party functions across the country, including the possibility of some face time with the party leader. Corporations are banned from buying memberships, but their CEOs, presidents, board members, and so on are not, and many of the individual members of the Laurier Club have corporate connections.

Between election campaigns, interest groups of all sorts are active in many ways, trying to influence the actions of government and the climate of public opinion. Much of this activity costs money, often a lot of money. The services of a high-powered, well-connected lobbying firm can easily run into hundreds of thousands of dollars. A public relations campaign that uses polling and focus groups, followed by some combination of electronic and print media advertising, may cost as much or more. Although spending money on such activities promises no guarantee of favourable political outcomes, a widespread and probably well-founded belief suggests that such an investment may yield impressive returns. Spending on such activities is quite unevenly distributed across groups in society. Some people conclude from

Governing Realities

Box 1.5 Measuring Freedom

In determining how well a particular country respects and protects civil liberties, an important component of its democracy index, Freedom House uses the following criteria:

- Are there free and independent media and other forms of cultural expressions?
- Are religious institutions and communities free to practice their faith and express themselves in private and public?
- Is there freedom of assembly, demonstration, and open public expression?
- Do the people have the right to organize in different political parties or other competitive political groupings of their choice, and is the system open to the rise and fall of these competing parties or groupings?
- Are there free trade unions and peasant organizations or equivalents, and is there effective collective bargaining? Are there free professional and other private organizations?
- Is there protection from political terror, unjustified imprisonment, exile, or torture, whether by groups that support or oppose the system? Is there freedom from war and insurgencies?
- Is government free from pervasive corruption?
- Is there open and free private discussion?
- Do citizens enjoy freedom of travel or choice of residence, employment, or institution of higher education?
- Do citizens have the right to own property and establish private business? Is private business activity unduly influenced by government officials, the security forces, political parties/organizations, or organized crime?
- Are there personal social freedoms, including gender equality, choice of marriage partners, and size of family?
- Is there equality of opportunity and the absence of economic exploitation?

These criteria are part of a Political Rights Checklist, whose purpose is to measure several key components of democracy.

Source: Freedom House <www.freedomhouse.org/template.cfm?page=384&key=216&parent=21&report=81>.

this that having more money buys, at a minimum, greater access to those in positions of political authority and the ability to get a wider and perhaps more sympathetic hearing for the issues and points of view that matter most to the group spending the money.

But it is not this simple. The issues that get onto the **public agenda**—the matters that have been identified by opinion leaders in the media and in government as ones that warrant some policy response, even if that response is a decision not to act—are not determined by the spending of self-interested groups alone. The American journalist H.L. Mencken once said that the proper role of his profession was to 'bring comfort to the afflicted and afflict the comfortable.' Some in the media, in Canada and elsewhere, take Mencken's counsel to heart. But whether what they report and how they report it 'afflicts the comfortable' or not, it is undeniably the case that the values and beliefs of those who shape public opinion—including teachers, journalists, television and radio producers, researchers, and even, in their minor way, textbook writers!—influence the stories they tell and how they are told.

In Canada, as in other capitalist democracies, there is a long-standing and ongoing debate over whether those in the media—an important segment of the opinion-shaping class—do more to afflict or comfort the privileged and the powerful. On one point, however, the evidence is clear: interests and points of view that are not those of the wealthy and the well-connected do find their way into the public conversation. Getting heard is not only or always a matter of money.

Is Democracy a Process or an Outcome?

Tocqueville warned about the tyranny of the majority, that the multitude might show little concern for the rights and interests of minorities and see little wrong in imposing their force of superior numbers on those whose values and behaviour are different from those of the majority. Most people agree that majoritarianism needs to be tempered by protections for individual and group rights. That is why constitutions like Canada's include express guarantees for rights and freedoms.

But it often happens that when the rights claims of a minority are upheld by the courts, in the face of unsympathetic or divided public opinion and in circumstances where elected officials have shown an unwillingness to legislate such protection, some will argue that this is undemocratic. What is undemocratic, these critics charge, is that unelected public officials—judges in this case—have usurped policy-making prerogatives that, in a democracy, should be exercised by the people's elected representatives. For example, when the Charter of Rights and Freedoms was agreed to in 1981 by Ottawa and the provincial governments, its equality section (s. 15) did not include sexual orientation among the banned grounds for discrimination. This omission was deliberate. The case for including a reference to sexual orientation had been made during the hearings on the Charter, but had been rejected by the governments representing Canadians and the 10 provincial electorates. Several years later, however, the Supreme Court of Canada decided that discrimination under the law on the basis of sexual orientation was *analogous* to discrimination based on religion, race, or colour—forms of discrimination that are expressly prohibited by s. 15 of the Charter—and that sexual orientation should have the same constitutional status under the equality rights provision of the Charter as those forms of discrimination that were expressly mentioned by those who drafted and agreed to this important part of Canada's Constitution.

You might agree that this was the right thing to do. Or you may not. The point is, however, that this case and many like it raise contentious issues about what processes are democratic. Is there a problem when unelected officials, who cannot be removed from office when they make unpopular decisions, determine such matters? Even if public opinion is divided, so that many people support the decisions of judges or other unelected officials, should some issues—by their nature or because of their importance—be resolved only by those who have been elected to govern? Does democracy involve a particular process, and if so what process? Or is it more about particular outcomes being produced—a destination rather than a journey—whether by politicians, bureaucrats, or judges?

On reflection, most of us would probably agree that democracy involves a bit of both. Throughout this book we will argue that formal institutions are only part of what makes a society's politics democratic or not. The activities of the media, interest groups, and political parties are at least as crucial to the quality of democracy. Likewise, the socio-economic and ideological backgrounds to democratic government have important effects on how the formal and informal features of the political system operate. Democracy, then, cannot be reduced to a simple constitutional formula, nor to some particular vision of social equality. Several complex elements come into play, so that defining the term 'democracy' is a perilous task. Someone is bound to disagree, either with what is included in the definition or with what has been left out. In full recognition of these hazards, we offer the following definition. **Democracy** is a political system based on the formal political equality of all citizens, in which there is a realistic possibility that voters can replace the government, and in which certain basic rights and freedoms are protected.

Political Identities

Identities are ideas that link individuals to larger groups. They are self-definitions, such as 'I am a Canadian' or 'Je suis québécois', that help us make sense of who we are and how we fit into the world around us. An identity is a state of mind, a sense of belonging to a community that is defined by its language, ethnic character, religion, history, regional location, gender experiences, belief system, or other factors (see Box 1.6).

Identities perform important psychological and emotional functions. They provide the moorings that connect us to places, beliefs, and other people. People who share an identity are more likely to feel comfortable together and understand one another than they are with those who are not part of their

Politics in Focus

Box 1.6 Identity Politics

In Canada, as elsewhere, individuals have long thought of themselves as members of groups with specific traits that set them apart from others. After the French defeat on the Plains of Abraham in 1759 and the final terms of surrender in the 1763 Treaty of Paris, which ceded New France to the British, French-speaking *canadiens* thought of their language and the Catholic religion as defining features of who they were and who they were not. From the late 1800s until the middle of the 1900s, religion was an important marker of identity in Canadian society, separating Catholics from Protestants. Regional identities acquired political significance from the time of Confederation, when it became apparent that the greater population and economic influence of Ontario and Quebec would ensure that their voices would be louder and their values and interests more prominent in Canadian politics.

But since the 1960s the number of identities that matter in Canadian politics, as in other democracies, has proliferated enormously. Part of the reason for this proliferation has been the emergence of a culture of rights—group rights, but also individual rights—that gained irresistible momentum after World War II. Various social movements, involving women's rights, Aboriginal rights, gay and lesbian rights, environmentalism, and multiculturalism, have provided the intellectual architecture and the organizational impetus for this culture of group rights. Older identities tied to religion, language, territory, and values systems have not been washed away. But some have faded in significance and all must contend with the fact that newer identities have assumed a social and political importance far beyond what they had a couple of generations ago.

identity group. Often we only become aware of the importance of identity when we find ourselves in a very unfamiliar place or set of circumstances. Responses ranging from disorientation and longing for home—'home' understood both physically and culturally—to hostility and xenophobia are common when we become unmoored from our familiar identities.

By nature, identities are exclusive. If, for example, I think of myself as a member of the working class, I implicitly acknowledge the existence of other groups with which I do not identify. It is possible to identify with a number of groups without causing a sort of multiple personality disorder. There is, for example, no reason why a person could not think of himself or herself as a Canadian and a Québécois(e) at the same time. And, indeed, the evidence shows that many do. Multiple identities are common, but some will be more significant in shaping a person's ideas and behaviour than others.

A shared identity is based on a perception of having common interests. But the fact of some number of people having interests in common does not necessarily generate a shared identity. Most of us have no difficulty in recognizing that corporations in the same industry, or consumers, municipal ratepayers, or university students, have identifiable interests in common. These interests are related to the conditions that promote or impair the material well-being of the members of these groups. They become political interests when they are organized under a collective association that claims to represent the members of the group and attempts to influence the actions of the state. Organization is expected to provide the group's members with more collective influence in politics than any individual member could hope to exercise alone. The number of possible political interests is virtually without limit. Of these, only a finite number actually become organized for collective political action, and an even smaller number achieve significant political clout.

A political interest brings together individuals who might otherwise have little in common in terms of their attitudes and beliefs. What they often have in common is a material stake in how some political conflict is resolved. Wheat farmers, automotive workers, university students, east-coast fishers, pulp and paper companies, and small business people are all examples of political interests. Their participation in politics as organized groups is based on considerations of material well-being. Indeed, the interests that the members of such groups have in common are primarily economic ones.

The desire to protect or promote one's material well-being, while an important basis for the political organization of interests, is certainly not the only one. Politically active interests may come together around ideas, issues, and values that have little or no immediate relationship to the incomes, living conditions, social status, or other self-interest of a group's members. Mothers Against Drunk Driving (MADD) is an example of a group whose political involvement is motivated by shared values rather than material self-interest. The Canadian Abortion Rights Action League and the Canadian Conference of Catholic Bishops are groups whose political involvement on the abortion issue is motivated by values—very different values in these cases—rather than strictly material concerns.

Interests and identities are not inevitably political. One can be a French Canadian, an Albertan, a woman, or the member of some other social or cultural group, and be conscious of the fact, without this having any special political relevance. Identities such as these become politically relevant when those who share them make demands on the state—or when the state recognizes their group identity as a reason for treating them in a particular way. Some political identities emerge spontaneously in society, while others are forged and promoted by the state. Governments in Canada have come to play an increasingly active role in defining and promoting political identities in this country, a role that has generated much controversy.

The **nation** has been a particularly crucial political identity in Canadian politics. It is probably the single most powerful political identity in the world today—although religious identity surpasses it in some societies. The meaning of the term 'nation' is a matter of dispute (see Box 1.7). These disputes are not merely academic. Most people would agree that a nation is a community with certain characteristics that distinguish it from other communities. The devil, however, is in the details. What traits are associated with nationhood? Are they racial, as in Hitler's 'Aryan nation'? Are they sociological, including the sorts of 'objective' and 'subjective' attributes referred to in the first definition offered in Box 1.7? Is shared citizenship enough, as former Canadian Prime Minister Pierre Trudeau apparently believed? Or is a nation simply an imagined community—not the same as an *imaginary* community—as Rupert Emerson's definition suggests?

In *Blood and Belonging*, Michael Ignatieff describes the consequences that can follow from ideas about who does and does not belong to the nation. His book examines the rise of ethnic nationalism in the former Yugoslavia after the end of the Cold War, leading to the violent breakup of the country and to a long chain of events that ultimately produced several ethnic states—Bosnia, Croatia, Kosovo, Macedonia, Montenegro, and Serbia—out of what had previously been a single country. Ignatieff, one of Canada's foremost intellectuals, reserves a chapter for Quebec and Québécois nationalism. He endeavours to explain how a society whose sons were Canada's prime ministers for over half of the twentieth century has produced a powerful nationalist movement whose goal is nothing less than the independence of Quebec.

Nationalism usually is accompanied by territorial claims. The nation is associated with some particular territory—'the homeland', 'la patrie'—that is argued to belong to the members of the nation. Quebec nationalists have asserted such claims, but so, too, have organizations representing Aboriginal Canadians, many of which are grouped together under the Assembly of First Nations. The

Politics in Focus

Box 1.7 What Is a Nation?

'A nation is a community of persons bound together by a sense of solidarity and wishing to perpetuate this solidarity through some political means. Contributing to this solidarity are common "objective" factors such as history, territory, race, ethnicity, culture, language, religion and customs and common "subjective" factors such as the consciousness of a distinct identity, an awareness of common interests and a consequent willingness to live together. Because of the existence of such factors, there is a special relationship among members of a nation which enables them to co-operate politically more easily among themselves than with outsiders.'

Canada, *Report of the Task Force on Canadian Unity* (1979)

'A nation . . . is no more and no less than the entire population of a sovereign state.'

Pierre Elliott Trudeau, 'Federalism, Nationalism, and Reason' (1965)

'Nationalism is not to be confused with patriotism. Both words are normally used in so vague a way that any definition is liable to be challenged, but one must draw a

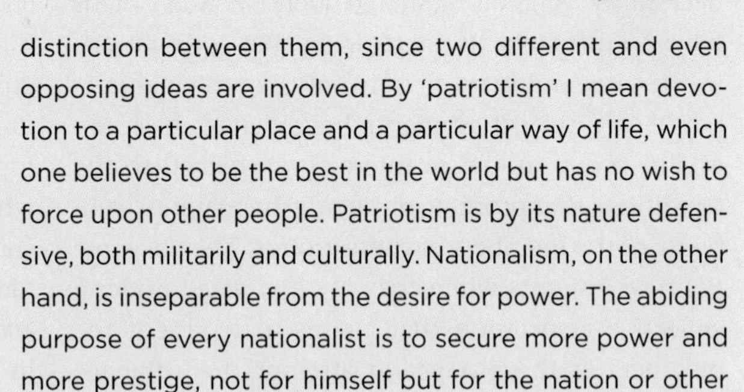

distinction between them, since two different and even opposing ideas are involved. By 'patriotism' I mean devotion to a particular place and a particular way of life, which one believes to be the best in the world but has no wish to force upon other people. Patriotism is by its nature defensive, both militarily and culturally. Nationalism, on the other hand, is inseparable from the desire for power. The abiding purpose of every nationalist is to secure more power and more prestige, not for himself but for the nation or other unit in which he has chosen to sink his own individuality.'

George Orwell, 'Notes on Nationalism' (1945)

'The simplest statement that can be made about a nation is that it is a body of people who feel that they are a nation; and it may be that when all the fine-spun analysis is concluded this will be the ultimate statement as well.'

Rupert Emerson, *From Empire to Nation* (1960)

'That this House recognize that the *québécois* form a nation within a united Canada.'

Motion passed by the Canadian House of Commons by a vote of 266 to 16, on 27 November 2006 territorial demands of organizations that claim to represent nations boil down to a demand for self-government, a demand that those making it usually justify as the democratic right of any 'people' to self-determination.

But a sense of place—a regional consciousness—may produce political demands that stop far short of independence and self-determination. A regional identity may be based on a variety of cultural, economic, institutional, and historical factors that distinguish the inhabitants of one region of a country from those of other regions. This identity may influence the political behaviour of those who share it, but their political demands generally will be less sweeping than those made by nationalist groups. When regionalism enters politics, it usually takes the form of demands for fairer treatment by the national government, better representation of the region in national political institutions, or more political autonomy for regional political authorities—all of which stop short of the usual catalogue of nationalist demands.

Cultural and social identities are not inherently political. The differences that exist between religious, ethnic, language, regional, or gender groups—to name only a few of the most important social-cultural divisions in the world today—may give rise to political conflicts when they are associated with inequalities in the economic status, social prestige, and political power of these groups. In other words, identities acquire political consequences when the members of a group, the 'identity-bearers', believe that they experience some deprivation or injustice because of their socio-cultural identity and when a 'critical mass' of the group's membership can be persuaded to take political action based on their self-identification as women, French Canadians, westerners, or whatever the identity happens to be. Political identities may not be primarily economic, but they usually have an economic dimension. Even when the stakes appear to be mainly symbolic—for example, the long-standing political debate over special status for Quebec in Canadian federalism—material considerations generally lurk behind the demands that the representatives of a social or cultural group make on the state.

Why particular identities surface in politics, while others remain 'pre-political', is a question that can only be answered by looking at the particular history and circumstances of any society. The persistence of regional, ethnolinguistic, and religious identities in the modern world and the emergence of gender inequality onto the political agendas of virtually all advanced industrial societies have confounded the earlier belief of many social scientists, and all socialists, that class divisions would come to dominate the politics of advanced capitalism. The term 'class' (like most of the concepts discussed in this chapter) means different things to different people. When used as in the labels 'upper class' or 'middle class', it refers to a social status that is determined by such measures as the societal prestige of a person's occupation, an individual's income, or one's lifestyle. Since Karl Marx's time, many social scientists have defined class as being primarily an economic concept. According to this usage, a person's class membership is determined by one's relationship to the means of economic production—the main division in society being between those who control the means of production and those who must sell their labour in order to earn a livelihood.

No one seriously argues that modern-day capitalism is characterized by a simple division between the owners of capital—the *bourgeoisie*—and their workers—the *proletariat*—as Marx predicted would happen. Advanced industrial/post-industrial democracies like Canada all have very large middle-class components. Moreover, the growth of pension funds and other large institutional investors has given a significant share of the middle class a direct ownership stake in their national economy and the economies of other countries. The last several decades have also seen a proliferation in the number of jobs that, while they involve dependence in the sense of relying on an employer for a salary, also are characterized by considerable personal freedom in terms of how work is done and even the nature of the work. These people—university professors, engineers, consultants of various sorts, physicians, and lawyers, to name a few—cannot reasonably be squeezed into a definition of the working class.

In recent years, however, the concept of class has experienced a comeback. This comeback has been linked to the phenomenon of **globalization**, which refers to the unprecedented integration of the world's economies through trade, capital flows, and internationalized production, as well as cultural integration through mass media, marketing, satellite- and computer-based information technologies, and migration. Critics argue that globalization has produced greater polarization between the affluent and the poor, both within advanced industrial democracies like Canada and between the wealthy developed countries and the poor developing countries. 'Globalization is creating, within our industrial democracies, a sort of underclass of the demoralized and impoverished', says a former United States Secretary of Labour, Robert Reich.[18] Moreover, critics argue that the ability of governments to protect the interests of society's poorest and most vulnerable groups, and to pursue policies that are unpopular with powerful corporate interests and investors, has been diminished by globalization.

In some societies class identity is a powerful force in politics. Political parties make calculated appeals to class interests and draw on different classes for their electoral support. This is not particularly true of Canada. The sense of belonging to a class is relatively weak in Canadian society. Other political identities, especially ethnolinguistic and regional identities, have overshadowed class in Canadian politics. Some commentators argue that this should be taken at face value—that the linguistic and regional interests of Canadians are simply more vital to them than is something as abstract as class. Others maintain that the consciousness of belonging to a class whose interests are at odds with those of other classes has been suppressed in various ways by political parties and elites who have vested interests in preventing the emergence of class awareness and action.

Political Fault Lines, Old and New

Some of the fault lines that shape the topography of Canadian politics extend back to the early years of this country, in some cases to the colonial era of Canada's history. The rift that separates French and English Canada is the oldest, going back to the military conquest of New France in 1759 and the subsequent domination of the francophone population by an English-speaking minority. The demographic balance would soon shift in favour of the anglophone population, a shift that lent even greater urgency to the fundamental issues of whether and how the language and distinct society of French Canada would be recognized and protected. These are fundamental questions, and they have not changed very much between the Conquest and the present-day possibility of Quebec separation.

A second fault line that reaches back to Canada's colonial past involves this country's relationship to the United States. The American Revolution and the victory of the Thirteen Colonies in the American War of Independence had a profound and enduring impact on Canada. At times this impact has been felt as a territorial threat from the United States. But for more than a century now, the economic, cultural, and political influences of the United States have replaced the fear of American troops and annexation. And over this entire period, from the Americans' Declaration of Independence in 1776 to the present day, a long shadow has been cast over Canadian politics and culture by the simple but primordially important fact of living alongside a much more powerful neighbour that resembles us in terms of historical origins, values, and dominant language but that, very clearly, is not us. David Bell argues that at the root of the identity dilemma in English Canada is a need—a need that goes back to 1776—to explain to ourselves who we are as Canadians and in what ways we are not Americans.

A third fault line of somewhat less ancient vintage than the French–English and Canada–United States ones involves regionalism. In a country as physically vast and diverse as Canada it was unavoidable that the economic and social characteristics of the regions would develop differently. Moreover, the concentration of most of the country's population and wealth in Ontario and Quebec, not surprisingly, led Ottawa to be more sensitive to the needs and preferences of the centre over those of the 'hinterland' regions.

Okay, now let's all think **asymmetrical** Triple-E...
Everything Ontario wants it gets,
Everything Quebec wants it gets,
Everyone else gets whatever is left over...
CONSTITUTIONAL CONFERENCE CALGARY
SENATE REFORM

In Canada, regional identity and its role in national politics often overshadow other identities, such as class.

Inter-regional conflict began to acquire a sharp edge in the late nineteenth century around such issues as high tariffs and railroads. This particular fault line quickly assumed an intergovernmental character, as provincial governments became the spokespersons for aggrieved regional interests in opposition to the federal government.

These three fault lines have been called by Donald Smiley the enduring axes of Canadian politics. They are not, however, the only fault lines that mark the Canadian political landscape. Some historically prominent ones, such as religious conflict and division between agrarian-rural and urban-industrial interests, have receded in importance (in the former case because of the diminished force of religion in Canadian life, and in the second because the rural and farm populations are today vastly outnumbered by those who live in urban centres and work in non-farm sectors of the economy). But other issues, including gender equality, Aboriginal rights, environmental protection, and multiculturalism, have traced new lines in Canadian politics.

The evidence of this may be seen in the issues profiled by political parties and their leaders in recent elections. Climate change, social justice, human rights, and environmental protection have become more prominent issues for all of the parties. The older issues associated with language, region, and Canada–US relations are still on the agenda, but they must compete for time and attention with these newer issues, particularly among citizens who reached voting age towards the end of the 1960s and later. The baby boomers and the generations who have followed them are more likely than older voters to be interested in issues that have to do with the quality of life rather than the standard of living. This is what Ronald Inglehart and his colleagues refer to as the post-materialist/materialist divide.[19]

In recent decades it has emerged as an important political cleavage—social scientists' term for the important lines of political division in a society—in all affluent democracies.

Recent years also have seen the re-emergence of a political fault line that, while quite prominent in the politics of many societies, has generally assumed a rather muted form in Canada and the United States: class conflict and the politics of the distribution of wealth. It is today widely believed that the forces of globalization have widened the gap between the affluent and the poor in Canada and in other advanced industrial democracies. 'A select group of wealthy Canadians are taking home fat pay cheques sweetened with bonuses and stock options. Meanwhile, a growing number of working people are seeing their incomes drop', says the Toronto-based Centre for Social Justice. 'Economic inequality is fundamentally tied to our market system', the study continues. 'This is why income inequality is at its largest spread . . . in the last generation. Additionally, when governments are in retreat . . . this bad dynamic gets even worse.'[20]

Stories and analyses linking globalization to claims of growing income inequality, increasing poverty, unemployment and homelessness, and a shrinking middle class have been common for over a decade. Leaving aside for now the fact that some of these claims are dubious at best (we will revisit this issue in Chapter 3), if they are true, or at least widely believed to be true, then we would expect to see some political fallout from such developments. In other words, the class fault line should become a more prominent feature of Canada's political landscape. To this point, however, the class polarization that many argue is taking place in Canadian society has not reached very deeply into the consciousness of most Canadians, nor has it affected very profoundly their political behaviour. Political parties that appeal to voters on class issues, notably the New Democratic Party, have not experienced a surge of support. The NDP's break-through in the 2011 federal election, which saw it win the second largest share of the popular vote and number of seats for the first time in its history, had more to do with leadership, the collapse of the Bloc Québécois and the feckless Liberal campaign than with class politics. Political protest and activism by labour unions and social justice advocacy groups probably have increased since the 1990s, in response to issues like free trade and the cutbacks to social spending that were front and centre in that decade. It is not clear, however, that such activism reflects an awakening sense of class-consciousness on the part of the general population. A more plausible argument can probably be made that the main manifestations of the new politics of class include the explosion in books, articles, and media coverage generally of globalization and class polarization, and the prominent coverage given to the ideas and activities of labour and social activists. But if behaviour at the ballot box is the litmus test of how deeply this fault line has cut into Canada's political landscape, one would have to conclude that class inequality remains a comparatively unimportant issue for most Canadians.

Listen to the 'Nouveau Politics' podcast on parties, branding, and political ideology, available at www.oupcanada.com/Brooks7e

Starting Points for Research

Mark O. Dickerson, Thomas Flanagan, and Neil Nevitte, *Introductory Readings in Government and Politics*, 4th edn (Toronto: ITP Nelson, 1995). This collection includes many excerpts from classic treatments of fundamental concepts in the study of politics, as well as a few more contemporary pieces.

George MacLean and Duncan Wood, *Politics: An Introduction* (Toronto: Oxford University Press, 2010). Written by two outstanding teachers, this introduction to the discipline situates its key concepts and issues within a Canadian perspective.

C.B. Macpherson, *The Real World of Democracy* (Toronto: CBC Enterprises, 1965). This somewhat dated classic—the references to the Cold War may disorient some readers—continues to perform the useful function of getting readers to think about the attributes of a democracy and whether there might be more varieties than the one we are familiar with in the West.

Jill Vickers, *Reinventing Political Science: A Feminist Approach* (Halifax: Fernwood, 1997). Vickers challenges readers to rethink conventional ways of understanding political life, viewed through a feminist lens.

Review Exercises

1. Nationalism is a powerful force in the modern world. From a website, a newspaper, or a magazine, find one or two stories that deal with nationalism outside of Canada. (Some websites that should prove helpful include the on-line *Globe and Mail* <www.globeandmail.ca> and the *National Post* <www.nationalpost.com>.) Would you say that the nationalist demands or actions in these stories are similar to or different from the nationalism you are familiar with in Canada? Why?
2. This chapter introduced some concepts and issues relevant to Canadian political life. An easy way to tell what political issues are current in Canada is to look at the political cartoons included in Canadian print journalism. Find a Canadian political cartoon that relates to a political issue with which you are familiar. One of the best sources is: <www.artizans.com>. Click on 'Political toons—CDN'. What message do you think the cartoonist is trying to communicate? Do you think the cartoonist's treatment of the subject is fair or biased? In what ways and why?
3. How does identity affect your political behaviour? If you were asked to describe who you are and what aspects of your self-image are most important to you, what would you list? When you see or hear a newsperson, a politician, or a professor do you notice his or her race, gender, signs of ethnicity, accent, or other features of the person? Do you think other people notice such traits?
4. Which country is more democratic, Canada or the United States? Canada or Sweden? You probably have an answer to the first comparison, but you may not be certain about the second. What criteria have you used in arriving at your conclusions and how would you set about measuring whether a society has more or less of the attributes that you associate with democracy? In order to guide your thinking about how the concept of democracy can be operationalized, go to the website for Freedom House: <www.freedomhouse.org>. Does Freedom House's ranking of Canada seem reasonable to you?

Part II
The Societal Context of Politics

In every society certain issues and divisions have a more prominent status and are more fundamental to an overall understanding of its politics and government than are others. In the United States, for example, the issue of race and the relations between white and black America are at the centre of that country's political history. In the case of France, the values of the French Revolution continue to shape the political conversation in that country, influencing policies and ideas that concern the integration of the large black, Maghreban (North African), and Muslim minorities that now live in France. In the case of Canada, the fact that English and French are spoken by large portions of the population and that the French-speaking population is concentrated largely in one region of the country, with a history that predates the emergence of an anglophone majority in Canada, continues to influence the politics of the country. The arrival of millions of immigrants from countries outside of Europe has changed Canadian demography in important ways over the last several decades, having a significant impact on Canadian politics. The country's long-standing relationship to the United States, a relationship that involves a complex web of interconnections through trade, investment, population, culture, and foreign policy, has always been a major factor affecting Canadian politics and government. In short, the societal context within which political life unfolds is crucial to an understanding of the nature of any country's politics and of the distribution of power and influence.

Some argue, however, that the actions of the state and their impacts on society are at least as important as the effects that societal forces have on the policies and institutions of government, and that sometimes these actions of the state are more important. State actors, including key political leaders and bureaucrats, often have a determining influence on what happens in politics, shaping the contours of the political conversation, the interests and voices that are listened to, and the outcomes that ensue. But only rarely are elected and appointed officials able to ignore the pressure of ideas and interests from the society around them. These ideas and interests, including the significant **political identities** in a society, its economic structure, and the major fault lines that cut across its landscape, provide the broader context within which political behaviour and policy-making take place. These societal factors are the subject of this next section of the book.

Many Canadians take pride in the values they feel distinguish them from other countries, most notably the United States, and consider symbols such as the Canadian flag outward representations of what they believe is their country's distinct political culture, including tolerance, compassion, and collectivity.

2 Political Culture

Ideas constitute an important element of political life. This chapter surveys some of the key issues pertaining to the role of ideas in Canadian politics and discusses the political ideas of Canadians. The following topics are examined:

- Ideologies, values, and institutions.
- Fragment theory.
- Formative events.
- Economic structures and political ideas.
- The political ideas of Canadians.
- The nature of Canadian and American value differences.
- Community.
- Freedom.
- Equality.
- Citizen expectations for government.
- How different are Canadian and American values?

There is no more Canadian pastime than reflecting on what it means to be a Canadian. Unlike the French, the English, the Chinese, the Russians, and the Americans, to name a handful of other peoples, Canadians have long obsessed over what it is in their values and beliefs that makes them distinctive, that sets them apart from others. In recent years some societies that have long been thought of as having quite confident self-identities seem to have acquired the Canadian penchant for introspection. The French government launched its Grand débat sur l'identité française in 2009. The issue of the consequences of multiculturalism for the American identity has roiled the waters of that country's politics and intellectual life for a generation. But in neither France nor the United States has the question of national identity been asked so urgently and often—and with answers seeming to be so elusive—as in Canada.

In fact, this long-standing and perennial search for the cultural essence of the Canadian condition has most often been about identifying and explaining the ways in which the values and beliefs of Canadians are different from those of Americans. Various answers have been given over the years. Until the latter half of the twentieth century, these answers more or less boiled down to this: Canadians believe in a more orderly, less individualistic society than that of the United States, in which the state is expected to engage in activities that promote the welfare of society and the development of an independent Canada. The affective tie to Great Britain remained strong well into the middle of the last century, and indeed many Canadians thought of themselves as British and of their country as more British than American in its institutions, values, and heritage.

This answer to the question of what it means to be a Canadian has seemed less plausible as Canada has become less British over the last couple of generations. Many still believe, however, that Canadian values continue to be less individualistic and less hostile to government than in the United States. Such words as 'tolerant', 'compassionate', and 'caring' are often used in comparisons between the two countries, always suggesting that Canadians have more of these qualities than Americans. And it is not just Canadians who make this claim. On the American left, Canada, for more than a generation now, has served the function of a sort of 'Nirvana to the north', a place that shows what is possible in public policy and social relations and a model to be emulated.[1] As the bonds joining Canada to the United States economically and culturally have multiplied and deepened, the question of what it means to be a Canadian continues to be a sort of national obsession.

This is not true, however, in French-speaking Canada, whose centre of gravity is Quebec, where over 90 per cent of Canadian francophones live. Insulated from American cultural influences by language and for much of their history by the strongly Catholic character of their society, French Canadians have been much less likely than their English-speaking compatriots to define themselves and their history with reference to the United States. They have long worried about anglicizing influences on their language and culture, but they have tended to see the challenge as coming chiefly from within Canada, with its English-speaking majority, rather than from the United States. This perceived challenge has provided the basis for the rise of, first, French-Canadian nationalism and, more recently, Quebec nationalism. Over the last generation, as non-traditional sources of immigration became increasingly important in Quebec, the question of what it means to be Québécois received greater attention. But in answering it, few French-speaking Canadians would think of using as a starting point the United States and what are believed to be American values and beliefs.

Ideologies, Values, and Institutions

Ideas assume various forms in political life. When they take the form of a set of interrelated beliefs about how society is organized and how it ought to function—an interpretive map for understanding the world—this is an **ideology**. An ideology spills beyond the boundaries of politics to embrace beliefs and judgements about other social relationships, including economic ones. This holistic character of ideologies distinguishes them from more limited political value systems. The fact that most people are not aware of having ideological leanings, and might be puzzled or even startled at being labelled a 'conservative', a 'liberal', or a 'socialist', does not mean that ideology is irrelevant to their political beliefs and actions. When the politics of a society is described as 'pragmatic' and 'non-ideological' this may simply indicate that a particular ideology dominates to such a degree that it has become the conventional wisdom.

Someone who regularly and consciously thinks about political matters and other social relationships in ideological terms is an ideologue, a person who is consciously committed to a particular interpretive map of society. Most people are not ideological in this sense of the word.

If ideology is the currency of the political activist, political culture is the medium of the general population. A political culture consists of the characteristic values, beliefs, and behaviours of a society's members in regard to politics. The very definition of what is considered by most people to be political and an appropriate subject for government action is an aspect of political culture. The relative weight that people assign to such values as personal freedom, equality, social order, and national prestige is another aspect of political culture. The expectations that citizens tend to hold for their participation in public life and the patterns of voter turnout, party activism, social movement activities, and other politically relevant forms of behaviour are part of political culture, as is the pattern of knowledge about political symbols, institutions, actors, and issues. Beliefs about whether government actions tend to be benign or malign, and towards whom, also are part of the political culture.

Obviously, people will not hold identical views on these matters, nor will their participation in politics conform to a single template. It is reasonable, nevertheless, to speak of a society as having certain core values or a belief system that is shared by most of its members. Political culture may be thought of as a cluster of typical orientations towards the political universe. The fact that in one society this cluster may be comparatively scattered and marked by division between different segments of society, while in another it is relatively compact, is in itself an observation about political culture.

In Canada, research on political culture has focused primarily on the differences that exist between the politically relevant attitudes and beliefs of French-speaking and English-speaking Canadians, and on the question of whether English-speaking Canada is characterized by regional political cultures. To determine whether significant and persistent differences exist, political scientists have attempted to measure such things as levels of political knowledge and participation, feelings of political efficacy (people's sense of whether their participation in politics matters) and alienation (variously defined as apathy, estrangement from the political system, or the belief that politics is systematically biased against one's interests and values), attitudes towards political authority and the different levels of government, and the sense of belonging to a particular regional or linguistic community.

A third way in which ideas are relevant for politics is through individual *personality*. One of the most often repeated claims about Canadians is that they are less likely to question and challenge authority than are Americans. Canadians are said to be more deferential. We examine this claim later in the chapter. Several of the standard questions used in studies of political culture, such as those dealing with political efficacy, trust in public officials, and emotional feelings towards political authorities, tap politically relevant dimensions of personality. Much of the research on the political consequences of individual personality traits has focused on the relationship between a person's general attitudes towards authority and non-conformity, on the one hand, and, on the other, his or her political attitudes on such issues as the protection of civil liberties, toleration of political dissent, the group rights of minorities, and attitudes towards public authorities. The main conclusion of this research is that general personality traits show up in an individual's political ideas and action.

One way of categorizing political ideas—perhaps the most popular way—is to describe them as being *left-wing*, *right-wing*, or *centrist/moderate*. These labels are used to signify the broader ideological premises believed to lie behind an action, opinion, or statement. For example, a newspaper editorial slamming welfare fraud and calling for mandatory 'workfare' would be called right-wing by some, as would a proposal to cut taxes for the affluent or to eliminate public funding for abortions. Proposals to increase the minimum wage, ban the use of replacement workers during a strike or lockout, or increase spending on assistance for developing countries are the sorts of measures likely to be described as left-wing. Centrist or moderate positions, as these terms suggest, fall between the right and left wings of the political spectrum. They attempt to achieve some middle ground between the arguments and principles of **left** and **right**. The **centre** is, virtually by definition, the mainstream of a society's politics, and those who occupy this location on the political spectrum are likely to view themselves as being non-ideological and pragmatic.

The right–left political spectrum is one way to map out the ideologies embedded in actions, opinion, and statements. Some would suggest, however, that the ideological gap between the principal 'right' and 'centre' parties in Canada, the Conservative Party and the Liberal Party, is quite small, and even the main party on the 'left', the New Democratic Party, if it ever attained power at the federal level, would drift to the centre, as has most often been the case in recent years with NDP governments at the provincial level.

'Right' and 'left' are shorthand labels for conflicting belief systems. These beliefs include basic notions about how society, the economy, and politics operate, as well as ideas about how these matters *should* be arranged. Generally speaking, to be on the right in Anglo-American societies means that one subscribes to an *individualistic* belief system. Such a person is likely to believe that what one achieves in life is due principally to his or her own efforts—that the welfare of society is best promoted by allowing individuals to pursue their own interests and that modern government is too expensive and too intrusive. To be on the left, however, is to prefer a set of beliefs that may be described as *collectivist*. A leftist is likely to attribute greater weight to social and economic circumstances as determinants of one's opportunities and achievements than does someone on the right. Moreover, those on the left have greater doubts about the economic efficiency and social fairness of free markets, and have greater faith in the ability of government to intervene in ways that promote the common good. Although those on the left may be critical of particular actions and institutions of government, they reject the claim that the size and scope of government need to be trimmed. Smaller government, they would argue, works to the advantage of the affluent and privileged, at the expense of the poor and disadvantaged.

In reality, the politics of left and right is more complicated than these simplified portraits suggest. For example, while opposition to abortion, same-sex marriage, and assisted suicide generally is viewed as a right-wing position, many who subscribe to all the elements of right-wing politics listed above may support these policies. Such people, sometimes labelled **libertarians**, believe that individuals should be allowed the largest possible margin of freedom in all realms of life, including those that involve moral choices. The libertarian right is, however, smaller and less of a political force than the socially conservative right. Social conservatives are distinguished by such stands as opposition to abortion and same-sex marriage, support for capital punishment and stiffer jail sentences, and rejection of forms of pluralism, which they believe are corrosive of traditional values. The wellsprings of their conservatism are quite different from those of libertarianism, but their shared antipathy for certain aspects of the modern welfare state cause libertarians and social conservatives to be grouped together on the right. The fissures in this alliance, and the limitations of the right–left categorization of political ideas, become apparent when the issue is one of personal morality (e.g., abortion, homosexuality, religious teachings in public schools).

Left versus right may also be of limited use, and even misleading, when it comes to environmental issues. It is true that the modern environmental movement and 'green' political parties are clearly on the left, as seen in their skepticism towards private enterprise and market forces, their support for state measures, from taxation and regulation to outright bans on certain behaviours, and their general opposition to military solutions to international conflicts. But support for protection of the environment and particularly for conservation of natural habitats and species may also be generated by values and beliefs that are usually thought of as conservative. Social conservatives, whose conservatism is linked to their religious beliefs, often believe that protection of the environment is a moral duty. They see human beings as the stewards of nature, entrusted with its use but also obliged to protect it and ensure that it is passed on to future generations in a state that enables those later generations to profit from nature's bounty. This sort of environmentalism has very different wellsprings from that based on the premises that there are physical limits to economic and population growth and that capitalist economics is the road to guaranteed environmental catastrophe.

The waters separating the ideological categories of left and right are further muddied by the exigencies of governing and what is required for re-election. Different parties may claim to be quite different ideological animals and may be clearly distinguishable during the heat of an election campaign. But once in power the pragmatics attached to future electoral success and to successful governance mean that the governing party moves to the centre to meet the needs and demands of the broader society rather than merely those of their core constituency.

Despite various limitations, and the fact that labels like 'right' and 'left' are more often used to dismiss and discredit one's opponents in politics than to inform in a dispassionate way, the right–left spectrum taps a crucial and enduring truth of modern politics. This involves the issue of the character of the good society and how best to achieve it. We have said that the underlying struggle is essentially one between collectivist and individualist visions of the good society. These visions differ in how they view the conditions that promote human dignity and in their conceptions of social justice. For example, it is often said that one of the cultural characteristics distinguishing Canadians from Americans is the greater propensity of Canadians to sacrifice individual self-interest for the good of the community. In this connection Canada's health-care system is invoked whenever Canadian–American cultural differences are discussed, and fears expressed by Canadian nationalists that Canada is sliding down the slope towards American values and public policies (see Box 2.1). What the watchdogs of Canadian-style health care are really saying is that the more collectivist Canadian health-care model provides greater dignity for individuals and is fairer than the more individualistic American system.

Defenders of the American health-care system often retort that Canadian health policy is a form of socialism. **Socialism** is one of a trio of

Politics in Focus

Box 2.1 Health Care and Canadian Culture: Two Views

In their discussions with me, Canadians have been clear that they still strongly support the core values on which our health care system is premised—equity, fairness, and solidarity. These values are tied to their understanding of citizenship. Canadians consider equal and timely access to medically necessary health care services on the basis of need as a right of citizenship, not a privilege of status or wealth.

Roy Romanow, from the Commission on the Future of Health Care in Canada, *Final Report* (2002), xvi

There is no greater fallacy than the idea that Canada's system of socialized medicine is essential to our system of national values. Without it, Roy Romanow and others tell us, we would not be Canadian.

This is intellectual hogwash.

Canada had existed as a distinct country for 101 years before the introduction of a form of socialized medicine in 1968. Millions upon millions of Canadians were born, flourished, received health care and died without giving a thought to the 'core value' of a state monopoly on the provision of essential health care. They defined their country sometimes as a rugged northern land, sometimes as a British kingdom, sometimes as a bastion of personal freedom, sometimes as an improvement on the US. Canadian lumberjacks, farmers and their wives, hockey players, and the men who seized Vimy Ridge in 1917 had no interest in the idea of a nanny state, and for the most part believed deeply in notions of personal responsibility and freedom.

Michael Bliss, 'Contrary History: Socialized Medicine and Canada's Decline', *Canadian Medical Association Journal* (July 2007)

ideologies that have greatly influenced the politics of Western societies since the American and French revolutions. The other two are **liberalism** and **conservatism**. The idea that Canada's health-care model both reflects and is vital to the protection of Canadian values has often found its way into election campaign advertising, particularly to attack parties and candidates who appear to favour significant reform of the system. They are portrayed as being un-Canadian and, worse, American in their sympathies and values.

The importance of these ideologies in defining the contours of political life is suggested by the fact that major and minor political parties in many Western democracies continue to use the names liberal, conservative, and socialist.

In Canada, the two parties that have dominated national politics for most of the country's history are the Liberal Party and the Conservative Party (the Conservative Party was renamed the Progressive Conservative Party in 1942; since December 2003, when it merged with the Canadian Alliance, it is once again known as the Conservative Party of Canada). They have their roots in the ideological divisions of the nineteenth century. Over time, however, the labels have lost much if not all of their informative value. Today, the ideological distance between a Liberal and a Conservative is likely to be small. Indeed, at the beginning of the twentieth century the astute French observer André Siegfried had already remarked that the Liberal and Conservative parties were virtually indistinguishable in terms of their ideological principles. They and their supporters shared in the dominant liberal tradition that pervaded Canada and the United States.

At the heart of this tradition was the primacy of individual freedom. *Classical liberalism*—liberalism as understood until the middle of the twentieth century—was associated with freedom of religious choice and practice, free enterprise and free trade in the realm of economics, and freedom of expression and association in politics. These liberal values constituted a sort of national ethos in the United States, where they were enshrined in the Declaration of Independence and in the American Bill of Rights. In the colonies of British North America, which would become Canada in the late nineteenth century, liberalism's dominance was somewhat more tentative than in the United States. This was due to the streak of conservatism kept alive by some of the elites in colonial society, notably the Catholic Church, the Church of England, and the British colonial authorities.

Classical conservatism was based on the importance of tradition. It accepted human inequality—social, political, and economic—as part of the natural order of things. Conservatives emphasized the importance of continuity with the past and the preservation of law and order. They were wary of innovation and opposed such basic liberal reforms as equal political rights for all men (even liberals did not come around to the idea of equal political rights for women until the twentieth century). Unlike liberals, who located the source of all just rule in the people, conservatives maintained that God and tradition were the true founts of political authority. Consequently, they supported an established church and were strong defenders of the Crown's traditional prerogatives against the rival claims of elected legislatures.

Although no party having the label 'socialist' has ever achieved the status of even an important minor party in either Canada or the United States, socialist ideology has been influential in various ways. *Classical socialism* was based on the principle of equality of condition, a radical egalitarianism that distinguished socialist doctrine from liberalism's advocacy of equality of opportunity. Socialists supported a vastly greater role for the state in directing the economy, better working conditions and greater rights for workers vis-à-vis their employers, and reforms like public health care, unemployment insurance, income assistance for the indigent, public pensions, and universal access to public education that became the hallmarks of the twentieth-century welfare state.

The usefulness of these three 'isms' as benchmarks for reading the political map is no longer very great. There are two main reasons for this. First, all three of these classical ideologies, but especially liberalism and conservatism, mean something quite different today from what they meant 100–200 years ago. For example, contemporary liberalism does not place individual freedom above all else. Instead, modern liberals are distinguished by their belief that governments can and should act to alleviate hardships experienced by the poor and the oppressed. They are more likely to worry about the problems of minority group rights than individual freedoms, or at any rate to see the improvement of the conditions of disadvantaged minorities as a necessary step towards the achievement of real freedom for the members of these groups. Modern liberalism also has become associated with support for multiculturalism and openness towards non-traditional lifestyles and social institutions.

The doctrine of classical conservatism has disappeared from the scene in contemporary democracies, leaving what has been called the conservative outlook or 'conservative mind'.[2] Modern conservatives tend to embrace the economic beliefs that once were characteristic of liberals. And like classical liberals they defend the principle of equality of opportunity. They are more likely to place the protection of personal freedoms before the advancement of minority rights. As in earlier times, conservatism is generally viewed as the ideology of the privileged in society. It is worth noting, however, that conservative politicians and political parties receive much of their support from middle-class voters whose hands are far from the levers of economic power and social influence.

Of the three classical ideologies, the meaning of socialism has changed the least. There is today, however, much less confidence among socialists that state ownership of the means of economic production and distribution is desirable. Modern socialists, or *social democrats* as they often call themselves, temper their advocacy of an egalitarian society with an acceptance of capitalism and the inequalities that inevitably are generated by free-market economies. The defence of the rights of society's least-well-off elements, which has always been a characteristic of socialism, is today carried out largely under the banner of other 'isms', including feminism, multiculturalism, and environmentalism. In Canada and the United States these other collectivist–egalitarian belief systems have more of an impact on politics than does socialism.

A second reason why the traditional trio of 'isms' is no longer a reliable guide to politics has to do with the character of political divisions in modern society. The aristocracy of land and title and the deferential social norms that nurtured classical conservatism belong to the past. They live on as the folklore of castles and estates in the once rigidly hierarchical societies of Europe, in the continuing pomp of hereditary royalty, and in Britain's House of Lords. Otherwise, classical conservatism has no legitimacy in the middle-class cultures of Western societies. In the United States the structures and values that supported classical conservatism never existed, and in Canada they achieved only a precarious and passing toehold.

The struggles of liberalism in the eighteenth and nineteenth centuries, and of socialism in the nineteenth and twentieth, have largely been won. Liberals fought for free-market reforms and the extension of political rights and freedoms, first to the new propertied classes created by the Industrial Revolution and then more widely to the (male) adult population. They fought against conservatives who dug in to protect the political privileges of a hereditary aristocracy and the economic dominance of the traditional land-owning classes. Socialists fought for more government control over the economy, for workers' rights like collective bargaining and limits on the hours of work, and for the welfare state. They fought against both the vestiges of conservatism and liberalism's emphasis on individualism.

The classical ideologies were formed and evolved in response to one another as well as to the social and economic conditions in which they were rooted. Today, Canadians, Americans, and Western Europeans live in affluent, middle-class societies that bear little resemblance to those of the nineteenth century, when Europe was a tilting ground for the rivalries between conservatism, liberalism, and socialism. As the character of Western societies has changed, so too have the ideologies that slug it out in their politics.

Does this mean, as some have argued, that the traditional ideologies are obsolete, unsuited to the realities of modern society? This is the **'end of ideology'** thesis that American sociologist Daniel Bell put forward in the 1960s. 'In the western world', he argued, 'there is today, a rough consensus among intellectuals on political issues: the acceptance of a Welfare State; the desirability of decentralized power; a system of mixed economy and of political pluralism.'[3] Some commentators dismiss the traditional 'isms' and the left–centre–right ideological grid as outmoded ways of thinking about politics.

It is a great mistake, however, to underestimate the continuing importance of ideology in politics. Although the traditional ideologies now must jostle with feminism, environmentalism, multiculturalism, and other 'isms' on a more crowded playing field, and despite the changes that have taken place in the meanings of the classical ideologies, they continue to be useful, though certainly not infallible, guides to understanding political ideas. The right-versus-left or individualism-versus-collectivism dichotomy is probably the most useful. In the real world, however, we should seldom expect to find that the ideas of an individual, or those associated with a group or political party, can be neatly categorized as one or the other.

Those who would argue that the individualism/collectivism dichotomy has become obsolete and that politics has become largely a debate about means rather than ends underestimate the continuing vitality of the struggle between what we might call competing images of the moral order (see Box 2.2). Many of the most profoundly felt differences of opinion on issues of importance in contemporary public life, from abortion and same-sex marriage to issues of trade and taxation, are based on the different ideas that people have about what social, economic, and political arrangements are consistent with personal dignity, justice, social order, and the good society. Those on the right of the modern ideological divide are less likely than those on the left to look to state action for the advancement and protection of the moral order that they prefer. This may be seen in the ongoing debate over the consequences of globalization—a debate in which moral considerations are seldom far from the surface.

Explaining Ideas and Institutions

Explanations of Canadians' political ideas, and of the institutions that embody them, can be grouped into three main camps. They include **fragment theory**, the role of formative events, and economic explanations. Each of these perspectives stresses a different set of causes in explaining the origins of Canadians' political ideas and institutions, and the forces that have shaped their development down to the present.

Fragment Theory: European Parents and Cultural Genes

Canada, along with other New World societies, was founded by immigrants from Europe. Aboriginal communities already existed, of course, but the sort of society that developed in Canada had its roots and inspiration in the values and practices of European civilization. Those who chose to immigrate to the New World—or who were forced to, as were the convicts sent from Britain to Australia—did not represent a cross-section of the European society from which they came. They were unrepresentative in terms of their social class (the privileged tended to remain in Europe, although primogeniture traditions forced many of the younger scions of privilege to emigrate), their occupations, and in some cases in terms of their religion. Moreover, immigration tended to occur in waves, coinciding with particular epochs in the ideological development of Europe. New World societies were 'fragments' of the European societies that gave birth to them. They were fragment societies because they represented only a part of the socio-economic and cultural spectrum of the European society from which they originated, and also because their creation

Governing Realities

Box 2.2 European vs American Models of Society?

The economic crisis that began in 2008 and that pulled the global economy into recession was widely blamed on the American housing market. Years of very low interest rates and lending policies that allowed for the accumulation of enormous and ultimately unsustainable levels of private indebtedness collapsed like a house of cards once it became clear that the assets of many banks and investment firms were grossly overvalued. The crisis was seen as provoked by unbridled greed—CEO and other management compensation became a lightning rod for criticism—and a failure of governments to adequately regulate financial markets. The American model—individualistic, capitalistic, and anti-statist—came in for a pummelling in the United States and especially abroad.

Two years later the crisis morphed into something rather different. It began with Greece and the inability of that country's government to pay its debts. These debts were, it was discovered, rather formidable and had been made possible by the fact that as a member of the euro zone—the 17 European Union (EU) countries who share a common currency—Greece had been able to borrow money for many years at rates of interest more favourable than its economic conditions warranted. This would not have been seen as calamitous if the only victims of default were expected to be some banks and other private investors. But the prospect of Greece defaulting on its loans had wider implications for the status of the euro, leading the other euro-zone countries, but especially Germany, and the IMF to put together a bailout plan for Greece and a contingency fund in the event that another euro-zone country also became incapable of paying its creditors. Spain, Italy, and Ireland were among the countries whose finances appeared to teeter on the brink.

This was a different crisis that had nothing to do with American housing markets and CEOs receiving gargantuan compensation packages. It was a crisis provoked by state spending, not private lending. By the late spring coincided with a particular ideological epoch. The timing of settlement is crucial. Along with whatever material possessions immigrants brought with them, they also brought along their 'cultural baggage': values and beliefs acquired in Europe and transplanted into the New World. As David Bell and Lorne Tepperman observe, 'the "fragment theory" sees the culture of founding groups as a kind of *genetic code* that does not determine but sets limits to later cultural developments.'[4]

But why should the ideas of the founders carry such weight that they shape the political values and beliefs of subsequent generations? Fragment theory is rather weak on this point, arguing that the fragment's ideological system 'congeals' at some point—the ideology of the founders becomes the dominant ideology—and that immigrants who arrive subsequently have little choice but to assimilate to the dominant values and beliefs that are already in place. The transmission of the fragment culture from generation to generation presumably depends on social structures and political institutions that date from the founding period, and embody the dominant ideas of the founding immigrants.

Canada has been characterized as a two-fragment society. French Canada was founded by immigrants from France who brought with them their Catholicism and *feudal* ideas about social and political relations. Feudal society is characterized by the existence of fairly rigid social classes, connected to one another by a web of mutual rights and duties based on tradition, and by the exclusion of most people from the full right to participate in politics. According to French-Canadian historian Fernand Ouellet, this was the ideological and social condition of New France when the colony was conquered by British forces in 1759.[5] Cut off from the social and political developments unleashed by the French Revolution (1789)—emigration from France, with the exception

of 2010 the European story had acquired dimensions far beyond tiny Greece and its messy finances. It was, observers now said, the European model itself that was in question. That model was based on a more generous welfare state, shielding individuals and families from a greater number of risks that were experienced under the American model. Retirement ages in Western Europe came in for particular criticism. In some countries the average age of retirement was below 60. In France, the Socialist government of François Mitterand in the early 1980s had legislated 60 as the age at which one became eligible for a full public pension. But populations were aging across the EU, with proportionately fewer workers supporting proportionately more pensioners. The left dug in its heels in defence of existing retirement ages and benefits, while the European right argued that they were unrealistic and unsustainable.

Right versus left: the American model of smaller, less generous government versus the Western European welfare state. It was clear that what some had argued was an old and outdated way of viewing political conflict was still very much alive and relevant.

Where did Canada fit into this debate? It is usual to say that Canada falls somewhere between the American and Western European models, being somewhat more statist and collectivist in thinking and policies than the United States, but not as left-leaning as such societies as France, the Netherlands, the Scandinavian democracies and others. Canada did not fare as badly as most capitalist democracies in the crisis that began in 2008, avoiding the housing collapse that afflicted the United States and the huge unemployment—20 per cent in Spain—experienced in some countries. So the conversation about right versus left tended to be somewhat more muted than in these other societies where the scale of economic hardship and its social costs focused attention more sharply on the ideological nature of the economic crisis and its solutions.

Not a separatist BQ MP around!
Not a St. Jean Baptiste Day leftover or
Quebec City rioter in sight! Make
it quick man!
Happy Canada Day...eh?

The long-standing division between French and English Canada has been one of the chief obstacles to the development of a confident national identity in Canada.

of some priests, virtually dried up—French Canada's ideological development was shaped by its origins as a feudal fragment of pre-revolutionary France. Institutions, chiefly the Catholic Church, the dominant social institution in French Canada until well into the twentieth century, operated to maintain this pre-liberal inheritance.

The 'cultural genes' of English Canada are, according to fragment theory, very different. English Canada was originally populated by immigrants from the United States. These were the so-called Loyalists; those who found themselves on the losing side of the American War of Independence (1776). They migrated north to British colonies that were overwhelmingly French-speaking.[6] The 'cultural baggage' they carried with them has been the subject of much debate, but the general view seems to be that they held predominantly *liberal* political beliefs. The liberalism that emerged in the eighteenth century was built around the idea of individual freedom: freedom in politics, in religion, and in economic relations. One of its crucial political tenets was the idea that government was based on the consent of the people. So why did the Loyalists leave the United States, a society whose political independence was founded on liberal beliefs?

The defenders of fragment theory offer different answers to this question. Some argue that the liberalism of the Loyalists was diluted by *conservative* or *Tory* political beliefs: deference towards established authority and institutions, an acceptance of inequality between classes as the natural condition of society, and a greater stress on preserving social order than on protecting individual freedoms.[7] Others reject the view that Tory values were ever a legitimate part of English Canada's political culture, arguing that this belief system had no roots in the pre-revolutionary Thirteen Colonies and therefore

TABLE 2.1 Liberalism, Conservatism, and Socialism: Classical and Contemporary Versions

I.	CLASSICAL	Liberalism	Conservatism	Socialism
a.	Characteristics of the Good Society	Individual freedom is maximized; politics and economics are free and competitive; achievements and recognition are due to personal merit and effort; a capitalist economy will produce the greatest happiness for society and maximize material welfare; personal dignity depends on the individual's own actions.	The traditional social order is preserved; individuals are members of social groups that are linked together by a web of rights and obligations; those born in privileged circumstances have an obligation to those below them on the social ladder; there is a natural social hierarchy based on inherited status; personal dignity depends on one's conformity to the norms and behaviour of one's social group.	Social and economic equality are maximized; private ownership of property is replaced by its collective ownership and management; competition is replaced by co-operation; the welfare of society is maximized through economic and social planning; personal dignity depends on work and one's solidarity with the working class.
b.	Nature of Government	All just government rests on the consent of the governed; party system is competitive; the state is subordinate to society; government should be small and its scope limited; the elected legislature is the most powerful component of the state; separation between church and state.	The rights and responsibilities of those who govern derive from God and tradition; the state's fundamental role is to preserve social order; the state is superior to society and is owed obedience by all citizens and groups; the Crown is the most powerful component of the state; the size and scope of government are small by modern standards, but are not limited by liberalism's suspicion of the state; the state recognizes an official church.	All just government rests on the consent of the governed and the principles of social and economic equality; the state should control crucial sectors of the economy; government has a responsibility to redistribute wealth from the wealthy to the less fortunate social classes; government is large and its scope wide; a socialist state is the embodiment of the will and interest of the working class; no officially recognized religion.
c.	Chief Supporters	Industrialists, merchants, property-owning individuals.	Landed aristocracy, established church, military officers and agents of the Crown whose status and income depended on maintenance of the traditional social hierarchy.	Organized workers; intellectuals.
II.	**CONTEMPORARY**	**Liberalism**	**Conservatism**	**Socialism**
a.	Characteristics of the Good Society	Individual freedom is balanced by protection for disadvantaged elements in society and recognition of group rights; capitalism must be regulated by the state to ensure the social and economic well-being of the majority; social diversity should be recognized and promoted through public education, hiring, and the policies of governments; social entitlements are respected, including a certain standard of living and access to decent education, health care, and accommodation; personal dignity is based on freedom and social equality.	Individual freedom is more important than social equality and should not be sacrificed to the latter; state regulation of capitalism should be kept to a minimum and should not be used to promote any but economic goals; social diversity is a fact, but is not something that should be actively promoted by government; individuals should be responsible for their own lives and policies that encourage dependency on the state should be avoided; personal dignity depends on one's own efforts and is undermined by collectivist policies and too much emphasis on promoting social and economic equality.	Social and economic equality values; individual rights must be subordinated to collective goals; small-scale capitalism has its place, but state economic planning and active participation in the economy are still necessary to promote both economic competitiveness and social fairness; the environmental consequences of all public and private actions must be considered; systemic discrimination based on gender, race, and ethnicity is eliminated through government policies; personal dignity depends on social and economic equality.

continued

TABLE 2.1 continued

b.	Nature of Government	The state has a responsibility to protect and promote the welfare of the disadvantaged; the post-WWII welfare state is a necessary vehicle for ensuring social justice; government should reflect the diversity of society in its personnel and policies; the state should not be aligned with any religious group.	The state's primary function should be to maintain circumstances in which individuals can pursue their own goals and life plans; government should be small and the level of taxation low in order to minimize interference with individual choice; government should not remain neutral between different systems of morality, but should promote traditional values through the schools and through support for the traditional family.	The state should redistribute wealth in society and ensure the social and economic equality of its citizens; some modern socialists argue that political power should be decentralized to community-level groups as the best way to ensure democratic responsiveness and accountability; the state should reflect the society in its personnel and policies; traditional value systems are based on systemic discrimination and oppression, and government has a responsibility to eradicate these values.
c.	Chief Supporters	Many middle-of-the-road advocacy groups within the feminist, environmental, and multicultural movements; public-sector workers; middle-class intellectuals in the universities and the media; the national Liberal Party and much of the Bloc Québécois; think-tanks, including Canadian Policy Research Networks, the Institute for Research on Public Policy, and the Canada West Foundation.	Business groups; middle-class workers in the private sector; the mainstream of the Conservative Party of Canada; think-tanks, including the Fraser Institute, the Atlantic Institute for Market Studies, and the C.D. Howe Institute.	More extreme advocacy groups within the feminist environmental, and multi-cultural movements; some elements in the NDP and within organized labour; the Green Party; think-tanks, including the Canadian Centre for Policy Alternatives, the Caledon Institute of Social Policy, and the Canadian Council on Social Development; some university-based intellectuals; the Council of Canadians.

could not have been exported to English Canada through the Loyalist migration.[8] The Loyalists were 'anti-American Yankees' who had rejected American independence because of their loyalty to the British Empire and to the monarchy, and their dislike of republican government (or, as they were more likely to put it, 'mob rule'). Their quarrel was not with liberal ideology, as shown by the fact that they immediately clamoured for elected assemblies and the political rights they had been used to in America. Bell and Tepperman thus argue that:

> Forced to leave their country, the Tories, or Loyalists, suffered profound doubts. Expulsion kept the Loyalist from basing a fragment identity on the liberal principles of John Locke. Made to give up his real identity, the Canadian Loyalist invented a new one. As a substitute, it was not quite good enough, of course. How could it be, when he had continuously to deny its true nature, liberalism? 'The typical Canadian', an Englishman observed a hundred years ago, 'tells you that he is not, but he is a Yankee—a Yankee in the sense in which we use the term at home, as synonymous with everything that smacks of democracy.' The Loyalist in Canada is thereafter always a paradox, an 'anti-American Yankee'. Only one path leads out of his dilemma: creating a myth that helps him survive. In this myth, he insists that he is British.[9]

The debate over how important non-liberal values were among the Loyalists is not merely academic. Contemporary analyses of English Canada as a more deferential and conservative society than the United States often trace this alleged difference back to the original ideological mixtures of the two societies. A second reason why the debate matters involves the explanation for Canadian socialism. Some of those who contend that conservative values were an important and legitimate component of English Canada's original cultural inheritance go on to argue that the emergence of socialism in Canada was facilitated by, first, the fact that liberalism never achieved the status of an unchallenged national creed (as it did in the United States) and, second, the fact that social class was not a foreign concept in English Canada.[10] Conservatism and socialism, according to this view, are two varieties of collectivism.

Formative Events: Counter-Revolution and the Conquest

Societies, like human beings, are marked by certain major events at critical periods in their development. These events are 'formative' in the sense that they make it more probable that a society will evolve along particular lines, instead of along others. In the world of politics, these formative events are associated both with ideas and with institutions. For example, the American Revolution was fought in the name of liberal values and was followed by the adoption of a constitution and structures of government that enshrined the victors' preference for dispersed political power, a weak executive, and guarantees for individual rights. The institutions put in place after the Revolution embodied eighteenth-century liberal values of individual freedom and limited government. They shaped the subsequent pattern of American politics by promoting and legitimizing behaviour and issues that conformed to these values.

The main exponent of the formative events theory of political culture is American sociologist Seymour Martin Lipset. He first introduced it by arguing that the political development of the United States has been shaped by its **revolutionary origins**, while that of English Canada has been shaped by its **counter-revolutionary origins**. Lipset writes:

> Americans do not know but Canadians cannot forget that two nations, not one, came out of the American Revolution. The United States is the country of the revolution, Canada of the counterrevolution. These very different formative events set indelible marks on the two nations. One celebrates the overthrow of an oppressive state, the triumph of the people, a successful effort to create a type of government never seen before. The other commemorates a defeat and a long struggle to preserve a historical source of legitimacy: government's deriving its title-to-rule from a monarchy linked to church establishment. Government power is feared in the south; uninhibited popular sovereignty has been a concern in the north.[11]

Many of those who found themselves on the losing side of the American Revolution—the Loyalists—migrated north. They were the founders of an English-speaking society that originated in its rejection of the new American republic. This original rejection would be repeated several times: in the War of 1812; in the defeat of the American-style democratic reforms advocated by the losers in the 1837–8 rebellions in Lower and Upper Canada; in the 1867 decision to establish a new country with a system of government similar to that of Great Britain. The political history of Canada, including many of the major economic and cultural policies instituted by Canadian governments, reads largely as a series of refusals in the face of Americanizing pressures.

Is rejection of American political values and institutions proof of the greater strength of conservative values in English Canada? Some of those who agree with Lipset about the importance of formative events do not agree that counter-revolutionary gestures signify *ideological conservatism*. David Bell and Lorne Tepperman have argued that **Loyalism** concealed an underlying *ideological liberalism*. They acknowledge that the Loyalists were not anti-government, and that Canadians ever since appear to have been more willing to use the state for social, economic, and cultural purposes than have their American neighbours. But, they argue, a fondness for government is not inconsistent with liberal values. It is only in the United States, where the Revolution was directly about the tyranny of government, that liberalism acquired a strongly anti-government character.[12]

If Loyalism was not a conservative ideology, what was it? Bell and Tepperman argue that Loyalism was essentially a self-justification for not being American. Faced with the paradox of being cast out of a society whose political values they shared, the Loyalists had a serious identity crisis. They resolved it by insisting on their Britishness, and by constant criticisms of American values and institutions. This anti-Americanism is a component of Loyalism that endures even today. It explains, according to Bell and Tepperman, English Canada's centuries-old national identity puzzle.

What 1776 represents for English Canada's political development, the British Conquest of New France in 1759 represents for that of French Canada. The Conquest has always occupied a central place in French-Canadian nationalism, testifying to French Canadians' own awareness of its significance. The motto on Quebec licence plates, 'Je me souviens' ('I remember'), is in fact an oblique reference to the time before the Conquest, when French-speaking Canadians presumably were free from the oppression of Ottawa and English Canadians. Particularly under Parti Québécois governments in Quebec it has been common for the Conquest to be mentioned in official government documents on subjects ranging from language to the economy and constitutional reform.

There is no agreement as to how the Conquest has affected the ideological development of French Canada. Some, like historian Michel Brunet and sociologist Marcel Rioux, have argued that the Conquest cut off the development of a French-speaking bourgeoisie—francophones were rarely found in Canada's corporate elite until only a few decades ago—thereby depriving French Canada of the class that elsewhere was the main carrier of liberal political values. The mantle of social leadership, and the task of defining French-Canadian society, eventually fell on the Catholic Church and the ideologically conservative politicians who accepted the clerics' interpretation of that society as Catholic, French-speaking, non-liberal, and agrarian—in about that order of importance.

Others, like historian Fernand Ouellet and political scientist Louis Balthazar, maintain that there was no fledgling bourgeoisie, and therefore no catalyst for liberal political reform, in the first place. French Canada, they argue, was essentially a feudal society at the time of the Conquest. It fixated at this pre-liberal/pre-capitalist stage because of the fact that it was cut off from the future, not because French Canada was deprived of something that it once possessed.

History did not, of course, stop at the Conquest. The crushed 1837 rebellion in Lower Canada (Quebec) signalled the defeat of the politically liberal *patriots*, and consolidated the dominance of the conservative ideology in French Canada. This ideology would ultimately collapse by the end of the 1950s, finally brought down by the weight of the enormous social and economic transformations that the conservatives had ignored and even denied. Since then, conservative ideology has had little credibility in Quebec, but the memory of the Conquest continues to be a favourite starting point for Quebec nationalists. The protests generated in 2008 by plans (ultimately cancelled) to re-enact the 1759 Battle of the Plains of Abraham, as part of Quebec's 400th anniversary celebration, showed how raw this nerve remains.

Economic Structures and Political Ideas

From a class analysis perspective, both fragment theory and the formative events explanation are 'hopelessly idealistic'.[13] This is because they locate the sources of political values and institutions primarily in ideas—the 'cultural baggage' of fragment theory and the cultural mindset and symbols associated with the notion of formative events. An economic interpretation, by contrast, explains culture and the institutions that embody and perpetuate it as the products of class relations. These class relations are themselves rooted in the particular system of economic production and distribution—the *mode of production* as Marxists generally call it—that is found in a society at any point in time. Ideas and institutions change in response to transformations in the economic system and in the class relations associated with this system. The dominant ideas and existing political arrangements of a society are not, however, merely the shadows cast by economic phenomena. But what sets this approach apart from the other two we have examined is the belief that *culture and institutions are the embodiments of power relations whose sources lie in the economic system.*

How is political culture produced? By whom? For whom? With what effects? How do political institutions embody and reinforce the power relations that characterize society? These are the questions addressed by those who approach political values and institutions from the angle of economically determined class relations. They argue that the dominant ideas of a society are inevitably those of its most powerful class, i.e., those who control the system of economic production and distribution. This is due to the fact that important means of forming and disseminating ideas and information, such as the privately owned mass media, are controlled by the dominant class. Others, including the schools, mainstream religious organizations, and the state, accept and propagate the values of this class for reasons more subtle than ownership. Chief among these reasons is their support for *social order*, and their rejection of tendencies and ideas that fundamentally challenge the status quo. None of these major institutions is in the business of overturning society. They depend on a stable social order to carry out their respective activities and to satisfy their particular organizational needs. But the social order they support, and whose values they accept, is one that embodies a particular economic system and the power relations it produces. Defence of established institutions and values is not, therefore, a class-neutral stance.

Why would the members of subordinate classes embrace values and beliefs that, according to this class perspective, are basically justifications for the self-interest of the dominant class? The answer has two parts. First, those who are not part of the dominant class—and this would by definition include the majority of people—may be the victims of **false consciousness**. This concept, first used by Karl Marx, involves the inability of the subordinate classes to see where their real interests lie. For example, deference to established authority and belief in a hereditary aristocracy's 'natural right to rule', ideas that defend the privileges of the dominant class in a feudal society, would seem to reinforce the subordinate social position of those who are not fortunate enough to be born into the ruling aristocracy. Similarly, the widespread support for military interventions halfway around the globe by the working classes in Canada and the United States can hardly be said to be in their best interest, given that it is the sons and daughters of the working class who give up their lives, limbs, and long-term mental stability in these conflicts. In liberal societies, the widespread belief that opportunities to move up the socio-economic ladder are relatively open to those who are willing to work hard is argued by some to reinforce the dominant position of that small minority who control the economy and who account for most of society's wealth. After all, they argue, there is abundant empirical evidence that significant barriers to socio-economic mobility exist, that a good deal of poverty is passed on from generation to generation, and that those at the top of the socio-economic pyramid constitute a largely self-perpetuating elite. And yet we learn in school, through the mass media, and in countless other ways that equality of opportunity, not systemic inequality, is a characteristic feature of our society.

The second reason why, according to this class perspective, members of subordinate classes accept the ideas of the dominant class as 'common sense' is because these ideas conform, to some significant extent, to their personal experience. Democratic claims about the fundamental equality of all persons have a false ring in societies where some people are denied a share of this equality because they are black or female, for example. But in a society in which, under the constitution, there are no second-class citizens, and where everyone has the right to vote and participate in politics and enjoys equal protection under the law, claims about equality may appear to be valid. Or, consider the liberal belief, discussed earlier, that opportunities to acquire wealth and social standing are relatively open. There is, in Canada and in other liberal societies, enough evidence of this mobility to make the proposition appear true (see Chapter 3 on social mobility). The election of Barack Obama as President of the United States—the son of a Kenyan goatherd!—is evidence of mythic proportions. While some people never escape the socio-economic circumstances they are born into, many others do. There is enough proof that hard work and/or intelligence pays off in terms of material success to make liberalism's claim about what determines a person's socio-economic status a credible one. As Patricia Marchak observes, 'the propagation of an ideology cannot occur in a vacuum of experience; there must be a fair amount of congruence between personal experience and ideological interpretation for the propaganda [read, 'dominant ideology'] to be successful.'[14] Where this congruence is either weak or totally absent, the dominant class must rely on force to uphold its rule.

This idea is important: a certain degree of congruence must exist between the dominant values and beliefs of a society and the lived experience of most of its members, for otherwise the ideas of the dominant class will be exposed as pure self-interest. It means that what some have called 'false consciousness' cannot be totally false. Ideological systems not anchored in the social and economic realities of those subject to them are just not viable. We can understand this better by looking at the case of Quebec and the ideological changes associated with that province's 'Quiet Revolution' of the 1960s.

As recently as the 1950s, the dominant ideology in French-speaking Quebec was conservative. It was an ideology based on the concept of *la survivance* (survival): conserving the religious and linguistic heritage of French Canada in the face of assimilationist pressures. While possessing the formal structures of political democracy, Quebec's political life was dominated by autocratic politicians, rampant patronage, and social institutions—notably the Church and conservative newspapers—that encouraged submission to established authority.[15] Functions like education and social services that, in virtually all industrial democracies, were already under state control, were still in the hands of the Church. Even the province's francophone labour unions were predominantly confessional, linked to a Church whose ideas about industrial relations were shaped largely by its concern for preserving social harmony. In short, the dominant ideology and the social institutions that embodied it were conservative.

This conservatism, linked as it was to the social dominance of the Church and to a sharply limited role for the provincial state, was increasingly out of step with the industrial society that had been evolving in Quebec throughout the twentieth century. Those who advocated reforms that entailed a more interventionist role for the Quebec state, such as public control over education and social assistance, and whose vision of Quebec was of a secular industrial society necessarily found themselves in conflict with the spokespersons for the conservative ideology. By the 1950s, however, as the reformist elements in Quebec politics were quick to point out, the typical Québécois was a city-dweller who worked in a factory, store, or office,[16] and a new middle class of university-educated francophone professionals was gaining numerical strength in the province.[17] This new middle class was the leading force behind the expansion of the Quebec state that took place in the early to mid-1960s. Ultimately, the lack of 'congruence' between the values of the conservative ideology and the personal experience of most Québécois brought about the collapse of one dominant ideology and its replacement by one more in tune with those social groups—the new middle class and the growing francophone business community—who have dominated Quebec politics since the Quiet Revolution.

The Political Ideas of Canadians

What do Canadians believe about politics? Is it true that they value social order more, and individual freedom less, than their American counterparts? Does French Canada, and more particularly French-speaking Quebec, constitute a 'distinct society' in terms of its values and beliefs? Is it reasonable to talk about the political ideas of English-speaking Canadians, or are the regional differences in political culture too great to warrant such an approach?

In the following pages we will organize our analysis of political culture under four themes: community, freedom, equality, and attitudes towards the state. These tap crucial dimensions of political culture and at the same time allow us to explore the differences and similarities between French- and

English-speaking Canadians, between different regions of the country, and between Canadians and Americans. The evidence we will use is drawn from history, survey research data on attitudes, and measures of actual behaviour of individuals, groups, and governments from which values can be inferred.

Community

'Canadians', someone has said, 'are the only people who regularly pull themselves up by the roots to see whether they are still growing.' This search for a national identity unites successive generations of Canadians. Indeed, as the above remark suggests, it may be that the obsessive and often insecure introspection of Canadians is itself one of the chief characteristics of the Canadian identity (in English Canada, at least).

The roots of this preoccupation with national identity go back to the Conquest and the American War of Independence. The Conquest formed the basis for a society in which two main ethnolinguistic communities would cohabit—communities whose values and aspirations would often be at cross-purposes. The American War of Independence, as explained earlier, was followed by the emigration of Loyalists from the United States to the British colonies that would become Canada. Founded by those who rejected the republican democracy to the south, English Canada would constantly compare itself to that society and seek to explain and justify its separate existence.

In more recent years these two historical pillars of Canada's identity 'crisis' have been joined by newer challenges to the political community. These have come from Aboriginal Canadians and from some ethnic minorities who reject what they argue is their marginalization within Canadian society. Lacking a confident unifying sense of national identity, Canadian society has been buffeted by identity politics and the often irreconcilable definitions of Canada—sometimes proposing the dismemberment of the country as we know it—advanced by various groups.

The term 'political community' implies, quite simply, a shared sense of belonging to a country whose national integrity is worth preserving. This is something less than nationalism, which defines a community by its language, ethnic origins, traditions, or unique history. And it is not quite the same as patriotism, which one associates with a more fervent and demonstrative love of country and its symbols than is usually considered seemly in Canada. Political community is, rather, what historian W.L. Morton once described as 'a community of political allegiance alone'.[18] National identity, in such a community, is free from cultural and racial associations. Instead, national identity is essentially political—a sense of common citizenship in a country whose members have more in common with one another than with the citizens of neighbouring states and who believe that there are good reasons for continuing to live together as a single political nation. The term 'political nationality' is used by Donald Smiley to refer to precisely this sort of non-ethnic, non-racial sense of political community.[19]

The importance of national identity and a sense of political community in politics is nowhere better illustrated than in the breakup of the former Soviet Union and Yugoslavia after the end of the Communist Party's monopoly over power. Nationalist aspirations and bitter animosities that had been kept in check under totalitarian rule were unleashed, undermining any possibility that these countries could retain their pre-reform boundaries. There was, quite simply, no popular basis for political community in these formerly communist political systems. Once democratic institutions were in place, their breakup was inevitable.

The spectre of Canadian troops laying siege to Gatineau, across the river from Ottawa, or of armed barricades where the Trans-Canada Highway crosses the border between Ontario and Quebec, probably seems like a lurid fantasy to the minds of most Canadians. The great national bust-up, if it comes about, would almost certainly be acrimonious, but it is unlikely that the sort of civil war that was unleashed by the breakup of Yugoslavia would occur if Quebec were to declare its independence. Not everyone agrees. In public statements towards the end of 1991, Gordon Robertson, former Chief Clerk of the Privy Council under Pierre Trudeau and a rather conservative person by temperament, raised precisely the spectre of the former Yugoslavia in arguing that the breakup of Canada could very well be violent.

Prediction is perilous. What is clear, however, is that Canada's sense of community has often seemed terribly fragile, threatened by French–English tensions, western grievances against Ontario and Quebec, and, most recently, conflicts between the aspirations of Aboriginal Canadians and the policies of federal and provincial governments. This apparent fragility needs to be viewed alongside evidence suggesting that the country has been relatively successful in managing (repressing, critics would say) the tensions that have threatened it. The existing Constitution dates from 1867, making it one of the oldest and most durable in the world. Moreover, the territorial integrity of the country has (so far) remained unshaken by either civil war or secession. This is not to understate the importance of the rifts in Canada's sense of community. But the problems of Canadian unity and identity should be viewed from a broader perspective.

In recent years, the Canadian political community has faced and continues to face three major challenges:

- managing French–English relations;
- responding to Aboriginal demands for self-government;
- addressing the American influence on Canadian culture.

The first two have occasionally been associated with political violence and calls for the redrawing of territorial boundary lines. They represent clear challenges to the Canadian political community, as defined earlier. The challenge of American influence has assumed forms that are less obviously territorial. Nevertheless, American impact on the Canadian political community has been great. We will examine American influences separately in the section on 'Independence' in Chapter 3.

Some commentators would include regional conflict as a fourth challenge to the Canadian political community. Such conflict certainly has deep roots in Canadian history and has generated regionally based movements and parties of protest. But these regional grievances and conflicts have never threatened the territorial integrity of Canada. Westerners and, less stridently, eastern Canadians have long complained about policies and institutions that favour the interests of Ontario and Quebec. They also have complained about an idea of Canada that often has seemed to relegate their regional histories and realities to the margins. But their resentment has never boiled over to produce politically significant separatist movements in these regions, nor popular defection from the *idea* of Canada. The importance of regionalism will be discussed in Chapter 4.

For most of Canada's history, relations between the francophone and anglophone communities have not posed a threat to the political community. The differences and tensions between Canada's two major language groups have been managed through political accommodations between their political elites. This practice arguably goes back to the Quebec Act of 1774. Official protection was extended to the Catholic Church and Quebec's civil law system just when the British authorities were worried about the prospect of political rebellion in the American colonies spreading north. The tradition of deal-making between French and English Canada acquired a rather different twist in the couple of decades prior to Confederation, when the current provinces of Ontario and Quebec were united with a common legislature. The practice of dual ministries, with a leader from both Canada East (Quebec) and Canada West (Ontario), quickly developed, as did the convention that a bill needed to be passed by majorities from both East and West in order to become law. The federal division of powers that formed the basis of the 1867 Confederation continued this deal-making tradition. The assignment to the provinces of jurisdiction over education, property, civil rights, and local matters was shaped by Quebec politicians' insistence on control over those matters involving cultural differences.

This tradition of elitist deal-making has continued throughout Canada's history at two different levels. Nationally, the federal cabinet and national political parties, particularly the Liberal Party of Canada, have been important forums where the interests of Quebec could be represented. But with the rise of a more aggressive Quebec-centred nationalism in

© The Canadian Press/Chuck Mitchell

In Canada to attend Expo 67, then French President Charles de Gaulle roused—and stunned—a crowd assembled at Montreal's city hall on 24 July 1967 when he spoke from a small hotel balcony and exclaimed, 'Vive Montréal! Vive le Québec! Vive le Québec libre!' ('Long live free Quebec!'). The slogan became a rallying cry for those organizing around a growing Quebec sovereignty movement at the time.

the 1960s, the ability to represent the interests of French and English Canada within national institutions has become less important than whether compromises can be reached between the governments of Canada and Quebec.

The modus vivendi that for a couple of centuries prevented French–English conflicts from exploding into challenges to the idea of a single Canada seemed to come unstitched during the 1960s. Quebec independence, which previously had been a marginal idea that surfaced only sporadically in the province's politics, became a serious proposition advocated by many French-speaking intellectuals and apparently supported by a sizable minority of Québécois. The independence option spawned a number of organized political groups during the 1960s. In 1968, most of them threw their support behind the newly formed pro-independence Parti Québécois (PQ). Since then, the debate over whether the province should remain in Canada, and if so on what terms, has been one of the chief dimensions of Quebec political life.

In attempting to understand how great a threat Quebec separatism has posed to the Canadian community, we will consider two aspects of the issue: political violence and public attitudes.

Political Violence

Canadians are not accustomed to the violent resolution of political disputes. There have been only two political assassinations since Confederation, the first when D'Arcy McGee was shot down on the muddy streets of Ottawa in 1868 and the second in 1970 when Quebec's Minister of Labour, Pierre Laporte, was strangled to death by members of the Front de Libération du Québec (FLQ). *The World Handbook of Social and Political Indicators* ranks Canada well down the list of countries in terms of riots, armed political attacks, deaths from domestic political violence, and government sanctions to repress or eliminate a perceived threat to the state. Non-violent protest has occupied a more prominent place in Canadian politics, as one would expect in any genuine democracy. But even in this regard, protest demonstrations historically have been much rarer in Canada than in most other advanced industrialized democracies.[20]

Violence has not, however, been either absent or unimportant in Canadian politics. Much of that violence has involved labour disputes or workers' protests where the police or military were called in to protect the interests of employers and the capitalist social order. The violent suppression of the Winnipeg General Strike in 1919 and the use of the Royal Canadian Mounted Police in Regina in 1935 to break up the 'On-to-Ottawa Trek' of unemployed workers during the depth of the Depression are perhaps the two most noteworthy instances of such violence. The forcible detention of many Japanese, German, and Italian Canadians during World War II is another instance of state political violence. Indeed, in most of these cases it was the state that decided to use violence to settle some conflict or deal with some perceived menace. The most significant instances of political violence instigated by groups or individuals against the state have been related to the French–English conflict and, more recently, the status of Canada's Aboriginal population.

The almost tribal animosities that have existed between French and English Canadians have crystallized around violent events on several occasions. The hanging of the francophone Métis leader Louis Riel in 1885, after the military defeat of the Northwest Rebellion in the territory of present-day Saskatchewan, provoked denunciations of the Conservative government and its leader, Sir John A. Macdonald, from many francophone leaders. Although they did not sympathize with the rebellion that Riel led, francophones felt that the government's unwillingness to commute Riel's execution sentence was influenced by anti-French prejudice. Violence broke out again in 1918 over the conscription issue. French Canadians believed that Canada's involvement in World War I was motivated by the colonial attachments that English Canadians still felt for Britain, and they opposed the imposition of conscription. Anti-conscription riots broke out in Quebec City during the spring of 1918, the culmination of simmering recriminations and animosities between French and English Canadians over Canada's relationship to the British Empire.

Violence flared up in the streets of Montreal in 1955 when Maurice 'Le Rocket' Richard was suspended by the president of the National Hockey League, Clarence Campbell. French-Canadian supporters of Les Canadiens and their star player saw the suspension as more than punishment for a stick-swinging incident. They saw it as yet another example of ethnically motivated discrimination on the part of 'les maudits anglais' (the damned English).

The 1960s saw renewed violence, this time a spate of bombings and vandalism directed at symbols of the federal government's authority and anglophone domination in the province of Quebec. This was mainly the work of the FLQ, a very small group of people who achieved national prominence when they kidnapped British trade commissioner James Cross and Quebec cabinet minister Pierre Laporte in October 1970. The federal government reacted by invoking the War Measures Act, under which normal civil liberties were suspended. About 500 people were detained under the authority of the Act, although none of them were ultimately charged. Laporte's body was found shortly after imposition of the Act. Cross was released by the FLQ a few weeks later in exchange for safe passage out of the country for his captors.

The October Crisis, as the affair came to be called, was unique in Canada's political history. It was the only occasion when the War Measures Act has been invoked during peacetime. The government of Pierre Trudeau, which acted on the urging of the Quebec Liberal government of Robert Bourassa, argued that civil order was teetering on the verge of collapse in Quebec and that there existed a state of 'apprehended insurrection'. Most commentators argue that Ottawa's reaction was excessive, even in the unfamiliar circumstances of political kidnappings and uncertainty that existed at the time. Excessive or not, the October Crisis needs to be placed in its proper perspective. The political kidnappings were the work of a tiny band of political extremists whose tactics enjoyed little support among Quebec nationalists. Although there was some sympathy for the goals of the FLQ, this evaporated after their murder of Pierre Laporte.

In recent years political violence has been linked most often to unresolved disputes between groups of Aboriginal Canadians and public authorities. During the summer and autumn of 1990—a time now known as the 'Indian summer of 1990'—a group of Mohawk Warriors, protesting the planned expansion of a golf course on land they claimed as their own, barricaded a road leading to the golf course. The confrontation eventually escalated, resulting in the death of one Quebec police officer, a sympathy blockade by Mohawks at Kahnawake of the Mercier Bridge leading into Montreal, an important commuter route for the city, and other sympathy blockades of rail lines and roads by other Indian bands in communities across the country. Eventually, the standoff at Oka led to riots involving the white townspeople and members of the local Mohawk band of Kanesatake, intervention by thousands of Canadian troops, and even United Nations observers.[21] Fears of another Oka were raised in 1995 when small groups of Natives occupied land that they claimed was sacred at Gustafsen Lake, BC, and Ipperwash Provincial Park in Ontario. Violence broke out in both cases and a Native was shot dead at Ipperwash.

Since then a number of violent episodes, but no deaths, have occurred in New Brunswick, Ontario, and Quebec (see Table 2.2). Although the circumstances of each case were unique, they all had one element in common: resistance by Aboriginal Canadians against laws, policies, or property claims based on what they maintained to be their distinct status and rights. In the case of the ongoing standoff at Caledonia, Ontario, some spokespersons for the Six Nations Reserve have stated bluntly that the rulings of Canadian courts do not apply to their people. Some non-Aboriginal Canadians agree. Such attitudes, regardless of whether we agree with them, represent a significant challenge to the notion of a single Canadian political community.

Political violence has not been limited to clashes that have their roots in language conflict or in the tensions and unresolved issues that have occasionally pitted Aboriginal Canadians against political authorities and sometimes against non-Aboriginal citizens. The 2010 meeting of the G20 in Toronto set off anti-globalization protests. Several vehicles were set afire, store and bank windows were smashed, and over 400 arrests were made. Although not frequent, violent episodes involving clashes of ideologies and economic interests have occurred in Canada, including the Winnipeg General Strike of 1919 and some smaller conflicts between workers and employers that ended in violence, such as the 1973 Artistic Woodwork dispute in Toronto and the 1978 Fleck Manufacturing conflict near London, Ontario. These episodes of violence raised questions about the political neutrality of the state and the legitimacy of its actions. But unlike the cases involving Aboriginal Canadians and violence arising from the French–English conflict, they did not challenge the idea of the legitimacy of the Canadian community.

Public Attitudes

'Égalité ou indépendance!' ('Equality or independence!') The sentiment is familiar to any contemporary Quebec-watcher. The slogan did not, however, originate with the PQ. *Égalité ou independence* was the title of a booklet written by Daniel Johnson, leader of the Union Nationale and Premier of Quebec between 1966 and 1968, and served as his party's campaign slogan in the 1966 election. But neither Johnson nor the Union Nationale was committed to separatism. With the birth of the Parti Québécois in 1968, the province acquired a political party whose leader, René Lévesque, and platform were committed to taking Quebec out of Canada. Daniel Johnson's rhetoric and René Lévesque's commitment represented and helped catalyze an important change in Quebec politics. This change involved the idea of Quebec independence. Before the mid-1960s independence was a marginal idea in the province's politics, supported by many Québécois intellectuals but not taken seriously by the main political parties or by the public. Since then, independence has attracted the support of a sizable minority of Québécois.

According to public opinion polls, the level of popular support for Quebec independence has ranged between a low of about 20 per cent to a high of nearly 60 per cent over the last few decades (see Figure 2.1). Without reading too much into the numbers, we may say that there appears to be a durable core of support for the idea of Quebec independence. The level of support varies over time and also depending on what sort of independence is envisaged by the pollster's question. Support is always higher for 'sovereignty-association'—a term generally understood to mean a politically sovereign Quebec that would be linked to Canada through some sort of commercial union or free trade agreement—than for outright political and economic separation. It is clear that many Québécois are conditional separatists. Indeed, even among PQ supporters there has always been much less enthusiasm for complete separation than for separation with economic association.

When the PQ was first elected to office in 1976, it was clear that Quebec voters were not casting their ballots for separatism. The PQ was committed to holding a referendum on Quebec independence, so that non-separatists and soft separatists were able to vote for the party without fear that a PQ government would necessarily mean Quebec independence. Indeed, a survey conducted during the 1976 campaign revealed that only about half of those intending to vote for the PQ actually favoured independence.[22] When the PQ sought re-election in 1981, following a decisive referendum defeat the previous year, it ran on its record in office rather than on its continued goal of Quebec independence. In fact, the PQ promised not to hold another referendum during its next term. As in 1976, the PQ's 1981 victory could not be interpreted as a vote for separatism. Similarly, in 1998 the PQ won re-election after a campaign in which such issues as unemployment and health-care reform clearly overshadowed the issue of Quebec's future in or out of Canada. At that time, Premier Lucien Bouchard felt constrained to admit that the 43 per cent of votes cast for the PQ, versus 44 per cent for the Quebec Liberal Party, could in no way be viewed as a mandate for independence nor even for another referendum in the near term.

The first direct challenge to the Canadian political community came in May of 1980, when the PQ government held its promised referendum on sovereignty-association. The referendum was very carefully—some would say trickily—worded. It stressed that what was being proposed was not a radical break from Canada, but a negotiated political independence for Quebec that would maintain economic ties to Canada.

> The Government of Quebec has made public its proposal to negotiate a new arrangement with the rest of Canada, based on the equality of nations; this arrangement would enable Quebec to acquire the exclusive power to make its laws, administer its taxes and establish relations abroad—in other words, sovereignty—and at the same time to maintain with Canada an economic association including a common currency; no change in political status resulting from these negotiations will be effected without approval by the people through another referendum; on these terms, do you give the Government of Quebec the mandate to negotiate the proposed agreement between Quebec and Canada? Yes. No.

Despite the PQ's careful strategy, Quebec voters rejected the sovereignty-association option by a vote of 59.6 per cent ('Non') to 40.4 per cent ('Oui'). Even among francophones, a majority voted against Quebec independence.[23] Advocates of Quebec separatism were quick to point out that sovereignty-association was more popular among younger than older voters. Time, they argued, would turn the tide in favour of independence. Others argued that the greater popularity of the 'Oui' option among those who entered adulthood in the nationalist 1960s and early 1970s—Quebec's 'baby boomers'—reflected the exceptional politically formative experiences of this generation, and that subsequent generations, not raised in the intensely nationalist ferment that

'If a referendum was held today regarding Quebec sovereignty, would you vote for or against Quebec sovereignty?'

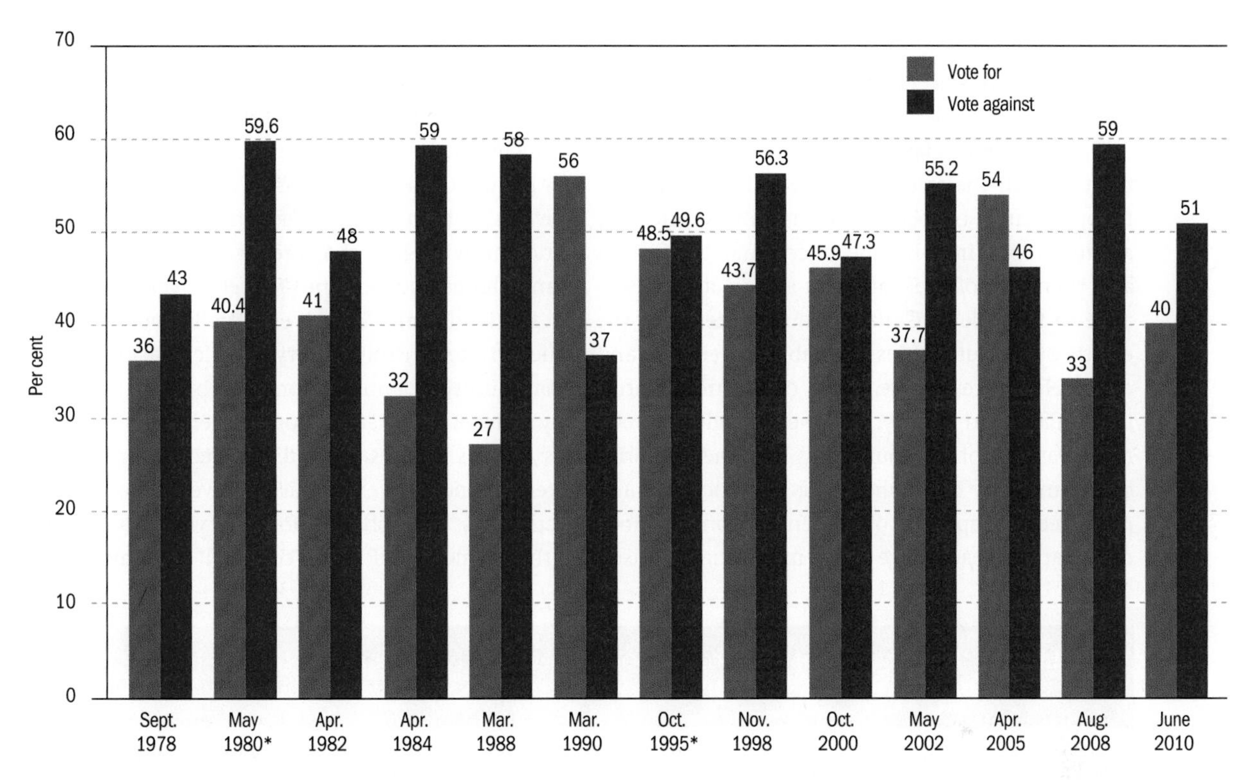

FIGURE 2.1 Support for Quebec Independence, 1978–2010

*The results for 1980 and 1995 are based on the referendum questions for each of those years.

Note: The columns for each year may not add up to 100 per cent because 'don't know' and 'no response' are not included.

Sources: Adapted from Simon Langlois, *La société québécoise en tendances, 1960–1990* (Québec: Institut québécois de recherche sur la culture, 1990), 649. Percentages for 1998–2005 and 2010 are based on polls conducted by Léger Marketing. Data for 2008 from La Presse / crop, 'Le climat politique au Québec', 14–28 août 2008.

characterized the 1960s in Quebec, would find separatism less appealing.

It does not appear, however, that Quebec separation is less popular among young francophone Québécois than it was among their counterparts in the 1960s and 1970s. On the contrary, support for separatism is stronger among younger cohorts of Quebec's francophone electorate than among other voters. Support for separatism is especially strong among young, highly educated Québécois, as was also true in the 1960s. Studies of the subsequent 1995 Quebec referendum, which, on a differently worded question, the 'Non' side won by the narrowest of margins (49.6 per cent to 48.5 per cent), show that a solid majority of younger francophone voters, between the ages of 20 and 30, voted for independence. Separatists draw the conclusion that support for independence will grow over time, as older cohorts of the electorate are replaced by younger, pro-independence ones. Skeptics note, however, that political preferences often change as one grows older and that there is no reason to assume that the younger generation's support for Quebec sovereignty will remain firm.

Accustomed to the challenge that Quebec separatism poses to the political community, most Canadians probably were surprised when the Oka crisis revealed the existence of another challenge to the idea of a single Canada. In fact, however, the armed confrontation at Oka had several precedents. Violent confrontations between Natives and whites punctuate Canadian history, going back to before the extermination of the Beothuk Indians of Newfoundland in the 1700s (the last Beothuk died in 1829). Some of the major episodes of violence between Natives and whites are described in Table 2.2.

These violent clashes are linked by a common thread: the struggle between the traditional independence of Native communities and the authority of, first, European colonial authorities and then that of the Canadian state. Native resistance to the rule of Canadian authorities, and the efforts of the authorities to establish their rule and crush Native resistance, span over three centuries of Canadian history. But the struggle between Native aspirations for autonomy and the authority of the majority community has only occasionally produced flashpoints of violence. Long periods of apparent peace have been more characteristic of Aboriginal–non-Aboriginal relations. We say 'apparent peace', because even during these periods the conflict between the aspirations of many Native communities and the demands and restrictions imposed on them by the Canadian state was only dormant, waiting for the catalyst of some issue or incident. The confrontation at Oka turned out to be just such an incident, galvanizing Native groups and throwing into sharp relief the issues of Native land claims and demands for self-government.

The land claims issue is essentially about who has the right to control territory to which various Native communities claim a historical right. Treaties signed by Ottawa and Native groups after Confederation, as well as treaties prior to Confederation—which were intended to extinguish Native claims to these territories in exchange for reserves, money, and other benefits—do not cover all of Canada. In

TABLE 2.2 Major Violent Confrontations between Natives and Non-Natives and/or Political Authorities

Date	Native Group and Location	Event
1700s	Beothuk (Newfoundland)	Many were killed by Europeans.
1763	Seneca, Ojibway, and other tribes (area near Detroit)	Led by Odawa war chief, Pontiac, a confederation of tribes rebelled against British rule in several bloody confrontations.
circa 1794	Shawnee and other tribes (Ohio River Valley)	Led by Shawnee war chief Tecumseh, several Indian tribes attempted unsuccessfully to resist white settlement and control of the Ohio Valley.
1869–70	Métis (Manitoba)	In the Red River Rebellion, Métis fought for provincial status and guaranteed land and cultural rights.
1885	Métis and Plains Indians (Saskatchewan)	In the Northwest Rebellion, a series of battles took place between Métis and Indian forces, on one side, and white militia volunteers and soldiers, on the other.
1990	Mohawk (Quebec)	This armed confrontation at Oka resulted in one death and riots against Natives protesting the expansion of a golf course on land that they claimed was theirs by historical right.
1995	Shuswap (British Columbia) Chippewa (Ontario)	Armed confrontations took place at Gustafsen Lake, BC, and Ipperwash Provincial Park in Ontario. In both cases a small group of Natives occupied land they claimed was sacred. Dudley George of the Kettle and Stoney Point First Nation was killed at Ipperwash.
2000	Mi'kmaq (Burnt Church, NB)	Conflict between Aboriginals and non-Aboriginals over fishing rights flared up in vandalism, boat ramming, and shots fired.
2004	Mohawk (Quebec)	Anti-police riot took place when 67 Aboriginal officers, authorized by Grand Chief James Gabriel and the Mohawk band council and financed by the federal Solicitor-General, were trapped in the Kanesatake police station for three days by armed protestors from the local Mohawk community.
2006	Six Nations (Ontario)	Police arrests of 16 Six Nations protestors at Caledonia in southern Ontario were responded to by fires and the blockade of a major highway by hundreds of Natives who claimed that land being developed for houses rightfully belonged to them, dating back to the Haldimand Grant of 1784, although an Ontario court decision had ruled otherwise.

fact, an enormous area encompassing much of the North and both the western and eastern extremities of the country were not covered by historic (pre-1975) treaties. Moreover, about 40 per cent of status Indians[24] are not members of bands that have signed treaties with Ottawa. Having never been vanquished militarily or given up their territorial rights through a treaty, they claim that the land their ancestors inhabited still belongs to them. This and other issues related to Canada's Aboriginal population are examined in Chapter 16.

Land claim negotiations progressed at a snail's pace for decades, leading most Native groups to conclude that Ottawa really had not been serious about settling these claims, many of which related to government misuse and misappropriation of lands that had been reserved for Indians who had signed historic treaties. With the Oka confrontation, when the Mohawk Warriors claimed to be an independent nation with a historical right to the land on which the local municipality planned to extend a golf course, the issue truly became part of the public consciousness. This claim to be a sovereign nation, outside the authority of Canadian law, was more extreme than most Native demands for self-government. And it was a claim that was steadfastly rejected by the federal government and most Canadians. 'Native self-government', Prime Minister Brian Mulroney declared, 'does not now and cannot ever mean sovereign independence. Mohawk lands are part of Canadian territory, and Canadian law must and does apply.'[25] A few years later, Liberal Prime Minister Jean Chrétien also rejected the claims of some Natives that they stand outside the authority of Canadian law.

Recent land claim settlements that include structures for Aboriginal self-government, notably the creation of Nunavut in the eastern Arctic and the Nisga'a Treaty in British Columbia, state explicitly that laws of general application continue to apply to those who inhabit these Native lands and that the Charter of Rights and Freedoms applies to their governments. Nevertheless, a sort of de facto acceptance of separate communities, defined by their Aboriginal ethnicity and heritage, now exists within Canada. This is discussed more fully in Chapter 16.

Freedom

'Live free or die' reads the motto on licence plates in the state of New Hampshire. Individual freedom is said to be part of the American political creed, symbolized in such icons as the Statue of Liberty, Philadelphia's Liberty Bell, the Bill of Rights, and the Declaration of Independence. Canadians, it is usually claimed, are more willing than Americans to limit individual freedom in pursuit of social order or group rights. Is this true?

The greater stress on individual freedom and stronger suspicion of government control in the United States than in Canada are corroborated by many types of evidence. One of these is literature. Writers like Henry David Thoreau, Jack Kerouac, and Allan Ginsberg embody a powerfully individualistic current that runs through American culture. There is no Canadian equivalent to Thoreau, whose writings about civil disobedience and the need to resist the demands of society as the price to be paid for a life of virtue and freedom have had an important influence on the libertarian tradition in American politics. Individualism and freedom are also powerful themes in American popular culture, as epitomized in the early radio and television program, *The Lone Ranger*. Hollywood's portrayal of the loner who is indifferent to social conventions and the law, whose virtue and attractiveness rest on these traits, has long been one of the most successful genres in popular film. Marlon Brando's brooding performance in *The Wild One* (1953) and Peter Fonda in *Easy Rider* (1969) maintained this tradition. Clint Eastwood, Sylvester Stallone, Charles Bronson, Harrison Ford, Bruce Willis, and Denzel Washington are among those actors whose film characters have embodied this against-the-grain individualism.

Americans' more passionate love affair with freedom is evident in the very different character of the gun control debate in Canada and the United States, as was depicted with considerable irony in Michael Moore's Academy Award-winning documentary, *Bowling for Columbine* (2002), and as was heard in the shrill dialogue that immediately followed the attempted assassination of an Arizona congresswoman in January 2011. When former Liberal Justice Minister Allan Rock introduced a law proposing tougher restrictions on gun ownership and a national registry for all firearms, opposition in Canada focused on such matters as whether the legislation would really reduce the use of guns in committing crimes and whether the legislation reflected urban Canada's insensitivity and even hostility to the values and lifestyles of hunters and rural communities. Few people argued, and not many seriously believed, that a fundamental freedom was jeopardized by this legislation.

In the United States, however, proposals to restrict the sale and ownership of firearms invariably face objections from those who see these restrictions as threatening individual freedom. It is a mistake to assume that these objections are merely the cynical ravings of National Rifle Association devotees and white supremacists who wrap themselves in the Second Amendment's guarantee of the 'right to bear arms'. Many Americans believe that gun ownership is a right, not a privilege that governments bestow on citizens. One sometimes hears the argument that restrictions on gun ownership will leave citizens helpless to defend themselves, not simply against criminals but against the state! This argument would be met with blank stares of incomprehension in Canada. Americans are more likely than Canadians to believe that gun ownership is part of their right to protect themselves and their property, instead of relying on the state to do this for them.

Mistrust of the state is as old as the American War of Independence. It is woven into the American Constitution's systems of checks and balances; it was behind the adoption of a Bill of Rights scarcely before the ink had dried on that Constitution; and it was also part of the case for federalism, which, as James Madison argued in the famous *Federalist Papers*, no. 51, was expected to help check the emergence of any political majority large enough to threaten individual and minority rights. In the American political culture, pride in their system of government and greater patriotism than in most other democracies have coexisted with a mistrust of government that has its roots in both the revolutionary experience and in the individualistic spirit of Americans. Thus, many Americans—and not just those who dress in khaki on the weekends and participate in the civilian militias that are a distinctly American phenomenon—understand the argument that government may be the problem and the enemy and that citizens have a right to defend themselves and should not have to rely on government to do it for them. Canadians are much less likely to share these views.

In Canada the state is viewed as more benign. As Seymour Martin Lipset observes, 'If [Canada] leans towards communitarianism—the public mobilization of resources to fulfill group objectives—the [United States] sees individualism—private endeavour—as the way an "unseen hand" produces optimum, socially beneficial results.'[26] Canadian writer Pierre Berton made the same point when he maintained that 'We've always accepted more governmental control over our lives than . . . [Americans] have—and fewer civil liberties.'[27]

Attitudinal data also provide a basis for generalizations about the value attached to freedom in the two societies. Using questions that require people to choose between the protection of individual liberty and the defence of social order, a survey conducted in the 1980s found that Americans consistently gave more freedom-oriented responses.[28] This pattern of difference between Canadians and Americans has persisted over time. The 1991 World Values Survey (WVS) found that Americans (75 per cent) were considerably more likely than Canadians (61 per cent) to say that, if required to choose, they would opt for liberty over equality. Unfortunately, this question was not asked of Americans and Canadians in either the 2001 or 2006 round of the WVS. Nonetheless, on other questions related to individualism in the 2006 survey (Figure 2.2), Canadians are hardly differentiated from Americans in their belief that people are responsible for their own success and happiness. In the selected European countries (Germany, France, Britain, Italy, and Spain) shown in this figure, in most instances there is somewhat less faith expressed in the 'pull yourself up by your own bootstraps' mentality that many North Americans espouse.

Americans' greater stress on individual freedom is often credited to their individualist culture. Canadians, on the other hand, are often portrayed as less assertive about their rights as individuals, and more concerned than Americans with social

A. Individuals should take more reponsibility for providing for themselves. (percentage agreeing)

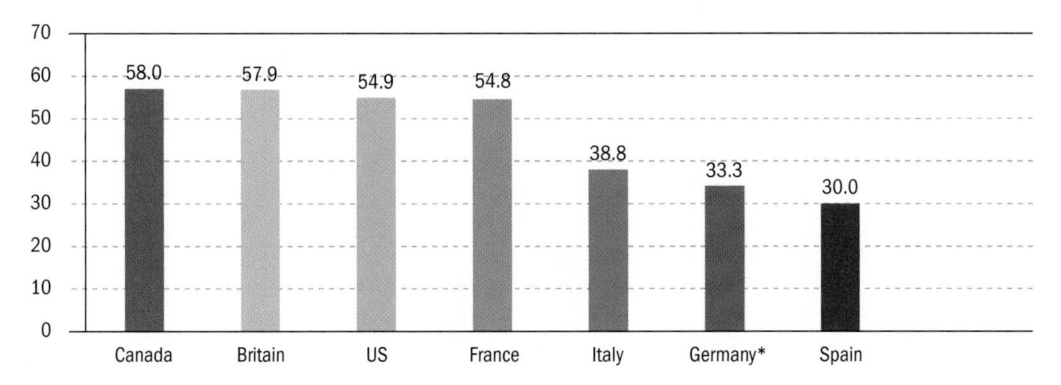

B. In the long run, hard work usually brings a better life. (percentage agreeing)

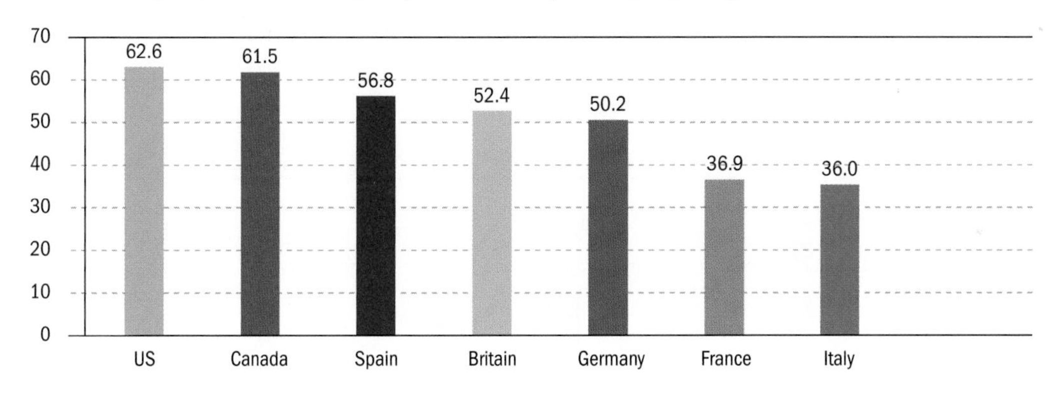

C. Some people feel they have completely free choice and control over their lives, while other people feel that they have no real effect on what happens to them.
(percentage expressing a great deal of freedom)

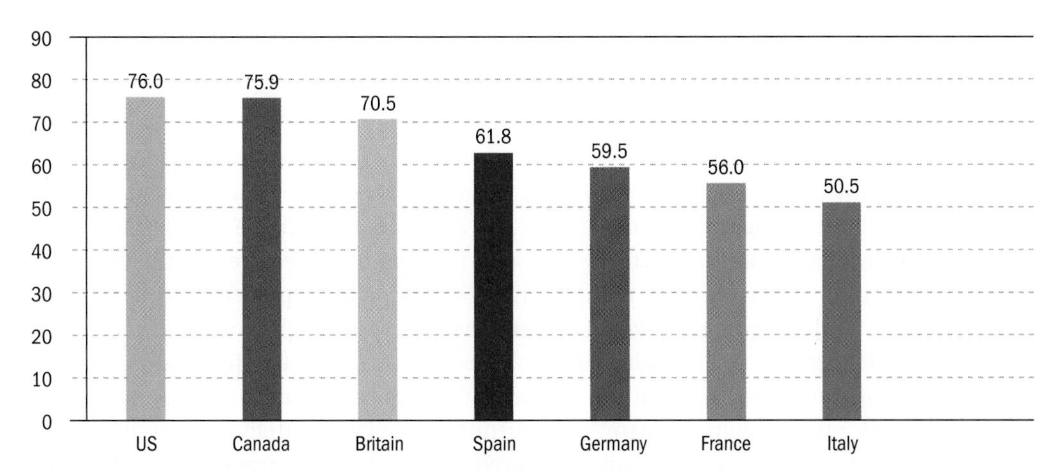

FIGURE 2.2 Individualism: A Cross-National Comparison

D. Why are there people who live in need? (percentage choosing 'because of laziness and lack of will power' as their first choice)*

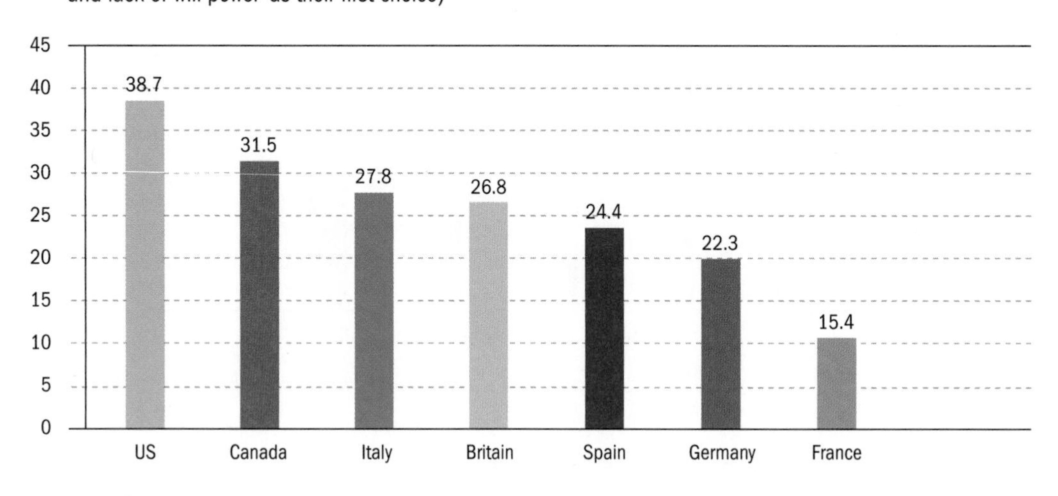

E. Competition is good. It stimulates people to work hard and develop new ideas. (percentage agreeing)

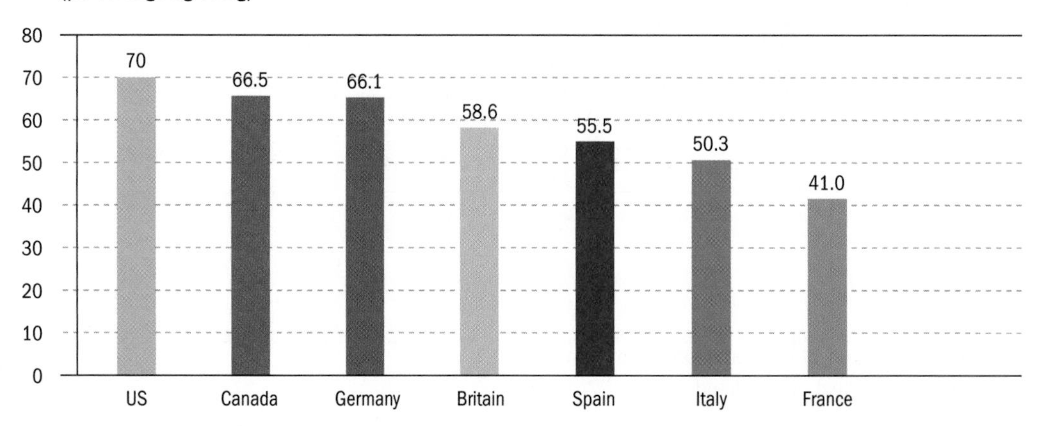

FIGURE 2.2 continued

*Data from the 2000 wave of the WVS. This question was not asked in 2006.

Source: World Values Survey, 2006, at: <www.worldvaluessurvey.org>.

order. Attitudinal data provide some support for these claims. Some people object to this characterization of Americans as being more respectful of individual freedoms than Canadians on the grounds that Americans' understanding of 'freedom' as 'the absence of restraint, or individual behaviour'—what is sometimes called 'negative freedom'—actually denies real freedom to many people. Canadians' greater willingness to permit government restrictions on individual behaviour does not mean that they value freedom less, but that they are more likely than Americans to believe that real freedom often requires that government interfere with individual property rights and economic markets. Moreover, governments should guarantee to all citizens such things as public education and health care in order to help equalize the opportunities available both to the well-off and the less-privileged. Canadians, some argue, have what might be characterized as a positive conception of freedom, one that requires that governments act rather than get out of the way.

The notion that the American conception of freedom attaches greater weight to individual self-reliance and the Canadian conception to positive state action that makes it more likely that individuals will be able to achieve their goals is given some support by the results of a 2009 survey on economic mobility in these two countries. Canadians, it was found, were more likely than Americans to express the belief that government does more to help people move up the economic ladder (46 per cent of Canadians agreeing, compared to 36 per cent of Americans), whereas Americans were more likely than Canadians to believe that government did more to hurt mobility (46 per cent vs 39 per cent). This is, it should be said, not a particularly large gap between the beliefs of Canadians and Americans.[29]

The somewhat weaker attachment of Canadians to what might be characterized as an individualistic notion of freedom is corroborated by the words and symbols that parties and candidates use in their attempt to win the support of voters. If we think of these words and symbols as being a sort of connective tissue between citizens and those who wish to represent them, it is clear that the key to electoral success lies in the use of ideas, images, words, and symbols that resonate positively with a large number of voters. A study of the campaign rhetoric of Canadian party leaders and the American presidential candidates in the 2000 elections held in their respective countries found that the core values and unifying themes expressed in the George W. Bush/Republican Party message were clearly more individualistic than those of any national leader and party in Canada.[30] This confirms the picture that emerges from attitudinal data and other evidence from which cultural values may be inferred: the defence of individual freedom can be a harder sell in Canada than in the United States (see Box 2.3).

In the wake of the terrorist attacks of 11 September 2001, both the American and Canadian governments passed laws that involved greater restrictions on individual rights and freedoms. Public opinion surveys showed that Canadians were considerably less likely than Americans to believe that such restrictions were necessary, but at the same time polls showed that Canadians were about as accepting of security measures that involved some loss of privacy safeguards as were Americans.[31] In 2008 the CBC launched a prime-time drama called *The Border*, which portrays Americans as more concerned with security and the protection of social order and Canadians as more vigilant in defending individual rights. A sort of role reversal has taken place, argue some, such that Canada is now the society that cares more about freedom and the United States has become the country obsessed with threats to its security.

The evidence for this claim is less than clear. The post-9/11 spike in American support for measures that appeared to purchase security at the cost of reduced freedoms and rights for some has dissipated over time. Moreover, opposition to limitations on freedoms and rights existed in the United States from the moment the Patriot Act was passed in 2001 and this opposition gained strength and won victories in both Congress and the courts as time went on. Although it is arguable that 9/11 produced a short-term gap between Canadian and American attitudes concerning the security/freedom trade-off, it is not certain that the core beliefs of Americans became less freedom-oriented as a result of these terrorist attacks.

Listen to the 'Security and Sovereignty: Perspectives on the World's Longest Undefended Border' podcast, available at www.oupcanada.com/Brooks7e

Equality

If the Loyalists have left a Tory imprint on Canadian politics, we would expect to find that Canadians place a lower value on equality than do Americans. Tories, after all, believed that the organization of society along class lines was a natural and desirable state of affairs. They were apt to sneer at American democracy as 'mobocracy'. A long line of sociologists, political scientists, and historians, going back to Alexis de Tocqueville and other Europeans who visited North America in the nineteenth century, have generally agreed that America's political culture is more egalitarian and Canada's more hierarchical.

Whatever the historical accuracy of this characterization might have been, it is no longer obviously true. As Figure 2.3 on page 64 shows, Canadians

Politics in Focus

Box 2.3 Should Offensive Speech Be Protected? The 'Town Square Test'

The former Soviet Union dissident Natan Sharansky offers a simple and practical test of whether a person lives in a free or fear society. 'If a person cannot walk into the middle of the town square and express his or her views without fear of arrest, imprisonment and physical harm', he says, 'then that person is living in a fear society.' Are there views that one would not be able to freely express in public places in Canada, without fear of being punished? Is offensive speech more or less likely to be tolerated in Canada than in the United States? Consider the following case.

In March of 2010 the American pundit Ann Coulter was scheduled to give a talk at the University of Ottawa. Coulter is a well-known conservative commentator who is often described as being 'controversial'. Coulter's books have often been best-sellers in the United States and she is a regular on both Fox and CNN. She has given talks on university campuses for many years, where she is frequently greeted by protestors and hostile listeners. This occasion was rather different. The presence of a crowd of angry protestors—some of whom were students and faculty, but many of whom had no connection to the University of Ottawa—led the university to cancel the talk, apparently based on fear of violence. But even before Coulter's scheduled talk the university had prohibited posters on campus advertising the event (although posters condemning her scheduled talk were allowed) and the academic vice-president, François Houle, saw fit to send Coulter the following letter:

> I understand that you have been invited by University of Ottawa Campus Conservatives to speak at the University of Ottawa this coming Tuesday. We are, of course, always delighted to welcome speakers on our campus and hope that they will contribute positively to the meaningful exchange of ideas that is the hallmark of a great university campus. We have a great respect for freedom of expression in Canada, as well as on our campus, and view it as a fundamental freedom, as recognized by our Canadian Charter of Rights and Freedoms.
>
> I would, however, like to inform you, or perhaps remind you, that our domestic laws, both provincial and federal, delineate freedom of expression (or 'free speech') in a manner that is somewhat different than the approach taken in the United States. I therefore encourage you to educate yourself, if need be, as to what is acceptable in Canada and to do so before your planned visit here.
>
> You will realize that Canadian law puts reasonable limits on the freedom of expression. For example, promoting hatred against any identifiable group would not only be considered inappropriate, but could in fact lead to criminal charges. Outside of the criminal realm, Canadian defamation laws also limit freedom of expression and may differ somewhat from those to which you are accustomed. I therefore ask you, while you are a guest on our campus, to weigh your words with respect and civility in mind.
>
> There is a strong tradition in Canada, including at this university, of restraint, respect and consideration in expressing even provocative and controversial opinions and [I] urge you to respect that Canadian tradition while on our campus. Hopefully, you will understand and agree that what may, at first glance, seem like unnecessary restrictions to freedom of expression do, in fact, lead not only to a more civilized discussion, but to a more meaningful, reasoned and intelligent one as well.
>
> I hope you will enjoy your stay in our beautiful country, city and campus.

Did Canada, or perhaps just the University of Ottawa, fail the town square test in this case, or is this test not a reasonable measure of an important democratic freedom? (Postscript: A few days later Coulter visited the University of Calgary, where she was greeted by jeering protestors as well as admirers, and where she was allowed to speak.)

appear to value equality *more* than do Americans. They are much more likely to support public policies, like a publicly funded health-care system and a guaranteed minimum income, that are intended to narrow the gap between the poor and the well-off. A comparative study of the development of the welfare state in Canada and the US corroborates this difference. Robert Kudrle and Theodore Marmor argue that ideological differences between the two societies are the main reasons for the earlier enactment and more generous character of welfare state policies in Canada, observing that 'In every policy area it appears that general public as well as elite opinion . . . [has been] more supportive of state action in Canada than in the United States.'[32] At the same time, some observers caution that too much is often attributed to cultural differences in explaining differences between social policies in these countries. Gerard Boychuk argues that the significance of race politics in the United States and of territorial politics in Canada explains more of the difference in the health policies of the two countries than does political culture.[33]

In Canada, egalitarianism has its roots in a more collectivist tradition; in the United States it draws on a more individualistic tradition. But the value differences between the two societies are shaded rather than starkly contrasting, as Figure 2.3 shows. Nevertheless, they help to explain Canadians' apparently greater tolerance—historically at any rate—for state measures targeted at disadvantaged groups and regions. Lipset's conclusion seems a fair one: 'Canadians are committed to redistribution egalitarianism, while Americans place more emphasis on meritocratic competition and equality of opportunity.'[34]

This difference between the two societies, however, should not be pushed too far. If Americans care more about equality of opportunity and Canadians about equality of condition, then we would expect to find greater acceptance of economic inequalities among Americans. But the evidence is unclear. Although the average CEO-to-worker earnings ratio was about twice as great in the United States as in Canada—44 to 1 compared to 21 to 1 in the manufacturing sector, as of 2001[35]—Canadians and Americans are almost identical in their beliefs about what would constitute a 'fair' ratio of maximum-to-minimum earnings. Respondents from both countries say that it should be about 10 to 1.

It has often been said that the American concept of equality stresses equality of opportunity, whereas the Canadian concept of equality is more likely to emphasize equality of condition. A good deal of evidence, including government policies, suggests that this claim is valid. At the same time, the extent of this difference is easily and often exaggerated. When asked whether they thought it was more important to reduce inequality or to ensure that everyone has a fair chance to improve their economic standing, 71 per cent of Americans and 68 per cent of Canadians chose ensuring a fair chance (see Figure 2.3).[36] If Canadians are truly more oriented towards equality of condition, and if this is an important difference between the values of Canadians and Americans, then one would expect to find a greater gap. The author of the Economic Mobility Project study, Statistics Canada's Miles Corak, observes that 'Both Americans and Canadians feel strongly that individual characteristics, like hard work, ambition, and [education], lead to upward economic mobility. In both countries, factors external to the individual, outside of his or her control, rank much lower.'[37] And majorities in both countries expressed the view that all of their fellow citizens had a fair chance of moving up the economic ladder. Corak notes that Canadians were about as likely as Americans to support merit-based differences, including the right of hard workers to make more than others, the limited role of luck, gender, and race in determining one's economic fortunes, and the fairness of inequalities when there is equality of opportunity.

In Canada, more than in the United States, debates over equality historically have been about group rights and equality between different groups in society, not about equality between individuals. This difference goes back to the founding of the two societies. While the American Constitution made no distinction between groups of citizens, the Quebec Act of 1774 incorporated protection for religious rights and the British North America Act of 1867 provided protections for both religious and language rights.

A by-product of Canada's long tradition of recognizing group rights, many have argued, is greater tolerance of cultural diversity than one finds in the

A. The government has a responsibility to take care of the poor. (percentage agreeing)

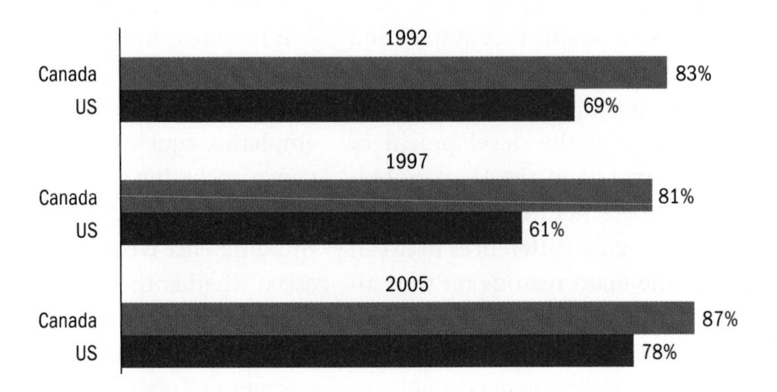

B. Incomes should be made more equal. (percentage expressing high agreement)

C. Both freedom and equality are important, but I would say that personal freedom is more important.

D. Immigrants improve society by bringing in new ideas and cultures. (percentage agreeing)

E. People from different racial and cultural backgrounds would be better off if they became more like the majority. (percentage agreeing)

F. Homosexuality is never justifiable. (percentage expressing high agreement)

G. Do you approve of interracial marriages between whites and blacks? (percentage* approving)

FIGURE 2.3 Dimensions of Equality in Canada and the United States

*This is the percentage of white Americans who approve of interracial marriage. The figure for Canada includes people of all races.

Sources: World Values Survey, 2000; Ipsos-Reid, 'A Public Opinion Survey of Canadians and Americans', May 2005; Carleton University International Social Survey Program, 2004; Gallup Poll, June 2007; Reginald Bibby, 'Racial Intermarriage: Canada and the U.S.', Project Canada Press Release #9, University of Lethbridge, 29 Aug. 2007, at: <www.reginaldbibby.com/images/PC_9_RACIAL_INTERMARRIAGE_AUG2907.pdf>.

United States. This is the familiar, if exaggerated, theme of the Canadian 'mosaic' versus the American 'melting pot'. Although considerable historical evidence suggests that non-French, non-British groups have felt less pressure to abandon their language and customs in Canada than have non-English-speaking groups in the United States, rates of cultural assimilation have been high in both societies. Moreover, Canadian governments have shown themselves to be as capable as their American counterparts of discriminating against ethnic and religious communities. For example, in both countries many people of Japanese origin were deprived of their property and kept confined to camps during World War II. The religious practices of Doukhobors, Hutterites, Mennonites, and Jehovah's Witnesses have at various times brought them into conflict with either Ottawa or provincial governments. And in both Canada and the United States immigration policy until the 1960s discriminated against non-white, non-European peoples—although this is no longer characteristic of policy in either country.

Despite evidence that, in Canada, too, tolerance of cultural diversity has known limits, these limits have been less restrictive than in the United States. The treatment of Canada's Aboriginal peoples, for example, has been less harsh and less violent than that of America's Native minorities. And there is nothing in Canada's history that compares to the official discrimination and the physical violence directed against American blacks for much of that country's history. An official policy of **multiculturalism** has existed in Canada since 1971 and was entrenched in the Constitution in 1982.[38] Moreover, Canada's Constitution appears to provide a firmer basis for affirmative action programs and other state activities that have as their goal 'the amelioration of conditions of disadvantaged individuals or groups including those that are disadvantaged because of race, national or ethnic origin, colour, religion, sex, age or mental or physical disability.'[39]

The thesis of the Canadian mosaic versus the American melting pot should not be pushed too hard. Despite the fact that cultural assimilation seems historically to have been part of the American ethos, to the point that it is even expressed in the national motto 'E pluribus unum' (from the many, one), a combination of government policies and court decisions in that country has steered that country away from the melting pot and towards a mosaic society. An extensive system of Spanish-language schools has been created in parts of the United States, particularly California, over the last two decades. Affirmative action policies, from university admission quotas to 'minority set asides' (minority quotas in the allotment of government contracts), and congressional boundary lines drawn to maximize the proportion of minority voters began earlier and arguably have been taken further in the United States than in Canada. Universities and other schools in the United States pioneered the concept and practice of minority-oriented curricula (African-American studies, for example), and this dimension of cultural pluralism is well established there, even while some other aspects of multicultural policy appear to be under assault. Indeed, the very intensity of controversy over multiculturalism, affirmative action, and ascription-based policies in the United States is to some degree a reflection of just how successful the mosaic model has been in influencing public life in that society. The backlash attests to the inroads it made.

At the same time, we should not imagine that the idea of multiculturalism and the programs and structures that seek to implement the mosaic model have gone unchallenged in Canada. Neil Bissoondath's best-selling book, *Selling Illusions: The Cult of Multiculturalism in Canada*,[40] and Reginald Bibby's *Mosaic Madness: The Poverty and Potential of Life in Canada*[41] are two of the salvoes launched against official multiculturalism (as opposed to tolerance of diversity and pluralism that are not sponsored and reinforced by the state). Moreover, part E of Figure 2.3 suggests that a significant number of Canadians believe that the retention of minority cultural identities may not be such a good thing.

In view of how deeply the distinction between the Canadian mosaic and the American melting pot is embedded in the collective psyche of Canadians, it seems surprising that there has been little effort to test empirically this article of faith. But perhaps this is not so surprising. After all, the thing about articles of *faith* is that they do not require proof. They are assumed to be so self-evidently true that searching examination of the evidence on which they rest is considered a waste of time. Moreover, there may appear to be something sacrilegious in questioning a belief that is so central to Canadians' ideas of what distinguishes their society from that of the United States.

Raymond Breton and Jeffrey Reitz risk this sacrilege in what is the most ambitious and systematic attempt to test the proposition that Canadians are more tolerant of diversity than their allegedly more assimilationist neighbours to the south. In *The Illusion of Difference* they review existing studies of the mosaic versus melting pot thesis and examine a number of comparative surveys and census data from the two countries. They conclude that the differences between Canada and the United States are 'more apparent than real'. The Canadian style, they argue, 'is more low-key than the American; moreover, Canadians have a conscious tradition of "tolerance" that Americans do not have.' These differences in the way multiculturalism and ethnic diversity have been thought of in the two societies 'have not produced less pressure towards conformity in Canada, or less propensity to discriminate in employment or housing.'[42] Comparing rates of language retention, ethnic group identification, participation in ethnically based social networks, and attitudes and behaviour towards racial minorities, Breton and Reitz make the case that there is almost no empirical basis for Canadians' cherished self-image of their society as being more tolerant and less assimilationist than that of the United States. Their conclusion is supported by a more recent study of language retention based on Statistics Canada's 2002 Ethnic Diversity Study.[43]

Perhaps in response to the public's growing sense that cultural mosaic policies have contributed to national disunity, in late 1998 the federal government proposed changes to the Immigration Act that would require prospective immigrants to Canada, other than those in the family and refugee classes, to know either French or English. This proposal was criticized by some as having the effect, if not the intention, of discriminating against prospective immigrants from countries—mainly less developed countries—where the likelihood of knowing either English or French is relatively low.

Gender equality is another dimension of group rights that has acquired prominence in recent decades. In both Canada and the United States attitudes concerning the appropriate roles and behaviour of men and women have changed sharply in the direction of greater equality. The visible signs of this change are everywhere, including laws on pay equity, easier access to abortion, affirmative action to increase the number of women employed in male-dominated professions, the ways in which females are portrayed by the media, and greater female participation in the political system. All of these are indirect measures of attitudes towards gender equality. Although they do not provide a direct indication of cultural values, we might reasonably infer these values from the actions of governments and private organizations. Comparing Canada to the United States using such measures, we come up with a mixed scorecard. The differences between the two societies tend not to be very large, Canada being 'more equal' on some counts, and the United States on others. The percentage of female elected officials in each country's legislature is not very different: in 2010, 21.4 per cent of members in Canada's House of Commons were female, while 17.2 per cent of those in the US House of Representatives were female. According to the data collected by the World Values Survey, public opinion is almost identical in the two countries regarding relations between the sexes and the roles appropriate to each.

As in the case of the other dimensions of equality we have examined, no evidence supports the claim that Canadians value equality less than Americans do. Indeed, in terms of recognizing group rights, it is fair to say that Canadian governments have gone at least as far as their American counterparts. In one important respect, however, Canadians are unequivocally more committed to an egalitarian society than are Americans. This involves racial equality. Part G of Figure 2.3 suggests that racist sentiments are somewhat more pervasive in the United States than in Canada. Although it is tempting to infer from the statistics on racial segregation, income differences associated with race, crime and sentencing data, and a host of other measures that Americans tend to be more racist than Canadians, such an inference may not be warranted. To come

In Canada, all citizens' health care is administered via a public system in which a pool of funds provides for medical costs. Those funds are collected via taxation and are managed and paid out by government. During the recent health-care debate in the United States, many protested proposed reforms for a similar universal system, claiming that health-care management should be determined by a private system composed of users, medical providers, and insurers—not governments. The pros and cons of each system continue to be debated in both countries. Right: Republican Michele Bachmann speaks during a rally against the US health-care reform bill in 2009 (© AP Photo/Alex Brandon); left: Friends of Medicare chairperson Christine Burdett speaks about Alberta's proposed health-care reform in 2001 (CP Photo/*Edmonton Journal*/Larry Wong).

at this a bit differently, should one infer from the election of a black American as President of the United States in 2008, while no black has ever been the leader of a Canadian political party, that Americans are more tolerant of racial difference? Or does the fact that a much higher percentage of blacks hold public office in the United States than in Canada, or that the number of blacks among the CEOs of the largest 1,000 companies in the United States is greater than for the largest 1,000 companies in Canada, suggest that the United States, not Canada, is the more racially tolerant society? The answer, most would agree, is no. The enormous differences in the historical circumstances shaping race relations in the two societies and the much greater relative size of the black population in the United States will be cited by most as reasons for being wary of drawing such conclusions. The fact is that these two factors ensure that race and racism are far more central to American political life than to politics in Canada.

But before we jump to conclusions about current attitudes towards race in the two societies, we should keep in mind that the average incomes of black Canadians are about 80 per cent of those for white Canadians, roughly the same as in the United States, and that the likelihood of blacks and whites intermarrying is about the same (5 per cent) in both societies. As well, if our focus is the degree of racial and ethnic tolerance among the majority populations (and these 'majorities' are dwindling), we also would need to examine other groups—South Asians, Aboriginal peoples, Chinese, Koreans, Hispanics, etc.—using numerous demographic variables.

Citizen Expectations for Government

Canadians, it has often been argued, are more likely than Americans to look to government to meet their needs. They are, moreover, more likely to accept state actions that they dislike, instead of mobilizing against such policies and the governments that institute them. Thomas Jefferson's declaration, 'That government is best which governs least', has an oddly foreign tone to Canadians. The mistrust of government and implicit celebration of individualism that inspired Jefferson's aphorism are not sentiments that have resonated in Canada the way they have throughout American history.

This view of Canadians as both more demanding of the state and more passive towards it appears to be backed by a good deal of evidence. On the expectations side, Canadian governments do more than American ones to redistribute wealth between individuals and regions of the country. They have been resistant to the expansion of a private presence in health care and post-secondary education. They own corporations whose activities range from producing electricity to television broadcasting, while American governments have generally been content to regulate privately owned businesses in these same industries. And Canadian governments are much more actively involved in promoting particular cultural values, especially those associated with bilingualism and multiculturalism, than are most governments in the United States. In Canada the state accounts for a larger share of gross national expenditure than in the United States—and spends more on redistributive social programs and also takes a larger share of citizens' incomes in taxes. Overall, government appears to be more intrusive in Canadian society than in the United States.

What about the evidence for Canadians' alleged passivity in the face of government actions that they dislike? Is it true that Canadians are more deferential to authority, including political authority, than their American counterparts? It was once fairly common to hear Canadian political experts intone that 'freedom wears a crown', meaning that the more orderly society and the stability that Canadians experienced through this country's parliamentary system and titular monarchy, compared to the rather chaotic 'mobocracy' to the south, provided a sort of protective mantle under which citizens were better able to enjoy their democratic rights and freedoms. 'We've always accepted more governmental control over our lives than . . . [Americans] have—and fewer civil liberties', argued Pierre Berton, Canada's foremost popular historian. But, he added, 'the other side of the coin of liberty is license, sometimes anarchy. It seems to us that . . . Americans have been more willing to suffer violence in . . . [their] lives than we have for the sake of individual freedom.'[44]

Canadians' apparent greater faith in government, compared to the more skeptical attitudes of Americans, owes a good deal to a collectivist ethos that sets Canadians and their history apart from the United States. It is this ethos that Canadian nationalists are invoking when they argue that Canada's public health-care system and more generous social programs reflect the 'soul' of this country, and that their dismemberment would send Canadians down the allegedly mean-spirited path of American individualism. Some of Canada's most prominent thinkers, including George Grant and Charles Taylor, have argued that the collectivist ethos and greater willingness of Canadians than Americans to use the state to achieve community goals are central to the Canadian political tradition.

In *Lament for a Nation*, Grant argued that the Canadian political tradition was marked by a communitarian spirit that rejected the individualism of American-style liberalism. He traced the roots of this spirit to the influence of conservative ideas and the British connection, which helped to keep alive a benign view of government as an agent for pursuing the common good. This distinctive national character was, Grant believed, doomed to be crushed by the steamroller of American liberalism and technology, which, he maintained in later works, would ultimately flatten national cultures throughout the capitalist world.

Grant's 'lament' was in the key of what has been called **red Toryism**. Red Tories are conservatives who believe that government has a responsibility to act as an agent for the collective good, and that this responsibility goes far beyond maintaining law and order. Grant and others in this tradition are in favour of state support for culture as, for example, through the Canadian Broadcasting Corporation. Red Tories since Grant are comfortable with the welfare state and the principle that government *should* protect the poor and disadvantaged. Red Toryism, its critics would claim, involves a rather paternalistic philosophy of government and state–citizen relations. Defenders, however, maintain that it is compassionate and a true expression of a collectivist national ethos that distinguishes Canadians from their southern neighbours.

Charles Taylor is not a red Tory. Canada's most internationally acclaimed living philosopher is firmly on the left of the political spectrum. He agrees with Grant about the importance of collectivism in Canada's political tradition. Taylor has always been extremely critical of what he calls the 'atomism' of American liberalism, a value system that he believes cuts people off from the communal relations that nurture human dignity. Like most Canadian nationalists, he believes implicitly in the moral superiority of Canada's collectivist political tradition.

Taylor is one of the leading thinkers in the contemporary movement known as **communitarianism**. This is based on the belief that real human freedom and dignity are possible only in the context of communal relations that allow for the public recognition of group identities and that are based on equal respect for these different identity-groups. Taylor argues that the key to Canadian unity lies in finding constitutional arrangements that enable different groups of Canadians to feel that they belong to Canada and are recognized as constituent elements of Canadian society. 'Nations . . . which have a strong sense of their own identity,' says Taylor, 'and hence a desire to direct in some ways their common affairs, can only be induced to take part willingly in multinational states if they are in some ways recognized within them.'[45] He calls this the recognition of 'deep diversity'. The realization of deep diversity would require, at a minimum, official recognition of Quebec as a distinct society and probably constitutional acknowledgement of an Aboriginal right to self-government. To some this might sound like a recipe for dismantling whatever fragile sense of Canadian community already exists. Taylor insists, however, that one-size-fits-all notions of community do not work in the modern world.

The characterization of Canada as a deferential society, or at least one where citizens are less likely to question political and other sources of established authority than in the United States, has been challenged in recent years. In *The Canadian Revolution*, Peter C. Newman argues that the historically elitist tenor of Canadian life collapsed during the years 1985–95 under the pressure of developments in Canada and in the world at large. Newman speaks of the rise of a 'new populism' and of what he calls the 'breakdown of trust between the governors and the governed'.[46] The growth of the underground cash economy in reaction to the GST, the breakdown of the old two-party dominance in the 1993 election, the rejection of the elite-supported Charlottetown Accord by Canada citizens, the violent clash between Natives and white authorities at Oka in 1990, and the near-victory of Quebec separatists in 1995 are, Newman argues, indications of Canadians' passage from deference to defiance. He attributes their transition to a constellation of factors that includes the arrogance of politicians, the more competitive global economy, the inability of Canadian government to continue financing the system of entitlements that Canadians came to take for granted in the 1960s and 1970s, and the decline in religious faith, among other things.

A more quantitative treatment of the same phenomenon is offered by Neil Nevitte in *The Decline of Deference*.[47] Nevitte agrees that Canadians are less deferential today than in the past. He attributes this to the post-materialist values of those born in the post–World War II era. **Post-materialism** attaches comparatively greater importance to human needs for belonging, self-esteem, and personal fulfillment than does **materialism**, which places greater stress on economic security and material well-being. Such issues as employment and incomes matter most to materialists, whereas post-materialists are likely to place higher value on so-called quality-of-life issues such as the environment, human rights, and group equality. Materialists are more likely than post-materialists to have confidence in public institutions and to trust in the judgements of elites.

Nevitte shows that Canadians' confidence in government institutions, a category that included the armed forces, police, Parliament, and public service, declined during the 1980s and that high levels of confidence are much less likely to be expressed by those between the ages of 25–54 than among older citizens. He also finds that Canadians are, if anything, slightly more skeptical of government institutions than are Americans—not what one would expect to find if the traditional stereotype of deferential Canadians versus defiant Americans holds true.

We should not be too quick to conclude, however, that the old characterization of Canadians as being more deferential towards political authority and trusting of government than Americans is no longer accurate. What Nevitte and others call post-materialism may be more pervasive in Canada than in the United States. But data from the 2000 and 2006 waves of the World Values Survey show that only with respect to the armed forces do Americans express much more confidence than Canadians. Levels of confidence in the police, Parliament/Congress, the public service, and government are not very different in the two countries. An important lesson that may be drawn from this is a cautionary one: be careful not to read too much significance into data collected at one point in time.

Asking people how much confidence they have in state institutions is one possible measure of deference. But another involves behaviour that requires people to act in a defiant manner towards authority or at least to behave in ways that require them to take a public position on a divisive issue. Signing petitions, joining boycotts, and attending lawful demonstrations are acts that, while not necessarily defiant towards authority, are not characteristic of a deferential population. Figure 2.4 shows that Canadians and Americans are not very different when it comes to such behaviour. The evidence certainly does not support the revisionist claim that Canadians, emboldened by the experience of life under the Charter, have become less deferential than Americans.

Another angle on citizen expectations for government is provided by what political scientists call **social capital**. This involves the fabric of connections between members of a community. It is made up both of norms, such as trust in one's neighbours, and of behaviours, such as voting and participating in community organizations. The roots of this concept can be found in Alexis de Tocqueville's observations on the propensity of mid-nineteenth-century Americans to join together in voluntary associations in order to achieve communal goals. Tocqueville believed that these voluntary associations were the connective tissue of American democracy. They reminded citizens in immediate and practical ways of the fact that they belonged to a community and depended on one another.

Many commentators on American society argue that social capital in that country has been in serious decline for years. The evidence for this claim is not, however, rock solid. But what is clear is that Americans continue to be more likely than Canadians and the citizens of other rich democracies to belong to voluntary associations and to participate in their activities. Figure 2.5 shows that a much larger share of the American population

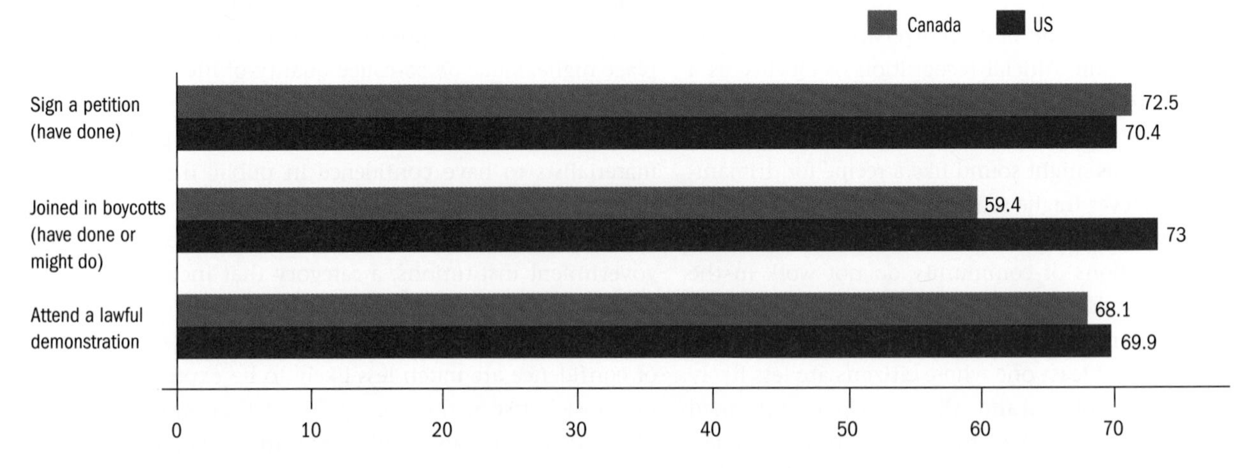

FIGURE 2.4 Engaged Citizen Behaviour, Canada and the United States
Source: World Values Survey, 2006.

devotes some of their time to unpaid work for religious, youth, sports and recreation, educational, and cultural groups. These are activities that, in Canada, are more likely to be the responsibility of state agencies and financed by public revenues. One might conclude from this difference that Americans are more likely than Canadians to believe that private citizens and the voluntary associations they create—not the state—should be responsible for meeting many of society's needs. Canadians are more likely to see these activities as the responsibility of government.

Some significant part of the civic and communal engagement of Americans is due to the far greater strength of traditional religious values in the United States compared to Canada. Canada is, quite simply, a more secular society than the United States, though not nearly as secular as some Western European democracies. **Secularization** involves a decline in the belief that religion and religious authorities should be looked to for guidance about how to behave and how to evaluate behaviour, and an increase in the social, cultural, and political influence of elites whose expertise is not based on religious faith.

For most of their respective histories, Canada and especially French-speaking Canada were generally thought of as being more traditionally religious than the United States. Religious elites certainly appeared to have more influence in Canada, at least until the 1960s. Since then, the process of secularization has advanced more rapidly in Canada and other Western democracies than in the United States. Figure 2.6 shows that on a range of measures Americans tend to be more traditionally religious than Canadians. France and Great Britain, the two European countries that colonized Canada, are included for purposes of comparison.

The more secular character of Canada's political culture helps to explain why issues with important moral dimensions, such as abortion and stem cell research using human embryo cells, have been more controversial in the United States than in Canada and why Canadian legislation recognizing same-sex marriage was passed in 2005 while in the United States this particular battle rages on. The more secular nature of Canadian culture also helps to explain why Canadian politicians, unlike their American counterparts, infrequently invoke religious references or even mention God in their public statements. Being perceived as too religious can even be a liability in Canadian politics, as Canadian Alliance party leader Stockwell Day discovered when his born-again Christianity made him a target for sniping from the media and rival parties in the 2000 federal election.

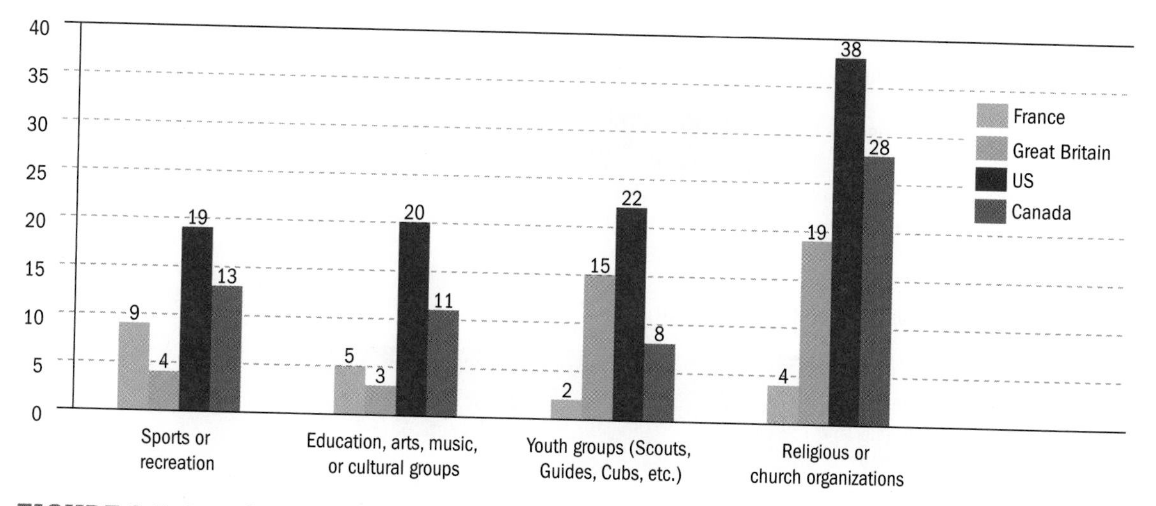

FIGURE 2.5 Social Capital in Canada, the United States, France, and Great Britain

Note: Percentages indicate those claiming to be active members of each type of organization. All figures are from the 2000 survey except for religious organizations, for which the data are from the 2006 survey.

Source: World Values Survey, 2000, 2006.

A. God is very important in my life. (percentage agreeing)

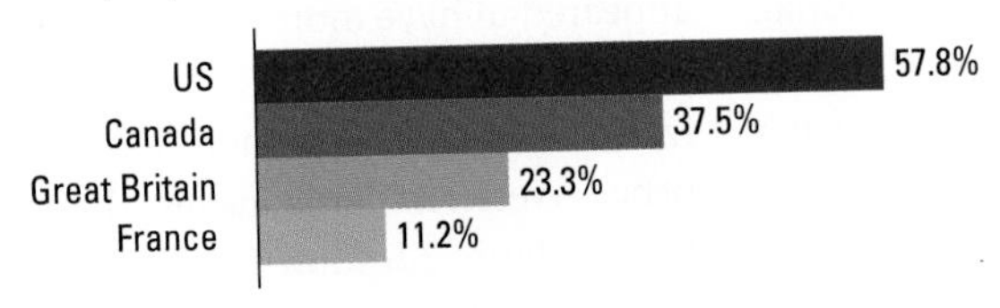

B. I do unpaid voluntary work for a religious or church organization. (percentage agreeing)

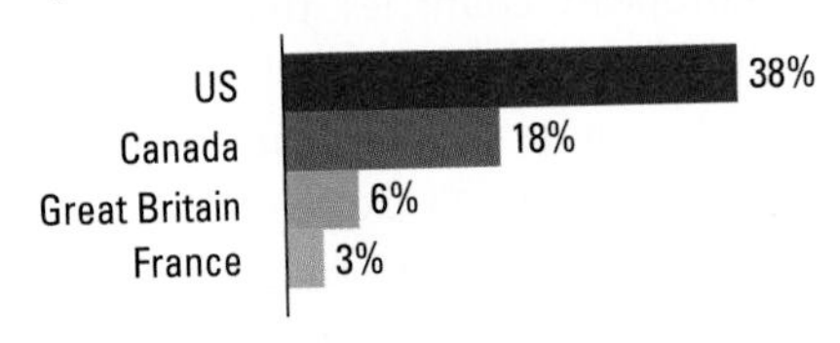

C. I agree that marriage is an outdated institution. (percentage agreeing)

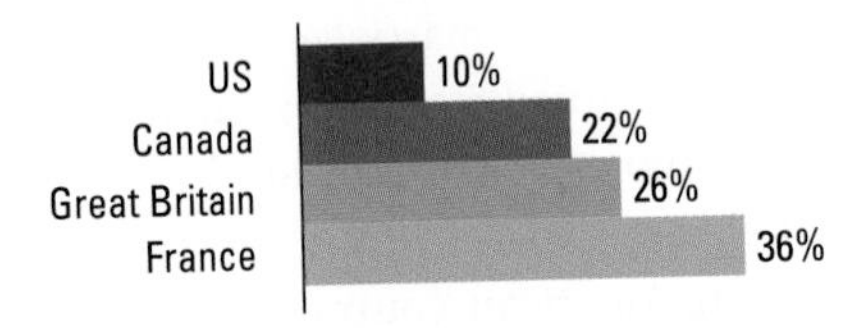

D. It would be better for the country if more people with strong religious beliefs held public office. (percentage disagreeing)

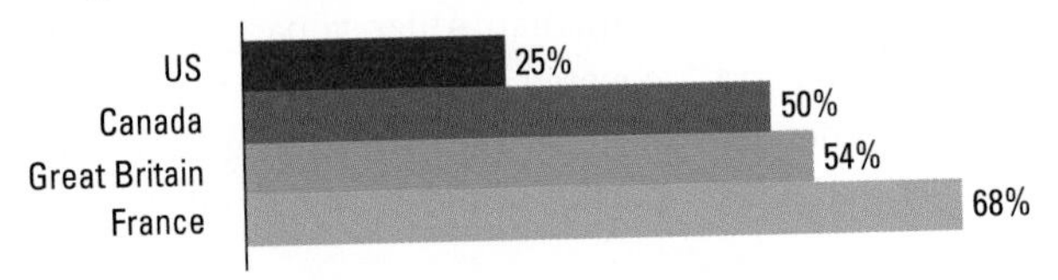

E. There are absolutely clear guidelines about what is good and evil. (percentage agreeing)

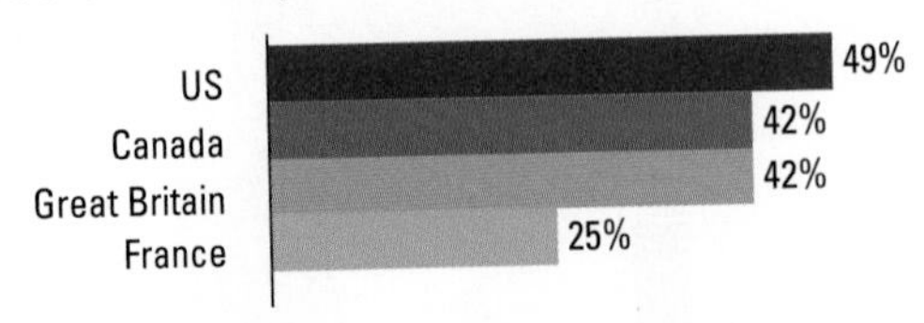

F. I believe in sin. (percentage agreeing)

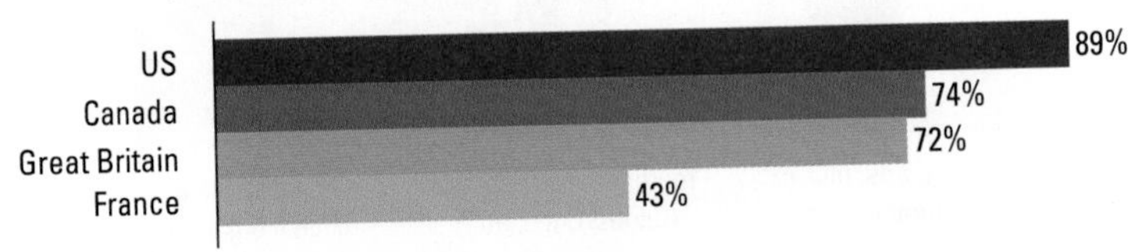

FIGURE 2.6 Strength of Traditional Religious Values: Canada, the United States, France, and Great Britain, 2000

Sources: World Values Survey, 2000 (B–F) and 2006 (A).

How Different Are Canadian and American Values?

Observing English Canada and the United States about 100 years ago, the French sociologist André Siegfried argued that the differences between them were relatively small and certainly insignificant by European standards. Siegfried was one of the first to weigh in on a question that has been at the centre of the comparative study of political culture in Canada and the United States: which are politically more significant, the similarities or differences in the values and beliefs of these two societies?

One hundred years after Siegfried, Michael Adams[48] and Philip Resnick[49] are among those who argue that these value differences are significant

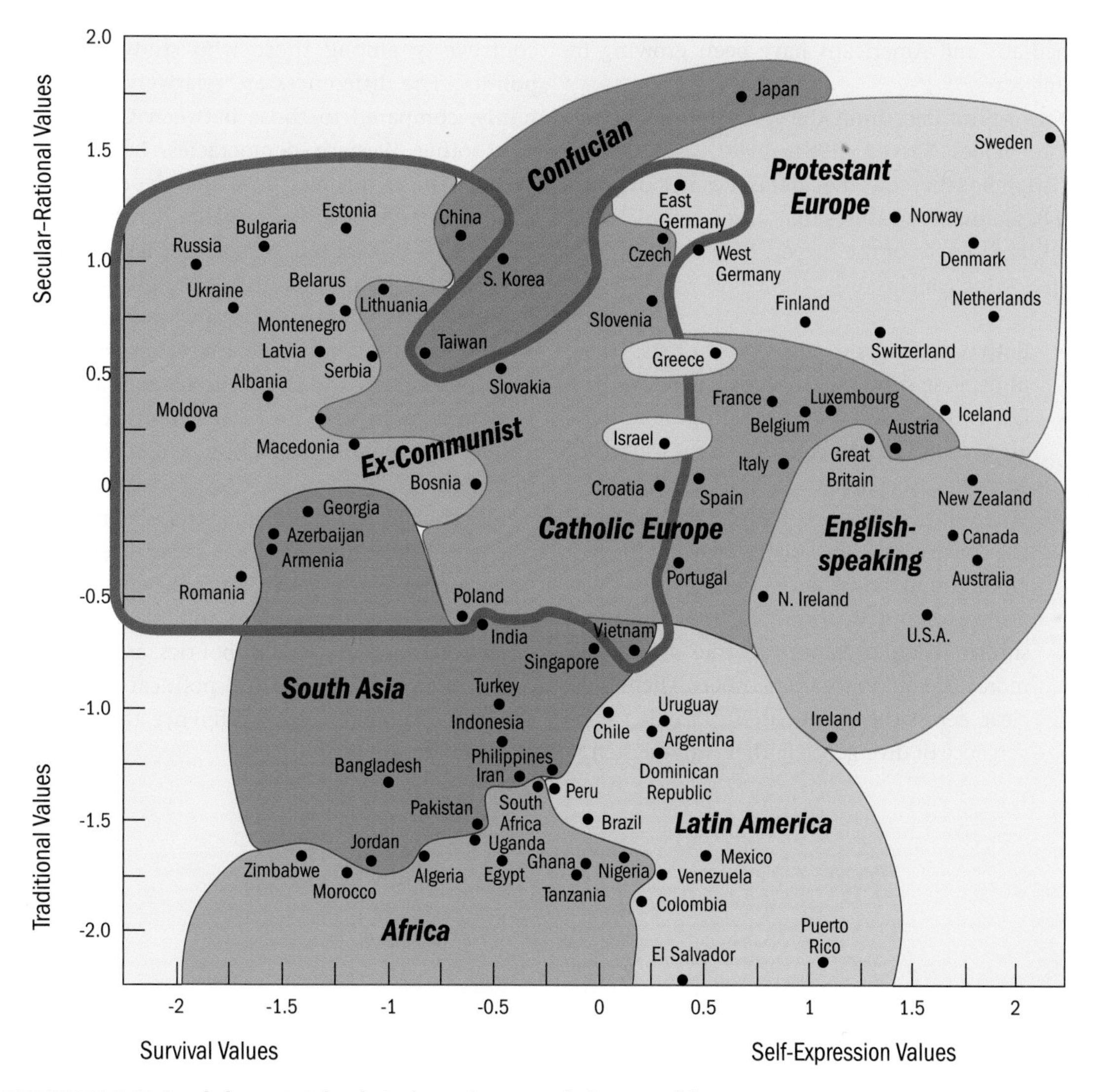

FIGURE 2.7 Inglehart-Welzel Cultural Map of the World

This map shows that many basic values are closely correlated. The scale on the vertical axis represents a continuum from traditional to secular values; the horizontal scale, ranging from survival values to self-expression values, reflects the fact that increasing wealth in many societies since the 1960s has meant that, as Ronald Inglehart puts it, 'priorities have shifted from an overwhelming emphasis on economic and physical security toward . . . subjective well-being, self-expression and quality of life.'

Source: Adapted from World Values Survey, 2000.

and growing. Adams goes so far as to conclude that Canada and the United States are fundamentally different and maintains that this has always been the case. Resnick is more cautious. He acknowledges the undeniable similarity between Canadian and American culture but argues that, in many important ways, Canadians have more in common with Western Europeans, such as the French, than they do with Americans. Moreover, Resnick believes that this affinity with Europeans and the gap between Canadians and Americans have been growing in recent years.

Drawing on data from the three rounds of the World Values Survey (1981, 1990, and 2000), Christian Boucher tests the Adams–Resnick hypothesis. Based on 28 measures that have been included in all three waves of the survey, Boucher arrives at the following conclusions:

- Both Canada and the United States have undergone substantial value change over the last two decades, both becoming more 'progressive and secular regarding some aspects of economic, social, political and moral issues'.
- 'The values differences between Canada and the United States are small . . . except for religious and moral issues.'[50]
- Canadians and Americans are becoming more similar when it comes to some values and more different in regard to others. There is no clear, across-the-board pattern of either convergence or divergence in their value systems.

Data from the 2006 wave of the World Values Survey provide further confirmation of Boucher's three conclusions. Indeed, the finding that is most striking is how much more similar Canadian attitudes and beliefs are to those of Americans, compared to the citizens of Western European societies.

In the end, what may be most significant about this debate over the extent of the value differences between Canada and the United States is that it has gone on so long and continues to generate controversy among those who study Canadian politics. The differences are relatively small, certainly, compared to those between Canada and most other Western democracies. But this is a debate whose survival does not depend on the reality of large or growing value differences (see Figure 2.7). It is rooted, instead, in the precariousness of the national identity of English-speaking Canada. This identity has always been based on the premise of significant value differences between Canada and the United States, a premise used to explain why these two countries are not united under one constitution and *should not* be so united.

It is probably fair to conclude that the magnitude of these value differences has never been, and is not at present, very great. But neither is it inconsequential. It is also certain that this issue very often becomes embroiled in politics, as politicians, commentators, citizens—and political scientists—allow their preferences to influence their reading of the evidence.

Starting Points for Research

David Bell, *The Roots of Disunity*, rev. edn (Toronto: Oxford University Press, 1992). This revised edition of Bell and Tepperman's 1979 book presents an excellent analysis of the historical roots of English Canada's long-standing identity crisis, French–English conflict, and the rise of regionalism in Canada.

Seymour Martin Lipset, *Continental Divide: The Values and Institutions of the United States and Canada* (Toronto: C.D. Howe Institute, 1989). This remains one of the best surveys of the voluminous work done on the differences and similarities in the political cultures of Canada and the United States, written by one of the most astute observers of political culture in these two countries.

Neil Nevitte, *The Decline of Deference: Canadian Value Change in Cross-National Perspective* (Peterborough, Ont.: Broadview Press, 1996). Nevitte examines the changing Canadian value system in a cross-national context that includes American and European societies.

Philip Resnick, *The European Roots of Canadian Identity* (Peterborough, Ont.: Broadview Press, 2005). In this wide-ranging analysis Resnick argues that the fundamental values and beliefs of Canadians are more like those of Western Europeans than of Americans and that the European affinity of Canada became more evident and was reinforced by the war in Iraq.

David Thomas and Barbara Boyle Torrey, eds, *Canada and the United States: Differences That Count*, 3rd edn (Peterborough, Ont.: Broadview Press, 2008). This collection includes many useful essays on differences in Canadian and American values, behaviour, institutions, and policies, ranging from health care to crime.

Nelson Wiseman, *In Search of Canadian Political Culture* (Vancouver: University of British Columbia Press, 2007). Although much of this book's focus is on the nature of regional political cultures, it includes several excellent chapters that deal more generally with Canadian political culture.

Review Exercises

1. Look at Figure 2.1, Support for Quebec Independence, 1978–2010. Can you suggest some reason(s) for the wide fluctuations in the percentage of Quebecers saying they would vote for Quebec sovereignty? Why was it so high in 1990 and 1995? Why was it comparatively low in 1984, 1988, 2002, and 2008?
2. Where would you place each of the parties represented in the federal Parliament on a political ideology scale ranging from far left to far right? Where would you place the party that governs your province? Where would you place yourself? In each case, explain why you chose a particular place on the scale for a party or yourself.
3. Choose any three organizations from the following list. From the information included in their websites, decide whether each organization advocates mainly collectivist or individualistic ideas. Do you think these organizations represent the ideas of significant numbers of Canadians? Why?

   Fraser Institute: <www.fraserinstitute.ca>

   Centre for Social Justice:
   <www.socialjustice.org>

   Canadian Centre for Policy Alternatives:
   <www.policyalternatives.ca>

   Canadian Labour Congress:
   <www.clc-ctc.ca>

Sierra Club Canada: <www.sierraclub.ca>

C.D. Howe Institute: <www.cdhowe.org>

National Citizens' Coalition: <www.morefreedom.org>

Council of Canadians: <www.canadians.org>

4. Canadians often compare their values and beliefs to those of Americans. In 2005 the Dominion Institute published a series of five articles on 'American Myths' <www.dominion.ca/americanmyths/>, which argued that the beliefs that many Canadians hold about Americans and how Canadians differ culturally from their southern neighbours are wrong in fundamental ways. Are you convinced by the arguments and evidence in this series? Why or why not?

Canadians are among the most satisfied people in the world and have long been so. According to the 2006 World Values Survey, they are almost as satisfied with their lives as Mexicans, Colombians, and Guatemalans. Obviously, affluence is not the determining factor when it comes to satisfaction and happiness (although all studies show that it helps). © Sergeibach/Dreamstime.com

3 The Social and Economic Setting

Politics unfolds against a backdrop of social and economic conditions. This chapter focuses on the following aspects of Canadian society:

- Material well-being.
- Equality.
- Discrimination.
- Quality of life.
- Poverty.
- Independence.

After President George W. Bush's 2004 re-election, many Canadians were gratified to read stories claiming that thousands of Americans were inquiring into the possibility of moving to Canada. This seemed to them to be the surest confirmation of their belief—a belief shared by most Canadians—that Canada is superior in important ways to the powerhouse to the south, the benchmark against which we always compare ourselves and our achievements. The Canadian self-image is one of compassion, tolerance, and prosperity. Canadians tend to see themselves as being more compassionate and more tolerant than Americans. Their neighbours may be richer, but most Canadians believe that their country's prosperity is more equally shared. And they believe that this is as it should be.

Canadians are indeed fortunate. But that good fortune is not shared by all Canadians. Roughly three million Canadians fall below what is conventionally called the 'poverty line', the low-income point established by Statistics Canada. In recent years, anti-globalization protestors, poverty activists, and spokespersons for the homeless have all been critical of conditions in Canada and the performance of government in this country.

In this chapter we will examine the social and economic setting of Canadian politics. At various points comparisons will be made between Canada and other countries, between regions in Canada, between various points in Canada's history, and between actual conditions and some idealized standards that have been applied to the performance of Canada's political system. Our goal in this chapter is not, however, chiefly to judge. Instead, our main purpose is to understand the societal context that influences, and is influenced by, politics and public policy. In doing so we will be selective, focusing on aspects of Canadian society and the economy that are closely associated with several values that most Canadians consider to be important. These include the following:

- material well-being;
- equality;
- quality of life;
- independence.

Obviously, these values will be interpreted differently by different people. Disagreements aside, these values are of special importance for two related reasons. First, they represent public purposes that most of us expect governments to preserve or promote. Second, political controversies are frequently about one or more of these values—disagreements over how to achieve them; over what value(s) should give way, and by how much, when they conflict; about whether they are being adequately met; and so on. It makes sense, therefore, to focus on these dimensions of the social and economic setting of Canadian politics.

Political issues and outcomes are not determined in any simplistic manner by such things as the extent and nature of inequalities in Canadian society or the level of material well-being, any more than political ideologies and institutions translate directly into political behaviour and public policy. Like ideology and institutions, the social and economic settings of politics establish boundaries to political life. They do so by determining the sorts of problems a society faces, the resources available for coping with these problems, the nature and intensity of divisions within society, and the distribution of politically valuable resources between societal interests.

Material Well-Being

Canada is an affluent society. This simple fact is sometimes obscured by the news of fresh layoffs, plant closings, slipping competitiveness, and pockets of poverty. For most of the last generation, the average real purchasing power of Canadians was the second highest in the world, topped only by Americans. In the last decade Canada has slipped significantly, so that today 15 OECD countries rank ahead of it in terms of average real purchasing power, or **purchasing power parities** (see Figure 3.1). On a global scale, however, Canadians remain relatively wealthy. Affluence affects both the opportunities and problems faced by policy-makers. The problem of poverty, for example, assumes a very different character in an affluent society like Canada from that in a poorer society like Mexico or a destitute one like Sudan. Not only does Canada's poverty problem look rather enviable from the standpoint of these other countries, but the means that governments in Canada have available to deal with this problem are far greater than those that can be deployed by the governments of poorer societies. The very definition of what constitute public problems, warranting the attention of government, is also influenced by a society's material conditions. Environmental pollution, a prominent issue on the public agendas of affluent societies, tends to be buried under the weight of other pressing social and economic problems in less affluent societies.

Within the elite club of affluent societies, cultural and institutional differences are probably more important as determinants of the public agenda and government response to them than are their differences in material well-being. But the particular characteristics of a national economy, factors upon which material affluence depends, are significant influences on the politics and public policies of any society. These characteristics include the sectoral and regional distribution of economic activity, the level and distribution of employment, characteristics of its labour force, the profile of its trade with the rest of the world, and so on. Despite enjoying one of the highest standards of living in the world, Canadians have seldom been complacent about their affluence. Fears that Canada's material well-being may rest on fragile footings have long been expressed. These fears have become increasingly urgent since the 1980s, as Canadians have attempted to come to grips with what global economic restructuring means for their future.

A secure job at a decent rate of pay is desired by most people. It enables one to plan for the future

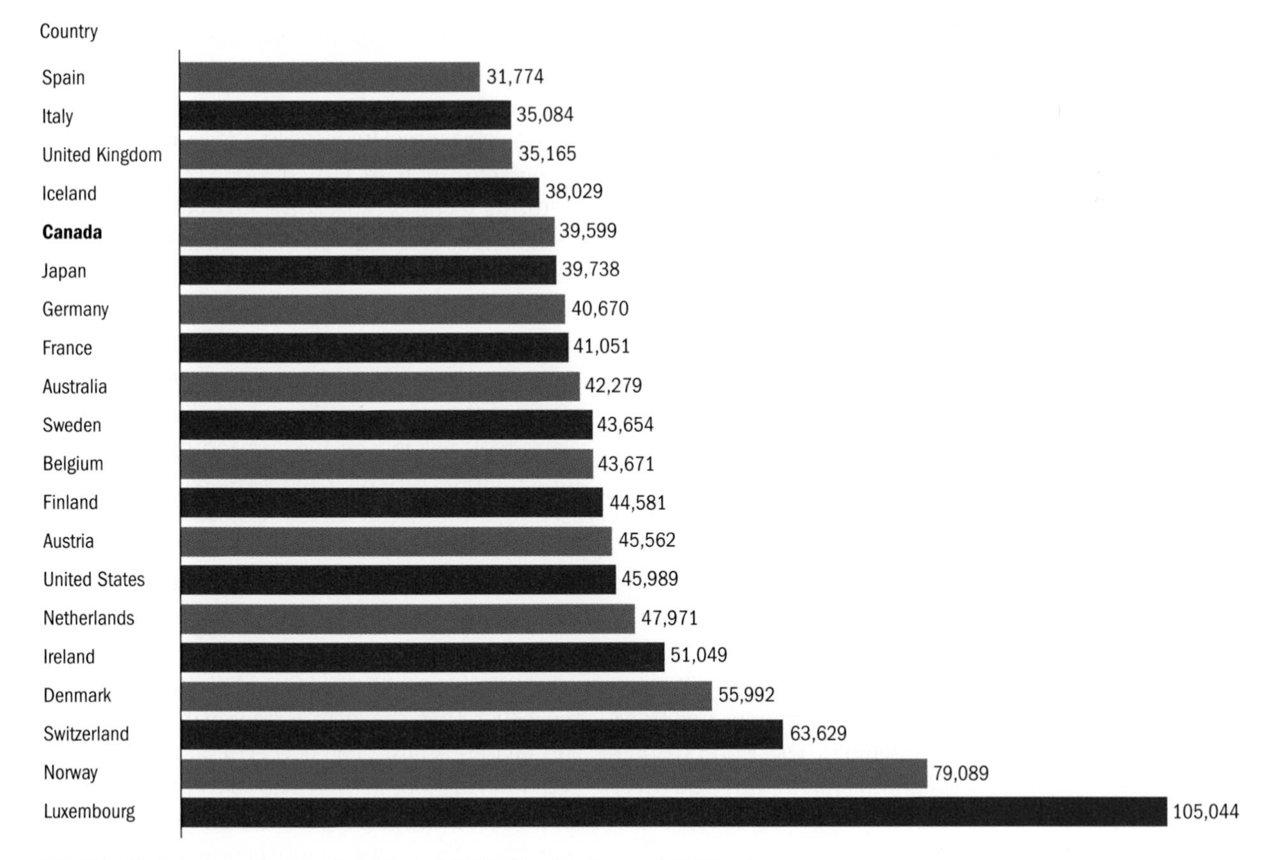

FIGURE 3.1 Per Capital PPPs* ($US) for Richest OECD Countries, 2009

*Purchasing power parities.

Source: International Bank for Reconstruction and Development / The World Bank: World Development Indicators Database, 9 July 2010. At: <data.worldbank.org/indicator/NY.GDP.PCAP.CD/countries/1W?display=default> (13 Feb. 2011).

and achieve the goals that one has for oneself and one's family. Unemployment can be personally and socially devastating. The political importance of the employment issue is seen in the fact that it is regularly mentioned by Canadians as one of most important issues facing the country. Governments react with rhetoric, gestures, and policies. These policies may not succeed in maintaining employment at a socially acceptable level—indeed, they may not even be expected to reduce unemployment—but no government would pass up an opportunity to express its commitment to increasing jobs and its sympathy for the unemployed.

What does Canada's employment record look like? Compared to other advanced industrialized democracies, Canada has done fairly well. Over the past 30 years the national level of unemployment has fluctuated between a low of 6 per cent (2007) and a high of 12 per cent (1983), averaging about 7–9 per cent during most of this period. This may not impress Americans, whose unemployment rate generally has been a few percentage points below Canada's (although, since the recession that began in late 2008, this is no longer the case). Canadians, however, are used to dismissing the superior employment record of the US as being bought with lower wages and greater income inequality than most Canadians would tolerate (the claim about lower wages is simply not true if one compares real wages and net after-tax incomes). Canada's unemployment rate has been close to the average for the more affluent OECD countries. Moreover, the economy's ability to create new jobs has been among the best. Between 1999 and 2009 it was about 50 per cent greater than in the United States, twice the average rate in Western Europe, and exceeded only by Australia's rate of job growth.

Looking at the distribution of employment across sectors of the Canadian economy, one finds that Canada closely resembles the world's other major capitalist economies. About three-quarters of workers are in service industries (sales, communications, transportation, tourism, finance, public administration, etc.), about 14 per cent are employed in the manufacturing sector, roughly 4 per cent work in primary industries like farming, fishing, forestry, and mining, and the remaining 6 per cent work in construction (2009). These shares are similar to those of our major trading partner, the United States, as well as in the economies of the UK and Sweden. Over time, the service sector's share of total employment has grown dramatically, from about 40 per cent in the mid-twentieth century to the current level of almost 8 in 10 jobs. The shares in the primary and secondary sectors have obviously declined, more sharply in primary industries than in manufacturing. These employment trends have led many to worry that the Canadian economy is 'deindustrializing'. In fact, however, these trends are broadly similar to those that have characterized all of the world's major capitalist economies over the last several decades.

The past two decades have seen the emergence of a politically important debate over the relative value to an economy of service versus manufacturing jobs. Some argue that service industries, particularly in regard to generating knowledge and distributing information, also produce value, and so there is no reason to worry about a shrinking manufacturing base. Others argue that the manufacturing sector is especially important, and that a point can be reached—and may already have been reached in economies like Canada's and that of the United States—where further decline of the manufacturing base undermines the overall competitiveness of the economy and drags down real incomes.[1] Much of this argument hinges on the often-heard claim that new jobs in the burgeoning service sector tend to be unskilled and low-paying—'McJobs', as they are often derisively called. These jobs, it is said, have increasingly replaced better-paying manufacturing sector jobs that have been exported to low-wage economies. That unskilled and low-skilled manufacturing jobs have migrated to developing economies is beyond dispute. However, the belief that the new economy primarily creates McJobs is false. The new economy also creates better-paying jobs in information technology, communications, financial services, and other service industries. These jobs require education and expertise, whereas McJobs do not. What have been lost in the new economy are the low-skill/high-paying manufacturing jobs characteristic of the factory economy of the 1950s, 1960s, and 1970s. Their disappearance has heightened the importance of education and skills as necessary qualifications for well-paying jobs. The case of a Ph.D. driving a taxi or an engineer flipping burgers will always be the one reported by the media, as will the relocation of a manufacturing business to China (although the latter hardly qualifies as news anymore!). The reality, however, is that education and training generally translate into higher incomes and better job security—a relationship confirmed by virtually all studies of education and income—in both developed economies like Canada's and in the developing world.

Fears over the export of low-skill manufacturing jobs have been replaced in more recent years by worries that more highly skilled jobs, including those requiring a good deal of education, have been moving abroad to some developing countries. Much of the work in the computer programming and financial services sectors has moved to India. An increasing share of the production of machine tools, dies, and moulds for manufacturing has relocated to China. This is known as **outsourcing**. Unlike the earlier movement of textile, footwear, and repetitive low-skill jobs to developing countries, outsourcing also includes the loss of more highly skilled and highly paid jobs.

Media Spotlight

Box 3.1 The Best of Times?

As the American economy sank deeper into the quagmire of the sub-prime crisis in financial markets, dragging down Canada and other Western economies, and the price of a barrel of oil and a number of other natural resources reached vertiginous levels in 2007–8, Brookings Institution policy analyst Greg Easterbrook made what almost everyone found to be a startling claim. 'We have never been as well off as we are today', he told Americans. Although his analysis and supporting data concerned the United States, Easterbrook's argument applies to Canada as well.

It goes like this. The real income of a typical person or household has never been higher. The percentage of people attending and graduating from university has never been greater. The amount of space per person in the average home is at an all-time high. The likelihood of being a crime victim has been falling steadily. All forms of pollution, with the exception of greenhouse gases, are in decline. And rates of cancer, heart disease, and stroke have also fallen. But despite what Easterbrook claims is irrefutable and overwhelming evidence of improvement in most people's lives, the public mood is often downcast and pessimistic.

This is what Easterbrook calls *The Progress Paradox*, the title of a book he published in 2005. He blames the media, arguing that the incentive system within which most reporters, producers, writers, and other media personnel operate tends to reward bad news stories and punish, or at least discourage, the coverage of good news. And so, in the midst of what Easterbrook argues are the best of times, a steady bombardment of negative and pessimistic news reporting causes us to believe that these are in fact the worst of times.

You may be dubious about Easterbrook's argument, or at least about some of the data he offers in support of his claim that things have never been so good for Americans, Canadians, and the citizens of other capitalist democracies. But at the very least Easterbrook's 'progress paradox' encourages us to open our minds to the possibility that the rich diet of doom and gloom we are fed by much of the media system, much of the time, may reflect something other than the facts on the ground.

Examples are easy enough to find, all the way from the telephone call that you receive from India on behalf of a Canadian bank or other financial services company trying to sell you new products to the software design that contributed to the latest video game that you may be thinking of buying.

These fears are probably unfounded. Canada's job creation rate has been one of the best in the developed world for over a decade and virtually all labour economists project that as the country's population continues to age, the supply of workers, including those needed to fill highly skilled and well-paying jobs, will not meet the projected demand. But even if it could be shown that outsourcing has and will continue to result in a hemorrhage of jobs, one could still make the case that sharing employment opportunities with people in less affluent parts of the world is preferable to providing them with foreign aid. If Canadians truly believe that the world's wealth should be shared more equally—which is what they regularly tell pollsters—then they should applaud the redistribution of economic activity from the rich countries of the world to those that aspire to a higher standard of living. But most do not.

Equality

> One of the most persistent images that Canadians have of their society is that it has no classes. This image becomes translated into the assertion that Canadians are all relatively equal in their possessions, in the amount of money they earn, and in the opportunities which they and their children have to get on in the world. . . .
>
> That there is neither very rich nor very poor in Canada is an important part of the image. There are no barriers to opportunity. Education is free. Therefore, making use of it is largely a question of personal ambition.[2]

This may well have been the image held by most Canadians when sociologist John Porter wrote these words in *The Vertical Mosaic* (1965). It is doubtful whether Canadians today are as confident that their society is one without serious inequalities. Stories about homelessness, food banks, poverty, and growing income inequality have become routine. Moreover, charges of discrimination made by women's groups, Native Canadians, visible minorities, gays and lesbians, and other minorities—charges that were muffled until a few decades ago—are common today. The passage of provincial human rights codes and of the Charter of Rights and Freedoms and the proliferation of human rights officers—ombudsmen, race relations officers, equity officers, and so on—have contributed to this sharpened awareness of inequality. But these reforms were themselves inspired by a growing sense that existing policies and institutions did not adequately protect the equality of citizens and that, in some cases, laws and institutions actually perpetuated inequality.

For various reasons, then, Canadians are probably more aware of inequalities today than they were a few decades ago. But despite this heightened awareness, most Canadians still cling to the belief that their society is basically middle class. This belief—which, we hasten to add, is by no means false—springs from the dominant liberal ideology. Individualism and a belief that opportunities to get ahead in life are open to those with the energy and talent needed to take advantage of them are at the core of this liberal ideology. To say that society is basically middle class means, from this ideological perspective, that the barriers to upward mobility are relatively low for the vast majority of people. The fact that some people are extraordinarily wealthy and others are quite destitute needs to be set alongside an even more prominent fact, i.e., that most Canadians occupy a broad middle band in terms of their incomes and lifestyles.

Wealth is unevenly divided in all societies. Few people believe that the sort of levelling implied by Karl Marx's aphorism, 'From each according to his abilities, to each according to his needs', is desirable. But many people are disturbed by the jarring contrast between conspicuous luxury and destitution in their society. The gap between rich and poor is not as great in Canada as in some other industrialized democracies. Nevertheless, it is considerable and persistent. Moreover, some groups bear the brunt of poverty much more heavily than others.

In 2007 the richest one-fifth of the population received about 47 per cent of all income, while the poorest one-fifth accounted for about 4 per cent. These shares are not dramatically different from what they were four decades earlier. In 1957 the bottom quintile of Canadians accounted for 4.2 percent of all money income compared to 41.4 percent for the top quintile. If social security benefits are left out of the picture, the inequality gap is much wider, the bottom fifth of Canadians accounting for barely 1 per cent of earned income. Compared to the distribution of income in other advanced capitalist societies, Canada's is fairly typical. The distribution of income is more equal than in some countries, such as the United States, but less equal than in others, including France and Sweden.

In recent years, news stories and academic studies purporting to show a growing gap between the rich and the poor in Canada have contributed to a widespread belief that inequality has worsened. Figure 3.2 shows that *every* income group experienced an increase in real income between 1996 and 2007, but the wealthiest Canadians (the top quintile in Figure 3.2) benefited from the greatest percentage increase in their average incomes. Some household types have done better than others in terms of improvement in their average incomes over time, but *every* family type experienced improvement in average real incomes over the last three decades. Figure 3.3 shows the current (2007) median after-tax income for various family types.

The distribution of income is only part of the story in any assessment of equality. The other part involves the extent of poverty. 'Poverty' is to some degree a relative concept, meaning something different in an advanced industrialized society like Canada than in a developing country like Nigeria. In Canada, poverty is usually measured using Statistics Canada's definition of what constitutes an income that is so low that an individual or household lives in 'straitened circumstances'. Statistics Canada's low-income cut-offs (LICOs) are generally referred to by the media, academics, politicians, and others as the poverty line. This low-income threshold, with some variation depending on family size, region of the country, and city (or rural) population, is reached by a household that spends over 20 per cent more of their annual family

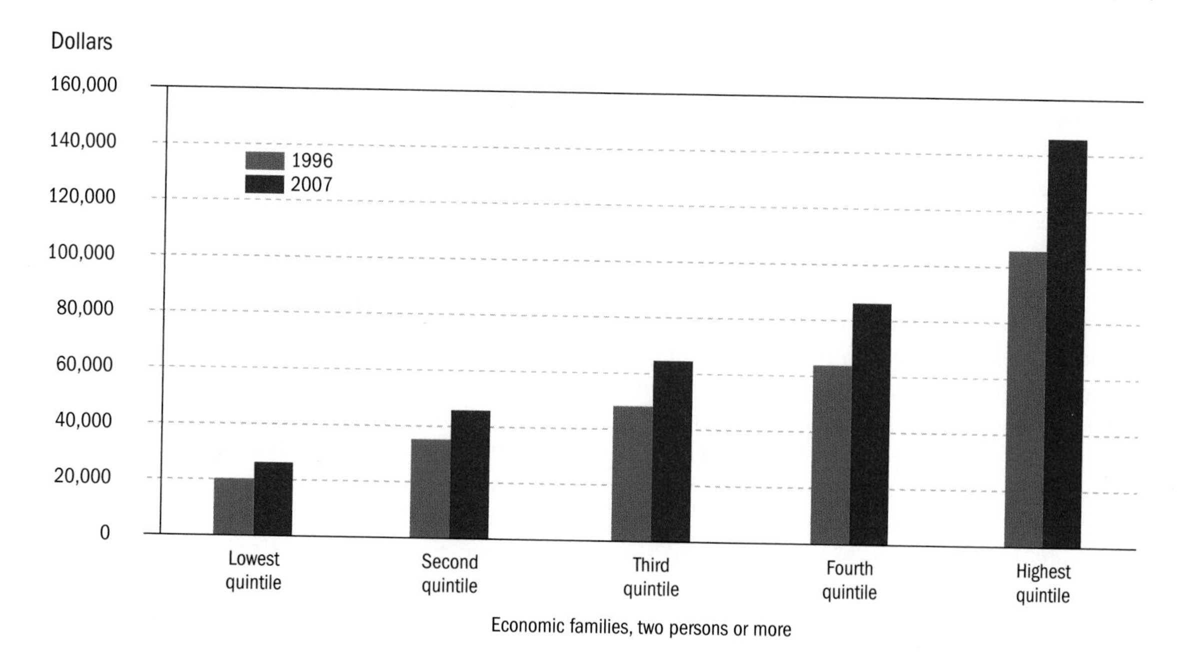

FIGURE 3.2 Average After-Tax Income Quintiles, Canada, 1996 and 2007

Source: Statistics Canada, *Income in Canada, 2007*, Catalogue no. 75-202-X, adapted from chart 9, p. 17.

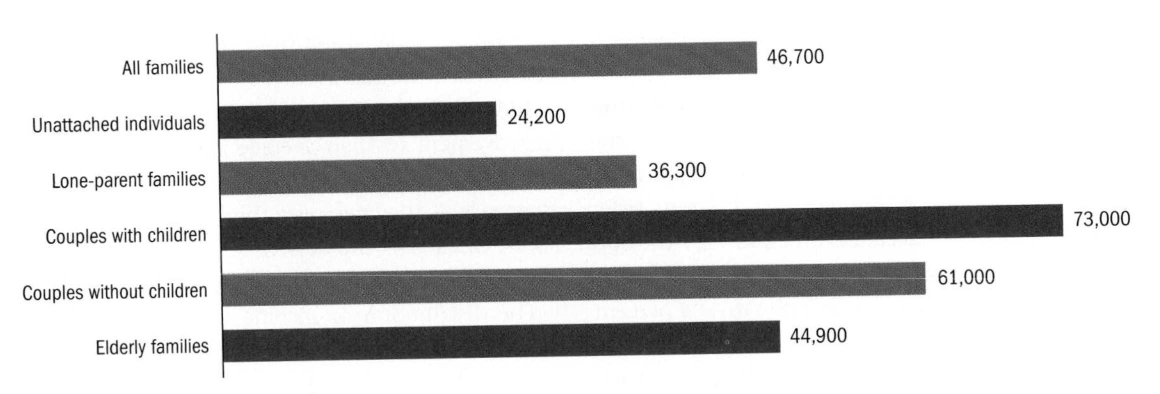

FIGURE 3.3 Median After-Tax Income by Family Type, 2007 (dollars)

Source: Statistics Canada, *Income in Canada, 2007*, Catalogue no. 75-202-X.

income on the basic necessities of living (food, clothing, and shelter) than does the national average household. Because the term 'poverty line' has become an established part of Canada's political vocabulary, evoking images of need and destitution in the minds of many if not most Canadians, it is important to recognize the limitations of Statistics Canada's low-income cut-offs. According to a study of **poverty lines** by the National Council of Welfare,[3] these limitations include the following:

- Poverty lines are relative.
- All poverty lines are arbitrary.
- Poverty lines are a research tool for measuring the incomes of *groups* of people, not a measure of *individual* need.
- Some poverty lines are better than others, but none of them are perfect.

Although the number of Canadians whose incomes fall below the poverty line varies from year to year, the figure has fluctuated over the past few decades between a high of about 16 per cent (1996) and a low of 9–10 per cent in recent years. The likelihood of being poor is not, however, evenly distributed across the population. Two of the groups most likely to be at risk are Native Canadians and women. Consider the following facts:

Native Canadians

- The employment rate for Aboriginal Canadians is the lowest of any ethnic group, at about two-thirds of the national level. To put this a bit differently, the unemployment rate among Native peoples is usually between two and two and one-half times the national level.
- The employment rate for Aboriginal people living on reserves is only half the Canadian rate.
- About one-half of all status Indians obtain most of their income from employment, compared to roughly 70 per cent of all Canadians.
- The incomes of Aboriginal people are about two-thirds the Canadian average.
- Close to half of Aboriginal Canadians living off reserve fall below the poverty line, a figure that is about three times greater than for the general population.

Women

- Women are more likely than men to be poor. The poverty rate for women is about one-third higher than that for men.
- Elderly women are about three times more likely than elderly men to fall below the poverty line.
- Over 40 per cent of single-parent families headed by women fall below the poverty line (post-tax income), a rate several times higher than for two-parent families and three times greater than for single-parent families headed by men.

- The poverty rate among single-parent families headed by young mothers is absolutely crushing. For mothers under 25 it is close to 70 per cent (post-tax income). Among those aged 25–44 it is roughly 40 per cent.

Why are these groups particularly susceptible to poverty? There is no single or simple answer. A few of the contributing causes are fairly clear, however. In the case of Aboriginal Canadians, discrimination certainly plays a role in explaining their higher jobless rate and lower incomes. Lower levels of education also are a factor. But as John Price notes, these causes are considerably less important than 'cultural heritage, choice of occupation and residence far from the main centres of the economy'.[4] Likewise, poverty among women results from a complex set of causes. Most of the difference in the poverty levels of women and men is due to the comparatively high poverty rates of single-parent mothers with children under 18 and unattached women. The lower incomes of women are chiefly due to their segregation in lower-paying occupations and the greater number of women than men who work part-time. Of course, these conditions also have causes, some of which we examine in Chapter 15.

Inequality also has an important regional dimension in Canada. Income levels and employment rates vary dramatically and persistently between provinces, as well between regions within provinces. Personal incomes in what have traditionally been the poorest provinces (Newfoundland and Labrador, New Brunswick, and PEI) are about 80–5 per cent of the Canadian average. The citizens of these provinces have been much more dependent on various transfer payments from government for part of their incomes than have Canadians in wealthier provinces. For example, the median government transfer to a family of two persons or more was slightly above $12,000 in Newfoundland and Labrador in 2006, compared to about $3,000 in Alberta and $4,000 in Ontario.[5] Figure 3.4 shows that inter-regional variation in average personal incomes has narrowed over the last few decades, although it is still quite wide. This has been due mainly to government transfers that provide greater income benefits to the residents of the poorer provinces than to those of the richer ones. On the other hand, the gap between the highest and lowest

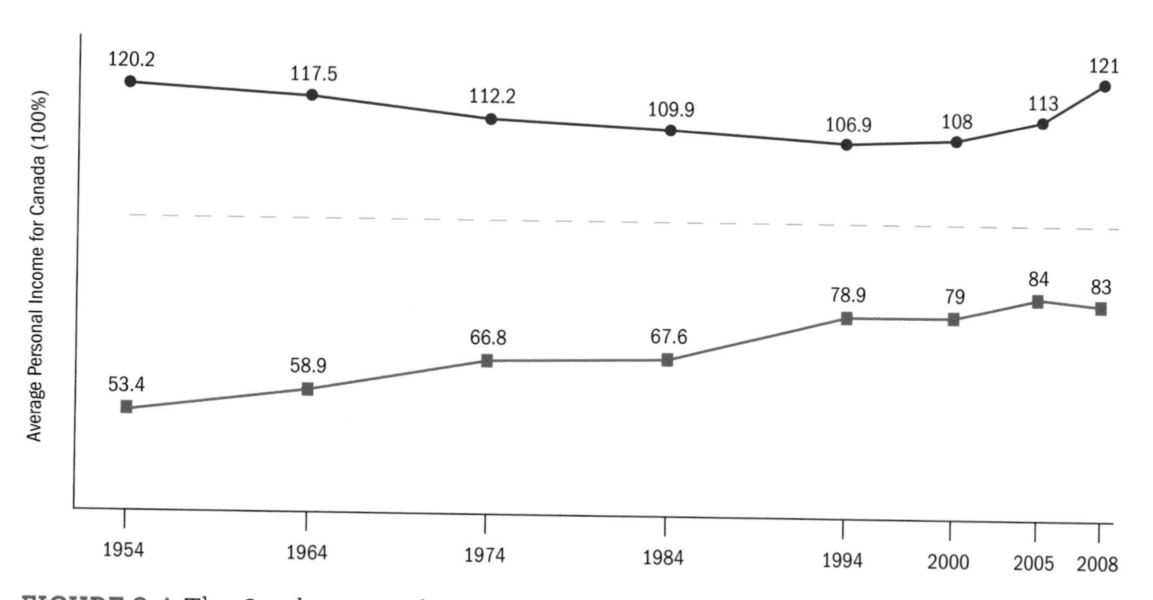

FIGURE 3.4 The Gap between the Richest and Poorest Provinces, 1954–2008

Note: The two provinces used in this comparison are Ontario and Newfoundland and Labrador, for all years except 2005, when Alberta was the wealthiest province, and 2008, when Alberta was the wealthiest province and Nova Scotia was the poorest province.

Source: Statistics Canada, *Provincial Economic Accounts*.

FIGURE 3.5 Regional Unemployment Rates, 1966–2010

Sources: Statistics Canada, *Canadian Economic Observer*, Historical Statistical Supplement, 1994, Catalogue no. 11-210; Statistics Canada Labour Force Survey, special tabulations, CANSIM Table 109-5304.

regional rates of unemployment has widened (see Figure 3.5).

One of the important dimensions of equality, and one of the chief influences on it, is **socio-economic mobility**. This refers to the ability of individuals, families, and groups to move from one social or economic position to another. Socio-economic mobility implies the existence of hierarchically arranged differences in society, such as those that exist between income groups and occupations. These differences exist in all societies, to a greater or lesser extent. Where socio-economic mobility is high, movement up and down the social ladder is common and the barriers to entry into high-paying occupations, prestigious status groups, or powerful elites are relatively low. This is what students of mobility call an open society. In a closed society there is relatively little intergenerational movement on the social ladder and barriers to entry into privileged social and economic groups are high.

Most Canadians believe that theirs is a relatively open society, and compared to most rich countries it is. Miles Corak has examined how closely sons' rankings on their society's income ladder is related to the earnings of their fathers.[6] He reports that intergenerational mobility in Canada is surpassed by that in only a small number of wealthy democracies, and then just marginally (see Figure 3.6). At the same time, however, an abundance of evidence shows that social stratification in Canada remains high and real opportunities to climb the socio-economic ladder are perhaps lower than the conventional wisdom suggests. The **vertical mosaic** that John Porter analyzed over four decades ago has been opened up, but gender, ethnicity, race, and family background continue to exert a significant downward pull on mobility.

Of these factors, family background appears to be the most important. More specifically, the education, occupation, and income of one's parents—these three factors being highly correlated—have a significant impact on the likelihood that a person's income and class position will be better or worse than that of his or her parents. (Mobility is a two-way street and includes the possibility of slipping down the income ladder between generations, not just climbing it.) Corak reports that the probability of a son born to a father whose income is in the lowest 20 per cent of income earners reaching the upper half of all Canadian income earners is 38 per cent. This compares favourably to the United States, where the probability of someone from this same rung of the income ladder reaching the upper half of income earners is 30 per cent. On the middle rungs of the income ladder the likelihood of moving up a rung or two (one or two deciles on the income ladder) is about 50 per cent in both countries. But at both the top and the bottom of the income ladder there is a lower probability of mobility in the United States than in Canada.[7]

So the good news is that intergenerational social mobility in Canada appears to be higher than in the United States, Great Britain, France, and some other wealthy democracies.[8] Moreover, Canada does a better job than many other societies in terms of how quickly immigrants and their children are able to climb the socio-economic ladder.[9] Smooth integration into the labour force often does not happen immediately, despite the fact that the Canadian economy has needed highly skilled immigrants for decades. Indeed, a mountain of evidence demonstrates that immigrants' skills are often underutilized, at least for a certain period of

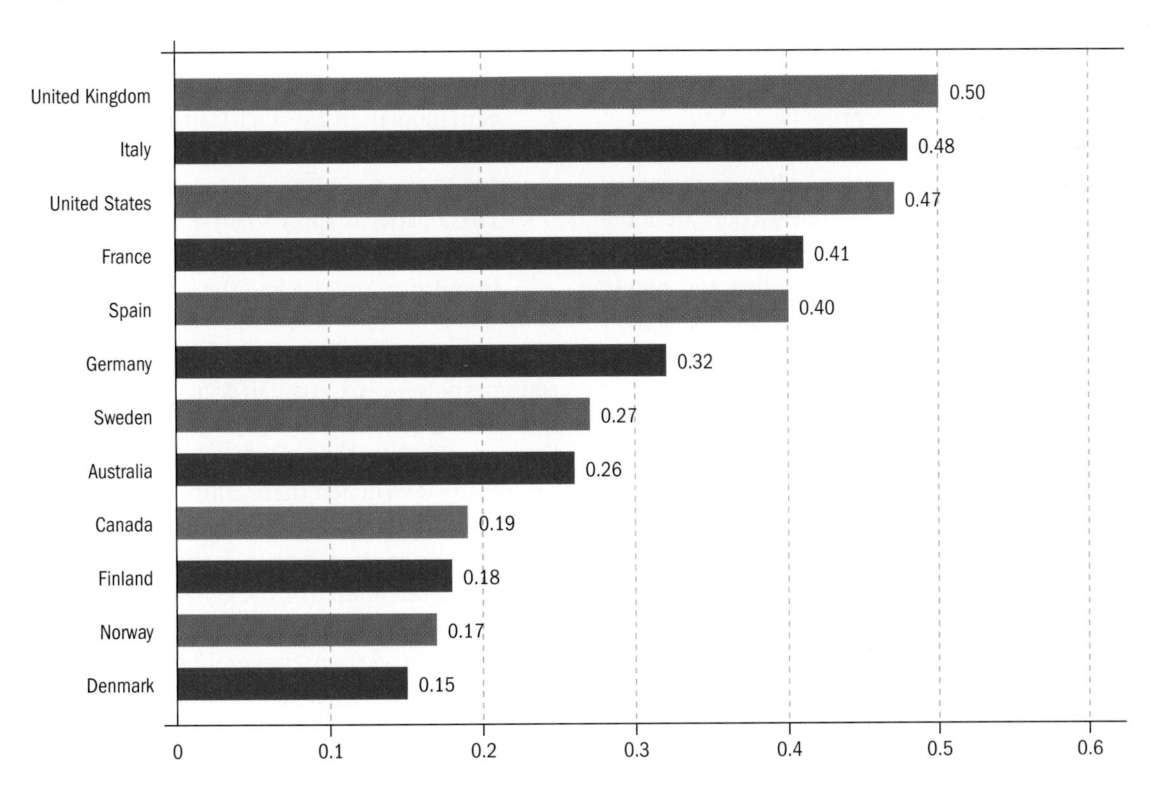

FIGURE 3.6 Intergenerational Elasticity of Earning between Fathers and Sons, Selected Countries

Note: The higher the intergenerational elasticity of earnings, the more highly correlated one's income is with that of one's parents.

Source: Miles Corak, 'Chasing the Same Dream, Climbing Different Ladders: Economic Mobility in the United States and Canada', Economic Mobility Project of the Pew Charitable Trusts, Jan. 2010, at: <www.economicmobility.org/assets/img/EMP_US_Canada_Fig1.jpg>.

time after their arrival in Canada. A 2003 study by Statistics Canada found that six in 10 immigrants were working in different occupational fields in Canada than they had been, or for which they were trained, in their home country.

Immigrants' job prospects do, however, improve over time. The employment rate of those between the ages of 25 and 44, who arrived in Canada between 1991 and 1996, was 61 per cent, but the employment rate for the members of this group increased to 74 per cent by 2001. Although this was still several percentage points below the employment rate for native-born Canadians, it clearly was a significant improvement over a relatively short period of time. Some immigrants simply need to spend some time in school, upgrading, acquiring language skills, or becoming certified in their occupational field. The fact that an increasing number of immigrants in Canada's labour force are non-European and members of what in Canada are called *visible minorities* raises the issue of whether some of the barriers facing immigrant workers are due to discrimination.

It seems likely, however, that problems of assessing foreign credentials, lack of Canadian work experience, and language and cultural barriers are more significant in explaining the underemployment and underutilization of highly skilled and highly educated immigrants. Indeed, in some parts of Canada being an immigrant is about as common as being Canadian-born. The foreign-born comprised about 46 per cent of the population of the Greater Toronto Area as of the 2006 census and about 40 per cent of the population of the Vancouver metropolitan region. Visible minorities constitute significant shares of the population in these cities, and Statistics Canada has projected that within a few years visible minorities will be in the majority in Toronto and Vancouver and that by 2031 they will comprise 63 per cent and 59 per cent, respectively, of the populations of these two cities.[10] Although no one would claim that prejudice no longer exists in their workplaces, what might be described as cultural diversity is now firmly anchored in these and other major urban centres in Canada.

In such countries as France, the United Kingdom, Germany, and Belgium, those who have been born in the country to immigrant parents continue to lag far behind the native-born in education and income. This is not true of Canada. Consider the following findings from a recent Statistics Canada study, based on 2006 census data:

- Second-generation Canadians, both of whose parents were immigrants, are more educated than the Canadian-born whose family roots in Canada go back at least three generations. This is true for both males (21 per cent of the Canadian-born children of immigrants have at least a BA, compared to 14 per cent for 'old-stock' Canadians) and females (24 per cent vs 15 per cent).
- The Canadian-born children of immigrant parents are more likely than old-stock Canadians to hold managerial or professional jobs (among males, 38 per cent vs 31 per cent; among females, 37.5 per cent vs 34 per cent).
- Both men and women who were born in Canada to immigrant parents are likely to earn more than old-stock Canadians (among males, $41,490 vs 39,098; among females, $27,127 vs $24,819).
- These patterns apply to all main immigrant communities with the exception of those from Latin America and the Caribbean.[11]

What about the elite—those with political and economic power—in Canadian society? John Porter argued that they were largely self-perpetuating, recruiting new members chiefly from those groups that already dominated them. Does this continue to be true? Academic and journalistic writing on Canada's **corporate elite** agrees that this group is highly unrepresentative of the general population and that access to it appears to be much greater for those from certain backgrounds than from others. The most systematic studies of the social characteristics of the corporate elite have been carried out by sociologists John Porter and Wallace Clement. Porter's study was based on data for 1951 and Clement's on data for 1972.[12] They both found that this elite (which they defined as the directors of Canada's dominant corporations) was overwhelmingly male, about a third had attended private schools like Upper Canada College or Ridley, many had upper-class backgrounds (50 per cent in 1951 and 59.4 per cent in 1972), those with non-Anglo-Saxon ethnic origins were under-represented (comprising 13.8 per cent of Clement's 1972 group, compared to 55.3 per cent of the Canadian population), and about half (51.1 per cent in 1972) belonged to one or more of the six most prominent private clubs in Canada. The picture they sketched was one of a self-perpetuating group whose social backgrounds and adult activities set them sharply apart from the general population.

The corporate elite operates as a social network that reproduces itself largely through self-recruitment. Education at elite schools adds to what John Porter called the 'social capital' of its members, reinforcing elite ties that are maintained in the adult world of business. Club membership provides a complement to the boardroom, a social setting that is very much part of the personal relations essential in business life. For this reason the question of private club membership became a matter of political controversy during the 1980s. Women's groups especially charged that the exclusively male character of these clubs reinforced men's dominance of the business world by excluding women from its social network.

Using data from 1991, Milan Korac replicated the analysis of Porter and Clement. He reported findings almost identical to those of these two earlier studies. For example, men constituted 92 per cent of the corporate elite; 42 per cent had attended exclusive private schools; those from non-Anglo-Saxon backgrounds were still grossly under-represented (only 22.1 per cent of the economic elite, compared to 74.7 per cent of the population); and well over half of the economic elite belonged to one or more of the Toronto Club, the Mount Royal Club, the Rideau Club, and the St James Club.[13] Although the corporate elite today is far from mirroring Canadian society, there are indications that having been born into this elite is somewhat less important in gaining entry than in the past (see Box 3.2).

Access to the political elite is certainly more open than in the past. Traditionally, Canada's major political parties were dominated by males of either British or French ethnic origins. They still are, but the representation of females and Canadians of non-British, non-French origins has increased sharply over the last couple of decades. The election of Audrey McLaughlin as NDP leader in 1989 marked the first time a woman had been chosen to lead a national political party, followed by the 1993 selection of Kim Campbell as leader of the Conservative Party and of Alexa McDonough as leader of the NDP in 1994. Over the last two decades a number of provincial political parties have had female leaders and one, Catherine Callbeck of PEI, was elected premier of a province. Several of Canada's major cities have had female mayors, going back to the middle of the last century.

The domination of Canada's political elite by males of British and French ethnic origins is less striking than in the past. Jerome Black's study of the ethno-racial background of members of Parliament elected in 1993, 1997, and 2000 found that about one-quarter of them had minority (non-British, non-French) ancestry and another 10 per cent had mixed majority–minority ancestry. Most of this minority ethnic group membership involved ancestral ties to other European groups. Visible minorities constituted only about 6 per cent of MPs elected over these three elections, which was about half their share of the Canadian population. At the same time, evidence suggests that this segment of the political elite is more diverse today than when Porter documented the overwhelming dominance of males from the two 'founding peoples', British and French. About 13 per cent of MPs sitting in 2010 were born outside of Canada, a higher percentage than in any developed democracy with the exception of Australia. Women accounted for just over one in five members of the House of Commons, a figure far below the female share of the population but significantly greater than it was a generation ago.

Why do inequalities like those that we have described in the preceding pages exist? What consequences do they have for Canadian politics and society? These are complex questions that cannot be fully dealt with here. We may, however, suggest some of the elements of their answers. Several factors contribute to inequality, including deliberate discrimination, systemic discrimination, choice, and politics.

Media Spotlight

Box 3.2 The Corporate Elite: Where Everyone Looks the Same

John Gray, writing in *Canadian Business* a few years ago, described the remarkable extent to which leading CEOs in Canada are representative of a single demographic group: middle-aged white men.

> These are the leaders of Canada's biggest companies by market cap [the investment community's assessment of a company's net worth, calculated by multiplying its share price by the number of shares in circulation], ranked from one to 50 . . . . With one exception, they're all white, middle-aged males. If corporate Canada was an ice cream, it would be vanilla—make that two scoops. That in itself shouldn't be surprising, but what is rather shocking is the almost complete absence of any kind of diversity. Not one woman heads up a Top 50 company, despite women making up half the workforce. Only one visible minority—John Lau at Husky Energy—found his way to the top, even though at least 13.4 per cent of the population identifies themselves as such. . . .
>
> Aside from being white, the men at the top of Canada's corporate food chain are middle-aged, with the typical exec being almost 53, and very well educated. Oddly enough, though, it turns out a business degree isn't the path to fame and fortune: turns out your average Canadian CEO is more likely to have a bachelor of science degree. Roughly a fifth of them reported having an MBA. Roughly half have multiple degrees. . . .
>
> Hard work, and biding your time while rising the ranks, can also pay off. Telus's Darren Entwistle started out a telephone lineman for Bell Canada; Canadian National Railway's Hunter Harrison's first job was crawling under box cars to oil wheel bearings; and Canadian Pacific Railway's Fred Green has been with the company since 1978. Clearly, this group is bright and hard-working—positive signs of meritocracy at work. Now, the challenge is to get that culture of meritocracy to extend beyond white middle-aged men.

Source: Andy Holloway. 'The Big 50: The CEO's of Canada's Largest Companies.' May 22–June 4, 2006. *Canadian Business*.

Deliberate Discrimination

The prejudice that one person feels towards the members of some group or groups becomes deliberate discrimination when it is acted upon. For example, the landlord who refuses to rent to someone he suspects of being homosexual is discriminating against that person and against all members of that group. Deliberate discrimination is characterized by the intent to treat the members of some group in an unequal manner. The intent that underlies social prejudice and bigotry, however, is often hard to prove. While this sort of discrimination certainly still exists in Canadian society, and against the members of some groups more than others, it is probably much less important in explaining inequality than the following three causes.

Systemic Discrimination

This is discrimination without conscious individual intent. It is the discrimination that inheres in traditions, customary practices, rules, and institutions that have the effect of favouring the members of one group over another. For example, in 1999 the British Columbia Human Rights Commission ruled that the section of the province's Highway Act requiring motorcyclists to wear helmets discriminated—albeit unintentionally—against male Sikhs, whose religion requires the wearing of a turban. Another example would be height and/or weight requirements for certain jobs. Because women are typically smaller than men, it could be argued that these requirements are discriminatory. Everyone recognizes, of course, that some job requirements may be reasonable and cannot be jettisoned even if they have the effect of discriminating against certain groups.

The examples mentioned above merely scratch the surface of **systemic discrimination**. A further example will help to demonstrate just how deeply rooted systemic discrimination may be. In

Values and ideals can be influenced by one's stage of life. The student activists of the 1960s are in their sixties today, and many are now more interested in RSPs and drug benefits than in the causes and ideas that brought them into the streets when they were in university.

our society most people learn that child-rearing is primarily a female function. This assumption is deeply embedded in our culture and social practices, and is even reinforced through the law (why else would about 85 per cent of child custody orders in cases of separation and divorce assign sole custody to the mother?). What results is a situation where the opportunities effectively open to men and women are not equal. They may appear to be the product of individual choice, particularly where the Constitution proclaims the equality of men and women. But these individual choices are shaped by the weight of social practices and cultural values that have the effect of discriminating between males and females.

Choice

Individual choice also contributes to inequality. For example, a status Indian who decides to stay on the reserve reduces his or her opportunities of finding a job, and if one does find employment it probably will pay less than a job in the city. First Nation reserves are usually far from centres of population and economic activity, so an economic cost accompanies the choice of life on the reserve. Likewise, if one decides to live in Cape Breton, northern Ontario, New Brunswick, or many other regions of Canada, there is a greater probability that one will be unemployed or earn less than someone else who went down the road to Toronto or Calgary.

Mobility choices like these are not always easy. A person who grows up in the poverty and deprived environment that characterize most First Nation reserves may neither perceive nor have much choice about his or her future. Only by applying a rather generous meaning to the word may one conclude that someone from a second-generation welfare family has much individual choice regarding education and future career opportunities. Nevertheless, individual choice is a factor that contributes to inequality.

Politics

Although debates over equality generally draw on the rarefied language of rights and justice, this should not conceal the fact that they are essentially political struggles. How much inequality is acceptable, or, to put it differently, how much equality is enough? Are there circumstances where some forms of discrimination might be reasonable because they are necessary to protect or promote other values? What groups should be targeted for affirmative action—why, for example, do many affirmative action schemes consider Punjabis to be a visible minority but not Chinese?

Fairness and equality are cultural notions. A century ago only a small minority of Canadians regretted the fact that women were without most of the rights that are taken for granted today. Poverty was once believed to be primarily the fault of the person suffering from it—an explanation that absolved society, the economic system, and governments from blame for the suffering of many whose greatest offence was to be born into the sort of circumstances that make a life of poverty very likely. As values and beliefs change, a society's notions of what is fair may also be transformed.

Value shifts of this sort are almost certain to be accompanied, and influenced, by political struggles. If Canadians are more conscious today of the discrimination that has been practised against the country's Aboriginal peoples it is because of the efforts of Aboriginal groups to bring these inequalities to the public's attention and influence government policy. The social policies that redistribute wealth from more affluent to less affluent Canadians did not emerge overnight: they have been built up (and, more recently, chipped away at) gradually over time in response to struggles between conflicting interests and values. Political parties, interest groups, individuals, and various parts of the state may all be participants in these struggles.

The structure of the state matters, too, affecting what sorts of inequalities are dealt with by governments and influencing the opportunities and resources available to different interests. It is likely, for example, that Canadian governments have long targeted more money at regional economic inequalities than have American governments because of the particular division of powers between Ottawa and the provinces under Canada's

Constitution and the relatively greater leverage of the provincial governments than of the state governments in the United States. To use another example, the entrenchment of the Charter of Rights and Freedoms in the Canadian Constitution has had an enormous impact on the prominence of equality rights issues, the strategies that groups use to achieve their goals, and the treatment of certain groups. The interplay of interest, ideas, and institutions that is politics plays a key role in determining what inequalities get on the public agenda and how they are dealt with.

Quality of Life

The United States, the world's wealthiest society, has one of the world's highest rates of homicide and a drug problem that costs thousands of lives and billions of dollars annually, to say nothing of the enormous misery associated with it. It also has a high rate of alcoholism, many thousands of homeless people, and a high level of marriage breakup (which translates into many single-parent families, usually headed by women, and a high incidence of child poverty), to mention only a few of the social pathologies of that rich society. Racism, urban blight, and the environmental and other costs associated with suburban sprawl are a few of the other dilemmas with which the world's richest country must cope. Canadians often take smug pride in being less afflicted by these problems. But Canada's high standard of living, like that of the United States, is also tarnished by problems that undermine the **quality of life (QOL)** experienced by millions. These problems often become politicized as groups demand that governments take action to deal with them. In some cases government policies are blamed for having caused or contributed to a QOL problem. For example, Native groups and those sympathetic to their demands argue that the appallingly bad quality of life experienced by many Native Canadians is due to unjust and discriminatory policies. While the QOL in Canada is comparatively high, the picture is not uniformly bright for all groups. Aboriginal Canadians, in particular, experience conditions far below what most Canadians would consider decent and acceptable in a society as wealthy as ours.

One way of measuring the QOL in a society is to ask people how happy they are. Pollsters have done this for decades. What they find is that Canadians are by and large happy: most of them, most of the time, and in general terms. Interestingly, however, they are less likely to say that they are very happy than Trinidadians or Mexicans, people from countries that are much poorer and where life expectancy is considerably shorter than in Canada or other rich countries.[14] People in comparatively rich countries such as Italy, Spain, and Finland report being even less happy with their lives—much less—suggesting that there is no invariable correlation between the happiness of national populations and material well-being.

There is, however, a clear correlation between material well-being and the level of satisfaction with life expressed by a nation's population. Canadians and the citizens of other wealthy countries are far more likely to express a high degree of satisfaction with their lives than to say that they are very happy. Indeed, the 2005–6 World Values Survey found three comparatively poor countries, Mexico, Colombia, and Guatemala, among the 25 countries whose populations expressed the highest levels of satisfaction with life. Four out of five Canadians said they were highly satisfied. But a persistent and significant minority of Canada's population is not satisfied. Attitudinal data like these tell one nothing about the causes of dissatisfaction or the sorts of problems that actually undermine the QOL in a society. To get at these one must rely on objective measures that may reasonably be construed as reflections of QOL. We will look at mortality, crime, suicide, alcoholism, and destitution.

Compared to other advanced industrialized societies, Canada does relatively well on all of these measures. Its mortality rate of about 7 per 1,000 members of the population and the infant mortality rate of just under 6 per 1,000 are about average for such societies. Life expectancy is above average, at about 75 years for males and 81 years for females.

In terms of violent crime, Canada is unexceptional. Canada's current homicide rate is somewhat below 2 homicides per 100,000 population, compared to a rate of about 9 per 100,000 in the United States. Although rates vary marginally from year to year, the statistics do not support the popular assumption that murders have become more common. Canada's homicide rate has actually declined since the mid-1970s.

Statistics on other violent crimes, such as rape, domestic violence, and assault, are difficult to interpret. This is partly because of changes in reporting procedures that can produce an increase or decrease from one year to the next without there being any real change in the actual incidence of the offence. Changes to the law and public attitudes may also affect crime statistics. For example, rape charges and convictions are dramatically higher today than a generation ago. This increase is mainly due to the greater willingness of victims to come forward, a willingness that results from changed social attitudes and reforms to the law on sexual assault. Comparison between countries is complicated by variations in policing practices, the definition of offences, and the manner in which crime statistics are collected. Interpretation problems aside, the data do not suggest that Canada is an exceptionally dangerous place to live. At the same time, the widespread belief that Canada is a much less crime-ridden place than the United States is not supported by the empirical evidence. While it is true that Americans are more likely than Canadians to be the victims of homicide, victimization rates for other violent offences and crimes against property are not lower across the board in Canada than in the US, and in some cases are even higher (see Figure 3.7). Moreover, only about one-quarter of Canadians say that they feel very safe on the street after dark, about the same percentage as in the United States.[15]

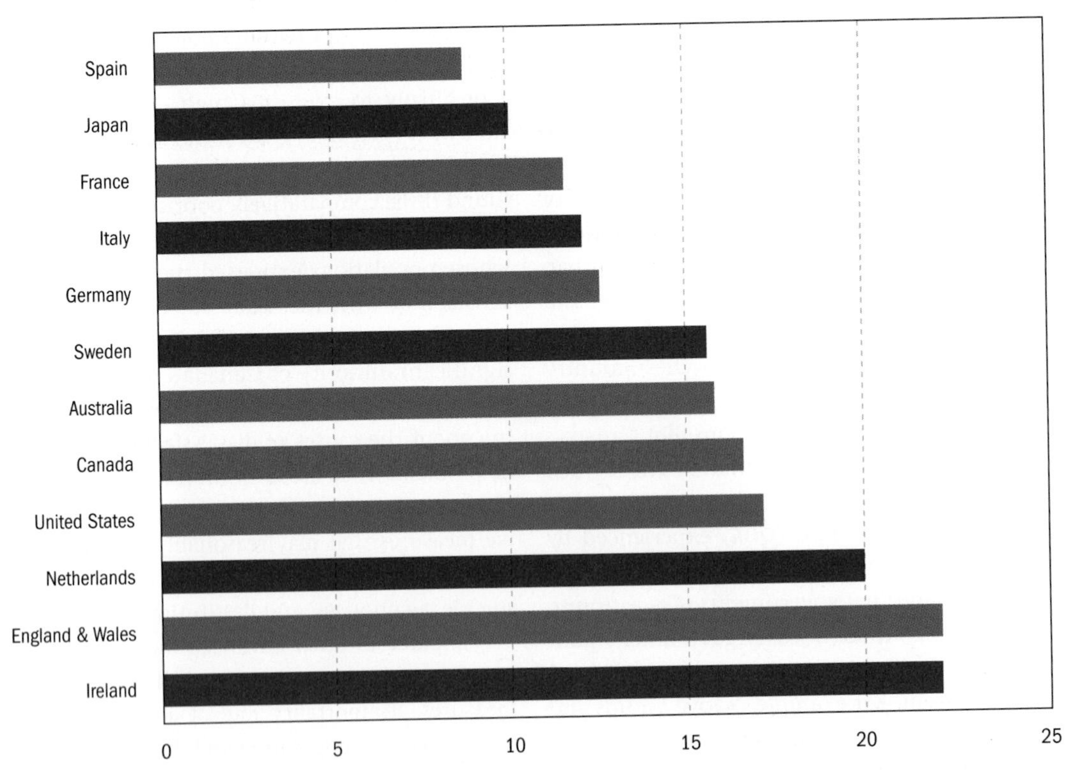

FIGURE 3.7 Overall Victimization Rates for 10 Crimes*, Selected Countries, 2004 (as percentage of population)

*The 10 crimes rage from petty theft to more serious crimes such as car theft, assault, and sexual assault. They do not include rape.

Sources: Adapted from Jan van Dijk, Jan van Kesteren, and Paul Smit, *Criminal Victimization in International Perspective* (Tilburg, Netherlands: Tilburg University and the UN office on Drugs and Crime. 2008), at: <rechten.uvt.nl.icvs/pdffiles/ICVS2004_05.pdf>. The Canadian percentage is based on statistics supplied by the Federal Department of Justice.

Suicide and alcoholism and other drug abuse are social pathologies that are symptomatic of a low QOL. Suicide accounts for about 5 per cent of deaths among Canadians between the ages of 15 and 69, exceeded only by cancer (36 per cent), circulatory system malfunction (30 per cent), and accidents (10 per cent). As in other countries, the rate of successful suicide is considerably higher among men than women, at about 20 per 100,000 population for men compared to 5 per 100,000 for women. And although the rate has remained stable for females, it has increased by about 30 per cent for males since the 1960s. On the other hand, Canada's suicide rate is only about one-third that of Hungary and a little over half the Swiss rate. There is enormous international variation even when levels of national wealth are controlled for, suggesting that suicide is closely related to culture. For example, Mexico's rate is just over 1 per 100,000, Italy and the United Kingdom have rates around 8 per 100,000, while Hungary and Austria top the list at about 40 and 25, respectively. Canada's rate of about 13 per 100,000 falls in the middle.

It is conservatively estimated that about 4–5 per cent of adult drinkers in Canada, or over 600,000 people, are alcoholics.[16] This figure is based on the mortality rate from cirrhosis of the liver, national cirrhosis rates being highly correlated with alcohol consumption levels. Alcoholism in Canada is about average for Western industrialized countries. The level is dramatically lower than in such countries as Hungary, Germany, Italy, and France. Abuse of other non-medical drugs generally is not considered to be a major problem in most of Canadian society, although particular cities, including Vancouver and Toronto, and some isolated Native communities have been well-publicized exceptions. On the whole, the social and economic costs associated with illegal drug use in Canada are probably less than those produced by alcohol and tobacco consumption, although the lack of hard data makes it difficult to reliably assess the costs inflicted on individuals and society by drug abuse.

Advanced industrial societies all have in place a 'safety net' of social programs intended to protect individuals and households from destitution. Nevertheless, some people fall between the cracks. When the safety net fails to catch a significant number of those who, for one reason or another, cannot make ends meet, this is surely an indication that the QOL experienced by some people falls below acceptable standards of human decency. Homelessness and the demands placed on food banks are two indicators of holes in the social safety net.

The extent of homelessness is difficult to pin down for the obvious reason that the homeless, unlike those who have a fixed address, cannot be enumerated, telephoned, or otherwise kept track of with any accuracy. The 2008 Senate report, *Poverty, Housing and Homelessness*, acknowledges the difficulties and does not even attempt to attach a number to this problem. Statistics Canada's first attempt to count the homeless came up with the implausibly low figure of 14,145, based on the number of people nationwide sleeping in emergency shelters the night of 15 May 2001. At the other extreme, the Calgary-based Sheldon Chumir Foundation for Ethics in Leadership estimates that the number is somewhere between 200,000–300,000, figures that were widely reported by the media even though their reliability is suspect. As Canada's largest city, with housing prices that in recent years have been surpassed only by Vancouver, Toronto experiences homelessness on a scale and with a visibility probably greater than elsewhere in Canada. It is not, however, a problem unique to Toronto, Vancouver, or other larger cities where the cost of accommodation is relatively high.

The number of Canadians who rely on food banks for part of their needs has also increased. The Canadian Association of Food Banks (CAFB) estimates that Canada's nearly 900 food banks provided food to roughly 800,000 people during a typical month in 2009. About three-quarters of food bank users rely on welfare or Old Age Security as their main source of income. Refugees, the disabled, and those with no income, and often no home, account for another 10 per cent. Slightly more than 10 per cent of users have employment income. According to the CAFB, the number of food bank users has more than doubled since 1989.[17]

Demands on food banks are largely cyclical, increasing during periods of higher than usual unemployment. But a more permanent component to food bank demand appears to have grown larger in recent years, even when the economy has been expanding and the rate of unemployment has been falling. This component, many argue, is created by the gap that exists between the income that social assistance provides and the cost of paying for life's necessities. The width of this gap varies across the country, first, because social assistance benefits are determined by the individual provinces and, second, because of regional variations in the cost of living. But the gap is wide in all provinces (see Figure 3.8). As social assistance benefits fail to keep pace with increases in the cost of living, the demand on food banks inevitably increases. Given the growth in the 'normal' use of food banks, an increase in the level of unemployment pushes an already strained system to the breaking point.

Not everyone agrees, however, that a **welfare gap** exists, let alone with the claim that it is widening. We have already alluded to the limitations of Statistics Canada's low-income cut-offs—poverty lines as they are commonly called—as measures of poverty. As an alternative to Statistics Canada's relative approach to what it means to be poor, some researchers have proposed measures that would be based on the actual spending needs of Canadians. Economist Chris Sarlo of the Fraser Institute has developed such measures, which he calls Basic Needs Lines. They are based on the cost of maintaining long-term physical well-being, including shelter, a nutritious diet, clothing, personal hygiene, health care, transportation, and a telephone. BNLs are considerably lower than Statistics Canada's LICOs, and unlike LICOs they do not automatically rise as average personal income increases. If BNLs are used to measure poverty instead of LICOs, a very different picture emerges. The welfare gap narrows and virtually disappears in some provinces. Using Sarlo's measure of income assistance, which includes the value of all forms of income assistance, including federal and provincial tax credits and supplementary benefits whose value varies between provinces,

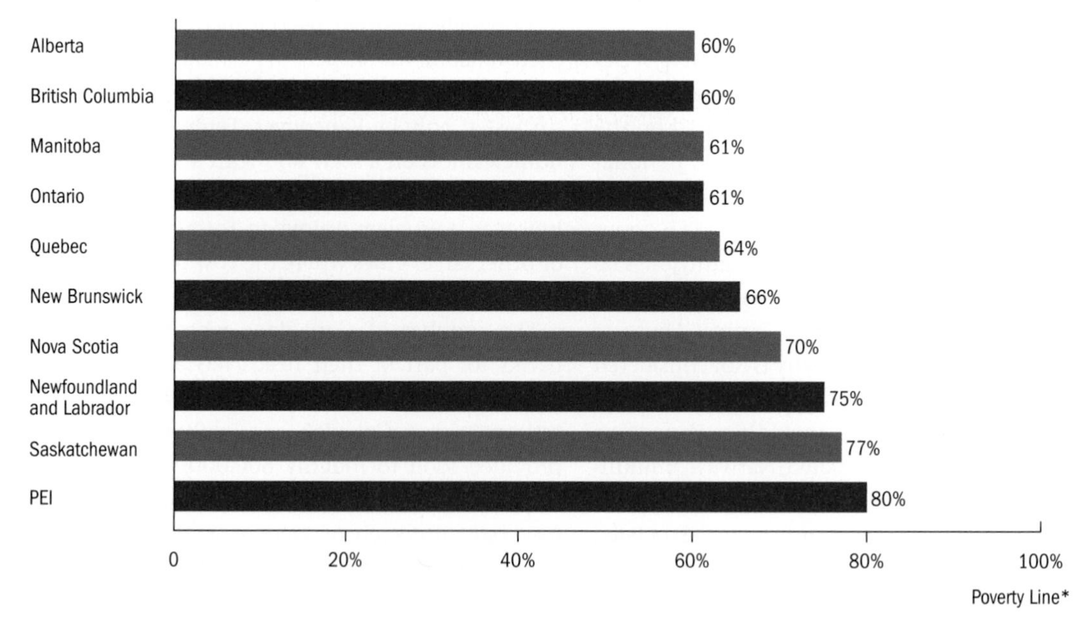

FIGURE 3.8 The Welfare Gap, 2008

*Based on Statistics Canada's low-income cut-off line for a couple with two children.

Note: The welfare gap is the difference between total welfare income (social assistance benefits, child tax benefits, and federal and provincial sales tax credits) and the Statistics Canada low-income cut-off line for each province. It does not take into account the value of welfare benefits such as subsidized accommodation, daycare, dental care, etc. Thus, for example, total welfare income in Alberta is 60 per cent of the LICO, so that a shortfall of 40 per cent exists, and in PEI it is 80 per cent, with a 20 per cent shortfall.

Source: Based on data from National Council of Welfare, *Welfare Incomes 2008*, Bulletin no. 4, at: <www.ncwcnbes.net/en/research/welfare-bienetre.html>.

the poverty picture appears much less bleak (see Figure 3.9).

Many readers will consider absurd the conclusion that welfare benefits are in fact generous enough to meet the basic needs of many categories of recipients. It is important to keep in mind, however, that this measure of basic needs does not take into account either self-esteem or the incapacity of many people to spend efficiently on life's necessities. Whether a measure of poverty should take these factors into account is part of the ongoing debate over how poverty should be measured and how extensive it really is in Canada.

Canada is an affluent society. Its social pathologies are fairly typical of those experienced by other advanced industrial societies. The surrogate measures of the QOL we have examined suggest that the United Nations is certainly right in rating Canada as one of the world's best countries in which to live. But the QOL is sharply lower for one group, namely, Native Canadians. Consider these facts:

- Life expectancy for status Indians is about 10 years less than for the Canadian population as a whole.
- Infant mortality rates are twice as high among Natives as among non-Natives.
- Native death, illness, and accident rates are all about three times greater than national levels. Most deaths of status Indians under 45 are caused by violence rather than illness.
- Although less than 3 per cent of the population are Aboriginal Canadians (defined to include Indians, Inuit, and Métis), about 18 per cent of those in prisons are Native. Natives also comprise almost one-fifth of all murder victims and over one-fifth of all murder suspects in Canada.

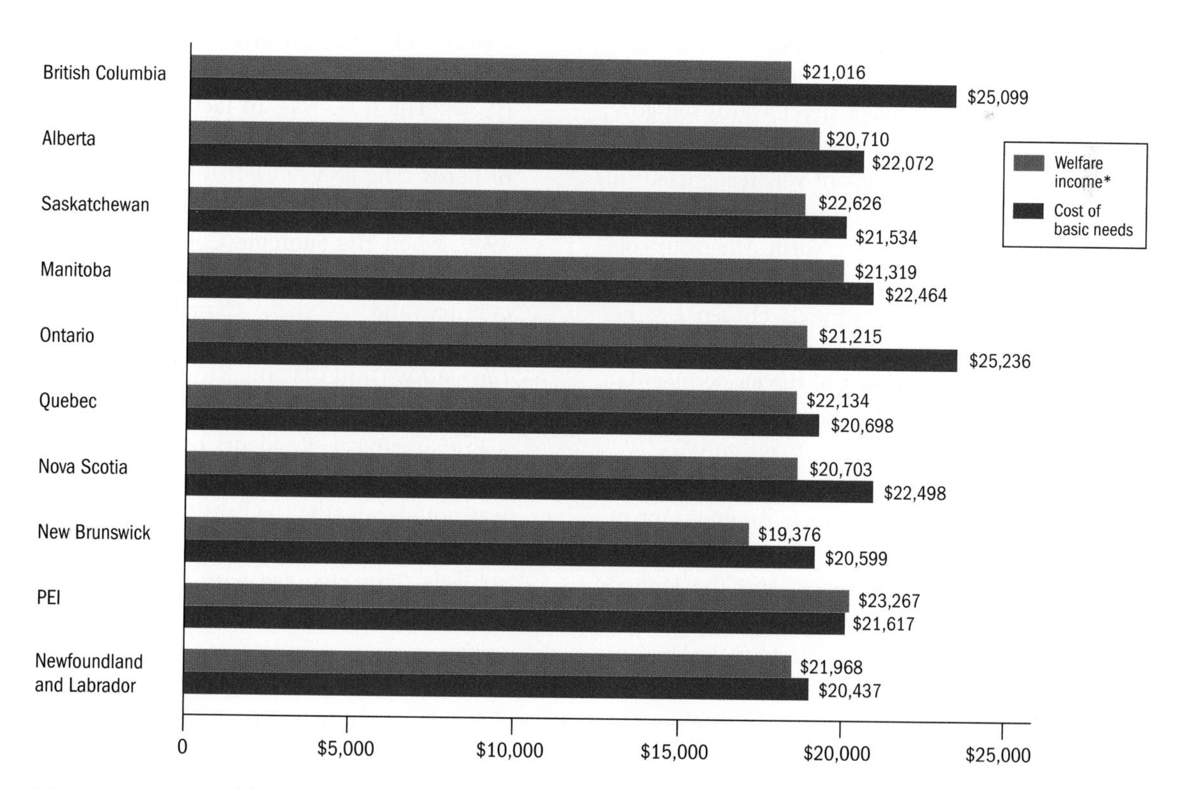

FIGURE 3.9 Welfare Adequacy, Using Basic Needs Lines, 2008

*Based on a family of four. This dollar figure represents the value of income assistance, consisting of general and supplementary welfare assistance, child benefits, and tax credits for each province.

Sources: Adapted from 'Measuring Poverty in Canada', at: <www.fraserinstitute.ca>, and National Council of Welfare, *Welfare Incomes* 2008, adjusted for cost-of-living increase between 2004 and 2008.

- The suicide rate among Aboriginal Canadians is well over twice the Canadian rate. For the Inuit it is about six times the national rate.
- Alcoholism is much more prevalent among Natives than non-Natives. It has been estimated that 50–60 per cent of accidents and deaths among status Indians are alcohol-related.
- Many Natives live in overcrowded conditions. About one-fifth of Indian dwellings are crowded (defined as more than one person per room), the figure rising to about one-third on reserves. This is several times greater than the Canadian rate.

Independence

A democracy requires self-government. This means that public policies affecting the lives of citizens should be taken by people whom these same citizens have elected and who are accountable to them for their policies. The first major step towards self-government in Canada was taken in 1848, when the principle of responsible government was recognized in the colonies of Nova Scotia and the United Canadas (followed by the other British North American colonies soon afterwards). Responsible government meant that the governor, himself chosen by the British Colonial Office, was obliged to select cabinet ministers who were members of the elected legislature. A cabinet without the support of a majority in the legislature would be required to resign.

Self-government advanced another step with Confederation. The British North America Act of 1867 created a new country out of the colonies of Nova Scotia, New Brunswick, and the United Canadas, and transferred to its federal and provincial legislatures the exclusive right to make laws for Canada and its provinces. Full self-government was almost achieved. We say 'almost' because certain powers were withheld from Canadian governments and, therefore, from the voters who elected them. These included:

- *The power to enter into foreign treaties.* Under section 133 of the BNA Act this remained the responsibility of the British government. Treaty-making power was formally transferred to Canada in 1931 by the Statute of Westminster.
- *The power to amend the Constitution.* This also remained in the hands of the British Parliament. The BNA Act that created Canada, and which established the powers of the federal and provincial governments, was a British law. It could only be changed by passing another British law. This situation remained unchanged until 1982, when the BNA Act and all its amendments were patriated and renamed the Constitution Act, 1867. Britain's authority to pass laws applying to Canada was ended, and a procedure for amending the Constitution in Canada was established (see Chapter 5).
- *The power to interpret the Constitution.* At Confederation, the highest court for the colonies of British North America was the Judicial Committee of the Privy Council (JCPC). The JCPC was, in fact, a committee comprised of members of the British House of Lords. The BNA Act left intact the JCPC's authority over Canada. This continued until 1949, when the Supreme Court of Canada became the final appellate court for this country and, as such, Canada's constitutional umpire.
- *Citizenship.* Until 1947 there was no Canadian citizenship status that did not involve being a British subject. Residents of Canada who were born in Canada carried a passport that was not identical to the British passport, but it nevertheless declared them to be British subjects. This changed with the passage of the Canadian Citizenship Act, 1947.

Step by step the Canadian state achieved the full powers of self-government that it exercises today. With the passage of the Constitution Act, 1982, the last formal impediment to political sovereignty was removed. But the issue of political sovereignty, although it still arises in relationship to the policies and preferences of the American government, sometimes has been less controversial in the modern politics of Canada than those of economic and cultural sovereignty. The real limitations on Canadian independence, many have argued, have not come from the vestiges of colonialism that have gradually been removed from Canada's Constitution, but have been and are imposed by economic **dependence** on, first, Great Britain and then the United States and by the 'colonization' of Canada by American cultural industries. Formal political sovereignty, according to Canadian nationalists, is empty so long as the country's economic and cultural destinies are controlled by others.

In the real world, however, no self-governing democracy is totally independent of external influences. Trade, military alliances and animosities, and contemporary mass media are some of the chief factors that create a web of interdependence between modern societies. The question is not, therefore, whether political life in Canada or in any other country is unaffected by influences from outside. Instead, the question is whether the nature and extent of these external influences undermine the political independence of a country.

If one looks at Canada's economic relations with the rest of the world, both historically and today, there is no denying our enormous dependence on foreign sources of investment capital, imports, and markets for Canadian exports. Some of the main features of Canada's international economic relations are listed in Box 3.3.

This dependence must, however, be put into perspective. Several advanced industrial democracies, including the Netherlands, Belgium, Sweden, Britain, and Germany,

Governing Realities

Box 3.3 Canada's Economic Links to the World

Past . . .

- Much of the money used to build the roads, railways, and canals of Canada's early commercial economy was borrowed from foreign, mainly British, investors.
- At Confederation, Canada was already heavily in debt to foreign investors.
- It is estimated that about 450 American companies had established subsidiaries in Canada by 1913.
- By the 1920s, the United States surpassed Britain as the major source of foreign investment in Canada.
- The level of foreign ownership in Canada peaked in 1971 at 37 per cent of corporate non-financial assets. The level was close to 60 per cent for manufacturing industries.

Present . . .

- Foreign investors, mainly American, control about one-fifth of corporate non-financial assets in Canada.
- Over half of all American investment in Canada is located in Ontario, although since the dramatic escalation in the world price of petroleum from 2005 to late 2008, the rate of new American investment in Alberta has been greater than in any other region of Canada.
- Close to 30 per cent of Canada's GDP comes from trade. In 2009, roughly 75 per cent of that trade was with the United States (about 75 per cent of our export trade and roughly 55 per cent of import trade).
- Canada went from being a net importer of investment capital to a net exporter around 1996. As of 2009, the estimated market value of foreign direct investment in Canada was $549 billion and the market value of Canadian direct investment abroad was about $593 billion. Canada is one of the top 10 sources of foreign investment in the United States economy.[18]

rely on trade for about as great a share of their national income as does Canada. Some are even more dependent on trade. These countries are members of the European Union, which imposes considerably greater limitations on the policy-makers of its member states than the Canada–United States Free Trade Agreement and the North American Free Trade Agreement (NAFTA) impose on Canadian and American governments. What is unique about Canada is the extent to which our trading relations depend on a single partner, i.e., the United States. Among advanced industrialized economies, only Japan comes close to this level of dependence on a single trading partner (close to half of Japanese exports are purchased by the United States).

In terms of investment, Canada remains heavily dependent on foreign capital. But this dependence has weakened over the last couple of decades at the same time as Canadian investment abroad—and therefore our penetration of other economies—has increased. Indeed, as a result of the increasing globalization of business and investment, Canada has come to look more and more like several other advanced industrial economies in terms of its level of foreign ownership. Again, however, Canada is rather unique in the degree to which it is dependent on a single source of foreign investment, i.e., the United States. With the global crisis in financial markets that was finally recognized in late 2008 and the media- and politician-driven panic that has ensued, particularly in regard to the auto industry, it is difficult to know what the shape of the future will be in regard to foreign investment in Canada and Canadian investment abroad.

Culturally, Canada, especially English-speaking Canada, has always lived in the shadow of the United States (see Box 3.4). Physical proximity, a common language, and shared values have facilitated the flow of cultural products—books, magazines, films and DVDs, television programs, music recordings, computer software—between the two countries. Economics has ensured that this flow has been mostly from the United States to Canada. This is because of the much greater domestic audience/readership available to American producers, which enables them to produce high-quality mass-appeal products that are attractive to advertisers. Advertising revenue is the main or sole source of income for most privately owned media businesses (films, compact discs, DVDs, video games, and books are the chief exceptions). It just makes economic sense for Canadian broadcasters to buy a product that is demonstrably popular with viewers, at a cost that is a fraction of what it would be if the same sort of program, with the same advertising budget, stars, writers, and production team, were to be produced in Canada.

The result has been predictable. American-made films, television programs, video games, popular music, and magazines spill over into Canada's English-language market. In fact, they dominate all of these Canadian markets. American books also do very well in the English-Canadian market, with authors like John Grisham, Stephen King, Stephenie Meyer, and Ken Follett featuring on the best-seller lists both north and south of the border. Newspapers are the main exception to the rule of American dominance. This is because of provisions in Canada's Income Tax Act that heavily favour Canadian-owned newspapers and because, for most people, newspapers are primarily sources of local information.[19]

Let us return to our initial questions. Is Canada's political independence undermined by the country's economic dependence on the United States and by the enormous influence of American mass media in English Canada? In what ways? Is the Canadian predicament so different from that faced by many other industrialized democracies in today's interdependent world?

The answer to the first question is clearly 'yes'. Canadian policy-makers, at all levels, must be sensitive to the actions and possible reactions of governments in the United States. Moreover, many of the public policy matters they deal with, from transboundary pollution to interest rates, are affected by circumstances in the United States, circumstances over which Canadians and their governments can exert little, if any, control. Canada's economic and cultural linkages with the United States affect us in too many ways to be listed here. The fact that roughly 75 per cent of our export trade is with the United States obviously means that our economy will be highly vulnerable to the state of the American economy and to changes in the exchange rate between the Canadian and American dollars. The fact that Canadians are raised on a heavy diet of Hollywood films, television, magazines, and an Internet dominated by American websites will certainly affect the images and ideas in their heads. To the extent that these American cultural imports erode distinctively Canadian values (whatever these may be, or might have been), one may argue that they also erode the cultural basis for a Canadian society and public policies that are different from those of the United States.

Faced with a challenge from a larger, more powerful economy and a predatory mass culture, governments typically respond with protectionist policies. They attempt to protect domestic industries or local culture through import restrictions, subsidies to domestic producers, regulations affecting business practices and cultural industries, and so on. Canadian policy-makers have resorted to all of these measures, as have policy-makers elsewhere. To cite but one example, Canadian cultural policy is determined largely by the rules that the Canadian Radio-television and Telecommunications Commission (CRTC) imposes on broadcasters. The CRTC establishes and enforces a dense thicket of regulations governing Canadian content over radio and television, and these regulations have a very simple bottom line: to ensure that more Canadian music and television programming reaches the airwaves than would be the case if market forces were allowed to operate without restriction.

Finally, is the Canadian 'dilemma' really so different from that of other small and middle-sized democracies? After all, Hollywood's *Avatar* and *Harry Potter and the Half-Blood Prince* were the box office hits of 2009 throughout much of the world, just as they were in North America. All world top-grossing films have been American for about three decades. McDonald's restaurants span the globe, so much so that the standardized cost of a 'Big Mac' is used by the respected business newspaper, *The Economist*, as a measure of the cost of living in different countries. As of the summer of 2008 there were 67 Starbucks locations in Toronto, but there were 34 in Paris and 100 in China. The US-dominated Internet, direct broadcast satellites,

Media Spotlight

Box 3.4 The Long Shadow of American Culture

- American magazines account for close to two-thirds of magazine sales in English Canada.
- About two-thirds of television viewing time in English Canada is spent watching American programs. This increases to about 90 per cent in the case of drama and comedy viewing time.
- During a fairly typical week in May 2010, 23 of the 30 most-watched television programs in English Canada were American. The exceptions included two Stanley Cup hockey games, a hockey pre-game telecast, and four newscasts. In contrast, only 2 of the top 30 in the French-language market for that week—*Criminal Minds* and *Desperate Housewives*—were American.
- Canada's feature film and television production industries depend on a life-support system of government subsidies, channelled through the Income Tax Act and Telefilm Canada, and through the production activities of the Canadian Broadcasting Corporation and National Film Board. Despite this, few genuinely Canadian films reach the box office market.

the cable news networks, international credit cards, and the multinational corporations have shrunk the globe, so that no country is free from some other's cultural or economic incursions. Is Canada really such a special case?

The answer to this question will inevitably be coloured by one's own values. How much dependence on another economy is too much? Is dependence on one of the world's economic powerhouses preferable to a more diversified trade profile with weaker or less reliable economies? Has Canada had much choice but to rely on the British economy and then the American economy?

On the cultural front, if most Canadians prefer American films, television programs, magazines, and music over homegrown alternatives, should their governments interfere? It stretches credulity to suggest that protectionist measures like the Canadian content quotas imposed on radio stations are a response to listener demands. Obviously they are not. And anyway, what are the differences in Canadian culture that policy-makers want to preserve? Does protectionism preserve these values, or just the industries that depend on the state's cultural life-support system?

All countries are subject to external influences that limit the independence of their elected governments. Canada is not unique in this regard. Nevertheless, one may fairly say that these influences are felt somewhat more powerfully in Canada than in most other countries. We would not go as far, however, as those Canadian nationalists who claim that economic and cultural ties to the United States undermine Canadian democracy. A self-governing democracy does not require the freedom from external influence that nationalists argue would be desirable for Canada. If it did, then none of the members of the European Union would qualify! An element of anti-Americanism—a dislike of American culture, institutions, and, especially, public policies—certainly contributes to the Canadian nationalist critique of American influence. More importantly, however, the nationalist arguments are based on an outdated ideal of national autonomy that bears increasingly little resemblance to today's world of interdependent states.

Starting Points for Research

Patrick James and Mark Kasoff, *Canadian Studies in the New Millennium* (Toronto: University of Toronto Press, 2008). Includes several excellent chapters on aspects of Canadian society.

Ernie Lightman, *Social Policy in Canada* (Toronto: Oxford University Press, 2003). Focusing on the distributional impacts of government policy, this book examines the nature and extent of poverty, the role of ideology in framing social policy discourse and shaping choices, and the ways through which social policies are financed.

Julie McMullin, *Understanding Social Inequality: Intersections of Class, Age, Gender, Ethnicity and Race in Canada* (Toronto: Oxford University Press, 2004). A widely used textbook that explores the complex relationships among various dimensions of inequality in Canada.

Michael Ornstein and H. Michael Stevenson, *Politics and Ideology in Canada: Elite and Public Opinion in the Transformation of the Welfare State* (Montreal and Kingston: McGill-Queen's University Press, 1999). The authors examine the relationship between public and elite opinion and declining support for the welfare state in Canada.

William Watson, *Globalization and the Meaning of Canadian Life* (Toronto: University of Toronto Press, 1998). Watson argues that, contrary to the widely held view, globalization does not seriously undermine the ability of Canadian governments to pursue policies, including taxation and social policies, different from those of the United States. Compare this with the pessimistic assessment of Stephen McBride in *Globalization and the Canadian State*, 2nd edn (Halifax: Fernwood, 2005).

Review Exercises

1. Education is one of the principal ladders for upward socio-economic mobility. How accessible is post-secondary education in Canada compared to other wealthy democracies? A good starting point might be 'Beyond the 49th Parallel: Affordability of University Education', at: <www.educationalpolicy.org>. Go beyond Canada–US comparisons to examine university accessibility in some Western European countries.
2. How much food bank use is there and how many homeless people are in your community? How would you go about finding answers to these questions? (Suggestions: Call a member of your city or town council and ask for the names of persons or organizations that operate food banks and shelters. Alternatively, you might call your local office of the United Way or a religious organization like the Salvation Army to ask about these matters.)
3. How would you define poverty? Calculate a monthly budget for a single person—including expenditures for food, shelter, clothing, transportation, and entertainment—that you think is the minimum necessary to ensure a decent standard of living. What annual income is necessary to maintain this standard of living? Ask a friend or family member to do the same exercise (don't give him or her any hints about your own calculations).
4. Who are the most influential people in your town or city? Make a list of the 10 most influential people. Once you have put together your list, think about why you have included these particular people. Are they politicians? Business people? Journalists? Activists? Labour leaders? In each case, what is the basis for their influence and who is able to hold them accountable for their actions?

A former Prime Minister, Joe Clark, once described Canada as a 'community of communities', a characterization that often seems confirmed in the regionally fractured nature of Canadian politics. © Richard Wong/GetStock.com

4 Regionalism and Canadian Politics

Regionalism and regionally based political conflict are enduring aspects of the Canadian political condition. This chapter looks at several important aspects of regionalism in Canadian politics, including the following topics:

- Predictions of the demise of regionalism.
- Reasons for the persistence of regionalism.
- The boundaries of Canada's regions.
- Regional political cultures.
- Regional grievances and western alienation.
- Western versus central Canadian 'visions' of the country.

'Canada has too much geography', declared the country's longest-serving Prime Minister, Mackenzie King. By this he meant that the vastness of the country and the diversity in the natural endowments and interests of its regions produced conflicts that would either not exist in a more compact country or whose resolution would be less difficult. Canadians have always accepted the truth of King's dictum, believing that the challenges of **regionalism** and inter-regional conflict are a central part of the Canadian story. Indeed, as we noted in Chapter 1, one of the most astute observers of Canadian politics, Donald Smiley, once identified regionalism as one of the three fundamental axes of Canadian politics. It was, he rightly noted, the source of major political divisions and controversies throughout Canada's history. And it continues to be one of the defining features of Canada's political landscape today.

Along with King, most Canadians have viewed regionalism as a problem. Aside from occasional patriotic celebrations of Canada's regional diversity and sheer size, as in the spate of songs that emerged around Canada's centennial year and in the speeches of politicians and after-dinner speakers, few have argued that size and regional diversity are positive attributes in political life. Students of American politics will know, however, that some of the founders of the United States believed these attributes to be positive, perhaps even necessary, characteristics of a political system respectful of freedom. In the *Federalist Papers*, James Madison argued that a larger territory encompassing a greater diversity of regional interests was more likely to provide protection for personal freedoms, group rights, and sectional interests than would a smaller, more homogeneous country. Madison reasoned that as the physical size of a country increased and the scope of its social and especially economic interests was enlarged, the likelihood of any particular group being able to dominate others or of being able to form a coalition with other interests to achieve such domination would decline. Small countries with comparatively homogeneous populations were, he thought, incapable of maintaining respect for individual and minority rights. The majority would inevitably exercise a sort of tyranny, using their superior numbers to oppress the rights of others. This was less likely to happen in a larger, more diverse country.

Madison's argument has never resonated very positively in Canada, with the exception of some supporters of this view in western Canada. The debates on Confederation contain no echoes of this argument for a vast republic to ensure the protection of rights. The expansion of Canada was seen by most as a necessary pre-emptive action to reduce the possibility of the vast western territories being annexed by a United States where the idea of Manifest Destiny and the fact of territorial expansion were riding high. Surprisingly, perhaps, one of the few Canadians to theorize about the consequences of regionalism in the style of Madison was Pierre Trudeau, usually thought of as being a prime minister with a strong preference for centralized federal power. Trudeau's thoughts on the political virtue of regionalism were, however, formulated before he entered federal politics. Aside from the early Trudeau and some disgruntled westerners, few Canadians have disagreed with Mackenzie King's assessment that regionalism has been primarily a burden on the back of Canadian politics.

The Unexpected Persistence of Regionalism

The last few decades have seen an upsurge in regionalism in Canada, a trend mirrored in many other parts of the world. The signs of this upsurge can be seen in the party system, western alienation, regional economic disparities, and intergovernmental conflict.

The party system. For most of Canada's history the two historically dominant parties, the Liberals and Conservatives, competed with each other across Canada. Although they did not draw equally well from all regional segments of the electorate—the Liberal Party did much better than the Conservatives in Quebec for most of the twentieth century and the Conservative Party tended to be stronger than the Liberals in the West for most of the second half of that century—both were very clearly national political parties with significant support across Canada.

Since the 1993 general election, the character of Canada's party system has appeared to be more regionally than nationally based. This is most obvious in the case of the Bloc Québécois, which only runs candidates in Quebec and which elected more MPs from that province than any other party in the 1993, 1997, 2004, 2006, and 2008 elections and ran a strong second to the Liberals in the 2000 election. The Canadian Alliance, formerly the **Reform Party**, won almost all its seats west of Ontario and received the greatest share of the popular vote of any party in the combined four western provinces during the 1993, 1997, and 2000 federal elections. The Progressive Conservative Party, long a truly national party in terms of the regional breadth of its support, elected more of its MPs from the Atlantic provinces in these three elections than from any other part of the country. The Alliance and the Progressive Conservatives merged into the Conservative Party of Canada before the 2004 election, a union that delivered less than a handful of seats in Ontario and none from Quebec in that election. Only the Liberal Party appeared capable of claiming significant support in all regions of the country over these four national elections, although even its regional levels of support were very uneven.

The 2006 and 2008 elections saw a continuation of very weak Liberal support west of Ontario, but a resurgence of Conservative support in Ontario and even in Quebec. Nevertheless, recent elections, including that of 2011, have produced party representation in Parliament that is strikingly fragmented along regional lines.

Western alienation. Western grievances against Ottawa and the Ontario–Quebec axis that has dominated the national political scene have existed for as long as the western provinces have been part of Canada. But in the 1970s there was a sharp upward ratcheting in the rhetoric associated with these grievances. At this point the term 'western alienation' entered the lexicon of Canadian politics. As had always been the case, economics was at the root of this discontent. Spokespersons for the western provinces argued that Ottawa treated the resources with which the West was well endowed, and which formed the basis for western prosperity, differently and less favourably than those located primarily in provinces like Ontario and Quebec. Although Albertans were the most vocal in making this case, politicians and industry leaders in British Columbia and Saskatchewan provided a supportive chorus.

The concept of 'western alienation' has tended to be most pronounced in Alberta and British Columbia. However, with Ontario receiving federal equalization payments for the first time in 2008, earning it the label of a 'have-not' province, the complexion of historical disparities between provinces is changing.

Economic disparities. The gap between the real prosperity of the richest and poorest provinces of

Canada has not grown narrower. Indeed, if the federal government transfers intended to narrow this gap are excluded, the disparity has increased between wealthy provinces like Alberta and Ontario and the less affluent provinces like New Brunswick and Nova Scotia. By itself, such disparity does not necessarily mean greater inter-regional conflict if the central government is able to subsidize incomes and public services in the poorer regions and if taxpayers in the wealthier regions are willing to pay for this regional redistribution of wealth. These conditions have been eroded. The last two decades have shown that the political will to maintain these redistributive transfers has become weaker.

Intergovernmental conflict. The pendulum of federal–provincial power has swung from Ottawa to the provinces and back again several times since Confederation. Sir John A. Macdonald's hope and expectation that the provincial governments would become little more than 'glorified municipalities', deferring to Ottawa on all matters of national importance, was stymied from the beginning by provincial politicians who had other ideas and by judges whose interpretation of the division of powers in Canada's Constitution did not accord with Macdonald's. Today, intergovernmental conflict is alive and intense on a number of fronts that include such important matters as environmental policy, health care, taxation, cities, and post-secondary education. Judging from these conflicts, regionalism continues to mark the Canadian political landscape.

The persistence and even resurgence of regionalism, in Canada and elsewhere, took many by surprise. One of the few points of agreement among most twentieth-century social and political observers was that as the conditions of people's existence became more alike, their values, beliefs, and behaviour would converge. As modern transportation, mass media, public education, and consumer lifestyle habits broke down the barriers that previously separated regional communities and nurtured their distinctiveness, regionalism would become a weaker force in social and political life. Those on the left predicted that region, like religion and ethnicity, eventually would be replaced by class as the dominant fault line in the politics of modernized societies. Indeed, some went so far as to argue that only the obfuscations and manipulations of the dominant class, exercised through their control of the mass media, political parties, and such agents of cultural learning as the schools and the churches, kept alive the fiction that region, and not class, was more important in shaping the interests and identities of average people.

Contrary to these expectations, and despite the undeniable fact that in many important ways the lives of people across the rich industrialized societies of the world are more alike today than a generation or two ago, regionalism and its even more robust cousin—nationalism—continue to be important forces in political life. This certainly is true

Governing Realities

Box 4.1 Modernization and Regionalism

The expectation . . .

In . . . modernizing societies, the general historical record has spelled centralization. . . . [T]he main reasons for this change, the major grounds of centralization and decentralization are to be found not in . . . 'ground rules' [the Constitution and court rulings] . . . [or] in the personal, partisan or ideological preferences of officeholders, but in the new forces produced by an advanced modernity.

Samuel Beer, 1973

The Canadian reality . . .

Modernization had not led to centralization in the Canadian federal system but rather to the power, assertiveness, and competence of the provinces. Furthermore, the provinces where modernization has proceeded most rapidly are insistent about preserving and extending their autonomy.

Donald Smiley, 1984

in Canada, as the signs of the vitality of regionalism discussed above attest, and as the persistence of a significant nationalist movement in Quebec demonstrates. Three principal factors help to explain the attraction and persistence of regionalism.

First, traditional thinking underestimated the degree to which regionally based states and elites may invest in regionalism—and regionally based nationalism, too, as in the case of Quebec—when this investment either serves their own interests or, more charitably, promotes their vision of what is in the best interests of the regional community that they purport to represent. During the 1970s Canadian political scientists began to use the term **province-building** to describe the phenomenon of powerful provincial governments using the various constitutional, legal, and taxation levers available to them in order to increase their control over activities and interests within their provincial borders and, in consequence, their stature vis-à-vis Ottawa. Alberta and Quebec were the two provinces most often cited as illustrations of this drive on the part of provincial state elites to extend the scope of their authority.

Although these two provinces may have been the outstanding examples of province-building in action, the phenomenon was not limited to them. Alan Cairns argued that the strength of regionalism in Canada was, in fact, primarily due to a Constitution that gave Canada's provincial governments considerable law-making and revenue-raising powers, reinforced by what he saw as the natural tendency of those who controlled, worked for, or depended on provincial states to protect and extend their turf. We will have more to say about this later in the chapter.

A second factor not anticipated by those who predicted the demise of regionalism involves the failure of national institutions—political, cultural, and economic—to produce levels of national integration and identity that would overcome regionally based ways of thinking and acting in Canadian politics. To put this a bit differently, many Canadians, particularly in Quebec and in the West, have remained unconvinced that the institutions of the national government and its policies have their best interests in mind. Students of federalism have made a distinction between *inter*-state federalism, where conflict and co-operation are played out between the national and regional governments, and *intra*-state federalism, where these forces are contained within the institutions of the national state. There certainly has been no shortage of national structures and policies intended to accommodate regional interests and perspectives. A short list of these, past and present, would include the following:

Structures

- The Senate incorporates the principle of regional representation, with Ontario, Quebec, the four western provinces, and the three Maritime provinces all being assigned the same number of seats.
- The Supreme Court Act requires that at least three of the nine justices be members of the Quebec bar. Moreover, the custom has developed over time whereby it is expected that three of the judges will be from Ontario and at least one from each of the western and eastern regions of the country.
- The federal cabinet has always been at the centre of attempts to ensure regional representation in federal decision-making. Every prime minister has given careful consideration to the representation of each region and, insofar as it is possible, each province in putting together his or her cabinet.
- Section 36 of the Constitution Act, 1982 commits the federal government to the principle of 'making equalization payments to ensure that provincial governments have sufficient revenues to provide reasonably comparable levels of public services at reasonably comparable levels of taxation.' Although the practical significance of this constitutional commitment is far from clear, the spirit of it clearly involves a federal obligation to assist the less affluent provincial governments in paying their bills.

Policies

- For about two decades, and in response to criticism that the Canadian media system

and federal cultural policy were strongly biased towards central Canada, Ottawa has attempted to 'regionalize' its cultural activities in various ways. One of these involves regional programming through the Canadian Broadcasting Corporation and a conscious policy of ensuring that regional points of view are expressed in its national programming. Another involves the programs and spending activities of the Department of Canadian Heritage, which, like the CBC, has a mandate to express the diversity of Canada.
- Federal support for regional economic development has a long and much-criticized history in Canada. These activities were given an organizational focus and a major spending boost through the 1968 creation of the Department of Regional Economic Expansion, which has morphed into departments and agencies by other names over the years. Today, Ottawa's support for the economies of the less affluent provinces is channelled mainly through the Atlantic Canada Opportunities Agency and Western Economic Diversification Canada, both under the Department of Industry.
- When making decisions that have important regional spending and employment implications, from the awarding of contracts to the location of government offices, Ottawa is always sensitive to the probable reactions of citizens and their spokespersons in regions competing for a share of the federal pie.

Although it would be unfair to write off these structures and policies as amounting to a complete and abject failure, they clearly have not succeeded in neutralizing regionalism. It is always possible, of course, that regional grievances and the acrimony that often accompanies intergovernmental relations in Canada might have been worse in the absence of these efforts at intra-state federalism.

A third factor whose importance was overlooked by those who anticipated the decline of regionalism involves the persistence of differences in the economic interests and social characteristics of regions. It is undeniably true that, in many respects, how people in Ontario and Saskatchewan live, the sorts of jobs they are likely to do, the programs they watch on television, and the cultural milieu in which they live are more alike today than two generations ago. But differences persist and their political importance, often fanned by politicians or other regional spokespersons, is considerable. For example, about one-quarter of Alberta's GDP is accounted for by the petrochemical industry, a level of dependence on this particular industry that is unrivalled in Canada. Ontario's economy is far more dependent than any other province on the automobile industry, with close to 40 per cent of all provincial exports, representing about 12 per cent of Ontario's GDP, accounted for by automotive vehicles and parts. Almost all of this goes to the United States, a fact that injects a great deal of urgency into the uncertainty associated with the future of the industry in Ontario.

If we shift from economics to demography we also find some significant differences between provinces and regions. On the whole, and with one major exception, the political impact of these demographic differences tends to be considerably less than that of the different economic interests of Canada's regions. The major exception is, of course, Quebec. It is the only majority francophone province, with over 80 per cent of the provincial population claiming French as their mother tongue and a majority having French ancestry. Nunavut, where about 85 per cent of the population is Aboriginal, represents another case of a region whose ethnic character is dramatically different from the rest of Canada. This is not to say that there are not enormous differences in the demographic character of provinces like British Columbia, which has been a magnet in recent decades for non-European immigrants, most of them from Asia, and Nova Scotia, where the predominance of people whose ancestry is from the British Isles remains undiminished. But the political significance of these demographic differences is less than in the case of Quebec or Nunavut. The ethnic character of Nova Scotia does not get expressed in Canadian politics in the way that Quebec's francophone character does.

Mapping Regionalism in Canada

How many regions does Canada have? The answer depends on our definition of region. A map with boundaries drawn along economic lines will look different from one drawn along lines of demography or history. Some have argued that the only sensible way to conceive of regions in Canada is along provincial lines, such that each province constitutes a separate region. More commonly, however, political observers have tended to combine certain provinces into the same region, particularly the western and easternmost provinces. But here, too, there are difficulties. The justification for lumping Manitoba and British Columbia into a common region designated the 'West' is not obvious. Aside from both being west of Ontario they may appear to have no more in common than Manitoba and Nova Scotia. Difficulties aside, it has been common to speak of four or five main regions in Canada: the West (or British Columbia and the Prairies), Ontario, Quebec, and the Atlantic provinces. From the point of view of both physical and cultural geography, as well as economics, the Canadian North comprises another significant region.

Listen to the 'Is It Time to Redraw the Regional Map of Canada?' podcast, available at www.oupcanada.com/Brooks7e

There are three principal ways of determining the boundaries of regions, all of them useful. They involve economics, values, and identity.

Canada's Economic Regions

Common economic interests, often linked to physical geography, may provide a basis for the classification of regions. Atlantic Canada's greater dependence on fisheries, Ontario and Quebec's greater manufacturing base, and the West's comparatively greater reliance on grain production and natural resources are economic interests that have provided a basis for thinking of these parts of Canada as constituting distinctive regions. As Table 4.1 shows, the economic characteristics of Canada's provinces vary considerably.

The regional variation that exists in Canada's industrial structure has often been at the root of major political conflicts between regions of the country and between Ottawa and the provinces. The Kyoto Protocol on limiting greenhouse gas emissions, which requires policies that would reduce the use of carbon-based fuels, pitted Ottawa against Alberta for over a decade. Albertans and their government knew that the environmental gains envisaged by advocates of the Kyoto Protocol would be achieved at the expense of the industry that is central to their province's economic well-being. The federal government was able to point to public opinion polls showing that a clear majority of Canadians favoured the ratification of the Kyoto agreement. As it turned out, the victory of the Conservative Party in the 2006 national election rendered the issue moot, given the party's lack of sympathy for the Kyoto guidelines and different approach to dealing with global warming.

Historically, the federal government's major economic policies have been slanted towards the interests of central Canada. On occasion the discrimination against and even exploitation of other regions of the country, particularly the West, has been egregious. Examples include the following.

Tariffs. For most of Canada's history a cornerstone of economic policy was high tariffs on manufactured imports, the costs and benefits of which were distributed unequally between the country's regions. The cost for western farmers to ship grain by rail to the Fort William railhead (today's Thunder Bay), despite federal subsidies, always seemed greater than it should have been to those in the West, and shipment of eastern manufactures to the West made prices higher than they might have been if trade, protected by the high tariffs of the National Policy beginning in 1879, could have followed more natural north–south lines to contiguous American states and regions. The extensive prime lands controlled by the Canadian Pacific Railway as part of its original agreement with the government in the nineteenth century also rankled western sensitivities.

One study of tariff impacts prior to the Canada–US Free Trade Agreement concluded that the per capita benefits for Ontario were about equal to the per capita costs in the West and Atlantic Canada. Quebecers were also net beneficiaries, but the decline of that province's manufacturing base by

TABLE 4.1 Selected Economic and Population Characteristics, by Province

Province	Median Family Income (2007)* ($)	Unemployment Rate (May 2010) (%)	Percentage of Labour Force in Manufacturing (2008) (%)	Most Important Industries	Average Annual Population Growth, 2004-2009 (%)	Median Government Transfers to Families (2007) ($)
NL	61,750	14	6.4	Fishing, mining, oil & gas, newsprint	-0.3	11,500
PEI	64,880	9.6	8.7	Fishing, mining, oil & gas, newsprint	0.5	9,000
NS	66,670	9.1	8.6	Forestry, agriculture, tourism, fishing	0.0	5,800
NB	63,230	9.9	9.6	Forestry, mining, agriculture	0.0	7,800
Que.	67,430	7.8	14.0	Manufacturing, mining, hydroelectric power	0.8	7,200
Ont.	76,510	9.3	13.5	Motor vehicles & parts, manufacturing, finance	1.1	4,500
Man.	69,490	5.6	11.3	Manufacturing, agriculture	0.8	4,500
Sask.	73,830	5.0	6.0	Agriculture, mining	0.6	3,400
Alta	89,720	7.0	7.2	Oil & gas, agriculture	2.6	1,700
BC	71,880	7.7	8.1	Forestry, tourism, mining	1.4	3,700
Canada	73,420	8.3	11.5		1.1	4,900

*Households consisting of a couple living together, with or without children.

Sources: Various on-line publications of Statistics Canada, at: <www.statcan.ca>.

the 1980s reduced the level of these benefits from what it had been for most of the previous century.[1]

Terms of entry into Confederation. Outside of Alberta and Saskatchewan, few Canadians know that when these provinces entered Canada in 1905 they did not immediately receive all of the law-making powers held by the other provinces. Specifically, they did not have control over natural resources within provincial borders, a power that sections 92 and 109 of the Constitution Act, 1867 assigns exclusively to the provinces. The reason for this discriminatory treatment involved, quite simply, Ottawa's desire to retain control over the economic development of the Prairies, a part of the country that was being settled rapidly in the early 1900s and whose expansion was essential to the National Policy goal of building a larger domestic market for the manufacturers of Ontario and Quebec.

The National Energy Policy (1981). A generation after it was abolished by the Conservative government of Brian Mulroney in 1984, the **National Energy Program (NEP)** remains vivid in the memory of Albertans. It involved, they quite reasonably believed, an enormous transfer of wealth from Alberta to the rest of Canada, and chiefly to the consumers and industries of Canada's industrial heartland, perpetrated by a Liberal government that they saw as being hostile to western, and especially Alberta's, interests. The NEP placed a limit on the price that could be charged in Canada for oil and gas from Canadian sources. This price was considerably below the going world price. Canadian producers' ability to export their petroleum at the higher world price was limited by the fact that any energy exports had to be approved by the National Energy Board. Albertans saw the NEP as a thinly disguised subsidy that their province was made to pay to central Canada. These fears were rekindled when the price of oil and gas rose dramatically in 2005, leading to proposals from some eastern Canadian politicians that Alberta's energy 'windfall' be shared more equitably with the rest of Canada (see Box 4.2).

When world oil prices doubled in 2007–8, there was somewhat less talk about the rest of Canada getting a slice of Alberta's growing revenue pie. Part of the reason for this change was probably the fact of a Conservative government in power, holding all 28 of Alberta's seats in the House of Commons, and led by a prime minister from that province. But another part of the reason was that the issue of energy costs was now framed largely in environmental terms. How to wean consumers and industry from dependence on fossil fuels and reduce CO_2 emissions had become a far more prominent issue than whether the good fortune of some

Politics in Focus

Box 4.2 'Everything for Alberta and Nothing for the Rest of Us?'*

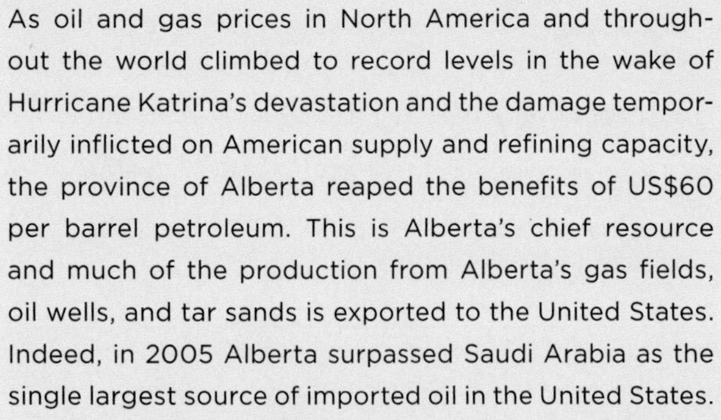

As oil and gas prices in North America and throughout the world climbed to record levels in the wake of Hurricane Katrina's devastation and the damage temporarily inflicted on American supply and refining capacity, the province of Alberta reaped the benefits of US$60 per barrel petroleum. This is Alberta's chief resource and much of the production from Alberta's gas fields, oil wells, and tar sands is exported to the United States. Indeed, in 2005 Alberta surpassed Saudi Arabia as the single largest source of imported oil in the United States.

Already the richest Canadian province with the lowest rates of taxation, Alberta went from its usual prosperity to boom times. This led some to ask, 'Who will benefit from the Alberta boom?' (Qui profitera du boom albertain?), as did the headline on the 1 October 2005 issue of Quebec's news and public affairs magazine, *L'Actualité*. Quebecers were not the only ones to ask this question. So, too, did federal government officials, some journalists, and many Canadians outside Alberta, judging from public opinion polls taken at the time.

This question enraged many in Alberta. It appeared to suggest that their province's resources and prosperity somehow belonged to all regions of Canada in a way that revenue from Quebec's hydroelectric exports, Ontario's automotive sector exports, or British Columbia's lumber exports did not. The response of most of Alberta's opinion leaders was that the Constitution gave their province control over the resources, which it does, and that the rest of Canada already was reaping the benefits of boom time in Alberta through employment opportunities in their province, economic spinoffs generated in the engineering, manufacturing, and construction sectors of other provinces, and even the investments of provincial public pension funds in Alberta's thriving petroleum industry.

Albertans certainly are not opposed to sharing their prosperity with the rest of Canada. On a per capita basis, more money is transferred via the federal government from Alberta to other parts of Canada than from any other province—$2,500 per Albertan as of 2004.[2] Public opinion surveys show that most Albertans believe that this is fair. But proposals to treat their resources and the basis of Alberta's economic prosperity differently from those of other provinces fuel their long-standing belief that there is one standard for eastern Canada and another for the West.

When eastern politicians and opinion leaders talk about how Alberta needs to do more to share its wealth, Albertans are reminded of the old saying, *le plus ça change, le plus c'est la même chose.*

*This title is from Pierre Fortin, 'Tout à l'Alberta, rien pour les autres?', *L'Acualité*, 1 October 2005, 50–2.

provinces meant that they should be expected to share the wealth.

This shift in how the energy issue, and particularly Alberta oil, was framed did not put an end to inter-regional conflict. Criticisms of Alberta the greedy were replaced by those of Alberta the despoiler of the environment and major source of global warming. This criticism came largely, but not exclusively, from Quebec. The Bloc Québécois and its leader, Gilles Duceppe, and Premier Jean Charest were outspokenly critical of the impact on the environment of oil sands development. Various public opinion polls taken between 2008 and 2010 found that Quebecers were significantly more likely than other Canadians to believe that the environmental costs associated with the oil sands outweighed the economic benefits to the country and to their province.

Canada's Cultural Regions

In what is perhaps the most widely cited—and disputed—study of regional political cultures in Canada, Richard Simeon and David Elkins conclude that 'there are strong differences among the citizens of Canadian provinces and those of different language groups in some basic orientations to politics.'[3] They go on to argue that these regional variations cannot be totally explained by demographic and socio-economic differences between Canada's regions. The sources of these differences in basic political orientations are, Simeon and Elkins admit, unclear. But their existence, they insist, is undeniable.

Other researchers have arrived at very different conclusions about the nature and extent of regional political cultures in Canada. Indeed, if there is anything approaching a consensus on this question—and it is a shaky consensus at best—it is that regional variations in basic and enduring political values and beliefs are not very great in English-speaking Canada, and while the differences between French-speaking Quebec and the rest of Canada appear to be more significant, they are not enormous.

A survey conducted in 2002 by Environics Research Group appears to support this consensus. Based on this survey of Canadians' attitudes towards the Charter of Rights and Freedoms, the study's authors note the 'lack of any significant regional differences of opinion on the Charter's legitimacy or the relationship between Parliament and the courts'[4] (see Figure 4.1). Moreover, they observed that there does not appear to be any difference across regions of Canada in support for such Charter principles and values as bilingualism and minority language, education rights, multiculturalism, the appropriateness of 'reasonable limits' on freedom of expression, and the rights of the accused. The one outlier, however, was Quebec. While sharing with other Canadian regions support for the Charter and its general principles, Quebecers are considerably more likely than other Canadians to value equality over personal freedom and consistently more likely than their compatriots in other regions to support the extension of equality rights to disadvantaged groups (see Figures 4.2 and 4.3).

These findings seem to confirm the widely held view of Quebec as being a more collectivist society than other regions of Canada. Further confirmation is provided by those aspects of personal freedom where Quebecers are more supportive than Canadians in other regions. When it comes to restricting police powers and guaranteeing the legal rights of vulnerable groups, Quebecers are somewhat more likely to come down on the side of civil liberties. For example, in the 2002 Environics survey 71 per cent of Quebecers said that the police *should not* be allowed to enter and search a criminal suspect's home or office without a search warrant, compared to 63 per cent in the rest of Canada. Similarly, only 61 per cent of Quebecers expressed the view that the police and courts have to spend too much time worrying about the rights of criminals, compared to 72 per cent of Canadians living outside Quebec. On the matter of the rights of refugee claimants, Quebecers were again more likely than other Canadians to come down on the side of protecting individual rights (85 per cent compared to 75 per cent).[5] Arguably, all these items tap support for 'underdogs' and the vulnerable—those accused of crimes, refugees, etc.—and so Quebecers' greater support for civil liberties intended to protect those who fall into these groups may reasonably be

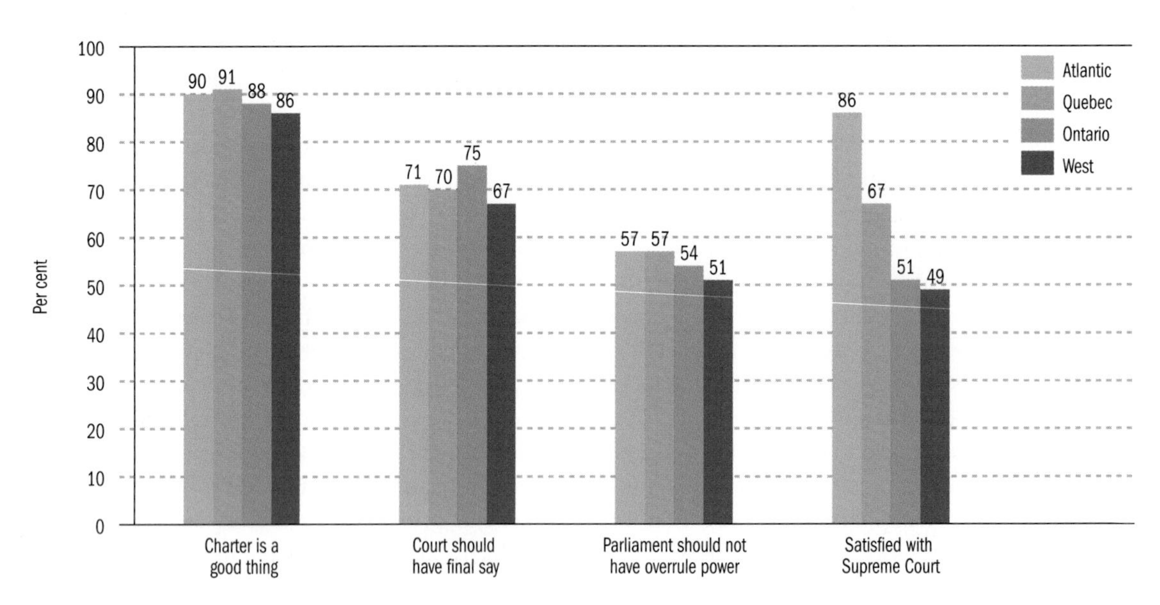

FIGURE 4.1 Opinion on the Charter and the Courts, by Region, 2002

Source: Centre for Research and Information on Canada (CRIC), *The Charter: Dividing or Uniting Canadians*, Apr. 2002, 30. Available at: <www.ccu-cuc.ca>.

A. Both freedom and equality are important. But I consider personal freedom to be more important, that is, everyone can live in freedom and develop without hindrance.

B. Both freedom and equality are important. But I consider equality to be more important, that is, nobody is underprivileged and social class differences are not so strong.

FIGURE 4.2 Support for Freedom versus Equality, by Region, 2002 (percentage agreeing with the statement)

Source: Adapted from CRIC, *The Charter*, Table 6, 30.

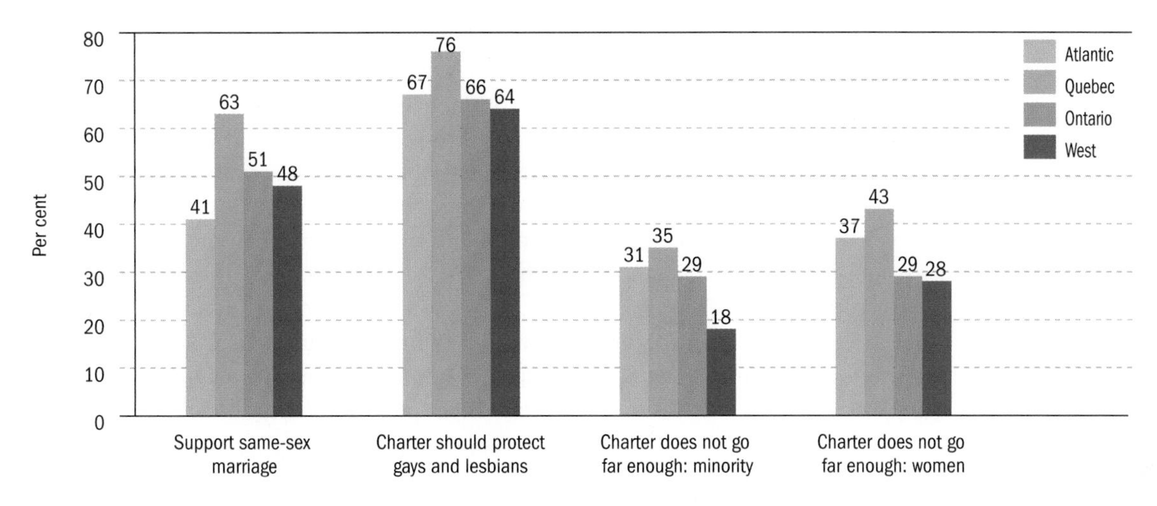

FIGURE 4.3 Attitudes on Equality, by Region, 2002

Source: CRIC, *The Charter*, 31.

interpreted as consistent with the characterization of Quebec as a more collectivist society.

One of the most thorough examinations of popular ideology in Canada corroborates the conclusion that, Quebec aside, the regional variations in political culture that exist in the rest of Canada are not very great.[6] Based on a large national survey Michael Ornstein and Michael Stevenson measured Canadians' support for social programs, redistributive policies, foreign investment, labour unions, and large corporations. Their examination of the variation in the ideological profiles of the provinces reveals that the differences are, for the most part, small and that Quebec stands out as the one province that is clearly to the left of the others. Moreover, contrary to the findings of Simeon and Elkins 20 years earlier, Ornstein and Stevenson do not find any significant variation between the provinces, Quebec included, in levels of political efficacy or political participation. 'Not one province', they argue, 'differs significantly from the national mean for the measure of efficacy',[7] and the small provincial variations in participation do not conform to the pattern found by Simeon and Elkins.

The Simeon and Elkins thesis of significant cultural variation between the predominantly English-speaking provinces is dealt another blow by data from the General Social Survey carried out by Statistics Canada. Here are some of its findings:

- Provincial populations are broadly similar in terms of levels of trust in individuals. The one exception is Quebec. In the majority anglophone provinces, levels of trust range from 54 per cent in New Brunswick to 67 per cent in PEI. In Quebec only 34 per cent of respondents agreed that people can be trusted.
- Provincial levels of charitable giving are linked to average provincial income, citizens in the wealthier provinces from Ontario west to BC giving more than those in the less affluent Atlantic provinces. Quebec is the exception. Although wealthier than their fellow citizens in the four Atlantic provinces, Quebecers give considerably less than residents of any other province, on average about half of what other Canadians give.
- Quebecers are also less likely to engage in volunteer activity. In the predominantly English-speaking provinces the percentage of people who said that they volunteered ranged from 46 per cent in Newfoundland and Labrador to 59 per cent in Saskatchewan. It was 37 per cent in Quebec (2007).

- Rates of involvement in organizations—sports, recreational, union, professional, cultural, service club, political, etc.—are broadly similar in all of the provinces. The only exception is religious involvement. In the majority anglophone provinces about 20 per cent are actively involved in a religious organization, except in BC where it is slightly lower at 16.8 per cent. But Quebec again stands out: only 6.3 per cent of Quebecers said that they were active in a religious organization in 2008.

The case for the existence of several regional political cultures in English-speaking Canada is salvaged a bit if, instead of ideological values, one looks at how regional populations view Ottawa, its treatment of their region, and policies intended to redistribute wealth between regions of the country (Figures 4.4–4.7). Albertans stand out as those least likely to believe that the federal government deserves their trust and confidence or that Ottawa gives them value for their tax money. They also appear to be less committed than other Canadians to the long-standing policy of equalization, whereby money is transferred by Ottawa from the richer to the poorer provinces. And they are among those least likely to believe that their province is treated with the respect it deserves. Atlantic Canada, on the other hand, displays greater trust and confidence in the federal government than other regions of the country and is the only part of the country where citizens are more likely to name Ottawa than their provincial government as providing them with value for their money.

These findings corroborate those of Ornstein and Stevenson, who found dramatic variation between provincial populations in their responses to the question of whether the federal government treated their province fairly and whether either Ottawa or their provincial government should have more power. For example, 64 per cent of Ontarians agreed that Ottawa treated their province fairly and only 22 per cent expressed the view that their provincial government should have more power. The percentages for PEI were almost identical. But Alberta, Saskatchewan, and Newfoundland offered a mirror image of this picture. In Newfoundland, for example, only 12 per cent agreed that Ottawa treated their province fairly and 58 per cent said that their provincial government should have more power.[8]

Despite this evidence of significant interprovincial differences in how citizens view the federal government, there is very little variation between provincial populations when it comes to their

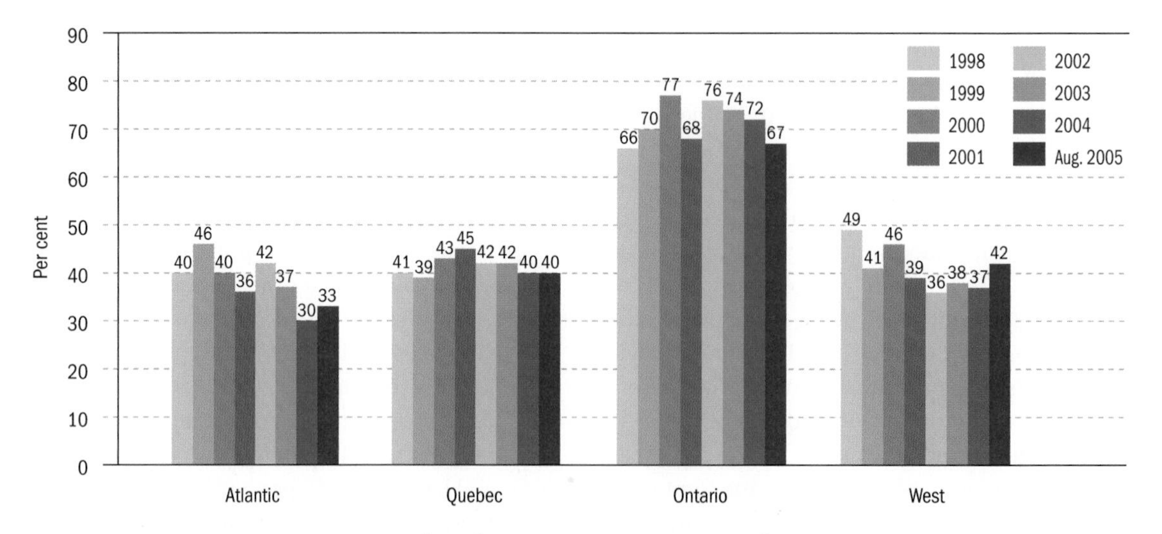

FIGURE 4.4 Province Is Treated with Respect It Deserves, by Region, 1998–2005

Source: CRIC, <www.ccu-cuc.ca/>.

sense of belonging to Canada. The exception is Quebec. Figure 4.8 shows that close to two-thirds of Canadians in the mainly anglophone regions of Canada say they have a very strong sense of belonging to Canada. Only about one-third of Quebecers express a strong sense of belonging to the country.

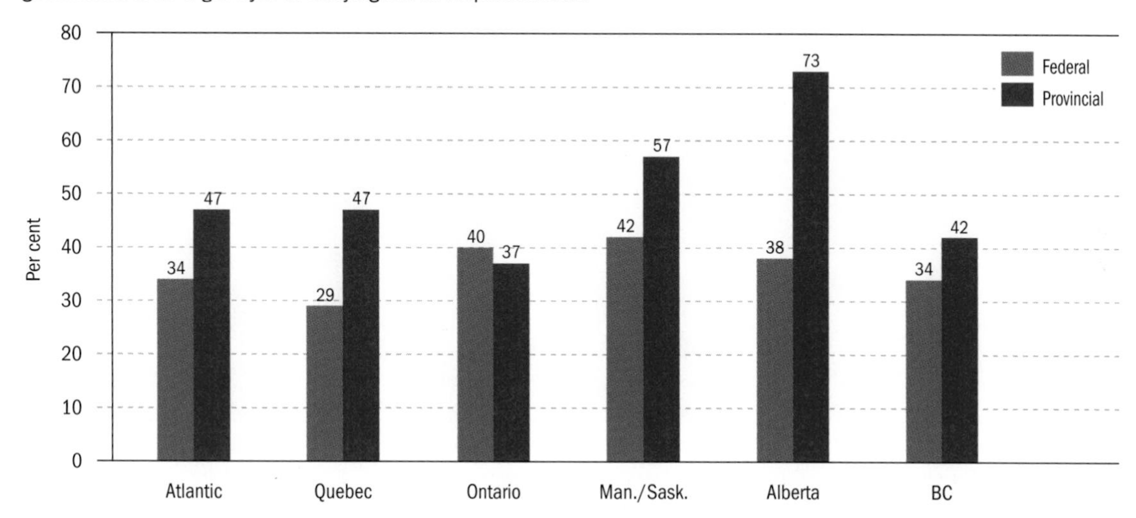

FIGURE 4.5 Trust and Confidence in Federal and Provincial Governments, by Region, 2004 (percentage saying they have a great deal or a fair amount)

Source: CRIC, Canada-US-Mexico Comparative Federalism Survey (June 2004).

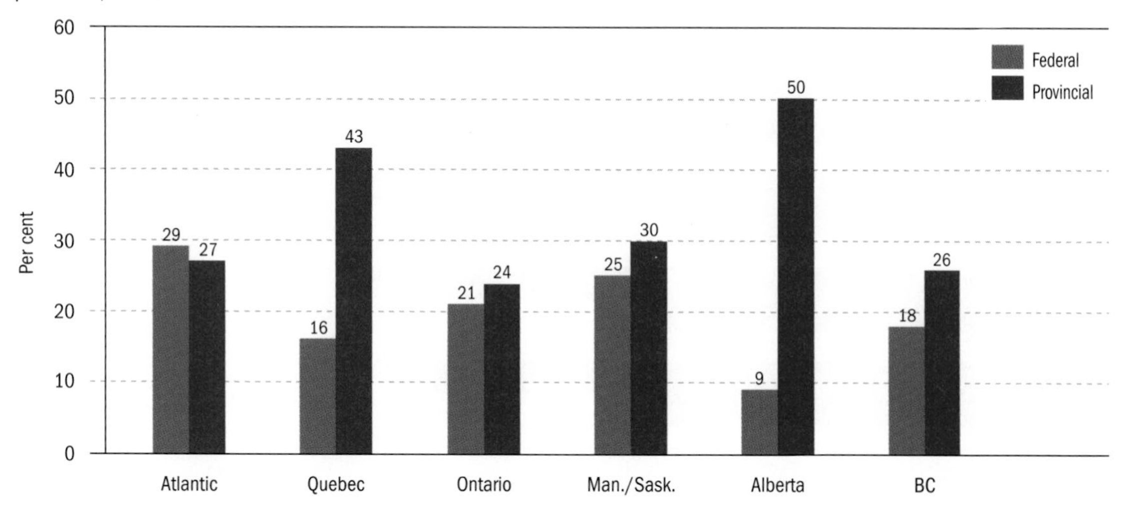

FIGURE 4.6 Level of Government That Gives You Most for Your Money, by Region, 2004

Note: Responses for 'local government' not shown.

Source: CRIC, Canada-US-Mexico Comparative Federalism Survey (June 2004).

Question: As you may know, under the federal equalization program money is transferred from the richer provinces to the poorer ones, in order to ensure that Canadians living in every province have access to similar levels of public services. Do you strongly support, moderately support, moderately oppose or strongly oppose the equalization program? (Percentage supporting)

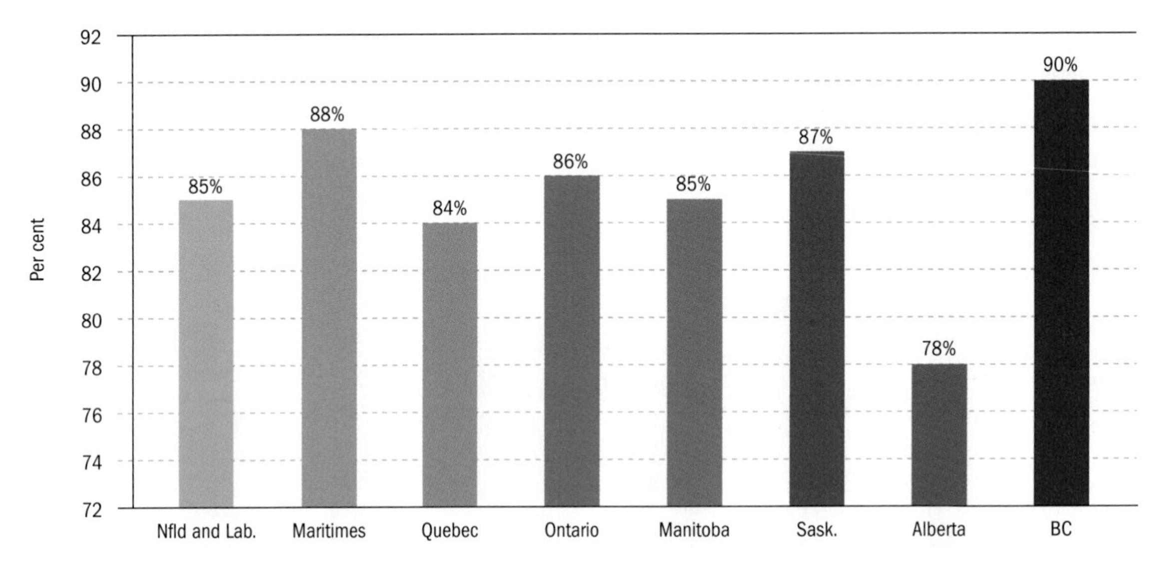

FIGURE 4.7 Support for Equalization, by Region, 2004

Source: CRIC, Portraits of Canada 2004, at: <www.ccu-cuc.ca>.

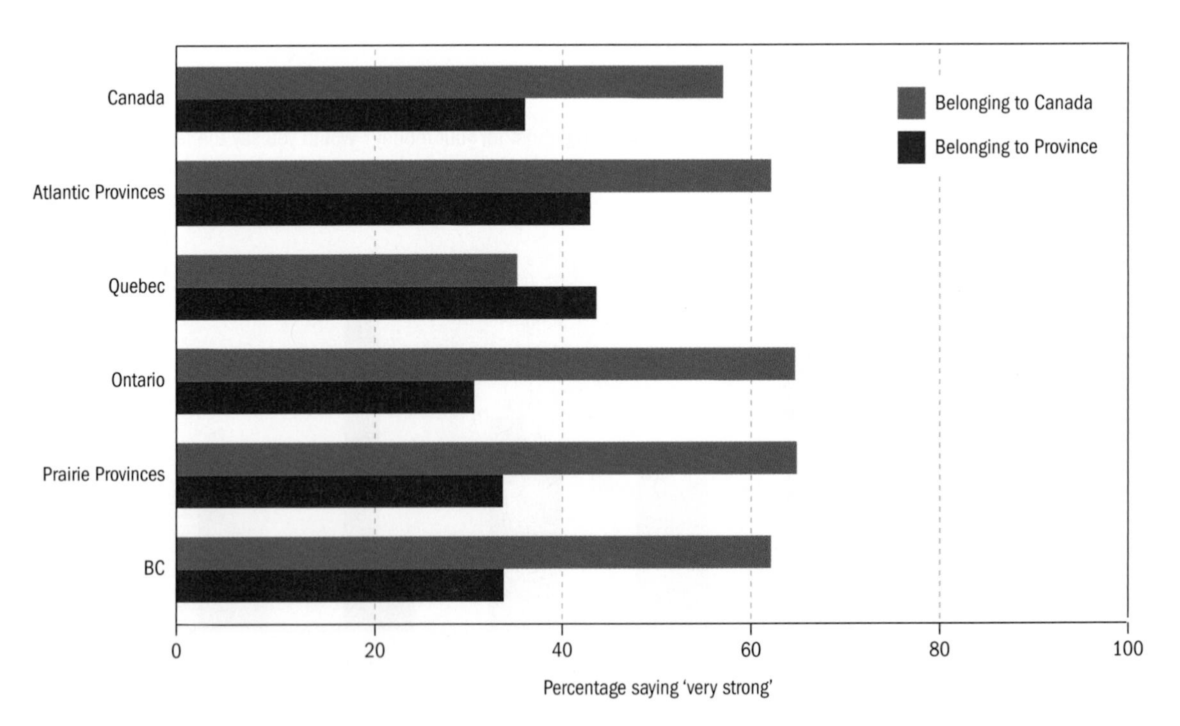

FIGURE 4.8 Sense of Belonging to Canada and to Home Province, 2008

Source: Adapted from Statistics Canada, *General Social Survey*, at: <www.statcan.gc.ca/pub/89-640-x/2009001/tab/tab4-6-eng.htm>.

Cross-Border Regions

A more recent method of mapping regions is suggested by Debora VanNijnatten and her colleagues in their work on **cross-border regions (CBRs)**. They define a CBR as a distinct grouping of neighbouring and nearby provinces and states whose economic, cultural, and institutional linkages create commonalities between the members of this binational (Canada–US) grouping and set it apart from other regions. Dense ties of trade and investment between the provinces and states that comprise a CBR is a fundamental characteristic of such regions. They give rise to physical infrastructure such as roads, rail lines, bridges, tunnels, and shared water routes. They also provide the impetus for cross-border institutions and processes—both public, between subnational governments, and between non-governmental groups—whose functions are to co-ordinate, plan, promote, and resolve conflicts related to the economic linkages between the members of a CBR. A significant degree of shared values and even a sense of regional identity characterize some of the CBRs that span the Canada–US border.

Based on an analysis of the density of economic, institutional, and socio-cultural ties between adjacent and nearby provinces and states, VanNijnatten and her colleagues propose a rather different map of regionalism (see Figure 4.9). It includes the following regions:

- *The West*. This CBR consists of British Columbia, Alberta, Yukon, Alaska, Washington, Idaho, Oregon, and Montana. It is characterized by a feeling of remoteness from the central governments of each country and a strong sense of regional identity,

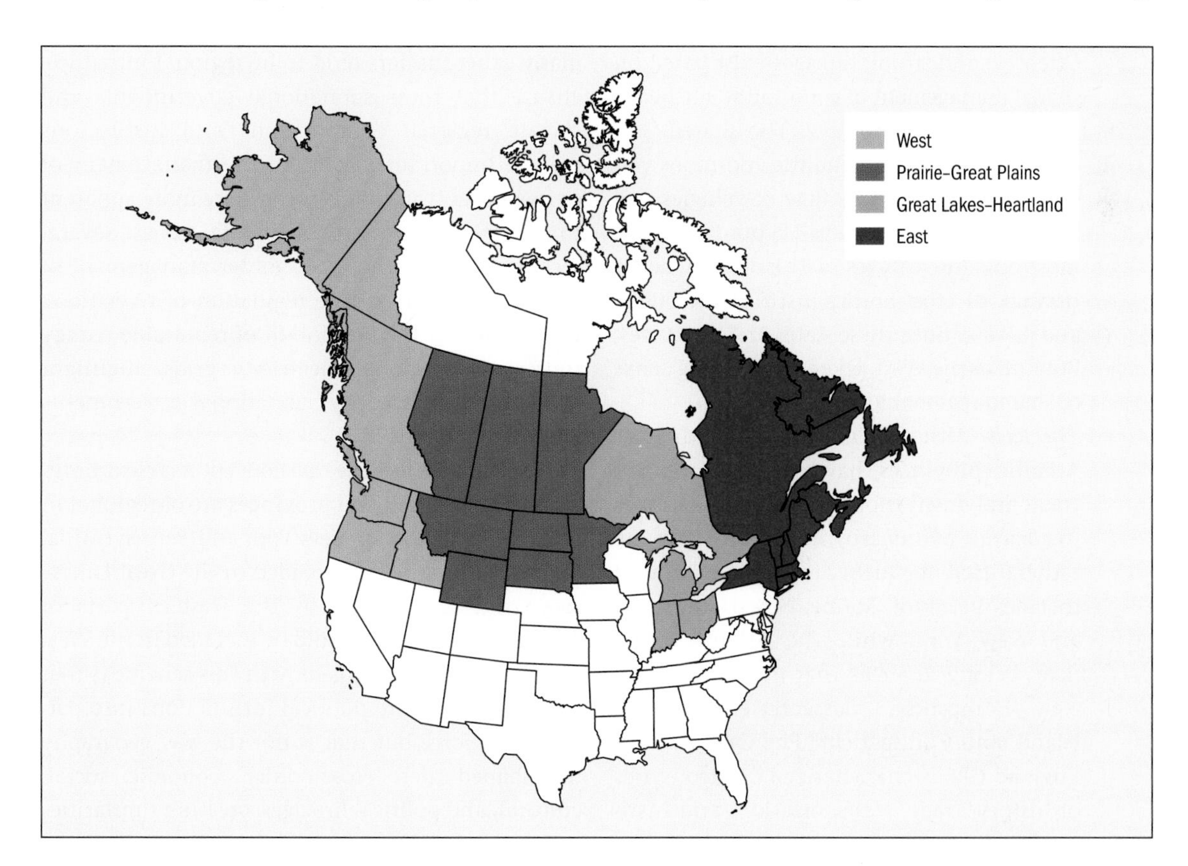

FIGURE 4.9 Cross-Border Regions

Source: Adapted from Debora VanNijnatten, 'Canada–US Relations and the Emergence of Cross-Border Regions', Government of Canada, Policy Research Initiatives, 2006, at: <www.policyresearch.gc.ca>.

such that residents of this CBR may be more alike in their values than they are with their compatriots in other regions of their respective countries. A dense network of private and public institutional linkages spans the Canada–US border and more emphasis is placed on shared environmental issues than characterizes other regions.

- *The Prairie–Great Plains.* This CBR includes Alberta, Saskatchewan, and Manitoba on the Canadian side, and Montana, Wyoming, North Dakota, South Dakota, and Minnesota on the US side (Alberta and Montana were identified by the CBR project as belonging to both this CBR and the West). Although the institutional linkages between these relatively sparsely populated and natural resource-dependent provinces and states are less deeply entrenched than is true of the other CBRs, the economic ties between them are extensive and strong linkages exist based on shared management of common watersheds.
- *The Great Lakes–Heartland.* The shared waters of the Great Lakes and the enormous volume of trade and daily flow of vehicles and people across the Canada–US border are the most obvious features of this CBR. A dense network of cross-border institutions, public and private, links these states and provinces. But unlike the West, there is no strong sense of shared regional identity.
- *The East.* Although Quebec and Canada's Atlantic provinces have some significant trade and institutional linkages, their ties to adjacent and nearby American states are rather different. Quebec is part of a CBR that includes Vermont, Maine, New Hampshire, and New York, while the Atlantic provinces belong to a CBR that includes Maine, New Hampshire, Massachusetts, Rhode Island, and Connecticut. The Quebec–New England CBR is characterized by strong ties of history, trade, transportation, and institutions, but nothing much in the way of a shared regional identity. The Atlantic–New England grouping within the East is based on ties of history, trade, environmental and energy co-operation, a rich network of institutional linkages, and a strong sense of regional identity.

Thinking about Canadian regions in a way that takes into account these cross-border linkages is useful in various ways. First, it enables us to better understand the causes and nature of integration between Canada and the United States, much of which has taken place through regionalized networks. Canada–US economic integration is perhaps more accurately described as integration between the states and provinces of each of these four CBRs. As VanNijnatten puts it, North American integration is a bottom-up phenomenon.[9] Second, the significant powers held by provincial, state, and local governments on both sides of the border, and the fact that transportation, environmental, security, energy supply and distribution, and many other matters tend to be regional in nature, ensure that these subnational governments and private regional organizations and institutions will be important players in the management of cross-border issues. This is nowhere more apparent than in the case of environmental issues. Several recent studies of the cross-border management of issues, ranging from the regulation of river flows to schemes for the promotion of renewable energy sources for regional electricity grids, highlight the key role played by subnational governments and organizations.[10]

At the same time, the CBR concept has clear limitations. Some states and provinces are bi-regional in this scheme. Most of New York and Pennsylvania, for example, could be included in the Great Lakes–Heartland region, just as the western parts of Alberta and Montana could be included in the West region. A possible problem with this scheme is that it seeks to fit entire political jurisdictions into particular regions, but that is not the way geography has shaped these cross-border economic, social, cultural, and political linkages, creating similarities within and differences between border regions. Natural geography and jurisdictional realities may not pull in the same direction.

Regional Identities and Western Alienation

If, instead of looking for significant and enduring regional differences in fundamental political values and beliefs—the sorts of orientations that Ornstein and Stevenson look for and do not find, except in the case of Quebec—we ask whether citizens of Canada's regions view their history in different ways and hold different aspirations for their country and their region's role in it, we then find rather compelling evidence for the existence of what, arguably, deserve to be called regional political cultures. In particular, we find that the West has long been characterized by sentiments of resentment towards and alienation from Ottawa and what westerners perceive to be the political preoccupations of central Canada. These sentiments vary in intensity across the western provinces and also fluctuate in response to specific circumstances and events. Gibbins and Arrison argue that it is reasonable to speak of 'national visions' in the West that, in their words, 'address not simply the place of the West within the Canadian federal state, but also the nature of *Canada* as a political community.'[11] These visions are not merely reactions to citizens' sense of being unfairly treated and marginalized within Canadian politics—the resentment captured in the Reform Party's founding slogan, 'The West wants in'—but are deeply rooted in regional histories that have forged a collective consciousness and memories that are not the same as those of central and eastern Canada.

Starting in a major way in the 1950s with W.L. Morton, western Canadian historians began to react against what they saw as a narrative of Canadian history told from a central Canadian perspective, with little allowance for the distinctive experiences and cultures of the West. This perspective, said Morton, 'fails to take account of regional experience and history and makes coherent Canadian history seem an "imperialist creed", an imposition on Maritime, French-Canadian, Western and British Columbian history of an interpretation which distorted local history and confirmed the feeling that union with Canada had been carried out against local sentiment and local interest.'[12] Morton and many others have attempted to counter the centralist bias of Canadian history writing, but the belief lives on that the West's stories are not given fair weight by a Canadian academic and cultural establishment whose centre of gravity is in the Toronto–Ottawa–Montreal triangle (see Box 4.3).

Writing during the height of the struggle between Pierre Trudeau, championing a bilingual vision of Canada, and René Lévesque, who advocated Quebec independence, George Woodcock fulminated about the 'betrayal' of Confederation, which he argued was based on 'the long campaign of the centralists in Ottawa to recover the power that in recent decades has rightfully flowed to the regions'.[13] Woodcock accused 'centralizers' like Pierre Trudeau of having no appreciation of or sympathy for the distinctive history and consciousness of the West.

In a broadly similar vein Barry Cooper, a Calgary-based political scientist, argues that a distinctive political tradition exists in western Canada, the roots of which lie in the history of that region. '[D]ualism', he observes, 'is not the political issue in the West that it is in central Canada. Moreover, multiculturalism does not mean the same thing to a third or fourth generation non-French, non-British Westerner as it does to someone from the Azores or Calabria living on College Street in Toronto.'[14] What is referred to as **western alienation**, Cooper argues, is not in fact a psychological, sociological, or economic condition experienced by those in the West. Rather, it is the awareness that the public realm—whose voices are heard and what counts as legitimate political discourse—belongs to others. These others are the citizens of central Canada and the elites who purport to speak on their behalf.

Of course, the history of the West and the political traditions that have evolved in western Canada are not disconnected from those of the rest of Canada. Likewise, as Gibbins and Arrison observe, 'western visions' of the nature of the Canadian political community and their region's place in it are not restricted to the West. They identify a

Politics in Focus

Box 4.3 The West as Canada's Internal Colony

To trace the decreasing sensitivity of the national government to influences which are specifically provincial or regional would be to write the history of Canadian political institutions over more than a century.

Donald Smiley, 1976

Unfortunately, federal policies, the attitudes of Central Canadian governments and the biases of so-called national institutions, such as the Canadian Broadcasting Corporation, have painted regionalism with the brush of divisiveness, disunity and even treason. Influences tending to strengthen regional power are 'balkanizing', while those working to increase the central power are 'in the national interest'. But this is true only if what is good for Central Canada is also good for Canada.

David Jay Bercuson, 1977

Western Canada has paid for the development of Canadian nationality, and it would appear that it must continue to pay.

Harold Innis, 1923

The West has never felt in control of its own destiny. None of the wealth of recent years has eased this feeling. In fact, the tremendous wealth of the region merely sharpens the contrast with the political powerlessness that exists on the national level.

Doug Owram, 1980

set of core values that they believe are more solidly anchored in the West than in other regions of Canada, but the same values also find support among Canadians in other regions, including French-speaking Quebec. The difference is one of degree. Western visions of Canada are more likely to embrace the *individual* equality of all Canadians, the equal status of all provinces, and a populist style of doing political business.

Regarding the first of these values—individual equality—Gibbins and Arrison rightly note that opposition to the official recognition and even constitutionalization of multiculturalism and a group rights concept of Canada has come largely from such popular western spokespersons as John Diefenbaker, Preston Manning, and, one would add more recently, Stephen Harper.

The election of ideologically conservative provincial governments, such as those of Ralph Klein, followed by Ed Stelmach, in Alberta and Gordon Campbell in British Columbia, and the impressive support in western Canada for Reform/Alliance, and now the Conservative Party, in federal elections appear to corroborate this argument that westerners are more receptive to what might be characterized as a classically American conception of equality. This involves the equal treatment of all individuals, without taking group membership into account, and formal equality of opportunity. On the other hand, it must be said that there is little in the way of survey evidence to support the claim that westerners are significantly different from their compatriots in other regions when it comes to what they think about equality. Moreover, the quite different histories of Saskatchewan and Alberta should give pause to anyone who wishes to generalize about a *western* conception of equality.

The second core value of the western vision that Gibbins and Arrison identify is provincial equality. This really has two components. One is the sense that Canadian federalism would operate more fairly if the West had more influence on decisions taken by Ottawa. The idea of an elected Senate in which each province has an equal number of senators is one that has been spearheaded by western spokespersons since the 1980s. The other component of this core value involves opposition to any arrangement that appears to treat Quebec differently from and more favourably than the western provinces. Opposition to the Charlottetown Accord in the

1992 referendum was significantly higher in the four western provinces than in the rest of English-speaking Canada (Figure 4.10). Constitutional recognition of Quebec as a distinct society and other provisions that may well have been interpreted as providing special status for Quebec were, of course, among the most controversial sections of the Charlottetown Accord. Observers of the western political scene know that westerners have often felt resentment against Quebec, believing it to be the 'spoiled child' of Confederation. The West's enthusiasm for the idea that the provinces are all equal in their rights and powers clashes with Quebecers' preference for a binational vision of the country in which Quebec, as the home of 90 per cent of French-speaking Canadians, and the rest of Canada are equal partners.

The third component of the western vision involves a populist style of politics. **Populism** arose in the American West and Midwest in the late 1800s out of the perception that economic and political elites, often far from where the people affected by their decisions lived, were too powerful and unsympathetic to the people's interests. The western Canadian version of populism was a combination of imported ideas and homegrown conditions that made the American message resonate in a farm and resource-based economy where people were constantly reminded by the railroads, the banks, the tariffs, and the grain elevator companies that they did not control their own destiny.

Populism, in its simplest form, seeks to return power to the common people. It sees elected politicians as delegates of those who elected them and therefore is hostile to party discipline and aspects of parliamentary government that reduce a public official's ability or willingness to be a direct tribune of his or her constituents' preferences. Populists favour recall votes to remove unfaithful public officials from office, plebiscites and referendums to give people a more direct say in the decisions that affect them, short terms of office, and term limits for public officials. In what is probably the best study of referendums in Canada, Patrick Boyer shows that this favoured instrument of populist democracy has been used far more extensively in the West than in other parts of Canada.[15] The Reform Party's original platform placed a heavy

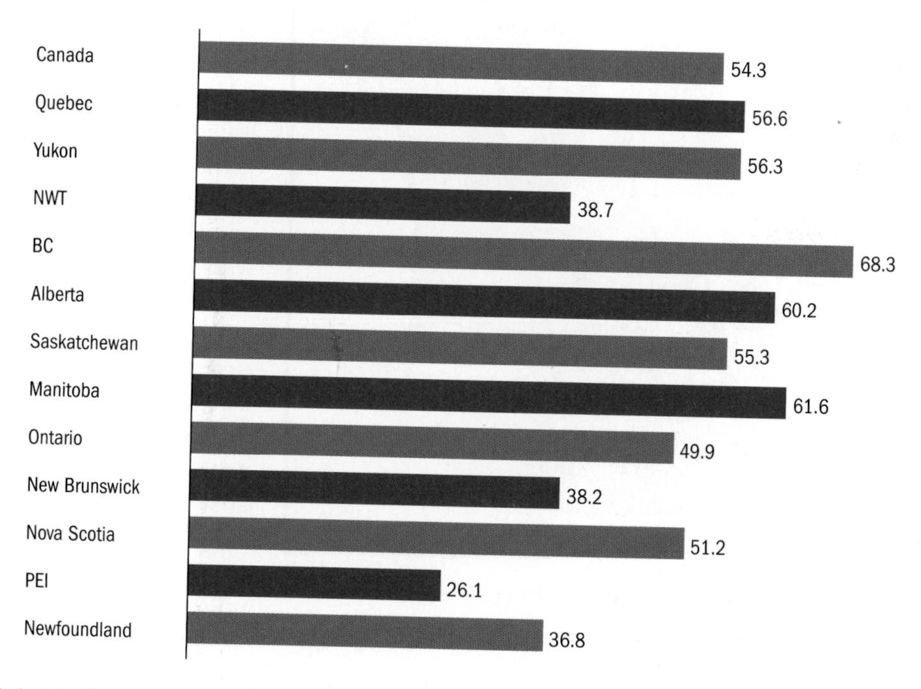

FIGURE 4.10 Percentage of Voters Rejecting the 1992 Charlottetown Accord, by Province and Territory

emphasis on referendums and recall votes, although this became a less prominent feature of the Alliance Party's platform. After Alliance morphed into the Conservative Party, it would seem that such an emphasis had lost any cachet it formerly had among the western conservative elite. When former Liberal cabinet minister David Emerson switched from the Liberals to the Conservatives immediately after the 2006 election in order to take a plum cabinet position in the new Harper government, despite his having won an overwhelming victory as a Liberal in a Vancouver riding where the Conservative candidate finished a poor third, both Emerson and his new Conservative colleagues quickly dismissed any possibility of recall or a new by-election despite popular protest.

At the provincial level, British Columbia passed a recall law in the 1990s—the first province to do so—and the British Columbia government of Gordon Campbell held a 2002 referendum on the highly contentious question of Native land claims and treaty negotiations in the province. All of the four western legislatures have laws requiring that proposals for constitutional amendment be submitted to the people in a referendum, although Canada's Constitution does not require this. In short, there have been strong indications that populist values are more solidly rooted in the West than in the rest of Canada. On the other hand, however, as the recently reconstituted Conservative Party, shaped and led by westerners, has successfully sought power at the federal level, its commitment to an egalitarian populism has waned.

As Canada's poorest region with its own list of grievances towards the federal government and central Canada, one might have expected that the Maritime provinces would have generated an eastern version of western alienation. In fact, however, the easternmost provinces have produced occasional leaders, such as Newfoundland Premiers Joey Smallwood (1949–72), Brian Peckford (1979–89), and Danny Williams (2003–10), who have taken a back seat to none in being outspoken critics of what they saw as unjust treatment of their province by Ottawa. A radical-populist Maritime rights movement—the Antigonish Movement centred at St Francis Xavier University—swept the region in the 1930s, and proposals for Maritime union have existed since before Confederation, continuing to surface as ideas, though with little political support, from time

© Roy Peterson, *Vancouver Sun*

Toronto is Canada's largest city. But in the 2008 election the party that formed the government did not elect a single MP from central Toronto, leaving Torontonians to experience the sort of exclusion that some of the western provinces came to think of as normal during periods of Liberal government.

to time. But the dissatisfaction of Maritimers has never produced a major political vehicle for the expression of alienation and resentment, such as the Progressive movement of the 1920s, the Social Credit Party from the 1930s to the 1970s, and the Reform Party in the late 1980s and 1990s represented in western Canada. Why not?

The answer is complex, but two elements are certainly crucial. First, the populist values that have been linked to western alienation from its beginnings a century ago have been comparatively weak in the Maritime provinces. The reasons for this involve a combination of demographic and economic differences between the eastern and western regions of Canada, but also differences in the political histories of the two regions. Whereas Alberta and Saskatchewan did not achieve provincial status until 1905—and then, without control of their natural resources for 25 years—Nova Scotia and New Brunswick, despite some loud and articulate anti-Confederation voices in the region, were original members of the Confederation pact, and PEI soon followed. The historically dominant parties have deep roots in the Maritimes, stretching back to Confederation. **Protest parties** have always found it difficult to break through the two-party domination in the East. The Progressives failed to win a single seat from the region even in 1921, when they emerged from the general election as the official opposition, and Social Credit and the Reform Party did no better. It was not until 1974 that the NDP won a seat from the region. In more recent years the NDP's fortunes have improved in the Maritimes, but it is dubious whether that party, after several decades on the Canadian political scene, is still a party of protest.

Economically and demographically the Maritimes have been in decline, relative to the rest of Canada, since the late nineteenth century. The region's population as a share of the national population has plummeted since Confederation; and, as shown earlier in this chapter, the economies of the eastern provinces are among the weakest in Canada. This remains true, despite Newfoundland and Labrador's impressive resource-fuelled growth of recent years. (The province experienced a net loss of over 10,000 persons from 2004 to 2007, notwithstanding dramatic increases in its provincial GDP and government revenues.) Most of the eastern provinces depend on money redistributed by Ottawa from more prosperous regions of the country in order to pay for public services. This stands in stark contrast to the prosperity that Alberta and British Columbia have experienced during most of the last half-century, and that Saskatchewan now enjoys as a result of higher world prices for natural resources found in the province, and to the dramatic population growth experienced in the two westernmost provinces.

The much more assertive attitude of western than eastern Canadians and their greater willingness to reject the traditional political parties in favour of protest parties surely is linked to some degree to confidence in the economic future of their region. 'The West wants in', the founding slogan of the Reform Party, was not the plea of a weak and supplicant region. Rather, it was the demand of a region whose population believed that Canadian politics needed to adjust to the reality of their economically powerful and growing provinces.

Conclusion

It may be true, as Michael Bliss argues in an essay on multiculturalism and Canadian identity,[16] that the populations of Ontario and Nova Scotia are more similar today than they were at the time of Confederation. Nonetheless, regionalism continues to cut deep grooves across Canada's political landscape, but for reasons that have far more to do with political and bureaucratic rivalries, different economic interests, and inequalities between the provinces in their political and economic clout. The importance of these factors has not diminished over time, ensuring that regional conflict remains, as Donald Smiley once described it, one of the three major axes of Canadian politics.

Starting Points for Research

Keith Archer and Lisa Young, eds, *Regionalism and Party Politics in Canada* (Toronto: Oxford University Press, 2002). This is an excellent collection of essays on the regional nature of Canada's party system, with a particular emphasis on western Canada.

Christopher Dunn, ed., *Provinces: Canadian Provincial Politics*, 2nd edn (Toronto: University of Toronto Press, 2006). The chapters in this collection offer the best single-volume coverage of political institutions, public administration, public policy, and political attitudes and behaviour in Canada's provinces.

Roger Gibbins and Loleen Berdahl, *Western Visions, Western Futures* (Peterborough, Ont.: Broadview Press, 2003). This is arguably the best short survey of the special characteristics of western Canada's political value system and the roots and consequences of western alienation. The authors make extensive use of attitudinal data.

Nelson Wiseman, *In Search of Canadian Political Culture* (Vancouver: University of British Columbia Press, 2007). Wiseman examines the distinctiveness of regional political cultures and emphasizes their importance in Canadian politics.

Review Exercises

1. Compare media coverage in three different regions of the country. You may do this by consulting hard copies or on-line versions of three daily papers in three different provinces—one from the West, one from Ontario, and one from an eastern province. Check the front page, the editorial page, and letters to the editor. Do you find any indication of a different news agenda or different perspectives in different provinces?
2. Go to journalist Andrew Coyne's website (www.andrewcoyne.com), click on 'columns' and then on May 12, 2007. Coyne argues that interprovincial barriers to trade in Canada continue to be very strong. Is he right? What barriers can he be talking about? Is it possible to find measures of their economic impact?
3. Who were Amor de Cosmos, Henry Wise Wood, Louis Robichaud, and Joseph Howe? What is the significance of each for his region of the country?

Part III
The Structures of Governance

The root of the word *government* is the Latin verb *gubernare*, meaning to guide or direct. And, indeed, what government does is to provide direction for a society through the management of the public's business. This general function is performed through a number of more specialized institutions, including a country's legislature, head of state and head of government, system of courts, and bureaucracy. Their authority and roles within a country's structure of government will depend in large part on the constitution. Laws are made, implemented, and enforced, and redress is provided to aggrieved citizens on the basis of the written and unwritten rules embodied in a country's constitution. This, at any rate, is the ideal of democratic governance.

Constitutions and structures of government are reflections of the societies in which they are embedded. In the case of Canada, the Constitution adopted in 1867 and the country's parliamentary system of government may be understood as responses to particular societal and historical circumstances. The same is true for the important revisions that took place as a result of the Constitution Act, 1982. But once in place, constitutions and institutions of government tend to have what political scientists call an *independent effect* on political outcomes. In other words, the issues that get onto the political agenda, how they are framed, what voices are listened to, and what ultimately happens are influenced to some degree by the structures of government. Societal factors are important—the environment of ideas and interests that press on those who exercise public authority—but political outcomes will depend on the nature of the constitutional and governmental systems through which they are processed.

One of the most difficult challenges in political analysis is to separate from the influence of *societal factors* the influence that *structural factors*—constitutions and government institutions—have on politics and policy. There is no one-size-fits-all answer to this question. The balance between structural and societal factors depends on the issue in question. But most of the time governmental structures play a role in the determination of political outcomes.

Prime Minister Pierre Elliott Trudeau signs the 17 April 1982 constitutional proclamation that patriated Canada's Constitution, giving the country full political independence from the United Kingdom. The Constitution of Canada outlines the country's system of government and the rights of citizens. © CP Photo/stf

5 The Constitution

Constitutions are at the heart of democratic politics. This chapter examines key features of the Canadian Constitution. It includes the following topics:

- Functions of a constitution.
- Rights and freedoms.
- Parliamentary government.
- Responsible government.
- Ministerial responsibility.
- Parliamentary and constitutional supremacy.
- Judicial independence.
- The House of Commons and the Senate.
- The biases of British parliamentary government.
- Changing the Constitution.
- Citizen participation in constitutional reform.
- Does Quebec have the right to separate?

A constitution is an essential ingredient of democratic politics. But the existence of a constitution does not by itself ensure that politics is democratic. South Africa, for example, for decades had a constitution that denied the black majority of that country rights equal to those of the white minority. The People's Republic of China has a constitution under which the violent suppression of peaceful protest and the arrest and imprisonment of people who challenge the Communist Party's monopoly on power are perfectly lawful. Closer to home, the fact that constitutional government was well established in Canada did not prevent the federal government from depriving thousands of Japanese Canadians of their rights as citizens during World War II, nor did it stop Alberta's provincial government from allowing the forced sterilization of people deemed to be mentally retarded in the 1950s. A constitution is no guarantee that human rights will be respected, that group rights will be protected, or that political opposition to those who govern will be tolerated. Without a constitution, however, the concepts of rights and limited government have no secure protection.

A **constitution** is the fundamental law of a political system. It is 'fundamental' because all other laws must conform to the constitution in terms of *how they are made* and in terms of their *substance.* A constitution is a necessary condition for democratic politics. Without it there is no civilized way of resolving conflicts and no way of predicting either the powers of government or the rights of citizens.

A constitution is expected to establish order, allowing for the peaceful settlement of differences. Early liberal thinkers like Thomas Hobbes, John Locke, and Jean-Jacques Rousseau all used the concept of the 'state of nature' to illustrate the impulse behind constitutional government. The state of nature, wrote Hobbes, was a state of chaos in which no individual could feel secure in the possession of his property or life. It is this insecurity that leads people to demand a constitution where there is none, and to accept the necessity of a constitution even if they find it difficult to agree on its precise components.

In modern societies the alternatives to constitutional government are anarchy—the sort of chaos and civil strife that broke out in some of the newly independent republics created after the dissolution of the former Soviet Union—or totalitarianism. Where anarchy reigns, there are no generally accepted rules for resolving the differences between factions of the population. The state does not exist. Under totalitarianism the state exists. But because its powers are unlimited and all realms of social and economic life are subordinate to it, it makes no sense to talk of a constitution. If the rules of a board game can be changed at will by one of the players then it is nonsense to speak of rules. So, too, with a constitution: if its terms are purely arbitrary it ceases to be a constitution in anything other than name.

The rules that make up a constitution deal with two sets of relations. One of these involves the relationship between citizens and the state. A constitution *empowers* the state to act, to pass laws on behalf of the community. At the same time most constitutions *limit power.* They do this by identifying those individual rights, and in some cases group rights, that the state cannot infringe. The other set of relations encompassed by a constitution involves the distribution of functions and powers between different parts of the state. After all, modern government is a complex mechanism. This mechanism is often analyzed under three main functional headings: the legislature (making the law); the executive (implementing the law); and the judiciary (interpreting the law). But the reality of the modern state is more complicated than this tripartite division of powers suggests. Whatever the degree of complexity is, the rules that govern the relations between the various parts of the state are an important component of the constitution.

In a federal state like Canada, where the Constitution divides law-making powers between a national government and regional governments, the rules governing the relations between these two levels are also part of the Constitution. This third aspect of the Constitution has overshadowed the other two for most of Canada's history. Indeed, before 1982, when the Charter of Rights and Freedoms was entrenched in the Constitution, the relations between individuals and the state in Canada were defined by the courts mainly in terms of federal and provincial legislative powers.

A constitution, then, is a set of rules that govern political life. These rules may take three forms: written documents, the decisions of courts (called the **common law**), or unwritten conventions. **Constitutional conventions** are those practices that emerge over time and are generally accepted as binding rules of the political system. An example would be the convention that the leader of the party that captures the most seats in a House of Commons election is called on to form a government. In Canada the first two components of the Constitution—written documents and the common law—together comprise *constitutional law*. Conventions, while part of the Constitution, do not have the status of constitutional law, at least not in Canada. This distinction was made by the Supreme Court of Canada in a 1981 ruling (see Box 5.1). It should not be interpreted to mean that constitutional law is more important than constitutional conventions. What it does mean, however, is that the rules of constitutional law are enforceable by the courts, whereas constitutional conventions are not.

Constitutional Functions

A constitution does more than provide a basis for non-violent politics. It also performs several more specific functions that include the following.

Representation

All modern democracies are representative democracies, in which politicians make decisions on behalf of those who elect them. But this still leaves enormous room for variation in how the population is represented, who is represented, and how representatives are selected.

A constitution describes both the *basis* of political representation and the *method* by which representatives are chosen. The basis of democratic representation may be by population, by territory, or by group. Representation by population is based on the principle of 'one person, one vote'. Under such a system, all elected members of the legislature should represent approximately the same number of voters. This arrangement is most likely to allow the preferences of a simple majority of the population to be translated into law. Although virtually all modern democracies incorporate some form of 'rep by pop' in their constitutions, many temper majority rule by representing regions as well. For example, the American Constitution gives each state the right to two senators, despite the fact that the population of the largest state is about 60 times that of the smallest. Representation in Canada's Senate is also by region: Ontario, Quebec, the western provinces, and the Maritime provinces each have 24 seats, Newfoundland has six, and the northern territories are represented by three senators. Federalism is a form of government that embodies the principle of territorial representation. It does so by giving regional governments the exclusive right to pass laws on particular subjects.

A constitution may also accord representation to groups. New Zealand's constitution, for one, guarantees a certain number of seats in that country's legislature to representatives of the Maori minority. In Canada, suggestions for Senate reform have sometimes included proposals to guarantee seats for women and for the representatives of Aboriginal Canadians. The defeated 1992 Charlottetown Accord would have ensured that Quebec, whose share of Canada's population has been falling steadily, would maintain one-quarter of all seats in the House of Commons, which is about the province's current share. This was, one might argue, a thinly disguised guarantee for francophone group representation. Proposals like these are based on a collectivist political philosophy.

A constitution also establishes the methods by which the holders of public office are selected. Election and appointment are the two basic methods, but each allows for a wide variety of procedures that affect who is represented and how responsive public officials are to the popular will. For example, it is typical for members of the judiciary to be appointed for life, a practice that is expected to insulate them from popular passions and the transitory preferences of elected governments. An elected legislature is a standard feature of democratic political systems and, for that matter, of non-democratic ones. But many constitutions divide the legislative power between an elected chamber and an appointed one, as in Canada, the United Kingdom, and Germany.

Finally, the electoral process itself has a crucial influence on representation. As we will see in Chapter 10, the single-member constituency system used in Canada discourages political parties from directing their appeals at a narrow segment of the national electorate. Unless that segment happens to be concentrated in a particular region, such a strategy will not pay off in elected members. A system of proportional representation, whereby a party's percentage of the popular votes translates into a corresponding share of seats in the legislature, has a very different effect. It promotes a splintering of the party system and allows for the direct representation of such interests as ardent environmentalists in Germany, orthodox Jews in Israel, and anti-immigration elements in the Netherlands. In a system like Canada's, these groups would have to rely on whatever influence they could achieve within one of the larger political parties or else turn to non-electoral political strategies. The failure of the Green Party to win any seats in the 2008 federal election, despite gaining 6.8 per cent of the popular vote, is a case in point.

Power

The simple fact of constitutional government means that the state is empowered to act and that its actions may be backed up by the full weight of public authority. A constitution, therefore, provides the basis for the legitimate exercise of state power. But it also *limits* and *divides* power, at least under a democratic constitution. For example, a constitutional requirement that elections periodically be held restrains state power by making those who wield it accountable to, and removable by, the electorate. The existence of separate branches of government under the constitution, or of two levels of government as in the case of federalism, divides state power between different groups of public officials. How power is divided among the various parts of the state, or between the national and regional governments, is not determined solely by the constitution. But constitutional law and conventions affect both the extent and distribution of state power.

Rights

A right is something that a person is entitled to, like the right to vote or

Governing Realities

Box 5.1 What Is a Constitutional Convention?

. . . [M]any Canadians would perhaps be surprised to learn that important parts of the Constitution of Canada, with which they are the most familiar because they are directly involved when they exercise their right to vote at federal and provincial elections, are nowhere to be found in the law of the Constitution. For instance it is a fundamental requirement of the Constitution that if the Opposition obtains the majority at the polls, the Government must tender its resignation forthwith. But fundamental as it is, this requirement of the Constitution does not form part of the law of the Constitution. . . .

The main purpose of constitutional conventions it to ensure that the legal framework of the Constitution will be operated in accordance with the prevailing constitutional values or principles of the period. . . .

The conventional rules of the Constitution present one striking peculiarity. In contradistinction to the laws of the Constitution, they are not enforced by the courts. . . .

It is because the sanctions of convention rest with institutions of government other than courts, such as the Governor General or the Lieutenant-Governor, or the Houses of Parliament, or with public opinion and, ultimately, with the electorate that it is generally said that they are political.

Source: Supreme Court of Canada, *Attorney General of Manitoba et al. v. Attorney General of Canada et al.*, 28 Sept. 1981.

the right not to be held against one's will without a reason being given. Constitutions vary greatly in the particular rights that they assign to individuals and to societal groups. At a minimum, a democratic constitution establishes the basic right of citizens to choose their government. But most constitutions go beyond this to guarantee—although not without limit—such rights as the individual's right to free speech, freedom of association, and freedom of religion and conscience, as well as legal rights such as freedom from arbitrary detention and illegal search and seizure. These are rights that limit the state's power vis-à-vis the individual either by making that power dependent on popular consent (democratic rights) or by establishing an individual's right not to be interfered with by the state (personal liberty).

Rights may also empower individuals by requiring the state to either protect or promote their interests. For example, a right to equal treatment under the law provides individuals with a constitutional remedy in cases where they have been discriminated against because of their sex, race, ethnic background, or whatever other basis of discrimination is prohibited by the constitution. The state is obliged to protect their interests. As a practical matter this may involve judicial decisions that remedy a private wrong (for example, requiring a minor hockey association to permit females to play in the same league with males). But the protection of equality may also see the state involved in more sweeping activities like affirmative action or racial desegregation on the grounds that these steps are necessary to alleviate discrimination.

Constitutions may also recognize the special status of particular groups, thereby giving special rights to their members that are not enjoyed by others. For example, Canada's Constitution declares that both French and English are official languages with 'equality of status and equal rights and privileges as to their use in all institutions of the Parliament and government of Canada.'[1] This is a *positive* right in the sense that it obliges the state to assume particular linguistic characteristics, and, therefore, to protect actively the rights of French- and English-speakers—at least in matters that fall under Ottawa's jurisdiction. A constitution that recognizes the special status of particular religious denominations, as the Israeli constitution recognizes the Jewish religion, the Iranian constitution the religion of Islam, or the British constitution the Church of England, empowers the members of these religious groups to varying degrees by giving them state-protected rights that are not held by other denominations.

Community and Identity

When Pierre Trudeau wrote that 'A nation is not more and no less than the entire population of a sovereign state',[2] he was arguing that a constitution establishes a community. And in an obvious sense it does. A constitution is the set of fundamental rules that govern political life *in a particular territory*. Its rules are operative within that territory and not elsewhere, so that it establishes a shared condition among all those who live in that territory. Individuals in Rimouski, Quebec, and in Kitimat, British Columbia, are part of the same constitutional system and share a formal political status as Canadians. Even if they perceive their differences to be more important than what they share, this does not diminish the fact that they have legal membership in the same constitutional community.

Carrying the same national passport and being eligible to vote in the same elections may seem a rather weak basis for a *sense of community*, a sentiment that transcends the cold, formal ties of common citizenship. The fact of being citizens of the Soviet Union, for example, did not erase the strongly nationalist sentiments of Ukrainians, Estonians, and other ethnic communities within that former country. For these groups the Soviet constitution and the political community it created were things to regret, not to rejoice over. Likewise in Canada, a significant minority of the population—Quebec separatists—rejects the Canadian political community and would prefer to live under a different constitution creating an independent Quebec.

A constitution, therefore, may inspire negative or positive feelings among the members of a political community. Or it may leave them feeling indifferent. These feelings may be associated with the political community that a constitution creates, but they may also be associated with the particular institutions, values, and symbols embedded in a constitution. For example, the monarchy and other institutions and symbols redolent of Canada's colonial past have historically been an aspect of the Canadian Constitution that has divided Canadians of French origin from those of British origin.

Official bilingualism and constitutional proposals that would recognize Quebec as a 'distinct society' within Canada have been two of the most divisive constitutional issues in recent decades. On the other hand, some features of the Constitution unite, rather than divide, Canadians. There is, for example, overwhelming support among all regions and social groups for the Charter of Rights and Freedoms. In general, we may say that a constitution generates a shared identity among the citizens of a country to the extent that most people have positive feelings towards the political community it creates and the values it embodies. On these counts, Canada's Constitution has had a mixed record of successes and failures.

National Purpose

When the first permanent white settlement was established at what today is Quebec City in the early seventeenth century, it operated under a royal charter that proclaimed the Catholic mission of the French colony. Aside from being an outpost of political and economic empire, it was to be a beachhead of Christianity, from which Catholicism would spread to the rest of the continent. The constitution of New France was therefore linked to a communal goal, to a sense of purpose and direction for society.

This is not so rare. The constitution of the People's Republic of China starts with a very long preamble that describes the country's path to socialism. The constitutions of the Islamic Republic of Iran and of Pakistan both declare that society should conform to Muslim religious teachings. The most controversial part of the failed Meech Lake reforms to Canada's Constitution, the recognition of Quebec as a 'distinct society', would have transformed Quebec nationalism from a political reality to a constitutionally entrenched fact. This was because the Quebec legislature and government would have been constitutionally required to 'preserve and promote' the distinct character of the province, which the distinct society proposal made clear was the French-speaking character of Quebec.

The constitutional document that created Canada, the Constitution Act, 1867, also included a number of provisions that embodied a national purpose. This purpose was the building of a new country stretching from the Atlantic to the Pacific oceans, and an integrated economy tying together this vast territory. The nation-building goal is evident in the anticipation that other parts of British North America eventually would be admitted into Canada,[3] in the prohibition of barriers to trade between provinces,[4] and even in the constitutional commitment to build the Intercolonial Railway, a project described as 'essential to the Consolidation of the Union of British North America, and to the assent thereto of Nova Scotia and New Brunswick.'[5] The Constitution Act, 1982 commits Ottawa and the provinces to the promotion of equal opportunities for Canadians and the reduction of economic disparities between regions of the country.[6] It is hard to know, however, if such declarations of national purpose are merely symbolic recognitions of current policy or whether they might someday be used as the basis for requiring that governments pursue particular policies.

Canada's Constitution

As constitutional documents go, Canada's is a fairly lengthy one. In fact, it is not one document but a series of laws passed between 1867 and 1982. Together they are both longer and more detailed than the United States Constitution. Even so, the written documents of Canada's Constitution provide only a fragmentary and even misleading picture of how the Constitution actually works. Many of the most basic features of the Constitution—including most of those that deal with the democratic accountability of government to the people—are nowhere to be found in these documents. On the other hand, some of what is included in the written

The crafting of a constitution and implementation of constitutional reform are processes that require participation, co-operation, and compromise among many stakeholders.

Constitution would, if acted on, probably result in a constitutional crisis! For example, the Queen is formally the head of state in Canada and has the constitutional authority to make decisions of fundamental importance, such as when an election will take place and who will be appointed to cabinet. No one expects, however, that she will actually make such decisions.

Canada's Constitution, like all constitutions, embodies values and principles that are central to the political life of the country. In its 1998 decision on the constitutionality of Quebec separation, the Supreme Court of Canada referred to these values and principles as the 'internal architecture' of the Constitution,[7] or what, in an earlier ruling, the Court had called the 'basic constitutional structure'.[8] These basic principles, although not necessarily part of the written Constitution, 'form the very foundation of the Constitution of Canada'.[9] The principles that the Supreme Court identified as making up the internal architecture of Canada's Constitution included federalism, democracy, constitutionalism and the rule of law, and respect for minority rights.

Federalism

'The principle of federalism', declares the Supreme Court, 'recognizes the diversity of the component parts of Confederation, and the autonomy of provincial governments to develop their societies within their respective spheres of jurisdiction.'[10] In other words, provinces are not constitutionally subordinate to the federal government, and Ottawa is not dependent on the provinces for the exercise of those powers assigned to it by the Constitution.

The written Constitution distributes law-making and revenue-raising authority between the central and regional governments, and this distribution reflects the underlying federal principle that some matters properly belong to provincial societies and their governments to decide, while others are national in scope and properly decided by the Parliament and government in Ottawa. We will explore more fully the nature and development of Canadian federalism in Chapter 7.

Democracy

Democracy has always been one of the fundamental, if unwritten, givens of Canada's constitutional system. A literal reading of Canada's written Constitution before the inclusion of the Charter of Rights and Freedoms in 1982 might well lead someone who knows nothing of Canada's history and culture to draw a very different conclusion. Aside from the fact that periodic elections were required under the Constitution Act, 1867, there were few other explicit indications that the Constitution adopted by the founders was democratic. On the contrary, while the authority of governments was detailed painstakingly, the Constitution was remarkably silent when it came to the rights of citizens. Why was this so?

In explaining the silence of the pre-Charter Constitution, the Supreme Court states that to have declared explicitly that Canada was a democracy, and to have specified what that entailed, would have seemed to the founders 'redundant' and even 'silly'. 'The representative and democratic nature of our political institutions', the Court writes, 'was simply assumed.'[11] This assumption was suggested in the preamble to the Constitution Act, 1867, which states that Canada has adopted 'a Constitution similar in Principle to that of the United Kingdom'. The very centrality of the democratic principle and the fact that it was simply taken for granted as the baseline against which government would operate explain why the framers of the written Constitution did not perceive the need to state what all assumed to be obvious.

But the precise meaning of the democracy principle, as we saw in Chapter 1, is not obvious and has evolved over time. Women did not have the vote for more than 50 years after Confederation, and only a small minority of the population found anything undemocratic in this exclusion. Even when the meaning of democracy is specified in a written constitution, as it was to a very considerable degree in the United States Constitution and the Declaration of Independence that preceded it, expectations and understandings change over time, as they have over the course of American history. What meaning is properly attributed to the democratic principle of Canada's Constitution today?

The Supreme Court's 1998 decision answers this question by distinguishing between process and outcomes. On the process side, the Court observed that majority rule is a basic premise of constitutional democracy in Canada. The fact that Canada has a federal constitution means, however, that 'there may be different and equally legitimate majorities in different provinces and territories and at the federal level.'[12] In other words, a nationwide majority does not trump a provincial majority if the matter in question belongs constitutionally to the provinces or requires the approval of some number of provincial legislatures (e.g., most constitutional amendments).

In a 1986 Charter decision,[13] the Supreme Court had expressed the view that the democratic principle underlying the Charter and the rest of Canada's Constitution is also linked to substantive goals. Among these are the following:

- respect for the inherent dignity of every person;
- commitment to equality and social justice;
- social and cultural diversity, including respect for the identities of minority groups' social and political institutions that enhance the opportunities for individuals and groups to participate in society.

This view was echoed in the Supreme Court's 1998 ruling. In words that were directly relevant to the issue of Quebec separation, the Court said that 'The consent of the governed is a value that is basic to our understanding of a free and democratic society.'[14] Democratic government derives its necessary legitimacy from this consent. Moreover, the legitimacy of laws passed and actions taken by a democratic government rests on 'moral values, many of which are imbedded in our constitutional structure'.[15] The Supreme Court did not expand on these moral values.

Constitutionalism and the Rule of Law

'At its most basic level', declares the Supreme Court, 'the rule of law vouchsafes to the citizens and residents of the country a stable, predictable and ordered society in which to conduct their affairs.'[16] It guarantees, therefore, that all public authority must ultimately be exercised in accordance with the law and that there will be one law for all persons. When it comes to light that some public official has overstepped the bounds of his or her office, regardless of the office-holder's intentions, or that someone has been accorded preferred treatment under the law because of personal connections, we rightly are offended. Such actions violate the premise of the rule of law, namely, that ours is a government of laws, not of men and women, and that everyone is entitled to equal treatment under the law.

Like the rule of law, the constitutionalism principle involves predictable governance that has its source in written rules rather than in the arbitrary wills of individuals. The constitutionalism principle is expressed in s. 52(1) of the Constitution Act, 1982, which states that the Constitution is the supreme law of the land and that all government action must be in conformity with the Constitution. Before the Charter was entrenched in the Constitution and the constitutionalism principle was expressly stated, the final authority of the Constitution was less certain. The pre-Charter era was one of **parliamentary supremacy**, which essentially meant that so long as one level of government did not trespass onto jurisdictional turf that the Constitution assigned to the other level, it was free to do as it liked. The principle of parliamentary supremacy is captured in the old saying that 'Parliament could do anything except change a man into a woman and a woman into a man.' The constitutionalism principle, by contrast, places certain matters relating to rights and freedoms beyond the reach of any government.

Constitutionalism and the rule of law temper and modify the principle of majority rule in a democracy. They do so by ensuring that the mere fact that a majority of citizens—even an overwhelming majority—supports a particular government action does not mean that such an action will be either lawful or constitutional. Together, they constitute a sort of bulwark against what Tocqueville called the 'tyranny of the majority'.

Protection of Minorities

The recognition of group rights has a history in Canada that goes back to the beginnings of British colonial rule. The Royal Proclamation of 1763 includes considerable detail—the meaning of which is a matter of dispute—on the rights of the 'several Nations or Tribes of Indians . . . who live under our protection'. The Quebec Act of 1774 recognized the rights of Catholics in Quebec and guaranteed the overwhelmingly French-speaking population the enjoyment of their 'Property and Possessions, together with all Customs and Usage's relative thereto, and all other their Civil Rights', concessions that most historians agree were intended to ensure the support of the Catholic Church authorities in Quebec at a time when rebellion was simmering in the American colonies. Group rights were recognized again through the 'double majority principle' that operated when Canada East (Quebec) and Canada West (Ontario) were joined together through a common legislature during the period 1841–67. Under this principle any bill touching on matters of language or religion in either Canada East or Canada West had to be approved by majorities of legislators from both Canada East—mainly French and Catholic—and Canada West—mainly English and Protestant. In practice this gave a veto to each ethnolinguistic community in regard to legislation affecting minority rights.

The Constitution Act, 1867 entrenched the principle of minority rights through the section 93 guarantee of minority religious education rights and the section 133 declaration that French and English were to have official status in the

Parliament of Canada, the legislature of Quebec, and courts created by either of those bodies. 'The protection of minority rights', declares the Supreme Court, 'was clearly an essential consideration in the design of our constitutional structure even at the time of Confederation.'[17] The principle acquired a new level of prominence as a result of the Charter of Rights and Freedoms. The Charter enlarges the scope of official-language minority rights, explicitly recognizes Aboriginal rights, opens the door to a multitude of group rights claims through the equality section of the Charter (s. 15), and provides a basis for a variety of minority rights claims through other sections, including the legal rights and democratic rights provisions of the Charter.

A useful way of analyzing a constitution is to approach it from the angle of each of the relationships governed by constitutional rules. As noted earlier, these relationships include: (1) those between individuals and the state; (2) those between the various institutions of government; and (3) those between the national and regional governments. The first category involves rights and freedoms, the second deals with the machinery and process of government, and the third category is about federalism. A constitution also includes a fourth category of rules that establish what procedures must be followed to bring about constitutional change. Federalism is dealt with in the next chapter. We turn now to an examination of the other three dimensions of Canada's Constitution.

The Charter of Rights and Freedoms

Since 1982 Canada's Constitution has included formal distinctions between fundamental political freedoms, democratic rights, mobility rights, legal rights, equality rights, and language rights. These are the categories set down in the Charter of Rights and Freedoms. Most of the rights and freedoms enumerated in the Charter were, however, part of Canada's Constitution before 1982. In some cases they can be found in the Constitution Act, 1867. In others, they were established principles of the common law. The inclusion of these rights and freedoms in the Charter, however, has made an important difference in Canadian politics. Groups and individuals are far more likely today than in the pre-Charter era to reach for the judicial lever in attempting to protect their rights. Second, these rights have been more secure since the Charter's passage. This has been due to the courts' willingness to strike down laws and practices on the grounds that they contravene the Charter's guarantees of rights and freedoms.

Fundamental Freedoms

Fundamental political freedoms are guaranteed in section 2 of the Charter. These include freedom of religion, belief, expression, the media, assembly, and association. During the pre-Charter era these freedoms, or *political liberties* as they are sometimes called, were part of the common law and of Canada's British parliamentary tradition. Individual freedoms were part of the British constitution, and thus became part of Canada's. Even before the Charter, then, political freedoms occupied a place in the Canadian Constitution. Their protection by the courts, however, was rather tenuous. Except in a few instances, the courts were unwilling to rule that a freedom was beyond the interference of government. Instead, political liberties were defended using the federal division of legislative powers as the basis for striking down a particular government's interference with individual freedom.

Democratic Rights

The basic democratic right is the opportunity to vote in regular elections. This right predated Confederation. It was embodied in the Constitution Act, 1867 through those sections that establish the elective basis of representation in the House of Commons and in provincial legislatures (ss. 37 and 40), through the requirement that the legislature meet at least once a year (ss. 20 and 86), through the right of citizens to vote (s. 41), and through the five-year limit on the life of both the House of Commons and provincial legislatures, thereby guaranteeing regular elections (ss. 50 and 85). All of these sections are now 'spent', having been superseded by ss. 3–5 of the Charter.

Mobility Rights

Mobility rights were not explicitly mentioned in Canadian constitutional law before 1982. Section 121 of the Constitution Act, 1867 prohibits the provincial governments from imposing tariffs on commodities coming from other provinces, but there is no mention of restrictions on the movement of people. Such restrictions are now prohibited by section 6 of the Charter. This guarantee of individual mobility rights was prompted by Ottawa's fear that some provincial governments were undermining the idea and practice of Canadian citizenship by discriminating in favour of their own permanent residents in some occupational sectors and by imposing residency requirements as a condition for receiving some social services. The Charter does, however, permit both of these types of discrimination. It allows 'reasonable residency requirements as a qualification for the receipt of publicly provided social services'[18] and permits affirmative action programs favouring a province's residents 'if the rate of employment in that province is below the rate of employment in Canada'.[19] The impact of section 6 on provincial practices limiting the mobility of Canadian between provinces has been marginal.

Legal Rights

Most rights-based litigation, both before and since the Charter's passage, has been based on individuals' and corporations' claims that their legal rights have been violated. Legal rights involve mainly procedural aspects of the law, such as the right to a fair trial, the right not to be held without a charge being laid, and the right to legal counsel. Before these rights were entrenched in the Constitution through the Charter, they were recognized principles of the common law and constitutional convention. For example, the field of administrative law was based largely on the principles of *natural justice*: hear the other side, and no one should be a judge in his own case. These were accepted parts of Canada's democratic tradition and Constitution even before they were entrenched in section 7 of the Charter. And like political freedoms, democratic rights, and equality rights, these legal rights were included in the Canadian Bill of Rights passed in 1960. In addition, the rights of accused parties were set forth in Canada's Criminal Code. It is apparent, however, that the constitutional entrenchment of legal rights has made an important difference. The courts have been much bolder in striking down parts of laws and in overturning administrative and police procedures than they were in the pre-Charter era. For example, a successful legal challenge to Canada's abortion law became possible only when the right to 'security of the person' was explicitly recognized in section 7 of the Charter.[20] More generally, Charter decisions have expanded the legal rights of the accused, convicted criminals, and immigrants.

Equality Rights

Equality rights are entrenched in the Constitution through section 15 of the Charter. They embody the **rule of law** principle that everyone should be treated equally under the law. But the Charter extends this principle to expressly prohibit discrimination based on race, national or ethnic origin, colour, religion, sex, age, or mental or physical disability.[21]

The particular headings in this list are important, given that Canadian courts historically have preferred to base their rulings on the precise text of laws and the Constitution. Women's groups and those representing the physically and mentally disabled clearly believed that the wording of the Charter made a difference, and both fought hard—and successfully—to have the original wording of section 15 changed. The 1960 Canadian Bill of Rights, which applied only in areas of federal jurisdiction, did not include age or mental/physical disability in its catalogue of equality rights.

The Charter explicitly declares that affirmative action is constitutional.[22] Thus, the equality rights section of the Canadian Constitution is designed to cut two ways. It provides individuals with grounds for redress if they believe that the law discriminates against them. But it also provides a basis for laws that treat different groups of people differently—some would say that this is the definition of discrimination—in order to improve the condition of disadvantaged individuals or groups.

Equality rights also are important features of provincial bills/charters of rights. Since 1975 every province has had such a bill. Quebec's is probably the most extensive, including even certain economic and social rights. These rights are administered and enforced by provincial human rights commissions.

Language Rights

At Confederation, the issue of language rights was dealt with in three ways. Section 133 of the Constitution Act, 1867 declares that both English and French are official languages in the Parliament of Canada and in the Quebec legislature, and in any court established by either the national or Quebec government. Section 93 of that same Act declares that rights held by denominational schools when a province became part of Canada cannot be taken away. As a practical matter, Catholic schools in Manitoba or even Ontario were often French-speaking, and most English-language schools in Quebec were Protestant. Consequently, what were formally denominational rights in section 93 were effectively language rights as well. This did not help when it came to their protection—or non-protection (see Chapter 13). The third approach—and in practical terms the most important language rights provision of the Constitution Act, 1867—is put forth in section 92. This assigns to the provinces jurisdiction over 'all Matters of a merely local or private Nature in the Province' (s. 92.16). Combined with exclusive provincial jurisdiction over education (s. 93), this has given provincial governments the tools to promote or deny, as the case may be, the language rights of their anglophone or francophone minorities.

The Constitution Act, 1982 extends language rights in several ways. These include the following:

- The declaration of the official equality of English and French, found in section 133 of the Constitution Act, 1867, is repeated and broadened to encompass 'their use in all institutions of the Parliament and government of Canada' (s. 16.1) and services to the public (s. 20).
- The New Brunswick legislature's earlier decision to declare that province officially bilingual is entrenched in the Constitution Act, 1982. The official status of English in the legislature and courts of Quebec and Manitoba is reaffirmed (s. 21).
- The right of anglophones and francophones to have their children educated in their mother tongue is entrenched, subject to there being sufficient demand to warrant the provision of such services out of public funds (s. 23).

Language rights would have been given an additional twist if the Meech Lake Accord (1987) or Charlottetown Accord (1992) had become constitutional law (see Chapter 7). The most controversial feature of both accords was the recognition of Quebec as a 'distinct society'. The wording of this section clearly linked this distinctiveness to the predominantly French-speaking character of Quebec. The 'distinct society' clause went on to oblige the province's legislature and government to 'preserve and promote the distinct identity of Quebec'. Some critics of the 'distinct society' clause argued that it would promote the concentration of French in Quebec, with harmful consequences for the status of the French-speaking minorities in the other provinces and for the English-speaking minority in Quebec (see Box 5.2).

Aboriginal Rights

Aboriginal rights are also included in Canada's Constitution. Their explicit recognition dates from the passage of the Charter in 1982. Section 25 declares that the rights and freedoms set forth in the Charter shall not be construed so as to 'abrogate or derogate' from whatever rights or freedoms the Aboriginal peoples of Canada have as a result of any treaty or land claim settlement. It also entrenches in the Constitution 'any rights or freedoms that have been recognized by the Royal Proclamation [of 1763]'. Section 35(1) appears to limit Aboriginal rights to the status quo that existed in 1982, stating

Politics in Focus

Box 5.2 The End of Bilingualism? Former Prime Minister Pierre Trudeau's View of the 'Distinct Society' Clause

Those Canadians who fought for a single Canada, bilingual and multicultural, can say goodbye to their dream: we are henceforth to have two Canadas, each defined in terms of its language. And because the Meech Lake accord states in the same breath that 'Quebec constitutes, within Canada, a distinct society' and that 'the role of the Legislature and government to preserve and promote [this] distinct identity . . . is affirmed', it is easy to predict what future awaits anglophones living in Quebec and what treatment will continue to be accorded to francophones living in provinces where they are fewer in number than Canadians of Ukrainian or German origin.

Indeed, the text of the accord spells it out: In the other provinces, where bilingualism still has an enormously long way to go, the only requirement is to 'protect' the status quo, while Quebec is to 'promote' the distinct character of Quebec society.

In other words, the Government of Quebec must take measures and the Legislature must pass laws aimed at promoting the uniqueness of Quebec. And the text of the accord specifies at least one aspect of this uniqueness: 'French-speaking Canada' is 'centred' in that province. Thus, Quebec acquires a new constitutional jurisdiction that the rest of Canada does not have, promoting the concentration of French in Quebec. It is easy to see the consequences for French and English minorities in the country, as well as for foreign policy, for education, for the economy, for social legislation, and so on.

Source: Pierre Elliott Trudeau, 'Say Goodbye to the dream of one Canada', *Toronto Star*, 27 May 1987, A7. Reprinted by permission of the Pierre Elliott Trudeau Estate.

that 'The *existing* aboriginal and treaty rights of the aboriginal peoples of Canada are hereby recognized and affirmed' (emphasis added). In fact, however, this has been less a limit than a boost for Aboriginal rights, which have been effectively constitutionalized by the 1982 Constitution Act. We examine this in greater detail in Chapter 16.

Parliamentary Government in Canada

The whole edifice of British parliamentary government is built on profound silences in constitutional law. These silences touch on the most fundamental principles of democracy and on practices that are essential to the orderly functioning of government. Such matters as the selection of the Prime Minister, which party has the right to form a government, the relationship between the Crown and the government and between the government and the legislature, the rights of the political opposition, and the role of the judicial branch of government cannot be understood from a simple reading of the Constitution. Nevertheless, for all of these matters certain rules are generally agreed upon and are vital parts of the Constitution—so vital, in fact, that when they are challenged the political system faces a crisis.

British parliamentary government was exported to Canada during the colonial period. Its main features have remained largely unchanged since the middle of the nineteenth century, when the British North American colonies achieved the right to self-government in their domestic affairs. As we have seen, the Constitution Act, 1867 explicitly reaffirms this British parliamentary inheritance. While the declaration that Canada has adopted 'a Constitution similar in Principle to that of the United Kingdom' might appear to be somewhat nebulous, Canada's founders understood very clearly what it meant. The Constitution of the United Kingdom was, and remains today, a set of political traditions rather than a series of constitutional documents. Those who founded Canada took these traditions as their starting point and grafted onto them certain institutions and procedures—particularly federalism—for which British parliamentary government provided no guide.

Parliament

The distinguishing feature of British-style parliamentary government is the relationship between the various institutions that together comprise Parliament. Parliament consists of the monarch and the legislature. The monarch, currently Queen Elizabeth II, is Canada's head of state. According to the strict letter of the Constitution, the monarch wields formidable powers. These include which party will be called upon to form the government, when Parliament will be dissolved and a new election held, and the requirement that all legislation—federal and provincial—must receive royal assent before it becomes law. In fact, however, these powers are almost entirely symbolic, and the role is primarily a ceremonial one. When the monarch is not in Canada (which is most of the time), her powers are exercised by the Governor General. At the provincial level, the lieutenant-governors are the Queen's representatives.

The power that resides formally in the monarchy is in reality held by the Crown's advisers, the Privy Council. The **Privy Council** formally includes all members of the present and past cabinets. However, only present members of cabinet exercise the powers of the Privy Council, and these people are usually elected members of the legislature. At the head of the cabinet is the Prime Minister. The structure of Canada's Parliament is shown in Figure 5.1.

Parliament comprises, then, both the *executive* and *legislative* branches of government. Those who actually exercise the executive power are drawn from the legislature. In deciding who among those elected members of Parliament (MPs) and appointed senators will become members of the government, the rule is quite simple. The leader of the political party with the most seats in the elected House of Commons has the right to try to form a government that has the support of a majority of MPs. If at any time the government loses its majority support in the House, tradition requires that it resign. At this point a fresh election would be called or, if there is a possibility that another party could put together a government that would be supported by a majority of MPs, the Governor General could call on the leader of that party to try to form a government.

Responsible Government

In order to govern, therefore, the Prime Minister and cabinet require the confidence of the elected House of Commons. This constitutional principle is called **responsible government**. If a government loses the confidence of the House—through either a defeat on an important piece of legislation (i.e., the annual budget or legislation related to government spending) or on a motion of non-confidence proposed by an opposition party—it loses the right to govern. This may appear to place enormous power in the hands of MPs, capable of making and breaking governments at will. It does not. The reason why the constitutional theory of responsible government does not translate into governments tremulous before their legislatures is **party discipline**. This is another tradition of British parliamentary government, according to which the MPs of a party generally vote as a unified block in the legislature. In Canada, however, party

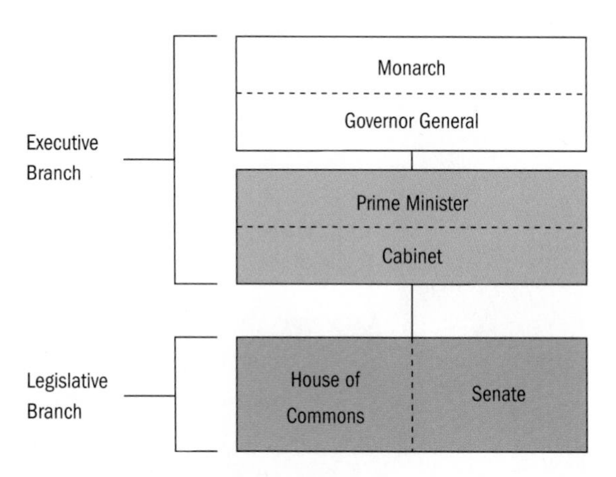

FIGURE 5.1 The Structure of Parliament in Canada

Note: The structure is basically the same at the provincial level, with two differences. The monarch's powers are exercised by a lieutenant-governor and the legislature consists of a single elected chamber.

discipline is conformed to more rigidly than in the British Parliament.

Of the 40 governments that were elected between 1867 and 2008 only six fell because of a defeat in the legislature. In all six cases these were *minority governments*: governments that depended on the support of another party's MPs in order to win votes in the legislature. But even in these apparently precarious circumstances, it was usually the government that finally determined when an election would occur. On only one occasion has a government been defeated in the Commons and then had its request for dissolution of Parliament and a fresh election denied. That was in 1926, and the denial provoked a constitutional crisis over the appropriate role of the Governor General. There was at least the chance of history repeating itself when the Progressive Conservative government's budget was defeated in 1979. The government had been in office a mere nine months, and the possibility of a minority Liberal government supported by the NDP was not totally outrageous. As it happened, however, Governor General Ed Schreyer granted Prime Minister Clark's request for a new election, although Schreyer claimed afterwards that he seriously considered asking the leader of the opposition to try to form a government.

The possibility that MPs, and not Canadian voters, might bring about a change in government appeared very real in the late autumn of 2008, just weeks after a federal election produced a Conservative minority government. The three opposition parties reached an agreement to bring down the government and replace it with a Liberal–NDP coalition that would have been led by then Liberal leader Stéphane Dion. The Conservative government cried foul, pointing out that an election had been held only weeks before and that it had won a significantly greater share of the popular vote than any of the opposition parties. Rather than turn over the reins of power to a Liberal–NDP coalition, backed by the Bloc Québécois, the Conservatives would have requested

In January 2010, faced with the second prorogation of Parliament since 2008, many Canadians voiced their displeasure at the premature shutdown of government, claiming the decision was politically, rather than practically, motivated.

a dissolution of Parliament and fresh elections. The Governor General, Michaëlle Jean, was saved from being a twenty-first-century Lord Byng by the government's decision to prorogue Parliament (see Box 5.3), preventing a vote that could have brought down the government. Opponents of the government now had their opportunity to cry foul, but public opinion showed that most Canadians opposed the idea of a Liberal–NDP coalition propped up with BQ support.

Responsible government is not just a constitutional relic. It operates today, but not in the narrow sense of legislatures making and defeating cabinets. Instead, it suffuses the parliamentary process in the form of the *rights of the legislature* and the corresponding *obligations of the government*. The legislature has the right to scrutinize, to debate, and to vote on policies proposed by the government. In order to carry out these activities the legislature has the general right to question the government and to demand explanations for its actions and for those of bureaucratic officials who act in the government's name. The government, for its part, has a constitutional obligation to provide opportunities for legislative scrutiny of its policies and to account for its actions before Parliament. These rights and obligations are to a large extent codified in the *standing orders*—the rules that govern parliamentary procedure.

Listen to the 'Perspectives on Proroguing' podcast, available at www.oupcanada.com/Brooks7e

Responsible government, then, is part of the living constitution. But its formal definition bears little resemblance to the reality of modern parliamentary government. Disciplined political parties and dominant prime ministers ensure that cabinets

Governing Realities

Box 5.3 Prorogation: When the Banal Becomes Controversial

Until fairly recently—December of 2008 to be more exact—few Canadians had heard the word 'prorogue'. It comes from the Latin, *prorogare*, meaning to defer. The procedure it refers to is used by the government to end a session of Parliament. Essentially, the business of the legislature shuts down until Parliament resumes sitting. Whatever legislative business was left unfinished when Parliament is prorogued dies. This business may or may not be reintroduced when the legislature is recalled, but the point is that the new session of Parliament will be a fresh start in terms of legislation, committee business, and other activities.

In some ways it is odd that Canadians were not more familiar with the word and what it involves. Every session of Parliament ends as a result of prorogation or, alternatively, dissolution. Dissolution ends the life of a Parliament and new elections for the House of Commons result. Between 1868 and 2009 Parliament was prorogued 105 times. So it is hardly a rare occurrence.

On most occasions prorogation is used when the government believes it is time to reconfigure its legislative agenda. A new Speech from the Throne, in which the Governor General reads the government's legislative plans for a new session of Parliament, announces this fresh beginning. The use of prorogation has been controversial only when it was perceived by critics to be a way of avoiding politically damaging circumstances in the legislature and thereby of evading the government's accountability to the voters who elected it.

The Harper government was not the first to use prorogation in such circumstances. Canada's first Prime Minister, John A. Macdonald, prorogued Parliament in 1873 to shut down an inquiry into a scandal that was probably the cause of his party's defeat in the election held later that year. The Liberal government of Jean Chrétien prorogued Parliament in 2003, critics charged, to avoid having Parliament receive a damning report from the Auditor General on improprieties and possible illegalities in the spending of public money in Quebec under a federal sponsorship and advertising program. Clearly, prorogation may sometimes be used for partisan advantage. But most of the time its use is far more banal and unnoticed.

seldom are defeated at the hands of unco-operative legislatures. But if the ultimate sanction that underlies the notion of responsible government has been lost—it really only operated for a brief period in Canadian history, between 1848 and 1864 in the legislature of the United Canadas—the practice of cabinet government that is accountable to the elected legislature remains.

Ministerial Responsibility

The accountability of the government to the legislature is the reason behind another principle of British parliamentary government, that of **ministerial responsibility**. It entails the obligation of a cabinet minister to explain and defend policies and actions carried out in his or her name. This individual accountability of cabinet ministers rests on a combination of constitutional law and parliamentary tradition. Section 54 of the Constitution Act, 1867 gives to cabinet the exclusive right to put before the legislature measures that involve the raising or spending of public revenue. In practice, such measures are introduced by particular members of the government. For example, changes to the tax system are proposed by the Minister of Finance. The Constitution also requires that any legislation that involves raising or spending public money must originate in the elected House of Commons. This reflects the liberal-democratic principle of no taxation without representation. Only the people's elected representatives, legislators who can be removed in a subsequent election, should have the right to propose laws that affect voters' pocketbooks. The accountability of ministers is, therefore, to the people's elected representatives.

Two fundamental principles of British parliamentary government, i.e., strong executive authority and democratic accountability, come together in the concept of ministerial responsibility. Strong executive authority is a tradition that dates from an era when the monarch wielded real power and the principle that these powers depended on the consent of the legislature was not yet established. When the legislature finally gained the upper hand in the seventeenth century, the tradition of strong executive power was not rejected. Instead, it was tamed and adapted to the democratic principle that government is based on the consent of the governed. Since then, individual ministers and cabinet as a whole have exercised the powers that, symbolically, continue to be vested in the Crown. But they do so in ways that enable the people's elected representatives to vote on their proposals and to call them to account for their policies (see Figure 5.2).

In recent times the constitutional principle of ministerial responsibility has come under increasing pressure. The enormous volume of decisions taken in a minister's name and the fact that much of the real power to determine government policy has passed into the hands of unelected officials mean that no minister can be well informed about all the policies and actions undertaken in his name. According to some, the solution is to locate accountability where decision-making power really lies. This strategy is reasonable for most actions and decisions. But elected members of the government must remain directly accountable for the general lines of policy and for major decisions; otherwise, a vital link in the chain of accountability that joins the people to those who govern is lost (see Box 5.4).

Parliamentary Supremacy versus Constitutional Supremacy

Another central feature of British parliamentary government is that of **parliamentary supremacy**. This means that Parliament's authority is superior to that of all other institutions of government. In concrete terms, this means that the courts will not second-guess the right of Parliament to pass any sort of law, on any subject. Parliament embodies the popular will, and unpopular laws can always be defeated by changing the government at the next election. In a federal system like Canada's there is one complication. Law-making powers are divided between the national and regional governments. But so long as Ottawa acts within its spheres of constitutional authority, and the provincial governments within theirs, both the federal and provincial parliaments are supreme.

Such was the situation in Canada until 1982. When called on to determine whether a law was constitutional or not, the courts almost always referred to the federal division of powers set down in the Constitution Act, 1867. If a legislature was not intruding onto the constitutional territory of the other level of government, its actions were by definition constitutional. The only exception to this rule was in the case of laws or actions that ran afoul of procedural rules of the common law, like the principles of natural justice. The substance of laws, on the other hand, would not be questioned.

Parliamentary supremacy was dealt a major blow by the Charter. Those who opposed the Charter argued that entrenching rights and freedoms in the written Constitution would result in a transfer of power from legislatures to the courts. This, indeed, is what has happened. Since 1982 the Supreme Court has struck down numerous federal and provincial laws on the grounds that they violate the guarantees set forth in the Charter. The defenders of parliamentary supremacy claim that a system of court-protected rights and freedoms is fundamentally undemocratic. Their reasoning is that it substitutes the decisions of non-elected judges for those of the people's elected representatives.

What is beyond doubt is that parliamentary supremacy has been replaced in Canada by **constitutional supremacy**. The Constitution Act, 1982 makes this very clear. Section 32 declares that the Charter applies to both the federal and provincial governments and to all matters under their authority. Section 52(1) of the Charter is even more categorical. It states that 'The Constitution of Canada is the supreme law of Canada, and any law that is inconsistent with the provisions of the Constitution is, to the extent of the inconsistency, of no force or effect.' A vestige of Parliament's former superiority is retained, however, through s. 33 of the Charter. This is the so-called 'notwithstanding clause'. It enables either Parliament or a provincial legislature to declare that a law shall operate even if it violates the fundamental freedoms, legal rights, or equality rights sections of the Charter. Such a declaration must be renewed after five years; otherwise, the Constitution reasserts its supremacy.

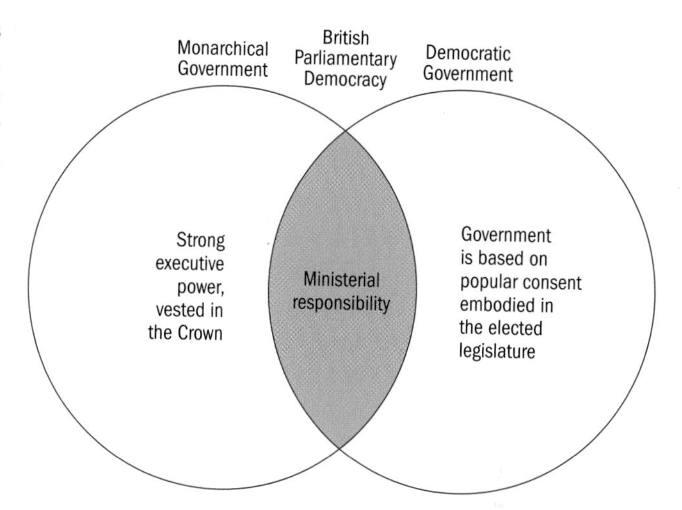

FIGURE 5.2 The Constitutional Roots of Ministerial Responsibility

Politics in Focus

Box 5.4 The Gomery Report on Ministerial Responsibility

I believe that the proposition that Ministers and their political staff have no responsibility for the proper implementation and administration of government programs and policies is an inadequate and incomplete expression of the principle of ministerial responsibility. The Minister should take steps, in consultation with the Deputy Minister, to see that trained personnel are available to administer any new initiatives and to establish proper procedures and oversight mechanisms. The Minister should give sufficient directions to the Deputy Minister so that the latter will be able to properly supervise the actions of the subordinate personnel. Willful ignorance of administrative inadequacies will not absolve a Minister from responsibility for failures within the department.

Source: Canada, Commission of Inquiry into the Sponsorship Program and Advertising Activities, *Final Report: Who Is Responsible?* (Ottawa, 1 Feb. 2006), 18–19.

Judicial Independence and the Separation of Powers

The role of the judicial branch of government is based on constitutional convention rather than law. The Constitution Act, 1867 includes several sections that deal with the system of provincial courts, including how judges shall be selected, how they may be removed, when provincial Superior Court judges must retire (age 75), and who will determine judicial salaries.[23] But there is no mention of the Supreme Court of Canada or of any other federal courts. Instead, section 101 authorizes Parliament to establish a 'General Court of Appeal for Canada', which it did in 1875 (the Supreme Court of Canada) and again in 1970 (the Federal Court of Canada).

Canadian constitutional law is silent on the powers, indeed on the very existence and composition, of this country's highest court of appeal. Nor is the relationship between the judicial and other branches of government described in much detail. This stands in sharp contrast to the American Constitution, in which lengthy descriptions of the powers of Congress (the legislative branch) and the President (the executive branch) are followed by Article III on the judicial branch of government. In Canada, however, the role of the judiciary is based largely on constitutional convention and statute law. The fundamental principles that underlie that role are judicial independence and separation of powers.

Judicial independence means that judges are to be free from any and all interference in their decision-making. Former Chief Justice Brian Dickson declared that the core of this principle involves 'the complete liberty of individual judges to hear and decide the cases that come before them'.[24] It is particularly important that judges be protected from interference by the government. Despite the fact that the principle of judicial independence is deeply embedded in Canada's political culture and enshrined in laws on contempt of court and in guidelines for ministerial conduct, doubts have been raised over whether these protections are adequate. The fact that court budgets are determined by governments represents, in the eyes of some, a potential limitation on judicial autonomy.[25]

The principle of **separation of powers** guarantees the special role of the judiciary. This role is to interpret what the law and the Constitution mean when disputes arise. As in the case of judicial independence, this principle relies more on cultural norms, statute law, and constitutional convention than it does on constitutional law. There is, however, at least one important reference to the role of the judicial branch in the Constitution. This is section 24 of the Constitution Act, 1982, which declares that the enforcement of the Charter shall be through the courts. The perception that the courts represent a check on the powers of Parliament and the provincial legislatures—a perception that has taken hold since the Charter's passage in 1982—reflects an Americanizing trend in Canadian politics. The concept of checks and balances between the three branches of government is basic to the American Constitution. It is not, however, part of British parliamentary democracy.

The separation of the judiciary's role from that of Parliament is not watertight. The ability of the federal and provincial governments to refer a resolution or draft legislation to the courts for a decision on its constitutionality does not, strictly speaking, respect the principle of separation of powers. These constitutional reference cases enable governments to use the provincial and Canadian supreme courts to receive advisory opinions before acting or to thrust a politically volatile issue into the hands of judges. The separation of powers is also breached when judges step outside their role as interpreters of the law's meaning to advocate some position or reform. Since the mid-1980s the justices of Canada's highest court, in public speeches and interviews, have occasionally weighed in on matters of public controversy, including the funding of bilingualism, gender bias in the law and justice system, multiculturalism, and the appropriate role of the judicial branch in Canada's parliamentary system (see Box 5.5).

Relations between the House of Commons and the Senate

When the founders designed Canada's Parliament, they took the bicameral structure of Britain's legislature as their model. Accordingly, the legislative branch was comprised of two bodies, an elected House of Commons (the lower house) and an appointed Senate (the upper house). A literal reading of the Constitution suggests that their powers are roughly equal. The major difference is that money bills must be introduced in the House of Commons. In fact, however, the superiority of the elected House of Commons has been clear from day one. The unelected character of the Senate has always sat uneasily in Canada's democratic political culture. This fact, along with the brazen patronage of most government appointments to the Senate, undermined its legitimacy.

The superiority of the House of Commons over the Senate is reinforced by several constitutional

Politics in Focus

Box 5.5 Chief Justice McLachlin Weighs In on Canadian Identity

We have achieved a common national space, a space that reflects our history and our shared values. But it has not been easy. Our shared history is not one of continuous bliss and harmonious interaction between diverse groups. Viewed from the perspective of Aboriginal peoples, ethnic minorities, disabled people or women, it is a history marked by profound mistakes. Despite the dark chapters of our history, an ethic of respect and inclusion has been part of Canada's fabric from its beginnings. Canadian history is replete with the efforts of men and women who sought to define their identity in terms that included the other.

I believe that this distinctively Canadian ethic of inclusion and tolerance, this distinctively Canadian definition of self and of citizenship is what continues to help us overcome the feelings of loss and alienation that can readily emerge in communities transformed by immigration. In Canadian terms, individual identity is a multi-layered thing. The values of inclusion and tolerance expressed in what I have called our common national space do not establish a constellation of mutually exclusive communities, each isolated from the other. Rather, our history is the story of citizens who belong to multiple communities at once. We all share membership in communities that accept the possibility of multiple allegiances. The presence of others, even many others, who are different from me does not require me to abandon what I hold dear. I can be French-speaking *and Canadian*. I can be Haida, Aboriginal *and Canadian*. I can be Métis, from Toronto, *and Canadian*. I can be Muslim, Christian or Jewish, a Quebecker, *and still Canadian*. Our history is the story of citizens who struggle with the different layers of their identities, and somehow manage to reconcile their overlapping commitments.

In that sense, part of the solution to the predicament of difference, at least in Canada, lies in the recognition that diversity is not a phenomenon that is external to our selves, something that is around us. Diversity is within each of us, not just around us. The distinctively Canadian formulation of the principle of equal respect and dignity of each individual is one which neither obliterates nor glorifies difference. Rather, we think of equality as the natural by-product of the ties that bind each of us to multiple groups, from the family to humankind.

This recognition of the intrinsic diversity of all Canadians provides an avenue for sustainable public discourse within a political community marked by cultural pluralism. In terms of governance, in terms that matter to you as public servants, the task is to uphold communities and institutions where the overlapping commitments of participants are fostered. In a country of diversity, successful communities are those that serve both as refuge and as springboard—those communities that are the 'anchor for self-identification and the safety of effortless secure belonging', but also the catalyst of broader civic duties to larger communities. Much like a family, successful communities and institutions should push us to encounter the world, while remaining shelters of comfort and warmth.

Source: 'Remarks at a Conference on Globalization, Citizenship and Identity', 26 Oct. 2004. From Supreme Court website: <www.scc-csc.gc.ca>.

conventions. Probably the most important of these involves the selection of the Prime Minister and other members of the government. Constitutional law does not require that they be drawn from the House of Commons, but it is unthinkable today that the Prime Minister not be an elected MP. Occasionally, one or two senators are appointed to cabinet, but this often has been because the party in power had few (or no) MPs from a particular region of the country. The appointment of Michael Fortier to the Senate after the Conservatives' 2006 election victory (with the promise that he would run for a seat in the House of Commons in the next federal election) was such a case. Fortier was an influential lawyer and financier from Montreal, a city in which the Conservatives did not win a seat in 2006, and was immediately appointed to the cabinet position of Minister of Public Works and Government Services. Occasionally, the Prime Minister will appoint to cabinet someone who is neither an MP nor a senator. By tradition, however, this person will very soon afterwards seek election to the House of Commons. The whole system of democratic accountability would crumble if the Prime Minister and other members of the government were not elected officials, removable by the electorate.

Another convention that reinforces the House of Common's superiority is found in the legislative process itself. All bills must pass both the Senate and the House of Commons before they become law. Moreover, the stages through which a bill must pass are identical in both houses of Parliament. Until recently, it was generally accepted that the Senate did not have the right to obstruct or reject the will of the elected House of Commons. On occasion, the Senate would suggest minor revisions to legislation, sending it back to the House of Commons for reconsideration. However, after the 1984 election of the Progressive Conservative government the Senate—dominated by people appointed during over two decades of almost unbroken Liberal government—became more recalcitrant. On legislation dealing with such matters as drug patents, government spending, Unemployment Insurance, the Goods and Services Tax, and the Canada–United States Free Trade Agreement the Senate delayed and in some cases rejected bills coming from the House of Commons. Senate unwillingness to pass bills sent to it by the elected House put the two chambers at loggerheads again in 2010. Opposition members of the Senate Finance committee deleted several sections from a budget bill that had been passed by the House of Commons. Constitutional law gives senators this right: constitutional convention suggests that they should not try to exercise it.

The Biases of British Parliamentary Government

Along with people, pop music, and the English language, Westminster-style parliamentary government has been one of Britain's chief exports to that country's former colonies, Canada included. We have described the major features of British parliamentary government, as adapted to Canadian circumstances. Let us consider whether this system tends to favour certain interests and outcomes more than others. In discussing ministerial responsibility we noted that the pre-democratic tradition of strong executive authority never was abandoned under British parliamentary government. Instead, it was adapted to the democratic principle that government is based on the consent of the people, a principle embodied in the powers of an elected legislature and in the doctrine of responsible government. When we recall that the legislature that embodied the popular will originally was elected by and accountable to only a fraction of the people, i.e., property-owning males, this adaptation does not appear very revolutionary or particularly democratic. Of course, universal male suffrage arrived by the latter half of the 1800s, and females were enfranchised early in the twentieth century, extending participatory rights to all people and not simply a privileged group of them. This democratization of citizenship rights did not, however, fundamentally alter the non-participatory biases that were already embedded in the structure of British parliamentary government.

Following Philip Resnick's arguments in *Parliament vs. People*, we may label these biases *statism*. A statist political tradition is one characterized by a relatively strong political executive and by a population that tends to be deferential towards those in power. The adoption of British parliamentary government, first in the colonial legislatures during the mid-1800s and then through the Constitution Act of 1867, mainly reaffirmed the tradition of centralized executive authority that had existed before the elected legislature's approval was needed to pass laws. This reaffirmation of strong executive power is, Resnick argues, apparent throughout Canada's founding Constitution Act. 'What our Founding Fathers were doing', he maintains:

> was consolidating an orderly . . . move from direct colonial rule to House Rule. . . . They had a particular kind of [political] order in mind, the parliamentary system as it had evolved in Britain, combining the interests of monarchs, lords and commoners. If by the latter part of the 19th Century this system was increasingly responsive to the wishes of an electorate, restricted or enlarged, it was by no means a servant of the electorate.[26]

Some might say, that was then but this is now. Yet, the institutions of government adopted through the Confederation agreement and, equally important, the expectations of the political elites who controlled the levers of state power reached forward to shape the future course of Canadian politics. Parliament was sovereign, but Parliament was not merely the people. It included the Crown, the traditional seat of state authority whose powers came to be exercised by a prime minister and cabinet with few checks from the legislature. 'Parliamentary sovereignty', Resnick argues, 'fostered attitudes in the population which were nominally participatory but maximally deferential towards those exercising political power. The mystique of British Crown and Constitution helped make illegitimate all forms of political activity not sanctioned or channeled through parliamentary institutions.'[27] This is an important point. Resnick is arguing that the more deferential political culture of Canada, as compared to the United States, did not simply happen. It was generated to some degree by parliamentary institutions that discouraged popular participation in politics beyond the rituals of voting and enshrined a sort of top-down philosophy of governance.

The evidence suggests that Resnick is right. Of course, there have been influential currents of participatory politics in Canadian history, particularly coming out of western Canada. But these populist urges have had to struggle against a parliamentary tradition that concentrates political power in the hands of the Prime Minister (or premiers) and cabinet. This style of governance is epitomized in the long tradition of elite deal-making that has characterized federal–provincial relations. But it also surfaces when this country's political leaders reject referendums or constituent assemblies on constitutional change as being 'un-Canadian' or foreign to our political tradition. Indeed, the statist political tradition fostered by British parliamentary government is apparent in a multitude of ways, large and small. 'Our governments', argues Resnick, '. . . become the organizers of our civic consciousness. National celebrations like Expo have to be staged; nationalist propaganda is transmitted across the airwaves, through the newspapers, along with our social security cheques.'[28] Many argue that the Canadian state's orchestration of culture has been a defensive response to the Americanizing pressures from mass media industries centred in the United States. To some degree this is true. But this explanation of state-centred nationalism in Canada does not pay adequate attention to the possibility that the state's efforts may pre-empt those of groups in civil society, and encourage a climate of dependence on government to, in Resnick's words, 'organize our civic consciousness'. If governments had done less, and private citizens had done more, to construct the identities that are part of Canadian culture, perhaps national unity would have been less fragile throughout much of the country's history.

To the extent that the Charter of Rights and Freedoms modifies British parliamentary government in Canada by replacing parliamentary supremacy with constitutional supremacy and by helping to generate a greater consciousness of rights among members of the public, it has shifted Canadian politics away from its elitist past towards a more participatory model. Indeed, it is now commonplace to claim that the Charter ushered in a new era in Canadian politics characterized by far less deference to elites. There is some truth in this claim, but the impact of the Charter on Canada's political culture is often exaggerated. The British parliamentary system that operates in Canada, albeit modified by the Charter and the principle of constitutional supremacy, continues to concentrate power in the hands of the Prime Minister and cabinet and still provides few opportunities for direct public participation in governance beyond voting in elections. More importantly, the statist culture of governance that Resnick associates with the British parliamentary system is not fundamentally challenged by the fact that, because of the Charter, the courts have become more important venues for resolution of political issues and thus many groups now bypass electoral and legislative politics. Politics waged in the courts is not necessarily more democratic and accessible than these other forms and forums for politics, as many, on both the left and right of the political spectrum, concede.

Back to Resnick's argument: does Canada's constitutional model, involving an adaptation of the British parliamentary system, continue to have statist biases that centralize power and that discourage popular participation? The answer is not simple. Other constitutional arrangements in other countries also have been criticized for promoting or, at least, permitting centralized power. The European Union has elaborate and extensive mechanisms for citizen participation in EU governance, under the terms of the Lisbon Treaty. Notwithstanding these strategies, complaints of a 'democratic deficit' in EU governance are as loud and frequent as at any time in the past. Resnick is probably right that the parliamentary model adopted in Canada has, throughout most of the country's history, promoted a top-down style of governance and discouraged—even delegitimized—forms of political participation that were not focused on and channelled through Parliament. But institutional arrangements are only part of the story. Even without the undeniable impact that the Charter has had on governance and citizen expectations regarding their relationship to the state, the culture of governance in Canada would almost certainly have become less deferential over the last generation. This has happened in democracies throughout the world, with and without major constitutional changes.

Changing the Constitution

Constitutions are meant to last a very long time, but they seldom do. Among the 47 countries whose independence predates 1900, only about a third have constitutions that date from before 1950. Canada's Constitution Act, 1867 is one of the oldest and most durable. Only the United States (1789), Sweden (1809), the Netherlands (1814), and the United Kingdom (1832) have older constitutions.

A *coup d'état* is one way of changing a constitution. More peaceful means may also accomplish dramatic change, including the wholesale replacement of one constitution by a fundamentally different one; but radical alteration of the fundamental rules and structures of government is much less common than is constitutional reform. Reform aims at changing some aspect(s) of the existing constitution, leaving the basic constitutional structure intact. Limited change of this sort is generally accomplished through a formal procedure set down in the constitution. Reforms that result from such a process are called *constitutional amendments*.

When does constitutional reform become constitutional upheaval? This is difficult to pinpoint, but the line has certainly been crossed when, as a result of change, a constitution is no longer recognizable as what it was. For example, the 1982 Constitution Act did three main things: (1) transformed Canada's written Constitution from a set of British laws into Canadian constitutional law; (2) entrenched the Charter of Rights and Freedoms in the Constitution; and (3) established formal mechanisms for changing the Constitution. As important as these changes are, they did not amount to a new Constitution. Most features of parliamentary government and of federalism remained the same. On the other hand, the replacement of parliamentary government by American-style congressional government, the elimination of federalism, or—least far-fetched of all—the political independence of Quebec would in each case represent a radical transformation of Canada's Constitution.

Constitutional change may also come about through the gradual evolution of principles and practices. For example, the principle that the Governor General should accept the advice of the

Prime Minister on when Parliament should be dissolved and a new election called was one that emerged imperceptibly as Canada shook off the vestiges of its colonial relationship to Great Britain. It was only when this principle was breached by Governor General Lord Byng in 1926 that it became clear that this relationship between the Prime Minister and the Governor General was part of the Constitution. The clear superiority of the House of Commons over the Senate on matters of legislation is another constitutional convention that became clearer with the passage of time. Those appointed to the Senate in 1867 primarily were prominent politicians from the new provinces. It was during this early period that the Senate became known as the chamber of 'sober second thought'. Over time, however, the practice of patronage appointments, the emergence of assertive provincial governments as spokespersons for regional interests, and changing ideas about democracy and representation all contributed to the Senate's decline vis-à-vis the Commons.

Amending the Constitution before 1982

The Constitution Act, 1867 gave Ottawa a very modest power to amend the Constitution of Canada regarding matters that concerned only the federal government.[29] In practical terms, all this power amounted to was the ability to change electoral districts and boundary lines. The Act gave the provincial governments a similar power.[30] Canada's founders, however, did not establish an amending procedure that could be used to change the division of powers and all the other important matters that could not be changed using the very limited amendment powers conferred by sections 91(1) and 92(1) of the Constitution Act, 1867. They did not even discuss such a procedure, a curious oversight in view of the fact that the federal Constitution of the United States—the only federal model that existed at the time—was very clear on the amendment procedures that had to be followed. In Canada, the only clear requirement was that a request would have to be made to the British Parliament in order to change the Constitution. The reason for this was, of course, that the Canadian Constitution was a British law, originally passed as the British North America Act, 1867.

What was not clear was who would have to agree here in Canada before a resolution could be sent to London. Would all provincial governments have to agree if a proposed amendment affected their powers? Did Quebec or Ontario or any other province enjoy a special right to veto amendments? Just how much provincial consent was needed to change the Constitution? It was not even clear what would happen if all 10 provincial legislatures and the House of Commons agreed to an amendment, but the Senate rejected it. Formally, at least, the Senate appeared to have the power to block constitutional change.

After decades of uncertainty, the issue was decided by the Supreme Court in 1981. The background to this decision was the stalemate in constitutional negotiations between Ottawa and the provinces. The Liberal government of Pierre Elliott Trudeau wanted to patriate the Constitution, entrench in it a Charter of Rights and Freedoms, and establish a formal procedure for future constitutional amendments. Only the governments of Ontario and New Brunswick supported Ottawa's proposal. The conflict ended up in the courts when the governments of Manitoba, Newfoundland, and Quebec each decided to ask their provincial supreme courts whether Ottawa's actions were constitutional. There was some variation in the questions and wording of these provincial references. Nonetheless, they all asked: (1) whether Ottawa's proposed amendments affected provincial powers; and (2) if provincial consent was constitutionally required in order to make such changes. Quebec's reference also asked if that province had a special veto over amendments. These decisions were then appealed to the Supreme Court of Canada.

In its *Reference on the Constitution*[31] the Court made the following points:

- Some level of provincial consent was required for changes affecting provincial powers. This requirement was a constitutional convention, not part of constitutional law. It could not, therefore, be enforced by the courts.

- The level of required provincial consent was not at all clear. It was the Court's view that a majority of the provinces certainly had to agree, but unanimous consent was not necessary.
- In constitutional law, no province had a special right of veto over constitutional change. The Court did not give an opinion on whether such a right existed as a matter of constitutional convention.
- Ottawa did not need provincial consent before requesting the British Parliament to change Canada's Constitution in ways affecting provincial powers. If the federal government chose to act without the consent of the provinces, or with the support of only a few of them, this would be legal—but at the same time unconstitutional!

Both Ottawa and the dissenting provinces claimed victory as a result of the Court's decision. Legally, the way was clear for Ottawa to act with or without the consent of the provinces. Politically, unilateral action remained a very risky option, particularly in light of the Court's acknowledgement that some level of provincial consent was required by constitutional convention. All 11 governments returned to the bargaining table, each side conscious of the constitutional turf occupied by itself and its opponents. In November of 1981, 10 of them were able to reach agreement on a compromise document that became the Constitution Act, 1982. Only the Parti Québécois government of Quebec rejected the proposed changes. Despite Quebec's refusal to sign the 1981 agreement, the Constitution Act, 1982 is constitutional law in that province just as it is elsewhere in Canada. A 1982 Supreme Court decision confirmed this.[32]

Amending the Constitution since 1982

The uncertainties surrounding constitutional amendment have been largely dispelled by the Constitution Act, 1982. Part V of the Act sets out the amendment procedures. In fact, it establishes four different procedures, each of which applies to certain types of constitutional change. These procedures and when they are used are explained in Table 5.1.

Any of the four amendment procedures may be set in motion by either Ottawa or a provincial government (s. 46[1]). But because intergovernmental agreement is crucial to the success of most amendments, the most likely scenario is that the Prime Minister and the provincial premiers will first reach an agreement, which will then be submitted to their respective legislatures. This procedure led to the Meech Lake Accord, the first proposal for constitutional amendment under the 1982 rules. Negotiations and deal-making between governments—the pre-legislative stage of the amendment process—are as crucial now as when the amendment process was governed by convention. The new procedures have not formally expanded the opportunities for public participation, nor have they enlarged the legislature's role in the process.

Not content with the distinction of having four different procedures for amending the Constitution, the 10 governments that agreed to the 1982 Constitution Act included another extraordinary feature in the amendment rules. This is the 'opting-out' section (s. 40). Under this section, a provincial government that does not agree to an amendment that transfers powers relating to education or other cultural matters from the provinces to Ottawa is not obliged to give up this power. Moreover, Ottawa is required to provide 'reasonable compensation' to any dissenting province. The Meech Lake and Charlottetown Accords would have expanded the opting-out section, guaranteeing a dissenting province the right to reasonable compensation in the case of any transfer of legislative powers from the provinces to Ottawa. In fact, this would only have enshrined in the Constitution a practice that has existed in Canada since 1964.

The first effort at amending the Constitution, using the 1982 rules, ended in acrimonious failure. The proposed amendment was in fact a group of changes collectively known as the Meech Lake Accord. The Accord was a 1987 agreement between Prime Minister Brian Mulroney and the 10 provincial premiers. It was a response to a series of five

TABLE 5.1 Amending the Constitution

Procedure	Requirement	Application
1. General (ss. 38, 42)	· Resolution passed by the House of Commons and the Senate* · Two-thirds of the legislatures of the provinces that together comprise at least half the population of all the provinces	· Reduction or elimination of powers, rights, or privileges of provincial governments or legislatures · Proportionate representation of the provinces in the House of Commons · Senate · Supreme Court of Canada (except its composition) · Extension of existing provinces into the territories · Creation of new provinces
2. Unanimous consent (s. 41)	· Resolution passed by the House of Commons and the Senate* · Resolution passed by every provincial legislature	· Queen · Governor General · Lieutenant-Governors · Right of each province to at least as many seats in the House of Commons as it has in the Senate · Use of the English or French language (except changes that apply only to single province) · Composition of the Supreme Court · Changing the amending procedures of the Constitution
3. Ottawa and one or more provinces (s. 43)	· Resolution passed by the House of Commons and the Senate* · Resolution passed by the legislature of each province where the amendment applies	· Alteration of boundaries between provinces · Use of French or English in a particular province or provinces
4. Ottawa or a province acting alone (ss. 44, 45)	· If Ottawa, a resolution passed by the House of Commons and the Senate* · If a province, a resolution passed by its legislature	· Executive government of Canada, the Senate, and the House of Commons, subject to the limits established by ss. 41 and 42 of the Constitution Act, 1982

*If after 180 days the Senate has not passed a resolution already passed by the House of Commons, Senate approval is not necessary.

demands that the Quebec Liberal government of Robert Bourassa wanted met before it was willing to sign the 1981 agreement that produced the Constitution Act, 1982. The main changes proposed by the Meech Lake Accord included: recognition of Quebec as a distinct society; constitutional recognition of a provincial (i.e., Quebec) right to control its own immigration policy (something Quebec had had since a 1978 agreement between Ottawa and Quebec); provincial power to nominate justices for the Supreme Court of Canada; constitutional entrenchment of a provincial right to opt out of federal–provincial shared-cost programs and to be reimbursed for running parallel programs of their own; certain changes to constitutional amendment procedures and categories (see Table 5.1).

After three years of wrangling marked by both an anti-French backlash in parts of English Canada and a revival of separatist nationalism in Quebec, the Accord expired when the legislatures of Manitoba and Newfoundland failed to ratify it by the 23 June 1990 deadline imposed on the process by the Constitution.

Both the birth and the death of the Accord suggested that not much had changed as a result of formalizing the amendment process. The proposed changes that made up the Accord represented a deal struck by 11 heads of government with no public participation or legislative debate. In fact, the Prime Minister and some of the provincial premiers were very insistent that their agreement could not be altered in any respect. It was submitted to their legislatures for ratification, not for possible modification. Public participation was solicited very late in the process, and then only because the Accord seemed destined for defeat. Indeed, there was little

Bob Bierman/© Simon Fraser University

The failure of the Meech Lake Accord is a testament to the difficult realities of amending the Constitution.

to suggest that any of the governments saw public participation as anything more than a resource to use when convenient. Groups and individuals opposed to the Accord's provisions denounced this process as being undemocratic.

The critics may have been right. But it was also clear that any change to the 1987 first ministers' agreement would have required that a new resolution be submitted to Parliament and all the provincial legislatures, and the ratification process would have to start over again. Debate and popular participation *after* an amendment resolution has been agreed to by governments are almost certain to prolong the amendment process, and probably reduce the chances of reaching an agreement.

The death of the Meech Lake Accord likewise suggested that the process of constitutional amendment remained largely as it was before 1982. The final several months leading up to the ratification deadline were marked by acrimonious debate and some ad hoc efforts to salvage the Accord, and finally ended with Quebec being largely isolated from the other provinces. There was a sense of déjà vu about the whole affair. Quebec had been similarly isolated in 1971 when the first Bourassa government suddenly withdrew its acceptance of the Victoria Charter amendments, and then again in 1981 when René Lévesque claimed to have been betrayed by a last-minute deal concocted between the other provinces and Ottawa. In each case agreement ran aground because the Quebec government and some of the governments of English Canada were unable to settle their differences on Quebec's status within Canada. Meech Lake came to grief because of the same obstacle that had blocked previous efforts at constitutional change.

The next two years saw dozens of government-organized public hearings on the Constitution and hundreds of conferences and forums organized by academics, political parties, and interest groups. Ottawa and the provinces were determined to avoid the charges of elitist deal-making that had been levelled at the Meech Lake process. In this they failed. Although there were ample opportunities for citizens and groups to express their views on constitutional reform, the proposals presented to Canadians in the 26 October 1992 referendum were widely viewed as yet another instance of the elites cutting a deal and trying to foist it on the public.

The Charlottetown Accord, as these proposals were referred to, represented the culmination of what the federal government rather misleadingly called the 'Canada round' of constitutional negotiations (the period leading up to Meech Lake having been labelled the 'Quebec round'). In fact, however, the desire to get the Quebec government's political agreement to the constitutional changes of 1982 and the worry over the post-Meech Lake resurgence of support for separatism were the chief reasons why the constitutional issue dominated Canadian politics with a vengeance between 1990 and 1992. Moreover, the deal ultimately struck at Charlottetown in August 1992 bore a striking resemblance to the Meech Lake Accord in some important respects. Besides certain carry-overs from Meech, such as Quebec's 'distinct society' status, Supreme Court nominations, and provinces' ability to opt out of shared-cost programs without penalty, the main features included:

- a Canada clause listing the fundamental characteristics of Canadian society;
- entrenchment of the right to Aboriginal self-government;
- an elected Senate with equal representation from the provinces and, eventually, special seats for Aboriginal representatives;
- francophone veto in the Senate regarding bills affecting the French language or culture;
- a guarantee to Quebec of at least 25 per cent of the seats in the House of Commons;
- confirmation of the provinces' exclusive jurisdiction in several policy areas, and some decentralization of powers to the provinces in the areas of immigration and labour policy.

A sense of the potentially far-reaching changes proposed in the Charlottetown Accord is conveyed by the Canada Clause (see Box 5.6). This provision sought to express the fundamental values of Canadians. Had the Accord been passed the Canada Clause would have been included as section 2 of the Constitution Act, 1867 and would have given the courts guidance in their interpretation of the entire Constitution, including the Charter of Rights and Freedoms. It is impossible to know how judges would interpret many of the provisions of the Canada Clause. What is certain, however, is that it would have given to the courts a whole new field of opportunity, on top of that already provided by the Charter, to involve themselves in the policy-making process. It requires little imagination to predict that subsection (1)f of the proposed Canada Clause, committing Canadians to 'respect for individual and collective human rights and freedoms of all people', could become the legal basis for challenges to social spending cuts, or that subsection (1)b on the Aboriginal peoples of Canada could become the basis for legal claims on tax resources and distinctive legal rights for Aboriginal Canadians. The Canada Clause, whatever its impact on Canadian society would have been, was certainly a constitutional lawyer's paradise.

In the national referendum on the Charlottetown Accord, a majority of Canadians (54.5 per cent) rejected the proposed reforms, including provincial majorities in British Columbia, Alberta, Saskatchewan, Manitoba, Quebec, and Nova Scotia, as well as the Yukon. The result in Ontario was virtually a dead heat. During the impassioned referendum campaign it was clear that many English Canadians said 'no' to the Charlottetown Accord because they thought it gave Quebec too much, while many francophone Quebecers rejected the deal because they believed it gave them too little! Indeed, the only serious question asked by members of the Quebec media and the province's politicians during the campaign was 'Did Quebec get enough in the Charlottetown Accord?' Although the 1992 agreement provided the Quebec government with more than had been proposed by the Meech Lake Accord, this was not enough in the nationalist political climate that prevailed in the post-Meech years.

On the other hand, a further decentralization of powers to the provinces and special status for Quebec proved to be more than most English Canadians could stomach. While it is always treacherous and somewhat misleading to talk about Quebec or any society as though it has a single set of aspirations, the failure of the Meech Lake and Charlottetown Accords confirmed that a wide gap existed between those of francophone Quebecers and their compatriots in the rest of the country.

Citizen Participation in Constitutional Reform

For most of Canada's history the only direct actors in constitutional reform were governments. This changed during the negotiations and debates that led to the Constitution Act of 1982, when a number of citizens' interest groups played an active role through lobbying government and attempting to influence public opinion. These groups, and many others inspired by the opportunities created by the Charter, were instrumental in bringing about the death of the 1987 Meech Lake Accord, which had been agreed to by the 11 first ministers in the old pre-1982 style. During the two years of consultation and negotiation that preceded the signing of the 1992 Charlottetown Accord these citizens' interest groups were very much part of the process. Informally, at least, Ottawa and the provincial governments appeared to have conceded the legitimacy of a more inclusive style of constitution-making.

What they did not concede, however, was a direct role for public participation and consent. Under the old elitist policy-making style popular consent was mediated by the heads of government. Under the more inclusive policy-making style that emerged in the early 1980s popular consent was mediated by these heads of government *plus* certain citizens' interest groups claiming to speak on behalf of women, ethnic and racial minorities, Aboriginal Canadians, the disabled, official-language minorities, and so on. But not until the decision was taken in the late summer of 1992 to submit the Charlottetown reforms to the people in a national referendum were popular consent unmediated and the public given a direct role in the constitutional amendment process. This represented a remarkable break from Canada's elitist tradition of constitution-making. With few exceptions, mainly from western Canada, the idea of a referendum to approve constitutional change had been rejected throughout Canada's history. When a formal procedure for constitutional amendment was being debated in the 1930s one of the country's most prominent constitutionalists dismissed the suggestion of a referendum as being inconsistent with cabinet government and a device for 'passing the buck'.[33] Frank Underhill, expressing the views of most intellectuals, argued that average citizens were generally incompetent to decide matters of constitutional change

Governing Realities

Box 5.6 The Canada Clause

(1) The Constitution of Canada, including the *Canadian Charter of Rights and Freedoms*, shall be interpreted in a manner consistent with the following fundamental characteristics:

a) Canada is a democracy committed to a parliamentary and federal system of government and to the rule of law;

b) the Aboriginal peoples of Canada, being the first peoples to govern this land, have the right to promote their languages, cultures and traditions and to ensure the integrity of their societies, and their governments constitute one of three orders of government in Canada;

c) Quebec constitutes within Canada a distinct society, which includes a French-speaking majority, a unique culture and a civil law tradition;

d) Canadians and their governments are committed to the vitality and development of official language minority communities throughout Canada;

e) Canadians are committed to racial and ethnic equality in a society that includes citizens from many lands who have contributed, and continue to contribute, to the building of a strong Canada that reflects its cultural and racial diversity;

f) Canadians are committed to a respect for individual and collective human rights and freedoms of all people;

g) Canadians are committed to the equality of female and male persons; and,

h) Canadians confirm the principle of the equality of the provinces at the same time as recognizing their diverse characteristics.

and that their elected representatives usually held more advanced views on public affairs. Legislatures, not citizens, he argued, should be required to ratify constitutional reforms.[34]

The idea of a referendum on the Meech Lake Accord surfaced from time to time in the English-language media. It was dismissed, however, by Prime Minister Mulroney and most of the provincial premiers as being alien to Canada's political tradition. This view was as likely to be expressed by those on the social democratic left, such as the national New Democratic Party leader Ed Broadbent and Manitoba's NDP Premier Howard Pawley, as by those more to the right of the political spectrum.

But in the flood of condemnation that followed the death of the Meech Lake Accord the idea gathered force that popular ratification should be sought in any future attempt to change the Constitution. Quebec's provincial government committed itself to holding a provincial referendum on whatever agreement it reached with Ottawa. British Columbia also passed a law requiring provincial ratification of reform proposals. However, most politicians remained steadfast in their opposition. Ottawa's decision, after much hesitation and obvious reluctance, to introduce legislation enabling Parliament to authorize a referendum (more precisely, a plebiscite, in that the vote would be formally non-binding) reflected practical necessity more than principled conviction. The powerful Quebec caucus of the governing Conservative Party opposed such legislation. The Minister of Intergovernmental Affairs, Joe Clark, had often expressed serious reservations about a referendum. But the fact was that Quebec and British Columbia were committed to holding a referendum, and there was a good chance that the reform proposals would be rejected in both provinces. A national referendum campaign and a favourable vote in most regions was a possible way of legitimizing reform proposals in this divisive climate.

The decision to hold a referendum on the Charlottetown Accord and the decision to abide by what was, legally speaking, a non-binding popular vote, appeared to mark the beginning of a new era in Canadian constitution-making. Most commentators believed so, arguing that governments in the future would find it impossible to ignore the 1992 precedent of a popular ratification vote.

Such predictions may be premature. A country's political culture and ways of conducting politics do not change abruptly as a result of a single experience. First ministers will continue to be the key players in any future effort at constitutional reform. Both political tradition and the formal amendment procedure ensure their dominance. But a repeat of the Meech Lake process—an accord negotiated and agreed to without public consultation—has become virtually unthinkable. It is fair to say that a process of consultation and opportunities for public participation in some form have become necessary preconditions for any future agreement.

It remains to be seen, however, whether governments will feel obliged to submit future agreements to the electorate for ratification, or whether the Charlottetown experience was an aberration that has left no mark on Canada's political culture. In British Columbia and Alberta, which have a more populist tradition, the political pressure for constitutional referendums may be irresistible. In the case of Quebec, the idea that any major change in that province's constitutional status must be approved by the electorate is now firmly established. These provinces are the ones most likely to insist on popular ratification of constitutional reform. If they do, it becomes very awkward for Ottawa not to concede a role for direct public participation through a national referendum, as happened in 1992.

Does Quebec Have the Constitutional Right to Secede? (and Does It Matter?)

On 20 August 1998 the Supreme Court of Canada handed down its much awaited decision on the constitutionality of Quebec separation. In the eyes of some, the most remarkable aspect of the ruling was that it was made at all. The separation of Quebec, if and when it comes about, is a political matter that will be determined by politicians and the people, not by nine appointed judges in Ottawa. This was certainly the view of most Quebec nationalists and of Quebec's Parti Québécois government, whose disdain for the process was such that it refused to send lawyers to argue the case for the constitutionality of Quebec secession. Indeed, the Supreme Court's involvement in this matter was widely viewed by francophone Quebecers as unwarranted meddling in the internal affairs of the province.

Ottawa's decision to refer the issue of the constitutionality of Quebec secession to the Supreme Court was prompted by the actions of Montreal lawyer Guy Bertrand. A one-time separatist, Bertrand had already begun legal proceedings in Quebec challenging the constitutionality of unilateral secession by Quebec. Ottawa's 1996 decision to refer the question to the Supreme Court of Canada was, in part, due to the simple fact that Bertrand's private action had already released the genie from the bottle. Nonetheless, there were political risks associated with Ottawa's involvement in a court challenge to Quebec secession. The Liberal government's decision to push forward, despite these risks, was consistent with what had come to be known as the 'Plan B' approach to Quebec separatism. Whereas Plan A had involved efforts to satisfy moderate Quebec nationalists with promises of distinct society status for Quebec and some decentralization of powers to the provinces, Plan B was a hardline approach that relied on convincing Quebecers that separation would carry significant economic costs and that some parts of the territory of Quebec might not fall under the authority of an independent Quebec state (this was the partition threat, made by predominantly anglophone communities and Aboriginal groups in Quebec, and occasionally expressed by Stéphane Dion, the Liberal Minister of Intergovernmental Affairs). The court challenge to Quebec secession became a major component of the Plan B strategy.

In the reference submitted by Ottawa to the Supreme Court, three questions were asked:

- Question 1: Under the Constitution of Canada, can the National Assembly or government of Quebec effect the secession of Quebec from Canada unilaterally?
- Question 2: Does international law give the National Assembly or government of Quebec the right to effect the secession of Quebec from Canada unilaterally? In other words, is there a right to self-determination in international law that applies to Quebec?
- Question 3: If there is a conflict between international law and the Canadian Constitution on the secession of Quebec, which takes precedence?

The Court decided that there is no conflict, and so only the first two questions were addressed.

The Court's answer to the first question was a model of ambiguity that provided both federalists and separatists with congenial arguments. In strictly legal terms, said the Court, the secession of Quebec involves a major change to the Constitution of Canada that 'requires an amendment to the Constitution, which perforce requires negotiation.'[35] However, the Constitution of Canada consists of more than the Constitution Acts passed between 1867 and 1982. 'Underlying constitutional principles', said the Court, 'may in certain circumstances give rise to substantive legal obligations . . . which constitute substantive limitation upon government action.'[36] These underlying constitutional principles provided the basis for the Court's argument that if a clear majority of Quebecers voted 'yes' to an unambiguous question on Quebec separation, this would 'confer legitimacy on the efforts of the government of Quebec to initiate the Constitution's amendment process in order to secede by constitutional means'[37] (see Box 5.7). These underlying constitutional principles also impose on Ottawa and the provincial governments outside of Quebec an obligation to negotiate the terms of secession, if and when Quebecers and their provincial government express the democratic will to separate.

So who wins on the first question? The answer is that both federalists and separatists found enough in the Supreme Court's ruling to allow them to claim victory. Federalists emphasized that, legally speaking, Quebec has no constitutional right to secede unilaterally, and that even if separatists were to win a referendum the Court specified that a 'clear majority' on an 'unambiguous' question would be required before such a vote could be considered an expression of the democratic will of Quebecers on so weighty a matter. Separatists—or at least those who were even willing to acknowledge the Court's

Politics in Focus

Box 5.7 Can Quebecers Vote Their Way Out of Canada?

Although the Constitution does not itself address the use of a referendum procedure, and the results of a referendum have no direct role or legal effect in our constitutional scheme, a referendum undoubtedly may provide a democratic method of ascertaining the views of the electorate on important political questions on a particular occasion. The democratic principle identified above would demand that considerable weight be given to a clear expression by the people of Quebec of their will to secede from Canada, even though a referendum, in itself and without more, has no direct legal effect, and could not in itself bring about unilateral secession. Our political institutions are premised on the democratic principle, and so an expression of the democratic will of the people of a province carries weight, in that it would confer legitimacy on the efforts of the government of Quebec to initiate the Constitution's amendment process in order to secede by constitutional means. In this context, we refer to a 'clear' majority as a qualitative evaluation. The referendum result, if it is to be taken as an expression of the democratic will, must be free of ambiguity both in terms of the question asked and in terms of the support it achieves.

Source: Supreme Court of Canada, *Reference re the Secession of Quebec* (1998).

ruling—emphasized that the Court had agreed that the democratically expressed will of Quebecers had to be taken into account in determining whether unilateral secession was constitutional, and that if Quebecers were to express their clear support for separation the rest of Canada would be constitutionally bound to respect this decision and negotiate the terms of secession.

The Court's answer to the second question—whether international law gives Quebec the right to secede—was both shorter and less ambiguous. The Court said 'no'. While acknowledging that the right of self-determination of peoples exists in international law, the Supreme Court held that this right did not apply to Quebec.

The Court did not answer the contentious question of whether the Quebec population, or a part of it, constitutes a 'people' as understood in international law. It argued that such a determination was unnecessary because, however the Quebec people might be defined, it is clear that Quebecers are neither denied the ability to pursue their 'political, economic, social and cultural development within the framework of an existing state',[38] nor do they constitute a colonial or oppressed people (a claim that is a staple of contemporary Quebec historiography). The Court's pronouncements on these matters are found in Box 5.8.

Does the Supreme Court ruling make a difference? Probably not, or at least not much of one, as the Court seemed to acknowledge at various points in its decision. On the issue of what would constitute a 'clear majority' and an 'unambiguous question' in a referendum on Quebec independence, the Court admitted that 'it will be for the political actors to determine what constitutes a "clear majority on a clear question".'[39] Likewise, the practical meaning of what the Court said was that the constitutional obligation of the rest of Canada to negotiate the terms of separation with Quebec, if Quebecers express the democratic will to secede, would be for political actors to settle. Finally, in response to the argument that a unilateral declaration of independence by Quebec would be effective regardless of whether the Court's test of a clear majority on a clear question was met, the judges could say only that this might well be true, but the action would be unconstitutional nonetheless. One suspects that separatists would not lose much sleep over the constitutionality of such a declaration, particularly if France and certain other countries were to immediately recognize the new Quebec state.

Politics in Focus

Box 5.8 International Law and the Self-Determination of Quebec

There is no necessary incompatibility between the maintenance of the territorial integrity of existing states, including Canada, and the right of a 'people' to achieve a full measure of self-determination. A state whose government represents the whole of the people or peoples resident within its territory, on a basis of equality and without discrimination, and respects the principles of self-determination in its own internal arrangements, is entitled to the protection under international law of its territorial integrity.

The Quebec people is not the victim of attacks on its physical existence or integrity, or of a massive violation of its fundamental rights. The Quebec people is manifestly not, in the opinion of the *amicus curiae*, an oppressed people.

For close to 40 of the last 50 years, the Prime Minister of Canada has been a Quebecer. During this period, Quebecers have held from time to time all the most important positions in the federal Cabinet. During the 8 years prior to June 1997, the Prime Minister and the Leader of the Official Opposition in the House of Commons were both Quebecers. At present, the Prime Minister of Canada, the Right Honourable Chief Justice and two other members of the Court, the Chief of Staff of the Canadian Armed Forces and the Canadian ambassador to the United States, not to mention the Deputy Secretary-General of the United Nations, are all Quebecers. The international achievements of Quebecers in most fields of human endeavour are too numerous to list. Since the dynamism of the Quebec people has been directed towards the business sector, it has been clearly successful in Quebec, the rest of Canada, and abroad.

The population of Quebec cannot plausibly be said to be denied access to government. Quebecers occupy prominent positions within the government of Canada. Residents of the province freely make political choices and pursue economic, social, and cultural development within Quebec, across Canada, and throughout the world. The population of Quebec is equitably represented in legislative, executive, and judicial institutions. In short, to reflect the phraseology of the international documents that address the right to self-determination of peoples, Canada is a 'sovereign and independent state conducting itself in compliance with the principle of equal rights and self-determination of peoples and thus possessed of a government representing the whole people belonging to the territory without distinction'.

Source: Supreme Court of Canada, *Reference re the Secession of Quebec* (1998).

Ottawa's response to the 1998 Supreme Court ruling was to pass the Clarity Act in 2000. This law empowers Parliament to review the wording of any future referendum question to determine whether it complies with the Supreme Court's requirement that such a question be 'unambiguously worded' or that the margin of victory for the separatism option does not constitute the 'clear majority' required by the 1998 ruling. Under this law the Parliament of Canada could, conceivably, refuse to enter into negotiations on separatism with Quebec if it determined that one or both of these conditions were not met. 'Conceivably' is the key word here. There are strong reasons to think that Ottawa's rejection of a referendum question designed by a sovereignist Quebec government, or of even a fairly narrow margin of victory for those in favour of independence, could well backfire, playing into the hands of separatists who would be quick to accuse the federal government and the rest of Canada of meddling in Quebec's affairs. The aim of the Clarity Act was doubtless to strengthen the federalists' hand in a future Quebec referendum, but the actual result could prove to be quite the opposite.

Starting Points for Research

Alan Cairns, *Constitution, Government, and Society in Canada: Selected Essays* (Toronto: McClelland & Stewart, 1988). Several of Cairns's most insightful and widely cited articles are here, including his 1977 presidential address to the Canadian Political Science Association on the impact of political and bureaucratic self-interest and the Constitution on federalism and intergovernmental conflict.

Peter W. Hogg, *Constitutional Law of Canada* (Scarborough, Ont.: Carswell, 2007). This is perhaps the leading text on Canadian constitutional law, widely used in political science and law courses alike.

Peter Russell, *Constitutional Odyssey: Can Canadians Become a Sovereign People?*, 2nd edn (Toronto: University of Toronto Press, 1993). One of Canada's leading constitutional scholars gives an excellent survey of constitutional struggles in Canada, culminating in the failed Charlottetown Accord.

F.R. Scott, *Essays on the Constitution* (Toronto: University of Toronto Press, 1977). This somewhat dated classic is unsurpassed in the quality of insight that Scott, among Canada's foremost constitutionalists and poets, brings to the analysis of Canada's constitutional history.

Review Exercises

1. What are the pros and cons of the comparatively strict form of party discipline practised in Canada's House of Commons? How do you think our constitutional system would change if all votes in the House of Commons were free votes?
2. Draft a 'Canada Clause' to be added at the beginning of the Constitution Act, stating in no more than 100 words the core principles and values that Canada stands for and that should guide interpretation of the Constitution. Compare yours to those drafted by other members of your class and to similar sorts of clauses at the beginning of the United States and French constitutions.
3. Compare the topics, controversies, and key terms covered in this chapter to those in the constitution chapter of an American politics text (for example, Wilson and Dilulio's *American Government*, published by Houghton & Mifflin, the table of contents for which is available at: <www.hmco.com/college/polisci/index.html>, or Stephen Brooks, *Understanding American Politics* (Toronto: University of Toronto Press, 2009), at: <www.utphighereducation.com>. Identify some of the similarities and differences in coverage.

CANADIAN CHARTER OF RIGHTS AND FREEDOMS

Whereas Canada is founded upon principles that recognize the supremacy of God and the rule of law:

Guarantee of Rights and Freedoms

1. The *Canadian Charter of Rights and Freedoms* guarantees the rights and freedoms set out in it subject only to such reasonable limits prescribed by law as can be demonstrably justified in a free and democratic society.

Fundamental Freedoms

2. Everyone has the following fundamental freedoms: (*a*) freedom of conscience and religion; (*b*) freedom of thought, belief, opinion and expression, including freedom of the press and other media of communication; (*c*) freedom of peaceful assembly; and (*d*) freedom of association.

Democratic Rights

3. Every citizen of Canada has the right to vote in an election of members of the House of Commons or of a legislative assembly and to be qualified for membership therein. 4.(1) No House of Commons and no legislative assembly shall continue for longer than five years from the date fixed for the return of the writs at a general election of its members. (2) In time of real of apprehended war, invasion or insurrection, a House of Commons may be continued by Parliament and a legislative assembly may be continued by the legislature beyond five years if such continuation is not opposed by the votes of more than one-third of the members of the House of Commons or the legislative assembly, as the case may be. 5. There shall be a sitting of Parliament and of each legislature at least once every twelve months.

Mobility Rights

6. (1) Every citizen of Canada has the right to enter, remain in and leave Canada. (2) Every citizen of Canada and every person who has the status of a permanent resident of Canada has the right (*a*) to move to and take up residence in any province; and (*b*) to pursue the gaining of a livelihood in any province. (3) The rights specified in subsection (2) are subject to (*a*) any laws or practices of general application in force in a province other than those that discriminate among persons primarily on the basis of province of present or previous residence; and (*b*) any laws providing for reasonable residency requirements as a qualification for the receipt of publicly provided social services. (4) Subsections (2) and (3) do not preclude any law, program or activity that has as its object the amelioration in a province of conditions of individuals in that province who are socially or economically disadvantaged if the rate of employment in that province is below the rate of employment in Canada.

Legal Rights

7. Everyone has the right to life, liberty and security of the person and the right not to be deprived thereof except in accordance with the principles of fundamental justice. 8. Everyone has the right to be secure against unreasonable search or seizure. 9. Everyone has the right not to be arbitrarily detained or imprisoned. 10. Everyone has the right on arrest or detention (*a*) to be informed promptly of the reasons therefor; (*b*) to retain and instruct counsel without delay and to be informed of that right; and (*c*) to have the validity of the detention determined by way of *habeas corpus* and to be released if the detention is not lawful. 11. Any persons charged with an offence has the right (*a*) to be informed without unreasonable delay of the specific offence; (*b*) to be tried within a reasonable time; (*c*) not to be compelled to be a witness in proceedings against that person in respect of the offence; (*d*) to be presumed innocent until proven guilty according to law in a fair and public hearing by an independent and impartial tribunal; (*e*) not to be denied reasonable bail without just cause; (*f*) except in the case of an offence under military law tried before a military tribunal, to the benefit of trial by jury where the maximum punishment for the offence is imprisonment for five years or a more severe punishment; (*g*) not to be found guilty on account of any act or omission unless, at the time of the act or omission, it constituted an offence under Canadian or international law or was criminal according to the general principles of law recognized by the community of nations; (*h*) if finally acquitted of the offence, not to be tried for it again and, if finally found guilty and punished for the offence, not to be tried or punished for it again; and (*i*) if found guilty of the offence and if the punishment for the offence has been varied between the time of commission and the time of sentencing, to the benefit of the lesser punishment. 12. Everyone has the right not to be subjected to any cruel and unusual treatment or punishment. 13. A witness who testifies in any proceedings has the right not to have any incriminating evidence so given used to incriminate that witness in any other proceedings, except in a prosecution for perjury or for the giving of contradictory evidence. 14. A party or witness in any proceedings who does not understand or speak the language in which the proceedings are conducted or who is deaf has the right to the assistance of an interpreter.

Equality Rights

15. (1) Every individual is equal before and under the law and has the right to the equal protection and equal benefit of the law without discrimination and, in particular, without discrimination based on race, national or ethnic origin, colour, religion, sex, age or mental or physical disability. (2) Subsection (1) does not preclude any law, program or activity that has as its object the amelioration of conditions of disadvantaged individuals or groups including those that are disadvantaged because of race, national or ethnic origin, colour, religion, sex, age or mental or physical disability.

Official Languages of Canada

16. (1) English and French are the official languages of Canada and have equality of status and equal rights and privileges as to their use in all institutions of the Parliament and government of Canada. (2) English and French are the official languages of New Brunswick and have equality of status and equal rights and privileges as to their use in all institutions of the legislature and government of New Brunswick. (3) Nothing in this Charter limits the authority of Parliament or a legislature to advance the equality of status or use of English and French. 16.1 (1) The English linguistic community and the French linguistic community in New Brunswick have equality of status and equal rights and privileges, including the right to distinct educational institutions and such distinct cultural institutions as are necessary for the preservation and promotion of those communities. (2) The role of the legislature and government of New Brunswick to preserve and promote the status, rights and privileges referred to in subsection (1) is affirmed. 17. (1) Everyone has the right to use English or French in any debates and other proceedings of Parliament. (2) Everyone has the right to use English or French in any debates and other proceedings of the legislature of New Brunswick. 18. (1) The statutes, records and journals of Parliament shall be printed and published in English and French and both language versions are equally authoritative. (2) The statutes, records and journals of the legislature of New Brunswick shall be printed and published in English and French and both language versions are equally authoritative. 19. (1) Either English or French may be used by any person in, or in any pleading in or process issuing from, any court established by Parliament. (2) Either English or French may be used by any person in, or in any pleading in or process issuing from, any court of New Brunswick. 20. (1) Any member of the public in Canada has the right to communicate with, and to receive available services from, any head or central office of an institution of the Parliament or government of Canada in English or French, and has the same right with respect to any other office of any such institution where (*a*) there is a significant demand for communications with and services from that office in such language; or (*b*) due to the nature of the office, it is reasonable that communications with and services from that office be available in both English and French. (2) Any member of the public in New Brunswick has the right to communicate with, and to receive available services from, any office of an institution of the legislature or government of New Brunswick in English or French. 21. Nothing in sections 16 to 20 abrogates or derogates from any right, privilege or obligation with respect to the English and French languages, or either of them, that exists or is continued by virtue of any other provision of the Constitution of Canada. 22. Nothing in sections 16 to 20 abrogates or derogates from any legal or customary right or privilege acquired or enjoyed either before or after the coming into force of this Charter with respect to any language that is not English or French.

Minority Language Educational Rights

23.(1) Citizens of Canada (*a*) whose first language learned and still understood is that of the English or French linguistic minority population of the province in which they reside, or (*b*) who have received their primary school instruction in Canada in English or French and reside in a province where the language in which they received that instruction is the language of the English or French linguistic minority population of the province, have the right to have their children receive primary and secondary school instruction in that language in that province. (2) Citizens of Canada of whom any child has received or is receiving primary or secondary school instruction in English or French in Canada, have the right to have all their children receive primary and secondary school instruction in the same language. (3) The right of citizens of Canada under subsections (1) and (2) to have their children receive primary and secondary school instruction in the language of the English or French linguistic minority population of a province (*a*) applies wherever in the province the number of children of citizens who have such a right is sufficient to warrant the provision to them out of public funds of minority language instruction; and (*b*) includes, where the number of those children so warrants, the right to have them receive that instruction in minority language educational facilities provided out of public funds.

Enforcement

24. (1) Anyone whose rights or freedoms, as guaranteed by this Charter, have been infringed or denied may apply to a court of competent jurisdiction to obtain such remedy as the court considers appropriate and just in the circumstances. (2) Where, in proceedings under subsection (1), a court concludes that evidence was obtained in a manner that infringed or denied any rights or freedoms guaranteed by this Charter, the evidence shall be excluded if it is established that, having regard to all the circumstances, the admission of it in the proceedings would bring the administration of justice into disrepute.

General

25. The guarantee in this Charter of certain rights and freedoms shall not be construed so as to abrogate or derogate from any aboriginal, treaty or other rights or freedoms that pertain to the aboriginal peoples of Canada including (*a*) any rights or freedoms that have been recognized by the Royal Proclamation of October 7, 1763; and (*b*) any rights or freedoms that now exist by way of land claims agreements or may be so acquired. 26. The guarantee in this Charter of certain rights and freedoms shall not be construed as denying the existence of any other rights or freedoms that exist in Canada. 27. This Charter shall be interpreted in a manner consistent with the preservation and enhancement of the multicultural heritage of Canadians. 28. Notwithstanding anything in this Charter, the rights and freedoms referred to in it are guaranteed equally to male and female persons. 29. Nothing in this Charter abrogates or derogates from any rights or privileges guaranteed by or under the Constitution of Canada in respect of denominational, separate or dissentient schools. 30. A reference in this Charter to a province or to the legislative assembly or legislature of a province shall be deemed to include a reference to the Yukon Territory and the Northwest Territories, or to the appropriate legislative authority thereof, as the case may be. 31. Nothing in this Charter extends the legislative powers of any body or authority.

Application of Charter

32. (1) This Charter applies (*a*) to the Parliament and government of Canada in respect of all matters within the authority of Parliament including all matters relating to the Yukon Territory and Northwest Territories; and (*b*) to the legislature and government of each province in respect of all matters within the authority of the legislature of each province. (2) Notwithstanding subsection (1), section 15 shall not have effect until three years after this section comes into force. 33. (1) Parliament or the legislature of a province may expressly declare in an Act of Parliament or of the legislature, as the case may be, that the Act or a provision thereof shall operate notwithstanding a provision included in section 2 or sections 7 to 15 of this Charter. (2) An Act or a provision of an Act in respect of which a declaration made under this section is in effect shall have such operation as it would have but for the provision of this Charter referred to in the declaration. (3) A declaration made under subsection (1) shall cease to have effect five years after it comes into force or on such earlier date as may be specified in the declaration. (4) Parliament or a legislature of a province may re-enact a declaration made under subsection (1). (5) Subsection (3) applies in respect of a re-enactment made under subsection (4).

Citation

34. This Part may be cited as the *Canadian Charter of Rights and Freedoms*.

"We must now establish the basic principles, the basic values and beliefs which hold us together as Canadians so that beyond our regional loyalties there is a way of life and a system of values which make us proud of the country that has given us such freedom and such immeasurable joy."

P.E. Trudeau 1981

Entrenched in the Constitution and designed to unify Canadians around its set of principles, the Canadian Charter of Rights and Freedoms guarantees certain rights, both political and civil, to Canadian citizens and residents of Canada.

6 Rights and Freedoms

In modern democracies political demands often are expressed in the language of rights and freedoms. This chapter examines some of the controversies associated with rights and freedoms, and discusses the impact of the Canadian Charter of Rights and Freedoms on Canadian politics. Topics discussed include:

- What do 'rights' and 'freedoms' mean?
- The origins and meanings of rights.
- The pre-Charter era: 1867–1981.
- The Charter and constitutional supremacy.
- The 'notwithstanding' clause.
- Applying the Charter.
- Individual rights and freedoms.
- Equality and the Charter.

Like the Ten Commandments, rights and freedoms usually are expressed in uncompromising language. Those who argue the case for a woman's right to control her body, a fetus's right to life, a person's freedom of conscience, or an individual's right not to be discriminated against on the basis of race, gender, or some other personal attribute that is beyond one's control, typically advance their claims as moral absolutes. Moral absolutes, like Biblical injunctions, are non-negotiable. Either a right or freedom exists or it does not. And if it exists, it must be respected in all cases and not simply when governments or the majority find it convenient to do so.

In reality, however, no right or freedom is absolute. There are two reasons for this. One is that rights and freedoms may collide, necessitating some compromise. For example, does freedom of expression protect the right of an individual to shout 'Fire!' when there is none in a crowded theatre? This hypothetical case was used by American Supreme Court Justice Oliver Wendell Holmes to explain when and why limits on free speech are justified. Holmes established the 'clear and present danger' test,[1] according to which freedom of expression could legitimately be curtailed when it posed an unmistakable and immediate danger to others. Falsely shouting 'Fire!' in a crowded theatre obviously endangers the safety of those in the room. To guarantee an individual's freedom of expression in such circumstances is unreasonable because it could jeopardize the right of other individuals to be protected from danger.

The trade-offs between competing values in the body politic are seldom as simple as in the preceding example. Should freedom of expression protect people who publicly communicate statements that 'willfully promote hatred'[2] against some group distinguished by race, ethnicity, language, or religion? When do national security considerations or society's interest in preventing trafficking in drugs warrant wiretaps and other violations of the individual's right to privacy? How far should the public's interest in minimizing fraudulent claims on the public purse be allowed to justify intrusions into the homes and lives of welfare recipients or of those in public office? Is affirmative action a legitimate means for promoting social equality, or is it reverse discrimination against those who are not members of the groups targeted for special consideration? When does one right or freedom 'trump' another? Who should determine these issues: the courts or the people's elected representatives?

A second reason why no right or freedom can be treated as an absolute is because to do so would be impractical. If, for example, a constitution guarantees the right of official-language minorities to public education or services in their mother tongue, does that mean that all government services everywhere in the country should be available in each of the official languages? Does it mean that minority-language education should be provided in a community where only a very few families are demanding a school? Common sense suggests that there are limits to how far, and in what circumstances, the principles of linguistic equality and minority rights should apply.

What about administrative procedures that are determined by budget and personnel restrictions, but which impose hardship on individuals? For example, in 1990 an Ontario superior court judge decided that the time spent by many accused persons in jail or on bail while waiting for their trial date violated s. 11(b) of the Charter, i.e., the right 'to be tried within a reasonable time'. Given the existing number of judges and the limits on court resources, enormous backlogs had accumulated. He proceeded to dismiss hundreds of cases that had been in the dock for months. Can the bureaucratic procedures and budget constraints that led to these delays and that had inflicted real hardship on individuals be justified as 'practical limitations' on rights? Or are they matters of mere administrative convenience or policy that should not take precedence over individual rights?

Even in what may appear to be the most straightforward of circumstances, in which no compromise seems possible, the reality is that a balancing act between rights and other values may take place. Consider the case of human life and the measures that should be taken to preserve it. A 30-year-old person who needs a liver transplant in order to stay alive is more likely to receive this organ than an 80-year-old. Most, but not all of us, would find this preference for the younger person to be entirely reasonable. We might be even more likely to approve it if we learn that the 30-year-old is the mother of two young children and her family's main breadwinner, whereas the 80-year-old has a history of serious health problems and is considered unlikely to survive very long after a liver transplant operation. For most people, at least, the determination of whether one person's right to life ought to be protected more vigilantly than another's will be influenced by knowledge of surrounding circumstances like these.

Dilemmas await us at every turn. Despite this, and despite the passions unleashed by such controversies, rights and freedoms have had a low profile in Canadian politics for most of this country's history. The courts were reluctant to question the authority of elected legislatures to pass laws, whatever their content and effects, except to decide whether the matter in question constitutionally belonged to Ottawa or the provinces. As a result, civil liberties issues were transformed—deformed, some would say—into squabbles over the federal–provincial division of powers.

This changed with the passage of the Charter of Rights and Freedoms in 1982. As we noted in Chapter 5, the Charter entrenched various rights and freedoms in the Constitution. Moreover, by establishing the principle of constitutional supremacy (sections 32 and 52[1] of the Constitution Act, 1982), the 1982 constitutional reforms placed these rights more or less beyond the interference

"I'm trying to see you, Albert, in the light of our new Charter of Rights and Freedoms . . ."

No right or freedom is absolute. Questions such as *When should one individual's rights and freedoms be diminished to protect those of others?* and *Should one right or freedom supersede another?* are raised when applying a document such as the Charter to everyday situations.

of governments because section 1 of the Charter states that these rights and freedoms are 'subject only to such reasonable limits prescribed by law as can be demonstrably justified in a free and democratic society', and section 33(1) enables either Parliament or a provincial legislature to declare that a particular law or provision of a law shall operate even if it violates rights or freedoms guaranteed in sections 2 or 7 to 15 of the Charter. Together, sections 1 and 33 operate to maintain some measure of parliamentary supremacy over the courts and the Charter.

There is little doubt, however, that the Charter has decisively changed the face of Canadian politics. The authority of elected legislatures has receded before the authority of the Constitution and the courts. A transformation has taken place in the venues and language of Canadian politics. The discourse of 'rights', always a part of the political scene, has assumed much greater prominence since passage of the Charter. Individuals, organized interests, and even governments have turned increasingly to litigation as a means of influencing public policy. During the first decade after the Charter's passage, about 1,000 Charter cases a year were decided by Canadian courts,[3] reflecting the increased importance of the courts as a forum for political conflict. About 20–30 Charter rulings were handed down by the Supreme Court each year, including many that had major effects on public policy. The pace of such judicial interventions has slowed in recent years. Only 14 of the 62 Supreme Court rulings issued in 2009 involved Charter issues. Nevertheless, Michael Mandel's early judgement that 'the Charter has legalized our politics'[4] still seems apt.

What have been the consequences? Which groups (leaving aside lawyers) have won as a result of Charter politics, and which have lost ground? Has Canadian society become more democratic as a result of the unprecedented prominence accorded to rights and freedoms since the Charter's passage? These are crucial questions for which there are no easy answers. Let us begin by examining the concepts of rights and freedoms. We will then examine the history of rights and freedoms in Canada, pre- and post-Charter.

Coming to Terms: What Do Rights and Freedoms Mean?

Although there is a long tradition in Western constitutional law of distinguishing between rights and freedoms, often the distinction is not so straightforward in practice. An individual's freedom to believe something or to behave in a particular way may be expressed in terms of a right. 'I have a right to picket this employer' (freedom of assembly), or 'I have a right to distribute pamphlets explaining that the [you fill in the blank] are responsible for most of the evils that beset the world' (freedom of expression). Likewise, the right to fair and equal treatment by the law is often framed in terms of the conditions necessary to ensure an individual's freedom. For example, an accused person's right to be tried within a reasonable time—a right guaranteed by section 11(b) of the Charter—probably is violated if he or she has to spend a year in prison or 'free' but under onerous bail restrictions. Obviously, this individual's personal freedom is seriously compromised in such circumstances. Or consider the case of abortion. Those who argue against legal restrictions on a woman's access to abortion claim that such laws violate a woman's right to control her body, an important dimension of the right to privacy. In this case the right being claimed is nothing less than freedom from interference by the state, or what Alan Borovoy, for many years the general counsel for the Canadian Civil Liberties Association, has called the 'right to be left alone'.[5]

Rights and freedoms are not, therefore, watertight compartments in reality. Nevertheless, constitutional experts usually reserve the term 'rights' for those individual and group **entitlements** that 'are considered so fundamental to human dignity that they receive special protection under the law and usually under the constitution of a country.'[6] Freedoms involve an individual's liberty to do or believe certain things without restraint by government. Whereas the defence of rights often requires some government action, the protection of freedoms requires that government refrain from interfering in certain matters. 'Rights' suggests an active role for government, 'freedoms' a limited one.

Civil liberties or civil rights are terms sometimes used to refer to all the basic rights and freedoms of citizens. Under the influence of the United Nations' **Universal Declaration of Human Rights** (1948), the term **human rights** has become the more commonly used designation for this bundle of rights and freedoms. Included among them are the following:

- *Political rights/fundamental freedoms.* These include freedom of association, assembly, expression, the media, conscience, and religion, and the right to privacy.
- *Democratic rights.* Among these are the rights of all adult persons to vote and stand for public office. Requirements that elections periodically be held and that the law apply equally to those who govern and those who are governed are also important democratic rights.
- *Legal rights.* These are essentially procedural rights intended to ensure the fair and equal treatment of individuals under the law. They include, *inter alia*, the right to due process of law, freedom from arbitrary arrest, the right to a fair hearing, the right to legal counsel, and the right not to be subjected to cruel or unusual punishment.
- *Economic rights.* Although they usually are not listed as a separate category of entrenched rights, economic rights occupy an important place in all capitalist democracies. They include the right to own property and not to be deprived of it without fair compensation, the right to withhold one's labour, and freedom of contract.
- *Equality rights.* This is the most recent and probably the most controversial category of rights. The American Constitution, the first modern constitution to include an entrenched guarantee of equality rights, refers only to every person's right to 'equal protection of the laws'.[7] The more recent tendency, however, has been to enumerate the proscribed bases of legal discrimination, such as race, religion, ethnicity, gender, and age. Canada's Charter also includes mental or physical disability and has been interpreted by the courts to prohibit discrimination based on sexual orientation.

These five categories by no means exhaust the rights that may be protected by law. *Language rights* represent an important category of group rights in many societies, Canada included. Other group rights, such as for religious minorities or Native peoples, may also be protected by law. Some argue that *social rights*, or what are sometimes called *entitlements*, including the right to a job, economic security, decent housing, and adequate health care, should also have the status of entrenched constitutional rights. *Environmental rights*, including citizens' rights to clean air and water, to the preservation of wilderness areas, and to the protection of species diversity, are advocated by some groups, including the Canadian Bar Association. Some go even further, calling for the protection of animal rights and the dignity of plant life (see Box 6.1).

In Canada, many of the main categories of human rights are entrenched in the Charter. Table 6.1 identifies the sections of the Charter that correspond to each of them. A word of warning: this classification should be read as a general guide to the location of specific rights in the Charter. Due to the imagination of lawyers, the complex circumstances of particular cases, and the inevitable overlap that exists between different rights claims, the basis for a particular right may be found under what appears to be an unrelated heading.

For example, unions have argued that collective bargaining is a right that belongs to working people. They have claimed (successfully) that it should be implied by and protected under section 2(d) of the Charter, which guarantees 'freedom of association'. Business interests have argued (also successfully) that section 8 of the Charter, which guarantees 'the right to be secure against unreasonable search and seizure', limits the search powers that were being exercised by a government agency with responsibility for investigating collusive business practices.[8] Protection for the tobacco's industry's right to advertise its product was found under the Charter's guarantee of 'freedom of expression' (s. 2[6]).[9] The

Politics in Focus

Box 6.1 Should Trees and Pigs Have Constitutionally Protected Rights?

In 2009 the Swiss changed their constitution to include protection for animal and plant life, the preservation of their natural environment and diversity, and the protection of endangered species from extinction. A year later the country's voters massively rejected a proposed amendment that would have guaranteed publicly paid lawyers to advocate on behalf of animal rights across the country and to represent their rights in cases involving allegations of abuse and loss of dignity, a system that already existed in Zurich.

Including such protections in a constitution involves a fundamental shift in thinking about rights. Historically, rights have been based on ideas about human dignity and happiness. The notion that non-human life forms should be invested with rights that do not depend on the needs and desires of human beings is radically different. It is based on a rejection of what are referred to by the advocates of plant and animal rights as anthropocentric—human-centred—and species-specific notions of justice that unfairly privilege human beings. To get a better sense of the reasoning and world view on which such arguments rest (if you don't already share them) visit the website of People for the Ethical Treatment of Animals (www.peta.org).

basis for an economic right was found to rest on a fundamental freedom enshrined in the Charter. But perhaps the most striking case of one sort of right—again an economic one—being claimed under a different category of rights involved business's successful challenge to the federal Lord's Day Act.[10] Hardly anyone seriously believed that the case had anything much to do with the Charter's guarantee of freedom of religion (s. 2[a]). It had a lot to do, however, with the right to make money on Sundays.

It is no accident that cases involving what obviously are economic claims are packaged in the language of other rights. Except for the Charter's reference to mobility rights, a right intended to guarantee the free movement of Canadian citizens

TABLE 6.1 Human Rights and the Charter

Rights Category	Pre-Charter Protections	Charter Protections
1. Political rights/ fundamental freedoms	Common-law protections implied in the preamble of the Constitution Act, 1867	s. 2
2. Democratic rights	Constitution Act, 1867, ss. 41, 50, 84, 85	ss. 3–5
3. Legal rights	Common law; Criminal Code	ss. 7–14
4. Economic rights	Common-law rights re: contract, property, mobility, etc.	s. 6 (and implied under some other sections)
5. Equality rights	Common law; s. 93 of Constitution Act, 1867, guaranteeing educational rights of religious denominations	ss. 15, 28
6. Language rights	Constitution Act, 1867 s. 133	ss. 16–23
7. Aboriginal rights	Treaties	ss. 25, 35
8. Social rights	None	Although not mentioned directly, some court rulings suggest that some social rights are implied

between provinces, it is silent in regard to economic rights. Moreover, the Supreme Court of Canada has declared on a number of occasions that the Charter does not include economic and property rights. '[T]he overwhelming preoccupation of the Charter', declared the majority in a 1987 decision denying the right to strike, 'is with individual, political, and democratic rights with conspicuous inattention to economic and property rights.'[11] This interpretation of the Charter has also worked against business interests on occasion. In particular, business's efforts to find some protection for property rights in the Charter's guarantee of security of the person (s. 7) have been expressly rejected by the Court.[12]

Denied explicit constitutional recognition of their rights, economic interests have urged their claims under what appear to be non-economic provisions of the Charter. This has produced some curious distortions, as the protagonists to a political conflict attempt to fit their claims into the categories available under the Charter and the interpretative tendencies of judges. Michael Mandel refers to this process as the 'legalization of politics'. Legalized politics, he argues, inevitably favours established interests and serves to reinforce the status quo because of what he and other critics claim to be biases built into the law and the legal/judicial profession. But 'the legalization of politics' does not express strongly enough the occasional *deformation* of politics that the Charter has encouraged. By this we mean that the issue is framed and arguments are advanced so that they fit the categories and concepts embedded in the Charter. In a non-judicial setting where the parties to a conflict

Media Spotlight

Box 6.2 Amnesty International on Human Rights Violations

For several decades Amnesty International has operated as a watchdog for human rights violations in countries throughout the world. Here are some excerpts from its 2004 report on one country:

- Indigenous women and girls, who have long been socially and economically marginalized in [this country], continued to suffer a disproportionately high incidence of violence. The authorities failed to implement measures to reduce the marginalization of these women and ensure that police understand and are accountable to indigenous peoples.
- Six men died in separate incidents after they were subdued by police using a Taser gun. Autopsies were pending in some cases. The authorities announced reviews of the use of Taser guns, but failed to suspend their use until an independent study was carried out.
- There was no response to Amnesty International's call for an inquiry into allegations of racially motivated violence against Albert Duterville, a prisoner at Port-Cartier penitentiary.
- Six men remained in detention pending deportation, pursuant to security certificates issued under the Immigration and Refugee Protection Act. In five of the cases the individuals faced a serious risk of torture if deported. Under security certificate proceedings, detainees only have access to summaries of the evidence against them and have no opportunity to challenge key witnesses.

The country is, of course, Canada. Are you surprised by this? Should Amnesty International's report on Canada be cause for concern?

are not obliged to make their case in strictly legal terms, but instead can rely on arguments about the public interest, efficiency, social and economic benefits, and so on, the political conversation and its resolution may be quite different.

On the Origins and Meanings of Rights

There is no inevitability to either the precise rights recognized by a constitution or the meanings that come to be associated with them. Rights, like a society's notions of justice, are constructed out of concrete historical circumstances. The rights that are claimed in present-day Canada and the rights discourses that emerge around these claims and counterclaims are very different from those of even a generation ago. And much of Canadian rights discourse would be unrecognizable in a society like Iran, where very different religious, cultural, and economic forces have contributed to the recognition of and meaning ascribed to rights. There are, therefore, no absolute rights that may be adduced from human history. What may appear to be the most obvious and uncontroversial rights claims—for example, the right to vote or the right to express one's personal beliefs—are denied in many societies.

Rights come from political struggles. A claim made by an individual or a group will be expressed as a right only when it is denied or placed in jeopardy by the words or actions of some other party. For example, the claim that a woman has a right to abort her pregnancy arises because of legal and practical restrictions on access to abortion. The experience of limitations on freedom of speech, religion/conscience, or association produced calls for their constitutional protection. Likewise, when a linguistic group claims the protection or promotion of their language as a right, this is an indication that conflict exists between linguistic groups in that society.

Political struggle is a necessary condition for rights claims. It is not, however, a sufficient condition. Only some political conflicts acquire the character of rights issues. To be recognized as legitimate, a rights claim must be successfully linked to one or more of a society's fundamental values. These fundamental values operate as limits on rights discourse.

Consider the familiar issue of abortion. Those who argue for a woman's right to abort her pregnancy when she chooses have often linked this rights claim to individual freedom of choice, a fundamental value in liberal-democratic society. Those who oppose abortion, or who favour serious restrictions on access to it, often argue that the human fetus has a right to life, the most fundamental of rights in any civilized society. Those who favour access to abortion would, of course, object to the imputation that they do not value human life, just as those who oppose abortion would deny that they undervalue individual freedom. Behind these rights, as behind all of the rights that are widely recognized in democratic political systems, rests one (or more) fundamental values, such as the equality of human beings, the autonomy of the individual, and, most importantly, the nature of the good society.

The abortion issue illustrates well the way in which rights claims tend to be squeezed into existing ideological and legal categories, and how unconventional political discourses are discouraged by legalized politics. When individual women, women's organizations, and abortionists like Henry Morgentaler have been successful in challenging legal restrictions on access to abortion, this has been because their case has been framed in legal arguments and moral claims that fall within the dominant ideology. Beginning in the 1970s, Morgentaler was involved in a number of court cases where he was charged with violating section 251 of Canada's Criminal Code, which placed limits on a woman's access to abortion. He was acquitted by juries on a number of separate occasions, each time successfully invoking the 'defence of necessity'. This is a common-law principle that, applied to medical procedures, provides immunity from criminal prosecution if the procedure is necessary to save the life of the patient. Pregnancy was treated, in these cases, as an illness and abortion as a medical procedure necessary to deal with it.

The passage of the Charter opened up new legal avenues to abortion advocates. In a 1983 Ontario trial, Morgentaler's lawyer argued that Canada's existing abortion law violated a long list of rights and freedoms that the Charter had entrenched in Canada's Constitution. These included freedom of conscience and expression; the rights to life, liberty, and security of the person; and the right not to be subjected to cruel and unusual treatment. Anti-abortion activist Joe Borowski invoked some of the same rights, i.e., the Charter's section 7 guarantee of life, liberty, and security of the person, arguing that the unborn fetus should be considered a legal person entitled to these rights.[13] Canada's abortion law was eventually ruled unconstitutional by a 1987 Supreme Court decision in which the majority ruled that it violated security of the person. But the same majority agreed that the state has an interest in protecting the fetus, although at what stage of fetal development and in what circumstances the Court did not say. This acknowledgement of fetal rights provided some encouragement to the anti-abortion coalition, whose political strategy focused increasingly on claiming the personhood of the unborn.

When appealing to public opinion and in arguing their case before the courts, both pro- and anti-abortion forces have resorted to symbols and values that are well-established parts of the dominant ideology. The temptation to do so is overwhelming. But there may be unintended consequences to fitting a group's objectives into the available framework of rights discourse and the concepts and interpretations that the legal system provides.

First, the issue may be incorrectly defined or, what amounts to the same thing, defined in terms that conform to prevailing notions of what rights are legitimate and what strategies are appropriate for pursuing them. This delegitimizes alternative ways of conceptualizing the issue—and even what is really at issue—and the discourses associated with these alternatives. For example, is the abortion issue primarily about 'security of the person' and about procedural fairness in the application of the law, the rights that have provided the basis for successful legal challenges to Canada's abortion law? Or is the struggle over abortion just an element in a larger political struggle involving competing notions of the good society and/or male domination of women? Most feminists would take the latter position, arguing that legal restrictions on access to abortion and the tendency in law to treat abortion as a health problem are manifestations of the social dominance of males; in this instance, of males defining female experiences. Frontal attacks, like those of the feminists against laws and traditions they consider patriarchal, tend to be labelled—and largely dismissed—as radical and unrepresentative of majority opinion. Not all women by any means accept the feminist viewpoint on abortion. Moreover, the sweep and general character of such critiques pose a strategic dilemma. 'Patriarchy' is not a concept that is directly recognized by the law. The law does, however, recognize various individual rights. Strategically, then, feminist women's groups have used the legal tools that are available in order to make a difference in the short term. But in succumbing to what Carol Smart calls the 'siren call of law',[14] the sweep and character of feminist demands may undergo change.

The second way in which recourse to rights discourse and the law may result in unintended consequences involves the idea that legal solutions to a problem are possible and desirable. '[I]n engaging with law to produce law reforms', argues Smart, 'the women's movement is tacitly accepting the significance of law in regulating social order. In this process the idea that law is the means to resolve social problems gains strength and the idea that the lawyers . . . are the technocrats of an unfolding Utopia becomes taken for granted. . . . [W]hile some law reforms may benefit women, *it is certain that all law reforms empower law*.'[15] (See Box 6.3.)

Smart's point is that law is only one of the possible means through which such matters as gender relations, energy consumption, lifestyles, and many other issues may be regulated. They may also be regulated by societal norms, by institutions such as the family, churches, the media, and schools, and by processes such as the market. None of these depend on the special knowledge of lawyers, the sanctions and rewards of legislation, or the power of judges. There may be very good reasons to believe that only a law-based policy can deal with a particular problem. At the same time, most of what we know about human motivation and the behaviour of institutions suggests very strongly

Politics in Focus

Box 6.3 Lawyers and the Charter

The support of legal academics for the Charter is part of the modern trend of the transfer of political influence to professional 'experts'. Keren has observed that all professionals 'derive their status from their possession of esoteric and easily monopolized skills and their political engagement may be seen as a means to increase the scope of issue areas in which those skills can be demonstrated. . . . The more social matters are discussed in professional terms, the more symbolic assets are translated into economic and political gains.' In the context of the Canadian Charter (and 'rights instruments' in other Western democracies), lawyers have a vested interest in redefining policy issues as rights issues, since the latter call into play their 'expertise' and marginalize the non-expert opinions of most legislators and voters.

Source: F.L. Morton and Rainer Knopff, *The Charter Revolution and the Court Party* (Peterborough, Ont.: Broadview Press, 2000), 145. Reprinted by permission of Broadview Press.

that legislators, lawyers, and judges will be inclined to view problems and their resolution through the lens of their particular training and interests. But reliance on the law may not always be the 'best' solution from the standpoint of efficiency, fairness, durability, general public satisfaction, or other criteria that we might consider important.

Rights and Their Protection

During the 1980–1 debate on constitutional reform, critics of an entrenched charter of rights warned that entrenchment would lead to the Americanization of Canadian politics. Since then, they have lamented that their prediction has come true. The 'Americanization' that they warned of, and that many still regret, has two main aspects. One involves a more prominent policy role for unelected judges, and a related decline in the status of elected legislatures. The other is an increase in recourse to the courts to solve political disputes.

Some of those who opposed entrenched rights argued that rights and freedoms are better protected by elected legislatures, accountable to the electorate for their actions, than by unelected judges. By 'better', they meant that the decisions of elected politicians are more likely to correspond with the sentiments of citizens—or at least that if they do not there exists a democratic mechanism, i.e., elections, to hold politicians accountable for their choices. Rights, the opponents of entrenchment argued, should not be interpreted independently of popular opinion. Nor should important political controversies be determined by unelected officials.

What the critics denounced as the undemocratic flaws of entrenchment, advocates of the Charter acclaimed as its virtues. Rights, they argued, should not be subject to the vicissitudes of public opinion as registered in the legislature. The fact that judges are not elected and are virtually immune from removal before the age of 75 serves to protect, not undermine, democracy. What sort of democracy, entrenchment advocates ask, would permit rights and freedoms to depend on shifting popular sentiments and politicians' calculations of political expediency?

The difference between the opponents and advocates of entrenchment is not over the importance of rights. It is not even primarily about the appropriate balance between the rights of individuals and minorities versus those of the majority. As unflinching a civil libertarian as Alan Borovoy argues against the entrenchment of rights.[16] The difference between these two positions is over how best to *protect rights*. Those who advocate the American model of entrenched rights prefer to put their faith in the Constitution and the judges who interpret it. Those who prefer the British model of parliamentary supremacy are more dubious about judge-made law and more inclined to place their trust in the prudence and democratic responsiveness of elected governments. (It is perhaps worth noting here that even in Britain the British model has been adapted to the contemporary reality of international law and norms that operate to influence domestic policy and erode the supremacy of elected lawmakers.)

Does the record of rights enforcement in other countries permit us to draw conclusions about whether the American or British model is 'best'? Has the Charter made a difference in how well rights are protected in Canada? There are no easy answers to these questions. Rights activists are themselves divided in their assessment of entrenchment's impact. But if definitive answers are elusive, we can at least attempt to understand how rights have been argued and enforced in Canadian politics. The Charter, we will see, represents an important watershed.

The Pre-Charter Era: 1867–1981

There is not a single reference to the subject of rights in R. MacGregor Dawson's *Constitutional Issues in Canada, 1900–1931*, published in 1933.[17] In Dawson's *The Government of Canada* (1947), the first textbook on Canadian government, one finds a mere handful of references to fundamental rights and liberties.[18] J.A. Corry and J.E. Hodgetts's *Democratic Government and Politics* (1946)[19] pays greater attention to rights, devoting an entire chapter to a comparison of civil liberties in Britain, the United States, and Canada. Generally, however, rights issues occupied a distinctly marginal place in Canadian political science and even in legal circles until the middle of the twentieth century.

A couple of factors were responsible for blunting the profile of rights questions. The most important undoubtedly was federalism. The Constitution Act, 1867 contains very few references to the rights and freedoms of Canadians. It does, however, include a very detailed catalogue of the 'rights' of governments, i.e., the legislative and fiscal powers of Ottawa and the provinces. Faithful to the principle of parliamentary supremacy, the courts were unwilling to overrule the authority of elected legislatures. As a result, throughout most of Canada's history issues that clearly involved the protection of rights and freedoms were dealt with by the courts as federalism questions. To have a chance at success, therefore, rights claims had to be packaged in the constitutional categories of federalism. In retrospect, the resulting jurisprudence was bizarre, to say the least. Consider the following cases:

- *Reference re Alberta Statutes* (Alberta Press case, 1938).[20] The law in question was the Accurate News and Information Act, passed by the Alberta legislature in 1937. It imposed censorship restrictions on the province's newspapers, based on the Social Credit government's belief that the press was unfairly critical of its policies. Ottawa referred this and two other pieces of Social Credit legislation to the Supreme Court for a ruling on their constitutionality. The Court was unanimous in striking down the press censorship law. Two of the judgements in this case referred to the 'right of free public discussion of public affairs' as being a right fundamental to parliamentary democracy and implied under the preamble to the Constitution Act, 1867, which states that Canada is adopting 'a constitution similar in principle to that of the United Kingdom'. But both of these judgements, although using somewhat different reasoning, suggested that the federal government possessed the authority to impose restrictions on freedom of the press. The Alberta law was, therefore, struck down essentially on federalism grounds.
- *Saumur v. City of Quebec* (1953).[21] The City of Quebec had passed a bylaw forbidding the distribution in the streets of any printed material without the prior consent of the Chief of Police. Without explicitly singling out any group, this bylaw was intended to curb proselytizing activities by the Jehovah's Witnesses sect, whose activities and teachings strongly offended Catholic Church

authorities. In a five-to-four decision, the Court struck down the bylaw. An analysis of the judges' reasoning reveals how disinclined they were to place the protection of fundamental freedoms over the authority of government. On the majority side, four of the five justices decided that the bylaw was **ultra vires** (i.e., beyond the legal authority of the government in question). The fifth was willing to concede that the regulation fell within provincial jurisdiction, but felt that the right to disseminate religious material was protected by Quebec's Freedom of Worship Act. On the dissenting side, two of the judges argued that the bylaw fell within the province's jurisdiction over civil rights. No one suggested that freedom of religious expression ought to be protected from interference by any level of government.

- *Switzman v. Elbling* (Padlock Case) (1957).[22] In 1937 the Quebec government had passed a law declaring illegal the use of a house for the propagation of Communism, authorizing the Quebec police to put a padlock on premises where such activities were suspected. The Supreme Court of Canada ruled that the impugned Act had the effect of making the propagation of Communism a crime. But criminal law is under the exclusive jurisdiction of Ottawa, and so the 'Padlock Law' was struck down as being ultra vires. The issue of political censorship was raised by a couple of justices, but this was not the basis for the Court's ruling.
- *Attorney General of Canada and Dupond v. Montreal* (1978).[23] This case involved a Montreal bylaw that restricted freedom of assembly in public places. The bylaw was used during the 1960s to prevent public demonstrations during a period of political turmoil and occasional terrorist incidents. By a five-to-three vote the Supreme Court upheld the constitutionality of this restriction. The majority argued that the impugned bylaw regulated matters of a local or private nature and therefore came under the authority of the province. Interestingly, the dissenting judges did not focus on the issue of freedom of assembly. Instead, they argued that the Montreal bylaw was ultra vires because it represented a sort of 'mini-Criminal Code' and thus intruded upon Ottawa's exclusive authority to make criminal law. As a final note, the judgement in this case was unequivocal in dismissing the relevance of the Canadian Bill of Rights (1960). 'None of the freedoms referred to', wrote Justice Beetz, 'is so enshrined in the constitution as to be above the reach of competent legislation.'[24]

Federalism was not the only factor responsible for the relatively low profile of rights issues until well into the twentieth century. Public opinion was generally sanguine about the treatment of rights and freedoms in Canada. The thinking of most informed Canadians was probably that rights were best protected by legislatures, the common law, and a vigilant public: the system that Canada had inherited from the United Kingdom. But increasing doubts about the adequacy of these guarantees were being expressed during the 1940s and 1950s. These doubts were sown by apparent rights violations like Quebec's infamous 'Padlock Law' (1937), the Alberta government's attempt to censor the press (1937), the threatened deportation of Japanese-Canadians in 1945–6, and the arbitrary measures taken during the Gouzenko spy affair of 1946. These constituted, according to political scientist Norman Ward, 'disturbing signs of a weakening concern by Dominion and provincial governments for personal rights and liberties'.[25] Corry and Hodgetts agreed, arguing that the protections provided under British parliamentary government were not sufficient in a young country facing the challenge of absorbing large numbers of persons of diverse ethnic origins and cultural backgrounds.[26]

This growing concern over civil liberties was shared by influential groups like the Canadian Bar Association. The solution, they argued, was a bill of rights that would be entrenched in the Constitution. Canada's participation in the United Nations, and the human rights commitments entered into through the UN, reinforced the voices of those calling for constitutionally entrenched rights. When the Conservative Party came to power in 1957 under the leadership of John Diefenbaker, who had long been an outspoken advocate of entrenched rights, the timing for a Bill of Rights seemed propitious.

But there was a major snag. A constitutional Bill of Rights would affect the powers of both Ottawa and the provinces and, it was believed, would therefore require provincial consent. It was clear that some of the provinces would oppose entrenchment; consequently, the Conservative government chose to introduce the Bill of Rights as a statute, requiring only the approval of the House of Commons and the Senate. The **Canadian Bill of Rights** became law on 10 August 1960.

The Bill of Rights proved to be a major disappointment for civil libertarians. The first Supreme Court decisions on its application were very conservative. In a case involving a challenge to the federal Lord's Day Act, the Court took the position that the Bill of Rights only reaffirmed the rights and freedoms status quo that existed at the time it became law (1960). Speaking for the majority, Justice Ritchie declared that '[The Canadian Bill of Rights] is not concerned with "human rights and fundamental freedoms" in any abstract sense, but rather with such "rights and freedoms" as they existed in Canada immediately before the statute was enacted.'[27]

After nearly a decade of judgements that, to paraphrase Saskatchewan former Chief Justice Emmett Hall, whittled away at the Bill of Rights,[28] the Supreme Court suddenly gave evidence of abandoning its cautious approach. The case involved an Indian, Joseph Drybones, who was convicted under section 94(b) of the Indian Act. This provision of the Act made it an offence for an Indian to be intoxicated off a reserve. In challenging this provision, Drybones's lawyer argued that it conflicted with the Canadian Bill of Rights guarantee of 'equality before the law', subjecting Indians to criminal sanctions that other people were not exposed to. This was obviously true. But if the Court remained faithful to its earlier interpretation, this would not be sufficient to render the discrimination unconstitutional.

By a five-to-three vote the Supreme Court used the Bill of Rights to strike down section 94 of the Indian Act.[29] This proved, however, to be an aberration. Perhaps realizing the Pandora's box they were opening through this more activist interpretation of the Bill of Rights, a majority of the judges retreated from this position after *Drybones*. This became crystal clear a few years later in the *Lavell* case,[30] where the majority upheld the constitutionality of another provision of the Indian Act against a challenge that it denied equality before the law.

Another nail was hammered into the Bill of Rights' coffin by the Court's decision in *Hogan v. The Queen* (1975).[31] In *Hogan*, a person suspected of driving while intoxicated refused to take a breathalyzer test before seeing his lawyer. He ultimately took the test and this evidence was instrumental to his conviction. The question before the Supreme Court was whether evidence should be excluded if it has been obtained in an improper manner. Under the common law, Canadian judges had followed the rule that such evidence would be admitted so long as it was relevant to the case at hand. But the Canadian Bill of Rights included a number of legal rights, including the right of an accused or detained person 'to retain and instruct counsel without delay' (s. 2[c][ii]).

The Supreme Court was unwilling to apply the Bill of Rights in this case. It appeared, therefore, that not only could the Bill of Rights not be used to strike down conflicting federal legislation—at least laws on the books before 1960—it did not take precedence over established rules of the common law. Chief Justice Laskin's dissenting argument that the Bill of Rights should be interpreted as a 'quasi-constitutional instrument' was never supported by a majority of his colleagues. The glimmer of hope that the *Drybones* decision had sparked was extinguished during the 1970s, producing renewed calls for constitutionally entrenched rights.

Before passage of the Charter, the only rights entrenched in Canada's Constitution were associated with religion and language. Section 93 of the Constitution Act, 1867 declares that the educational rights of denominational minorities may not be diminished from what they were when a province entered Confederation. Section 133 establishes the equal standing of French and English in Parliament and in federal courts, and in the Quebec legislature and in the courts of that province. Neither of these sections proved to be very effective in protecting minority rights.

The major test of section 93 involved the Manitoba Public Schools Act. This law eliminated the Catholic and Protestant schools that had existed in the province and replaced them with a single public school system. In *Barrett*,[32] the Judicial Committee of the Privy Council decided that this law did not violate the educational rights of the Roman Catholic minority because Catholics, like the members of any religious denomination, were free to set up their own private schools. Of course, they would have to pay for them out of their own pockets, in addition to having to pay the local and provincial taxes that financed the public schools. This, in the JCPC's view, did not diminish the rights they had enjoyed when both Protestant and Catholic schools were financed out of public revenues.

In two other cases involving section 93, the courts refused to accept the argument that this section also protected the educational rights of language minorities. The argument had at least a ring of plausibility because of the fact that, historically, the Roman Catholic schools in Manitoba were predominantly francophone and in Ontario they were often francophone, while Quebec's Protestant schools were anglophone. Thus, when in 1913 the Ontario government issued regulations banning the use of French as a language of instruction in both public and separate (Catholic) schools, this had a negligible impact on public schools but dealt a major blow to the predominantly francophone Catholic schools of eastern Ontario. The issue arose again in the 1970s when the Quebec government passed Bill 22, restricting access to the province's English-language schools, most of which were under the control of Protestant school boards. In both instances the courts rejected outright the claim that section 93 should be read as a protection for linguistic rights in addition to denominational ones.[33]

From the standpoint of promoting bilingualism outside of Quebec, the courts' unwillingness to read language rights into section 93 represented a real setback. On the other hand, the 'victories' for language rights in a pair of Supreme Court decisions handed down in 1978 and 1979 produced little in the way of practical consequences. Both of these decisions involved the limited guarantee of bilingualism established by section 133 of the Constitution Act, 1867. In both cases the Court declared that this guarantee was beyond the interference of governments, thus repudiating the idea that no action lay outside the competence of Parliament or a provincial legislature so long as it did not encroach on the constitutional powers of the other level of government.

In *Attorney General of Quebec v. Blaikie*,[34] the Court upheld a Quebec Superior Court decision that had ruled unconstitutional those sections of Quebec's Bill 101 that attempted to make French the sole official language in that province. While Bill 101 did not ban the use of English from the legislature and the province's courts, and the Quebec government continued to print and publish laws and legislative documents in both languages, the law's clear intent was to make French the only official language for all government activities and the dominant language in the province's courts. This, the courts decided, violated the spirit—if not the strict letter—of section 133.

The issue in *Attorney General of Manitoba v. Forest* (1979)[35] was essentially the same, although the circumstances were quite different. In 1890, the Manitoba legislature had passed a law making English the sole official language of the province's government and courts, and went the further step of actually banning the use of French in the legislature and the courts. This flatly contradicted the Manitoba Act, 1870 (an Act of the British Parliament creating the province of Manitoba), which imposed on Manitoba the same language requirements that section 133 of the Constitution Act, 1867 imposed on Quebec. Ironically, Manitoba's Official Language Act, 1890 had been ruled unconstitutional by a lower court judge in 1892 and then again in 1909. These rulings apparently were ignored by the provincial government. The successful challenge in the *Forest* case was a hollow victory, to say the least. In the words of René Lévesque, Quebec's Premier at the time, the decision came 90 years too late to make a difference for Manitoba francophones.

Life in the Charter Era

It probably is fair to say that the changes generated by the Charter have far exceeded the expectations of all but a few of the politicians and experts who presided at its birth. On a quantitative level, the Charter has been the direct stimulus for explosive growth in the number of rights cases that come before the courts. Hundreds of Charter cases are decided by Canadian courts each year, and in a typical year about two dozen of these have been rulings by the Supreme Court or one of the provincial superior courts. Between 1982 and 2003, 64 statutes or parts of statutes were struck down by the Supreme Court on the grounds that they violated the Charter,[36] but the Court is more likely to uphold the validity of a challenged law, as it has two-thirds of the time over the past two decades.[37] In the case of some laws, for example, the Immigration Act, the Income Tax Act, and the Criminal Code, dozens of Charter-based rulings have been handed down by the Supreme Court. An even greater number of provincial laws have been the subject of Supreme Court Charter rulings. Over the last few years about one-fifth of the rulings handed down by the Supreme Court involved constitutional matters based on the Charter.[38]

In terms of 'quality', the change produced by the Charter has been no less pronounced. The previous pattern of deciding rights issues as federalism cases, asking only whether a government was transgressing the jurisdictional turf of the other level of government, has been abandoned. Rights issues are now dealt with head on, argued by litigants, and decided by judges on the basis of the Charter. Moreover, the courts have shed most of their traditional reluctance to question the substance of duly enacted laws and regulations. Emboldened by the Charter's unambiguous declarations that the 'Constitution is the supreme law of Canada' and that the courts have exclusive authority to interpret and enforce the Charter's guarantees, judges have struck down provisions in dozens of federal and provincial statutes. As we will see, although judges are quite aware of the expanded role they play in the political process, most of them insist that there is nothing undemocratic in this and that it is quite incorrect to assert, as some do, that judges now have too much power.

Since the Charter of Rights and Freedoms was entrenched in the Constitution, the Supreme Court of Canada has assumed a much more prominent role in our political system.

Reasonable Limits and the Charter

The courts are 'invited' to exercise self-restraint, commonly called **judicial restraint**, by the opening words of the Charter. Section 1 declares that the guarantees set forth in the Charter shall be 'subject only to such reasonable limits prescribed by law as can be demonstrably justified in a free and democratic society'. What are these **reasonable limits**? The Supreme Court established a test in the case of *The Queen v. Oakes* (1986).[39] The first part of this test asks whether a government's objective in limiting a right is of sufficient importance to warrant such an encroachment. The second part of the test asks whether the extent of the limitation is proportionate to the importance of the government's objective. In order to satisfy this second criterion, a limitation must meet three conditions: (1) it must be rationally connected to the government's objective; (2) it should impair the right in question as little as is necessary to meet the government's objective; and (3) the harm done to rights by a limitation must not exceed the good that it accomplishes.

In *Oakes*, the Court was called upon to determine whether a 'reverse onus' provision in the Narcotic Control Act violated the presumption of innocence set forth in section 11(d) of the Charter. Under that Act, a person found guilty of possessing drugs was automatically considered guilty of trafficking unless he could prove his innocence on this more serious charge. The Court did not question the importance of the objective associated with this provision of the Act, i.e., to prevent drug trafficking. But in applying the second part of the test that they developed in *Oakes*, the justices decided that the means was disproportionate to the end.

The separation of legislative ends, part one of the ***Oakes* test**, from an assessment of the means used to accomplish them may appear to be a way around the thorny problem of judges second-guessing the decisions of duly elected governments. In fact, however, it is not possible to answer such questions as whether a right is impaired as little as possible in the circumstances, or whether the means are proportionate to the ends without trespassing into the realm of political value judgements. Since *Oakes*, the courts have been reluctant to question the ends associated with laws and regulations limiting rights. But they have not been shy about using the second part of the *Oakes* test to dismiss governments' section 1 justifications.

This was apparent in the Supreme Court's decision in *Ford v. Attorney General of Quebec* (1988).[40] The case involved a challenge to those sections of Quebec's Bill 101 that prohibited commercial advertising in languages other than French. The Quebec government argued that this limitation was necessary in order to preserve the economic value of the French language and the predominantly French character of the province. The Court accepted that this was a perfectly legitimate policy goal (it passed part one of the *Oakes* test), but argued that the Quebec government had not shown that 'the requirement of the use of French only is either necessary for the achievement of the legislative objective or proportionate to it.'[41] Not content to let matters rest here, the Court suggested what the Quebec government perhaps should have done to accomplish its legislative purpose in a way acceptable under section 1 of the Charter. 'French could be required', it suggested, 'in addition to any other language or it could be required to have greater visibility than that accorded to other languages.'[42]

In fairness to judges, why shouldn't they give legislators an idea of how the law needs to be changed to bring it into line with their interpretation of the Constitution? The point is, however, that means and ends are not neatly separable in the real world of politics. Moreover, tests like means being proportional to the ends just beg the question of *who* should determine how much or little is enough? Is proportionality an appropriate matter for unelected judges to decide, or should this be determined by elected legislatures?

These questions resurfaced with a vengeance when the Supreme Court ruled on 21 September 1995 that the federal ban on tobacco advertising violated the Charter's guarantee of freedom of expression. The total ban did not, in the eyes of the majority of the Court, satisfy the second part of the *Oakes* test. 'The government had before it a variety of less intrusive measures when it enacted the total ban on advertising', observed Madam Justice Beverley McLachlin. Commenting on the government's refusal to allow the Court to see documents pertaining to advertising and tobacco consumption, including one on the alternatives to a total ban on advertising, she added, 'In the face of this behaviour, one is hard-pressed not to infer that the results of the studies must undercut the government's claim that a less invasive ban would not have produced an equally salutary result.'[43] Anti-smoking groups responded to the decision by calling on Ottawa to use the notwithstanding clause to override Charter protection for tobacco advertising. Many staunch Charter boosters became skeptics overnight. They were awakened by the tobacco advertising decision to a basic truth of constitutionally entrenched rights: the price of entrenchment is that judges assume a more important role in political life.

The Notwithstanding Clause: Section 33

'What the Charter gives, the legislature may take away.' This appears to be the meaning of section 33 of the Charter, the **notwithstanding clause**. It states that either Parliament or a provincial legislature may expressly declare that a law shall operate even if it offends against section 2 or sections 7–15 of the Charter. This provision was not part of Ottawa's original Charter proposal, but was inserted at the insistence of several provinces. Indeed, it appears that federal–provincial agreement on the constitutional deal that produced the Charter would have died without this concession.[44]

Although the notwithstanding clause appears to provide governments with a constitutional escape hatch from much of Charter, it is not clear that it actually has this effect. It has been resorted to on only a handful of occasions. Why have governments generally been reluctant to use section 33 to avoid or reverse court decisions declaring their laws to be in violation of the Charter? In the words of civil libertarian Alan Borovoy, 'The mere introduction of a bill to oust the application of the Charter would likely spark an enormous controversy. . . . Without solid support in the legislature and the community, a government would be very reluctant to take the heat that such action would invariably generate.'[45]

Borovoy's confidence that public support for the Charter and vigilant media provide adequate protection against section 33 is not shared by everyone. Civil liberties groups and the legal profession have generally been outspokenly critical of the notwithstanding clause, to the point that a court challenge was launched against it immediately after the Charter was proclaimed.[46] The basis of this challenge was that if the Constitution is the supreme law of the land, as the Constitution Act declares, then no part of it should be placed beyond the powers of judicial review. By this reasoning, a legislature's decision to invoke section 33 should itself be reviewable, and therefore able to be overturned, by the courts. In a 1985 ruling, the Quebec Court of Appeal agreed. This decision was, however, overruled by the Supreme Court of Canada in *Ford v. Attorney General of Quebec* (1988). The Court pronounced in favour of a literal interpretation of section 33—which also happens to correspond to the intentions of those provincial governments that insisted on the notwithstanding clause—requiring only that a legislature expressly declare its intention to override the Charter.

It appears, therefore, that there are no serious legal roadblocks in the way of a government using section 33 to circumvent the Charter. But in fact, it has been invoked on only a couple of occasions—if one does not take into account the PQ's policy, between 1982 and 1985, of inserting the notwithstanding clause into all laws passed by the Quebec legislature and retroactively into all existing provincial statutes. (These actions were part of a symbolic and legal strategy against the constitutional reforms of 1982, to which the PQ government had not agreed.) This suggests that there are significant political barriers to its use. Quite simply, governments do not want to give the appearance of denying rights to their citizens. There are, however, circumstances where the denial of rights inflicts little political damage on government and may even produce political dividends.

This effect was certainly true of the Quebec Liberal government's decision to use the notwithstanding clause to re-pass, with some modifications, the provisions of Bill 101 that had been ruled unconstitutional by the Supreme Court (see Chapter 12). Public opinion, the province's francophone media, and the opposition PQ all were strongly supportive of legislative restrictions on the use of languages other than French. While the government's move precipitated the resignation of three anglophone cabinet ministers and drove many English-speaking voters into the arms of the newly formed Equality Party in the next provincial election, there is no doubt that the political costs of not overriding the Charter would have been far greater.

The political costs were negligible also when Saskatchewan's Conservative government inserted section 33 in a 1986 law passed to force striking public servants back to work. The government feared that, without the notwithstanding clause, the courts might rule that back-to-work legislation infringed the freedom of association guaranteed by section 2 of the Charter. Rather than run this risk, it chose to act pre-emptively to override this right. (As it turned out, the Supreme Court later decided that collective bargaining and strike action are not protected by the Charter.) Denying government employees the right to strike is popular with the public. Some analysts suggest that the Saskatchewan Conservatives' use of section 33 against public servants may even have produced a net gain in votes for the party in the election that followed about a year later.[47]

Do public opinion and vigilant media provide adequate protection against legislative abuses of the notwithstanding clause? Ultimately, the answer depends on our expectations for democracy. For some, the mere fact that public opinion may be overwhelmingly supportive of a law that denies rights to some persons is not a legitimate basis for invoking section 33. They would argue that if the Charter does not protect rights when they are vulnerable, guarding them from the 'tyranny of the majority', then it fails what should be the real test of its worth. Rights are either entrenched against popular passions and legislative assault, they would insist, or they are not. But for others, the notwithstanding clause is a mechanism for asserting the popular will in exceptional circumstances. The only other way of overcoming an unpopular court decision on the Charter would be to amend the Constitution, a difficult and time-consuming process. The controversy over section 33 is, in the final analysis, nothing less than the familiar debate over parliamentary versus constitutional supremacy.

Applying the Charter

News stories of yet another attempt to use the Charter to challenge some law or administrative procedure have become routine. These attempts range from matters whose social importance is obvious to challenges that appear trivial, even by charitable standards. Only a small fraction of the hundreds of trial court rulings on the Charter ultimately reach the provincial superior courts, and fewer still are appealed to the Supreme Court. Even so, a large share of the workload of these courts is now consumed by cases requiring them to apply the Charter. More than two decades after its passage it is possible to identify the main tendencies in judicial interpretation of the Charter.

To understand these tendencies, three issues are of special significance. First, how have the courts interpreted the Charter's scope and authority? Second, what difference has the Charter had on the relationship between the state and individuals? Third, what have been the Charter's effects on equality in Canada? The last two issues are, of course, fundamental to our assessment of Canadian democracy.

Scope and Authority

In its first Charter decision, *Law Society of Upper Canada v. Skapinker* (1984), the Supreme Court made clear its position on judicial review of the Charter. In this case, Joel Skapinker, a South African citizen living in Canada, had sought admission to the Ontario bar but had been denied because he was not a Canadian citizen. After an appeal court in Ontario ruled that he had been wrongfully denied on the basis of the mobility rights section of the Charter (s. 6), the case moved on to the Supreme Court, which, taking a cautious approach, ruled against Skapinker. Consciously modelling its position along the lines of *Marbury v. Madison* (1803), the landmark American Supreme Court ruling that established that Court's supervisory role over the US Constitution, the Supreme Court of Canada declared its intention to assume a similar role in applying the Charter. 'With the Constitution Act 1982', wrote Justice Willard Estey, 'comes a new dimension, a new yardstick of reconciliation between the individual and the community and their respective rights, a dimension which, like the balance of the Constitution, remains to be interpreted and applied by the Court.'[48]

How far would the Court be willing to go in using the Charter to strike down laws passed by elected legislatures? Here, too, the ruling in *Skapinker* borrowed from *Marbury v. Madison*. Although the Constitution must be considered the supreme law of the land, judges should interpret it in ways that 'enable [the legislature] to perform the high duties assigned to it, in the manner most beneficial to the people.'[49] In other words, judges should not be too quick to second-guess elected lawmakers.

Skapinker was more a broad statement of intent than a clear signpost. But a year later the Court was given the opportunity to show how activist it was prepared to be in applying the Charter. The case involved a challenge to procedures under Canada's Immigration Act, whereby applicants for political refugee status were not given automatic right to a hearing. By a 6–0 vote, the Supreme Court decided that this violated fundamental principles of justice. However, three of the justices based their ruling on a section of the Canadian Bill of Rights that guarantees the 'right to a fair hearing', while the other three went further in arguing that the right to a hearing is implied under section 7 of the Charter, guaranteeing 'the right to life, liberty and security of the person and the right not to be deprived thereof except in accordance with the principles of fundamental justice'. Justice Bertha Wilson took the most aggressive approach to the Charter, arguing that 'the guarantees of the Charter would be illusory if they could be ignored because it was administratively convenient to do so.'[50] At least some of the judges, then, demonstrated their willingness to take a hard-line approach to the Charter, whatever the administrative and political effects on government policy might be. As it transpired, the *Singh* decision resulted in thousands of additional cases being added to what was already a huge backlog of refugee claims, and precipitated the introduction of a new law whose intent was to limit refugees' access to Canada.[51]

Singh was followed by a string of 1985 rulings that defined in sharper hues the Supreme Court's approach to the Charter. In *The Queen v. Big M Drug Mart* (1985), the Court struck down the federal Lord's Day Act on the grounds that it violated the Charter's guarantee of freedom of religion. From the standpoint of the interpretive rules being developed by judges in applying the Charter (see Boxes 6.4 and 6.5), the most significant feature of the *Big M* case was the willingness of all of the justices to inquire into the purposes associated with the rights and freedoms set forth in the Charter. The Court signalled its readiness to go beyond the simple words of the Charter and the stated intentions of those who drafted it to interpret the historical meaning and social purposes of a concept like, in this particular case, freedom of religion. This approach is the very hallmark of judicial activism.

The issue of what the Charter's drafters actually intended was raised again in *Reference re B.C. Motor Vehicle Act* (1985).[52] In this case, British Columbia's Attorney General argued that section 7 protection for the 'principles of fundamental justice' was meant by the governments who agreed to the Charter to be a guarantee of procedural fairness (the issue raised in *Singh*). It was not, he argued, intended to enable the courts to assess the fairness of the 'substance' of laws. In rejecting the government's argument, the Court quite correctly reasoned that it is not always possible to separate substance and procedure. For example, a law whose substance is the denial of a procedural right associated with the principles of fundamental justice is both procedurally and substantively unfair. The majority was quick to add, however, that judicial review under section 7 should be limited to the criminal law and legal rights, and should not extend to general public policy. This declaration was intended to prevent section 7 from being used by any individual or group who believed that a law treated them unfairly.

On the question of what the Charter's drafters had intended for section 7, the Court ruled that arguments about intentions could not be binding for two reasons. First, it is not possible to state categorically what legislative bodies intended for the Charter as a whole or for particular provisions of it. Second, if the original intentions were treated as binding on the courts, then 'the rights, freedoms and values embodied in the Charter in effect becomes [*sic*] frozen in time to the moment of adoption with little or no possibility of growth, development and adjustment to changing societal needs.'[53] This implies, of course, that judges will determine what constitute 'changing societal needs' (see Box 6.5).

As reasonable as these arguments about legislative 'intentions' sound, it should be pointed out

Politics in Focus

Box 6.4 When the Charter and Crown Prerogatives Collide

The case of Omar Khadr is well known in Canada. Khadr is a member of a family that immigrated to Canada from Egypt in 1977. The family had ties to Osama bin Laden and several members fought against the NATO forces in Afghanistan. Omar Khadr was 15 years old when he was captured by American troops after allegedly having killed a soldier with a grenade. After recovering somewhat from severe wounding he suffered in the firefight with NATO forces, Khadr was sent to the Guantanamo Bay detention camp in Cuba, where he has remained since 2002. During much of this time he was not provided with legal counsel. His demands that the Canadian government intervene on his behalf and request his repatriation to Canada were rejected by successive Canadian governments.

Khadr's case eventually reached the Supreme Court of Canada. Here are some key excerpts from its June 2010 ruling:

> Canada actively participated in a process contrary to its international human rights obligations and contributed to K's ongoing detention so as to deprive him of his right to liberty and security of the person, guaranteed by s. 7 of the *Charter*, not in accordance with the principles of fundamental justice . . . . While the US is the primary source of the deprivation, it is reasonable to infer from the uncontradicted evidence before the Court that the statements taken by Canadian officials are contributing to K's continued detention. The deprivation of K's right to liberty and security of the person is not in accordance with the principles of fundamental justice. The interrogation of a youth detained without access to counsel, to elicit statements about serious criminal charges while knowing that the youth had been subjected to sleep deprivation and while knowing that the fruits of the interrogations would be shared with the prosecutors, offends the most basic Canadian standards about the treatment of detained youth suspects.
>
> K is entitled to a remedy under s. 24(1) of the *Charter*. . . . The appropriate remedy in this case is to declare that K's *Charter* rights were violated, leaving it to the government to decide how best to respond in light of current information, its responsibility over foreign affairs and the *Charter*.[54]

Khadr was awarded costs by the Court, but challenging the government's prerogative to make foreign policy decisions was a step that the justices were unwilling to take. After a plea bargain before an American military tribunal to avoid lifetime imprisonment by the US, Omar Khadr remained incarcerated at Guantanamo with the expectation of being repatriated to Canada in late 2011 to complete the last seven years of a reduced prison sentence.

that the Court has sometimes taken lawmakers' intentions very seriously. This was true in the *Quebec Protestant School Boards* (1984)[55] ruling, where the Court relied on the drafters' intentions for section 23 of the Charter in striking down the education provisions of Quebec's Bill 101. It has also been evident in other decisions, including *Re Public Service Employee Relations Act* (1987).[56] In denying that the right to strike is protected by the Charter, the Court argued that the drafters of the Charter were deliberately silent on economic rights. (The court changed its mind on this in the 2001 *Dunmore* decision, discussed below.) It appears, then, that legislative intentions do matter when judges find them convenient.

The issue of the Charter's scope was the focus of another of the Court's 1985 decisions, *Operation Dismantle v. The Queen*.[57] A coalition of groups opposed to testing the cruise missile in Canada argued that these tests violated the Charter's guarantee of the right to life and security of the person by making nuclear war more probable. The Court rejected this argument on the grounds that the alleged facts in the plaintiff's claim were in fact unprovable speculations. But the other question before the Court was whether cabinet decisions—the decision to allow cruise missile tests was taken by cabinet—and foreign policy defence issues are reviewable by the courts. The federal government argued that cabinet decisions are 'Crown prerogatives' and therefore off limits to the courts. The Supreme Court disagreed. It argued that section 32 of the Charter should be interpreted to apply to all government actions. On the precise question of whether foreign policy and defence issues are inherently political and beyond the reach of judicial review, the Court did not express an opinion. Twenty-five years later, confronted with a somewhat

Governing Realities

Box 6.5 Some General Principles of Interpretation That Guide the Courts in Charter Cases

The Charter is designed and adopted to guide and serve the Canadian community for a long time. Narrow and technical interpretation, if not modulated by a sense of the unknowns of the future, can stunt growth of the law and hence the community it serves. It is clear that headings were systematically and deliberately included as an integral part of the Charter for whatever purpose. At the very minimum a court must take them into consideration when engaged in the process of discerning the meaning and application of the provisions of the Charter.

The task of expounding a constitution is crucially different from that of construing a statute. A constitution is drafted with an eye to the future. Its function is to provide a continuing framework for the legitimate exercise of governmental power and, when joined by a bill or a charter of rights, for the unremitting protection of individual rights and liberties. It must be capable of growth and development over time to meet new social, political, and historical realities often unimagined by its framers. The judiciary is the guardian of the constitution and must, in interpreting its provisions, not 'read the provisions of the Constitution like a last will and testament lest it become one.'

Neither before nor after the Charter have the courts been enabled to decide upon the appropriateness of policies underlying legislative enactments. In both instances, however, the courts are empowered, indeed required, to measure the content of legislation against the guarantees of the Constitution.

It was never intended that the Charter could be used to invalidate other provisions of the Constitution, particularly a provision such as s. 93 of the Constitution Act, 1867, which represented a fundamental part of the Confederation compromise.

In *The Queen v. Big M Drug Mart*, Dickson J. elaborated on how the interests that are intended to be protected by a particular Charter right are to be discovered: 'in my view this analysis is to be undertaken, and the purpose of the right or freedom in question is to be sought by reference to the character and the larger objects of the Charter itself, to the language chosen to articulate the specific right or freedom, to the historical origins of the concepts enshrined, and where applicable, to the meaning and purpose of the other specific rights and freedoms with which it is associated within the text of the Charter.'

A hierarchical approach to rights, which places some over others, must be avoided, both when interpreting the Charter and when developing the common law. When the protected rights of two individuals come into conflict, as can occur in the case of publication bans, Charter principles require a balance to be achieved that fully respects the importance of both sets of rights.

Source: Excerpt from *Canadian Charter of Rights Decision Digest*, Appendix A, Box 5.6. Department of Justice Canada, 2006. Reproduced with the permission of the Minister of Public Works and Government Services Canada, 2011.

similar question, the Supreme Court ruled that when it comes to foreign policy and defence issues, 'the government must have flexibility in deciding how its duties under the royal prerogative over foreign relations are discharged [but] *the executive is not exempt from constitutional scrutiny*' (emphasis added; see Box 6.4).

An additional feature of the Court's approach to the Charter's scope deserves mention. This involves its insistence that the Charter applies only to relationships between the state and citizens, not to private-sector relationships. Thus, the Charter cannot be used by someone who believes that he has been denied a job or an apartment because of his race, or by a person whose private-sector employer requires that she retire at the age of 65. Forms of discrimination like these are pervasive throughout society, but they are not inequalities that can be overcome using the Charter. The Supreme Court has on several occasions articulated this distinction between public (covered by the Charter) and private, as in *Dolphin Delivery* (1986):[58] '[The Charter] was set up to regulate the relationship between the individual and the government. It was intended to restrain government action and to protect the individual.'[59] This position is, in fact, faithful to the intentions of those who framed and agreed to the Charter.

The Court's refusal to recognize economic rights is related to this public/private distinction. As noted earlier, the Charter is deliberately silent on economic and property rights, except for the qualified protection it extends to the right to live, work, and be eligible for social benefits in any province. Claims that certain economic rights are implied by provisions of the Charter have generally received a cold reception. For example, the courts have expressly rejected business's arguments that corporations should fall within the ambit of section 7 of the Charter, which guarantees the 'right to life, liberty and security of the person'. The economic rights claims of workers have fared no better at the hands of judges. In a 1987 ruling on whether a right to strike exists, the Supreme Court declared that 'The constitutional guarantee of freedom of association . . . does not include, in the case of a trade union, a guarantee of the right to bargain collectively and the right to strike.'[60] The right to bargain collectively and to strike are not, the Court ruled, fundamental rights or freedoms that deserve the constitutional protection of freedom of association under the Charter. 'They are', the majority declared, 'the creation of legislation, involving a balance of competing interests',[61] and their scope and limitations are appropriately determined by legislatures. To put it very simply, economic rights were viewed as subordinate to political ones.

It is sometimes said that today's dissent becomes tomorrow's law. This appears to be true in the matter of the Supreme Court's interpretation of freedom of association, guaranteed by section 2(d) of the Charter, and worker's rights. In *Dunmore* (2001),[62] the Court struck down as unconstitutional an Ontario law that excluded agricultural workers from collective bargaining rights that were available to other groups of workers. In reaching this decision the majority borrowed from the reasoning of the dissent in the 1987 *Re Public Service Employee Relations Act* decision, rejecting the view that the fundamental freedoms in the Charter are intended to protect political freedoms, but not economic ones. Then, in 2007, the Court did a complete about-face from its 1987 ruling in *Health Services and Support v. British Columbia*, accepting that collective bargaining rights are protected by the Charter's guarantee of freedom of association (see Box 6.6).

It may seem, then, that the courts have not strongly favoured either business or labour in their interpretation of the Charter, supporting arguments for economic rights in some limited instances, but denying them in others. In fact, this appearance of neutrality is deceiving for two reasons. First, business interests have been able to use some of the 'political' rights in the Charter to protect property rights, in some cases arguably at the expense of workers, consumers, or other community interests. Second, much of the inequality that exists in society is generated by private economic relations—relations between employers and employees, men and women in the workplace, landlords and tenants, buyers and sellers. To declare that the Charter recognizes only 'political' and 'democratic' rights but not 'economic' ones, as the courts have occasionally done, could have the effect of freezing the inequalities that currently exist in society and in the economy. Dominant groups tend to win from this public/private distinction, which places important sources of inequality beyond the authority of the Charter, while subordinate groups lose. The *Dunmore* ruling and *Health Services* suggest, however, that the Supreme Court has become less conservative in the matter of economic rights than it was in the past.

It is true, of course, that every major Supreme Court ruling on the Charter serves to clarify the scope and authority of judicial review. We have focused on several early Charter decisions in order to demonstrate that the Court very quickly assumed the mantle of judicial activism. How far judges go in using the Charter to strike down laws and administrative practices is, to a large extent, up to them. There are, however, two provisions of the Charter that were intended to rein in the courts' authority. One is the 'reasonable limits' clause (s. 1) and the other is the 'notwithstanding clause' (s. 33). In practice, however, neither of these has been very effective in limiting the scope of judicial activism.

Individual Rights and Freedoms

Some individual rights and freedoms are better protected today as a result of the Charter. Court decisions have expanded the rights of, among others, those accused of crimes, immigrants, women seeking abortions, and of business people wanting to advertise in English in Quebec. On the other hand, Supreme Court decisions (1) have declared that the Charter's freedom of association does not provide unionized workers with the right to strike; (2) upheld the constitutionality of terribly vague provincial anti-hate laws against claims that they violate freedom of expression;

Governing Realities

Box 6.6 On Freedom of Association and Collective Bargaining Activities: The Supreme Court Changes Its Mind

Freedom of association guaranteed by s. 2(*d*) of the *Charter* includes a procedural right to collective bargaining. The grounds advanced in the earlier decisions of this Court for the exclusion of collective bargaining from the s. 2(*d*)'s protection do not withstand principled scrutiny and should be rejected. The general purpose of the *Charter* guarantees and the broad language of s. 2(*d*) are consistent with a measure of protection for collective bargaining. Further, the right to collective bargaining is neither of recent origin nor merely a creature of statute. The history of collective bargaining in Canada reveals that long before the present statutory labour regimes were put in place, collective bargaining was recognized as a fundamental aspect of Canadian society, emerging as the most significant collective activity through which freedom of association is expressed in the labour context. Association for purposes of collective bargaining has long been recognized as a fundamental Canadian right which predated the *Charter*. The protection enshrined in s. 2(*d*) of the *Charter* may properly be seen as the culmination of a historical movement towards the recognition of a procedural right to collective bargaining. Canada's adherence to international documents recognizing a right to collective bargaining also supports recognition of that right in s. 2(*d*). The *Charter* should be presumed to provide at least as great a level of protection as is found in the international human rights documents that Canada has ratified. Lastly, the protection of collective bargaining under s. 2(*d*) is consistent with and supportive of the values underlying the *Charter* and the purposes of the *Charter* as a whole. Recognizing that workers have the right to bargain collectively as part of their freedom to associate reaffirms the values of dignity, personal autonomy, equality and democracy that are inherent in the *Charter*.

Source: *Health Services and Support v. British Columbia*, [2007] S.C.C. 27.

and (3) ruled that secularly worded Sunday closing laws have the effect of being an 'indirect and unintentional' violation of freedom of religion, but that they qualify as 'reasonable limits' under section 1 of the Charter. In fact, the Court's record has been quite mixed. It came down on the side of freedom of expression over anti-hate restrictions in the *Zundel* decision (1992) and over the federal ban on tobacco advertising (1995). In a major ruling on obscenity, the Supreme Court decided that Criminal Code restrictions on the distribution and sale of obscene materials violated freedom of expression, but that this restriction could be justified under the reasonable limits section of the Charter (*R. v. Butler*, 1992; see Box 6.7). In a 2001 decision the Court ruled that the Criminal Code's prohibition on possession of child pornography could in some circumstances violate the individual's right to privacy and could not be justified under s. 1 of the Charter. However, while indicating that possession of child pornography is in some instances protected by section 2 of the Charter, the thrust of the Supreme Court

Politics in Focus

Box 6.7 When Are Limitations on Freedom of Expression Reasonable? The Case of Obscenity

The *R. v. Butler* case involved a store owner accused of selling and renting hard-core videotapes and magazines, as well as 'sex toys' and devices, in contravention of s. 163 of the Criminal Code. Section 163 states that 'any publication a dominant characteristic of which is the undue exploitation of sex, or of sex and any one or more of . . . crime, horror, cruelty and violence, shall be deemed to be obscene.' The key words here are 'undue exploitation'.

The majority of the Court agreed that s. 163 of the Criminal Code infringes the Charter's guarantee of freedom of expression, but that this was a reasonable limitation on the grounds that governments have a legitimate responsibility to protect the community and groups in the community from harmful behaviour. Here is part of what they said:

> There is a sufficiently rational link between the criminal sanction, which demonstrates our community's disapproval of the dissemination of materials which potentially victimize women and restricts the negative influence which such materials have on changes in attitudes and behaviour, and the objective. While a direct link between obscenity and harm to society may be difficult to establish, it is reasonable to presume that exposure to images bears a causal relationship to changes in attitudes and beliefs. Section 163 of the Code minimally impairs freedom of expression. It does not proscribe sexually explicit erotica without violence that is not degrading or dehumanizing, but is designed to catch material that creates a risk of harm to society. Materials which have scientific, artistic or literary merit are not caught by the provision. Since the attempt to provide exhaustive instances of obscenity has been shown to be destined to fail, the only practical alternative is to strive towards a more abstract definition of obscenity which is contextually sensitive. The standard of 'undue exploitation' is thus appropriate. Further, it is only the public distribution and exhibition of obscene materials which is in issue here. Given the gravity of the harm, and the threat to the values at stake, there is no alternative equal to the measure chosen by Parliament. Serious social problems such as violence against women require multi-pronged approaches by government; education and legislation are not alternatives but complements in addressing such problems. Finally, the effects of the law do not so severely trench on the protected right that the legislative objective is outweighed by the infringement.

Source: *R. v. Butler*, [1992] 1 S.C.R.

ruling in *Sharpe* was to uphold the constitutionality of the general decriminalization of possession as a reasonable limit of free speech. Although the courts have not unleashed a torrent of individualism on Canadian society, it is fair to say that individual rights claims tend to do better, and certainly do no worse, under the Charter than previously.

This was certainly true in the *Big M* case, when the Supreme Court was called upon to decide whether the federal Lord's Day Act violated the freedom of religion guarantee set down in section 2 of the Charter. The Court had little trouble in deciding that it did. What could not be achieved using the Canadian Bill of Rights became possible under the Charter.

The courts' rulings on legal rights challenges to Canada's criminal law provide another clear illustration of the more liberal treatment of individual rights in the Charter era. Charter decisions have produced many important changes in law enforcement practices, including the following:

- 'Reverse onus' provisions, requiring a defendant to prove his innocence of a charge, have been ruled unconstitutional.
- Evidence obtained by inappropriate means, such as confession obtained without informing an accused person of his right to legal counsel, cannot be used to help convict that person.
- Writs of assistance, under which the police were able to enter premises at any time without a search warrant, were ruled unconstitutional.
- Search and seizure powers have been restricted.
- Thousands of persons accused of criminal offences have had the charges against them dismissed because of an Ontario Superior Court ruling that lengthy delays in getting them to trial contravened their s. 11(b) right 'to be tried within a reasonable time'.

In one of the most publicized Charter decisions to date, the Supreme Court struck down Canada's 20-year-old abortion law. Under section 251 of the Criminal Code a woman wanting an abortion required the approval of a hospital's therapeutic abortion committee. In most communities, however, the local hospital(s) did not have such a committee and did not perform abortions. Even in communities where hospitals performing abortions existed (about 20 per cent of all hospitals at the time), there was considerable difference between them in the likelihood that an abortion would be permitted. The majority in *Morgentaler* (1988)[63] ruled that the obvious practical inequalities in the application of the law violated section 7 of the Charter, guaranteeing the principles of fundamental justice.

The Court has shown, however, that it is prepared to override individual rights when other values appear to be at stake. This is certainly true in the case of the Supreme Court's willingness to uphold hate speech provisions of Canada's Criminal Code in the case of *R. v. Keegstra* (1990).[64] James Keegstra was an Alberta high school teacher who taught his students that the Holocaust was a hoax and that an international Jewish conspiracy pulled much of the world's political, economic, and cultural strings. He was charged under s. 319(2) of the Criminal Code, which makes it a punishable offence to communicate statements, other than in private conversation, that wilfully promote hatred against any identifiable group. In a 4–3 ruling the majority on Canada's highest court held that the content of speech, in and of itself, could be considered so offensive as to place it outside the protection of s. 2 of the Charter. They reasoned that the 'pain suffered by target group members', Canada's 'international commitments to eradicate hate propaganda', Canada's 'commitment to the values of equality and multiculturalism in ss. 15 and 27 of the Charter', and 'our historical knowledge of the potentially catastrophic effects of the promotion of hatred' combined to make section 319(2) of the Criminal Code a reasonable limit on freedom of expression.

The Supreme Court's ruling in *Keegstra* paid virtually no attention to the question of whether the messages communicated by the accused placed anyone or any group of persons in imminent peril. Such a test was considered to be wholly unnecessary. Instead, the majority accepted the argument that some speech is quite simply inconsistent with the sort of society that Canada is or ought to be and therefore should not be tolerated by law and protected by the Constitution.

Individual freedom of expression, as guaranteed by section 2 of the Charter, was again the issue in *Harper v. Canada* (2004).[65] The case originated as a challenge brought by Stephen Harper in 2000, when he was president of the National Citizens' Coalition, to legislated restrictions on the right of so-called 'third parties'—groups and individuals other than registered political parties and their candidates—to spend money on political advertising during election campaigns. In its 2004 ruling the Supreme Court upheld these restrictions by a 6–3 majority. The decision is particularly interesting because of the conception of democracy that underpins the majority's ruling, one that sees unfettered freedom of speech as a danger to the equality rights of citizens (see Box 6.8).

Four years later the Supreme Court returned to the issue of free speech in the case of *WIC Radio Ltd. v. Simpson* (2008). A radio talk show host and former British Columbia politician, Rafe Mair, compared the ideas of a local conservative activist, Kari Simpson, to those of Hitler and the Ku Klux Klan. Mair made the comparison in a radio broadcast that attacked Simpson's views opposing the use of

Politics in Focus

Box 6.8 Does the Ability to Spend Money during an Election Campaign Jeopardize Democracy?

The majority said . . .

In the absence of spending limits, it is possible for the affluent or a number of persons pooling their resources and acting in concert to dominate the political discourse, depriving their opponents of a reasonable opportunity to speak and be heard, and undermining the voter's ability to be adequately informed of all views. Equality in the political discourse is thus necessary for meaningful participation in the electoral process and ultimately enhances the right to vote.

[Third-party advertising spending limits] prevent those who have access to significant financial resources, and are able to purchase unlimited amount of advertising, to dominate the electoral discourse to the detriment of others; they create a balance between the financial resources of each candidate or political party; and they advance the perception that the electoral process is substantively fair as it provides for a reasonable degree of equality between citizens who wish to participate in that process. . . . The limits set out in [the law] allow third parties to inform the electorate of their message in a manner that will not overwhelm candidates, political parties or other third parties while precluding the voices of the wealthy from dominating the political discourse.

The minority said . . .

The effect of third-party limits for spending on advertising is to prevent citizens from effectively communicating their views on issues during an election campaign. The denial of effective communication to citizens violates freedom of expression where it warrants the greatest protection—the sphere of political discourse. Section 350 [of the Canada Elections Act] puts effective radio and television communication beyond the reach of 'third party' citizens, preventing citizens from effectively communicating their views on election issues, and restricting them to minor local communication. Effective expression of ideas thus becomes the exclusive right of registered political parties and their candidates.

There is no evidence to support a connection between the limits on citizen spending and electoral fairness, and the legislation does not infringe the right to free expression in a way that is measured and carefully tailored to the goals sought to be achieved. The limits imposed on citizens amount to a virtual ban on their participation in political debate during the election period, except through political parties . . . the Attorney General has not demonstrated that limits this draconian are required to meet the perceived dangers.

Source: *Harper v. Canada* (2004).

school materials and lessons that conveyed a positive portrayal of homosexual lifestyles. Simpson claimed that Mair's comments were defamatory and not protected by section 2 of the Charter.

Defamation—the impugning of someone's character or actions in a manner that results in real damage being done to that person's reputation, including such consequences as impairment of his or her ability to earn a living—is a private law matter. Like slip-and-fall accidents on private property or odours from a pig barn that a neighbour claims reduce his enjoyment of his property and its market value, such matters do not fall directly under the Charter. They are covered by the common law that emerges from judicial rulings on actual cases. However, as the Supreme Court stated in the *Simpson* decision, 'the evolution of the common law is to be informed and guided by Charter values.'[66] Mair argued that the doctrine of fair comment protected him against the charge of defamation. The Supreme Court agreed. Its ruling used the Charter values of freedom of expression and freedom of the media to broaden the defence of fair comment and limit the ability of plaintiffs to intimidate those who would make controversial public statements. The result of this 2008 ruling is that it is more difficult for public figures or organizations to successfully sue, arguing that their reputation has been damaged, and therefore less likely that journalists and broadcasters will censor themselves out of fear of incurring such lawsuits.

Is there an identifiable pattern in the Court's interpretation of the individual rights guaranteed by the Charter? Aside from what most commentators characterize as a moderately activist approach, the Court has shown few sharply pronounced tendencies. In the *Morgentaler* case, for example, the Court's decision was supported by three distinct sets of reasons. This is not uncommon, nor is it rare for the Court to be sharply divided in its interpretation of important provisions of the Charter. Even where the Court has adopted what appears to be a clear interpretation rule, it is difficult to predict how it will be applied in particular circumstances. Finally, it needs to be kept in mind that the Court is sometimes sharply divided in its approach to individual rights, as was seen in its 1995 ruling on Ottawa's tobacco advertising ban and in the 1990 *Keegstra* ruling on hate speech (see Box 6.9), where the minority on the Court claimed that freedom of expression 'does not protect only justified or meritorious expression. If a guarantee of free expression is to be meaningful, it must protect expression which challenges even the very basic conceptions about our society.'[67]

Equality and the Charter

Some Charter decisions have contributed to greater equality in Canadian society, but others clearly have not. Any attempt to assess the Charter's overall impact on equality is fraught with difficulties. But given that its supporters have always claimed that the Charter represents a major victory for democracy in Canada, and given the undeniable importance of many Charter rulings for public policy, the issue needs to be addressed.

Section 15 of the Charter deals explicitly with equality rights. Those who drafted this section, whose precise wording provoked as much controversy as anything in the Charter, expected that it would have significant consequences for the laws and administrative practices of governments. For this reason the equality section did not become operative until three years after the Charter was proclaimed. But in fact, section 15 has had less of an impact on equality in Canada than some other sections of the Charter and less impact than the federal and provincial human rights codes.

First and most importantly, it does not extend to discrimination in private-sector relationships. We have already discussed the practical consequences of limiting the Charter to abuses of governmental power. As constitutional expert Peter Hogg puts it:

> The real threat to civil liberties in Canada comes not from legislative and official action, but from discrimination by private persons—employers, trade unions, landlords, realtors, restaurateurs and other suppliers of goods or services. The economic liberties of freedom of property and contract, which imply a power to deal with whomever one pleases, come into direct conflict with egalitarian values.[68]

Although section 15 cannot be used to fight these private forms of discrimination, provincial human rights codes enforced by commissions do cover private-sector relations.

The potential impact of section 15 is also limited by the courts' unwillingness to treat equality rights as superior to other rights in the Charter or to other parts of the Constitution. Not only must the courts balance equality rights against the 'reasonable limits' provision of the Charter—this is a tightrope they must walk with all of the rights set forth in the Charter—they must also weigh section 15 rights against other rights and freedoms. How to strike this balance was the issue before the Supreme Court in *Re Education Act* (1987),[69] dealing with the constitutionality of an Ontario law extending full public funding to that province's Roman Catholic schools.[70] The Supreme Court ruled that the equality of religion guaranteed by section 15 did not override provincial governments' authority to grant special educational rights to Catholics and Protestants under section 93 of the Constitution Act, 1867.

In the final analysis the Charter and the courts send out mixed and sometimes confusing signals about equality. The same can be said, of course, about governments. Despite the courts' willingness to go beyond formal legal equality to see whether the effects of a law meet the requirements of the Charter (as the Supreme Court did in *Morgentaler*), the usefulness of the Charter as an instrument for overcoming the most prevalent and deeply rooted forms of social and economic inequality is limited.

Nevertheless, there have been cases where the equality guarantees of the Charter have provided the basis for fairly dramatic and controversial reversals of long-standing public policy. This was true of the Supreme Court's ruling in *M. v. H.* (1999), a case that involved a challenge to the heterosexual definition of spouses in the Family Law Act. In earlier decisions the Court had ruled that discrimination on the basis of sexual orientation is analogous to the enumerated grounds for discrimination proscribed by s. 15 of the Charter (*Egan v. Canada*, 1995). It came as no surprise, therefore, when the Supreme Court decided that the heterosexual definition of a cohabiting couple under the Family Law Act was unconstitutional, because it denied the same status and rights to homosexual couples. The Court determined that the exclusion of same-sex relationships from the spousal support provisions of the Family Law Act was not rationally connected to the objectives of the Family Law Act and thus could not be justified under the reasonable limits section of the Charter. Federal Justice Minister Allan Rock had already announced the government's intention to change the law so as to provide same-sex couples with the same status as heterosexual ones. The ruling in *M. v. H.* simply made this job easier.

After a decade and a half of considering equality cases without a systematic and consistent framework for assessing s. 15 claims, the Supreme Court developed just such a framework in *Law v. Minister of Human Resources Development*.[71] At the heart of the three-part test is the question of whether the differential treatment of the members of a group under the law is demeaning to human dignity. Recall that the Supreme Court has been very explicit since the early years of the Charter in insisting that the rights and freedoms guaranteed by the Charter should not become tools that the advantaged and wealthy can use to protect their status. In the Charter, especially its equality sections, the Court has suggested what might be described as an 'ameliorative' or 'progressive' purpose. The interpretive framework articulated in the *Law* decision is another step in the direction of the courts interpreting the Constitution with an eye to its impact on social relationships.

On balance, there is little doubt that what Morton and Knopff call 'equality seeking groups', a category that includes women, visible and religious minorities, the mentally and physically disabled, and homosexuals, have won victories using s. 15 of the Charter that probably could not have been won in a non-judicial forum and without the benefit of constitutionally entrenched equality rights.

In their interpretation of s. 15 of the Charter, judges have been sensitive to the social and economic context of the inequalities that appear before them as Charter claims. Indeed, many of the major Charter rulings read like sociological or historical treatises,[72] which is precisely what alarms many of the Charter's critics, who recoil at what they see as judicial usurpation of the legislature's function.

Judicial sensitivity to the broader societal and historical context of their interpretations of equality rights was very clear in the Supreme Court's 2008 ruling in *R. v. Kapp*. The case involved a group of non-Aboriginal fishermen who were charged with salmon fishing during a 24-hour period reserved under federal law to three Aboriginal bands. The non-Aboriginal fishermen claimed that the law violated their equality rights under the Charter by making legal distinctions based on race. The Supreme Court agreed that this law made such distinctions, but held that they were constitutionally protected by the affirmative action clause, s. 15(2), of the Charter. In arriving at this decision the Court reiterated its long-held view that s.15 guarantees substantive equality for Canadians, not identical treatment. This decision opens the door to the judicial consideration of evidence and arguments based on history, economics, and sociology. Indeed, this particular ruling included references to over 50 books, articles, and other publications on equality matters. This circumstance is not uncommon.

In 1991, Delwin Vriend was dismissed from his teaching position at an Alberta college on the basis of his sexual orientation. A series of courts cases ensued, with the Supreme Court of Canada eventually providing a landmark ruling in 1998. Under section 15 of the Charter, provincial governments cannot exclude lesbian, gay, bisexual, and transgendered individuals from human rights legislation. The case confirmed that though entrenched rights and freedoms are sometimes at odds with certain public opinions, the interpretation of the Constitution and the protection of rights is not a matter to be determined by popularity.

What is clear, however, is that the issue of when and how far judges should involve themselves in the determination of public policy has become increasingly prominent. Critics from both the right and the left of the spectrum have attacked what they believe to be over-willingness on the part of many judges to use the Charter to strike down government policies. By 1998 the chorus of criticism had become so loud and frequent that Chief Justice Antonio Lamer stated publicly that 'court-bashing' was damaging the reputation of the judicial system. Like their counterparts on the United States Supreme Court during the 1960s and 1970s—an era that saw America's highest court expand the rights of the criminally accused, declare that women had a constitutional right to abortion, ban prayer from public schools, and require the busing of children to achieve racial integration in schools—the justices of Canada's Supreme Court have discovered that judicial activism is not always received well by the public.

In an apparent response to a downdraft of negative media commentary about judges alleged to be arrogant and indifferent to public sentiment, eight of the nine members of the Supreme Court took the unprecedented step of travelling together to Winnipeg in April 1999. Their trip was widely perceived as a public relations exercise, intended to show that the Court was willing to break out of the cocoon of the nation's capital and get closer to the people. The current Chief Justice, Beverley McLachlin, regularly gives speeches in which she explains the Court's role to a wider public audience.[73]

But in fairness to the judges of the Supreme Court and of all the other courts in Canada, interpreting the Constitution is not supposed to be a popularity contest. If minority rights were to be protected by the courts only when it is popular to do so, these rights would be extremely precarious. Similarly, it is notoriously the case that the works and deeds of 'degenerate' artists, political 'radicals', religious 'oddballs', and all manner of non-conformists enjoy little sympathy in the court of public opinion. Entrenching rights and freedoms in the Constitution and then assigning judges the role of deciding when the actions of elected governments infringe these constitutional guarantees is fundamentally at odds with majoritarian democracy. It enables the views of a minority to triumph over public opinion—and sometimes the public reaction is one of outrage.

At the same time, however, it must be acknowledged that public support for the Charter has remained high across Canada. When judges use the Charter to make unpopular decisions, public ire is directed chiefly at judges rather than at the Charter. Critics too seldom realize that the phenomenon of 'judicial imperialism', a phenomenon that is far from being uniquely Canadian, is to some degree an unavoidable result of entrenching rights in the Constitution. In France and Germany, both of which have constitutionally entrenched bills of rights, criticisms that judges have encroached on the policy-making prerogatives of elected governments are not uncommon. This is, of course, a long-standing complaint in the United States, particularly from conservatives.

But why, one might ask, don't judges show greater deference to elected governments, as section 1 of the Canadian Charter of Rights and Freedoms would allow them to do? The answer to this question is complex and would require an analysis of the sociology and psychology of the legal profession from law school to the bench. Suffice it to say that under the influence of the Charter a new generation of lawyers and judges has acquired a more activist conception of the appropriate role of judges than existed in the past. Whether this is a good or bad thing is for each of us to decide.

Has the Charter 'Americanized' Canadian Politics?

Early critics of the Charter said that it would 'Americanize' Canadian politics. By this they meant that it would do three things that they believed were regrettable. First, it would elevate the importance of unelected judges and the courts, giving them a much more prominent role in determining important policy matters. Second, it would undermine the operation of parliamentary government in Canada by diminishing the authority of Parliament to determine the law and to be held accountable to the people, not to the courts, for its decisions. Third, it would generate a more litigious society in which individuals and groups are more likely to base their claims and political arguments on rights, making compromise more difficult and bypassing such political processes as elections and lobbying in preference for the courts. If a victory can be won in court, the critics charged, there will be less need to worry about winning victories in the court of public opinion. The end result of all this, the critics lamented, would be the Americanization of Canadian politics.

For better or for worse—and there are many people on both sides of this divide—much of this prediction has come to pass. Judges are far more prominent in policy-making than they were in the pre-Charter era. Parliamentary supremacy has been replaced by constitutional supremacy, with the Supreme Court as chief arbiter. And important and controversial issues are often decided in the courts or as a result of court decisions pushing governments in a particular direction. Despite these important changes, the Charter has not resulted in a wholesale Americanization of Canadian politics. Judges in Canada have tended to interpret the Charter's guarantees in distinctively Canadian ways, anchored in aspects of Canada's political culture that are different from those of the United States (Box 6.9).

This is demonstrated by the case of hate speech targeting a particular group. In Canada, the law and judicial interpretation of section 2 of the

Politics in Focus

Box 6.9 Is Hate Speech Protected by Free Speech?

Canada

Hate propaganda contributes little to the aspirations of Canadians or Canada in either the quest for truth, the promotion of individual self-development or the protection and fostering of a vibrant democracy where the participation of all individuals is accepted and encouraged. . . . Consequently, the suppression of hate propaganda represents impairment of the individual's freedom of expression which is not of a most serious nature . . . .

Indeed, one may quite plausibly contend that it is through rejecting hate propaganda that the state can best encourage the protection of values central to freedom of expression, while simultaneously demonstrating dislike for the vision forwarded by hate-mongers. In this regard, the reaction to various types of expression by a democratic government [and the criminalization of certain forms of speech] may be perceived as meaningful expression on behalf of the vast majority of citizens.

Source: *R. v. Keegstra*, [1990] 3 S.C.R. 697.

United States

The First Amendment generally prevents government from proscribing speech, or even expressive conduct, because of disapproval of the ideas expressed. Content-based regulations are presumptively invalid. From 1791 to the present, however, our society, like other free but civilized societies, has permitted restrictions upon the content of speech in a few limited areas, which are 'of such slight social value as a step to truth that any benefit that may be derived from them is clearly outweighed by the social interest in order and morality.'

. . . One must wholeheartedly agree . . . that 'it is the responsibility, even the obligation, of diverse communities to confront [hateful] notions in whatever form they appear', but the manner of that confrontation cannot consist of selective limitations upon speech. . . . The point of the First Amendment is that majority preferences must be expressed in some fashion other than silencing speech on the basis of its content.

. . . [T]he reason why fighting words are categorically excluded from the protection of the First Amendment is not that their content communicates any particular idea, but that their content embodies a particularly intolerable (and socially unnecessary) mode of expressing whatever idea the speaker wishes to convey.

Source: *R.A.V. v. St Paul*, 505 U.S. 377 (1992). <www.findlaw.com>

Charter stresses the *content of speech*, whereas in the United States the test of whether hateful speech directed at the members of a group is protected by the First Amendment is the *probability that actual harm may result*. Judges in Canada and the United States have taken significantly different approaches towards hate speech and its relationship to the guarantee of freedom of expression found in the constitutions of their respective countries. That difference boils down to this. In the United States, just because you say something demonstrably false and odious about the members of a group does not mean that you lose the Constitution's protection to speak your mind. If, however, this speech becomes what lawyers call 'fighting words', liable to incite violence, then it loses the protection of the First Amendment. But in Canada, some speech is considered to be so nasty that, by its very nature, it promotes hatred and is undeserving of constitutional protection, as is demonstrated by the majority opinion in *Keegstra*. Embedding protection for free speech in Canada's Constitution has not resulted in Canadian judges simply aping the interpretations of their American counterparts, at least not when it comes to hate speech. Moreover, the greater willingness of Canadian courts—as well as legislatures—to restrict hate speech on the grounds that some ideas and their expression contribute nothing to democratic life, and therefore can be restricted without doing any harm to freedom, is consistent with a cultural difference between these countries that predates the Charter era.

Starting Points for Research

Donald Abelson, Patrick James, and Michael Lusztig, eds, *The Myth of the Sacred: The Charter, the Courts and the Politics of the Constitution in Canada* (Montreal and Kingston: McGill-Queen's University Press, 2002). This collection of critical perspectives on the Charter challenges the idea of judges as neutral arbiters of the Constitution and argues that the Charter has been used by various groups to institutionalize their particular notions of justice and rights.

Alan Cairns, *Disruptions: Constitutional Struggles, from the Charter to Meech Lake* (Toronto: McClelland & Stewart, 1991). These essays of one of Canada's pre-eminent political scientists focus on the consequences of the Charter for Canadian politics and were written between the 1976 election of the Parti Québécois and the 1990 demise of the Meech Lake Accord.

Gerald Kernerman and Philip Resnick, eds, *Insiders and Outsiders: Alan Cairns and the Reshaping of Canadian Citizenship* (Vancouver: University of British Columbia Press, 2005). Many of the chapters in this collection deal with rights issues and the Charter's impact on Canadian politics and society.

Christopher Manfredi, *Judicial Power and the Charter: Canada and the Paradox of Liberal Constitutionalism*, 2nd edn (Toronto: Oxford University Press, 2001). Manfredi examines the tension between the political accountability of elected legislatures and the increasing power of the courts in this analysis of Charter decisions.

F.L. Morton and Rainer Knopff, *The Charter Revolution and the Court Party* (Peterborough, Ont.: Broadview Press, 2000). In this highly critical account of how the Charter has affected Canadian politics, Morton and Knopff argue that state-funded interest groups, an activist component of the legal profession, and judges themselves have been successful in using the Charter to advance a minority agenda.

Review Exercises

1. Find a story in the media that deals with the Charter. Summarize it, covering as many of the following points as are relevant:
   (a) What are the circumstances?
   (b) Who are the people or organizations involved?
   (c) What law/regulation/action/practice is being challenged?
   (d) At what stage is the challenge?
   (e) Are lawyers or other experts interviewed? Who are they?
   (f) What right or freedom of the Charter is at stake in this story?
2. What is the background of a Supreme Court judge? Visit the Supreme Court of Canada's website <www.scc-csc.gc.ca>. Click on 'About the Court', then, under 'Member of the Court', click on the name of a particular judge. In a paragraph or two, provide a profile of one of the current justices. (If you prefer, you may use a recent edition of *Who's Who* to acquire this information.)
3. What are the pros and cons of requiring that at least some judicial nominations—e.g., those for the Supreme Court and for provincial appeals courts—should be subject to open public scrutiny? The Conservative government held committee hearings on the 2006 nomination of Justice Marshall Rothstein to the Supreme Court of Canada. Is this model an improvement on the process that existed prior to Rothstein's nomination? Would some other model be preferable?

4. Compare the Charter of Rights and Freedoms to some of its counterparts in other democracies (simply type into your search engine the words 'constitution' and the countries that you are interested in—for example, France, Germany, and the United States—and you will find websites that provide this information). What are the main similarities between them? Are there any aspects of these other rights documents that you think should be adopted in Canada?

The view of what is best for Canada is not always the same from Ontario and Quebec as it is from other parts of the country, a fact that westerners in particular have often claimed is ignored by Ottawa.

7 Federalism

Canada's Constitution establishes two levels of government—national and provincial—both of which have important law-making and taxation powers. This system of divided jurisdiction is known as federalism. In this chapter some of the major issues associated with federalism are discussed, including the following:

- What is federalism?
- The origins, maintenance, and demise of federal states.
- The origins of Canadian federalism.
- The federal division of powers.
- The courts and federalism.
- Quebec's impact on federalism.
- Centre-periphery relations.
- Intergovernmental relations.
- Financing federalism.
- The federal spending power and national standards.

When the proposal to create an independent Canada was discussed at Charlottetown (1864) and Quebec (1867), the main subject of debate was the relationship between the new national and regional governments. Two decades of self-government and the constitutional traditions imported from Britain provided the colonies with ready guideposts for most other features of the Constitution. Federalism, by contrast, was uncharted territory. Most of the practical knowledge of the principles and operation of federalism held by Canada's founders was based on their observation of the United States. The lessons they took from the American experience were mainly negative. Secession of the Confederacy and the bloody Civil War of 1861–5 did not inspire much confidence in the American model. Despite all this, Canada's founders opted for a federal system of government.

What Is Federalism?

In a federal system of government the constitutional authority to make laws and to tax is divided between a national government and some number of regional governments. Neither the national government acting alone nor the regional governments acting together have the authority to alter the powers of the other level of government. They are co-ordinate and independent in their separate constitutional spheres. Citizens in a federal state are members of two political communities, one national and the other coinciding with the boundaries of the province, state, canton (the name given to the regional units of a federal state vary between countries) in which they reside.

'Federalism' is a legal term, and its existence is based on the constitution. If a single government controls all legislative and taxation powers in a country, then no amount of administrative decentralization or variation in the economic, social, or cultural characteristics of its regions will make it a federal state. Federalism is chiefly a property of constitutions, not of societies. Nonetheless, some political scientists refer to 'federal-type' societies, a tendency that has been labelled the *sociological approach* to federalism. Its most prominent advocate, American political scientist William S. Livingston, argues that 'the essence of federalism lies not in the constitutional or institutional structure but in the society itself.'[1] 'Federalism', Livingston declares, 'is a function of societies.'[2]

Which understanding of federalism is correct, the constitutional or sociological one? The answer must be the constitutional approach, for two reasons. First, if federalism is primarily a quality of societies, not of constitutions, then relatively few countries would *not* be federal. After all, most societies have politically significant ethnic or linguistic minorities, often concentrated in a particular region of the country. In fact, of those political systems with federal constitutions, only India places in the world's top 10 countries ranked according to their level of ethnic and linguistic diversity. Canada is 19th, Belgium is 49th, Switzerland and the United States tie at 54th place, and Australia comes in at 69th.[3] Thus, federalism does not appear to be an intrinsic characteristic of pluralistic societies but of those with federal constitutions.

The second reason for preferring the constitutional approach to federalism involves the dynamic of state power. A federal constitution institutionalizes regional divisions by associating them with different governments. The regionalism that is responsible for the adoption of a federal constitution in the first place is reinforced by political and administrative rivalries between the national and regional governments. Regional politics can certainly take place in the absence of a federal constitution. But the political significance of regional differences tends to be elevated by associating them with different political jurisdictions and the governments' bureaucracies that preside over them.

Federalism divides political authority along territorial lines. It is not, however, the only form of government to do so. Important policy-making and administrative powers may be exercised at the regional level even in a unitary state. The extent to which these activities are *decentralized*, i.e., placed in the hands of regional officials, or remain *centralized* at the national level is determined by the particular social, geographic, and political conditions of a country. This is also true of federal states, where the constitution provides only a partial and sometimes very misleading guide to the real division of powers between governments. Political authority is also linked to territory in *confederations* and *economic communities*. These are formal groupings of independent states that have agreed to assign certain legislative and administrative functions to a common institution or set of institutions. All member states have a say—though not necessarily an equal say—in the decision-making of such a body, while at the same time retaining their ultimate sovereignty (see Box 7.1).

The Origins, Maintenance, and Demise of Federal States

Only about two dozen of the 192 member countries of the United Nations have a federal system of government. This is an estimate of the actual number of federal states because the determination of whether a political system is federal is not an exact science (see Figure 7.1). For example, Mexico, Argentina, and Russia generally are included in the club of federal states, but the central governments of these countries have sometimes interfered with the autonomy of state governments. How many countries actually belong to the federalism club is less important than the fact that the club is a small one, although it does include some of the world's largest and most powerful countries. Unitary government is far more popular, even in countries where regionally based political conflicts are strong.

What are the circumstances that lead to the adoption of a federal political system? Although there is no simple answer, it is possible to identify a very general condition that is present at the birth of all federal states, and vital to the continued health of a federal union. This condition involves agreement among the regional components of the federal state that the benefits of being part of the union exceed whatever costs membership may impose. A federal state is based, therefore, on a *consensus of regions*. Students of international law and federalism disagree over whether any part of a federal state has a legal right to break away from the union. But the political facts are that when a region no longer shares the

Governing Realities

Box 7.1 Territory and Political Authority

In the *unitary* form of government, even when there is a good measure of administrative or legislative devolution or decentralization, sovereignty, or competence resides exclusively with the central government, and regional or local governments are legally and politically subordinate to it.

In the *federal* form of government, sovereignty or competence is distributed between central and provincial (or state) governments so that, within a single political system, neither order of government is legally or politically subordinate to the other, and each order of government is elected by and exercises authority directly on the electorate.

In the *confederal* form of government, even where there is a considerable allocation of responsibilities to central institutions or agencies, the ultimate sovereignty is retained by the member-state governments and, therefore, the central government is legally and politically subordinate to them. Furthermore, the members of the major central institutions are delegates of the constituent state governments.

An *economic association*, when it has common organizing institutions, is a confederal type of government in which the functions assigned by the participating states to the common institutions are limited mainly to economic co-operation and co-ordination.

Source: Canada, Task Force on Canadian Unity, *Coming to Terms: The Words of the Debate* (Hull, Que.: Supply and Services Canada, 1979), 21–2; emphasis added.

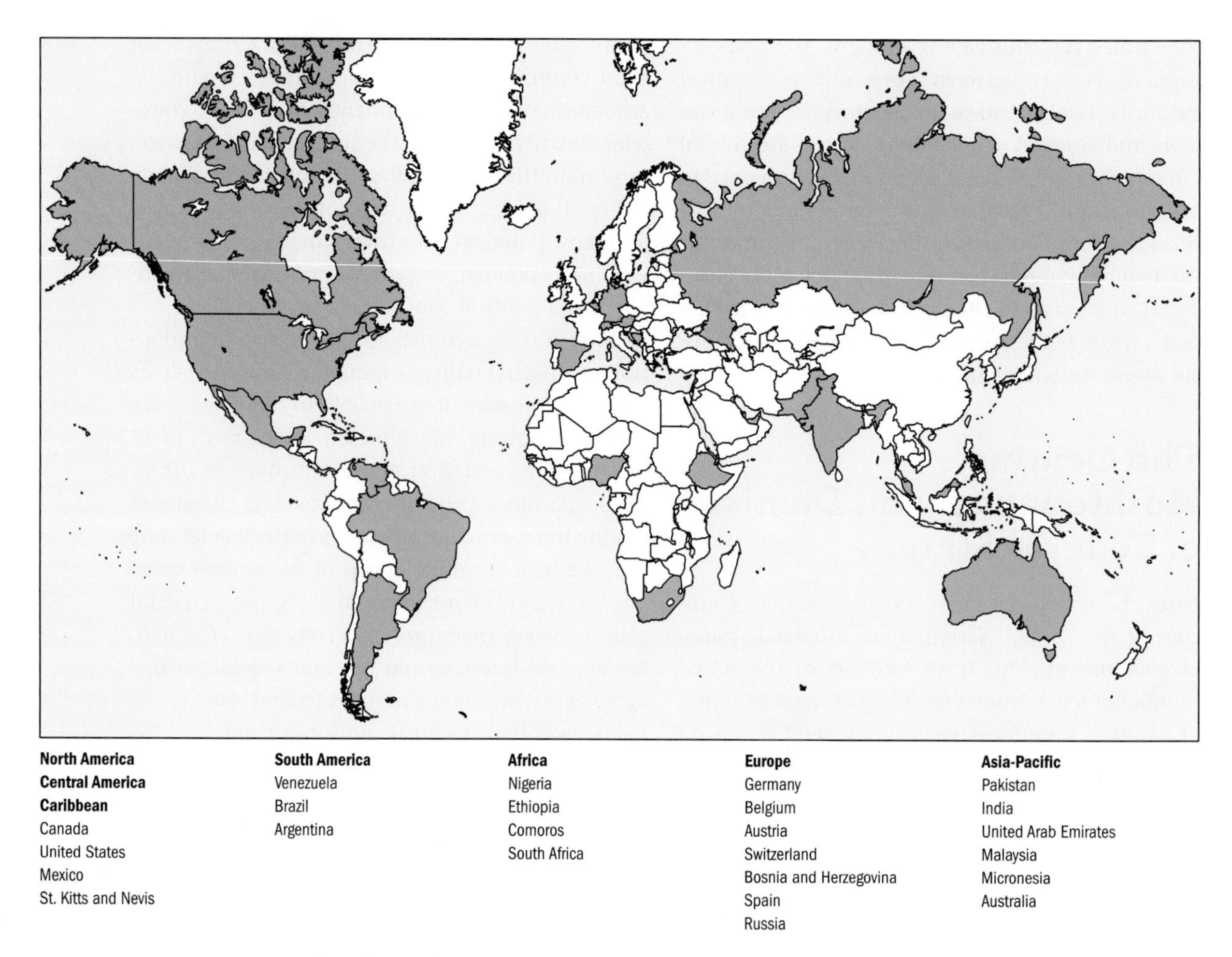

FIGURE 7.1 Federalism throughout the World

Source: Privy Council Office website, 'Federation Maps and Fact Sheets' at: <www.pco-bcp.gc.ca/>.

national consensus on which federalism is based, its separation becomes a real possibility.

'Federalism', declared Pierre Trudeau, 'has all along been a product of reason in politics. . . . it is an attempt to find a rational compromise between the divergent interest groups which history has thrown together; but it is a compromise based on the will of the people.'[4] This is why federal unions often are referred to as 'pacts', 'contracts', or 'bargains'. The key role of consent may be seen in the case of the former Soviet Union. As part of the post–World War II deal between the Soviet Union and the US-led Western democracies, the countries of Estonia, Latvia, and Lithuania were made members of the Soviet 'federal' state against their will. Their unwilling entry into the Soviet Union, combined with the fact that Moscow dominated the regional republics through the Communist Party's monopoly on power, exposed the hollowness of the Soviet Union's federal pretensions. But with the 1989 abolition of the Communist Party's legal monopoly on power and the greater autonomy enjoyed by the regional republics, the Soviet Union fell apart. Without even a minimal consensus on the desirability of maintaining the central government, and without the Communist Party and Red Army to keep them in check, republic after republic declared national independence.

Trudeau's argument that federalism is the product of reason will not convince Quebec separatists, whose view of 1867 is of a sell-out by an elite of 'cannibal kings'[5] who were willing to collaborate with the Anglo-Saxon oppressor. Nor does reason appear to be the chief factor explaining why disgruntled regions remain part of a federal union when their politicians and their people clearly believe that they are treated unfairly and exploited for the benefit of other regions—a century-old view in western Canada. Some argue that the 'reason' that leads to federal union or that sustains it may indeed be in the self-interest of some groups, but that federalism may not be reasonable from the standpoint of other groups' self-interest.

Nevertheless, federal democracies originated in compromise. The fact that some regions are more enthusiastic than others about the federal compromise—indeed, some may enter it only in despair at the lack of viable alternatives—does not diminish the voluntary consent of the regions forming the basis of a federal union. Once established, however, a federal state may achieve a new dynamic. The existence of a national government and the idea of national citizenship can be centralizing factors that offset the decentralizing pull of regional interests. Federalism is sustained, then, not by sheer rational calculations on the part of regional populations and politicians. Instead, it is sustained by a *sense of political nationality*. According to Donald Smiley, who for two decades was Canada's foremost expert on federalism, political nationality 'means that Canadians as such have reciprocal moral and legal claims upon one another that have no precise counterparts in their relations with others, and that Canadians as such have a continuing determination to carry out a significant number of important common activities together.'[6] It is, in short, a sense of political community that transcends regional, ethnic, and linguistic identifications, although it does not replace or necessarily overshadow the other identities that citizens have of themselves.

Federalism ultimately is sustained by the sense of political nationality—or community—that develops around the national state. By the same token, the breakup of a federal state is sure to be presaged by the deterioration of this sense of community. Sometimes a sense of political nationality is never solidly established in the first place, as it was not in post-independence Nigeria, whose post-colonial federal system immediately came under stress and collapsed from within shortly after having been adopted. In other cases a fragile political nationality may be destroyed by a particularly divisive regional conflict, as American federalism was split asunder by the slavery issue. The most stable federal systems are those where regional communities share in a sense of political nationality that dampens the decentralizing tendencies produced by regional differences. Switzerland, the contemporary United States, and Austria are good examples of such stability. The Swiss case in particular demonstrates regionally based ethnolinguistic divisions that do not necessarily prevent the development of a durable political nationality.

To say that a weak sense of political nationality is associated with unstable federalism really is tautological: What determines the strength of political nationality? Why do regional divisions acquire the status of independence movements in some federal states but not in others? Several factors come into play, but the most basic is regional inequality. If the citizens of a particular region feel strongly that existing federal structures discriminate against their interests economically and politically, this inequity places a strain on the sense of political nationality. Sentiments like these are very common. A 2005 survey by the Centre for Research and Information on Canada found that Ontarians were almost twice as likely as Canadians in most other provinces to believe that their province was treated with the respect it deserved.[7] Studies show, however, that there is no direct correlation between the answer to such a question and the level of affection and loyalty that provincial populations feel towards Canada. Nor do strong provincial identities appear to prevent their holders from identifying also with Canada. As Roger Gibbins has observed, it is probably a mistake to think of national and provincial loyalties as competitive, although the case of Quebec is the exception to this rule.

The likelihood that regional grievances may threaten the stability of federalism is greatest when they are linked to a nationalist movement. Nationalism usually is accompanied by territorial claims. These claims can range from demands for outright independence to more moderate calls for greater autonomy for the region where members of the national community are concentrated. What distinguishes nationalism from regionalism is that nationalism makes its demands on behalf of both a territory and a community that shares some ethnic, linguistic, or other cultural traits. This is far more difficult to accommodate within a federal state than is a region's complaints of unfair treatment. Indeed, nationalism that is linked to the social and cultural characteristics of a group is fundamentally at odds with the concept of political nationality on which a viable federal state depends (see Box 7.2).

The Origins of Canadian Federalism

Canada's federal Constitution was a compromise. Most of the anglophone Fathers of Confederation favoured a unitary system of government under which all power would be in the hands of a new national parliament. They were opposed, however, by two groups. The strongest opposition came from the French-Canadian representatives of Canada East, what today is Quebec. This group, led by George-Étienne Cartier, insisted on constitutional protection for their cultural community. They believed that the most effective way to protect their

Politics in Focus

Box 7.2 Language, Nationalism, and Federalism

This country has two major language communities that have coexisted sometimes on uneasy terms since the country achieved independence in the nineteenth century. One of these communities has a significant nationalist movement that includes a couple of political parties committed to independence for their national community. Many of this country's citizens believe that their language community and region has subsidized public services and incomes in the other community for decades and they feel resentful. This resentment is deepened by historical memories of social and political inequality between the two communities. As of 2010, the prospects for their continued cohabitation seem weak. The country described here is Belgium.

Over the years Belgium has been compared frequently to Canada, facing some rather similar challenges and attempting to manage conflict between its two main language communities, French and Flemish (Belgium also has a very small German-speaking official-language community), through a federal constitution. Unlike Canada, however, the nationalist movement that aspires to break up the country is associated with the wealthier majority community—the Flemish-speaking north of the country. In the national election of 2010 the most popular political party in the Flemish region of the country was the Flemish Nationalist Party (N-VA), a party committed to independence and led by a multilingual historian whose victory speech began with the words, 'Nil volentibus arduum' (For those who have the will, nothing is impossible).

Comparisons between Belgium and Canada can be misleading. Nevertheless, political scientists and constitutionalists from each country have looked to the other to find answers about what does and does not work in managing inter-community relations in a federal state. If recent developments in Belgium hold any lessons for Canada, the main one probably is this: when the ties of identity and shared cultural values that bridge the language gap between communities are weak, and when one group believes that existing state institutions treat it unfairly, federalism is in trouble. The compromise at the heart of federalism's viability ultimately depends on the sentiment of the people or, more precisely, the *peoples* who live together under a federal constitution. This is what the French historian Ernest Renan meant when he said that federalism is a daily referendum of the popular will.

interests was through a federal union that gave exclusive jurisdiction over linguistic and cultural matters to the provincial governments. Federalism was also the preferred constitutional option of Maritime politicians. Maritimers had developed strong local identities that they were unwilling to see submerged under unitary government. Besides, in an era when politics and patronage were virtually synonymous it was only reasonable that provincial politicians would want to retain control over such important sources of contracts as roads and public works, as well as bureaucratic sinecures.

Although the anglophone politicians of Ontario and Quebec tended to be much less enthusiastic about federalism, some of them saw merit in the idea of dividing legislative powers between two levels of government. For example, Grit politician George Brown expressed the view that conflict between the English Protestant and French Catholic communities—conflict that had produced government instability and political deadlock in the legislature of the United Canadas and that was one of the reasons behind the Confederation movement—would be reduced by assigning local matters to the provincial legislatures.[8] Ottawa would deal with matters of national interest, like trade and commerce, immigration, defence, and transportation. The presumption that sectional rivalries and local interests would not enter into deliberations on these national issues was naive, to say the least.

The forces pushing the colonies of British North America towards political union required a strong national government. Commercial interests, particularly railroad promoters, wanted unification because their ability to raise investment capital abroad was linked to Canada's credit worthiness. A larger union with a wider revenue base and an integrated national economy was crucial to the railroad promoters' interests and to those of the Canadian financial institutions linked to them. Likewise, a strong central government was needed if British North America was to assume the burden of its own military defence and if expansion into the sparsely populated region between Ontario and British Columbia was to be accomplished. Tugging in the opposite direction were the facts of cultural dualism and the existence of colonial administrations and regional societies that were unwilling to be completely submerged in a unitary state that would inevitably be dominated by Ontario and Quebec. Federalism was a necessary compromise between these contradictory tendencies.

What sort of federal union did the founders envisage? Obviously, politicians had various expectations. Some, such as Canada's first Prime Minister, John A. Macdonald, anticipated that the provincial governments would be little more than glorified municipalities, subordinate to Ottawa. Others, like Oliver Mowat, who as Ontario's Premier led the movement for provincial rights during the 1870s and 1880s, clearly did not share this centralist vision.[9] Individual expectations aside, the agreement the founders reached gave the most important legislative powers and sources of public revenue of the time to the federal government. Ottawa was given authority over trade and commerce, shipping, fisheries, interprovincial transportation, currency and banking, the postal service, and several other areas of endeavour related to managing the economy. Responsibility for immigration and agriculture was divided between the federal and provincial governments, but in the event of a conflict Ottawa's legislation would prevail. The federal government was assigned the duty to build an intercolonial railway connecting Montreal to Halifax. Together, these powers appeared to establish Ottawa's clear superiority over the provinces in economic matters. When we consider that promoting economic growth and military defence (also a federal responsibility) were two of the chief functions of the nineteenth-century state—maintaining public order was the third, and responsibility for this was divided between Ottawa and the provinces—there is little doubt that Ottawa was assigned the major legislative powers of that era.

Ottawa's superiority was clear on the taxation front. Donald Smiley notes that customs and excise taxes—indirect forms of taxation—accounted for about three-quarters of colonial revenues prior to Confederation. The Confederation agreement made these the exclusive preserve of the federal government, which could '[raise] Money by any

Mode or System of Taxation' (s. 91[3]). The provinces were restricted to the less developed field of 'Direct Taxation' (s. 92[2]), as well as royalties on provincially owned natural resources (s. 109). Not only were provincial revenue sources meagre compared to those of the federal government, the Confederation agreement also established the practice of federal money transfers to the provinces (s. 118, repealed in 1950). The dependence of the economically weaker provinces on subsidies from Ottawa began in 1867 and continues to this day (see the discussion later in this chapter).

In addition to all this, the Confederation agreement included several provisions that have been described as *quasi-federal*. They appear to establish a nearly colonial relationship between Ottawa and the provinces by permitting the federal government to disallow laws passed by provincial legislatures. Sections 55, 56, and 90 of the Constitution Act, 1867 give provincial lieutenant-governors, appointees of Ottawa, the authority to reserve approval from any Act passed by a provincial legislature for a period of up to one year, or to disallow the Act at any time within a year of its passage. These were widely used powers during the first few decades after Confederation and were used periodically during the first half of the twentieth century. In most instances Ottawa was reacting to provincial economic policies that challenged its own priorities and jurisdiction. Moreover, section 92(10c) gives the federal government the authority to intervene in a provincial economy by declaring that the construction of a 'public work' (this could be anything from a road to an oil field) is in the national interest. This power has been used 470 times, but has not been used since 1961. Finally, section 93(3)(4) actually gives Ottawa the power to pass laws respecting education, an area of provincial jurisdiction. It may do so where education rights that denominational minorities held when a province entered Confederation are abrogated by provincial law. This power has never been used.

Assuming that it is even possible to sort out the founders' intentions, do they really matter? Legally, no. In interpreting the federal division of powers the courts have generally been unreceptive to arguments about what the Fathers of Confederation really had in mind.[10] Indeed, the Supreme Court of Canada's ruling in the 1981 Patriation Reference, *Re Constitution of Canada*, declared flatly that 'arguments from history do not lead to any consistent view or any single view of

George P. Roberts/Library and Archives Canada/C-000733

The Fathers of Confederation at Charlottetown. Canada's entrance into federalism was far from a unanimous decision; rather, the system of divided jurisdiction was a compromise that made Ottawa the seat of national power to control collective issues such as defence, immigration, and trade, while leaving the provinces to preside over issues of a more local nature, such as culture and education.

the nature of the British North America Act. So, too, with pronouncements by political figures or persons in other branches of public life. There is little profit in parading them.'[11]

Politically, however, arguments about intentions can matter. The argument most frequently made about Canadian federalism is that it represents a compact between French and English Canada or, alternatively, a contract among the provinces that agreed to give up certain powers to a new national government of their creation. Both the compact and contract theories of federalism maintain that the federal 'bargain' cannot be changed without the mutual consent of those who agreed to it. In the case of the compact theory, this means that Quebec—the province in which most francophones reside and the only province in which they are in the majority—should have a veto over any constitutional change that affects either the federal distribution of powers or the relative weight of Quebec in Parliament and on the Supreme Court (where three of the nine justices must be members of the Quebec bar). This argument was rejected by the Supreme Court of Canada in the 1981 Patriation Reference.

Those who argue that federalism is a contract among the provinces claim that each of them has the right to veto constitutional change that affects provincial powers or national representation. In fact, there are three variants of contract theory. One would restrict the right of veto to the original signatories (Nova Scotia, New Brunswick, Quebec, and Ontario). A second extends it to all provinces, regardless of when they joined Canada. The third takes the position that the unanimous consent of the provinces is not required to change the federal distribution of powers, but that 'substantial provincial agreement' is necessary. Like compact theory, none of these variants of contract theory has any legal foundation.

The political importance of these compact/contract theories may be seen in the fact that for nearly 50 years Canadian governments were unable to agree on a formula for amending the Constitution. Between the first serious attempt in 1935 and the 1982 promulgation of the Constitution Act, it proved impossible to get all the provincial governments to agree to an amendment formula. Unanimous provincial consent appeared to be a political requirement for enacting such a formula (although if one or two of the smaller provinces had been the only dissenters this 'requirement' might have been overcome). Moreover, many constitutionalists and political scientists came to assume—wrongly, it turned out—that unanimity or something close to it was also a legal requirement.

The compact interpretation of Canadian federalism continues to carry political weight. The Quebec government's refusal to agree to the Constitution Act, 1982 was widely viewed as a serious blow to the Constitution's legitimacy. Former Prime Minister Brian Mulroney regularly, if misleadingly, spoke of bringing Quebec into the Constitution. Legally, of course, the 1982 reforms applied right across Canada. But politically the Prime Minister had a point. The government of Quebec, whose claim to speak on behalf of one of the country's two founding nations rests on the fact that the province is home to about 90 per cent of Canadian francophones, did not consent to far-reaching constitutional changes. Both of Quebec's major provincial political parties, the Parti Québécois and the Quebec Liberal Party, insist that Canadian federalism must be viewed as a compact between founding nations, a view that enjoys diminishing support in the rest of Canada. Indeed, diminished support for the idea of Canada as a binational compact is precisely the problem, claimed Claude Ryan, former leader of the Quebec Liberal Party. 'If the movement in favour of sovereignty was able to put down its roots and develop itself in Quebec,' Ryan argued, 'it is precisely because more and more Quebecers came to the conclusion that this equality, which had been the dream of many generations, will never be realized with the Canadian federation.'[12]

The contract theory of Canada lives on politically in the idea of the formal equality of the provinces. Section 2 of the Calgary Declaration, an agreement on the parameters for future constitutional negotiations that all of the provinces, except Quebec, agreed to in 1997, states that 'All provinces, while diverse in their characteristics, have equality of status.' The Declaration also stated that any constitutional amendment that confers powers on one province must make these powers available to all provinces. This involves a fundamentally different view of Canadian federalism than that which flows from the compact theory. The idea that provinces are and ought to remain formally equal—a contract theory view of federalism—is not easily squared with the notion of Quebec as a distinct society—a compact theory perspective on federalism.

The Federal Division of Powers

Whatever the intentions of the founders may have been when they drafted the Constitution Act, 1867, it is clear today that both levels of government exercise wide-ranging legislative and taxation powers. Their ability to do so ultimately rests on the responsibilities assigned to them by the Constitution. Canada's founders took exceptional pains to specify the responsibilities of each level of government. But a literal reading of the division of powers they decided on and of the formal changes that have been made to it since then provide at best a partial and at worst a misleading guide to Canadian federalism. In some cases policy areas were unimagined when the federal division of powers was framed—electronic communications, air transportation, and environmental protection would be examples—and so are not explicitly assigned either to Ottawa or to the provinces. In other cases what were minor responsibilities in the nineteenth and early twentieth centuries have assumed greater importance as a result of economic and societal changes, and of changes in the state itself.

The heart of the federal division of powers is found in sections 91 and 92 of the Constitution Act, 1867. Each of these sections contains a detailed list of enumerated powers that belong exclusively to Parliament (s. 91) or the provincial (s. 92) legislatures. Combined with several other sections that also deal with the division of powers, this is the constitutional foundation of Canadian federalism. An examination of who holds what powers reveals that both Ottawa and the provinces have the capacity to act in most of the major policy fields (see Table 7.1 and Box 7.3).

Some of the constitutional powers listed in Table 7.1 could reasonably have been placed under more than one policy heading. The authority to tax, for example, has been used to promote economic growth, to redistribute income between groups, and to subsidize all sorts of special interests. Unemployment insurance is both an economic policy, tied to manpower retraining and a claimant's job search activities, and a social policy that has the effect of redistributing income to less affluent regions of the country. Immigration policy has always been harnessed to the needs of the Canadian economy and has also been tied to cultural policy through citizenship services and language training for immigrants.

At the same time, governments have sometimes found the authority to legislate through powers that are implied, rather than stated, in the Constitution. The most important example of this involves the federal government's spending power. Ottawa spends billions of dollars annually on programs that fall under the jurisdiction of provincial and municipal governments. The feds also provide money to universities (for research and student scholarships) and to school boards (for language instruction), even though these organizations fall under the constitutional authority of the provinces, and to individuals for purposes that might appear to fall under provincial jurisdiction (e.g., tax benefits for child care). Ottawa's constitutional 'right' to spend money for any purpose has never been definitely established in the courts.[13] Nevertheless, the spending power today provides the constitutional basis for such major federal grants to the provinces as the Canada Health Transfer (CHT) and Canada Social Transfer (CST) and equalization payments.

The Courts and Federalism

Only the layperson expects constitutional terms like 'trade and commerce', 'property and civil rights', and 'direct taxation' to have straightforward meanings. This view has not been shared

TABLE 7.1 The Federal Division of Powers Under the Constitution Acts

	Ottawa	Provinces
Public finance	(1867) · 91(3): authority to raise money by any 'Mode or System of Taxation' · 91(4): authority to borrow money (1982) · 36(2): commits Ottawa to the principle of equalizing public revenue levels in the provinces	(1867) · 92(2): authorizes direct taxation within the province · 92(3): authority to borrow money · 92A(4): permits provinces to use 'any mode or system of taxation' in the case of non-renewable natural resources, forestry resources, and electrical energy
Managing the economy	(1867) · 91(2): regulation of trade and commerce · 91(2A): unemployment insurance · 91(5): post office · 91(10, 12): navigation, international waters, and offshore resources · 91(14, 15, 16, 18, 19, 20): national monetary system · 91(17, 22, 23): commercial standards · 92(10.c): authority to intervene in a provincial economy by declaring a public work to be in the national interest · 95: agriculture · 121: prohibits provincial taxes on imports from other provinces, thus reinforcing the concept of a national economic union (1982) · 6(2): guarantees the economic mobility of citizens anywhere within Canada, reinforcing the concept of a national economic union	(1867) · 92(9): authority to issue commercial licences · 92(10): public works within the province · 92(11): incorporation of companies with provincial objects · 92(13): property and civil rights · 92A: reaffirms provincial authority over natural resources within their borders · 95: agriculture, but federal law takes precedence · 109: establishes provincial ownership of natural resources within their borders (1982) · 6(4): permits provinces to favour provincial residents in hiring if the rate of unemployment in that province is above the national average
Social policy and the quality of life	(1867) · 91(24): Aboriginal Canadians · 91(26): marriage and divorce · 93(3, 4): authority to protect the educational rights of denominational minorities · 94A: old age pensions, but provincial law prevails · 95: immigration	(1867) · 92(7): hospitals · 92(12): solemnization of marriage · 93: education · 94A: public pensions · 95: immigration, but federal law prevails
Cultural policy	(1867) · 133: official bilingualism of Parliament (1982) · 16(l), 19, 20: establishes official bilingualism in all institutions of the federal government	(1867) · 92(16): all matters of a merely local or private nature · 93: education · 133: official bilingualism of Quebec legislature (1982) · 16(2), 17(2), 18(2), 19(2), 20(2): establishes official bilingualism in all institutions of the New Brunswick government
Administration and enforcement of law	(1867) · 91(27): criminal law · 91(28): penitentiaries · 96: appointment of judges of provincial courts · 100: authority to set judicial salaries · 101: authority to establish a general court of appeal for Canada, and other federal courts	(1867) · 92(14): administration of justice and the organization of courts within the province · 92(15): authority to establish penalties for violations of provincial laws
International relations and defence	(1867) · 91(7): military and defence · 132: authority to enter foreign treaties and perform obligations under them	(1867) · Since the Supreme Court's decision in the Labour Conventions case of 1937, it appears that provincial consent is required to implement foreign treaty obligations involving matters of provincial jurisdiction. There is, however, no consensus on this.

continued

TABLE 7.1 continued

Other legislative authority	(1867) · 91 (preamble): authorizes Parliament to make laws for the 'peace, order, and good government' of Canada · 91(29): matters not falling under the enumerated powers of the provinces come under Ottawa's jurisdiction	(1867) · 92(8): municipal institutions · 92(16): all matters of a local or private nature in the province
Environmental policy	(1867) · 91: peace, order, and good government of Canada (this basis for federal power is suggested in the Canada Water Act) · 91(10): navigation and shipping · 91(12): sea coast and inland fisheries · 91(27): criminal law · 95: agriculture · 132: foreign treaties	(1867) · 92(5): management and sale of public lands · 92(10): local works and undertakings · 92(13): property and civil rights · 92(16): matters of a merely local or private nature (1982) · 92A: non-renewable natural resources, forestry resources, and electric energy

by constitutional lawyers, governments, and the private interests that have challenged federal and provincial laws. For these groups the federal division of powers is a dense thicket of contradictory and contested meanings and opportunities, and the interpretation attached to a particular enumerated power is often a matter to haggle over in the courts. The judicial decisions that have resulted from these disputes have played an important role in shaping the evolution of Canadian federalism. Among the many contentious sections of the Constitution, the courts' interpretation of Ottawa's authority to 'make laws for the peace, order, and good government of Canada' (POGG) and the federal government's 'trade and commerce' power have had the greatest impact on the division of powers. We will look briefly at each of these.

Peace, Order, and Good Government

The courts have tended to place a narrow interpretation on the federal Parliament's general authority to make laws for the **'peace, order, and good government of Canada'**. This has been reduced over time to an emergency power that can provide the constitutional basis for federal actions in special circumstances. It cannot, however, be used to justify federal laws during 'normal' times. This narrow interpretation of POGG began with the *Local Prohibition* case (1896). The Judicial Committee of the Privy Council ruled that POGG could not be used by Ottawa to override the enumerated powers of the provinces. The decision also marked the introduction into Canadian constitutional law of the 'national dimensions' test. Lord Watson wrote:

> Their Lordships do not doubt that some matters, in their origin local or provincial, might attain such dimensions as to affect the body politic of the Dominion, and to justify the Canadian Parliament in passing laws for their regulation or abolition in the interest of the Dominion.[14]

When does a matter acquire 'national dimensions'? This question was dealt with in a series of three decisions handed down in 1922, 1923, and 1925. In *Re Board of Commerce Act and Combines and Fair Prices Act 1919* (1922), the JCPC struck down two federal laws introduced after World War I to prevent business monopoly and hoarding of essential commodities. For the first time the 'emergency doctrine' was articulated, according to which Parliament could pass laws under the authority of POGG only in the case of a national emergency. Writing for the majority, Viscount Haldane declared that:

> Circumstances are conceivable, such as those of war or famine, when the peace, order and good Government of the Dominion might be imperilled under conditions so

exceptional that they require legislation of a character in reality beyond anything provided for by the enumerated heads in either s. 92 or s. 91.[15]

Essentially, the JCPC ruled that some national crisis must exist before federal laws can be based on POGG. The fact that a matter has acquired 'national

Governing Realities

Box 7.3 Who Has Authority over Water?

When the Constitution Act of 1867 came into effect, water was considered to be significant in three main ways. It was important for navigation, as a source of fish, and for irrigating farmland. In fact, the third of these was not yet particularly important in Canada, although the building of dams and the diversion of rivers for irrigation had begun to be a contentious issue in the United States. The supply of fresh water for drinking was taken for granted. Water pollution was not an issue. No one had heard of invasive species. The issues surrounding hydroelectric power did not yet exist. And the idea that Aboriginal rights and interests should be taken into account when it came to water would have been greeted with incredulity.

It is hardly surprising, then, that water is not one of the enumerated legislative powers under sections 91 and 92 of the Constitution Act, 1867. Over time, however, it acquired enormous importance and the question of which level of government held the constitutional authority to regulate its use was asked more often and with greater urgency. Ottawa based its case on a clutch of constitutional provisions, including the 'peace, order, and good government' clause, the trade and commerce provision, jurisdiction over coastal and inland fisheries, as well as over navigation and shipping, and its authority to enter into foreign treaties (though not necessarily to implement the terms of such treaties). More recently the federal government's exclusive jurisdiction over criminal law has been advanced as a basis for a federal role in water policy.

The provinces have had their own list of constitutional claims to authority over water. These have included jurisdiction over property and civil rights, municipal institutions, local works and undertakings, the authority conferred by s. 92(5) regarding the management of public lands, and 'all matters of a merely local or private nature in the province' (s. 92[16]). Conflict over who has jurisdiction has occasionally led to court battles over pollution, the building of dams, and the management of fisheries.

In the 1960s and the 1970s governments in developed economies throughout the world, Canada included, became more active in matters concerning water pollution, passing laws and creating environmental bureaucracies to manage this issue. What Ottawa immediately discovered was that provincial and local governments already claimed responsibility for providing clean water, dealing with sewage, regulating agricultural, industrial, and residential activities that influence water supply and quality, and managing recreational and commercial fishing in their lakes and rivers. There were, of course, some things these provincial and local governments could not do, including negotiating water treaties with foreign governments, regulating water that flowed across provincial boundaries, and managing the waters off Canada's coasts. But most of the key regulatory functions that relate to water supply and quality, and that have immediate impacts on Canadians' lives and on their communities, were and continue to be under the control of provincial and local governments.

Some water experts lament the decentralized and divided reality of authority over water in Canada and believe that a more robust federal presence and national standards would be preferable. Whether or not they are right—and it is not obvious that a dominant federal role would produce better water policy, whatever 'better' might be understood to mean—the fact is that the constitutional authority to regulate water is divided and overlapping. The 'watertight compartments' metaphor of Canadian federalism, proposed by the Judicial Committee of the Privy Council in the 1930s, is never leakier than when applied to water.

dimensions' would not, by itself, be sufficient to justify such exceptional legislation.

Despite the JCPC's admission that peacetime circumstances could conceivably warrant Ottawa acting under the authority of POGG, subsequent rulings suggested that POGG was really a wartime power. In the first of these decisions, *Fort Frances Pulp and Power Co. v. Manitoba Free Press* (1923), the JCPC declared that war-related circumstances were sufficient to warrant legislating under POGG. Moreover, Viscount Haldane's opinion in *Fort Frances* indicated that the courts should be reluctant to question Parliament's judgement that a war-related emergency exists. Rulings in 1947 by the JCPC and in 1950 by the Supreme Court of Canada repeated this view.[16]

In those cases where the courts have rejected POGG as a valid basis for federal legislation, the impugned laws were intended to deal with peacetime circumstances. The first of these was the decision in *Toronto Electric Commissioners v. Snider* (1925). Relying on the 'emergency doctrine' it had developed in the *Board of Commerce* case, the JCPC struck down Canada's major industrial relations law, the Industrial Disputes Investigation Act, 1907. The JCPC again rejected peacetime recourse to POGG in the 1937 reference decision on Ottawa's Employment and Social Insurance Act, 1935.[17] The federal government's attempt to justify this law under POGG, on the grounds that unemployment was a matter of national concern and, moreover, that it threatened the well-being of the country, was considered inadequate by the JCPC.

Confronted with broadly similar reasoning in the 1970s, the Supreme Court of Canada found that POGG could be used to justify federal laws during peacetime. The Court was asked to rule on the constitutionality of Ottawa's Anti-Inflation Act, 1975. A majority of the Court accepted the federal government's argument that mounting inflationary pressures constituted an emergency justifying legislation that encroached on provincial jurisdiction. Not only was the 'emergency doctrine' liberated from war-related circumstances, the Court also indicated its reluctance to challenge Parliament's judgement on when emergency circumstances exist. The result, according to constitutionalists like Peter Russell, is that Ottawa now appeared to have fairly easy access to emergency powers under this doctrine.[18] Constitutionally this may be so. Politically, however, any federal government would think twice before legislating under this contentious power. In the three decades since Ottawa won this constitutional victory there has not been a single instance where the federal government has relied on POGG as the basis for an alleged intrusion into provincial jurisdiction.

Trade and Commerce

On the face of it, Ottawa's authority over the regulation of trade and commerce (s. 91[2])[19] appears rather sweeping. Any economic activity or transaction would seem to fall within its scope. In fact, however, court decisions have construed the trade and commerce power to be much narrower, limited largely to interprovincial and international trade. At the same time, provincial jurisdiction over property and civil rights in the province (s. 92[13])[20] has been interpreted as the provinces' own 'trade and commerce' power. This line of judicial interpretation began with the decision in *Citizens' Insurance Co. v. Parsons* (1881). Based on its view that a broad, literal interpretation of s. 91(2) of the Constitution Act, 1867 would bring any and all aspects of economic life under the authority of Ottawa, leaving the provinces powerless to affect business, the JCPC interpreted 'regulation of trade and commerce' to include 'political arrangements in regard to trade requiring the sanction of parliament, regulation of trade in matters of interprovincial concern, and it may be that they would include general regulation of trade affecting the whole Dominion'.[21] To construe Ottawa's trade and commerce power otherwise, the JCPC argued, would be to deny the 'fair and ordinary meaning' of s. 92(13) of the Constitution Act, 1867, which assigns property and civil rights in the province to the provincial governments.

The legacy of *Parsons* has been that Ottawa's authority to regulate trade and commerce has been limited to interprovincial trade, international trade, and general trade affecting the whole of Canada. But even this definition of federal jurisdiction has presented problems of interpretation. For example, what about a federal law whose principal goal is to regulate trade that crosses provincial borders, but which has as an incidental effect the regulation of some transactions that occur wholly within a province? Is such a law constitutional under s. 91(2)? Until the 1950s the courts' answer was 'no'.[22]

But a series of Supreme Court decisions, culminating in *Caloil v. Attorney General of Canada* (1971), signified a broader interpretation of Ottawa's power to regulate interprovincial trade.[23] In *Caloil*, the Court acknowledged that a federal law prohibiting the transportation or sale of imported oil west of the Ottawa Valley interfered with local trade in a province. Nevertheless, the Court upheld the federal law on the grounds that its 'true character' was 'the control of imports in the furtherance of an extraprovincial trade policy'.[24] Ottawa's authority was given an additional boost by a 1971 reference decision of the Supreme Court. In the *'Chicken and Egg' Reference*—no kidding, 'Chicken and Egg'—the Court ruled unconstitutional a provincial egg-marketing scheme that restricted imports from other provinces on the grounds that it encroached on Ottawa's trade and commerce power. Justice Bora Laskin, who would later become Chief Justice of the Supreme Court, referred specifically to the trend towards a more balanced interpretation of federal and provincial jurisdiction over trade.[25] Laskin argued that, 'to permit each province to seek its own advantage . . . through a figurative sealing of its borders to entry of goods from others would be to deny one of the objects of Confederation . . . namely, to form an economic unit of the whole of Canada.'[26] The situation since these rulings may be described as *Parsons* + *Caloil* = 'trade and commerce'.

What of the *Parsons* allusion to general trade affecting the whole of Canada? Constitutional expert Peter Hogg suggests that its meaning remains obscure, but that it could conceivably provide the basis for federal laws regulating business.[27] In both *MacDonald v. Vapor Canada Ltd.* (1977) and *Attorney General of Canada v. Canadian National Transportation* (1983), the court raised the question of when trade affects the whole country, thereby justifying, per *Parsons*, federal regulation under the trade and commerce power. The answer was given in *General Motors of Canada v. City National Leasing* (1989) when the Supreme Court laid down five criteria that must be met before Ottawa may regulate commerce under the 'general trade' provision of s. 91(2) of the Constitution. They include the following:

> (1) the impugned legislation must be part of a general regulatory scheme;
>
> (2) the scheme must be monitored by the continuing oversight of a regulatory agency;
>
> (3) the legislation must be concerned with trade as a whole rather than with a particular industry;
>
> (4) the legislation should be of a nature that the provinces jointly or severally would be constitutionally incapable of enacting; and
>
> (5) the failure to include one or more provinces or localities in a legislative scheme would jeopardize the successful operation of the scheme in other parts of the country.[28]

In May of 2010 the federal government referred to the Supreme Court for an advisory opinion on the proposed Canadian Securities Act. Prompted by the financial crisis that swept across the United States and other capitalist economies in 2008–10, the Act was intended to strengthen Ottawa's regulatory role in Canadian capital markets. The Supreme Court's interpretation of the federal trade and commerce power was expected to be a key part of its eventual opinion on the constitutionality of this proposed law. The Court's decision is not expected until 2011 or 2012.

The Impact of Judicial Decisions

Court rulings seldom put an end to conflicts between Ottawa and the provinces. Instead, they typically become part of the bargaining process between governments. Consider the following examples:

- *Employment and Social Insurance Act Reference* (1937). The JCPC struck down a federal statute establishing a program to deal with national unemployment. This was followed by negotiations between the federal and provincial governments, leading to a 1940 constitutional amendment that gave Ottawa authority over unemployment insurance.

- *Public Service Board v. Dionne* (1978). The Supreme Court confirmed Ottawa's exclusive jurisdiction to regulate television broadcasting. Immediately after the decision was handed down, the federal Minister of Communications announced Ottawa's willingness to negotiate some division of authority with the provinces.
- *CIGOL v. Government of Saskatchewan* (1978). In *CIGOL*, a provincial tax on natural gas was found to be a direct tax and therefore outside the jurisdiction of the province. When Ottawa and the provinces were negotiating constitutional reform in 1980–1, the issue of provincial control over natural resources was on the table. The result was s. 92A of the Constitution Act. It appears to permit the form of resource taxation that was ruled ultra vires in the *CIGOL* decision.
- *Re Constitution of Canada* (1981). The Supreme Court ruled that Ottawa's proposal to patriate the British North America Act and to change it in ways affecting provincial powers was legal, but that it was unconstitutional in the conventional sense (see Chapter 5). The decision gave the federal government a legal victory, at the same time as the provinces were given the moral high ground. Within weeks all governments were back at the table trying to find a negotiated solution.
- *Reference re Secession of Quebec* (1998). On the face of it, this appeared to be a victory for Ottawa and federalist forces generally. The Supreme Court ruled that neither the Canadian Constitution nor international law confer on the government and National Assembly of Quebec the right to secede from Canada unilaterally. The Court added, however, that a 'clear majority vote in Quebec on a clear question in favour of secession would confer democratic legitimacy on the secession initiative which all of the other participants in Confederation would have to recognize.' So who really won, the separatists or the federalists? As was also true of the Court's ambiguous 1981 pronouncement in the Patriation Reference, both sides were able to claim a victory of sorts. The 1998 ruling did not resolve the issue of Quebec separation—indeed, no one expected that this would be its result. Instead, by clarifying some of the constitutional questions associated with Quebec secession the Court provided all sides in this ongoing political struggle with ammunition for future sniping.

Evolving Federalism

It is generally believed that judicial decisions decentralized Canadian federalism in a way that the Fathers of Confederation had not planned, but that this tendency has been attenuated since 1949 when the Supreme Court became Canada's highest court of appeal. Some bemoan the judiciary's decentralizing influence, particularly that of the JCPC during Canada's first half-century. Others maintain that the limits placed on Ottawa's general legislative authority (POGG) and trade and commerce power, and the broad interpretation of provincial authority over property and civil rights, have reflected the political reality of Canada. As Pierre Trudeau observed, 'it has long been the custom in English Canada to denounce the [Judicial Committee of the] Privy Council for its provincial bias; but it should perhaps be considered that if the law lords had not leaned in that direction, Quebec separatism might not be a threat today: it might be an accomplished fact.'[29]

Judicial review is only one of the factors that have shaped the evolution of federalism. In fact, legal disputes over the division of powers are only symptomatic of underlying tensions that are at the root of intergovernmental conflict. These tensions have three main sources: (1) the status of Quebec and the powers of the Quebec state; (2) relations between the more heavily industrialized and populous centre of the country and the outlying western and eastern regions; and (3) the political and administrative needs of governments.

Quebec

'What does Quebec want?' The question has been asked countless times over the years by English Canadians, some of whom genuinely wanted to know and by others who asked it out of exasperation, believing all along that the answer would be unacceptable. The complementary question, 'What does English Canada want?' has seldom been posed. Yet neither question makes sense in isolation from the other. In order to understand what Quebec wants from Canada it is also necessary to consider what the rest of Canada expects from, and is willing to concede to, Quebec. Quebec's unique role in Canadian federalism derives from two factors. One is its predominantly French-speaking character. Over 80 per cent of the provincial population claims French as their mother tongue, and about 90 per cent of all Canadian francophones reside in Quebec. The second factor is Quebec's size. At Confederation it was the second most populous province and Montreal was the hub of Canada's commercial and financial industries. Although its weight relative to the rest of Canada is much less today, Quebec is still Canada's second most populous province, accounting for slightly less than one-quarter of Canada's population. Economically, Quebec's gross provincial product and its importance as a centre for finance and manufacturing are surpassed only by Ontario.

Quebec's distinctive social and cultural fabric explains why it has made special demands on Canadian federalism. Because it is a large province with the second largest bloc of seats in the federal Parliament and because francophones have always been able to control Quebec's provincial legislature, the demands of Quebec have had a significant impact on the evolution of Canadian federalism. This impact has been experienced on two main fronts: the Constitution and the financial and administrative practices of federalism. We will examine Quebec's impact on the financial and administrative dimensions of federalism later in this chapter.

Quebec's influence on the Constitution predates the Confederation agreement. Between 1848 and 1867 Ontario and Quebec formed the United Canadas, governed by a single legislature in which the two colonies held equal representation. It was during this period that the *double-majority* practice developed. To become law, a bill had to be approved by a majority of members on both the Ontario and Quebec sides of the legislature. This was Canada's first experience with the federal principle of regional representation. Predominantly francophone Quebec and predominantly anglophone Ontario were joined in a legislative partnership that required the agreement of both regional communities in order to work. It turned out to be a failure. Quebec's influence on the Constitution was strongly evident in the Confederation agreement. Its representatives were the most insistent on a federal constitution for Canada, under which the provincial government would have authority over those matters considered vital to the preservation of the language, religion, and social institutions of Quebec. Indeed, for decades the clerical and political leaders of French Canada were unanimous in viewing Canadian federalism as a pact between two peoples. 'Canadian Confederation', declared Henri Bourassa, 'is the result of a contract between the two races in Canada, French and English, based on equality and recognizing equal rights and reciprocal duties. Canadian Confederation will last only as long as this equality of rights is recognized as the basis of the public right in Canada, from Halifax to Vancouver.'[30]

The equality Bourassa had in mind did not last very long. It was violated in Manitoba, where the status of French in the provincial legislature and the educational rights of francophone Catholics were swept away a couple of decades after that province entered Confederation. It was also violated in Ontario, where Regulation 17 (1913) banned French instruction from the province's public schools. These developments contributed to the identification of French Canada with Quebec, the only province in which francophones were in the majority and where they could effectively defend their rights and preserve their culture.

The constitutional consequences of limiting French Canada to the boundaries of Quebec became apparent by the middle of the twentieth century. As Ottawa became increasingly involved in areas of provincial jurisdiction, particularly through its spending power but also by monopolizing the field of direct taxation between 1947 and 1954 under a tax rental agreement with the provinces, the Quebec government became more and more protective of what it argued were exclusive provincial powers under the Constitution. Indeed, the Quebec government of Maurice Duplessis was the first among the provinces to reject Ottawa's exclusive occupation of the personal income tax field, imposing its own provincial income tax in 1954. But not until the Quiet Revolution of the 1960s, marking the eclipse of the conservative anti-statist nationalism that had dominated Quebec politics for more than a century, was Quebec's resentment towards Ottawa's encroachment onto provincial territory matched by aggressive constitutional demands. The first major indication of this occurred during the federal–provincial negotiations on a public old-age pension scheme (1963–5). Quebec Premier Jean Lesage stated that his government would only agree to a constitutional amendment giving Ottawa the authority to pass pension legislation if Quebec were able to opt out of the federal plan. Ottawa agreed, and thus was born the Canadian practice of provinces being able to opt out of a federal shared-cost program without suffering any financial loss.

Quebec's constitutional demands appeared to become even more ambitious a few years later. The 1966 provincial election saw the Union Nationale party run on the slogan 'Québec d'abord!' (Quebec first!) The party's leader, Daniel Johnson, had authored the book *Egalité ou indépendance* and in the election campaign the Union Nationale called for major constitutional reform that included the transfer of virtually all social and cultural matters to the province, constitutional recognition of Canada's binational character, and exclusive provincial control over the major tax fields then shared with Ottawa. In fact, however, these demands were not pursued with much vigour during the party's five years in power (1966–70). The one constitutional issue on which the Union Nationale government did confront Ottawa was that of international representation for Quebec. But as Kenneth McRoberts observes:

> In purely symbolic terms Quebec's demands seemed very significant; Quebec was seeking to assume what many regarded as the trappings of sovereignty. Yet . . . these demands did not directly attack the real distribution of power and responsibilities to the extent that various Lesage demands, such as a separate Quebec Pension Plan, had.[31]

Despite the lack of substantive change in Quebec's constitutional status and powers during this period, the province's nationalist undercurrent was gaining momentum. The creation of the Parti Québécois (PQ) in 1968, under the leadership of René Lévesque, brought under one roof most of the major groups committed to the eventual political independence of Quebec. The Liberal Party of Quebec (LPQ) remained federalist, but advocated what amounted to special status for Quebec within Canadian federalism. 'Un fédéralisme rentable' (profitable federalism) was the passionless way in which Liberal leader Robert Bourassa explained Quebec's commitment to Canada.

Constitutional negotiations between Ottawa and the provinces had been ongoing since 1968. The 1970 election of a Liberal government in Quebec appeared to provide an opportunity to bring these talks to a successful conclusion. But when the 11 governments got together at Victoria in 1971, it became apparent that Quebec's price for agreeing to a constitutional amendment formula and a charter of rights was higher than Ottawa was willing to pay.[32] The impasse was over social policy. Quebec demanded constitutional supremacy in an area in which Ottawa operated several major programs, including family allowances, unemployment insurance, manpower training, and old-age pensions. Moreover, the Quebec government wanted the fiscal means to pay for provincial policies in these fields. Ottawa went some way towards meeting these demands. The Trudeau government refused, however, to concede the principle of provincial supremacy over social policy and would not provide a constitutional guarantee that provinces would receive financial compensation for operating their own programs in these areas. The federal–provincial compromise reached in Victoria fell apart days later in Quebec, where the deal was widely seen as constitutional entrenchment of an unacceptable status quo.

After Quebec's rejection of the Victoria Charter, the Bourassa government adopted a piecemeal strategy for changing federalism, negotiating with Ottawa on single issues like family allowances, social security, and telecommunications. It was unsuccessful, however, in extracting any major concessions from a federal government that believed provincial powers were already too great, and that was staunchly opposed to special status for Quebec.

A rather different strategy was followed by the PQ government of René Lévesque after it came to power in 1976. The PQ was committed to holding a provincial referendum on its option of political sovereignty for Quebec, combined with some form of economic association with the rest of Canada. But instead of simple confrontation with Ottawa, the Lévesque government pursued an *étapiste* (gradualist) strategy of providing 'good government'—which required some degree of co-operation with Ottawa because of the intricate network of intergovernmental programs and agreements—while attempting to convince the Quebec population that its best interests lay in **sovereignty-association**. The two governments co-operated on dozens of new capital spending projects, on management of the economy, and on immigration policy. The PQ government even participated in federal–provincial talks on constitutional reform in 1978–9. All of this occurred against the background of the looming referendum on the PQ's separatist option.

Sovereignty-association was rejected by Quebec voters in May 1980. But they re-elected the PQ to office in 1981. It was thus a PQ government that participated in the constitutional negotiations towards 'renewed federalism' that the federal Liberal government had initiated after the Quebec referendum. But it was also a PQ government that refused to sign the final product of these talks, the November 1981 accord that became the Constitution Act, 1982. The PQ's refusal was hardly surprising in light of the fact that none of the demands that Quebec governments had made since the 1960s were included in the 1981 constitutional accord. Indeed, the province's Liberal opposition also found the accord to be unacceptable. The Constitution had undergone its most dramatic reform since its passage in 1867, but the provincial government of the country's second largest province and home to 90 per cent of Canada's francophones had not agreed to these changes. Although the legality of the Constitution Act, 1982 was not in doubt, its political legitimacy was.

This was the situation when Robert Bourassa and the provincial Liberals were returned to power in 1985. Their election appeared to reflect the muted tenor of Quebec nationalism in the post-referendum era. Change had also taken place in Ottawa. Prime Minister Brian Mulroney, elected in 1984, did not share Pierre Trudeau's view that the provinces were already too powerful for the good of the national economy and political unity. Nor was he viscerally opposed to some form of special status for Quebec, as Trudeau was. Conditions seemed propitious, therefore, for 'bringing Quebec into the constitutional family'—a phrase favoured by Prime Minister Mulroney.

It was not to be. The Quebec government put forward a package of five demands that had to be met before it would agree to the constitutional reforms passed in 1982. These proposals were agreed to by Ottawa and all of the provincial premiers on 30 April 1987, forming the basis for what became known as the Meech Lake Accord. As we have seen in Chapter 5, these constitutional proposals died on the drawing board, and two years later, in 1992, the Charlottetown proposals for constitutional reform, which offered Quebec even more and also brought Aboriginal Canadians to the table, were defeated in a national referendum.

In the wake of the Charlottetown Accord's rejection, politicians of all stripes fled from the constitutional issue. Indeed, the whole question of constitutional reform was conspicuously absent from the Liberal Party's 1993 'Red Book', its official statement of policy positions and promises. Nor was it an issue in the 1993 federal election campaign, at least not outside Quebec. In Quebec, however, these matters were kept before the voters by the Bloc Québécois, under the leadership of Lucien Bouchard. The Bloc's raison d'être was, of course, to achieve political independence for Quebec. Their success in capturing 54 of Quebec's 75 seats in the House of Commons may not have been a surrogate vote for separation, but it certainly demonstrated the depth of Quebec voters' dissatisfaction with the federal government and existing constitutional arrangements.

Despite their obvious wish to avoid the constitutional quagmire, the Liberals were forced to confront the issue as a result of the 1994 election of the PQ in Quebec. The PQ was committed to holding a referendum on Quebec independence within a year of their election. When the referendum campaign began in September of 1995, the *indépendantiste* side got off to a sputtering start. There appeared to be a little enthusiasm among Québécois for the PQ's separatist vision, and the early polls showed the 'no' side to be leading by a margin of as much as 20 percentage points. The federalist campaign relied on messages intended to convince Quebecers that they would suffer economically if the province voted 'yes'. Federal Minister of Finance Paul Martin and prominent business spokespersons warned Quebec voters that the days after separation would be dark ones.

About halfway through the campaign, however, leadership of the 'yes' side passed from Quebec Premier Jacques Parizeau to Bloc Québécois leader Lucien Bouchard. Support for independence took off, no doubt due in large measure to Bouchard's charismatic style and unsurpassed ability to connect emotionally with francophone Quebecers, but also due to what in retrospect can be seen to have been a terribly uninspired campaign by the federalists. Prime Minister Jean Chrétien chose to stay on the sidelines until the last couple of weeks of the campaign when polls showed the 'yes' side to be leading. His previous refusal to make any concrete constitutional offer to Quebec wavered during the period before the vote, when he suggested that he supported constitutional recognition of Quebec as a distinct society and a Quebec veto over constitutional reform. On 30 October 1995, the 'no' side emerged with the narrowest of victories: 49.6 per cent against independence, 48.5 per cent for, with spoiled ballots accounting for the rest.

The federal government's reluctance to deal with the issue of constitutional reform and with Quebec's demands before the 1995 referendum forced its hand was due in great measure to its realization that Canadians' reactions to the constitutional issue tended to range from indifference to deep hostility. But as their uncertain performance in the referendum campaign showed, the Liberals' silence may also have been due to their inability to formulate a positive response to the sovereignty option proposed by Quebec nationalists.

This inability can be traced to the Liberal model of federalism that took shape during the Trudeau

'Oui' supporters rally on the floor of the Palais des congrès in Montreal as they wait for the results of the 1995 referendum vote (left); 'Non' supporters react to poll results as the pro-Canada vote inches up to 50 per cent en route to a slim victory in the 1995 sovereignty referendum (right). Left: © CP Photo/stf—Tom Hanson; right: CP Photo/stf—Jacques Bossinot era. Although not centralist in any absolute sense—Canada has surely been among the least centralized federal systems in the world in recent decades—it assumes that a strong central government is essential to the maintenance of Canadian unity. Moreover, this model is in general opposed to what is called 'asymmetrical federalism', i.e., the constitutional recognition of differences in the status and powers of provincial governments; in particular, it is against constitutional entrenchment of special status for Quebec. The Constitution Act of 1982, particularly the Charter and the denial of a right of constitutional veto to any single province, embodies this vision of federalism.

This model is, of course, hotly contested. The main challenge comes from Quebec nationalists, not only from separatists but also from Quebec's nationalist-federalists. This latter group, which includes the Liberal Party of Quebec, maintains that constitutional reforms, including, at a minimum, recognition of Quebec's special responsibility for the protection and promotion of the French language in Canada and a Quebec veto over constitutional change, are necessary to keep Quebecers interested in Canadian federalism. The federal Liberals, since Trudeau stepped down as party leader in 1984, have shown a willingness to concede much of what the nationalist-federalists demand, as seen in the party's support for the Meech Lake and Charlottetown Accords. However, their enthusiasm for these constitutional reforms has been tempered both by a realization that they receive mixed reviews among voters in Ontario and generate downright hostility in western Canada, and by a vestigial loyalty among some Liberals to Trudeau's brand of no-special-status-for-Quebec federalism.

In the wake of the close call experienced by federalists in the 1995 Quebec referendum, where a clear majority of francophones voted for the sovereignty option, the federal Liberal Party showed that it was ready to cut the cord connecting it to the Trudeau era. Only weeks after the referendum the Liberal government introduced a motion recognizing Quebec as a distinct society, assigning the province a veto over constitutional change, and transferring to Quebec some authority for job training. Ontario and British Columbia also were assigned veto power, as were the Prairie and Atlantic regions if at least two provinces representing more than 50 per cent of the regional population opposed a proposed amendment. The first two of this trio of reforms have clear constitutional implications. The federal motion did not, of course, change the written Constitution. However, to the extent that Ottawa allows its behaviour to be governed by what the Liberal government of the time characterized as a constitutional offer to Quebecers, it does change the Constitution in an informal way. Likewise, the resolution introduced by the Conservative government and passed by the House of Commons in 2006, recognizing Quebec as a nation within a united Canada, does not change the constitutional status of Quebec in any formal way. But it may be argued to confer a sort of de facto special status on Quebec in matters of constitutional reform.

These federal actions marked a return to a tradition of flexibility in Canadian federalism that predates Pierre Trudeau's entry into federal politics. It is a tradition familiar to students of the British Constitution and of Canadian federalism alike, whereby constitutional change is not the result of formal amendments to the written Constitution but of developments in policy and practice whose status is greater than that of ordinary laws but not quite that of constitutional reform.

Centre–Periphery Relations

Canada spans five and a half time zones and occupies the second largest land mass of any country, and yet the narrow belt that runs between Windsor and Montreal—the 'industrial heartland' of Canada—is home to over 55 per cent of Canada's population and generates about 60 per cent of national income and production. Ontario and Quebec together account for just under 60 per cent of the 308 seats in the House of Commons. No national political party can hope to form a government without considerable support from the voters of at least one, and usually both, of these provinces. They comprise Canada's centre, in terms of their political and economic power.

Predictably, the provincial governments of Ontario and Quebec carry greater weight in

Canadian federalism than do those of the other provinces. The other eight provincial governments preside over regions whose interests usually have been subordinated by Ottawa to those of central Canada. In this sense these other provinces constitute Canada's *peripheries*, situated on the edge—sometimes precariously so—of national politics. Resentment towards central Canada and the federal government has deep roots in the politics of these provinces, particularly in the West. Their litany of historical grievances includes, to mention only a few: tariff policy that for a century protected manufacturing jobs and corporate profits in Ontario and Quebec; the perceived insensitivity of the country's Toronto- and Montreal-based financial institutions when it comes to western interests; Ottawa's treatment of the petroleum resources that are concentrated in the West; investment and spending decisions by the federal government; official bilingualism and what westerners in particular perceive to be Ottawa's favouritism towards Quebec's interests. No one can seriously doubt that the peripheral provinces have a case. As Donald Smiley has written, 'there are dangers that Canadian problems will be resolved almost entirely within the framework of the heartland of the country with the progressive alienation from national affairs of those who live on the peripheries.'[33]

The federal principle of regional representation is embodied in the Canadian Senate and is practised assiduously by prime ministers in selecting cabinet ministers and in making certain other federal appointments, yet this federal deference to regionalism has not provided these regions with what they believe to be an adequate voice in national politics. **Intrastate federalism**—the representation and accommodation of regional interests within national political institutions—has been an abysmal failure in Canada. Deprived of significant influence in Ottawa, the peripheral regions of the country have tended to rely on their provincial governments for the protection and promotion of their interests.

The fact that more MPs are elected from Ontario and Quebec than from all the other provinces combined has always been the root cause of Ottawa's tendency to favour central Canadian interests. This political factor has been reinforced by the ideological bias of Canadian politics, a bias that has tended to interpret Canadian history and identity in terms of experiences that are more germane to central Canada than to the peripheral regions. The very concept of 'Canada' has been associated with a counter-revolutionary or Loyalist tradition based on a rejection of the values and political institutions of the United States and on the cultural dualism so important to the political history of central Canada. Neither of these experiences is central to the identity and political consciousness of western Canadians.[34] In the East, too, the national myths, symbols, and identities associated with 'Canada' often have had little relationship to the experience of Maritimers.[35]

The dominance of Ontario and Quebec in national politics and the subordinate status of the interests and cultural values of the peripheral regions of the country have always been reflected in relations between Ottawa and the provincial governments of the peripheries. For example, although Ottawa has exercised its constitutional power to disallow provincial laws 112 times, only a few of these were laws passed by Ontario or Quebec.[36] When Manitoba joined Confederation in 1870 it did so without control over public lands situated in the province.[37] Ottawa retained control in order to promote its own nation-building strategy relating to railway construction and western settlement. Similarly, when Saskatchewan and Alberta became provinces in 1905 they did not immediately acquire control over public lands and natural resources within their borders.[38] Ottawa kept these powers to itself, using the argument that this was necessary to accomplish its immigration and settlement objectives for western Canada. All of these provinces received subsidies from Ottawa as compensation for the revenue they were deprived of by not controlling public lands and, in Alberta and Saskatchewan, natural resources. Their governments did not consider this to be adequate recompense for the quasi-colonial status imposed on them by Ottawa.

There is nothing subtle about the disallowance power, or about denying some provinces constitutional powers possessed by other provincial governments. Today's list of grievances against

Ottawa is comprised of less blatant forms of policy discrimination against the interests of the peripheries. Among the items perennially on this list are claims that Ottawa does too little to support prairie grain farmers or the east coast fishing industry, and that the federal government's spending decisions unfairly favour Ontario and Quebec. Even in provinces like Alberta, British Columbia, and Saskatchewan, which are wealthy by Canadian standards, a sense of powerlessness in the face of central Canadian dominance is a major component of their provincial politics. 'The West', observes Alberta historian Doug Owram, 'has never felt in control of its own destiny. None of the wealth of recent years has eased this feeling. In fact, the tremendous wealth of the region merely sharpens the contrast with the political powerlessness that exists on the national level.'[39] Although the fact of having an Albertan, Stephen Harper, as Prime Minister has taken the edge off this sentiment, it has not disappeared entirely. The outraged reaction of Albertans, several weeks after the 2008 election, when the opposition parties attempted to dislodge the Conservatives from power and replace them with a coalition government supported by the Bloc Québécois, showed that the region is still very conscious of the long decades when it was on the outside of federal politics, looking in.

This contrast between the economic strength and political weakness of the West, or at least of British Columbia and Alberta, is more likely to sharpen than diminish in the future. Between 1996 and 2009 British Columbia's population grew by about 600,000 persons, Alberta's by roughly 859,000, but Quebec's by only about 506,000. These westernmost provinces have for many years been among Canada's fastest-growing regions, and their combined population is now larger than that of Quebec. Moreover, the economic muscle of these provinces has increased in recent years. About one-third of the 100 largest industrial firms in Canada have their head offices in either British Columbia or Alberta, compared to about 60 per cent in Ontario and Quebec. The West's share has increased significantly over the last decade. At the level of major cities, the economic prosperity and buoyant growth that have characterized Vancouver and Calgary for most of the last two decades contrasts sharply with the relative economic decline of Montreal, the hub of Quebec's economy.

It would appear unlikely that the West, aware of its economic strength and its growing population, will become less resentful of what it perceives to be the domination of national politics by Ontario and Quebec. Under Prime Minister Stephen Harper, the Conservative government has embraced a policy that it calls 'open federalism', intended to satisfy what have often been seen as the mutually exclusive viewpoints and interests of Quebec and the West. As Box 7.4 explains, the policy is not without its critics.

State Interests and Intergovernmental Conflict

The fact that Quebec is overwhelmingly francophone, while the other provinces are not, gives it a special set of interests that any Quebec government feels bound to defend. Likewise, grain farming and resource extraction in Saskatchewan, petroleum in Alberta, the automotive industry in Ontario, and forestry in British Columbia shape the positions taken by the governments of these provinces on taxation, trade, and other policies affecting these interests. Each province comprises a particular constellation of economic, social, and cultural interests that together influence the demands its provincial government makes on federalism. Intergovernmental conflict, then, is to some extent the clash of conflicting regional interests.

This is, however, only part of the explanation. Governments do not simply reflect societal interests. They actively shape these interests through their policies, sometimes deliberately and other times inadvertently. Moreover, governments have their own political and administrative interests, the pursuit of which may have nothing to do with the interests of those they represent. 'Canadian federalism', Alan Cairns has argued, 'is about governments, governments that are possessed of massive human and financial resources, that are driven by purposes fashioned by elites, and that accord high priority to their own long-term institutional self-interest.'[40] This state-centred interpretation

Politics in Focus

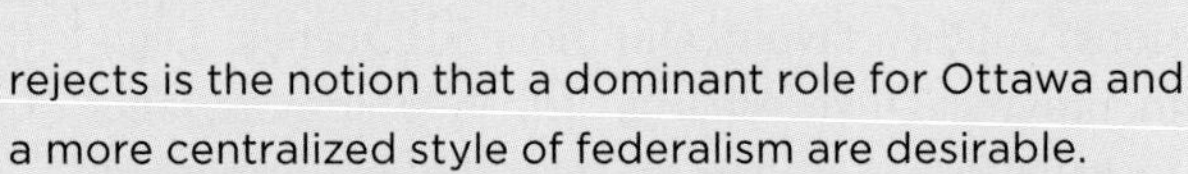

Box 7.4 'Open Federalism': Ideology, the Constitution, and Intergovernmental Style

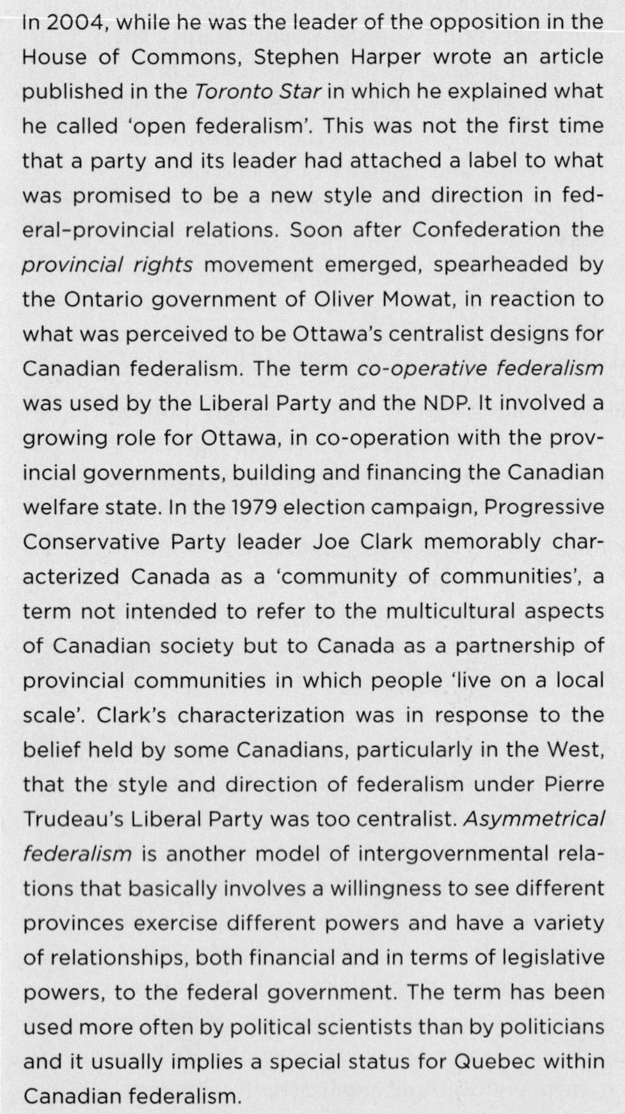

In 2004, while he was the leader of the opposition in the House of Commons, Stephen Harper wrote an article published in the *Toronto Star* in which he explained what he called 'open federalism'. This was not the first time that a party and its leader had attached a label to what was promised to be a new style and direction in federal-provincial relations. Soon after Confederation the *provincial rights* movement emerged, spearheaded by the Ontario government of Oliver Mowat, in reaction to what was perceived to be Ottawa's centralist designs for Canadian federalism. The term *co-operative federalism* was used by the Liberal Party and the NDP. It involved a growing role for Ottawa, in co-operation with the provincial governments, building and financing the Canadian welfare state. In the 1979 election campaign, Progressive Conservative Party leader Joe Clark memorably characterized Canada as a 'community of communities', a term not intended to refer to the multicultural aspects of Canadian society but to Canada as a partnership of provincial communities in which people 'live on a local scale'. Clark's characterization was in response to the belief held by some Canadians, particularly in the West, that the style and direction of federalism under Pierre Trudeau's Liberal Party was too centralist. *Asymmetrical federalism* is another model of intergovernmental relations that basically involves a willingness to see different provinces exercise different powers and have a variety of relationships, both financial and in terms of legislative powers, to the federal government. The term has been used more often by political scientists than by politicians and it usually implies a special status for Quebec within Canadian federalism.

Open federalism, advocated by Conservative Prime Minister Stephen Harper, borrows elements of the provincial rights movement, Joe Clark's vision of Canada as a community of communities, and asymmetrical federalism, without being reducible to any one of these models of federalism. What open federalism most assuredly rejects is the notion that a dominant role for Ottawa and a more centralized style of federalism are desirable.

The Conservative Party's 2005 policy declaration identified several features of open federalism. These included a shift in the federal-provincial balance towards the provinces, greater respect for what the Constitution says about the division of powers, reining in the federal spending power, a commitment to redressing the fiscal imbalance between Ottawa and the provinces, and willingness to accept special arrangements for Quebec (this last feature is inferred rather than stated outright). According to some critics, the real goal is smaller government, which is expected to be achieved by limiting and even reducing Ottawa's legislative and spending powers. Open federalism, they claim, is a flimsy cover for a hidden agenda of less federal involvement in social policy and retreat from environmental matters on the pretext that they are mainly in the provinces' domain.

This attribution of deceitful cleverness could be correct. But it may also be far off the mark. The Prime Minister and many of his closest and most trusted advisers are westerners who have long resented what they believed to be a sort of father-knows-best style of federalism. Westerners have never accepted the vision of themselves as junior partners in Canadian federalism, bound to defer to a national government whose priorities and agenda have most often favoured Ontario and Quebec. Those who airily dismiss the case for open federalism as an ideological smokescreen ignore the fact that there is a long history of opposition to centralizing visions of federalism in Canada going back to the early years of the country and John A. Macdonald's expectation and hope that the provincial governments would be mere 'glorified municipalities'. Much of this opposition—perhaps even most of it—has had little to do with the issues of left versus right, but a lot to do with whether regional or national interests and values should prevail.

of federalism maintains that conflicts between governments are likely to be generated, or at least influenced, by the 'institutional self-interest' of politicians and bureaucrats.

The evidence in support of this view is overwhelming. Intergovernmental turf wars, over their respective shares of particular tax fields and over which level will have jurisdiction over what matters, often seem remote from the concerns of Canadian citizens. For example, in 1998 the federal government proudly announced the creation of the Millennium Scholarship to provide financial assistance to university students. Provincial governments immediately cried foul, pointing out that education falls under provincial jurisdiction and that Ottawa had not even consulted them on this new initiative. One suspects that for the students eligible to receive the money, its source was a matter of total irrelevance. But looked at from the state's point of view, how revenue sources and legislative competence are divided between levels of governments affects the ability of politicians to pursue their interests in re-election, career advancement, and personal prestige, and their own conception of the public interest. So, too, in the case of bureaucratic officials, we may assume that they, also, are not indifferent towards matters that influence the future of the organizations and programs to which their personal careers, fortunes, and ambitions, and their own conception of the public interest, are tied.

When the political administrative needs of governments are reinforced by the demands of province-oriented economic interests this may give rise to what has been called **province-building**. As the very term suggests, this is the provincial counterpart to the nation-building orientation of Sir John A. Macdonald's post-Confederation government. Province-building has been defined as the 'recent evolution of more powerful and competent provincial administrations which aim to manage socioeconomic change in their territories and which are in essential conflict with the central government.'[41] The concept generally has been associated with the provincial governments of Alberta and Quebec.[42] The Ontario government is as 'powerful and competent' as these other provincial states, and no one would accuse Ontario governments of being indifferent towards the direction of 'socio-economic change' within their borders. Ontario's pivotal status in Canadian politics, however, based on its large population and economic importance, has meant that it generally has been able to count on a sympathetic hearing in Ottawa. With the exception of the NDP government of Bob Rae (1990–5) and more recent complaining by the Liberal government of Dalton McGuinty about the **fiscal imbalance** between what Ontario contributes to federal coffers and what it receives back in federal transfers and spending, aggressive and persistent 'fed-bashing' has not been a popular blood sport among that province's politicians simply because it has not been necessary for the achievement of their goals. In other respects, however, Ontario governments have not lagged behind their more aggressive counterparts, and frequently have been at the forefront in expanding the political and administrative reach of the provincial state.

Intergovernmental Relations

The Constitution, we have seen, does not establish a neat division of legislative and taxation powers between Ottawa and the provinces. All of the chief sources of public revenue—personal and corporate income taxes, payroll taxes, sales taxes, and public-sector borrowing—are shared between the two levels of government. Likewise, both the federal and provincial governments are involved in all the major policy fields. Defence and monetary policy come closest to being exclusive federal terrain, although provincial governments do not hesitate to express their views on such issues as the location of armed forces bases, major defence purchases, and interest rates. On the provincial side, snow removal, refuse collection, and sidewalk maintenance are the sorts of local activities that supposedly are free from federal involvement. But not entirely: the money that Ottawa transfers annually to the provinces affects the amounts that provincial governments pay to their municipalities, thereby having an impact on municipalities' ability to carry out these local functions.

Divided jurisdiction has given rise to a sprawling and complicated network of relations linking the federal and provincial governments. This network has often been compared to an iceberg, only a small part of which is visible to the eye. The 'visible' tip of intergovernmental relations involves meetings of the Prime Minister and provincial premiers (first ministers' conferences) and meetings of provincial premiers. These meetings, which have become less frequent in recent years, always generate considerable media attention and some part of their proceedings usually takes place before the television cameras (see Figure 7.2). Less publicized, but far more frequent, are the hundreds of annual meetings between federal and provincial cabinet ministers and bureaucrats. Many of these meetings take place in the context of ongoing federal–provincial structures like the Continuing Committee on Economic and Fiscal Matters, established in 1955, and the Economic and Regional Development Agreements negotiated between Ottawa and the less affluent provinces. Others are generated by the wide range of shared-cost activities that link the two levels of government, from major spending programs such as the Canada Health and Social Transfer to smaller federal subsidies such as for official minority-language education. In the six-month period from January to June 2010, 36 federal–provincial meetings took place at the ministerial and senior bureaucratic levels.[43]

Executive federalism is a term sometimes used to describe the relations between cabinet ministers and other high-ranking officials of the two levels of government. The negotiations between them and the agreements they reach are usually undertaken with minimal, if any, input from either legislatures or the public. The secrecy that generally cloaks this decision-making process, combined with the fact that the distinction between federal and provincial responsibilities is often blurred by the deals it produces, has generated charges that executive federalism is undemocratic. It is undemocratic because it undermines the role of elected legislatures whose role, if they have one at all, is usually limited to ratifying *faits accomplis*. Second, an agreement to finance jointly the cost of a program or to share a particular tax field or legislative power makes it difficult for citizens to determine

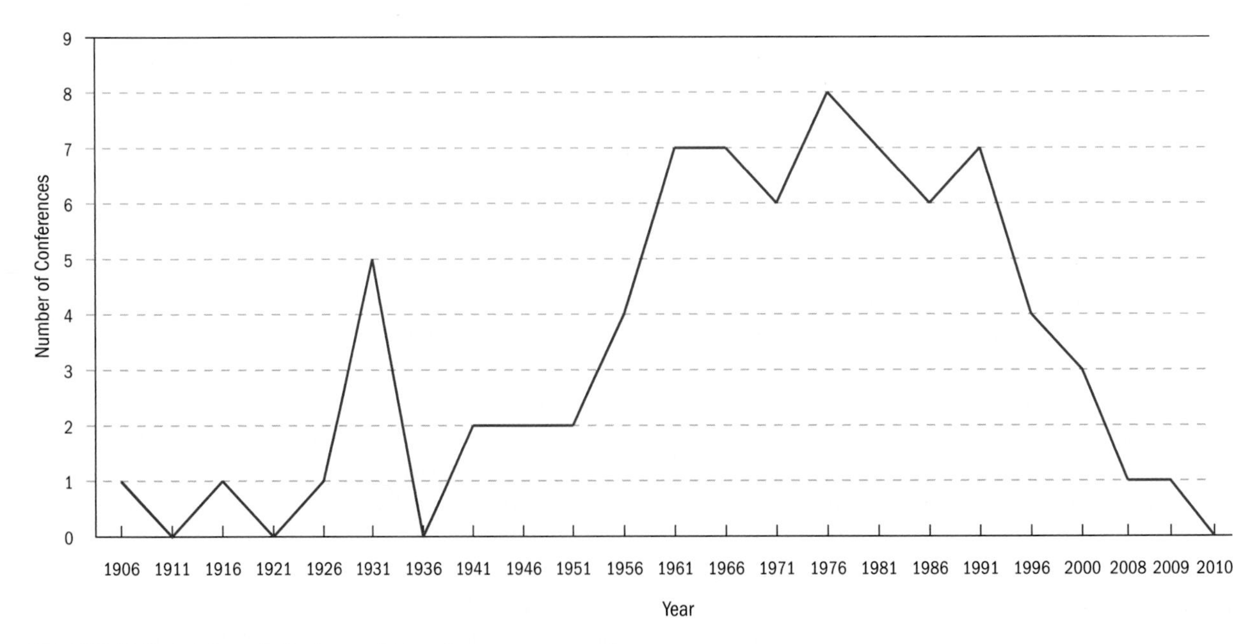

FIGURE 7.2 First Ministers' Conferences, 1906–2010

Source: Adapted with author updates from Canadian Intergovernmental Conference Secretariat, 'First Ministers' Conferences, 1906-2004', at <www.scics.gc.ca/CMFiles/fmp_e.pdf>.

which level of government should be held responsible for what policies. Third, executive federalism provides no meaningful opportunities for public debate of intergovernmental issues that affect the standard of health-care services, welfare, post-secondary education, local taxation, and other matters of real concern to citizens. Political parties, interest groups, and individual Canadians generally are excluded from a decision-making process dominated by cabinet ministers and intergovernmental affairs specialists of the two levels of government.

In addition to these indictments of executive federalism, Donald Smiley lists three others.[44]

- *It distorts the political agenda.* Executive federalism has a territorial bias. It reinforces the significance of territorially concentrated interests and of the provincial governments that represent them, at the same time as it undervalues the importance of other interests.
- *It fuels government expansion.* Competitive relations between Ottawa and the provinces have produced inefficient duplication, as each level of government has its own bureaucracy to pursue similar goals.
- *It perpetuates intergovernmental conflict.* The increasing sophistication of executive federalism, conducted through specialized bureaus staffed by intergovernmental affairs specialists, reduces the likelihood of resolving federal–provincial disputes. This is because specialized intergovernmental affairs bureaus, which exist in all provinces and at the federal level, and the experts who staff them tend to perceive issues in terms of the powers and jurisdiction of their particular government. Intergovernmental conflict is in a sense institutionalized by the fact that what is perceived to be at stake are the power, resources, and prestige of one's government.

In the face of this lengthy catalogue of allegations, executive federalism and its practitioners are left to rely on the defence of necessity. 'Overlapping powers' is an unavoidable fact of life under Canada's federal Constitution. In light of this, is it realistic to imagine that complex administrative and financial agreements can be negotiated in public forums? And besides, much of policy-making is carried on in a closed fashion, dominated by cabinet ministers and bureaucratic elites. Why condemn executive federalism for traits that are deeply embedded in Canadian policy-making generally? The fact of the matter is, however, that the characteristics of executive federalism are out of sync with the less deferential political culture that has evolved in Canada over the last generation. Governments will continue to conduct much of their negotiations behind closed doors and the constitutional division of powers will continue to be characterized by overlap, competition, and ambiguity. But public acceptance of this and other elitist forms of policy-making is today much weaker than in decades past.

Financing Federalism

From the very beginning, money has been at the centre of intergovernmental relations. The Confederation agreement included an annual per capita subsidy that Ottawa would pay to all provincial governments.[45] Moreover, the new federal government agreed to assume liability for the debts of the provinces as they stood in 1867.[46] Taxation powers were divided between the two levels of government, with Ottawa receiving what were at the time the major sources of public revenue.

These financial arrangements have never been adequate. At the root of the problem is the fact that the provinces' legislative responsibilities proved to be much more extensive and expensive than the founders had anticipated. This has been referred to as the *fiscal gap*. Provincial governments attempted to fill this gap between their revenues and their expenditure requirements through an increasing array of provincial taxes. Licence fees, succession duties, and personal and corporate income taxes all were used to increase provincial revenues. In addition, the provinces pressed Ottawa for more money. Indeed, only two years after Confederation the federal subsidy paid to Nova Scotia was increased. An important precedent was thereby established: federal–provincial financial relations are determined by governments, not by the Constitution.

Today, combined provincial and local revenues exceed those of the federal government (see Figure 7.3). The revenue position of the provinces improved steadily between the 1950s and the 1970s, as Ottawa conceded *tax room*—i.e., an increasing share of particular revenue sources like the personal income tax—to aggressive provincial governments. But at the same time, provincial dependence on subsidies from Ottawa remains high in several provinces. In the case of the poorest provinces, money from Ottawa currently accounts for about half of their total revenue. Part of this dependence has been encouraged by Ottawa through **shared-cost programs**, provincially administered programs where Ottawa's financial contribution is geared to how much a province spends. In the past Ottawa agreed to match provincial spending dollar for dollar. Until 1995 the major shared-cost program in Canada was the Canada Assistance Plan (CAP), which financed welfare and other provincial social services. The federal budget of that year replaced CAP with the Canada Health and Social Transfer to the provinces, the amount of which is not geared to provincial spending. Federal grants for health care and post-secondary education also were launched on a shared-cost basis, but were converted by Ottawa into **block funding** programs through the Federal–Provincial Fiscal Arrangements Act of 1977. The federal government argued, reasonably enough, that the shared-cost formula did not encourage the provinces to control program costs. Under block funding, Ottawa's financial contribution is geared to the previous year's subsidy plus an amount calculated on the basis of growth in the recipient province's gross product. Ottawa is not obliged to match provincial spending, and indeed the effect of the switch to block funding has been to transfer an increasing share of the burden of health care and post-secondary education costs onto the shoulders of the provinces.

What could possibly be wrong with the provinces carrying more of the costs for programs that fall under their constitutional jurisdiction? First, provincial governments argue that Ottawa encouraged them to spend more on social services by offering to share program costs on a matching basis. It is unfair, they claim, for the federal government to try to back out of financing policy areas whose growth it encouraged. Second, the provinces' ability to increase their own source revenues in order to compensate for reduced federal transfer payments is limited by the fact that they share all of the major taxes fields with Ottawa. Unless the federal government is willing to give up some tax room (i.e., some of its share of total tax revenue from a particular source) to the provinces, provincial governments face the hard choice of increasing the total tax burden on their citizens, charging or increasing user fees (e.g., tuition fees), or cutting back on program expenditures. Third, any reduction in Ottawa's commitment to financing provincial social services hurts the poorer provinces more than it does the wealthier ones. The Maritime provinces in particular are dependent on federal transfers in order to offer a level of social services comparable to that in other provinces. Figure 7.4 shows federal transfers to the provinces in 2008–9 as a percentage of provincial gross revenues.

Some of the money that Ottawa transfers to the provinces carries conditions as to how it must be spent. These are called conditional grants. Transfers that have no strings attached to them are called unconditional grants. Important examples of both include the following:

- Provincial social assistance programs must be based exclusively on need, and must not make previous residency in the province a condition for receiving benefits.
- The block transfer that Ottawa makes to the provinces under the Canada Health Transfer (CHT) and the Canada Social Transfer (CST) must be spent on health care and post-secondary education, and social services previously covered under CAP.
- The Canada Health Act, 1984 includes a provision that reduces Ottawa's payment to provincial governments that permit physicians to extra-bill their patients. The terms of the CHT and CST also specify that provinces must respect the principles of the Canada Health Act, 1965 (portability of coverage between provinces, comprehensiveness of provincial plans, universality, public funding, and public administration). Ottawa's contribution to

provincial health-care spending is, therefore, subject to some conditions.

- Equalization grants are paid to provincial governments whose per capita tax revenues (according to a complex formula negotiated between Ottawa and the provinces) fall below the average of the two most affluent provinces. **Equalization** accounts for about one-quarter of all federal cash transfers to the provinces, and about a quarter of the total revenue of the poorest provincial governments. It carries no conditions as to how it must be spent. Figure 7.5 provides a breakdown of federal transfers to the provinces.

The adequacy of federal transfers is not the only issue that has set Ottawa against the provincial governments. Another long-standing complaint of the provinces is that shared-cost programs distort provincial spending priorities because of the enticement of matching federal grants. Ottawa's spending power, they argue, permits undue federal interference in matters of provincial jurisdiction. The government of Quebec has been most insistent about this. Indeed, during the 1950s the provincial government of Maurice Duplessis refused to accept federal money for the construction of Quebec's portion of the Trans-Canada Highway and for universities, and was not even compensated for the fact that Canadian taxpayers residing in Quebec were paying for these programs in the other provinces. In 1965 the Quebec government of Jean Lesage opted out of the new Canada Assistance Plan (although Quebec has never been freed from the fairly minimal program

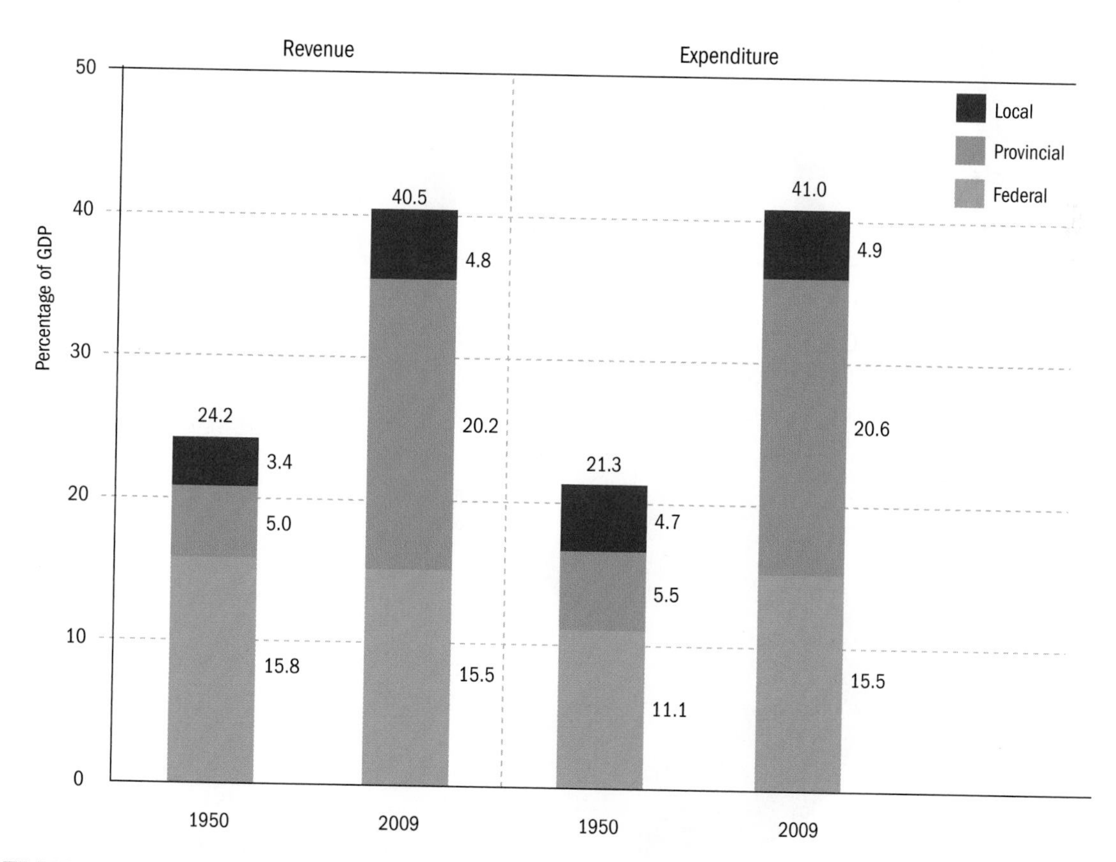

FIGURE 7.3 Public Finance in Canada: Revenue and Expenditure as Percentages of GDP for Each Level of Government, 1950 and 2009

Source: Based on data from Canada, Department of Finance, Fiscal Reference Tables, 2009; Statistics Canada, *Canadian Economic Observer*, Historical Statistical Supplement 1994–5, Catalogue no. 11-210.

standards that Ottawa sets) and some other conditional grant programs, receiving compensation in the form of tax room surrendered by Ottawa to the province. Both the Meech Lake and Charlottetown Accords included a provision that would have obligated Ottawa to provide 'reasonable compensation' to any provincial government choosing not to participate in a new national shared-cost program, so long as the province's own program was 'compatible with the national objectives'. Critics argued that this opened the door for an erosion of **national standards** in social policy. Defenders claimed that this particular section just constitutionalized a long-standing practice in Canadian federalism.

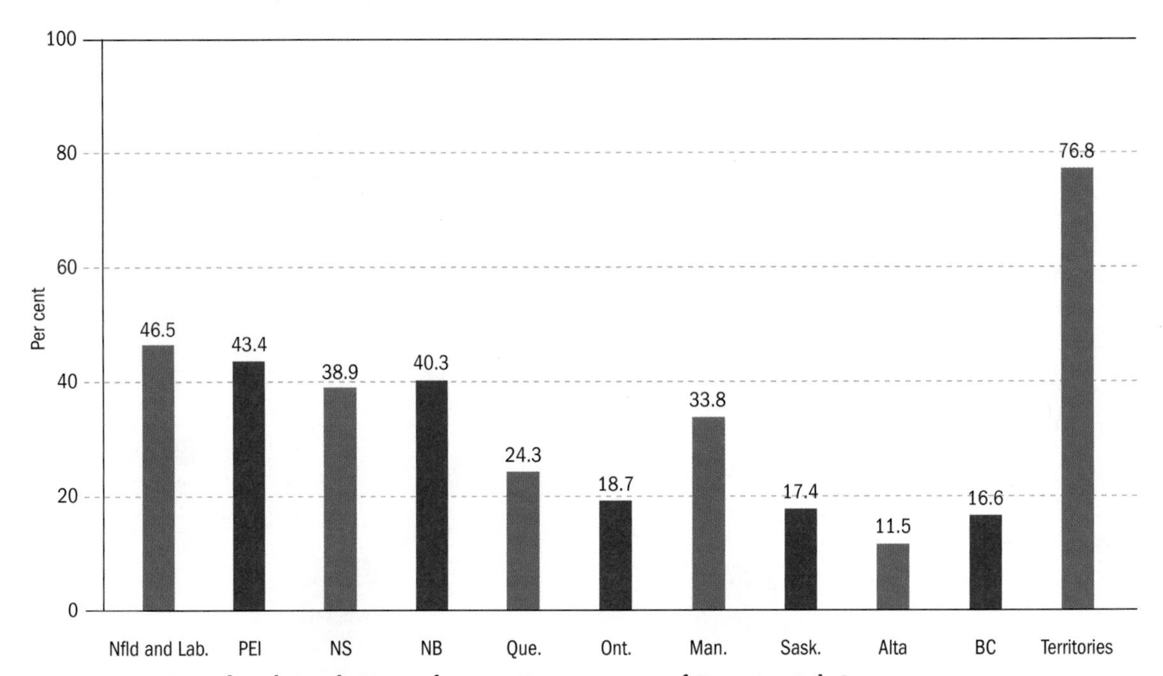

FIGURE 7.4 Federal Cash Transfers as Percentage of Provincial Government Expenditures, 2008–9

Source: Canada, Department of Finance, Fiscal Reference Tables, 2009.

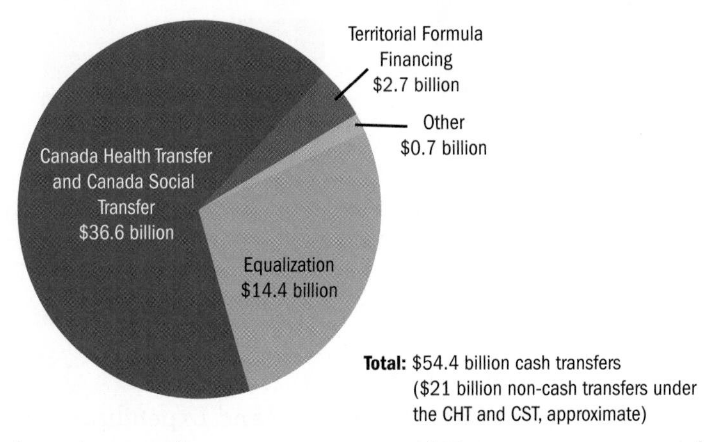

FIGURE 7.5 Federal Cash Transfers to Provinces and Territories, 2010–11 (estimated)

Source: Department of Finance, 'Government of Canada Support to Provinces and Territories at All-Time High', 18 Dec. 2009, at: <www.fin.gc.ca/n08/09-119-eng.asp>.

The Federal Spending Power, National Standards, and the Social Union

In the 1990s it became popular to vilify certain provincial governments, particularly the Conservative governments of Ralph Klein in Alberta and Mike Harris in Ontario, for having undermined national standards in social programs. In fact, however, one of the major threats to national standards came from Ottawa's shrinking financial commitment to provincially administered social programs. Federal transfers as a share of provincial program spending fell from 21 per cent in 1986–7 to 16 per cent in 1996–7.[47] The wealthier provinces, including Ontario, Alberta, and British Columbia, faced the largest burden of these federal cuts, starting with Ottawa's 1990 decision to limit the annual increase in CAP payments to these provinces to 5 per cent.

Ottawa's retreat from financing provincial social programs became unmistakable with the 1995 federal budget. Described as a 'new vision of confederation' by Liberal Finance Minister Paul Martin, the 1995 budget replaced the shared-cost programs that pay for welfare and social services under the CAP and EPF funding for health and post-secondary education with a single block transfer called the Canada Health and Social Transfer (CHST). The CHST institutionalized the ad hoc freezes and caps on transfers that both Liberal and Tory governments imposed from the early 1980s. It did so, in Ottawa's words, by ensuring that 'the amounts transferred will not be determined by provincial spending decisions (as under cost-sharing).'[48] Caps and freezes also had this effect, the difference being that Ottawa could always excuse what were effectively transfer cuts by citing their 'temporary' nature. The CHST appeared to put the decisive nail in the coffin of shared-cost programs and thus to mark a retreat from Ottawa's commitment to maintaining national standards in social policy, a commitment that has always depended on the federal spending power. In 2004 the CHST was divided into the Canada Health Transfer and the Canada Social Transfer, a change that provided greater transparency in identifying how much money was being transferred for what provincial spending purposes.

The appearance may, however, be deceptive. The Liberals' determination to rein in federal transfers to the provinces was not matched by a corresponding rhetoric of decentralization. On the contrary, the Liberal government refused to concede ground on the issue of national standards, particularly in regard to the health-care system (see Box 7.6). Their message to the provinces was this: we will give you fewer and fewer dollars with which to pay for your health-care services, but we will continue to set conditions on how those services must operate.

The Liberals' resolve was put to the test by the Conservative government of Alberta, which allowed the establishment of private clinics for certain health services like cataract operations, where patients, for a price, can jump the queue that they would otherwise face in the publicly funded system. At the end of the day, however, all Ottawa could do was withhold some of the health-care dollars Alberta received from the feds. For a wealthy province like Alberta, where federal cash transfers amount to less than 10 per cent of the provincial health-care budget, this is a penalty without much sting.

In explaining the advantages of the CHST, the 1995 budget documents stated that it would 'end the intrusiveness of previous cost-sharing arrangements'.[49] More specifically, the transition to block funding under the CHST was argued to have the following beneficial effects:

- Provinces will no longer be subject to rules stipulating which expenditures are eligible for cost-sharing or not.
- Provinces will be free to pursue their own innovative approaches to social security reform.
- The expense of administering cost-sharing will be eliminated.
- Federal expenditures will no longer be driven by provincial decisions on how, and to whom, to provide social assistance and social services.[50]

Provinces would not, however, be free to do whatever they please under the new fiscal arrangements.

The Liberal budget mentioned health care and social assistance as two areas where national standards would be maintained. In the case of social assistance this amounted only to an interdiction on minimum residency requirements. In regard to health care, the Liberals insisted that provinces

Politics in Focus

Box 7.5 Two Former Premiers and Two Views on Federal Transfers

For . . .

No Canadian should have his or her life chances determined solely by geography. Canadians enjoy a political culture much like a family; we are all responsible for each other. These principles, enshrined in our Constitution, differentiate us from our friends in the United States where no such program exists. The vehicle for leveling the national playing field is the country's equalization program. Because of equalization, the gap between richer and poorer provinces has been reduced. The Canadian people understand the principle. [Polls demonstrate] that overwhelming majorities in each province support equalization.

Still, ideological opponents of equalization argue that such a program is wrong; they claim that it interferes with the operation of market forces and perpetuates poverty in some regions of the country. These claims are demonstrably wrong. Equalization has never prevented provinces from developing their own natural resources. Saskatchewan's oil and natural gas industries were developed even though that province's equalization payments declined as a result. Equalization did not obstruct the mining of potash in Saskatchewan, nickel in Manitoba, and hydroelectric development in Quebec, Manitoba, and Newfoundland and Labrador. There is no reason for it to be otherwise in the future. Furthermore, Ontario has always supported equalization, recognizing as it does that a strong Canada also strengthens that province.

Howard Pawley, former Premier of Manitoba (1981–8) and Adjunct Professor, University of Windsor, in *Opinion Canada* 7, 10 (17 Mar. 2005). Reprinted by permission of the author.

Against . . .

I think it was Karl Marx who once said that religion is the opiate of the masses. Well, I can tell you that federal dependency is the opiate of this region, Atlantic Canada. Dependency—unemployment insurance, welfare cheques, transfer payments—have all become a narcotic to us to which we have become addicted. And there is not a person in this room that can tell you and me that we have not been influenced and affected, and had our behaviour modified by being part of that culture, because it shaped everything that we are. We know it to be true. We know it better than anybody else in Canada.

Looking at experience from all over the world, I can tell you that those jurisdictions which establish low and predictable corporate tax regimes end up resulting in much better growth, and long-term growth, and a much better environment for business to prosper.

What we need to do is get rid of all of the make-work projects and the money we spend transferring people to federal unemployment. We need to get rid of all those programs and either get rid of the taxes low income people pay or offer income supplementation so they are always better off working in a job. If we do that, if we change that incentive system, it will have a powerful impact on Atlantic Canada.

I despise the people who whine and snivel about their lot in life within this country. People who tell us that, unless they get their lighthouses saved, they're going to separate from Canada, have no time in my book. We may not like base closures in Atlantic Canada, and we certainly don't like transfer payment cuts . . . but we will not—we will not—consider that an act of alienation or humiliation.

Frank McKenna, former Premier of New Brunswick (1987–97), in a speech to the Atlantic Vision Conference of Atlantic Canadian Premiers in Moncton, NB, 9 Oct. 1997. Reprinted by permission.

would have to respect the principles of the Canada Health Act. But even if Ottawa was able to enforce national standards on the provinces, critics noted that the lumping together of Ottawa's transfer for health care, social assistance, and post-secondary education under the CHST would permit provinces greater room to redistribute their spending between politically unpopular welfare programs and more popular health care and education spending.

Ottawa's retreat from its financial commitment to provincially administered social programs—a retreat, it should be said, that was motivated more by the Liberal government's desire to reduce its budget deficit rather than by what Finance Minister Martin grandly called a 'new vision of federalism'—was not received well by provincial governments. Ottawa's success in transforming budget deficits into surpluses was largely due to cuts in transfers to the provinces, the use of Employment Insurance fund surpluses as general revenue, and increased federal tax revenues during the mid- to late 1990s. Very little of

Governing Realities

Box 7.6 Health Care and Federalism: Canada's Second Longest-Running Soap Opera

After the issue of Quebec's constitutional status, health care has a reasonable claim to being Canadian federalism's second longest-running soap opera. Elements of intrigue, betrayal, good, and evil intermingle in a story that reveals much about the nature of intergovernmental relations.

A 'soap opera digest' summary of how the story has unfolded might go something like this. Ottawa and the provincial governments co-operated during the 1960s to create a national health-care system that would be administered by the provinces, but where they would share the costs with the federal government. Ottawa, flush with revenue in the 1960s and disposed to encourage provinces to spend money on social programs that fell under provincial jurisdiction, agreed to match provincial spending on health care, a formula that provided little incentive for the provinces to control costs. The feds began to back away from this open-ended commitment to health care in the late 1970s. Over the next 20 years the federal contribution to health care, as a share of total public spending on health, would drop dramatically from about 50 per cent to 20 per cent.

Provincial cries of betrayal were met with federal accusations of provincial treachery, as Ottawa accused some of the provinces of allowing creeping privatization and the importation of 'American-style' health care. No one could agree on the numbers. Ottawa protested that its contribution was much greater than the provinces claimed, if the mysterious phenomenon of 'tax points' were included. Ottawa threatened to withhold dollars from the province of Alberta in a struggle that it characterized as nothing short of good, compassionate Canadianism versus evil individualistic conservatism.

By the end of the 1990s Ottawa and several of the provinces launched major studies of the health-care system, producing duelling reports on what was wrong and what to do about it. Alberta's Mazankowski Report recommended greater room for private elements to operate alongside the public health-care system. Ottawa's Romanow Report recommended more spending—much more spending—as a major part of the solution to the system's woes. In early 2003, Ottawa and the provinces reached a deal whereby $12 billion in new health-care funding would be transferred to the provinces during the period 2003–8.

Well into its fourth decade, there is little likelihood that the Canadian health-care soap opera will disappear from the prime-time schedule anytime soon. It became an important campaign issue in the 2004 and 2006 federal elections. If there is a federalism lesson to be learned from the last 30 years of intergovernmental conflict over health care it is this: sharing the costs of an expensive policy area is a prescription for political and bureaucratic rivalry, muddied accountability, and mutual recriminations.

the turnaround in federal finances was due to cuts in Ottawa's program spending, although the Liberal government certainly conveyed this impression. From the provinces' point of view, Ottawa's deficit-cutting strategy was at their expense, leaving provincial governments with the politically difficult choices between raising taxes or cutting services or doing a bit of both. Moreover, the Liberal government's insistence that national standards for health care and welfare would have to be respected was particularly galling, ignoring the old adage that he who pays the piper calls the tune.

This was the background to the idea of a Canadian *social union*, a concept that emerged in the wake of the transfer cuts announced in Ottawa's 1995 budget. Although the meaning attributed to the term depends on who is defining it, it is fair to say that the social union involves some new set of arrangements for funding and determining program standards in the areas of health, welfare, and post-secondary education. Provinces like Alberta and Ontario, whose per capita payments under the CHT and CST are the lowest in Canada, tend to see the social union as a commitment to national standards in social policy that are not federally imposed standards, negotiated between the provinces and Ottawa in a spirit that reflects each province's constitutional authority in matters of social policy. This is a decentralized version of the social union, under which the balance of control over and money to fund social programs would shift to the provinces. Ottawa and some of the more transfer-dependent provinces have viewed the social union differently, insisting on a central role for the feds in maintaining the interprovincial uniformity of social program standards, limiting provincial barriers against citizens from other provinces when it comes to social services (for example, provincial residency requirements such as those BC maintains as a condition for welfare eligibility or the higher tuition fees that Quebec universities charge out-of-province Canadian students), and continuing a strong federal role in financing social programs. The Quebec government kept its distance from the formal social union negotiations, insisting on a principle that has long been defended by provincial governments of various

In a 2004 initiative on health care struck between then Liberal Prime Minister Paul Martin and the provincial premiers, Quebec negotiated a separate deal in acknowledgement of its unique health-care system. Some Canadians felt this 'special treatment' was unfair, particularly since attempts by Alberta to introduce new elements into its system, such as limited private care, had previously been opposed by the federal government.

party stripes in Quebec, namely, that neither Ottawa nor the other provinces have any constitutional authority to interfere with Quebec's autonomy in setting its standards for social policy.

Ideology was never very far from the surface of debates on the social union. To the degree that the social union was associated with a redistribution of power and money away from Ottawa and towards the provinces, it was often characterized as being part of a market-oriented agenda that was hostile to entitlements and the welfare state. This characterization, however, was always overly simplistic and misleading. While it certainly is true that the ideologically conservative governments of Ontario and Alberta in the later 1990s preferred a version of the social union that would increase their autonomy in determining standards in provincial social policy and that, as a consequence, would weaken Ottawa's ability to set and enforce national standards, the NDP government in British Columbia and the PQ government in Quebec—neither of which were ideological soulmates of their Ontario and Alberta counterparts—also supported more provincial autonomy.

On 4 February 1999, Prime Minister Chrétien and nine of the 10 provincial premiers agreed to the Social Union Framework Agreement (SUFA). Quebec's separatist Premier Lucien Bouchard was present but refused to sign the agreement, maintaining that Ottawa's retention of the right to set national standards in social policy and penalize provinces that refused to conform to those standards represented an unconstitutional intrusion into matters of provincial jurisdiction. In taking this stand Premier Bouchard remained faithful to a position that all Quebec governments, separatist and non-separatist, have insisted on since the 1960s.

The willingness of Alberta, Ontario, and British Columbia to agree to such a social union pact, with Ottawa formally retaining its right to withhold money from any province that, in its view, violates the principles of the social union and to initiate new federal programs in the area of social policy, was probably due to money. Ottawa promised all

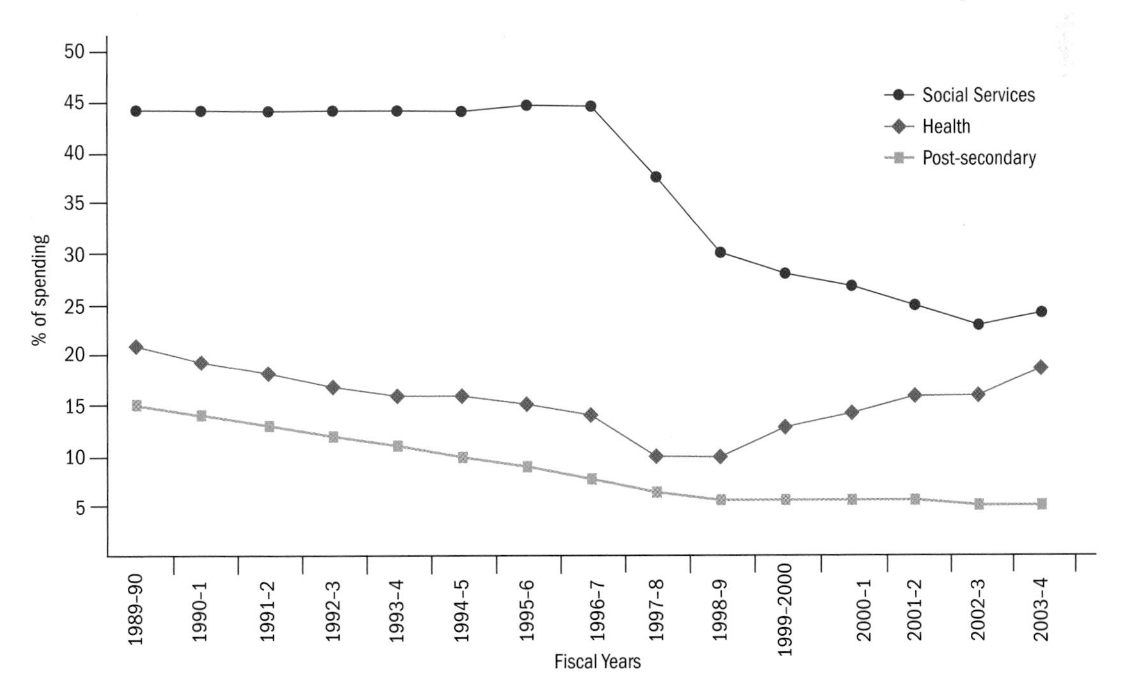

FIGURE 7.6 Federal Social Transfers as a Percentage of Provincial Program Spending, 1989–2003

Source: France St-Hilaire, 'Fiscal Gaps and Imbalances: The New Fundamentals of Canadian Federalism', 20 May 2005, at: <www.irpp.org>.

of the provinces more money—about $2.5 billion per year in new health-care funding—which really amounted to a reinstatement of federal transfers that had been cut over the previous few years, said the deal's critics. Only Quebec, for political reasons, was able to reject this enticement. The Quebec government was alone in insisting that the SUFA include the right of a province to get out of new national social programs with financial compensation to operate its own programs free of federal dollars and standards. Ottawa insisted that the social union pact is binding on Quebec, despite that province's unwillingness sign it. In this case 'binding' meant that the Quebec government received some new health-care funding, just like the other provinces, but beyond this Ottawa lacked any serious levers that could be used to compel an unco-operative Quebec government into complying with the other provisions of the deal.

Until the recession that began in late 2008, which sent many national economies into a tailspin, the federal government experienced large annual budget surpluses for several years, totalling over $61 billion between 1997 and 2005. But anyone who expected that this would lead to a return to the older model of fiscal federalism, whereby Ottawa would use financial transfers to the provinces to achieve its social policy objectives, has been disappointed. 'Since 1997', observes France St-Hilaire, '[Ottawa] has clearly preferred to reinvest in direct spending initiatives over which it is able to maintain full control and gain visibility.'[51] This has been particularly so, St-Hilaire notes, in the fields of post-secondary education and social services where most federal spending now takes the form of programs administered by Ottawa rather than money transferred to the provinces to finance their programs in these fields. The exception—and it is an important exception—involves health care. As Figure 7.6 shows, the federal share of provincial spending on health care rebounded after the trough experienced in the late 1990s. In 2005 Parliament legislated an automatic escalator of 6 per cent per year in the value of cash payments to the provinces under the Canada Health Transfer. This annual increase, negotiated with the provincial governments in 2004, is to continue until 2013–14. Unlike post-secondary education and social services, where Ottawa has been able to create and administer its own programs, this simply is not possible on a significant scale in the area of health care. In order to maintain some leverage over policy in the health field, Ottawa has had no choice but to increase its financial contribution to provincial health-care programs. Nonetheless, the scale of federal transfers is today significantly less than it was in the decades when the public health-care system was constructed on the basis of the 50/50 financing formula.

Starting Points for Research

Herman Bakvis and Grace Skogstad, eds, *Canadian Federalism: Performance, Effectiveness, and Legitimacy*, 2nd edn (Toronto: Oxford University Press, 2008). This is the best recent reader on Canadian federalism and intergovernmental relations.

Alan Cairns, *Charter versus Federalism: The Dilemmas of Constitutional Reform* (Montreal and Kingston: McGill-Queen's University Press, 1992). The essays in this collection examine the demise of the older elite accommodation-style politics and the dominance of federalism issues and the ascendance of what Cairns calls 'Charter Canadians', whose identities and demands on government are powerfully influenced by the Charter.

Thomas Courchene and John R. Allan, eds, *Canada: The State of the Federation 2009: Carbon Pricing and Environmental Federalism* (Montreal and Kingston: McGill-Queen's University Press, 2010). This recent edition of an annual publication of the Institute of Intergovernmental Relations at Queen's University focuses on issues of shared jurisdiction in environmental regulation.

Alan Maslove, ed., *How Ottawa Spends 2008–2009: A More Orderly Federalism?* (Montreal and Kingston: McGill-Queen's University Press, 2008). In this annual issue of a long-standing series produced by Carleton University's School of Public Administration, the focus is on federal–provincial relations under the Harper government.

Ian Peach, ed., *Constructing Tomorrow's Federalism: New Perspectives on Canadian Governance* (Winnipeg: University of Manitoba Press, 2007). Includes chapters by some of Canada's foremost experts on federalism.

Richard Simeon, *Political Science and Federalism: Seven Decades of Scholarly Engagement* (Kingston, Ont.: Institute of Intergovernmental Relations, Queen's University, 2002). This is a highly readable survey of the study of federalism in Canada since the Great Depression.

Donald Smiley, *The Federal Condition in Canada* (Toronto: McGraw-Hill Ryerson, 1987). Although somewhat dated, this survey of the development, nature, and challenges associated with Canadian federalism, written by arguably the most astute observer of the subject, remains worthwhile reading.

Pierre Elliott Trudeau, *Federalism and the French Canadians* (Toronto: Macmillan, 1968). In these classic essays, written before he became Prime Minister, Trudeau considered the meaning and significance of Canadian federalism, the protection of French language rights, the role of Quebec in Canadian federalism, and the development of nationalism in French Canada.

Review Exercises

1. Go to <archives.cbc.ca/politics/elections/clips/14735/>. What does this piece on the 2007 re-election of Newfoundland Premier Danny Williams indicate about the relationship of that province to the federal government? Would you say that this relationship is mainly similar to or different from that between Alberta and Ottawa?
2. Visit the primary website for the government of Canada <www.gc.ca>. Click on 'About Government' and then 'Provincial and Territorial Governments'. Click on a province or territory that is not your own. Make a list of the main public issues discussed at the site. What information is provided about the relationship of the province's/territory's finances and programs to Ottawa?
3. Draw up a list of issues that would have to be resolved if Quebec were to separate from the rest of Canada. Attach a level of difficulty to each, ranging from 1 (very easily resolvable) to 10 (almost impossible to resolve).
4. Does it matter which level of government pays for what share of health-care costs and which level or levels set the rules for health policy? In answering this question be sure to address the issues of constitutionality, political accountability, Canadian values, and taxpayer interests.

The House of Commons represents the principle of government by popular consent, as it is the scene for debate among the representatives elected to office by citizens. In the House on Parliament Hill and next door at the Supreme Court many important decisions affecting the lives of Canadians are made. © Tektite/ Dreamstime.com

8 The Machinery of Government

Modern government is complicated. This chapter examines the key components of the machinery of government, including the following topics:

- The monarch and Governor General.
- The Prime Minister and cabinet.
- Central agencies.
- The legislature.
- The influence and activities of MPs.
- A democratic deficit?
- The courts.
- How a law is passed.

Like a Rube Goldberg invention, modern government appears to be an unwieldy and complicated apparatus. Many of its parts seem to perform no useful function, and the overall impression may sometimes seem to be one of unco-ordinated and often pointless activity. It appears to have been assembled piece by piece, without much planning and without discarding old parts to make room for new ones. The purpose of the machinery is easily lost sight of in its Byzantine complexity and it seems certain that there must be a more efficient way of doing whatever the apparatus is intended to accomplish.

But for all its inelegance and appearance of muddling, the machinery does produce results. Laws are passed, regulations are applied, applications are dealt with, cheques are issued, and the innumerable other specific tasks performed by government are carried out. How well these tasks are done, whether some of them should be done at all, and what other things should be done by public authorities are important questions. But before we can answer them, we need an understanding of the machinery itself—of its individual parts, the functions they perform, and the relations between them.

In these next two chapters we will focus on state institutions at the national level. But Canadians also encounter the machinery of government at the provincial and local levels, where the state's activities affect their lives in ways that often seem more direct and significant. Hospitals, doctors' services, schools, rubbish collection and disposal, water treatment, police, roads, and urban mass transit: these are all primarily the responsibilities of provincial and local governments. Together, provincial and local governments out-spend and out-tax the federal government.

The formal organization of the government of Canada is shown in Figure 8.1. Portrayed this way, the structure appears to be quite simple—deceptively simple, as it turns out! The three branches of government coincide with three major functions of democratic governance: the legislature makes the laws; the executive branch implements the laws; and the judicial branch interprets the laws.

In reality, however, these compartments are not watertight. The legislature does indeed debate and pass laws, but these laws typically originate in the executive branch as bills that are seldom expected

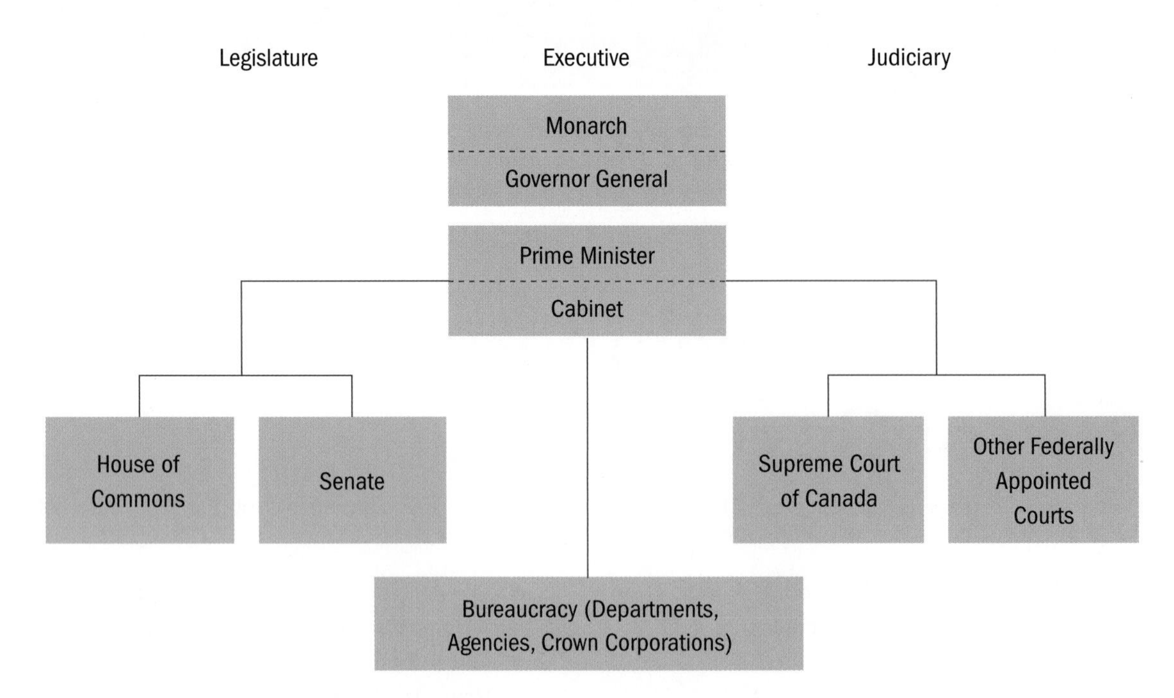

FIGURE 8.1 The Formal Organization of Canadian Government

to change much, if at all, as they make their way through the legislative mill. The legislature, in fact, is dominated by a small group of its members—the Prime Minister and cabinet—who oversee the executive branch. The judicial branch of government does not, strictly speaking, involve itself in the making of laws. In recent times, however, Canadian courts have played a major role in the determination of policy on such matters as Sunday shopping, abortion, Aboriginal landownership, the collective bargaining rights of workers, and same-sex benefits such as pension rights for gays and lesbians and the legal definition of marriage. The courts may truly be said to have made policy on many important public issues. Is the distinction between making policy and making law really a distinction without a difference and, if so, can we say that through their responsibility for interpreting the law the courts become involved in what amounts to law-making? The bureaucrats whose job it is to implement the laws passed by their political masters in the executive branch often have enormous discretion in determining the actual meaning of laws that provide them with only vague guidelines about what they are expected to do. When elected officials delegate discretion to non-elected bureaucrats are they not also delegating part of their law-making function?

While the actual operations of the machinery of Canadian government are more complex than its formal organization suggests, nevertheless, the respective roles of the legislative, executive, and judicial branches are significantly different and their differences are rooted in our expectations for democratic government. These expectations can be briefly summarized as follows:

The legislative branch shall . . .

- represent the people and be accountable to them through periodic elections;
- debate public issues and provide a forum for competition between political parties;
- make laws.

The executive branch shall . . .

- implement the laws;
- ensure that the public's business is carried out efficiently, accountably, and in accordance with the law;
- be non-partisan at the bureaucratic level, such that non-elected officials faithfully carry out the policies of whatever party forms the government of the day.

The judicial branch shall . . .

- be non-partisan and free from interference by the government;
- interpret the law's meaning;
- not substitute its preferences for those of elected public officials in matters of public policy, as distinct from legal and constitutional interpretation.

Democratic expectations are not, however, immutable. Today, many people expect that the bureaucracy should be representative of the population it serves, an expectation that may affect bureaucratic recruitment and promotion policies. Some argue that it is neither realistic nor desirable to expect non-elected officials to be politically neutral, and that accountability for policy (as distinct from its implementation) should be shared between politicians and bureaucrats. The elevated status of Canadian courts in the political process since the Charter of Rights and Freedoms was passed in 1982 has been welcomed by those who see judges as more likely than politicians to protect rights and promote democracy. Others, clinging to more traditional expectations, lament that the courts have come to trespass on turf that properly belongs to the people's elected and accountable representatives. The courts are also expected by many to be representative, instead of being dominated by white males. The under-representation of women and minorities on the bench, these critics say, undermines the courts' ability to reflect the diverse interests and values of Canadians.

Expectations for our institutions of government are not chiselled in stone. In this chapter we will discuss the main characteristics and roles of the institutions that comprise the machinery of Canadian government, including the changes that have taken place in their roles and the controversies associated with these changes.

The Executive Branch

The Monarch and Governor General

Canada is a constitutional monarchy. The monarch, currently Queen Elizabeth II, embodies the authority of the Canadian state. Any action of the government of Canada is taken in the Queen's name.[1] The monarch is responsible for appointing the Prime Minister and for deciding when Parliament will be dissolved and a new election held. When she is not in Canada, which is, of course, most of the time, her duties are carried out by the Governor General, currently David Johnston, a former university president. Although the strict letter of the Constitution suggests that the role of the monarch in Canada's system of government is a formidable one, most Canadians realize that the Queen and Governor General perform mainly symbolic functions. The real decision-making powers of the executive are exercised by the Prime Minister, who is the head of government, and cabinet.

Listen to the 'Who Is Canada's Head of State? (and Does It Matter?)' podcast, available at www.oupcanada.com/Brooks7e

In matters such as the selection of the Prime Minister and the dissolution of Parliament, constitutional convention is far more important than the discretion of the monarch. For example, when one party wins a majority of the seats in an election, the choice of Prime Minister is automatic. Even when no party has a majority, it is understood that the leader of the party with the most seats will be given the first opportunity to try to form a government that has the support of a majority in the legislature. If, however, it is clear that the members of the other parties will not support a government led by this person, the monarch's representative may turn directly to the leader of another party. This happened in Ontario after the 1985 provincial election. Whatever the legislative scenarios appear to be, it is understood that a newly elected legislature must at least be given the opportunity to meet. The monarch's representative cannot simply decide that there is no point in convening the legislature and that a new election should be held straightaway.

Likewise in the case of dissolving Parliament, the monarch's discretion is limited by constitutional conventions that have developed over time. Normally, the Prime Minister's request that Parliament be dissolved and a new election held will be granted automatically. It is remotely conceivable, although highly improbable, that in circumstances of minority government the monarch's representative could refuse such a request and instead ask the leader of another party to try to form a government. The last time this happened was in 1926, when Governor General Lord Byng refused Prime Minister Mackenzie King's request for a new election. This refusal provoked a minor constitutional crisis. Since then, the view of most constitutional experts has been that the monarch's representative is required to accept the 'advice' given by the Prime Minister.

The Byng precedent suddenly and rather unexpectedly became relevant several weeks after the federal election of 2008, which produced a Conservative minority government. Although the factors that precipitated the affair are a matter of dispute—some claim that the opposition parties were outraged at what they saw as the government's failure to pay proper attention to the economy in the Minister of Finance's economic statement, while others argued that the Conservatives' proposal to eliminate public funding for political parties was the real trigger for the unexpected unity among the opposition parties—the opposition parties agreed to bring down the government on a motion of non-confidence in the House of Commons. They also agreed to a coalition pact whereby the Liberals and NDP would form a coalition government for a period of at least two years, supported by the BQ. But before they could replace the Conservatives as the government, the Governor General would have to refuse Prime Minister Harper's request for a new election, instead calling on Liberal leader Stéphane Dion to form a government. Constitutional experts were divided on the question of whether the Governor General would be breaking an important unwritten rule of the Constitution in turning down such a request. In the end, the question became moot when Prime Minister Harper decided to request a prorogation of Parliament until late January 2009, when the government planned to introduce a budget.

The monarch and Governor General play no significant role in setting the government's policy agenda or in the subsequent decision-making process. Royal assent to legislation is virtually automatic. It has never been withheld from a law passed by Parliament. On the occasions when the monarch's provincial representatives, the lieutenant-governors, used the disallowance and reservation powers, this was almost always at the behest of the elected government in Ottawa.[2]

What role, then, does the monarchy play in Canada's system of government? We have said that the monarch's role today is primarily a symbolic one. This does not mean that the functions performed by the Queen and Governor General—and lieutenant-governors at the provincial level—are unimportant. The ceremonial duties that are part of government must be performed by someone, and it may be that assigning them to a head of state who is above the partisan fray reduces the possibility of too close an association between the political system itself—the state—and the leadership of particular political factions within it. As James Mallory argues, '[the monarchy] denies to political leaders the full splendor of their power and the excessive aggrandizement of their persons which come from the undisturbed occupancy of the centre of the stage.'[3] Perhaps, but it must be admitted that these state functions are performed by an elected president in countries such as the United States and France without there being much evidence that this has imperilled those democracies. On the other hand, both the American and French political systems have legislative checks on executive power that do not exist in a British parliamentary system. Mallory may be correct, therefore, in his belief that a non-elected head of state serves as a buffer against the self-aggrandizing tendencies of elected politicians. Paradoxically, then, a non-democratic institution, i.e., an unelected head of state, may contribute to the protection of a democratic social order.

But the monarchy has not always been an uncontroversial pillar of stability in Canadian politics. Despite the constitutional fact that the monarch's status in Canada's system of government is that of the King or Queen of Canada, not of the United Kingdom, the institution of monarchy has been perceived by some as an irritating reminder of Canada's colonial ties to Britain and of the dominance of Anglo-Canadians in this country's politics. This was particularly true during the 1960s, when royal visits to Quebec acted as lightning rods for the anti-federalist grievances of Quebec nationalists. Ancient memories of English domination and French subordination have faded, but they have not disappeared. The failure of the Meech Lake Accord in 1990 led many francophone politicians to call for the cancellation of the Queen's scheduled visit to Montreal. When French–English tensions run high, the issue of which groups in Canada are symbolically represented by the monarch resurfaces.

Despite occasional imbroglios over royal visits, we should not exaggerate the institution's contribution to national disunity. The summer 2010 tour of Canada by Queen Elizabeth II avoided Quebec entirely. This may have been due to competing demands on her time. But the decision not to visit Quebec might also have been influenced by the fact that the November 2009 visit to Montreal of Prince Charles and Lady Camilla Parker-Bowles occasioned egg-throwing, chants of 'le Québéc pour les québécois', and several arrests of demonstrators who were mainly associated with the ultra-nationalist/leftist Réseau de résistance du québécois. The incident suggested that the institution of the monarchy has not entirely lost its power to excite passions in Canada.

A new sort of controversy was associated with the position of Governor General during the tenure of Adrienne Clarkson (1999–2005). Clarkson's spouse, John Ralston Saul, is a well-known philosopher-historian and author. Saul's writing and public pronouncements on contemporary issues, as when he was critical of the American reaction to the terrorist attacks of 11 September 2001 and expressed skepticism about George W. Bush's competence as a leader, focused attention on the question of whether his relationship to the Governor General ought to have limited his forays into political matters. While his defenders noted that he was a private citizen, entitled to the same freedom of speech to which any other citizen is entitled, this was somewhat disingenuous. Like Governor General Clarkson, Saul was referred to as 'His Excellency' and made use of the publicly financed staff and other facilities that are part of the office of Governor General. Whether this reality ought to have limited his participation in the more controversial side of public life was a matter on which there was disagreement.

Perhaps more importantly, Governor General Clarkson showed occasional signs of wanting to reshape the boundaries of the office's role in public life. For example, in 2001 she sent a message of congratulations to a gay couple in Ontario who were wed in Toronto's Metropolitan Community Church, at a time when there was much public controversy over the legal definition of marriage. Critics charged that as a non-elected and non-partisan head of state, Clarkson should not have expressed views that could have been construed as critical of existing law and therefore politically divisive. Michaëlle Jean, Clarkson's successor as Governor General, was not averse to wading into potentially controversial waters (see Box 8.1).

Listen to the 'Who Should Represent Canada and Why?' podcast, available at www.oupcanada.com/Brooks7e

The Prime Minister and Cabinet

In contrast to the passive and principally symbolic roles of the monarch and Governor General, the Prime Minister (PM) and cabinet are at the centre of the policy-making process. The PM is the head of government in Canada. By convention, this person is the leader of the dominant party in the House of Commons. One of the PM's first duties is to select the people who will be cabinet ministers. In the vast majority of cases these will be other elected members of the House of Commons, although it occasionally happens that a senator or two are appointed to cabinet in order to give the government representation from a region where the governing party has elected few or no members, or because of the special abilities of a senator. In the British parliamentary tradition, cabinet members always are drawn from the same political party as the PM (but see Box 8.2). In recent years, the size of the federal cabinet has ranged from a low of 20 to a high of almost 40 members. Provincial cabinets are somewhat smaller.

The power of the PM and cabinet rests on a combination of factors. One of these is the written

Politics in Focus

Box 8.1 The Governor General Urges Alberta's Legislature to Share the Wealth

The pioneer spirit of independence and resourcefulness in this province is legendary. And yet your deserved reputation for fierce individualism and economic self-reliance belies another lesser-known aspect of Alberta's character: your people are among the most generous of Canadians. Eighty-five per cent of you make financial contributions to charitable and non-profit organizations. Combined with those who volunteer their time, 94 per cent of your citizens believe in giving back.

Alberta's tremendous prosperity affords you the opportunity to make the most of this attitude of sharing. Surely a prime benefit to be derived from such communal wealth is the ability it gives us: to ensure that no one is left behind, and that each among us has a voice.

The health and prosperity of every society is compromised by the people within it who suffer from poverty, who are disadvantaged by birth, who fight against discrimination of all kinds.

Here in this House, at a time of unprecedented prosperity in your province, you have a golden opportunity to continue this tradition. Your capacity to make a difference in the lives of others through your actions and decisions is limitless.

Source: From 'Her Excellency the Right Honourable Michaëlle Jean Speech on the Occasion of the Official Welcoming Ceremony at the Legislative Assembly', 4 May 2006. At: <www.gg.ca/media/doc.asp?lang=e&DocID=4750>. Office of the Secretary to the Governor General of Canada 2006. Reproduced with the permission of the Minister of Public Works and Government Services 2006.

Constitution. Section 11 of the Constitution Act, 1867 states that 'There shall be a Council to aid and advise in the Government of Canada, to be styled the Queen's Privy Council for Canada.' Section 13 of that Act goes even further to specify that the actions of the monarch's representative in Canada, the Governor General, shall be undertaken 'by and with the Advice of the Queen's Privy Council for Canada'. The Privy Council is, of course, the cabinet, under the leadership of the PM. Although, formally, anyone who has ever been a member of cabinet retains the title of privy councillor after leaving government, only those who are active members of the government exercise the powers referred to in the Constitution.

These powers include control over the budget. Section 54 of the Constitution Act, 1867 requires that any legislation or other measure that involves the raising or spending of public revenue must be introduced by cabinet. In fact, cabinet dominates the entire legislative agenda of Parliament, not just money matters. MPs who are not members of the cabinet do have the right to introduce private members' bills. But the meagre time allocated to considering these bills and the operation of party discipline combine to kill the prospects of most of these initiatives.

More important than these written provisions of the Constitution, however, are constitutional conventions relating to the PM and cabinet. Although the position of Prime Minister is not even mentioned in the written Constitution, it is understood that the person who leads the dominant party in the House of Commons has the power to decide the following matters:

- who will be appointed to, or removed from, cabinet;
- when a new election will be held;
- the administrative structure and decision-making process of government;

Governing Realities

Box 8.2 Adapting Parliamentary Tradition to New Realities

The 2010 British election produced no clear winner. It did, however, produce a clear loser. Gordon Brown's Labour Party went from forming the government with 349 of the 650 seats in the House of Commons to a second-place finish with 258 seats and only 29 per cent of the popular vote. The Conservative Party, led by David Cameron, won 307 seats based on 36.1 per cent of the vote and the Liberal-Democratic Party of Nick Clegg won 57 seats and 23 per cent of the vote.

In the past these might have been seen as the ingredients for minority government. Instead, Conservative leader Cameron did something that few had expected. He entered an agreement with Liberal-Democrat leader Clegg to form a coalition government in which the Lib-Dems would be given seats in cabinet. This is a true coalition government of the sort that is common across much of Western Europe. It marked a dramatic break from the British parliamentary tradition of single-party rule. And perhaps the most remarkable fact associated with this sharp break with tradition was how little fuss it generated. Citizens and political commentators, for the most part, took it in stride.

If this sort of change is possible in the 'mother of parliaments', could it happen in Canada? Possibly. It would require particular circumstances, including an election that produces no clear winner and the willingness of two parties, with enough seats between them to command a majority in the legislature, to share the reins of power. This second condition is more elusive than it might appear, particularly in the case of a historically dominant party that might see such co-operation as carrying risks for its future election prospects. But as the British case shows, it is not out of the question; indeed, the British precedent can now be invoked in support of such a departure from parliamentary tradition.

- the selection of persons to a wide array of appointive positions, including deputy ministers, judges of all federal and provincial courts, senators, members of federal regulatory agencies and of the boards of directors of federal Crown corporations, ambassadors, etc.

These are formidable powers. They help to explain why the PM is always the pre-eminent figure in Canadian government, even when his or her decision-making style is a collegial one that encourages the participation of other members of cabinet. The PM's pre-eminence is reinforced by constitutional conventions on accountability. Although individual cabinet ministers are separately accountable to Parliament for the actions of their departments and the entire cabinet is collectively accountable for government policy, the PM cannot avoid personal accountability for the overall performance of government and for all major policies. The opposition parties and the media ensure that the PM takes the heat for these matters.

Responsible government is another constitutional convention that strengthens the power of the PM and cabinet. As we noted in Chapter 5, responsible government encourages party discipline. This means that the elected members of a party will tend to act as a unified bloc on most matters, particularly when voting on budget measures and important government legislation. If the members of the governing party break ranks, the government will fall. Party discipline, therefore, ensures that members of the governing party will normally be docile in their support of the government's policies. And when the government has a majority in both the House of Commons and the Senate, the automatic backing of the government party's backbenchers (i.e., MPs who are not cabinet ministers) enables the PM and cabinet to move their legislative agenda through Parliament without serious impediment. Cabinet dominance may be attenuated, however, during periods of minority government (see Box 8.3) and when different parties control the House of Commons and the Senate.

The weakness of Canada's political party organizations is another factor that reinforces the dominance of the PM and cabinet. Parties, particularly the Liberal and Conservative parties, are geared primarily towards fighting election campaigns. Neither the Conservative Party nor the Liberal Party is what one would consider a social movement party with extensive ties to and dependence on organizations and groups in civil society. These parties are much more concerned with raising money, selecting candidates, and contesting elections than they are with formulating policy. They usually have little influence on the policies adopted by the party leadership when it forms the government. There are two main reasons for this emphasis. One is the parties' efforts to attract a broad base of support. This requires that the party's leadership be allowed a large margin to manoeuvre in communicating the party's policies to different groups. A second reason involves the absence, except in the case of the NDP, of formal affiliations between the parties and organized interests. Since 1961 the NDP has been formally affiliated with the Canadian Labour Congress. Formal affiliations usually have the effect of narrowing a party's electoral appeal and increasing the weight in a party's internal affairs—including leadership selection and policy-making—of the affiliated group(s). Some, including prominent labour activist Buzz Hargrove, argue that it also has the effect of limiting organized labour's influence with other political parties that are more likely to win in particular constituencies or to form a government, and that labour should abandon its formal ties to the NDP in favour of strategic support for candidates and parties. In any case, history shows that when in power, NDP provincial governments have not been willing to tie themselves rigidly to the party's platform and have occasionally been willing to incur the ire of their union backers.

Statute law is not an important source of prime ministerial power. It provides, however, a significant legal basis for the authority and responsibilities of individual cabinet ministers. The statute under which a government department, agency, or Crown corporation operates will always specify which minister is responsible for the organization's actions. Legislation may also assign to a particular minister special powers over a part of the bureaucracy, such as a right of approval or veto of all or some category of the organization's decisions, or the right to order an agency or Crown corporation to base its decisions on particular guidelines or to act in a specific way. In fact, however, this sort of intervention is more likely to come from the PM and cabinet acting collectively rather than being the initiative of an individual minister.

The constitutional and statutory foundations of prime ministerial and cabinet powers are reinforced by the

Governing Realities

Box 8.3 Responsible Government: The Case of the 19 May 2005 Confidence Vote

The June 2004 general election produced Canada's first minority government since 1979. The Liberal Party held 135 of the 308 seats in the House of Commons. In order to have the confidence of the House, Paul Martin's government needed the support of all the 19 NDP members and at least one additional member to achieve a majority. Failure to muster a majority on an important vote in the Commons would require, according to the conventions of responsible government, that the Liberal government resign.

But did they? The precariousness of the Liberal government's position in the Commons and the steady stream of evidence of Liberal Party corruption coming out of the Gomery Commission created a situation where the government's defeat seemed imminent. Between them, the opposition Conservatives and Bloc Québécois had the numbers to defeat the Liberals. They had an election issue—the scandal over the misappropriation of public money by the Liberal Party in Quebec—and they had popular momentum. It appeared that the government had lost the confidence of the House. 'In Canada,' says Senator Eugene Forsey, one of the country's foremost constitutional experts, 'the Government and the House of Commons cannot be at odds for more than a few weeks at a time. If they differ on any matter of importance, then, promptly, there is either a new government or [an election].'[4] This is what responsible government is all about.

In practice, however, the constitutional waters are not quite so clear. When the opposition Conservatives made clear their intention to use one of their opposition days—days allotted to opposition parties when they determine the business that will be dealt with by the House—to introduce a motion of non-confidence in the government, the Liberals promptly declared that they would suspend opposition days for an unspecified period. Was this consistent with the spirit of responsible government? Finally, the Conservatives managed to force two votes on the government's budget. The government was defeated on both of these votes, but declared that these motions involved 'procedural' matters and were not tantamount to confidence motions. Was this faithful to the spirit of responsible government?

Some Canadians will remember how the story finished. The governing Liberals managed to peel off the votes of a couple of independent MPs—a former Conservative and a former Liberal—and in a spectacular last-minute coup enticed Belinda Stronach, who a year earlier had run for the Conservative Party leadership, into the Liberal fold with an immediate position in cabinet. When the vote on the second reading of the Liberal budget took place on 19 May 2005, the House was deadlocked: 152 to 152. The Speaker, Peter Milliken, cast the deciding vote. He voted for the Liberal budget.

Some observers saw in this a vindication of Canada's system of government. The House decided: the government survived. Others concluded that the weeks leading up to the budget vote of 19 May revealed just how murky the rules were on the question of when the government has lost the confidence of the House and its right to govern. And the deal-making and promises that kept the Liberal government in power led many to conclude that responsible government was no match for old-style, bare-knuckles, backroom politics.

relationship between the political executive and the media. This relationship is close and mutually dependent. The PM and members of cabinet regularly speak 'directly' to the people or to targeted publics via the media. Even when presenting or defending the government's policies in the House of Commons, they are aware of the wider audience to whom their words and behaviour are communicated by television cameras and the parliamentary press corps. For their part, journalists typically turn first to the PM and the responsible ministers when reporting on politics. In doing so, the media contribute to the personalization of politics and, more particularly, to the popular identification of government with the PM and cabinet. These tendencies have become even more pronounced as a result of the visual character of television—the medium that most Canadians depend on for national news—and modern electioneering techniques that focus on the party leaders.

The reality of direct communications between the PM and cabinet and the public has undermined the role of the legislature and political parties. When public sentiment can be gauged through public opinion polls and when the PM and cabinet ministers can speak to either the general public or targeted groups via the media and personal appearances, there is no perceived need to communicate through government MPs and the party organization. The result is that Parliament often seems to be little more than a procedural sideshow. This infuriates some constitutional purists, for whom Parliament is the proper conduit between the state and society. They argue that the practice of responsible government, the bedrock of the British parliamentary system, is subverted by direct communications between the government and the people. But the fact is that responsible government is already attenuated by party discipline. And, in any case, there is no reason to believe that a diminished communications role for Parliament and MPs has reduced the democratic accountability of government from what it was before images of the PM and other government members flickered nightly across television screens.

The communications role of the PM and cabinet is related to their representative functions. From the beginnings of self-government in Canada, cabinet formation has been guided by the principle that politically important interests should, whenever possible, be 'represented' by particular cabinet ministers. Adequate representation of different regions and even particular provinces has always been

It does look a bit like Central Canada!
And some of them speak english!
A few look almost like us!
One or two are friendly!
And they pay taxes expecting nothing in return!
Daring to leave Ottawa, the federal cabinet visits B.C.

Creating a cabinet that adequately represents all of the country's regions is a formidable challenge for any prime minister, and almost every sitting cabinet runs the risk of being perceived as under-representing certain provinces.

considered important, as has representation of francophones (see Figure 8.2).

The numerical dominance of anglophones has always ensured that they would be well represented in any government. Representation from the business community—the Minister of Finance has often been a person with professional connections to either the Toronto or Montreal corporate elite—and the inclusion of ministers perceived to be spokespersons for particular economic interests, particularly agriculture and occasionally labour, have also been significant factors in making appointments to particular cabinet positions. Some representational concerns, such as the inclusion of various religious denominations, have diminished in importance while others, such as the representation of women and non-French, non-British Canadians, have become increasingly significant.

Representational concerns also surface in the case of the PM. These concerns are particularly important when a party is choosing its leader. Candidates are looked at, by party members and the media, in terms of their likely ability to draw support from politically important regions and groups. At a minimum, an aspiring leader of a national political party cannot be associated too closely with the interests of a single region of the country. Moreover, he or she must be at least minimally competent in French. In practical terms, this means being able to read parts of speeches in French and answer

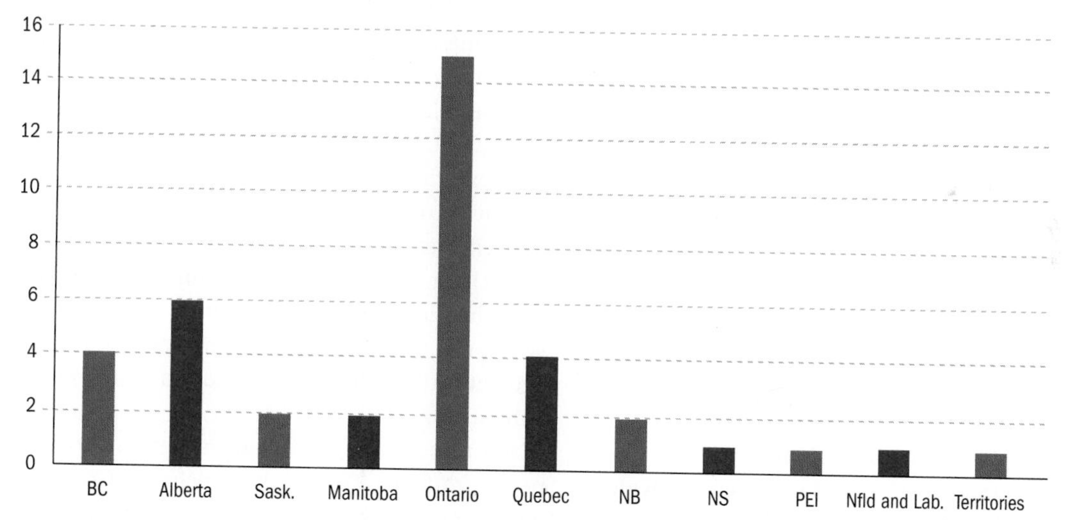

B. 1985 Mulroney Cabinet

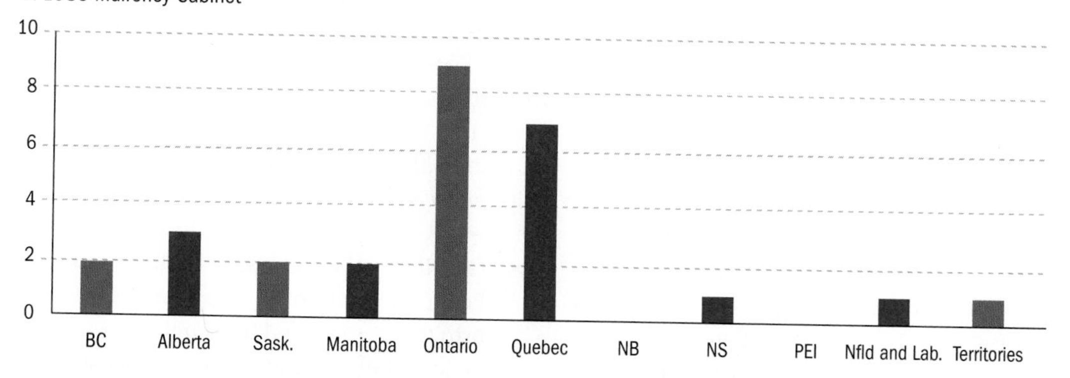

FIGURE 8.2 Regional Representation in the 1985 Mulroney and 2011 Harper Governments

*May.

questions in French. Given the numerical superiority of anglophone voters, it goes without saying that any serious leadership candidate must be able to communicate well in English.

Being the leader of a national political party or even PM does not automatically elevate a politician above the factional strife of politics. Conservative Prime Minister John Diefenbaker (1957–63) was never perceived as being particularly sensitive to Quebec's interests, despite the fact that his party held a majority of that province's seats in the House of Commons between 1958 and 1962. Liberal Prime Minister Pierre Elliott Trudeau (1968–79, 1980–4) was never able to convince western Canada—not that he always tried very hard—that he shared their perspectives on Canadian politics. For westerners, Trudeau and the Liberals represented the dominance of 'the East' and favouritism towards Quebec. Conservative Prime Minister Brian Mulroney was more successful than Trudeau in drawing support from all regions of the country. But he, too, came under attack, particularly from the West, for allegedly neglecting western interests in favour of those of central Canada, especially Quebec. In the end, the political weight of Ontario and Quebec is such that any PM, regardless of his or her background, is bound to be accused of favouring central Canada. The alternative is to risk losing the support of the region that accounts for 60 per cent of the seats in the House of Commons.

Liberal Prime Minister Jean Chrétien was widely perceived as being more successful than his predecessors in attracting the support of both French and English Canadians. In fact, however, under Chrétien's leadership the Liberal Party did less well in Quebec than during the Trudeau years—the Liberals were outpolled by the Bloc Québécois in both 1993 and 1997, and in 2000, while the Liberals gained 44.2 per cent of the vote to the BQ's 39.8 per cent, the BQ garnered 38 seats to 36 for the Liberals. The Liberals ran a distant second to the Reform Party/Canadian Alliance west of Manitoba in 1993, 1997, and 2000. Chrétien's popularity and the success of the Liberal Party under his leadership rested largely on Liberal strength in Ontario and on the fact that the right-of-centre vote was divided between the Reform/Alliance and Conservative parties.

A prime minister whose party's representation in the House of Commons from a key region is relatively weak can attempt to convey a message of inclusion by appointing a high-profile cabinet minister from that region. This is precisely what Conservative Prime Minister Stephen Harper did after the 2006 election. His party won only 10 of Quebec's 75 seats, but he moved immediately to appoint to the Senate and to cabinet Quebec's Michael Fortier. Fortier had been the co-chair of the 2005–6 Conservative federal election campaign and had run unsuccessfully as a Tory candidate in Quebec. He was made Minister of Public Works, the government department that had been at the heart of the advertising scandal in Quebec that arguably led to the Liberals' downfall in the election. At the same time, Harper appointed four newly elected MPs from Quebec to his cabinet, three of these to the perennially important portfolios of Industry, Labour, and Transport.

Representation is about power. The PM and cabinet wield considerable power over the machinery of government, which is why representation in the inner circle of government is valued by regional and other interests. This power is based on the agenda-setting role of the PM and cabinet and on their authority within the decision-making process of the state.

Each new session of Parliament begins with the Speech from the Throne, in which the Governor General reads a statement explaining the government's legislative priorities. This formal procedure is required by the Constitution.[5] Although a typical Throne Speech will be packed with generalities, it will also contain some specific indications of the agenda that Parliament will deal with over the ensuing months. For example, the 2010 Throne Speech included the following goals and promises:

- Continue the stimulus policies of the Economic Action Plan adopted in 2009, bringing it to an end by March 2011.
- Reduce the government deficit that stood at about $56 billion at the time of the March 2010 Throne Speech by winding down

economic stimulus spending as the economy recovered and through more general cutbacks in government spending.
- Freeze the salaries of the Prime Minister, MPs, and senators.
- Increase penalties for sexual offences against children.
- Reduce barriers to foreign ownership in Canada's telecommunications sector.
- Make some changes to the Canadian symbolic order, including the declaration of a national Seniors Day, possible changes to the lyrics of 'O Canada' to make it more gender-neutral, and the creation of a monument to the victims of communism and a Holocaust memorial.

Budgets represent a second way in which the PM and cabinet define the policy agenda. Every winter, usually around late February, the Minister of Finance tables the **estimates** in the House of Commons. This is what students of public finance call the *expenditure budget*. It represents the government's spending plans for the forthcoming fiscal year (1 April–31 March). Given that most public policies involve spending, changes in the allocation of public money provide an indication of the government's shifting priorities. The government can also use the expenditure budget to signal its overall fiscal stance. Increased spending may be part of an expansionary fiscal policy. Spending restraint and cutbacks, as during the 1990s, may signal the government's concern that the total level of public spending and the size of the public-sector deficit are damaging the economy.

From time to time, usually every two years, the Minister of Finance will present in Parliament either a **revenue budget** or a major *economic statement*. The former outlines the government's plans to change the tax system. An economic statement provides the government's analysis of the state of the economy and where the government plans to steer it. Both revenue budgets and economic statements are major opportunities for the government to shape the economic policy agenda.

Even when the bills and budget proposals of government have not originated in cabinet—they often have been generated within some part of the bureaucracy—or when they appear to be simple reactions to politically or economically pressing circumstances, these initiatives must still be accepted and sponsored by the government. In deciding which initiatives will be placed before Parliament, the priorities among them, and the strategies for manoeuvring policies through the legislature and communicating them to the public, the government influences the policy agenda. As Figure 8.3 shows, cabinet and cabinet committees, particularly the Treasury Board, are central players in the budget-making process.

Agenda-setting is part of the decision-making process in government. It is a crucial part, being that early stage during which public issues are defined and policy responses are proposed. The role of the PM and cabinet at this and other stages of the policy process is institutionalized through the formal structure of cabinet decision-making. Between 1968 and 1993 the key committee of cabinet in terms of establishing the government's policy and budget priorities was the Priorities and Planning (P&P) Committee. It was chaired by the Prime Minister and included only the most influential members of cabinet. This formal distinction between a sort of inner and outer cabinet was abolished under Prime Minister Kim Campbell (1993). Gone, too, is the elaborate system of formal committees created during the Trudeau years. The structure of cabinet decision-making was streamlined under the Chrétien Liberals to include only five permanent subcommittees of cabinet: Economic Union, Social Union, Treasury Board, the Special Committee of Council, and Government Communications. Under Stephen Harper, the Committee on Priorities and Planning, chaired by the Prime Minister, has been reinstituted. There are seven additional committees: Operations (day-to-day co-ordination of the government's agenda and issue management); Social Affairs; Economic Growth and Long-Term Prosperity; Treasury Board; Foreign Affairs and Security; Environment and Energy Security; and Afghanistan.

The formal structure of cabinet decision-making, including its committee structure, has never been more than an imperfect guide to who has influence over what within the government of the day.

The one reliable rule of thumb is this: ministers are influential to the degree that the Prime Minister allows them to be influential and supports their favoured projects and initiatives. A minister who has a reputation for having the PM's ear and being part of his favoured circle acquires enhanced status among his or her colleagues in Parliament and in the eyes of the media. Other factors are important, too, such as a base of support within the party or being in charge of a powerful part of the bureaucracy, but the personal relationship between the PM and a minister is always a significant determinant of a minister's influence. The decision-making process in cabinet does not occur only through formal committee meetings. One-on-one conversations in the corridors of the Langevin Building (the location of the Privy Council Office), in the PM's office in the West Block, over the phone, or however and wherever they may take place have always been crucial in the decision-making process. No organization chart can capture this informal but crucial aspect of ministerial influence. Nor can it convey the extent to which the Prime Minister is the dominant player in this decision-making process. Political observers have long characterized the PM's status in cabinet as *primus inter pares*—first among equals. But as Donald Savoie notes, there is no longer any *inter* or *pares*. There is only *primus*, the PM, when it comes to setting the government's agenda and taking major decisions.[6]

Ministerial control over the bureaucracy is another dimension of cabinet's decision-making authority. The word 'control' should be used carefully, however. Ministers are virtually

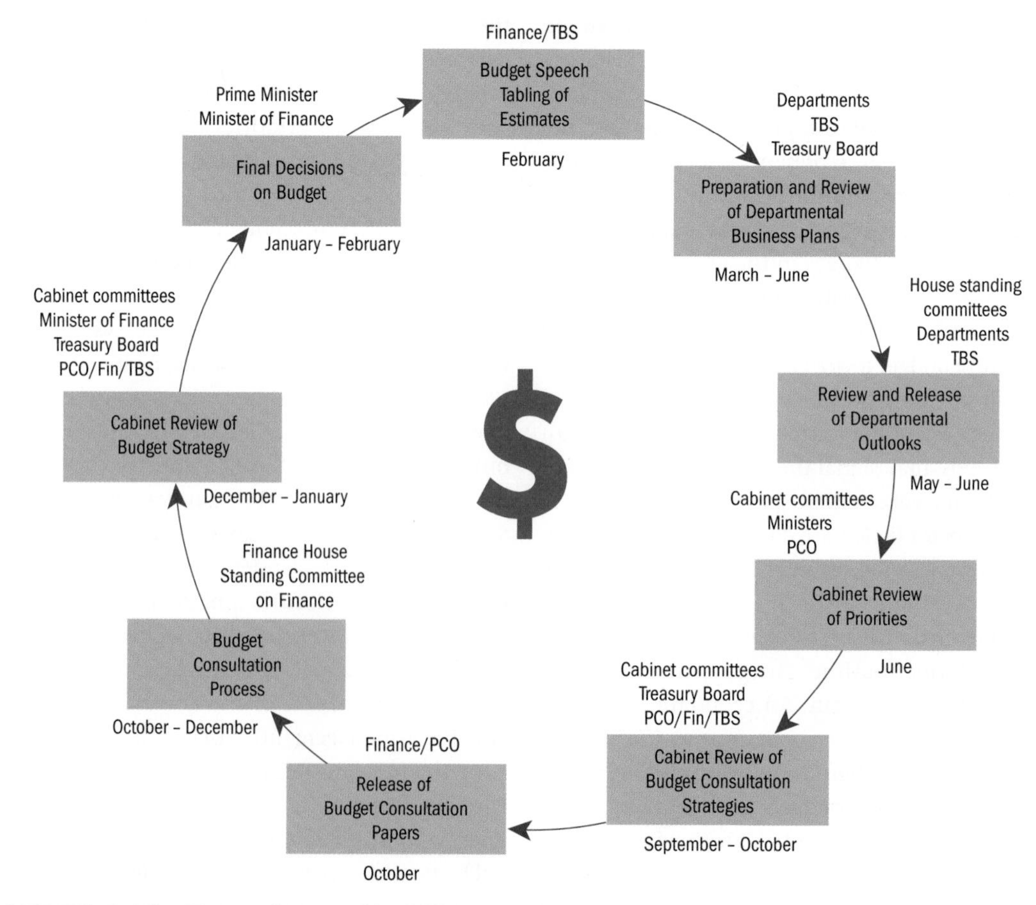

FIGURE 8.3 The Expenditure Management System

Source: Canada, Treasury Board, 'The Expenditure Management System of the Government of Canada', at: <www.tbs-sct.gc.ca/pubs_pol/opepubs/TB_H/figure1e.gif>.

never involved in the day-to-day running of the departments that fall under their nominal control. Moreover, policy initiatives are more likely to be generated within the bureaucracy than to spring from the fertile imagination of the responsible minister. There are, of course, exceptions. Stéphane Dion, when he was the federal Minister of Intergovernmental Affairs, was the principal author of the 2000 **Clarity Act**, an idea that he had championed from the time of the 1995 Quebec referendum. Under the Conservative government of Stephen Harper, it appears that unelected advisers in and around the Prime Minister's Office have played a greater role than is usual in shaping the government's policy agenda, and the role of the permanent bureaucracy, which some argue is mistrusted by the Conservatives as too liberal, has been weaker than is usually the case. As a general rule, however, most ministers, most of the time, act as cabinet advocates for the interests of their department, its budget and programs, and the groups that depend on them. We should not succumb, however, to the caricature of wily, powerful bureaucrats manipulating their hapless political 'masters'. Departments and other parts of the bureaucracy are created and restructured as a result of cabinet initiatives, and changes to their budgets and programs are often undertaken in spite of bureaucratic opposition. Anyone who doubts this need only look at the restructuring of the federal bureaucracy carried out under Kim Campbell in 1993 and the major program cuts instituted by Prime Minister Chrétien and Finance Minister Paul Martin in the mid-1990s.

Central Agencies

Cabinet has always been a decision-making body. But when John A. Macdonald and the first cabinet met in 1867, they dealt with a workload that was only a fraction of that facing government today. There were only a handful of departments and no Crown corporations or regulatory agencies; and federal–provincial relations were still relatively uncomplicated. The scope and complexity of contemporary government are vastly wider. In order to deal with the sheer volume of information that comes before cabinet and the hundreds of separate decisions that it takes annually, cabinet needs help. This help is provided by central agencies.

Central agencies are parts of the bureaucracy whose main or only purpose is to support the decision-making activities of cabinet. More concretely, this means that they perform such functions as providing cabinet with needed information, applying cabinet decisions in dealing with other parts of the bureaucracy, and communicating cabinet decisions and their implications to the public, provincial governments, or other organizations within the federal state. The general character of their policy role, their direct involvement in cabinet decision-making, and their ability to intervene in the affairs of departments led political scientists Colin Campbell and George Szablowski to refer to the senior officials of central agencies as 'superbureaucrats'.[7] The main organizations that are usually considered to have central agency status are the Department of Finance, the Privy Council Office (PCO), the Treasury Board Secretariat, the Prime Minister's Office, and, within the PCO, Intergovernmental Affairs.

Department of Finance

The Department of Finance plays the leading role in the formulation of economic policy. Its formal authority is found in the Department of Finance Act, 1869 and in the Financial Administration Act. The authority that the law confers on Finance is reinforced by the department's informal reputation within the state. Although comparatively small—it employs about 700 persons—Finance has always been a magnet for 'the best and the brightest' within the public service because of its unrivalled status in all aspects of economic policy-making.

The Finance Department has what amounts to almost exclusive authority over the preparation of the revenue budget, budget speeches, and economic statements delivered in Parliament by the Finance Minister. Whatever input other parts of the bureaucracy and interests outside of government have is at the discretion of the Minister of Finance and the department.[8] New initiatives in taxation and trade policy and in managing the level of government spending and debt will often be generated within Finance. Even when a new policy idea originates elsewhere, it is unlikely to reach the legislation stage if Finance is steadfastly opposed.

Finance officials are able to influence the entire spectrum of government policy through their role in the annual formulation of the expenditure budget. They are involved at the very beginning of the expenditure budget process, providing projections on the future state of the economy and the fiscal framework within which spending choices will have to be made. A Finance forecast of weak economic activity and lean taxation revenues will impose across-the-board restraint on departments jostling for scarce funds. But in addition to this macro-level influence on policy, Finance officials may also be involved in micro-level decisions about programs and in setting the policy agenda. In the words of one senior federal bureaucrat:

> Budget cutting tends not to be 'take 10 percent off your budget and do what you will.' The Department of Finance tends to say 'you will take so much off such-and-such a program in such-and-such a way, in such-and-such a time frame, and once they've said all of those things, you really have a fairly small box to start playing in. . . . The Speech from the Throne might be a Speech from the Throne, but I can tell you that there is an awful lot of Finance finger in the pie . . . [and t]here's nothing in there that they haven't figured out how to finance.[9]

The dominant status of Finance was reinforced during the 1990s, once deficit reduction and debt management became Ottawa's overriding priorities. When Ottawa turned the corner on the deficit issue and began to accumulate considerable budget surpluses during the late 1990s, many believed that Finance's stranglehold on the government's agenda would loosen under pressure from those who believed that Ottawa could afford to restore spending on some of the programs that had been cut during the mid-1990s. In fact, however, Finance had lost none of its authority at the centre of the policy-making universe. As Donald Savoie observes:

> the budget has come to dominate policy and decision-making in Ottawa as never before. This holds significant advantages for the centre of government. It enables the prime minister and the minister of finance to introduce new measures and policies under the cover of budget secrecy and avoid debate in Cabinet—and perhaps, more importantly, long interdepartmental consultations and attempts to define a consensus.[10]

In other words, the unrivalled status of Finance within the federal bureaucracy is one of the factors that effectively reinforces the power of the PM, who, along with his or her Minister of Finance, is the only member of the government to be intimately involved in the process that leads up to the making of a budget or economic statement in the House of Commons.

Finance has only a handful of programs for which the department is directly responsible, but they are important, big-ticket ones. One of these is *fiscal equalization*, under which unconditional payments are made to provincial governments whose revenues fall below a level agreed to by Ottawa and the provinces. These payments amount to over $14 billion per year. Finance oversees the entirety of federal transfers to the provinces, of which equalization is a part, including the Canada Health Transfer and Canada Social Transfer (which used to be combined into the Canada Health and Social Transfer before these were split up in 2004). Combined CHT and CST cash transfers to the provinces were worth about $36.6 billion in 2010–11, with another $21 billion in tax room ceded by Ottawa to the provinces. Changes in the conditions under which these and other transfers are made and in the size of the transfer do not happen without the close involvement of Finance.

The Privy Council Office

The Privy Council Office is the cabinet's secretariat and a principal source of policy advice to the Prime Minister. Donald Savoie characterizes it as 'the nerve centre of the federal public service'.[11] The PCO was formally created by Order-in-Council in 1940. The position of Chief Clerk of

© CP Photo/Tom Hanson

Prime Minister Jean Chrétien congratulates Minister of Finance Paul Martin after delivery of the 2001–2 federal budget. The reading of a new budget is a ceremonial affair in Ottawa, and though no one knows its origin, there is a long-standing tradition of the Finance Minister purchasing and wearing a new pair of shoes for the occasion. Though he delivered eight Liberal budgets, Paul Martin claims never to have worn new shoes on budget day.

the Privy Council was put on a statutory basis in 1974, without any specification of the duties associated with this position. The authority of this person, who is the head of the Public Service, and the influence of the PCO derive mainly from their intimate and continuous involvement in cabinet decision-making.

In the first comprehensive study of central agencies, Campbell and Szablowski argue that the PCO is the lead agency for 'strategic planning and formulation of substantive policy'.[12] The PCO's role is 'strategic' because it is situated at the confluence of all the various policy issues and decisions that come before cabinet.

In terms of its organization, the PCO is divided into a number of secretariats that provide support services for the various committees of cabinet. These services range from such mundane functions as scheduling and keeping the minutes of committee meetings to activities that carry the potential for real influence, such as providing policy advice and dealing directly with government departments. Perhaps more than any other single component of the bureaucracy, the PCO is capable of seeing 'the big picture' of government policy. This picture embraces policy *and* political concerns. A former head of the PCO, Gordon Robertson, has summarized the different roles of the PCO and the Prime Minister's Office in the following way: 'The Prime Minister's Office is partisan, politically oriented, yet operationally sensitive. The Privy Council Office is non-partisan, operationally oriented, yet politically sensitive.'[13] Although Robertson's characterization of the different roles of the PCO and PMO was made three decades ago, it continues to be apt. As Donald Savoie observes, 'the office briefs the prime minister on any issue it wishes, controls the flow of papers to Cabinet, reports back to departments on the decisions taken, or not taken, by Cabinet, advises the prime minister on the selection of deputy ministers . . . on federal–provincial relations and on all issues of governmental organization and ministerial mandates.'[14] If the government of Canada is a railway, the PCO is Grand Central Station.

Savoie argues that the title 'Clerk of the Privy Council' is in some ways a misnomer as this most senior member of the federal bureaucracy in fact serves and reports to the PM, not to cabinet as a whole. Along with the PM's chief of staff in the PMO, the Clerk of the PCO is the only official who meets almost daily with the PM when he is in Ottawa. 'The clerk', Savoie observes, 'has direct access to the prime minister as needed.'[15] The Clerk of the Privy Council is, effectively, a sort of deputy minister to the Prime Minister, and as such is always one of the most influential persons in the federal government.

The Treasury Board Secretariat

The Treasury Board Secretariat (TBS) is an administrative adjunct to the Treasury Board, which in turn is the only cabinet committee that has a statutory basis, going back to 1869. The Treasury Board is, in a sense, guardian of the purse strings, but it performs this function in more of a micro fashion compared to Finance's macro authority in relation to spending matters. The Treasury Board is also the government's voice on employment and personnel matters and on administrative policy within the federal government. Its authority is, in a word, extensive. But although the responsibilities of the TBS are wide-ranging and important, it occupies the shadows of the policy-making and agenda-setting process when compared to Finance and the PCO. Donald Savoie quotes a senior federal official who compares the roles of Finance, the PCO, and the TBS this way: 'PCO looks after the broad picture and resolves conflicts between ministers and departments. Finance looks after the big economic and budgeting decisions. The Treasury Board looks after the little decisions.'[16]

'Little', however, should not be confused with 'unimportant'. Particularly from the standpoint of program managers within the federal bureaucracy, the activities and decisions of the Treasury Board and TBS are quite significant. The TBS includes the Office of the Comptroller General of Canada (OCG), whose functions include departmental audits, establishing and enforcing accounting standards in government, and the evaluation of particular programs. As government employer, the Treasury Board negotiates with federal public-sector unions, establishes the rules for recruitment and promotion, is involved in implementing the terms of the Official Languages Act relating to the representation of francophones in the public service and the availability of services to the public in both official languages, and is responsible for setting rules for increasing the representation of women, visible minorities, disabled persons, and Aboriginal people in the Canadian public service. These clearly are important functions.

TBS officials formulate the expenditure outlook that, along with the economic outlook and fiscal framework developed by Finance, is the starting point in the annual expenditure budget exercise. The expenditure forecasts provided by TBS are used by cabinet in making decisions on the allocation of financial resources between competing programs. The involvement of TBS officials does not stop here. Along with the spending committees of cabinet, they assess the spending proposals and plans that departments are required to submit each year. Preparation of the main estimates, the detailed spending plans that the government tables in the House of Commons each winter, is the responsibility of the Treasury Board. Because the TBS has the deepest ongoing knowledge of government spending programs of all central agencies, it is often turned to by the PCO and Finance—its more muscular and glamorous cousins—for information and advice.[17]

The Prime Minister's Office

Unlike the other central agencies, the Prime Minister's Office (PMO) is staffed chiefly by partisan appointees rather than by career public servants. These officials are the Prime Minister's personal staff, performing functions that range from handling the PM's correspondence and schedule to speech-writing, media relations, liaison with ministers, caucus, and the party, and providing advice on appointments and policy. Gordon Robertson's observation that the PMO is 'partisan, politically oriented, yet operationally sensitive'[18] captures well the role of this central agency. It serves as the PM's political eyes and ears, and has the added distinction of being able to speak on behalf of the PM. The PMO is headed by the PM's chief of staff. No other non-elected official is in such regular contact with the PM.

Since the expansion in the PMO that took place under Pierre Trudeau nearly four decades ago, the size of the Prime Minister's staff has varied between about 80 to 120 persons. Some people may wonder what could possibly justify such a large staff, but the demands on the Prime Minister's time are enormous and the process of co-ordinating his activities, providing him or her with briefing and advice, and dealing with the volume of communication that flows into and from the Prime Minister's Office are daunting, to say the least. The bottom line for all staffers in the PMO, from the chief of staff to those who answer the phones, is summed up by a former PMO staff member in these words: 'Our job is quite simple really, we make the PM look good.'[19] This can, of course, be a challenge.

To give but one example of how PMO officials perform this job, let us consider the preparation that takes place before Question Period in the House of Commons. In Canada the Prime Minister is expected to attend Question Period, held shortly after 2:00 p.m. on Monday through Thursday and just after noon on Fridays, when the House is sitting and when he or she is in Ottawa. Moreover, the Prime Minister is expected to remain in the House for all of Question Period. The PM is the star of the show and Question Period occupies the central place in media coverage of Parliament and in Canadians' idea about the process of government because of this understanding that the Prime Minister should be present to answer questions about the activities and policies of his or her government.

Question Period is, potentially, a political minefield, a fact attested to by the presence of journalists in the gallery, few of whom ever bother to be physically present for any of the debates or committee proceedings that take up most of Parliament's working day. Given the stakes, preparation of the PM and his or her ministers is crucial. Within the PMO a handful of staffers arrive each day before sunrise to begin the process of sifting through the day's newspapers and the broadcast media's coverage from the previous day and that morning, identifying those issues that the opposition parties are most likely to pounce on during Question Period. But their job does not stop there. They also craft responses to the anticipated questions, a process that involves considerable partisan and tactical thinking. The most successful response to an opposition member's question is, of course, one that turns the tables and puts the opposition on the defensive or in some way embarrasses the questioner and his or her party. Staffers in the PMO have done their job well when they provide the boss with the ammunition for just such a response.

Although the PMO is clearly the most partisan of the central agencies, it would be quite wrong to think of the PMO as being unconcerned with policy matters. Protecting the Prime Minister and making him look good necessarily involve PMO officials in issues of policy, large and small. 'Senior PMO staff', says Savoie, 'will get involved in whatever issue they and the prime minister think they should.'[20] It simply is not possible to draw a line between the drafting of a speech for the Prime Minister, a function that typically will take place in the PMO, and providing policy advice. But how involved PMO officials are in the shaping of policy and what their influence is vis-à-vis other central agency officials and departmental managers will, as always, depend on the Prime Minister. Ultimately, the Prime Minister decides from whom to seek advice and who will be a player on any particular issue.

Intergovernmental Affairs (formerly the Federal–Provincial Relations Office)

Perhaps the most surprising thing about this central agency is that it did not exist before 1975. Federal–provincial relations did not suddenly become complex and the political stakes high in the 1970s. Before the Federal–Provincial Relations Office (FPRO) was created, its functions had been carried out within the PCO. What, then, prompted Prime Minister Pierre Trudeau to create a new agency to deal with intergovernmental affairs? According to Colin Campbell, the reason had to do with a staffing problem. Trudeau wanted to appoint Michael Pitfield as Chief Clerk of the Privy Council, but was faced with the dilemma of what to do with Gordon Robertson, Pitfield's predecessor and perhaps the most widely respected official in the public service. The solution was to create the Federal–Provincial Relations Office and to appoint Robertson as the first Secretary to the Cabinet for Federal–Provincial Relations.[21] The episode provides a nice illustration of the role played by serendipity in government decision-making.

After its launch, and despite the prestige of its first head, the FPRO never achieved the influence of other central agencies like Finance, the TBS, and the PCO. Indeed, only two years after the FPRO was established, the cabinet position of Minister for Federal–Provincial Relations and the cabinet committee on federal–provincial relations were abolished. The FPRO was to have been the support staff for this minister and the secretariat to this committee. Their elimination did not result in the dismantling of the FPRO. It continued to provide information and advice to cabinet committees on issues that had an intergovernmental dimension. The precise functions performed by the FPRO depended on the PM. For example, the FPRO played a major role in the development of the Meech Lake Accord proposals. Its lesser stature in the universe of central agencies was largely due to the fact that the FPRO did not hold a monopoly over advice on federal–provincial matters.

The FPRO was restructured under Prime Minister Chrétien after the Liberals returned to power in 1993. The functions of the FPRO were reintegrated into the PCO through its Intergovernmental Affairs Office. Intergovernmental Affairs provides policy advice to the Prime Minister and the Minister of Intergovernmental Affairs on issues ranging from health and social programs to national unity and Aboriginal matters. The mandate of the office includes the following objectives:

- To provide advice and strategic planning related to national unity, federal–provincial relations, and constitutional and legal issues.
- To provide communications support on issues with federal–provincial dimensions.
- To work with the provinces and provide advice on the basis of provincial priorities, by monitoring files with intergovernmental dimensions and seeking to forge broader partnerships and new agreements with the provinces and territories to renew the federation.
- To develop policies with respect to Aboriginals and ensure that Aboriginal concerns are taken into consideration in Canadian constitutional development.[22]

The influence of the Intergovernmental Affairs Office waxes and wanes, depending in large measure on the stature of the minister with responsibility for intergovernmental relations and on the nature of the issues it is permitted to deal with. 'Permitted' is the key word because whether Intergovernmental Affairs and its minister take the lead or a leading role on an issue will depend on the Prime Minister. With Stéphane Dion as minister, the Intergovernmental Affairs Office played an important role in the communications—negotiations they were not!—with Quebec over the future terms of a referendum on Quebec independence, which eventually produced the Clarity Act. Likewise, Dion and the Intergovernmental Affairs Office played important roles in the federal–provincial negotiations that produced the 1999 Social Union Framework Agreement. Under a minister with less clout on Ottawa–Quebec relations—Dion was recruited into the Liberal Party with the promise of a cabinet post precisely because of his views on Quebec's place in Canadian federalism—it is entirely imaginable that Intergovernmental Affairs would find it difficult to make its voice heard and its presence felt in the central agency universe.

Prime Ministerial Government

For decades various commentators on the Canadian political scene have asked whether Canadian prime ministers were becoming more 'presidential' in their stature and power. The question, however, was always based on the false premise that an American President is more powerful in relation to the country's legislation and his own party than is a Canadian Prime Minister. In fact, there have always been fewer checks on the behaviour of a Canadian Prime Minister than on an American President, and any occupant of the White House would envy the sort of constitutional latitude enjoyed by the leader of the Canadian government. Canadian commentators who purported to see creeping presidentialization occurring in Canada's system of government were, in fact, mistakenly attributing to the American head of state powers beyond those actually held by the US President.

In recent years this wrong-headed debate has come to a close. Indeed, it is now widely recognized that the Canadian Prime Minister has far more clout within the Canadian system of government than the President has in the American system and, moreover, that power has become increasingly centralized in the hands of the PM and those around him. These days, if one looks for counterweights to the PM's power, they are more plausibly found in the courts, the media, and in some of the provincial capitals than in Parliament. This centralization of power has advanced to such a degree that some of Canada's most astute political commentators now characterize Canada's system of government as *prime ministerial* rather than *parliamentary* government.[23] Donald Savoie and Jeffrey Simpson are among those who argue that not only has the influence of Parliament been effectively eclipsed by the growth of **prime ministerial government**, but cabinet, too, has been left on the margins of the policy-making process, 'a kind of focus group for the prime minister', in the words of a recent Liberal cabinet minister,[24] or what Jeffrey Simpson calls a 'mini-sounding board'[25] where decisions already approved by the PM and his advisers in key central agencies are rubber-stamped (see Box 8.4).

The greater influence of the Prime Minister within the Canadian system of government than the President in the American system is due to structural differences between these two governmental systems. But the high degree of centralization of power that commentators such as Savoie and Simpson argue has occurred under recent prime ministers—a trend that was not reversed when Stephen Harper came to power—may be explained by a combination of personal style and the political incentives to choose more rather than less centralization. The individuals who occupy the role of Prime Minister all have their own preferences when

Governing Realities

Box 8.4 The Reality of Prime Ministerial Government

Cabinet has now joined Parliament as an institution being bypassed. Real political debate and decision-making are increasingly elsewhere—in federal-provincial meetings of first ministers, on Team Canada flights, where first ministers can hold informal meetings, in the Prime Minister's Office, in the Privy Council Office, in the Department of Finance, and in international organizations and international summits. There is no indication that the one person who holds all the cards, the prime minister, and the central agencies which enable him to bring effective political authority to the centre, are about to change things. The Canadian prime minister has little in the way of institutional check, at least inside government, to inhibit his ability to have his way.

Source: Donald Savoie, *Governing from the Centre: The Concentration of Power in Canadian Politics* (Toronto: University of Toronto Press, 1999), 362.

it comes to decision-making. Some prefer a more participatory process, as was true of Lester Pearson (1963–8) and Pierre Trudeau (1968–79, 1980–4), at least during Trudeau's earlier years. Marc Lalonde, one of the most influential ministers during the Trudeau era, has described cabinet meetings under Trudeau as resembling university seminars during which the Prime Minister often remained silent for much of the time while the members of his government expressed their views. This is the decision-making style, as noted earlier, in which the Prime Minister has been depicted as 'first among equals'. The historical evidence from politicians' memoirs and journalistic accounts, however, suggests that this style has been relatively rare. More common, certainly in recent times, has been a more centralized decision-making style in which priorities are effectively set and decisions are made by the Prime Minister and a relatively small group of advisers, only some of whom may be cabinet ministers.

While it is tempting to locate the roots of what Savoie calls prime ministerial government in the personalities of such leaders as Brian Mulroney, Jean Chrétien, and Stephen Harper, it is also worth asking what a prime minister would gain by choosing a more participatory decision-making style characterized by greater opportunities for involvement and influence on the part of all members of cabinet and more delegation of policy-making responsibility to individual cabinet ministers. The pluses seem nebulous and hard to pinpoint. They might include the gratitude of the cabinet ministers empowered by the *primus inter pares* style and the plaudits of old-style purists who believe that this is the decision-making ideal that all prime ministers should strive for. But the various risks that a prime minister would take by adopting a significantly more decentralized and collegial approach are fairly easy to identify. They include the following:

- The decisions or publicly expressed views of individual cabinet ministers might be perceived to be in conflict with other government actions, promises, or policies and thus cause embarrassment to the government.
- Ministers will often have their own strongly held preferences on issues, but it is also well known that most ministers soon see their role at the cabinet table as that of defender of 'their' department, programs, budget allocation, etc. The *primus inter pares* style of collective cabinet decision-making probably has a built-in bias towards protection of the status quo and against change that appears to threaten the programs, prestige, and budget interests of a significant number of ministers.
- A collegial cabinet decision-making style also is more likely to allow for the emergence of powerful, high-profile cabinet ministers who may be seen by the media, within the governing party, and by the public as rivals to the Prime Minister.

The Legislature

The legislature is a study in contrasts. Its physical setting is soberly impressive, yet the behaviour of its members is frequently the object of derision. Its constitutional powers appear to be formidable, yet its actual influence on policy usually is much less than that of the cabinet and the bureaucracy. All major policies, including all laws, must be approved by the legislature, but the legislature's approval often seems a foregone conclusion and a mere formality. One of the two chambers of the legislature, the House of Commons, is democratically elected. The other, the Senate, has long had an unenviable reputation as a sinecure for party hacks and other appointed unworthies.

The contradictions of the legislature have their source in the tension between traditional ideas about political democracy and the character of the modern state. Representation, accountability to the people, and choice are the cornerstones of liberal democratic theory. An elected legislature that represents the population either on the basis of population or by region—or both—and party competition are the means by which these democratic goals are to be accomplished. But the modern state, we have seen, is characterized by a vast bureaucratic apparatus that is not easily controlled by elected politicians. Moreover, while the Prime Minister's power has always been vastly greater than that of other members of Parliament, the concentration of power in and around the office of the Prime Minister appears to have reached unprecedented levels. As the scale and influence of the non-elected parts of the state have grown and prime ministerial government has been consolidated, the inadequacies of traditional democratic theory—centred on the role of the legislature—have become increasingly apparent.

Is there an alternative? A more representative and democratically responsive bureaucracy is sometimes viewed as the solution to the problem of power without accountability. Reforms in this direction are certainly useful. They cannot, however, substitute for elections that enable voters to choose those who will represent them. If one begins from the premise that the free election must be the cornerstone of political democracy, the role of the legislature is crucial.

One way of ensuring that the legislature better performs its democratic functions is to improve its representative character. Possible ways through which this could be done include reform of the political parties' candidate selection process, instituting a system of proportional representation electoral system, or a reformed Senate. Another option is to tighten the legislature's control over the political executive and the non-elected parts of the state. This may be done by increasing the legislature's access to information about the intentions and performance of the government and bureaucracy, providing opportunities for legislative scrutiny and debate of executive action, and enabling legislators to influence the priorities and agenda of government.

Canada's legislature has two parts, the House of Commons and the Senate. Representation in the elected House of Commons is roughly according to population—roughly, because some MPs represent as few as 20,000 constituents, while others represent close to 200,000. Each of the 308 members of the House of Commons is the sole representative for a constituency, also known as a 'riding'.

Senators are appointed by the government of the day when a vacancy occurs. They hold their seats until age 75. Representation in the Senate is on the basis of regions. Each of the four main regions (Ontario, Quebec, the four western provinces, and the Maritimes) has 24 seats. Newfoundland has six, and there is one from each of the Yukon, Northwest Territories, and Nunavut for a total of 105 seats.

En route to taking office in 2006, Stephen Harper's Conservative government expressed the intent to introduce legislation on Senate reform. Their proposed overhauls of the Senate process included an eight-year limit on the term of Senate service and, eventually, the requirement that senators be elected to their seats rather than appointed. To date those reforms have not come to pass.

Eight temporary seats were added by the Mulroney government in 1988 to overcome Liberal opposition in the Senate to the Goods and Services Tax (GST), thus raising the total number of senators for a while from 104 to 112.[26] In recent years there have been suggestions that senators be elected, and some have proposed that a certain number of Senate seats be reserved for women and Aboriginal Canadians.

In law, the powers of the House of Commons and Senate are roughly equal. There are, however, a couple of important exceptions. Legislation involving the spending or raising of public money must, under the Constitution, be introduced in the House of Commons. And when it comes to amending the Constitution, the Senate can only delay passage of a resolution already approved by the Commons. But all bills must pass through identical stages in both bodies before becoming law (see the Appendix at the end of this chapter).

Despite the similarity of their formal powers, the superiority of the elected branch is well established. For most of its history, the Senate has deferred to the will of the Commons. This changed after the 1984 election of a Progressive Conservative majority in Parliament. On several occasions the Liberal-dominated Senate obstructed bills that had already been passed by the Commons. When the Senate balked at passage of the politically unpopular GST the government decided it had had enough. Using an obscure constitutional power it appointed eight new Conservative senators, thereby giving the Conservative Party a slender majority. Under the Chrétien government the partisan balance in the Senate shifted back to a Liberal majority. The squabbles that often occurred after 1984, when the House of Commons was controlled by one party and the Senate by another, became increasingly rare during the years 1993–2006, when the Liberals formed the government and re-established a Liberal majority in the Senate through the filling of vacancies.

This Liberal majority posed a problem for the minority Conservatives of Stephen Harper, blocking and delaying several pieces of legislation sent to it from the House of Commons. Instead of filling Senate seats with Conservative Party loyalists as vacancies occurred, Harper allowed these vacancies to accumulate before appointing 18 new senators in December 2008. The government explained this delay as having been due to its commitment to Senate reform and, in particular, the election of senators. It was, however, unable to win enough support in the House of Commons for such reform and, in any case, it was not clear that direct election and term limits for senators could be accomplished without changing the Constitution.

The legislature performs a number of functions that are basic to political democracy. The most fundamental of these is the passage of laws by the people's elected representatives. Budget proposals and new policy initiatives must be placed before Parliament for its approval. The operation of party discipline ensures that bills tabled in the legislature are seldom modified in major ways during the law-passing process. This does not mean, however, that Parliament's approval of the government's legislative agenda is an empty formality. The rules under which the legislature operates ensure that the opposition parties have opportunities to debate and criticize the government's proposals.

Writing a generation ago, Robert Jackson and Michael Atkinson argued that those involved in the pre-parliamentary stages of policy-making anticipate the probable reactions of the legislature and of the government party caucus before a bill or budget is tabled in Parliament.[27] While this may have been true in the past, it no longer appears that those who actually take policy decisions and draft legislation lose much sleep over what they think will be the reaction of backbench MPs. On the influence of **caucus**, Savoie states that '[government party MPs] report that they are rarely, if ever, in a position to launch a new initiative, and worse, that they are rarely effective in getting the government to change course. They also do not consider themselves to be an effective check on prime ministerial power.'[28] In the words of one government party MP, 'We simply respond to what Cabinet does, and there are limits to what you can do when you are always reacting.'[29] In short, there is little evidence from recent years to suggest that the Prime Minister and those around him who are involved in making policy pay much attention to the preferences of those in the legislature, on either the government or opposition side of the aisle. They are, however, very likely to pay serious attention to the results of surveys and focus groups that have been commissioned to gauge public reaction to a policy.

Although the legislature may often, indeed usually, play second fiddle to more direct means used by government to take the public pulse on issues, it is far from being irrelevant in the policy-making process. Functions performed by the legislature include scrutiny of government performance, constituency representation, debate of issues, and legitimation of the political system.

Oversight of Government Performance

Various regular opportunities exist for the legislature to prod, question, and criticize the government. These include the daily Question Period, the set-piece debates that follow the Speech from the Throne and the introduction of a new budget, and Opposition Days, when the opposition parties determine the topic of debate. Committee hearings and special parliamentary task forces also provide opportunities for legislative oversight of government actions and performance, although the subjects that these bodies deal with are mainly determined by the government. Party discipline is a key factor that limits the critical tendencies of parliamentary committees, particularly during periods of majority government.

Earlier we said that Question Period, for better or for worse, has become both the centrepiece of Parliament's day and the chief activity shaping the ideas that most Canadians have of what goes on in Parliament. The introduction of television cameras into the legislature in the late 1970s has reinforced the stature of Question Period as the primary forum through which the opposition can scrutinize and criticize the government on matters big and small. This is the opposition parties' main chance to influence the issues that will be discussed in the media and the way the government will be portrayed by the press.

In fact, however, the dynamic of Question Period involves reciprocal influences between the media and opposition parties. It has often been said that this morning's *Globe and Mail* or *National Post* headline becomes this afternoon's leading volley in Question Period, but things are not this simple. Journalists also react—although not always in the way that opposition parties may like—to the questions and lines of attack that opposition parties launch against the government. For example, during the spring of 2002 the opposition parties, particularly the Alliance and the Progressive Conservatives, carried out a sustained assault on the government and, in particular, a handful of its members, charging that there was widespread evidence of corruption and influence-peddling in the awarding of government advertising contracts. This was clearly part of an opposition campaign to generate as much negative publicity for the Chrétien government as possible and create (or reinforce) a public perception of the government as corrupt. To what degree this issue was media-driven as opposed to opposition party-driven is impossible to say. What is clear is that this sort of critical scrutiny of the government serves the interests of both the opposition parties, who wish to see the government embarrassed and its popular support drop, and the media, who know that controversy and the scent of wrongdoing attract more readers and viewers than do reports that all is well with the world.

Committees of the House of Commons, whose membership is generally limited to about 20 MPs, may appear to be a forum where the leash of party discipline can be loosened and backbench MPs may acquire some expertise in particular policy areas that will enable them to assess the merits of legislation in a more informed and less partisan manner. Students of American politics know that congressional committees are where the real action is in Congress, and that what enters one end of the committee sausage-grinder may not bear much resemblance to what emerges from the other end, if it emerges at all. In Canada's Parliament, however, committees seldom modify in more than marginal ways what is placed before them and virtually never derail any bill that the government has introduced in the House. Far from being a source of opportunity and satisfaction for MPs who wish to see themselves as being truly engaged in the law-making process, much evidence suggests that committees are a source of frustration for many MPs and that they do not provide a serious vehicle through which the legislature can scrutinize the activities of government and call it to account for its actions. In his study of MPs' behaviour and perceptions of their jobs, David Docherty states that 'several rookie Liberals indicated that the failure of their own executive to treat committee work and reports seriously was the single most frustrating (and unexpected) aspect of their job as an MP.'[30] Docherty found that frustration with House committees was not limited to government party members. Opposition MPs also expressed disappointment with the inability of committees to make more than a marginal and occasional difference.

Party discipline is at the root of this dissatisfaction. Despite some tinkering over the last couple of decades, the ostensible goal of which was to increase the independence of committees and thereby augment the influence of the legislature, the fact that party discipline operates in committees just as it does on the floor of the House of Commons undoes all of these reforms. Moreover, all but a small fraction of what committees do is reactive—responding to a bill tabled in Parliament by the government, examining spending proposals submitted by the government, or pursuing some investigative task assigned to a committee by the government. Within this straitjacket there can be little wiggle room for non-partisan accounting of the government's record and proposals.

Senators argue that life is different in the red chamber. They point to the Senate's long string of committee and task force studies on topics ranging from corporate concentration in Canada's media industries to the decriminalization of marijuana possession. Being appointed to serve until the age of 75, most of them argue, loosens the constraint of party discipline. Not having to worry about whether their party leader will sign their nomination papers at some future election and being unconcerned with how their actions will affect their prospect of being appointed someday to cabinet, senators can behave with far greater independence than their House of Commons colleagues (see Box 8.5).

This argument, while not totally false, is both naive and self-serving. It is naive in that it ignores the palpable reality that most senators have demonstrated pretty firm and unswerving loyalty to the party, and especially the Prime Minister, that appointed them. This is not surprising when one looks at who becomes a senator and why. Most are people who have served their party long and well, and it would be more than a bit unusual if they were suddenly, after appointment to the Senate, to change the patterns of loyalty that got them there in the first place. That there are mavericks and 'characters' in Canada's Senate whose idiosyncrasies and speechifying in that chamber would not be tolerated by their party in the House is beyond question. But how many Canadians know or care about this? The truth is that the media seldom report this side of the Senate and, to senators' disappointment, few are paying attention but themselves.

The self-serving aspect of the argument about senators' greater independence enabling them to scrutinize and criticize the government to a degree not permitted in the House of Commons is pointed out by Jeffrey Simpson.[31] Simpson notes that senators routinely point to their many committee reports on important policy matters, undertaken at arm's length from the government, as proof of the significant role the unelected Senate performs in Canada's system of government. This is, Simpson rightly observes, a sort of *faute de mieux* argument. Lacking other plausible justifications for the existence of an unelected Senate stuffed with those whose appointments represent a form of patronage bestowed by the present Prime Minister and his/her predecessors, senators point to their committees and their products. While their committee reports have often influenced the contours of public debate on an issue—and the independence often associated with them could not have occurred in the House—there is no reason to believe that only the Senate as currently constituted could make this contribution to the process of scrutinizing government policy, investigating important issues, and proposing legislative change. Indeed, the committee work that senators point to as their proudest accomplishment and chief raison d'être usually just covers the same ground that think-tanks, academic studies, and government-commissioned studies have mapped.

Politics in Focus

Box 8.5 Edmund Burke and the Canadian Senate

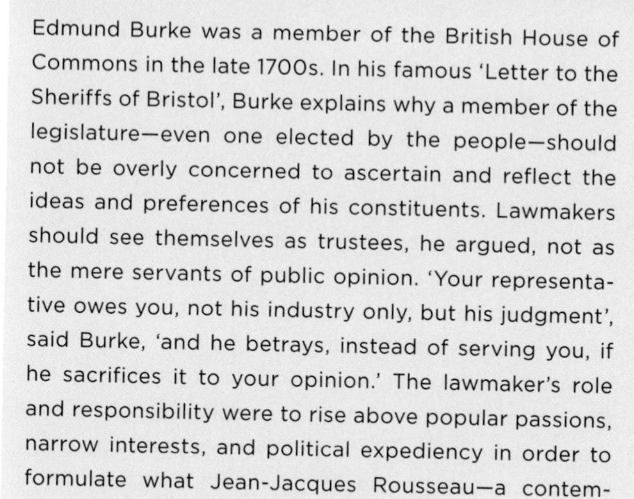

Edmund Burke was a member of the British House of Commons in the late 1700s. In his famous 'Letter to the Sheriffs of Bristol', Burke explains why a member of the legislature—even one elected by the people—should not be overly concerned to ascertain and reflect the ideas and preferences of his constituents. Lawmakers should see themselves as trustees, he argued, not as the mere servants of public opinion. 'Your representative owes you, not his industry only, but his judgment', said Burke, 'and he betrays, instead of serving you, if he sacrifices it to your opinion.' The lawmaker's role and responsibility were to rise above popular passions, narrow interests, and political expediency in order to formulate what Jean-Jacques Rousseau—a contemporary of Burke's, though not particularly a soulmate in matters of governance—called the general will. Lawmakers who thought of themselves as delegates of the people were, Burke felt, merely pandering to the mood of the moment. Their real duty was to their conscience and to an idea of the national interest that was not determined by simply adding those in support of a proposal, subtracting those against it, then acting based on the result.

Burke's trustee lives on in the Canadian Senate, many of whose members are quite proud to acknowledge that they feel beholden to no one and to nothing except their conscience and their own ideas about what is in the best interests of the country. Notwithstanding the caricature of senators as lazy party hacks, many if not most of them are intelligent, thoughtful men and women who care deeply about Canada and who take their responsibilities very seriously. But do these qualities buy them a pass from the sort of accountability that most people expect in a modern democracy? Although a handful of other Western democracies have non-elected upper houses as part of their legislatures, only Canada does not set term limits on its non-elected senators. Edmund Burke at least had to explain himself to the citizens of Bristol and persuade them that his self-image as a trustee was worthy of their votes.

The legislature's oversight function also operates through the Office of the Auditor General. Created in 1878, the modern history of the office dates from 1977 when the Auditor General Act broadened its responsibilities from what were essentially auditing and accounting functions to examining how well programs and governments were being managed. This has proven to be a wide-ranging mandate. The Auditor General reports to the House of Commons and is authorized to issue up to three reports per year in addition to an annual report (Box 8.6). The first annual reports of the Auditor General tended to focus rather narrowly on the question of whether money appropriated by Parliament was spent in authorized ways and followed required accountability guidelines. Since passage of the 1977 Act, the concept of 'value for money' has been part of the Auditor General's terms of reference. In 1995 the Auditor General Act was changed again, creating the position of Commissioner of the Environment and Sustainable Development within the Office of the Auditor General, thereby broadening its mandate to include the environmental audit of government programs and institutions. The statute also allows the Auditor General wide discretion in the selection of particular aspects of government spending for special scrutiny.

The result of all this has been that the Office of the Auditor General is today much larger and does much more than was the case several decades ago. Its annual reports and special studies often generate extensive and unfavourable media coverage of particular aspects of government performance. But even more often this spotlight goes out rather quickly. This is less the fault of the Auditor General than a commentary on a media system that has a short attention span, in which few stories have a shelf life of more than a week or two.

Politics in Focus

Box 8.6 Casting a Spotlight on Government Mismanagement

The Office of the Auditor General's reports seldom produce more than temporary discomfort for the government of the day. There have been exceptions, the most significant in recent years being the sponsorship scandal, involving millions of dollars in advertising government sponsorship contracts in Quebec for services that were not provided or were at grossly inflated prices. Auditor General Sheila Fraser blew the whistle on this pattern of misspending in her February 2004 report. A Royal Commission, headed by Justice John Gomery, was created to examine the affair and charges were laid.

More typically, however, the Auditor General's reports highlight mismanagement, inefficiency, and ineptitude, not criminality. For example, the 2008 annual report was critical of the Canada Border Services Agency for failing to keep track of the whereabouts of 41,000 people who had been ordered to leave the country, and also brought attention to supply line inefficiencies in getting needed goods to Canadian troops in Afghanistan. In 2010 some squirming among politicians occurred when the Auditor General revealed that MPs had refused her request to audit about $533 million in annual parliamentary spending. Faced with a barrage of public and media criticism, MPs relented.

But the effectiveness of the Office of the Auditor General cannot be measured by the number of 'gotcha!' cases it reports or the amount of embarrassment it creates for the government. Knowing that the Auditor General performs an ongoing oversight function and that program inefficiencies and mismanagement may be brought to light in her reports is already a serious incentive for senior managers to do what they can to avoid being caught in the crosshairs of a negative audit.

Representation

The House of Commons is both symbolically and practically important as a contact point between citizens and government. Symbolically, the elected House embodies the principle of government by popular consent. The partisan divisions within it, between government and opposition parties, have the additional effect of affirming for most citizens their belief in the competitive character of politics. At a practical level, citizens often turn to their elected representatives when they experience problems with bureaucracy or when they want to express their views on government policy.

Unlike the elected Commons, the Senate does not perform a significant representational role in Canadian politics. This is despite the fact that senators are appointed to represent the various provinces and regions of Canada. The unelected character of Canada's upper house and the crassly partisan criteria that prime ministers have usually relied on in filling Senate vacancies have undermined whatever legitimacy senators might otherwise have achieved as spokespersons for the regions. Provincial governments, regional spokespersons in the federal cabinet, and regional blocs of MPs within the party caucuses are, in about that order of importance, vastly more significant in representing regional interests.

Debate

The image that most Canadians have of Parliament is of the heated exchanges that take place across the aisle that separates the government and opposition parties. Parliamentary procedure and even the physical layout of the legislature are based on the adversarial principle of 'them versus us'. This principle is most clearly seen in the daily Question Period and the set-piece debates that follow the Speech from the Throne and the introduction of a new budget. At its best, the thrust and riposte of partisan debate can provide a very public forum for the discussion of national issues, as well as highlight the policy differences between the parties. Unfortunately for the quality of political discourse in Canada, parliamentary debate is more often dragged down by the wooden reading of prepared remarks, heckling and personal invective, and occasional blatant abuses of either the government's majority or the opposition's opportunities to hold up the business of Parliament.

It is a mistake to imagine that the purpose of parliamentary debate is to allow for a searching discussion of issues in a spirit of open-mindedness. Generally, MPs' minds are made up when a measure is first tabled in Parliament. So what is the point of the long hours spent criticizing and defending legislative proposals and the government's record, all at taxpayers' expense?

Legislative debate is important for two reasons. First, outcomes are not always predictable. Even when the government party holds a commanding majority in Parliament, or when the policy differences between government and opposition are not significant, the dynamic of debate on an issue is not entirely controllable by the government or by Parliament. Media coverage of the issue, reporting of public opinion polls, the interventions of organized interests, other governments, and even individuals who have credibility in the eyes of the media and public all will have a bearing on the trajectory of parliamentary debate.

Parliamentary debate is also important because it reinforces the popular belief in the open and competitive qualities of Canadian democracy. The stylized conflict between government and opposition parties, which is the essence of the British parliamentary system, emphasizes disagreements and differences. Adversarial politics obscures the fact that these partisan disagreements usually are contained within a fairly narrow band of consensus on basic values and that the words and deeds of the opposition, when it holds power, usually bear a strong resemblance to those of its predecessor. Parliamentary debate, therefore, produces an exaggerated impression of the open and competitive qualities of Canadian politics. It is exaggerated because the sound and fury belies the fact that the positions of the government and at least some of those who sit on the opposition benches are seldom diametrically opposed, a reality that may be confirmed by perusing the policy platforms at the parties' respective websites.

Legitimation

Parliament is both a legislative and a legitimizing institution. Laws must pass through the parliamentary mill before being approved, and thus Parliament is the legislative branch of government. But it is also the legitimizing branch of government because most of the mechanisms of democratic accountability are embodied in the structure and procedures of Parliament. It represents the people. It scrutinizes the actions of government. And it debates public issues. Along with elections and judicial review of the Constitution, Parliament appears to be one of the chief bulwarks against the danger that government will abuse its powers.

How well Parliament performs its democratic functions is another matter. But the structures and procedures of the legislature are built around the ideas of open government and popular consent, and the constitutional requirement that the actions of government must be approved by Parliament. These factors help to legitimize the political system and the policies it produces. If most people held the view that the legislature is a farce, however, then its contribution to the perceived legitimacy of Canadian government would be undermined. Canadians do not hold this view. Their cynicism about the integrity of politicians does not appear to undermine their faith in parliamentary institutions.

Although the concentration of power in and around the Prime Minister has reached unprecedented levels, the legislature is not the helpless pawn of the executive. Using the rules of parliamentary procedure, opposition parties are able to prod, question, and castigate the government all in front of the parliamentary press gallery and the television cameras in the House of Commons. The opposition's behaviour is usually reactive, responding to the government's proposals and policies. Nevertheless, the legislature's function as a talking shop—the *parler* in 'parliament'—enables it to draw attention to controversial aspects of the government's performance. MPs are not quite the 'nobodies' that Pierre Trudeau once labelled them. But they are far from having the policy influence of their American

Listen to the 'Political Parties and the Parliamentary System' podcast, available at www.oupcanada.com/Brooks7e

counterparts, who, because of loose party discipline and very different rules governing the law-making process, are often assiduously courted by interest groups and the President himself.

Earlier, we said that caucus, the body of elected MPs belonging to a particular party, generally does not have much influence on the party leadership, at least not in the government party. When Parliament is in session, it is usual for a party's caucus to meet at least weekly. Caucus is not, however, considered unimportant by party leaders. The Prime Minister regularly attends caucus meetings, as do members of his or her cabinet when they are in Ottawa. These meetings often amount to little more than what one MP describes as 'bitching sessions', but almost never do MPs challenge the Prime Minister behind the closed doors of the party's weekly meeting.[32]

Some insiders argue, however, that the government caucus provides a real opportunity for backbench members to influence government policy through frank debate away from the peering eyes and ears of the media and the opposition. This may occasionally be true. But the limits on the influence of caucus are readily apparent from two facts. First, extremely unpopular policies, as was the GST, that are priorities of the government are not affected by caucus opposition. The same is true of policies that create sharp divisions in a party's caucus, such as the Liberal government's 1995 gun control law. If the policy is a high priority, the prospect that a caucus revolt will defeat or substantially change it is extremely remote. Members who fail to toe the line are likely to experience the fate of those Liberal MPs who voted against the government's gun law in 1995: the loss of committee assignments. Expulsion from caucus is another sanction that may be used to punish recalcitrant backbenchers. Second, the caucus of the governing party—like the legislature as a whole—usually enters the policy-making process late, after much study, consultation, and negotiation have already taken place. Embedded in the legislation that the members of the government party caucus are asked to vote for is a complex fabric of compromises and accommodations between government and interest groups, different agencies of government, or even Ottawa and the provinces. It is unlikely that the government will be willing to see this fabric come unravelled because of caucus opposition.

Bob Krieger/© Simon Fraser University

Although Canadians are often cynical about politicians, believing them to be overpaid, the majority of MPs work very long hours both in Ottawa and at home in their constituency offices.

What Does an MP Do?

It is almost certainly true that most Canadians believe that their MPs are overpaid and underworked. Stories of 'gold-clad' MPs' pensions and of senators who slurp at the public trough while living in Mexico help to fuel this widespread but generally unfair charge. Most backbench MPs work very long hours, whether in Ottawa or at home in their constituencies (see Box 8.7). The demands on their time ratchet upward in the case of members of the government and party leaders, all of whom are required to travel extensively in carrying out their jobs. But what does a typical MP do? For most MPs, the single largest block of their working day is devoted to taking care of constituency business. David Docherty reports that the MPs he surveyed from the thirty-fourth (1988–93) and thirty-fifth (1993–7) parliaments claimed to devote just over 40 per cent of their working time to constituency affairs. The second largest block of time was spent on legislative work, such as committee assignments and attending Question Period and debates. These activities run a fairly distant second, however, to constituency work, as shown in Figure 8.4.

In performing their functions, all MPs are provided with a budget that enables them to hire staff in Ottawa and in their riding office. How they allocate these resources is up to them, but most MPs opt to have two staffers in Ottawa and two in the constituency office. MPs are also provided with public funds to maintain their constituency office and are allowed an unlimited regular mail budget and four mass mailings to constituents—known as 'householders'—per year. Although these resources are paltry compared to those at the disposal of US congressional representatives and senators, they are superior to those of legislators in the United Kingdom, Belgium, France, and many other democracies. And while they are adequate to enable an MP to carry out his or her constituency duties, they are not sufficient to pay for high-powered policy analysts and other research staff.

Docherty found that MPs who were new to Parliament tended to spend more time on constituency work than those who had been in the legislature for a longer period of time. '[T]he longer members serve in office,' he observes, 'the less time they will devote to constituency work.'[33] This shift from constituency to policy-oriented work does not, however, mean that a veteran MP's constituents are less well served than those of an MP who is new to Parliament. Docherty found that the Ottawa staffs of veteran MPs tended to make up the difference, spending more of their time on constituency business as their MPs' focus shifted to policy concerns. 'No matter what stage of their career,' Docherty states, 'members of parliament see helping individuals as their most crucial duty.'[34] In this, MPs show themselves to be realistic about the limits on their ability to be lawmakers.

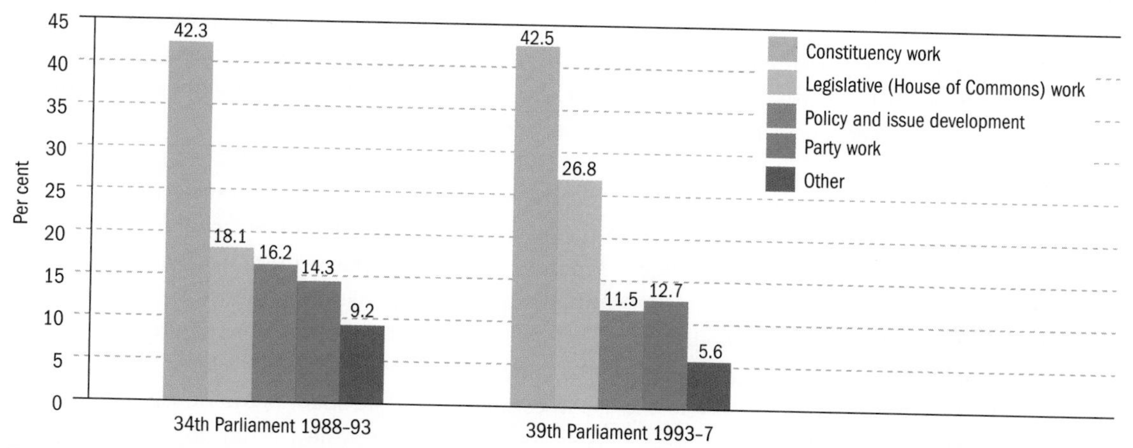

FIGURE 8.4 How an MP Spends the Day (per cent of working time devoted to different tasks)

Source: This figure is reprinted with permission of the Publisher from *Mr. Smith Goes to Ottawa: Life in the House of Commons* by David Docherty © University of British Columbia Press 1997. All rights reserved by the Publisher.

The Democratic Deficit?

During the 1990s it became increasingly popular to speak about a **democratic deficit** in Canadian politics, resulting from what critics believed to be the excessive centralization of power in and around the Prime Minister and cabinet and the marginalization of the legislature to little more than an occasionally entertaining, more often embarrassing, but almost always irrelevant sideshow. Jeffrey Simpson's book, *The Friendly Dictatorship*, made the case for significant reform of the way in which Parliament

Politics in Focus

Box 8.7 Parliament: An MP's View

There really is no such thing as a typical day in the life of an MP: they work in Ottawa when Parliament is in session; they travel back and forth to their constituencies and to conferences and meetings of various kinds; and they work in their constituencies. For some MPs, such as Dr Keith Martin from British Columbia, the job is gratifying but increasingly frustrating because of the extent to which party discipline and partisanship have created a democratic deficit whereby members must 'toe the party line' or risk ostracism.

Canada's Parliament is a child of the British Westminster system where the party in power tries to implement their agenda while opposition parties hold the government to account. Canada is supposed to be a democracy yet fundamental democratic principles and rights, such as the right to freedom of speech, are consistently violated in the nation's senior governing body. As a result the ability of our citizenry to have their wishes expressed in Parliament by the MPs they elect has been dramatically compromised over the last 30 years and especially over the last four.

Today, MPs are expected to parrot what is given to them by the leader of their party regardless of what their constituents want. The position a party takes is made by its leader and a small number of advisers in their office who are not elected by the people and thus are not accountable to them. MPs have little or no say in what a party does. Their role is to represent their party to the people and not their constituents to Parliament.

MPs who advocate for the will of their constituents over that of the party will be penalized by the party. They will not be allowed to speak in Parliament. They will be removed from any position they hold, and can be banished from caucus and forced to sit as independents (see the cases of MPs Michael Chong and Bill Casey). This significantly harms an MP's ability to represent his or her constituents and produces very difficult ethical dilemmas for the member. Do you support the will of the people over that of the leadership of your party and weaken your influence within your party, or do you buckle under, go against the will of the citizens you represent but maintain whatever influence you may have within your party?

No democratically elected leader in the West has as much power as a Canadian Prime Minister. This role was described by Quebec Supreme Court Justice John Gomery as, 'one-man government'.

Against this backdrop is the press, which in Canada has become concentrated in very few hands. Fighting for a shrinking advertising dollar, the media have resolved to increase their readership or viewership by focusing on 'infotainment'. Reality TV and *People* magazine trump news and informative documentaries.

Into this milieu enters the member of Parliament, a person who has chosen to seek and successfully attained public office to better his or her community and the country as a whole. What a shock it is when that person enters the hallowed halls of the House of Commons.

When they are in Ottawa, MPs' day-to-day work in Parliament revolves around the House of Commons and committees. Time spent in the House of Commons (House duty), where they listen to speeches, give speeches, and ask questions about legislation, is poorly attended. There are usually fewer than 15 MPs, out of 308, sitting in the House at any one time and fewer conducts its business, as did many other political commentators. Prime Minister Harper's prorogation of Parliament in November 2008 and December 2009, each time in circumstances that appeared likely to bring down his government, fuelled charges that the democratic deficit was deeper than ever.

Is there a democratic deficit in Canada? Those who think that the Prime Minister should have a relatively unfettered hand in shaping the legislative agenda and moving it through Parliament will not think so. But revelations by the federal Auditor General in her 2004 annual report

people sit in the public galleries. The debates, however, are televised.

Most speeches are written by the party for their MPs, who stand up and read them. Their speeches toe the party line with a heavy emphasis on criticizing other parties for real or imagined failures. Personally, I write my own speeches and use them to advance new solutions on the subject under debate.

MPs also spend four to six hours per week on committees that they are appointed to sit on. Committees used to be a place where partisanship was kept to a minimum and discussions revolved around important issues of the day. Today, Parliament's committees are highly dysfunctional and are simply an extension of the partisan bickering found in the House of Commons. Studies are done, but rarely does anyone pay any attention to them. Committees are a colossal waste of time and money and are meant to keep MPs busy and unproductive. The rest of the time members meet with groups who wish to lobby them on an issue.

MPs generally work 10 hours a day Monday to Thursday when Parliament is in session. They travel back to their home ridings Thursday night and work Friday, Saturday, and Sunday in their ridings, where they attend community functions and deal with constituency problems. If an MP tries to create and implement solutions to problems, then the workload can easily reach 80 hours a week or more.

When an MP comes to Parliament, he or she has some decisions to make. If MPs want to advance up the ladder within their own party they should do exactly what they are told to do and engage in rabid, partisan attacks against other parties. An MP should not think independently and work collaboratively with MPs from other parties in order to move ideas forward. To do so is to run the risk of being labelled a maverick or not being seen as a team player. This is unfortunate, as failing to engage in the independent, critical analysis of problems weakens our political system, and fails the nation.

A tough road, but one that is very gratifying, is for the MP to have an agenda of initiatives to pursue and build partnerships with citizens, NGOs, activists, the private sector, and other MPs to implement these solutions. Building coalitions, advancing ideas, and leading is the purview of an MP. This approach will make the individual MP run afoul of the party leadership, but, in the end, why have this job unless you are willing to take chances and be courageous in the pursuit of solutions that will make our world a better place to live?

Parliament can change, but it will require courage. Leaders will have to stare down the status quo and champion the innovations that will address the big challenges we face.

Democracy and party discipline make strange bedfellows. Enforcing oppressive discipline over MPs in the manner that is done today corrodes our democracy by severing the will of the people from being exercised in Parliament. In this environment an MP faces difficult challenges, but he or she was elected by the people, and for the people. They must do what they have to do to live with themselves and be able to look into the eyes of the people they represent with a clear conscience.

Dr Keith Martin, MD, PC, was the member of Parliament for Esquimalt-Juan de Fuca in British Columbia. First elected to office in 1993 as a member of the Reform Party of Canada, he sat as a Liberal from 2004 to 2011, when he chose not to stand for re-election.

to Parliament seemed to illustrate at least one important dimension of the problem. She claimed that millions of dollars of taxpayer money were channelled to Quebec advertising agencies with Liberal Party connections during the years after the 1995 referendum, for services that were often not provided. There appeared to be no transparency in the awarding of these contracts, little in the way of public accountability for the spending of the money, partisan favouritism in their allocation, and a high probability of illegal behaviour on the part of many of those who distributed and received this money. Although there was no evidence that either Prime Minister Chrétien or his successor, Paul Martin, personally knew about or authorized any of these payments, the affair seemed to corroborate the view that corrupt practices were made possible by a system of government that did not provide adequate checks on the actions of some public officials, particularly in the Prime Minister's Office.

In 2004 the Liberal government appointed the Commission of Inquiry into the Sponsorship Program and Advertising Activities under the direction of Justice John Gomery. The Commission's final report touched directly on the issue of this alleged democratic deficit, suggesting that the malfeasance and illegal activities associated with the sponsorship program in Quebec were allowed to happen because of inadequate lines and methods of accountability and an abdication of responsibility for subordinates' actions on the part of those at the top of the bureaucratic and political hierarchy. In other words, the problem was one of systemic failure and not just or even primarily of bad people doing bad things (although there was clearly a good deal of this). The research studies carried out for the Commission argued that the oversight of government programs by parliamentary committees is, most of the time, pathetically weak. The Commission made a large number of recommendations for reforming the relationship of Parliament to the government and its public servants, increasing transparency in financial matters and program administration, and clarifying the roles and responsibilities of cabinet ministers and their deputies. Such recommendations, particularly those proposing a more robust role for Parliament, have been made before. But the Conservative government elected in 2006 put its Accountability Act, influenced by the Gomery Commission's recommendations, towards the top of its list of priorities and the bill received royal assent in December of that same year. Predictably, opinion is divided on the effectiveness of these reforms.[35]

The Courts

Responsibility for Canada's judicial system is divided between Ottawa and the provinces. While the Constitution gives the federal government the exclusive right to make criminal law, it assigns responsibility for the administration of justice and for law enforcement to the provinces. Consequently, all provinces have established their own systems of courts that interpret and apply both federal and provincial laws.

The Constitution also gives Ottawa the authority to create courts. This authority was used in 1875 to create the Supreme Court of Canada. Since 1949 the Supreme Court has been Canada's highest court of appeal. Ottawa again used this constitutional power in 1971 to create the Federal Court of Canada. It has jurisdiction over civil claims involving the federal government, cases arising from the decisions of federally appointed administrative bodies like the Immigration Appeal Board, and matters relating to federal income tax, copyrights, and maritime law—all of which fall under the legislative authority of Ottawa. The structure of Canada's court system is shown in Figure 8.5.

Courts apply and interpret the law. They perform this role in matters ranging from contested driving offences to disputes over the most fundamental principles of the Constitution. The decisions of judges often have profound implications for the rights and status of individuals and groups, for the balance of social and economic power, and for the federal division of powers. It is, therefore, crucial that we understand the political significance of the judicial process and the methods of interpretation typically used by the courts.

The independence of judges is the cornerstone of the Canadian judicial system. Judges are appointed by governments. But once appointed they hold their office 'during good behaviour'[36]—or to age 75. What constitutes a lapse from 'good behaviour'? A criminal or a serious moral offence could provide grounds for removal, as could decisions of such incompetence that they undermine public respect for the law and the judiciary. In such circumstances the appointing government may launch removal proceedings against a judge. In fact, however, this has seldom happened. Formal proceedings have rarely been initiated and have never been prosecuted to their ultimate conclusion, i.e., the actual removal of a judge by resolution of Parliament or a provincial legislature. Judicial independence is also protected by the fact that judges' salaries and conditions of service are established by law. Consequently, governments cannot single out any individual judge for special reward or punishment.

But as Ralph Miliband puts it, to say that judges are 'independent' begs the question, 'Independent of what?' As members of the societies in which they live—usually successful members of the middle and upper-middle classes—they cannot be neutral in the values they bring to their task. Judges, observes Miliband, 'are by no means, and cannot be, independent of the multitude of influences, notably of class origin, education, class situation and professional tendency, which contribute as much to the formation of their view of the world as they do in the case of other men.'[37] Thus, when one says that the judiciary is 'independent' this should be understood as a description of its formal separation from the executive and legislative branches of the state. When it comes to the dominant value system of their society, judges are no more independent than are the members of any other part of the state elite. Leaving aside the socio-economically unrepresentative character of the legal profession and the effects of formal training in the law, in British parliamentary systems all judges are appointed by governments.[38] One would hardly expect these governments to appoint radical critics of society, even supposing that a significant number of such individuals existed within the more respected ranks of the legal profession from which judges are selected. Moreover, governments control promotion within

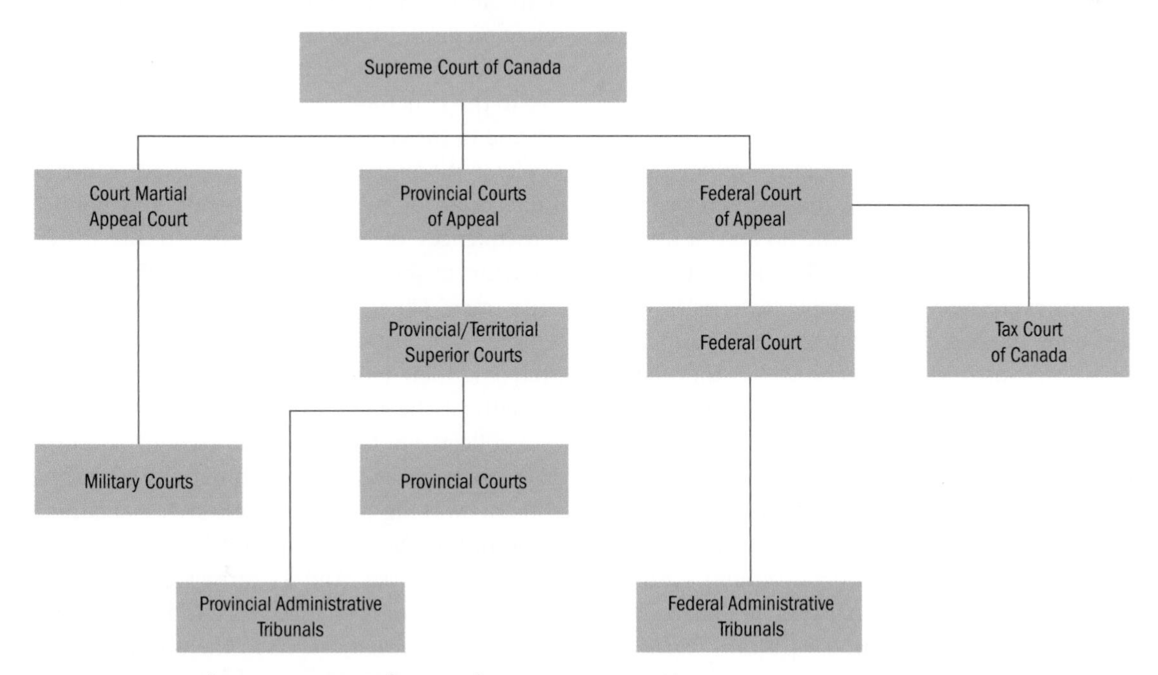

FIGURE 8.5 The Structure of Canada's Court System

Source: *Canada's Court System*, Department of Justice Canada, 2005. Figure: Outline of Canada's Court System, page 16, at <http://canada.justice.gc.ca/eng/dept-min/pub/just/img/courten.pdf>. Reproduced with the permission of the Minister of Public Works and Government Services Canada, 2011.

the system of courts—who will be promoted from a district court to a superior court, and so on. This fact may also exert a chilling effect on unconventional judicial behaviour.

The socio-economic background of judges and the process by which they are selected have been argued by some to introduce conservative tendencies into the judiciary. But they are not the only factors, nor are they necessarily the most important ones, that may incline the courts towards protection of the status quo. The law itself is often a powerful conservative force. We are used to thinking of the law as simply 'the rules made by governments' that 'apply to everybody in society'.[39] But the law is more than this. It represents values that have accumulated over a long period of time. The concepts, meanings, precedents, and interpretive rules that shape judicial decision-making tend to inhibit sharp breaks with the past.

Judges work within the embedded premises of the law. Among the most important of these premises, in terms of their impact on the distribution of power in society, are the rights of the individual, the rights associated with private property, and the concept of the business corporation. Individualism is woven throughout the legal fabric of Canadian society. As a practical matter, respect for individual rights tends to be more important for the privileged than for the disadvantaged. While this is obviously true in the case of property rights—protection for these rights matters more to those who have something to lose than to those who do not—it has also tended to be true in matters like individual freedom of expression. For example, a series of court decisions handed down between 1983 and 2001 ruled unconstitutional sections of the federal Elections Act that prohibited advertising by organizations other than registered political parties during federal election campaigns. In the abstract this represented a victory for freedom of expression. Critics charged, however, that these victories mattered most to well-heeled organizations with the means to pay for such advertising, such as the ideologically conservative National Citizens' Coalition that led the challenges to these restrictions. (In the end, these restrictions were upheld by the Supreme Court of Canada in a 2004 ruling.)

The powerful tug of liberal individualism on judicial reasoning was clearly demonstrated in a 1987 Supreme Court of Canada decision on the right to strike. A majority of the justices decided that 'The constitutional guarantee of freedom of association . . . does not include, in the case of a trade union, a guarantee of the right to bargain collectively and the right to strike.'[40] The right to bargain collectively and to strike were not, the Court ruled, fundamental rights or freedoms that deserved the constitutional protection of section 2(d) of the Charter. 'They are', the Court said, 'the creation of legislation, involving a balance of competing interests',[41] and their scope and limitations are appropriately determined by legislatures. To put it very simply, economic rights were viewed as subordinate to political ones. The Court said as much: 'the overwhelming preoccupation of the Charter is with individual, political, and democratic rights with conspicuous inattention to economic and property rights.'[42] But what 'conspicuous inattention' meant in practical terms was that the existing balance of power and rights between employers and workers was considered to be correct, and that workers and unions could not count on the courts to defend their rights against governments intent on diminishing them.

On the other hand, judges are not always insensitive to the structural inequalities that exist in society and in the economy. Particularly at the highest levels of the judicial system, judges are generally quite aware of the socio-economic and political consequences of their decisions. In his dissent from the majority decision in the 1987 right-to-strike case, Chief Justice Dickson observed that 'Throughout history, workers have associated to overcome their vulnerability as individuals to the strength of their employers. The capacity to bargain collectively has long been recognized as one of the integral and primary functions of associations of working people.'[43] Collective bargaining, according to Dickson, requires that workers have the right to strike. And as we saw in Chapter 6, the Supreme Court changed its mind in later decisions that essentially reversed the position that it had taken in 1987. Moreover, in a 1989 decision the Supreme Court rejected the traditional liberal notion of equality as identical treatment before the law in favour of what is sometimes called **substantive equality**. This requires that individuals be looked at in terms of their group characteristics and the possible advantages or disadvantages they may have experienced as a result of these attributes. Liberal individualism does not have the field all to itself in Canadian society and it is far from being uncontested in legal and judicial circles.

Aspects of liberal individualism are also embedded in the judicial process. While all judicial systems are adversarial, in the sense that one party (the plaintiff in civil cases; the prosecution in criminal ones) brings an action against another (the defendant), common-law systems like Canada's represent the most extreme form of this adversarial process. In civil cases the onus is placed on the individual parties—plaintiff and defendant—to make their respective cases before the court. In criminal proceedings the state is responsible for prosecuting the case against an individual or organization, but that individual or organization is responsible for the defence. In both civil and criminal proceedings, the role of the court is to hear and weigh the evidence, not to participate actively in the development of either side to the action.

It is up to a plaintiff or defendant to make his or her most persuasive case. Their ability to do so will depend, in part, on their access to competent legal counsel. In criminal proceedings, the state will pay for legal counsel for defendants who cannot afford to hire a lawyer. Legal aid is available in all provinces for those who cannot afford the legal costs of a civil action. But these forms of subsidized legal assistance by no means equalize access to effective legal counsel. The difference between an Edward Greenspan and a court-appointed lawyer is not simply, or even mainly, their skills in the courtroom. The high-priced Edward Greenspans of the legal profession are backed up by the resources of a large law firm. A large corporation or a wealthy individual can afford to pay for these resources, but they are beyond the means of most people.

Although the judicial system is hardly a level playing field, it would be wrong to suggest that it serves only the interests of the wealthy and powerful. Indeed, particularly since the addition of the Charter of Rights and Freedoms to Canada's Constitution, groups representing women, Aboriginal Canadians, the disabled, gays and lesbians, and other interests that could hardly be described as being near the epicentre of power in Canadian society have frequently achieved successes in the courts that were not possible in legislative and electoral forums. For example, the Supreme Court's unanimous 1997 *Delgamuukw* decision on Native landownership produced a victory for the Gitksan and Wet'suwet'en peoples, and by extension for other Aboriginal communities claiming a historic right of occupancy and use to land not covered by a treaty, that years of political negotiation had not been able to achieve.

Some argue that recourse to the courts to achieve ends that cannot be accomplished through the political process is fundamentally undemocratic. It is simply wrong, however, to conceive of the courts as being outside the political process. Even before the Charter, the courts were very much a part of politics and policy-making in Canada. Their rulings on the federal–provincial division of powers and on all manner of policy questions have always been part of Canadian politics. Quebec nationalists have long complained that the Supreme Court of Canada has a pro-federal bias, a claim that—true or not—reflects the inescapable involvement of the Court in the politics of federalism. The fact that by law three of the Supreme Court's nine judges must be members of the Quebec bar, and that by tradition three should be from Ontario, two from the West, and one from Atlantic Canada, shows that the essentially political issue of regional representation has been considered important for the judicial branch, just as it is important in the executive and legislative branches of government.

In recent years the issue of representation on the bench, particularly on the Supreme Court, has become even more politically charged. The 1998 retirement of Justice John Sopinka unleashed a flurry of behind-the-scenes lobbying and public advocacy on behalf of particular candidates for the vacancy on Canada's highest court. The formal retirement of Justice Peter Cory in 1999 likewise was preceded by active lobbying in legal circles, particularly on behalf of female candidates for the job. Gender and judicial ideology appear to have become more prominent criteria in the Supreme

Court selection process, at least in the eyes of many advocacy and rights-oriented groups.[44] Many critics argue that the judicial selection process is mired in partisanship and a lack of transparency and should be reformed.[45]

If we accept, then, that the courts are unavoidably part of the political process, is there any basis for the claim that recourse to the courts may be undemocratic? The short answer is 'yes'. Several decades before the Charter, James Mallory argued that business interests cynically exploited the federal division of powers in the British North America Act to oppose increased state interference in their affairs, regardless of which level of government was doing the interfering.[46] Respect for democratic principles and the Constitution was the cloak behind which business attempted to conceal its self-interest.

In the Charter era similar criticisms have been expressed. Charter critics like Ted Morton and Rainer Knopff argue that recourse to the courts by abortion rights advocates, gay and lesbian rights groups, and Aboriginals, among others, have produced rulings that often elevate the preferences of special interests over more broadly held values. More importantly, from the standpoint of our examination of the machinery of government, they agree with Michael Mandel's argument that the Charter era has witnessed the 'legalization' of Canadian politics. Emboldened by the entrenchment of rights in the Constitution and the declaration of constitutional supremacy in section 52 of the Constitution Act, 1982, judges have been less deferential to governments and legislatures than in the past. Moreover, a network of rights-oriented advocacy groups, law professors, lawyers, journalists, and bureaucrats working within the rights apparatus of the state (from human rights commissions to the ubiquitous equity officers found throughout the public sector) has emerged, and which, in the words of Morton and Knopff, 'prefers the policy-making power of the less obviously democratic governmental institutions.'[47] The institutions they are referring to are the courts and quasi-judicial rights commissions and tribunals.

As we saw in Chapter 6, the era of judges deferring to the will of elected officials is over. The Charter was the catalyst for what both critics and supporters see as an enormous increase in the policy role of the courts. While acknowledging that the courts now play a vastly greater role in the policy process, including matters of social policy, Chief Justice Beverley McLachlin argues that judges do so in a spirit of impartiality (see Box 8.8). She is, of course, correct that judges are not political in the sense of being representatives of one or another party and its agenda. But with all due respect to the Chief Justice and her colleagues on the bench, it is disingenuous or at least naive to suggest that judges are impartial in the sense of being apolitical, i.e., without political beliefs, values, and preferences. We are back to Ralph Miliband's observation that judges are no more independent of the value system of their society than any other part of the state elite. We expect them to be independent of party influence, but until the law contains its own self-evident meanings—in which case we would have no need for courts—judges will not be politically impartial.

Appendix: How a Law Is Passed

The law takes various forms. A statute passed by the House of Commons and the Senate, and given royal assent by the Governor General, is clearly a law. But decisions taken by cabinet that have not been approved in the legislature also have the force of law. These are called 'Orders-in-Council'. Thousands of them are issued each year, and they are published in the *Canada Gazette*. The decisions of agencies, boards, and commissions that receive their regulatory powers from a statute also have the force of law. Finally, there are the regulations and guidelines issued and enforced by the departmental bureaucracy in accordance with the discretionary powers delegated to them under a statute. These also have the force of law.

In a strictly numerical sense the statutes passed annually by Parliament represent only the tip of the iceberg of laws promulgated each year. Nevertheless, virtually all major policy decisions—including budget measures and the laws that assign discretionary power to the bureaucracy—come before the legislature. The only exception has been when the normal process of government was suspended by passage of the War Measures Act. This happened during World War I, again during World War II, and briefly in 1970 when Ottawa proclaimed the War Measures Act after two political kidnappings in Quebec by the Front de libération du Québec. The War Measures Act was replaced by the Emergencies Act in 1988.

During normal times the law-making process involves several stages and opportunities for debate and amendment. The steps from the introduction of a bill in Parliament to the final proclamation of a statute are set out in Figure 8.6.

There are two types of bills, namely private members' bills and government bills. Private members' bills originate from any individual MP, but unless they get the backing of government they have little chance of passing. Government bills dominate Parliament's legislative agenda. When major legislation is being proposed, a bill is sometimes preceded by a *white paper.* This is a report for discussion, based on research by the bureaucracy (and sometimes the legislature as well), and serves as a statement of the government's legislative intentions. Major legislation may also follow from the recommendations of a Royal Commission, a task force, or

Governing Realities

Box 8.8 Chief Justice McLachlin Defends the Court's Involvement with Questions of Social Policy

The fact that judges rule on social questions that affect large numbers of people does not, however, mean that judges are political. There is much confusion on this point in the popular press. Judges are said to be acting politically, to have descended (or perhaps ascended) into the political arena. Judges, on this view, are simply politicians who do not need to stand for election and can never be removed.

This misapprehension confuses outcome with process. Many judicial decisions on important social issues—say affirmative action, or abortion, or gay rights—will be political in the sense that they will satisfy some political factions at the expense of others. But the term 'political' is used in the context to describe an outcome, not a process. While the outcomes of cases are inevitably political in some broad sense of the term, it is important—critical, even—that the process be impartial. It is inescapable that judges' decisions will have political ramifications. But it is essential that they not be partisan. In their final form, judgments on social policy questions are often not all that different from legislation. It is the process by which the judgments are arrived at that distinguishes them. Legislation is often the product of compromise or conflict between various political factions, each faction pushing its own agenda. The judicial arena does not, and should not, provide simply another forum for the same kind of contests. Judges must *maintain the appearance and reality of impartiality.* It is impartiality that distinguishes us from the other branches of government, and impartiality that gives us our legitimacy.

. . . [Our] changing society affects the work of judges. The nature of the questions they decide, and the public expectation that they will decide them fairly and well, place new demands on judges. It no longer suffices to be a competent legal scholar and a fair arbiter. To perform their modern role well, judges must be sensitive to a broad range of social concerns. They must possess a keen appreciation of the importance of individual and group interests and rights. And they must be in touch with the society in which they work, understanding its values and its tensions. The ivory tower no longer suffices as the residence of choice for judges.

Source: Remarks of the Right Honourable Beverley McLachlin, PC, Chief Justice of Canada, on 'The Role of Judges in Modern Society', given at the 4th Worldwide Common Law Judiciary Conference in Vancouver, BC, 5 May 2001. At: <www.scc-csc.gc.ca/aboutcourt/judges/speeches/role-of-judges_e.html>.

some other consultative body that has been created by the government to study and make recommendations on an issue.

Once a bill has been drafted by government, it is introduced into the Senate, or more usually, into the House of Commons. Here, it is given *first reading*, which is just a formality and involves no debate. Then the bill goes to *second reading*, when the main principles of the bill are debated and a vote is taken. If the bill passes second reading it is sent to a smaller legislative committee, where the details of the bill are considered clause by clause. At this committee stage, amendments can be made but the principle of the bill cannot be altered. The bill is then reported back to the House, where all aspects, including any amendments, are debated. At this *report stage* new amendments also can be introduced. If a bill passes this hurdle it then goes to *third reading* where a final vote is taken, sometimes after further debate. Once a bill has been passed in the House, it is then sent to the Senate where a virtually identical process takes place. If a bill was first introduced in the Senate, then it would now be sent to the House. Finally, a bill that has been passed in both the House and the Senate can be given royal assent and become law.

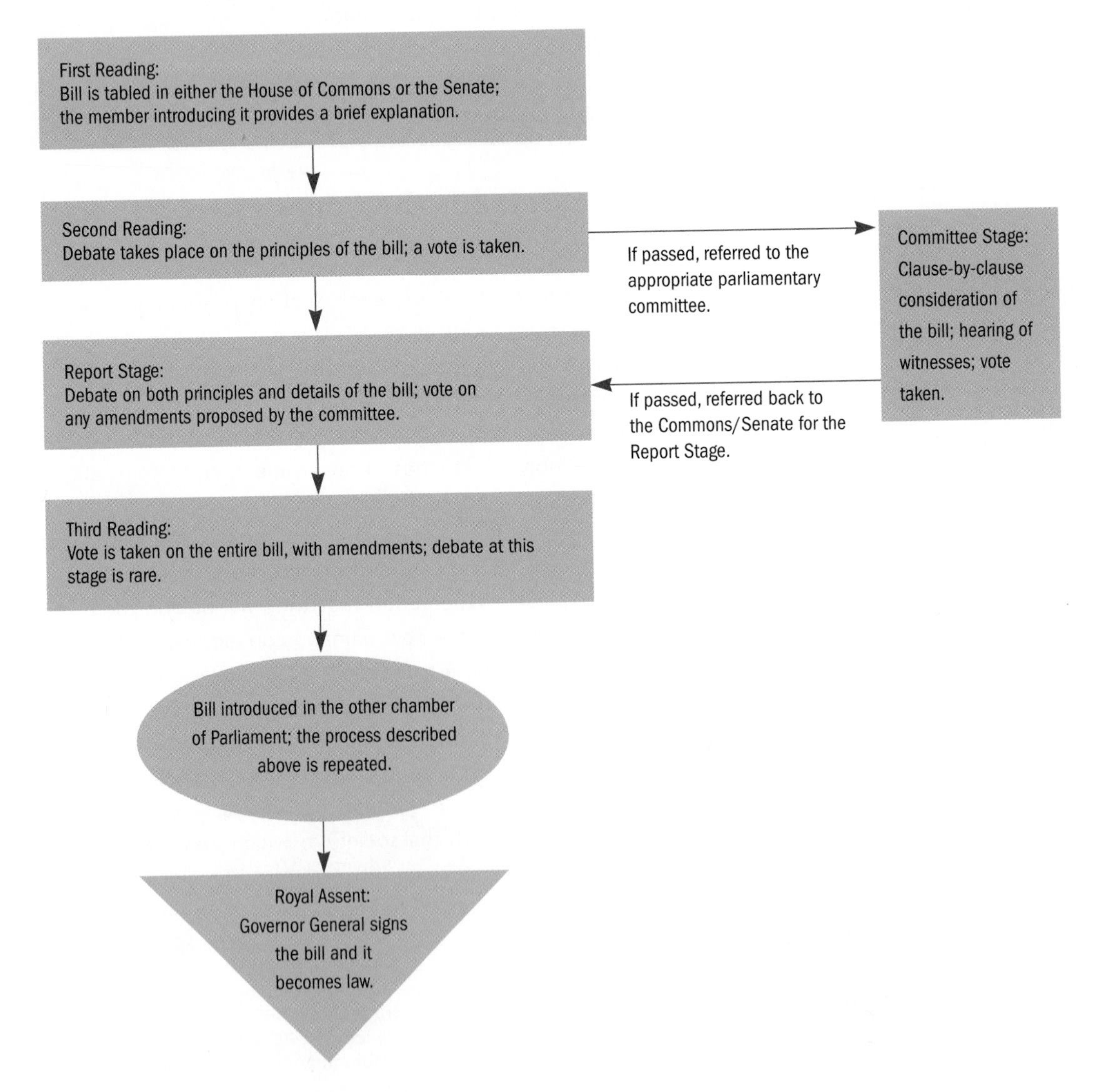

FIGURE 8.6 From Bill to Statute

Starting Points for Research

David Docherty, *Mr. Smith Goes to Ottawa: Life in the House of Commons* (Vancouver: University of British Columbia Press, 1997). Based largely on surveys of MPs, this is the best analysis of legislative behaviour and influence in the House of Commons to be written in last 20 years.

G. Bruce Doern and Christopher Stoney, eds, *How Ottawa Spends 2010–2011* (Montreal and Kingston: McGill-Queen's University Press, 2010). This annual publication of the School of Public Administration at Carleton University includes contributions on various structures, processes, and current issues relating to the federal government.

Lydia Miljan, *Public Policy in Canada*, 5th edn (Toronto: Oxford University Press, 2008). This text examines the forces that shape Canadian public policy and surveys several policy fields, including health, Aboriginal, social, economic, family, and environmental policy.

Donald Savoie, *The Politics of Public Spending in Canada* (Toronto: University of Toronto Press, 1990). Savoie, who served as the director of research for the Gomery Commission, unpacks and lays bare the structural factors within the bureaucracy, cabinet, and federal–provincial relations that pull in the direction of increased public spending.

Donald Savoie, *Governing from the Centre: The Concentration of Power in Canadian Politics* (Toronto: University of Toronto Press, 1999). Here Savoie makes the case that the concentration of power in and around the Prime Minister's Office has reached unprecedented and undemocratic levels. This is a 'must read' for those interested in the inner workings of the machinery of government.

Review Exercises

1. The Gomery Commission made far-reaching recommendations regarding the selection of deputy ministers and their relationship to the government of the day. You can find these and the reasoning behind them at: <www.cbc.ca/news/background/groupaction/gomeryreport_phasetwo_full.html>. (See in particular Chapter 5 in the phase 2 report, 'Restoring Accountability'.) Summarize the arguments in favour of these changes and explain why you think such reforms would or would not be desirable.
2. Put together a list of the various governmental organizations (federal, provincial, municipal) you have been in contact with during your life and the reasons for the contact(s). Think hard—the list is probably longer than you imagine at first.

The Canadian Broadcasting Corporation (CBC), along with the Bank of Canada, Canada Revenue Agency, Canada Post Corporation, Export Development Canada, Parks Canada, and a whole host of other government institutions, make up the federal bureaucracy and are responsible for carrying out the policies set by the government of Canada. © *Toronto Star*/GetStock.com

9 The Administrative State

For policies to have an impact they must be implemented. This is the role of the bureaucracy. Implementation, however, is not an automatic process of converting laws into actions. Unelected officials often wield enormous discretion in applying laws and administering programs. Moreover, their influence is felt at numerous points in the decision-making process preceding the actual introduction of a bill in Parliament. This chapter examines the federal bureaucracy, focusing on the following topics:

- The development of the administrative state.
- Professionalization of the public service in Canada.
- The political rights of public servants.
- The functions of the bureaucracy.
- Departments.
- Public enterprise.
- Regulatory agencies.

In 1867 the Canadian state had a budget of $15 million. Its major source of revenue was customs duties (tariffs), accounting for $9 million or about two-thirds of all federal revenue. Of the $15 million spent that year, interest on the public debt was the single largest expenditure ($4 million), followed by payments to provincial governments ($3 million), expenditures on transportation infrastructure ($2 million), economic development ($2 million), employee salaries and other administrative costs ($2 million), defence ($1 million), and miscellaneous odds and ends ($1 million). We do not have hard numbers on government employment for the first few decades after Confederation, but by 1900 there were only about 3,000 federal public servants. This was a mere fraction of the Canadian labour force, which included roughly 2.5 million workers at that time. As part of the agreement that produced the Constitution Act, 1867, the new national government assumed the debts of the original four provinces. Ottawa owed $94 million in 1867, or about $27 per inhabitant of the country. Even if we add provincial and municipal budgets and employment to this picture, the state was by any measure quite small.

Statistics like these, however, tell only part of the story. When the American writer Henry David Thoreau visited Canada in 1850 he was struck by the statist culture that he observed: 'in Canada you are reminded of the government every day. It parades itself before you. It is not content to be the servant but will be the master.'[1] For Thoreau, remnants of the British aristocratic system and of the French feudal system gave to Canada an Old World character where hierarchy, distinction, and deference were woven through the culture. Although the state was not large in terms of its resources, its influence was more pervasive and the awe—understood as a combination of fear and respect—that it elicited from citizens was greater than in the United States. So Thoreau believed.

A statist mentality may have existed in nineteenth-century Canada, although the testimony of Thoreau needs to be placed alongside that of others, such as fellow writer Susanna Moodie. She believed that the arrival of the 'lower orders' in the New World caused them to abandon the proper deference that they owed their social superiors and adopt an 'I'm as good as you, Jack' mentality.[2] But whether Thoreau or Moodie comes closer to the mark in characterizing the mentality of the times, the state in Canada was puny. It employed comparatively few people, accounted for but a small share of the country's economy, and did many fewer things than it does today.

It was different from the contemporary state in another important way. Today we take for granted that most state officials will be bureaucrats who are hired and promoted according to job-relevant criteria and who keep their positions regardless of which party controls the government. We expect, in other words, that **patronage**—the practice of making decisions about the distribution of public resources based on friendship, family, loyalty, or in exchange for benefits of various sorts—will be very limited. It may still be all right if the prime minister appoints a loyal friend and partisan ally to a position in the PMO, but we would find it unacceptable if he stuffed the bureaucracy, the courts, the higher rungs of the military, or the RCMP with such people. And, indeed, laws and staffing rules exist in order to reduce the possibility of such practices occurring. Nor would most of us consider appropriate the awarding of public contracts based on political favouritism. Patronage continues to exist, but the point is that in the nineteenth century such practices were both common and believed by many to be normal and acceptable. The gears of the state were lubricated with generous amounts of patronage to a degree and in circumstances that today would be considered unethical and sometimes even illegal.

Professionalization of the Public Service

The adoption of the **merit principle**, whereby hiring and promotion decisions were expected to be based on such qualifications as relevant experience, academic degrees, professional credentials and certification, and other attributes deemed to be relevant to the competent performance of the job, did not occur until passage of the Civil Service Amendment

Act, 1908. Prior to this reform, the practice of patronage-based appointments was rampant, as was also true in most other democracies and certainly in the United States, where pressures for public service reform also were building. The Royal Commission to Enquire into and Report on the Operation of the Civil Service Act and Kindred Legislation stated that 'patronage seems to run more or less through every department of the public service. It was the universal feeling among the officials who gave evidence before the Commissioners that this patronage evil was the curse of the public service.'[3]

But the reforms instituted by the 1908 law were quite limited, extending the merit principle in hiring only to what was called the 'inside service' in Ottawa but not to the thousands of federal civil service positions elsewhere in the country. This changed 10 years later when the Conservative government of Robert Borden passed the Civil Service Act, 1918, extending merit principle hiring and the authority of the non-partisan Civil Service Commission (today called the Public Service Commission of Canada) to federal positions outside of Ottawa.

The merit principle was a key part of a larger process of professionalization of the public service. Another reform involved various prohibitions on the political activities of unelected state officials. The reasoning was quite simple. Bureaucrats should be able to serve whatever party formed the government, uninfluenced by their own political beliefs and partisan preferences. A politically neutral public service was considered essential to a modern, professional bureaucracy. This reasoning was premised on the **politics–administration dichotomy** that was an important aspect of progressive thought about the democratic state in the late nineteenth and early twentieth centuries. It held that only elected politicians should make choices between competing values and interests, choices that would be embodied in the laws. The proper function of non-elected state officials was to implement these choices without regard for their personal views and preferences. It is worth observing at this point that even some of those who supported the politics–administration dichotomy worried about what would eventually be seen as the dehumanizing and even totalitarian implications of viewing state bureaucrats as, in Max Weber's words, 'specialists without spirit, sensualists without heart'.[4]

In any case, the 1908 and 1918 reforms to the Civil Service Act placed strict limits on the rights of public servants to participate in politics beyond voting. They could not contribute money to a party or a candidate for public office and, although the law was not entirely clear on these matters, it appeared that they could not put campaign signs on their lawns, make public speeches or publish articles in newspapers or elsewhere in which they expressed their political views, or even belong to a party and attend its meetings.

This changed in 1967 when the Public Service Employment Act was passed. The Act specifically omitted attending political meetings and contributing money from the political activities that were off limits to public servants. It also gave to the Public Service Commission the authority to grant unpaid leaves of absence to public servants running for office. Increasingly, however, the inherent tension between the obligation of political neutrality imposed on public servants and their political rights as citizens was viewed as a problem, at least by those whose right to participate in the political process was restricted on account of their employment status. Their demands for the same rights enjoyed by other citizens were part of the broader movement towards the expansion and recognition of rights that produced human rights codes in the 1960s and 1970s and the Charter of Rights and Freedoms in 1982. Armed with the Charter, public servants have gone to court to challenge what they believed to be unconstitutional limitations on their political rights. Here is what the courts have said in three of these cases.

Fraser v. PSSRB

Neil Fraser was a public servant with Revenue Canada's Kingston office. He was outspoken and even vitriolic in his criticism of the federal government's adoption of the metric system and also of the Charter of Rights and Freedoms. After repeated warnings and suspensions by his employer, Fraser was dismissed from his job. In challenging his dismissal, Fraser did not argue that his right to free speech under the Charter had been violated (not only would this have been hugely ironic, but the Charter was not part of the Constitution when his dismissal occurred). Instead, he argued that federal law concerning the dismissal of employees made a crucial distinction between job-related and non-job-related criticism and that a public servant ought to be as free as any private citizen to criticize policies unrelated to his or her job or department. The government responded that public criticism by an employee of any government policy may have the effect of undermining the actual and perceived neutrality and impartiality of the public service.

The Supreme Court, in its 1985 ruling, agreed with Fraser's contention that public servants should be allowed non-job-related criticism of government policy. But it held that, in this case, his criticisms crossed the line and could, in fact, be considered job-related. Here is the key section of the Court's ruling:

> . . . As a general rule, federal public servants should be loyal to their employer, the Government of Canada. The loyalty owed is to the Government of Canada, not the political party in power at any one time. . . . In some circumstances a public servant may actively and publicly express opposition to the policies of a government . . . if, for example the Government were engaged in illegal acts, or if its policies jeopardized the life, health or safety of the public servant or others, or if the public servant's criticisms had no impact on his or her ability to perform effectively the duties of a public servant or on the public perception of that ability. But, having stated these qualifications . . . it is my view that a public servant . . . must not engage, as the appellant did in the present case, in sustained and highly visible attacks on major Government policies.[5]

Osborne v. Canada (Treasury Board)

Bryan Osborne was a public servant working in the Actuarial Branch of the Department of Insurance within the Treasury Board. He was elected by his Liberal Party riding association to serve as a delegate at the party's 1984 leadership convention. Osborne resigned as a delegate after his employer warned him that he would face disciplinary action if he failed to do so. But subsequently, when a by-election was called in his riding, Osborne requested and received a leave of absence from his job in order to stand as a candidate for the Liberal Party nomination. He admitted that he did this to be free to attend the party's leadership convention, after which Osborne withdrew from the nomination race and requested that he be reinstated in his job. His political leave was terminated and Osborne did, in fact, return to his job.

Other public servants were also involved in this case, but the issue was the same: did s. 33(1) of the Public Service Employment Act, which prohibits public servants from engaging in work for or against a candidate, violate their Charter rights? Osborne and the other public servants in this case argued that their rights of free speech and freedom of association were infringed. In a 1991 judgement, the Supreme Court agreed. It ruled that these prohibitions were 'over-inclusive and went beyond what is necessary to achieve the objective of an impartial and loyal civil service.' The government's argument that these were reasonable limits on Charter rights was rejected. Only the requirement that a public servant must take an unpaid leave in order to stand as a candidate and the restrictions on the political activities of deputy ministers were upheld by the Court.[6]

Haydon v. Canada (Treasury Board)

Dr Margaret Haydon was a veterinarian with Health Canada. In 2001 she was given a 10-day suspension after having told a *Globe and Mail* reporter that a ban imposed by the Canadian government on imports of Brazilian beef was motivated more by political factors than genuine health concerns. Prior to this incident Dr Haydon had been publicly critical of government health policies on two occasions, one of which resulted in a warning from her employer.

This case involved issues similar to those in *Fraser*. In the 2004 *Haydon* ruling, the Federal Court of Canada reiterated what the Supreme Court had said in that earlier decision on the employee's duty of loyalty and the reasons for this duty. It then elaborated on the balance between a public servant's free speech rights and his or her duty of loyalty:

> The following factors are relevant in determining whether a public servant in speaking out has breached his loyalty duty: the employee's level within the hierarchy; nature and content of the expression; visibility of the expression; sensitivity of the issue; truth of the statement made; steps taken to determine the facts prior to speaking; efforts to raise concerns with the employer; extent of damage to employer's reputation and impact upon employer's ability to conduct business.
>
> Where disciplinary action is taken against a public servant, the employer must demonstrate that the comments were inappropriate and harmful. . . .
>
> The duty of loyalty constitutes a reasonable limit on freedom of expression. . . .[7]

If Dr Haydon had been engaged in what is called **whistleblowing**—bringing public attention to government actions or policies that she believed endangered public health or safety, based on her careful examination of the facts—the balance between her right to free speech and her duty of loyalty would have tipped in favour of the former. But that was not what she was doing, the Court decided.

Efficiency and Accountability

When the state was small and its functions fewer than today, the need for expertise was felt less strongly. Some positions required special skills and training, such as government surveyors, statisticians with the Dominion Bureau of Statistics (rechristened Statistics Canada in 1971), and accountants working for the Treasury Board. But most positions in the bureaucracy did not require much, if anything, in the way of formal education, specialized credentials, and professional certification. The long struggle for adoption of the merit principle in public-sector hiring and promotion was in large part a response to the obvious inefficiencies likely to result from staffing decisions made on the basis of friendship, family, and service rendered. But it was also connected to an important shift taking place by the late nineteenth century in ideas about the state, its proper functions, and its potential.

These ideas are sometimes referred to as the **positive state**: a state that is active in attempting to shape society and influence its direction. It was championed by liberal intellectuals such as John Dewey in the United States (*The Public and Its Problems*, 1927), socialist thinkers in the United Kingdom, most prominently the members of the Fabian Society, and in Canada by Progressive movement intellectuals such as Adam Shortt, a University of Chicago–educated economic historian at Queen's University and an original member of the Civil Service Commission. Shortt expressed the intellectual spirit of his times when he wrote, 'One does not attempt fine work through the instrumentality of a mob. . . . It is through a select, active minority that the most effective and progressive ideas as to political and social welfare must be introduced.'[8] The state, thinkers like Shortt believed, needed to be staffed by people with expert training in order to meet the challenges of a modern society in which policy problems were typically complex and not capable of being understood, let alone solved, by non-experts.

One of the first of such experts to make an important mark on the federal public service was Oscar Douglas Skelton. Like Shortt, he had been educated at the University of Chicago and taught at Queen's University. It is part of the lore of Canadian intellectual history that Skelton's *Socialism: A Critical Appraisal* (1911) received the backhanded compliment of being referred to by Lenin as a sophisticated embodiment of intellectual power in the service of capitalism. Skelton's insistence that Canadian foreign policy should be determined independently of the British Empire, and that Canada's most important external relationship was with the United States, coincided with the views of the Liberal Prime Minister, Mackenzie King. In 1925 Skelton was appointed by King as Under-Secretary of State for External Affairs, and until his death in 1941 Skelton was beyond doubt the most influential figure in the determination of Canada's foreign policy, an influence acknowledged by King in several passages from his diaries. Indeed, J.L. Granatstein dates the beginning of the modern civil service in Canada from Skelton's entry into the Ottawa bureaucracy. Skelton recruited into External Affairs several highly educated individuals, many of whom had done post-graduate work at Oxford or at an American university. In addition, he was the director of research for the Royal Commission on Dominion–Provincial Relations (1937).

Another professor from Queen's, the economist W.C. Clark, was appointed in 1932 as Deputy Minister of Finance. Clark's role as one of the key architects of Keynesian economic policy after World War II is well known. He was at the centre of a group of Queen's economists who were prominent members of the bureaucratic elite through their positions in the Department of Finance and the Bank of Canada. This group included W.A. Mackintosh and John Deutsch, both of whom served as Deputy Minister of Finance and ultimately became Principal of Queen's. Indeed, Queen's developed a reputation as a recruiting ground for the senior levels of the bureaucracy.

The links between the federal bureaucracy and academe during this period when the administrative state was being consolidated have been examined by John Porter. He found that in 1953 just under a fifth of the bureaucratic elite (comprised of the 243 senior officials of federal government departments, agencies, and Crown corporations) had taught in a university at some point, and an even greater proportion of the highest-ranking bureaucrats (9 out of 40 at the deputy minister level) were former university teachers.[9] The unrivalled dominance of the Department of Finance in economic policy and in the developing field of social policy meant that this group, and the economics profession generally, had a relationship to public policy and the state not enjoyed by other social scientists. This certainly was evident in the formation and activities of the Royal Commission on Canada's Economic Prospects (Gordon Commission, 1956). In the words of one commentator, 'The Gordon Commission was like a vast wind tunnel with the door accidently left open: it sucked up practically every available economist in the country.'[10]

The special relationship of economics to public policy and the state already had begun to take shape in the 1930s. The recruitment of university-trained economists for the Department of Finance and the research department of the Bank of Canada, created in 1935, as well as for the economic studies commissioned for the Nova Scotia Royal Commission on the Economy (1934), the National Employment Commission (1936), and the Royal Commission on Dominion–Provincial Relations (1937–40), provided the institutional opportunities for the increasing integration of the economics profession into the state. In terms of intellectual developments, it is clear that even before John Maynard Keynes's ideas on the manipulation of aggregate demand by government became the orthodox view among economists and policy-makers, providing what appeared to be an irrefutable intellectual foundation for the positive state, there existed widespread skepticism about what had been thought to be the self-correcting markets of classical economic theory and a willingness to rely on trained professionals to advise governments on how to influence macroeconomic activity.

World War II saw state planning on a level never previously experienced in Canada, with increasing recruitment of university economists into such government bodies as the Department of Finance and the Wartime Prices and Trade Board. They formed the core of what Mackenzie King referred to as the 'intelligentsia', a group of experts for whom wartime planning provided opportunities to influence policy from within the state. Their influence and the special relationship of the economics profession to public policy were consolidated by the federal government's formal acceptance of Keynesian economic policy in the White Paper on Employment and Income (1945) and in the governing Liberal Party's 1945 election platform.

These decades stretching from the 1925 appointment of Skelton as Under-Secretary of State for External Affairs to the 1950s saw the rise of what historian Doug Owram has called 'the government generation'.[11] Trained in the modern social sciences, often holding graduate degrees from American universities, they represented a new breed of senior bureaucrat for whom government was viewed as the necessary instrument for maintaining economic prosperity and solving social problems. They were, in an important sense, the architects of the positive state in Canada, a state characterized by professionalism and an increasingly influential role for the bureaucracy.

By the end of the 1950s some were of the opinion that the senior bureaucracy had become, in fact, too influential. The election of the Progressive Conservative Party in 1957 under John Diefenbaker, after 22 uninterrupted years of Liberal government, presented a challenge to the model of an impartial and politically neutral bureaucracy. Would senior bureaucrats, who had worked with Liberal politicians for almost a generation developing the modern Canadian state, be willing and able to transfer their loyalty to a new set of political masters and to whatever changes in policy they might insist upon? It is well known that Prime Minister Diefenbaker and some of his cabinet ministers mistrusted the bureaucracy, suspecting many senior officials of Liberal sympathies and of being subtly unco-operative with the Conservative government and its policies. In *Lament for a Nation*, the philosopher George Grant famously accused the senior Ottawa bureaucrats of being complicit with the Liberal Party and the representatives of American capital in a continentalist vision of the Canada–United States relationship that Diefenbaker rejected.

Ironically, soon after the 1963 defeat of Diefenbaker and the return to power of the Liberal Party, the power of the 'Ottawa mandarins' whom Diefenbaker so mistrusted began to decline. The Canadian administrative state was entering a new phase in its development, characterized by dramatic growth in revenue, expenditure, personnel, and programs. Between 1965 and 1975, the number of federal public servants increased by 50 per cent, from 203,419 to 307,390.[12] The growth was greatest in the Department of Health and Welfare, National Revenue, and the Unemployment Insurance Commission, but also took place because of the creation of new departments, each with its own raft of programs to administer. These included Communications (1970), Consumer and Corporate Affairs (1968), the Environment (1972), Regional Economic Expansion (1970), and Science and Technology (1973). Federal revenue increased between 1965 and 1975 by almost 400 per cent, from $9.3 billion to $34.7 billion. Expenditures grew from $8.6 billion to $36.8 billion. Spending increased most rapidly on social services, including health, social welfare, and education, as well as transfers to the provinces, much of which went towards financing their rapidly growing social spending.

As the administrative state grew in size and complexity, the influence of the so-called mandarins declined. Influence within the state became more diffuse and, in a sense, impersonal. Of course, some officials would continue to be found at the top of the administrative food chain, including the deputy ministers of Finance and Justice, the governor of the Bank of Canada, and the chief clerk of the Privy Council. But the days when the bureaucratic power-brokers could be gathered around a medium-sized table in the dining room of the Château Laurier were definitely over.

The 1970s marked the beginning of what some social and political commentators, particularly on the left, began to call the **crisis of the state**. This referred to what appeared to be the inability or unwillingness of governments to finance the welfare state policies put in place over the preceding four decades. The Keynesian consensus—the belief that governments could and should manage their economies by using a repertoire of fiscal policy measures, notably taxation and government spending—was increasingly challenged in the economics and policy-making communities and was largely discredited in many Western democracies by the 1980s. The reason had to do largely with debt—the accumulation of government spending deficits over two or more years. Federal deficits increased during the 1970s and 1980s, a trend that was not reversed until the late 1990s. Year after year of deficit spending, financed through borrowing, necessarily

"I preface my requests by informing you that my father is in government and talk of restraint and lowering expectations will not necessarily inhibit me . . ."

Len Norris/© Simon Fraser University

The late 1970s might be remembered as the beginning of an era of diminished expectations for the Canadian state, but many—politicians and citizens alike—remain steadfast in their belief that the state is necessary for the promotion of social justice, environmental protection and improvement, and economic prosperity distributed equally among all Canadians.

produced an increase in the stockpile of government debt. Public debt charges that amounted to $1.9 billion in 1970, or about 13 per cent of total federal expenditures, reached $30 billion, or 16 per cent of total spending, in 1980 and about $41 billion (27 per cent of total spending) in 1990, peaking at 30 per cent of total federal expenditure in 1997.

The term 'crisis' is often used too casually and often for ideological purposes. Whether there was a crisis of the state during these decades depends on what one means by crisis. What is certain, however, is that the optimism associated with the Keynesian welfare state declined and government spending increasingly was seen to be a problem. But state spending in Canada as a share of GDP did not decline until the late 1990s (see Figure 9.1), nor was there any significant slashing of government programs and regulation during this same period. Healthy economic growth in Canada over most of the past quarter-century has produced significant growth in government revenues. This, rather than spending cuts, has been the key factor that transformed years of government deficits into surpluses starting in 1997, ending only in 2008 when the

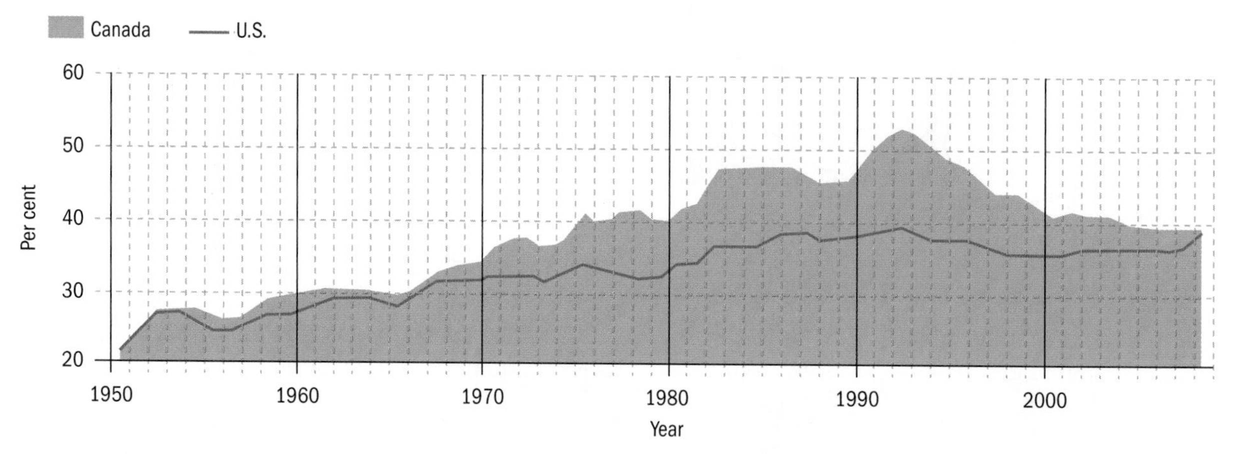

FIGURE 9.1 State Spending as Share of GDP, Canada and the US, 1950–2008

Source: Niels Veldhuis and Jason Clemens, 'Canada's Advantage', *Financial Post*, 28 Apr. 2009, based on data from *OECD Economic Outlook*, Statistics Canada, and the US Department of Commerce. <www.network.nationalpost.com/np/blogs/fpcomment/archive/tags/Jason+Clemens/default.aspx>

Canadian economy followed the American and other Western economies into recession.

The last couple of decades, perhaps even extending as far back as the late 1970s, might be characterized as an era of diminished expectations for the Canadian state. It is difficult to imagine that, a few decades ago, proposals for a guaranteed annual income and full employment that would be guaranteed by the state were talked about quite seriously by policy-makers and commentators who were not dismissed as 'radical'. Nor was the idea of governments 'fine-tuning' their economies through a judicious spending increase here or a timely tax measure there likely to be greeted with skepticism and even derision. The neo-liberal ideology of smaller government, less regulation, and a greater reliance on markets has, according to many observers, replaced the Keynesian welfare state consensus of the post–World War II era.

But this claim is not entirely true. To begin with, not everyone shares in the diminished expectations for the state that have become more prevalent over the past few decades. The NDP, labour unions, the Council of Canadians, much of the social sciences and social services community, a significant number of those in the media, the environmental movement, and others remain optimistic, to varying degrees and depending on the circumstances, about the ability of the state to solve problems. Moreover, they see the state as a necessary instrument for the promotion of social justice, environmental protection and improvement, and economic prosperity, the benefits of which do not accrue mainly to a few. It is simply incorrect to argue that a consensus about an activist state has been replaced by the view that a diminished state is preferable. The mood of lesser expectations of the state surely has had the upper hand in recent decades, but it has been vigorously contested.

Finally, it is simply not the case that the administrative state has been downsized significantly over this same period of time. The public sector's share of the Canadian labour force today is about as large as it was in 1980, with about one in five workers employed either directly or indirectly by the state.[13] Although some of Canada's most prominent public enterprises have been sold to private investors since the 1980s, including Petro-Canada, Air Canada, and Canadian National, the role of the federal and provincial governments in the Canadian economy, through direct ownership but more significantly through regulation, taxation, and purchasing, remains very important. Human rights codes, pay equity rulings, and environmental laws have made the state more rather than less intrusive in some ways over the past couple of decades. So is the downsized neo-liberal state that some claim exists in Canada a myth or reality?

It may be a bit of both. Despite widespread public skepticism about bureaucracy and the effectiveness of government, most people continue to demand that government 'do something' when a perceived problem arises. When the Canadian economy slid into recession in late 2008, the reaction of most Canadians was not that the government should stand back and let market forces take their course. On the contrary, most expected the government to act—to spend money, pass laws, bail out industries, and protect jobs. Although there was no agreement about what industries should be helped and whose jobs should be protected, there appeared to be a widespread sense that government actions were needed. And when the economy is doing well, even ideologically conservative governments, such as the Conservative government of Stephen Harper, produce a long 'to do' list that the Governor General reads in the Speech from the Throne. In other words, they see themselves and the state apparatus over which they preside as being in the problem-solving business.

Globalization and the State

The administrative state arose over time in response to changes in the nature of society and the economy. It is unrealistic to assume that its particular form will remain fixed as conditions around it change. Foremost among these changes has been the process of globalization. It has affected the Canadian state in regard to the capacity, structure, and the idea of the state.

State Capacity

For the administrative state to carry out its many functions it must have the resources to do so. In turn, this requires an adequate stream of revenue to cover the cost of paying bureaucrats' salaries and benefits, building and maintaining roads, funding for schools and hospitals, paying those on state pensions, social assistance, and all the other expenditures of government. This is what is meant by state capacity. It has been affected by the unprecedented ease and speed of capital movements between countries, provinces and states, and even between cities.

The consequences have been twofold. Governments have become more sensitive to the demands of businesses whose activities create jobs and thereby contribute to state revenues in various ways, from the payroll taxes (i.e., Employment Insurance and Canada Pension Plan premiums) paid by employers and employees to the sales taxes paid when workers and their families make purchases. They are also more sensitive to the expectations of investors, a category that often includes foreign governments and institutional investors like large pension funds, who buy their bonds. It is easy to exaggerate the degree of this sensitivity. Governments in Canada and elsewhere obviously have not scrapped all of those laws and regulations that are unpopular with various parts of the business and investment community. The mobility of capital, while greater during the last few decades than at any other time in history, is limited by a number of factors. These include the economic costs associated with relocating production facilities or services. Such costs involve more than mothballing existing facilities and opening new ones. Much more significant may be the cultural friction that results when services, in particular, are moved to another country where labour may be cheap, but proficiency in the language of clients and understanding of the myriad cultural nuances that contribute to satisfactory service may be weaker than in the country where these services were originally based. Political costs and obstacles also may be associated with the moving of jobs and facilities, as well as investment capital. The Conservative government's 2010 rejection of the takeover of Potash Corporation of Saskatchewan by Australia-based BHP-Billiton was a high-profile example of such obstacles.

A second consequence of the ease with which capital and jobs move around the globe is that, in order to maintain state capacity, governments have become less dependent on revenue generated by the direct taxation of businesses and more dependent on revenue from the taxation of individuals. Income taxes, sales taxes, payroll taxes, and user fees all have become more important as sources of state revenue (see Figure 9.2).

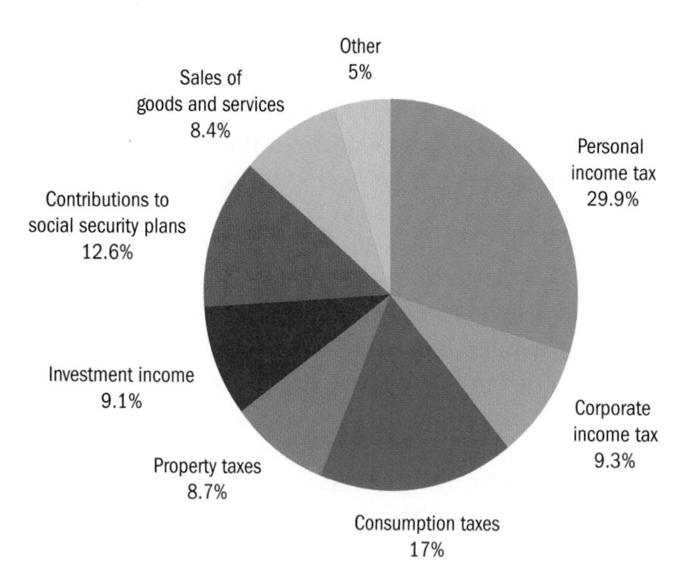

FIGURE 9.2 Relative Importance of Various Sources of State Revenue, All Levels of Government, 2009

Source: Adapted from Statistics Canada data, at: <www.statcan.gc.ca/daily-quotidien/090616/t090616a-eng.htm>.

State Structure

It is often said that globalization has contributed to the downsizing of the state, but this is too simplistic and rather misleading. Certainly, the privatization of some services and the sale of some state enterprises to private investors have occurred in Canada, as in many other countries, as the state searches for infusions of money or seeks to offload costs. And in some cases privatization very clearly has been motivated by ideology. The outsourcing of certain functions also may be a way of reducing the influence of public-sector unions, which, in turn, is expected to reduce costs. All of these policy shifts involve changes to the structure of the state, and are aimed at making it leaner, whether motivated by considerations of costs or ideology, or both.

Nevertheless, the state has hardly withered away, to paraphrase Marx (and change the context of his well-known prediction!). In 1991 total public-sector employment in Canada was 2.7 million. In 2010 it was 3,599,471. But the structure of the state has changed, and some functions that used to be carried out directly by government have been outsourced.

At the same time, globalization has contributed to the state taking on new or expanded functions or legitimizing its actions based on ideas and institutions that have been generated by this process. Although we tend to associate globalization with economics, this is only part—albeit a very important part—of what it involves. Fundamentally, globalization is about interdependence and the various ways in which the world has become a 'smaller' place. One of these ways involves the development of an international architecture of policy-making and globalized networks of interests and ideas that influence domestic state officials and civil society. Human rights commissions and courts in Canada regularly refer to international agreements and developments concerning rights. Canadian state officials involved with matters of Arctic sovereignty and economic development participate in negotiations with other Arctic states, sometimes bilaterally and other times in multilateral forums. Energy and environment officials in Canada are very aware that they do not operate in isolation from the rest of the world when it comes to oil sands development, climate change measures, species at risk, and so on. Officials in the Department of Defence and Canada's intelligence services are influenced by their participation in international missions, organizations, and policy communities. The same may be said of officials in health care, education, immigration, and other fields.

The Idea of the State

At the risk of drifting into the realm of philosophy and world history—surely no crime for students of politics—globalization has contributed to important changes in how we think about state sovereignty. The 1648 Treaty of Westphalia, which ended the Thirty Years' War, ushered in the era of the nation-state. Interference in the domestic affairs of a sovereign state was considered verboten. Today, the United Nations and its various covenants and declarations, particularly the Universal Declaration of Human Rights and the Convention on the Crime of Genocide, the UN Security Council, the International Criminal Court, and the International Court of Justice are important parts of the architecture of an international political community—'system of global governance' is too strong a term—that challenges this idea that nation-state sovereignty is inviolable.

Canadians, it appears, are open to this notion that the nation-state's sovereignty should not be thought of as sacrosanct. Asked whether they see themselves as 'world citizens', Canadians were considerably more likely to agree (85.8 per cent) than were Americans (68.6 per cent), Germans (53 per cent), and Italians (61.9 per cent), slightly more than Spaniards (79.3 per cent), but somewhat less than the Japanese (93.7 per cent).[14] Although it is unlikely that more than a minority of Canadians would be ready to exchange national autonomy for global governance, popular support for multilateralism and Canada's long tradition of generally enthusiastic participation in international organizations suggest that Canadians' idea of the state is not tied to older notions of national sovereignty.

The Structure of Canadian Bureaucracy

The federal public sector employs roughly 486,000 people working in close to 400 different organizations (all figures as of 2007). Just over 60 per cent of them work directly for government departments and agencies. They are public servants, in the narrow legal sense of this term. Their employer is the Treasury Board and the organizations they work for fall directly under the authority of a cabinet minister. Close to 20 per cent are employed by federally owned Crown corporations and the remainder (another 20 per cent) work in some capacity in the Canadian Forces. The organizations they work for receive all or part of their funding from the federal government and are subject to rules that it sets, but these organizations operate with some degree of autonomy.

Public-sector employment is even greater at the provincial, territorial, and local levels. In 2007, the combined employment of these governments came to about 753,000 persons. This figure does not include hospitals and other health-care facilities, schools, or enterprises owned by these levels of government, which together add another 1,986,000 employees to the public-sector total. If we define the public sector broadly to include those organizations that receive all or a major part of their operating revenues from one or more levels of government, then 20–5 per cent of Canadian workers fall within this sector. It includes nurses, teachers, firefighters and police officers, workers for Children's Aid Societies and at some women's shelters, and so on.

Despite frequently heard claims that the welfare state has been replaced by a new reality of downsized government, the public sector remains quite extensive. That part of it often labelled the 'bureaucracy' may be divided into three main components: the public service (chiefly departments); independent and semi-independent agencies and tribunals; and Crown corporations.

Public service. About half of the federal public sector falls under this category. It includes all statutory departments and other organizations whose members are appointed by the Public Service Commission (PSC) and are employees of the Treasury Board. This is the part of the bureaucracy most directly under the authority of cabinet.

Agencies and tribunals. These organizations perform a wide variety of regulatory, research, and advisory functions. Among the most widely known federal regulatory agencies are the Canadian Radio-television and Telecommunications Commission (CRTC, which regulates communications and broadcasting), the National Transportation Agency (air, water, and rail transportation), and the National Energy Board (energy when it crosses provincial and international boundaries). Many important areas of regulation, including trucking, public utilities within provincial boundaries, and most labour relations, are controlled by provincial governments.

These organizations have a greater degree of independence from government than those that fall under the public service. With few exceptions their members are not appointed by the PSC, nor are they employees of the Treasury Board. The precise degree of autonomy enjoyed by an agency or tribunal varies, but in some cases it is almost total.

Crown corporations. These organizations, in most cases, perform commercial functions and typically operate at 'arm's length' from the government of the day. They hire their own employees, determine their own internal administrative structures, and in many instances behave much like privately owned businesses. Over the last couple of decades some of the largest of these corporations, notably Air Canada, Canadian National, and Petro-Canada, have been privatized.

These three categories do not cover the entire federal bureaucracy. Some relatively small but important parts of that bureaucracy, including the Auditor General's Office (discussed in Chapter 8) and the Commissioner of Official Languages, are independent of cabinet, reporting directly to Parliament. The Royal Canadian Mounted Police also has a distinct legal status, as does the Canadian Forces.

Together, this vast administrative apparatus has responsibility for implementing public policy. At the most prosaic level—the level where virtually all of us have made personal contact with the state—officials deal with passport applications, meat inspections, public queries regarding Employment Insurance benefits, job seekers at Canada Employment centres, and a vast number of similarly routine administrative tasks. But at the top of the bureaucratic pyramid are women and men whose relationship to public policy is much more active. Senior officials within the departmental bureaucracy, particularly deputy ministers and assistant deputy ministers, interact frequently with cabinet ministers and senior officials in central agencies. They are called on to testify before committees of the legislature. These officials often deal directly with the representatives of organized interests. They are universally acknowledged to have influence in shaping public policy, although the extent of their influence is a matter of debate.

The bureaucracy is not a uniform structure. One can identify several different functions performed by organizations within the administrative system. These include:

- the provision and administration of services to the public, often to narrow economic, social, or cultural clientele groups;
- the provision of services to other parts of the bureaucracy;
- the integration of policy in a particular field, or the generation of policy advice;
- the adjudication of applications and/or interpretation of regulations (such as product safety standards, or the determination of what constitutes morally offensive scenes of sex or violence in films);
- the disbursement of funds to groups or individuals, as with the grants to artists and cultural organizations administered by the Canada Council;
- the production of a good or the operation of a service that is sold to buyers.

These functions are not mutually exclusive. A large and organizationally complex department like the federal Department of Transport is involved in service delivery, the regulation of transport standards, and the development of policy. Almost all government departments, regardless of their primary orientation, have a policy development capacity. During the 1970s this was formalized—although not necessarily enhanced—with the creation of policy analysis units, usually at the assistant deputy minister level. An informal policy advisory capacity, however, has always existed at the level of senior officials. This role is based on their expert familiarity with the programs administered by the department and on the fact that, typically, they remain within a particular policy field longer than their nominal superiors in cabinet. The turnover rate for deputy ministers and other senior bureaucrats has increased since the era of the Ottawa mandarins, from the 1940s to the 1960s, when a coterie of top officials whose careers were associated with particular parts of the bureaucracy exercised an extraordinary influence on the direction of federal policy. The more recent emphasis has been on senior officials as managers, whose management skills are transferable across policy fields. Combined with the more rapid turnover of deputy ministers since the early 1980s, it is often argued that the policy influence of senior bureaucrats has diminished.

In fact, it would be more accurate to say that this power has become more diffuse. The days when a mere handful of key deputy ministers could dominate the policy-making process are gone. Today, bureaucratic influence is distributed more widely, in large part because of the increased importance of central agencies like the Privy Council Office and the Treasury Board Secretariat, but also because it is rare for a deputy minister to remain in charge of a particular department for more than a few years. Nevertheless, there is little doubt that senior bureaucrats continue to be key players in policy-making (see Box 9.1).

The passing of the era of the Ottawa mandarins and the emergence of central agencies as an alternative source of expert policy advice to cabinet have not undermined the fundamental basis of bureaucratic influence on policy. This influence rests on the following factors:

- Departments are repositories for a vast amount of information about current and past programs and about the day-to-day details of their administration. While the aphorism 'Knowledge is power' is too simplistic and implies a sort of rationality that usually is not characteristic of policy choices, ministers invariably depend on the permanent bureaucracy for advice on policy. Senior bureaucrats occupy strategic positions in the policy process because of their ability to shape the information and recommendations reaching the minister.
- The relationship of a department to the social or economic interests that benefit from the programs it administers is a source of departmental influence on policy. Departmental officials clearly are not indifferent in their sympathies towards conflicting societal interests. Moreover, the bureaucracy is an important target for professional lobbyists and interest group representatives who wish to influence policy.
- 'Ministers', observes Donald Savoie, 'do not manage.'[15]

Governing Realities

Box 9.1 The Role of the Deputy Minister

The deputy minister's mission is to serve the minister in non-partisan fashion, competently, impartially, diligently and loyally. So as to optimize the management of the minister's time and to inform him in his decisions and projects, the deputy minister provides professional, non-partisan advice concerning the development and implementation of policies, prepares the tools that will enable the minister to take a discerning stand in public, and manages the compliance of the decisions he makes. On a daily basis, he ensures the sound operational management of the department.

The deputy minister also acts as the senior adviser to the minister concerning all the responsibilities exercised by him. In addition to having responsibility to Parliament for the agencies in his portfolio, the minister receives special mandates from the Prime Minister and Cabinet. The deputy minister acts as his chief adviser in all such matters.

Generally speaking, he comments on draft policies of the Council of Ministers and ensures that the agenda and priorities of the government are properly reflected in his department's action plan. He also ensures that all of his department's employees act to fulfill the objectives of the government of the day. In addition, he organizes interministerial consultations on any issue liable to affect the general responsibilities of the other ministers. The manner in which the deputy minister supports his minister is another way of serving the government, overall; sound projects make the government look good, and timely cautions keep it from getting into trouble.

Source: Jacques Bourgault, 'The Deputy Minister's Role in the Government of Canada: His Responsibility and His Accountability', in Commission of Inquiry into the Sponsorship Program and Advertising Activities, *Restoring Accountability*, Research Studies, vol. 1 (2006), 258–9.

Their deputy ministers perform this job. Given the competing pressures on a minister's time, the deputy minister inevitably assumes the job of senior manager of the department over which a cabinet minister nominally presides. In many instances the chief responsibility for policy direction also will be assumed by the deputy minister.

- Most laws contain provisions delegating to bureaucrats the authority to interpret the general terms of the law in its application to actual cases (see Box 9.2). This is also true of other statutory instruments that have the force of law (for example, the thousands of Orders-in-Council that issue from cabinet each year). The task of implementation—applying the law to actual cases—is not a neutral one. In some cases this discretion is exercised at a low level in the bureaucratic hierarchy (for example, decisions by local custom officials on whether a particular DVD constitutes obscene material and therefore should be prohibited entry into Canada).

To summarize, the bureaucracy enters the policy process both early and late. Bureaucrats are the people who actually administer the programs established by law. In doing so they regularly exercise considerable discretion, a fact that often leads special interests to focus at least part of their attention on the bureaucracy. Departmental officials are also involved in the early stages of the policy process because of the intimate knowledge they have of existing programs and the daily contact between bureaucrats and the groups directly affected by the programs they administer. Moreover, the annual expenditure budget, which provides a fairly reasonable indication of a government's policy priorities, is based largely on the information provided by departments. New legislation is invariably influenced by the input of senior permanent officials. These officials are both managers and policy advisers, and they are very clearly part of the inner circle of policy-making that extends outward from cabinet.

Representative Bureaucracy

On top of all the other expectations held for bureaucracy in democratic societies, it is also expected to 'represent' the population. This means that the composition of the bureaucracy should reflect in fair proportion certain demographic characteristics of society. Affirmative action programs and quota hiring are the tools used in pursuit of this goal. The basic reasoning behind arguments for 'representative' bureaucracy is that it will have greater popular legitimacy than a bureaucracy that does not reflect the nation's demography (e.g., women and men, ethnic groups, Aboriginal peoples, the disabled) and that its representative character will help ensure that the advice bureaucrats give to politicians and the services they provide to their clienteles are sensitive to the values and aspirations of the governed.

As reasonable as this may sound, the idea and implementation of **representative bureaucracy** have always been problematic. Which groups should be singled out for representation? What constitutes 'fair proportion'? To what extent are other values like efficient performance and equal rights for all compromised by such a policy? Can the idea of a representative bureaucracy be squared with that of a politically neutral one?

Problems aside, it is clear that a grossly unrepresentative bureaucracy can pose problems. The fact that comparatively few French Canadians were found at the senior levels of the federal bureaucracy was already a controversial matter in the 1940s, 1950s, and 1960s, and led to major public service reforms and Canada's first policy of representative bureaucracy under Lester B. Pearson and Pierre Elliott Trudeau. On the other hand, most students of British bureaucracy agree that the strongly upper-class character of that country's public service did not prevent it from co-operating with the post–World War II Labour government in implementing reforms opposed by the upper class. Nor has the unrepresentative and elitist character of the French bureaucracy been considered a major problem in that country.

One thing is certain: governments that have instituted policies of affirmative action and quota hiring have done so chiefly for political reasons, not because the intellectual arguments offered in support of such policies are demonstrably true. Among the most important political reasons is national unity. In Canada it has long been recognized that the merit principle, which ignores the ascriptive characteristics of individuals and looks only at their job-related achievements and skills,

Politics in Focus

Box 9.2 The Delegation of Discretion

The Broadcasting Act is the key law regulating television, radio, and telecommunications in Canada. Like many laws it delegates to non-elected officials the power to make rules that flesh out the very general terms of the statute they implement. For example, officials with the Canadian Broadcasting Corporation, a Crown corporation, and with the Canadian Radio-television and Telecommunications Commission, the regulatory agency that licenses broadcasters, must determine the meaning of the following vague objectives set down in the Broadcasting Act:

3. (1) It is hereby declared as the broadcasting policy for Canada that . . .
   - (d) the Canadian broadcasting system should
     - (i) serve to safeguard, enrich and strengthen the cultural, political, social and economic fabric of Canada,
     - (ii) encourage the development of Canadian expression by providing a wide range of programming that reflects Canadian attitudes, opinions, ideas, values and artistic creativity, by displaying Canadian talent in entertainment programming and by offering information and analysis concerning Canada and other countries from a Canadian point of view,
     - (iii) through its programming and the employment opportunities arising out of its operations, serve the needs and interests, and reflect the circumstances and aspirations, of Canadian men, women and children, including equal rights, the linguistic duality and multicultural and multiracial nature of Canadian society and the special place of aboriginal peoples within that society, and
     - (iv) be readily adaptable to scientific and technological change; . . .

And moreover,

- (l) the Canadian Broadcasting Corporation, as the national public broadcaster, should provide radio and television services incorporating a wide range of programming that informs, enlightens and entertains;
- (m) the programming provided by the Corporation should
  - (i) be predominantly and distinctly Canadian,
  - (ii) reflect Canada and its regions to national and regional audiences, while serving the special needs of those regions,
  - (iii) actively contribute to the flow and exchange of cultural expression,
  - (iv) be in English and in French, reflecting the different needs and circumstances of each official language community, including the particular needs and circumstances of English and French linguistic minorities,
  - (v) strive to be of equivalent quality in English and in French,
  - (vi) contribute to shared national consciousness and identity,
  - (vii) be made available throughout Canada by the most appropriate and efficient means and as resources become available for the purpose, and
  - (viii) reflect the multicultural and multiracial nature of Canada. . . .

Source: Broadcasting Act, Chapter B-9.01, section 3 (1991).

'What's the point of them going to all this trouble if you won't put in for Senator, join the RCMP or run a crown corporation?'

As we will see in Chapter 15, women have not always been represented proportionally in government, particularly not at senior levels.

should not interfere with what one writer called 'a tactful balance of national elements'.[16] Until fairly recently, this balancing act chiefly involved ensuring adequate francophone representation in the management ranks of the bureaucracy. Indeed, it is fair to say that until the 1970s this was the only serious representational factor taken into account in public service recruitment and promotion. John Porter's analysis of the senior federal bureaucracy during the 1950s showed that only the British, French, and Jewish ethnic groups were significantly represented, and those of British origin were clearly dominant.[17] Women and visible minorities were almost completely absent from the senior levels of the public service.

As the ethnic composition of Canadian society has changed—people of non-British, non-French ancestry now comprise over 30 per cent of the population[18]—and especially as the discourse of collective rights and group identities has achieved greater prominence, the old concern with 'fair' linguistic representation has been joined by efforts to recruit and promote women, visible minorities, Aboriginal Canadians, and the disabled. Affirmative action programs are established by the Treasury Board and monitored by the Public Service Commission. During the 1980s their programs relied mainly on a system of employment targets rather than on mandatory quotas for group representation. Ottawa and the provincial governments continue to use targets and incentives to encourage senior managers to hire and promote members of designated groups. In 2002 the federal government, through the Treasury Board, issued an employment directive to departmental managers that required them to increase the proportions of visible minorities—defined by the Treasury Board as someone other than an Aboriginal person who is non-white—on their staffs to 20 per cent and for one out of every five appointments to the executive category of the public service to be from visible minorities by 2005. The line separating targets from quotas is always a matter of debate, as is the determination of what groups should be represented in what proportion. Some interpret 'fair representation' as a proportion of the bureaucracy equal to a group's share of the population. This is, for example, the position taken by the New Democratic Party and feminist organizations in Canada. To this day, however, Canadian governments have not attempted to implement this vision of fairness.

Starting Points for Research

Christopher Dunn, ed., *The Handbook of Canadian Public Administration* (Toronto: Oxford University Press, 2002). Virtually all key aspects of the structures and processes of Canadian public administration are covered in this fine collection, with contributions from some of the foremost students of Canadian bureaucracy and policy-making.

David Good, *The Politics of Public Management: The HRDC Audit of Grants and Contributions* (Toronto: University of Toronto Press, 2003). Written by a former assistant deputy minister, this is an award-winning insider's account of the complex circumstances leading to what was believed, at the time, to be an enormous scandal involving lack of accountability in spending by Human Resources and Development Canada.

David Good, *The Politics of Public Money* (Toronto: University of Toronto Press, 2007). A worthy successor to the spenders and guardians analysis found in Donald Savoie's 1990 book, *The Politics of Public Spending in Canada*.

David Johnson, *Thinking Government: Public Sector Management in Canada* (Toronto: University of Toronto Press, 2006). An excellent textbook on public administration in Canada.

Donald Savoie, *Breaking the Bargain: Public Servants, Ministers and Parliament* (Toronto: University of Toronto Press, 2003). Arguably Canada's foremost scholar of bureaucracy and governance explores, in his own words, 'the territory between elected and permanent government officials—a kind of no man's land'.

Review Exercises

1. Visit the government of Canada website <www.gc.ca>. Click on 'About Government'. Now click on 'Government of Canada Institutions' (listed alphabetically). Choose a government institution and click on its website. Find the following information for the institution you have chosen:
   (a) number of employees
   (b) budget
   (c) cabinet minister responsible for the department/agency/Crown corporation
   (d) major programs or functions.
2. Most Canadians believe that public-sector organizations are less efficient than those in the private sector. How would you set about measuring efficiency in private and public organizations? Put together a list of the criteria you would use and how straightforward or difficult each would be to measure. How have you defined 'efficiency'? Are there other qualities that should be taken into account in assessing the performance of public and private organizations? What might they be and can they be measured?
3. Do unelected officials have too much discretion? Can you think of instances where you have encountered public-sector bureaucrats whose decision(s) seemed to have been based on their personal judgement rather than simply and entirely on rules? Can anything be done about such cases? Should anything be done?

Part IV
Participation in Politics

Politics does not stop at the doors of Parliament. It spills out onto the streets and into community halls and corporate boardrooms, involving citizens, organized interests, and the media. What is sometimes referred to as *civil society* both acts on and in turn is acted on by the institutions of the state, making demands, organizing resistance, and providing support in various ways.

The participation of groups in civil society assumes many forms. Individual citizens play a role as voters and collectively through what is described as public opinion. Some of them are involved in more active ways, belonging to and working for political parties or participating in groups that attempt to shape the political conversation and government policy. Organized interests often attempt to influence the actions of government, through a range of techniques that include lobbying, legal action, and attempting to influence public opinion. The media's specialized function involves reporting and framing the political conversation. Most of what we know about the political world is mediated by those whose job involves selecting information (i.e., news) for print and broadcast and then interpreting it.

In the following three chapters we will examine some of the most important forms of participation in Canadian politics. The focus is on parties, elections and voters, organized interests, and the media. In any democracy these elements of civil society must be largely independent of the state. Indeed, the extent to which they are able to act autonomously, setting their own agendas and behaving free of direct control or indirect manipulation by the state, is one of the tests of any democracy. At the same time, we need to be alert to the possibility that concentrated power in civil society can pose the same sort of danger to democracy that government by the few and mainly for the few can represent.

The 2011 federal election produced a Conservative majority and saw the NDP surge into second place in the popular vote and in its share of seats in the House of Commons. The Liberal Party experienced the worst election result in its history and the Bloc Québécois saw its support collapse. The Green Party's national support declined rather sharply, but its leader was elected to Parliament for the first time. © Canadian Press/Bayne Stanley

10 Parties and Elections

Political parties and elections are essential features of modern democracy. This chapter examines the characteristics and influence of these institutions in Canadian political life. The following topics are covered:

- The origins and evolution of Canada's party system.
- Brokerage politics.
- The role of minor parties.
- Recent elections.
- Is the party system undergoing fundamental realignment?
- Party leadership selection.
- The electoral system and its consequences.
- Voting behaviour.
- Party finances and special interests.

Elections and the political parties that contest them represent the main contact points between most citizens and their political system. Most adult citizens vote at least some of the time, although perhaps not in every election and probably more often federally than in provincial and local elections. This may be, in fact, the extent of their participation in politics, short bursts of attention to candidates and their messages and occasional visits to the polls, interspersed around lengthier periods of inattention and political inactivity. Only about six of 10 eligible voters actually cast their ballots in the last few federal elections, but even among those who did not vote we can probably assume that most were at least aware that an election was taking place.

Elections remind us that we live in a democracy in which those who wish to govern must win the support of the governed—or of some considerable number of the governed. Elections are the cornerstone of democratic governance, yet it is widely believed they have become meaningless and even farcical affairs in which political parties and their candidates serve up sound bites instead of sound policy in campaigns orchestrated by the same people who put together marketing campaigns for cars and deodorants. Political parties have for years ranked among the lowest of social institutions in public esteem. It would seem, therefore, that democracy's cornerstone suffers from some worrisome cracks.

Doubts about the democratic qualities of democracy's showpiece are not new. One of the oldest fears is that those with money are more likely than those without it to be able to influence voter behaviour. In the nineteenth century the influence of money often took such petty forms as candidates buying beer or whisky for voters, a practice facilitated by the fact that voters cast their ballots in public. But the role of money also assumed more dramatic forms, as when Hugh Allan essentially bankrolled the Conservative Party in the 1873 federal election in exchange for a promise from John A. Macdonald that Allan would be made president of the railroad company chartered to build a transcontinental railroad linking Ontario to the Pacific coast. Over a century ago Liberal cabinet minister Israël Tarte remarked that 'Elections are not won with prayers', a fact of political life that has become even truer in the age of television campaigning. But fact of life or not, if parties and votes can be purchased by those with deep pockets, this surely undermines the democratic credibility of the electoral process.

Money is not the only factor that stands accused of defiling democracy's temple. Political parties and candidates have often been criticized for avoiding important issues and framing electoral discourse in ways that deflect attention from major divisions in society, oversimplifying the issues, or trivializing politics by substituting style and image for substance. The 'dumbing down' of public life has been facilitated—some would argue necessitated—by the fact that modern elections are fought largely through the medium of television, a medium that by its very nature elevates images over ideas. But the claims that parties and candidates avoid certain divisive issues and attempt to frame electoral discourse in ways that privilege certain interests while marginalizing others are long-standing ones in Canada.

The criticisms occasionally levelled at parties and elections in Canada may appear petty when viewed alongside the problems of one-party states and the practices of ballot fraud, voter intimidation, and bribery that are routine in many countries where elections are held. But Canadians are not used to comparing their democratic institutions and processes to those of Côte d'Ivoire, Haiti, Russia, or Egypt. We place the bar higher than this and measure the performance of our political parties and our electoral system against ideas of equality and participation that have evolved out of our liberal democratic tradition. Judged against these values, the Canadian experience is not perfect, although critics differ over the nature and extent of its shortcomings.

Parties: Definition and Functions

Political parties may be defined as organizations that offer slates of candidates to voters at election time. To this end they recruit and select party candidates, raise money to pay for their campaigns, develop policies that express the ideas and goals their candidates stand for, and attempt to persuade citizens to vote for their candidates. In a democracy parties are not created by nor are they agents of the state. They are, in Eugene Forsey's words, 'voluntary associations of people who hold broadly similar opinions on public questions'.[1]

It is usual to give as one of the distinguishing characteristics of political parties their attempt to 'elect governmental office-holders'.[2] This is, however, somewhat misleading. While most parties do hope to elect candidates to office, and some even have a realistic prospect of electing enough candidates to form a government, other parties may contest elections chiefly to get their ideas onto the public stage, without any expectation of garnering more than a small fraction of the vote. This would seem to be true of the Marijuana Party, whose stated mission is the decriminalization of cannabis, and the Marxist-Leninist Party, whose quixotic advocacy of global revolution by the proletariat remains largely unchanged from Karl Marx and Friedrich Engels's *Communist Manifesto* of 1848. The now defunct Rhinoceros Party ran candidates in many Canadian ridings during the 1970s and 1980s, injecting welcome humour into elections—the party stood for the repeal of the law of gravity, among other things—without any serious expectation of electing candidates to office.

John Meisel, one of Canada's foremost experts on parties and elections, identifies seven functions that political parties play in a democracy.[3]

1. *Integrating citizens into the political system.* Historically, parties have served as important linkages between citizens and the governmental system. Through voting for parties and thinking about public affairs in terms of policies and ideologies represented by parties, citizens develop attachments to the political system more generally. This connection, Meisel argues, has weakened as political parties have fallen in public esteem and have come to be perceived by many as simply another distant and unaccountable institution in a political system characterized by alienating institutions.

2. *Developing policy.* In many democracies different parties represent clear ideological and policy options. Moreover, party members and their deliberations are important sources of the policies that a party will seek to implement when in power. Canada's historically dominant parties, the Liberal and Conservative parties, have seldom been sharply different from one another in either ideological terms or in their behaviour when in power. They have occasionally stood for significantly different policies during election campaigns, as was true in 1988 when the Liberals opposed the Canada–United States Free Trade Agreement that had been negotiated by the Conservative government. Neither party, once in office, has felt tied to the policy platforms developed by the extra-parliamentary wing of the party—witness the Liberal government's refusal to either scrap or reform the GST after winning the 1993 election, despite what was generally perceived to be a firm commitment to do so in the party's 'Red Book' of election promises.

The New Democrats—and the Reform Party before it morphed into the present Conservative Party—provide voters with clearer policy choices than do the historically dominant parties. The NDP has also been, of all Canada's national parties, the one characterized by the greatest involvement of the party's extra-parliamentary membership in policy development.

3. *Elite recruitment.* With rare exceptions, those elected to federal and provincial office in Canada are associated with a political party and run as the official candidates of their parties. Parties choose their candidates and their leaders, and in doing so they determine the pool of persons from whom elected public officials, including members of the government, will be drawn. In most democracies the bar to participation in the selection of party leaders is fairly low, requiring interest and personal motivation as much as anything else. The fact of the matter is, however, that in virtually all democracies those with more formal education, higher incomes, and jobs that carry greater social status are much more likely than their fellow citizens to participate in the selection of party candidates and leaders, let alone being candidates themselves.

4. *Organization of government.* Governing parties propose; opposition parties oppose. This somewhat oversimplified formula expresses an important fact about the role that parties play within the system of government. They provide a partisan structure to the process of law-making and the debate of public

affairs. Under the British parliamentary system that exists in Canada, this partisan structure is by design an adversarial one, from the physical layout of the legislature, in which the government benches face those of the opposition parties, to the traditions and procedures observed in conducting the business of Parliament.

5. Structuring the vote. Just as parties lend structure to the activities of the legislature and allow for the identification of the government with a particular party (or coalition of parties in some democratic systems), they also serve to structure the vote in elections. The fact that only a handful of political parties are serious contenders for citizens' votes simplifies enormously the information-gathering task facing voters. Instead of having to determine what every individual candidate stands for they can—and most people do—rely on party labels as a sort of shorthand for the ideas and policies that a candidate represents. Each party represents, in a sense, a particular selection on a limited menu. The parties will differ from one another in their voter appeal with different segments of the population, and most voters can be said to have most-favoured and least-favoured political parties. These partisan inclinations, at the weak end, or loyalties and identifications, at the strong end, provide a degree of continuity in voting behaviour. This continuity can, however, be quickly shattered, as the 1993 collapse of the federal Conservative vote and the dramatic growth of the Reform Party and its successor, the Canadian Alliance Party—since December 2003 reconstituted as the Conservative Party of Canada—and of the Bloc Québécois vote showed.

Until the 1993 election it had been common to characterize Canada as having a two and one-half party system. The Liberal and Conservative parties both had a realistic chance of forming a government, and between them usually accounted for about 85 per cent of the popular vote. The NDP accounted for the balance. This fairly stable structure to the vote and to the parliamentary status of the parties dissolved in 1993, for reasons discussed later in this chapter.

6. Organizing public opinion. Parties are often characterized as right-wing, left-wing, or centrist; as liberal, conservative, or socialist; or by some other set of labels signifying that they occupy particular places on the ideological map. Parties reflect, but may also help create or at least reinforce, divisions within society. They do so through the issues they identify as important, the way they frame these issues, and the policies they propose.

Canada's two historically dominant political parties have avoided ideological appeals in favour of a flexible centrist style of politics that is often labelled **brokerage politics**. They have avoided talking the language of class politics—rich vs poor, bosses vs workers, corporations vs unions—and have attempted to accommodate the preferences of major interests, regions, and communities through their flexible policy style. Of course, politics has to be about something, and even the most centrist and waffling of parties cannot avoid taking positions on some divisive issues. Historically, language, religion, and region have been among the key issues distinguishing the Liberals from the Conservatives, the Liberals doing better among francophones, Catholics, and in the provinces east of Manitoba, and the Conservatives doing better among Protestants and western Canadians. These differences have helped to organize Canadian public opinion on religious (in the past), linguistic, and territorial lines. The NDP and its predecessor, the **Co-operative Commonwealth Federation (CCF)**, have been the only significant parties presenting voters with a class-based definition of Canadian politics. In recent years the ability of the historically dominant parties to organize public opinion in ways that preserve their dominance by bridging major divisions in Canadian politics was challenged by the Reform Party/Canadian Alliance, which emerged out of westerners' dissatisfaction with the older parties, and the Bloc Québécois, whose success in Quebec is testimony to the failure of brokerage politics to accommodate Quebec nationalism.

7. Interest aggregation. Organizations that represent secondary school teachers, gays, or advocates for wetlands preservation may be influential in politics. However, the narrowness of their respective agendas and the fact that each represents only a small segment of the population mean that they could not hope to elect a Teachers' Party, Gay Rights

Len Norris/© Simon Fraser University

'Then it's settled. We model ourselves on Canada and use a four-party system.'

There are advantages and disadvantages to Canada's multi-party approach to politics. One clear advantage is that it provides more opportunities for disparate viewpoints to be heard, as evidenced by issues brought forward by parties such as the Reform/Alliance, NDP, Bloc Québécois, and Green Party. Disadvantages of a multi-party state are discussed later in the chapter.

Party, or Save-the-Ducks Party to power. Parties, especially parties that hope to form a government, must aggregate different interests. This requires that they be willing to reach compromises on issues, bringing together under the party roof a coalition of different interests sufficiently broad to win election.

In order to be electorally successful it is not necessary that a party bring all major groups or regions under its roof. The Liberal Party, the most successful of Canada's national parties during the twentieth century, often formed a government with little representation from western Canada. In fact, history shows that it is seldom possible to avoid playing off one region against another in Canadian politics. Interest aggregation that produces a winning result in a federal election does not always promote unity. Paradoxically, the practice of interest aggregation may reinforce regional division.

The Origins and Evolution of Canada's Party System[4]

The Nature of Brokerage Politics

The origins of Canada's two major political parties—the Conservatives and the Liberals—can be traced back to the shifting coalitions and alignments in the United Province of Canada in the 1840s and 1850s. Although these groups were much more amorphous and unstable than modern political parties, and would not really coalesce into cohesive organizations until the 1880s, they did represent distinct political tendencies. On the one hand was the governing coalition of Liberal-Conservatives (which would eventually drop the 'Liberal' from its official name) under the leadership of Sir John A. Macdonald in Canada West and his French-Canadian counterpart, George-Étienne Cartier, in Canada East. This disparate organization encompassed a number of distinct groups: moderate Reformers from what was to become Ontario, moderate Conservatives (the *bleus*) from Canada East (Quebec), the commercial and industrial interests of English-speaking Quebec, and the remnants of the old ruling oligarchies in Upper and Lower Canada, the Family Compact and the Château Clique. Many of these groups had potentially conflicting interests (Catholics and Protestants, French and English, urban and rural elements), but the organization was held together largely by the political dexterity of Macdonald and by the gradual development of a unifying vision, one based on the nation-building program eventually enshrined in the **National Policy** of 1878–9. The key elements of this program were the implementation of a protective tariff designed to promote the growth of indigenous manufacturing in Ontario and Quebec, the encouragement of western settlement to open up a market for the products of central Canadian industry and to protect this territory from American encroachment, and the creation of a transcontinental railroad to ship the manufactured goods of the centre to the newly opened western territories.[5]

On the other hand was an even looser opposition coalition, comprising the Clear Grits of Canada West and the *rouges* of Canada East. Both of these groups shared a common admiration for the republican and individualist ideas of the United States and both advocated free trade with the Americans. They also shared an unrelenting hostility to the commercial and banking interests linked to Macdonald's governing party. But the two groups made for rather uneasy partners, since the Grits were vocally critical of the Roman Catholic Church. So were the *rouges*, for that matter (and their anticlericalism placed serious obstacles in the path of electoral success in their home province of Quebec), but there was nonetheless considerable ethnic and religious tension between the two groups. It was only when Wilfrid Laurier assumed the leadership of the Liberal Party in 1887 that these diverse elements were moulded into a relatively cohesive political organization.

It would be a mistake to make too much of the doctrinal differences between Liberals and Conservatives during the formative years of the Canadian party system (roughly 1880 to 1920). Admittedly, the Liberals were identified with free trade and provincial rights, and after 1885 (when Louis Riel was hanged for treason following the failed Northwest Rebellion) they appeared to be 'more sensitive to the interests of French Canada' than the Tories.[6] They were also more sympathetic to the plight of the farmer than were the Conservatives. The latter, meanwhile, were generally thought of as the party of the British connection, the party of privilege—in the sense that its leading spokesmen claimed that all healthy and stable societies are ruled by a *natural* governing elite—the party of centralization and economic protection. But these ideological differences, far from constituting fundamental clashes of world outlooks on which the two sides sought to mobilize their supporters, were almost always subordinated to the central preoccupation of Canadian politics: **patronage**.

The scramble to control the distribution of government largesse was undoubtedly the dominant feature of Canadian politics during the 1860s and 1870s, when a number of provisions in our electoral law helped to force political life into that mould. In particular, the use of the open ballot, whereby voters simply declared their choice at the polls in the presence of a government official (and anybody else who happened to be in the room at the time!), provided numerous opportunities for bribery, coercion, and intimidation, and made it difficult for anybody whose livelihood depended on government contracts to vote against candidates supported by the ruling cabinet (see Box 10.1). Non-simultaneous or staggered elections, which permitted the government to call elections in safe ridings before having to work its way into more doubtful territory, forced candidates in many ridings to be *ministerialists*, so called because their 'politics were not to support a party but a ministry and any ministry would do.'[7] This non-partisan stance was the surest way to provide for a steady flow of government patronage into the successful candidate's constituency.

The elimination of the open ballot and deferred elections by the late 1870s, along with the gradual standardization of electoral regulations across the different provinces, did not reduce the importance of patronage in federal politics—far from it. Despite the removal of some of the crasser forms of electoral corruption by the 1880s, the two federal parties still operated in a political environment characterized by the absence of civil service reform (the merit principle), a highly restricted franchise, and a weak working class (there were plenty of workers, but they tended to be unorganized and did not share a collective political identity). All of these factors, it has been suggested, predispose political parties to appeal to potential supporters through networks of patron–client relations (where votes are exchanged for certain 'favours') rather than on the basis of collectivist or solidaristic appeals (class-based ideologies).[8]

This is precisely the situation described by the French political sociologist, André Siegfried, when he visited Canada just over 100 years ago. Siegfried complained that the preoccupation with questions of 'material interest' and 'public works' tended to 'lower the general level of political life' in Canada. He also noted that Canadian politics was hardly lacking in substantive issues—rivalries between Catholics and Protestants, French and English, for example—that could have been addressed by the two major parties, but that the party leaders 'prefer that they should not be talked about. The subjects which remain available for discussion are not numerous. In addition, the parties borrow one another's policies periodically, displaying a coolness in this process that would disconcert us Europeans.'[9]

Siegfried's comments on the nature of party competition in Canada are still remarkably relevant (see Box 10.2). If Siegfried were somehow transported to present-day Canada, he would probably conclude that there have been few substantive changes in our party system since he published his work in 1906. The emphasis on accommodating the diverse interests—regional, linguistic, ethnic, class, religious—of the electorate through the prudent employment of 'public works' and individual material incentives is still a characteristic feature of federal and provincial politics. Elections are usually preceded by a barrage of new government programs and spending initiatives in various parts of the country—ill-disguised attempts by the party in power to purchase electoral support in

Governing Realities

Box 10.1 The Open Ballot

The Liberals, for reasons that are not hard to discern, favoured the secret ballot, and every year after 1869 saw a Liberal motion for the adoption of the ballot fall by the wayside. The opportunities for bribery of voters, the coercion of employees by their superiors and of civil servants by the Conservatives, and the open interference of the clergy in Quebec all were cited as arguments by the Liberals. The Conservatives tacitly admitted the justice of the opposition's case, but yielded nothing. One staunch party man went so far on one occasion as to observe with commendable frankness that, after all, elections could not be carried on without money, and 'under an open system of voting, you can readily ascertain whether the voter has deceived you.' The Prime Minister thought the [secret] ballot 'un-British'. Another was critical of it on the ground that it would let a dishonest elector sell his vote to two or three different parties, instead of just one. With these and other cogent reasons for preserving electoral purity, the open system of voting was allowed to last until 1874.

Source: Norman Ward, *The Canadian House of Commons*, © University of Toronto Press, 1950, p. 158.

key ridings. As well, the nonchalant borrowing of elements of one party's program by another party, which Siegfried found so disconcerting, is still going on today. Among the more flagrant modern examples of this habit we might mention the 1974, 1984, and 1993 federal elections. In the first case, Pierre Trudeau's Liberal government implemented wage-and-price controls in an attempt to cure inflation, only a few months after an election in which the Liberals had castigated the Conservatives and their leader, Robert Stanfield, for proposing just such a policy. In 1984, the new leader of the Conservatives, Brian Mulroney, is widely thought to have scored a decisive win in the television debate with his Liberal counterpart, John Turner, on the issue of patronage appointments. Voters were seemingly impressed by the Tory leader's display of moral outrage at Turner's feeble attempt to justify appointing a raft of Liberals to plum positions at the tail end of the Trudeau dynasty. But not long after the election, the Tories themselves were practising pork-barrel politics on a scale that made their predecessors look like rank amateurs.

During the 1993 election campaign the Liberal Party under Jean Chrétien promised to eliminate the despised GST and reopen negotiations with the Americans on the Free Trade Agreement (FTA), both of which were part of the Conservatives' legacy. To no one's surprise the Americans indicated that they were not interested in renegotiating the FTA, and the Liberals retreated from their campaign bravado. In the case of the GST, after two years in power it

Politics in Focus

Box 10.2 An Early Illustration of the Brokerage Theory of Canadian Politics

The fact that in the Dominion parties exist apart from their programs, or even without a program at all, frequently deprives the electoral consultations of the people of their true meaning. In the absence of ideas or doctrines to divide the voters, there remain only questions of material interest, collective or individual. Against their pressure the candidate cannot maintain his integrity, for he knows that his opponent will not show the same self-restraint. The result is that the same promises are made on both sides, following an absolutely identical conception of the meaning of power. Posed in this way, the issue of an election manifestly changes. Whoever may be the winner, everyone knows that the country will be administered in the same way, or almost the same. The only difference will be in the personnel of the government. This is the prevailing conception of politics—except when some great wave of opinion sweeps over the whole country, covering under its waters all the political pygmies. . . .

The reason for this . . . is easy to understand. Canada, we know, is a country of violent oppositions. English and French, Protestant and Catholic, are jealous of each other and fear each other. The lack of ideas, programs, convictions, is only apparent. Let a question of race or religion be raised, and you will immediately see most of the sordid preoccupations of patronage or connection disappear below the surface. The elections will become struggles of political principle, sincere and passionate. Now this is exactly what is feared by the prudent and far-sighted men who have been given the responsibility of maintaining the national equilibrium. Aware of the sharpness of certain rivalries, they know that if these are let loose without any counter-balance, the unity of the Dominion may be endangered. That is why they persistently apply themselves to prevent the formation of homogeneous parties, divided according to race, religion, or class—a French party, for instance, or a Catholic party, or a Labour party. The clarity of political life suffers from this, but perhaps the existence of the federation can be preserved only at this price.

Source: *The Race Question in Canada* by André Siegfried. ed. and trans. Frank Underhill became apparent that what the Liberals really meant by elimination of the GST was the harmonization of this tax with its provincial counterparts into a single sales tax. This was not exactly what voters had been led to believe. These kinds of flip-flops by the older parties on key issues—and many more examples could be cited—only serve to fuel the electorate's cynicism about politics in general and their distrust of politicians in particular.

The electoral opportunism exhibited by both the Liberals and the Tories in recent decades should not to be taken to mean that the two older parties have no principles or ideological commitments whatsoever. Just as was the case when Siegfried was studying the Canadian party system, in recent times Canada's oldest parties have represented somewhat distinct traditions, particularly on matters concerning federalism and Canada–US relations. With the accession of Pierre Trudeau to the party leadership in 1968, the Liberals became identified in the minds of most Canadian voters with a strong central state (hence the ongoing battles between Ottawa and the provinces over control of natural resource revenues), with economic nationalism (Petro-Canada, the National Energy Program, the Foreign Investment Review Agency [FIRA]), and with 'French power'. The Tories, meanwhile, came increasingly to be associated with political decentralization: Joe Clark, when he was leader of the party and briefly Prime Minister in the late 1970s, described Canadian federalism as a 'community of communities', which Trudeau sarcastically rejected as 'shopping-mall' federalism. The Conservatives also came to embrace the notion of free trade with the United States; this represented a reversal of the party positions on the subject in the late nineteenth and early twentieth centuries, when the Liberals strongly advocated continentalist economic policies. Finally, the neo-conservatism of the 1980s, spearheaded by British Prime Minister Margaret Thatcher and US President Ronald Reagan, found its most receptive audience among the Conservatives during the Mulroney years. In recent years the federal Liberal Party has been associated with a somewhat more centralist vision of federal–provincial relations and a brand of mild to occasionally hotter anti-Americanism, while the Conservatives have branded themselves as a more decentralist party in matters of federal–provincial relations and more sympathetic to Washington than their Liberal rivals. The 2011 pre-election Tory attack ad, which showed Liberal leader Michael Ignatieff, when he was a US-based academic, saying how much he loves America and speaking as if he were an American, presents an ironic twist to party tendencies that still are true today.

Despite these apparent differences in the policy orientations of the two older parties in recent times, Siegfried's central contention about the Canadian party system remains indisputable. Our historically dominant parties have continued to be much more flexible, opportunistic, dominated by their leaders (see Box 10.3), and wary of ideological appeals to the electorate than those in most European nations. The nature of our electoral system and the norms that govern party competition in this country are such that the Liberals and Conservatives can usually fight elections without having to worry too much about keeping their principles intact or consistent. Many observers of the Canadian party system have attached a specific label to this type of flexible, non-ideological party system: it is a *brokerage* party system. That is, the two older parties at the federal level act as 'brokers of ideas . . . middlemen who select from all the ideas pressing for recognition as public policy those they think can be shaped to have the widest appeal'.[10] Each of the parties attempts to cobble together a winning coalition of voters at election time; the voting support for the two major parties, therefore, does not come from stable, well-defined social groups, as is the case in many Western European countries. Most importantly, politics in Canada lacks an obvious *class* dimension. Conflicts between the working class and capitalists over the political and economic rights of workers, and over the distribution of national wealth, take a back seat to other issues—those arising out of linguistic and regional rivalries, for instance, or divisions that are not obviously linked to social class such as age, gender, environmental views, or attitudes towards the United States.

This peculiarity of Canadian politics led some observers to describe the Canadian party system as less developed or less modern than those of most other industrial nations. Robert Alford, for example, declared in his classic study of voting behaviour in four Anglo-American democracies (the United States, Canada, Great Britain, and Australia) that Canada had the lowest level of class voting among the nations he examined.[11] Alford's explanation of this situation echoed the one advanced by Siegfried almost 60 years earlier: 'Class voting is low in Canada because the political parties are identified as representatives of regional, religious, and ethnic groupings rather than as representatives of national class interests, and this, in turn, is due to a relative lack of national integration.'[12] Class divisions and antagonisms are certainly not absent in Canada, Alford observed, and he predicted that once the issue of national unity had been resolved, class voting would increase and Canada would come to resemble other modern democracies—Great Britain, for instance.

In the almost 50 years since Alford's book was written, it should be noted, his prediction has simply not come true: the issue of class is still subordinated to questions of national unity and regional or ethnic grievances. The two older parties do not normally appeal to specific class constituencies and still evade class issues when possible. Moreover, the self-described left-wing party in Canada, the NDP, historically has received nowhere near a majority of the votes of blue-collar workers. This may have changed in the 2011 election, although we won't know until the Canadian Election Study data for that election become available.

Brokerage theory, then, makes two fundamental claims about Canada's two historically dominant political parties: first, they do not appeal to specific socio-economic groupings, and they lack cohesive ideological visions (especially those based on class interests and identity); second, the parties are flexible and opportunistic because this sort of behaviour is necessary to preserve the fragile unity of the nation. This brings to mind Siegfried's observation that there are all kinds of pressing issues in Canadian politics, but that the prudent and cautious leaders of the two main parties do not want them to be discussed, for fear of inflaming group jealousies and thereby jeopardizing the stability of the country.

An alternative explanation of the absence of class politics in Canada is advanced by Janine Brodie and Jane Jenson in *Crisis, Challenge, and Change*.[13] They argue that brokerage theory tends to view political parties as more or less passive transmission belts for societal demands. In the vocabulary of empirical social science, brokerage theorists consider parties to be *dependent variables*: their behaviour is shaped by the divisions that exist in society—in Canada's case, the most important divisions being those of language, ethnicity, region, and religion. Brodie and Jenson call for a more nuanced view of parties, one that treats them simultaneously as *dependent* (influenced by society) and *independent* (actively shaping societal demands) variables. The most important aspect of the independent, creative function of political parties in liberal democracies like Canada is their role in creating a *definition of politics*:

Governing Realities

Box 10.3 The Historical Importance of the Leader in Canadian Party Politics

. . . it is of the first importance to the success of a party that it should be led by someone who inspires confidence, and whose mere name is a program in itself. As long as the Conservatives had Macdonald for their leader, they voted for him rather than for the party. So it is with Laurier and the Liberals of today. If Laurier disappeared, the Liberals would perhaps find that they had lost the real secret of their victories. . . . Canadians attach themselves rather to the concrete reality than to the abstract principle. They vote as much for the man who symbolizes the policy as for the policy itself.

Source: *The Race Question in Canada* by André Siegfried. ed. and trans. Frank Underhill

> through which people make sense of their daily lives. Because issues are raised and choices provided in particular ways, this cultural construction defines the content and sets the limits of partisan politics. Social problems never included within the bounds of partisan political debate remain invisible and confined to the private sector or private life for resolution. From a myriad of social tensions the definition of politics identifies and selects those susceptible to 'political' solutions. Political parties, in other words, by defining the political, contribute to the organization and disorganization of groups in the electorate.[14]

Brodie and Jenson argue that in the period immediately following Confederation, class, religion, language, and other social differences competed with each other—more or less equally—as potential support bases for the two federal parties. Since both of these parties drew the bulk of their support from the same social group—property-owning males—they tended to avoid the issue of class in their competition for votes. As a strategy for differentiating their 'product' from that of the governing Conservatives, the Liberals gradually seized on the issue of ethnic, religious, and linguistic differences and 'became the party of French Quebec (and later of other ethnic minorities) while the Conservatives solidified their base among Anglophone Canadians.'[15] In later years, the authors claim, the two traditional parties would frequently try to avoid discussing class issues such as the rights and place of workers in Canadian society by redefining them as regional or cultural concerns. The NDP, they contend, has not been able or willing to challenge the prevailing definition of politics in Canada, and therefore is forced to compete with the Liberals and Conservatives under conditions that permanently handicap it and leave a significant portion of the Canadian electorate effectively disenfranchised.

Brodie and Jenson's explanation of the non-class nature of the Canadian party system is an important contribution to our understanding of politics in this country. Nevertheless, it does seem somewhat overdrawn, since it appears to downplay or minimize the pre-eminence of religious and ethnic divisions in Canadian society in the late nineteenth century and to exaggerate the extent to which the parties have been able to play up the issues of language and culture for their own electoral advantage. One important reason that class identity came so slowly and unevenly to Canadian workers was precisely the role played by religious institutions—the Catholic Church and the Orange Order, most notably—in organizing the working class. The Orange Order appealed to workers as Scottish or Irish Protestants, while the Catholic Church stressed the spiritual mission of French-Canadian workers and was reluctant to define society in terms of antagonistic classes (as socialists did). All of this helped to ensure that for large numbers of Canadian workers, their class identity was intermingled with their ethnic and religious allegiance. A large part of the explanation of the relative unimportance of class issues in Canadian politics, therefore, must be found in the social organization of the working class itself, and not simply attributed to the major parties' manipulation of the definition of politics.

The Role of Minor Parties in the Brokerage System: The Case of the Reform Party

By the summer of 1991, almost three years into its second mandate, the Progressive Conservative government of Prime Minister Brian Mulroney had sunk to historic lows in public opinion polls, with barely 15 per cent of Canadians claiming that they would vote for the Tories if an election were held at that time. In fact, the Conservatives were being rivalled in voter popularity by a fledgling organization that was beginning to capture a great deal of voter and media attention: the Reform Party of Canada. Under the leadership of Preston Manning, the son of the former Social Credit Premier of Alberta, Ernest Manning, the Reform Party was founded in late 1987 primarily as a vehicle for western discontent (its original slogan was 'The West Wants In'). The Reform Party, which became the Canadian Alliance Party in 2000, was the latest in a string of Western protest movements—its most successful predecessors having been the Progressives in the 1920s, Social

Credit and the CCF in the 1930s and 1940s, and the Western Canada Concept in the early 1980s—that have tapped into the powerful feelings of economic and political alienation in the western provinces. These feelings originate in the firm conviction that the West is getting the short end of the stick, economically speaking: many westerners believe that existing federal arrangements allow Ontario and Quebec to siphon off the resource wealth of the West in order to fuel growth and prosperity in the centre. The two major parties have been seen as co-conspirators in this vicious circle of exploitation, since they are beholden to the powerful economic interests in the metropolitan areas and are compelled to enact policies that favour those regions where the bulk of the seats are to be won in a federal election.

This deep-seated suspicion among westerners of central Canada and national political institutions was briefly dispelled by the 1984 federal election. Although the new Prime Minister, Brian Mulroney, was himself a bilingual Quebecer, for the first time since the Diefenbaker interlude of the 1950s a large number of prominent westerners were placed in key cabinet positions. 'At last,' western voters seemed to be saying to themselves, 'we're getting a government that will understand and respond to our concerns, and not treat us like second-class citizens.' Gradually, however, this guarded optimism gave way to a shattering disillusionment, as the Conservative government made a number of policy decisions that were viewed as detrimental to western interests. Without a doubt the most publicized instance of 'biased' government decision-making was Ottawa's awarding of a multi-million dollar maintenance contract for the CF-18 fighter aircraft to a Quebec-based firm, despite the fact that Bristol Aerospace of Winnipeg had presented what federal officials acknowledged was a technically superior bid. 'This enraged not only Manitobans, but most westerners, and the CF-18 decision quickly joined the National Energy Program as a symbol of regional resentment and injustice.'[16] Many westerners drew the conclusion from this affair that no matter how many representatives they sent to the House of Commons, the system itself—especially the 'national' parties—was biased against the West. A new voice, therefore, that of a regionally based protest party like the Reform Party, was necessary to extract favourable policies from central Canada.

Although the Reform Party began its life as a strictly regional organization—its constitution originally even included a prohibition on fielding candidates east of Manitoba—it quickly capitalized on the public's growing disenchantment with so-called 'traditional' political parties to make inroads into Ontario, the bastion of central Canadian power. The percentage of Canadians expressing 'a great deal' or 'quite a lot' of confidence in political parties had dropped from 30 per cent in 1979 to only 7 per cent in 1991.[17] Reform attacked existing political institutions as being unresponsive, unaccountable, and elitist, and attempted to portray itself as a populist movement rather than a political party. Rigid party discipline—which various governments have promised to relax, without much noticeable effect—was singled out by both voters and the Reform Party alike as one of the biggest culprits in driving a wedge between the individual citizen and the political system. Under the Mulroney Conservatives, two Tory backbenchers who were publicly critical of the GST found themselves expelled from the party's caucus. Likewise, and despite Jean Chrétien's promise to relax party discipline, those Liberal MPs who opposed the government's 1995 gun control law were stripped of their parliamentary committee assignments. Such incidents remind voters that under the traditional parties those they elect to Parliament are expected to vote as the party brass decides, even if this collides with the strongly held desires of their constituents.

There is also a generalized suspicion, fuelled by occasional sordid conflict-of-interest scandals that befell governments in Ottawa and in many of the provincial capitals as well, that politicians had become overly concerned with furthering their own careers or lining their pockets, at the expense of their primary duty of representing the wishes and interests of their constituents. The issue of MPs' pensions was and continues to be a lightning rod for this popular sentiment. The Reform Party made much of its commitment to opt out of what it considered to be the unfairly generous terms of MPs' pensions, and in 1995 all but one of the party's MPs chose not to participate in the pension plan.

Finally, there was declining tolerance among voters for the kind of closed-door, elitist decision-making that traditionally had characterized Canadian politics under Liberal and Conservative governments.

Responding to the widely held demands among the electorate for greater accountability and a more democratic political structure, the Reform Party and then the Canadian Alliance followed in the path of their populist predecessors, the Progressives and Social Credit, and called for the implementation of a number of institutional reforms that would increase the individual citizen's control over his or her representatives. The Alliance advocated greater use of referendums and citizen initiatives; the right of constituents to recall their MPs, should they be deviating too obviously from their wishes; and relaxation of party discipline, so that most votes in Parliament would be 'free' votes. The Reform/Alliance ideology was conservative, and it regularly found itself alone as the sole political party advocating radical change to the policy status quo. For example, during the 1993 election campaign it was the only party to advocate a major reduction in Canada's annual intake of immigrants during times when the economy was weak. It was also the only party to insist that deficit reduction, to be achieved mainly through spending cuts, should be Ottawa's top priority (a policy that the Liberal government subsequently embraced). Reform Party MPs were the main critics in Parliament of the 1995 gun control law requiring the registration of all firearms. The party also stood alone in its opposition to official multiculturalism and bilingualism.

Although the Conservatives, Liberals, and NDP all initially tried to ignore or downplay the significance of the Reform Party, by the summer of 1991—when the report of the Spicer Commission was released, documenting the deep dissatisfaction of many Canadians with the functioning of their traditional democratic institutions, especially the political parties—this protest movement was simply too powerful to be casually dismissed as a sort of political chinook. If the Conservatives and the New Democrats hoped to hold onto at least some of their traditional electoral strongholds in the Prairies, then they had to respond to the policy concerns raised by Preston Manning's organization, no matter how distasteful or 'populist' they considered them to be. This is exactly what happened during previous cycles of regional protest: the major parties were eventually compelled to head off the electoral challenge of a nascent protest movement (whether it was the Progressives, the CCF, or Social Credit) by endorsing policies that appealed to the new party's supporters. In the case of the Progressives, for instance, the party was opposed to the National Policy tariff (which kept the price of central Canada's manufactured goods relatively high and drove up the costs of farming) and to the discriminatory freight rates charged by the CPR (which made it cheaper to ship manufactured goods from central Canada to the West than to send grain eastward). After the Progressives' meteoric rise to prominence in the 1921 federal election, however, the protest they represented was gradually dissipated by the skilful manoeuvring of the Liberal Prime Minister, Mackenzie King, who made relatively minor changes in the tariff and in freight rate policy and managed to buy off some of the Progressive leaders with offers of cabinet posts in his government. This was largely the fate of the Co-operative Commonwealth Federation as well: Mackenzie King sought to take the wind out of the socialist party's sails by implementing a number of social welfare policies that its supporters were advocating, including old-age pensions and unemployment insurance.

'Minor' parties like Reform/Alliance perform an important function in our brokerage party system: they provide a much-needed source of policy innovation, goading the major parties into acting on the concerns of regions, classes, or significant social groups that they have traditionally ignored or underestimated. Walter Young, in his history of the national CCF, described the contribution of third parties to the Canadian political system:

> By providing . . . the kind of ideological confrontation which is typically absent in contests between the two major parties, [minor parties] have served to stimulate the older parties and reactivate their previously dormant philosophies. . . . Two parties alone cannot successfully represent all the interests or act as a broker—honest or otherwise. At-

tempts to represent a national consensus have been usually based on the assessment of a few with limited access to the attitudes of the whole. The result has been that the national consensus has in fact been the view of the most dominant voices in the old parties. And these are the voices at the centre; historically, the voices of the elite or the establishment.[18]

Bob Krieger/© Simon Fraser University

Preston Manning, who founded and led the Reform Party of Canada from 1987 to 2000, helped to 'fan the flames' on western regional and social conservative issues, forcing the country's dominant parties into ideological debates that would not have surfaced otherwise.

The 1993 and 1997 Elections: The End of Brokerage Politics?

Before the 1993 election it was common to speak of Canada's 'two and one-half' party system. The Liberals and Progressive Conservatives were the parties with a realistic chance of forming a government, while the NDP was a stable minority party on the federal scene, regularly winning 15–20 per cent of the popular vote and occasionally holding the balance of power during a period of **minority government**. The distinction between major and minor parties was rooted in the realities of electoral competition.

The old certainties were shattered by the 1993 election results. The Liberals won a solid majority, taking 177 of the 295 seats in the House of Commons and 41.3 per cent of the popular vote. Neither the Conservatives nor the NDP elected enough MPs to qualify for official party status, which guarantees the opportunity to speak in the House during Question Period as well as automatic funding for research staff. On the other hand, the Reform Party jumped from one seat that had been won in a by-election to 52 seats. The Bloc Québécois (BQ), created in 1990 by the defections of several Tory and Liberal MPs, went from seven seats to 54. Not since 1921, when the Progressives came second to the Liberals, had the national party system received such a jolt by voters.

With the Conservatives and NDP reduced to near irrelevance in the Commons and two strong opposition parties, neither of which gave signs of being interested in brokerage-style politics, it was natural that political analysts should talk of the realignment taking place in Canada's national party system. Realignment suggests a durable change, not one caused by transient and unusual factors. Those who interpreted the 1993 election results as evidence of a realignment based this reading on what they saw as voters' dissatisfaction with brokerage-style politics, the weakness of party loyalties among voters, and erosion of the NDP's support across the country. This interpretation was greeted skeptically or even rejected by others. Critics of the realignment argument pointed to such factors as the monumental unpopularity of former Conservative Prime Minister Brian Mulroney, the erosion of NDP support in Ontario where an unpopular NDP government was in power, a wave of western disaffection with the major parties, and the unusual and presumably passing phenomenon of the Bloc Québécois, spawned in the bitter wake of the 1990 defeat of the Meech Lake Accord.

It appeared that the elements for a durable party realignment existed. One of these involved the low esteem in which parties and politicians were—and continue to be—held by voters. In the words of the Royal Commission on Electoral Reform and Party Financing:

> Canadians appear to distrust their political leaders, the political process and political institutions. Parties themselves may be contributing to the malaise of voters. . . . whatever the cause, there is little doubt that Canadian political parties are held in low public esteem, and that their standing has declined steadily over the past decade. They are under attack from citizens for failing to achieve a variety of goals deemed important by significant groups within society.[19]

The wave of cynicism that was building in the Canadian electorate weakened attachments to the traditional parties. This opened the door for newcomers on the party scene, the votes won by BQ and Reform candidates having gone mainly to Liberals and Conservatives before 1993.

A second element that seemed to presage a realignment of the party system involved what might be described as the shrinking centre in Canadian politics. The traditional dominance of the Liberals and Progressive Conservatives, centrist parties that differed very little from one another in terms of their principles and policies, depended on the existence of a broad popular consensus on the role of government and on the older parties' ability to keep political debate within the familiar confines of language, regionalism, and leadership. This popular consensus had become frayed and the traditionally dominant parties' ability to keep political conflict within 'safe' boundaries was diminished.

The consensus that developed during the post–World War II era was based on the welfare state, an active economic management role for government, and official bilingualism. The Liberals and Conservatives, but particularly the Liberal Party in its role as the government for most of this era, were the architects of the policies that were the practical expressions of this consensus. On constitutional issues, too, the traditional parties were capable of broad agreement. This was evident in the support that all three parties gave to both the Meech Lake Accord and the Charlottetown Accord, a unanimity that certainly was not found in the Canadian population.

Popular consensus on the Keynesian welfare state and activist government has unravelled since the 1980s. Issues like deficit reduction, welfare reform, and lower taxes became the rallying points for dissent from the post-war consensus. Opposition to what is perceived to be state-sponsored pluralism through official multiculturalism and bilingualism provided another pole for this dissent. In broadening its organization from the West to include Ontario and eastern Canada, the Reform Party was clearly attempting to provide a voice for this dissent that many voters believed was not being provided by the Progressive Conservative Party. Reform's second-place finish in Ontario in the 1993 election, capturing 20 per cent of the popular vote, cannot be explained in terms of 'western alienation'. These appeared to be voters who had defected from the Conservative Party in search of a party that defined the issues in a way they believed responded to the country's true problems. At the provincial level this dissent contributed to the election of the Conservatives under Ralph Klein in Alberta and under Mike Harris in Ontario, provincial Conservative governments that were much closer to the outlook of the Reform Party than they were to the national Progressive Conservative Party under Jean Charest (1993–8) and Joe Clark (1998–2003).

Only the Liberal Party succeeded in practising the old brokerage-style politics. It emerged from the 1993 election as the only truly national party, electing members from every province and territory and receiving no less than one-quarter of the votes cast in any province. The Liberals did only slightly less well in 1997, failing to elect a member only in Nova Scotia and the Yukon. In the 2000 election Liberal support ranged from a low of 20.7 per cent of the popular vote in Saskatchewan to a high of 51.5 per cent in Ontario. The party won seats in every province and territory, no other party coming close to this accomplishment. The lesson that some drew was that there no longer existed enough space in the centre of the Canadian electorate to support two centrist brokerage parties. It became increasingly evident that the Progressive Conservative Party would have to reposition itself ideologically if it wanted to regain the votes that Reform/Canadian Alliance siphoned off in the 1993, 1997, and 2000 elections. It could not afford to remain a near-clone of the Liberal Party, especially since the Liberals in power created some distance between themselves and the Keynesian welfare state they were instrumental in building. The electoral success of right-leaning Conservatives in Alberta and Ontario suggested that the future of the national party was in this direction.

The 1997 general election was a replay of 1993 in several important respects. The Liberals swept all but one of Ontario's 103 seats. The Reform Party dominated in the West, taking 57 of the 74 seats in Saskatchewan, Alberta, and British Columbia. The Reform share of the vote in Ontario remained stable at slightly less than 20 per cent, but the Conservative share of the Ontario vote recovered to almost equal that of Reform. The Bloc Québécois continued to be the most popular party in Quebec, but it lost some ground in both share of the vote and seats to the Liberals.

More significant than these nuanced changes were the election results in the Atlantic provinces. Twenty-one of the 32 seats in the four Atlantic provinces were won by the NDP and the Conservatives. Indeed, the Conservative Party emerged from the 1997 election appearing to be almost as much an Atlantic Canada party as Reform appeared to be a western Canadian party. Thirteen of the PC's 20 seats were won in Newfoundland, Nova Scotia, and New Brunswick. The NDP, which historically had achieved only minor inroads in Atlantic Canada, won eight seats in the region, representing about 40 per cent of the party's caucus in Parliament. The loss of several Liberal seats and the ascendance of the Conservatives and the NDP in the region were almost certainly due to voters' unhappiness with federal spending cuts, particularly in transfers to provincial governments, which were felt more deeply in their region than in more affluent parts of Canada. The message of fiscal conservatism that the Liberals preached, particularly after the 1995 federal budget, was an unnerving one in provinces whose job markets and public services have long been sustained by a life-support system of federal assistance.

The rise of the Reform Party in the West and of the Bloc Québécois in Quebec in the 1993 and 1997 elections tells us that the party loyalties of many Canadian voters are not very durable. The Reform Party, joined by some elements from the national and provincial Conservative parties, sought to capitalize on the apparent softness of party loyalties through a movement to create the United Alternative. Formally launched in 1998, the roots of the United Alternative go back to the 1993 election. The Liberals won a strong majority on the strength of only 41.3 per cent of the popular vote. Combined popular support for the PCs and Reform came to 34.7 per cent. While not all Reform voters were disaffected Conservatives, it is safe to conclude that most were. Those on the right of Canada's political spectrum were quick to lament the division of the conservative vote, a situation that enabled the Liberal Party to win seats that it probably would not have won, particularly in many Ontario ridings. The combined popular vote of the Conservative and Reform parties in 1997 came to 38.2 per cent, just a fraction less than the Liberals' 38.5 per cent of the vote.

At this point the talk of the need for a 'unite the right' movement to defeat the Liberals became more persistent. Spearheaded intellectually by conservative political writer David Frum and organized by the Reform Party, the United Alternative (UA) was created in 1998 and held its first national convention in February of 1999. The convention certainly gave the appearance of inter-party co-operation

TABLE 10.1 Summary of Election Results, 1940–2011

A. Percentage of Vote* and Candidates Elected by Political Party at Canadian General Elections, 1940–2011

Party	1940	1945	1949	1953	1957	1958	1962	1963
Liberal	54.9%	41.4%	50.1%	50.0%	42.3%	33.8%	37.4%	41.7%
	181	127	193	172	106	48	99	128
PC	30.6%	27.7%	29.7%	31.0%	39.0%	53.7%	37.3%	32.8%
	40	68	41	51	112	208	116	95
CCF/NDP	8.5%	15.7%	13.4%	11.3%	10.8%	9.5%	13.4%	13.1%
	8	28	13	23	25	8	19	17
Social Credit	2.7%	4.1%	3.9%	5.4%	6.6%	2.6%	11.7%	–
	10	13	10	15	19	–	30	–
Bloc Populaire	–	3.7%	0.8%	7.6%	5.0%	4.6%	1.7%	11.9%
	–	5	0	15	11	6	0	24
Others	3.3%	7.8%	2.9%	2.3%	1.3%	0.4%	0.2%	0.4%
	6	7	5	4	3	1	1	1
Total valid votes	4,620,260	5,246,130	5,848,971	5,641,272	6,605,980	7,287,297	7,690,134	7,894,076
Total seats	245	245	262	265	265	265	265	265

Party	1965	1968	1972	1974	1979	1980	1984	1988
Liberal	40.2%	45.5%	38.5%	43.2%	40.1%	44.3%	28.0%	31.9%
	131	155	109	141	114	147	40	83
PC	32.4%	31.4%	34.9%	35.4%	35.9%	32.5%	50.0%	43.0%
	97	72	107	95	136	103	211	169
NDP	17.9%	17.0%	17.7%	15.4%	17.9%	19.8%	18.8%	20.4%
	21	22	31	16	26	32	30	43
Créditistes	4.6%	4.4%	–	–	–	–	–	–
	9	14	–	–	–	–	–	–
Social Credit	3.7%	0.8%	7.6%	5.0%	4.6%	1.7%	0.1%	***
	5	0	15	11	6	0	0	0
Reform/Alliance	–	–	–	–	–	–	–	2.1%
	–	–	–	–	–	–	–	0
Others	1.2%	0.9%	1.2%	0.9%	1.5%	1.7%	3.0%	2.6%
	2	1	2	1	0	0	1	0
Total valid votes	7,713,316	8,125,996	9,667,489	9,505,908	11,455,702	10,947,914	12,548,721	13,175,599
Total seats	265	264	264	264	282	282	282	295

Party	1993	1997	2000	2004	2006	2008	2011
Liberal	41.3%	38.5%	40.8%	36.7%	30.2%	26.2%	18.9%
	177	155	172	135	103	77	34
PC**	16.0%	18.8%	12.2%	29.6%	36.3%	37.6%	39.6%
	2	20	12	99	124	143	166
NDP	6.9%	11.0%	8.5%	15.7%	17.5%	18.2%	30.6%
	9	21	13	19	29	37	103
Bloc Québécois	13.5%	10.7%	10.7%	12.4%	10.5%	10%	6.0%
	54	44	38	54	51	49	4
Reform/Alliance	18.7%	19.4%	25.5%	–	–	–	–
	52	60	66	–	–	–	–
Green Party	–	–	–	4.3%	4.5%	6.8%	3.9%
	–	–	–	0	0	0	1
Others	3.6%	1.6%	2.2%	0.3%	1.0%	1.1%	1.0%
	1	1	0	1	1	2	0
Total valid votes	13,667,671	12,985,964	12,857,774	13,489,559	14,815,680	13,832,972	14,720,580
Total seats	295	301	301	308	308	308	308

Note: The election of 1945 was the first in which the name Progressive Conservative was used. The New Democratic Party first participated in the election of 1962.

*Columns may not add up to 100 per cent due to rounding.

**In 2003 the Progressive Conservative and Canadian Alliance parties merged to form the Conservative Party. The 2004 and 2006 election results for this party are reported at this line.

***Less than 0.1 per cent.

TABLE 10.1 continued

B. Percentage of Vote* and Candidates Elected by Party and Province, 2011

Province	Liberal	Conservative	NDP	Green Party	Bloc Québécois	Others	Totals, Province
NL	37.9 4	28.4 1	32.6 2	0.9 0	–	–	215,874 7
NS	28.9 4	36.7 4	30.3 3	4.0 0	–	–	451,330 11
NB	22.6 1	43.9 8	29.8 1	3.2 0	–	–	388,437 10
PEI	41.0 3	41.2 1	15.4 0	2.4 0	–	–	79,048 4
Que.	14.2 7	16.5 5	42.9 59	2.1 0	23.4 4	–	3,798,430 75
Ont.	25.3 11	44.4 73	25.6 22	3.8 0	–	–	5,531,288 106
Man.	16.6 1	53.5 11	25.8 2	3.6 0	–	–	491,225 14
Sask.	8.6 1	56.3 13	32.3 0	2.7 0	–	–	455,053 14
Alta.	9.3 0	66.8 27	16.8 1	5.3 0	–	–	1,397,346 28
BC	13.4 2	45.5 21	32.5 12	7.7 1	–	–	1,871,665 36
Yukon, NWT, and Nunavut	26.4 0	36.4 2	27.7 1	9.2 0	–	–	39,881 3
Totals, Party	2,783,175 34	5,832,401 166	4,508,474 103	576,221 1	889,788 4	130,521 0	14,720,580 308

*Rows may not add up to 100 per cent due to rounding and the omission of candidates other than those of these five parties.

to unite conservative political forces against the governing Liberal Party. An Ontario cabinet minister, Tony Clement, was the convention co-chair. Conservative Premier Ralph Klein gave the keynote address. Prominent Quebecer and former Liberal Jean Allaire spoke to the convention. The fly in the ointment, from the standpoint of the UA and its goal of realigning Canada's national party system, was that with the exception of only a couple of Conservative MPs, the national Progressive Conservative Party kept its distance from the UA. Conservative leader Joe Clark repeatedly refused to respond to Preston Manning's public invitations to join forces in a new party. This was not surprising in light of Clark's long history as a product and practitioner of brokerage politics. Clark clearly nurtured the vision of re-establishing the Progressive Conservative Party's status as Canada's other brokerage party.

The 2000 Election: Alliance Stalled?

It is generally conceded by all but the most loyal supporters of Jean Chrétien that the 2000 election was called for no better reason than what appeared to be its winnability. The main opposition party, the Canadian Alliance, had just gone through a fairly divisive leadership race that resulted in the defeat of the party's founder, Preston Manning, and his replacement by another Alberta politician, Stockwell Day. The Alliance's new leader was a born-again Christian with a reputation for social conservatism. The Liberals could have continued in power for almost two more years before calling an election. But Day appeared vulnerable and so an election was called.

The rest, as they say, is history. The Liberals were re-elected with a larger majority than they held before the election. The Alliance failed to make its much desired breakthrough in Ontario and so continued to be seen as a party of western protest. Stockwell Day's performance in the campaign was generally seen as ineffective, leaving him open to criticism within his own party. This criticism continued to build during the year after the election until the pressure on Day to resign became irresistible. Day stepped down as leader and ran as a candidate in a new leadership race held less than two years after he had defeated Preston Manning. This time Day lost to Stephen Harper, another Albertan but one who was born and raised in Ontario.

What makes the story of the 2000 election and Stockwell Day's subsequent loss of the Alliance leadership strange are the following facts, virtually ignored by most members of the media and academic commentators:

- Alliance's share of the popular vote increased from 19.4 per cent in 1997 to 25.5 per cent in 2000.
- The party's share of the popular vote in Ontario increased from 19.1 per cent in 1997 to 23.6 per cent in 2000.
- Alliance increased its seats in the House of Commons from 60 to 66.
- Alliance's share of the popular vote in Ontario exceeded that of the NDP and Progressive Conservative Party combined.

Given these facts, the obvious question is why the 2000 election was widely interpreted as a setback for the Canadian Alliance and a personal defeat for its leader, Stockwell Day.

The answer to this question reveals much about Canadian politics. What an outsider, viewing the Canadian electoral scene for the first time, might interpret as clear progress by the Alliance Party was viewed as a setback by most of the country's opinion-makers because of Alliance's failure to pick up seats in Ontario. Winning only two out of Ontario's 103 seats, and nothing in the eastern reaches of Canada, seemed to reconfirm the party's image as just the latest in a line of western protest parties. Of course, the distortions created by Canada's electoral system (about which more will be said below) were largely responsible for this image of Reform/Alliance. Nevertheless, the bar had been set at an Ontario breakthrough. When this did not happen, due to the Alliance and the Conservative parties splitting the right-of-centre vote, it appeared that the Alliance was stalled. Three successive elections had left it pretty much where it began in 1993.

Why the blame for this should come to rest largely on the shoulders of Stockwell Day provides another insight into Canadian politics. During the election campaign *Maclean's* magazine ran an issue with Day's picture and the question, 'Are Canadians right to fear this man?' The cover story focused on the Alliance leader's religious beliefs and social conservatism, and included claims that Day believed in the literal truth of the book of Genesis and thus rejected evolutionary theory and evidence that the Earth is older than 5,000 years. The fundamental questions posed by the piece were, one, whether Day's ideas were significantly out of sync with those of most Canadians and, two, if he became Prime Minister, whether Day could be trusted not to try to foist an agenda of social conservatism onto Canadian society.

Most Canadians do not read *Maclean's* and it is probably a fair bet that among those who do, support for the Alliance was not very high to begin with. But the *Maclean's* story was only part of a broader pattern of media questioning of Day's religious beliefs and what the political implications of these might be. Questions like these are reasonable enough, but they were not asked in connection with any of the other party leaders. Day may have been singled out for scrutiny because his born-again Christianity placed him further from

Despite a campaign that tried to sell an image of Stockwell Day as 'every man'—even 'hip', as pictured here on Parliament Hill rollerblading with his son Logan—the media and the public questioned whether Day's religious beliefs were out of step with those of the average Canadian and if those beliefs would have political implications were he to become Prime Minister.

the safe centre of Canadian spiritual life than the other leaders. But this merely illustrates the point: the constituency for social conservatism is far from being large enough in Canada to elect a like-minded leader. Moreover, whether a majority of Canadians consider such a leader to be 'scary' is an open question, but there is not much doubt that most of their opinion leaders do and that they believe Canadians should as well. Once the social conservative label was stuck to him, Day was no longer considered viable in Ontario. For Alliance to eventually make its breakthrough beyond the comfortable confines of the West it needed a leader who could not be portrayed, by innuendo or otherwise, as a religious nut.

In terms of the more general implications of the 2000 election, it remained unclear whether the party *de*alignment that began in 1993 had been succeeded by a reasonably durable *re*alignment of the national party system and voter support. The odds appeared to be against it. The Bloc Québécois continued to capture a significant share of the Quebec electorate—about four of 10 voters—and support for both the NDP and the Progressive Conservatives remained weak. Indeed, the Conservative Party appeared to have become a party of Atlantic Canada, winning about one of every three votes in the four Atlantic provinces and nine of their 12 seats from this region. This was achieved by positioning the party *to the left* of the Liberals in Atlantic Canada, criticizing the Chrétien government's spending cuts and their negative impact on the region. The idea that the Progressive Conservative Party could re-establish itself nationally by outflanking the Liberals on the left was pretty far-fetched. Emerging from the 2000 election with the smallest share of the popular vote in its history on the national political stage, the PCs and their leadership seemed to be clinging pathetically to the hope that the Alliance would somehow implode and wayward Alliance MPs and voters would return to their proper home in the Progressive Conservative Party.

As for the NDP, 2000 marked the third consecutive election in which the party's national support was in the single digits. The long-simmering debate over whether the way out of marginal status in national politics could be found in moving the party further to the left or in recapturing the centrist orientation it had under former leaders Ed Broadbent and David Lewis eventually led to the resignation of NDP leader Alexa McDonough. The ensuing leadership race pitted a strongly left-wing Toronto city councillor, Jack Layton, against a less strident long-time Winnipeg MP, Bill Blaikie. Layton's victory suggested that the party was pinning its hopes on a shift to the left and on improving its fortunes in urban Canada.

The 2004, 2006, and 2008 Elections: A Divided Electorate

The 2003 merger of the Canadian Alliance and Progressive Conservative Party eliminated what many considered to be the conditions for permanent Liberal government in Canada. The right was now united and the prospect of making inroads in the Liberal stronghold of Ontario seemed within reach. When the 2004 election was called there were reasons for the opposition parties to feel optimistic. The federal Auditor General, Sheila Fraser, had focused attention in her annual report on what appeared to be inappropriate and probably unlawful misallocation of public dollars on advertising in Quebec. Money had gone to individuals and ad companies with little—and in some cases nothing—provided in exchange. A network of shady dealings and favouritism to Liberal operatives in Quebec was exposed. The Adscam scandal, as this affair was known, resulted in a sharp drop in Liberal support in Quebec and a corresponding boost in the popularity of the BQ. The recently chosen leader of the Liberal Party, Prime Minister Paul Martin, attempted to distance himself from the scandal, but it clearly cast a shadow over what many had expected would be the Liberals' fairly effortless march to another majority government.

The new Conservative Party and the NDP were also going into the 2004 election with new leaders. The stakes were different for these parties. In the case of the Conservatives, a breakthrough in Ontario was the goal. For the NDP, emergence from the near irrelevance that the party had experienced federally since the 1993 election was the objective. Both parties achieved their goals, but neither to the degree that its leader and supporters had hoped for in an election that produced Canada's first minority government in a quarter of a century.

Halfway through the campaign public opinion polls were showing a steady deterioration in Liberal support in English Canada. It appeared that the Conservatives were on the cusp of being swept into power with a minority government on the strength of gains in Ontario. At this point the Liberal campaign went heavily negative with a barrage of attack ads on television and radio. These ads targeted a number of fears about the Conservatives and their leader that many voters clearly held. The Conservatives had a 'hidden agenda', it was claimed. This agenda involved the privatization of health care, chipping away at abortion rights, dragging Canada into American-led military adventures, scrapping the Kyoto Accord and other environmental protections, and, in sum, transforming Canada into a northern extension of the United States.

The Liberal strategy appeared to work. The party's share of the national popular vote fell by about four percentage points but it held on to power with a minority government. The Conservatives made gains in Ontario, winning 24 of the province's 106 seats, but this was still far from what it needed to defeat the Liberals. The BQ and NDP both experienced significant gains in their respective shares of the popular vote and number of MPs. It was clear that this was a Parliament unlikely to last more than a year or two.

The 2004 election was a reminder that campaigns do matter. What had appeared to be a probable Conservative victory evaporated in the last weeks of the campaign and, according to some analysts, even in the last few days when the Liberal advertising assault appeared to produce its intended effect in Ontario. Going into the 2006 campaign the polls placed the Liberals comfortably ahead of the Conservatives but the undecided share of the electorate was large, ensuring that this, too, would be a campaign that would matter.

And matter it did. Like the French defending the Maginot Line at the start of World War II, the Liberals attempted to use a familiar strategy that in the end proved ill-suited to the times. The Liberal campaign relied on attack ads from the beginning and tried to portray the Conservatives and their leader very much as they had done in 2004. The Conservatives countered with a strategy of introducing a new policy promise each day. This placed the Liberals on the defensive, responding to such Conservative promises as a reduction in the GST, providing parents with a child-care allowance, improving government accountability, and so on. The Conservatives were able to dominate the issue agenda and, of at least equal importance, avoid the sorts of embarrassing and potentially damaging statements from candidates that had been used against them in previous campaigns. The disciplined and focused character of the Conservative campaign contrasted with the uncharacteristically bumbling and increasingly desperate one waged by the Liberals as that party saw its lead in the polls slip away.

The final result was a Conservative minority government, achieved on the strength of significant gains in the party's popular vote and seat total in Ontario, but also, and surprisingly, because of a breakthrough in Quebec. The Conservatives won almost one-quarter of the popular vote in that province—more than the Liberals—and 10 seats. In order to consolidate these gains Prime Minister Harper moved quickly to appoint five Quebecers to cabinet, including to such important posts as Transport, Industry, and Labour.

The Conservative victory in 2006 was widely interpreted as a rightward shift in Canadian politics. This may have been so, but the magnitude of the shift was not very great and its staying power was uncertain. Barely more than 36 per cent of the electorate voted for Conservative candidates in an election where Stephen Harper and his party were careful not to rely on ideologically polarizing language or messages. The Liberals continued to be handicapped by the lingering effects of the Adscam scandal, as well as by the perception of many voters that they had become arrogant in power. The NDP increased its share of the popular vote and number of MPs back to levels that it had typically enjoyed before the party's collapse in the 1993 election. It was far from clear, therefore, that the Conservative victory signified a move to the right in Canadian politics. Such a judgement would have to wait until the next federal election, which, given the fragmented party standings in the legislature, appeared to be no more than a couple of years away.

The 2008 election failed to confirm this rightward shift. The Conservatives managed to increase their share of the popular vote by a couple of percentage points, mainly at the expense of sagging national support for the Liberal Party under the uncertain leadership of Stéphane Dion. The Bloc Québécois held onto its status as the dominant federal party in the Quebec, denying the Liberals one of the pillars they had long counted on to win national elections and preventing the Conservatives from capturing the seats they needed to form a majority government. The centre–left of Canadian politics appeared to be undiminished in strength. But unlike the years before the 1993 election, the votes on the centre–left of the spectrum are now distributed between four parties—the Liberals, NDP, the Bloc, and the Green Party—instead of being divided between the Liberal Party and the NDP. The Conservative Party controls the centre–right of the

Politics in Focus

Box 10.4 Unite the Left?

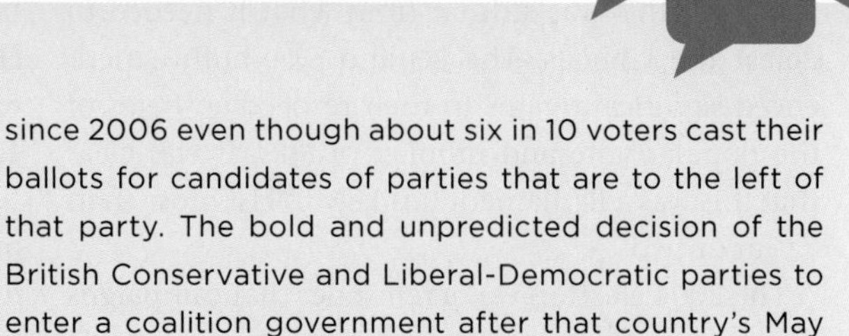

'The lady doth protest too much, methinks.' So says the Queen in Shakespeare's *Hamlet*, suggesting that the repeated protestations of an actor whose performance she has just witnessed may in fact conceal exactly what she so insistently denies. Canadian politics is hardly the tragic psychodrama that is *Hamlet*. But when former Ontario NDP leader and current Liberal MP Bob Rae was asked in June 2010 about rumours of high-level talks concerning a possible merger of the national NDP and Liberal Party, his categorical dismissal of such rumours sounded a bit like the Queen's protests.

Whether or not party heavyweights had sat down in the same room to discuss the idea of a unite-the-left merger of the national Liberal Party and the NDP, the idea of such a marriage had been circulating since the 2006 election of the Conservative minority government. Former Liberal cabinet minister Lloyd Axworthy publicly advocated such a merger after the 2008 election, arguing that it was necessary to defeat the Conservative Party of Stephen Harper. Several former NDP politicians, including Roy Romanow, Ed Broadbent, and Lorne Calvert, have spoken in support of the merger concept. No less a figure than former Liberal Prime Minister Jean Chrétien admitted in June 2010 to having had informal discussions with former NDP leader Ed Broadbent about ways of uniting the centre-left vote in order to defeat the Conservatives. And then there is the fact that the Liberals and the NDP, with the support of the BQ, signed a formal agreement in 2008 to bring down the Conservative government on a confidence vote and support a Liberal government for an agreed period of time. Such an agreement was far from a merger, but it showed how desperate the parties were to find a way to dislodge the Conservatives from power, something that neither the Liberals nor the NDP appeared capable of doing on their own at the polls.

On the face of it, the unite-the-left idea may appear to make sense. Axworthy, Broadbent, and others tirelessly point out that the Conservatives have governed since 2006 even though about six in 10 voters cast their ballots for candidates of parties that are to the left of that party. The bold and unpredicted decision of the British Conservative and Liberal-Democratic parties to enter a coalition government after that country's May 2010 election seemed to make the idea of an inter-party merger in Canada a bit more credible, at least in the eyes of some.

So why don't the parties just merge? There are many reasons why such a step would be difficult to accomplish and would not necessarily achieve the goals of those who advocate it. Here are three big ones:

- Some supporters of both the NDP and the Liberal Party hate the idea. Many NDP activists argue that it would pull their party away from what should be its proper left-wing agenda. From the Liberal side, not all activists and certainly not all Liberal voters are left of centre. Many are more comfortable with the ideas and policies of the Conservatives than they are with those of the NDP.
- A merger of the party cannot be achieved just because some leaders want it to happen. The parties operate under constitutions that require that their respective memberships be given a say in the matter, as happened in 2003 when the Canadian Alliance and Progressive Conservative parties merged to form the Conservative Party of Canada.
- Egos are at stake. Who would lead this new party? How would the career and leadership prospects of politicians and officials in the two parties be affected by a merger? Is their desire to defeat the Conservatives powerful enough for them to risk losing position and influence within their own party?

None of this means that a merger of the NDP and Liberal Party is impossible. Nor does it mean that some important people in the parties have not talked seriously about it. But the obstacles are huge and, even if overcome, there is no guarantee that the result would be the one that unite-the-left advocates would hope to see.

political spectrum, but there do not appear to be enough votes in this electoral space to deliver the party a majority government.

The years between the 1993 and 2008 elections, which produced such dramatic changes in the parties' representation in the House of Commons, were not accompanied by the sorts of shifts in party support that are generally associated with a period of realignment. A **realignment election**, or series of elections, produces a durable change in the parties' bases of support. Perhaps the classic illustration of this was the emergence of the New Deal coalition in American politics during the 1930s, when blue-collar workers, Catholics, black Americans, and southerners lined up solidly behind the Democratic Party, ensuring its domination of Congress for the following several decades. In Canada the 1896 election comes closest to deserving the realignment label, as French-Canadian Catholics, a voting bloc that had leaned towards the Conservative Party, shifted to the Liberals after the execution of the Métis leader Louis Riel and the selection of the francophone Wilfrid Laurier as the Liberal leader. The huge vote swings that occurred in 1958, when Quebecers massively shifted their support to the Conservative Party, and again in 1984 proved not to be durable.

The most significant and enduring shift that took place beginning with the 1993 election was that a large share of the Quebec electorate voted for the separatist Bloc Québécois in six consecutive elections. Although the demise of the BQ and the re-absorption of most of its supporters into the Liberal Party vote column were confidently predicted at various points, this did not happen. Until 2011, the 1993 election brought about a temporary realignment in Quebec. With the 2003 merger of the Canadian Alliance and the Progressive Conservative Party, it appeared to be business as usual in the rest of Canada. The two historically dominant parties competed to form a national government, with the NDP back in its familiar role as a third party capable of tipping the balance between the larger parties and exercising leverage over a minority government. But business as usual ended with the 2011 election.

The 2011 Election: A 60/40 Country?

Canadian elections have often produced a change in government, but only occasionally have the results redrawn the party map. The election of 1921 was one such case, when the Progressive Party, which had no seats in the House of Commons prior to the election, became the official opposition. By the 1926 election things were back to normal and the Liberal–Conservative duopoly in Canadian party politics had been re-established. The election of 1993, when the Conservative Party's support collapsed and the Bloc Québécois and Reform Party surged into second and third place, respectively, in the House of Commons standings was another case where the party map was redrawn in dramatic fashion.

No such surprises were expected when, on 26 March 2011, the 40th Parliament was dissolved and an election was called. The conventional wisdom was that not very much was likely to change in the party standings. Most of the speculation involved whether the governing Conservative Party would manage to eke out a narrow majority this time. In the absence of a clear issue dividing the parties and galvanizing voters, what excitement existed was generated in large part by the prospect of yet another Conservative minority government. It was widely expected that if this were to happen, the opposition parties would take the first opportunity to defeat the Conservatives in the House and install a coalition government of the sort that they had contemplated in 2008 and again in 2009.

Listen to 'The 60/40 Country?' podcast, available at www.oupcanada.com/Brooks7e

And then the unexpected happened. The election of 2011 was a jolting reminder that campaigns matter. No one predicted at the outset that the once mighty Liberal Party, Canada's 'natural governing party', as it came to be known in the latter half of the twentieth century, would fall to third place with the support of fewer than one out of five voters. Nor did anyone imagine that the NDP would vault into second place, winning more than twice as many seats as its previous election high of 43 in 1988 and doubling its share of the popular vote. These would have been surprises enough for one election. But perhaps the greatest surprise in this election full of startling results was the almost total collapse of the BQ in Quebec—a party that was comfortably in the lead in that province when the election was called—and the emergence of the NDP as Quebec's leading party. In its entire history the NDP, going back to its original incarnation as the CCF, had elected only two MPs from Quebec. On 2 May 2011, the party captured 59 of the province's 75 seats.

Explanations for these seismic changes in Canadian party politics focused on two major factors: leadership and what was believed to be Quebecers' fatigue with the sovereignists and their goal of Quebec independence. The NDP leader, Jack Layton, was said to have caught the imagination of Canadians, including Quebecers, appearing confident, compassionate, and articulate. Of course, some voters thought that he already showed these leadership qualities in 2004, 2006, and 2008. Layton's death in August of 2011 demonstrated the breadth and depth of the admiration that many Canadians, including those who did not share his social democratic ideology, felt for him. Not since the death of Pierre Trudeau in 2000 had the passing of a public figure provoked such an outpouring of grief and tributes. Layton's rivals for the centre-left vote in the 2011 election, the Liberals' Michael Ignatieff and the BQ's Gilles Duceppe, failed to connect with many of their respective parties' usual supporters. The reasons were different in each case. Ignatieff proved unable to shake the narrative that the Conservatives had done so much to instill in the minds of Canadians from the time of his selection as Liberal leader in 2009. He seemed, according to the critics, aloof and uninspiring after his 35 years spent outside of Canada. In the case of Gilles Duceppe, it was not that his style or personal story—a story that Quebecers knew very well and seemed to approve of in the five previous elections—alienated voters. Rather, his message no longer seemed to resonate with *les québécois*. Ideologically, in terms of such issues as taxation, social spending, the environment, and Canadian troops abroad, the BQ and the NDP were not very different. From its inception in the wake of the failed Meech Lake Accord, the BQ's competitive advantage was its special relationship to Quebec nationalism. That advantage no longer seemed to matter to voters in 2011.

Over the years Quebecers have shown themselves to be capable of dramatic change in how they cast their votes. In 1958 they abandoned the Liberal Party in droves for the Conservatives—a party that had done poorly in the province since the end of the nineteenth century—only to return to the Liberals in next election. With a Conservative victory imminent in 1984, Quebec voters again swung their allegiance from the Liberals to the Conservative Party. But only nine years later the Conservatives could not elect a single member from Quebec and the BQ, which had existed for only a couple of years, won most of the seats from the province and received close to half of the popular vote. Support for the BQ was widely seen as a means whereby nationalist Quebec voters could leverage their province's influence within the House of Commons without having to make the compromises with English-speaking Canada that were necessary in the Liberal and Conservative parties. These dramatic swings in Quebecers' party preferences have been interpreted by many as evidence of strategic voting in a province whose citizens recognize that it is *pas comme les autres*.

The fact that four out of 10 Quebec voters cast a ballot for the NDP in 2011 was seen as the latest instance of this putative tendency towards strategic voting. When the NDP edged closer to the Liberals in the polls and then appeared to be about level with them just after the midpoint of the campaign, media speculation on the possibility of a coalition government led by the NDP became rampant. We cannot know for certain whether a significant number of voters who usually would have voted either Liberal or BQ decided to vote for the NDP for strategic reasons, thinking that Jack Layton's party might actually head a coalition government. We do know, however, that polls in Quebec showed Layton to be more popular than the other party leaders. If strategic reasoning was an important part of the mix of factors that contributed to the massive shift in Quebecers' party preferences in 2011, the gamble did not pay off. The Conservatives won a clear majority nationally and the possibility of an NDP-led coalition melted away along with the last snow in the province of Quebec.

The 2011 election appeared to be all about change and, indeed, the changes were significant. But buried underneath the focus on the NDP surge, the BQ collapse, and the Liberals' worst showing in the party's history were two important elements of continuity. First, issues appeared to take a back seat to the leaders and their perceived strengths and shortcomings. As we saw earlier in this chapter, this is something that André Siegfried remarked upon over 100 years ago: the tendency for Canadian elections to be contests between the parties' leaders rather than struggles between rival ideas and ideologies. This is only partly correct, however. It is not that ideas do not matter in Canadian elections, but rather that they become associated with and absorbed into images that voters have of the party leaders and, in the process, lose some of their independent force. The electoral conversation is not bereft of policy ideas and promises. But these are refracted through perceptions of the party leaders. Leadership becomes the pre-eminent issue and this necessarily focuses attention on what are believed to be the personal attributes of the men and women who lead the parties.

Second, the election results demonstrate that Canada is a 60/40 country. The Conservative Party, the only party with a centre-right platform, won with about 40 per cent of the popular vote. The four centre-left parties, the Liberals being the most centrist of this group, together accounted for about 60 per cent of the vote. This has been the pattern for the past three decades, with the exception of 1984 when the Conservative Party won 50 per cent of the popular vote. Otherwise the electorate has tended to divide ideologically on a 60/40 basis, centre-left parties receiving the majority of the votes cast in these elections. Of course, we can quibble about whether the Liberal Party became a more right-leaning than left-leaning party during the mid- to late 1990s, when Paul Martin was Minister of Finance and leaner government appeared to be the priority. But ideological characterizations are relative and the Liberal brand, as most commentators agree, has always been a bit to left of the Conservative brand on the Canadian ideological spectrum. In the eight elections from 1988 to 2011 the percentage of the vote received by centre-right parties (a category that includes the Progressive Conservative Party, the Reform Party, the Canadian Alliance, and the Conservative Party of Canada) has ranged between 29.6 per cent (2004) and 43 per cent (1988), averaging just over 37 per cent.

Canada is a country in which the balance of the electorate leans towards the centre-left of the Canadian political spectrum. History will show whether the 2011 election results and the surge of the NDP is a one-off affair or the harbinger of realignment in the party system. Some believe that victory for the left in Canada now requires that the centre-left parties unite, as the right united in the 2003 merger of the Canadian Alliance and the Progressive Conservative Party. What is overlooked in this scenario is that some of those who run for office as Liberals and who vote for that party would find life more congenial under the Conservative Party banner than in a centre-left party that includes and might be dominated by activists and supporters of the NDP. As mentioned earlier in this chapter, some prominent members of both the Liberal Party and the NDP have talked openly about what they see as the need to unite the left to take electoral advantage of the fact that most Canadians appear to cluster around the centre-left of the ideological spectrum. But as the dust settled after the 2011 election, it did not appear that a merger of any sort was imminent.

Selecting Party Leaders in Canada

When Wilfrid Laurier was chosen as the first French-Canadian leader of the Liberal Party in 1887, about 80 men did the choosing. They were the Liberal MPs in Canada's Sixth Parliament. Laurier's candidacy was promoted by Edward Blake, then leader of the party, after Blake's poor showing in the 1887 general election. Some prominent members of the Liberal Party opposed Laurier as leader, but in the end he had no serious opposition for the post. The rules that were followed in this leadership selection process were not written down in any formal document. It was simply understood that, following the British parliamentary tradition, it was the prerogative of caucus to choose who among its members would be the party leader.

When the Liberal Party of Canada chose Stéphane Dion as its new leader on 3 December 2006, 4,605 delegates cast ballots in Montreal's Palais des Congrès. About 850 of them were *ex officio delegates*, men and women who because of their positions in the Liberal Party—including elected MPs and provincial legislators, senators, and party officials—automatically had the right to attend and vote at the party's leadership convention. All of these delegates cast their ballots on the final day of a five-day party convention that was covered on live television, choosing among a field of eight candidates. It took four ballots to select the party's new leader, following formal rules laid down in the 23-page Rules of Procedure for the 2006 Leadership and Biennial Convention.

Shortly before the Liberals' 2006 leadership convention Jeffrey Simpson wrote a column entitled 'It's tough to be ahead'. And, indeed, in the wake of Michael Ignatieff's defeat and Stéphane Dion's unpredicted victory the conventional wisdom quickly became that there are serious drawbacks to being the frontrunner. The scrutiny is more intense, the analysis and criticism of every word and action more unforgiving. Being an underdog, on the other hand—but not too much of an underdog!—has the advantage of freeing a candidate from this unremitting media spotlight and, potentially, enabling him or her to profit from an 'anybody-but-frontrunner-X' movement on the convention floor.

As plausible as all this sounds, it is also incorrect. If one looks at all the Conservative, Liberal, and NDP leadership conventions that required more than one ballot to choose the leader—16 in total—13 were won by the candidate who led on the first ballot. The only exceptions were the Progressive Conservative Party conventions of 1976 (Joe Clark was third on the first ballot and won on the fourth) and 1983 (Brian Mulroney was second on the first ballot and won on the fourth) and the Liberal convention of 2006 (Dion was third on the first ballot and won on the fourth). If there is a lesson to be drawn from the history of leadership conventions in Canada it is that there is a huge advantage to being the frontrunner heading into the convention vote.

In particular circumstances, however, this frontrunner advantage may be absent, as was true in the case of the 2006 Liberal convention. Looking back on the three frontrunners who failed to hang onto their leads (Claude Wagner at the Conservative convention of 1976; Joe Clark at the Conservative convention of 1983; and Michael Ignatieff at the Liberal convention of 2006), the fact that stands out is *not* the wide distribution of initial delegate support between several candidates or the relatively small share of total votes received by the frontrunner on the first ballot. Joe Clark, for example, received 36.5 per cent of first ballot votes in 1983 and eventually lost, whereas Robert Stanfield received only 23.3 per cent in 1967 and Pierre Trudeau received 31.5 per cent in 1968, and the latter two ultimately won. Michael Ignatieff captured 29.3 per cent on the first ballot but was unable to build sufficiently on this initial delegate support.

What does stand out as the common factor running through the failed candidacies of Wagner, Clark, and Ignatieff was the polarizing nature of each man's candidacy. Wagner was a French Canadian running for the leadership of a party that had never had a leader from French Canada. By itself, this fact may not have been decisive. Nevertheless, media accounts at the time suggested that many English-speaking delegates, particularly from the West, resented the idea of choosing a French-Canadian leader from Quebec. Wagner's somewhat tenuous connection to the Progressive Conservative Party—he had been a long-time member of Quebec's Union Nationale—simply reinforced many delegates' perception of him as something of an outsider who did not truly represent the party and its values.

Joe Clark, the candidate who eventually defeated Wagner by a narrow margin on the fourth ballot, was in turn the polarizing candidate at the party's 1983 convention. That convention had been called as a result of Clark's insistence that anything less than an overwhelming endorsement of his leadership at the party's biennial conference in December 1982 would be tantamount to a vote of non-confidence in his leadership. He received the endorsement of only two-thirds of delegates at that 1983 Winnipeg convention, about the same level of support that he had received two years earlier at the party's Ottawa convention. Clark's leadership had been under fire by some within the party since the unexpected fall of his minority government in December 1979 and their subsequent defeat by the Liberals in the 1980 general election. A selection of his frontbench MPs, people who had served under him during his short-lived government, ran against him for the leadership. Many in the party and in the media saw Clark as a weak leader who lacked the ability to defeat the Liberals. An 'Anybody but Clark' ('ABC') movement developed during the campaign and continued onto the convention floor, where strategic voting benefited two of Clark's rivals, John Crosbie and Brian Mulroney, until Mulroney finally emerged victorious on the fourth ballot.

The defeat of Michael Ignatieff on the fourth ballot of the 2006 Liberal convention, as in the case of both Wagner and Clark, may be attributed to the polarizing nature of his candidacy. Ignatieff had lived outside of Canada for most of his adult life, in some of his writings he had expressed himself as though he were American, and he had returned to Canada and joined the Liberal Party only a couple of years before running for its leadership, but these were probably not the main reasons for the anti-Ignatieff sentiment that became increasingly apparent as the convention approached. More serious were the ideas and policies that he was seen to represent.

As an academic, documentarist, and public intellectual of considerable reputation, Ignatieff had left an extensive paper trail. His views on such controversial matters as the decision to depose Saddam Hussein in Iraq (he had supported it), rethinking post–Geneva Convention ideas about torture (like his erstwhile Harvard colleague, Alan Dershowitz, he was open to this), and maintaining a Canadian combat presence in Afghanistan (he was for this) put him on the wrong side of important issues in the eyes of many Liberal convention delegates. Related to all of these issues was a sense that Ignatieff was a bit too close to Americans, or at least not convincing enough in his Canadian nationalism (which inevitably requires distance between Canada and the United States and, usually, staking out an anti-American stand on key issues). Ignatieff was aware of this sentiment and even included a video on his campaign website in which he was critical of anti-Americanism.

In the end, however, Ignatieff's candidacy had too little potential for growth over a multi-ballot convention. Figure 10.1 shows that his vote total increased only gradually after the first ballot and that Stéphane Dion clearly was the chief beneficiary of the movement that took place once some delegates' preferred candidates dropped off the ballot. It is often said that governments lose elections; their opponents don't win them. The same may be said of at least some leadership races where the frontrunner's candidacy polarizes delegates. The 2006 Liberal convention was such a case. While it is indeed true that Stéphane Dion won the party's leadership, the story of his victory is, in an important sense, the story of Ignatieff's loss. It was, as well, a consequence of the fact that Ignatieff was not the only leading candidate carrying 'anyone-but' baggage. In second place through the first two ballots was Bob Rae, who normally might have been expected to capitalize from the negative attitudes

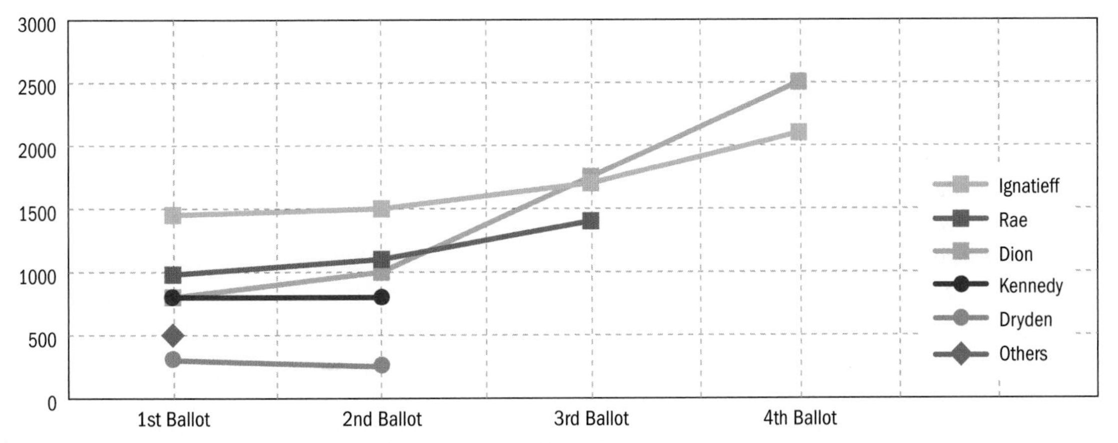

FIGURE 10.1 The Dynamic of the 2006 Liberal Convention Vote

of some delegates towards Ignatieff, his old college roommate. But Rae, as a former NDP Premier of Ontario and former NDP MP, also had turned to the Liberal Party for a run at the brass ring. His past NDP affiliation was a problem, to be sure, and he was an unacceptable alternative to many delegates who remembered unfavourably his term as Ontario Premier during the recession of the early 1990s.

Listen to the 'Who Is Michael Ignatieff? What Our Leaders' Stories Say about Canadian Politics' podcast, available at www.oupcanada.com/Brooks7e

Interestingly, a combination of factors following the 2008 election led to Ignatieff assuming the Liberal helm without a leadership convention:

- A coalition of Liberal and NDP members of Parliament, with the support of the Bloc, intended to topple the Conservative minority on a confidence vote and seek to form a coalition government.
- The proposed leader of the coalition, and, therefore, the Prime-Minister-in-waiting, was none other than Stéphane Dion, who had already announced he would step down following a Liberal leadership convention in May 2009.
- In early December, Conservative Prime Minister Harper convinced the Governor General to agree to the prorogation, or suspension, of Parliament until late January 2009 to avoid defeat on a confidence vote.
- The Liberals, as the largest parliamentary party in the proposed coalition, were loath to continue with Dion as the leader, given that, with the NDP and the Bloc, there still remained the possibility of defeating the Conservatives at the first opportunity, which would mean either a new election or the coalition taking control of the government.
- Finally, there was division within the Liberal Party over the wisdom of the coalition strategy. This division became apparent when the Conservative government managed to stave off a confidence vote through prorogation and public opinion polls showed that Quebec was the only province in which a majority of voters favoured the idea of a Liberal–NDP coalition backed by the BQ. Ignatieff had stayed carefully at the margins of the coalition plan, out of the media glare, whereas Bob Rae had been very active in its promotion.

The Liberals clearly could not wait until May 2009 for a new leader, and when it became obvious that Ignatieff was the favoured choice of the majority in the Liberal caucus and within the party's elite, Bob Rae, the only other high-profile candidate for the Liberal leadership, stepped aside. Ignatieff thus became interim leader of the party, and in all likelihood would be acclaimed leader at the May 2009 convention, if events by then had not thrust him into the prime ministership by one route or another. It was a case of a return to a distant past, as the Liberals effectively selected a leader in a manner they had not employed since the selection of Laurier in the late nineteenth century.

Three Models for Selecting Party Leaders

The 2006 Liberal leadership convention involved a method for choosing party leaders that began in Canada in 1919. That year marked the transition from the *caucus model*, where party leaders were chosen by other elected MPs of their party, to the *convention model* (see Table 10.2). In some ways this transition was a simple product of circumstances. Wilfrid Laurier had called a national convention of the Liberal Party in 1919 to discuss policy at a time when the party was reduced to mainly Quebec representation in the House of Commons. Laurier died soon after the convention was called and the party's national executive decided to use the Ottawa meeting as an opportunity to choose his successor. In doing so they were breaking new ground. In no other British parliamentary democracy were party leaders chosen in this manner. Presidential candidates in the United States were, of course, selected at conventions that brought together state delegations. In adopting the convention model for their party—a model that would also be followed by other Canadian parties—Liberals were aware of the American practice. But the Canadian convention model has always been different from the American one in important ways, from the process used to choose convention delegates to procedures on the convention floor.

Criticisms that the convention model was elitist and too easily dominated by money and backroom deal-making were heard with increasing frequency after the 1960s. When the Reform Party began to choose its leaders through a direct vote of all party members the pressure on other parties to follow suit was difficult to resist. In 1997 the Bloc Québécois chose Gilles Duceppe as its leader using the one-member, one-vote (OMOV) model. The Progressive Conservative Party followed in 1998, choosing Joe Clark as its leader using the OMOV model, and today all of the parties except the Liberals use some variant of the OMOV model.

Whether this model produces better results than the caucus or convention models depends on what one means by 'better'. The argument for OMOV is that it democratizes the leadership selection process, broadening the scope of participation and

TABLE 10.2 Three Models of Leadership Selection

Model 1	Model 2	Model 3
Party Caucus	Party Activists (narrow)	Party Activists (broad)
Few and closed ——	——	—— Many and open
Participants		
Elected members of the party (i.e., MPs)	Party members elected by members of their riding associations to serve as delegates at the leadership convention, plus ex officio delegates*	Party members
Procedures		
Selection takes place behind closed doors, often without competition between rival candidates	Selection takes place at a party leadership convention, often after several months of campaigning	Selection takes place through votes cast by party members: some voting may take place at a fixed convention site but most votes are cast electronically by party members who are elsewhere
Examples		
Liberal Party: Mackenzie, 1873; Blake, 1880; Laurier, 1887; Ignatieff, 2008	Liberal Party: King, 1919; St Laurent, 1948; Pearson, 1958; Trudeau, 1968; Turner, 1984; Chrétien, 1990; Martin, 2003; Dion, 2006	
Conservative Party: Macdonald, 1867; Abbott, 1891; Thompson, 1892; Bowell, 1894; Tupper, 1896; Borden, 1901; Meighen, 1920; Gutherie, 1926; Meighen, 1941	Conservative Party: Bennett, 1927; Manion, 1938; Bracken, 1942; Drew, 1948; Diefenbaker, 1956; Stanfield, 1967; Clark, 1976; Mulroney, 1983; Charest, 1995	Conservative Party:** Clark, 1998; Harper, 2004
CCF-NDP	CCF-NDP Woodsworth, 1933; Caldwell, 1942; Argue, 1960; Douglas, 1961; Lewis, 1971; Broadbent, 1975; McLaughlin, 1989; McDonough, 1995; McDonough, 2001	NDP Layton, 2003
Bloc Québécois Bouchard, 1990	Bloc Québécois Bouchard, 1991	Bloc Québécois Duceppe, 1997

*An ex officio delegate is one whose formal position entitles him or her to a vote in the choice of party leader. Elected MPs and party office-holders would be examples of these delegates.

**The Reform Party's successor, the Canadian Alliance Party, used Model 3 in choosing Stockwell Day as its leader in 2000.

thereby reducing the influence of elites within the party. Combined with limitations that all of the parties place on leadership campaign spending and the contribution limits and reporting requirements that have existed under Canadian law since 2004, this is expected to make leadership races more open, less about who has the most dollars and more about who has the most supporters within the rank and file of the party. It is hard to argue against such aims. At the same time, however, it is not yet clear that these reforms to the leadership selection process produce leaders who are more likely to be successful at winning elections and holding together the different elements that exist within any political party. Indeed, only one leader can win any given election, at least in regard to being able to form a government, and it might be argued that the many face-to-face meetings that are central to the convention model have been extremely important in creating nationwide unity and focus within Canadian political parties.

The Electoral System and Its Consequences

Many Canadians were shocked and even scandalized when George W. Bush was elected President of the United States in 2000, even though he received about one-half million fewer votes than Al Gore. What they did not realize is that such an outcome can and has happened in Canada. In 1979 the Liberal Party received about 4 per cent more of the popular vote than the Conservatives, but the Conservatives won 22 more seats and formed the government. In the 1998 provincial election in Quebec, the Quebec Liberal Party won 43.7 per cent of the popular vote compared to 42.7 per cent for the Parti Québécois. Despite this the PQ won a strong majority of seats in Quebec's National Assembly. It occasionally happens that the party that wins a provincial or federal election in Canada is not the party that wins in the popular vote. Even more common, however, is the situation where the governing party is elected on the strength of only 38–40 per cent of the popular vote. Canadians who were scandalized by George W. Bush's victory in 2000 would do well to consider that Bush won a larger share of the eligible electorate than did Jean Chrétien's Liberal Party in the Canadian election of that same year. But no one seriously contested the legitimacy of Chrétien's victory.

Canada's electoral system does not reward parties in proportion to their share of the popular vote. The Conservative Party, whose candidates garnered just under 40 per cent of the popular vote in the 2011 election, won 54.2 per cent of all seats in the House of Commons. On the other hand, the 12 per cent of the popular vote that the Conservatives received in the Greater Montreal area translated into none of the 34 seats from that metropolitan region. The Liberals received 18.9 per cent of the popular vote but only 11 per cent of the seats in the Commons while the NDP, for the first time in its history, was over-rewarded by the electoral system, winning 30.6 per cent of the popular vote but electing 33.1 per cent of all MPs. But the prize for apparent injustice was taken by the Green Party, whose 3.9 per cent of the popular vote produced only one seat in the House of Commons, and by the Bloc Québécois, whose 6 per cent of the popular vote translated into 1.3 per cent of all seats in the House of Commons.

To understand what happened in recent elections, we must first describe the Canadian electoral system, whose principal features are the same at both the federal and provincial levels. It is based on the **single-member constituency**: one person is elected to represent the citizens of a particular geographic area called a constituency or riding. The candidate who receives the most votes in a constituency election becomes the member of Parliament (or provincial legislator) for that constituency. This is called a **plurality system**. A majority of votes is not necessary for election and, given the fragmentation of votes between the three main parties, is the exception rather than the rule.

A political party's representation in the House of Commons will depend, therefore, on how well its candidates fare in the 308 constituency races that make up a general election today. It regularly happens that, nationally, the leading party's candidates may account for only about 40 per cent of the popular vote and yet capture a majority of the seats in the Commons. Indeed, the advocates of the single-member, simple plurality electoral system point to this as the system's chief virtue. It manages, they claim, to transform something less than a majority of votes for a party into a majority of seats, thereby delivering stable majority government. (In fact, however, the system's performance on this count has been rather mediocre. Nine of the 19 general elections from 1957 to 2011 produced minority governments, although majority governments do remain in power for a longer period of time before an election is called.)

The chief alternative to the single-member, plurality electoral system is some form of **proportional representation** (PR). Under a PR system, the number of members elected by each party about coincides with its share of the popular vote. This sounds eminently fair, but PR has its critics. Detractors criticize it on three main counts. First, they claim that it promotes a splintering of the party system, encouraging the creation of minor parties that represent very narrow interests and undermining the development of broad-based national parties capable of bridging sectional rivalries and the differences between special interests. Second, proportional representation is said to produce unstable government. The unlikelihood that any party will have a majority of seats and, therefore, the need to cobble together and maintain a coalition government result in more frequent elections. And even between elections, the inter-party deals necessary to maintain a coalition government may paralyze cabinet decision-making. Countries such as Italy and Belgium, where governments seldom lasted longer than a year or two during much of the post–World War II era, are said to illustrate the horrors of PR (curiously, proportional systems with a relatively low level of executive turnover, such as the Netherlands and Germany, are seldom mentioned by the critics).

A third standard criticism of PR systems is that they encourage ideological polarity and enable extremist parties to achieve representation in the legislature. There is no doubt that countries having proportional electoral systems do tend to have more political parties than those with plurality systems, and the ideological distance between the extreme ends of the party spectrum will inevitably be greater than that separating Canada's major parties, or Democrats and Republicans in the United States (another plurality electoral system). In fact, however, the ideological distance between those parties in proportional systems that are likely to be the senior partners of any government coalition tends to be no greater than between, say, the Liberal Party and the NDP in Canada. Moreover, not everyone would agree that more, rather than less, ideological dispersion between parties is a bad thing. One might argue that it improves voters' ability to distinguish between parties on the basis of the values and policies they represent. The prospect that extremist parties will infiltrate the legislature through a proportional system is also less worrisome than is claimed by detractors. Both theory and experience suggest that the closer a party gets to membership in a governing coalition, the more moderate its behaviour will be.[20]

The 'winner-take-all' electoral system that exists in Canada is not without its own detractors. In a classic analysis, Alan Cairns identifies several consequences for Canada's party system and national unity that flow from the single-member, simple plurality system.[21]

- It tends to produce more seats than votes for the strongest major party and for minor parties whose support is regionally concentrated.
- It gives the impression that some parties have no or little support in certain regions, when in fact their candidates may regularly account for 15–30 per cent of the popular vote.
- The parliamentary composition of a party will be less representative of the different regions of the country than is that party's electoral support.
- Minor parties whose appeal is to interests that are distributed widely across the country will receive a smaller percentage of seats than votes.

Cairns concludes that the overall impact of Canada's electoral system has been negative. The system has, he argues, exacerbated regional and ethnolinguistic divisions in Canadian political life by shutting out the Conservative Party in Quebec for most of the last century and giving the impression that the Liberal Party was the only national party with support in French Canada. Cairns's article on the electoral system's effects was written in the late 1960s. If it were written today it would also mention, among other consequences, the gross under-representation of the Liberals in western Canada over the last couple of decades, despite their receiving between one-quarter and one-third of western votes in most elections, and the failure of the Reform Party to elect a single member from Ontario in 1997 and Alliance's election of a mere two Ontario MPs in 2000, despite receiving more votes in that province than in the three westernmost provinces combined. As William Irvine observes, 'the electoral system confers a spurious image of unanimity on provinces. By magnifying the success of the provincial vote leader, the electoral system ensures that party caucuses will over-represent any party's "best" province.'[22] And this is not the only quirk of our electoral system.

Along with the distortions that Canada's electoral system produces, another argument for reform is that the present system leaves many voters feeling disempowered and contributes to low levels of voter turnout. This view has become increasingly popular in recent years, and is reflected in what has become known as 'strategic voting', whereby a voter in a particular riding will cast his or her ballot not for the party or candidate of choice but for the party or candidate with the greatest likelihood of defeating the projected frontrunner in that riding. Such a phenomenon might be a reasonably compelling argument for reform of the electoral system, but little evidence beyond the anecdotal suggests that it exists. Those who study voting behaviour have been unable to find evidence that any significant number of Canadians vote strategically—on the contrary, there appear to be many cases where labour groups have advocated such voting, without any indication that this has had the desired effect—although there is stronger evidence that voter disillusionment with the choices on offer may cause some to stay home on election day.

Voter turnout in federal elections declined over the last several elections until 2006, reaching bottom at about 58 per cent of the eligible electorate in 2004 before rebounding to 65 per cent in 2006. It fell off again to only 59 per cent in 2008 and then increased marginally to 61.5 per cent in 2011. However, this overall decline in voter participation could be caused by other factors, such as a generalized dissatisfaction with parties and politics, independent of any sense that one's vote may be futile because of the electoral system. There is absolutely no definitive proof that voters' perceptions of the electoral system's impact on the probable consequences of each person's vote influences the likelihood that they will go to the polls on election day.

Historically, the party that has stood to gain most from the replacement of Canada's electoral system by some form of proportional representation has been the CCF-NDP. It received a smaller percentage of total seats in the Commons than its share of the national vote in every general election until it was slightly over-rewarded by the electoral system in 2011. Irvine's point about the tendency of the electoral system to magnify the success of the most popular party in a province and punish those parties whose share of the vote does not achieve some critical mass has certainly been borne out by recent election results. Reform received 20 per cent of the Ontario vote in 1993, coming in second behind the Liberals' 53 per cent, but was rewarded with only one seat to the Liberals' 98. Reform's share of the Ontario vote dropped by only one percentage point in 1997, but it failed to elect a single member from the province. In the 2000 election Alliance candidates captured almost one-quarter of the votes cast in Ontario, good enough for almost 2 per cent of the province's seats! This helped fuel the misperception of Alliance as being merely a western party, when in fact over one million votes, representing about one-third of all votes cast for the Alliance Party, were received in Ontario. Given the realities of political life, however, there is no reason to imagine that either the Liberal or Conservative Party is likely to champion electoral reform, let alone adopt proportional representation. Their dominance would almost certainly be eroded by such a system, and strategic voting, which some believe has tended to draw votes away from the NDP and, more recently, perhaps the Green Party, would cease to be a factor in the ballot-box decisions of voters. It is too soon to know if the Liberal Party's disastrous showing in the 2011 election and the NDP's surge into second place will change how supporters of these parties view the existing electoral system.

Canadians probably will just have to live with the regionally divisive effects of the existing electoral system. The best hope for overcoming the negative consequences that Cairns, Irvine, and many others have pointed to may be reform of the Canadian Senate. An elected Senate whose members would be chosen according to some system of proportional representation within each province—so that a party's share of Senate seats for a province would be determined by its share of the provincial popular vote—could go some way towards overcoming the regionally unrepresentative character of parties' caucuses in the House of Commons. This would depend, however, on the Senate becoming a more respected and effective branch of the legislature than it is at present. A Senate with greater legitimacy in the eyes of Canadians, and in which members felt free to vote on the basis of regional and other interests, free of the tight leash of party discipline, could be a step towards the better representation of the regions within the institutions of the national government. In other words, it would be a Senate functioning more on the lines of the United States Senate. The obstacles to Senate reform in Canada, however, including the reluctance of the major federal parties to encourage a serious institutional rival to the powers of the Prime Minister and the House of Commons, are significant.

One of the critiques of Canada's single-member, plurality electoral system is that it leaves many voters feeling disempowered and leads to low voter turnout. The 2008 federal election saw the second lowest voter participation in the history of the country, with only 59.1 per cent of the eligible voters casting a ballot.

Giving it an elected basis would certainly increase its legitimacy in the eyes of Canadians and would probably improve the calibre of representatives found in the Senate. If this happened, it is easily conceivable that senators would routinely be appointed to cabinet, rather than exceptionally as is currently the practice. In such circumstances no major party should have difficulty in putting together a government with a fair share of representation from all regions of the country. At the same time, an unreformed House of Commons would have the virtue of retaining the Canadian tradition of individual representatives for citizens—MPs who are accountable to electors in local **constituencies**. Little in our recent political history, however, suggests that major reforms to the Senate are imminent.

Voting Behaviour

When it comes to the voting behaviour of Canadians, few generalizations withstand the test of time. During the first couple of decades after Confederation, the Conservative Party did better than the Liberals among Catholics and French

Canadians, but this changed after the 1885 execution of the Métis leader Louis Riel under a Conservative government and the 1887 selection of Wilfrid Laurier—a Catholic francophone from Quebec—as leader of the Liberal Party. For most of the following century the Liberal Party fared better than the Conservatives among francophones and Catholics, although their support among these groups temporarily weakened in the 1958 election and again in the 1984 and 1988 elections.

Regionally, the Conservative Party began its long association with western voters in 1957 with the election of the Diefenbaker government. Conservative candidates outpolled Liberals and the party elected more MPs from the four westernmost provinces in most elections after 1957. This

Politics in Focus

Box 10.5 The French Run-off System

Electoral systems are vitally connected to constitutions. Those who propose significant reforms to a country's system of electing politicians need to be aware that such changes may, and probably will, produce important domino effects throughout their system of government. Proportional representation, if adopted, would almost certainly guarantee that Canada would regularly have coalition governments, partnerships between two or more political parties that would divide cabinet representation between them. This would produce important changes in the dynamic of party relations in the legislature, in government accountability, and possibly even in election campaigning.

Another reform that may appear attractive, but that would also produce far-reaching changes, is the French run-off system. Along with several other countries, France elects its President separately from the members of its legislature, the elections taking place at different times. Moreover, in order to ensure that the President has the support of most people, French presidential elections involve two stages. The first is a run-off election in which several parties' candidates are on the ballot, although it is usually the case that only a couple of them receive more than about 20–30 per cent of the popular vote apiece. The two candidates receiving the most votes move on two weeks later to the decisive presidential election that will produce a majority for one of them. And thus does *la république française* elect a leader who has the support of a majority of the people.

There is something obviously appealing to the idea of a system guaranteed to produce majority support for the country's foremost leader in elections where voters are given the chance to vote directly for the person they want to lead the country. Other things being equal, it appears to confer on him or her much greater legitimacy than a leader of a party that won only 35–40 per cent of the popular vote, the percentage often received by the governing party in Canada. But such a system also requires that the head of government or head of state (in France, the President is the head of state and the Prime Minister, appointed by the President, is head of government, but the President is clearly the national leader) be elected separately from the legislature. Decoupling the executive from the legislative branch in this manner would involve a profound change in Canada's system of government. It might even seem to lead towards an American-style system of separation of powers. But this need not be so. The French preserve an important accountability and policy-making linkage between these branches of government by giving the President the authority to select the Prime Minister and other members of the government, who are elected members of the legislature.

As matters currently stand in Canada, only those who reside in the riding for which the Prime Minister is the member of Parliament have directly voted for (or against) him or her. And in choosing their MP, Canadian voters must weigh what they think about the local candidates against who they would like to be leader of the country. Would the greater Cartesian clarity of the French be an improvement, or might it bring along its own set of problems?

tendency was accentuated after the 1972 election. The Liberal Party's fortunes in the West sank dramatically under the leadership of Pierre Trudeau and the region became thought of as mainly Conservative and NDP turf. The Reform Party, we have seen, became the vehicle for this anti-Liberal resentment after many western voters became disappointed with the behaviour in office of the Conservative government of Brian Mulroney. A pox on both your houses, westerners seemed to say.

Quebec appeared to be an electoral stronghold for the Liberal Party over most of the last century. But this association was weakened with the emergence of the Bloc Québécois. The BQ has outpolled the Liberals in six of the seven general elections since 1993, and in 2006 a resurgent Conservative Party received more votes in Quebec than the Liberals and only two percentage points fewer in 2008, although winning fewer seats in both elections.

In regard to social class, differences between voters for the Liberal and Conservative parties have never been very great and certainly have been less important than regional and ethnolinguistic differences. The NDP's formal affiliation to organized labour might have been expected to reflect a preference among working-class Canadians for that party. But class is a complicated concept and, as we have seen, has never been a particularly strong political identity for most Canadians. Electoral studies carried out since the 1960s have shown that although NDP support generally is stronger among voters who belong to unions than among most other segments of the electorate, it has never been the case that a majority of working-class voters (whether this is defined by voter self-identification or by some objective measure of occupation) has opted for NDP candidates. This may have changed in the 2011 election, but we will not know until the results of the post-election voter surveys become available.

Figure 10.2 shows the breakdown of voter support for the Conservative, Liberal, and New Democratic parties along several dimensions for the 2008 election. Only voters outside Quebec have been included in this analysis. The two-party competition between the Liberals and the BQ between 1993 and 2004, and the continuing strong presence of the BQ in the subsequent 2006 and 2008 elections, made the Quebec case quite different from that among the rest of the Canadian electorate. Including Quebec voters in a national analysis of voting behaviour muddies the waters for the rest of Canada and so data for Quebec needs to be presented separately.

Two of the most widely accepted claims about Liberal/Conservative differences in voter support are that women are less likely than men to prefer the Conservative Party and that urban Canadians prefer the Liberals while rural voters tend to favour the Conservatives. The first claim is supported by the 2004 and 2006 election survey data, although an important qualification is required. As Figure 10.2 indicates, female voters were more likely to prefer the Conservative Party over either of the two other parties in English-speaking Canada. In 2006 the female vote was fairly evenly divided between the Liberal and Conservative parties, but male voters were significantly more likely to have voted Conservative. Regarding the second claim, urban voters were evenly divided between the Liberals and Conservatives in 2006, having given a slight edge to the Liberals in 2004, but rural voters were much more likely to have voted for the Conservatives.

This claim about the supposed rural/urban divide in Canadian politics had fresh wind blown in its sails by the results of the 2006 election. As evidence of this, the pundits—including many political scientists—pointed to the fact that the Liberals did well in Toronto, Montreal, and Vancouver, while the Conservatives did not win a single seat from these three cities and received slightly fewer than half the number of votes cast for their Liberal rivals.[23]

This interpretation was deeply flawed and provides a good illustration of how unfounded conclusions can be drawn from inadequate evidence. First of all, it is not true that all of Canada's largest urban centres were unsympathetic to the Conservative Party in 2006. The Halifax, Calgary, Edmonton, Winnipeg, Ottawa, Hamilton–Burlington, and Waterloo–Kitchener–Cambridge areas all elected Conservative MPs. Of the three cities cited as proof of urban Canada's hostility to the Conservatives, the case of Montreal, arguably, had far more to do with language and a decades-old history of voting Liberal than it did with the urban condition. Vancouver was also a weak reed on which to build

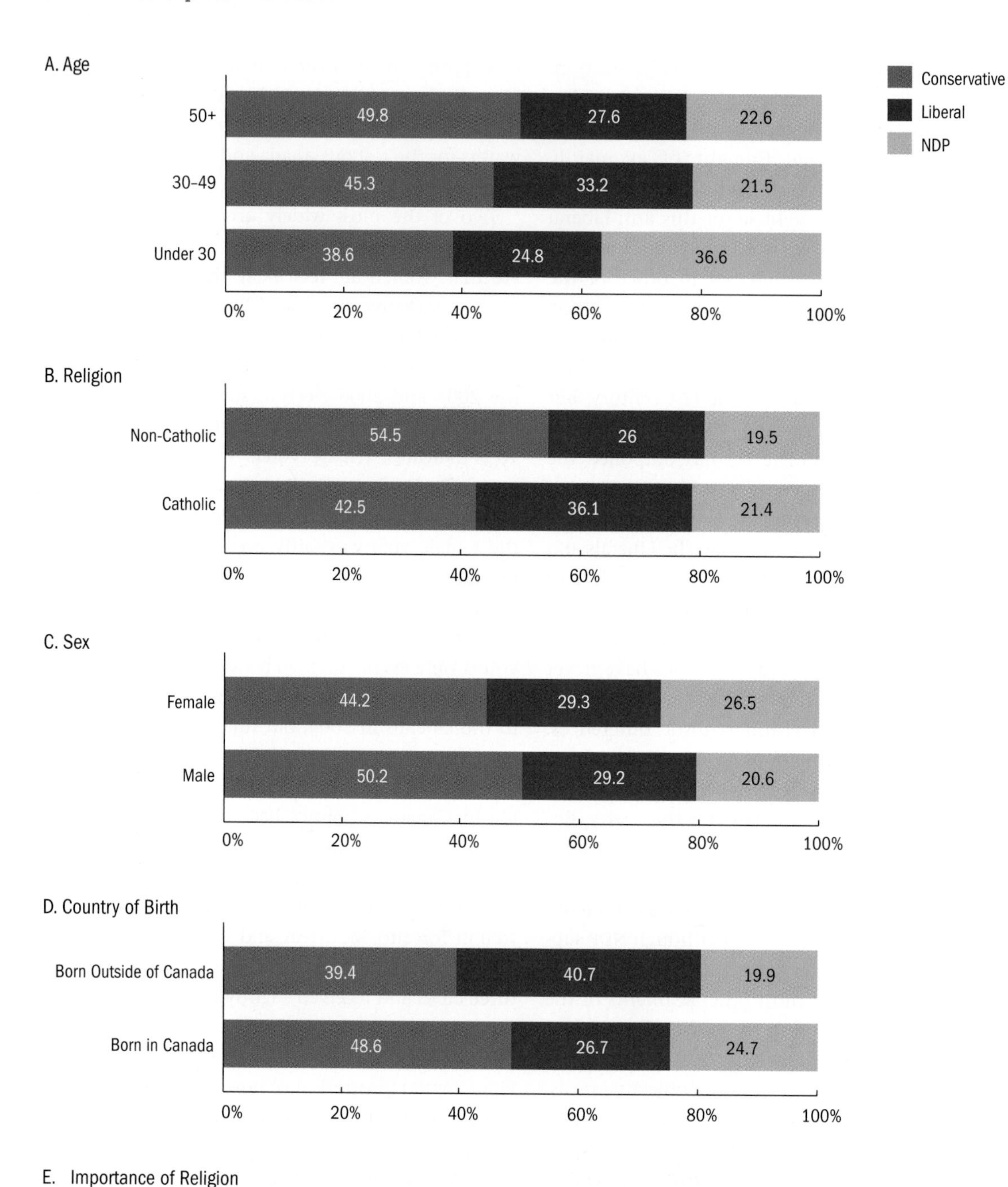

FIGURE 10.2 Voting Behaviour Outside Quebec, 2008 Election

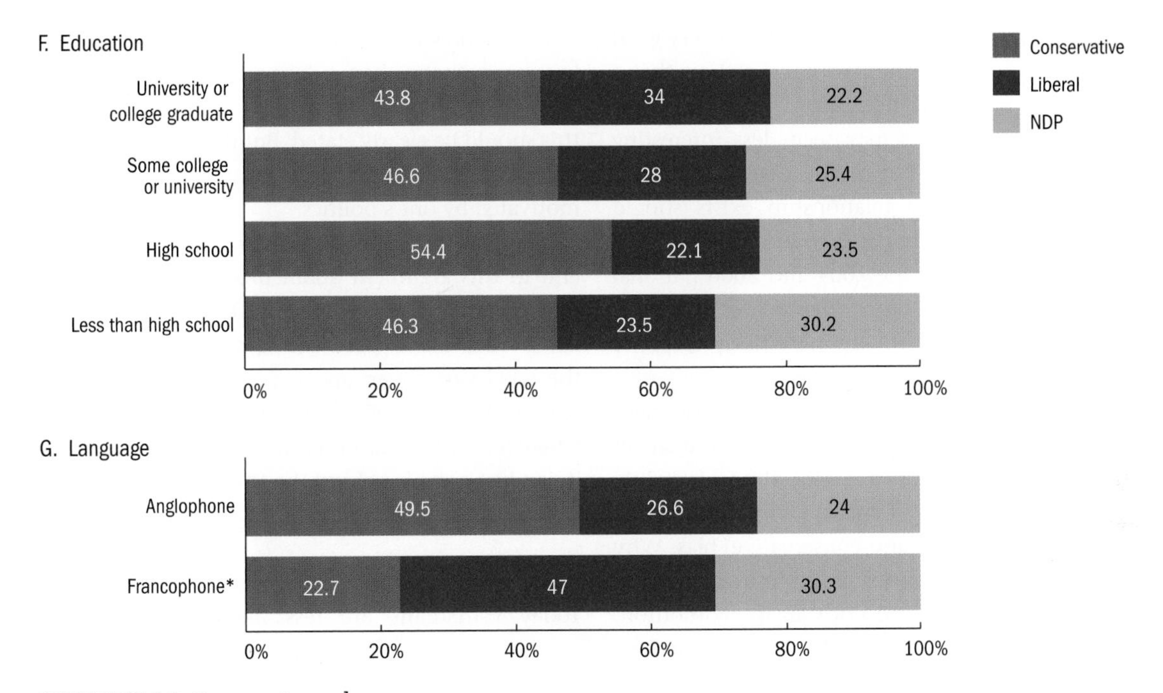

FIGURE 10.2 continued

*Of the 1,158 respondents outside Quebec, only 66 self-identified as francophones. Because of the small number of respondents in this category, caution is advised in interpreting results.

Source: Elections Canada. I am grateful to Professor Lydia Miljan for generating these cross-tabulations.

this argument about big cities being unsympathetic to the Conservative Party. The Vancouver results shown at the Elections Canada website that commentators relied on in making this claim about voter hostility towards the Conservatives included only the five ridings that make up the city of Vancouver, not the Greater Vancouver Regional District. Halifax is, in fact, larger than the Vancouver urban area covered by these five ridings, with almost 100,000 more registered voters and two more seats in Parliament, but analysts chose to focus on Vancouver.

The Greater Vancouver Regional District is, of course, far larger than the five constituencies included in the Elections Canada data, and some of the ridings outside the Vancouver core elected Conservatives, including Abbotsford, Delta–Richmond East, and South Surrey. And in a couple of the Vancouver area ridings that the Conservatives lost—Newton–North Delta and West Vancouver–Sunshine Coast—the Liberal margin over the Conservatives was slender. The same was true in several of the ridings on the edge of the Greater Toronto Area. The Conservatives tended to do much better in these ridings than in Toronto proper, winning in Burlington, Oshawa, Wellington–Halton Hills, Whitby–Oshawa, and York–Simcoe and losing by only a percentage point to the Liberals in Oakville. All of these constituencies are part of the wider Toronto conurbation.

What conclusions should one draw from the data on urban voting in 2006 and the conventional wisdom that voters in Canada's big cities were cooler than their small-town and country cousins to the Conservative Party? First, in their rush to be interesting and insightful, pollsters, pundits, and political scientists sometimes allow sloppiness to creep into their analysis. The idea that the conditions and demographics of big cities cause the values and partisan preferences of people who live in them to be significantly different from those who live in less urbanized settings seems reasonable and is certainly interesting. If the difference is, in fact, not very great or not consistently in the partisan direction that a theory of how urbanization affects values and voting would predict, this may seem less interesting and less newsworthy. But in any case, conclusions about whether such a relationship exists should be based on the polling data produced by national election surveys. Both the 2004 and 2006 national election surveys showed that urban voters in English Canada were only marginally more likely to prefer the Liberals over the Conservatives.

Second, the eagerness to accept the argument that the cities are on the left, politically, and small-town/rural Canada is on the right almost certainly reflected, on the part of many commentators, an anti-Conservative (and anti-conservative) bias. Why should Toronto, Vancouver, and Montreal be considered urban Canada and not Calgary, Edmonton, Halifax, Winnipeg, and Kitchener–Waterloo–Cambridge? Some will say that the reason is simply that Toronto, Vancouver, and Montreal are the three largest metropolitan areas in Canada. Fair enough, but then it would make sense to include the entire metropolitan region for each of these cities, which, as we have seen, was not done in the election results data reported by Elections Canada for Vancouver and relied on by commentators in their analysis of the alleged urban/rural divide. If one wants to argue that the cores of major Canadian cities tend to be less sympathetic than suburban and other regions to the Conservative Party—at least in 2006—then this should be clearly stated. But this is an argument that packs less punch, particularly if one's analysis is motivated by one's politics.

In any event, the 2008 and 2011 elections put an end to this argument about urban hostility to the Conservative Party. As Figure 10.3 shows, in 2011 the Conservatives were the most popular party in the GTA, Vancouver, and every other major urban region in Canada with the exceptions of Montreal, where it came in a distant fourth, and Halifax, where it was just a shade behind the NDP in popularity.

Political Participation

Today Canadians are less likely to vote than at almost any time since Confederation (see Figure 10.4). Indeed, in recent years they have been less likely to vote in national elections than have Americans in that country's presidential elections. Canadians are not, however, alone in staying away from the ballot box. Voter turnout has been slipping in Western democracies generally, a trend that has generated a good deal of hand-wringing about the health of democracies and various explanations for this decline in participation.

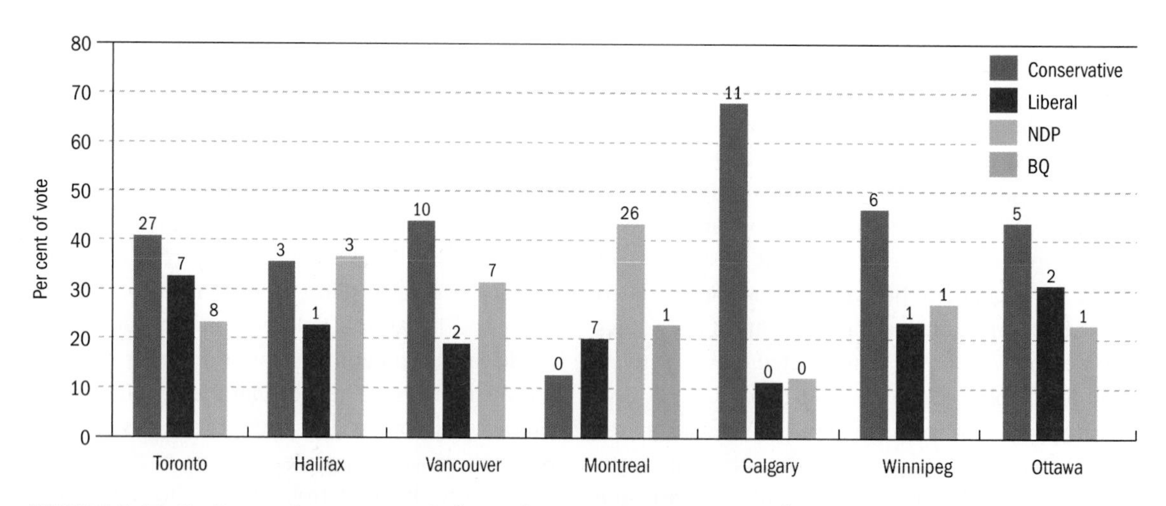

FIGURE 10.3 Party Support in Selected Major Cities, 2011 Election

Note: Numbers at top of bars indicate members elected.

Source: Elections Canada, at: <www.elections.ca>.

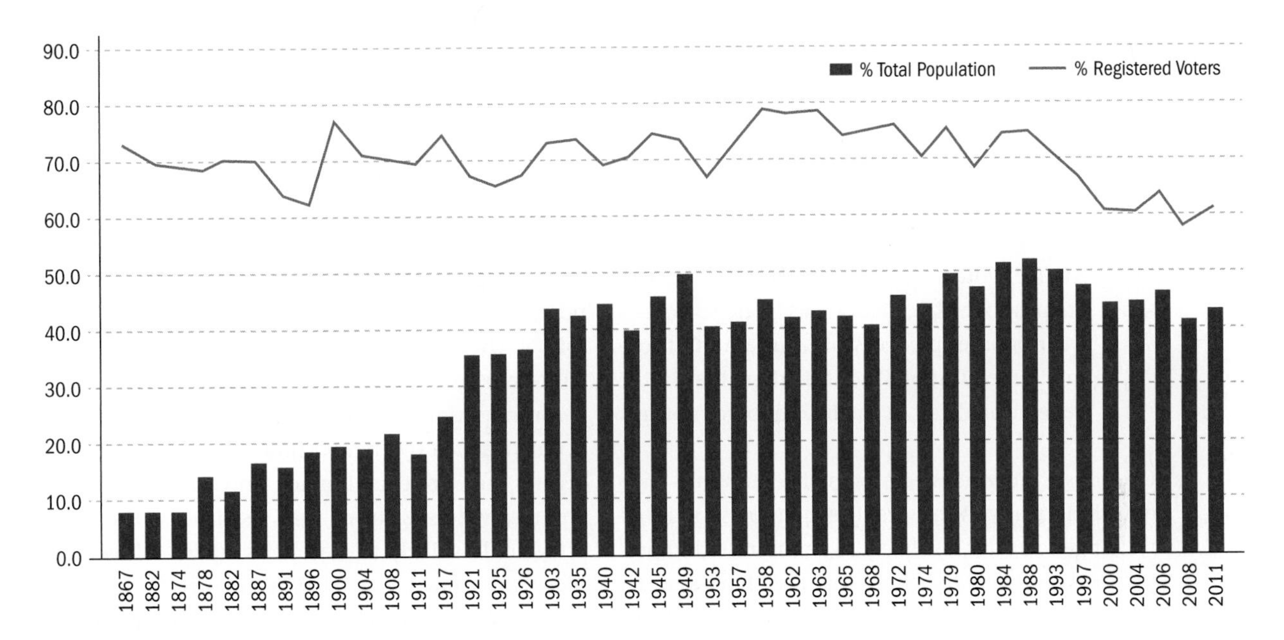

FIGURE 10.4 Voter Turnout, 1867–2011

Source: Website on Canadian elections maintained by Professor Andrew Heard, Department of Political Science, Simon Fraser University, at: <www.sfu.ca/~aheard/elections/historical-turnout.html>.

Two facts are clear, in Canada and elsewhere. Younger citizens are considerably less likely to vote than their older compatriots. Second, they vote at a lower rate than people their age did in the past. 'We know that age is the best predictor of voting,' write André Blais and his colleagues on the Canadian Election Study team, 'the older one is, the more likely one is to vote. The challenge is to unravel the meaning of that relationship, to ascertain whether this reflects a life cycle effect . . ., a generation effect . . . or both.'[24] The life cycle effect refers to the fact that people become more likely to vote as they grow older, a phenomenon generally attributed to changes in their life circumstances (entering a permanent relationship, having children, buying a home, establishing roots in a community) that cause them to feel more invested in their community and to recognize the relevance of government decisions to their own lives. The generation effect refers to the possibility that the members of a particular generation may be less likely than those of preceding ones to vote. This could be caused by various factors, such as a society-wide increase in cynicism about politics or a drop in those non-age factors known to be linked to the likelihood of voting, including years of formal education and political interest and knowledge.

Based on voter surveys between 1968 and 2000, Blais and his colleagues arrive at a number of conclusions with regard to declining voter turnout:

- There are important life cycle effects. For example, a person who is 30 is about 8–11 percentage points more likely to vote than someone 20 years old. The likelihood of voting increases by about 15 percentage points from age 20 to age 50.[25]
- There is a clear generational effect. Comparing voters in the same age cohort but belonging to different generations (for example, a 25-year-old baby boomer surveyed for the 1974 election study and a 25-year-old surveyed for the 2000 study), the generation effect on declining voter turnout is at least as significant as life cycle effects: 'age being held constant, the propensity to vote decreases by more than 20 points from the oldest to the most recent cohort.'[26]

- Blais and his colleagues note that 'younger generations view the act of voting differently' from previous generations.[27] They are less likely to see it as important and less likely to view it as a civic duty.
- The generational difference is not found among the university-educated. Controlling for age, voters with a university degree who are post-baby boomers are as likely to vote as their boomer predecessors. But among those in other educational cohorts there is a sizable generational gap in the likelihood of voting.

Of course, all of this just begs the question—two questions really. Why are the members of more recent generations less likely to be interested in politics and less likely to believe that they have a moral responsibility to vote? Second, does declining turnout matter?

The answer to the first question is unlikely to involve a single factor, but two rather different clusters of causes have been identified by researchers. One involves a lower level of deference towards authority and established institutions among post-baby boomers and a greater tendency to embrace values and beliefs associated with what has been called post-materialism (see Chapter 2). The weaker belief that voting is a civic duty is said to reflect the less deferential character of the more recent generation of voters. This explanation does not help to explain, however, why university-educated members of recent generations vote at about the same rate as earlier generations of voters with similar levels of education.

A second cluster of causes focuses on what are argued to be the failings of parties and politicians. Those who have entered the electorate during the last couple of decades are more likely than those who entered earlier to feel alienated from conventional politics, including parties and elections, and cynical about politicians and their craft. This alienation and cynicism has been produced, at least in part, by a failure of parties and politicians to convince these newer members of the electorate that what they do is relevant to the lives of citizens or that, on the other hand, any meaningful change can be effected by participating in the electoral process. In other words, what politicians and parties do may well be relevant, but it is seen as next to hopeless to imagine that voting will change anything. When all parties and leaders express concern about the environment but are perceived as doing nothing to address climate change and the pollution of some industries, or when they all act as cheerleaders for 'our' troops in far-off wars of poorly explained purpose, it is little wonder that cynicism and apathy follow. There are no black-and-white choices at the ballot box in a grey, homogenized political world.

An important variation of this argument has been advanced by Henry Milner and others. Milner argues that political literacy and interest among younger voters is lower than used to be the case. They are less likely to read newspapers, follow politics in the media, or be able to correctly identify political figures, institutions, and events than members of previous generations. They have less interest and less knowledge about politics, contributing to a reduced propensity to vote. Milner and most other commentators believe that the quality of democracy will suffer as more of society's members choose to abstain from voting.

But will society really suffer and are the non-voters truly abstaining from political participation? It is understandable that parties and voting are seen by most of us to be the essential linchpins in the relationship between the population and government. The struggle for universal voting rights was long and arduous and its achievement is only a few generations old. Quebec was the last province to grant women the right to vote in 1940 and Aboriginal Canadians did not have the right to vote if they maintained their Indian status until 1960. That the self-disenfranchisement of millions of citizens who choose seldom or never to vote might be treated with indifference is shocking to many.

But as important as voting is, it is not the only form of political engagement. A 2003 survey carried out by Statistics Canada[28] asked respondents whether they had engaged in any of the following political activities during the previous year:

- signing a petition;
- searching for political information;
- attending a public meeting;

- boycotting/choosing a product for ethical reasons;
- contacting a newspaper or politician;
- participating in a demonstration or march;
- volunteering for a political party.

The bad news is that almost half of all Canadians, 45 per cent, said that they did not participate in any of these non-voting activities. The good news is that this Statistics Canada survey found no evidence that younger Canadians were less likely than their older compatriots to participate in political activities. Just under six in 10 respondents between the ages of 15 and 24 said that they had participated in at least one of these non-voting activities in the previous year, the same rate of participation found for those in the 25–44 and 45–64 age groups. Participation among the oldest Canadians—those 65 years of age and older—dropped off to about four in 10.

It appears then that although younger Canadians are much less likely to vote than their older fellow citizens, they are as likely to participate in politics in other ways. Is boycotting or choosing a product on ethical grounds or signing a petition a less significant political act than voting in an election? Reasonable people will disagree on this matter. But perhaps we should at least be open to the possibility that declining voter turnout, particularly among the young, is not necessarily evidence that they are disengaged politically or that the health of democracy is imperilled by this decline.

Party Finances and Special Interests

Throughout their history, the Liberal and Conservative parties have relied heavily on corporate contributors to finance their activities. The NDP, by contrast, has depended mainly on contributions from individuals and on the financial support of affiliated trade unions. Corporate donations to the national NDP have always been minuscule.

It is difficult to attach precise numbers to party finances before 1974, for the simple reason that parties were not legally required to disclose their sources of revenue. A study done by Khayyam Paltiel for the federally appointed Committee on Election Expenses (1966) estimated that, before the 1974 reforms, the older parties were dependent on business contributions for between 75 and 90 per cent of their incomes,[29] a figure that did not even include the value of services in kind that they received from businesses, particularly from advertising and polling firms during election campaigns.[30] Not only were the Liberals and Conservatives dependent on business for all but a small share of their revenue, but most of this corporate money was collected from big businesses in Toronto and Montreal.[31] Other students of party finances have confirmed this historical pattern of dependence on big financial and industrial capital.[32]

Passage of the **Election Expenses Act, 1974** signalled a watershed in Canadian party finance. The Act included spending limits for individual candidates and political parties during election campaigns, changes to the Broadcasting Act requiring radio and television stations to make available to the parties represented in the House of Commons both paid and free broadcast time during election campaigns,[33] and a system of reimbursement for part of their expenses for candidates who receive at least 15 per cent of the popular vote. This last reform had the effect of subsidizing the three main parties at taxpayer expense, a consequence that can only be defended on the grounds that this public subsidy helps to weaken parties' financial dependence on special interests. As we will see below, this public subsidization of political parties was taken much further by reforms that took effect in 2004.

But from the standpoint of the parties' sources of income, the most important reforms brought in by the Election Expenses Act involved tax credits for political contributions and public disclosure requirements for candidates and political parties. On the first count, changes to the Income Tax Act allow individuals or organizations to deduct from their taxable income a percentage of their donation to a registered political party or candidate, up to a maximum tax credit of $650. Since 2007 the maximum amount that an individual may donate to a political party or candidate is $1,100. The maximum tax credit of $650 is reached once a donor has given $1,275 in total contributions during a single taxation year. On the second count, parties and candidates are required to provide the chief electoral officer with a list of all donors who have contributed $200 or more in money or services in kind, as well as an itemized account of their expenditures. Before the 2004 revisions to the Canada Elections Act, parties were not required to disclose how much they spent on important activities such as fundraising and polling between elections, although evidence has long suggested that these were very expensive functions.[34] Since 2004 the law requires much more transparency in the parties' reporting of their annual and election campaign expenditures.

Perhaps the most striking consequence of the 1974 reforms was the dramatic increase in the importance of donations by individuals. These contributions were always the mainstay of NDP finances. Spurred by the tax credit for political donations and the older parties' adoption of sophisticated direct-mail techniques of fundraising, first developed in the United States,[35] contributions by individuals became a major source of income for all three political parties. In fact, contributions from individuals exceeded business contributions to both the PC and Liberal parties in many of the years after the tax credit came into effect. The same was true of candidates' revenue. NDP candidates received very little from corporate donors, but depended heavily on trade union contributions. The Reform Party/Canadian Alliance relied overwhelmingly on contributions from individuals, as did the Bloc Québécois. Figure 10.5 shows the chief sources of revenue for the five parties represented in the House of Commons in 2003, the last year before the party financing rules were changed, and in 2004 following the changes. Figure 10.6 shows the breakdown of election spending by the parties in the 2006 general election.

The Liberal and Conservative parties' traditional financial dependence on business appeared to have been diluted under the post-1974 model for party and election financing. Nonetheless, corporate donations continued to be a tremendously important source of revenue for the older parties. They still accounted for close to half of total contributions during election years and roughly 40–50 per cent between elections. Moreover, very large corporate contributions represented a sizable share of the older parties' total revenues. If we define a large corporate donation as being at least $10,000, we find that these contributions accounted for about 15 to 30 per cent of total contributions for both the Liberal and Progressive Conservative parties over the 30-year period from the introduction of the 1974 Canada Elections Act to its overhaul in 2004. In 2003, the last year under which the old party financing rules applied, the 10 largest contributions to each of the Liberal, Progressive Conservative and Canadian Alliance (the latter two parties and their finances were merged towards the end of 2003), and New Democratic parties accounted for 16 per cent, 16 per cent, and 39 per cent of total party revenues, respectively. All of the leading 10 contributions to the Liberal and Conservative parties were from corporate donors and all 10 of the NDP's biggest donors were trade unions.

The most important consequence of special-interest contributions to parties and individual politicians was almost certainly the access to policy-makers it bought for contributors. Although cases of influence-peddling came to light from time to time, it was usually erroneous to think of political contributions as payments offered in the expectation of receiving some particular favour. There were, no doubt, instances where firms that relied on government contracts for some part of their revenue, or hoped to receive government business in the future, found it prudent to donate money to parties or candidates. But for most corporate contributors, and certainly for large donors like the banks and those leading industrial firms that were perennial contributors to the two older parties, there was no expectation of a specific quid pro quo.

So why did they bother? One explanation is that corporate political donations represented a sort of insurance premium. As the late Conservative strategist and political adviser Dalton Camp put it:

> For the wise donor, the financing of the political system may very well be a duty and an obligation to the system, but it is, as well, insurance against the unlikely—such as the ascendancy of socialism—or against occasional political aberration, a Walter Gordon budget,

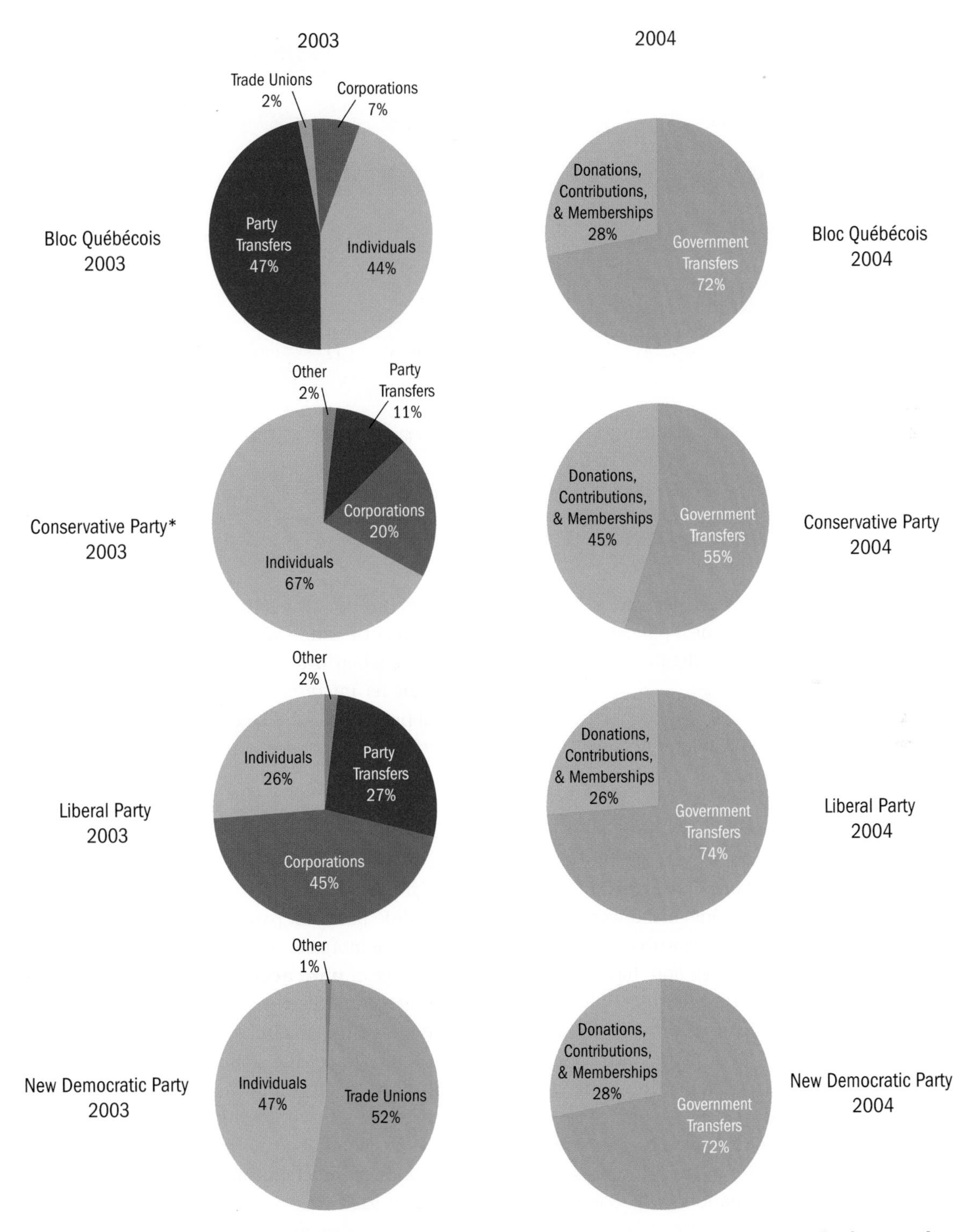

FIGURE 10.5 The Changing Sources of Revenue for the Four Main Parties, before and after the 2004 Reforms

*The Progressive Conservative Party and the Canadian Alliance Party formally merged to form the Conservative Party of Canada on 7 December 2003. Their 2003 financial statements have been combined in this chart.

Source: Data provided by Elections Canada, at: <www.elections.ca>.

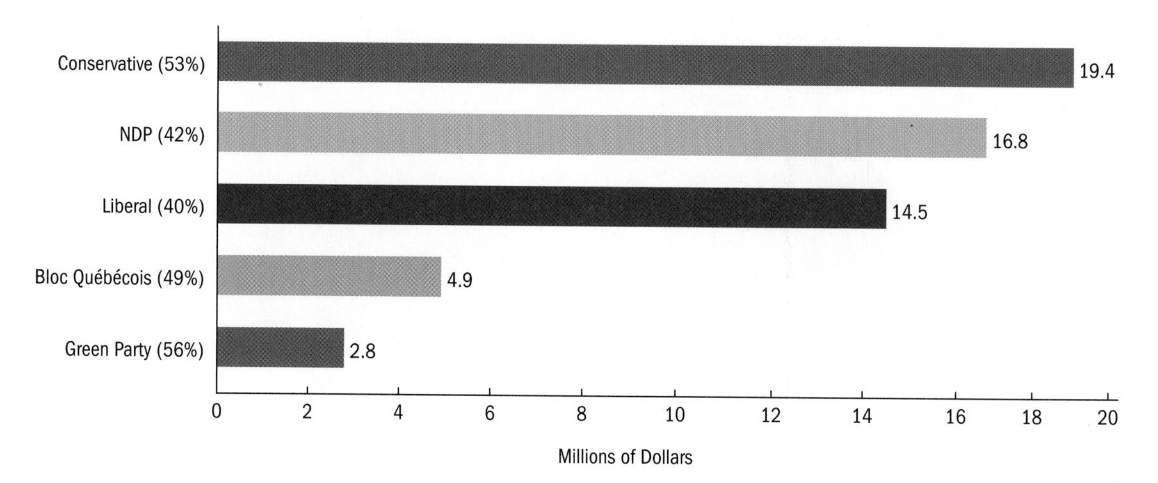

FIGURE 10.6 Election Spending by Political Parties, Including the Percentage Spent on Broadcast Advertising*, 2008

*The percentage spent on television and radio broadcasting advertising is shown next to party name.

Note: These amounts do not include spending by individual candidates.

Source: Elections Canada, at: <www.elections.ca>.

> say, or a Carter report on tax reform [both perceived to be anti-business policies]. When such contingencies arise, the price for access is modest indeed.[36]

What Camp called a 'duty and an obligation to the system' might also be described as an investment in two-party dominance. Business interests were often at loggerheads with both Liberal and Conservative governments over specific policies. But generally speaking, both of the two older parties were, and continue to be, congenial towards corporate enterprise. Business can live with either a Liberal or Conservative government and has a material interest in supporting the centrist politics that characterize the Canadian political system and in avoiding the polarization of party politics between the right and the left (as happened in the United Kingdom several decades ago).

In addition to helping finance a party system that is generally congenial to business interests, it was long understood that donations helped buy access. In the words of Dalton Camp: 'Toronto money merely maintains access to the parties, keeping open essential lines of communication, corporate hotlines, so to speak, to the right ears at appropriate times.'[37] In many cases the sheer size and importance of a corporation would be sufficient to ensure a hearing when the corporation's owners or managers felt its interests were at stake. In any given year about half of the largest 100 industrial firms in Canada did not even contribute to either of the two older parties. It would be ridiculous to conclude that their lack of generosity cut them off from direct access to political decision-makers. But all things being equal, contributions probably opened the door a bit wider.

The link between party contributions and access became more controversial with the increasing prominence of **paid access opportunities**. These are fundraising events such as dinners and cocktail parties where, for an admission price that can range up to several thousand dollars, donors receive the opportunity to rub shoulders and exchange views with party leaders who, if the party is in power, are also members of the government. Money obviously acts as a filter in determining who is likely to participate in such events, as does the party's invitation list. These events have been supplemented by an American invention—special clubs for large contributors. Both the Republican and Democratic parties have operated such clubs since the 1980s. For an individual contribution of thousands of dollars (higher for a corporate membership), the donor receives the chance to meet with important politicians, such as congressional committee chairpersons. The Progressive Conservative Party was the first to establish this sort of exclusive donor network in Canada, the '500 Club', which has been succeeded by the Conservative Party's Leader's Circle. Membership costs $1,000. The national Liberal Party also has this sort of paid-admission elite network through its Laurier Club. Admission to the club costs $1,100—half that amount for those under 35. Donations buy the privilege of invitations to exclusive meetings with party leaders, opportunities that are particularly valuable when the party in question forms the government and the party leader is the Prime Minister. It must be said, however, that the entry bar was set much higher before the limitations on political contributions brought in by the 2004 reforms to the Canada Elections Act. These special donor clubs are now less exclusive than they were when the price of admission was several thousand dollars.

In the eyes of some, paid access opportunities such as these raise an ethical question: at what point does the ability to pay for special access to political decision-makers subvert the democratic process by favouring those with the money to make their views known directly? Parties need funds to carry out their activities. Even with a tax credit for political contributions, only a small portion of all Canadian taxpayers contribute money directly to parties or candidates. The money has to come from somewhere, and such developments as paid access opportunities represent the parties' innovative search for stable sources of funds. One alternative would be to impose severe restrictions on how much money parties can spend, so that the relatively small contributions from individuals (publicly subsidized by the tax credit) and the public subsidy that candidates receive from the reimbursement provision of the Election Expenses Act would be sufficient to finance their activities. Shortly after its re-election in 2008 the Conservative government rather imprudently proposed the abolition of this public subsidy system—'imprudently' because this proposal was important in galvanizing the opposition parties' resolve to try to bring down the government at the first possible opportunity. Only the Conservative Party's finances were in good shape at the time, owing to its superior ability to raise private contributions. The Conservative government discovered the truth of the old adage that it is unwise to kick a dog that is already down.

Another alternative, one widely used in Western European democracies, is to increase the size of the public subsidies that parties receive, freeing them from their traditional dependence on contributions from special interests. This is the model that Canada adopted in 2004. The major elements of the post-2004 model for party and campaign financing in Canada include the following:

- Donations by special interests, including corporations and trade unions, are banned.
- Individuals may donate up to $1,100 in any year to a registered political party or candidate.
- Parties receive an annual public subsidy of $1.75 for every vote that they receive.
- Third parties—organizations and individuals other than registered political parties and their candidates—may spend no more than $187,650 in total, and no more than $3,753 in any single electoral district (as of 2010), on political advertising during an election campaign, effectively preventing them from having any significant impact on the national campaign.
- Candidates for the leadership of registered political parties must provide information on the identity of those who donate to their campaigns and, as of April 2006, no individual may contribute more than $5,400 in total to the contestants for the leadership of a particular political party. Contributions from corporations and unions are not permitted. The amount that leadership candidates may spend on their campaigns is set by the parties, not by Canadian law.

No restrictions are placed on spending by political parties, groups, or individuals during periods other than elections. As a result, considerable money is spent on fundraising, polling, consultants, and pre-campaign advertising before an election is called. A clear example of such non-election advertising is the extensive negative ad campaign that the Conservatives launched as soon as Stéphane Dion was chosen as the Liberal leader, portraying Dion as indecisive and without leadership qualities. Some argue that this type of pre-campaign spending undermines the intent of the 2004 reforms. Certainly, the Conservatives' attack ads undermined Dion's image among the Canadian public. Others maintain that the ability to spend money in order to craft a political message and communicate it to citizens is a basic democratic right that is already unjustifiably limited by these reforms. Whether legislation that restricts spending on political communications between election campaigns would be upheld by the courts is difficult to say. But as we saw in Chapter 6 in regard to the *Harper v. Canada* (2004) ruling by the Supreme Court, the majority of Canada's top justices take the view that unequal spending power undermines the equality of citizens and skews the political conversation towards the interests and values of those with deep pockets.

Regardless of what one thinks about the rights implications of the 2004 *Harper* ruling, it is undeniable that a party, candidate, private organization, or individual with a lot of money is able to purchase more media advertising time or space than one with only a little (and is better able to afford the services that are usually necessary to produce high-quality, effective advertising). In recognition of this potential for unequal access to the media, some believe that governments need to regulate who may purchase political advertising, when they may do so, and how much they may spend.

In some European democracies, including France and Germany, paid political advertising on television and radio is banned, as is campaign advertising by private organizations that might be construed as supporting or opposing a party or candidate. In the United Kingdom, the law regulates the permissible length of television ads—they must run for at least 2 minutes and 40 seconds and up to 4 minutes and 40 seconds—based on the apparent belief that longer ads are more likely than the 15–30 second spot ads that are the norm in Canada and the United States to communicate information and address issues in less manipulative ways. At the other extreme is the United States, where that country's courts have taken a dim view of legislative efforts to limit campaign spending on advertising on the grounds that this would violate the First Amendment's guarantee of free speech.

Canada falls between these positions. Since the mid-1970s Canadian law has empowered the CRTC, Canada's telecommunications regulator, to require television and radio broadcasters to provide a certain amount of air time to registered political parties for their ads during election campaigns. As explained above, campaign spending by so-called 'third parties' is sharply limited by Canadian election law. Federal law also limits the amount of money that registered political parties and their candidates may spend during campaigns, thus placing a ceiling on the amount of advertising a party can purchase. The communication activities of political parties via the Internet remain, so far, unregulated (though not for want of desire or effort from many quarters, including Elections Canada).

Starting Points for Research

R. Kenneth Carty and Munroe Eagles, *Politics Is Local: National Politics at the Grassroots* (Toronto: Oxford University Press, 2005). The authors examine the local dimension of Canadian party politics, including their finances, organization, candidate selection, campaigns, and media coverage.

William Cross, ed., *Political Parties, Representation, and Electoral Democracy in Canada* (Toronto: Oxford University Press, 2002). These essays, by many of Canada's leading students of political parties and elections, cover topics including leadership selection, western populism, television campaign coverage, and the relationship between parties and interest groups.

Alain-G. Gagnon and Brian A. Tanguay, eds, *Canadian Parties in Transition*, 3rd edn (Toronto: University of Toronto Press, 2007). A comprehensive reader on Canadian parties, with an appendix of federal election results from 1925 to 2006.

Hans Michelmann, Donald Story, and Jeffrey Steeves, eds, *Political Leadership and Representation in Canada: Essays in Honour of John C. Courtney* (Toronto: University of Toronto Press, 2007). Nine essays from a festschrift honouring the work of one of Canada's foremost students of political parties and party leadership selection.

John Pammett and Christopher Doran, eds, *The Canadian Election of 2006* (Toronto: Dundurn Press, 2006). With contributions from academics, journalists, and pollsters, this book includes good analyses of campaigning and voting in the 2006 election.

Review Exercises

1. Using data available at the website of the Chief Electoral Officer of Canada <www.elections.ca>, determine the following:
   (a) the number of seats each party would have received in the last general election under a straight proportional representation system; and
   (b) the number of votes and percentage of the vote received by each candidate in your constituency during the last federal election.
2. Visit the websites of two of the political parties represented in the House of Commons. Compare the depth and breadth of information provided about each party's history, current leader, and present policies.
3. How do Canadian political parties select their candidates? For information on this, visit the websites of a couple of the national political parties. Click on the party's constitution, looking for the rules on candidate selection.
4. Professor André Blais is one of Canada's foremost experts on voting behaviour. You can hear him speak on the factors that have contributed to declining voter turnout since the 1970s at: <www.citizensassembly.bc.ca/public/learning_resources/learning_materials/av> (go to Week 3, Session 2, 7 Feb. 2004, Part 15). What, according to Blais, is the leading cause of declining voter participation in elections? Is this phenomenon unique to Canada?

Every interest imaginable is represented by groups who often attempt to influence the government directly as a way to achieve their goals. Patty Jeffrey, whose father served in World War II, holds a sign thanking veterans during a demonstration on Parliament Hill in November 2010 in support of injured soldiers, veterans, and RCMP members and their families. © The Canadian Press/Pawel Dwulit

11 Interest Groups

Politics does not stop between election campaigns. Much of the effort to influence the actions of government is channelled through interest groups. This chapter examines their characteristics and the role they play in Canadian politics. Topics include the following:

- How many groups, representing what interests?
- The bias of the interest group system.
- Perspectives on interest groups.
- Factors in interest group success.
- The impact of federalism on interest groups.
- Strategies for influence.
- Advocacy advertising.
- Lobbying and lobbyists.

Elections are democracy's showpiece. Important as they are, however, the influence of elections on what governments do is usually rather blunt and indirect. Policies are far more likely to be determined by forces generated within the state and by the actions of organized groups outside of it than by the latest election results. Indeed, it may often seem that special interests dominate the policy-making process in democracies. Their attempts to influence government are unremitting. The resources they marshal often are impressive. And their access to policy-makers is, in the case of some organized interests, privileged. Compared to this, the role of elections and the influence of voters may appear feeble.

Interest groups or *pressure groups*—the terms can be used interchangeably—have been defined as 'private associations . . . [which] promote their interests by attempting to influence government rather than by nominating candidates and seeking responsibility for the management of government.'[1] They arise from a very basic fact of social life, the reality of diversity in the interests and values of human beings. This diversity, in turn, gives rise to what James Madison called **political factions**: groups of citizens whose goals and behaviour are contrary to those of other groups or to the interests of the community as a whole.[2] If these factions, or special interests as we are apt to call them today, appear to overshadow the public interest in democracies, there is a simple explanation for this. The tug of one's personal interests—as an automotive worker, teacher, farmer, or postal worker—tend to be felt more keenly than the rather nebulous concept of the public interest. Arguments that appeal to such general interests as consumer benefits or economic efficiency are unlikely to convince the farmer whose income is protected by the production quotas and price floors set by a marketing board. But economic interests are not the only basis for factionalism in politics. Group characteristics like ethnicity, language, religion, race, and gender or the sharing of similar values may also provide the basis for the political organization of interests.

Economically based or not, interest groups are distinguished by the fact that they seek to promote goals that are not shared by all members of society. Paradoxically, however, their success in achieving these goals often depends on their ability to associate their efforts with the broader public interest. 'What is good for General Motors is good for America'[3] may or may not be true. Nevertheless, the slogan makes good sense as a strategy for promoting the interests of GM, North American automobile producers, and business interests generally.

Charting the Territory

The world of interest groups is both vast and characterized by enormous variety. Although no unified reliable list of interest groups exists for Canada or any other democracy, some idea of the sheer number of groups may be had from a source like the directory, *Associations Canada*.[4] Its 2009 edition lists about 20,000 organizations, not all of which would meet the criterion of attempting to influence government action. Many groups focus exclusively on non-political activities like providing services and information to their members, but several thousand perform political functions for their members on a regular or occasional basis.

Almost every imaginable interest is represented by an organization. There are several hundred women's associations across Canada, close to 1,000 environmental groups, over 2,000 business associations, perhaps 500 organizations representing agricultural interests, about 200 that focus on Aboriginal issues[5]—the range of organized interests and the sheer number of groups within each general category of interests are enormous. Impressive as these figures may seem, they do not provide a complete map of Canada's associational system. They do not, for example, include those transitory groups that emerge briefly around a single issue and then disappear from the scene. Nor do they include international organizations that may attempt to influence the actions of Canadian governments. However we draw its boundaries, the universe of organized interests is vast.

While it is impossible to say exactly how many of these associations qualify as interest groups, no doubt a large number of them are politically active. One way to get a sense of this activity is to look at the list of groups that make representations to a legislative body or a government-sponsored commission considering some issue. For example, well over 1,000 groups made representations and submitted briefs to the Royal Commission on Aboriginal Peoples during its six months of public hearings (1993). The Commission on the Future of Health Care in Canada received submissions from 429 groups and associations during the public consultation phase of its work (2001). In Quebec, the Commission on Accommodation Practices Related to Cultural Differences (2008) received more than 900 briefs and heard testimony from 241 groups and individuals.

The amount of representation and activity in a single sector can be remarkable. Robert Wolfe reports that over 100 agriculture and food-processing groups participated in the Next Generation consultations organized in 2007 by Agriculture and Agri-Food Canada and that over 60 Canadian agri-food groups participated in at least one, and often several, of the WTO meetings on agricultural trade policy between 1996 and 2006.[6] Alternatively, one may look at the composition of some politically active organizations. The Canadian Labour Congress is the umbrella organization for hundreds of unions, including provincial and national federations of labour and 137 district labour councils that together represent about 3 million workers. The Canadian Chamber of Commerce, one of whose main functions is to influence government policies, represents over 500 community and provincial chambers of commerce and boards of trade; as well, close to 100 trade and professional associations and many international organizations are located in Canada. No matter how we measure it, the size of the interest group system is considerable.

The Bias of the Interest Group System

> The notion that the pressure system is automatically representative of the whole community is a myth. . . . The system is skewed, loaded and unbalanced in favor of a fraction of a minority.[7]

Obviously, some interest groups are more influential than others, but which are the most powerful? Why? Is the interest group system biased 'in favour of a fraction of a minority' as E.E. Schattschneider claims?

Schattschneider argues that the interest group system—he calls it the pressure system—has a business and upper-class bias. Writing about American politics in the early 1960s, he observed that business associations comprised the single largest group of organized interests in American society; they were far more likely than other interests to lobby government, and they tended to spend much more money on attempting to influence policy-makers than did other interest groups. Moreover, Schattschneider cites impressive evidence demonstrating that 'even non-business organizations reflect an upper-class tendency.'[8] Those persons with higher than average incomes and/or years of formal education are more likely to belong to organized groups than those lower down the socio-economic ladder. He explains the business and upper-class bias of interest-group politics as being a product both of superior resources and of the relatively limited size and exclusive character of these special interests. 'Special-interest organizations', he argues, 'are most easily formed when they deal with small numbers of individuals [or corporations] who are acutely aware of their exclusive interests.'[9] This awareness of special interests that are vital to one's material well-being or the well-being of one's organization is characteristic of trade associations like the Canadian Association of Petroleum Producers, the Canadian Bankers' Association, or a more broadly based business organization like the Canadian Manufacturers & Exporters (formerly the Canadian Manufacturers Association and the Canadian Exporters Association), and also characterizes producer and occupational groups like the Quebec Dairy Association and the Ontario Medical Association. It is less likely to characterize organizations that represent more general interests.

Most social scientists and political journalists agree with Schattschneider. Charles Lindblom argues that business occupies a 'privileged position' in the politics of capitalist societies. In his book *Politics and Markets*,[10] Lindblom attributes this pre-eminence to business's superior financial resources and lobbying organization, greater access than other groups to government officials, and, most importantly, propagandistic activities that—directly through political advertising and indirectly through commercial advertising—reinforce the ideological dominance of business values in society.

One of the key factors most often cited by those who argue that business interests are politically superior is the **mobility of capital**. Investors enjoy a wide although not absolute freedom to shift their capital between sectors of the economy and from one national economy to another. The epitome of this mobility is found in the transnational corporation—an enterprise whose activities span a number of national economies and whose international character often is used as a lever in dealing with the government of a particular country. In addition to being territorially mobile, investment capital also has the capacity to expand and contract in response to investors' perceptions of the political-economic climate for business. Short of imposing punitive tax rates on savings, governments cannot force business and private investors to invest. Governments in all capitalist societies are concerned with levels of business confidence and are reluctant to take actions that carry a high risk of causing a cutback in investment. The consequences of such a cutback are felt politically by governments. Weak economic activity tends to translate into popular dissatisfaction and a loss of political support.[11]

The mobility of capital gives rise, in turn, to concern with *business confidence*. Politicians need to care about business confidence because of the very real possibility that they will not be re-elected if business's unwillingness to invest causes unemployment and falling incomes. But another factor that gives pause even to governments that can count on strong popular backing is the state's financial dependence on business. A decline in the levels of investment or profit soon will be felt as a drop in government revenues from the taxation of corporate and employment income, payroll taxes, and from the taxation of consumption. The problem of falling revenues is almost certain to be compounded by an increase in state expenditures on social programs whose costs are sensitive to changes in the level of economic activity. Borrowing on the public credit is only a temporary solution to this dilemma, and one that experience has shown to be both costly and subject to the limits of international investor confidence.

Neither Lindblom nor anyone else would argue that business interests 'win' all of the time, or even that powerful business groups cannot experience major defeats. Instead, they maintain that there is a tendency to favour business interests over others because of systemic characteristics of capitalist societies. This is one of the few propositions about politics that manages to cut across the ideological spectrum, attracting support from the left and right alike (if rather more heavily from the left). There are, however, dissenters.

Those who teach or write for a business school audience, for example, are likely to view business interests as being simply one set of interests in a sea of competing interest groups making claims on government.[12] Business historian Michael Bliss argues that whatever privileged access business people may have enjoyed in the corridors of political power and whatever superiority business interests may have had in relation to rival claims on government had largely disappeared by the 1980s. 'Groups with powerful vested interests,' he writes, 'including trade unions, civil servants, tenured academics, and courtesanal cultural producers, perpetuated a hostility toward business enterprise rooted in their own fear of competition on open markets.'[13]

In his rebuttal to the 'privileged position' thesis, David Vogel argues that, on balance, 'business is more affected by broad political and economic trends than it is able to affect them.'[14] Although Vogel focuses on the United States, he develops a more general argument about the political power of business interests in capitalist democracies. Popular opinion and the sophistication of interest group organization are, he maintains, the keys to understanding the political successes and failures of business and other interest groups. Vogel argues that business's ability to influence public policy is greatest when the public is worried about the long-term strength of the economy and weakest when the economy's ability to produce jobs and to increase incomes is taken for granted.

The political organization of business interests is the second key to understanding the ebb and flow of business influence. Vogel maintains that the victories of environmental, consumer, and other public interest groups in the 1960s and 1970s were largely due to their ability to read the Washington map and work the levers of congressional and media politics. Business interests, by comparison, were poorly organized and amateurish. Since then, however, the political mobilization of business has been without equal. But despite its organizational prowess, divisions within the business community have generally served to check its influence on public policy.

Another factor that prevents business interests from dominating politics is what James Q. Wilson has called 'entrepreneurial politics'.[15] This involves the ability of politicians and interest groups to identify issues around which popular support can be mobilized in opposition to business interests. The opportunities for entrepreneurial politics are fewer in Canada than in the United States because of the tighter party discipline in Canada's legislature. Entrepreneurial politics is, however, practised by interest groups such as People for the Ethical Treatment of Animals (PETA) on issues involving farming practices and food industries and Equality for Gays and Lesbians Everywhere (EGALE) on issues involving discrimination on the basis of sexual preference. Astute use of the media and adept packaging of a group's message so as to generate public awareness and support for its goals are essential to entrepreneurial politics.

Are business interests perched securely atop the heap of the interest group system in capitalist societies, or do business groups have to slug it out in the political trenches just like other groups and with no more likelihood of victory? Perhaps neither position is correct—the conclusion suggested by much of the work on Canadian interest groups. Paul Pross calls this rather agnostic approach *post-pluralism* and others have called it a *neo-institutionalist* approach.

This approach is based on a simple observable fact: policy-making generally involves the participation of a relatively limited set of state and societal actors, a **policy community** that is centred around a sub-government; i.e., that set of state institutions and interest groups usually involved in making and implementing policy in some field. We will have more to say about the approach later in the chapter. For now, the point is simply that groups representing business interests may or may not be members of a sub-government or policy community. Whether or not they are and how influential they may be depends on the policy field in question and on the particular configuration of interests that are active in the policy community. Moreover, neo-institutionalists tend to emphasize the capacity of state actors to act independently of the pressures and demands placed on them by societal interests. This capacity will vary across policy sectors. But the bottom line of the neo-institutionalist approach is that state actors in some policy communities may be quite capable of resisting pressures coming from highly organized, well-heeled business interests—or from any societal interests, for that matter.

Analytical Perspectives on Interest Groups

Pluralism

Pluralism or group theory may be defined as an explanation of politics that sees organized interests as the central fact of political life and which explains politics chiefly in terms of the activities of groups. It is a societal explanation of politics in that it locates the main causes of government action in the efforts and activities of voluntary associations—trade associations, labour unions, churches, PTAs, etc.—outside the state. When it turns its attention to the role and character of the state in democratic societies, pluralist theory draws two main conclusions. First, the state itself is viewed as a sort of group interest or, more precisely, as an assortment of different interests associated with various components of the state. Second, despite the possibility that the state may have interests of its own, its chief political function is to ratify the balance of group interests in society and to enforce the policies that embody this balance of power. As Earl Latham graphically put it: 'The legislature referees the group struggle, ratifies the victories of the successful coalition, and records the terms of the surrenders, compromises, and conquests in the form of statutes.'[16]

The purest embodiment of group theory is found in the work of Arthur Bentley. Society, Bentley argues, can be understood only in terms of the groups that comprise it. He views government as simply a process of 'groups pressing one another, forming one another, and pushing out new groups and group representatives (the organs or agencies of government) to mediate the adjustments.'[17] This is an extremely reductionist approach. Pluralists after Bentley, figures like David Truman, Robert Dahl, and John Kenneth Galbraith,[18] have certainly been aware of the danger of trying to squeeze too much explanation out of a single cause. But they have remained faithful to two basic elements of pluralist theory, one empirical and the other normative. The empirical element is the claim that politics is a competitive process where power is widely distributed, there is no single ruling elite or dominant class, and the interaction of organized interests outside the state is the chief force behind the actions of government. The normative element suggests that the outcome of this competitive struggle among groups represents the public interest and, indeed, that this is the only reasonable way of understanding the public interest in democracy.

Pluralism begat *neo-pluralism*. The neo-pluralist assault took issue with both the empirical and normative claims of group theory. Writers like E.E. Schattschneider, Theodore Lowi, and Charles Lindblom had little difficulty in showing that the interest group system was much less open and competitive than the earlier pluralists had argued. Regarding pluralism's normative features, Lowi

PETA is known for evocative protests designed to mobilize popular public support. In this July 2010 protest a protestor is covered in red body paint to represent the blood shed by baby seals during Canada's annual cull in the Arctic.

took aim at its equation of the public interest with the outcome of struggles between special interests. He argued that the special interest state—what Lowi called interest group liberalism—actually trivializes the public interest and ends up undermining it by pretending that it is no more than the latest set of deals struck between the powerful through the intermediary offices of government. 'Interest group liberalism', he argued, 'seeks pluralistic government, in which there is no formal specification of means or of ends. In pluralistic government there is therefore no substance. Neither is there procedure. There is only process.'[19]

As if these indictments were not enough, pluralism also stands accused of misunderstanding the true character of political power. By focusing on group competition, their critics argue, pluralists are inclined to see political life as relatively open and competitive because they observe struggles between groups and the decisions of governments. But as Bachrach and Baratz suggest, 'power may be, and often is, exercised by confining the scope of decision-making to relatively "safe" issues.'[20] Non-decision-making—the ability to keep issues unformulated and off the public agenda—is a form of power. Looked at from this angle, the interest group system appears much less competitive.

Class Analysis

Viewed through the prism of class analysis, interest groups do not disappear, but their edges become blurred and they take a back seat to the class interests these groups are argued to represent. Some of the major works of contemporary Marxist scholarship do not even mention such terms as 'interest group', 'pressure group', or 'social group'.[21] In Canada the class analysis approach is generally referred to as 'political economy'.[22] Interest groups have been given scant attention in most of the work in the Canadian political economy tradition and are sometimes ignored entirely in preference for such categories as class factions within subordinate and dominant classes. A recent reader on Canadian political economy, *Changing Canada: Political Economy as Transformation*, includes very few direct references to interest groups.

This is not to say that the reality of organized interests in politics is either denied or ignored by class analysis. Ralph Miliband observes:

> Democratic and pluralist theory could not have achieved the degree of ascendancy which it enjoys in advanced capitalist society had it not at least been based on one plainly accurate observation about them, namely that they permit and even encourage a multitude of groups and associations to organize openly and freely and to compete with each other for the advancement of such purposes as their members may wish.[23]

Miliband's *The State in Capitalist Society* devotes an entire chapter to the role of organized interests in an attempt to refute the pluralist model that we discussed earlier. Some of the Canadian political economy literature includes examples of how class analysis can coexist with a careful analysis of interest groups. Wallace Clement's *The Challenge of Class Analysis*[24] and Rianne Mahon's study of Canada's textile industry fall into this category. Clement examines the complex network of unions, co-operatives, and associations in Canada's coastal fisheries in order to, in his words, 'lend understanding to the material basis of class struggle.'[25] In *The Politics of Industrial Restructuring*, Mahon develops a very sophisticated analysis of trade associations and labour unions in the textile sector, in terms of the fundamental class interests they represent, the organizational capacity of these interests, and their ideological characteristics.[26]

But interest groups, from the perspective of class analysis, are not the basic units of society and political life. Classes are. Thus, organized groups are seen as the bearers of more fundamental interests and ideologies, namely those of classes and their factions. This enables one to acknowledge the uniqueness of individual groups and associations while focusing on larger collective interests represented by individual groups. An association like the Canadian Council of Chief Executives, which represents 150 of the largest private-sector corporations in Canada, would be seen as a representative of 'monopoly capital'. The Canadian

Manufacturers & Exporters, although it represents over 3,000 corporations spanning virtually all manufacturing industries and ranging in size from thousands of employees to a handful, is viewed as an organizational voice for the manufacturing faction of the capitalist class. In fact, some class analyses characterize this organization as an instrument of the oligopolistic, American-oriented faction of the capitalist class. Labour unions, of course, are viewed from this perspective as representative of subordinate class interests and ideologies, as are groups representing women, Aboriginal peoples, and ethnic and racial minorities.

Corporatism

Corporatism is a political structure characterized by the direct participation of organizations representing business and labour in public policy-making. 'In its core', states Jurg Steiner, 'corporatism in a modern democracy deals with the interactions among organized business, organized labor, and the state bureaucracy. These three actors co-operate at the national level in the pursuit of the public good.'[27] Such structures are associated to varying degrees with several of the capitalist democracies of Western Europe, including Sweden, Austria, the Netherlands, Germany, and Switzerland.

The distinctiveness of corporatism as an interest group system is based on three characteristics. One is the existence of *peak associations* for business and labour. These are organizations that can credibly claim to represent all significant interests within the business and labour communities, respectively, and which have the ability to negotiate on behalf of the interests they represent. A second characteristic of a corporatist interest group system is the formal integration of business and labour into structures of state authority. Under corporatism, these interests do not simply have privileged access to state policy-makers, they have *institutionalized access*. A third characteristic of corporatism is its ideology of social partnership. As William Coleman says of corporatist ideology in Austria, 'There is a commitment to allow class conflict to grow only so far before it is internalized and addressed in ways judged a "fair" compromise.'[28] Compared to pluralism, which is characterized by an intensely competitive interest group system that stands outside the state, a corporatist system is more consensus-oriented and obliterates the barriers between the state and the societal interests represented through corporatist decision-making structures.

What possible relevance can the corporatist model have to an understanding of interest groups in Canada? The peak associations of business and labour necessary to make corporatism work do not exist in Canada. The most inclusive of Canadian business associations, the Canadian Chamber of Commerce (CCC), is just a loose federation of provincial and local chambers, individual corporations, and trade associations. The national organization exercises no control over its members, and the sheer range of interests represented within the CCC obliges it to focus mainly on very general issues—lower corporate taxation, cutting the level of government spending, reducing the amount of government regulation of business—where there is broad consensus among business people.[29] On labour's side, the ability of an association to claim to represent Canadian workers is weakened by the fact that fewer than four out of 10 members of the labour force belong to a union. The Canadian Labour Congress is the largest of Canada's labour associations, with close to 100 affiliated unions that represent about 2 million workers. This is only about 15 per cent of the total labour force. Unions representing mainly francophone workers have preferred to affiliate with the Confédération des syndicats nationaux.

The two other requirements for corporatism—tripartite decision-making structures bringing together the state, business, and labour and an ideology of social partnership between business and labour—are absent from the Canadian scene. Indeed, Gerhard Lehmbruch, one of the leading students of corporatism, places Canada in the group of countries having the fewest characteristics of corporatism.[30] Canadian political scientist William Coleman agrees with this assessment, although he notes that corporatist policy-making networks are found in the agricultural sector of the Canadian economy.[31] This is due, however, to the decades-old policies and structure in that industry—particularly in the eastern provinces and in the dairy and poultry sectors—rather than having much at all to do with culture and broader patterns of industrial relations.

Some observers have claimed to detect elements of corporatism in various tripartite consensus-building efforts launched by governments in Canada, and in the practice of labour and business organizations being invited to appoint representatives to various public boards and tribunals. Past examples have included the Economic Council of Canada and the Canadian Labour Market and Productivity Centre (both of which are now defunct) and task forces on industrial restructuring orchestrated by Ottawa between 1975–8. Some of the provinces, particularly Quebec, have experimented with tripartite consensus-building, and the periodic 'economic summits' organized by Ottawa and several of the provinces from time to time have been interpreted by some as signs of incipient corporatism.[32] None of these has produced any fundamental change in the process of economic policy-making. The obstacles to corporatism in Canada are enormous, including such factors as British parliamentary structures that centralize power in the hands of the Prime Minister and cabinet, a political culture that is not favourable to the interventionist planning associated with corporatism, the decentralization of authority that exists in both the business and labour communities, and the division of economic powers between Ottawa and the provinces. Whether or not corporatist-style interest mediation is desirable or not is a different question.[33]

Neo-Institutionalism

Neo-institutionalism is a perspective on policy-making that emphasizes the impact that structures and rules, formal and informal, have on political outcomes. '[T]he preferences and rules of policy actors', argue Coleman and Grace Skogstad, 'are shaped fundamentally by their structural position. Institutions are conceived as structuring political reality and as defining the terms and nature of political discourse.'[34] What does this mean and how does it help us understand the behaviour and influence of interest groups?

First, what has been called neo-institutionalism or the new institutionalism is not so much a model of politics and policy-making as a theoretical premise shared by an otherwise diverse group of perspectives. The premise is, quite simply, that institutions—their structural characteristics, formal rules, and informal norms—play a central role in shaping both the actions of individuals and of the organizations to which they belong. This 'insight' is neither very new nor very surprising. The founders of modern sociology knew very well the importance of institutions in determining behaviour, a relationship that is most pithily expressed in Robert Michels's aphorism, 'He who says organization, says oligarchy.'[35] Moreover, few of us would blink at the rather bland assertion that 'where you stand depends on where you sit.' So where is the 'neo' in 'neo-institutionalism', and what special contribution can it make to understanding interest groups? Let us begin by examining the diverse roots of the neo-institutionalist approach.

Economics

Rational choice theory forms the bedrock of modern economics. Beginning in the 1950s and 1960s, economists began to systematically apply the concepts of individual (limited) rationality and market behaviour to the study of elections, political parties, interest groups, bureaucracy, and other political phenomena.[36] The economic theory of politics that has developed from this work emphasizes the role played by rules, formal and informal, in shaping individual choices and policy outcomes. Viewed from this perspective, 'institutions are bundles of rules that make collective action possible.'[37]

Organization Theory

Appropriately enough, organization theory has been an important source of inspiration and ideas for the neo-institutionalist approach. One of the first political scientists to apply the behavioural insights of organization theory to Canadian politics was Alan Cairns. His 1977 presidential address to the Canadian Political Science Association relied heavily on organization theory. He argued that Canadian federalism is influenced mainly by state actors, the 'needs' of the organizations they belong to, and the constitutional rules within which they operate.[38] James March, Herbert Simon, and Johan Olsen are among the organization theorists frequently cited by neo-institutionalists.[39] The spirit of the organizational perspective is captured in Charles Perrow's declaration that 'The formal structure of the organization is the single most important key to its functioning.'[40]

Society-Centred Analysis

The rising popularity of neo-institutional analysis can be attributed in part to a reaction against explanations of politics and policy-making that emphasize the role of such societal factors as interest groups, voters, and social classes. This reaction has produced an enormous outpouring of work on the autonomy, or relative autonomy, of the state, i.e., the ability of state actors to act on their own preferences and to actively shape societal demands and interest configurations rather than simply responding to and mediating societal interests. Neo-institutionalism, which focuses on the structural characteristics of and relationships between political actors, has been inspired by this same reaction. This is not to say that neo-institutionalism is a state-centred explanation of politics. But in ascribing a key role to institutions—structures and rules—it inevitably takes seriously the structural characteristics of the state.

Neo-institutionalism deals intensively with what might be called the interior lives of interest groups: the factors responsible for their creation, maintenance, and capacity for concerted political action. James Q. Wilson identifies four categories of incentives that underlie the interior dynamics of interest groups:[41]

- *material incentives*—tangible rewards that include money and other material benefits that clearly have a monetary value;
- *specific solidarity incentives*—intangible rewards like honours, official deference, and recognition that are scarce, i.e., they have value precisely because some people are excluded from their enjoyment;
- *collective solidarity incentives*—intangible rewards that are created by the act of associating together in an organized group and which are enjoyed by all members of the group, such as a collective sense of group esteem or affirmation;
- *purposive incentives*—'intangible rewards that derive from the sense of satisfaction of having contributed to the attainment of a worthwhile cause'.

Economists also have attempted to explain what Mancur Olson first called the logic of collective action, including how the interior character of a group affects its capacity for political influence.

Neo-institutionalism tends to agnosticism when it comes to the old debate on whether societal or state forces are more important determinants of political outcomes. Such concepts as *policy communities*—the constellation of actors in a particular policy field—or **policy networks**[42]—the nature of the relationships between the key actors in a policy community—are the building blocks of the neo-institutional approach. Embedded in them is the irrefutable claim that 'the state' is in fact a fragmented structure when it comes to actual policy-making. So, too, is society. The interests that are active and influential on the issue of abortion, for example, are very different from those who are part of the official-language policy community. What Coleman and Skogstad describe as the 'diversity in arrangements between civil society and the state'[43] inspires agnosticism on the state-versus-society debate. The reality is that the relative strength of state and societal actors and the characteristics of policy networks vary between policy communities in the same society and, moreover, the line between state and society often is not very distinct. Paul Pross's visual depiction of what a policy community looks like conveys a good sense of the complexity and potential for fluidity in the relations between interest groups and the state (see Figure 11.1).

A group's capacity for influence within a policy community will depend on its internal characteristics and on its external relationships to the larger political system and the state. Philippe Schmitter and Wolfgang Streeck call these the logics of membership and influence, respectively.[44] We have already mentioned some of the factors that may be relevant to understanding a group's interior life. On the logic of influence, Coleman and Skogstad argue that the key determinant of a group's influence is 'the structure of the state itself at the sectoral level',[45] i.e., within a particular policy community. Perhaps. But *macro*-political factors like political culture, the dominant ideology, and the state system's more general characteristics also are important to understanding the political influence of organized interests. Policy communities are perhaps best viewed as solar systems that are themselves influenced by the gravitational tug of cultural and institutional forces emanating from the centre of the larger galaxy in which they move. The diversity of state–society relations between policy communities can be reconciled with larger generalizations about the interest group system, such as Lindblom's claim that business interests occupy a privileged position within this system.

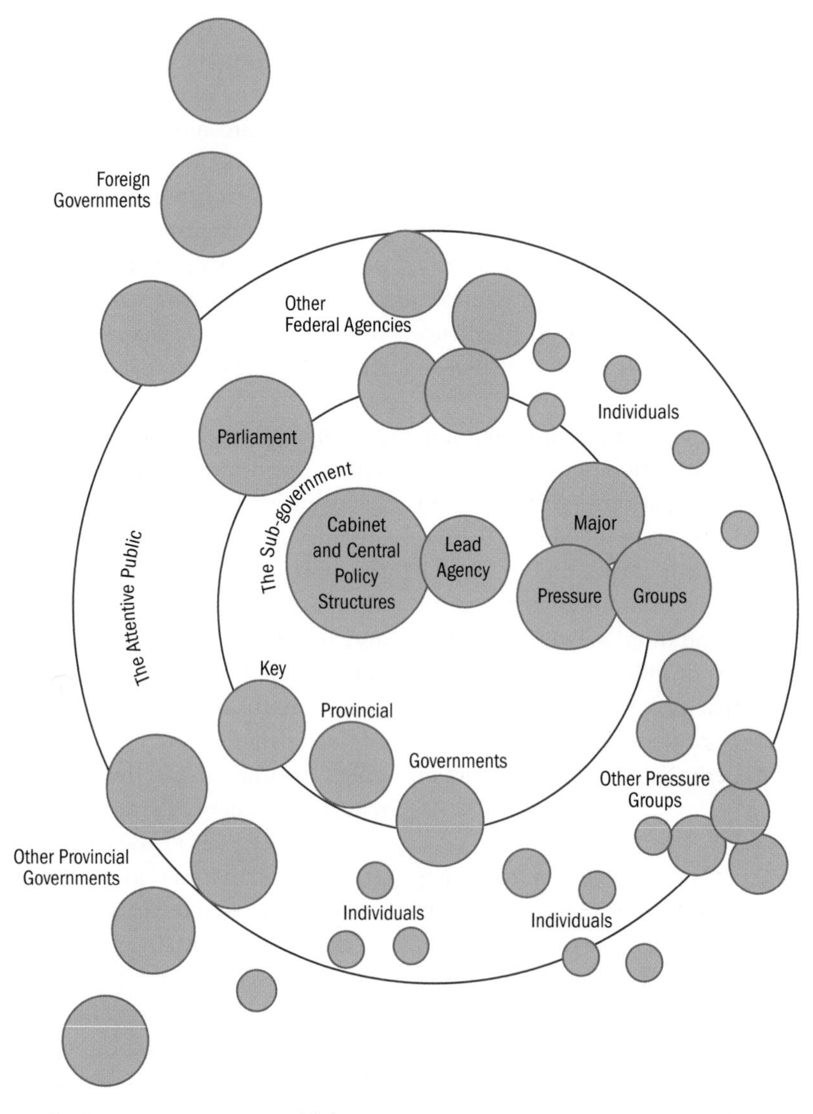

FIGURE 11.1 Policy Community 'Bubble Diagram'

Source: From Whittington, M.S. & Williams, G. *Canadian Politics in the 1990's*, 3E. © 1991 Nelson Education Ltd. Reproduced by permission. www.cengage.com/permissions

The Ingredients of Interest Group Success

There is no magic recipe for group influence. Successful strategies and appropriate targets depend on the issue, the resources and actions of other groups, the state of public opinion, and the characteristics of the political system. But although there is no single formula for influence, it is possible to generalize about the factors associated with powerful interest groups. As we will see, these factors are more likely to characterize business groups and their dealings with government than any other set of societal interests.

Organization

It may seem a trite observation, but organized interests are usually more influential than unorganized ones and are always better equipped to apply sustained pressure on policy-makers. A lone person who writes a letter to the Prime Minister demanding that the government act in a particular way is unlikely to have much impact, even if that person is someone of national stature. Tens of thousands of people writing to the Prime Minister and taking to the streets in front of television and cellphone cameras that bring their demonstrations to the screens viewed by millions of others are more likely to get the Prime Minister's attention. Their impact will be even greater if their demand is channelled through an organization or organizations that can credibly claim to speak on behalf of these thousands of like-minded people, especially if the organizations are skilled at media and government relations. The unco-ordinated efforts of individuals and the fury of a spontaneous mob can have an impact on policy-makers. But this impact is unlikely to be sustained without organization.

Paul Pross, one of Canada's most distinguished experts on interest groups, points to the character of modern government and the policy-making process in explaining why organization is crucial. Modern government, he observes, is a sprawling, highly bureaucratized affair in which the power to influence policy is widely diffused. When government was smaller, the number of policies and programs affecting societal interests were fewer, and power was concentrated in the hands of a small group of senior bureaucratic officials and cabinet. Groups did not require sophisticated organizational structures to manage their dealings with government. This was the era of the 'mandarins', the tightly knit group of deputy ministers who dominated the policy process.[46] Pathways to influence were relatively uncomplicated. A conversation with the minister or deputy minister in the restaurant of the Château Laurier or at the Five Lakes Fishing Club was the preferred method of communicating a group's views. Access at this rarefied level was, however, restricted to members of the corporate elite and those representing their interests.

This era began to pass into history during the 1960s. The more complex interventionist state that emerged was not as amenable to the informal, discreet style of influence that powerful economic interests had grown used to during the 1940s and 1950s. As the scope of state intervention widened and its regulation of economic and social matters deepened, it became increasingly desirable that groups have the ongoing capacity to monitor government and deal with it at those levels where power resided. Inevitably, a large, intrusive state means that power is more widely diffused throughout the administrative apparatus of government. It resides in officials who draw up regulatory guidelines and who interpret and administer technical matters delegated to them under the authority of vaguely worded statutes, and in those who provide advice on programs and policies that influences the options considered by those nominally in charge, i.e., the members of cabinet.

To deal with the reality of the modern administrative state, groups need to organize. And organize they have. A veritable explosion of associations representing business interests, environmental concerns, consumer interests, women, ethnic groups, official-language minorities, and other interests has taken place during the last few decades. Interest groups acquired prominence later in Canada than in the United States, and when they did it was largely due to a defensive reaction against a state that, like Kafka's castle, was fast becoming more impenetrable and mysterious—not to mention hostile from the standpoint of those in the business community.

The increasing size and complexity of the public sector spawned organized interests in another way. The active role of government in promoting the creation of associations that would in turn represent and articulate the interests of their group interests is well-documented. It is a phenomenon that appears to have begun in World War I, when the federal Department of Trade and Commerce encouraged the creation of trade associations to represent corporations in the same industry.[47] During the 1960s and 1970s, the Department of Secretary of State was instrumental in the creation and proliferation of a large number of organizations representing women, ethnic groups, and official-language minorities, particularly through the provision of core funding to finance the activities of these groups.[48] It appears that the motivation of the state agencies that encouraged the creation of interest groups was at least partly self-serving. They were helping to organize the interests that depended on their programs and budgets and thereby created constituencies whose support could be useful to the bureaucracy in protecting its policy and budgetary turf.[49]

This practice of state funding for organized groups continues today. For example, Canadian Parents for French, a group that is active in promoting French-language schools in English-speaking Canada, receives a large part of its budget from the Official Languages Support Programs Branch of the Department of Canadian Heritage. The Multiculturalism Program of Canadian Heritage funds a wide array of ethnic, racial, religious, and cultural organizations in Canada, many of which lobby government officials or attempt to influence public opinion on matters of concern to them. Many Aboriginal and human rights groups receive a large part of their funding from the Canadian government. The Court Challenges Program provided funding for almost 25 years to organizations representing 'members of historically disadvantaged groups' or official-language minorities. The Women's Legal Education and Action Fund (LEAF), a regular and prominent intervener in Charter cases involving alleged sexual discrimination, often received funding under this program, usually between $35,000 and $50,000 per case. The Conservative government disbanded the Court Challenges Program in 2006 but resurrected part of it in 2008, through the Program to Support Linguistic Rights.

Sophisticated organization has become a *sine qua non* for sustained group influence. Paul Pross uses the term **institutional groups** to describe those interests that possess the highest level of organization. These groups have the following characteristics:

- They possess organizational continuity and cohesion.
- They have extensive knowledge of those sectors of government that affect their clients and enjoy easy communications with those sectors.
- They have stable memberships.
- They have concrete and immediate objectives.
- The overall goals of the organization are more important than any particular objective.[50]

While many different types of groups can claim to have these characteristics, there is no doubt that business associations are more likely to conform to Pross's criteria for institutionalized groups than those representing other interests. Indeed, associations like the Canadian Council of Chief Executives, Canadian Manufacturers & Exporters, the Canadian Chamber of Commerce, the Conseil du Patronat du Québec, the Canadian Federation of Agriculture, the Canadian Federation of Independent Business, and many of the major trade associations in Canada are among the most sophisticated organizationally of interest groups in this country.

Resources

Money is no guarantee of interest group success—but it usually doesn't hurt. It is no accident that the most organizationally sophisticated groups, which enjoy easy access to policy-makers and have the best track records of success in protecting and promoting the interests they represent, tend also to be well-heeled. Money is necessary to pay for the services that are vital to interest group success. A permanent staff costs money—a good deal of money if it includes lawyers, economists, accountants, researchers, public relations specialists, and others whose services are needed to monitor the government scene and communicate both with the group's membership and with policy-makers. The services of public relations firms, polling companies, and professional lobbyists are costly and certainly beyond the reach of many interest groups.

Interest groups representing business tend to have more affluent and stable financial footings than other groups. Their closest rivals are major labour associations; some occupational groups, such as physicians, dentists, lawyers, university professors, and teachers; and some agricultural producer groups. The budgets and personnel of some non-economic groups may also appear to be considerable. For example, in 2009 Ecojustice (formerly the Sierra Legal Defence Fund) had a budget of about $3.9 million and a staff of 15 at its national office. Inuit Tapiriit Kanatami, representing Canada's Inuit population, had a 2010 budget of $8.1 million and a staff of about 40. These budgets are small, however, alongside those of such groups as the Canadian Bankers' Association, the Canadian Federation of Independent Business, and the Canadian Medical Association, all of which have annual spending budgets in excess of $25 million. The size of an association's staff is not always a reliable indicator of its probable influence with decision-makers—for example, the Canadian Council of Chief Executives has a full-time staff of only 12—but these more affluent interest groups tend also to have larger staffs with more specialized personnel. The Canadian Medical Association, for example, employs about 165 persons, the Canadian Bankers' Association about 75, and the Canadian Association of Petroleum Producers about 50. Moreover, there are three important differences between the monetary resources of the major business interest groups and those of other organized interests.

First, the members of business interest groups typically do not rely on their collective associations for political influence to the extent that the members of other interest groups do. Large corporations usually have their own public affairs departments that, among other functions, manage the organization's relations with government. Moreover, corporations will often act on their own in employing the services of a professional lobbying firm or other service that is expected to help them influence policy-makers. Indeed, the clientele lists of such firms as Hill & Knowlton, Government Consultants International, and Executive Consultants Ltd read like a 'Who's Who' of the Canadian corporate elite (with many non-Canadian corporate clients into the bargain). Corporations have traditionally been major contributors to the Liberal and Progressive Conservative parties—business associations seldom donated at all—and annual contributions in the $50,000–$100,000 range were not unusual before the 2004 overhaul of Canada's election and party finance legislation. This kind of contribution was another channel of influence—purchasing access is a better way of describing it—that could be afforded by the individual members of business associations but seldom by the members of other types of interest groups.

The second important difference in the monetary resources of business and non-business associations relates to stability. Simply put, business groups rest on more secure financial footings. They are less subject to the vicissitudes of economic recession and because they do not depend on government or charitable foundation funding they are not exposed to the vagaries of cutbacks and budgetary shuffles. Many other groups cannot make this claim. 'It's been painful', said the head of BC's Sierra Club in December 2008, as the Canadian economy slid more deeply into recession. Their annual budget for 2009 was about 60 per cent of what it had been in 2007, leading to significant cuts in staff and activity.[51] A 2009 survey by the Ontario Trillium Foundation reported that about two-thirds of non-profit groups, including social, cultural, and environmental organizations, said their funding had decreased compared to the previous year.[52] Ecojustice, one of the most important Canadian environmental groups, experienced a decline of about one-third in its foundation grants in 2009, from $1.25 million to $779,627, a story that could be told by social advocacy and environmental groups across the country.

A third difference involves the ability of business and non-business groups to raise money to deal with a 'crisis' issue. The issue of free trade in the federal election campaign of 1988 is a case in point. Although no hard numbers exist, no one seriously denies that business associations in favour of the Canada–US Free Trade Agreement outspent their opponents by a wide margin in an attempt to influence public opinion on the deal and thereby ensure the election of the Conservatives, the only party that supported the FTA. Much of the pro-FTA money was spent through the Canadian Alliance for Trade and Job Opportunities, an ad hoc association financed by 112 Canadian-based corporations. Most of the major contributors to the Alliance were members of the elite Business Council on National Issues, now known as the Canadian Council of Chief Executives (see Box 11.1). The Alliance spent a good deal of money, probably at least $2 million, purchasing television and newspaper ads in the year before the election.[53] When a Conservative victory seemed in doubt, the Alliance financed a media blitz during the last three weeks of the 1988 campaign. Deep pockets will not always get the job done. During the late 1990s the Canadian corporate elite and its lead association, the CCCE, lobbied hard for the Multilateral Agreement on Investment. The MAI was a proposed treaty among the wealthy industrialized countries that would have imposed serious restrictions on governments' ability to discriminate against foreign investors through, for example, requirements that they source materials locally or meet other conditions for investing in a nation's economy. In the end, opposition to the MAI from labour unions and anti-globalization groups in Canada and abroad led the governments who were championing the MAI to abandon their efforts. The superior resources of the corporate backers of the MAI were not enough to win this particular battle.

Money is not the only resource that is useful in promoting an interest group's objectives. John Kingdon identifies several other resources that enable a group to influence what gets on (or stays

Politics in Focus

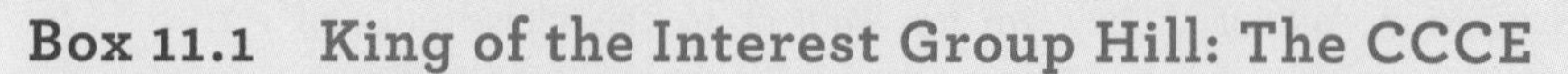

Box 11.1 King of the Interest Group Hill: The CCCE

The Canadian Council of Chief Executives, begun in 1976 as the Business Council on National Issues, was modelled after the Business Roundtable, created in the United States two years earlier. Like the Business Roundtable, the CCCE was created in response to the perception among the corporate elite that big business was under attack from consumers' groups, environmentalists, and governments wedded to tax and regulation policies. An organization representing the heavy hitters of the corporate world was needed to articulate big business's points of view and to defend its interests in the corridors of power.

The CCCE is composed of the 150 CEOs of major companies operating in the Canadian economy. Most of them do some part of their business outside of Canada and many are truly international in their production and sales activities. The CCCE has never included a government-controlled firm. As of 2010 member companies of the CCCE controlled about $4.5 trillion in assets, had yearly revenues of more than $850 billion, and employed close to 1.5 million Canadians.

As the senior voice of Canadian big business, the CCCE takes positions on a range of public policy issues, and not simply economic ones. It was, for example, supportive of the Charlottetown Accord in 1992. The CCCE is believed by many to have been instrumental in persuading the Conservative government to propose free trade talks to the United States in 1985. The Council's focus is, however, primarily on matters of trade and finance and it is a strong voice in favour of Canada–US economic integration and trade liberalization globally.

off) the policy agenda and the alternatives considered by policy-makers. These include electoral influence, the capacity to affect the economy negatively, and group cohesion.[54]

Electoral Influence

The perceived ability to swing a significant bloc of votes is an important group resource. While all interest-group leaders claim to speak on behalf of the group's membership, politicians know that the claim is more credible in some cases than in others. The sheer size of a group's membership can be an important resource, as can the status or wealth of its members and their geographic distribution. The distribution factor can cut two ways. In political systems like Canada's, characterized by the election of a single member from each constituency, the concentration of a group's members in a particular region, other things being equal, will increase the political influence of that group. Candidates and parties are likely to see the advantage of proposing policies that are attractive to such a regionally concentrated group, whose votes are crucial in order to win the seats in that region. On the other hand, geographic dispersion of a group's membership may also be advantageous, even under an electoral system like Canada's. A group's claim to speak on behalf of members who are found across the country, and who can be mobilized to vote in a particular way, can be an impressive electoral resource. It is, for example, an argument regularly used by the Canadian Federation of Independent Business, which has about 100,000 members across Canada.

Capacity to Inflict Damage on the Economy

The ability to 'down tools', close businesses, scale down investment plans, refuse to purchase government bonds, or in some other way inflict harm on the economy or public finances (or both!) can be a powerful group resource. It is a resource that is possessed mainly by business groups. Unions and such other occupational groups as physicians or agricultural producers have a more difficult time using 'economic blackmail' to influence policy-makers. There are two reasons for this. First, when a group such as nurses, teachers, dockworkers, postal workers, truckers, or doctors attempts to tie up the economy or some important public service by withholding their labour, the linkage between the behaviour of such a group and the social or economic consequences of their actions is extremely visible. Regardless of the factors that led to their action, the general public is likely to perceive the situation as one where the *special* interests of such a group stands in sharp contrast to the *public* interest. A union or other occupational group that attempts to use the threat of economic or social chaos to back up its demands should not count on favourable public opinion. On the contrary, public support for or indifference towards a group's demands is likely to change to hostility in such circumstances. In the case of unions, they suffer from the additional disadvantage of being held in very low esteem by Canadians. Surveys regularly show that public confidence in labour unions is lower than for most other major social institutions.

A second reason why business interests are better able than other economic interest groups to successfully use the threat of economic damage in pursuing their objectives has to do with culture. In a capitalist society like ours, the fundamental values that underpin the strength of business interests—the belief in private property, the importance of profits, and faith in markets as the best mechanism for generating and distributing wealth—lend legitimacy to the general interests of business. Particular industries or corporations may be perceived as being greedy or socially irresponsible, but the values generally associated with a capitalist economy enjoy widespread support. When workers lay down their tools to apply pressure in support of their demands there is a good chance that their action will be interpreted as irresponsible. But if a business refuses to invest in new plant and machinery, lays off workers, or relocates, the reactions of policy-makers and the public are likely to be quite different. Most of us accept that business is about making a profit. The damage that a failure of business confidence may do to an economy may be regrettable, but business people are less likely to be accused of being irresponsible because they are just acting in accordance with the rules of a system that most of us accept.

Group Cohesion

'United we stand, divided we fall' has always been an accepted rule of interest group influence. Other things being equal, an association's hand will be strengthened if it is able to convince policy-makers that it speaks with a single voice and genuinely represents the views of its membership. This is not always easy. We have already noted that both labour and business interests are highly fragmented in Canada and are represented by a large number of associations, not one of which can credibly claim to speak on behalf of all labour or business interests.

The same is true for many other collective interests in Canadian society. Hundreds of organizations represent different groups of agricultural and food producers. Native Canadians are represented by many associations, the largest of which is the Assembly of First Nations. Its ability to speak on behalf of all Native groups is limited, however, by the fact that it does not speak for Métis and non-status Indians (who are represented, respectively, by the Métis National Council and the Congress of Aboriginal Peoples) or for the Inuit (represented by the Inuit Tapiriit Kanatami). Cohesion once appeared to be greatest in the women's movement. Founded in 1972 and originally financed entirely by the federal government, the National Action Committee on the Status of Women was for many years the major umbrella association that at its peak represented about 700 smaller women's organizations. This appearance, however, was somewhat deceiving. By the late 1980s NAC was increasingly beset by internal divisions and the confrontational style that its leadership favoured was not supported by some groups within the women's movement. By 2004 NAC was insolvent and any claim it had to be the major organizational voice for Canadian women's groups was no longer credible.

Group cohesion typically becomes less problematic as the number of members represented by an organization grows fewer and the similarity between members increases. But what is gained in cohesion may, of course, be lost as a result of the perception that an association represents a narrow special interest. As well, it is easier to present a united front when an association is speaking on behalf of just one group. Alliances with associations representing other groups, however, may be politically useful. The downside, again, is the problem of submerging group differences in such a common front.

A rather different problem of cohesion involves the relationship between a group's leaders and its membership. Evidence of a gap between the goals of leaders and those they purport to represent will undermine an association's credibility in the eyes of policy-makers. A variation of this problem exists when an interest group claims to speak on behalf of a collectivity that is largely unorganized, or where there are good reasons for doubting that the group actually expresses the views of those they claim to represent. For example, women's groups like the NAC have sometimes been accused of not expressing the views of a large part of Canada's female population. Labour unions' claims to speak on behalf of Canadian workers are weakened, in the eyes of some, by the fact that they represent fewer than four out of every 10 workers.

The dynamics of group cohesion tend to favour certain types of interests more than others. As is also true of the other group resources we have examined, the winners are mainly business interest groups. To understand why this is the case, consider two widely accepted propositions about interest group cohesion.[55] First, as the number of members in an organization increases, the likelihood that some individuals will believe that they can reap the benefits of the organization's actions without having to contribute to it also increases. This is called the **free-rider problem**. Other things being equal, smaller groups are more cohesive than larger ones. Second, groups able to offer exclusive benefits to their members, i.e., benefits only available to members of the organization, will be more cohesive and more capable of concerted political pressure than those that rely on collective benefits, i.e., benefits that will accrue to society as a whole. A corollary of this second proposition is that organizations relying on material incentives to attract and retain members, which therefore can motivate members with the prospect of shared material benefits, will be more cohesive than groups that rely on non-material incentives.[56]

If we turn now to the actual interest group system, we find that business groups tend to be smaller than other interest associations. Indeed, some are quite small, particularly those that represent companies in oligopolistic industries. For example, the Canadian Vehicle Manufacturers Association represents only four companies, the Forest Products Association of Canada has only 18 members, and the Canadian Bankers' Association has 51 member organizations. Some business associations, such as Chambers of Commerce, the Canadian Federation of Independent Business, and Canadian Manufacturers & Exporters, have much larger memberships. But it is also true that these organizations represent more general interests of the business community, while the more specific interests of corporations are represented through trade associations that have smaller memberships.

Business groups are not the only ones to rely on exclusive benefits and material incentives to attract, maintain, and motivate members. Labour unions, agricultural producer groups, and professional associations do as well. But one needs to remember that cohesion is only one group resource. Farmers' groups or labour unions may be as cohesive as business associations but still inferior to business in terms of the other resources at their disposal.

Safety in the Shadows

Placard-carrying animal rights activists, a blue-suited spokesperson for an organization presenting a brief to a parliamentary committee, or a full-page newspaper ad promoting a particular policy are all highly visible manifestations of interest groups in action. They are not, however, necessarily the most effective pathways of group influence. Often it is what does not happen—the absence of visible signs of groups exerting themselves to influence policy—that tells us most about the strength of organized interests. In the jungle that is the interest group system, some seek safety in the shadows.

The fact that the status, privileges, or interests of some groups are not matters of public debate tells us something about the power of this group. As E.E. Schattschneider writes, 'The very expression "pressure politics" invites us to misconceive the role of special-interest groups in politics.'[57] 'Private conflicts', he argues, 'are taken into the public arena precisely because someone wants to make certain that the power ratio among the private interests most immediately involved shall not prevail.'[58] On reflection, the point is obvious and yet profoundly important. Society's most powerful interests would prefer to avoid the public arena where they have to justify themselves and respond to those who advocate changes that would affect their interests. They are safe in the shadows. But when the light of public debate is shone on them they become prey to attacks from other groups and they lose their security. Conflict, Schattschneider notes, always includes an element of unpredictability. Consequently, even private interests with impressive group resources may suffer losses in their status and privileges, depending on what alliances form against them, the shape of public opinion, and the behaviour of political parties. Indeed, when previously unquestioned interests have reached the public agenda and are recognized as group interests, this registers a loss of influence on the part of such a group.

When the security of the shadows is lost, the relative safety of a fairly closed policy community is a decent substitute. In the United States, the concept of an **iron triangle** has been used to describe the closed system of relations between an interest group and the administrative agencies and congressional committees with which it routinely deals. Most commentators agree that the 'iron triangles' that may have characterized policy-making in the United States have become less rigid over the last few decades. Moreover, because one of the corners in these triangular relationships involved Congress and its powerful committees, the 'iron triangle' concept never travelled very well beyond the United States. The terms 'sub-governments', 'policy communities', and 'policy networks' are now more commonly used in both the United States and elsewhere to describe the reality of relatively exclusive constellations of state and societal actors who dominate routine policy-making in a particular field. Indeed, the ability to maintain the routine nature of policy-making is vital to preserving the privileged status of the dominant actors in a policy community.[59]

The Impact of Federalism on Interest Groups

Hardly a corner of Canadian political life is unaffected by federalism, the interest group system included. Because the Constitution divides political authority between two levels of government, one of the first challenges facing an interest group is to determine where jurisdiction lies or, as is often the case, how it is divided between the national and provincial governments. An extensive literature has developed on federalism and interest groups in Canada.[60] We will examine three of the more general propositions that emerge from this body of work.

The first has been labelled the *multiple crack hypothesis*.[61] According to this interpretation, the existence of two levels of government, each of which is equipped with a range of taxing, spending, and regulatory powers, provides interest groups with an opportunity to seek from one government what they cannot get from the other. Business groups have been the ones most likely to exploit the constitutional division of powers, and in many well-documented cases they have done so successfully.[62]

A second interpretation of federalism's impact on interest groups argues that a federal constitution tends to weaken group influence by reducing the internal cohesion of organized interests. According to this argument, divided authority to make policy on matters that affect a group's interests will encourage it to adopt a federal form of organization.[63] Although this may seem a politically prudent response to the realities of divided legislative authority, it may reduce the ability of groups to speak with a single voice and to persuade governments that they have the capacity for collective action to back up their demands. A group's influence may be weakened even further when the two levels of government are in serious conflict, a situation that may spill over to create division within the group itself (for example, along regional lines) and between its representative associations.[64]

A third proposition about federalism and interest groups involves what might be called the statist interpretation of federalism's impact. According to this view, governments and their sprawling bureaucracies increasingly dominate the policy-making scene, particularly when jurisdictional issues are involved. Societal groups, even those with considerable resources, may be largely frozen out of the process of intergovernmental relations. Alan Cairns implies as much in arguing that modern Canadian federalism is mainly about conflicts between governments and their competing political and organizational goals.[65] Leslie Pal draws similar conclusions—although he is careful not to overgeneralize his findings—from his study of the historical development of Canada's Unemployment Insurance program. Pal finds that the impact of societal groups on the original form of UI and on subsequent changes to the program was minor compared to the role played by bureaucratic and intergovernmental factors.[66] Unlike the 'federalism as opportunity' view, this interpretation sees federalism—at least the modern federalism of large, bureaucratic state structures at both the national and regional levels—as a constraint on the influence of business and other societal interests.

The 'federalism as opportunity' and 'federalism as constraint' views are best thought of as representing the two ends of a continuum along which actual cases fall. Examples can be found to support either of these interpretations. Between them are other instances (probably the majority) where the federal division of powers and the intergovernmental rivalry that it sets up provide opportunities for interest groups (the 'multiple cracks' referred to earlier) but also place limits on their influence. Opportunity or constraint, federalism does have some influence on the way in which interests organize for political action, the strategies they adopt when trying to influence policy, and the likelihood of their success.

Strategies for Influence

There are three basic strategies open to interest groups. One is to target policy-makers directly, through personal meetings with officials, briefs, and exchanges of information. This is the *lobbying option*. Another strategy is to target *public opinion* in the expectation that policy-makers will respond to indications that there is considerable popular support for a group's position. The media play a crucial role here, because they are the channel by which a group's message will be communicated to the wider public. A variation of the public opinion option involves alliance-building. By building visible bridges with other groups on some issue, a group may hope to persuade policy-makers that its position has broad support. A third strategy involves *judicial action*. This confrontational strategy involves a very public challenge and an outcome that is likely to leave one side a winner and the other a loser. For some groups it tends to be an option of last resort, used after other strategies have failed. But for other groups, such as the Women's Legal Education and Action Fund (LEAF), Equality for Gays and Lesbians Everywhere (EGALE), Ecojustice (formerly the Sierra Legal Defence Fund), and the Canadian Civil Liberties Association, litigation is a basic weapon in their arsenal of pressure tactics (see Box 11.2).

These strategies are not mutually exclusive. A group may use more than one of them at once or switch from one strategy to another. Nor can one draw firm conclusions about the relative effectiveness of different influence strategies. Much depends on the nature of the issue and the character of the policy community within which a group's actions reverberate. Despite the contingent quality of group influence, a few generalizations are possible. They include the following:

- Everyone recognizes that one of the keys to influence is being involved early in the

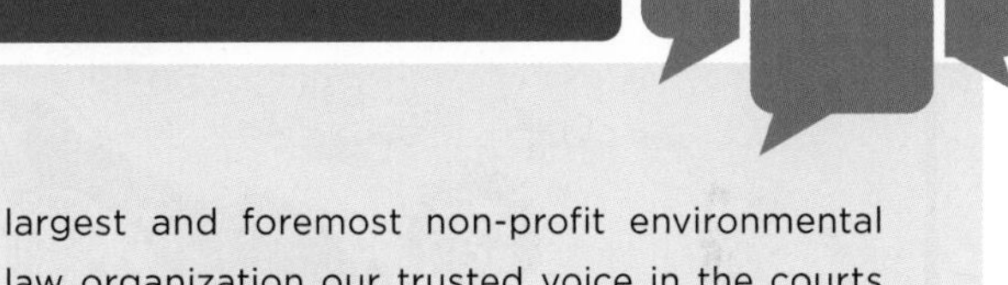

Politics in Focus

Box 11.2 Influence through Litigation

Ecojustice, for many years known as the Sierra Legal Defence Fund, maintains a robust staff that includes lawyers and scientists. The group's *2011 Victories Report* (http://www.ecojustice.ca/publications/2011-victories-report/attachment) lists 84 clients from virtually every region of Canada. LEAF's website lists about 80 cases where the organization has intervened since 1985. Between 1974 and 2008 the Canadian Civil Liberties Association was involved in 103 cases either as an intervener or a direct litigant. EGALE has had intervener status in every case dealing with sexual equality rights since *Egan v. Canada* in 1995. For these groups and others, litigation is a key tool in their efforts to influence public policy and shape the direction of Canadian society. Their impact goes far beyond the individual cases in which they become involved. If these cases are the battles, the war is the wider and longer-term effort to shape the interpretation of the law and the context of public opinion in which policy decisions are made. This is clearly expressed on the website of Ecojustice (www.ecojustice.ca):

> Ecojustice goes to court to defend the right of Canadians to a healthy environment. As Canada's largest and foremost non-profit environmental law organization our trusted voice in the courts enables citizens to expose lawbreakers and hold governments accountable, all while setting powerful precedents for clean water, natural spaces, healthy communities and for global warming solutions.
>
> . . .
>
> Ecojustice acts strategically. We take on cases with the potential to set legal precedents and strengthen laws in support of four goals: fighting global warming, the protection of clean water and natural spaces (parks, wilderness and wildlife), and the promotion of healthy communities. Our influence also extends beyond the courts and corridors of power. Since 1990, Ecojustice outreach campaigns, workshops, investigations and reports have strengthened the work of conservationists in Canada and abroad. As a leader in the courts, community and conservation movement, we aim to defend the right of Canadians to a healthy environment—now and for decades to come.

policy-making process, when ideas are just being considered and legislation has not yet been drafted. Lobbying is the generally preferred strategy at this stage of the policy process. Confrontation and visibility are relatively low, and the importance of thorough preparation and credible technical information is high.

- Groups that are well-established members of a policy community, routinely consulted by government officials, will tend to prefer a lobbying strategy. More public and confrontational strategies involve the risk of bringing unpredictable elements into the policy-making process and will be used only as measures of last resort.
- Groups that are not well established within a policy community are more likely to rely on confrontation, media campaigns, and other public strategies to get policy-makers to pay attention and respond to the interests they represent.
- Where a group's interests are significantly affected by regulation, lobbying strategies that rely on research and technical information supplied to the bureaucratic officials doing the regulating will be most successful.
- The era of vested interests relying on lobbying strategies has passed. Lobbying remains a very important influence strategy, but even groups enjoying regular high-level access to policy-makers now often find that lobbying is not enough.
- A successful influence strategy is usually quite expensive. This is true whether one is talking about lobbying (which often involves hiring a professional government relations firm), aiming at public opinion (which may involve the use of paid advertisements and the services of public relations and polling experts), or going to court. Business groups tend to be better able to pay for these expensive strategies than other groups.

Following the example of successful litigants in the United States, some Canadian interest groups have come to see the courts as the venue where they are most likely to achieve their goals.

Just what *is* the price of influence? It varies, but a legal challenge that makes its way to the Supreme Court can certainly cost millions of dollars in legal bills. If the case is one where much of the legal work has been contributed on a pro bono basis, as is often true of sexual equality or same-sex discrimination cases, the costs may be considerably less. Large business corporations and industry associations have the financial means to go to court in defence of their interests. For other groups, it is often necessary for a litigation-oriented advocacy group such as Ecojustice or LEAF to take on the burden of their representation. A recent example of this involves Ecojustice's lawsuit against the federal Department of Fisheries and Oceans, on behalf of nine conservation groups, challenging the department's decision to appeal a Federal Court ruling that protected killer whale habitats off the British Columbia coast.[67]

A campaign directed at influencing public opinion can also be costly. We have already mentioned the multi-million dollar campaign waged by the pro-FTA Canadian Alliance for Trade and Job Opportunities—probably over $2 million spent even before the final blitz during the 1988 federal election campaign. Although this case is two decades old and the amount of money may sound rather paltry by today's standards, its importance lies in the fact that it became the catalyst for reform of the law on third-party spending during election campaigns. But business groups are not the only ones to spend lavishly in an effort to shape public opinion. Quebec's Cree Indians spent an estimated $500,000 on paid advertisements and the services of a New York public relations firm in an effort to stop the construction of the Great Whale hydroelectric project in Quebec. The public opinion they were targeting was in New York, the people who would be the consumers of power generated by Great Whale and exported to the United States, and in 2002 the provincial government dropped its plans for the Great Whale portion of the massive hydroelectric developments in northern Quebec.

In recent years Alberta's oil sands have generated an enormous amount of spending in an effort to influence public opinion, mainly outside of Canada. In February 2009 an anti-oil sands ad was placed in *USA Today*, paid for by the Cree and Chipewyan communities of Alberta. A year later, San Francisco-based Corporate Ethics International (CEI) launched what it called its 'Rethink Alberta' anti-tourism campaign with billboards in Denver, Portland, Seattle, and Minneapolis. The billboards cost about $50,000, but were only the beginning of a much larger campaign whose costs were expected to reach hundreds of thousands of dollars. 'We're running flash and banner ads on major tourist websites', said Michael Marx, CEI's executive director. '[They] start with images of Banff and then morph into images of the tar sands.'[68] These sums, however, pale alongside the $25 million that the Alberta government announced it would spend over several years to tell Canadians, Americans, and others its side of the oil sands story. Similarly, following the massive oil spill in the Gulf of Mexico in the spring of 2010, the oil giant BP reported spending $93 million from April through July on advertising to 'polish the corporate image' in an attempt to convince customers (and perhaps, especially, investors) that it was committed to stopping the wellhead blowout and that it cared about the environment and the communities affected.[69]

It is usually extremely difficult to pinpoint the resources devoted to an advertising campaign that aims to influence public opinion in a way favourable to the interests of the organization paying for it. Wal-Mart is just one of many companies that has invested a significant amount of money over the years in television and other ads intended to convey the message that the company is a socially responsible and valued member of the communities where its stores are located. The beer and liquor industries have likewise invested large amounts of money in advertising that aims to create a favourable public image of them, as distinct from their products, presumably in order to preclude the sort of regulation and product advertising limits that have been imposed on the tobacco industry. None of this spending is related to election campaigns, and therefore does not fall under the rules set by the Canada Elections Act. Indeed, it is certain that the severe limits placed on interest group spending in election campaigns, going back to 2000, and the ban on corporate and union contributions to parties and candidates that came into effect in 2004 have had the effect of increasing the importance of group money spent between elections.

The purchase of newspaper/magazine space or broadcast time to convey a political message is called **advocacy advertising**. As the Great Whale and Alberta oil sands cases show, business interest groups are not the only ones to buy advertising in an effort to influence public opinion on some issue. But among societal groups, business uses advocacy advertising most extensively. The crucial question raised by any form of advertising that carries a political message is whether the ability to pay for media time/space should determine what views get expressed. The critics of advocacy advertising were

President Obama,
You'll never guess who's standing between
us and our new energy economy...

Canada's Tar Sands: the dirtiest oil on earth.
President Obama travels to Canada on February 19. We hope he'll discuss his vision for a new energy future with leaders there. The US and Canada can revive our economies, create green jobs, and build a better future for our children.
This is the best path forward.
Right now, Canada is not on that path. Producing oil from Canada's Tar Sands releases massive greenhouse gas emissions, consumes huge amounts of energy, contaminates fresh water and fish, produces toxic waste and destroys vast forests along with their birds and wildlife. And now, downstream indigenous communities are suffering higher than normal rates of cancer.
Prime Minister Harper and the government of Alberta continue to turn a blind eye to these problems.
Your voice counts. Please let President Obama know that he should ask Canada to clean up the Tar Sands.
Take action online today.
Visit ForestEthics.org

MIKISEW CREE
FIRST NATION

FORESTETHICS
VANCOUVER • TORONTO • SAN FRANCISCO • BELLINGHAM

ForestEthics teamed up with the Mikisew Cree and Athabasca Chipewyan First Nations to place this full-page ad in *USA Today*.

quick to denounce the blitz of pro-free trade advertising by business during the 1988 election campaign. They argued that the deep pockets of the corporate interests ranged behind free trade made a sham of the democratic political process and totally undermined the intention of the statutory limits on election spending by political parties. The Royal Commission on Elections agreed. Its 1992 report recommended that spending by organizations other than registered political parties be limited during elections. As we saw in Chapter 10, these restrictions have been passed and their constitutionality upheld by the Supreme Court of Canada.

The defenders of advocacy advertising claim that it is a way for business to overcome the anti-business bias of the media and to bridge the 'credibility gap' that has developed between business and the public. Mobil Oil, one of the pioneers of this advertising technique, responded to criticism by calling it a 'new form of public disclosure',[70] thereby associating it with freedom of information. Business and economic issues are complex, and advocacy advertising—most of which is done through the print media—provides an opportunity for business to explain its actions and to counter public misconceptions. And in any case, argue corporate spokespersons, the biggest spender on advocacy advertising is government, whose justification for this spending is essentially the same as that of business![71] There is no doubt that strategies aimed at influencing public opinion have become increasingly important to interest groups. In fact, in discussing advocacy advertising we have only scratched the surface of these strategies (see Box 11.3).[72] Important as they are, however, strategies that target public opinion usually take a back seat

Politics in Focus

Box 11.3 Think-Tanks and Interest Group Influence

A think-tank is an organization that carries out research on some matter of public importance and seeks to communicate its findings and recommendations for government policy to a wider audience that may range from citizens to policy-makers at the highest levels. Its goals tend to be broader and its influence strategies rather different from those of interest groups. Think-tanks are in the business of influencing the climate of ideas within which policy choices are discussed, as well as the particular options that are considered in dealing with an issue. Some of them are not anchored to an ideological agenda and seldom, if ever, advocate a particular policy option. But others resemble broad-based interest groups like the Canadian Labour Congress and the Canadian Chamber of Commerce in that they have a clear ideological orientation—for example, market-oriented in the case of the Fraser Institute and the Frontier Centre for Public Policy, or left-of-centre and anti-globalization in the case of the Centre for Social Justice and the Caledon Institute—and attempt to nudge public policy in a specific direction.

Many of the world's most prominent think-tanks, particularly in the United States where most such organizations are found, including such well-known ones as the Brookings Institution, the Hoover Institute, and the American Enterprise Institute, were created by donors in the expectations that they would work to influence the policy conversation in ways favourable to their benefactors. In Canada, the Fraser Institute was created in 1974 at a time when, in the organization's own words, 'the intellectual consensus was that government action was the best means of meeting the economic and social aspirations of Canadians.' The Institute was originally funded by corporate donations, and from its inception has had a strong business presence on its board of directors.

The Caledon Institute for Social Policy has a very different world view from that of the Fraser Institute. Created in 1992, it is funded mainly by the Maytree Foundation, a philanthropic organization headed by businessman and philanthropist Alan Broadbent. The Canadian Centre for Policy Alternatives was created in 1980. It shares the same ideological space as the Caledon Institute and, in its own words, is 'concerned with issues of social, economic and environmental justice'. The Centre's original funding came from trade unions and individual members.

to those that target policy-makers directly. These are lobbying strategies.

Lobbying may be defined as any form of direct or indirect communication with government that is designed to influence public policy.[73] Although the term conjures up images of smoke-filled rooms, 'old boy networks', and sleazy deal-making, this is a somewhat unfair caricature of lobbying on two counts. First, lobbying is a basic democratic right. When a group of citizens organizes to demand a traffic light at a dangerous neighbourhood corner and meets with their local city councillor to express their concerns, this is lobbying. When the president of a powerful business association arranges a lunch rendezvous with an official in the Prime Minister's Office with whom he went to law school, this, too, is lobbying. The fact that lobbying is often associated in the minds of the public and journalists with unfair privilege and even corruption should not obscure the fact that it is not limited to organizations representing the powerful or the fact that, in principle, there is nothing undemocratic about lobbying.

A second way in which the 'sleaze' caricature of lobbying conveys a wrong impression is by associating it with practices that, in fact, constitute only a small part of what lobbyists actually do. Direct meetings with influential public officials are certainly an aspect of lobbying. Likewise, there is no shortage of evidence that ethically dubious relations occasionally exist between lobbyists and policy-makers (see Box 11.4). But lobbying involves a much wider set of activities than simply buttonholing cabinet ministers or their senior officials.

Most professional lobbyists, whether they work for a company or interest group, or for a government relations firm that sells its lobbying expertise to clients, spend the better part of their time collecting and communicating information on behalf of the interests they represent. They monitor the political scene as it affects their client's interests. An effective lobbyist does not simply react, but instead is like an early warning system, providing information about policy when it is still in its formative stages and tracking public opinion on the issues that are vital to a client's interests. Lobbyists provide information about how and where to access the policy-making system and strategies for influencing policies or winning contracts. They may also provide advice and professional assistance in putting together briefs, press releases, speeches, and other communications, as well as public relations services such as identifying and targeting those segments of public opinion that influence policy-makers on some issue (see Boxes 11.5 and 11.6). Helping to build strategic coalitions with other groups is another function that lobbyists may perform.

Most interest groups lobby government on their own. But for those who can afford it, the services of a professional lobbying firm may also be purchased. The 2010 Ottawa telephone directory lists 34 firms under the 'Government relations' heading of the Yellow Pages. They range from large firms like Hill & Knowlton Canada, which employ dozens of professional staff and have annual billings in the tens of millions of dollars, to small operations that employ a handful of persons. In addition, many law firms and accounting companies, including such prominent ones as McCarthy Tétrault, Osler Hoskins & Harcourt, MacMillan Binch, and Pricewaterhousecoopers, do lobbying work. The line between legal representation and lobbying is often non-existent, a fact

Governing Realities

Box 11.4 The Potential Influence of Foreign Money

In June of 2010 the director of the Canadian Security Intelligence Service, Richard Fadden, testified before a parliamentary committee. What he said came as a shock to many Canadians. Their public officials, he said, were being targeted by foreign nationals who hoped to buy political goodwill and policy influence in Canada. One of the main ways this is done is through foreign corporations, governments, or associations funded by foreign governments paying for trips to visit their country. Canadian politicians at all levels of government frequently take such trips, often described as 'fact-finding missions', the ostensible goal of which is to nurture contacts and identify business possibilities. The hospitality is often lavish and spouses are frequently invited.

Such trips are not the equivalent of bribes. There is seldom an expectation of a specific quid pro quo. But the foreign government or organization footing the bill does so in the expectation that, at a minimum, it is buying goodwill that will ultimately translate into influence in Canadian political decision-making.

Should public officials be banned from accepting the largesse of foreigners? Perhaps. But the trips they make abroad *may** generate benefits, economic and otherwise, for their communities and constituents in Canada. Experience shows, however, that when they travel on the taxpayers' dime there is predictable outrage, and media stories suggest that they are off on foreign boondoggles. If Canadians want their representatives to be properly informed and to make the connections necessary in our globalized world, but at the same time keep their virtue intact, then some acceptable way for Canadians to pay for their representatives' travel abroad will need to be found.

*The word 'may' needs to be emphasized. A study by two University of British Columbia researchers, published in the August 2010 issue of the *Canadian Journal of Economics* and based on trade missions during the period 1993 to 2003, concluded that their effect amounted to zero.[74]

attested to by the presence of many law firms on the public registry of lobbyists.

Since 1989, those who are paid to lobby federal public office-holders have been required to register with a federal agency. The Lobbyists Registration Act provides for three categories of lobbyists:

- *Consultant lobbyists* are those who, for a fee, work for various clients. As of July 2010, there were 747 such individuals registered as active consultant lobbyists.
- *Corporate in-house lobbyists* are those who work for a single corporation and who lobby federal officials as a significant part of their duties. As of July 2010, there were 1,023 individuals registered as in-house corporate lobbyists.
- *Organization in-house lobbyists* are the senior paid officers and other employees of organizations—business, labour, environmental, charitable, etc.—whose activities would include lobbying federal officials. As of July 2010, there were 1,525 in-house organization lobbyists registered with the Lobbyists Registration Branch of Industry Canada.

The majority of active consultant and in-house organization lobbyists represent corporations and business associations (as do the in-house corporate lobbyists). The clientele lists of Canada's leading government relations firms include major players in the Canadian and international corporate world. Hill & Knowlton Canada, for example, boasts that it represents such clients as Microsoft,

Politics in Focus

Box 11.5 What Does a Government Relations Firm Sell?

Public Affairs

Governments have a profound impact on the way business is conducted, especially when they make changes to policies and regulations with little or no public consultation. These changes can alter the competitive landscape for Canadian businesses, raise or lower taxes, and impact the investment climate for companies operating in Canada or abroad.

Hill & Knowlton Canada's national public affairs practice is dedicated to working with clients to ensure they are prepared for the ever-changing environment and are equipped to affect government decisions and processes in a meaningful manner.

Our public affairs practitioners are the best in the business. They have firsthand experience with government decision-making structure and deep connections within government departments to assist their client's challenges. With years of experience, the PA team members have served in the offices of the Prime Minister and Premiers, at the executive branches of the public service, and as elected officials themselves, each consultant brings an in-depth understanding of how decisions are made, and how to engage in political debate in a meaningful way. Our strategic counsel and programs take into account the interplay between government departments, and the critical need to manage the internal and external debate through compelling arguments, strategically delivered—often through the inclusion of social media, outreach to key stakeholders, strategic media relations as well as political and bureaucratic influencers.

Whether it is securing a multi-billion dollar procurement contract, explaining opposition to a new tax, or mobilizing support for an infrastructure project, H&K's public affairs team helps clients succeed in every jurisdiction in Canada.

Hill & Knowlton Canada is also able to provide clients with global representation as it draws on the resources of its parent company, Hill & Knowlton Inc., a world leader in public affairs.

Source: Hill & Knowlton website: <http://www.hillandknowlton.ca/public-affairs-firm>. Used by permission of Hill & Knowlton Canada.

SHL Systemhouse, De Beers, Rio Algom, Kraft, Glaxo Wellcome, Deutsche Bank Canada, and Standard Life (www.hillandknowlton.ca/letter.htm). Box 11.7 lists some of Canada's most prominent consultant lobbyists and some of the clients they work for.

As the scope and process of governance have changed, so, too, has the character of lobbying. What was once a rather shadowy activity undertaken by well-connected individuals, who often worked for major law firms that relatively few Canadians had heard of, became increasingly complicated and characterized by a broader range of influence strategies and tools. The old model of lobbying as personal communications by a well-placed individual to a cabinet minister or high-ranking bureaucrat on behalf of a client morphed into an activity more akin to Sherpas guiding their climbers towards a destination. Personal contacts with key policy-makers continue to be a large part of what lobbying firms sell, but this is reinforced by extensive knowledge and intensive analysis of the policy matters of concern to clients. Under the

Politics in Focus

Box 11.6 What Do the Clients of a Government Relations Firm Get for Their Money? Expertise and Connections

Harry Near, Principal, Earnscliffe Strategy Group

Harry Near has spent over twenty-five years as a government affairs consultant advising private sector companies on strategies and tactics for best dealing with the federal government.

Prior to his government consulting career Mr. Near worked in business, government and also as a political volunteer. From 1970 to 1979 he worked for Imperial Oil Limited in a number of company departments. In 1979 and 1984 he was Senior Policy Advisor and Chief of Staff to the federal Ministers of Energy, Mines and Resources.

Through the 70s, 80s, 90s and continuing today he has been a political advisor to Progressive Conservative parties and governments at both the federal and provincial level. In 1984 and in 1988 he was the National Campaign Director for the Progressive Conservative party national election campaigns. He continues as an advisor to Conservative Party candidates today.

Ian Brodie, Senior Counsellor, Hill & Knowlton

Ian provides strategic advice to a range of local, national, and international clients on the positioning of their critical issues in a dynamic and complex public environment. Most recently, Ian served as Chief of Staff to the Prime Minister of Canada, where he dealt with competing interests and demanding stakeholder organizations and demonstrated his depth of knowledge of the public policy process. Ian was the founding Executive Director of the Conservative Party following the amalgamation of the Canadian Alliance and the PC Party. In that capacity, he was responsible for establishing a professional, national institution focused on organization and election readiness, fundraising, membership development and information technology.

David Angus, Senior Partner, Capital Hill Group

Prior to joining The Capital Hill Group in 1985, David was highly involved with key players in both the Ontario and Canadian governments. David has maintained these networks over the years, giving him a solid reputation for access to decision-makers in the civil service and in the political offices of ministers.

David has extensive expertise in procurement, defence and transport policy, and has consistently delivered results to clients in these areas. David has also been integral in connecting Information Technology (IT) clients to opportunities to participate in shaping government service delivery on an electronic basis.

David has been nominated to the North American Directory of 'Who's Who' for business and executives for several years running.

Sources: Earnscliffe website at: <www.earnscliffe.ca>. Hill & Knowlton website at <www.hillandknowlton.ca>. Used by permission of Hill & Knowlton Canada. Capital Hill website at <www.capitalhill.ca>.

Politics in Focus

Box 11.7 Who Do Government Relations Firms Represent?

Lobbyist	Company	Clients
Ronald Atkey	Osler, Hoskins & Harcourt	Time Canada Warner Brothers Viacom Canadian Motion Picture Distributors Association
Brian Mersereau	Hill & Knowlton	Eurocopter Northrop Grumman Amex Canada Rio Tinto General Dynamics
Charles King	Earnscliffe Strategy	Microsoft Canada Bell Canada Canadian Imperial Bank of Commerce General Motors Canadian Association of Broadcasters
David Angus	Capital Hill Group	Lockheed Martin Molson Canada Trillium Health Care Ducks Unlimited Royal Conservatory of Music Mackenzie Aboriginal Corp.
Steven Dover	Self-employed	Intuit Canada John Deere Limited Algoma Central Corp. Bombardier Aeronautique

Source: Industry Canada, Lobbyists Registration System, on-line public registry, at: <www.ocl-cal.gc.ca/eic/site/lobbyist-lobbyistel.nsf/eng/h_nx00274.html>. Reproduced with the permission of the Library of Parliament, 2010.

leadership of Allan Gregg, Decima Research played an important role in this transformation. It offered clients analysis of the public opinion environment in which their activities were situated and that affected the achievement of their goals. The *Decima Quarterly* provided clients with confidential and up-to-date information on public opinion. When Hill & Knowlton, already a world leader in the lobbying industry, acquired Decima the fusion of public opinion expertise, marketing skills, policy analysis, and personal access to government officials was achieved. A sort of one-stop-shopping model for public affairs advice and strategic communication became the new standard.

This remains the model in Canada, as practised by the heavyweights of the lobbying establishment. Most of the activities engaged in by these lobbyists on behalf of their clients involve economic affairs. The Lobbyists Registration Act requires that lobbyists identify the general subject matter of their activities as well as the government departments and agencies that they contact on behalf of those they represent. 'Industry', 'international trade', and 'taxation and finance' have, from the beginning of the registration system, been the most frequent subjects on which lobbyists have plied their trade. 'Environment' has moved steadily up the list and was ranked third in 2010, reflecting the increasing importance of environmental laws and regulations for corporations and business associations. Matters relating to health policy also have been among the most frequent subjects of lobbying in recent years. Lobbyists are required to indicate the government institutions they contact or expect to contact, and, since 2006, the particular public officials they lobby. The departments of Finance, Industry, and Foreign Affairs and International Trade, as well as the PCO and the PMO, are perennially among the most targeted institutions.

Starting Points for Research

Robert Campbell, Michael Howlett, and Leslie Pal, *The Real Worlds of Canadian Politics*, 4th edn (Peterborough, Ont.: Broadview Press, 2004). This book provides rich accounts of the policy-making process in Canada, including the behaviour and influence of interest groups.

William D. Coleman, *Business and Politics: A Study of Collective Action* (Montreal and Kingston: McGill-Queen's University Press, 1988). This remains one of the leading empirical contributions to the study of interest groups in Canada.

Geoffrey Hale, *Uneasy Partnership: The Politics of Business and Government* (Toronto: University of Toronto Press, 2006). This leading textbook on business–government relations in Canada provides a solid introduction to the factors that contribute to and limit the political influence of business interests.

Leslie A. Pal, *Interests of State: The Politics of Language, Multiculturalism and Feminism in Canada* (Montreal and Kingston: McGill-Queen's University Press, 1993). Testing various models of interest group influence, Pal explains the complex interaction between group interests and identity formation and the interests and goals of public officials.

Donley T. Studlar, *Tobacco Control: Comparative Politics in the United States and Canada* (Toronto: University of Toronto Press, 2002). This work presents an excellent comparative analysis of the actions and influence of the tobacco lobby in Canada and the United States.

Review Exercises

1. Find a newspaper story that discusses an interest group. Based on this article, answer as fully as you can the following questions:
   (a) What is the name of the group?
   (b) Who does the group represent?
   (c) Why is the group in the news?
   (d) Can anything about the group's demands or values be determined from the article?
2. How many organized groups do you or have you belonged to or contributed to in some way? Make a list. Which of these do you think attempt to influence public opinion or policy? If you are having trouble coming up with a list, just think about jobs that you may have had (were they unionized?), churches, clubs, or associations that you may have belonged to, causes to which you might have donated money, petitions you may have signed, etc.
3. Make a list of the various political activities engaged in by different interest groups. Which activities do you consider to be strongly democratic, somewhat democratic, and undemocratic? Explain your reasons.
4. When politicians or civil servants leave government to work for lobbying firms or interest groups that they had dealings with while they were in the public sector, the potential for unethical conduct exists. Examine the rules that apply to these circumstances at: <www.parl.gc.ca/ciec-ccie/en/default.asp>. Do you think that these regulations go far enough or too far, or are they about right? Why?

The media do not merely report political news; they are influential players in shaping the public agenda.

12 The Media

Media impact on modern political life is profound. In this chapter the following aspects of media influence on politics are examined:

- Shaping the political agenda.
- What do the media produce?
- What determines the mass media product?
- The economic filter.
- The technological filter.
- The legal-regulatory filter.
- The organizational filter.
- The ideological filter.
- The media and democracy.

Few readers of this book will have met the Prime Minister of Canada. Even fewer will have met the President of the United States. However, virtually all readers will have ideas about these two leaders and many will have strongly held views on their character, abilities, and performance, despite never having exchanged a word with them. What most of us know and believe about presidents and prime ministers, the facts upon which we form our ideas and judgements concerning them, is based on third-hand information, at best. The same may be said, of course, about how we acquire our knowledge and beliefs about most of the world outside of our own neighbourhoods. We rely on the edited images and information offered on television screens, in newspapers, over the radio waves, and via many other media in our information-saturated societies.

The fact that our ideas are based largely on third-hand information means that we should pay careful attention to the character of the 'hands' that communicate this information. Think for a moment about the typical political story on the evening television news. It may involve about 60–90 seconds of images of the Prime Minister, other cabinet ministers, and opposition leaders and critics, probably in the House of Commons during Question Period or in the foyer near the entrance to the Commons, where journalists and cameras await their daily feeding by politicians exiting Question Period. The story may include brief segments featuring politicians, experts, and interest group spokespersons commenting on the Prime Minister's remarks. Some portion of the story will consist of the reporter's narration of what is happening and what it means. The news clip has involved a large number of choices by those who assign stories to be covered and those who edit and package the story at the television network's newsroom. This is why the information is described as third-hand. The viewer is not personally a witness to the action or occurrence covered in the story. The reporter's account of what happened is shaped by the decisions of others who have been involved in packaging the story for the television news. Consequently, what the viewer ultimately sees has been influenced by a number of people whose choices contribute to what we call 'the news'.

Most citizens have always depended on the media for many of their ideas and information about the world they live in. What is more recent is our awareness of the possibilities for selection, distortion, and manipulation in the process of reporting the news. Long-standing fears that media might have a partisan bias or that propaganda might subvert democratic politics by depriving citizens of independent sources of information and varied perspectives on their societies have been joined in recent years by worries that the biases of the media are more deeply rooted and insidious than ever before. The 'seductions of language', says media expert Neil Postman, are trivial compared to the seductions and manipulative powers of the image-based media.[1]

The media are crucial to the health of democracy. The founders of the American republic knew this, which is why freedom of the press, along with freedom of speech, religion, and assembly, was specifically mentioned in the First Amendment to the United States Constitution. Freedom of the press was, in fact, already enshrined in several of the state constitutions. For example, Virginia's 1776 Bill of Rights stated 'That the freedom of the press is one of the great bulwarks of liberty, and can never be restrained but by despotick government.'[2] Canada's founders devoted little attention to freedom of the press, or other freedoms for that matter, assuming that these would be adequately respected under the system of parliamentary government they adopted from Britain and that a democratic society had no need to inscribe on tablets of stone the principles that it lived by. (Some of the American founders were of the same view. In the *Federalist Papers*, no. 84, Alexander Hamilton argued that freedom of the press ultimately depended on public opinion and 'the general spirit of the people and of the government', and that no explicit constitutional guarantee would be able to protect this or any other freedom in a hostile political culture.)

The ability of those in the media to report on public affairs as they see fit—within the limits of defamation law and recognizing that the public disclosure of some government information could be prejudicial to legitimate national security or policy-making interests that state officials are expected to protect—is crucial to democracy. If a broadcaster,

Internet site, newspaper, or other media organ can be shut down, censored, or punished because public officials do not like the information it conveys, the free discussion of public issues is diminished and democracy suffers. Likewise, when governments get into the business of broadcasting, publishing, and advertising, fears are often expressed that public dollars may be spent on partisan and propagandistic purposes.

At the same time, all countries regulate the media system in some way. This is particularly true of broadcasting, where the airwaves have been defined as public property throughout the world and where there have been technological reasons for restricting the number of broadcasters in order to protect the quality of the television or radio signals reaching consumers. But even this traditional argument for regulation has been challenged by newer technologies that rely on cables and satellites, which have produced an explosion in the quantity of messages that can be sent and received at any time. The proliferation of websites and blogs on the Internet is the most recent culmination of these technological developments, resulting in a situation where more information and a more diverse range of perspectives are available to more people than at any time in human history. In addition, this flood of information has meant that state regulation of information has become increasingly difficult.

But state regulation of the media is not, in the eyes of some critics, the only or even the main threat to freedom of the press and the health of democracy. A more serious threat than state control and censorship, critics argue, is the economic censorship that may result when too few owners control too many media organs that account for too great a share of the market. Moreover, they point to the dependence of most mass media organs on advertising as a key factor that operates to filter out certain forms of controversial, critical, and non-mainstream coverage of political, economic, and social affairs. Whether censorship results from governmental *diktat* or from the working of capitalist markets, they insist, it is censorship just the same.

The relationship of the media to politics is a subject that generates enormous controversy. Before we attempt to make sense of this relationship, let us begin by examining the mass media's role in social learning and the chief characteristics of Canada's media system.

'The Pictures in Our Heads'

The media are creators and purveyors of images and information. As such, they play a role in social learning—the process of acquiring knowledge, values, and beliefs about the world and ourselves. This is a role the media share with other agents of social learning: the family, schools, peer groups, and organizations that one belongs to.

While the family and other agents of social learning all contribute to what Walter Lippmann called 'the pictures in our heads', none of them rival the media in their impact on the political agenda. Lippmann wrote, 'The only feeling that anyone can have about an event that he does not experience is the feeling aroused by his mental image of that event.'[3] The contours of modern political discourse are largely determined by the mass media as they process and report on 'reality'. Moreover, when it comes to matters remote from one's personal experience and daily life—political turmoil in the countries of the former Soviet Union, global pollution, conflict in the Middle East, or the latest Canadian federal budget—the media provide the main source of images and information about the events, issues, and personalities involved. Politicians and generals realize the media's importance, which is why one of the first steps taken in any serious *coup d'état* is to seize control of broadcasting and either shut down or muzzle any newspapers not sympathetic to the new regime.

It has often been remarked that the media do not determine *what we think* so much as *what we think about*. If this were entirely true, it would be a formidable power. To what extent it may be true, media shape public consciousness by conveying certain images and interpretations and excluding others. Such power implies an enormous responsibility. A 'free press' has been viewed as a necessary ingredient of democratic politics since the

American Revolution. The reasoning is that all other groups and individuals—political parties, candidates for public office, corporations, labour unions, government officials, and so on—are self-interested. They cannot be counted on to give an objective assessment of their goals and actions. Too

John Larter/© Simon Fraser University

One of the discussions in Chapter 10 focused on the broad pattern of the media's questioning of Stockwell Day's religious beliefs and what political implications they might have had if he were to become Prime Minister. What does editorial cartoonist John Larter seem to be saying about the picture of Day the media helped shape in the public's mind?

often their interests will be best served through concealment, deception, and manipulation—by **propaganda** that espouses a particular ideology or policy through the public dissemination of selected information and/or misinformation. Only the media, so the argument goes, have an interest in presenting the facts. They may perform this function imperfectly, and particular media organs may have political biases that reflect the views of their owners, the values of their editors, producers, and journalists, or the prejudices of their readership/viewership. But competition ensures that all significant points of view reach the public.

Is this an accurate picture of the media's role in political democracies? How well do the media cover all significant points of view? Who determines 'the facts', or are they self-evident? Regardless of what the intentions of those in the media might be, what are the actual consequences for politics of their publishing or broadcasting particular stories in particular ways? Let us start by considering the 'products' of the mass media.

What Do the Media Produce?

Only a small portion of television and radio time is devoted to public affairs. Most programming, including during the prime-time periods when people are most likely to be watching or listening, aims to entertain rather than inform. Despite the existence of a hard-core minority who tune in mainly or exclusively for news and public affairs, television and radio are essentially entertainment media. Most television viewing and radio listening time is spent watching drama, comedy, game and talk shows, and sports, and listening to music. In the English segment of the television and radio market, most of this viewing and listening involves American programs and music. The overwhelming domination of American programming in the English-Canadian market has always existed (see Figure 12.1) and may be seen by perusing the top-ranked programs for any given week as recorded by the Bureau of Broadcast Measurement.[4]

The pattern is similar for radio. Private broadcasters account for about 90 per cent of the market, and most of what they offer is music. Although the Canadian Radio-television and Telecommunications Commission (CRTC), the industry's regulatory watchdog, requires all radio stations to carry news, only the largest privately owned stations generate any significant amount of news themselves. Most rely on information supplied by wire services, newspapers, and local sports and weather to meet their news quota. Only stations affiliated with the state-owned Canadian Broadcasting Corporation and Radio-Canada, its French-language counterpart, broadcast a significant amount of national and international public affairs programming that has been generated by their own staff.

Like most radio stations, newspapers are geared primarily to the local market. Although all dailies carry national and international news, much of their space is devoted to community affairs. Studies going back to one carried out in 1981 for the Royal Commission on Newspapers suggest that newspapers are considered to be better than either television or radio as a source of community information, while television is believed to be the best source of information for international, national, and even provincial news. Television is also judged to be most up-to-date, fair and unbiased, believable, influential, and essential to the country. A 2007 survey conducted for the Information Technology Association of Canada found that this preference for television as the most important and trustworthy medium continues.[5] Newspapers are relied on by most readers chiefly as a source of local information. A handful of Canadian dailies, including the Toronto-based *Globe and Mail* and the *National Post*, do not conform to this community paper model. They also are distinguished by having the greatest national circulations among Canadian newspapers. The emphasis on national and international news is greater in the *Globe and Mail* and the *National Post* than in other dailies, although such papers as the *Toronto Star*, *Montreal Gazette*, *Ottawa Citizen*, and *Vancouver Sun* also include more of such coverage than is typical of most dailies. The *Globe*'s daily 'Report on Business' section and the 'Financial Post' section of the *Post* also distinguish them from community-oriented papers; some of the other leading papers, including the *Toronto Star* and the *Montreal Gazette*, also provide much more extensive reporting on business and economics than is typical of Canadian dailies. The *Globe*'s long-standing reputation as English Canada's 'national' newspaper—a reputation that the *Post* has challenged since it began publication in 1998—has been acquired in part because of high-calibre journalism. The political columnists and editorial writers of both the *Globe* and the *National Post* are influential players in defining the country's political agenda. Montreal-based *Le Devoir* plays a similar role in Quebec.

Critics of Canadian newspapers have focused on a number of specific concerns relating to industry structure. First, concentrated ownership is seen as limiting the range of ideas and information that reach the public. We argue, however, that weak competition has less impact on the range of media information than do the need to make profits and the organizational structure of news-gathering and reporting. (The organizational filter through which the media product must pass is discussed in a subsequent section.)

As well, newspapers that are part of larger corporate networks that include non-media interests may be reluctant to cover stories and interpret events in ways that put their owners' other interests in a bad light. Again, however, the empirical proof for this claim is weak. Incidents of owner interference do occasionally happen, as does, more often, self-censorship that appears clearly to be based on media people's sensitivity to their owner's interests.[6] But as Edward Herman and Noam Chomsky argue, it is too simplistic to look for direct correlations between ownership and how the *particular* issues or stories are handled by the media. Instead, they maintain, owners exercise their influence more diffusely through 'establishing the general aims of the company and choosing its top management'.[7]

Finally, ownership is said to produce a degree of uniformity in the partisan orientations of newspapers within the chain. This claim, while superficially plausible, is not supported by the evidence. Studies carried out by researchers at the University of Windsor found no proof that chain ownership is associated with the patterns of news reporting or with editorial policy.[8] The differences one finds between newspapers are determined far more by their readership characteristics than by who owns them. Moreover, their market shares do not appear to coincide with political divisions, unlike the situation in countries like France, Belgium, Italy, and Spain where particular papers have distinct partisan or ideological readerships.

In the case of magazines, foreign ownership, rather than concentrated ownership, is the major

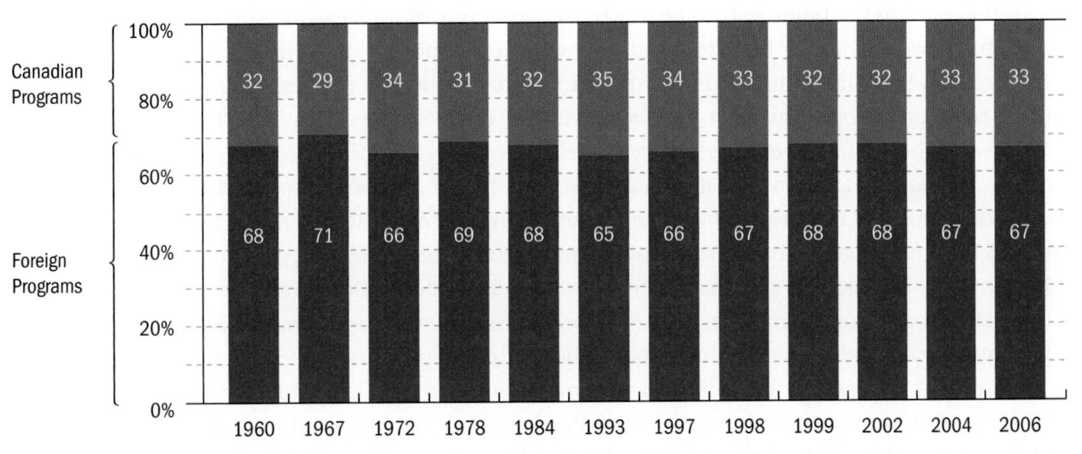

FIGURE 12.1 Prime-Time TV Viewing in English Canada, 1960–2006 (6 p.m.–midnight)

Note: The domination of foreign, overwhelmingly American, programming is even more striking during the heart of prime time. The 6 p.m. to midnight period includes suppertime and late evening news programming, which is popular with Canadian viewers.

Source: Canadian Media Research 'Trends in TV Audiences and Public Opinion, 1996–2006', 14 Mar. 2007.

political issue. The best-selling ones include scandal sheets like the *National Enquirer*, current affairs weeklies like *Newsweek*, *Time*, and *Maclean's*, and *Sports Illustrated*, monthlies like *National Geographic* and *Reader's Digest*, and magazines directed mainly at a female readership such as *Ladies' Home Journal*, *Cosmopolitan*, *Elle*, and *Chatelaine*. All of these sell hundreds of thousands of copies monthly or weekly. In fact, despite the enormous number of magazines sold in Canada, a mere handful representing a limited number of genres accounts for the majority of total magazine sales.[9] Most of them are not oriented towards coverage of politics and public affairs, and several of the most popular ones are American-based, including *Time*, *Newsweek*, *Sports Illustrated*, *Cosmopolitan*, *Elle*, and *Maxim*. Those that focus on 'hard news' and that have large circulations, such as *Time*, *Newsweek*, and *Maclean's*, occupy the conventional middle ground of Canadian and American politics.

Compared to the media we have discussed so far, film may appear relatively insignificant. The average Canadian goes to the cinema only about four or five times per year (more often among those who live in major cities). But some of the time he or she spends in front of the television is spent watching films. Cable television, direct broadcast satellites, pay-TV, VCR/DVD players, and iPods have increased the market penetration of films, freeing the film industry from the movie theatre and bringing its product directly into the home of the consumer. In a sense, this new technology has produced a new 'golden age' for the film industry, enabling it to recapture some of the prominence it held between the 1930s and the 1950s, before the television set became a standard feature of most households. Whether the quality of what the industry produces these days is better or worse than during the era of Hitchcock, Ford, and Capra is another matter.

Film is at the centre of the modern imagination. If a person has not read the book, he or she probably has seen its film adaptation. Indeed, recent years have seen the emergence of the ultimate tribute to the power of the visual medium, the book based on the motion picture. Blockbusters like the *Batman* and the *Star Wars* films, the adventures of Indiana Jones, *Spider-Man*, *Titanic*, *Avatar*, the Harry Potter films, and the *Lord of the Rings* trilogy are familiar to most of us. The stories they tell, the characters they contain, and the stereotypes they convey both shape and reflect our popular culture. At the extreme, life may imitate art, as when gangs of British youths copied the random violence seen in Stanley Kubrick's adaptation of *A Clockwork Orange*, and in the Littleton, Colorado, massacre where teenage members of the 'Trenchcoat Mafia' styled themselves after Leonardo DiCaprio's character in *The Basketball Diaries*. In the 1980s US President Ronald Reagan borrowed from *Star Wars* to label the Soviet Union the 'evil empire' and to call for a 'star wars' defence system (formally referred to as the Strategic Defense Initiative). The archetypes and icons of popular culture are more likely to be associated with movies than with any other mass medium.

What does the film industry offer the viewing public? With hundreds of new releases every year from the studios of Hollywood and thousands more from independents in the US, Canada, and elsewhere, one might assume that the industry produces a richly varied product. It does. But only a narrow band of the entire range of film production is backed by the marketing resources of the studios that produce them. This band represents the commercial feature film. The genre may vary, but what distinguishes such a film is the fact that it must appeal to a large mass audience to recoup the millions of dollars—often running to the tens and even hundreds of millions of dollars—spent on its production and marketing. (*Pirates of the Caribbean: At World's End* is thought to be the most expensive movie ever produced, at a cost of about US$300 million.) Documentary and artistic films generally cost much less to make, but they also generate smaller revenues. They usually are made by small independent film companies or by state-owned filmmakers like Canada's National Film Board. Little is spent on marketing them and public access to non-commercial films is limited by the fact that the distributors do not want to show them and relatively few video rental stores stock them.

The images and stories purveyed by the commercial film industry are often disturbing and occasionally critical of 'the system'. Indeed, one of the most popular motifs of popular film has long been the lone good man versus the bad system. Bruce Willis, Denzel Washington, Clint Eastwood, Sylvester Stallone, and Harrison Ford have been among the more successful actors portraying this stereotype. *It's a Wonderful Life* is a classic example of this simple theme, as are the archetypal westerns *Shane* and *High Noon*. Other examples of older and more recent vintage include *To Kill a Mockingbird, Places in the Heart, Silkwood, Grand Canyon,* and *Erin Brockovich*. On balance, commercial film does much more to reinforce dominant values and institutions than it does to challenge them. The economics of the industry make this inevitable, as we will explain later in this chapter.

Advertisements are another important part of the media product. Most people are exposed to hundreds of ads each day. Television and radio are heavily laced with them. Newspapers and magazines are layered with them. Even films have become vehicles for advertising, with companies willing to pay thousands of dollars for fleeting glimpses of their product in a favourable context. Billboards, storefront signs, pamphlets, flyers, the cinema, Internet banners . . . there is no escape. The estimated amount spent on mass media advertising worldwide exceeds the value of Canada's GNP. The advertising assault is so massive and unremitting that the vast majority of it fails to pierce our consciousness. Advertisers have long been aware of this and search continually for ways to capture the attention of the viewers, listeners, or readers to whom they want to sell something. Whether we pay attention or tune out, advertising constitutes a continuous 'buzz' in the background of our daily lives. What is it telling us?

In the case of most advertising, the intended message is 'buy this'. We say 'most' because some advertising aims to persuade people to vote or to think in particular ways, or simply provides them with useful information (much public service advertising by governments would fall into this last category). The vast majority of advertising, however, aims to affect our behaviour as consumers.

Commercial advertising conveys much more than the intended message, 'buy product X'. We are urged to buy, period. The high-consumption capitalist economy is sustained by the frenetic materialism that pervades our culture. This materialism, in turn, is reinforced by the mass media through advertising and entertainment programming. When the message 'buy this' is hurled at us hundreds of times a day from the time we are quite young, the cumulative impact is to instill and sustain a high-consumption mindset.

Consumerism is only one of the incidental messages communicated through commercial advertising. Gender stereotyping and the use of sexual imagery and innuendo are rampant. The youthful, the slender, the muscular, the large-breasted, the extroverted, the materially successful, and the 'cool' are far more likely to appear in television, magazine, and billboard ads than are those who appear to be deficient in these qualities. Who and what are excluded from visual advertising—and the same holds true for all visual media—are as important as who and what are included. The silences and blind spots of advertising and of all mass media include the poor, visible minorities, men and women who do not conform to fairly traditional stereotypes, the physically unattractive, and the socially nonconforming (as this is defined by the marketers of popular culture: a rebellious look may sell, but off-putting difference is avoided). There are, of course, exceptions. But in general, advertisers find it more profitable to appeal to conventional beliefs and prejudices and to very basic emotional needs and insecurities. This aspect of commercial advertising has not changed since the birth of Madison Avenue (see Box 12.1).

What Determines the Mass Media Product?

> The facts of modern life do not spontaneously take a shape in which they can be known. They must be given a shape by somebody.[10]

No one except the naive and those with a professional interest in self-deception believes that the mass media simply mirror reality. Confronted with more information than can possibly be conveyed to their readerships/audiences, those who produce the media product must choose what stories, images, and 'facts' to communicate. What ultimately is offered to the media consumer is a selective pastiche, an abridged and inevitably somewhat distorted version of a 'reality' that is constructed in the process of being communicated.

The choices made by reporters, editors, producers, and others who contribute to the media product are not random. Several factors influence how reality is processed and how news is reported by the media. These factors may be understood as a series of filters that are more likely to let through certain information and images than others. To oversimplify, information and images that threaten the privileges of dominant social and economic groups are less likely to make it through these media filters than those that are fairly orthodox and non-menacing. This claim will strike many readers as absurd, conditioned as most of us are to believe that the media are independent and frequently critical of the powerful. On balance, however, the media do much more to support the status quo, including the distribution of power in society and the economy, than they do to erode it. In other words, their role in politics is essentially conservative.

The Economic Filter

Most media organs are privately owned, and as such they are subject to the iron law of the marketplace. That law is very simple: they must be able to sell a product that will attract enough subscribers, advertisers, buyers, or patrons—the exact source of revenue depends on the media product—to cover production costs and, usually, earn a competitive return on invested capital. Given the high costs involved in producing a daily newspaper, a slick magazine, a television series, or a feature film, profitability requires a mass market. No media organ needs to appeal to everyone in order to survive, and none tries. But particularly when a marketplace is competitive, there will be a tendency to avoid programming or content that seems likely to have limited appeal in favour of that which will hold onto, or even increase, sales.

Media Spotlight

Box 12.1 The Art of Selling

The principles underlying this [commercial advertising] are extremely simple. Find some common desire, some widespread unconscious fear or anxiety; think out some way to relate this wish or fear to the product you have to sell; then build a bridge of verbal or pictorial symbols over which your customer can pass from fact to compensatory dream, and from the dream to the illusion that your product, when purchased, will make the dream come true. 'We no longer buy oranges, we buy vitality. We do not buy just an auto, we buy prestige.' And so with all the rest. In toothpaste, for example, we buy, not a mere cleanser and antiseptic, but release from the fear of being sexually repulsive. . . . In every case the motivation analyst has found some deep-seated wish or fear, whose energy can be used to move the consumer to part with cash and so, indirectly, to turn the wheels of industry. Stored in the minds and bodies of countless individuals, this potential energy is released by, and transmitted along, a line of symbols carefully laid out so as to bypass rationality and obscure the real issue.

Source: *Brave New World Revisited* by Aldous Huxley.

State ownership alters, but does not eliminate, the economic pressures to which the mass media are exposed. Publicly owned broadcasters must be sensitive to charges of elitism. This is particularly true of television broadcasting, where the costs of producing high-quality entertainment programming are great. Few politicians will be willing to risk the loss of votes in order to subsidize broadcasting that attracts a tiny audience. Market influences become even greater when a publicly owned broadcaster is required to raise some part of its revenues from advertising or viewer/corporate support.

Economic pressures have an important impact on what the mass media produce. They cannot, however, explain all media behaviour. What finally is offered to viewers, readers, and listeners is affected by regulatory requirements, the legal system, and the cultural norms of society.

The economic filter operates mainly through the influence that advertising and industry structure have on the media product. Without advertising dollars, privately owned and even (to a lesser degree) publicly owned media companies are not economically viable. These media companies are in competition for the advertising patronage of business. It follows, then, that they will be sensitive to their patrons' needs and will tend to avoid reporting or programming that reduces their attractiveness in the eyes of advertisers. In the words of an American network executive, television 'is an advertising-supported medium, and to the extent that support falls out, programming will change.'[11] The advertising base of a newspaper or radio broadcaster is typically more local than that of a television network, but the maxim still holds: advertisers' preferences cannot be ignored by an ad-dependent media system.

How is this commercially driven shaping of the media relevant to politics? First of all, dependence on advertising may reduce the likelihood that powerful economic interests will be portrayed in a negative light. This is not to imply that advertisers hold a power of economic blackmail over the heads of media organs. There have been occasions, however, when particular programs were boycotted by corporate sponsors or where their broadcast was followed by advertiser reprisals. In some instances, the anticipated reaction of corporate advertisers is enough to either kill a story or moderate its tone. But the influence of advertising is much more subtle and pervasive than these occasional incidents might suggest. When a typical 30-second commercial spot during prime time on a major American network costs roughly US$300,000–$400,000 (closer to $1 million if the program is *American Idol*, and US$3 million for 30 seconds in the case of the 2010 Super Bowl), the economic costs of broadcasting material that offends powerful corporate advertisers obviously are great. Those who make programming decisions certainly are aware of this.

Little evidence supports the occasionally expressed view that news reporting is 'censored' or slanted as a result of advertiser interference. In *News from Nowhere*, Edward Epstein declares that none of the hundreds of correspondents and production personnel he interviewed for his study could recall an incident of sponsor interference in a network news broadcast. On the contrary, Epstein observes that stories in direct conflict with the interests of major sponsors were not uncommon.[12] The fear that advertisers may withhold their business, he argues, has little impact on the content of national news programming, although it may occasionally affect news documentaries and other public affairs programs.

The influence of advertising operates in a second, more powerful way. Most television broadcasting and most viewing time are devoted to entertainment programming. Naturally, the most lucrative advertising slots are associated with this sort of programming. Therefore, an economic pressure is placed on ad-dependent broadcasters to maximize the amount of high audience-appeal programming during prime-time hours. Most public affairs programming does not have the draw of a popular sitcom or drama, and consequently is subject to pressures that it be marginalized (relegated to off-peak viewing times, or left up to state-owned or viewer-supported broadcasters) or that it adopt an entertainment format. The emergence of what has been called **infotainment** or 'soft news'—news that is packaged using an entertainment, celebrity journalist format—has become prevalent in the United States. Infotainment is clearly linked to the high price fetched by advertising spots during popular viewing hours. The Canadian industry may not have gone as far in breaking down the traditional barriers between entertainment and public affairs programming, although the local news programming model developed by Rogers's *CityNews* is essentially the same as the soft news format pioneered in the United States. But as in the United States, the economics of broadcasting in Canada work against the viability of programming that does not attract a mass audience and so the pressures to adopt the infotainment/celebrity newsreader format are great.

State-owned media organs like the CBC, TV Ontario, and Radio-Québec in Canada and the viewer-supported Public Broadcasting System (PBS) network in the United States are not immune from the influence of advertising. Both the CBC and Radio-Québec rely on advertising for part of their revenue. In the case of the CBC, advertising income accounts for about one-third of its annual budget. Viewer-supported broadcasters like the American PBS rely on state subsidies (directly and through the tax system) and on foundation and corporate sponsorship of programs for part of their revenue needs. Some critics have argued that corporate sponsorship, like advertising, tends to filter out socially divisive and controversial programming, including criticism of powerful economic interests and the capitalist system. This claim, however, is rather

Rick Mercer holds his award for the *Rick Mercer Report*'s win in the Best Comedy Program or Series category at the 24th Annual Gemini Awards in November 2009. Mercer's satirical news program is part of a growing phenomenon of shows, including Jon Stewart's *Daily Show* and Stephen Colbert's the *Colbert Report* in the US, that offer an alternative viewpoint on current events while ostensibly poking fun at the formats of the infotainment or 'soft news' channels.

dubious or at least exaggerated. One need only peruse some of the programming on PBS's *Frontline* and *American Experience* programs, among others, to find evidence that refutes this charge.

Dependence on state subsidies does not necessarily remove all constraints on media content. Public broadcasters must constantly be sensitive to charges of bias and ideological favouritism. Over the years CBC television programs like *This Hour Has Seven Days, the fifth estate, Marketplace, The Passionate Eye,* and the various programs hosted by environmentalist David Suzuki, notably *The Nature of Things,* have been accused of having a leftist political bias and of being anti-business. The in-house monitoring of CBC broadcasting for 'fairness' has reached unprecedented levels of sophistication. Much of this, as during election campaigns, is intended to ensure that the CBC is even-handed in its treatment of the major political parties and their leaders. But monitoring also focuses on the portrayal and coverage of social and economic groups, including business. In the world of public broadcasting, culturecrats' and politicians' aversion to controversy may substitute for the check that dependence on advertising imposes on private broadcasters.

Industry structure is the second component of the economic filter. As the costs associated with producing a newspaper have increased, competition has suffered. The daily newspaper industry in Canada (as in the United States) is characterized by local monopoly. In only eight Canadian cities (Quebec City, Montreal, Ottawa, Toronto, Winnipeg, Calgary, Edmonton, and Vancouver) is there competition between same-language, mass-circulation dailies that have different owners. Chain ownership is a feature of both the English- and French-language markets. Most daily newspaper circulation in English Canada is controlled by the Postmedia Network (formerly Canwest), and Quebecor chains. Quebecor controls the Osprey and Sun Media groups, which together account for 36 daily newspapers across Canada. Torstar Corporation papers also have a significant market share and CTVGlobemedia owns the influential *Globe and Mail.* In French-speaking Quebec all but a tiny share of the daily newspaper market is controlled by Quebecor (Péladeau family) and by Power Corporation (Paul Desmarais) through its Gesca group.

Television and radio markets, to say nothing of the Internet, are much more fragmented than the newspaper market. The days are long past when a handful of American broadcasters, plus the CBC, dominated television broadcasting. Cable and satellite technology and the development of the Internet have created unprecedented opportunities for niche programming targeted at more limited audiences than the traditional broadcasters require to ensure profitability. The economics of electronic media are significantly different from those of print media, such that concentrated ownership is not as prominent an issue in broadcasting as in newspaper markets.

Instead, the ownership issue in broadcasting and newer media like the Internet is framed chiefly as an issue of American penetration into Canadian markets. There may indeed be hundreds of television stations that Canadian viewers have access to through direct broadcast satellite (DBS), cable technology, or the Internet, but the fact remains that the most popular ones either originate in the United States or rely to a great extent on programming, often heavily promoted through advertising, produced in the United States. Issues of ownership in the United States and internationally are thereby imported into Canada.

One of these issues involves the new corporate convergence in mass media, particularly in electronic media industries. As the nationalist Friends of Canadian Broadcasting puts it, 'large media multinationals are getting larger, concentrating their market power, crossing over into new lines of [media] business and crossing national borders with unprecedented ease.'[13] One of the most prominent examples of such a multi-media giant is Time Warner, whose corporate empire spans the older media of books, magazines, television broadcasting, and films, the newer media of cable, pay-per-view, and shop-at-home TV, and the ownership of intellectual property rights. Critics argue that multi-media convergence and the growth of giants like Time Warner will accelerate the erosion of national cultures like that of Canada.

A world in which such multinationals as Time Warner, Sony, IBM, Philips NV, and Disney dominate the electronic media food chain, from the production of the entertainment and information products through the means for distributing and receiving them, is not likely to provide much opportunity for the expression of distinctively Canadian values, perspectives, and stories. Or is it? There is, after all, little doubt that more Canadian programming is produced and available today than ever before. This has been largely due to government regulation and subsidies, to which we now turn.

The Legal/Regulatory Filter

Print media in Canada and in most other democracies are basically free from direct regulation by government. Unlike radio and television broadcasters and cable system companies, they do not require a special licence to do business. Newspapers and magazines essentially regulate themselves through press councils created and operated by the industry. These councils receive and investigate complaints; they do not systematically monitor performance. Calls for greater state regulation of their behaviour invariably provoke cries of censorship from those in the newspaper and magazine business.

A number of indirect forms of regulation, however, may affect content in the print media. Most of these involve measures whose ostensible aim is to promote Canadian values through newspapers and magazines. For example, the federal Income Tax Act permits advertisers to deduct from their taxable income only the cost of ads placed in newspapers or magazines that are at least 75 per cent Canadian-owned. This explains why foreign ownership of Canadian newspapers has never been an issue, despite the fact that for most of its history the industry has been extremely profitable and might therefore have been expected to attract foreign capital.

It is doubtful, however, whether the provisions of the Income Tax Act favouring Canadian-owned publications has much of an impact on newspaper content. With the chief exceptions of the *Globe and Mail*, the *National Post*, and *Le Devoir*, newspapers are geared mainly to local markets. Community news and classified ads account for a large share of these papers. Their profitability depends on a large local readership that they can 'sell' to local advertisers. This, and not the nationality of their owners, will influence newspaper content.

One might argue, however, that the owner's nationality could influence the way a newspaper covers national and international news, as well as sports and comics—two of a paper's most read sections—but even Canadian-owned papers depend heavily on news that they purchase from foreign news agencies like the Associated Press wire service, particularly for international news and sports. Most comic strips—and we should not dismiss comics and cartoons as reinforcers and purveyors of values—are produced by American cartoonists. The economics of news-gathering, not the nationality of the owners, is responsible for this dependence on foreign sources of news. In the end, the Income Tax Act almost certainly does more to promote Canadian ownership than Canadian culture.

The situation in the magazine industry is quite different. Despite the fact that the Canadian ownership provisions of the Income Tax Act also apply to magazines, the English-Canadian market has been dominated by American magazines and, for a short time, **split-run publications**, where the magazine was based outside of Canada, most of its editorial and other production costs were incurred outside of Canada, and most of its circulation was non-Canadian. A split-run edition of such a magazine could be produced at a very low cost by importing the American version via satellite and adding a few pages of Canadian content, thereby qualifying for the lower Canadian advertising rates that Canadian magazines could offer to advertisers. This was done in 1993 by Time Warner's immensely popular *Sports Illustrated*, which in turn triggered changes in Canadian tax law to halt the practice. By the summer of 1999, following an earlier World Trade Organization ruling against Canada and a revised and punitive Canadian law, a compromise of sorts was negotiated, requiring that split-run editions include a majority of Canadian content in order to sell advertising space at the lower Canadian rate. In recent years this issue has largely dropped from public and government attention.

The split-run issue encapsulates the essential regulatory dilemma for Canadian policy-makers grappling to preserve Canadian culture and promote domestic cultural industries. It boils down to this: the much larger American market enables US magazine publishers to produce a glossier product and pay better rates for articles at a lower cost than their small-market Canadian counterparts. Moreover, Canadians have shown over the years that they like what American magazines offer. An estimated 80 per cent of the magazine titles available on Canadian newsstands are American, and US-based publications account for about 70 per cent of total magazine sales in Canada. Availability of Canadian magazines is not the problem. According to the Canadian magazine industry's own figures there are roughly 1,500 magazines published in Canada. But with low cultural barriers between English Canada and the United States, no language barrier, and a high level of consumer and media integration between the two societies, American magazines do not seem to be foreign in the way that British or other English-language ones do.

State regulation is much more intrusive in the case of the electronic media. The original reason for treating broadcasting differently from print media was the need to prevent chaos on overcrowded airwaves. Controlling entry in a market through the licensing of broadcasters seemed the only practical solution to this potential problem. At the same time, however, broadcasting policy has always been based on the assumption that only extensive state intervention can prevent complete American domination of the Canadian market.[14]

The American 'threat' is a matter of simple economics, and content regulations for both radio and television constitute one of the pillars of Canadian broadcasting policy. The CRTC establishes and enforces a complicated set of content guidelines that all licensed broadcasters must observe. The idea behind them is to ensure that more **Canadian content** reaches the airwaves than would be available without regulation (see Box 12.2).

Whether or not the system works depends on what one means by 'Canadian content'. If this signifies that some of the major people involved in the production of a television program or piece of music are Canadian, then the policy has been a success. But if Canadian content is taken to mean the subjects, values, and ideas conveyed through these media, then the verdict is rather different. Over two decades ago the *Report* of the Task Force on Broadcasting (1986) characterized the content system applied to television broadcasters as 'regulatory tokenism'. Many of the programs that qualify as Canadian content, it observed, 'could be mistaken for American productions and seem to have been made on the assumption that references to their Canadian origin would hurt their appeal to audiences outside Canada, particularly in the United States.'[15] This may be true in many instances, but the popularity over the years of such recognizably Canadian programs as *Traders*, *Corner Gas*, *Little Mosque on the Prairie*, and *The Border* shows that the American clone programming format complained of by the Task Force has not always been the recipe for success in Canadian television.

As in television, the economics of the recording industry encourage products that are marketable outside of Canada. Radio stations typically deal with Canadian content requirements by relying heavily on recordings by performers like the Barenaked Ladies, Céline Dion, Nelly Furtado, Avril Lavigne, and Justin Bieber, whose music seems as at home in Boston as Toronto, and, to the degree that regulations permit, by marginalizing much of their Canadian content to off-peak hours. The advent of satellite radio has presented Canadian regulators with a new version of the old challenge of Canadians' apparent appetite for American products over homegrown competitors.

Governments also affect the content of the electronic mass media through subsidies paid to Canadian film and television producers and through their direct participation in the industry as broadcasters and filmmakers. The Canadian content quotas established by the CRTC are, in the case of television, met largely through sports, news, and public affairs programming. But most viewing time is spent watching entertainment programs. Very few of these programs are Canadian, again, simply because it makes economic sense to purchase an American-made product for a fraction of its production costs—a product that, moreover, benefits from the inevitable spillover into Canada of advertising that American networks use to promote audience interest. In English-speaking Canada only the CBC broadcasts a significant amount of Canadian-made entertainment programming.

To compensate for the unfavourable economics of domestic production, Ottawa offers subsidies. This is done chiefly through Telefilm Canada, which helps to finance the production of Canadian-made feature films (over 200 of them since 1986), television programs (more than 1,500 television programs and series since 1968), documentary films, and animation. Telefilm Canada also invests in international co-productions. If you look closely at the credits that scroll across the screen at the end of a Canadian-made television documentary, dramatic series, or children's program, chances are good that you will see that it was subsidized by Telefilm Canada.

While the publicly owned CBC, Radio-Canada, TV Ontario, and Radio-Québec have been among the major recipients of money provided through Telefilm Canada over the years, private television and film producers have also drawn on this source of public money. Fears have long been expressed that private producers typically use these subsidies to produce films and television programs that are as unrecognizably Canadian as possible so as not

Media Spotlight

Box 12.2 What Is Canadian Content?

Radio

According to the Canadian Radio-television and Telecommunications Commission (CRTC), a musical selection qualifies as Canadian content if it meets any two of the following criteria:

- The music is composed entirely by a Canadian.
- The lyrics are written entirely by a Canadian.
- The music or lyrics are performed principally by a Canadian.
- The live performance is performed wholly in Canada and broadcast live in Canada or is recorded wholly in Canada.
- The musical selection was performed live or recorded after 7 September 1991, and a Canadian who has collaborated with a non-Canadian receives at least 50 per cent of the credit as composer and lyricist.

For AM radio, at least 35 per cent of all music aired must meet this definition of Canadian content. In recognition of FM radio's diversity of formats (and the corresponding supply of appropriate Canadian content recordings), the CRTC allows different levels of required Canadian music content. The quota is as low as 7 per cent in the case of ethnic radio stations.

In the case of French-language radio stations, at least 65 per cent of the music played must have French vocals, a quota that drops to 55 per cent between 6:00 a.m. and 6:00 p.m.

Television

To be considered Canadian, a television program must have a Canadian producer and must earn a minimum 6 of a possible 10 points based on key creative positions. The CRTC awards points when the duties of these positions are performed by Canadians. There are additional criteria regarding financial and creative control for programs involving foreign production partners. The CRTC requires that Canadian programs be used to fill at least 60 per cent of the overall schedules of both public and private television broadcasters. Moreover, Canadian content must fill at least 50 per cent of evening programming hours for private broadcasters and 60 per cent for public broadcasters.

to alienate potential American audiences—the copycat generic productions the 1986 Task Force on Broadcasting argued against. Again, the economies of profitability in broadcasting and film work against the goal of producing and promoting distinctively Canadian cultural products. Even with the maximum level of public support that Telefilm Canada is allowed to provide, the typically low licence fees paid by Canadian broadcasters still leave a production company with a significant share of production costs uncovered. There are, therefore, economic pressures to turn out an exportable product in order to recoup costs through foreign (this will usually mean American) sales. In the case of feature films the problem is largely that the sole major distribution chain, Cineplex Galaxy, does little to promote Canadian-made films, nor do the companies producing them have the resources to advertise widely to generate audience interest.

Despite the unfavourable economics of producing recognizably Canadian programs, a situation that subsidies appear not to correct, such programs do get produced. In the end it falls to public broadcasters and the National Film Board to carry most of the burden of showing Canadians what is distinctive about their society and culture. Indeed, this is what these organizations were intended to do. Under the Broadcasting Act the CBC is required to be 'a balanced service of information, enlightenment and entertainment for people of different ages, interests and tastes covering the whole range of programming in fair proportion'. The CBC, through its English- and French-language divisions, has done far more to Canadianize the airwaves than any other broadcaster, particularly when it comes to dramatic programming and during prime viewing hours. Its ability to do so, however, is threatened by budget cuts that began in the late 1970s. The CBC has responded by increasing its dependence on advertising. This places Canada's main public broadcaster between a rock and a hard place. On the one hand, the CBC is required to rely on Canadian programming. On the other hand, it is increasingly dependent on the revenues from the sale of advertising time, which requires that the CBC's programming achieve audience ratings that will attract and retain advertisers.

The NFB's mandate is to 'interpret Canada to Canadians and the rest of the world' (Film Act). For 70 years the NFB has done this to critical and international acclaim, turning out documentaries and serious drama that the private sector has been unwilling to produce. There is, of course, a very simple reason why private companies have not invested in these sorts of productions: the major theatre chains do not want to show them and ad-dependent television stations do not want to broadcast them. Their lack of interest in these productions, made in and about Canada, is due to their belief that they will be unprofitable. Without significantly large advertising budgets and deprived of access to commercial distribution, these films and documentaries live a sort of fugitive life in 'art house cinemas' and on public broadcasting stations.

Media content also is affected through federal and provincial laws dealing with obscenity, pornography, and what is called hate literature. None of these terms is defined very precisely in Canadian law, but the federal Criminal Code and the Customs Act, as well as provincial statutes dealing with hate literature, restrict the sorts of printed matter and films that may enter Canada or be distributed here, as well as the media products that individuals may possess. This last restriction became extremely controversial in January 1999 when a British Columbia Supreme Court judge ruled that a 1993 federal law prohibiting the possession of child pornography violated the right to individual privacy guaranteed under the Charter. A firestorm of protest greeted the ruling, which ultimately was upheld by the Supreme Court of Canada. Civil liberties groups were critical of the law for being too general.

The issue of when and how to restrict media content raises issues of censorship, individual privacy, freedom of expression, public morality, and the safety of certain groups, such as the children who become fodder for pornographic films, magazines, and Internet sites. These issues have become increasingly complex and traditional methods used to regulate media content have been challenged by the newer media of satellite communications and the Internet. Proposals to regulate media content on the Internet have ranged from making service providers responsible for the content of their websites and e-mail carried over their networks to a law that would require the labelling of all on-line information, identifying the degree of adult content. To this point, however, regulation of the Internet remains relatively slight in Canada and other democracies. Nonetheless, websites and those who communicate via cyberspace, and who fall under the jurisdiction of Canadian governments, are subject to the provisions of the Criminal Code and federal and provincial human rights laws, just as are those who communicate through traditional media.

The hand of Internet regulation weighs more heavily, however, in some other parts of the world. Not until 2002 did the government of Iraq allow citizens, other than authorized officials, Internet access. Political authorities in China and some countries of the Middle East routinely attempt to control and restrict access to websites they deem unacceptable. Some Western service providers have been willing to help them in restricting what their citizens can access, as when Google, the world's largest Internet search engine, agreed in 2006 to allow its service to be censored in China (searches for such words as 'Tiananmen' and 'democracy' would produce no hits). After announcing in January 2010 that it would no longer comply with the Chinese government's censorship requirements, Google backed down several months later. The Chinese authorities' regulation of the Internet was also an issue at the beginning of the 2008 Summer Olympic Games, when journalists found that access to certain sites was blocked. Not surprisingly, countries in which traditional media are state-controlled have been unwilling to let their populations have full and open access to web-based sources of information.

The Technological Filter

Few things date more quickly than news. The technology of broadcasting and Internet- and satellite-based communications is instantaneous. That of newspapers involves a matter of hours. The mass media are thus capable of providing their audiences with the latest developments, and indeed our general expectations are that they will communicate what is happening now. What is happening now, of course, can be reported in the context of the larger background against which events unfold. The practical problem is that stories must be edited to a length suitable for inclusion in a 30-minute news program or the pages of a newspaper.

Television, we have already noted, is the medium relied on by most people for their knowledge of national and international events. The visual character of this medium lends itself to the personalization of reality—an emphasis on individuals and personalities at the expense of ideas and broad social forces that cannot be related or captured by a camera. Consequently, the media, especially television, are disposed towards the personal, the immediate, and the concrete. 'Reality' is conveyed as a constantly shifting pastiche of images, as though those who produce the news assume that the average viewer has an attention span that lasts a minute or two at best. Entertainment programming tends to assume the same faster-than-life character. According to Morris Wolfe, this style reflects his First Law of Commercial Television: 'Thou shalt give them enough jolts per minute (JPMs) or thou shalt lose them.'[16] Too few **JPMs** and viewers will lose interest, change channels, and ratings will suffer. And if ratings suffer, advertising revenue will fall and profits will drop. But are the networks simply giving the viewers what they want? And what difference does it make for politics if, in Wolfe's words, 'all television increasingly aspires to the condition of the TV commercial'?[17]

Industry people are doubtless correct when they claim that many viewers are easily bored and that a rapid pace and frequent jolts are necessary to capture and hold their attention. But it may also be true that viewers have come to expect the sort of high JPM product at which commercial television and film excel. Morris Wolfe again: '[A] steady diet of nothing but high JPM television tends to condition viewers' nervous systems to respond only to certain kinds of stimulation. Their boredom thresholds are frequently so low that TV viewers find it difficult to enjoy anything that isn't fast-paced.'[18] Some psychologists argue that the explosive growth in what is labelled attention deficit disorder is, in fact, a result of the impact of television and videogames on the central nervous systems of children.[19] Whatever the cause, it can hardly be denied that most television shows (including news programs) and commercial films have the staccato rhythm and jumped-up energy level that Wolfe and countless other media watchers have commented on.

Wolfe's First Law of Commercial Television captures only part of the explanation for what he calls the 'TV wasteland'. The technology of television and film is also responsible. It is often said that one picture is worth a thousand words. This is doubtless true—sometimes. But it is often the case that the moving images on the screen capture only the surface of events, and this substitutes for an explanation that is more complicated and *non-visual* than the medium can deal with. The eye is engaged in preference to the ear, which has a profound effect on the intellect. Of course, people can turn to newspapers, magazines, and books to fill in those parts of the story that are not covered well by television pictures. But the shrinking size of newspapers, fewer magazines, and hard times in the publishing industry are good reasons for believing that most do not. We mentioned earlier that a clear majority of Canadians rely on television for their knowledge of national and international affairs and, furthermore, believe this medium to be the most unbiased and believable. In other words, they count on what is paraded before their eyes and briefly commented on.

Politicians and others who regularly come into the eye of the camera have long understood the biases of the visual medium. Photo opportunities and highly structured, controllable events are among their ways of using television's need for the immediate, the personal, and the visual to their own advantage. Television has had an enormous impact on how elections are fought, how special interests attempt to influence public policy, and how public officials communicate with the people. One of the masters of the medium, the American social activist Jesse Jackson, remarked over three decades ago on the importance of speaking in short memorable sentences—'sound bites' as they are called today. They conform to the needs of television technology; long, rambling, or complex statements do not (see Box 12.3).

Those who produce television programs, including the news, operate on the assumption that action and motion are far more likely to hold viewer attention than are 'talking heads'. There is, therefore, an exaggerated emphasis on action, and particularly on two-sided conflict. As Edward Jay Epstein explains:

> . . . the high value placed on action footage by executives leads to a three-step distillation of news happenings by correspondents, cameramen and editors, all of whom seek the moment of highest action. Through this process, the action in a news event, which in fact may account for only a fraction of the time, is concentrated together and becomes the central feature of the happening. This helps explain why news on television tends willy-nilly to focus on activity.[20]

The visual character of television introduces other biases as well, including dependence on stereotypes and emphasis on confrontation.

Dependence on a repertory of stereotypes. Writing over 80 years ago, Walter Lippmann argued that newspaper reporting consisted largely of fitting current news to a **'repertory of stereotypes'**. There are cultural reasons for this that we will discuss later. But in the case of a visual medium, there are also technological reasons for this dependence. 'Viewers' interest', observes Epstein, 'is most likely to be maintained through easily recognizable and palpable images, and conversely, most likely to be distracted by unfamiliar or confusing images.'[21]

Emphasis on confrontation. From the standpoint of a visual medium confrontation has two virtues. First, it involves action, which, we have already noted, is one of the requirements of most television news and public affairs coverage. Second, conflict helps to present a story in a way that viewers can easily grasp. Epstein notes that 'Situations are thus sought out in network news in which there is a high potential for violence, but a low potential for audience confusion.'[22] When the events themselves do not include the necessary visual drama, this can always be provided through the use of file films—action in the can and ready to go!

Media Spotlight

Box 12.3 The Philosophy behind the 30-Second TV News Story

Because the television commercial is the single most voluminous form of public communication in our society, it was inevitable that Americans would accommodate themselves to the philosophy of television commercials. By 'accommodate', I mean that we accept them as a normal and plausible form of discourse. By 'philosophy', I mean that the television commercial has embedded in it certain assumptions about the nature of communication that run counter to those of other media, especially the printed word. For one thing, the commercial insists on an unprecedented brevity of expression. One may even say, instancy. A sixty-second commercial is prolix; thirty seconds is longer than most; fifteen to twenty seconds is about average. This is a brash and startling structure for communication since, as I remarked earlier, the commercial always addresses itself to the psychological needs of the viewer. Thus, it is not merely therapy. It is instant therapy. Indeed, it puts forward a psychological theory of unique axioms: The commercial asks us to believe that all problems are solvable, that they are solvable fast, and that they are solvable fast through the interventions of technology, techniques, and chemistry. This is, of course, a preposterous theory about the roots of discontent, and would appear so to anyone hearing or reading it. But the commercial disdains exposition, for that takes time and invites argument.

Source: 'Reach Out and Elect Someone', from *Amusing Ourselves to Death* by Neil Postman, 130–1, copyright © 1985 by Neil Postman. Used by permission of Viking Penguin, a division of Penguin Group (USA) Inc.

Marshall McLuhan's adage, 'the medium is the message', reminds us of the unintended or at least not obvious consequences of change in the technology of communications. Morris Wolfe, Walter Lippmann, and Edward Jay Epstein are among those who have taken this reminder seriously. But it is likely that we are living through a new chapter in the evolution of communications technology with potentially profound consequences for how politics and the news are reported and how we perceive them (see Box 12.4).

The Organizational Filter

News-gathering and reporting are carried out by organizations. The needs and routine procedures of these organizations influence the content of the news: both what is reported and how it is covered. The organization's dilemma is that news developments are not entirely predictable, yet it does not have the resources to be everywhere news might break or to cover all stories equally well. News organizations rely on various strategies to deal with this dilemma.

In the case of television, several criteria help to impose predictability on the news. Those who have a reputation for being influential or who occupy an official position of some power are more likely to make the news than those whose public profile is lower or whose position does not, in the eyes of news gatherers, automatically confer on them a mantle of credibility. Prime ministers, premiers, and the leaders of opposition parties are assumed to be newsworthy, as are mayors and leading councillors when the news item is local. Spokespersons for what are considered to be important organizations—the Canadian Council of Chief Executives, the Canadian Labour Congress, Equality for Gays and Lesbians Everywhere (EGALE), the Catholic Church, and so on—are also considered to be newsworthy and can count on being sought out when an issue falls into their sphere of concern.

Government officials and powerful private interests understand that news organizations operate within a system of routines and requirements including, for example, the need to have the evening news film footage in the can by a certain hour to allow time for editing. Accommodating the media's needs through well-timed press conferences, photo opportunities, news releases, and staged events—what Daniel Boorstin has called 'pseudo-events'—is simple prudence from the standpoint of groups that want to affect public opinion. This practice has been called **news management**. Obviously, governments and the public affairs/media relations bureaucracies of the powerful are not able to control the news agenda. But they are able to influence news reporting.

Frankly, Kong, I'm much more frightened of those Liberal attack ads...
Me too!
CANADA

© Roy Peterson/*Vancouver Sun*

Television spot ads—usually only 20–30 seconds long—are one of the main vehicles for political communication during election campaigns. Some worry that the medium debases the message, dumbing down the political conversation.

Publicly acknowledged experts also are sought out by the media. What makes one a 'publicly acknowledged expert'? Affiliation with a respectable institution is one of the key determinants of this status. Specialists who are associated with an established institution like the C.D. Howe Institute, the Canadian Centre for Policy Alternatives, the Fraser Institute, or a university—particularly a university located in a city where a network has production facilities—are those most likely to be considered newsworthy. The point here is not that only 'establishment' voices will be heard on an issue, but that spokespersons for mainstream views are almost certain to receive a hearing because their institutional affiliation confers on them the status of 'acknowledged expert', while spokespersons for marginal groups and unconventional views are much less likely to be deemed newsworthy. As a result, creative, entrepreneurial, and innovative work outside of the mainstream is suppressed by being ignored.

The mass media's demand for the ideas and information generated by experts is based on a combination of factors. One of these is the media's self-image as dispenser of the news and reporter of the facts. Fulfillment of this role requires access to sources of information whose credibility is sound and whose claim to objectivity is generally accepted. Related to this is a second factor: the media's need for low-cost information and instant analysis. To conduct their own analysis would be expensive and time-consuming, and most journalists are in any case not professionally trained as economists, epidemiologists, constitutional lawyers, political scientists, or whatever other field of expertise a story may call for. It makes economic sense to tap the knowledge of those whose training, reputation, and/or institutional affiliation confer on them the social standing of 'expert'. Third, in

Media Spotlight

Box 12.4 Technology, Cognition, and How We Perceive the World

The year 2010 may be remembered as a watershed in the technology of communications. The social networking site Facebook recorded 500 million users. Apple launched its iPad, combining several functions in a medium that is something between a laptop and a cell phone. Twitter, which began in 2008 as a social network, acquired features of a news medium, a transition that may have dated from the Iranian elections of 2009 when Twitter was used by protestors to communicate news about their opposition to the fraud perpetrated by the regime.

The Pew Internet and American Life Project reported that the Internet had surpassed newspapers as a source for news. National and local television stations remained the top two sources of news. But changes appeared to be underway. One-third of cell-phone users said that they use the medium to get news and over one-third of those with Internet access claim to have contributed to the news food chain by commenting on a story or disseminating one via Twitter or Facebook. Nicholas Carr's *The Shallows: What the Internet Is Doing to Our Brains* argues that 'Whereas the Internet scatters our attention, the book focuses it. Unlike the screen, the page promotes contemplation.'[23] On-line media, Carr argues, may make us dumber in certain ways, reducing our capacity for creativity and the ability to make cognitive connections, on which intelligence largely rests.

Clearly, technology has transformed the processes by which news is gathered, reported, distributed, and consumed. But as the Pew Project for Excellence in Journalism observes in its 2010 annual report,[24] the impacts are neither simple nor quite what many people believe. The Pew Report identifies several trends driven by changing technology, including the following:

- 'Online consumers are not seeking out news organizations for their full news agenda. They are hunting the news by topic and by event and grazing across multiple outlets.'
- Old and new media are tied together. New media still have a limited capacity to generate content and rely on traditional media sources for reporting capacity.
- Reportorial journalism—what newspapers and other traditional news outlets do—is shrinking, but commentary and discussion in the media—what cable, radio, social media, blogs, and websites do—is growing.
- 'Technology is shifting power to newsmakers, and the newest way is through their ability to control the initial accounts of events.' The potential for the manipulation of public opinion through carefully crafted news management may be greater than ever.
- Ease of entry into the blogosphere, social networks, and Internet-based sites has produced enormous growth in the number and ideological range of those reporting, interpreting, and commenting on the news and vying for audiences.

What are we to make of all this? It appears that, for our information about and interpretation of the world, we increasingly rely on media that discourage reflection and contemplation. In turn, these new media rely for most of their content on old media that have fewer resources than in the past for reporting the news. Commentary, interpretation, and opinion comprise an increasingly large share of news coverage communicated through the new media. And the possibilities for news management may be greater today than ever before, as those who make the news are able to get their message framed and communicated directly to audiences via Twitter, Facebook, blogs, and cell-phone messages that do not depend on intermediaries. Of course, it is also easier than ever before for people to participate directly in the news system rather than depending on the top-down technologies of the past. So, should we worry about technological change and its consequences or welcome them?

order to protect themselves against charges of bias and lawsuits, media organizations and reporters need information 'that can be portrayed as presumptively accurate'.[25] Expert knowledge meets this criterion, and that provided by those with socially respected professional or institutional credentials is particularly useful. In fact, the media's need for expert opinion and information helps to confer this social respectability on individuals and institutions, and in many instances probably serves to reinforce the political status quo.

Predictability is important in determining what becomes 'news'. Any news organization operates within the framework of a budget and the limited resources—camera crews, journalists, researchers, and so on—that this implies. Other things being equal, it is cost-effective to concentrate organizational resources where news is most likely to happen: Parliament Hill, the provincial capitals, Toronto and Montreal, and internationally as resources permit. Of course, this strategy creates a self-fulfilling prophecy. The unplanned and unexpected happenings that occur too quickly or too far away to send a journalist and film crew are less likely to be covered than scheduled events that take place near where a news crew is stationed. As Epstein puts it, 'The more predictable the event, the more likely it will be covered.'[26]

Visual appeal is also important. Television obviously needs pictures. But some subjects are more telegenic than others. Epstein writes:

> . . . priority is naturally given to the story in a given category that promises to yield the most dramatic or visual film footage, other things being equal. This means, in effect, that political institutions with rules that restrict television cameras from filming the more dramatic parts of their proceedings are not routinely assigned coverage.[27]

Canadians see much more of what is happening in the House of Commons, particularly Question Period, than they do of the Supreme Court. And yet the Court's decisions have an enormous impact on public policy, in many instances more of an impact than the fairly predictable antics of parliamentarians. Likewise, closed meetings of first ministers, the proceedings of regulatory commissions, and the institutions of the bureaucracy generally are either inaccessible to cameras or lack the sort of visual spice considered a crucial ingredient of televised news. The result, therefore, is to overemphasize the importance of those actors and individuals who can be filmed in action—action that is often stage-managed by the actors themselves—and to underemphasize the significance of those who are more reclusive or who do not lend themselves to confrontational or sensational visuals.

A news organization's need for stories that are newsworthy, predictable, and visually appealing produces a situation where 'the news selected is the news expected.'[28] Along with the other filters that we have discussed, the organizational one creates biases that affect media content. Simple, dramatized confrontation, familiar players and issues, and a relatively narrow range of locales where most news happens are among these biases.

The Ideological Filter

Those who report the news are often accused by conservatives and business people of having liberal-left and anti-business biases. They are more likely, it is argued, to favour stories and groups that challenge established authority. The CBC in general and some of its programs in particular have occasionally been accused of ideological bias against conservatism and big business (especially American business). Similar charges have been heard in the United States, where Republicans, conservatives, Christians, and business interests have often accused the major networks, and journalists generally, of having liberal biases.

The evidence for this claim is mixed. An early American study that looked at the social backgrounds, personality traits, ideologies, and world views of business and media elites found that media respondents typically gave more liberal responses to such statements as 'Government should substantially reduce the income gap between rich and poor.'[29] The researchers concluded that 'leading journalists seem to inhabit a symbolic universe which is quite different from that of businessmen,

Is the introduction of new personalities such as outspoken entrepreneur and venture capitalist Kevin O'Leary one of CBC's strategies to combat critics claiming it has an ideological bias again conservatism and big business? Known for his philosophy 'Greed is good', O'Leary co-hosts the *Lang and O'Leary Exchange* on CBC Newsworld and sits on the investors' panel on CBC Television's *Dragon's Den*.

with implications for the manner in which they report the news to the general public.'[30] Several American studies have confirmed that those in the media, particularly the electronic media, tend to be more liberal than members of the general population. A study of CBC radio, directed by Barry Cooper, concluded that 'on the whole, [the CBC] adopted a left-wing, rather than right-wing critical stance.'[31] His study of CBC television news coverage arrives at a similar conclusion, although Cooper expresses it rather differently. 'The CBC,' he argues, 'like all modern media, has directed its energies towards the production of a specific configuration of opinion—namely progressive opinion—and not toward the provision of reliable information about the world.'[32]

This conclusion is reinforced by what is probably the most systematic study of Canadian journalists' values and beliefs to date.[33] Based on a survey of 270 electronic and print journalists and a sample of the general public (804 respondents), Cooper and Lydia Miljan draw two main conclusions. First, English-Canadian journalists tend to be more left-of-centre than the general public, a finding that corroborates Cooper's earlier studies. Second, the left-leaning proclivities of journalists affect the way news stories are reported, a finding that may appear unsurprising but does not exactly square with the media's credo of objectivity. Among the ways in which English-Canadian journalists differ from their audiences and readerships are the following:

- Journalists are less religious than the public, 57 per cent saying that they did not espouse a particular religious faith and 32 per cent saying that they definitely believed in God compared to 39 per cent (no religious affiliation) and 56 per cent (definitely believe in God) for the university-educated public.

- Although the ideas of private-sector journalists on the desirability of capitalism, free markets, and private property are broadly the same as those of the general public, the views of the public-sector CBC journalists are significantly to the left.
- The public is more conservative on social issues than those in the media. For example, journalists are more likely than the general public to believe that abortion should be considered a moral and legal right and a much greater share of the public than journalists believes that gay and lesbian issues receive too much media attention.
- Journalists are considerably more likely than the general public to vote for the NDP, the highest level of NDP support by far being among CBC radio journalists.

Miljan and Cooper also note that French-Canadian journalists are closer to their audience/readership in their political and social views than are English-Canadian journalists to theirs, a circumstance that may reflect a more secularized, libertarian, and left-leaning society in Quebec than is found in English Canada.

On the other hand, recent studies by researchers at McGill University found no evidence of a left-leaning partisan bias in the case of Canadian newspapers. Based on their analysis of campaign coverage in 2004 and 2006 in seven major dailies (*Globe and Mail, Calgary Herald, Vancouver Sun, Toronto Star, La Presse,* and *Le Devoir*), they found that reporting tended to be quite neutral between the parties and, on the whole, negative towards all of them. Editorial coverage, however, was characterized by partisan favouritism. The party most likely to be on the receiving end of positive editorial coverage was the Conservative Party, hardly the result one would expect to find if those in the media have a left-of-centre bias. Also worth mentioning is that in 2006 and 2008 all of the country's leading newspapers, with the exception of the *Toronto Star*, endorsed the Conservative Party.[34]

But even if it is the case that left-of-centre political and social views are more often found among those in the media than in Canadian society as a whole, this ideological gap needs to be understood in the context of what 'left' and 'right' mean in Canadian society. 'Left' does not mean fundamental opposition to the basic institutions of the capitalist economy. To be on the left in the predominantly liberal societies of Canada and the United States has always meant to be ambivalent about business—to distrust excessive concentrations of economic power and to believe that business must be regulated, while accepting the superiority (in most circumstances) of private property and the market system of allocation. But this is the ambivalence of family members who do not see eye to eye on all matters at all times.

News and public affairs reporting focuses on conflict and controversy, often that involving government officials and powerful private interests, which naturally gives the impression that those in the media are anti-establishment critics. The impression is somewhat misleading. Only a minority of those in the mass media—albeit a few colourful and occasionally influential ones—have strong left-wing or right-wing commitments. Those on the right, such as David Frum, George Jonas, and Mark Steyn, and those on the left, such as Linda McQuaig, David Suzuki, and Judy Rebick, are the exceptions rather than the rule in Canadian journalism. Most journalists occupy locations towards the middle of the ideological spectrum and generally experience little difficulty in accommodating themselves to the needs of the organization within which they work. 'They mostly "say what they like"', says Ralph Miliband, 'but this is mainly because their employers mostly like what they say, or at least find little in what they say which is objectionable.'[35]

It bears repeating that most of what the mass media produce does not fall into the categories of news and public affairs. It should not be assumed, however, that the entertainment and information products of the media industry carry no political messages or ideological biases. They do, both through the images, themes, and interpretations they communicate and through their silences. If the mass media are 'more important in confirming or reinforcing existing opinions than they are in changing opinions',[36] as studies generally suggest, this is partly due to the ideological orthodoxy of most writers, producers, editors, and others who have an influence on the media product.

This is not to suggest that there is no place in the mass media for people whose political views lie outside the safer familiar mainstream. The point is, rather, that those in media industries cluster mainly in the uncontroversial centre of the political spectrum. For these cultural workers the other four filters affecting media content are largely beside the point. The conformity of their value systems with that of society's dominant ideology ensures that they seldom, if ever, test the limits of what the system will allow.

In his website on journalism and democracy, *PressThink*, Jay Rosen argues that instead of thinking of those in the media as tilting the political playing field to the left or the right, their more important ideological function is 'to place certain people, causes and ideas within the deviant sphere' and therefore to deny them a place in the cultural and political conversation.[37] If these deviant ideas and their promoters are acknowledged at all, they are likely to be framed in a narrative that characterizes them as 'dangerous', 'fanatical', 'hateful', and 'extreme'—in short, illegitimate. This treatment was once the fate of communist ideas and thinkers, particularly in the United States during the Cold War.

We should not imagine that members of the media do not perform this ideological function in Canada, helping to reinforce a sphere of consensus. This does not mean that points of view that fall outside of this ideological consensus will not be heard, but their spokespersons will, Rosen says, 'experience the press as an opponent in the struggle for recognition'.[38] Spokespersons for 'deviant' points of view may nevertheless find a forum for their ideas via the Internet, where all manner of marginal and socially unrespectable ideas manage to thrive.

The Media and Democracy

> In regard to propaganda the early advocates of universal literacy and a free press envisaged only two possibilities: the propaganda might be true, or it might be false. They did not foresee what in fact has happened, above all in our Western capitalist democracies—the development of a vast mass communications industry, concerned in the main neither with the true nor the false, but with the unreal, the more or less totally irrelevant. In a word, they failed to take into account man's almost infinite appetite for distractions.[39]

The media, it often appears, have few friends except themselves. Politicians, business people, and those on the right of the political spectrum regularly accuse the media of having liberal-left biases, of irresponsible scandal-mongering, and of being inherently and unfairly opposed to established authority. Those on the political left, however, are no less critical of the media. They are apt to view the media as the servile handmaidens of powerful interests, particularly economic ones. Both ideological camps, right and left, accuse the media of having strongly anti-democratic tendencies. Conservatives argue that those in the media tend to be more liberal-left than society as a whole, but that they foist their interests and perspectives on the public behind a smokescreen of journalistic detachment and objectivity. Left-wing critics of the media claim that the media help to '**manufacture consent**'[40] for a social system—including political and economic structures—that operates mainly in the interests of a privileged minority. What the mass media foist on the public, leftist critics charge, are less their own ideological biases than the false consciousness of the dominant ideology.

In this chapter we have argued that the behaviour of the mass media is shaped by a number of filters. These filters cumulatively determine the sort of 'product' that is likely to reach the consuming public. Our conclusion is that the products of the mass media are generally supportive of established values and institutions. Thus, the media tend to reinforce the power of those groups whose interests are best served by the status quo. In order to play this role it is not necessary that the media avoid all criticism of powerful interests. This would be a ludicrous claim. All that is necessary is that an overwhelming preponderance of what appears on the page, screen, and over the airwaves conforms to mainstream values. This test is amply met.

On the other hand, the gains made in recent years by socially marginal, politically weak interests, such as Aboriginal Canadians, women, and environmental activists, have been in large measure due to media coverage of their demands and spokespersons. This, in turn, has raised public consciousness of the issues and discourse—'equal pay for work of equal value', 'Aboriginal self-government',

Media Spotlight

Box 12.5 Editorializing through Public Opinion Polls

'According to an Environics Research Group survey, 57 per cent of Canadians believe that gays and lesbians should be allowed to marry. The results are based on a telephone survey of 1,500 people and are considered to be accurate within a margin of error of plus or minus 2.5 per cent, 19 times out of 20.'

Statements like the one above are reported on a daily basis. In fact, polling results have become an indispensable part of media coverage of public affairs, along with the observations and analysis of 'experts'. Poll results, perhaps even more than the words of interviewed experts, seem to carry a sort of authority that is widely respected. For this reason, it is worth paying attention to why they are conducted, who pays for them, and where they are reported. It turns out that public opinion polling sometimes shades into editorializing when surveys of public opinion are deliberately used to push the public conversation on an issue in a particular direction.

Political parties, governments, and private organizations may commission surveys that are designed to tell a particular story about public opinion—that Canadians are 'fearful of American-style, two-tiered health care' or that they are dissatisfied with 'long waiting times for medical procedures' and believe that they should have a 'right to purchase private medical services in Canada'. Sometimes it is all in the phrasing, as pollsters know very well. These poll results are inconsequential until they are reported and commented on in the media. It would be naive to imagine that journalists, editors, and the news outlets they work for treat all polls, by all polling firms, in the same way. Indeed, it has become routine for particular television broadcasters, newspapers, and magazines to have a special relationship to a particular survey research firm. For example, the *National Post* and Global Television, both part of the CanWest media group, regularly commission polls carried out by Compas Research. *Maclean's* magazine has had the same sort of relationship with Environics. The *Toronto Star*'s pollster of choice is Ekos.

Particular political parties have their preferred pollsters to whom they regularly turn for data on issues and questions that they have chosen and framed according to not only what they want to learn about their support but what message and image they wish to convey about themselves and their opponents. Some of these polling data they will keep private for their own strategic and campaigning purposes. At other times the purpose of the polling enterprise is to make the data public, with appropriate interpretations provided, in order to shape public opinion. This requires that at least some journalists, producers, and news outlets will provide the opportunities for the public to learn what it is the party wants people to know about it, its leader, or an issue that plays to its popular strength. Such opportunities will generally exist.

When is a poll simply a poll—a mirror on public opinion—and when is it a sort of disguised editorial, intended to tell the public what they should think? If a poll is paid for and shaped by a political party or group sympathetic to it and reported to the public by a news outlet that is generally sympathetic to its policies, is this information or manipulation? Or both?

'sustainable development', 'social justice'—associated with their demands. Moreover, it can hardly be denied that the media usually do a better job of scrutinizing and criticizing government actions, to say nothing of those of powerful societal groups, than do the opposition parties. Indeed, it is precisely the critical and even irreverent tenor of much public affairs journalism that contributes to the widespread belief in the mass media's independent and anti-establishment character.

Most of what the mass media offer does not have this character. Frank Lloyd Wright's description of television as 'chewing gum for the eyes' is, in fact, a fairly apt characterization of much of the electronic and print media. Wright's judgement was basically an aesthetic one. But Aldous Huxley's argument that the 'mass communications industry is concerned in the main neither with the true nor the false, but with the unreal, the more or less totally irrelevant', expresses a political judgement about the mass media. Huxley is suggesting that the media—particularly their entertainment and advertising components—help foster a false consciousness among the public, the sort of pacified somnolence that characterizes the masses in his *Brave New World.* This judgement may seem rather harsh, but Huxley is certainly right in suggesting that one should not assume that only news and public affairs reporting has political consequences.

On balance, the media do an uneven job of providing Canadians with the information needed to make informed judgements about their society and its political issues. The biases of the mass media are towards familiar images and stories—what Lippmann called a 'repertory of stereotypes'—oversimplified conflict, the personalization of events, drama and action, and reliance on established opinion leaders. These biases are much more supportive than threatening of the status quo. At the same time, citizens cannot avoid shouldering some of the responsibility for whatever information deficit they experience and ill-founded views they hold. For all the problems surrounding the quality of information that beset the Internet, there is also no doubt that it has put within the reach of almost everyone an enormous range of information and interpretation concerning matters all the way from our own communities to the global community. Reliance on the same old sources of news and public affairs is a choice, not an inevitability.

Starting Points for Research

Barry Cooper and Lydia Miljan, *Hidden Agendas: How Journalists Influence the News* (Vancouver: University of British Columbia Press, 2003). This is one of the few empirical studies of the nature and causes of media bias, and probably the best.

Paul Nesbitt-Larking, *Politics, Society, and the Media: Canadian Perspectives*, 2nd edn (Toronto: University of Toronto Press, 2007). Nesbitt-Larking offers a comprehensive and critical examination of the characteristics and political and social impacts of Canada's media system.

Florian Sauvageau, David Taras, and David Schneiderman, *The Last Word: Media Coverage of the Supreme Court of Canada* (Vancouver: University of British Columbia Press, 2005). An analysis of media coverage, in French and English Canada, of a handful of major Supreme Court rulings.

Stuart Soroka, *Agenda-Setting Dynamics in Canada* (Vancouver: University of British Columbia Press, 2002). Following eight separate policy issues, this book examines the interaction of the media, public opinion, and policy-makers in setting and shaping the policy agenda.

Review Exercises

1. Keep a two-day record of your media consumption, being sure to write down all the television programs and films you watch, the amount and sorts of radio programming you listen to, the newspapers, magazines, and books you read, and your Internet activity. Try not to change what would be your normal pattern of viewing/listening/reading/surfing. Based on this record, answer the following questions:
   (a) What proportion of your daily media consumption is normally devoted to entertainment? News and public affairs? Other purposes?
   (b) Which medium (or media) do you rely upon most for news about your local community, your country, the international scene?
   (c) If and when you pick up a newspaper, which section do you read first? What else do you look at in the newspaper? What about the Internet? How often do you click on news stories? Do you rely on blogs or particular websites to keep you informed? Are they Canadian?
2. Watch the late-evening television news broadcast of one of the main Canadian broadcasters (CBC, CTV, or Global). Make a list of those stories where experts are interviewed, quoted, or referred to (for example, 'A study by the C.D. Howe Institute . . .'). Record the positions and, if possible, affiliations of the experts (e.g., professors, government officials, think-tank researchers, activists, etc.). Can you suggest other sorts of experts or organizations that could have been contacted for any of these stories?
3. Visit the websites of *The Guardian* <www.guardianunlimited.co.uk>, National Public Radio <www.npr.org>, the British Broadcasting Corporation's World Service <www.bbc.co.uk>, the *Western Standard* <www.westernstandard.ca>, and such popular blogs as smalldeadanimals.com and steynonline.com. Have you ever used any of these websites? Do you think many Canadians are aware of them? Do you think they provide perspectives or coverage of national or world affairs that is different from what is offered by the media outlets relied on by most people?

Part V
Contemporary Issues in Canadian Political Life

The complex interplay of ideas, institutions, and processes is best understood through the examination of particular issues that roil the waters of politics. For example, the long-standing conflict between French and English Canadians, a conflict historically rooted in language, ethnicity, values, and an imbalance in power, has been played out within the framework of particular institutions and managed through certain processes that have evolved over the nearly 250 years that francophones and anglophones have lived under the same political roof in what today is Canada. These institutions and processes have affected the relationship between the two communities, but the values and demographic characteristics and circumstances of these communities have also shaped the laws, constitutional changes, and processes that influence their relations. Case studies of particular issues enable us to untangle the complex web of cause and effect that exists between ideas, institutions, and processes in the real world of politics.

The next five chapters will focus on several important issues in Canadian politics, all of which are crucial to an understanding of what might be described as the Canadian condition. The first involves language politics and Quebec, home to about nine out of 10 French-speaking Canadians. This is the oldest continuing conflict in Canadian politics. The second issue is multiculturalism and the politics of diversity, focusing on how ethnic pluralism has been managed in Canada. After this we turn to women and politics, examining the developments that have taken place in laws, attitudes, and social conditions pertaining to women. The fourth issue, which in many ways is just as old as the ethno-linguistic conflict, although it was pushed below the surface of Canadian politics for most of the time Canada has been a country, involves Aboriginal Canadians and their relationship to other citizens and governments in Canada. The final chapter examines Canada's relations with the rest of the world, with a particular emphasis on Canada–US relations. Together, the study of these issues helps us to understand the Canadian political condition as it has evolved over time and as it exists today.

'The Quebec Question'—the status of Quebec and its language policy—remains central in the nation's politics. There are no easy solutions to the challenges raised by Quebec's claim to having a distinct culture (or, as this sign says, 'We have the right to be different'). © Megapress/Alamy

13 Language Politics

Conflict over language has always been a central feature of Canadian politics. This chapter explains why language and the status of Quebec are such prominent issues in Canada. It also examines the chief aspects of federal and Quebec language policies. Topics include the following:

- The demographics of language politics.
- The shift from French-Canadian nationalism to Quebec nationalism.
- The Quiet Revolution and its legacy.
- Language policy in Quebec.
- Federal language policy.
- Is Quebec a distinct society?

Like the theme of unrequited love in an opera, the status of Quebec is an issue that surfaces repeatedly when Canadians and their governments turn their thoughts to constitutional reform. And like an opera, elements of tragedy and comedy mingle freely when the related issues of Quebec's constitutional status and language rights are on the table. But unlike an opera, the 'Quebec question'—which might just as fairly be called the 'Canada question' (or at least one of the fundamental Canada questions, the other one being Canada's relationship to the United States)—has no neat finale. Even the scenario of a separate Quebec would not bring down the curtain on the 'Canada/Quebec' question. No one doubts that an enormous number of practical matters would have to be dealt with, including such thorny issues as the nature of economic relations between the remnants of *l'ancien Canada* to the status of the French language in a Canada without Quebec.

Why are Quebec and language so central to Canadian politics? Why is the issue of language rights so closely tied to that of Quebec's constitutional status? Why do Lord Durham's words about 'two nations warring in the bosom of a single state', words written 170 years ago, sound apt today? What does Quebec want from the rest of Canada, and the rest of Canada from Quebec? Why has nationalism always been the key to unlocking the mysteries of Quebec politics?

These are big questions, and despite all the attention paid to them throughout this country's history they are far from being settled. Let us at least try to understand why these particular questions have so often been asked and why answers have been so elusive.

The Demographics of Language Politics

When New France was formally placed under British control in 1763, francophones outnumbered anglophones by about eight to one in the territory that would become Canada. Forty years later, the two groups were of roughly equal size. During the mid-1800s the English language gained ground on the French because of the wave of immigrants from the British Isles, so that by the 1871 census—Canada's first—Canadians of French origin comprised about one-third of the population.[1] The extraordinarily high birth rate among French-Canadian women enabled francophones to hold their own until the end of the 1950s against an English-speaking population that was buoyed by immigration—immigrants of whatever language group overwhelmingly adopted English as their new language. Since then, birth rates have dropped precipitously in Quebec, where the vast majority of francophones reside, and the francophone share of Canada's population has nudged down to its present all-time low of about 22 per cent (see Figure 13.1).

The end of ***la revanche des berceaux***—the high birth rate that for close to a century enabled French Canada to maintain its numerical strength against English Canada—coupled with the fact that the vast majority of immigrants have chosen English as their adopted language, finally led to a decline in the francophone share of the Canadian population by the early 1960s. More worrisome from the standpoint of Quebec governments was the fact that demographers began to predict a fall in the francophone share of that province's population, particularly in Montreal where most new immigrants chose to establish themselves. Montreal, which proudly called itself the second largest French-speaking city in the world (after Paris), according to demographer Jacques Henripin, would be about equally divided between anglophones and francophones by the early twenty-first century.[2] The possibility that francophones would become a minority in Quebec was often raised by Quebec nationalists, although serious demographers like Henripin argued that this possibility was quite remote.[3] Nevertheless, this decline provided the impetus for provincial language laws intended to stem this tide.

The key factor in shifting the linguistic balance of Quebec, it should be emphasized, was immigration. Given that the province's anglophones were

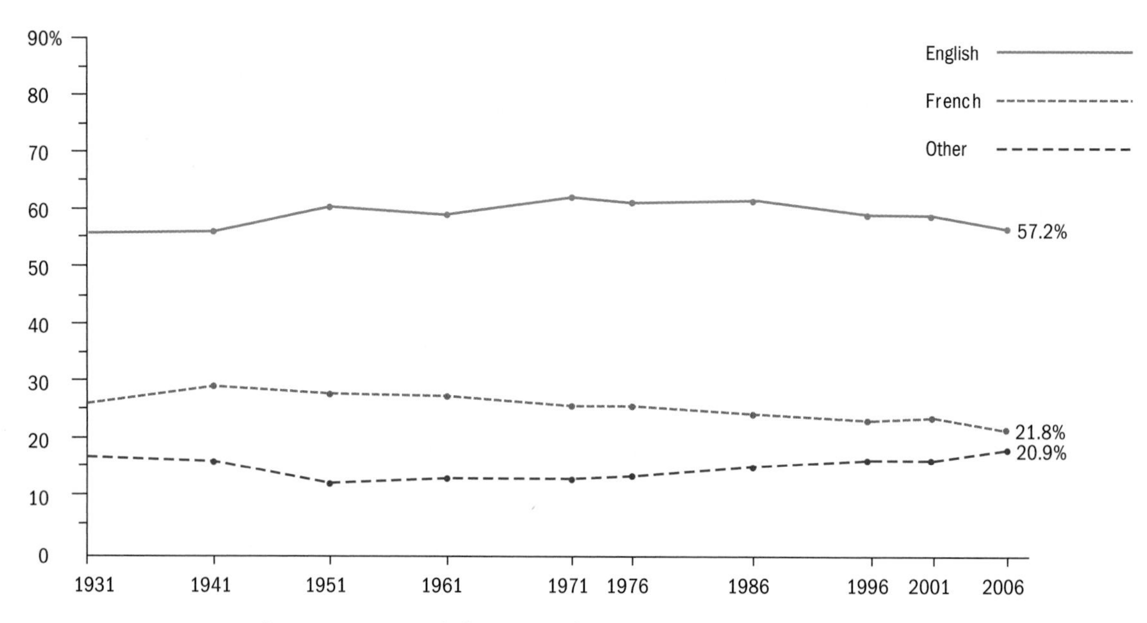

FIGURE 13.1 Mother Tongues of the Canadian Population, 1931–2006

Source: F.H. Leacy, ed., *Historical Statistics of Canada*, 2nd edn, Series A185-237 (Ottawa: Minister of Supply and Services Canada, 1983); Canada Year Book 1990, 2-25; Statistics Canada, *2006 Census of Population*, at: <www.statcan.ca/>.

no more fecund than francophones, the language choices of allophones—Canadian demographers' term for those whose native language is neither English nor French—would be crucial in shaping Quebec's future linguistic contours. Immigration became the sole reason for provincial population growth by the 1960s, given that the provincial fertility rate had fallen below the replacement level (i.e., the average number of births per female needed to offset the mortality rate).

With the exception of the relatively few immigrants whose native tongue was French, all other groups overwhelmingly adopted English for themselves and their children. As of the 1961 census, 46 per cent of foreign-born residents of Quebec spoke only English, another 25 per cent spoke English and French, and only 17 per cent spoke only French.[4] Despite provincial language laws that require immigrants to send their children to French schools, make French the sole official language for provincial public services, and promote the use of French in the Quebec economy, evidence indicates that many allophones still opt for English. Figure 13.2 shows that the percentage of Quebecers claiming French as their mother tongue is almost identical to the percentage who speak mainly French in the home. But the percentage speaking English in the home is greater than that which claims English as its mother tongue. The gains made by the English-speaking community can only be explained by the linguistic choices of those whose mother tongue is neither French nor English. New Quebecers have continued to find English an attractive choice, although less often than before the existing provincial language laws were put into place.

Inside Quebec, the current demographic picture includes the following characteristics.

- French is spoken at home by about 81 per cent of the population (2006 census).
- Contrary to projections made in the 1960s and early 1970s, Quebec has not become less francophone. The 81.1 per cent of the population speaking French at home compares to 80 per cent in 1901 and 81 per cent in 1961.
- Most of the province's population increase is due to immigration and consequently the linguistic choices made by newcomers to Quebec are crucial to the language balance in the province. According to the 2006 cen-

sus, 51 per cent of allophones who switched to one of Canada's official languages as their home language chose French, versus 49 per cent who adopted English as their home language.

- Quebec's share of Canada's total population has fallen over the last two decades, from 28 per cent in 1971 to about 23 per cent in 2010.

Outside Quebec the language picture looks very different. With the exceptions of New Brunswick and Ontario, the francophone populations of the other provinces are tiny. In fact, in certain provinces and in all but a handful of Canada's major metropolitan areas outside Quebec, some of the non-official-language communities are considerably larger than the French-speaking minority. For example, in Vancouver native speakers of Chinese outnumber those whose mother tongue is French by a ratio of more than ten to one and in Toronto by more than five to one, and in Hamilton, Ontario, native speakers of Italian outnumber francophones by a ratio of two to one. Even in the Ottawa–Gatineau urban region, native speakers of non-official languages now outnumber those whose mother tongue is French (2006 census).

In all provinces except Quebec, the French language community continuously loses some of its

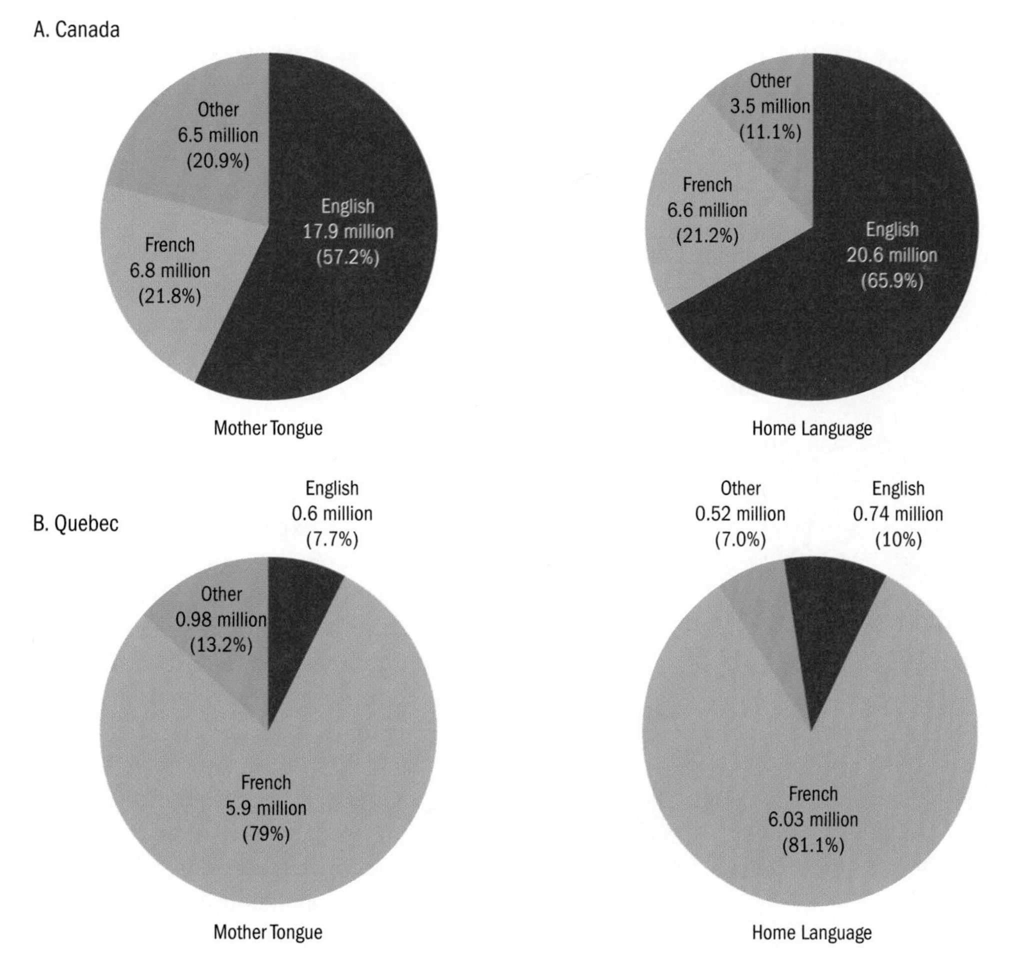

FIGURE 13.2 Mother Tongue and Language Spoken at Home, 2006

Note: The category 'Other' includes non-official languages and those who report French and English, or French or English plus a non-official language, as their mother tongue or home language.

Source: Statistics Canada, *Census of Canada*, 2006.

members to the English majority. This may be seen from the difference between the number of people for whom French is their mother tongue compared to the number for whom it is their home language. The difference represents the rate of language transfer to the dominant language group (see Table 13.1). Only in Quebec and, to a lesser degree, New Brunswick is the rate of French language retention high. By contrast, the rate of language retention among native English-speakers is high everywhere in Canada.

This is not a recent development. In *Languages in Conflict*, Richard Joy carefully documented the trend towards the assimilation of francophones outside Quebec. Joy was the first to make what today seems an obvious point, namely, that the rate of language transfer is greatest among the younger generations. For example, using data from the 1961 census he found that the transfer rate from French to English in the four western provinces was 25 per cent among those aged 45–54, but was 60 per cent for those aged 5–14 and 67 per cent among infants aged 0–4.[5] Only in what Joy called the **bilingual belt**, the narrow region running from Moncton, New Brunswick, in the east, to Sault Ste Marie, Ontario, in the west, was the rate of assimilation among all generations significantly lower. The reason, of course, was the ability to shop, work, go to church, and do the other things that keep a language alive. Outside the bilingual belt, this supportive milieu was seldom encountered. Indeed, the 2001 census showed that the francophone population in every province except Quebec and New Brunswick is older than in Canada as a whole, confirming Joy's prediction that the failure to retain young francophones would contribute to the steady erosion of the community's base.

At this point some readers may protest that the gloomy picture Joy drew three decades ago is no longer accurate. They will point to statistics that suggest bilingualism outside of Quebec has been increasing in recent years. Indeed, it is today highest among the young (see Figure 13.3), the very group that Joy argued was most likely to transfer to the dominant language group. The rapid expansion of French immersion schools since the 1980s, particularly in Ontario, which accounts for over half of all immersion students in Canada, is responsible for most of this increase. The future of French outside Quebec, they argue, is assured.

What is one to conclude from the fact that while the francophone share of Canada's population outside of Quebec has been declining, the proportion of the population claiming to be bilingual has been increasing? Does this represent a reprieve for French-language minorities? Or are they, as René Lévesque once said, 'dead ducks', or as Quebec writer

You ethnics are free to complain about Quebec's unjust language laws...
... just be sure that you complain twice as loudly in French as you do in English!
TONGUE TROOPER
COMMISSION de PROTECTION de la LANGUE FRANÇAISE
PQ
PQ

The portrayal of Quebec's language laws in English Canada is usually extremely critical. In this cartoon the character in the dark trench coat is evocative of a Nazi, an unflattering image if ever there was one!

TABLE 13.1 Percentage of Francophones Speaking English Most Often at Home: Canada, Provinces, Territories, and Canada Less Quebec, 1971, 1991, 2001, and 2006

Regions	1971	1991	2001	2006
Canada	6.0	6.0	6.2	6.3
NL	43.2	55.1	63.5	67.9
PEI	43.2	46.8	53.2	50.7
NS	34.1	41.7	45.6	48.3
NB	8.7	9.7	10.5	11.2
Que.	1.5	1.0	1.0	1.1
Ont.	29.9	36.9	40.3	41.8
Man.	36.9	50.1	54.6	55.5
Sask.	51.9	67.5	74.5	74.4
Alta	53.7	64.5	67.6	69.0
BC	73.0	72.8	72.6	72.0
Yukon	74.4	53.8	56.2	54.8
NWT	51.1	54.0	62.6	56.2
Nunavut	n.a.	n.a.	46.8	47.9
Canada Less Quebec	29.6	35.1	38.1	39.3

n.a. = not applicable
Source: Statistics Canada, at: <www12.statcan.ca/english/census06/analysis/language/tables/table9.htm>.

Yves Beauchemin characterized them, 'des morts vivantes' ('warm corpses' would be a reasonable translation)?

The pressures of assimilation continue unabated throughout most of the predominantly English-speaking provinces. A study by Roger Bernard of the University of Ottawa concludes that a combination of aging populations, low birth rates, marriage to non-francophones, and the general lack of supportive social and economic milieux for French speakers will lead to the collapse of many francophone communities outside Quebec within a generation or two.[6] The 2001 census found that about 50 per cent of married francophones living outside Quebec and New Brunswick had anglophone spouses. Generally, English becomes the lingua franca and the language of the children in such families. It appears, however, that the fate of larger francophone communities in northern and eastern Ontario and in New Brunswick may be less bleak. Already in 1988, Jacques Henripin cautiously suggested that official bilingualism in New Brunswick and the extension of French language services and education in Ontario may have slowed the assimilationist tide in those provinces.[7]

As for the increasing level of bilingualism in Canada, we would not conclude that the prospects for living in French outside of Quebec have improved. The census question that measures bilingualism ('Can you carry on a conversation in the other official language?') does not provide a measure of languages in use. The fact that increasing numbers of those whose mother tongue is English are 'functionally fluent' in French does not mean that French will be used more often in the home, the workplace, at the pub, and wherever else communication takes place. Indeed, there is a good deal of evidence suggesting that three decades of French

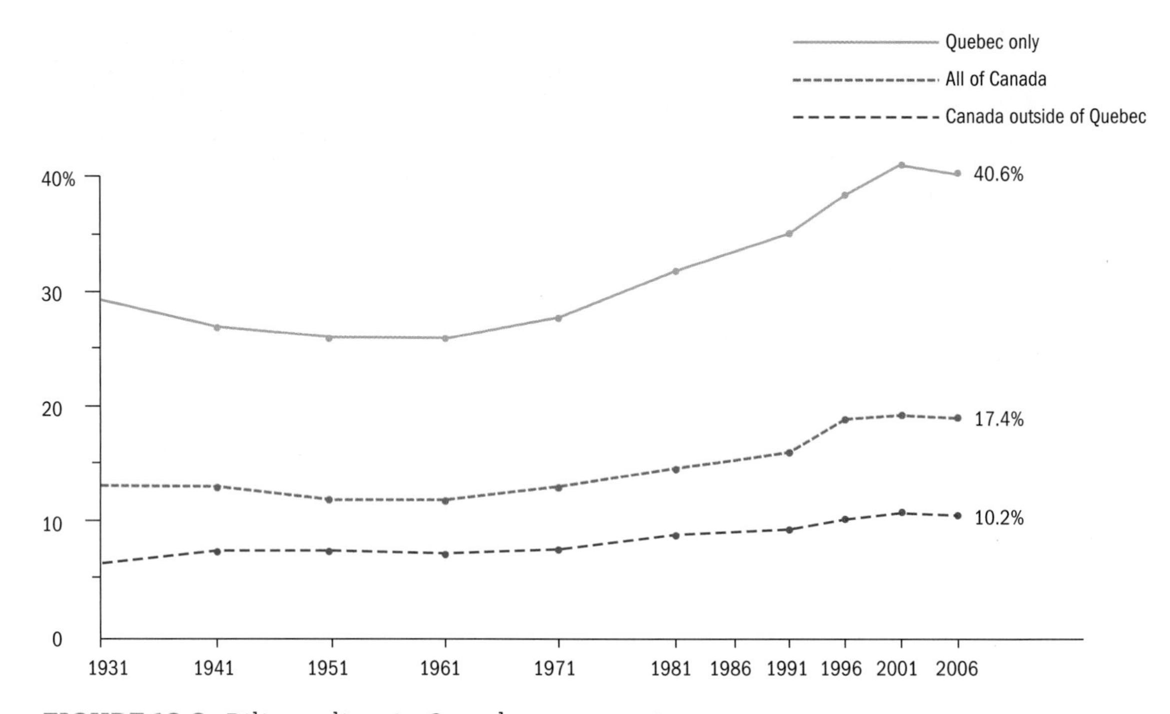

FIGURE 13.3 Bilingualism in Canada, 1931–2006

Source: Statistics Canada, *Census of Canada*, various years.

immersion education[8] has produced a wave of **receptive bilinguals**—people who are capable of responding to French communications but do not themselves initiate conversations in French, consume French language media, or seek out opportunities to live in their acquired second language. There is certainly nothing wrong with this and, indeed, much that is good about the expansion of bilinguals, receptive or otherwise! But the claims made for and conclusions drawn from the immersion experience should be viewed with a certain amount of caution.

Moreover, despite over 30 years of immersion education in Canada, the rate of functional bilingualism is still relatively low outside of Quebec, at about 10 per cent for the population as a whole and closer to 13 per cent for young people between the ages of 15 and 24 (down from closer to 16 per cent a decade ago). Over half of all bilingual Canadians reside in Quebec, where the rate of bilingualism is about four times greater than in Ontario. The increase in the level of bilingualism in Quebec since the 1960s has been sharper than in the rest of Canada. This is simply to say that Canadian bilingualism is to a considerable degree a predominantly Quebec phenomenon. In fact, the most recent census found that the level of bilingualism among anglophones outside Quebec declined in recent years.

The bottom line is that the social and economic milieux outside Quebec have not become more supportive for francophones. It is true that provincial government services for the francophone communities of Ontario have improved since the mid-1980s, and those in New Brunswick are quite good. But it is also true that few people outside the 'bilingual belt' can manage to shop, work, and do the other daily social activities in French that help keep a language alive. Even francophone schools in predominantly English-speaking communities experience the pressures of language erosion. René Lévesque's characterization of francophones outside Quebec as 'dead ducks' is somewhat overstated. Lame ducks might be closer to the truth.

The Trajectory of Nationalism

French-Canadian nationalism, Pierre Trudeau writes, was originally a system of self-defence. This was certainly true. Conquered by arms, the French-speaking people of New France found themselves subordinated to an anglophone minority about one-eighth their size. English was the language of the new political and commercial elites. The **Conquest** left French a second-class language within Quebec, and francophones largely excluded from the colony's structures of power.

Why did francophones not succumb to assimilationist pressures, as they did in Louisiana after it, too, passed from French control? The answer is complex, but three chief factors can be identified. One involved the policies of the British colonial authorities in New France. By the terms of the Quebec Act, 1774, they granted formal protection to the status of the Roman Catholic religion and the *code civil*, the basis of civil law in New France.[9] Faced with rebellion in the Thirteen Colonies, which two years later successfully declared their independence from Britain, this recognition for the rights of the French-Canadian population may have been motivated chiefly by the desire to ensure the allegiance of the clerical and civil leaders of that population. Regardless, it involved official recognition of the rights of the francophone Catholic majority and reinforced the leadership role of that community's clerical elite.

A second factor that explained the different fates of the French language and culture in Louisiana compared to Quebec was demography. French-speakers in the south of the United States were very quickly swamped by a rapidly growing anglophone population. But as we observed earlier in this chapter, although immigration of Loyalists from the United States and English-speakers from the British Isles tipped the linguistic balance in Canada towards English by the early nineteenth century, the high fertility rate among French Canadians enabled them to hold their ground at about one-third of Canada's population between Confederation and the 1950s.

The defensive posture that Trudeau argues was characteristic of French-Canadian nationalism is the third factor that explains the ability of French Canada to resist the pressures of assimilation. Under the guidance of a clerical elite whose leading social role was strengthened when anglophones occupied the political and commercial elites of the colony, French Canada met the challenge of English domination by remaining loyal to traditional values and institutions. The nationalist ideology that developed in French Canada after the Conquest is summed up in a famous passage from *Maria Chapdelaine*, the classic novel of traditional French Canada:

> Round about us strangers have come, whom we are wont to call barbarians; they have seized almost all the power; they have acquired almost all the money, but in the country of Quebec nothing has changed . . . [W]e have held our own, so that, it may be, after several centuries more, the world will turn to us and say: these people are of a race that knows not how to perish . . . . In the country of Quebec, nothing shall die, and nothing shall be changed.[10]

Traditional French-Canadian nationalism was guided by the idea of ***la survivance***—survival, against the pressures of a dominant culture that was anglicizing, Protestant, materialistic, liberal democratic, and business-oriented. In other words, this dominant anglophone culture was all the things that French Canada, according to the spokespersons for this ideology, was not and should not become. The main ideas expressed in the writings and public pronouncements of the exponents of the traditional nationalism can be summarized briefly:

- French Canada comprised a distinct nation, whose chief characteristics were the Catholic religion and the French language. Preservation of the French language and the Catholic religion were considered inseparable, as the title of Henri Bourassa's book *La langue, guardienne de la foi*[11] explicitly declared. 'The preservation of language', Bourassa wrote, 'is absolutely necessary for the preservation of a race, its spirit, character and temperament.'[12]

- French Canada had a mission, a special vocation as a people. The mission was to remain faithful to its roots, and to resist the lure of materialistic, English, Protestant pressures. The democratic belief in the separation of church and state was ludicrous. It was a lamentable heresy spawned by the French Revolution and the American Constitution.
- The character of the French-Canadian people was most secure in the province of Quebec, but French Canada was not restricted to the boundaries of that province. In other words, French Canada was defined by socio-cultural characteristics, not by the territory of Quebec.

While these were the chief characteristics of the nationalist ideology that became dominant in French Canada during the nineteenth century, a dominance that it maintained until the middle of the twentieth century, there were voices of dissent. In fact, sociologist Marcel Rioux argues that the idea of the French-Canadian nation was first developed by the secular elites of Quebec who espoused liberal and often aggressively anti-clerical views.[13] Political scientist Denis Monière concurs, noting that the authority of the Church was much weaker before and in the decades immediately following the Conquest than is usually believed (especially by English-Canadian historians).[14] He maintains that the 'victory' of the conservative traditional nationalism became assured only after the defeat of Louis-Joseph Papineau's liberal forces in the Lower Canada Rebellion of 1837. However, even after the ideological dominance of the Church and the voices of traditional rationalism were firmly established, liberal voices of dissent were occasionally heard.[15]

The traditional nationalism came under mounting pressure during the middle of the twentieth century. Its chief tenets were increasingly at odds with the economic and social reality of Quebec. The emigration of hundreds of thousands of French-speaking Quebecers to the northeastern United States during the 1800s demonstrated more clearly than anything else the weakness of the traditional nationalism's hymn to the pastoral vocation of French Canadians. There simply was not enough arable land to support the rural parish lifestyle that the ideologues of the traditional nationalism clung to so tenaciously. The urban population of Quebec surpassed the rural population in the 1921 census (56 per cent to 44 per cent). Between 1926 and 1950 the number of people employed in Quebec's manufacturing sector increased by about 220 per cent, slightly higher than the rate of increase for Canada as a whole (210 per cent), but significantly higher than the rate for the rest of the country if Ontario—where most new investment in manufacturing was located—is omitted from the picture.[16] By mid-century manufacturing workers outnumbered farm workers in Quebec by a large margin.[17] In short, by the early twentieth century the 'typical' Québécois lived in a city or town, worked in a factory, store, or office, and had family members who had left the province in search of employment opportunities.

Quebec was following the path of modernization, but the urbanization and industrialization that this involved also produced a political side effect of enormous importance. This was the increasing realization that francophones, despite accounting for about four-fifths of the Quebec population, were largely shut out of the centres of economic decision-making and controlled relatively little of the province's wealth. 'Is there any inherent or unavoidable reason why,' asked Abbé Lionel Groulx in 1934, 'with 2,500,000 French Canadians in Quebec, all big business, all high finance, all the public utilities, all our water rights, forests and mines, should belong to a minority of 300,000?'[18] Although the question was not new—Édouard Montpetit, Errol Bouchette, Étienne Parent, and others had raised basically the same issue in arguing that educated francophones needed to rid themselves of their apparent distaste for careers in industry and finance—it was being asked with increasing frequency between the 1930s and the 1950s.[19]

These decades saw the emergence of the first serious challenge to the conservative ideology since the crushed rebellion of 1837. It brought together a diverse group of university professors and students, journalists, union activists, liberal politicians, and even some elements within the Catholic Church (particularly Action catholique). They were united by their opposition to the so-called '**unholy alliance**' of the Catholic Church, anglophone capital, and the Union Nationale party of Maurice Duplessis—and, of course, to the conservative nationalism that sought to justify French Canadians' marginal economic status. Marcel Rioux calls this anti-establishment challenge the ideology of contestation and recoupment.[20] It contested the traditional elites' monopoly over power in the province and what was argued to be their backward characterization of French-Canadian society and culture. Its goal was to recoup lost ground; to bring Quebec's society, economy, and government up to date, a goal that became known in Quebec as ***rattrapage*** (catching up).

The nerve centre of this challenge to the conservative establishment and ideology included the Faculty of Social Sciences at Laval University; the intellectual revue ***Cité libre***, founded by such figures as Pierre Trudeau and Gérard Pelletier; and the provincial Liberal Party. As the political party attempting to depose Duplessis, it was natural that the Quebec Liberal Party would attract the energies of those who saw the Union Nationale under *le chef* as one of the principal obstacles to reform.

The traditional ideology and the interests it defended were doomed by their failure to adapt to a changing environment. As Marcel Rioux observes, '[T]he ideology and old power structure in Quebec were becoming anachronistic in the face of the demographic, economic, and social changes that Quebec was experiencing.'[21] They managed to hold on until the 1960s largely because of the tight web of patronage politics that Maurice Duplessis used to keep the ideologically conservative Union Nationale in power for most of the period from 1936 until his death in 1959. The death of Duplessis was followed by disorder within the governing Union Nationale. Paul Sauvé, who succeeded Duplessis as Premier, died suddenly within a year. The Union Nationale went into the 1960 provincial election under a leader, Antonio Barrette, who was opposed by many powerful members of the party. The Liberal Party's election victory probably owed as much to disorder within the Union Nationale as to popular support for change. Regardless, the opportunity for reform had come.

The Quiet Revolution and Its Legacy

The first several years of the 1960s are justly considered a turning point in the history of Quebec. Duplessis's death in 1959 and the election of the provincial Liberals under Jean Lesage in 1960 opened the way for the political reforms and social changes referred to as the **Quiet Revolution**. At the heart of these reforms lay an increased role for the Quebec state. It replaced the authority of the Catholic Church in the areas of social services and education, and also acquired a vastly broader range of economic functions. The provincial state was seen as the *moteur principal* of Quebec's attempt to modernize social and political institutions that were ill-suited to the urbanized, industrialized society that Quebec had become. The state, traditionally viewed as a second-class institution in a province where most social services were controlled by the Church and where government was associated with crass patronage, became the focus of nationalist energies.

The nationalism that emerged in the crucible of the Quiet Revolution marked a sharp break with the past. The traditional nationalism had emphasized preservation of the *patrimoine*—the language, the faith, the mores of a community whose roots went back to New France. Although some of its chief spokespersons, such as Abbé Lionel Groulx, associated this community with the region of the St Lawrence River and even with the vision of a Laurentian state whose territory would include what is today the southern region of the province, the essential elements of the traditional nationalism were not defined by either the territory or the powers of the Quebec state.

Rioux has characterized the traditional nationalism as an ideology of conservation. Its goals were the preservation of the traditional values and social structures of French Canada, including the leading

A man paints a fleur-de-lys—a symbol of Quebec—on a building under the words 'We know what we want' at the time of the 1980 referendum, which sought a mandate for the provincial government to negotiate with the rest of Canada a new status for Quebecers. The new nationalism that arose during the Quiet Revolution was—and still is—felt keenly by supporters of a sovereign Quebec.

role played by the Church in articulating these values and controlling these structures (i.e., the schools, hospitals, labour unions, etc.). The modern welfare state necessarily threatens the dominant social role of the Church and was generally rejected by spokespersons for the traditional nationalism. Although they insisted on constitutional protections for the province's exclusive right to make education policy and put limits on Ottawa's ability to interfere with social affairs in the province, they did not expect that the Quebec state would actively occupy these fields. The traditional nationalism attached no particular value to the Quebec state, except insofar as its powers could be used to ward off federal intrusions that challenged the status of conservative values and the power of the traditional elites—the clergy, anglophone business leaders, and provincial politicians.

Nationalism is always based on some concept of the nation: who belongs to it and who does not. The traditional nationalism did not identify *la nation canadienne-française* with *la société française du Québec*. The boundaries of *la nation* extended beyond Quebec to embrace French Canadians throughout Canada. There were two reasons for this. First, Catholicism and the role of the Church were important elements of the traditional nationalism. Obviously, neither of these stopped at the Quebec border. Second, the anti-statist quality of the traditional nationalism prevented it from associating the French-Canadian nation with the Quebec state.

History had shown that assimilationist pressures and unsympathetic governments faced francophones outside of Quebec. Nevertheless, to identify the *nation* with the Quebec state would have challenged the dominant social role of the Church. The survival of the nation did not depend, according to the traditional nationalism, on the activities of the Quebec state. Instead, it depended primarily on those institutions that were crucial to the continuation from generation to generation of the French language and the Catholic religion—family, school, and parish. Family and parish obviously fell outside the state's authority. And although the schools were under the constitutional jurisdiction of the provincial state, their control was mainly left in the hands of the Church. This did not change until the early 1960s.

The central elements of the traditional nationalism were located outside of the state. This would not be true of the new nationalism that both spurred and was influenced by the Quiet Revolution. Instead of defining *la nation* in terms of language and religion, the ascendant nationalism of the 1960s developed an understanding of Quebec's history, its economy, and its social structure that was based on language and dependency. The dependency perspective portrayed Quebec as a society whose evolution had been shaped and distorted by the economic and political domination of English Canadians.

This secularized version of French-Canadian history, and more particularly of francophone Quebec, cast an entirely different light on the future of the Quebec nation and its relationship to English Canada. If the problem was that Québécois were dominated economically and politically, then the solution required that they take control of their economic and political destiny. To do so, they would have to use the Quebec state. All of the major reforms of the Quiet Revolution—the establishment of a provincial ministry of education, the nationalization of privately owned hydroelectric companies, the creation of Crown corporations like la Caisse de dépôt et placement and la Société générale de financement, and passage of the Quebec Pension Plan—involved using the Quebec state in a newly assertive way.

The replacement of the traditional nationalism by the state-centred nationalism of the Quiet Revolution was not as abrupt as history might suggest, nor was this new nationalism unchallenged. The traditional social order and its values had been crumbling at the edges for at least a couple of decades before the death of Duplessis and then of Sauvé finally provided the opportunity for opposition groups to gain power. Once the doors were opened to reform, it quickly became apparent that the anti-Duplessis forces shared little more than a common antipathy towards the old order. They were divided on at least three main levels.

First, there was a split between the federalists and those who advocated either special status or independence for Quebec. The federalists included such prominent figures as Pierre Elliott Trudeau, Jean Marchand, and Gérard Pelletier, all of whom entered federal politics through the Liberal Party in 1965. Leadership of the Quebec autonomy side would fall on René Lévesque, formerly a popular television journalist who had masterminded the nationalization of the hydroelectric industry as a minister in the Lesage government and who became the first leader of the Parti Québécois in 1968.

The second division concerned the size and functions of the Quebec state. Even within the reformist Liberal government of Jean Lesage, sharp differences existed over such major policies as the nationalization of the hydroelectricity industry and the role of the province's investment agency, la Caisse de dépôt et placement. Agreement that the provincial state should play a larger role in Quebec society was not matched by consensus on what that role should be.

Finally, Quebec separatists were divided on ideological lines. Those who came to form the leadership of the *indépendantiste* Parti Québécois, such individuals as René Lévesque, Jacques Parizeau, and Claude Morin, were ideologically liberal. But there were others, within the PQ and in other pro-independence organizations, for whom Quebec independence was inseparably linked to the overthrow of what they argued to be a bourgeois state. PQ members Pierre Bourgault and Robert Burns, for example, wanted the end of *la domination anglaise* of the Quebec economy. Although the electoral strength of these left-wing groups never amounted to much, they managed to have a significant impact on political discourse in Quebec, particularly through the province's universities, labour unions, and in the extra-parliamentary wing of the PQ.

In view of these divisions, two developments justify the claim that a state-centred nationalism emerged out of the Quiet Revolution. First, the identification of French Canada with the territory of Quebec was a view shared by most nationalists. Indeed, the entry of Trudeau and his fellow federalists into national politics was chiefly a reaction to this Quebec-oriented nationalism. The provincial Liberals' 1962 campaign slogan, ***Maîtres chez nous***, captured a nationalist consensus that ever since has been an accepted tenet of Quebec politics. Second, key institutional reforms of the Quiet Revolution, including the Caisse de dépôt et placement, Hydro-Québec, and the jurisdictional terrain that the Quebec government wrested from Ottawa in the areas of social policy, immigration, and taxation, have left an important mark on Quebec nationalism. They constitute the core of the provincial state upon which the aspirations summed up in the phrase *Maîtres chez nous* depend.

The Unilingual Approach of Quebec

> We are Québécois. . . . At the core of this personality is the fact that we speak French. Everything else depends on this essential element and follows from it or leads us infallibly back to it.[22]

The origins of present-day language policy in Canada lie in developments in Quebec during the 1960s. With the election of the Quebec Liberal Party in 1960, the political obstacles to change were largely removed and the outdated character of the traditional ideology was exposed. It was replaced by an emphasis on catching up with the level of social and economic development elsewhere. As many commentators have observed, the construction of the Manicouagan dam in northern Quebec and the development of long-distance lines to transmit electrical power to southern markets—engineered and built by Québécois—became a popular symbol for the new confidence in the ability of French-speaking Quebecers to cope with a modern world and to compete economically. The state, traditionally viewed as a second-class institution in a province in which most social services were controlled by the Church and government was associated with crass patronage, became the focus of nationalist energies. The fact that the new nationalism of the Quiet Revolution turned to the provincial state, in which French-speaking Quebecers were unquestionably in the majority, reinforced the identification of French Canada with the territory of Quebec.

The ideology of *rattrapage* and the identification of French Canada with Quebec had important consequences for language policy in that province. As the instrument for economic and social development, the Quebec state assumed functions previously administered by the Church authorities and also expanded the scope of its economic activities. In doing so it provided career opportunities for the growing number of educated francophones graduating from the province's universities. Access to high-paying managerial and technical jobs in the private sector, however, remained blocked by anglophone domination of the Quebec economy. The relative exclusion of francophones from positions of authority above that of foreman and the concentration of francophone businesses in the *petites et moyennes enterprises* sector of the economy had long been known.[23] This situation ran directly counter to the expectations of the Quiet Revolution and became an important political issue when the capacity of the public sector to absorb the increasing ranks of highly educated francophones became strained.

Demographic trends comprised an additional factor that shaped provincial language policy in Quebec. Immigrants to the province overwhelmingly adopted the English language. This fact, combined with the dramatic reduction in the birth rate among francophones, lent credibility to a scenario where francophones might eventually become a minority even within Quebec. Along with evidence of the exclusion of francophones from much of the province's economic structure, these trends formed the basis for the policy recommendations of the Quebec Royal Commission of Inquiry on the Position of the French Language and on Language Rights in Quebec (the Gendron Commission, 1972). That Commission's recommendation that the provincial government take legislative action to promote the use of French in business and in the schools was translated into law under the Quebec Liberal government that introduced the Official Language Act[24] and in the Charte de la langue française[25]—or **Bill 101** as it was more commonly known outside Quebec—passed under the subsequent Parti Québécois government. Without going into the detailed provisions of this legislation, three principal features of Quebec language policy since the passage of Bill 101 can be identified as follows.

(1) French is established as the sole official language in Quebec, and therefore the exclusive official language for proceedings of the provincial legislature and the courts and the main language for public administration in the province. In a 1979 decision the Supreme Court of Canada ruled that this section of Bill 101 violated section 133 of the BNA Act, which guarantees the co-equal status of the French and English languages at the federal level and in the province of Quebec.[26] Nevertheless, the principal language of provincial government services in Quebec is French, and many provincial and local services are not available in English in much of the province.

(2) Through the requirement that businesses with 50 or more employees receive a *francisation* certificate as a condition of doing business in the province, the Quebec government seeks to increase the use of French as a working language of business in the province. The language charter does not establish linguistic quotas for corporations. Instead, it leaves the conditions of certification a matter for individual negotiations between a firm and the Office de la langue française. Despite some initial resistance from the anglophone business community, symbolized by the immediate move of Sun Life's head office from Montreal to Toronto in 1977, this section of Bill 101 has generally been accepted by employers. More controversial have been the provisions requiring that public signs and advertisements be in French only. This blanket prohibition was relaxed in 1983 to make exception for bilingual advertising by 'ethnic' businesses, and in a 1988 decision the Supreme Court ruled that it violated the freedom of expression guaranteed in the Charter of Rights and Freedoms.[27] The signage provisions of Quebec's language law were modified in 1989 through Bill 178, which required that exterior commercial signs be in French only, but allowed bilingual interior signs so long as the French language was more prominently displayed. These provisions were amended again in 1993 through Bill 86, which states that the rules governing when signs must be unilingual French and when other languages are allowed shall be established by government regulations—a more flexible approach than enshrining the rules in the statute.

(3) The provisions of Bill 101 that initially excited the most controversy were those restricting access to English-language schools in Quebec. Under this law, children could enrol in an English school if one of the following conditions was met: their parents had been educated in English in Quebec; they had a sibling already going to an English school; their parents were educated in English outside of Quebec but were living in the province when the law was passed (1977); they were already enrolled in an English school when the law came into effect. The intent, obviously, was to reverse the overwhelming preference of immigrants for the English language, a preference that demographers predicted would eventually change the linguistic balance in the province, and even more dramatically in Montreal, which attracted the vast majority of immigrants. In one of the first Supreme Court decisions on the Charter of Rights and Freedoms, the Court held that the requirement that at least one of a child's parents must have been educated in English in Quebec violated section 23 of the Charter, a section that clearly had been drafted with Bill 101 in mind. The practical importance of this ruling is small, given the low level of migration to Quebec from other Canadian provinces. More significant is the fact that the Supreme Court was unwilling to accept the Quebec government's argument that the demographic threat to the position of the French language justified this restriction on language rights under the 'reasonable limits' section of the Charter. In 1993 the

education provisions of Bill 101 were brought into conformity with s. 23 of the Charter.

Despite some setbacks in the courts, the principles on which Quebec's language policy rests have remained substantially unchanged since the passage of Bill 101. The most publicized reform of the province's language law occurred after the Supreme Court's 1988 ruling that the prohibition of languages other than French for commercial signs in Quebec violated the Charter's guarantee of freedom of expression. Within weeks the Quebec legislature passed Bill 178, which invoked the 'notwithstanding clause' of the Charter in order to reaffirm the ban on languages other than French for commercial signs outside a business. Bill 178 allowed, however, the use of other languages on signs inside a business, but French signs had to be predominant. Legal restrictions on commercial signs were removed in 1993 although they continue to be maintained through regulations (see Box 13.1). Judged according to its two main objectives—increasing the use of the French language in the Quebec economy and stemming the decline in the francophone share of the provincial population—Bill 101 must be judged a success.

Language policy in Quebec has been shaped by the idea that French Canada is co-extensive with the boundaries of that province. The Office de la langue française and the law it administers build on an approach to language promotion that can be traced back to the early 1960s. The Liberal government of Jean Lesage set out to increase francophone participation in the economy through such provincial institutions as la Société générale de financement, la Caisse de dépôt et placement, Sidérurgie québécoise, and an expanded Hydro-Québec.[28] The common denominator since then has been the use of the provincial state as an instrument for the socio-economic advancement of francophones.

The Bilingual Approach of Ottawa

A very different approach to language policy—one based on a conception of French and English Canada that cuts across provincial borders—has been pursued by successive federal governments since the 1960s. Responding to the new assertive nationalism of the Quiet Revolution, the signs of which ranged from Quebec's demands for greater taxation powers and less interference by Ottawa in areas of provincial constitutional responsibility to bombs placed in mailboxes and at public monuments, the Liberal government of Lester Pearson established the **Royal Commission on Bilingualism and Biculturalism**. As Eric Waddell writes, 'The federal government was facing a legitimacy crisis in the 1960s and 1970s and had the immediate task of proposing a Canadian alternative to Quebec nationalism.'[29] The B&B Commission was a first step towards the adoption by Ottawa of a policy of official bilingualism. This policy was to some degree intended to defuse the *indépendantiste* sentiment building in Quebec, especially among young francophones, by opening Ottawa as a field of career opportunities to rival the Quebec public service.

The alternative Ottawa offered, which was expressed in the federalist philosophy of Pierre Trudeau, was of a Canada in which language rights would be guaranteed to the individual and protected by national institutions. In practical terms this meant changing the overwhelmingly anglophone character of the federal state so that francophones would not have grounds to view it as an 'alien' level of government from which they were largely excluded. These changes have been carried out on two main fronts.

First, what Raymond Breton refers to as the 'Canadian symbolic order' has been transformed since the 1960s.[30] Through a new flag, the proclamation of 'O Canada' as the official national anthem, new designs for stamps and currency, and the language neutralizing of some federal institutions, documents, and celebrations (for example, Trans-Canada Airlines became Air Canada, the BNA Act is now officially titled the Constitution Act, 1867, and Dominion Day is now called Canada Day), a deliberate attempt has been made to create symbols that do not evoke Canada's colonial past and British domination.

Second, the passage of the Official Languages Act (1969) gave statutory expression to the policy of bilingualism that had been set in motion under Lester Pearson. This Act established the Office of the

Commissioner of Official Languages as a 'watchdog' agency to monitor the three main components of language equality set forth in the Act: (1) the public's right to be served by the federal government in the official language of their choice; (2) the equitable representation of francophones and anglophones in the federal public service; and (3) the ability of public servants of both language groups to work in the language of their choice. The situation that the Official Languages Act was intended to redress was one where francophone representation in the federal state was less than their share of the national population. Francophone under-representation was greatest in managerial, scientific, and technical job

Media Spotlight

Box 13.1 Do English-Language Posters in Pubs Threaten the French Language in Quebec?

Quebec's French-language watchdog is investigating a popular Montreal pub, which is cluttered with classic Irish signage and English-only posters. The owner of McKibbin's received a letter from the Office québécois de la langue française (OLF) earlier this month inquiring about the use of English signs inside. The wall hangings include vintage advertisements for Guinness and the St James Gate brewery in Dublin, posters the owners say add to the charm and ambience of their downtown establishment. An OLF inspector ruled McKibbin's bilingual menu, bar service and vintage posters do not respect article 58 of Quebec's language charter.

McKibbin's owner Rick Fon told CBC News he will not take the posters down because they serve as decoration, not to advertise beer.

The language office understands and will withdraw its order for McKibbin's to remove some of the posters, Montreal's *La Presse* newspaper reported. It quoted a spokesperson as saying the office accepts that most of the posters are decorative and therefore not covered by language laws. However, three posters are still considered to be ads and will be ordered to be taken down, the paper said.

'What we asked them were what measures would be taken to ensure that service would be offered in French, because we received two complaints', Gérald Paquette, a spokesman for the language watchdog, said on Friday.

'If the business says some of those pictures are decorative to give the pub an Irish flavour, it is certain we would exempt them', Paquette said. 'But there were other posters also, notably ones about contests and events, that were in English only.'

The brewhaha has prompted the pub's co-owners to extend an invite to Quebec Premier Jean Charest to stop by for a hearty meal and a pint and inspect the signs himself. Dean Laderoute and Rick Fon said they'll remove the posters if Charest believes they violate Quebec's language laws, which require French to be predominant on most commercial signs.

'An Irish pub without these decorations is just an empty box', Fon said in an interview. 'It's the décor, the pictures, the clutter—it creates the warmth.'

Fon also said they have bilingual menus and that his regulars, including a considerable French clientele, all agree the complaints are ridiculous.

'It makes no sense. It's silly', regular Suzette L'Abbé said.

'The staff, if not French-speaking to begin with, get by in French', L'Abbé added.

The pub could face fines as high as $1,500 for each infraction.

Source: CBC News, 'Quebec Language Police Pressure Montreal Bar over Posters', 14 Feb. 2008. Reprinted by permission of CBC and the Canadian Press.

categories (see Figure 13.4). Moreover, the language of the public service—the language that officials worked in and, in most parts of the country, the language that citizens could realistically be expected to be served in—was English. In view of these circumstances, Ottawa's claim to 'represent' the interests of francophones lacked credibility.

Among the main actions taken to increase the bilingual character of the federal bureaucracy have been language training for public servants, the designation of an increasing share of positions as bilingual, and the creation of the National Capital Region as the office blocks of the federal state spread across the Ottawa River into Hull (now Gatineau), Quebec, during the 1970s. Language training for public servants was perhaps the most controversial of these measures. In his annual report for 1984 a former Commissioner of Official Languages, D'Iberville Fortier, noted that a relatively small proportion of public servants in positions designated bilingual appeared to have acquired their second-language skills as a result of taxpayer-funded language training. This led Fortier to question the extent to which language training was capable of making public servants effectively bilingual, particularly anglophones who were the main consumers of federal language courses.[31] Fortier's successors occasionally have expressed similar reservations, and over the last couple of decades the focus has shifted away from training current public servants in the other official language to recruiting people who already have the language skills needed for particular positions.

In view of the fact that two of the objectives of the Official Languages Act have been to increase the number of francophones recruited into the public service and to improve francophones' opportunities for upward mobility within it, the designation of positions according to their linguistic requirements has been probably the most significant feature of Ottawa's language policy. As of 2008, about 44 per cent of positions in the federal public service were designated either bilingual or French (40 per cent bilingual; 4 per cent French essential). Bilingualism was most likely to be required for public service positions in the National Capital Region (Ottawa–Gatineau), Quebec, and outside Canada, at 65 per cent, 65 per cent, and 36 per cent, respectively.

Evidence on recruitment to the federal public service and upward mobility within it demonstrate that the linguistic designation of positions *has* worked to the advantage of francophones. In recent years close to one-third of new appointments to the federal public service have gone to those who claim French as their mother tongue, a level significantly higher than the approximately 22 per cent of the Canadian population comprised of native French speakers. A clear majority of appointments to bilingual positions are filled by francophones. This is true for both new appointments to the public service and for reappointments within the federal bureaucracy, about 70 per cent of each going to francophones. But as the Commissioner of Official Languages regularly observes, increased representation of francophones should not be taken as an indication that the French and English are approaching greater equality as *languages of work* in the federal state. Outside of federal departments and agencies located in Quebec, the language of work remains predominantly English. And inside Quebec, the ability of anglophone public servants to work in English is often limited. As the 1998 annual report of the Commissioner of Official Languages put it:

> Our experience in conducting audits and investigating complaints in this area over the past decade reveals that there has been little or no improvement on the language of work front; many public servants are still unable to exercise their right to work in French in the NCR [National Capital Region] and New Brunswick and, albeit to a lesser extent, in English in Quebec. This is not surprising when one considers that over one-third of federal government executives, to whom employees look for an example . . . do not meet the language requirements of their bilingual positions.[32]

According to the current Commissioner of Official Languages, Graham Fraser, not much has changed since this indictment of federal government inaction on one of the major objectives of the Official Languages Act. 'Managers don't realize', he states in the 2009 annual report, 'that maintaining

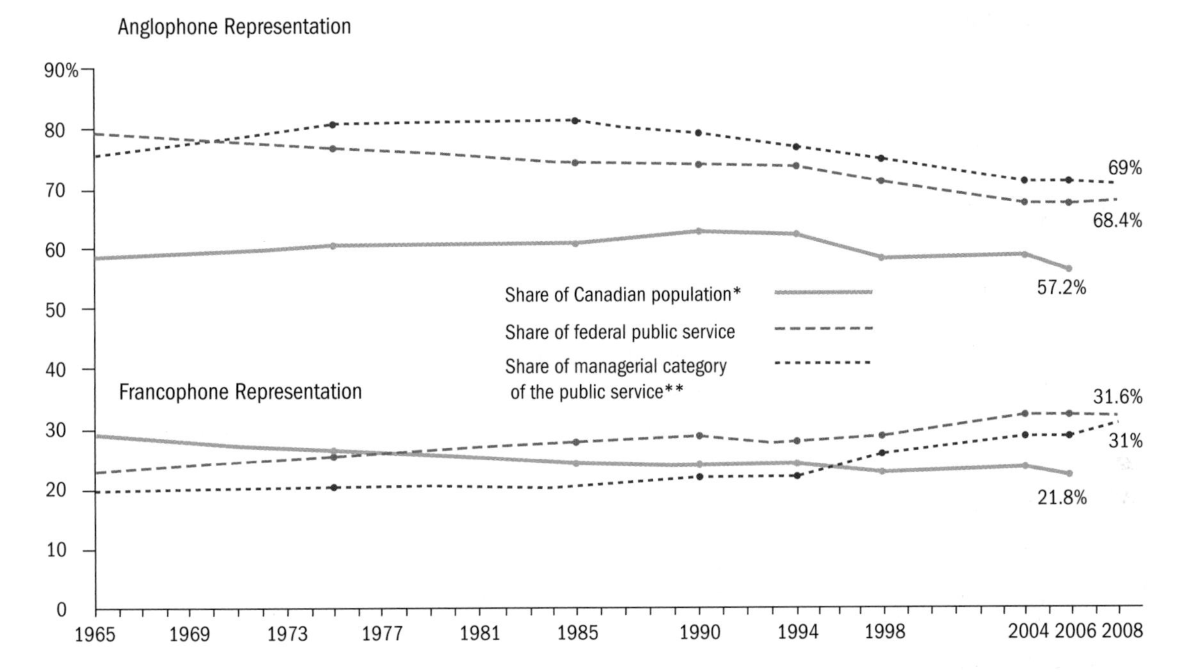

FIGURE 13.4 Anglophone and Francophone Representation in the Federal Public Service as a Whole, in the Management Category of the Public Service, and in the Canadian Population, 1965–2008

*Data for the representation of French and English language groups in the Canadian population are taken from the censuses for various years. The question refers to mother tongue, and therefore the figures do not add up to 100 per cent. The most recent census was conducted in 2006.

**The 1965 survey used to determine the language of those in the management category asked respondents to indicate their mother tongue; 5.2 per cent indicated a language other than English or French.

Sources: Figures provided in various annual reports of the Commissioner of Official Languages, the *Canada Year Book*, the *Report of the Royal Commission on Bilingualism and Biculturalism*, volume 3A (Ottawa: Queen's Printer, 1969), 215, table 50, and Canada, Public Service Human Resources Agency of Canada, *Annual Report on Official Languages 2006–07*.

a work culture that, in many cases, is totally unilingual hinders the public service's efforts to offer quality bilingual services to the public. The domination of English as the lingua franca of the bureaucracy persists even in the National Capital Region.'[33] This led a previous Commissioner of Official Languages to conclude that French has become a valuable attribute from the standpoint of career advancement, without becoming a working language on a par with English.[34] It appears that this continues to be a fair assessment of the situation.

Another annual report of the Commissioner's office points to a rather different development, the linguistic polarization of the federal public service on regional lines. It notes that there is 'virtually all-Anglophone recruitment in seven provinces and virtually all-Francophone recruitment in Quebec'.[35] New Brunswick and Ontario—and within Ontario, particularly the Ottawa region—are the only parts of the country where recruitment to the federal public service draws significantly on both official-language communities. This ought not to be surprising, given the very small size of francophone minorities in all provinces except Ontario and New Brunswick.

Ottawa's language policy acquired two additional thrusts in the 1970s. The first of these has involved financial assistance to organizations and individuals seeking to defend or expand the rights of official-language minorities and to local francophone cultural organizations outside of Quebec. Most significant in terms of results has been financial support for court challenges to provincial laws respecting language rights. These challenges have included Supreme Court decisions in 1979 and 1985 that established the official status of French in the province of Manitoba[36] and successful challenges to the restrictions on education and public signs and advertising contained in Quebec's Bill 101.[37] Until 1985, language rights cases were the only ones supported by Ottawa under its Court Challenges Program.

A second thrust of federal policy to promote bilingualism in Canadian society has been through financial assistance for second-language instruction and minority-language schools controlled by the provinces, including French immersion schools and support for summer immersion programs. The immersion phenomenon has seen the proliferation of French immersion schools in cities throughout English Canada. By 2008, about 300,000 students were enrolled in French immersion elementary and secondary schools outside Quebec, compared to roughly 75,000 in 1980. More than half of all French immersion schools and about half of all immersion students in Canada are in Ontario.[38]

The popularity of French immersion education has grown steadily over the last two decades, fuelled by non-francophone parents' perception that bilingualism will give their children an edge in the future competition for good jobs. This perception of greater opportunities for bilinguals, at least in the private sector, remains to be substantiated. Two decades ago, a study of bilingual job opportunities by the Commissioner of Languages answered the question, 'Do immersion graduates make good use of their French after high school?' with 'Yes, they do—in Ottawa.'[39] The 2006 census found that 4.1 per cent of anglophone Canadians claimed to use French most often or regularly at work. But half of these workers are anglophones in Quebec, the percentage being 2.1 for anglophones outside Quebec. Only among francophones did workers report that they often used the other official language—English—in the workplace: close to one-third of francophones in Quebec said that they used English most often or regularly and two-thirds of francophones outside Quebec reported using English most often at work. This hardly supports the picture of a Canadian work world in which the opportunities to use French are great, at least outside Quebec.[40]

Moreover, as noted earlier, studies of immersion graduates demonstrate that the experience tends to produce 'receptive' bilinguals—people who neither initiate conversations in French nor consume French-language newspapers, radio, or television after leaving immersion. Bilingualism becomes in some sense a badge of social distinction rather than a part of their lifestyle. This has led some to comment on the incidental effects of immersion on social class distinctions. Eric Waddell writes:

> There is much to suggest that the current fascination for French language education is more an expression of class (and indirectly of ethnic class) interests than of a concern to forge a new national identity. French immersion schools give the impression of constituting an elite system of education functioning within the public system. The state, through federal intervention, is in the process of elaborating a dual system, one for tomorrow's leaders and one for the followers. For this 'new' class, the bilingualism that mastery of the French language confers constitutes something profoundly Canadian in the sense of being sophisticated and more 'European'. Hence it serves increasingly to demarcate this class from other social classes and, strikingly, from our southern neighbours.[41]

Waddell's assessment was made a generation ago, after only about a decade into Canada's experiment in French immersion education. But it seems the class bias that he observed continues to exist, as more recent studies have shown.[42]

A Distinct Society?

Does Quebec comprise a **distinct society**? Is Quebec more distinct from the other nine provinces than any one of those other provinces is from the rest? What is the basis for Quebec's claim to be distinct? Even if Quebecers' claim to distinctiveness is valid, should distinct society status be entrenched in the Constitution? Is this necessary? Is it desirable?

Few Canadians had heard of 'distinct society' before the late 1980s, when the Meech Lake

Accord came to grief over the proposal to recognize Quebec as a distinct society within Canada. It is also reasonable to assume that most Canadians are today no wiser about what 'distinct society' means. This, it should be added, is after tens of millions of dollars were spent by a phalanx of federal and

Politics in Focus

Box 13.2 Another Model for Language Rights: The Case of Belgium

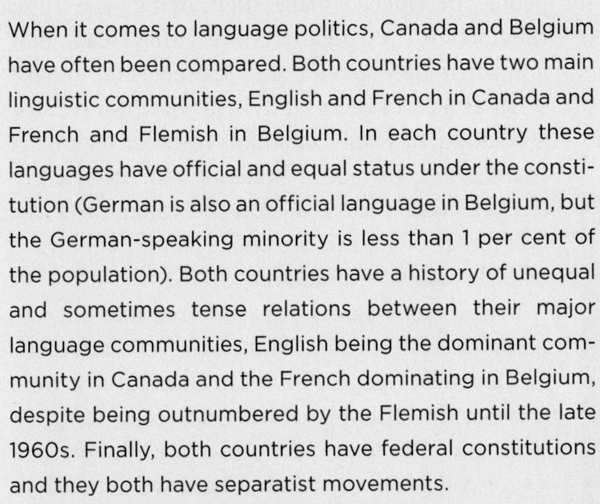

When it comes to language politics, Canada and Belgium have often been compared. Both countries have two main linguistic communities, English and French in Canada and French and Flemish in Belgium. In each country these languages have official and equal status under the constitution (German is also an official language in Belgium, but the German-speaking minority is less than 1 per cent of the population). Both countries have a history of unequal and sometimes tense relations between their major language communities, English being the dominant community in Canada and the French dominating in Belgium, despite being outnumbered by the Flemish until the late 1960s. Finally, both countries have federal constitutions and they both have separatist movements.

Given these similarities, comparison comes naturally. But Belgium has adopted a model of language rights that is quite different from Canada's. The Canadian model, we know, is based on the premise that every citizen, anglophone or francophone, has certain language rights that must be recognized anywhere in Canada and that French and English have equal constitutional status in national affairs across the country. The Belgian model is based on the idea that one's language rights depend on where a person lives. This is a *territorial* model of language rights, unlike the Canadian *personal* model.

Here is how the Belgian model works. In Flanders, the Flemish-speaking northern region of the country, public education, government services, election ballots, and signage on roads, at train stations, and for buses are in Flemish only. In Wallonia, the southern French-speaking region, French is the only official language. Brussels, the national capital, is officially bilingual, although French speakers outnumber Flemish speakers by a very wide margin. Citizens vote in national, regional, and local elections, as in Canada. But unlike Canada, there are no national political parties in Belgium. There is a Flemish socialist party and a French one, a Flemish Green party and a French one, and so on. Consequently, the party system cannot be counted on to help bridge the gap between the linguistic communities and their respective regions.

Over the years many Quebec nationalists have pointed to Belgium as a model to be emulated. But Canadian and Quebec federalists from Pierre Trudeau to the present day have always argued that the territorial model, instead of providing a better recipe for coexistence between the linguistic communities, would lead to greater division and ultimately to separation.

The federalists may be right. Although *indépendantisme* is far from dead in Quebec, a certain modus vivendi seems to have existed in Canada since the 1995 referendum. In Belgium, on the other hand, recent governments have been short-lived and have come to grief on the issue of relations between the language communities in the linguistically mixed periphery of Brussels. Then, in 2010, the Flemish Nationalist Party, under the leadership of a multilingual avowed separatist, won more seats than any other party in the Belgian legislature. Suddenly moderate Belgians were talking seriously about the possibility of separatism, although no one believed that it would happen tomorrow.

Belgians have sometimes looked to Canada for lessons in how to make language relations work, and Canadians have returned the gaze. But it is clear that there is no one-size-fits-all formula for peace between language communities. The particulars of a country's history and demography are crucial determinants of whether a certain language rights model will satisfy a country's linguistic communities, such that they prefer an occasionally uneasy cohabitation to divorce.

provincial task forces, commissions, and committees on the Constitution that sprang into existence in the two years after the failure of the Meech Lake Accord, and after countless hours and column-inches of discussion and debate in the media since the late 1980s. Average Canadians perhaps may be forgiven whatever confusion they have over the distinct society issue. Constitutional experts, political scientists, journalists, and politicians cannot agree on what it means!

What is clear is that the demand for constitutional recognition of Quebec as a distinct society has been a non-negotiable item on the agenda of Quebec's political elite since the late 1980s. It is also clear that the issue excites a popular emotional response both inside Quebec and in the rest of Canada that other constitutional proposals—reforming the Senate, tinkering with the Supreme Court, changing the amendment process, and so on—do not. Let us try to understand the controversy over a distinct society clause by addressing the questions posed at the beginning of this section.

The band Les Cowboys Fringants enjoys wild popularity in Quebec and is an important part of the Québécois néo-trad genre (modernized Quebec folk music with a rock sound). While Les Cowboys have garnered an international following in France and French-speaking Belgium and Switzerland, they remain relatively unknown to anglophones in the rest of Canada. Is such a cultural factor an indicator of Quebec's distinct nature or does it have little political relevance?

Whether or not Quebec is a distinct society depends on what criteria we use in comparing Quebec to the other provinces. In terms of how people in Quebec make their living, the films they watch, the popular novels they read, how and where they spend their vacations, and in most other aspects of their lifestyle they are not remarkably different from Canadians in other regions of the country. In fact, if material and lifestyle criteria are used, there is a good case for arguing that Quebec and Ontario are more similar than, say, Ontario and Newfoundland.

Not everyone agrees. And it is true that one can point to several important social characteristics of the Quebec population that distinguish it from those of the other provinces. Québécois marry less often and later than other Canadians; the percentage of couples living in common-law relationships is about twice the national average and higher than in any other province; a greater percentage of children (about half of first births) are born outside of marriage than in other provinces; a higher percentage of Quebecers than other Canadians report single ethnic origins (about 90 per cent, compared to 70 per cent for all of Canada); they are heavier smokers and drink more wine than their compatriots. Whereas English-Canadian television viewers prefer American-produced programs during prime time, French-speaking Quebecers are likely to be watching Quebec-made dramas and sitcoms. But to base an argument for constitutional recognition of Quebec as a distinct society on such social characteristics trivializes the meaning of distinct society. Many of these phenomena have no political relevance. Moreover, in some cases the differences between Quebec and the rest of Canada are too slight to warrant reading much significance into them.

Another possibility is that the beliefs and values of the Québécois set them apart from other Canadians. As we saw in Chapter 4, the evidence for this claim is mixed. Several early studies on regional variations in political culture concluded that Canada, in fact, is comprised of several distinctive regional political cultures. Richard Simeon and David Elkins found that levels of political trust, efficacy, interest in politics, and participation varied significantly between provinces and that this variation persisted even after eliminating the impact of socio-economic factors (i.e., levels of education and income) known to influence these attitudes/behaviours.[43] The implication is, of course, that while Quebec may be a 'special case' in terms of its politically relevant values, it is not the only regional special case.

Conversely, other studies of regionalism conclude that no significant attitudinal differences exist between citizens in different parts of the country. Either way, whether Quebec's political culture is argued to be broadly similar to that in the rest of Canada or if one takes the position that there are several distinct regional cultures in Canada, among them Quebec, the argument for constitutional entrenchment of distinct society status for Quebec is weakened.

Nonetheless, one's conclusions may depend on the questions asked and the values they tap. Surveys that ask Canadians whether they think of themselves as Canadians first or as citizens of their province reveal that those in Quebec are most likely to see their primary attachment as provincial. However, Newfoundlanders are just about as provincialist and Prince Edward Islanders are not terribly far behind. Anyway, this evidence of strong provincial loyalty may not matter very much because numerous surveys have shown that Quebecers and other provincial populations are capable of maintaining provincial and Canadian loyalties at the same time. Studies of Canadians' attitudes towards rights and freedoms and the Charter suggest much more similarity than difference between French-speaking Québécois and other Canadians.[44] On the other hand, one of the most rigorous empirical investigations of regional variations in political ideology concludes that 'the extent of ideological differentiation in English Canada is very small' and that 'the ideological difference between Quebec and English Canada is greater than the internal variation within English Canada'.[45] Michael Ornstein shows that ideological values in Quebec are considerably to the left of those in the other provinces.[46]

In view of these apparently contradictory findings can we conclude that Quebec comprises a distinct society in terms of the values and beliefs of its citizens? Possibly not. Differences between Quebec and the rest of Canada are sharpest on attitudes relating to language. A 1991 Gallup poll found that 78 per cent of Montrealers, compared to 28 per cent of Torontonians, thought that English language rights were well protected in Quebec. Asked about the protection of French language rights outside Quebec, 87 per cent of Torontonians thought they were well protected, compared to only 25 per cent of Montrealers. The two solitudes were perfectly balanced in their mutual mistrust! On other political issues, differences are often slight or non-existent. Even if we concur with those, like Ornstein, who argue that Quebec is more different attitudinally from the rest of Canada than the predominantly English-speaking provinces are from one another, it does not follow that this difference warrants constitutional recognition of special status. Values and beliefs are not set in stone, as any student of changes in Quebec society and French-Canadian nationalism over the last half-century knows.

A third possible argument for Quebec's distinctiveness relies on history. The outline of such an argument goes as follows. French-Canadian society goes back to the seventeenth century when the first immigrants came from France. Most French Canadians actually are descended from those who were already settled in New France at the time of the Conquest. Current generations of French Canadians are heirs to three centuries of tradition and resistance against assimilating pressures. This continuity can be seen in the distinctive French that is spoken in Quebec (and, for that matter, in the dialects spoken in the French-speaking communities outside of Quebec); in Quebec folksongs, popular music, films, and literature; in such social institutions as Quebec's distinctive system of civil law (based on the French civil code rather than on English common law); and in the history that children in Quebec learn in school—a history that has always told a rather different story from that learned by students in English schools across Canada.[47] For example, according to provincial curriculum guidelines in Quebec in 1999, for Grade 9 history, the only two Canadian prime ministers studied were Sir John A. Macdonald (1867–73, 1878–91) and Wilfrid Laurier (1896–1911); otherwise, the focus was exclusively on Quebec. In Ontario, by contrast, the history curriculum for this age group is far less provincially focused, emphasizing Canadian developments and consequences and including a unit on the development of western Canada.[48] It is this unique history as one of Canada's two 'founding peoples' that justifies distinct society status for Quebec. Moreover, history has demonstrated that only in Quebec, where francophones have always formed the majority and have been able to control the levers of provincial government, are the distinctive language and traditions of French Canadians secure against Anglicizing pressures and discrimination.

Variations on this basic argument are standard features of Quebec government documents on the Constitution and in the literature of both the Quebec Liberal Party and the Parti Québécois. It is a view that is widely shared by francophones in Quebec. Not only does this form the basis of demands for constitutional recognition of Quebec as a distinct society, but historical arguments also are used to make the case for a Quebec veto over constitutional amendments, as indicated by the 1991 *Report* of the Commission on the Political and Constitutional Future of Quebec:

> At its origin, Canada's federal system was founded, from Quebec's point of view, on Canadian duality [French/English] and the autonomy of the provinces. Canadian duality, which rests on the relationship between the French-Canadian and English-Canadian peoples, is seen as the founding principle of the federal system. The federal union is thus conceived of as a pact between these two peoples, that may only be changed with the consent of each of these parties.[49]

This reasoning was expressed in unequivocal terms in the Quebec legislature's response to the Clarity Act passed by Parliament in 2000. All parties in Quebec's National Assembly agreed that only the Québécois constituted a nation with a right to self-determination and, moreover, that only the citizens and legislature of Quebec had a legitimate voice in the determination of whether the province would become an independent state. The full text of the resolution passed by Quebec's legislature is very clearly based on the assumption that Quebec is a *province pas comme les autres* (see Box 13.3).

The problem with the historical case for constitutional recognition of Quebec as a distinct society is not that it is based on incorrect or flimsy evidence. Indeed, the historical record speaks for itself. Rather, some of the other provinces claim that their regional histories are equally distinct. Western Canadians and their governments are unimpressed by arguments that Quebec's history is somehow more distinctive than their own. Newfoundlanders are unlikely to be convinced. The unsympathetic reception that spokespersons for the predominantly English-speaking provinces give to the historical argument for Quebec as a distinct society has recently been joined by that of Aboriginal Canadians. They argue that if any community (or communities) has a historical right to distinct society status it is theirs. After all, their languages and traditions had been established for centuries and even millennia before the arrival of Canada's European 'founders'. No discussion of 'founding peoples' or 'distinct societies' is complete, they argue, without recognition of the historical status and rights of Aboriginal Canadians.

The final and most persuasive grounds for arguing Quebec's right to distinct society status is the province's linguistic character. As noted earlier, over 80 per cent of the Quebec population claims French as its mother tongue and an equal percentage reports speaking French at home. No other province comes close to this level of French language dominance; indeed, in no other province do francophones comprise a majority of the population. Close to 90 per cent of all Canadian francophones reside in Quebec. It was no accident that the Commission on the Political and Constitutional Future of Quebec, established by the Bourassa government after the failure of the Meech

Lake Accord, emphasized the distinctive linguistic character of Quebec as the first point in the section of its *Report* on Quebec's *identité proper* (special or unique identity).[50] Moreover, the distinct society clauses proposed by the Meech Lake Accord and the Charlottetown Accord, and more recently in the motion passed by Parliament in 1995 and in the **Calgary Declaration** of 1997, were explicit in declaring that what is distinct about Quebec society is primarily its linguistic character (see Appendix to this chapter).

This argument cannot be refuted. Of course, each province has its own distinctive linguistic character, but the remarkably unique linguistic character of Quebec within Canada and, for that matter, in all of North America is undeniable. In no other jurisdiction, provincial or state, is English not the language regularly spoken by a clear majority of the population.

But if the distinct society clauses of Meech Lake and Charlottetown are merely statements of demographic reality, why the fuss? There are a couple of reasons. One is that some people will readily acknowledge Quebec's distinctive linguistic character, but deny that this warrants constitutional recognition of Quebec as a distinct society any more than, say, Saskatchewan deserves to be recognized as a distinct society because of its special economy, history, and demographic character.[51] Why, they ask, should language be elevated above other social characteristics in determining which provincial societies are distinct and which are not?

A second and probably more important reason why some provincial governments and most English-speaking Canadians resist what might appear to be a compelling linguistic argument for a distinct society clause involves the consequences that would follow from entrenching this in the Constitution. Many English Canadians believe that this would give to Quebec legislative powers not possessed by other provinces. Some worry that minority rights—those of non-francophones in Quebec and those of francophones outside the province—would suffer from constitutional recognition of Quebec as a predominantly French-speaking society and of the rest of Canada as predominantly English-speaking. Fears have been expressed that a distinct society clause could undermine Charter guarantees of rights and freedoms in Quebec.

Above all, however, what probably bothers English-speaking Canadians outside of Quebec more than anything else is their gut sense that distinct society status for Quebec undermines their idea of Canada. A **two-nations theory** of Canada, while enjoying some popularity in certain political parties and among anglophone political scientists, has never been very popular with the English-Canadian public. In an unarticulated way they sense that distinct society recognition for Quebec is a sort of Trojan horse for a two-nations conception of Canada. This offends against a particular understanding of equality that—again, while usually inarticulate—objects to the idea that there are categories of Canadians instead of Canadians, period. Former Conservative Prime Minister John Diefenbaker probably expressed this best when he inveighed against what he called 'the Anglo-phonies, the Franco-phonies, and all the other phonies' whose insistence on defining Canada in linguistic and ethnic terms, he believed, undermined national unity.

Although many of Canada's national political elite have for years denied that the 'one Canada' aspirations of most English Canadians conflict with the recognition of Quebec as a distinct society, Québécois political leaders suffer from no illusions on this count. The *Report* of the Commission on the Political and Constitutional Future of Quebec made this very clear. The *Report* argued that the 'one Canada' and 'dual societies' conceptions have become increasingly irreconcilable since the passage of the Charter and the other constitutional reforms of 1982. This is because, the *Report* argues, the Constitution Act of 1982 is based on three principles that, while popular outside of Quebec, are fundamentally opposed to the recognition of Quebec as a distinct society. These principles are:

- The equality of all Canadian citizens, from one ocean to the other, and the unity of the society in which they live.
- The equality of all cultures and cultural origins in Canada.
- The equality of the 10 provinces of Canada.

Whatever a distinct society clause in the Constitution might mean in practice—and, notwithstanding the confident blustering of many politicians and constitutional experts, we should have learned from the experience with the Charter that it is often impossible to predict how Canadian judges will interpret important sections of the Constitution—there can be no doubt that the Quebec elites who insist on it expect it to make a difference. They reject the 'one Canada' vision that they argue is represented in the Charter and in the current procedure for amending the Constitution (whereby Quebec does not have a constitutionally entrenched veto). Distinct society is, in their eyes, a corrective against the centralizing implications of the Charter and, moreover, represents a return to the founding spirit of Canada.

Distinct society status and a veto over constitutional change may no longer be enough. Several weeks after the narrow defeat of the separatist option in the 1995 Quebec referendum, the Liberal government passed a motion recognizing Quebec as a distinct society and giving the province (as well as British Columbia, the Prairie provinces, Ontario, and the Atlantic provinces) a veto over constitutional reform. The PQ government in Quebec, the Bloc Québécois in Ottawa, and Quebec's French-language media were not particularly impressed

Governing Realities

Box 13.3 The Rights and Prerogatives of the Quebec People and the Quebec State

WHEREAS the Québec people, in the majority French-speaking, possesses specific characteristics and a deep-rooted historical continuity in a territory over which it exercises its rights through a modern national state, having a government, a national assembly and impartial and independent courts of justice;

WHEREAS the constitutional foundation of the Québec State has been enriched over the years by the passage of fundamental laws and the creation of democratic institutions specific to Quebec . . .

CHAPTER I

THE QUÉBEC PEOPLE

1. The right of the Québec people to self-determination is founded in fact and in law. The Québec people is the holder of rights that are universally recognized under the principle of equal rights and self-determination of peoples.
2. The Québec people has the inalienable right to freely decide the political regime and legal status of Québec.
3. The Québec people, acting through its own political institutions, shall determine alone the mode of exercise of its right to choose the political regime and legal status of Québec.

   No condition or mode of exercise of that right, in particular the consultation of the Québec people by way of a referendum, shall have effect unless determined in accordance with the first paragraph.
4. When the Québec people is consulted by way of a referendum under the Referendum Act, the winning option is the option that obtains a majority of the valid votes cast, namely fifty percent of the valid votes cast plus one.

CHAPTER II

THE QUÉBEC NATIONAL STATE

5. The Québec State derives its legitimacy from the will of the people inhabiting its territory.

   The will of the people is expressed through the election of Members to the National Assembly by universal suffrage, by secret ballot under the one person, one vote system pursuant to the Election Act, and through referendums held pursuant to the Referendum Act.

   Qualification as an elector is governed by the provisions of the Election Act.
6. The Québec State is sovereign in the areas assigned to its jurisdiction within the scope of constitutional laws and conventions.

by Ottawa's action. Even the Quebec Liberal Party argued that Ottawa's proposals—whose constitutional status was uncertain, to say the least—did not go far enough. Ottawa's hope, of course, was to satisfy the demands of enough 'soft nationalists' to undercut the separatists in the next referendum. For their part, the PQ and the BQ have been determined to shift the debate away from distinct society and constitutional vetoes, terms that imply a federalism framework, and onto a different plane. That plane involves political independence and economic association.

Quebec citizens, however, seemed to have grown weary of what were decades-old debates over political independence, distinct society status, and constitutional reform. Public opinion polls taken throughout 2001–2 showed that about six in 10 Quebecers were opposed to the idea of another referendum on Quebec sovereignty. The rise in the popularity of a new provincial party, Action Démocratique du Québec (ADQ), a right-of-centre populist party that was nationalist but not secessionist, was interpreted by many as a sign of Quebecers' dissatisfaction with the tired dialogue of the PQ and the Quebec Liberal Party. Independence and constitutional reform, according to what quickly became the conventional wisdom,

The Québec State also holds, on behalf of the Québec people, any right established to its advantage pursuant to a constitutional convention or obligation.

It is the duty of the Government to uphold the exercise and defend the integrity of those prerogatives, at all times and in all places, including on the international scene.

7. The Québec State is free to consent to be bound by any treaty, convention or international agreement in matters under its constitutional jurisdiction. No treaty, convention or agreement in the areas under its jurisdiction may be binding on the Québec State unless the consent of the Québec State to be bound has been formally expressed by the National Assembly or the Government, subject to the applicable legislative provisions.

The Québec State may, in the areas under its jurisdiction, establish and maintain relations with foreign States and international organizations and ensure its representation outside Québec. . . .

CHAPTER III

THE TERRITORY OF QUÉBEC

9. The territory of Québec and its boundaries cannot be altered except with the consent of the National Assembly. The Government must ensure that the territorial integrity of Québec is maintained and respected.
10. The Québec State exercises, throughout the territory of Québec and on behalf of the Québec people, all the powers relating to its jurisdiction and to the Québec public domain. . . .
13. No other parliament or government may reduce the powers, authority, sovereignty or legitimacy of the National Assembly, or impose constraint on the democratic will of the Québec people to determine its own future.
14. The provisions of this Act come into force on the dates to be fixed by the Government.

Source: From Bill 99, An Act respecting the fundamental rights and prerogatives of the Quebec People and the Quebec State (2000, c. 46, s. 10).

was yesterday's political agenda. Many went as far as pronouncing that Quebec separatism was dead when the ADQ became the official opposition, pushing the Parti Québécois to third place in the political pecking order in the 2007 Quebec election. A 2010 survey conducted for the pro-federalism think-tank, The Federal Idea, reported that 58 per cent of Quebecers believed that the sovereignty debate was over, compared to only 26 per cent who said that it was more relevant than ever. The survey also found that 47 per cent of respondents said there were fewer reasons to become independent than there were when the 1980 referendum was held, compared to 41 per cent who said that there continue to be at least as many reasons.[52]

This obituary is premature, to say the least. The ADQ tumbled in the December 2008 provincial election (won by the Liberals) from 41 seats to a mere seven in the National Assembly. The PQ experienced a strong comeback under its leader, Pauline Marois. At the federal level, the separatist Bloc Québécois continued to capture more seats than any other party in Quebec; in the 2008 federal election BQ candidates won 49 of the province's 75 seats. It was also common to pronounce Quebec separatism dead or at least harmless in the mid-1980s, until the failure of the Meech Lake Accord and the sudden upsurge in support for independence demonstrated the difference that exists between dead and dormant. It is not difficult to imagine circumstances, such as a major conflict between Ottawa and Quebec, that could trigger an increase in support for separatism among French-speaking Quebecers. The revelations of Liberal Party corruption that emerged from the Gomery inquiry in 2005 produced just such a spike in support for the BQ and in support for separatism. Moreover, the same poll that caused The Federal Idea think-tank to proclaim Quebec sovereignty 'outmoded' found that Quebecers were dissatisfied with the functioning of Canadian federalism. Fifty-six per cent said that federalism generally did not produce satisfactory agreements between Quebec and the rest of Canada, versus only 26 per cent who said that it did, and 57 per cent of respondents expressed the view that the French language was less secure in Quebec than it was 30 years earlier.

Listen to the 'Does Quebec Separatism Have a Future?' podcast, available at www.oupcanada.com/Brooks7e

The fact remains that Quebec is a province *pas comme les autres*, and one that continues to attract special attention from federal politicians: in 2006 the House of Commons passed a resolution affirming that the Québécois are a nation within the nation of Canada. One of the politically significant ways in which Quebec's difference may be seen is in French-speaking Quebecers' weaker attachment to Canada, particularly among younger citizens. A 2006 survey found that only 19 per cent of francophone Quebecers between the ages of 18 and 30 said that they felt 'very attached to Canada', compared to 71 per cent among anglophone Quebecers and 45 per cent among allophones. Young francophones also were far less likely than anglophones to believe that Quebec's economic situation would be harmed by independence (29 per cent versus 72 per cent). It comes as no surprise, therefore, that young French-speaking Quebecers were found to be strongly in support of Quebec assuming the status of a country (59 per cent) while support was very weak among young English-speakers (9 per cent) and allophones (30 per cent).[53]

History should teach us that complacency about Quebec's relationship to the rest of Canada is far from being warranted by the enduring facts of the situation. Foremost among these facts is the gap that continues to separate the one-Canada, equality of the provinces, and multicultural visions of the country, which dominate outside Quebec, from the insistence by Quebec's politicians and opinion leaders—federalists and separatists alike—that Quebec must be considered a province *pas comme les autres*. The art of national unity involves finding ways to bridge this gap.

Appendix: Proposals for a Distinct Society Clause

Version I: Meech Lake Accord (1987)

1. The Constitution Act, 1867, is amended by adding thereto, immediately after Section 1 thereof, the following section:
2. (1) The Constitution of Canada shall be interpreted in a manner consistent with: (a) The recognition that the existence of French-speaking Canadians, centred in Quebec but also present elsewhere in Canada, and English-speaking Canadians, concentrated outside Quebec but also present in Quebec, constitutes a fundamental characteristic of Canada; and, (b) The recognition that Quebec constitutes within Canada a distinct society;
   (2) The role of the Parliament of Canada and the provincial legislatures to preserve the fundamental characteristic of Canada referred to in paragraph (1)(a) is affirmed;
   (3) The role of the Legislature and Government of Quebec to preserve and promote the distinct identity of Quebec referred to in paragraph (1)(b) is affirmed;
   (4) Nothing in this section derogates from the powers, rights or privileges of Parliament or the Government of Canada, or of the legislatures or governments of the provinces, including any powers, rights or privileges relating to language.

Version II: Charlottetown Accord (1992)

The Constitution Act, 1867 is amended by adding thereto, immediately after Section 1 thereof, the following section:

2. (1) The Constitution of Canada, including the Canadian Charter of Rights and Freedoms, shall be interpreted in a manner consistent with the following fundamental characteristics:
   . . .
   (c) Quebec constitutes within Canada a distinct society, which includes a French-speaking majority, a unique culture and a civil law tradition;
   . . .
   (2) The role of the legislature and Government of Quebec to preserve and promote the distinct society of Quebec is affirmed.

Version III: Motion Passed by Parliament (1995)

THAT

Whereas the people of Quebec have expressed the desire for recognition of Quebec's distinct society;

(1) the House recognize that Quebec is a distinct society within Canada;
(2) the House recognize that Quebec's distinct society includes its French-speaking majority, unique culture and civil law tradition;
(3) the House undertake to be guided by this reality;
(4) the House encourage all components of the legislative and executive branches of government to take note of this recognition and be guided in their conduct accordingly.

Version IV: The Calgary Declaration (1997)

(Adopted by all provincial governments except that of Quebec)

In Canada's federal system, where respect for diversity and equality underlines unity, the unique character of Quebec society, including its French-speaking majority, its culture and its tradition of civil law, is fundamental to the wellbeing of Canada. Consequently, the legislature and the Government of Quebec have a role to protect and develop the unique character of Quebec society within Canada.

Version V: The 2006 House of Commons Resolution

That this House recognize that the Québécois form a nation within a united Canada.

Starting Points for Research

Ramsay Cook, ed., *French Canadian Nationalism: An Anthology* (Toronto: Macmillan, 1969). This work contains a wide selection of writings from French-Canadian nationalists and about French-Canadian and Quebec nationalists, from the mid-nineteenth century to the Quiet Revolution.

Alain-G. Gagnon, ed., *Quebec: State and Society*, 3rd edn (Toronto: University of Toronto Press, 2004). A comprehensive reader, this collection includes contributions from many of Canada's leading students of Quebec politics.

——— and Raffaele Iacovino, *Federalism, Citizenship, and Quebec* (Toronto: University of Toronto Press, 2007). A challenging book that examines the impact of Quebec nationalism on Canadian politics and proposes a multinational model for the future of the Canadian federation.

Kenneth McRoberts, *Quebec: Social Change and Political Crisis*, 3rd edn (Toronto: Oxford University Press, 1999). McRoberts provides an excellent account of Quebec's historical and political evolution.

Garth Stevenson, *Community Besieged: The Anglophone Minority and the Politics of Quebec* (Montreal and Kingston: McGill-Queen's University Press, 1999). This is a somewhat nostalgic examination of the history and current state of the anglophone minority in Quebec.

Charles Taylor, *Reconciling the Solitudes: Essays on Canadian Federalism and Nationalism* (Montreal and Kingston: McGill-Queen's University Press, 1993). Written by Canada's most internationally renowned philosopher, several of the pieces in this collection deal with Quebec and Quebec nationalism.

Review Exercises

1. Watch the following video segment at <archives.cbc.ca/>: click on 'Politics & Economy', then on 'Separation anxiety: the 1995 Quebec referendum', and finally on 'Money and the ethnic vote'. Are there any arguments that may be used to justify Premier Parizeau's referendum night remarks? What circumstances do you think would have to exist for a referendum on Quebec independence to succeed?
2. How bilingual is your community? Make an inventory of the indications that French (or English, if you are in Quebec) language rights are protected and the French language promoted. It might look something like this:

   A. Schools
   French schools
   - Monseigneur Jean Noël
   - Ste-Thérèse
   - Lajeunesse

   Immersion schools
   - Bellewood

   B. Media
   Newspapers
   - Le Rempart

   Radio
   - Radio-Canada (540 AM)

   Television
   - Radio-Canada (54)
   - TFO (19, cable)
   - TVA (69, cable)
   - TVO (70, cable)

   C. Signs
   - stores
   - traffic signs
   - billboards
   - product labels
   - government office

   D. Churches
   Catholic
   - St Jérome
   - Ste-Anne
   - St Joseph

E. Clubs, Bars, Community Centres
   - Club Alouette
   - Place Concorde

F. Employment
   Teaching jobs in French (or English in Quebec); businesses that require French-speaking employees; government agencies that hire French-speaking workers

G. Public services
   Can you communicate with officials of government agencies in both French and English? Which levels of government?

3. What would be the consequences of Quebec independence for official bilingualism in the rest of Canada? Move past the immediate emotion and backlash to consider what possible consequences separation might have for schools, political parties, government services, and the Constitution.

Rukhsana Khan reads to students from her book *Coming to Canada*. As Canadian society continues to become more diverse, there is a need to reflect the experiences and issues of all Canadians in public institutions such as schools and the political arena nationwide. © Toronto Star/GetStock.com

14 Diversity and Multiculturalism

Diversity is both a part of the social reality of Canada and one of the leading values associated with Canadian politics. In this chapter we examine the politics of diversity in Canada, paying special attention to issues of multiculturalism and equality. Topics include the following:

- The changing ethnic character of Canadian society.
- Increased awareness of diversity.
- The institutionalization of diversity.
- The political representation of ethnic groups.
- Other models of integration and accommodation.
- The economic integration of immigrants.

Over the last generation respect for diversity has joined equality and freedom as one of the core values of Canadian politics. Indeed, many would go so far as to say that it has become *the* pre-eminent Canadian cultural trait, the quality that more than any other defines Canada and how our society and political life are different from those of other countries, but particularly from the United States. Canada is, as former Prime Minister Joe Clark once put it, 'a community of communities'. Canadians, we are often told, are united by their differences. This claim appears to be at least paradoxical and possibly even contradictory. What it means, however, is that tolerance, respect, the recognition of group rights, and a belief in the equal dignity of different cultures are central to the Canadian ethos. Indeed, the very idea that there is such a thing as a Canadian ethos is comparatively recent, emerging at the same time as this image of Canada as the pluralistic society par excellence and a model of cultural coexistence.

This image of Canada is not without its ironies and skeptics. Foremost among the ironies is the fact that separatist sentiment in Quebec—support for which is far from extinguished—challenges this rosy picture of Canada as a model of cultural coexistence. On the skeptical side, many people maintain that the diversity-centred image of Canada, and policies and institutions based on it, does more to undermine Canadian unity than strengthen it. Others question whether multicultural democracy can work at all, in Canada or elsewhere, except in special circumstances. They note the resurgence of ethnicity-based nationalism in the modern world and the breakup or instability of many countries that combine different cultures within their borders.

Ironies and skepticism aside, there is no denying that the politics of diversity has moved to the centre of Canada's political stage in recent decades. The evidence ranges from official recognition of multiculturalism in the law and under the Constitution to public controversy over the impact of recent immigration on Canadian society. While diversity is nothing new in Canada—Canadian society has always been pluralistic and the official recognition of group rights goes back at least as far as the 1774 Quebec Act, under which the British authorities recognized the religious rights of French Canadians—what is relatively new is the level of awareness of diversity and the idea that it should be recognized, protected, and even promoted through the actions and institutions of the state.

In this chapter we will examine the politics of diversity and the policy of multiculturalism in Canada. The issues that will be examined include the following:

- how Canada's population characteristics have changed over time;
- the ways in which diversity politics has been institutionalized in state institutions and policies;
- controversies associated with the Canadian multicultural experience and comparisons to policies in other pluralist democracies.

From Founding Nations to Multiculturalism: The Changing Ethnic Demography of Canada

The Canada that we know today was built on two premises: the displacement and marginalization of Aboriginal Canadians and the settlement and development of the land by European immigrants. Not only were the vast majority of the immigrants who settled in Canada during the country's formative years European, they were overwhelmingly of French and British Isles origins, although many of the latter came to Canada via the United States in the wave of Loyalists and non-Loyalists who left America during the three decades after the War of Independence. The languages they established in Canada were mainly French and English. With very few exceptions their religion was Christian, either Roman Catholic or Protestant. For much of Canada's history they would be referred to without hesitation as the founding nations or **charter groups**, one French and Catholic and the other English and mainly Protestant.

At the time of Confederation the virtual monopoly of the French and English on Canadian public life was symbolized in the partnership of John A. Macdonald, the leading English-Canadian advocate of an independent Canada, and George-Étienne Cartier, the major spokesperson for French Canada. The first Canadian government under Macdonald did not include anyone who was *not* a member of these so-called charter groups (not to be confused with today's Charter groups!). This image of Canada as a partnership—albeit an unequal one—of two European charter groups survived well into the twentieth century. It was not until the 1960s and, more specifically, the work of the Royal Commission on Bilingualism and Biculturalism (the B&B Commission) that the two-nations image of Canada experienced any serious competition. Spokespersons for non-French and non-British groups in Canada argued that this image of Canada and the policies that were based on it excluded them from the Canadian picture. These groups were, in the main, also representative of Canadians of European origin. Ukrainian spokespersons, for example, were prominent among those who were critical of the two-nations, bicultural image of Canada. The demands of these dissenting groups stopped well short of equality of status with English and French for their groups and languages. What they demanded and won was official recognition of Canada as a *multicultural society*, not a bicultural one. This was achieved through the 1971 passage of the Multiculturalism Act and the creation of a new federal Ministry of State for Multiculturalism, a position that has morphed over the years and currently falls under the rubric of the Department of Canadian Heritage.

The image of Canada as a sort of New World extension of two European peoples and their value systems was being challenged by some Canadian intellectuals. John Porter's influential book, *The Vertical Mosaic*,[1] drew attention to the stratified nature of Canada's pluralistic society, in which English Canadians dominated virtually all of the important elites and controlled the channels of recruitment into them. The picture he painted was of a Canada in which influence, status, and wealth were held disproportionately in the hands of one of Canada's two charter groups and where the members of other groups were largely blocked from access to the opportunities monopolized by Anglo-Canadians. This situation, Porter argued, was inconsistent with the democratic values of openness, socio-economic mobility, and equality preached by Canadian politicians and believed in by the general population. His analysis of the systemic inequality and discrimination that characterized Canadian society would provide much of the inspiration for a generation of social critics who, unlike their predecessors, did not take for granted the domination of the British charter group and the exclusion of increasing numbers of Canadians from an image of Canada as consisting of two peoples, the French and English.

The challenges launched by intellectual critics such as Porter and by the groups that wanted the biculturalism in the B&B Commission to be replaced with multiculturalism would not have had much of an audience or impact had it not been for the changes to Canada's population characteristics that were well underway by the 1960s. These changes have accelerated since then and, moreover, have altered in ways that present even greater challenges to older notions of Canadian pluralism than those first launched in the 1960s. To put it simply, the share of Canada's population with neither French nor British Isles ethnic origins has increased quite dramatically. Immigrants from Eastern and Southern Europe became increasingly important within Canada's overall immigration picture between the 1950s and 1970s. They have been joined in recent decades by increasing numbers of non-European immigrants, many of whom come from non-Christian cultures. As Figure 14.1 shows, the ethnic composition of Canadian society has changed significantly over the last half-century. This change has been experienced most strikingly in Canada's largest metropolitan areas, magnets for new immigrants, where the new Canadians of neither British nor French ethnic origins have clustered and where the **visible minority** population has increased significantly in recent years (see Figure 14.2). In fact, as noted in Chapter 3, Statistics Canada has projected that Toronto's visible minorities will be in the majority by 2017 and that, by 2031, visible minorities in Toronto will comprise over 60 per cent of the total population and in Vancouver will be just under 60 per cent.[2]

Change in the ethnic distribution of Canada's population has been brought about by shifting patterns of immigration. For most of Canada's history the major sources of immigration were Europe and the United States. In recent years the leading sources of immigration have been Asia, the Middle East, and the Caribbean. Whereas just under 95 per cent of all immigrants to Canada before 1961 were born in Europe or the United States, that figure was only 22.3 per cent for the period 1991–2001. Immigrants from Asia, the Middle East, Africa, Latin America, and the Caribbean, who together accounted for only 5.5 per cent of all immigrants prior to 1961, grew to about 77.5 per cent of all immigration during the

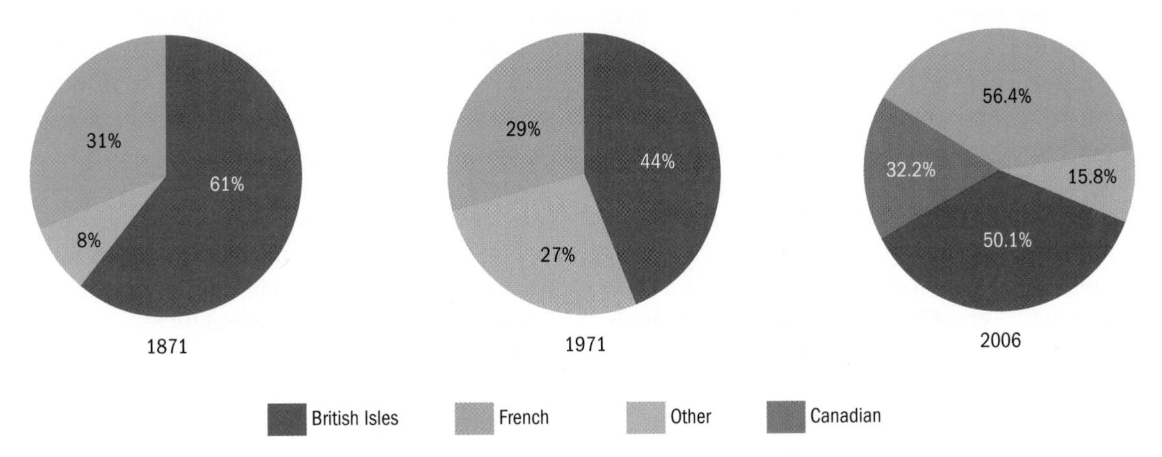

FIGURE 14.1 Ethnic Origins of the Canadian Population, Selected Years

Note: The comparability of the ethnic origins data from the 2006 census with answers prior to 1991 is affected by the fact that since 1991 respondents have been able to provide multiple ethnic origins. The percentages for 2006 add up to more than 100 because many respondents indicated more than one ethnic origin. In fact, the percentage of census respondents indicating multiple ethnic origins increased from 28.9% in 1991 to 41.4% in 2006.

Sources: F.H. Leacy, ed., *Historical Statistics of Canada*, 2nd edn (Ottawa: Minister of Supply and Services Canada, 1983); Statistics Canada, *Census of Canada*, 2006.

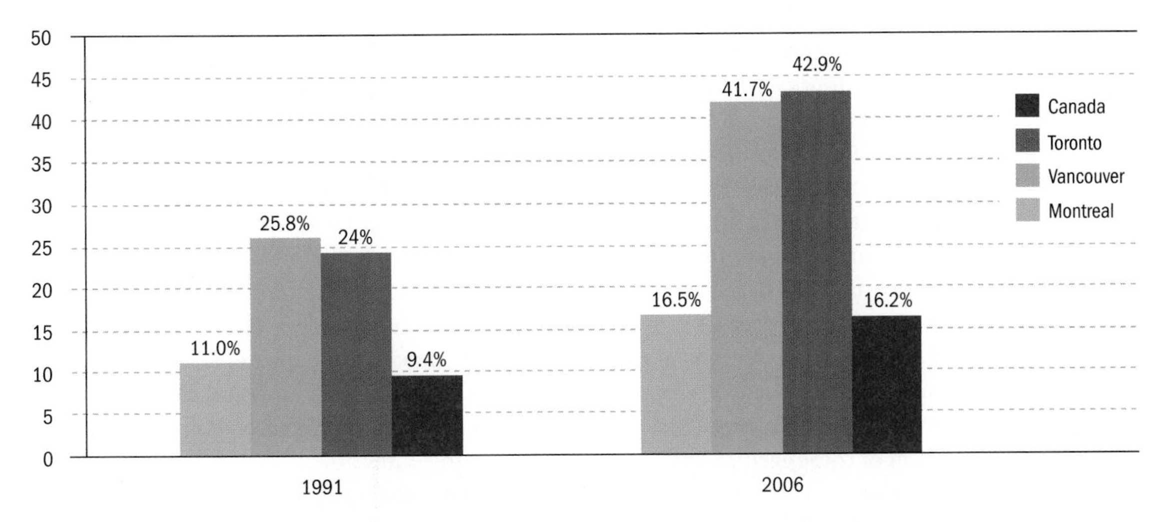

FIGURE 14.2 Visible Minorities in Canada and in Main Metropolitan Areas, 1991 and 2006

Sources: Statistics Canada, *Canada's Ethnocultural Portrait: The Changing Mosaic*, Catalogue no. 96F0030XIE2001008; Statistics Canada, *Census of Canada*, 2006.

1991–2001 decade and just under 80 per cent for the years 2001–6. The dramatic change that has taken place in the sources of immigration to Canada may be seen in Figure 14.3.

Canada remains, even after recent waves of immigration from non-European countries, a predominantly Christian society. As Figure 14.4 shows, about four out of five Canadians claim an affiliation with either the Catholic Church or a Protestant denomination. This is down from all but a sliver of the population at the time of Confederation and even represents some small slippage since 1971, about the time the profile of Canadian immigration began to shift away from traditional European sources. This slippage has been due chiefly to a sharp increase over the last generation in the number of people without a religious affiliation. People belonging to non-Christian religions continue to constitute a rather small minority, at about 6 per cent of the population. Their presence in particular cities, however, such as Sikhs and Hindus in Vancouver and Muslims in Toronto, is much greater than it is nationwide.

The growth of the non-European and non-Christian elements of Canadian society has not been entirely free from tensions and unease on the part of some (see Box 14.1). Most people appear to be accepting of the changes taking place in their society, but a 2004 survey of Canadians' attitudes towards cross-cultural and interracial marriage found that a significant minority of the population is uneasy with the idea of their children mixing with members of certain groups. Reservations were greatest in the case of marriage to Muslims, Pakistanis or East Indians, and blacks, in that order (see Figure 14.5). Older Canadians are much more likely to express disapproval of marriage with members of these groups than are younger Canadians. For example, 47 per cent of respondents aged over 60 said that they were not very or not at all comfortable with the idea of their child marrying a Muslim, compared to 24 per cent of those aged 18–29.

Interestingly, the region of the country where disapproval of marriage to Muslims was highest was Quebec, where 43 per cent—compared to the national figure of 35 per cent—said that they were not very or not at all comfortable with such marriages. Quebecers were also slightly more likely (33 per cent vs 27 per cent) to disapprove of their children marrying Pakistanis. These results do not seem to fit with the idea of Quebec as one of the most open and tolerant regions of the country. The explanation may have to do with the perception that these groups are less likely than others to integrate into Quebec's majority francophone society or, perhaps, that these groups are less likely than others to respect the idea of gender equality that Quebecers embrace more firmly than other Canadians. We will have more to say on this subject later in the chapter.

Along with greater diversity in the ethnic, religious, and racial composition of Canada, the demographic picture has become more recognizably varied in other ways, too, including family composition, sexual orientation, and disability.

Families. Families tend to be smaller today than they were a generation ago and considerably smaller than they were two generations ago. There are many more single-parent families than in the past (today, roughly one out of every six families) and many more couples who choose not to marry (over 10 per cent of all couples nationally, ranging from a low of about 7 per cent in some provinces to 20 per cent in Quebec). Same-sex couples are more frequent than in the past, although precisely how much more frequent is impossible to say as virtually no data were collected on such matters until recently.

Sexuality. There probably is no reason to assume that the ratio of those who are heterosexual compared to those who are gay/lesbian has changed significantly over time. What has changed, however, is the willingness of non-heterosexuals to proclaim openly their sexuality and the readiness of a growing number of Canadians to accept this in many, if not all, circumstances. Consequently, sexual diversity is much more apparent today than was the case when social pressures and the law discouraged all but a small number of non-heterosexuals from 'coming out'.

Times have changed, as the hundreds of thousands who annually line the streets and march in Toronto's Gay Pride parade attest. Canada has openly gay politicians, some of its churches ordain and marry homosexuals, and human rights codes and court interpretation of the Charter prohibit discrimination based on sexual preference. This is not to imply that this aspect of Canadian diversity is not controversial. These matters continue to divide Canadians. The struggle over the legal definition of marriage as excluding same-sex unions was seen by many as the last major legal barrier to the equality of gays and lesbians with heterosexuals. This struggle was waged in the courts and in the court of public opinion. Polls show that Canadians remain divided on this issue, but a combination of court rulings and legislation passed by Parliament in 2005 extended full legal status to same-sex marriages.

Governing Realities

Box 14.1 The Kirpan, Religious Freedom, and Canadian Multiculturalism

Beliefs and behaviours that are unfamiliar may or may not generate controversy. The fact that many Canadians of Ukrainian, Russian, and Serbian ancestry are members of the Orthodox Church and celebrate Christmas and Easter several days after the dates of these statutory holidays is probably unknown to many Canadians. Once known, most people will be indifferent. They might not be indifferent, however, if members of the Orthodox Church demanded forms of public recognition for their religious holidays, such as the right to a paid holiday.

Something of the sort was at issue in 2001 when a young Sikh male attending public school in British Columbia was told that he could not bring his kirpan to school. The kirpan is a metal ceremonial dagger that Sikh males are required to wear at all times after being baptized. It symbolizes religious loyalty. The parents of the boy in question were told by the school authorities that he would be permitted to wear a kirpan made of wood or plastic, some material that would eliminate or at least reduce its capacity to be used as a weapon. His parents refused, arguing that their son's religious freedom, guaranteed by the Charter, was violated by the school board's policy. Eventually the dispute reached the Supreme Court. In March 2006 the Court ruled that the wearing of a kirpan in schools for religious reasons is indeed protected by the Charter.

This case was about both religious freedom and multiculturalism. Indeed, the two values are intertwined, as the court said in its ruling:

> Religious tolerance is a very important value of Canadian society. If some students consider it unfair that G may wear his kirpan to school while they are not allowed to have knives in their possession, it is incumbent on the schools to discharge their obligation to instil in their students this value that is at the very foundation of our democracy. A total prohibition against wearing a kirpan to school undermines the value of this religious symbol and sends students the message that some religious practices do not merit the same protection as others. Accommodating G and allowing him to wear his kirpan under certain conditions demonstrates the importance that our society attaches to protecting freedom of religion and to showing respect for its minorities.[3]

Canadians are overwhelmingly supportive of multiculturalism in principle, but in practice their tolerance for accommodating difference has not always matched this support. As noted above and demonstrated in January 2011, this might be especially true in Quebec, where four members of the World Sikh Organization, who had been invited to testify before a legislative committee examining a proposed law on reasonable accommodation of ethnic minorities, were denied entry to Quebec's National Assembly because they wore kirpans. As one of the four, Balpreet Singh, said: 'Unfortunately, we weren't allowed to enter because we wear the kirpan, which is a bit ironic because we were here to speak upon the issue of accommodation and we weren't accommodated.'[4] Within weeks, the members of Quebec's National Assembly voted unanimously to ban the wearing of the Sikh ceremonial dagger from the province's legislative buildings.

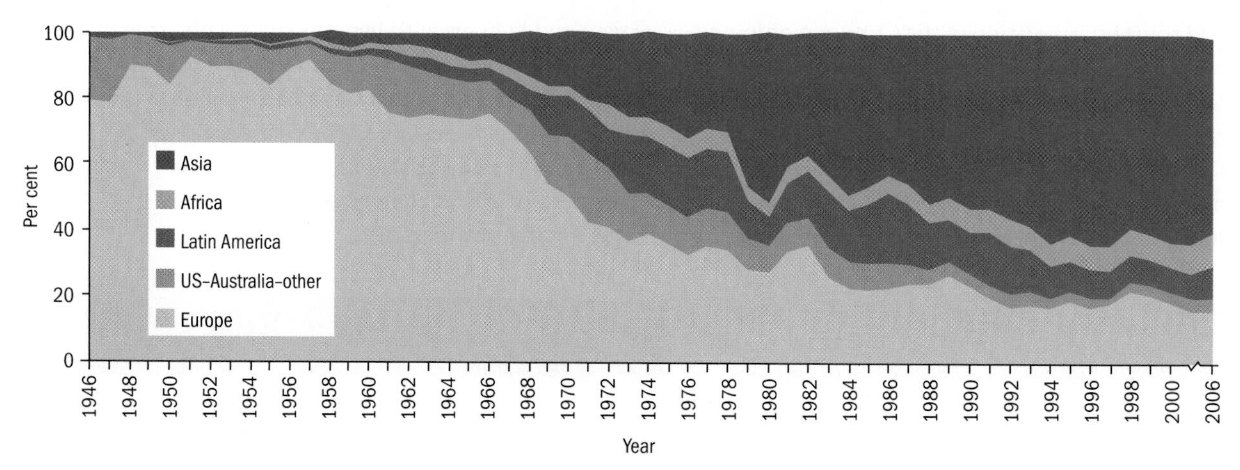

FIGURE 14.3 Place of Birth of Immigrants, 1946–2006

Sources: Roderic Beaujot, 'Effect of Immigration on Demographic Structure', discussion paper no. 02-09 (Oct. 2002), at <www.sociology.uwo.ca/popstudies/dp/dp02-09.pdf> and Statistics Canada, 'Immigration in Canada: A Portrait of the Foreign-born Population, 2006 Census', Figure 2, *Census of Canada*, 2006.

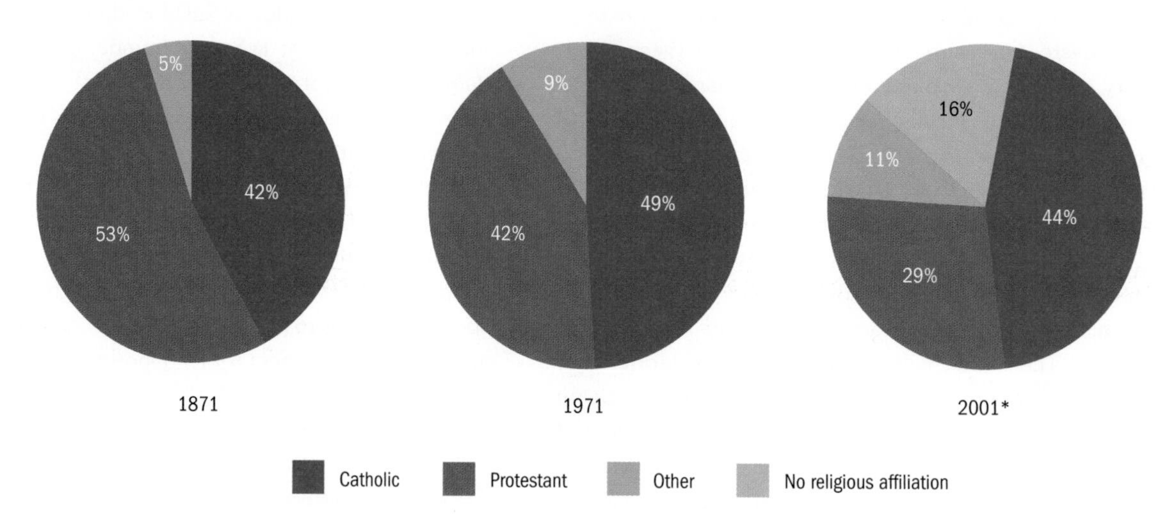

FIGURE 14.4 Religious Affiliations of the Canadian Population, Selected Years

*The 'Other' category for 2001 includes other Christians (2.6%), Christian Orthodox (1.6%), Muslim (2%), Jewish (1.1%), Buddhist (1%), Hindu (1%), and Sikh (0.9%).

Sources: F.H. Leacy, ed., *Historical Statistics of Canada*, 2nd edn (Ottawa: Minister of Supply and Services Canada, 1983); Statistics Canada, at <www.statcan.ca/english/Pgdb/demo32.htm>.

Disability. According to statistics, a greater proportion of the population is disabled today than at any point in Canada's history. Health Canada reports that about one in eight Canadians claims to experience either a mental or physical disability. But as in the case of sexuality, it is doubtful whether the actual incidence of Canadians suffering from various forms of disability is greater today than in the past. What has changed, however, is both our society's ideas about what constitute disabilities and the legal definition of what counts as a disability for purposes of pensions, workers' compensation, social assistance, employment, housing, and other matters. The recognition of disabledness has increased and, moreover, it has become one of the diversity criteria used by governments in making public policy.

Question: Please tell me whether you would be very, somewhat, not very, or not at all comfortable with having a son or daughter who married someone from each of the following groups. (percentage disapproving)

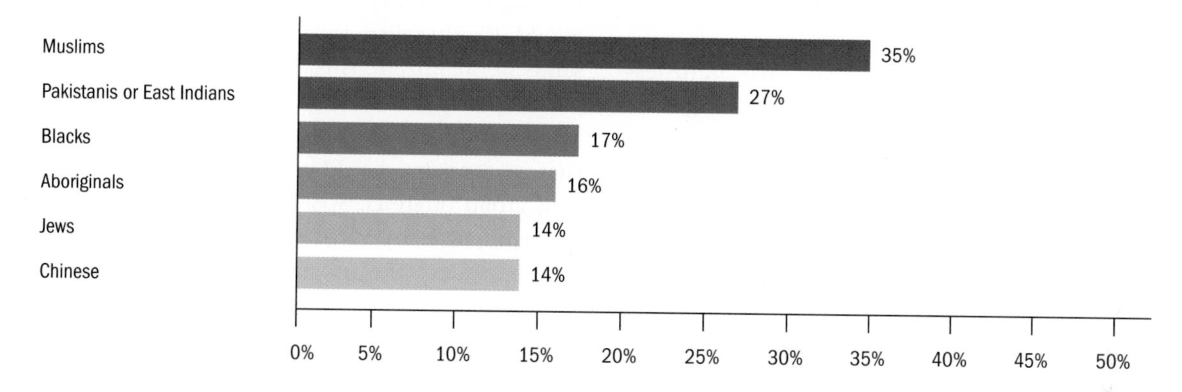

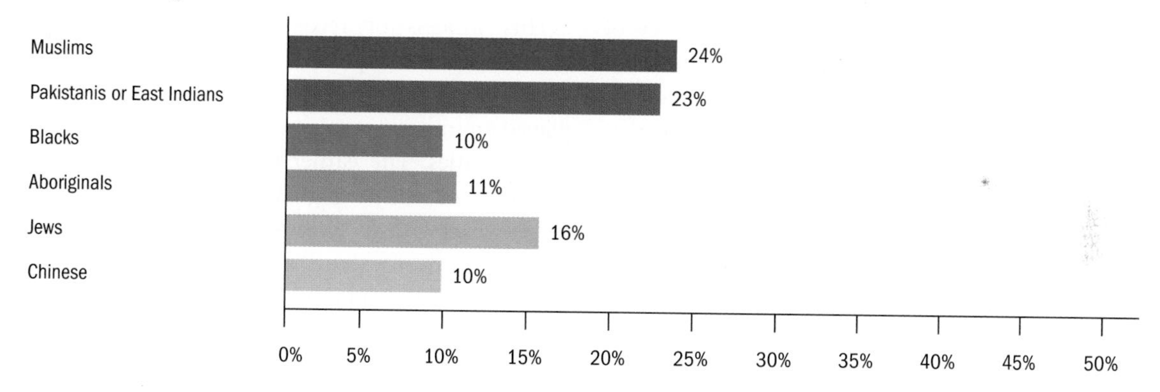

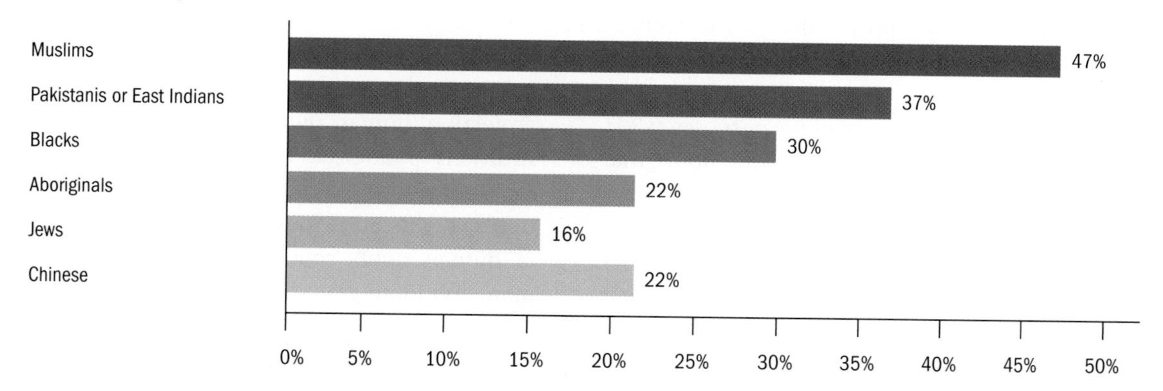

FIGURE 14.5 Canadian Attitudes towards Cross-Cultural Marriage

Source: Environics Poll conducted for the Department of Canadian Heritage, 29 Mar.–18 Apr. 2004.

Official Recognition and the Institutionalization of Diversity

Multiculturalism was given its own minister—albeit a minister of state, which is a rung down from a departmental minister—in 1972. But the official recognition of groups of Canadian citizens according to their group characteristics and the institutionalization of diversity go back much further. We have already mentioned that the Quebec Act of 1774 represented the first official confirmation of the status and rights of a particular segment of the population, in this case French-speaking Catholics. But the distinction of 'first' probably ought to be conferred upon the Royal Proclamation of 1763. This document recognized the presence and rights of 'the several Nations or Tribes of Indians with whom we are connected, and who live under our protection'. Aboriginal Canadians were recognized by the Proclamation as distinct rights-bearing peoples under the protection of the British Crown. This relationship continues to the present day—although the Canadian government long ago assumed the obligations that originally belonged to Britain—perpetuated and institutionalized through the Indian Act and s. 35 of the Constitution Act, 1982, which embeds the treaty rights of Aboriginal peoples in Canada.

There is, therefore, a long history of recognizing diversity in Canada. But until the 1960s that recognition extended principally to the French- and English-language communities (s. 133 of the Constitution Act, 1867), the Catholic and Protestant religions for schooling purposes (s. 93 of the Constitution Act, 1867), and Aboriginal Canadians. This changed as a result of the emergence of feminism as a political force in the 1960s and 1970s and the increasing popularity—first among some elites, spreading later to the general population—of multiculturalism and group-oriented thinking about rights.

Leslie Pal argues that the institutionalization of diversity in Canadian public life was leveraged during the late 1960s and throughout the 1970s and 1980s by the activities of a small organization, the Citizenship Branch, within the Department of Secretary of State (SOS).[5] The grants disbursed by the Citizenship Branch through its Official Language Minority Group, Women's Program, and Multiculturalism section helped finance thousands of organizations that, in time, made group-related policy demands on government, raised the profile of diversity issues, and reinforced the idea that government should be protecting and promoting group interests. SOS played a pivotal role in financing diversity advocacy. 'Measured in dollars,' Pal concludes, 'the programs were insignificant. Measured in increased tolerance for minorities and women, they were at best marginally successful.'[6] But their enduring significance, Pal argues, was to help reshape the structures of government and the relationship of the state to groups of citizens in ways that institutionalized diversity.

This process of recognizing and promoting diversity did not stop at SOS. Human rights commissions at both the federal and provincial levels have played an important role in expanding the concept of minorities. The earlier emphasis on language, religion, and ethnic origins has had to compete in recent years with such non-racial and non-cultural forms of minority status as gender, sexual orientation, dependence on alcohol and drugs, and social conditions. Human rights commission officials, as R. Brian Howe and David Johnson argue, have been at the forefront of the movement to extend the recognition of diversity through expanding the number of rights-bearing groups. As they say:

> By providing education about rights, and by publicizing the existence of a system of rights protection, human rights programs and institutions politicized Canadian society in the direction of making demands for wider rights. Rights consciousness and awareness of human rights commissions encouraged more and more groups to pressure for more and more rights. The result was a steady expansion of human rights protections, the entrenchment of human rights legislation, and the institutionalization of human rights commissions, embedded in an increasingly politicized society in which rights-conscious

human rights interest groups demanded ever-wider rights.[7]

At the federal level, the activities of the Canadian Broadcasting Corporation, including its Native language broadcasting operations, the National Film Board, and Telefilm Canada, all have contributed to the public projection of images of Canadian society that reflect the diversity of the country's population and history. The Department of Canadian Heritage has inherited the functions pioneered by the Citizenship Branch of SOS, providing grants to an enormous array of groups and operating as the leader within government for the promotion of Canadian pluralistic identity. For example, in the 2008–9 fiscal year Canadian Heritage disbursed close to $1.4 billion to hundreds of groups and projects, ranging from small one-time grants, such as support for the Calgary Coalition on Family Violence for a project on 'Improving Access and Quality of Services for Culturally Diverse Women and Their Families' and a grant to the Chinese Canadian National Council's Toronto chapter for 'Promoting good relations in the Markham and Richmond Hill areas', to expensive ongoing programs, including the Promotion of Official Languages and the Official Languages in Education programs. If Canada's Booker Prize-winning novelist Yann Martel is correct in his description of Canada as the 'world's greatest hotel', then the Department of Canadian Heritage may be considered its concierge.

Diversity and Political Representation

The 1878 cabinet of Sir John A. Macdonald had 14 members. All but one were born in Canada. About 80 per cent (11 of 14) had British Isles ethnic origins and the others were of French ethnic origin. All were either Catholic (4 of 14) or Protestant.

The 2010 cabinet of Stephen Harper was not as different from Sir John A.'s government as one might have expected, given the enormous demographic shifts that have occurred in Canadian society. Of its 32 members only a couple were born outside of Canada. The vast majority, about 85 per cent, had French or British ethnic origins. The religious affiliation of MPs is today more difficult to ascertain from public records than it was in the past, but only one or two of the members of cabinet may have had a non-Judeo-Christian religious affiliation. It is probable that a handful had no religious affiliation. On the whole, however, the demographic composition of Harper's 2010 cabinet was more similar to than different from the Macdonald cabinet of 1878, except in one striking respect. The Harper government included seven women and one Aboriginal Canadian, whereas Macdonald's included none.

Forty years ago John Porter remarked that Canada's political elite had been slow to change, failing to reflect the increasing ethnic diversity of the country. It was, he said, still an elite dominated by males from the two charter groups. Members of these groups continue to be disproportionately represented, at least if we define the political elite rather narrowly to include only the federal cabinet. In the late 1950s John Diefenbaker appointed to cabinet Canada's first female minister, Ellen Fairclough, and first non-charter group Canadian, Michael Starr, of Ukrainian origin. Canada's first Jewish member of cabinet was Herb Gray, appointed in 1969. But despite the election of increasing numbers of candidates from non-Judeo-Christian backgrounds over the last couple of decades, very few have been promoted to cabinet. People from non-European ethnic backgrounds, who today comprise about 12 per cent of the Canadian population, and even those of non-charter group European origins, continue to be under-represented at this highest level.

The situation is not different in the case of the judicial elite and the highest ranks of the federal bureaucracy. If we look at the 74 individuals who have been members of the Supreme Court since its creation, all but three have had British or French ethnic origins and all have had Judeo-Christian backgrounds. The same, broadly speaking, is true of the ranks of deputy ministers in Canada, although members of non-charter groups have made somewhat greater inroads into this elite. The main change to have occurred in both of these elites is the increased presence of women.

Ujjal Dosanjh served as the thirty-third premier of British Columbia from 2000 to 2001 and was a Liberal MP from 2004 to 2011, serving the riding of Vancouver South. His receipt of the Pravasi Bharative Samman, the Expatriate Indian Honour for persons of Indian origin demonstrating excellence across the world, speaks to his achievements in Canada, where visible minorities have not historically been proportionately represented in the political elite.

By bringing attention to the continuing dominance of these elites by members of the French and British charter groups, we are not suggesting that this is evidence of discrimination against those who come from other backgrounds. A couple of qualifying factors need to be taken into account. First, it takes time for demographic change to work its way through to the top of a political system. Most of the decline in the share of Canada's population claiming either French or British Isles ethnic origins has occurred since the 1970s. It is rare for one to become a member of one of the elites examined above before the age of 40, and most are in their fifties and sixties. As the size of the pool of non-charter group Canadians with the qualifications and other attributes necessary to become a member of one of these elites increases, we might expect to see more of these persons selected.

Second, the concept of 'charter group Canadians' has become increasingly problematic. Growing numbers of Canadians have mixed ethnic origins and a considerable share of the population now rejects the traditional ethnic identities, preferring to describe themselves as Canadian. Consequently, it may be more accurate to say that the political, judicial, and bureaucratic elites in Canada are dominated by persons of French, British, *and* Canadian origins, without intending 'Canadian' as a substitute for membership in one of the traditional charter groups.

Media Spotlight

Box 14.2 *Little Mosque on the Prairie*

Canadians who live in the Greater Toronto Area, Vancouver, Montreal, Windsor, or several other larger urban centres are aware that Muslims are part of the Canadian mosaic. Mosques, Islamic schools, traditional Islamic dress, and the controversies that inevitably accompany cultural difference, even in a society with a long history of cultural pluralism, are among the visible signs of this religious community. But a mosque and Muslims in small-town Saskatchewan?

This is the setting for the CBC's weekly situation comedy, *Little Mosque on the Prairie*. The incongruity of a Muslim community in a small prairie town, which does not appear to have had much experience with visible or religious minorities, gives the locale an edge that multicultural Toronto would not have. The premise of the show is straightforward: Muslims are different in terms of their religious beliefs and practices, and some of these differences spill over into lifestyle differences, but these differences are insignificant compared to the values that they share with other Canadians. While these differences provide the grist for the misunderstandings and minor conflicts that provide the basis for each week's story line, in the end everything works out. Indeed, the Muslims in this small town seem remarkably like other Canadians in most important ways. In one episode a Muslim female is shown playfully slapping her husband's bottom, a gesture that most viewers might imagine is frowned on by traditional Muslim standards of female modesty, but that seems very equality-of-the-sexes. The give-and-take between traditional and more liberal versions of Islam is, in fact, one of the program's leitmotifs.

The program was launched in 2007, at a time when the issue of what sort of accommodations should be made to cultural minorities, including Muslims, was increasingly part of the public conversation in Canada. It enjoyed considerable popularity during its first season, although the program's ratings slipped in its second year. Nonetheless, the concept caught the attention of television producers in the United States, where Fox Television announced in June 2008 that it would produce an American adaptation of the show. Although this hasn't happened, *La petite mosquée dans la prairie* has been picked up in France, where it is broadcast on one of the state channels. Many American and Canadian viewers will, of course, be familiar with the hit series, *Little House on the Prairie* (1974–83), and the works of Laura Ingalls Wilder upon which this series was based. Clearly, the title of *Little Mosque on the Prairie* contrasts the cultural pluralism of small-town twenty-first-century Saskatchewan with the comparative homogeneity of life in Wilder's *Little House*, set in the early twentieth-century American Midwest. Yet, the more things change, the more they stay the same, as many of the same values are to be found in both treatments of small-town life.

Other Models of Integration and Accommodation

The Canadian model of multiculturalism represents one possible regime for the accommodation and recognition of the ancestral cultures of minorities, including their languages and religious beliefs. Other models exist and it would probably surprise most Canadians to learn that some Western democracies have taken group recognition and the protection of cultural rights considerably further than in Canada. Table 14.1 shows a range of models for the accommodation and recognition of minority cultures. At one end is what we might call *deep diversity multiculturalism*, represented by the Netherlands until fairly recently; at the other is *integration without major accommodation*, as found in France. Between these extremes fall Canada and the United States. Quebec has its own rather different regime of integration and accommodation that also falls between these extremes. The Canadian version of multiculturalism is towards the middle of this scale in terms of the degree to which the state is obliged to protect and promote minority cultures and identities.

Listen to the 'Reasonable Accommodation of Cultural Differences' podcast, available at www.oupcanada.com/Brooks7e

The Dutch Experiment with Deep Diversity Multiculturalism

To understand how multiculturalism is viewed by a particular society and why certain institutions and policies exist, one needs to examine the historical circumstances and demographic conditions of that society. In the case of the Netherlands, increasing wealth and a shortage of unskilled labour led to an increase in immigration during the 1970s. 'Guest workers'—immigrants who were not given citizenship rights and who were expected to return to their countries of origin after a certain number of years in the Netherlands—arrived from Morocco and Turkey, along with non-European immigrants from former Dutch colonies. They were followed by refugees from Sri Lanka, Iran, Iraq, and Somalia in the 1980s and 1990s and by the relatives of Moroccan and Turkish workers already living in the Netherlands. This influx of non-European immigrants took place against the historical backdrop of World War II and the Holocaust, and a sense of what has been called 'Dutch guilt'. This involves a

TABLE 14.1 Models of Cultural Accommodation

	Deep Diversity Multiculturalism	Interculturalism	Official Multiculturalism	De Facto but Contested Multiculturalism	Universalism with Skeptical Acceptance of Some Aspects of Multiculturalism
Characteristics	· Allows and encourages groups to maintain their languages, religions, and identities · Provides public support for schools, religious organizations, community centres	· Advocates the official recognition of minority cultures and state measures to protect their rights and sustain their practices and beliefs	· Allows and even encourages the retention of minority cultural identities through state support for cultural organizations, heritage language instruction, inclusion in state symbols, ceremonies, etc.	· Allows for the retention of minority cultural identities with some state support · Opposed by some as divisive	· Discourages the official recognition of group cultural identities · The public space and state institutions are based on a universal set of values and a single national identity
Guiding Principles	· 'The larger society is obliged to support the institutions symbolizing and sustaining the identity of the majority.'*	· Mutual respect between the cultural majority and minorities and a willingness from both sides to accommodate the other and adapt	· Minority cultures deserve respect and recognition · Based on concept of reasonable accommodation	· Cultural pluralism is positive, but citizens should be encouraged to share a common civic identity	· Pragmatic recognition of culture minorities exists · Cultural minorities should be discouraged from retaining separate identities and should be encouraged to identify with the universal values of the society
Countries	· The Netherlands during the 1990s, until roughly 2004	· Recommended for Quebec by the Bouchard-Taylor Commission, 2008	· Canada	· United States	· France

*Paul Sniderman and Louk Hagendoorn, *When Ways of Life Collide: Multiculturalism and Its Discontents* (Princeton, NJ: Princeton University Press, 2007), 5.

widespread feeling, the Anne Frank story notwithstanding, that the country's population did not do enough to resist the Nazi occupation and the deportation of Dutch Jews. Therefore, the adoption of multiculturalism, mainly in the 1990s, was inspired by a constellation of factors. It was, in a sense, compensation for what was seen as a failure to stand up for minorities during the Nazi occupation. It was also a practical response to a labour market situation where guest workers were expected to return to their countries of origin eventually, so providing them and their children with education and public services in their own languages, and in various ways making it unnecessary for these immigrants to integrate into Dutch society, appeared to make sense. But the policy also accorded with the liberal politics that was ascendant among Western intellectuals and that was particularly strong in secular, tolerant Holland.

The result was a multicultural regime based on a principle that the Canadian philosopher, Charles Taylor, has called 'deep diversity'. It involves the idea that in a pluralistic society no single national identity is possible or even desirable without depriving some minority or minorities of equal status, recognition, and dignity. Taylor argues that different communities can belong to a country in different ways and that competing loyalties are not necessarily destabilizing for a society. This ethos underpinned the Dutch experiment with multiculturalism. Paul Sniderman and Louk Hagendoorn summarize the results as follows:

> In the Netherlands, as much as can be done on behalf of multiculturalism has been done. Minority groups are provided instruction in their own language and culture; separate radio and television programs; government funding to import religious leaders; and subsidies for a wide range of social and religious organizations; 'consultation prerogatives' for community leaders; and publicly financed housing set aside for and specifically designed to meet Muslim requirements for strict separation of 'public' and 'private' spaces.[8]

In short, Dutch multiculturalism went considerably beyond the Canadian model in the extent to which it supported and promoted minority cultural identities.

Although diagnoses of what went wrong vary, there is a general consensus that the Dutch model has failed. The fact that immigrant communities were not integrated into the wider Dutch society—on the contrary, the incomes of Muslims, Turks, and Moroccans remained the lowest in the country—permitted a situation to develop where members of these groups saw themselves, and were seen by the majority group, as being *in* the country without being *of* the country. The strong electoral showing of anti-immigration parties in the 2007 and 2010 Dutch elections led some to dismiss the rejection of the country's multiculturalism regime as the intolerant reaction of the xenophobic right. But this was far from the entire truth. Liberal intellectuals also have become disillusioned with multiculturalism and increasingly question whether their country's large Muslim minority is willing to accept such values as freedom of speech, gender equality, and tolerance of diverse lifestyles that are embraced by the liberal intelligentsia and, indeed, by most of Dutch society.

American Multiculturalism: Contested Institutionalization

Canadians, conditioned as they often are to believe that the United States is an assimilationist melting pot that actively discourages immigrants from retaining their ancestral cultural identities, are likely to be perplexed by the suggestion that there is any sort of multiculturalism regime in that country. In fact, however, the main difference between Canadian and American multiculturalism may be that in Canada it is enshrined in law and the Constitution and has become, since the 1970s, a central aspect of the story that Canadians tell themselves and others about who they are and what they are about culturally. Not coincidentally, this narrative serves the culturally and politically important function of establishing a frontier of difference between Canada and the United States.

What public authorities across the United States do to protect and in some ways even to promote minority cultural identities are not very different from policies and programs in Canada. Laws providing rights to public services in languages other than English—Spanish, for the large Latino population in the United States, but other languages, too—are common across the country. In California, the code governing state services requires that state agencies employ persons who speak minority languages, provide interpreters for non-English speaking citizens needing state services, and provide information about government services in minority languages. In practice, the minority language usually is Spanish, but the law does not limit this requirement to Spanish and services in many other languages are provided by some agencies. Most states offer driver examinations in foreign languages, many of them in multiple languages. New York is one of many states that provide publicly paid interpreters for all litigants and witnesses in both criminal and civil law proceedings.

When it comes to the incorporation of minority ethnic identities and cultures into their public life, Americans can hardly be said to lag behind Canadians. There may be less celebration of diversity in the institutions and activities of the US federal government than in Canada, but many state and local governments across the United States, as well as community activities that do not depend on government funding and initiatives, extensively recognize and celebrate ethnic diversity. An important difference is less agreement in American society that multiculturalism—which usually is referred to as 'diversity'—is a good thing. In Canada the idea of multiculturalism is widely accepted. In the United States it is a hot-button issue that divides liberals from conservatives. Moreover, there has been much more willingness in the United States, from researchers and not just ideological warriors, to consider the possibility that the official recognition of diversity may generate conflict and impede the economic progress of the recognized minorities.[9]

The area of American life where multiculturalism is most evident, institutionalized, and contested involves the country's educational system. Ethnic studies exploded onto American university campuses at the end of the 1960s. Even the most casual perusal of curricula, programs, and research centres in American higher education shows that diversity education is at least as pervasive in that system as in Canada. In words that most Canadian educators would find comforting and familiar, the curricular guidelines created for the National Council for Social Studies state:

> Multicultural education helps students understand and affirm their community cultures and helps to free them from cultural boundaries, allowing them to create and maintain a civic community that works for the common good. Multicultural education seeks to actualized the idea of e pluribus unum within our nation and to create a society that recognizes and respects the cultures of its diverse people. . . . A unified and cohesive democratic society can be created only when the rights of its diverse people are reflected in its institutions, within its national culture, and within its schools, colleges and universities.[10]

On the other hand, in May 2010 the state legislature of Arizona passed a law prohibiting courses in public schools that 'advocate ethnic solidarity instead of the treatment of pupils as individuals'. Clearly, the institutionalization of ethnic studies has not gone unchallenged.

Although Americans are less likely to embrace multiculturalism as an idea and see it as a defining characteristic of their society, their attitudes towards cultural minorities are not very different from those of Canadians. When asked whether the United States is 'a country with a basic American culture and values that immigrants take on when they come here', or 'a country made up of many cultures and values that change as new people come here', only one-third of non-immigrant Americans gave the first response, but two-thirds gave the second response that recognized one of the distinguishing features of a multicultural society.[11] The results were reversed when people were asked whether America should be a society with a basic culture and values that immigrants take on when they arrive.

An identical pair of questions has not been asked in Canada, so we do not know whether Canadians are different from their southern neighbours in their sentiments towards cultural accommodation. However, an Angus Reid survey carried out in 2009 asked Canadians whether they thought that laws and norms should not be modified to accommodate minorities. Over six in 10 respondents said that they should not be modified. It may be, therefore, that Canadians' ideas on the accommodations that should be made for minority cultures are not very different from those of Americans.

France: Where Multiculturalism Exists, But Is Not Officially Embraced

When you step out of the exit of Paris's Gare du nord train station you immediately see that the capital of France is a place where races and cultures meet. But they do not always mix. If you take the metro to the city's perimeter, where *les banlieux* (the suburbs) begin, you immediately sense that Paris is a highly segregated place. In Montreuil, for example, at Paris's eastern edge, the vast majority of the population is non-white and a significant portion is Muslim.

What percentage is non-white and what percentage is Muslim? No one knows for sure because French law prohibits state authorities from asking people their race, ethnicity, or religion. This prohibition exists because the official ideology of the French state, enshrined in the constitution, is based on universalist values of *liberté, égalité, et fraternité* (freedom, equality, and social solidarity). These values are at the heart of the French civic identity. Along with the French language they define what it means to be French.

Like many other countries of Western Europe, France has become culturally more diverse as a result of non-European immigration over the last several decades. Immigrants from France's former colonies in Africa and elsewhere have arrived in large numbers, some originally as guest workers, some as refugees, some because they had a right to residence and citizenship in France as a result of their colonial relationship to the metropole, and others illegally. Today it is estimated that about one-tenth of the French population is Muslim. The official ideology enforced by the state sees only citizens, regardless of their skin colour, religion, and ethnic ancestry. But the reality of French society is multicultural. And in response to that fact the state has grudgingly and to a limited degree provided some recognition of the existence and importance of minority cultural identities. It has done so within the framework of a classically liberal approach, focusing on cases of discrimination on the basis of ethnic origin, race, religion, and so on. The Haute autorité de lutte contre les discriminations et pour l'égalité is the key institution in this regard, operating much as a human rights commission does in Canada.

Tensions between the evolving multicultural reality of French society and the universalist ideology of the state have been increasingly evident in recent years. In the autumn of 2009 the government of President Nicolas Sarkozy launched what it called *le grand débat sur l'identité nationale*, creating a commission and soliciting input from individuals across the country. The idea that France, of all countries, would create a commission to study the *problem* of national identity would have been unthinkable a couple of decades earlier. Although some dismissed the national identity initiative as a politically motivated attempt to pander to the prejudices of right-of-centre voters, this interpretation ignores the widespread unease, cutting across the French ideological spectrum, regarding what are seen as challenges to the principles of gender equality and secularism in France. The debate about national identity was, in fact, a debate about the compatibility of Islam—or some forms of Islam—and the French civic culture.

Two of the measures taken by the French government, and widely supported by the French public, included what might be called 'citizenship-values contracts' for newcomers (*le contrat d'accueil et d'intégration*) and a ban on the wearing of the burqa and the niqab in public places (schools, government offices, public transportation, etc.). It should be said that France was not alone in enacting such measures. Citizenship-values contracts were also mandated in Germany, the Netherlands, the United Kingdom, and several other Western

©AP Photo/Bob Edme

For 20 nights beginning on 27 October 2005, civil unrest gripped the suburbs of Paris and other parts of France. In riots that saw the burning of just under 9,000 vehicles and nearly 3,000 arrests, the tensions that had been building among the country's youth population—particularly those from impoverished ethnic neighbourhoods—exploded. Media reported that discrimination against immigrants and French society's negative perception of practising Muslims may have played a role in inciting the riots.

European democracies and have been advocated by the Parti Québécois for newcomers to Quebec. Likewise, laws banning the burqa and niqab also exist in Belgium and Italy and are being contemplated elsewhere in Europe.

Quebec: Multiculturalism, Interculturalism, or Something Else?

Since the 1960s, when the preference of immigrants for the English language caused Quebec demographers to predict, and nationalist spokespersons to fret, that the French language and distinctive culture of Quebec would be placed under increasing pressure, immigrants have been an important part of the debate about language and cultural policy in Quebec. For decades, Quebec's birth rate has been below the level needed to reproduce the population. Immigration has long been crucial for population and labour market growth, as is also true in the rest of Canada. And as is true of the rest of Canada, the sources of immigration to Quebec have shifted from Europe to other parts of the world. According to the 2006 census, over 60 per cent of immigrants in Quebec came from countries outside of Europe and the United States. Africa, Asia, the Middle East, and the Caribbean have become major sources of immigration to the province.

The debate in Quebec has shifted somewhat from the impact of immigrants on the French language—after all, many of these immigrants come from former French colonies and speak French—to the integration of newcomers into Quebec culture and society. Tensions in the province were crystallized in the highly publicized case of Hérouxville, a small town 180 kilometres north of Montreal whose local government adopted a declaration of cultural standards that newcomers were expected to respect.[12] This apparently xenophobic resolution from the heart of rural Quebec—the former bastion of traditional Quebec nationalism—targeted Muslims, Sikhs, North Africans, South Asians, and Middle Eastern Arabs, stating that immigrants were unwelcome in their community of less than 2,000 if they covered their faces, carried weapons to school, practised genital mutilation, or stoned or burned women to death. The furor that the publication of this code of behaviour incited—the story was widely covered throughout the world, including in France, Great Britain, and the United States—eventually led the Quebec government to appoint a consultative commission on 'reasonable accommodation', under the leadership of philosopher Charles Taylor and sociologist Gérard Bouchard.

Their report seemed to some to recommend that the Quebec government and Quebec citizens adopt a form of multiculturalism within the province rather similar to that which has been embraced by the federal government for decades. The report's reception was not enthusiastic. Most French-speaking Quebecers, and not simply the folks in Hérouxville and communities like it, felt that the emphasis in the Bouchard-Taylor report leaned too far in the direction of accommodation and openness to change on the part of old-stock Québécois—sometimes called ***les québécois de souche***—and not enough on the need for newcomers to adapt and accept not only the language of the French majority, but their culture and mores as well (see Box 14.3 and the Appendix to this chapter).

What the Bouchard-Taylor report recommended was called **interculturalism**. This was proposed as an alternative to the Canadian multicultural regime, about which Quebecers are more skeptical than their compatriots in the rest of the country. Multiculturalism is about accommodating the different values and practices of minorities and imposes an obligation of tolerance on the majority, if, in fact, a 'majority' even can be identified in such a pluralistic society. Indeed, some would argue that the concept of multiculturalism as it has evolved, and as Canada's many minorities have increased in number, does not posit a majority but simply many different cultures and peoples. Interculturalism, on the other hand, as explained by the Bouchard-Taylor Commission, is about reconciliation and mutual adaptation on the part of both the dominant majority and minorities: both sides must be prepared to make cultural concessions. Quebec, historically and today, has a clearly identifiable majority population; urban Canada, especially outside Quebec, increasingly does not.

Quebec nationalism has always been uneasy with the Canadian concept of multiculturalism, which is often seen to be in competition with the notion that Canada ought to be viewed as a partnership between two founding peoples, one French-speaking and the other English-speaking. Interculturalism was proposed by the Bouchard-Taylor Commission as an alternative to the Canadian multicultural model. But many Quebecers and their nationalist leaders were skeptical, believing that interculturalism requires too much accommodation from the French-speaking Québécois and too little from newcomers to the province. The separatist Parti Québécois argued that the emphasis on compromise and mutual adaptation that interculturalism involves sidesteps what for most Quebecers is the real problem: the protection and preservation of their French identity. 'It is not necessary to be born here to be part of our collective journey', said PQ leader Pauline Marois, 'but you have to get on the train.'[13] The province's Liberal government distanced itself from the Bouchard-Taylor report and little was done to implement its ambitious and extensive recommendations.

As in the case of France, Belgium, and some other Western European countries, Quebec introduced legislation that would deny public employment and government services to women wearing

Politics in Focus

Box 14.3 The Bouchard-Taylor Report and Its Political Reception

Our deliberations and reflections have firmly convinced us that integration through pluralism, equality and reciprocity is by far the most commendable, reasonable course. Like all democracies in the world, Québec must seek to reach a consensus against a backdrop of growing diversity, renew the social bond, accommodate difference by combating discrimination, and promote an identity, a culture and a memory without creating either exclusion or division.

From *Building the Future: A Time for Reconciliation*, the report of the Bouchard-Taylor Commission on Reasonable Accommodation, p. 241.

Quebec's Premier Jean Charest responded immediately to the report and its recommendations.

No society can succeed by withdrawing or turning in on itself. Our nation and economy can only grow by continuing to welcome others.

Immigration is not a right. Immigrating to Quebec is a privilege. And welcoming immigrants is a responsibility shared by all Quebecers.

There is a line to be drawn between the two. Quebecers have every right to decide the kind of society we want to live in. We have values that are not negotiable, and those values come with responsibilities.

As Premier of Quebec, I assume the supreme responsibility of protecting and promoting the French language. New Quebecers and members of cultural communities must speak it. The language is a meeting point for minorities and the majority.

As citizens, we must also respect the personal convictions of each individual. And for its part, the state, which serves all members of society, must affirm the secular nature of our institutions.

Today, I am announcing that the actions of my government, as inspired by the Bouchard-Taylor Commission, will:

- Reinforce francization prior to the arrival of immigrants.
- Provide for a signed statement by potential immigrants committing to the common values of our society.
- Develop a mechanism to help decision makers handle questions of *accommodation* while respecting the secular character of our institutions.
- I am also asking members of the National Assembly to collaborate in adopting Bill 63, which would amend the Charter of Rights and Freedoms to affirm the equality of men and women.

Declaration by Premier Jean Charest, 22 May 2008. At: <www.premier-ministre.gouv.qc.ca/actualites/communiques/2008/mai/2008-05-22.asp>.

face coverings such as the burqa or the niqab. This policy has the support of the Quebec Council on the Status of Women and the Muslim Canadian Congress, although it is opposed by such Muslim associations as the Canadian Islamic Congress and is clearly contrary to the spirit of the Bouchard-Taylor Commission. 'Multiculturalism is not a Quebec value', said Louise Beaudoin, the Parti Québécois's designated spokesperson for secularism. 'I think a lot of the onus is being placed on us, telling us how we have to accept this and that. It seems to me a different question should be asked and it should be asked of the people who absolutely insist on wearing either the burqa or the niqab, or the kirpan in the National Assembly.'[14]

Immigration and Economic Integration

Immigration has long been a crucial factor contributing to the growth of Canada's population. Although more people have left Canada than have entered at various points in the country's history, the balance over time has strongly favoured immigration over emigration (see Table 14.2). As the fertility rate in Canada has fallen over the last several decades to the current rate of about 1.6 (the population replacement rate is 2.1), immigration has become crucial for population maintenance and growth.

We have seen that the sources of immigration to Canada have changed dramatically since the 1970s. This is partly due to the fact that several of the European countries that previously had been major sources of immigration were becoming more affluent. Economics has always been a main driver of population migrations, with people fleeing impoverished circumstances and moving towards places that they believed would provide them and their families with a better life and more opportunities. The economic recovery and increasing affluence of Western Europe reduced the incentives for people to leave for Canada, the United States, and Australia, all of which were main destinations for European immigrants.

But another factor contributing to the change in the pattern of immigration to Canada was the reform of immigration law. Prior to the 1960s the law had discriminated in favour of European nationals and essentially held the door wide open to immigrants from the United Kingdom. Moreover, immigration policy actively discriminated against certain non-European groups at various points in Canada's history, notably against Chinese immigrants beginning in 1885 through the imposition of a head tax. The tax began at $50 per person but increased 20 years later to $500. The Immigration

TABLE 14.2 Immigration, Emigration, and Contribution to Population Growth, Canada, 1851–2006

	Population (at end of period)	Immigration	Average Immigration (% of population)	Emigration	Contribution to Population Growth
1851	2,523,000				
1851-61	3,230,000	352,000	1.22%	170,000	23.0%
1861-71	3,689,000	260,000	0.75%	410,000	-32.6%
1871-81	4,325,000	350,000	0.87%	404,000	- 8.5%
1881-91	4,833,000	680,000	1.49%	826,000	-28.7%
1891-1901	5,371,000	250,000	0.49%	380,000	-24.2%
1901-11	7,207,000	1,550,000	2.46%	740,000	44.1%
1911-21	8,788,000	1,400,000	1.75%	1,089,000	19.7%
1921-31	10,376,700	1,200,000	1.25%	970,000	14.5%
1931-41	11,506,700	149,000	0.14%	241,000	- 8.1%
1941-51	14,009,400	548,000	0.43%	379,000	7.9%
1951-61	18,238,200	1,543,000	0.96%	463,000	25.5%
1961-71	21,962,082	1,429,000	0.71%	707,000	21.7%
1971-81	24,820,382	1,429,000	0.61%	636,000	28.6%
1981-91	28,030,864	1,381,000	0.52%	490,000	27.7%
1991-8	30,300,422	1,556,000	0.67%	328,000	54.1%
1991-2001 (est.)	31,048,284	1,881,000	0.64%	428,000	48.2%
2001-6	31,613,000	1,446,080	0.46%	237,418	65%

Sources: Roderic Beaujot and Deborah Matthews, 'Immigration and the Future of Canada's Population', Table 1, 30 Jan. 2000, at <www.sscl.uwo.ca/sociology/popstudies/dp/dp00-1.pdf> and updated with data from Statistics Canada, *Census of Canada, 2006*.

Act, 1967 eliminated racial discrimination and ethnic favouritism and established a points system that has been used since then. With this system, immigrants who apply under the economic category—the law also recognizes family reunification and refugee status as grounds for immigration, as well as business class immigrants who bring capital and entrepreneurial skills—receive points for their level of proficiency in one or both of Canada's official languages, years of formal education, years of work experience, age (most points are awarded to those between 20 and 50 years of age), having arranged employment in Canada, and adaptability (this includes having family already in Canada and a number of other factors). Immigrants who arrive under the points system are much more likely than family-class immigrants or refugees to have the education, language skills, and job-related qualifications that enable them to integrate more quickly into the labour force and the Canadian middle class (see Figure 14.6). Language proficiency, which is linked in subtle and not so subtle ways to familiarity with cultural norms in the host society, is a key factor affecting employment prospects and earnings. Figure 14.7 shows that immigrants who mainly or always use a language other than French or English at work are essentially trapped in a lifetime of much lower incomes.

In view of the criteria that need to be met to qualify as an economic-class immigrant, it is not surprising that these new Canadians tend to be more educated than Canadian-born citizens of the same age. But education, professional certification and years of work experience abroad do not necessarily produce easy entry into the Canadian labour force, at least not right away. A recent longitudinal study of immigrant employment in Canada found that about 90 per cent of prime working-age immigrants (25–44) who arrived in the economic class found work within their first two years in the country. Roughly half found work in their intended occupation, 40 per cent within their first year in Canada.[15] This means, of course, that about half of these highly educated, highly qualified immigrants were not successfully integrated into the Canadian labour force after two years. Why?

The answer sometimes given is 'discrimination', in systemic forms and in subtle and more overt forms; but the explanation is far more complex than this and raises the question, 'What do we mean by discrimination?' Research by Jeffrey Reitz and others points to four main factors that slow or even block the entry of highly educated, skilled immigrants into the professions they held in their countries of origin. They include the following:

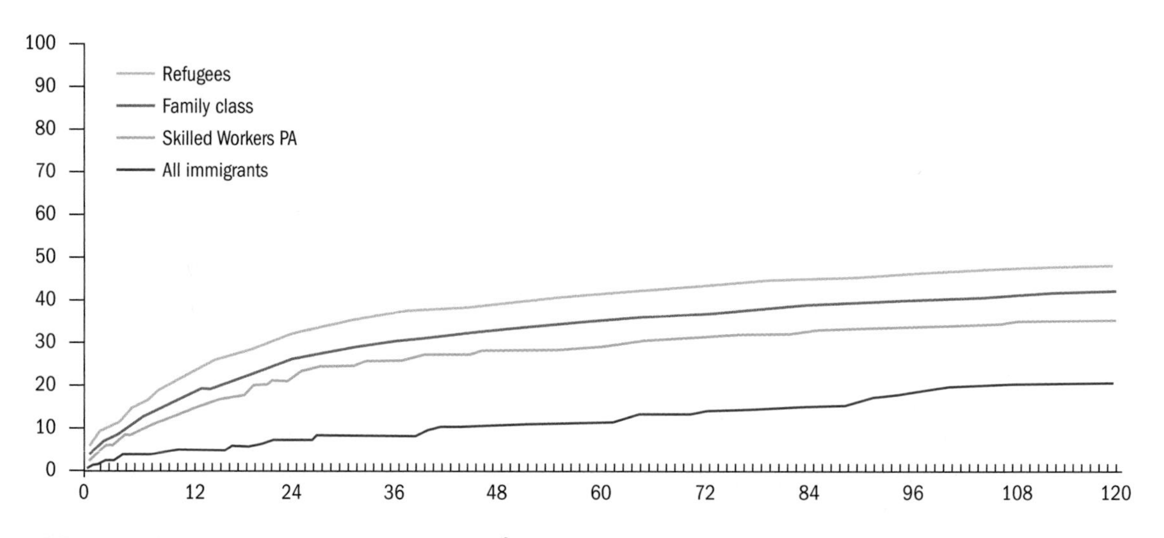

FIGURE 14.6 Economic Integration of Immigrants

Source: Statistics Canada, *Longitudinal Survey of Immigrants to Canada Progress and Challenges of New Immigrants in the Workforce 2003*, Chart 2, 89-615-XwE2005001, October 2005. <www.statcan.gc.ca/pub/11-008-x/2009001/article/10771-eng.htm>

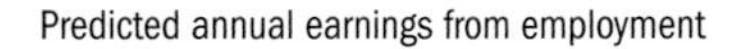

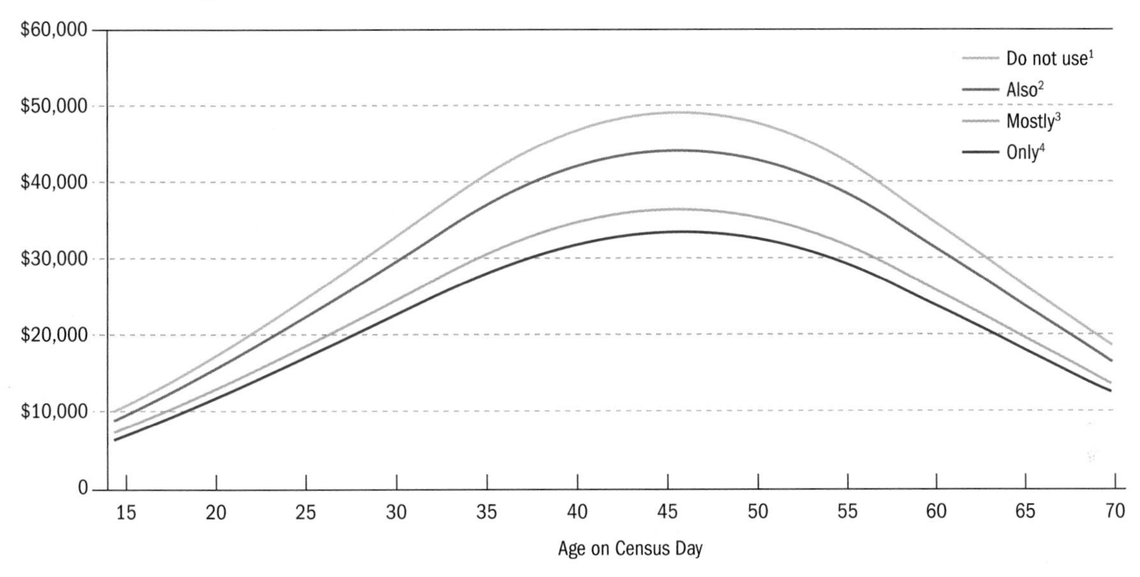

1. Does not use a non-official language at work.
2. Uses an official language most of the time at work, but also regularly uses a non-official language at work.
3. Mostly uses a non-official language at work.
4. Only uses a non-official language at work.

FIGURE 14.7 Predicted Earnings for Married Male Immigrants, Five Years in Canada, with University Education Obtained outside Canada, the US, or Europe: By Use of Non-Official Language at Work

Source: Derrick Thomas, 'The Impact of Working in a Non-Official Language on the Occupations and Earnings of Immigrants in Canada,' *Canadian Social Trends* (2009), Statistics Canada, at <www.statcan.gc.ca/pub/11-008-x/2009001/article/10771-eng.htm>.

- *Language proficiency.* Being proficient in the official language of one's community of residence and workplace is positively correlated with the likelihood of being employed in one's intended occupation. Not being fluent in one of the official languages—and this can include having an accent that interferes with the ability of clients, patients, or co-workers to understand the speaker—can limit an immigrant's employment prospects.
- *Cultural norms.* This is often associated with language proficiency. Communication is not only about understanding the words spoken by someone else. It is also about the unspoken meanings and messages transmitted in everything from a face-to-face conversation to an e-mail message. Not having been raised in the language community and associated culture of the majority may be a disadvantage in terms of communications skills. At any rate, there is little doubt that some Canadian employers will believe this to be the case and may be reluctant to hire an immigrant worker for fear that customers, clients, or patients may not 'connect' with him or her as well as with someone who is more fluent in the mainstream culture.
- *Work experience.* Having worked for 14 years with two employers in Lahore (Pakistan) or for seven years with an employer in Posdan (Poland) may not be viewed seriously by a Canadian employer who has never heard of these places. Even if the places of previous employment are recognized, it would not be surprising if an employer in, say, Calgary placed more confidence in work experience with a company that he or she knows, in Toronto or Victoria, than in a company that

he or she has not heard of, in a market far away. This Catch-22 situation often is the experience of highly educated, skilled immigrant workers. To get the job in Canada one needs experience. But the experience one has is not recognized in Canada. So how is one to acquire the experience needed if what one has is not on a par with experience in Canada or the US?

- *Credentials.* Degrees and professional certification are usually required for a professional or other skilled occupation; however, degrees and certification earned abroad are often not recognized in Canada (sometimes those earned in one province are not recognized in another!). Once in Canada, a highly educated immigrant may have to return to school to acquire a degree, certification, or training that will qualify him or her for the anticipated job. These barriers to the recognition of foreign degrees and certification are not always, and perhaps not even usually, arbitrary and without reasons associated with the competencies expected of a person in a given profession in this country. But in some cases they may be. Ottawa and the provinces have taken steps in recent years to improve the process whereby degrees and qualifications earned abroad are evaluated.[16]

Do these four factors add up to discrimination? This may depend on what one means by discrimination. If one means norms and rules that have as their consequence the differential treatment of individuals on the basis of characteristics that tend to be associated with a person's country of origin—the likelihood of speaking English or French proficiently; the probability that one will have degrees or work experience that are not as readily acknowledged as those earned in Canada—then these rules certainly count as discrimination. Some might argue, however, that these criteria are relevant to a person's ability to perform a job at a high or even reasonable level of competence or in a manner satisfactory to some customers, clients, or patients. Is it discriminatory, they might ask, to place more confidence in one person over another because one understands him or her better or is familiar with the background and credentials of one person but not at all with those of the other? We make choices on the basis of these sorts of considerations all the time. Indeed, in a world of imperfect information, where we cannot know everything that might be relevant to a decision that we need to make and where the costs of acquiring such information may be high, we necessarily rely on what is familiar to us. Just because a decision is based on what does and does not fall into our comfort zone, the range of what we think we know and that is familiar to us, does that make it discriminatory? Here, the answer will depend in part on ideology—conservative or liberal; individualist or communitarian—and in part on which side of the hiring desk one is seated.

Appendix: *Building the Future: A Time for Reconciliation*

(From Bouchard-Taylor Commission, *Rapport de la commission de consultation sur les pratiques d'accommodement reliées aux differences culturelles*, mai 2008, 40–2)

. . . [I]nterculturalism seeks to reconcile ethnocultural diversity with the continuity of the French-speaking core and the preservation of the social link. It thus affords security to Quebecers of French-Canadian origin and to ethnocultural minorities and protects the rights of all in keeping with the liberal tradition. By instituting French as the common public language, it establishes a framework in society for communication and exchanges. It has the virtue of being flexible and receptive to negotiation, adaptation and innovation.

The 11 proposals below allow us to define Québec interculturalism even more precisely.

1. Québec as a nation, as recognized by all Québec political parties and the federal government, is the operational framework for interculturalism.
2. In a spirit of reciprocity, interculturalism strongly emphasizes interaction, in particular

intercommunity action, with a view to overcoming stereotypes and defusing fear or rejection of the Other, taking advantage of the enrichment that stems from diversity, and benefiting from social cohesion.

3. Members of the majority ethnocultural group, i.e. Quebecers of French-Canadian origin, like the members of ethnocultural minorities, accept that their culture will be transformed sooner or later through interaction.
4. Cultural, and, in particular, religious differences need not be confined to the private domain. The following logic underpins this choice: it is healthier to display our differences and get to know those of the Other than to deny or marginalize them.
5. The principle of multiple identities is recognized, as is the right to maintain an affiliation with one's ethnic group.
6. For those citizens who so wish, it is desirable for initial affiliations to survive, since ethnic groups of origin often act as mediators between their members and society as a whole. A general phenomenon arises in this regard: almost without exception, each citizen integrates into society through a milieu or an institution that serves as a link, e.g. the family, a profession, a community group, a church, an association, and so on.
7. Multilingualism is encouraged at the same time as French as the common public language. The debate that opposes the language of identity and the common language (as a simple communication tool) is hardly promising.

   What is important, first and foremost, is the broadest possible dissemination of French, in whatever form.
8. To facilitate the integration of immigrants and their children, it is useful to provide them with the means to preserve their mother tongue, at least at the outset. This helps them to mitigate the shock of immigration by affording them a cultural anchor. It is also a means of preserving the enrichment that stems from cultural diversity.
9. Constant interaction between citizens of different origins leads to the development of a new identity and a new culture. This is what has been happening in Québec in recent decades without altering the cultural position of the majority group or infringing on the culture of minority groups.
10. Under a recent, highly promising orientation from the standpoint of pluralism, the groups present in Québec define themselves with reference to common, often universal, values stemming from their history rather than their ethnic traits. Québec is thus part of an international trend whereby societies choose to integrate diversity in light of shared values.
11. The civic and legal dimensions (and everything that concerns, in particular, non-discrimination) must be regarded as fundamental in interculturalism.

To summarize, we could say that Québec interculturalism *a*) institutes French as the common language of intercultural relations; *b*) cultivates a pluralistic orientation that is highly sensitive to the protection of rights; *c*) preserves the creative tension between diversity and the continuity of the French-speaking core and the social link; *d*) places special emphasis on integration; and *e*) advocates interaction.

Starting Points for Research

Yasmeen Abu-Laban and Christina Gabriel, eds, *Selling Diversity: Immigration, Multiculturalism, Employment Equity and Globalization* (Peterborough, Ont.: Broadview Press, 2002). The editors and contributors argue that social justice objectives associated with diversity have been hijacked by a neo-liberal agenda that views the value of diversity through an economic lens.

Neil Bissoondath, *Selling Illusions: The Cult of Multiculturalism in Canada* (Toronto: Penguin, 2002). The author challenges the prevailing belief that official multiculturalism benefits the ethnic, racial, and other minorities that it purports to help.

Raymond Breton and Jeffrey Reitz, *The Illusion of Difference: Realities of Ethnicity in Canada and the United States* (Toronto: C.D. Howe Institute, 1994). This is one of the very few works that actually attempts to test whether the rate of ethnic assimilation is faster in the United States than in Canada. A useful update is Martin Turcotte, 'Passing on the Ancestral Language', *Canadian Social Trends* 80 (Spring 2006): 20–6.

Will Kymlicka, *Multicultural Odysseys: Navigating the New International Politics of Diversity* (Toronto: Oxford University Press, 2007). This is a very different analysis of multiculturalism from that provided in Bissoondath's *Selling Illusions*. Kymlicka argues that Canadian history equips this country to deal with the challenges of multiculturalism and to successfully pioneer new arrangements, including ways of thinking about citizenship, more appropriate to the sort of society Canada has become.

Phil Ryan, *Multicultiphobia* (Toronto: University of Toronto Press, 2010). A lively analysis of Canadian multiculturalism and its critics.

Review Exercises

1. In January 2003 Statistics Canada announced that it would be asking Canadians to declare their sexual orientation in a national survey. In its 2001 census, Statistics Canada for the first time asked how many people in common-law relationships were of the same sex. Why do you think Canada's official statistics agency would attempt to collect such information? Do you think the information collected on such matters could make a difference for politics and policy?
2. Ethnic and racial profiling involves the practice of singling out people for different and disadvantageous treatment because of their ethnicity or race. Find two or three cases where this has been alleged to be a systematic practice in Canada. You might start by going to the websites of the Canadian Race Relations Foundation <www.crr.ca>, the Canadian Bar Association <www.cba.org>, and the Canadian Civil Liberties Association <www.ccla.org>.
3. Canadians and their leaders usually attribute the comparatively good relations between ethnic communities in Canada to the country's policy of multiculturalism. But some experts on immigration, diversity, and integration argue that Canada's immigration policy, which for several decades has favoured immigrants with higher levels of education and job skills, is the main factor explaining why Canada's pluralist model appears to work better than those in some other democracies. How would you set about testing these claims? Where would you find the data needed to test these propositions?

On 11 June 1929, women were finally declared 'persons' under Canadian law thanks to efforts led by five Alberta women activists known as the 'Famous Five': Emily Murphy, Irene Parlby, Louise McKinney, Henrietta Muir Edwards, and Nellie McClung. Identical sculptures commemorating the five women, by Canadian artist Barbara Paterson, stand on Parliament Hill in Ottawa and in Calgary's Olympic Plaza. Pictured here is the statue of Nellie McClung. © Greg Vickers

15 Women and Politics

In 1929 the Supreme Court of Canada, in the *Persons* case, addressed the question of whether women had the status of persons under certain laws, including those determining who could be a judge. Today, four of the nine justices of the Supreme Court are women. Gender equality was a major issue in Canadian politics from the 1970s to the 1990s. Although the issue may not appear to be as controversial today, this is because of legislative and court victories and important changes in public opinion. Topics in this chapter include the following:

- The extent and causes of female under-representation in politics.
- Early feminism.
- Contemporary feminism.
- Organization.
- Strategies.
- Achievements.
- Attitudes regarding gender.

The Social Construction of Gender Differences

Men and women are biologically different. Although obvious, the social implications of this simple fact have been the subject of enormous controversy. Until a few decades ago, both popular opinion and scientific consensus agreed that the biological attributes of the sexes played a major role in the determination of their respective personality traits, intellectual aptitudes, general abilities, and social roles. Males were considered to be more aggressive, rational, analytical, adventurous, and active than females—and more fitted to leadership roles. Females were generally believed to be more nurturing, emotional, intuitive, cautious, and passive. Nature, not nurture, was considered to be the primary reason for the behavioural and attitudinal differences between males and females and for the social superiority of men over women.

This view was even shared by the first wave of the women's movement. Beginning in the late 1800s, the objectives of this movement focused on extending voting rights to women and on legal and social reforms geared towards the protection of the family and traditional values. The arguments used to support these demands emphasized fairness and morality. Extending voting rights to women and eliminating some of the grosser forms of legal discrimination against them—such as the common law's ambiguity about whether a woman was a person in law, or the law's failure to ensure a woman's right to property acquired during the course of married life—were matters of fundamental justice based on the equal humanity of the sexes. This argument, however, did not challenge the conventional wisdom on the biological determination of gender differences.

Suffragists often allied themselves with organizations promoting such causes as temperance, educational reform, child labour laws, and public service reform (to eliminate corruption). These causes were central to the character of the early women's movement. Groups like the Woman's Christian Temperance Union (WCTU), the National Council of Women of Canada (NCWC), and the Women's Institutes comprised the movement's organizational hub. These organizations supported female suffrage on the grounds that women voters would inject a morally uplifting element into the grubby business of politics. It was in a woman's nature, they argued, to care more about life and the conditions that nurtured it. Extending full democratic rights to women would immediately elevate the prominence of those issues that most concerned the women's movement, including mothers' pensions, minimum wage laws for women, better industrial health and safety standards, prison and family law reform, and more public spending on education. Women were the morally superior sex, and their participation in politics would make the world a better, more civilized place.

These arguments formed the basis of what has come to be called *social feminism* or *maternal feminism*. Far from challenging the notion that gender role differences are the inevitable product of biology, maternal feminists accepted this assumption wholeheartedly. But they turned it from an argument against political rights for women into the basis of their case for political equality. Some of the leaders of the feminist movement, such as Nellie McClung, in fact used both contemporary-sounding and maternal feminism arguments in demanding the vote and social reforms.[1] The mainstream of this first wave of the women's movement, however, was dominated by the more moderate arguments of social feminism and by traditional family and Christian values. Indeed, looking back on women's struggle to achieve political rights, the wonder is that female suffrage was resisted so vigorously and for so long. Although it challenged men's monopoly on public life, the early women's movement did not threaten the social and economic pillars of male dominance.

But the second wave of feminism did. Simone de Beauvoir's declaration that 'One is not born, but rather becomes, a woman'[2] suggests that gender role differences are not inherent. They are socially constructed—passed on and relearned from generation to generation. This is the basic premise of the second wave of the women's movement.

If the real roots of gender inequality lie in the institutionalized practices and cultural norms of society, then the solution must go beyond the formal political equality of the sexes. Anything that promotes stereotyped gender roles that are not based on inherent differences between males and females restricts individual freedom. If one learns that certain careers are not for the members of one's sex, or that child-rearing and homemaking are primarily female responsibilities, this limits one's freedom to choose and to act. Moreover, because many of these stereotyped differences are linked to power relations between men and women, their existence undermines human equality.

This is not the place to attempt the perilous task of resolving the nature versus nurture controversy. It is clear, however, that the inherent differences between males and females are much less significant than used to be believed. In one of the most frequently cited studies on the subject, Maccoby and Jacklin claim that scientific research provides firm support for only four non-physiological differences between the sexes.[3] Three of these differences involve cognitive skills: verbal ability (females better), mathematical ability (males better), and visual-spatial ability (males better). The fourth involves personality: males are more aggressive than females. In the case of both verbal and mathematical ability, differences between the sexes only appear during adolescence, suggesting that social learning may play a role in the development of these skills. All of the four differences claimed by Maccoby and Jacklin are matters of tendency only: for example, males tend to be more aggressive than females and females are more likely than males to excel in verbal ability. A good deal of recent research, however, points to the impact of hormonal changes on the development of male and female brains and suggests that the tendencies identified by Maccoby and Jacklin are more rooted in biology than in social learning.[4]

The debate continues. One of its most controversial aspects involves the relationship of males and females to children. In virtually all societies throughout recorded history women have assumed primary responsibility for raising children. Are females more nurturing and child-oriented by nature? Or is this gender role difference a product of social learning?

Yousuf Karsh, Yousuf Karsh fonds, Library and Archives Canada

Agnes Macphail was elected to the House of Commons for the riding of Grey Southeast in the 1921 federal election, making her the first female MP in Canada. Throughout her political career, Macphail advocated for rural issues, penal reform, and seniors' and workers' rights. Macphail founded the Elizabeth Fry Society of Canada to work on the behalf of women and girls in the criminal justice system, and was the first woman delegate to the League of Nations in Geneva, Switzerland.

The evidence is inconclusive. As prominent an anthropologist as Margaret Mead is cited by both sides of this debate. Based on her study of three primitive societies in New Guinea, the 'early' Mead argued that:

> Many, if not all, of the personality traits which we have called masculine or feminine are as lightly linked to sex as are the clothing, the manners, and the form of headdress that a society at a given period assigns to either sex. . . . the evidence is overwhelmingly in favor of the strength of social conditioning.[5]

But the 'later' Mead had this to say on the subject:

> The mother's nurturing tie to her child is apparently so deeply rooted in the actual biological conditions of conception and gestation, birth and suckling, that only fairly complicated social arrangements can break it down entirely. . . . women may be said to be mothers unless they are taught to deny the child-bearing qualities. Society must distort their sense of themselves, pervert their inherent growth-patterns, perpetrate a series of learning-outrages upon them, before they will cease to want to provide, at least for a few years, for the child they have already nourished for nine months within the safe circle of their own bodies.[6]

The different roles played by men and women in the family and the social learning that prepares them for these roles contribute to the under-representation of women in public life. The question is, are the duties and roles associated with motherhood and homemaking mainly the products of what Mead calls the 'inherent growth-patterns' of females or are they chiefly determined by social learning?

This is an old question. Nearly 150 years ago John Stuart Mill commented on the hypocrisy of society's attitudes towards women. Stripped of its moral pretensions, this attitude, Mill argued, could be summarized as follows: 'It is necessary to society that women should marry and produce children. They will not do so unless they are compelled. Therefore it is necessary to compel them.'[7] Mill was not suggesting that women did not have biological impulses or nurturing tendencies that perhaps in most cases would cause them to assume a disproportionate share of child-rearing and household tasks. His argument was simply that the weight of the law and social convention left them with no choice.

Mill's explanation had two parts. He argued that the subservient condition of a married woman—her lack of rights, standing, and personhood in relation to a husband whom the law and society treated as her master—would not be voluntarily chosen by many women, and certainly not by women capable of doing something else. But at the same time, this form of legalized 'slavery' or 'impressment'—the analogies are Mill's—provided men with a free source of domestic labour. Rather than pay women the 'honest value of their labour',[8] male-dominated society chose to institutionalize this sexual exploitation, at the same time claiming that woman's condition was naturally and even divinely ordained.

According to Mill, men wanted to deny women equal recognition and fair compensation for their domestic labour, simply because most men preferred the status and privileges of master, even if their mastery was limited to the confines of their home. This, argued Mill, was an egotism that inflicted costs on society. By depriving women of opportunities outside of marriage and the home, male-dominated society deprived itself of the talents, intelligence, and contributions of half the population.

Mill's arguments on the social construction of gender differences and the subordination of women were in the tradition of liberal utilitarianism. A rather different angle on women, the family, and power was provided at about the same time by Karl Marx's collaborator, Friedrich Engels.[9]

Engels sought to show that the subservience of women to men within the family and, by extension, in society is based on economic foundations. He argued that the free domestic labour provided by women subsidized capitalist production by reducing the wages that employers had to pay to attract the services of male employers. The male breadwinner/female homemaker family served the interests of the capitalist class because it ensured the reproduction of the working class at low cost. Marxists ever since have pointed out that the values associated with the traditional family also perform an ideological function, helping to ensure the acceptance by subordinate classes and by women of a social system that ensures their subordination. The state actively promoted the sexual exploitation of women within the family through laws restricting the legal and property rights and opportunities of females.

Within the institution of marriage, Engels contended, the relationship between man and woman was analogous to that between the bourgeoisie and the proletariat in society. The property relations that provided the basis for inequalities in power between social classes were mirrored in the relations between husband and wife. It followed from this, he argued, that the emancipation of women required their full integration into society and the economy in order to eliminate their dependence on male wage-earners. Women cannot be dependent and equal at the same time, an argument that became an important part of second-wave feminism.

The Under-representation of Women

Women constitute about 52 per cent of the Canadian population and a slightly larger percentage of the electorate. Despite their numerical superiority, only one female, Kim Campbell, has held the office of Prime Minister, and three, Rita Johnson and Christy Clark in BC and Catherine Callbeck of PEI, have been provincial premiers. Of these four only Callbeck led her party to election victory, although Clark, who gained the premiership in late February 2011 by winning the party leadership after Liberal Premier Gordon Campbell stepped aside, has yet to face the electorate in a general election. The number of women who have been elected to the leadership of political parties in Canada can be counted on the fingers of a couple hands. There are, however, some signs of change. The percentage of female candidates nominated by the major political parties has never been as high as it is today. Women have comprised almost one-quarter of all candidates for the main parties in the five elections since 1993. Just over one-third of all NDP candidates in 2008 were women and an even greater percentage—37 per cent—of Liberal candidates were women (Figure 15.1). In 1989 the NDP became the first major political party to elect a woman as its leader, again choosing a female leader in 1994.

A similar pattern of under-representation is found in the case of non-elected positions within

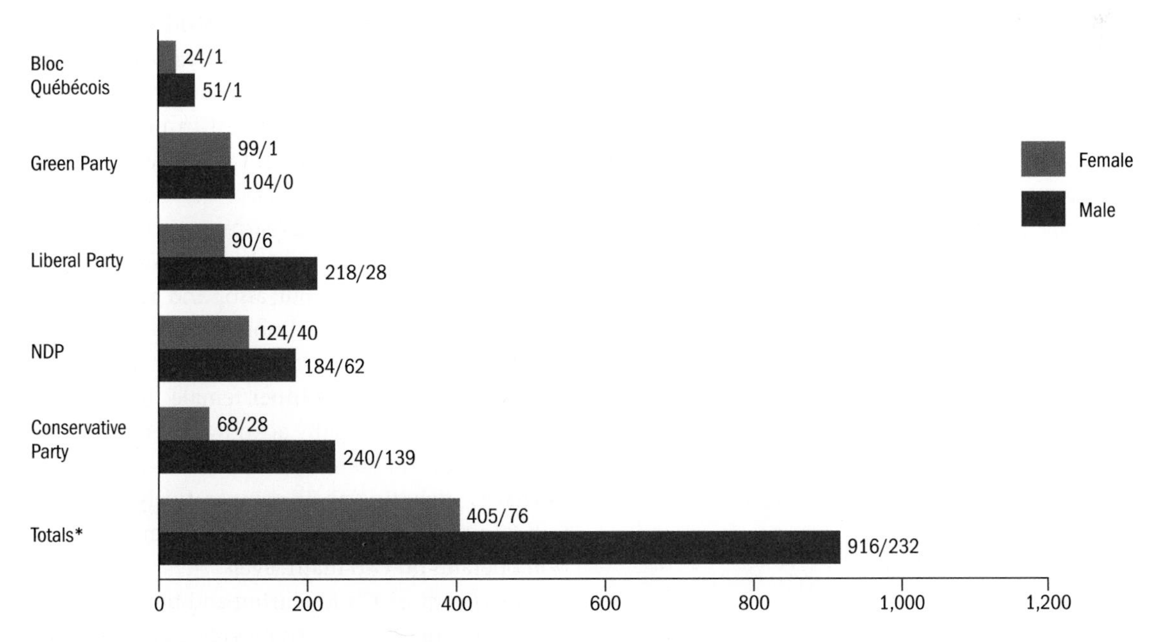

FIGURE 15.1 Gender of Candidates for the Five Main Parties in the 2011 Election

*These totals include only the candidates of these five registered parties in the 2011 election.

Note: The number of male and female candidates for each party is indicated to the right of each bar, followed by the number of male or female candidates actually elected.

Source: Based on data provided in the Report of the Chief Electoral Officer of Canada, 41st General Election (2011).

the state. Before the 1982 appointment of Justice Bertha Wilson, no woman had ever been a member of the Supreme Court of Canada. Since then Justice Claire L'Heureux-Dubé (1987), Justice Beverley McLachlin (1989), Justice Louise Arbour (1999), Justice Marie Deschamps (2002), Justice Rosalie Abella (2004), and Justice Louise Charron (2004) have been appointed to the Supreme Court. Currently, four of the nine Supreme Court justices—Deschamps, Abella, Charron, and Chief Justice McLachlin—are women. Overall, about 40 per cent of federally appointed judges (353 of 863 as of 2010) are women. Significant inroads also have been cut into the senior ranks of the bureaucracy. Women account for about 30 per cent of senior management personnel in the federal public service, and their presence is no longer rare on the topmost rungs of the bureaucratic ladder (deputy ministers and equivalent positions). While it is not uncommon for women to be appointed to the boards of directors of Crown corporations and to hold officer positions in these companies—about one-quarter of senior positions in federal Crowns were held by women as of 2008[10]—few women have ever been the CEOs of major commercially oriented Crowns at either the federal or provincial level. In this respect, Crown corporations such as VIA Rail, the Canadian Wheat Board, Hydro One Networks in Ontario, Hydro-Québec, and the Caisse de dépôt et placement du Québec simply mirror the pattern of female exclusion that characterizes the pinnacle of Canada's corporate elite.

Why are females under-represented in political life? Does it matter that the levers of the state are overwhelmingly in the hands of men? These questions are not new. The reasons behind female under-representation are, however, more easily explained than are its consequences. Let us begin with the relatively uncontroversial part.

Why Aren't More Women Involved in Political Life?

At a superficial level, the riddle of women's under-representation in public life may appear to be simple: they have been less interested than men. Female participation levels have long been about the same as men's for political activities like voting and campaigning, but have been much lower for more demanding activities, such as holding office in a political party and running for office. **'The higher, the fewer'** is how Sylvia Bashevkin describes the political participation gap between males and females.[11] This gap has narrowed over time, but it continues to exist.

If interest is one of the key determinants of participation, what explains different levels of interest? The answer lies in social learning. Traditionally, females learned from the world around them that politics was a predominantly male occupation. The signals were unmistakable. The Prime Minister/President was a man. So, too, were all but a handful of cabinet ministers and elected representatives. More subtle than the evident maleness of the political profession, but probably more important in discouraging most females from seeing themselves in political roles beyond those of voter and perhaps member of the women's auxiliary of Party X, was the sheer weight of social customs and expectations, communicated in the family, in school, in churches, and through the media. Leadership and an active involvement in the world beyond the family and neighbourhood were associated with masculinity. If females were not actively discouraged from developing an interest in politics, they generally were not encouraged to apply their energies and time to such matters.

The influence of social learning was reinforced by the sexual division of labour in society, particularly in the family but also, and relatedly, in the workplace. The traditional male breadwinner/female homemaker family and the more contemporary two breadwinner/female homemaker household are universally acknowledged by feminists as important sources of female subordination to males, including their comparatively marginal status in politics. This subordination/marginalization operates on two main levels.

1. Psychological. Child-rearing and housework are useful and necessary activities. Society's attitude towards them, however, is ambivalent. Because they are forms of unpaid labour, at least when carried out by a household member, no objective yardstick exists for determining their value. And so they tend to be undervalued, particularly in comparison to paid work outside of the home. A good deal of evidence suggests that society's general failure to recognize the value of domestic work, or to praise it while labelling it 'woman's work', generates frustration and low self-esteem among many women.[12] Moreover, the traditional roles of mother and homemaker have often operated to limit women *spatially* (tied to the physical demands of the domestic routine), *cognitively* (the relevant world and its activities are more likely to centre on the family and household than in the case of men), and *emotionally* (expressive, nurturing, caring functions are associated with the homemaker, while instrumental, active, and rational qualities are associated with the breadwinner). In brief, the consciousness that is likely to be produced by the traditional roles of mother and homemaker is not likely to generate the motivations, interests, and personal resources for political activism.

2. *Status and professional achievements*. Traditionally, women have been under-represented in precisely those occupations from which political office-holders tend to be drawn: law, business, and the liberal professions. In the past, their formal educational attainments tended to be less than those of men, and even today they are not found in significant numbers in fields like finance, economics, and engineering, which are important professional backgrounds for many senior positions in the public service. But even when women have made what were and (in some cases like engineering) still are viewed as non-traditional career choices, the likelihood has been great that they have had to take time out from their career and/or not pursue opportunities that would make greater demands on their time or require them to uproot their families because of the expectation that the nurturing of children and household duties will fall primarily to women.

The sexual division of labour within the household, therefore, has worked to reduce women's opportunities to achieve the sorts of experience and professional status that often provide the basis for recruitment into parties and other political organizations. If, however, a woman has the motivation and the status achievements to break into public life, there is still a good chance that the competing pressures of household responsibilities will limit the scope of her aspirations. It is certainly true that males are less likely to feel the constraining tug of these responsibilities than females. The 2001 census found that females accounted for about 65 per cent of all those who claimed to spend at least 15 hours per week on unpaid child care and that females were twice as likely as males to say that they spent at least 15 hours per week on unpaid housework (45 per cent vs 23 per cent).[13]

The traditional male breadwinner/female homemaker family is, of course, much less common than it used to be. About 63 per cent of Canadian women over the age of 15 are in the workforce, and for women 25–44 years old the participation rate climbs to 82.4 per cent (2009), higher than in any other affluent democracy. Canada is followed by Sweden, Australia, the Netherlands, and the United States, all of which had rates between 59 and 61 per cent in 2009. The labour force participation rate for married women with children under six years old is about two-thirds, compared to barely more than one-quarter in 1971. Whereas 65 per cent of Canadian families were one-earner/male-breadwinner families in 1961, barely more than 10 per cent conform to this model today. Although the average female income for full-time workers is still less than three-quarters of that for men (71.3 per cent in 2008, up from 58.4 per cent in 1967), the proportion of women in relatively high-status professions such as law, accounting, and university teaching, and in middle management positions in both the private and public sectors, has increased significantly during the last generation. Labour market experience and time spent with a particular employer are often pointed to as two factors that explain much of the gap between the pay of males and females holding similar jobs. The impact of these factors is minimized by comparing the earnings of younger male and female workers who have recently entered the labour market. According to the 2006 census, females between the ages of 25 and 29 earned about 85 per cent of what their male counterparts earned, up from 75 per cent in 1980. Nonetheless, the traditional sexual division of household labour still places limits on women's opportunities for political participation that men are less likely to experience.

Women in Politics

Women were active in politics before being entitled to vote and run for office. Much of this activity was aimed at achieving full citizenship rights for women. But this was far from being the sole concern of women's groups during the pre-suffrage era. They were also active in demanding a long list of social reforms ranging from pensions for widowed mothers to non-militaristic policies in international relations. By contemporary standards, however, the early women's movement was small and politically weak. Moreover, its demands and values—although radical in the context of the times—today appear to have been quite moderate and in some cases even reactionary.

Although the women's movement of today looks and sounds very different from early versions, elements of continuity span the movement's history. In tracing the history of women's political involvement in Canada, we will focus on the social and ideological forces that have influenced the women's movement, as well as the issues, organizations, strategies, and accomplishments that have characterized the movement at different points in time.

Phase One: The Contradictions of Democracy and Industrialization

Feminist writings and occasional incidents of women mobilizing around particular events or issues before the nineteenth century were quite

Although all political parties today nominate many more female candidates than a generation ago, almost three-quarters of all candidates for the four main parties in the 2008 election were men.

rare. The democratic impulses released by the overthrow of absolute monarchy in Britain (1688) and by the American (1776) and French revolutions (1789) generated some agitation for equality of political rights, but their consequences in regard to social change were negligible. One early feminist, Olympe de Gouges in France, argued in *Declaration of the Rights of Women and the Citizen* (1791) that patriarchy was the source of society's ills, but for challenging the patriarchal assumptions inherent in the French Revolution she received the equality of the guillotine during the 1793 Reign of Terror.[14] Although married women did have the right to vote in some societies, they were expected to follow the lead of their husbands—particularly during an era before the secret ballot. In matters of law and property, a woman was subsumed under the person of her father and, after marriage, her husband. This state of affairs had been the focus of calls for reform by late eighteenth-century feminists such as de Gouges and England's Mary Wollstonecraft.

The origins of the women's movement as social action usually are located in the mid-nineteenth century. As Sheila Rowbotham writes, 'Feminism came, like socialism, out of the tangled, confused response of men and women to capitalism.'[15] The progress of capitalism produced both affluence and misery. As more and more people crowded into the cities whose growth was spawned by factory production, a new set of social problems arose. Working-class women, girls, and children were employed in many industries. In fact, their cheap labour provided the basis for the profitability of such industries as textiles, clothing, footwear, and cigar-making. As historian Terry Copp observes:

> Large numbers of working class women were 'emancipated' from the bondage of unpaid labour at home long before their middle class counterparts won entry into male-dominated high income occupations. There was no need to struggle against an exclusionist policy, since employers were only too happy to provide opportunities for women in the factories, shops, and garment lofts of the city.[16]

Hard numbers on female participation in the workforce do not exist before twentieth-century census-takers began to keep track of such things. It has been estimated, however, that women comprised about 20 per cent of the labour force in Montreal during the 1890s. There is no reason to think that the percentage was lower in other cities. The low wages they were invariably paid put downward pressure on the wages of all unskilled working people.

Working conditions in most manufacturing establishments were hard, to say the least. There were no laws regulating the hours of work, minimum wages, or safety and sanitation in the workplace. A disabling injury on the job usually meant personal financial disaster. While both men and women suffered under these conditions, the exposure of women—usually single—to the harsh environment of the factory and sweatshop was considered more serious because of the era's views on femininity. A woman's natural place was considered to be the home, and her participation in the wage economy was believed, by political reactionaries and social reformers alike, to be 'one of the sad novelties of the modern world . . . a true social heresy'.[17]

Early industrialization took its toll on women in other ways as well. The brutal grind and crushing squalor that characterized the lives of many working people could be numbed through drink. And in an era before heavy 'sin taxes', beer and spirits were very cheap. Alcohol abuse, although by no means restricted to the working class, was one of the side effects of the long hours of work, inadequate wages, and sordid workplace conditions characteristic of workers' lives. It not only contributed to the ruin of individuals, but to the suffering of their families. Poor sanitation, overcrowding in improperly ventilated housing, and improper diet combined to produce low life expectancy—tuberculosis was a major killer among the urban working class—and high infant mortality.

The harshness of early industrialization was experienced by both men and women. Its manifestations—child labour, poverty, alcohol abuse—became central issues in the early women's movement because of their perceived impact on the family and on prevailing standards of decency. The

Woman's Christian Temperance Union, the Young Women's Christian Association, and the Women's Institutes that sprang up in cities across Canada starting in the late nineteenth century were keenly aware of the clash between the material conditions of working-class women and prevailing notions of femininity and family. The social reforms they urged on government were intended to protect women and the family from what they saw as the corrosive influences of industrial life.

Early feminism, however, was not merely a response to the contradictions that industrialization created for women. The achievement of democracy was also full of contradictions. If democracy was a system of government based on the will of the people, that recognized the equal humanity and dignity of human beings, half of the population could not be denied the rights and status enjoyed by the other half.

As John Stuart Mill observed in his essay *On the Subjection of Women*, arguments against the political and legal equality of the sexes took several forms. The principal arguments, and Mill's refutations (*in italic*), included the following:

- Unlike the slavery of one race by another, or the subordination of a defeated nation by its military conqueror, the subjection of women to men is natural. *When hasn't the subordination of one category of the human race by another been labelled 'natural' by members of the dominant group? What is said to be natural turns out to be, on closer examination, merely customary.*
- Unlike other forms of domination, the rule of men over women is accepted voluntarily by the female population. *This is not true. Some women do not accept the subordinate lot of their sex. And if a majority appear to acquiesce in their second-class status, this should surprise no one. From their earliest years women are trained in the habits of submission and learn what male-dominated society expects of them.*
- Granting equal rights to women will not promote the interests of society. *What this means, in fact, is that equality will not promote the interests of male society. It is a mere argument of convenience and self-interest.*
- What good could possibly come from extending full political and legal rights to women? *Leaving aside the good that this would produce for women—for their character, dignity, and material conditions—all society would benefit from a situation where the competition for any particular vocation is determined by interest and capabilities. Society loses when any group is barred from contributing its talents to humanity. Finally, equality for women would improve the character of men, who would no longer enjoy the sense of being superior to one-half of the human race because of an accident of birth, rather than to any merit or earned distinction on their part.*

Despite Mill's compelling arguments for equality, men who would have been shocked at the imputation that they were anything but democratic continued to ignore and resist demands that women be treated as full citizens. The arguments used to deny political rights for women were intellectually flabby and often amounted to nothing more than 'nice women do not want the vote' or 'my wife doesn't want the vote'.[18] But the logic of democratic rights is universal, and the exclusion of the female half of the population from the enjoyment of these rights was one of the major contradictions of most democracies until well into the twentieth century (see Table 15.1).

The early women's movement focused mainly on three sets of issues: political rights, legal rights, and social reform. Anti-militarism was a fourth, but less prominent, issue on the political agenda of feminists. The social feminism mainstream of the movement was concerned chiefly with what it perceived as threats to the security of women and the family and to the traditional values associated with them. The demands made by organizations like the WCTU and YWCA and by prominent feminists like Nellie McClung were based solidly on the middle-class morality of the times.

The dominant middle-class morality could, and eventually did, accommodate itself to political rights for women. 'Respectable' feminists were those who consented to play by the rules of the game as they found it. Political rights for women were expected to make the political parties and government more sensitive to issues of concern to women, such as working conditions for females, child labour, alcohol abuse, and pensions for widowed mothers. Legal rights enabling a married woman to own property in her own name or protecting her from disinheritance in the event of her husband's death were demanded in order to provide more economic security for women and their dependent children. Such social reforms as the prohibition of alcohol sales, family allowances, more humane conditions in women's prisons, and labour legislation dealing with women and children were expected to produce a more civilized, compassionate society. Finally, peace issues within the women's movement were tied directly to the image of woman as the giver and nurturer of life, to what were believed to be the maternal instincts of women.

The mainstream of the women's movement was represented by organizations like the Woman's Christian Temperance Union, the Young Women's Christian Association, the National Council of Women of Canada, and the Federated Women's Institutes. They were politically moderate organizations in terms of both their goals and their strategies for attaining them. Indeed, it would be fair to say that the goals of social feminism were fundamentally conservative, aimed at protecting women and the family from the corrosive influences of the industrial age. The political discourse of the movement drew upon the middle-class morality of the times. Even Nellie McClung, who was considered a firebrand of the movement, did not in the least suggest that the social roles of man the provider and woman the nurturer be changed. Instead, McClung and most other leaders of the early women's movement wanted to put women's role on a more secure material footing.

The political tactics employed by mainstream women's groups hardly ever strayed beyond the familiar bounds of accepted practice. Unlike their sisters in Great Britain and the United States, Canadian **suffragists** did not resort to such confrontational methods as chaining themselves to the fences surrounding Parliament, physically resisting the police, or hunger strikes. Instead, they relied on petitions to government and efforts to persuade public opinion.

TABLE 15.1 Women's Suffrage

Year	Number of countries where men and women could vote in national elections on equal terms
1900	1
1910	3
1920	15
1930	21
1940	30
1950	69
1960	92
1970	127
1975	129
2010	Almost all*

*Elections are held in all but a handful of the world's countries. Only Saudi Arabia, among countries that hold elections, denies women the vote.

Sources: Kathleen Newman, *Women in Politics: A Global Review* (Washington: Worldwatch Institute, 1975), 8; Inter-Parliamentary Union, at: www.ipu.org>.

After about 40 years of campaigning, the first success came in Manitoba in 1916. The other three western provinces and Ontario followed suit within about a year. In the Maritimes, where the suffrage movement was comparatively weak, the achievement of political rights for women was preceded by much less agitation than in the West. Nova Scotia (1918), New Brunswick (1919), PEI (1922), and Newfoundland (1925) extended political rights to women, although in the case of New Brunswick, women were granted only voting rights. They could not hold provincial public office until 1934. Quebec was the straggler among Canada's provinces. Opposition from the Catholic Church blocked political rights for women until 1940.

Nationally, women became citizens between 1917 and 1919. The Wartime Elections Act of 1917 extended voting rights to the relatively small number of women serving in the military and to the much larger pool of females whose male relatives were in military service. This was broadened in 1918 to include all women aged 21 years and over. The right to hold office in the House of Commons followed a year later, although women appeared to be barred from entry into the non-elected Senate and from holding other appointive public offices, such as judgeships, by virtue of not qualifying as 'persons', as this term was understood in law.

Absurd though it may seem, the personhood of women was considered to be dubious in the years following their enfranchisement.[19] Two prime ministers rejected calls for the appointment of a woman to the Senate on the grounds that women, not being persons as understood in law, were not eligible. The right of females to sit as judges was challenged in the handful of cases where they were appointed to the bench. After a couple of provincial rulings in their favour, the question was placed before the Supreme Court of Canada in 1927. Feminists were shocked when the Court ruled that the legal meaning of 'persons' excluded females.

This decision was reversed on appeal by the Judicial Committee of the Privy Council. Its ruling was blunt: 'The exclusion of women from all public offices is a relic of days more barbarous than ours . . . and to ask why the word [person] should include females, the obvious answer is, why should it not?'[20] While logic and justice won the day in this particular legal battle, women have lost a number of others in the courts. Indeed, some contemporary feminists express strong doubts about the courts and law as vehicles for achieving the movement's goals. Voting rights for women and formal access to the male world of politics and the professions did not change the fact that society still viewed a woman's place as being in the home. Social feminists never really challenged this belief.

Political rights for women might have provided the basis for the reforms envisaged by feminists if two conditions had existed: (1) a sufficient number of voters were prepared to cast their ballots for candidates and parties who supported the reforms advocated by the women's movement; and (2) a political vehicle existed to articulate the movement's agenda and provide a feminist alternative in electoral politics. Indeed, it appears to have been the belief of many in the women's suffrage movement that the major political parties either would crumble when a flood of independent candidates was elected or would tremble submissively before the demands of reform-minded female voters. But in fact the parties continued to set the agenda of electoral politics along the familiar lines that had long served them so well. That the parties felt no need to respond to the agenda of the women's movement or to recruit more women into their inner circles showed how slight was the impact of feminism on public consciousness.

The major parties' indifference to the demands of the women's movement was matched by the movement's distrust of the party system. Early feminists were reluctant to rely on the established political parties as vehicles for reform. There were two main reasons for this. One involved the attitude of

Library and Archives Canada/C-008408

Cairine Wilson became Canada's first woman senator after her appointment by Prime Minister William Lyon Mackenzie King in February 1930, four months after the 1929 ruling in the case initiated by the Famous Five declared women persons under the law, thereby making them eligible to sit in the Senate. She served until her death in 1962.

the parties. It was not simply that the Liberal and Conservative parties showed little enthusiasm for the goals of the women's movement, including political rights for women; they were often dismissive and even hostile towards women's concerns and those expressing them. So after achieving the same formal political rights as men, women found that little of substance had changed. They were marginalized within parties dominated by men who, in the words of Canada's first female MP, Agnes Macphail, 'Want to Hog Everything'.[21] This was not surprising. The parties reflected the dominant beliefs of the time, beliefs that made women in public life—or in any of what were traditionally male preserves—appear an oddity. Even the more egalitarian of Canada's male politicians were not immune from sexism when it came to women in politics. J.S. Woodsworth, at the time a Labour MP from Winnipeg, probably summed up male politicians' grudging acceptance of women in *their* game when he said, 'I still don't think a woman has any place in politics.'[22]

A second reason why early feminists were reluctant to work within the framework of the party system was that their movement, like the farmers' movement of the same era, was issue-based. The organizations that formed the core of the movement took hard, uncompromising positions on issues like prohibition, political rights for women, and social reform. Political parties, the two major ones at least, were based on principles that rejected the issue-based approach. One of these principles was partisan loyalty, the chief manifestation of which was the sheep-like obedience of elected members to the policy positions established by their party's leaders. Feminists wanted to be able to take positions based on their perception of what was in the interests of women without having to compromise the movement's goals. This concept of direct representation was shared by the farmers' movement of the time but was discouraged by the partisan rules of British parliamentary government.

The anti-party inclinations of feminists were reinforced by the parties' tendency to avoid if possible, and fudge, if avoidance was not possible, issue stances that might alienate important groups of voters. This has been called 'brokerage politics' (see Chapter 10). It is an approach that had no appeal to single-issue groups like prohibitionists and suffragists, or to the reform-minded women's movement more generally.

But working outside the established party system and the legislature, in an era when the media were less effective channels for political influence than they are today, carried heavy costs. A legislator who sits as an independent is marginalized in British parliamentary government, not sharing in the opportunities for participation available to the members of political parties. Moreover, the organizational and financial resources of the parties are important advantages that their candidates have over independents. It very quickly became apparent that non-partyism could not be made to work in practice.

Phase Two: After the Vote, What?

'Is Women's Suffrage a Fizzle?' asked a 1928 article in *Maclean's*. The question reflected the disillusionment experienced by many in the women's movement only years after having won the vote. Little, it seemed, had changed. Men still dominated the political process. The issues that interested women's groups, with the exception of prohibition, were no more prominent than before women's suffrage. And despite having the same formal political rights as men, women were still viewed as a not-quite-appropriate oddity in public life, rather like a dog walking on its hind legs. The dog can do it, but it's unnatural and, anyway, what is the point?

Part of the disappointment felt by feminists was due to their unrealistic expectations. Those who spearheaded the fight for women's suffrage believed—wrongly as it turned out—that the vote would be the tool that women would use to change the world. As Nellie McClung put it, 'Women have cleaned up things since time began; and if women ever get into politics there will be a cleaning out of pigeon-holes and forgotten corners, on which the dust of years has fallen, and the sound of the political carpet-beater will be heard in the land.'[23] When the millennial expectations of social feminists were not met, worse than this, when hardly anything appeared to have changed after the victory that was supposed to change so much, frustration and gloom were natural reactions.

It is usual to treat the period from suffrage to the new feminism that gained momentum in the 1960s as one long hiatus in the women's movement.[24] A small number of women did run for public office, and an even smaller number won election. Of those elected or appointed to public office, some achieved national prominence. Among them were Ottawa mayor Charlotte Whitton, five-term MP and two-term Ontario MPP Agnes Macphail, British Columbia judges Emily Murphy and Helen Gregory MacGill, and Conservative cabinet minister Ellen Louise Fairclough. But the distinction of being the first woman to enter what had been an exclusive preserve of men, or to achieve recognition for one's talents and capabilities, had little impact on the political and social status of women in general. The breakthroughs and accomplishments of a few stood in sharp contrast to the unchanged status of the many. A number of plausible reasons help to explain this lack of change, chief among them the nature of early feminism, the party system, and societal attitudes.

The nature of early feminism. The mainstream of the women's movement was essentially

'I don't object to women running for prime minister . . . as long as it's just to kiss him.'

One significant obstacle for women's participation in politics has been overcoming traditional thinking about gender roles.

conservative. Far from wanting to break down traditional **gender roles**, social feminists wanted to protect the social values and family structure on which they rested. Early feminists tended to believe that the political subordination of women was based on their inferior political and legal rights. What they failed to see was that traditional gender roles in the family, the workplace, and other social settings prevented women from participating more fully and effectively in public life.

The party system. We have already explained how the anti-party stance of feminist reformers proved difficult to maintain once they became part of a parliamentary process that was based on partisanship. This was not, however, the only impact that the party system had on women's political involvement. Within the two traditional parties, as well as the CCF-NDP, women's involvement was organized around support services. The women's auxiliary or club was the symbol of the complementary role that women were encouraged to play in political parties dominated by men. These separate organizations for women actually predated women's suffrage by a few years.[25] By the 1960s, this segregation of active male roles from supportive female roles—essentially an extension of the gender relations that existed within the family and society—was increasingly seen as an impediment to the equal and effective participation of women in politics.

Societal attitudes. Feminism failed to make a greater mark on social attitudes in part because the social feminist mainstream of the women's movement did not challenge conventional ways of thinking about appropriate gender roles. Outside of the mainstream was a more radical feminist fringe, what William O'Neill calls 'hard-core feminists',[26] who were not satisfied with the political rights and the social reforms that constituted the agenda of social feminism. Hard-core feminists such as Flora MacDonald Denison demanded the legal emancipation of women and sexual equality in education, employment, the family: in short, wherever women were systematically subordinated to men.[27] Their ideas were not, however, considered to be 'respectable'.

If mainstream feminism was a weak force in Canadian politics, which it was, hard-core feminism barely scratched the surface of public life and political discourse. Its more radical critique of female subordination was marginalized in left-wing political organizations, which themselves were on the near-irrelevant periphery of Canadian politics. Even within the CCF, the only left-wing political organization that managed to occupy an important place in Canadian politics, hard-core feminism ran up against some intransigent barriers. As historian Joan Sangster writes:

> [E]vidence indicates that women were channelled into [the CCF's] social committees; that women's feminine character was often described as emotional and sensitive, implying a female inability to cope with the 'rational' world of politics; and that women were seen as more apathetic and politically backward than men. Perhaps most important of all, because women's primary responsibility for the family was never questioned, an essential barrier to women's wholehearted participation in politics remained unchallenged and unchanged.[28]

But this raises the question of why social attitudes about gender roles were slow in changing. It is a complex issue that cannot be reduced to a single explanation. We would argue, however, that the ability of women to exert some greater degree of control over their reproductive role was a chief factor contributing to this change. Fairly reliable contraceptive devices became widely available and used during the 1950s (mainly condoms and diaphragms) and the 1960s (the birth control pill). It was no coincidence that women began to have fewer children. Smaller families and the ability to be sexually active without fear of becoming pregnant provided the opportunity for women to stay in school longer or participate in the workforce for more years of their reproductive lives. Choice in the realm of reproduction was a crucial material condition for **women's liberation** in other aspects of life.

The pill made it possible, but not inevitable. We still need to understand why the second wave of feminism that became a political force in the 1960s—it already was something of an intellectual force, influenced by writers like Margaret Mead and Simone de Beauvoir—was more critical and, as it turned out, more effective than the early women's movement. The explanation has three parts: sexuality, secularism, and economics.

Sexuality had been the deafening silence of the first wave of feminism. The entire topic of sexuality was shrouded in mystery and taboo before the 1960s. The decades since then have been marked by a much greater willingness to talk about sexuality and acknowledge its importance in social relationships. This was a necessary step that opened the way for public debate on such matters as reproductive rights and women's control of their bodies, pornography's possible impact on violence against women, and sexual stereotyping in education and the media.

Sexuality was not entirely in the closet before the 1960s. The subject had received considerable attention from intellectuals since Sigmund Freud based the totality of human experience on males' and females' different struggles to resolve the conflict between their libidinal drives (sexual energy) and the demands of the super-ego (society's expectations and taboos on behaviour). It is no accident that virtually every major intellectual leader of feminism's second wave took direct aim at Freud and what they saw as the patriarchal bias of twentieth-century psychology.[29] Essentially, they argued that Freudian psychology was phallocentric, and that concepts like the 'castration complex', 'penis envy', and 'masculinity complex' were pseudo-scientific justifications for male dominance, not biologically rooted facts of the human condition.

Once conventional beliefs about sexuality were challenged, this opened the door to a re-examination of traditional gender roles and stereotypes throughout society. The position taken by modern feminists was that these roles and their accompanying stereotypes were mainly social constructions rather than facts of nature. This was the reasoning that underlay the movement's slogan, **'The personal is political'**. Conventional beliefs about female passivity, maternal instincts, and home-centredness were argued to be the ideological foundations, and the traditional division of labour in the home, workplace, church, and other supposedly non-political settings were the structural foundations, of women's political subordination. Differences that had been largely accepted and even promoted by women espousing **maternal feminism** earlier in the century were flatly rejected by the new feminism of the sixties.

Secularism was a second factor that contributed to the changed character of second-wave feminism. Many of the leading individuals in the first wave of feminism had been women of strong religious conviction and even fervour. As well, some of the key organizations in the suffrage and social feminism movements, such as the WCTU, the Imperial Order of the Daughters of the Empire, and the National Council of Women of Canada, had either direct links or an affinity of views with some of the Protestant churches. Early feminism had strong ties to the social gospel movement of the period between the 1890s and the 1930s, a movement that 'attempt[ed] to apply Christianity to the collective ills of an industrializing society'.[30] Those in the social gospel movement, like the early feminist leaders, believed that a New Jerusalem could be created on earth through social reforms. Their Christianity was secular insofar as it focused on changing conditions in the here and now. But their vision of reform was inspired by traditional Christian ideals.[31]

The second wave of the women's movement was secular in both its goals and inspiration. Its worldly character was broadly in tune with the changed social climate of the post-fifties world, where the traditional moral authority of religion was weaker than previously. In fact, traditional religious values regarding the family, procreation, and appropriate behaviour for males and females, as well as the patriarchal authority structures of most churches, were targets of feminist criticism. While some of the women's movement's earlier leaders, for example, Nellie McClung,[32] had been outspokenly critical of certain church teachings and practices, they had generally embraced traditional moral values, not seeing them as impediments to equality for women.

Economic change was a third factor that influenced the second wave of the women's movement. Women had long constituted an important part of the labour force. Single women in particular provided a pool of very cheap labour in some manufacturing and service industries. The unpaid domestic work of women helped to subsidize the private economy by reducing the price that employers would otherwise have had to pay to male employees. Moreover, women constituted what has been called a 'reserve army' of labour that could be mobilized in unusual circumstances, as during the two world wars. Their participation in the wage economy was limited, however, by two conventional beliefs: women should not take jobs that could be held by men, and outside employment was fine for single women but should stop after marriage.

These constraints began to weaken during the 1950s and 1960s. As Figure 15.2 shows, the labour force participation rate of women (i.e., the percentage of working-age women who hold jobs or are looking for jobs outside the home) increased dramatically between 1951 and 1971. Most of this increase was the result of an explosion in the number of married women working outside the home. Their participation rate increased 300 per cent over these 20 years. Women's share of the total labour force also increased sharply.

A number of explanations have been offered for this increased participation rate. Economists have favoured three main arguments:

- Falling real family incomes have compelled women to enter the workforce to maintain the household's purchasing power. (This explanation is more plausible for the period since the 1980s. Real incomes for individual workers increased between the 1950s and the 1970s, the period during which the greatest increase in female labour force participation occurred.)
- Labour-saving household appliances and higher female educational attainment have produced feelings of boredom and dissatisfaction in the home, leading more and more women to seek outside employment.
- As the real wages associated with some 'female' jobs increased, outside employment appeared increasingly attractive to women.

There is doubtless some truth in each of these explanations. But as is so often true of conventional economics, it misses the mark by ignoring the obvious. Women had become increasingly restive with their traditional role. Betty Friedan called this 'the problem that has no name'.[33] Although difficult to label and express in a culture that told women they should feel fulfilled in the home, the problem amounted to this: 'I want something more than my husband and my children and my home.'[34] A paying job was often seen to be that

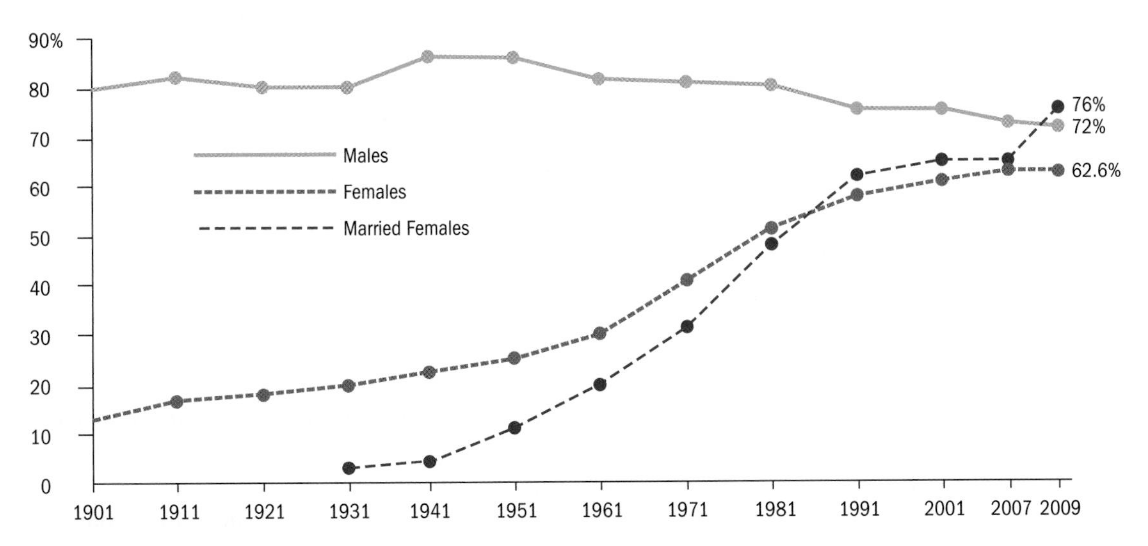

FIGURE 15.2 Labour Force Participation Rates, Ages 15 and Older, 1901–2009

Source: F.H. Leacy, ed., *Historical Statistics of Canada*, 2nd edn (Ottawa: Supply and Services Canada, 1983), D107–22 and D31–48; Statistics Canada, *Labour Force Annual Averages*, Catalogue no. 71-220 annual; Statistics Canada on-line data at: <www.statscan.ca>.

'something more'.

Yet another factor, however, should not be ignored. Most of the new jobs created in advanced industrial economies since World War II have been in service industries. Many of these jobs have been relatively low-paying ones that have been traditionally viewed as female occupations. Expansion of the service economy thus produced an increase in the supply of the clerical, secretarial, retail sales, cashier/teller, and food service jobs that were predominantly held by females. Many economists have a difficult time dealing with this factor because their model of the economic world says that if the demand for something increases, in this case secretaries and so on, the price should also increase. This did not happen—underpaid 'female' occupations remained underpaid—because of conventional beliefs that undervalued the work performed by women, seeing it as temporary or merely a supplement to the main (male) breadwinner's income. The world of work is a central part of modern feminism's reform agenda.

Of course, the exploitation of female workers had been an important concern of social feminists, but they never questioned the belief that a married woman's proper place was in the home and that marriage was the most desirable estate for a woman. By the 1960s, the material basis of these conventional views had become shaky. The economic forces that caused a growing number of married women to seek wage employment, combined with the psychological impetus for women to seek fulfillment beyond their homemaker role, changed the nature of women's involvement in the economy. The reality of their segregation into low-pay, low-prestige occupations[35] became less and less palatable to women as their participation in the wage economy increased.

Phase Three: The Personal Is Political

The decade of the fifties was like the quiet before the storm. Post-war economic growth and the 'baby boom' combined to reinforce traditional gender roles and stereotypes. Television sitcoms, films, and popular magazines almost unfailingly portrayed the male breadwinner/female homemaker family as the pinnacle of human happiness. Once women had achieved political rights, it seemed that equality was no longer an issue.

The syrupy bliss of the era, it turned out, was an illusion. By the early sixties voices of discontent were being increasingly heard. Women were challenging the deep-seated beliefs and social structures that limited their participation in the male-dominated world. The 'problem that has no name' was being named, and the name was **sexism**. This word is not found in dictionaries before the 1970s, a fact that reflected the unconscious acceptance by most people of gender role differences as natural and even desirable. 'Sexism' was coined in the 1960s as a label for behaviour that treated males and females unequally for no better reason than their sexuality. Sexism in its numerous forms and wherever it took place was the target of the women's movement that emerged during these years.

The revival of the women's movement was the result of several factors. Intellectually, writers like Simone de Beauvoir in France, Germaine Greer in Britain, and Betty Friedan and Gloria Steinem in the United States were developing a powerful analysis of women's subordination to men. Their critique went far beyond matters of political and legal rights and social reform, the chief concerns of earlier feminists. Instead, they exposed the social, cultural, and economic roots of inequality. Friedan's approach was typical in its range. In *The Feminine Mystique* (1963) she traced the causes of female subordination to the family, the social sciences (particularly psychology, sociology, and anthropology), education, advertising and the media, mass consumption capitalism, and sexual mores.

Anti-establishment ideas always face an uphill struggle. They never triumph by their intellectual weight alone. What saved the feminist critiques of Beauvoir, Friedan, and company from the fate of many interesting but ultimately ineffectual intellectual movements were the supportive material conditions and social climate of the 1960s. With about one out of every three women of working age employed outside the home, including about one out of five married women (1961), and increasing numbers of women enrolled in post-secondary education,[36] sexual double standards were increasingly apparent to more women than ever before. Articles on the dilemmas facing the 'new woman', telling her how to juggle family, romance, and job, became standard fare in women's magazines like *Chatelaine* and *Redbook*. Terms such as 'women's lib' and 'women's libbers' were more frequently said with a sneer than not, and most women (and men) probably would not have recognized the names of people like Betty Friedan and Germaine Greer. Nevertheless, modern feminism's argument that the personal is political, that the fight for gender equality had to be waged in the workplace, the media, the schools, and over women's bodies, struck a responsive chord with many.

What the lived experience of women confirmed, the social climate of the 1960s encouraged. This was the era of the civil rights movement in the United States, mounting opposition to American military involvement in Vietnam, and anti-establishment political causes generally. Attacks on the 'establishment' and its values were common. Student radicalism, protest marches, sit-ins, and occasional violence were the visible signs of a reaction against the status quo. While the feminist movement did not spearhead the protest movements of the 1960s, it profited from the tendency of these movements to see all established power relations as unjust.

The protest politics of the 1960s affected the women's movement in a second, more enduring way as well. Civil rights advocates in the United States argued that **affirmative action** programs were necessary to provide real equality of opportunity for blacks. Quotas and preferential hiring policies for targeted minorities were justified, they reasoned, because these groups were the victims of a systemic discrimination that ensured that few of them would acquire the formal qualifications—degrees, professional school admission scores, job-relevant experience—needed to compete with the members of more advantaged groups. The opponents of affirmative action—reverse discrimination as they were more likely to call it—charged that such a policy just shifted the burden of injustice onto the shoulders of the qualified members of advantaged groups who were not personally responsible for the plight of the minority groups targeted for special treatment. But despite considerable opposition, affirmative action policies were widely adopted by governments and educational institutions in the United States.

The arguments and demands of the North American women's movement bear a strong resemblance to those that emerged during the struggle to advance the rights of American blacks. Affirmative action does not have nearly the same prominence in several of the Western European democracies. Part of the explanation for this may have to do with lower barriers to the participation of women in politics and the professions in some European societies than in North America. Also, many European countries have more supportive structures, such as publicly financed schools that accept children from the age of two or younger, enabling women to continue their careers with minimal interruption. But an important part of the answer is the influence that the American civil rights movement has had on the demands of the women's movement and the response of policy-makers. Affirmative action for women borrows arguments and policy measures that were pioneered in the struggle to increase the economic and social status of blacks in the United States.

Although Canada had no first-hand experience with racially based affirmative action policies before the 1960s, the concept and practice were not totally imported. Language policies adopted in Quebec during the 1970s aimed to increase the representation of francophones in the managerial ranks of that province's economy through agreements negotiated between the government and private companies. At the federal level, the period from the early 1970s saw an increasing number of administrative positions designated officially bilingual. This policy had the practical effect of favouring francophones who, more often than anglophones, had bilingual skills. During the 1980s, Ottawa began the practice of setting 'targets'—the word 'quotas' was and continues to be rejected—for the representation of particular groups in specified categories of the public service, and eventually of linking the performance evaluation of senior bureaucrats to their success in hitting these targets.

The logic of affirmative action was not, therefore, foreign to Canada. Language policies, in

Quebec and nationally, incorporated elements of such an approach by the mid-1970s. Not only was the discourse of group rights already familiar in Canada, largely because of the struggles over language policies and Quebec's constitutional status, but the logic and machinery of targeting groups for preferred treatment were already embedded in the Canadian state.

Contemporary feminism is different from the first wave of the women's movement in more than its analysis and aims. The organizational network of women's groups became much more developed than when female suffrage and social reform were the key issues. Moreover, the movement's strategies have distinguished it from its predecessor. We turn now to an examination of the organizations, strategies, and achievements of modern feminism.

Organizing for Influence

Women have long been active in Canadian politics. As may be seen in Appendix 1 to this chapter, several important women's organizations date from the pre-suffrage era. Moreover, the political parties provided a channel—though not a very effective one—for women's participation in political life. Over the last several decades these organizations have been joined by hundreds more, as the organizational network of the women's movement has proliferated. This proliferation has generated, in response, new state structures to deal with 'women's issues' and the groups expressing them.

While the network of women's groups has become denser, some argue that a focus on formal organizations and the structures of women's political involvement is misleading. Historian Anne Firor Scott suggests that there has been a long but 'invisible' history of women's struggles against practices and conditions they wanted changed.[37] Many Canadian feminists agree.[38] They maintain that a female political culture operates through contacts and consciousness at the community level—based around issues that affect women in their daily lives—and that it does not rely on the formal political institutions and decision-making processes dominated by men. These grassroots activities tend to be overlooked and undervalued because the dominant political culture 'puts a premium on formal, institutionalized political processes, predictable and regulated levels and types of participation and both bureaucratic and hierarchical structures.'[39] Some argue that women's influence diminishes and their perspective on issues becomes blunted when they play by the rules of a political game established by men.

Although it is common to refer to the women's or feminist movement, such a label conceals the often profound divisions that exist between women's groups on matters ranging from ideology to political tactics. Just as there is an enormous range of perspectives within feminism, the real world of women's organizations reflects diversity rather than a monolithic bloc. Perhaps the most prominent and arguably the most crippling division within the Canadian women's movement in recent years has been between the predominantly white middle-class feminists, who led the movement since the 1960s, and non-white feminists whose ties are to less privileged ethnic groups and classes. This second group emphasizes race and class as central themes of their feminist vision. In the words of prominent Canadian feminist and social activist Judy Rebick, 'an organization like NAC, which has been dominated by white middle class women, must transform almost everything we do to respond to the needs of doubly oppressed women.'[40] At the extreme, some have argued that white middle-class feminists are incapable of truly understanding and representing the circumstances and aspirations of women who are black, Aboriginal, poor, or from some other historically oppressed group.

This claim has generated considerable controversy within the feminist movement and in particular organizations such as the **National Action Committee on the Status of Women** (NAC) and the Women's Legal Education and Action Fund (LEAF). After Judy Rebick's departure in 1993 the NAC's presidents were members of visible minorities and the orientation of the organization very definitely shifted towards an emphasis on the special problems of poor women from such groups. Whether this was a laudable change of direction is not the point. What is clear, however, is that the

NAC's redefinition of the feminist project and division among feminists themselves made it easier for governments to question whether the organization truly represented the concerns and values of a majority of Canadian women. By 2004, this once influential voice for feminist concerns no longer had enough money to staff a permanent office and answer its phones.

The decline of NAC is sometimes seen as indicative of a more widespread decline in the organizational power of women. Indeed, over the past two decades some writers and intellectuals within the women's movement have parted company with their liberal and radical sisters to become what has been called a 'third wave', with an emphasis on individual empowerment and on personally claiming the gains of the second wave rather than continuing to repeat what they see as the self-defeating narrative of 'victimhood'. Nonetheless, consolidating and extending the achievements of the second wave is the central task of a number of vibrant organizations today. Important groups including LEAF, la Fédération des Femmes du Québec, and the National Association of Women and the Law continue to exist and to be active in politics. But even more significantly, women's issues and representation have been institutionalized in many labour unions, professional associations, and departments and agencies of the state at all levels. Although some will disagree, it may simply be that an umbrella organization like NAC is no longer necessary. Many of the battles that it fought and that provided its raison d'être have been won or have seen significant progress. Moreover, the organizational voice of women is today far more pervasive and entrenched in institutions across Canadian society than was true only a generation ago.

Strategies

'There are fifty-six whooping cranes in Canada and one female federal politician.'[41] So began a 1971 article by Barbara Frum in *Chatelaine*. Half a century after winning the same political rights as men, the inroads made by women in Canada's political parties were pitifully small. Their participation was still channelled mainly into the activities of women's auxiliaries/associations, whose role was to provide support services for the mainstream of the parties. Although vital to the parties, these activities—social, administrative, fundraising, and campaigning—had low prestige and were remote from the policy- and strategy-oriented structures of the parties. Separate women's associations were singled out by the 1970 Royal Commission on the Status of Women as a serious barrier to the full participation of women in party politics. The Commission recommended that they be abolished.

Support-oriented women's associations within the parties were redolent of the sexual division of labour that modern feminism condemned. They have been eliminated at the national and provincial levels in all of the major parties. The trend since the late 1960s has been to replace the traditional women's associations with new women's groups dedicated to increasing women's representation and policy influence. As Sylvia Bashevkin notes, this transition has not been frictionless.[42] Nevertheless, if men still dominate within Canada's political parties—which they do—and if the feminist political agenda is still resisted—which it is to varying degrees in all of the main national parties except the NDP—the internal structures of the parties are no longer to blame.

Attempting to increase the representation and influence of women in parties that aspire to govern is a rather blunt strategy for achieving feminist goals. Parties in power, or even within sight of being elected to govern, are disinclined to alienate those voters and organized interests who object to such elements of the feminist agenda as the elimination of legal restrictions on abortion, affirmative action in hiring, and a national program of publicly subsidized daycare. Consequently, the women's movement has sought influence by other means.

One of these means has been the courts. Litigation in support of sexual equality claims has a long history in Canada, going back to the turn of the century when women challenged barriers to their entry into certain professions. But with the notable exception of the 1929 ***Persons* case**, in which the JCPC overruled Canadian courts in determining that women were persons in law, most of the pre-Charter litigation on sexual equality resulted in defeats for

© TorontoStar/GetStock.com

A member of Equal Voice (www.equalvoice.ca), a group advocating for the election of more women at all levels of government, demonstrates in front of the Ontario legislature in 2007. Organizations such as Equal Voice strive to break down the barriers to women's participation in politics through such avenues as recruiting and training; working to create family-friendly work environments; advocating for electoral reform, including proportional representation; and spearheading public awareness campaigns.

women's claims.[43] Given this dismal track record in the courts, plus the high cost of litigation—several pre-Charter cases reached the Supreme Court only because certain lawyers were willing to freely donate their time[44]—it comes as no surprise that this strategy was seldom chosen by women.

The Charter was expected to change all this. Indeed, women's groups fought hard and successfully for the inclusion of section 28 of the Charter, which states that 'the rights and freedoms referred to in [the Charter] are guaranteed equally to male and female persons.' Their efforts had already ensured that the equality section of the Charter (s. 15) proscribed discrimination based on sex. With sections 15 and 28 in hand, it appeared that women's groups would turn to the courts as never before.

They have, but with mixed results. In the first four years after the equality section came into effect (1985–9), 44 cases of sexual discrimination under section 15 were decided by the courts. Most of these cases were instigated by or on behalf of men. In only nine cases were equality claims made by women. Despite victories in some of these cases, feminist legal scholars quickly became dubious about the usefulness of section 15. Michael Mandel uses the term 'equality with a vengeance' to describe the early tendency of courts, and of governments responding to court decisions, to interpret the Charter's equality provisions in ways that can backfire against women.[45]

Feminists have argued that the sexual equality guarantees of the Charter are undermined by two aspects of judicial interpretation. One is the courts' unwillingness to elevate equality rights over other rights and freedoms guaranteed in the Charter. For example, in *Casagrande v. Hinton Roman Catholic*

Separate School District (1987),[46] a Catholic school board's decision to fire an unmarried pregnant teacher was upheld on the grounds that section 15 equality rights took a back seat to the rights of 'denominational, separate or dissentient schools' that are also guaranteed by the Constitution. Second, and more serious according to feminists, is the tendency of judges to interpret equality in **formal** rather than **substantive** terms. What they mean by this is that judges will be satisfied that no discrimination has occurred if laws treat similarly persons who are similarly situated. This is an 'equality before the law' approach that, according to feminists, fails to understand the real mechanisms through which discrimination occurs. Systemic discrimination—the inequality created and maintained through social practices and beliefs—cannot be overcome by ensuring that the law is blind to the sex or other group characteristic of a section 15 claimant. Substantive equality, they argue, requires that judges determine whether a claimant belongs to a disadvantaged group and, second, 'whether the impugned law, policy or practice is operating to the detriment of [that disadvantaged group]'.[47]

In fact, however, this claim is not entirely fair. As early as 1984 the Supreme Court of Canada had declared its intention to look beyond the formal words of Charter sections to consider the interests they were meant to protect.[48] In *Edwards Books* (1986),[49] the majority expressed the view that 'the courts must be cautious to ensure that [the Charter] does not simply become an instrument of better situated individuals to roll back legislation which has as its object the improvement of the condition of less advantaged persons.'[50] A year later, Justices Dickson and Wilson argued that one of the important purposes of the Charter was to assist social and economic 'underdogs'.[51] These intimations of judicial activism were acted on in the *Morgentaler* abortion decision (1988), where the majority was willing to look at the actual effects of Canada's abortion law to determine whether it violated the 'liberty' and 'security of the person' guarantees in section 7 of the Charter.

Then, in *Law Society of British Columbia v. Andrews and Kinersley* (1989),[52] which dealt with a resident non-citizen having been rejected for admission to the British Columbia bar because of BC statutory law, Canada's highest court showed that it was prepared to go beyond the wooden requirements of formal equality in interpreting section 15 of the Charter. Although this case did not directly relate to the rights holders enumerated in s. 15, a number of these groups, including LEAF, presented interventions.[53] The Supreme Court argued that the Charter's equality section prohibits laws that have had a discriminatory impact on the members of some group or groups. The decisions written by Justices Wilson and McIntyre both cited approvingly an American Supreme Court precedent that identified 'discrete and insular minorities' as groups requiring the protection of constitutional equality guarantees. In fact, the formal equality test so maligned by feminist legal scholars was explicitly rejected by all of the Supreme Court justices.[54] The substantive equality test is now routinely used by the courts in applying s. 15 of the Charter (see Box 15.1).

Activist Penney Kome identifies several political strategies, including legal action, that are open to women's groups. They range across grassroots organizing to deal with emergencies (e.g., a rash of sexual assaults in a neighbourhood) or chronic local problems (e.g., inadequate public transportation or pollution), representations through official channels, lobbying campaigns directed at decision-makers and potential supporters, and use of the media.[55] Lacking the financial resources and the personal access that characterize many business and professional interest groups, the women's movement has made extensive use of all of these political action strategies.

Like many groups that lack the financial resources and personal access to the corridors of power to carry on effective behind-the-scenes lobbying, women's organizations have often resorted to very public and sometimes confrontational strategies intended to generate media coverage of their issues and demands. Such strategies come with no guarantee of success. The representations that the NAC and other women's groups have made over the years to the United Nations Committee on Economic, Social and Cultural Rights and to international meetings on women's issues have often received considerable media attention in Canada. This helps to maintain public awareness of feminist demands, at least within a certain segment of public opinion. But attempts to embarrass governments through public reproaches and protests can backfire, as NAC discovered. NAC revenues fell by about 40 per cent between 1993 and 1999, a drop that was largely due to cuts in federal government grants to an organization that, in the 1980s, was probably the single most influential women's group in Canada.

When NAC representatives reproached the Liberal government at its annual meeting with the Minister of Justice in 1997, Stéphane Dion chastised its spokespersons for being unable to communicate any part of their presentation in French or answer questions in Canada's other official language. It had become clear that the confrontational strategies NAC had long favoured, and that for years had generated favourable coverage in at least some parts of Canada's media system, no longer worked. Or perhaps what had happened was that such strategies were no longer necessary as a result of changes in public opinion on gender matters and the institutionalization of feminist ideas and concerns throughout the state.

Achievements

The achievements of modern feminists can be grouped into three types: legislative reform; changes in the process of decision-making; and improvements in the material/social conditions of women. Together they add up to a mixed record of success and failure.

Let us begin with changes to the law. Some of the most celebrated achievements of the women's movement have been on this front. Sex was not one of the proscribed grounds of discrimination in the draft Charter proposed by the Liberal government in 1981. It became part of the Charter after the vigorous representations made by women's groups before the Special Parliamentary Committee on the Constitution. Likewise, the section 28 guarantee of legal equality for men and women was a direct product of intense lobbying by women's groups.[56] And in perhaps the most publicized of court decisions on the Charter, the Supreme Court of Canada struck down the section of the Criminal Code dealing with abortion, a decision greeted as a major victory for the women's movement.

Governing Realities

Box 15.1 When Is a Sexual Double Standard Protected by the Charter?

Note: This case involved a male prisoner who objected to cross-sex frisk searches and the presence of female guards when being strip-searched. Male searches of female prisoners were already prohibited. A detailed explanation of the guidelines used by the court in the interpretation of s. 15 is found in Law v. Canada (Minister of Employment and Immigration), *[1999] 1 S.C.R. 497.*

> The jurisprudence of this court is clear: equality does not necessarily connote identical treatment and, in fact, different treatment may be called for in certain cases to promote equality. Given the historical, biological and sociological differences between men and women, equality does not demand that practices which are forbidden where male officers guard female inmates must also be banned where female officers guard male inmates. The reality of the relationship between the sexes is such that the historical trend of violence perpetrated by men against women is not matched by a comparable trend pursuant to which men are the victims and women the aggressors. . . . Viewed in this light, it becomes clear that the effect of cross-gender searching is different and more threatening for women than for men. The different treatment to which the appellant objects thus may not be discrimination at all.

Source: *Conway v. Canada (Attorney General)* (1993), 83 C.C.C. (3d) 1.

Several other rulings by Canada's courts have also been generally received as victories by the women's movement. These include: *Blainey* (1986), a decision that opened boys' sports leagues to girls; *Daigle* (1989), in which the Supreme Court ruled that a potential father does not have the right to veto a woman's decision to have an abortion; a 1998 Canadian Human Rights Tribunal decision that found the federal government liable for roughly $5 billion in back pay owed primarily to female public servants under pay equity legislation; and *Ewanchuk* (1999), where the Supreme Court ruled that no defence of implied consent to sexual assault exists under Canadian law.

Other legislative breakthroughs include the maternity leave provisions written into the Canada Labour Code in 1970; the 1983 amendment to the Unemployment Insurance Act that eliminated discrimination against pregnant women; and the pay equity laws passed by Ottawa and the provinces. Human rights codes and commissions to enforce them exist nationally and in all of the provinces. They have provided opportunities to challenge discriminatory employment and commercial practices in the private sector, practices that the courts have deemed to fall outside the ambit of the Charter.

So have the main legal barriers to sexual equality been eliminated? Not nearly, claim women's groups. They point to inaction on what they believe to be government's inadequate response to such issues as daycare, affirmative action, female poverty, pay equity, and pornography. Today, many feminists argue that a popular backlash has enabled governments to roll back some of the gains made in the past. This may well be true, but it is also true that groups may understate their gains and influence for the possible reason that public crowing about the gains experienced by those they purport to represent may cause their public constituency to doubt whether these groups are still needed.

A second measure of feminism's achievements involves the decision-making structures of the state. Among the striking characteristics of the modern women's movement are its financial and organizational links to government. The 1970 *Report* of the Royal Commission on the Status of Women was followed by the creation of the Canadian Advisory Council on the Status of Women, now called Status of Women Canada (SWC), and the creation of a women's portfolio in the federal cabinet. Similar advisory councils have been created by all provinces, and some have also established special cabinet positions. Within government departments and agencies it is now common to have special divisions devoted to 'women's issues' or affirmative action. For example, the Public Service Commission of Canada has a Program Development (Affirmative Action) branch that monitors the representation of women, indigenous Canadians, disabled persons, and visible minorities in the federal bureaucracy. The Treasury Board Secretariat has an Affirmative Action Group and an Employment Equity section within its Human Resources Division. As Penney Kome observes, the creation of status of women councils was followed by a 'deluge of equal-opportunity officers, women's directorates, grant officers, labour specialists, and other women's advocates attached to various branches of government'.[57] Since 1995 the federal government has required that all of its departments and agencies apply a gender-based analysis to new policies and legislation in order to identify any gender-specific and potentially inequitable consequences that might be expected to result from such policies.

Financially, the women's movement, which from the early 1970s until the mid-1990s was led by NAC, has depended on government money. This dependence has operated through two main channels. One is the budget of the Secretary of State for the Status of Women, within Heritage Canada, which has responsibility for SWC. Similar public funding is also available from provincial governments. The second channel involves social spending, part of which takes the form of transfers from Ottawa to provincial governments. Much of the money that ultimately reaches the hands of rape crisis centres, women's counselling services, halfway houses for battered women, and the vast network of services geared to meeting women's needs, as well as women's research and information organizations, is buried in the budgets of the Canada Health Transfer and Canada Social Transfer to the provinces. When Ottawa has cut back on transfers to the provinces, and to social spending generally, this has had the effect of squeezing the financial lifeline of grassroots women's groups that depend on public money.

Those on the left of the women' s movement have often criticized the organizational and financial ties between women's groups and the state, arguing that such ties have the effect of co-opting feminists into the state. The demands of these groups will perforce be more moderate and their influence strategies less confrontational—and perhaps less effective—than if they resisted the siren call of money and a seat at the table. On the other hand, the independent resources available to voluntary associations are often meagre and so the temptation to seek and accept state support is strong. Likewise, direct representation on a government body provides an opportunity to be part of the process and to express women's perspectives from inside the state.

In fact, despite the financial dependence of women's groups on government, little evidence suggests that this has made them more 'polite' towards the hand that feeds. Based on his examination of the Secretary of State's support for voluntary groups since the 1960s, Leslie Pal concludes that that these groups have not been co-opted into an agenda set by the bureaucrats and politicians. On the contrary, he argues, women's groups in particular did not hesitate to criticize and embarrass the governments that have provided them with the means to publicize the alleged failures of government policy.[58] Sylvia Bashevkin's study of NAC's strong opposition to the free trade initiative of the Mulroney Conservative government confirms this view. Bashevkin argues that the depth of Ottawa's cuts in funding for NAC was certainly influenced by its vigorous opposition to free trade, in alliance with other critics of the Conservative government.[59] Janine Brodie argues that although the voices of feminist criticism inside and outside the Canadian state are more muted today than in the late twentieth century, it is incorrect to conclude that gender politics and identities have been erased by neo-liberal ideology.[60]

What about the social conditions of women? Has the women's movement managed to improve the material circumstances of women or change social attitudes towards men and women? Reforming the law and the state is fine, but do women believe that they have achieved equality? For that matter, does everyone want equality?

Here, the record of achievement is mixed. There is no doubt that social attitudes regarding appropriate roles and behaviour for males and females have changed over the last two generations. For example, the vast majority of Canadians believe that a woman could run most businesses as well as a man. Most Canadians claim that the sex of a political party leader does not influence the likelihood of their voting for that party (a tiny minority say that a female leader would make them less inclined to support the party, but a considerably larger minority say that a woman at the helm would make them more likely to support such a party). On such issues as abortion and equality of job opportunities for men and women, there is a little evidence of a significant gender gap. As shown in Table 15.2, Canadians' attitudes towards gender equality are more progressive than those of the populations of most other affluent democracies.

Alongside the evidence of changed attitudes there are signs that considerable sexism persists. These signs include gender characterizations in commercial advertising and entertainment programming, the child-rearing practices of many, indeed probably most, parents, the unequal division of domestic responsibilities between men and women, and the relative infrequency of women's career choices taking precedence over men's even in this age of two-earner households. Changed attitudes towards gender roles need to be weighed against the empirical evidence of persistent inequality.

When one turns to the material conditions of women the record is mixed and shows evidence of a significant class divide. Today there are more women lawyers, professors, accountants, and even engineers than in the past, and females are more likely than males to attend university (among university graduates in 2006, 60 per cent were female and 40 per cent were male). Indeed, in 2010 the widely respected public affairs and culture magazine, *The Atlantic*, included as a feature article an analysis of gender accomplishments and current trends entitled, 'The End of Men: How Women Are

TABLE 15.2 Attitudes towards Gender Equality, Selected Countries, 2006

Country	'When jobs are scarce, men should have more right to a job than women.' (% who disagree)*	'On the whole, men make better leaders than women.' (% who agree)	'A woman has to have a child in order to be fulfilled.' (% who agree, 2000 survey)	'A man's job is to earn money; a woman's job is to look after the home and family.'**
Australia	64.7	24.6	20	26
Britain	76.1	19.7	21	25
Canada	77.9	18.3	19	10
Germany	66.8	18.8	54	36
Italy	59.2	19.2	56	32
Japan	17.9	43.9	66	40
Netherlands	81.4	17.6	7	18
Norway	88.6	14.5	19	15
Sweden	94.1	7.7	25	11
US	82	24.7	15	20

*In some countries, the percentage of those agreeing or choosing neither was very high. In Japan it was 77.1 and in Italy it was 40.8.
**This question was part of the 2002 International Social Survey Programme.
Source: Adapted from 2000 data at the website for the World Values Survey: <www.worldvaluessurvey.org>.

Taking Control of Everything'. Such an analysis, and its conclusion that the gender equality pendulum now swings in favour of females in affluent democracies such as the United States and Canada, would have been unimaginable 20 years ago. But for over a decade, studies showing a clear and even increasing trend for females to outperform males academically, in many respects at least, and stories asking what the longer-term consequences of these trends might be have been common. But the breakthroughs made by middle-class women have not been matched by their less privileged sisters. Consider the following facts:

- About 60 per cent of working women are employed in clerical, sales, and service jobs where the pay tends to be lower. This is almost exactly the same percentage of women employed in these occupations as was the case five decades ago.
- The average income of a full-time female worker is not quite three-quarters of what the average male earns. This represents 'progress' when one considers that the figure was below 60 per cent a generation ago. Most of this difference is accounted for by three factors: the segregation of women into low-paying occupations; more women than men having part-time jobs (when both full- and part-time workers are taken into account, the average income of female workers falls to about 62 per cent of males); and the greater seniority of male employers.
- Women are more likely to be poor than men. Approximately 60 per cent of those below the poverty lines established by Statistics Canada are women. Over time, poverty has assumed an increasingly feminine aspect. For example, in 1961 only about 15 per cent of low-income families (i.e., families with incomes below the poverty line) were headed by women. Today the share is over one-third, as higher levels of marital breakdown have produced many more female single-parent households. Single-parent families headed by women constitute the most poverty-prone group in Canada, with about 60 per cent of them living below the poverty line.

Media Spotlight

Box 15.2 Understanding the Glass Ceiling

A study of high-powered business school graduates from the University of Chicago found that males and females made similar incomes after graduation. But 15 years later the average income of a female graduate was 75 per cent of what a male earned. This was not true, however, in the case of females who did not have children. Their incomes were about the same as those of their male counterparts 15 years after graduation. Daniel Indiviglio asks, '[Is this] really something that should concern us, or just a symptom of the choices we make as a society?' Here's his answer:

> . . . [L]et's redefine the disparity that the studies point out. Imagine there was no classification of men or women, just primary caregivers and primary professionals. Each family with children has one of each. Would anyone really care if primary caregivers didn't climb the corporate ladder as quickly as primary professionals if gender weren't involved? Wouldn't that just make logical sense? If men more often take on the primary professional role, consequently working more intensely and taking fewer vacations than women, then they *should be* promoted more aggressively.
>
> In this case, gender is actually coincidental to the issue outlined above. Imagine if society developed differently instead. What if men regularly took paternity leave, while women returned immediately to work without significant time off? What if men chose to work part time to make sure they were at the house when the kids arrived home from school, while women preferred to work full time? What if men drove the children to soccer practice, while women worked late on the presentation for tomorrow's board meeting?
>
> Certainly, there are households where the couple takes on these non-traditional gender roles today—but they're the exception, rather than the norm. Should we lament that society hasn't embraced such progress towards equality? Maybe. But there's also a possibility that most men and women in traditional gender roles are perfectly content with the current arrangement. After all, if they aren't, then it's often within their power to live their lives differently.[61]

To be sure, such a perspective as that expressed by Indiviglio must make feminists of all political stripes cringe (except, perhaps, for libertarian third-wave feminists such as Camille Paglia), and to suggest that individuals and couples *often* have the 'power to live their lives differently' certainly is debatable. Is it more a question of 'damned if you do and damned if you don't'? And what middle-class assumptions are built into this analysis? What do you think?

The *Financial Post* annually publishes 'The Financial Post 500', a survey of the leading companies in the Canadian economy. Two women made the 2010 list of the CEOs of the top 50 companies. Nineteen of the leading 500 companies had female CEOs. Of the 25 most respected corporations in Canada, based on a 2005 poll of Canadian CEOs conducted by Ipsos Reid for KPMG, none was headed by a woman. A 2009 study by the consulting firm Catalyst found that 15 per cent of all directorships on the boards of directors of Financial Post 500 companies in Canada were held by women. By whatever measure one cares to use, women are rare at the highest rungs of the business ladder. Moya Greene, appointed CEO of Canada Post in 2007 (she left in May 2010 to become the CEO of the

Royal Mail in the UK), points to two factors that she believes are key to understanding what is often referred to as a 'glass ceiling' for women in the corporate world. One is that ambition continues to be seen as more of a masculine than feminine trait, admired when it is associated with men and often looked at askance when displayed by women. The other factor is that of balancing the demands of a high-powered job with family commitments. 'It is simply not possible to commit to a major leadership job and be the kind of mother my mother was', Greene observes, adding that this ideal of balance—which is not generally expected of or by male CEOs—is not realistic (see Box 15.2).[62]

The continuing exclusion of women from Canada's corporate elite, at the same time as their participation in the political elite has been increasing, may thwart some of the gains achieved by the women's movement. As economies become internationalized, domestic politics matters less and business matters more. Increasingly, decisions with major social implications are taken by the corporate elite, from which women are still largely excluded. The general opposition of the women's movement to globalization, though it cannot be explained by this factor alone, certainly is influenced by the realization that a relative decline in the power of states and an increase in that of transnational corporations and markets tend to reduce the political clout of women's groups. The feminist criticism of the under-representation of women in the corporate elite is premised in large part on a belief that more women CEOs would make a difference in the sorts of decisions taken by major corporations. This may well be a false premise.

Appendix 1: Selected Women's Organizations in Canada

Year Established	Name
1870	Young Women's Christian Association (YWCA)
1874	Woman's Christian Temperance Union (WCTU)
1893	National Council of Women of Canada
1897	Federated Women's Institutes of Canada
	National Council of Jewish Women
1908	Canadian Nurses' Association
1918	Federation of Women Teachers Association of Canada
1919	Canadian Federation of University Women
1920	Canadian Teachers' Federation
1930	Canadian Federation of Business and Professional Women's Clubs
1939	Canadian Association of Elizabeth Fry Societies
1960	Voice of Women
1967	Fédération des Femmes du Québec
1971	Women for Political Action
1972	National Action Committee on the Status of Women (NAC)
	Canadian Congress for Learning Opportunities for Women
1974	Canadian Abortion Rights Action League (CARAL)
	National Association of Women and the Law
1976	Canadian Research Institute for the Advancement of Women
1983	REAL Women (Realistic, Equal, and Active for Life)
1985	Women's Legal Education and Action Fund (LEAF)

Appendix 2: Dates in Women's Progress towards Legal and Political Equality

Year	Event
1916	Alberta, Saskatchewan, Manitoba give vote to women.
1918	Women given franchise in federal elections.
1921	Agnes Macphail first woman elected to Parliament.
1928	Supreme Court rules women are not 'persons' and cannot be appointed to Senate.
1929	Judicial Committee of the British Privy Council overturns Supreme Court decision in the *Persons* case.
1930	Cairine Wilson first woman appointed to the Senate.
1940	Quebec gives vote to women.
1947	Married women restricted from holding federal public service jobs.
1955	Restrictions on married women in federal public service removed.
1957	Ellen Fairclough sworn in as first female federal cabinet minister.
1967	Royal Commission on Status of Women established.
1971	Canada Labour Code amended to allow women 17 weeks' maternity leave.
	About one-third of university graduates are female.
1973	Supreme Court upholds section of Indian Act depriving Aboriginal women of their rights.
	Supreme Court denies Irene Murdoch right to share in family property.
1977	Canadian Human Rights Act passed, forbidding discrimination on basis of sex.
1981	Canada ratifies UN Convention on the Elimination of All Forms of Discrimination against Women.
	Just under half of university graduates are female.
1982	Bertha Wilson becomes the first woman appointed to the Supreme Court of Canada.
1983	Affirmative action programs mandatory in the federal public service.
1984	Twenty-seven women elected to Parliament, six appointed to cabinet.
1985	Section 15 of Charter of Rights and Freedoms comes into effect.
	Employment Equity legislation passed.
	Indian Act amended to remove discrimination against Aboriginal women.
1988	*Morgentaler* decision strikes down Canada's abortion law.
1989	*Andrews* decision introduces the concept of 'substantive equality' in applying section 15 of the Charter.
	Audrey McLaughlin chosen to lead the national NDP.
1991	Ontario passes pay equity law that applies to the private sector (repealed in 1995).
1993	Kim Campbell becomes Canada's first female Prime Minister.
1995	Alexa McDonough chosen to lead the national NDP.
1997	Sixty-one women elected to House of Commons, eight appointed to cabinet.
2000	Right Honourable Beverley McLachlin appointed Chief Justice of the Supreme Court of Canada.
2001	Just under 60 per cent of university graduates are female.
2002	Justice Marie Deschamps appointed to the Supreme Court of Canada.
2004	Justices Rosalie Abella and Louise Charron appointed to the Supreme Court of Canada, bringing the number of female judges on the nine-person court to four.
2008	Sixty-nine women elected to the House of Commons; seven appointed to cabinet.
2011	Christy Clark is the third woman to become a provincial Premier when she wins the leadership of British Columbia's Liberal Party in late February.

Source: CACSW, 'Progress toward Equality for Women in Canada' (Feb. 1987), 15, with author's additions.

Starting Points for Research

Sylvia Bashevkin, *Women, Power, Politics: The Hidden Story of Canada's Unfinished Democracy* (Toronto: Oxford University Press, 2009). This engaging book, written by one of Canada's foremost feminist scholars, argues that women's progress in Canadian politics has stalled in recent years.

Jacquetta Newman and Linda White, *Women, Politics, and Public Policy: The Political Struggles of Canadian Women* (Toronto: Oxford University Press, 2006). This book provides a feminist analysis of the history of the women's movement in Canada and the gender dimensions of public policy.

Manon Tremblay and Linda Trimble, eds, *Women and Electoral Politics in Canada* (Toronto: Oxford University Press, 2003). The selections in this collection examine various aspects of women's participation in the electoral process, including how they vote, their participation in political parties, the portrayal and coverage of female leaders in the media, and generational differences in the political attitudes of women.

Review Exercises

1. How many women hold public office in your community? What about members of visible minorities? Make a list of public office-holders on your local city, town, or township council, your mayor, your MP, and your provincial representative. Include MPs and provincial representatives from a couple of adjoining constituencies. You can find all this information by going to websites or with a telephone book and a little bit of resourcefulness.
2. Read the first three sections of the document entitled 'An Integrated Approach to Gender-Based Analysis' at <www.swc-cfc.gc.ca/pol/gba-acs/guide/2007/index-eng.html> and respond to the following questions:
   (a) Is this an appropriate approach to analyzing and making policy recommendations? Why or why not?
   (b) How influential would this approach be if applied to issues like trade, national security, agriculture, fisheries, and economic growth? Why?
   (c) On what sorts of issues might this approach be most influential? Why?
3. The World Values Survey (www.worldvaluessurvey.org) asks respondents in countries throughout the world a number of questions that have to do with gender relations and ideas about appropriate roles for men and women. Go to its website, click on 'online data analysis' (left-hand column), then on the box that reads 'Begin analysis'. What differences and similarities do you find between Canada and other affluent democracies?

A wide gap exists between the Aboriginal symbols and culture that have become integrated into the Canadian identity and the bleak reality of life in many of the country's First Nations, Métis, and Inuit communities. Consequently, Aboriginal politics remains a critical aspect of governance in Canada. © David P. Lewis/iStockphoto.com

16 Aboriginal Politics

For most of Canada's history Aboriginal affairs were relegated to the dim corners of public life. Politicians and most Canadians paid them little attention. This has changed. Native groups have become much more sophisticated in their political strategies and tactics, and the issues that concern them, from landownership to abuse and discrimination, have become important parts of the political conversation in Canada. In this chapter we will examine the following topics:

- Aboriginal demographics: who and how many?
- The language of Aboriginal politics.
- Who is an Indian?
- The reserve system.
- Assimilation, integration, self-determination.
- The White Paper of 1969.
- The Royal Commission on Aboriginal Peoples.
- Organizing for political influence.
- Sovereignty, landownership, and Aboriginal rights.
- The institutionalization of Aboriginal affairs.
- Second thoughts or citizens plus?

The Museum of Civilization sits on the edge of the Ottawa River in Gatineau, Quebec, across from the Parliament buildings. Its sinuous curves and striking vistas are the creation of Douglas Cardinal, a Métis and one of Canada's foremost architects. Visitors to the museum start their tour in the Grand Hall where several totem poles tower over them in an atmosphere of quiet grandeur.

The Innu community of Sheshatshiu, population 1,600, is situated in south-central Labrador, about 20 kilometres north of the Canadian Forces base at Goose Bay. Fewer than 200 members of the community are employed, almost all of them in service industries. Among adults, about half the population has less than a Grade 9 education and only about a dozen have completed university. In 2004 this isolated community made national headlines when its chief, Paul Rich, talked about the problem of rampant substance abuse among its people. Gas-sniffing by teenagers and children as young as six was singled out as a particular problem. The plight of the Innu of Sheshatshiu brought back dark memories of a spate of youth suicides among the Innu of Davis Inlet in 1993.

The contrast between the incorporation and celebration of Aboriginal symbols and culture in the official life of Canada and the bleak reality that characterizes the lives of those who live in communities like Sheshatshiu is jarring. Many Canadians are often puzzled by the fact that circumstances like those at Sheshatshiu exist. After all, government expenditures per Aboriginal person in Canada are estimated to be about 50 per cent more than that for all Canadians.[1] And Canadians also are sometimes perplexed by news stories showing the continuing tensions that exist, and that occasionally break out in violence, between some Aboriginal communities and their neighbours or the political authorities. Why, they wonder, after years of treaties, legislation, government programs, inquiries, restitution, and financial settlements, does it appear that so much remains unresolved in relations between Aboriginal Canadians and the rest of the country?

Aboriginal Demographics: Who and How Many?

Aboriginal Canadians are those who can trace their ancestry back to before the arrival and permanent settlement of Europeans in what would become Canada. The actual size of this population has been a matter of some controversy over the last couple of decades. Some estimates place the number at 2–3 million, or about 7 to 9 per cent of the national population, while others estimate that the actual number is closer to one-third to one-half of this. Professional demographers are inclined to accept the lower figures, while some Aboriginal spokespersons and politicians maintain that the higher figures are the true ones. Using a definition of 'Aboriginal' that comprises those persons who report identification with at least one Aboriginal group—North American Indian, Métis, or Inuit—Statistics Canada provides the following numbers from the 2006 census:

- 1,678,200 people, or about 5.4 per cent of the national population, gave as their ethnic origins North American Indian, Métis, Inuit, or a combination of one of these with some other ethnic origin.
- 1,172,790 people, representing about 4 per cent of the Canadian population, reported identifying with an Aboriginal group.
- 763,555, or just under 2 per cent of the population, are status Indians, i.e., those to whom the Indian Act applies. Slightly more than half of these people live on reserves or in other recognized Aboriginal settlements.

The regional distribution of those who identify themselves as Aboriginal Canadians is shown in Figure 16.1.

As we saw in Chapter 3, the social and economic conditions of Aboriginal Canadians tend to be considerably less favourable than those of the general population. This is regularly brought home by news reports of substance abuse or high rates of

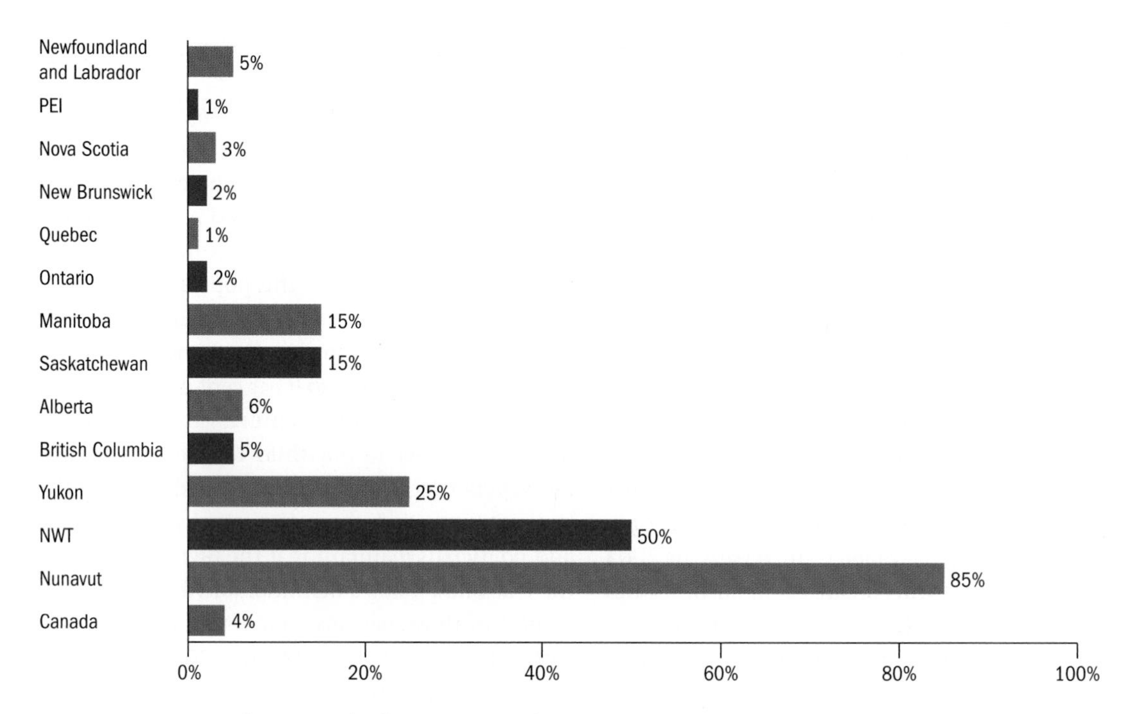

FIGURE 16.1 Aboriginal Identity Population as Percentage of Total Population, Provinces and Territories, 2006

Source: Statistics Canada, *Census of Canada*, 2006, Figure 1, at <www12.statcan.gc.ca/english/census06/analysis/aboriginal/surpass.cfm>.

suicide among young Aboriginal Canadians living in isolated communities. Statistics confirm that the members of this segment of Canadian society are less well off than their fellow Canadians. Average full-time employment incomes among members of the Aboriginal identity population are about 70 per cent those of non-Aboriginal Canadians. The median per capita income for the Aboriginal population in 2006 was $18,962, compared to $27,097 for non-Aboriginals. Government transfer payments make up about one-fifth of Aboriginal income, compared to about one-tenth of income for non-Aboriginal Canadians. The incidence of low incomes is about two and a half times higher for the Aboriginal population. According to the 2006 census, about one-third of Aboriginal Canadians between the ages of 25 and 64 have not completed high school (about 50 per cent among those living on reserves), compared to 15 per cent of other Canadians, and only 8 per cent have graduated from university, compared to 23 per cent for other Canadians.

The Language of Aboriginal Politics

The words used to describe those who trace their ancestry back to the period before the arrival of Europeans in North America provide a useful starting point for understanding the politics of Aboriginality. For most of Canada's history these people and their communities were acknowledged in only a marginal way in the official life of the country and were barely visible in mainstream interpretations of Canadian history and society. The terms 'Indians', 'Métis', and 'Eskimos' were used to describe various segments of the Aboriginal population. The legal meanings and implications of these terms were sometimes contested in the courts, as in the case of the 1939 Supreme Court ruling that the people known as Eskimos did not fall under the meaning of 'Indians' as set down in the Indian Act of 1876. On the whole, however, there was little controversy over the terms used to characterize the Aboriginal population of Canada and virtually no sense that the language made a significant difference.

This began to change by the 1960s. Labels that previously had been considered appropriate and unobjectionable and the concepts and assumptions associated with them were increasingly brought into question. These challenges resulted from an important change that was underway in Western thought. **Communitarianism**—the belief that communities and communal identities are essential to individual dignity and the maintenance of truly democratic societies—was gaining ground among intellectuals. At the street level this belief system was embodied in those elements of the black civil rights movement that called for greater awareness of black identity as something separate and apart from that of American society's white majority. There were echoes of this in the Quebec nationalism of that era, from Pierre Vallières' polemic *White Niggers of America* (*Les Nègres blancs d'Amérique*) to René Lévesque's insistence that Quebecers needed their own independent state in order to form a free and democratic society.

These years saw the emergence of black, ethnic, and women's studies at universities across North America, a development that would gain momentum in the 1970s. The intellectual premise underlying these programs proved to be far-reaching in its practical implications. It was that groups within society should be recognized as having rights and a status different from others and, moreover, that they should think about themselves and be thought of by others in terms of their cultural and other differences from the majority. An additional and crucial feature of this new communitarian model involved inequality. Virtually all calls for greater group self-awareness and demands for official recognition of this collective identity were linked to an analysis and historical narrative of discrimination, exploitation, and unjust treatment—in brief, inequality—in relations between the group in question and the state. Much of the intellectual impetus for this new analysis came from the writings of such colonial and post-colonial authors as Edward Said and Frantz Fanon as the European imperial colonies in Africa, the Middle East, and Asia disintegrated in the two decades following World War II.

This was a full frontal challenge to what had been thought of as progressive liberal thinking in the decades after World War II. Liberal opinion leaders during this era trained their sights on the eradication of poverty, socio-economic inequality, and discrimination, but believed that the ways to achieve these goals involved the full and equal integration of all people, as individuals, into society and the dismantlement of laws, norms, and practices that treated people differently on the basis of skin colour, ethnicity, or religion. The idea that the path to progress could be found in official recognition and institutionalization of difference represented a radical change in thinking.

In the case of Native Canadians, the first step involved rejection of the language of integration and liberal notions of equality that prevailed in the mid-twentieth century. Whatever the motives behind such proposals, their consequences were said to be assimilation and cultural genocide. The term 'Indian' was not immediately rejected by Aboriginal leaders, despite the historical fact of this being an obvious misnomer applied by the early European explorers to those who live in the lands that they mistakenly assumed to be the Far East. Indeed, the label 'Indian' continues to be regularly used by the members of some of these communities and their leaders.

By the late 1970s and certainly by the 1980s, 'Indian' had lost favour in preference for 'Native', 'Aboriginal', and 'First Nations', a shift that was both intellectual and political. Intellectually, the change in language reflected a reappropriation of the identities and histories of those to whom the descriptions applied. Whereas the word 'Indian' inevitably carried historical baggage of conquest, displacement, and subordination, in addition to the fundamental fact of having one's identity named by others, these more recent terms did not. Politically, the terms '**First Nations**' and 'First Nations peoples' carried connotations of communal status and rights as well as prior claims. The language of nationalism and the claims of nations—particularly nations that had been colonized by foreign powers—were familiar and powerful in the post–World War II

Library and Archives Canada, Acc. No. R9266-318/Peter Winkworth Collection of Canadiana

Mi'kmaq woman making a basket, Nova Scotia, *circa* 1845 (attributed to Mary R. McKie). In Canada, naming convention begins with the collective term used to describe the original people of North America and their descendants (e.g., Aboriginal peoples), then moves to a specific group within that collective (e.g., First Nations, Métis, Inuit), then specifies community (e.g., Mi'kmaq, Woodland Cree, Algonquin, etc.).

era. The dismantlement of the colonial empires of the European powers and the 1960 United Nations Declaration on the Granting of Independence to Colonial Countries and Peoples both reflected and reinforced nationalist claims and the idea that, in the words of the UN Declaration, 'All peoples have the right to self-determination.'

Quebec nationalist intellectuals were enthusiastic supporters of this doctrine of national self-determination. They argued that the Québécois constituted a nation or people within any reasonable meaning of these terms and, moreover, that the Quebec nation had experienced 'alien subjugation, domination and exploitation [constituting] a denial of fundamental human rights', in contravention of the 1960 UN Declaration.

If such claims could be made on behalf of the Quebec nation or people, then surely they applied in the case of Aboriginal Canadians. This, at any rate, was the reasoning of many Aboriginal leaders and intellectuals sympathetic to their demands. Indeed, it is difficult to argue that Aboriginal peoples are somehow less deserving of nation status than the Québécois. They certainly can make a more compelling case for having experienced 'alien subjugation' and 'domination' within the plain meaning of these words in the UN Declaration.

The question of whether Aboriginal communities are nations is not one on which everyone agrees. But the same may be said of the question of whether there is such a thing as the Québécois nation. More important than the judgements of philosophers and other scholars, however, is whether the language used to describe Aboriginal communities has practical consequences. There can be no doubt that the widespread acceptance of the terms 'First Nations', 'First Nations peoples', 'original peoples', and 'indigenous peoples' has had important consequences through the greater perceived legitimacy that such terms confer on a group's claims.

Grown accustomed to hearing Aboriginal groups in Canada referred to by public officials, journalists, and academics as First Nations, many Canadians probably assume that there is some obvious inevitability to this description. But there is not. In fact, the terms 'First Nations' and 'Aboriginals' are seldom used in the United States, where 'Native Americans' and 'Indians' are the terms commonly used to designate the members of these groups. In Australia the words 'native' and 'aboriginal', used as nouns, are widely considered to be offensive and derogatory. Even 'aborigines' is rejected by many on the grounds that it has inevitable associations with colonialism. 'Indigenous Australians', for the last couple of decades, has been the generally accepted description for those whose ancestry in Australia predates the arrival of European settlers.

The term 'Eskimo'—a Native American word that, by popular account, means 'eaters of raw meat'—was long used to refer to the indigenous peoples who inhabit the Arctic coasts of Canada, Alaska, Russia, and Greenland. It has been pushed aside, in Canada at least, in preference for **Inuit**. But the indigenous peoples of Alaska and Russia prefer to be called 'Yupik' or 'Eskimo', again demonstrating that there is no inevitability to the terms used in the conversation on Aboriginal politics.

Relations between Aboriginal communities and the Canadian state were long about treaty obligations and reserves, at least for those groups under treaty. Those who had never signed treaties with the British or Canadian government, such as the Inuit of the Far North and the Innu of Labrador, were often ignored. The language of treaty obligations continues to be important and reserves still exist, but several other terms and the issues associated with them have become part of the policy conversation on Aboriginal affairs. These include 'sovereignty', 'self-government', 'self-determination', and 'nation-to-nation'. These additions to the vocabulary of Aboriginal politics in Canada reflect the enormous change that has taken place over the last four decades in the scope and nature of Native demands, which rest on a communitarian ethos that has become increasingly influential in Canada over the last generation.

Who Is an Indian?

It has become unfashionable in some circles to use the word 'Indian' when speaking of the descendants of those who occupied North America before the arrival of Europeans. There are, however, practical reasons for not banning the word 'Indian' from a discussion of government policies towards Aboriginal peoples. Under Canada's Indian Act, which has been on the statute books since 1876, a person who qualifies as an Indian under the law has certain entitlements that do not apply to non-Indians. Moreover, those Indian bands that live on land referred to in law as Indian **reserves** are subject to special legal provisions concerning such matters as individual landownership and transfer, a prohibition against mortgages on reserve land, and numerous restrictions on permissible economic activities. Until the Indian Act and the legal status of 'Indian' are abolished, any analysis of Aboriginal policies cannot avoid using these terms.

In law, an Indian or status Indian is anyone who has been registered or is entitled to be registered under the Indian Act, including those who belong to communities covered by treaties. The defining characteristics are both biological and social. The Indian Act of 1876 stipulated that an Indian was any male person of Indian blood who belonged to a band recognized by the federal government, and any child of such a person or a woman married to such a person. An Indian woman who married a non-Indian lost her legal status as an Indian and the entitlements associated with that status.

This changed in 1985. In response to pressure from Aboriginal women, Canada's obligations under the United Nations International Covenant on Civil and Political Rights, and, most importantly, the sexual equality provisions of the Charter of Rights and Freedoms (sections 15 and 28), the federal government eliminated this obviously discriminatory section of the Indian Act. Since then female Indians, women who marry male Indians, and the children of such women enjoy the same rights under the Act as male persons. Women who lost their Indian status under the pre-1985 provisions of the Indian Act were permitted by this amendment to apply for reinstatement of band membership and re-registration as status Indians.

The fact that non-Native women married to Native men and, since 1985, non-Native men who marry Native women acquire the right to Indian status indicates that ancestry is not the only criterion determining who is an Indian under the law. Indeed, the courts have long recognized that a person's 'associations, habits, modes of life, and surroundings' may weigh more heavily in the balance than the ethnicity of one's forebears in determining legal status as an Indian.[2] Writing in 1972, Cumming and Mickenberg observed that 'The questions of how much Indian blood a person must have, and of how closely an individual must be associated with a native community before he will be considered a "native person", have not been answered.'[3] This remains true today.

Canadian law also recognizes the Métis and Inuit as two other categories of Aboriginal peoples of Canada. Although the Constitution Act, 1867 speaks only of 'Indians, and Lands reserved for Indians' (s. 91[24]), a 1939 decision of the Supreme Court of Canada pronounced the Inuit to be Indians within the meaning of the Constitution,[4] which meant that the federal government had a (paternalistic) responsibility for the welfare of these people. They are excluded, however, from the provisions of the Indian Act. **Métis**, a term originally understood to be limited to the mixed-blood descendants of unions between Indian women and Scots or French-speaking traders and settlers in the Red River region of Manitoba, may also be considered Indians under the law if they are the descendants of Métis who were part of Indian communities that fell under treaties. Descendants of Métis who received scrip (certificates that could be used to purchase land) or lands from the federal government are excluded from the provisions of the Indian Act. Nevertheless, Métis are considered to be Aboriginal people within the meaning of the Constitution, and so Ottawa has the authority to pass laws concerning the members of this group. Although there is not much in the way of such legislation, an example is the Legal Studies for Aboriginal Peoples Program, under which the Department of Justice provides financial assistance for Métis and other non-status Indian law students. The Inuit and Métis are grouped with the Indian people of Canada by section 35 of the Constitution Act, 1982, which recognizes and affirms the 'existing aboriginal and treaty rights of the aboriginal peoples of Canada'.

Today, for largely political, legal, and economic reasons, some people of mixed Aboriginal and European ancestry, such as the Labrador Métis Nation, have appropriated the term 'Métis' although their origins are not related to the early fur trade and their lifestyle, arguably, is not so different from that of many non-Aboriginal people.

The Reserve System

Indian reserves have been called by some Canada's own system of apartheid. Indeed, a South African delegation came to Canada early in the twentieth century to study the pass system then used on Canadian reserves as a means of social control.[5] On the face of it the apartheid label seems a fair one. Average life expectancy and incomes of those who live on reserves are significantly lower than the Canadian norms. Rates of suicide, alcoholism, violent death, unemployment, crowded housing conditions, and infant mortality are all higher than the Canadian average, in some cases dramatically higher. Moreover, although being of Aboriginal descent is not a necessary condition for residence on a reserve, the reserve system was created to provide small, fixed homelands for Indians—mostly in remote areas at or beyond the agricultural fringe—and the vast majority of those residing on reserves today are in fact status Indians. This combination of enormous disparity between life on reserves compared to the mainstream of society and the racial basis for the physical segregation of Indians does sound a lot like apartheid. (This was especially true under the pass system that lasted on some reserves in the Prairie provinces into the 1940s, when Indians were not allowed to leave their home reserve without the written permission of the Indian agent.) Non-Aboriginal Canadians who have seen first-hand the squalor and obvious destitution that characterize many of this country's reserves often wonder how such a system has been allowed to survive in a country that prides itself on being a compassionate democracy.

But when the Liberal government's 1969 White Paper proposed the abolition of reserves along with all the other legal structures that have treated Indians differently from other Canadians, the leadership of Canada's Native communities responded with a vehement 'No', despite the fact that everyone acknowledged that the reserves involved a paternalistic control by Ottawa over the lives of Indians living on reserves. This paternalistic, racially based system, whose origins in Canada appear to go back to New France, continues today, as does Native resistance to its abolition. If the system is truly a form of apartheid, as many of its critics have charged, why then is it not rejected outright by the very people who are its 'victims'?

The answer is complex. To understand how a racially based system of segregation manages to survive in a liberal democratic society one must examine the origins and operation of Indian reserves in Canada. We also need to consider the goals of today's Aboriginal leaders, who in important ways are opposed to the dismantling of the reserve system.

The Indian Act of 1876 defines reserves in the following way:

> The term 'reserve' means any tract or tracts of land set apart by treaty or otherwise for the use or benefit of or granted to a particular band of Indians, of which the legal title is in the Crown, but which is unsurrendered, and includes all the trees, wood, timber, soil, stone, minerals, metals, or other valuables thereon or therein.

At the heart of this definition and central to the quandary of the reserve system is the guardianship relationship established between the federal government and Indians living on reserves. The legal ownership of reserve land belongs to the Crown, but the land and all the resources appertaining to it must be managed for the 'use or benefit' of the people residing there. In practice this has meant that virtually no legal or commercial transaction of consequence could be undertaken by those living on a reserve without the permission of the federal Department of Indian Affairs, although in recent years these restrictions have been eased somewhat. This is what critics are referring to when they speak of the Indian Act's paternalism. For example:

- Band members may not sell any part of the reserve.
- The federal government retains the ultimate authority to grant timber-cutting licences and to establish their terms.
- Reserve land may not be used as security for loans.

There are over 2,700 Indian reserves in Canada, about two-thirds of them—and of a considerably smaller size—in British Columbia. Together they comprise about 10,000 square miles, an area roughly half the size of Nova Scotia. About three-quarters of all reserves are uninhabited, since many bands have leased their reserve land to non-Indians for purposes that include resource exploitation, rights of way, farming, and recreational uses. Reserve populations vary from two to just under 20,000 (the Six Nations Reserve in southern Ontario), and most inhabited reserves have populations of fewer than 1,000 people. Roughly 400,000 Indians live on reserves—it is impossible to arrive at a more precise number because census enumerations of the population have not been permitted on many reserves over the last couple of decades, including on some of the larger ones representing close to 60 per cent of all status Indians. Although there are reserves in all regions of the country, most reserves and the vast majority of those living on them are located in rural and remote areas. This has important social and economic consequences. Job opportunities are fewer, those residing on reserves are generally required to leave home to acquire secondary and post-secondary education, and physical isolation impedes the integration of reserve populations into the rest of society. This last effect is not considered to be a bad thing by many in the Indian community. As Harvey McCue explains:

> To many Indians, reserves represent the last visible evidence that they were the original people of this country. The reserve nurtures a community of 'Indianness' and reinforces spiritual unity among Indians. Despite the manifest poverty, ill health, poor housing and lack of services, the life-style on reserves, traditional values, kinship affiliations and the land itself all contribute to an Indian's identity and psychological well-being. The relative isolation of most reserves enables Indians to socialize their children to values important to their culture: reticence and non-interference, consensus decision-making and non-verbal communication. Reserves, since they are set apart both physically and legally, help Indians to maintain an ethnic identity within Canada.[6]

The pressures on Native Canadians to assimilate to the dominant culture are, as McCue suggests, powerful. Language loss is considered to be one of the key indicators of assimilation. Only three of Canada's roughly 53 Aboriginal languages—Cree, Inuktitut, and Ojibway—continue to be spoken by significant numbers of Native Canadians. A survey conducted by the Assembly of First Nations in the early 1990s found that even in those Aboriginal communities considered to be flourishing—where over 80 per cent of the population claimed to be fluent in their native language—the rate of fluency was sharply lower among younger members of the community. Figure 16.2 shows the gap between the percentage of the Aboriginal-origins population who claim a native language as their mother tongue and the percentage who say it is their home language for Canada's three largest Aboriginal language groups. Despite apparent language loss, however, some Aboriginal groups, recognizing the importance of their language to how they understand themselves and the world, are making impressive attempts at language learning and retention within their communities.[7]

Assimilation, Integration, Self-Determination

Although some of the major components of present-day Aboriginal policy were in place prior to Confederation, the principles underlying federal policy have undergone important transformations. Under French colonial rule there was no official recognition of any Aboriginal title to, or other proprietary interest in, the lands they had long occupied and used before European settlement. France laid claim to territory in the New World by right of discovery and conquest. As G.F.G. Stanley wrote:

> The French settler occupied his lands in Canada without any thought of compensating the native. There were no formal surrenders from the Indians, no negotiations, and no treaties such as marked the Indian policy of the British period. . . . Whatever rights the Indians acquired flowed not from a theoretical aboriginal title but from clemency of the crown or the charity of individuals.[8]

Conversion of the Native population to Christianity was a central objective of French colonial policy, implemented through the missionary work of the Jesuits and the Recollets. While clearly based on the premise that Indians were uncivilized, economically backward, and morally inferior to Europeans, French policy did not consider the Native population to be subhuman and beyond redemption. On the contrary, the 1627 Charter of the Company of One Hundred Associates declared

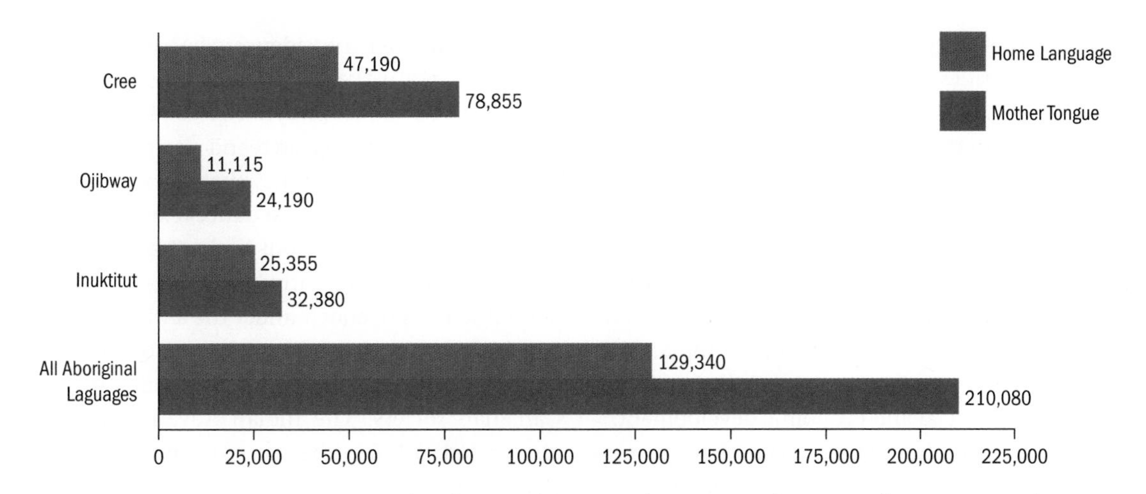

FIGURE 16.2 Language Transfer from Aboriginal to Non-Aboriginal Languages*, 2006

*Only the three most-spoken Aboriginal languages are shown here. The transfer rates for other Aboriginal languages are, for the most part, even higher.
Source: Data from *Census of Canada*, 2006.

that a converted Native had the status and rights of a naturalized French citizen. Assimilation and non-recognition of any Native proprietary interest in the lands claimed by France were, therefore, the two key principles underlying Aboriginal policy in New France.

With the transfer of French territories in Canada to the British, the foundation was laid for Aboriginal policies that would span the next two centuries. The **Royal Proclamation of 1763** and the treaties entered into between the colonial authorities and Indian tribes very clearly were based on the assumption that Natives had fallen under the protective stewardship of the British state. A proprietary Aboriginal interest in the land was acknowledged, but within the broader context of British sovereignty and the colonial authorities' expectations that European settlement would continue to expand onto land traditionally occupied by Native peoples. Moreover, as both the Royal Proclamation and early dealings between the British and Indians show, the British believed that they were required to compensate the Native population for land that was formally alienated through treaties and purchase agreements. This was an important departure from colonial policy under the French regime.

Efforts at assimilating the Native population were much less rigorous under the British than under the French. There is some truth in Francis Parkman's observation that 'Spanish civilization crushed the Indian; English civilization scorned and neglected him; French civilization embraced and cherished him.'[9] The British colonial authorities were much less concerned with the state of Natives' souls than with ensuring that the indigenous population did not impede the growth and development of the colonies they administered. To this end the policy of reserving certain lands for occupation and use by Indians was practised by the British. The policy of establishing Indian reserves was continued after Confederation.

Under the British North America Act (now called the Constitution Act, 1867), Ottawa was assigned exclusive legislative authority over Indian affairs, and within a decade of Confederation the federal government passed the Indian Act, a sweeping piece of legislation that consolidated the dependency relationship that already had been developing between Aboriginal peoples and the state. Under the Act, Indians living on reserves were placed under the almost total control of the Superintendent-General of Indian Affairs, whose god-like powers would be exercised by federal bureaucrats in Ottawa and by officials in the field referred to as Indian agents. Little of importance could be done by status Indians without the authorization of the Indian agent. All money paid by the federal government to members of a reserve or generated from economic activities on reserve lands was controlled by the federal authorities. To give an idea of how this system operated, if a licence to cut timber on reserve land was issued to a company, that licence could be granted by Ottawa only upon the recommendation of the Indian agent in whose agency the reserve was located, after which payments from the timber company would be received by the federal authorities in trust for the Indian residents of the reserve. The Indian Act made it impossible for Indians living on reserves to assume responsibility and control over their social and economic development.

The extremely limited powers of self-government assigned by the Act to reserve bands (powers that were always subject to approval by Ottawa) were to be exercised through band councils and chiefs elected for three-year terms (see sections 61–3 of the Act). This method for selecting chiefs reflects the assimilationist thinking of the time, whereby democratic practices of European origin were expected to replace Native traditions of governance that involved traditional and inherited leadership. The goal of assimilation is even more apparent in those sections of the Indian Act dealing with enfranchisement. The Act laid out a procedure whereby an Indian could request to become a full and equal Canadian citizen. While enfranchisement was automatic for Indians who acquired a certain social rank, including those with university degrees, lawyers, ordained ministers, and physicians, there was no automatic right to Canadian citizenship for status Indians before 1960, when an amendment to the Act extended Canadian citizenship to all Aboriginal people.

Until well into the latter half of the twentieth century it was believed by most that Aboriginal Canadians would gradually abandon their language, customs, and lifestyles and be absorbed into Euro-Canadian society. Speaking in 1950, Minister of Indian Affairs Walter Harris expressed this view. 'The ultimate goal of our Indian policy', he said, 'is the integration of the Indians into the general life and economy of the country. It is recognized, however, that during a temporary transition period special treatment and legislation are necessary.'[10] Integration progressed slowly, however, despite various prohibitions and inducements intended to eradicate what were considered to be backward practices and to reward bands that behaved in what were deemed to be suitable ways. The 1884 ban on the potlatch ceremony (repeated and clarified in 1895) and on religious ceremonies that involved dances (e.g., the sun dance or thirst dance) exemplifies the sanctions used to stamp out Native traditions. The prohibition on using Native languages in the residential schools operated under the authority of the federal government was another method of assimilating Aboriginal people into the mainstream of Canadian society. The Indian Advancement Act, also passed in 1884, whereby much more extensive powers could be delegated to a band by Ottawa, was an example of the carrot approach to encouraging compliant Native leadership and advancing the goal of integration. The extension of voting rights to Natives in 1960 brought their political status closer to that of other Canadians, but their legal and social status, and their civil rights, remained quite distinct. Moreover, instead of disappearing from the scene as the early architects of Canada's Indian policy doubtless hoped and expected, Indian reserves continued to exist as islands of shame within an affluent and democratic society.

The government of Pierre Trudeau set out to change this. Within a year of taking office Trudeau's Minister of Indian Affairs, Jean Chrétien, introduced the 1969 **White Paper** on Aboriginal reform. It proposed nothing short of the total dismantling of the Indian Affairs bureaucracy, an end to the reserve system, the abolition of different status for Indians under the law, and the transfer of responsibility for the education, health care, and social needs of Native citizens to the provinces, in line with provincial responsibilities for all other citizens.

The background to these dramatic proposals involved an elevated awareness of social inequality and discrimination during the 1960s. The black civil rights movement in the United States and the student activism that arose during those years took aim at the exclusion of minority groups from the rights and opportunities available to the majority. The remedy that social activists and civil libertarians proposed was integration, whereby barriers to the full economic, social, and political participation of historically disadvantaged minorities would be abolished. Integration was, in fact, the banner under which the civil rights movement marched in the 1950s and 1960s. It was not believed to be synonymous with assimilation, much less with 'cultural genocide' and 'extermination' that some critics have since equated with the liberal integrationist vision.

Nonetheless, the reaction to the 1969 White Paper from Canada's Aboriginal leadership was swift and overwhelmingly negative. 'Now, at a time when our fellow Canadians consider the promise of the Just Society, once more the Indians of Canada are betrayed by a programme which offers nothing better than cultural genocide' was the verdict of Chief Harold Cardinal of the National Indian Brotherhood. 'For the Indian to survive,' he said, 'the government [says] he must become a good little brown white man.'[11]

While much in the White Paper proved to be controversial, nothing galvanized Aboriginal opposition more than its proposals concerning treaty obligations and land claims. The government acknowledged that the lawful obligations of the Canadian government must be respected. However, it went on to argue that a 'plain reading of the words used in the treaties reveals the limited and minimal promises which were included in them' and that they should not be expected to define in perpetuity the relationship between Natives and the government of Canada. Moreover, the very concept of a treaty between one part of society and the government of all the people was morally and philosophically repugnant to Pierre

Ingrid Rice/© Simon Fraser University

Despite a vision for self-government rooted in the idea of Aboriginal sovereignty, the *Report* of the Royal Commission on Aboriginal Peoples has not moved the federal government to implement such a structure of governance except in piecemeal fashion.

Trudeau and the vision of inclusive integration laid out in the White Paper.

This vision and the premises on which it was based survive today as a minority point of view among Canada's political and intellectual elites. They have been refuted by numerous court decisions on treaty rights and Native land claims. Indeed, the trajectory of government policy since the ill-fated 1969 White Paper has been in the direction of recognizing, in the law and in the Constitution, the separate and distinct status of Aboriginal communities within Canadian society. Self-government for Native communities, a concept that was almost unheard of a couple of generations ago, is endorsed by the Assembly of First Nations, Canada's leading Aboriginal organization, and accepted as both fair and desirable by many Canadians—although most have little idea of what it might involve in practice.

This newer vision for Aboriginal Canadians was set forth in the 1996 *Report* of the **Royal Commission on Aboriginal Peoples**. The Commission started from the premise that Aboriginal Canadians constitute First Peoples whose sovereignty should be respected by the government of Canada. Its *Report* called for the creation of an Aboriginal third order of government whose existence would be based on the acknowledgement by Ottawa and the provinces that the inherent right to self-government is a treaty right guaranteed by the Constitution of Canada. A form of dual citizenship for Aboriginal Canadians, who would be both Canadian citizens and citizens of Aboriginal communities, was proposed by the Commission. The philosophical premises and policy proposals of the Royal Commission could hardly have been further from those of the 1969 White Paper. Among the most prominent of its 440 recommendations were the following:

- The government should issue an official admission of the wrongs done to Aboriginal people.
- The inherent right of Aboriginal self-government should be recognized by all governments as a right that exists under the Constitution.
- Natives should hold dual citizenship, as Canadians and as citizens of Aboriginal communities. The *Report* proposed, instead of the hundreds of Indian reserves and bands and over 1,000 Aboriginal communities in the country, that about 60–80 self-governing groups be created through the political merger of these communities.
- An Aboriginal parliament should be established with an advisory role concerning all legislation affecting Aboriginal Canadians.
- The government should negotiate with Métis representatives on self-government and the allocation to the Métis people of an adequate land base.
- Aboriginal representatives should be participants in all future talks on constitutional reform, with a veto over any changes that affect Aboriginal rights.
- Much more money should be spent on Aboriginal programs.

Running through all of the RCAP *Report* was a simple and fundamental premise: the original sovereignty of Native peoples and their ownership of the land to which they lay historical claim must be acknowledged and their continuing right to a land base and self-government must be embedded in the Constitution. Moreover, the survival and development of Aboriginal cultures can only be achieved through policies that recognize Aboriginal people as distinct communities with special rights and powers. The problem with federal policies for over a century is not, according to this view, that they have treated Indians differently from other Canadians. It is that these policies have not provided the Native population with either the decision-making autonomy or financial resources to take control over their lives and escape the cycle of dependency that the Indian Act and the reserve system have perpetuated (see Box 16.1).

Some of the Commission's recommendations have been acted on. Steps towards various forms of self-government for many Native communities—though not a one-size-fits-all model enshrined in the Constitution—were already underway before

Politics in Focus

Box 16.1 Chief Matthew Coon Come Compares Canada to South Africa under Apartheid

At the end of August 2001, Matthew Coon Come, at the time the National Chief of the Assembly of First Nations, spoke at the World Conference Against Racism in Durban, South Africa. His words, and the significance of this global gathering, soon were overshadowed by the terrorist attacks on the United States of 9/11 and subsequent events.

Canadians, and the government of Canada, present themselves around the world as upholders and protectors of human rights. In many ways, this reputation is well-deserved. In South Africa, the government of Canada played a prominent role in isolating the apartheid regime. In many other countries, Canada provides impressive international development assistance.

However, at home in Canada, the oppression, marginalization, and dispossession of indigenous peoples continue.

Every year, the Canadian government's own federal Human Rights Commission draws attention to this discriminatory situation, one that stunts and takes the lives of thousands and thousands of people. Yet little progress is made in addressing the fundamental, underlying cause of our poverty, hopelessness, and despair.

This root cause is the one that the South African anti-apartheid representative described [to us] over 20 years ago: landlessness, dispossession, and the social marginalization and exclusion of our peoples.

The lesson for me is that colonial and discriminatory policies and practices are not restricted to less-developed parts of the world. They are also to be found in Australia, Canada, New Zealand, the United States, and Scandinavia, to name a few examples. Indigenous peoples everywhere are being 'pushed to the edge of extinction'—even in Canada, where the plentiful land, resources, and capacity exist to correct these ongoing injustices.

Source: From 'Remarks of National Chief, Matthew Coon Come', World Conference Against Racism, Durban, South Africa, 30 Aug. 2001.

the RCAP made its recommendations, and some innovative models have been developed, such as the public model adopted for Nunavut and for Nunavik (Arctic Quebec), and the exclusionary model employed by the Aboriginal peoples of Yukon. Reparations have been paid to thousands of Aboriginal survivors who experienced mistreatment and abuse in the residential schools they were sent to, a practice begun in earnest in the late nineteenth century, and in June 2008 Prime Minister Stephen Harper issued a formal apology to the victims of these schools on behalf of the Canadian government (see Box 16.2). But no federal government has been willing to concede the division of sovereignty that seemed to be at the heart of the Commission's approach to Aboriginal reform. The notion of self-government that it proposed was premised on the idea that Aboriginal sovereignty must exist alongside and in no way inferior to the sovereignty that Ottawa and the provinces enjoy under the Constitution.

Organizing for Political Influence

Between 1867 and 2008 only 28 Aboriginal Canadians were elected to the House of Commons. That represents slightly more than half of 1 per cent of all MPs elected since Confederation. The picture is about the same in the Senate, where 15 Aboriginal members have sat, or 1.5 per cent of all senators over the course of Canadian history. Only

Media Spotlight

Box 16.2 The Lasting Legacy of Assimilation

Ottawa's apology to the victims of the residential schools that thousands of Aboriginal Canadians attended and the roughly $2 billion earmarked for reparations did not cover all of those who were victimized by a policy of assimilation. The article below describes the ongoing case of several Inuit who were selected for what the architects of this particular program doubtless would have described as a beneficial experience.

Inuit who as children were taken south as part of Ottawa's so-called 'Eskimo experiment' are suing the federal government, demanding compensation and an apology.

Seven Inuit children were used as 'guinea pigs' in the 1950s and 1960s when the government brought them from the Arctic to live with families from Alberta to Nova Scotia.

There they attended southern schools, without a chance to speak Inuktitut, learn traditional practices and eat country food.

'If you just said to the government "You used us as an experiment, I think you should pay us for that"', said Peter Ittinuar, who lived with a family in suburban Ottawa. '"You used us unwittingly, you didn't ask our parents, you just took us and in official documents you employed us as experimentees to determine how policy would be written about educating Inuit kids in Canada."'

Statements of claim filed in the Nunavut Court of Justice allege Canada denied the seven former students the right to communicate with their famil[ies] for long periods.

The court documents allege the seven Inuit were forbidden from practicing their culture, and were 'taught that their native language, cultural practices, customs and spiritual beliefs were inferior, wrong, sinful and shameful.'

That led to 'a loss of cultural identity and sense of belonging within their own community and within Canadian culture', and 'a loss of Inuit skills that are necessary to traditional living in the North'.

One of the plaintiffs, Zebedee Nungak, described in a 2000 article in *Inuktitut Magazine* his life in suburban Ottawa as growing up alongside 'textbook Dicks, Janes and Sallys' while taking part in judo and swimming, playing in rock bands and going to the cottage on summer weekends.

'Here we were, literate Eskimos, able to read and write English, and relate to the works of Shakespeare, yet no longer able to cut snow blocks with a pana (snow knife)', Nungak wrote. 'Well versed in calculus, we didn't know how to remove the sungaq (bile sac) from a seal's liver.'

Nungak wrote this 'cultural starvation' crippled his 'sense of identity'.

'These scars are hidden from the eye, but cut deep into our souls.'

The seven plaintiffs are seeking a total of $350,000 each in damages. More importantly, Ittinuar said, they're looking for an apology, much like former residential school students, who received cash payouts and, last month, an apology from the federal government.

'I think we deserve no less', Ittinuar said.

Yellowknife lawyer Steven Cooper, who's representing the seven, said Ottawa must make amends to groups left out by the residential school settlement. Social experimentation was common in the 1950s and 60s, he said, and part of the reason his clients are suing the government is to ensure their story is documented.

'These were kids who were considered by southern governments to be the best and the brightest and were expressly removed from their communities, not unlike residential school students, but with the intent of experimenting with them', Cooper said.

Source: Chris Windeyer, '"Eskimo Experiment" Claimants Seek Cash, Apology', *Nunatsiaq News*, 4 July 2008.

a couple of Aboriginal parliamentarians have been members of cabinet. The Charlottetown Accord on constitutional reform would have guaranteed an unspecified number of Aboriginal members of the Senate, somewhat along the lines of the representation that has been guaranteed since 1867 to the Maori minority in New Zealand's parliament. Of course, the Charlottetown Accord was rejected by the Canadian people in a 1992 referendum and the parliamentary path to Native influence remains weak.

Parliament, however, is only one of the venues where Aboriginal issues are debated and decisions are taken. The mere fact that Native Canadians have had little direct representation in Parliament is not conclusive evidence of anything. Influence may be exercised in other ways and through other forums. This has certainly been the case for Native Canadians, whose ability to affect policy has depended far more on their use of the courts, on public opinion, and on what might be called the institutionalization of Aboriginal rights and issues in the structures of the state.

The reaction to the federal government's 1969 White Paper on Indian Policy marked the real beginning of the politicization of the Native movement in Canada, although earlier efforts had been made by Aboriginal leaders to create pan-Canadian and provincial Indian organizations to lobby for their rights (see Box 16.3). Before the dramatic mobilization of opposition to the White Paper, Canada's Aboriginal communities were represented by a small number of ineffective organizations that had difficulty co-operating with one another and in managing their internal divisions. In fact, the federal government, through the control that the Indian agents exercised over spending by indigenous communities, had long discouraged the political organization of Aboriginal Canadians beyond the band or tribal level, and even at this grassroots level any organizing, as we have seen, was to occur according to terms established by Indian Affairs. Nevertheless, some efforts at broader political organization were made throughout the twentieth century, leading up to the formation of the Assembly of First Nations in 1982.

Sovereignty, Landownership, and Aboriginal Rights: The Battle in the Courts

> It has always been our belief that when God created this whole world he gave pieces of land to all races of people throughout this world, the Chinese people, Germans and you name them, including Indians. So at one time our land was this whole continent right from the tip of South America to the North Pole. . . . It has always been our belief that God gave us the land . . . and we say that no one can take our title away except He who gave it to us to begin with.[12]

Disputes over land—who owns it, who has the right to live on it, to benefit from it, to make laws that apply to those within the boundaries of a particular territory—are among the most intractable. Only recently have more than a small minority of non-Aboriginal Canadians come to realize that the crux of Native demands involves land. Phrases like 'self-government for Canada's Aboriginal peoples' have inoffensive and even positive associations for many Canadians until they are linked to exclusive Native ownership of land and political sovereignty in territory that the majority of Canadians assume to be part of Canada. The words of James Gosnell, quoted above, have been repeated in one form or another by many Native leaders, from Louis Riel to many of the current generation of Aboriginal leaders. Their message is simple: the land belonged to us, much of it was never lawfully surrendered by us, and much of what was surrendered under the terms of treaties was little more than a swindle of major proportions. Ownership and control over lands to which Aboriginal peoples claim a historic right are argued to be necessary for the survival of Aboriginal culture. In highlighting what are said to be the chief differences between Aboriginal and European-based cultures, nothing is invoked more often than how these respective cultures view the land and their relationship to it. Clearly, the land was crucial to the traditional lifestyles of Native peoples. For this reason such matters as Native hunting and fishing rights were recognized in the treaties entered into between Aboriginal peoples and the governments of European settlers. However, these rights were often restricted or ignored by federal and provincial governments and private citizens. Somewhat more controversial are claims to control mineral or other resources that are important to the lifestyles and economic activities imported into North America by Europeans, but which have little or no relationship to traditional Aboriginal cultures. This is an issue that Canadian courts have addressed in recent years.

Landownership is one thing. Sovereignty is another. The fact that a person or group of persons owns a particular parcel of land, regardless of its size and other characteristics, does not exempt them from the obligation to obey the law of the sovereign country within which their land is located. But many leaders within Canada's Native communities deny the sovereignty of the

Governing Realities

Box 16.3 Major Organizations Representing Native Canadians

1870–1938 *Grand General Indian Council of Ontario.* Created by missionaries' efforts to organize the Ojibwa tribes, the Council was conciliatory in its dealings with the Indian Affairs bureaucracy.

1915–27 *Allied Tribes of British Columbia.* An organization of BC bands, one of whose chiefs had travelled to England in 1906 to petition King Edward VII concerning a land claim, the Allied Tribes took up this cause and others, petitioning the Canadian government and Prime Minister Laurier and Britain's Judicial Committee of the Privy Council in the hope of gaining Aboriginal right and more and larger reserves. They did not succeed.

1918 *League of Indians.* Spearheaded by Fred Loft, a Mohawk veteran of World War I, this was the first real attempt to establish a national political organization representing Native Canadians. Loft's efforts were actively opposed by the Department of Indian Affairs, and after some initial organizing success in western Canada the League had failed by the early 1940s.

1945 *North American Indian Brotherhood.* Created by Andrew Paull, a BC Native leader, the Brotherhood advocated the extension of voting rights to Indians without the loss of their status rights under the Indian Act, an end to intoxication offences under the Indian Act, and better income support programs for Natives. It never achieved national support among Aboriginal Canadians and was disbanded by the early 1950s.

1961–8 *National Indian Advisory Council.* This was a classic example of the state creating an interest group in the expectation of being able to channel and to some degree control the demands it made. Although the stated goal of the Council was to promote 'unity among all First Nations people', it soon fell apart because of statutory differences among the three groups that it brought together: status Indians, non-status Indians, and Métis. The Council did not purport to represent the Inuit.

1968–82 *National Indian Brotherhood.* The breakup of the NIAC was followed by the creation of the National Indian Brotherhood, representing status Indians, and the Congress of Aboriginal Peoples, which represented non-status Indians and the Métis. Despite the fact that it did not speak for all Native Canadians, the NIB was the first national Aboriginal organization to achieve high public visibility and to be recognized by the Canadian state as the principal voice on Indian affairs. But the NIB had problems of internal cohesion, as was apparent when the organization split over the Canadian government's 1980 proposal to patriate the Constitution.

Canadian state over them and their land. Former AFN National Chief Ovide Mercredi's comment is fairly typical: 'We will not allow some other society to decide what we can do and determine the limits of our authority.'[13] Native assertions of sovereignty are sometimes more belligerent than this. Bargaining rhetoric and bottom lines are not always the same, of course. It needs to be said that while virtually all spokespersons for Native groups express support for the principles of **Aboriginal self-government** and rights, most advocate some form of self-determination that would be realized within the context of the Canadian state. The nature of such an arrangement, however, is the subject of much dispute.

The issues of sovereignty and landownership are obviously intertwined. These are matters that have been contested and determined largely through the courts, based on the interpretation of treaties. Indeed, it is usual for those who make the case for Aboriginal sovereignty to begin with the Royal

1968	*Congress of Aboriginal Peoples*. The 1968 breakup of the NIAC led to the formation of the Canadian Métis Society, which a year later was renamed the Native Council of Canada. The NCC brought together organizations representing Métis and non-status Indians. When the Métis National Council emerged in 1983 as a separate voice for the Métis, the NCC adjusted its focus and in 1993 it was rechristened the Congress of Aboriginal Peoples. CAP is a confederation of provincial and territorial organizations that seeks to represent Canada's urban Aboriginal population. In recent years CAP has had something of a rivalry with the Assembly of First Nations over which group best represents Aboriginal Canadians, with CAP taking a more conciliatory stance on some issues, as reflected by the fact that its National Chief, Patrick Brazeau, was appointed as a Conservative senator by the Harper government in 2009.
1971	*Inuit Tapiriit Kanatami*. Until the 1999 creation of Nunavut, Inuit Tapiriit (originally named Inuit Tapirisat of Canada) was the leading organizational voice for the Inuit. Its origins go back to the mid-1960s when the Indian and Eskimo Association was formed. When Inuit Tapiriit was founded, its initial funding was provided through the federal Secretary of State. Its efforts led to the creation of the territory of Nunavut in the eastern Arctic, about 85 per cent of whose population is Inuit.
1974	*Native Women's Association of Canada*. This organization, which speaks nationally for 13 regional Native women's groups, has as its mandate the promotion and enhancement of the political, economic, social, and cultural well-being of First Nations and Métis women. The NWAC, currently led by Beverley Jacobs, has been an important voice in seeking respect for Aboriginal communities, families, and women.
1982	*Assembly of First Nations*. Since its creation the AFN has been the country's foremost interlocutor with government on Aboriginal issues. Its leaders have included several of Canada's most prominent Native spokespersons, including Georges Erasmus, Ovide Mercredi, Matthew Coon Come, and Phil Fontaine. The current National Chief, elected in 2009, is Shawn A-in-chut Atleo, a hereditary chief from Vancouver Island with a background in education and community activism. Although the AFN does not represent the Inuit, Innu, or Métis, its credibility as a national voice for Aboriginal Canadians is unsurpassed. In addition to being regularly consulted by government officials, the AFN has often been an intervener in court cases involving Aboriginal rights.

Sources: Based on information provided in *The Canadian Encyclopedia* (Edmonton: Hurtig, 1988); <www.afn.ca>; <www.nwac-hq.org/>; and <www.itk.ca>.

Proclamation of 1763. The Proclamation dealt with the North American territories that were formally surrendered by France to England under the terms of the Treaty of Paris. It included detailed provisions regarding relations between the British and the Native inhabitants of these territories (see Box 16.4).

Aboriginal leaders generally view the Royal Proclamation as an affirmation of their existing right to the lands they occupied. Georges Erasmus, a former National Chief of the Assembly of First Nations (1985–91) and co-chair of the Royal Commission on Aboriginal Peoples, argues that 'by virtue of that Proclamation, it can be said that First Nations became protected states of the British, while being recognized as sovereign nations competent to maintain the relations of peace and war and capable of governing themselves under this protection.'[14] Regarding the treaties subsequently entered into between Aboriginal communities and the British and then Canadian authorities, Erasmus writes, 'First Nations did not perceive the treaties as being a surrender of authority.'[15]

In fact, however, it is not entirely clear that the Royal Proclamation of 1763—which was formally incorporated into the Canadian Constitution through section 25 of the Charter of Rights and Freedoms—recognizes Native sovereignty. What is clear, however, is that the Proclamation speaks of the 'Sovereignty, Protection, and Dominion' of the Crown in relation to the Native inhabitants who 'live under our protection'. That the Royal Proclamation recognizes Aboriginal rights is indisputable.

In the case of *St Catherine's Milling and Lumber Company v. The Queen*, decided by the Judicial Committee of the Privy Council in 1888, the Proclamation was interpreted as establishing for Indians 'a personal and usufructuary right, dependent on the good will of the sovereign'. In other words, according to this early interpretation the Proclamation neither established nor recognized Indian sovereignty over their traditional lands, but quite clearly referred to the sovereignty of the British Crown over these lands. While one might wish on various grounds to question the legitimacy of this assertion of British sovereignty, the point is simply that there was no explicit recognition of Indian sovereignty, at least according to this ruling of the JCPC.

But perhaps there is an implicit recognition of Aboriginal sovereignty in the Proclamation. This seems to be the argument of those who characterize it as a nation-to-nation agreement, a characterization that seems to receive some support from the Proclamation's use of the words 'the several Nations or Tribes of Indians', and also from the fact that the Proclamation states clearly that certain lands are reserved for the use of Indians and may not be purchased by private individuals or organizations, but only by the Crown. This restriction on the alienation of what the Proclamation refers to as 'Lands of the Indians' might be interpreted as an acknowledgement of Aboriginal sovereignty. At the very least it seems to establish an Indian right to compensation for land transferred by them to the Crown.

The legal case for Aboriginal sovereignty, which today is often expressed in the form of demands that the inherent right of self-government should be recognized in the Constitution, and for Native landownership draws significant inspiration from a case that was not even decided by a court with jurisdiction over Canadian affairs. The 1832 decision of the United States Supreme Court in *Worcester v. Georgia* is often cited approvingly by advocates for Aboriginal sovereignty. Although this case has no official standing in Canadian jurisprudence it nevertheless has been influential in a number of important Canadian decisions on Native rights.

Writing for the majority in *Worcester v. Georgia*, Chief Justice John Marshall distinguished between the right of discovery and possession that European powers could enforce against one another in the New World and the right of historical occupancy enjoyed by the Aboriginal populations that already inhabited land 'discovered' and claimed by Europeans. The right of discovery and possession, said Marshall:

> gave to the nation making the discovery, as its inevitable consequence, the sole right of acquiring the soil and of making settlements on it. It was an exclusive principle, which shut out the right of competition among

those who had agreed to it; not one which could annul the previous rights of those who had not agreed to it. It regulated the right given by discovery among the European discoverers; but could not affect the right of those already in possession, either as aboriginal occupants, or as occupants by virtue of a discovery

Governing Realities

Box 16.4 From the Royal Proclamation of 1763

And whereas it is just and reasonable, and essential to our Interest, and the security of our Colonies, that the several Nations or Tribes of Indians with whom We are connected, and who live under our protection, should not be molested or disturbed in the Possession of such Parts of Our Dominions and Territories as, not having been ceded to or purchased by Us, are reserved to them or any of them, as their Hunting Grounds — We do therefore, with the Advice of our Privy Council, declare it to be our Royal Will and Pleasure, that no Governor or Commander in Chief in any of our Colonies of Quebec, East Florida, or West Florida, do presume, upon any Pretence whatever, to grant Warrants of Survey, or pass any Patents for Lands beyond the Bounds of their respective Governments, as described in their Commissions; as also that no Governor or Commander in Chief in any of our other Colonies or Plantations in America do presume for the present, and until our further Pleasure be Known, to grant Warrants of Survey, or pass Patents for any Lands beyond the Heads or Sources of any of the Rivers which fall into the Atlantic Ocean from the West and North West, or upon any Lands whatever, which, not having been ceded to or purchased by Us as aforesaid, are reserved to the said Indians, or any of them.

And We do further declare it to be Our Royal Will and Pleasure, for the present as aforesaid, to reserve under our Sovereignty, Protection, and Dominion, for the use of the said Indians, all the Lands and Territories not included within the Limits of Our Said Three New Governments, or within the Limits of the Territory granted to the Hudson's Bay Company, as also all the Lands and Territories lying to the Westward of the Sources of the Rivers which fall into the Sea from the West and North West as aforesaid;

And We do hereby strictly forbid, on Pain of our Displeasure, all our loving Subjects from making any Purchases or Settlements whatever, or taking Possession of any of the Lands above reserved, without our especial leave and Licence for the Purpose first obtained.

And, We do further strictly enjoin and require all Persons whatever who have either wilfully or inadvertently seated themselves upon any lands within the Countries above described, or upon any other Lands which, not having been ceded to or purchased by Us, are still reserved to the said Indians as aforesaid, forthwith to remove themselves from such Settlements.

And Whereas Great Frauds and Abuses have been committed in purchasing Lands of the Indians, to the Great Prejudice of our Interests, and to the Great Dissatisfaction of the said Indians; In order, therefore, to prevent such Irregularities for the future, and to the End that the Indians may be convinced of our justice and determined Resolution to remove all reasonable Cause of Discontent, We do, with the Advice of our Privy Council strictly enjoin and require, that no private Person do presume to make any Purchase from the said Indians of any Lands reserved to the said Indians, within those parts of our Colonies where, We have thought proper to allow Settlement; but that, if at any Time any of the said Indians should be inclined to dispose of the said Lands, the same shall be Purchased only for Us, in our Name, at some public Meeting or Assembly of the said Indians, to be held for the Purpose by the Governor or Commander in Chief of our Colony respectively within which they shall lie; and in case they shall lie within the limits of any Proprietary Government, they shall be purchased only for the Use and in the name of such Proprietaries, conformable to such Directions and Instructions as We or they shall think proper to give for the Purpose. . . .

> made before the memory of man. It gave exclusive right to purchase, but did not found that right on a denial of the right of the possessor to sell.[16]

Marshall's pronouncement on the prior right of occupancy enjoyed by Native populations—a right that he argued the discovery claims of European powers could not in law impair—is generally construed as an argument supportive of Native land claims and even sovereignty. But the Chief Justice also had this to say:

> In the establishment of [relations between whites and Natives] the rights of the original inhabitants were, in no instance, entirely disregarded; but were, necessarily, to a considerable extent, impaired. They were admitted to be the rightful occupants of the soil, with a legal as well as a just claim to retain possession of it, and to use it according to their own discretion; but their rights to complete sovereignty, as independent nations, were necessarily diminished, and their power to dispose of the soil, at their own will, to whomsoever they pleased, was denied by the original fundamental principle, that discovery gave exclusive title to those who made it.[17]

This part of *Worcester v. Georgia* is, at the very least, inconvenient for those who purport to find a legal basis for Native claims to unrestricted landownership and sovereignty in that judicial decision. The legal principles that emerge from this much-cited ruling may be summarized as follows:

- Aboriginal peoples enjoy a right of occupancy and land use that predates the arrival of Europeans.
- Legal title to New World territory claimed by a European power belongs to the discovering nation.
- Aboriginal rights of occupancy and land use are not unrestricted, but rather are limited by the fact that discovery and possession gave the European authorities legal title to and sovereignty over these lands.

Marshall went on to say that the alienation of Indian land could be only to the state or Crown, and that Indian title to lands they claimed by historic right of occupancy and use could be extinguished by either conquest or legal purchase. The Chief Justice made specific reference to the Royal Proclamation of 1763, which, as we have seen, sets down precisely these conditions for the alienation of Indian lands.

The nature of Aboriginal interest in lands they occupied and used, and which had never been alienated by either military conquest or surrendered under the terms of a treaty, was elaborated further in *St Catherine's Milling and Lumber Company v. the Queen* (1888). In this case, the Judicial Committee of the Privy Council characterized the Crown's interest in the land under dispute as 'proprietary' and the Native interest as a 'mere burden' on this legal title.[18]

The land title issue was centre stage in the 1973 case of *Calder et al. v. Attorney General of British Columbia*. Although the Nisga'a claim to have unfettered legal title to land that they had occupied before the arrival of Europeans was dismissed on procedural grounds, the Court did express itself on the matter of Aboriginal title. One judge denied that it existed; three others recognized original Aboriginal title that, they argued, had been extinguished; and three others argued that Aboriginal title continued to exist. So while six of the seven judges recognized the concept of Aboriginal title, the majority determined that it did not exist in the case of the Nisga'a.

Because the *Calder* decision is so often cited as the legal basis for a right of Aboriginal landownership, it is worth quoting from the two sets of arguments given in this case. '[W]hatever property right may have existed,' said Mr Justice Judson for the majority, 'it had been extinguished by properly constituted authorities in the exercise of their sovereign powers.' In case there was any doubt regarding the Court's meaning, he went on to say that:

> [Crown] Proclamations and Ordinances reveal a unity of intention to exercise, and the legislative exercising of, absolute sovereignty over all the lands of British Columbia and such exercise of sovereignty is inconsistent

> with any conflicting interests, including one as to 'aboriginal title'.[19]

Why, then, is *Calder* generally viewed as a victory for the advocates of Aboriginal title? After all, since the *Calder* ruling successive governments in Ottawa and Victoria have preferred to emphasize the arguments of the three judges who maintained that Aboriginal title still existed. Their reasons for doing so probably involved a combination of factors. Most importantly, of course, six of the seven Supreme Court justices recognized the concept of Aboriginal title. Also, a shift in elite and public opinion towards greater sympathy for the territorial claims of Native Canadians was encouraged during the 1970s by the high-profile northern gas pipeline inquiry of 1974–7 headed by Justice Thomas Berger of the British Columbia Supreme Court, who a short time before had been chief counsel for the Nisga'a in the *Calder* case. This sentiment was expressed by Mr Justice Emmett Hall in the Nisga'a ruling:

> This aboriginal title does not depend on treaty, executive order or legislative enactment but flows from the fact that the owners of the interest have from time immemorial occupied the areas in question and have established a pre-existing right of possession. In the absence of an [explicit] indication that the sovereign intends to extinguish that right the aboriginal title continues.[20]

In view of the fact that no treaty or other legal instrument specifically extinguished the Nisga'a title in the land they claimed, it continued to be theirs. The practical ramifications of such a legal opinion, expressed by a minority on the Court, were potentially enormous given that virtually none of British Columbia was covered by treaties between the Crown and Native communities. Subsequent court rulings alluded to the Nisga'a decision and gave governments little choice but to acknowledge the new reality of a stronger legal basis for Aboriginal land claims.

The issue of Aboriginal title has been addressed in a number of cases since *Calder*. In *Hamlet of Baker Lake et al. v. Minister of Indian Affairs* (1980), the Federal Court of Canada appeared to accept the spirit and reasoning of the minority in *Calder*, arguing that 'The law of Canada recognizes the existence of an aboriginal title independent of the Royal Proclamation of 1763 or any other prerogative Act or legislation. It arises at common law.' While acknowledging, as has every other court decision on the issue, that the Crown exercises sovereign authority over Native lands, the *Baker Lake* ruling repeated the view, expressed by the minority in *Calder*, that Aboriginal title continued to exist until explicitly extinguished by legislation passed by Parliament.

A decade later, in *Regina v. Sparrow* (1990), the Supreme Court of Canada again addressed the issue of Aboriginal rights, including property rights. This decision continued the line of reasoning found in the *Calder* dissent and the *Baker Lake* ruling, holding that Aboriginal rights are pre-existing rights that are not created by government legislation and that such rights continue to exist until such time as they are explicitly extinguished. 'Historical policy on the part of the Crown', said the Court, 'can neither extinguish the existing aboriginal right without clear intention nor, in itself, delineate that right. The nature of government regulations cannot be determinative of the content and scope of an existing aboriginal right. Government policy can, however, regulate the exercise of that right but such regulation must be in keeping with s. 35(1) [of the Constitution Act, 1982].'[21]

The specific issue in *Sparrow* was whether the right to fish was an inherent Aboriginal right. Buried in the Supreme Court's ruling was a warning that common-law notions of property are not always appropriate in cases involving Aboriginal rights. 'Courts must be careful to avoid the application of traditional common law concepts of property as they develop their understanding of the "sui generis" nature of aboriginal rights.'[22] What does this mean? It could, one might argue, be interpreted as an argument against an unrestricted right of use and sale of a resource like fish or timber, if that use were to be inconsistent with the traditional practices and values of a Native community.

Calder, *Baker Lake*, and *Sparrow* were, in a sense, preliminaries to the main event that took place in the courts from 1987 to 1997. In *Delgamuukw v. Attorney General of British Columbia* the issue of Aboriginal title was addressed head on. A group of Gitksan and Wet'suwet'en chiefs argued that they owned an area in British Columbia roughly the size of the province of Nova Scotia. In their Statement of Claim they asked the Court to make three specific findings:

- The Gitksan and Wet'suwet'en owned the territory in question.
- They had the right to establish their own laws for this territory, and these laws would supersede those of the province.
- They were entitled to compensation for all the resources exploited and removed from the territory since 1858.

The stakes could hardly have been greater, nor the issues of Aboriginal title and the inherent right to self-government more squarely put.

Following rejection of the claim by the British Columbia Supreme Court in 1991 and the subsequent upholding of this judgement in the BC Court of Appeal, the Supreme Court of Canada in 1997 ruled in a unanimous decision that the Gitksan and Wet'suwet'en are the owners of the land to which they claim a historic right of occupancy and use. Where Aboriginal title to land has not been extinguished by the terms of a treaty—and this would include most of British Columbia as well as parts of Atlantic Canada—Aboriginal communities able to prove that they historically occupied and used the land continue to have property rights. Did this mean that non-Aboriginal families living in the Okanagan Valley on pieces of land that they thought they owned were in fact illegal squatters? Would a flurry of eviction notices hit residents of Vancouver? Did a forestry company like MacMillan Bloedel (taken over by the American lumber giant Weyerhaeuser in 1999) now have to renegotiate leases that it signed with the BC government that cover land rightfully owned by its original occupants?

In fact, the decision generated more questions than answers. What is clear from the *Delgamuukw* decision, however, is that the Supreme Court's interpretation of Aboriginal title means that at the very least Aboriginal communities like the Gitksan and Wet'suwet'en have a right to compensation for land determined to be theirs by historical right. The ruling strengthens the hand of Aboriginal groups who previously went into negotiations with governments armed with a rather nebulous concept of Aboriginal title, but who now can say that they have a constitutionally protected right of ownership that can only be extinguished through the terms of a treaty with the Crown. Landownership issues aside, the Supreme Court's 1997 decision did not establish a constitutional right to self-government for Aboriginal communities. It did, however, establish that the oral historical accounts of a people are admissible in court as proof of land occupancy and use, something that the lower courts had refused to accept.

The essential character of treaties between Aboriginal peoples and the Crown is another matter that has arisen in the courts, with some arguing that the treaties and other agreements between Aboriginal peoples and the Crown are tantamount to international treaties. If this is so, then it would seem to follow that these Aboriginal peoples have been recognized as sovereign nations capable of entering into agreements with other nations on a basis of legal equality. But as Cumming and Mickenberg say in what is generally a sympathetic treatment of Native rights, historically and legally there is little basis for interpreting treaties as international treaties. They note that the Supreme Court of Canada has expressly rejected this view of treaties. Moreover, they note that 'the Government did not consider the Indians to be independent nations at the time the treaties were made . . . and both the Government representatives and the Indian negotiators indicate that they considered the Indian peoples to be subjects of the Queen.'[23]

Despite the courts' lack of sympathy for the interpretation of Indian treaties as international agreements, Native spokespersons and some governments have insisted that treaties be viewed in this light. Speaking of those Native people who agreed to treaties with European powers, Georges Erasmus and Joe Sanders state, 'The way [our people] dealt with the Europeans is ample proof of their capacity to enter into relations with foreign powers.'[24] On the same subject they write:

> Our people understood what the non-native people were after when they came amongst our people and wanted to treaty with them, because they had done that many times amongst themselves. They recognized that a nation-to-nation agreement, defining the specific terms of peaceful coexistence, was being arranged.[25]

Not only are treaties agreements between sovereign nations, according to this view, they are emphatically not real estate transactions comparable to, say, the US purchase of Alaska from Russia. This point is crucial, because the position taken by the courts and most governments in Canada has been that any Aboriginal right to ownership of the land covered by the terms of a treaty is *extinguished* by such an agreement. The nation-to-nation view of treaties denies that any extinguishment occurred, on the grounds that this was not how treaties were understood by the Aboriginal peoples who agreed to them. That non-Natives understood these agreements differently does not, Native leaders argue, mean that their view, rather than that of Aboriginal people, should be considered the correct one.

A Native protestor stands at a barricade with the two-row wampum flag near Caledonia, Ontario, in April 2006, blocking a planned housing development on disputed land. The two-row wampum belt, two rows of purple beads set against a background of white beads, signifies the treaty made between the Five Nations of the Iroquois and Dutch settlers in 1613. The purple rows signify parallel life courses—together but never touching, the peaceful coexistence of two peoples. Today the two-row wampum is often used as a symbol of this broken treaty between the First Nations and government.

On a number of occasions courts have interpreted Indian treaties as contractual agreements. They certainly resemble contracts in that they typically include a rather detailed enumeration of mutually binding obligations. '[T]hey constitute mutually binding arrangements which have hardened into commitments that neither side can evade unilaterally.'[26] The courts, however, have recognized that Indian treaties constitute a rather unique sort of contractual agreement. This may be seen in the courts' tendency to interpret any ambiguous terms of treaties in favour of Aboriginal rights. As the British Columbia Supreme Court said in *Regina v. Cooper* (1969), 'The document embodying this larcenous arrangement must have been drawn by or on behalf of the Hudson's Bay Company and so any ambiguity must be construed in favour of the exploited Chiefs.'[27] The Supreme Court of Canada repeated and expanded on this rule of treaty interpretation in a 1983 decision. The Court declared that 'Indian treaties must be construed, not according to the technical meaning of their words, but in a sense in which they would naturally be understood by the Indians.'[28]

However treaties were viewed by the Aboriginal people who agreed to them, there is little doubt as to how the colonial officials and, later, Canadian authorities interpreted these agreements. As Cumming and Mickenberg write:

> The language of real property law as used in the treaties and the reports of the Government negotiators indicate that the purpose of the treaties was to extinguish Indian title in order that lands could be opened to white settlement. The treaties, therefore, can be best understood, from both a legal and historical point of view, when considered as agreements of a very special nature in which the Indians gave up their rights in the land in exchange for certain promises made by the Government.[29]

The question of how treaties negotiated centuries ago should be interpreted today does not provide easy answers. After all, the treaties were negotiated in very different circumstances, by parties of very unequal power and resources who spoke different languages and operated from very different cultural premises, and they were written in the language of only one of the parties. In *R. v. Marshall* (1999), a case involving the claimed right of a Mi'kmaq Indian, Donald Marshall Jr, to fish in contravention of federal fishery regulations, the Supreme Court said that 'extrinsic evidence of the historical and cultural context of a treaty may be received even if the treaty document purports to contain all of the terms and even absent any ambiguity on the face of the treaty.' The majority added that 'where a treaty was concluded orally and afterwards written up by representatives of the Crown'—a practice that was common—'it would be unconscionable for the Crown to ignore the oral terms while relying on the written ones.'[30]

The issue of Aboriginal title to lands and the conditions necessary to satisfy such title to ownership was revisited in *R. v. Marshall* (2005). In this case, Stephen Marshall (not related to Donald Marshall Jr) and 34 other Mi'kmaq Indians were charged with cutting timber on Crown lands without a licence to do so. They argued that they held title to the land and therefore did not require authorization to log it and sell the timber. They also argued that commercial logging represented a natural evolution in the trading activities that their forebears engaged in at the time (1760–1) the treaties in question were entered into.

The Supreme Court rejected both claims. While acknowledging, per the *Delgamuukw* decision, that both European common law and Aboriginal perspectives must be considered in assessing a claim of Aboriginal title and that 'evidence of oral history is admissible, provided it meets the requisite standards of usefulness and reasonable reliability', the majority found that the Mi'kmaq claim to having exercised exclusive occupation of the land in question before the arrival of Europeans was unsubstantiated.

On the separate issue of whether modern commercial logging represents a logical evolution of the trading practices the Mi'kmaq engaged in over 200 years ago, the Supreme Court acknowledged that 'ancestral trading activities are not frozen in time.' But these treaty-guaranteed trading rights did not, it decided, extend to commercial logging. This was not surprising in view of what the Court had said on this question in previous cases. '[T]reaty rights are limited to securing "necessaries" (which should be construed in the modern context as equivalent to a moderate livelihood), and do not extend to the open-ended accumulation of wealth.'[31]

The Institutionalization of Aboriginal Affairs

Treaties and the federal Indian bureaucracy that has existed since even before the 1876 passage of the Indian Act ensured that Aboriginal affairs were embedded in the activities of the Canadian state. Government transfers to Aboriginal communities under the terms of treaties, which were administered through the Indian agents, and transfers to individual Natives through welfare spending (Native

Canadians living off-reserve are about three times more likely than other Canadians to receive social assistance) created a web of financial dependency on the state that continues to exist. Historically, the institutionalization of Aboriginal affairs into the structure and activities of the Canadian state has also involved the creation and perpetuation of dependency relations. This continues to be the case, despite some important reforms whose ostensible goal is to break this cycle of dependence.

Sally Weaver has examined Ottawa's funding of the National Indian Brotherhood after the failure of the 1969 White Paper.[32] A former Liberal Minister of Indian Affairs, Hugh Faulkner, has argued that the motive behind his government's deliberate policy of funding selected interest groups, including Native organizations, was progressive and intended to strengthen the political voice of such groups.[33] Others have been more skeptical. Noel Starblanket, a former president of the National Indian Brotherhood, accused Ottawa of using money as part of a divide-and-conquer strategy for dealing with Native groups.[34] Roger Gibbins and Rick Ponting agree that the potential for the co-optation and control of Native organizations certainly existed as Ottawa became increasingly involved in the funding of these groups. '[T]he provision of money is deemed to carry the right to specify how, for what, and by whom it will be spent', they write. 'Other rights deemed to accompany the provision of money are the right to demand proof that the funds have been spent in accordance with the stipulations just cited, and the right to withdraw or terminate the funds.'[35] Gibbins and Ponting provide examples of money being used as a lever to control the behaviour of Native groups.

The leading organizational voices for Aboriginal Canadians continue to depend on public funding provided mainly through the budget of Indian and Northern Affairs Canada. There is not much evidence to suggest, however, that this dependence has muted their criticism of government policies or co-opted them into anyone else's agenda. Indeed, over the last couple of decades the criticisms from various leaders of the Assembly of First Nations and other groups have frequently been scathing. These attacks have often been made at international forums, ensuring that the shame factor would be magnified. Moreover, money spent on legal proceedings against the Canadian state, on retaining the services of some of Canada's most high-powered lobbying firms, and on advertising campaigns to influence public opinion in order to change government policy has come, at least in part, from state funding.

The institutionalization of Aboriginal affairs and identity within the Canadian state has also occurred through broadcasting. The early beginnings go back to 1960 when the CBC Northern Service broadcast the first Aboriginal-language program from its Montreal studios. This was followed by some Aboriginal programming through the CBC Northern Television Service, established in 1972, and by $40 million earmarked for Aboriginal-language television and radio programming in the Far North for the period 1983–7. Many other radio and television broadcasting initiatives were launched between 1960 and the mid-1990s, but the consensus is that the major impact of broadcasting to the North, where most viewers and listeners were Native Canadians, was to 'accelerate the process of cultural and language loss, particularly among the young.'[36]

The last decade has seen greater state involvement in support for Native broadcasting. Support for Aboriginal-language broadcasting was mentioned in the revised Broadcasting Act passed in 1991, but major new steps in this direction were not taken until the *Report* of the RCAP strongly emphasized the importance of such services to the cultural survival of Native communities. Telefilm Canada began to fund Aboriginal-language television productions in 1996. Since then, about 70 per cent of this funding has gone to documentary programs. The Nunavut Film Commission is another source of money for Aboriginal television productions. Ottawa also provides funding for the Aboriginal Peoples Television Network, launched in 1999, for radio broadcasters that serve the Arctic, including CBC Radio North, and for Aboriginal-language broadcasting in southern regions of Canada. The amount of Aboriginal-language programming broadcast by these networks and local stations varies considerably, but even the Inuit Broadcasting Corporation, whose programming is entirely in Inuktitut, offers only a few hours of television programming per day. The airwaves in Aboriginal communities continue to be dominated by English programming and, as discussed earlier in this chapter, the use of Aboriginal languages continues to decline.

A third way in which Aboriginal concerns and issues have been institutionalized through the Canadian state involves employment. Aboriginal representation in the federal public service, negligible for most of Canada's history, today is about proportional to the size of the Aboriginal identity population of the country. Native Canadians comprise about 3 per cent of the public service in the National Capital Region, but closer to one-quarter in the combined territories of Yukon, the Northwest Territories, and Nunavut. About 40 per cent of all Aboriginal federal employees work in the North or in the provinces west of Ontario. The largest employer of Native Canadians is Indian and Northern Affairs Canada (INAC). Almost one-third of its employees are Aboriginal, ensuring that the organizational culture of INAC is sensitive to the values and backgrounds of those it serves. Since 1997 the department has had an official target of 50 per cent Aboriginal employment.

Second Thoughts or Citizens Plus?

In 2000, two of Canada's leading political scientists weighed in on the debate regarding the place of Native peoples in Canadian society in a pair of books that offer very different analyses of Aboriginal politics and policy in Canada. Thomas Flanagan's *First Nations? Second Thoughts* staked out what today would be described as the conservative position on Aboriginal policy, attacking the idea of a distinctive and separate status for Aboriginal Canadians as both doomed to failure and unjust, and proposing instead a return to the sort of integrationist philosophy that informed the ill-fated 1969 White Paper. This was once considered a progressive approach to Aboriginal policy, emphasizing values of universalism, equality before the law, and the removal of barriers to the movement of marginalized groups into society's mainstream. But as liberalism has morphed into a more group-oriented ideology that sees universalism to be an obstacle to the equal participation and status in society of historically disadvantaged minorities, Flanagan's position and those who share it are generally labelled conservative (or something less kind!).

In fact, Flanagan is a close friend and former chief policy adviser of Canadian Prime Minister Stephen Harper. In 2004, when Flanagan headed the Conservative Party's national election campaign, the leaders of the three principal national Aboriginal organizations—the Assembly of First Nations, the Métis National Council, and Inuit Tapiriit Kanatami—called on Harper to disavow himself and his party of Flanagan's 'antiquated, ill-informed, regressive and offensive writings'. Harper chose not to. As AFN National Chief Phil Fontaine said:

> The reality is that if Flanagan was making these kinds of statements about any other group in Canada . . . he would not be given a senior role in a major political party and would more likely be exiled into the political wilderness.[37]

Within months of the publication of Flanagan's broadside launched at what he called 'the Aboriginal orthodoxy', Alan Cairns weighed in with his book, *Citizens Plus*. Cairns puts forward an analysis and proposals for reform that are very much in the spirit of the communitarian liberalism that Flanagan rejects. He accepts the argument that Aboriginal Canadians deserve to be treated as first nations with a sort of dual citizenship status within Canada. At the same time Cairns rejects the view, advanced by some spokespersons for the Aboriginal community, that Native Canadians can or should exist as fully sovereign communities outside of the Canadian constitutional and citizenship umbrella. **'Citizens plus'** is Cairns's formula for satisfying what he argues are Native Canadians' just demands for a restoration of dignity through the recognition that they are simultaneously Canadian citizens and rights-bearing members of Aboriginal communities. This is, as Cairns demonstrates, already the situation in Canada for many Native Canadians.

The Flanagan/Cairns debate crystallizes the points of difference that have existed in Canada since the rejection of the 1969 White Paper. Cairns distinguishes between what he calls the assimilationist integrationist perspective—he insists, contentiously some would say, that it does not matter whether you call it assimilation or integration: the harm to Aboriginal dignity is the same—and the institutionalized parallelism approach embodied in the analysis and recommendations of the Royal Commission on Aboriginal Peoples. This second approach is strongly supportive of Aboriginal self-government, a third constitutionally recognized level of Aboriginal government, and, at the extreme, full Aboriginal sovereignty. Cairns describes his own position as a moderate compromise between these two approaches, arguing that a one-size-fits-all citizenship for all Canadians, Native and non-Native, will never satisfy the legitimate demands of Aboriginal Canadians, but rejecting the idea that Aboriginal people should not share in a common citizenship with other Canadians. On the whole, however, Cairns's position clearly is much closer to what he calls the institutionalized parallelism position than it is to the integrationist model defended by Flanagan.

The case for 'citizens plus' is based on both history and current realities. In terms of history, Cairns argues, the primordial fact is that 'the majority built a flourishing, wealthy society on the dispossession of Aboriginal, especially Indian, peoples.'[38] Although many Canadians will agree with Pierre Trudeau's sentiment that we are only obliged to be just in our time, Cairns maintains that in Canada, as elsewhere in the world, there is a real need to come to terms with our past as an imperialist settler society built on the dispossession and marginalization of indigenous people.

Cairns notes that Canada's laws and institutions already include numerous instances of what he calls 'the positive recognition of difference'. He lists the following as examples:

- state funding of Aboriginal organizations;
- legal recognition of Aboriginal title to lands that they have traditionally occupied;
- entrenchment of Aboriginal rights in the Constitution through sections 25 and 35 of the Constitution Act, 1982;
- court decisions that have acknowledged a number of Aboriginal rights relating to land use, fishing, hunting, etc.;
- the creation of Nunavut;
- the use by governments and the wide acceptance in the population of the term 'First Nations' to describe Aboriginal communities.

Native Canadians, Cairns notes, are already 'citizens plus'. The key, he says, is to not lose sight of the 'citizen' component of their status—that which they share with all Canadians—while being open to the sorts of policies that satisfy Aboriginal Canadians' legitimate demands for recognition of their difference. He rightly notes that experiments in various forms of self-government are underway in Native communities across Canada. This, he argues, is the crucible where the concrete meaning of 'citizens plus' is being hammered out (see Box 16.5).

Flanagan does not disagree that Native Canadians already enjoy a different status from that of the non-Aboriginal majority. But this fact, he argues, makes less and less sense as Indians, Métis, and Inuit have become more like other Canadians in the way they live. '[T]he plain and simple fact is that aboriginal people now live very much like everyone else.'[39] The fact that Native demands to be recognized as distinct have been responded to sympathetically by policy-makers, courts, and some segment of the general public has far less to do with the inherent distinctiveness of Aboriginal Canadians—distinct subcultures and identities are not uncommon in Canada—and much more to do with the successful politicization of Aboriginal identity.

What Cairns calls the 'positive recognition of difference', Flanagan calls, borrowing from Thomas Sowell, 'government-mandated preferences for government-designated groups'.[40] He agrees with Cairns that such forms of recognition are extensive, but disagrees that they are a good thing. Instead

Politics in Focus

Box 16.5 Two Justice Systems or One?

Although Aboriginal Canadians comprise less than 3 per cent of the population, they represent roughly 20 per cent of the country's prison population. This is the background to section 718.2(e) of the Criminal Code, passed in 1996. It states that in considering the appropriate punishment for an Aboriginal offender, all available sanctions other than prison must be considered by the sentencing judge. This requirement applies, the Supreme Court has said, whether or not the Aboriginal offender lives on a reserve. This is one of the few sections of the Criminal Code that distinguishes between categories of citizens based on a group attribute, in this case ethnicity.

In *R. v. Gladue* (1999), the Supreme Court explained how this provision of the Criminal Code ought to be interpreted:

> Section 718.2(e) directs judges to undertake the sentencing of such offenders individually, but also differently, because the circumstances of aboriginal people are unique. In sentencing an aboriginal offender, the judge must consider: (a) the unique systemic or background factors which may have played a part in bringing the particular aboriginal offender before the courts; and (b) the types of sentencing procedures and sanctions which may be appropriate in the circumstances for the offender because of his or her particular aboriginal heritage or connection. . . .
>
> If there is no alternative to incarceration the length of the term must be carefully considered. The jail term for an aboriginal offender may in some circumstances be less than the term imposed on a non-aboriginal offender for the same offence.

Polls have shown that Aboriginal Canadians support this system, although not by overwhelming margins, while other Canadians tend to be opposed. The case against differential treatment for offenders from different ethnic groups is expressed by social and political commentator Naomi Lakritz:

> A separate aboriginal justice system might be a feel-good exercise for those involved with setting it up, and it will salve some consciences concerned with righting historic wrongs. But it will create an even greater wrong—race-based law and order. It will do nothing toward remediating that socio-economic disadvantage noted by the Canadian Criminal Justice Association—poverty, unemployment, substance abuse, domestic violence, lack of education. And it can never address the bottom line, which is that regardless of socio-economic circumstances, people are equal in one key way—everyone is free to make the choice not to commit a crime.[41]

What do you think? Is a one-size-fits-all justice system necessarily just, even when the life chances, world views, and ways of knowing of identifiable groups within society are very different? Should section 718.2(e) apply to other minorities as well?

Source: Excerpts from *R. v. Gladue* (1999); ('Why race-based justice is always wrong,' *Calgary Herald*, 2010.

of promoting the dignity of Aboriginal Canadians and providing their communities with a basis for economic autonomy and prosperity, Flanagan believes that the more probable consequences of 'citizens plus' include the following:

- An ever-increasing flow of public money will go to the governments of Native communities.
- More money for reserves will encourage more Native Canadians to stay or return

there, which is fine in the case of the relatively few reserves that are close to centres of employment and economic opportunity, but will merely keep the majority of more remote communities on a sort of government life-support system that chiefly perpetuates dependence.
- 'Citizens plus', which in practice means more money and more self-governance, 'will reinforce the already overwhelming presence of government in the lives of reserve residents.'[42]

Not everyone will see this as being a negative thing. Many Aboriginal leaders reject what they characterize as white notions of individual freedom and private property. But for those like Flanagan, for whom the individual's freedom to choose is a chief litmus test for determining the goodness of a policy or institution, the notion that Aboriginal communities should become more state-centred is abhorrent. Moreover, predicts Flanagan, 'On each reserve, the aboriginal elite will do well for itself by managing the cash flow of government programs, but most people will remain mired in poverty and misery.'[43]

Cairns and Flanagan offer two very different perspectives on where Aboriginal policy ought to go, based on their rather different readings of the past and current state of Aboriginal peoples' relations with government and the rest of Canadian society. They agree, however, that the idea of some sort of Native sovereignty that excludes or somehow overshadows Canadian citizenship is a disastrously bad idea. Policy should be crafted, they concur, so as to ensure that Aboriginal Canadians are part of the wider Canadian community. Beyond that, however, their analyses and recommendations are widely divergent.

Starting Points for Research

Yale D. Belanger, *Aboriginal Self-Government in Canada: Current Trends and Issues*, 3rd edn (Saskatoon: Purich Publishing, 2008). An excellent collection of contributions on various theoretical, legal, and practical aspects of Aboriginal self-government.

Olive Patricia Dickason, with David T. McNab, *Canada's First Nations: A History of Founding Peoples from Earliest Times*, 4th edn (Toronto: Oxford University Press, 2009). Dickason has been one of Canada's leading Aboriginal scholars for many years. This history, which draws on research in political science, anthropology, archaeology, biology, and sociology, spans the first peopling of the Americas to contemporary land claim settlements and conflicts.

James S. Frideres, *First Nations in the Twenty-First Century* (Toronto: Oxford University Press, 2011). Frideres, a sociologist and one of Canada's leading scholars on indigenous peoples and ethnicity, examines the various aspects of government–First Nations relations within a framework of epistemology, Aboriginal languages, and the residential schools and the intergenerational trauma the schools caused.

Paul Robert Magocsi, ed., *Aboriginal Peoples of Canada: A Short Introduction* (Toronto: University of Toronto Press, 2002). This volume includes chapters on the socio-cultural characteristics and histories of Canada's Aboriginal communities.

Review Exercises

1. How do the status and conditions of Aboriginal Canadians compare to those of their counterparts in the United States or Australia? You may find it useful to consult the data in the tables at: <www.dfait-maeci.gc.ca/aboriginalplanet/resource/canada/documents/diversityindigpolicy-en.asp>.
2. Should the Charter of Rights and Freedoms apply to all Aboriginal communities in all respects and at all times? Or should Aboriginal rights and the concept of self-government be construed so that they take precedence over the Charter in some circumstances? Formulate an argument on each side of this issue.
3. Identify an Aboriginal community that operates its own justice system, including law enforcement and Native sentencing. Explain how this system operates.
4. Watch the video segment at: <archives.cbc.ca/>. Click on 'Politics & Economy', then 'The Battle for Aboriginal Treaty Rights', and finally 'One paddle at a time', where Cree leader Matthew Coon Come explains why a hydroelectric development in northern Quebec should not take place. Explain why you find his arguments to be mainly convincing or unpersuasive.

Symbol of the close ties between Canada and the United States, the Ambassador Bridge joining Windsor and Detroit is North America's busiest border crossing, carrying close to 10,000 trucks and over half a billion dollars in goods each day. ©CP Photo/*Windsor Star*–Jason Kryk

17 Canada in the World

Canadian politics has always played out within the context of issues that transcend national boundaries, and this is especially true today. In this chapter we examine Canada's place in the world, focusing on the possibilities and limits available to Canada's policy-makers as they navigate a turbulent and fast-changing international scene. Topics include the following:

- How Canadians view their place in the world.
- How the world sees Canada and Canadians.
- The meaning of globalization.
- Arguments made about the consequences of globalization.
- Globalization and the intensification of Canadian–American relations.
- The asymmetrical relationship between Canada and the United States.
- Is more integration with the US the answer?
- Multilateralism versus the tug of continentalism.
- Soft power: option or illusion?

'The twentieth century will belong to Canada.' This was the bold prediction of Sir Wilfrid Laurier, Liberal Prime Minister of Canada from 1896 to 1911. Laurier's forecast of greatness for Canada was made against the backdrop of the enormous growth that had occurred in the United States over the previous century, when Canada's southern neighbour went from being a cluster of states hugging the Atlantic seaboard to a continent-wide power with the world's largest economy. In the heady years of the early 1900s, as the nation-building strategy launched by Sir John A. Macdonald in 1879 appeared to be fulfilling its promise and about 200,000 immigrants arrived in Canada each year, Laurier's prediction that something similar would happen in Canada probably appeared to many to be more than the rhetoric often expected from politicians.

Over 100 years later it is clear that the twentieth century did not 'belong' to Canada. The friends and foes of the United States would probably agree that it was the American century, for better or worse. By century's end the economic, cultural, and military dominance of the US was such that, in the eyes of many, comparisons to previous empires understated the sheer scale of America's global influence. The term 'hyperpower' entered the modern lexicon.

Notwithstanding the continuing global power of the United States, even today in a time of economic and military ambivalence, some Canadians believe that their country has achieved the greatness predicted by Laurier, though in a form that Canada's first French-Canadian Prime Minister did not imagine. 'For generations', says philosopher Mark Kingwell, 'we have been busy creating, in [the shadow of the United States], a model of citizenship that is inclusive, diverse, open-ended and transnational. It is dedicated to far-reaching social justice and the rule of international law. And we're successfully exporting it around the world . . . by seeing [the UN] for the flawed but necessary agency it is.'[1] Canada is, according to many of its opinion leaders, the cosmopolitan, multicultural, equality-oriented, internationalist face of the future. The Canadian model, as it has come to be thought of by some, is the real achievement of the last century and the one that is most likely to shape the direction of history in the twenty-first century.

Perhaps so, although Canadians might be surprised to learn that when the world's thoughts turn to the future of democracy, the evolving new world order, or the trajectory of world history, few people other than Canadians mention this country as charting the course. John Ralston Saul, one of Canada's most prominent public intellectuals, argues that 'Canada is above all an idea of what a country could be, a place of the imagination . . . it is very much its own invention.'[2] Canada is, he has argued, a successful model of accommodation and flexible ways of thinking about citizenship. But a survey of books written in recent years by leading Western intellectuals on democracy—excluding those written by Canadians—turns up very few references to Canada and certainly no sense that the rest of the world is watching, much less emulating, whatever the Canadian model might involve. Indeed, accustomed as we are to hearing that Canada is loved and admired by the rest of the world and that we are often looked to for wise counsel and assistance on troublesome issues far from our shores, it probably comes as something of a surprise to learn that not only our American neighbours, but other national populations as well, appear to know hardly anything about us (except that we are like the Americans in some ways, without being the Americans).

In a public lecture at Carleton University in February 2003,[3] Michael Ignatieff challenged his fellow Canadians to think about the ideas that most Canadians hold about their country and its role in the world. 'Are we what we seem to be?' he asked. 'Are the images that we have of ourselves true in the world?' Most Canadians, prompted by their opinion leaders, subscribe to a view of themselves and their country's place in the firmament of nations that has the following main elements:

- We are a peace-loving people.
- We are respected, listened to, and admired abroad.
- We stand for multilateralism and reliance on the United Nations and its agencies to solve global conflicts.
- We 'hit above our weight' in international affairs.

In addition to this short list of national characteristics, most Canadians probably would agree with the sentiment expressed by 'Joe Canada' in the hugely popular Molson beer commercial, released in 2000, known as 'The Rant'. Canadians stand for tolerance, not assimilation, says 'Joe', suggesting that the Canadian idea of citizenship is quite dramatically different from that of our southern neighbours. And as definers of the Canadian identity and interpreters of Canada's role in the world such as John Ralston Saul and Mark Kingwell argue, this Canadian idea of citizenship is perhaps our greatest contribution to world history.

For the most part, Canadians feel very good about themselves, their lives, and the state of their country. In the 2002 report of the Pew Global Attitudes Project,[4] involving a cross-national survey of 44 countries, only Guatemalans expressed a higher level of satisfaction with their lives. Canadians expressed slightly higher levels of life satisfaction than Americans and markedly higher levels than those in the other wealthy industrialized countries surveyed for this study. (It needs to be said, however, that other surveys have produced different rankings. Nevertheless, Canadians are always among the populations expressing the greatest satisfaction with their lives.) They were also far more likely than Americans and the citizens of several other wealthy nations to express satisfaction with the state of their country. When prompted to say whether one or more problems from a list of 10 was a 'very big' problem in their country, Canadians appeared to be remarkably complacent. The leading vote-getter was 'corrupt political leaders', which about one-third of Canadians agreed was a 'very big' problem. And yet by any reasonable standard corruption in Canadian government and economics is quite low, a conclusion that is supported by the annual corruption rankings produced by Transparency International.[5]

Canadians pride themselves on the maple leaf being a 'passport of goodwill'—that is, a symbol representing characteristics such as tolerance, compassion, prosperity, and politeness, making Canadians the envy of, and welcome all around, the world. Just how accurate is that self-perception?

Complacency and self-congratulations may be appropriate in some circumstances. They are not, however, particularly useful in regard to understanding Canada's role in the world. The conventional wisdom that most Canadians subscribe to when thinking about themselves and their country is flawed in many important ways. In this chapter we will consider some of the hard realities of Canada's relations with and influence in the world.

The Meaning and Consequences of Globalization for Canada

The central feature of Canada's economic condition is the degree to which it is dependent on markets outside Canadian borders. This has always been true (see Appendix at the end of this chapter). From the arrival more than 500 years ago of European fishermen who trolled the cod-rich waters off the coast of Newfoundland until the middle of the twentieth century, the economic prosperity of the northern reaches of North America depended on the exploitation and export of a succession of natural resources—fish, fur, timber, and wheat—to markets abroad, and on the import of people, capital, and finished goods. From the time Europeans began to be seriously interested in what would become Canada by sending ships, settlers, and goods, the Canadian economy was integrated into greater patterns of trade and shaped by forces beyond its borders.

At some point, however, there developed a hope and even an expectation that Canada would shake off this dependence and become the master of its economic destiny. One sees this already in Sir John A. Macdonald's ambitious National Policy of 1879, the first and only coherent and explicit economic development strategy that Canada had known before the decision to embrace free trade in the late 1980s, and therefore dependence, as the Canadian fate. One sees it also in Sir Wilfrid Laurier's optimistic prediction that the twentieth century would belong to Canada. And one sees it in the rise of economic nationalism in Canada, particularly from the 1950s to the early 1980s, the path of which was marked by a series of policies and institutions designed to limit American influence in the Canadian economy and promote indigenous capital.

Media Spotlight

Box 17.1 Canada's Image Abroad

As national 'brands' go, Canada's is a good one. An international survey carried out in 2005 by an international marketing firm found that Canada and Australia topped the table of affluent industrialized democracies in how well they were viewed by people in the 50 countries included in the survey. The warm feelings that foreigners generally have towards Canada are not matched, however, by much in the way of knowledge about the country or its people. Focus groups organized by Canada's Department of Foreign Affairs in 2003 found that many Parisians had no idea why French was widely spoken in Canada! For their part, Americans, as John Bartlet Brebner famously said, are 'benevolently uninformed' when it comes to Canada. Canadians tend to resent this. But they are quite wrong to assume that the rest of the world is either better informed about or more interested in their country than are Americans.

You may be dubious. After all, Canadians are regularly told that our health-care system is the 'envy of the world'. In recent times we have also been told by some politicians and opinion leaders that we 'punch above our weight' in international affairs and that Canada is looked to by other countries as a model of a 'post-national society'. Some of these claims are simply wrong and others are vastly exaggerated.

The truth is that, like most middle-sized countries throughout the world, Canada is seldom on the radar screen when it comes to media coverage in other societies, including those with which it has close economic, diplomatic, and cultural ties. During eight months spent in France I recall only two occasions when Canada was the subject of a story on the evening news: the deaths in Quebec due to buildings that collapsed under the heavy snowfalls of 2008 and Governor General Michaëlle Jean's visit to Paris in May of that same year. Those of my French students who believed that they knew something about Canadian health care and the country's social safety net had learned it from Michael Moore's films, *Sicko* and *Bowling for Columbine*.

Despite our intimate ties to the United States, Americans are not much better informed about Canada than the citizens of other countries. A 2005 survey of newspapers in five American regional markets plus the *New York Times* found that coverage of Canada was scant. Coverage of Canadian affairs was greatest in the *San Francisco Chronicle*, which featured more stories on same-sex marriage in Canada than did other papers. When Canada is in the news the story is not always good. Driving through Cheyenne, Wyoming, on the Fourth of July, 2004, I bought the local newspaper. A story about Canada as a launching point for terrorists to enter the United States was on the front page. *The Cell Next Door*—as in terrorist cell—was the title of a documentary shown on the highly regarded Public Broadcasting System in 2006. Staying out of the headlines and off the American news radar screen may sometimes be to Canada's benefit.

In the United States, France, and many other countries Canada is well known by a small segment of the population. These are 'Canadianists', mainly academics, who teach courses, carry out research, write articles and books, and give interviews on aspects of Canada in which they have acquired expertise. Since the mid-1980s the Canadian government has invested considerable resources in support of this international network of knowledge about and goodwill towards Canada, most of it going to the United States and the EU. This investment represents a form of what is called public diplomacy. Although the consequences are seldom immediately apparent and the returns are never easy to measure, there is little doubt that encouraging informed awareness of Canada and expert contacts abroad provide real benefits for the country. Of course, those benefits might be lessened when the government promotes Canadian stereotypes to the world, as it did with a fake Muskoka lake at the media centre in downtown Toronto during the G20 summit in June of 2010, and with a rustic shack peddling beaver tail pastries, complete with red-coated Mounties as greeters, at the World Economic Forum in Davos, Switzerland, in January 2011. Nor, perhaps, does it help Canada's standing when its political leaders show little knowledge of their near neighbour, as when Defence Minister Peter McKay, in late January 2011, spoke of the border shared by British Columbia and California.

Some of these nationalistic hopes still survive, although they have come to appear increasingly atavistic in a world characterized by unprecedented levels of economic interdependence and global communication. Today, the serious debate is not about whether the forces of globalization can be rolled back, but how and in what instances they should be controlled. In Canada the question of globalization is inseparable from that of Canada's relationship to the United States. For Canada, at least, globalization has meant an intensification in economic and other ties to the world's only (but some would say fading) superpower. Whether, on balance, this is a good thing is certainly one of the leading issues in Canadian public life.

What Is Globalization?

In some ways, globalization may appear to be a very old phenomenon. The Spice Road that snaked from the ports of the eastern Mediterranean across the Middle East and Asia to China 2,000 years ago was an early precursor of the massive flow of goods and services that today knits together all corners of the globe. A characteristic of today's globalized world that usually is thought to distinguish it from international trade in earlier times is the unprecedented volume and speed of the economic exchanges in the contemporary global economy. According to Harvard economist Jeffrey Sachs, only about one-quarter of the world's population, accounting for about half of global production, was linked by trade in 1980. He estimates that, two decades later, this had grown to closer to 90 per cent of the world's population, whose economies accounted for all but a tiny fraction of the world's wealth.[6]

Economists point to two chief factors that have driven globalization in recent decades. One is technology. Developments in transportation, telecommunications, and manufacturing have made it profitable to assemble in Mexico appliances designed in Canada or the United States, with parts and component systems from perhaps several different countries, and destined for sale in many different national markets. The global integration of goods production was accompanied by increased transnational flows of investment capital, leading inevitably to a greater integration of financial markets as banks, investment funds, and companies increasingly realized that their activities and opportunities spilled across national borders. Since the end of World War II, policy-makers in the developed countries have generally favoured a more open trading environment that has encouraged this process. Although the world economy is still far from the level playing field that free trade boosters often talk about, there can be no doubt that protectionist barriers have declined over the last several decades, through bilateral agreements like the **Canada–US Free Trade Agreement** (FTA), regional free trade such as that which occurs under NAFTA and in the European Union, and more comprehensive trade liberalization under the aegis of the General Agreement on Tariffs and Trade, which has now become the more formalized and institutionalized World Trade Organization (WTO). National subsidies and protectionism in various guises are still practised to varying degrees by all governments, but the overall trajectory of trade policy in Canada, as elsewhere, has been in the direction of more open markets.

The fact that free or freer trade has become the fashionable norm among the developed countries does not mean that doubt has been silenced or dissent squelched. The 1999 Seattle meeting of the WTO, the 2001 Organization of American States (OAS) Summit of the Americas in Quebec City, the G8 meetings in Genoa in 2001 and in Rostock, Germany, in 2007, and the 2010 G20 meetings in Toronto all were accompanied by violent clashes between anti-globalization protestors and police. Protestors in the streets have been complemented by various other forms of anti-globalization that range from intellectual attacks to political parties, social movements, and interest groups for whom the critique of globalization is a central ideological principle, or even *the* central principle. In Canada these forces include many—very likely most—of those who teach in the social sciences, a significant part of the country's media elite, much of the leadership of the labour movement, the NDP, many religious organizations, environmental groups, and nationalist groups like the Council of Canadians. Their criticisms of globalization receive considerable coverage, from the television screen to the classroom. Indeed, the critique of globalization is probably better known to most Canadians and, for that matter, citizens in other wealthy countries than is its defence.

But globalization is not simply about economics and trade. It also involves the unprecedented movement of people between countries of the world, exchange in cultural values, the more rapid and widespread diffusion of diseases across the world, new security concerns that reach across borders, the introduction of animal and vegetable species in parts of the world that did not previously know them, and the emergence of the virtual global village made possible by modern telecommunications technology. Again, some of these phenomena are not new. When the Romans conquered and ruled over far-flung parts of their empire, they also introduced and left a legacy of cultural values. The migration of peoples between different territories is a story as old as human history. When Europeans arrived in the New World they brought with them diseases for which the indigenous peoples lacked immunities, leading to the decimation of many of these populations. And the spread of species between distant parts of the world has a long history. The horse was introduced in the Americas by the Spanish in the sixteenth century and the potato was brought to Europe by them from South America. As in the case of trade, however, all of these flows have increased in volume, reach, and, in many instances, in their consequences for the people and natural environments affected by them. What we today call **globalization** may be defined as the historically unprecedented speed and scope of exchanges between different societies and regions of the world. Its consequences have been the subject of enormous debate.

CORPORATE GLOBALIZATION
Neither one of them has been elected to anything...
...and yet they blame us for never voting.

© Roy Peterson/*Vancouver Sun*

From 'the Battle in Seattle' to other clashes over globalization, all sides have attempted to wrap themselves in the flag of democracy, claiming to represent the interests of the people.

The Anti-Globalization Indictment

In many ways the anti-globalization movement and the analysis that underpins it represent the latest edge of a tradition whose origins go back to the critique of capitalism developed by Karl Marx in the middle of the nineteenth century. Marx made several claims that sound familiar today:

- Market economies necessarily create competitive and mutually exclusive interests, most importantly between those who control the means of producing and distributing wealth—the capitalist class—and those who must sell their time, talents, or skills to make a living—the working class.
- As capitalism achieves ever higher stages of development, an increasing polarization of class interests occurs and the gap separating the rich from the poor grows.
- The saturation of domestic market opportunities drives capitalists in search of opportunities abroad, and thus other countries and populations are drawn into the cycle of exploitation, of workers and resources, upon which advanced capitalism depends.
- Governments in the capitalist world—and this would include international organizations like the WTO, the International Monetary Fund (IMF), the World Bank, and the G8 and G20—are essentially and unavoidably instruments for the repression of subordinate class interests and the protection of capitalism and capitalists.

With only some minor tweaking this is, of course, pretty much the core of the modern condemnation of globalization. Globalization is blamed by its critics for exacerbating the income gap between the affluent and the poor in developed societies, widening the divide between standards of living in the developed and underdeveloped world, undermining indigenous cultures, weakening the ability of governments everywhere to regulate business in the public interest, and reducing governments' willingness and ability to finance social programs. To this list may be added such additional sins as degradation of ecosystems across the globe, child labour and forced labour in parts of the world, international conflict in regions of the world such as the Gulf War of 1991 and the Iraq War of 2003, and the rise of global terrorism. Some of these claims are more plausible than others. Some are almost certainly false. Almost all of them are difficult to prove with any certainty.

The pros and cons of globalization cannot be sorted here. Nevertheless, because these issues are hotly debated in Canadian politics, and because the broader consequences of globalization are related to its effects in Canada and affect the international system of which Canada is a part, we need to at least consider the evidence for these various claims. Moreover, a fair assessment of globalization's impact on Canada and throughout the world should also be open to the possibility that globalization has been, on balance, a good thing, or at least that the balance sheet is not entirely red.

Let us review the charges made concerning the general consequences of globalization and the specific impacts alleged by some to have been experienced in Canada.

1. *Inequality between the rich and the poor in Canada and the number of people living in poverty have increased due to globalization.*

Contrary to the conventional wisdom purveyed by probably most academics and journalists, and many politicians, these claims are not self-evidently true. First of all, the distribution of income in Canada is not more unequal today than it was 30 years ago, at least if one compares the share of national income received by those in the top quintile of all families to that received by those in the bottom quintile. There are, granted, various ways of measuring the distribution of income. By some of these measures it appears that income inequality has increased over time. Other measures, however, tell a different story. And in any case, the causal linkage between globalization and developments in the distribution of income is not as clear as many contend. Income inequality may change or remain the same in response to numerous factors, including government policies, shifting demographic patterns, economic restructuring caused by factors other than globalization, and so on. Globalization may be part of an explanation, but ideology more than analysis often elevates it to the status of the primary cause of income inequality.

What about poverty? The argument is often made that globalization has increased the ranks of the marginalized, producing more who are unable to afford a decent standard of living. Child poverty, the phenomenon of the working poor, and an apparent increase in visible destitution—homelessness, begging, reliance on food banks, etc.—are argued by some to be at least partially due to economic globalization.

There are at least two problems with such claims. The first is the one of wrongly attributed causality. As in the case of the distribution of income, change may be the result of a number of factors that have little or nothing to do with economic globalization. For example, it is demonstrably true and known to all serious students of family policy that the sharp increase over the last generation in the number of single-parent households—usually headed by women—has been a major factor driving the increase in child poverty. As a group, single mothers tend to have lower-than-average incomes. Consequently, they and their dependent children are at a greatly elevated risk of falling below the poverty line, however that line is defined. This has a lot to do with ideas about marriage, divorce laws, and income supports for single parents, but not much to do with globalization.

The other problem involves the very claim that poverty has increased. The truth of this claim is at least open to dispute. Using Statistics Canada's definition of what constitutes a low income, a smaller share of the population falls below what is often called the 'poverty line' at present than was the case 40 years ago. Moreover, claims about the extent of poverty are often confused with developments in the distribution of income, so that greater inequality in income is assumed—mistakenly—to signify an increase in poverty. Increased inequality within the society may increase the self-perception of poverty for those less well-off, but it does not mean that a greater proportion of the population is in dire straits. Although poverty is an undeniable problem in a rich country like Canada, it requires a rather imaginative and contestable definition to conclude that the scale of poverty has increased.

2. *Economic globalization has increased the income gap between the rich and poor countries of the world.*

There is no doubt that the income gap has been exacerbated in recent decades. This has been due not so much to poor countries becoming even poorer in some absolute sense—although some have reached new lows of destitution, due often to such factors as drought, civil war, bad policies, corrupt regimes, and other factors—but mainly because the rich world has become richer, and thus the gap has widened. But is this due to globalization?

The answer is mixed. Increased trade between such countries as China, India, Mexico, Malaysia, the Philippines, Vietnam, and the developed world has contributed to rising incomes in these countries and the growth of a middle class that, while very small by Western standards, is usually thought to be a crucial ingredient if a society is to acquire democratic institutions. Countries such as Bangladesh, Pakistan, and virtually all of Africa remain desperately poor, but the examples of the countries where living standards have improved suggest that it is not increasing participation in the global economy that causes countries to remain mired in destitution. Some argue that the loan conditions of the IMF and the World Bank and the subsidies that rich countries often provide to domestic industries—especially agriculture and natural resources—which might otherwise be export opportunities for developing countries, are among the reasons for the large and even widening gap between the rich and poor countries of the world. Even assuming that there is some truth to these claims, increasing participation in the world economy has generated higher average standards of living in many countries that, until a couple of decades ago, were miserably poor.

3. *Globalization undermines indigenous cultures, producing broadly homogeneous Western values and lifestyles in societies across the world.*

At one level this claim is obviously—but deceptively—true. Robert Reich, Secretary of Labor during the first several years of Bill Clinton's presidency, many years ago wrote about the new class of highly educated professionals generated by the knowledge-based economy.[7] These people, he observed, are at home almost anywhere in the world. The work they do and the lifestyles they lead are very similar in New York, Toronto, Brussels, or Tokyo. The experience of travelling abroad and switching on CNN International in hotel rooms across the world, seeing American products and corporate logos virtually everywhere, and being able to carry on with one's work and life through an Internet system dominated by Western- and especially American-based sites certainly seems to corroborate the claim that globalization has swamped local cultures in its wake. And at the level of general populations, there can be no doubt that some significant convergence has taken place in the music people listen to, the films they watch, the clothing styles they favour, and the food they eat.

These signs of cultural convergence in the direction of a Western norm are not merely superficial. But at the same time they are probably not nearly as profound or, for that matter, as insidious as critics claim. If one examines social and political institutions from the family to structures of local and national governance, there is little evidence that globalization has eroded differences and pushed different societies and cultures towards a common norm. On the contrary, students of contemporary nationalism and of the upsurge in radical Islam routinely argue that the resurgence of these communities is, in fact, a reaction to cultural homogenization. In other words, economic integration and the cultural consequences that inevitably accompany it may actually generate an affirmation of distinctive cultural identities. This affirmation is partly because national and regional communities—and especially their elites—may be motivated to resist the displacement of their languages, values, and institutions by those of the dominant global culture, but also because the strength of local customs and institutions is often underestimated. As Francis Fukuyama observes, 'if you look beneath the surface and ask people in different countries where their loyalties lie, how they regard their families, and how they regard authority, there will be enormous differences. When people examine a culture, they pay too much attention to aspects like the kinds of consumer goods that people buy. That's the most superficial aspect of culture. A culture really consists of deeper moral norms that affect how people live together.'[8] Most young people in the Netherlands speak English; Hollywood films routinely top the box office charts in Europe; American soap operas—significantly edited—are enormously popular in Egypt; and wealthy Saudis often send their sons to be educated at American universities. These are not inconsequential indications of globalization, or rather, of the Americanization of the world. They should not, however, be interpreted as signs that the pillars of local cultures are being washed away by globalization.

4. *Globalization has undermined the resolve and the ability of governments to regulate business in the public interest, to finance social safety needs, and, generally, to act as a counterweight to markets and rampant individualism.*

Despite being widely believed, little solid evidence supports any of these related claims. Taking the case of Canada as an example, the size of government, as measured by the share of GDP accounted for by the public sector, is about 40 per cent today, compared to about 45 per cent 20 years ago. Public spending on health care, education, and income maintenance programs (public pensions, employment insurance, social assistance, disability payments, etc.) accounts for as great a share of all program expenditures today as it did 20 years ago. While it is true that no new 'big ticket' social spending programs have been added over the last couple of decades, none of the major ones have been eliminated (though some, such as unemployment insurance and mothers' benefits for children, have been significantly overhauled). The decline in the government share of GDP is largely due to the fact that the growth of the economy has outpaced the increase in public spending. Overall levels of individual taxation have increased in Canada over this period, as they have in most affluent countries. And despite the privatizations and deregulation that have taken place in some sectors, if the sheer volume of health, consumer, and workplace safety and environmental and rights-based regulation is examined, as well as the number of regulatory bodies, one would be hard-pressed to conclude that the state's regulatory function is in decline. Indeed, many argue that regulation, before direct spending, has become increasingly popular as policy-makers' instrument of choice in dealing with policy problems.

A recent report carried out by the United Nations acknowledges that economic globalization has not produced, across the board, a decline in what the report calls **state capacity**.[9] On the contrary, the UN report concludes that, among developed countries, the state's capacity to maintain social safety nets and pursue such non-market goals as protection of the environment remains solid. The report argues that, notwithstanding what has become the conventional wisdom, 'there is no evidence that globalization weakens the State. On the contrary, increased globalization goes hand in hand with higher [public] expenditure.'[10]

The story is quite different in the case of many developing countries, but the authors of this report do not point the finger of blame at globalization. Rather, they blame 'state capacity deficit' in these countries—ineffective public administration characterized by low levels of professionalism, high levels of unethical conduct, inadequate technology, and weak social policies—for their failure to take advantage of the economic opportunities that globalization offers. In other words, the fundamental problem that besets many developing countries is governance, not economic globalization.

5. *Globalization has rendered the health of developed countries' economies more precarious than in the past.*

The old industrial model, pioneered by Henry Ford, was all about vertical integration. Coal, steel, rubber, and workers would enter the factory at one end, and vehicles would roll off the assembly line at the other. The new post-industrial model spawned by globalization is all about outsourcing. At the extreme, huge companies like communications equipment manufacturer Cisco Systems and computer manufacturer Dell 'exert a sort of postindustrial "Command Control" over [a] vast network of outsourced production',[11] depending on minimal parts inventories to keep costs down. Cisco Systems and Dell are not particularly exceptional, differing from such important companies operating in Canada as Bombardier, Chrysler, and Magna only in the extent of their dependence on a complex chain of outsourcing that extends across the world.

The problem with this, argues Barry Lynn, is that it introduces a vulnerability in the economies of rich countries that is far more significant in its potential implications than dependence on foreign sources of oil. Disruption at a crucial link or links in the supply and distribution network of the globalized economy, argues Lynn, could bring entire industries to a screeching halt because the globalized supply chain is more specialized than is often believed. This is particularly true of the flagship industries of the post-industrial economy—electronics and telecommunications. The effects of political upheaval or even natural disaster in a country far from Canada could send shock waves reverberating through Canadian industries.

The validity of Lynn's argument hinges on his claim that, faced with something like a catastrophic earthquake in Taiwan or a new anti-capitalism revolution in China, companies in developed countries like Canada would not be able to adjust their sources of supply quickly enough to avert a sort of meltdown in their production activities. Lynn probably overstates the extent of this dependence and, therefore, of the vulnerability to which globalization exposes the economies of the developed world. Nevertheless, he raises a question worth considering: 'As our companies continue to scatter industrial capacity to the far corners of the globe, then to trim slack at home until they come to depend on that distant capacity, are we not witnessing the creation of a new strategic commodity like oil, control of which can be exploited to wrangle away our wealth and security?'[12]

The supply and price of commodities on which the prosperity of the Canadian and other developed economies depend have long been affected by events in distant and not so distant parts of the world. Lynn's argument is that our exposure to such disruptions and the amplitude of their consequences are greater these days than in the past. He may be right. In recent years we have seen the price of oil and other natural resources spike dramatically in response to natural disasters like hurricanes and also in response to political circumstances. At the same time it may be the case that globalization and outsourcing have also increased the ability to substitute one source of supply for another. Canadians had a glimpse of the scenarios that Lynn argues have become increasingly possible after the terrorist attacks of 11 September 2001. Traffic at all border crossings to the United States ground to a halt, costing businesses on both sides of the border millions of dollars. At the Detroit–Windsor bridge crossing, the busiest transportation link in the world's largest trading partnership, truck traffic was backed up for over 20 kilometres at one point. The crisis brought home to Canadians and their governments just how precarious their economic prosperity has become (see Box 17.2).

Globalization and Canada–US Relations

The Chrysler minivan that rolls off the assembly line at Windsor, Ontario, appears to be the very embodiment of what economic globalization is about. Assembled in Canada by a Canadian workforce, the vehicle includes parts and component systems from the United States, Mexico, and China. The plastics and metals in these parts come from an even broader set of countries. Many of these components move across the Canada–US border on the hundreds of trucks whose daily destination is the Windsor minivan plant. Decisions about the design and marketing of the vehicle are made principally at Chrysler headquarters, about an hour's drive away in Michigan. General Motors' Chevrolet Equinox, assembled in Ingersoll, Ontario, has an engine from China, a transmission produced in Japan, and an estimated 55 per cent Canada–US content. For eight years, between 1999 and 2007, the company was owned by the German automaker Daimler-Benz. Since 2009 it has been owned by the Italian automaker Fiat.

Globalized production, sourcing, and investment have forced us to rethink what were, until fairly recently, firmly established ideas about what is Canadian. The case of the Chrysler minivan is merely one example—though a particularly important one in terms of its employment and income implications—of the new economic realities that characterize Canadian industry. Products exported from companies operating in Canada routinely

Politics in Focus

Box 17.2 Globalization's Real Soft Spot?

Barry Lynn's argument that globalization has increased the exposure of the economies of developed countries to events far beyond their borders appeared to be confirmed in 2008. But it was not a natural catastrophe in South Korea or political upheaval in China that sent economies in Europe and elsewhere into a downward spiral. Rather, it was the financial sector meltdown triggered by the billions in dollars of bad loans made by American banks and other lenders in what became known as the 'sub-prime crisis'. The crisis began in the United States, as millions of homeowners in a soft economy found themselves in default on their mortgages and housing prices plummeted, resulting in worthless loans on the books of financial companies. It was compounded when these same companies, fearful that others in their industry were teetering on the verge of insolvency or were already there, refused to loan to each other, strangling the supply of credit in the economy.

The crisis quickly spread to other economies in Western Europe, Japan, Russia, and China. Stock values tumbled, some banks and commercial investors had to be bailed out by their governments, and the belief that the health of these economies had been 'decoupled' from events in the United States—a belief that had recently become the conventional wisdom—was put back in the closet. Talk of a depression on the scale of the Great Depression of the 1930s was heard on both sides of the ocean.

Although Canada's financial sector did not experience the high-profile bank closings and bailouts seen in Europe and the United States, Canadians were not untouched by the crisis. As the world economy slowed dramatically, demand for some of the natural resources that had powered the growth of the Canadian economy over the previous several years and produced an increase in the value of the Canadian dollar softened and prices went down. Moreover, the drop in consumer demand in the United States, Canada's major export market, resulted in the further weakening of an already enfeebled manufacturing sector in Ontario and Quebec.

On the face of it this crisis resembled that of the stock market crash of 1929 and the Great Depression of the 1930s. Over-exuberant growth and unrealistically inflated values were followed by a financial sector collapse and a dramatic decline in consumer demand and business investment. But this latest crisis was different in important ways, both of which are linked to globalization. First, the impact of the financial meltdown in the United States on foreign financial markets, and ultimately on the economies of these countries, was faster and more far-reaching than in the 1930s. The world's financial markets are much more integrated and mutually dependent now than they were earlier in the century. Second, the possibility of governments being able to deal with the crisis appeared to be greater than during the decade of the Great Depression. The architecture of international co-operation among governments, as inadequate as it doubtless is in important respects, simply did not exist two and three generations ago. When Canada, the United States, Great Britain, the European Central Bank, and a handful of other national banks agreed in October 2008 to implement a co-ordinated cut in interest rates across these national economies, this was an unprecedented instance of globalized policy-making—albeit crisis policy-making—in response to an economic situation whose scope and depth were also linked to globalization.

Lynn was right in arguing that the interconnected world produced by economic globalization is one in which the health of many economies may be imperilled by circumstances in one of them. Where he was off the mark was in focusing on the suppliers of natural resources and cheap labour inputs for manufacturing as the weak link in the chain.

include foreign content, and imported products will often include content produced in Canada. Moreover, every Canadian provincial economy, with the exception of PEI, does more business with economies outside of Canada than it does with the rest of Canada. Thus, not only is the old idea of a made-in-Canada product cast in doubt, but the very notion of a Canadian economy seems a bit outdated given the reality of this country's enormous dependence on international or, more accurately, American trade.

The essential fact to keep in mind, however, is that in Canada's case economic globalization has meant greater integration with and dependence on the economy of the United States. The numbers are quite astounding. The total value of Canada–US trade in merchandise, services, and investment makes this easily the largest bilateral trading relationship in the world (although the China–US relationship is poised to surpass it in the near future). About 75 per cent of Canadian exports go to the United States, accounting for over one-quarter of Canada's total GDP. A somewhat lower share of Canada's substantial import trade comes from the United States, at about 60 per cent of total imports. This is down from about three-quarters of total imports a decade ago, a decline due largely to the increased importance of imports from China and a drop in cross-border automotive vehicle and parts trade. Canada has been the major export market for American goods for over half a century and is today the leading export market for about three-quarters of all state economies. The United States has long been the largest source of foreign investment in Canada, currently accounting for close to two-thirds of all foreign investment, and is the location for about half of all Canadian direct investment abroad.

This bilateral trading relationship has a long history, but in recent years it has achieved an unprecedented level of intimacy. The real value of local transactions between the Canadian and American economies has more than doubled since the FTA took effect in 1989, increasing gradually at first and then more dramatically since NAFTA came into effect in 1994 (see Figures 17.1 and 17.2). The fact that exports to and imports from the United States have sagged in recent years has been due to the increased value of the Canadian dollar vis-à-vis the American dollar (an increase resulting in large measure from the rising price of petroleum on world markets, Canada's currency being very much a 'petro-dollar') and to weakened demand in the recession-buffeted US economy. Over the longer term, however, more trade with the rest of the world has, in fact, meant more trade with the United States.

This relationship has never been one of equals and is not more so today than in the past. Revealingly, when the Canadian media were full of stories about the imposition of American duties on Canadian softwood lumber imports in 2005, there was barely any attention to the issue in the American media. Nor did the 2006 agreement ending this long-standing dispute receive more than passing notice on the US side, whereas it was hugely controversial in Canada. Canada–US trade disputes that lead the national news in Canada are lucky if they receive a mention in the American press, particularly outside border states that might be more immediately affected. The trading relationship is not only huge; it is hugely asymmetrical, affecting Canada's vital interests far more than it does those of the United States (see Table 17.1).

It would be an overstatement to say that Canada has no leverage in this relationship. After all, Canada—not Saudi Arabia!—is the single largest source of energy imports to the US and is the destination for over half the value of all US automotive exports. The Canadian economy is extremely important, and even strategically important, to the United States. Canada is the major source of foreign imports for 35 of the 50 American states and for many years has been the single largest foreign supplier of energy to the United States. But the influence that this might otherwise give Canadian negotiators in trade disputes with Washington is diluted by Canada's far greater across-the-board dependence on the American economy. To give but two examples, an end to petroleum exports from Alberta to the United States would bring Alberta's economy to its knees and ripple through the rest of the Canadian economy in various ways, but this would represent only a drop of roughly 8 per cent in the total supply of petroleum consumed in the

United States. Likewise, if the American border were to be closed to automobiles, trucks, and auto parts from Canada, this would represent a loss of almost 30 per cent of total Canadian exports, or about one-tenth of GDP. The impact on the Ontario economy would be as devastating as the hypothesized loss of Alberta's oil and gas exports to the US. State economies like those of Michigan and Ohio would experience serious losses from the end of automotive trade with Canada, but the total value

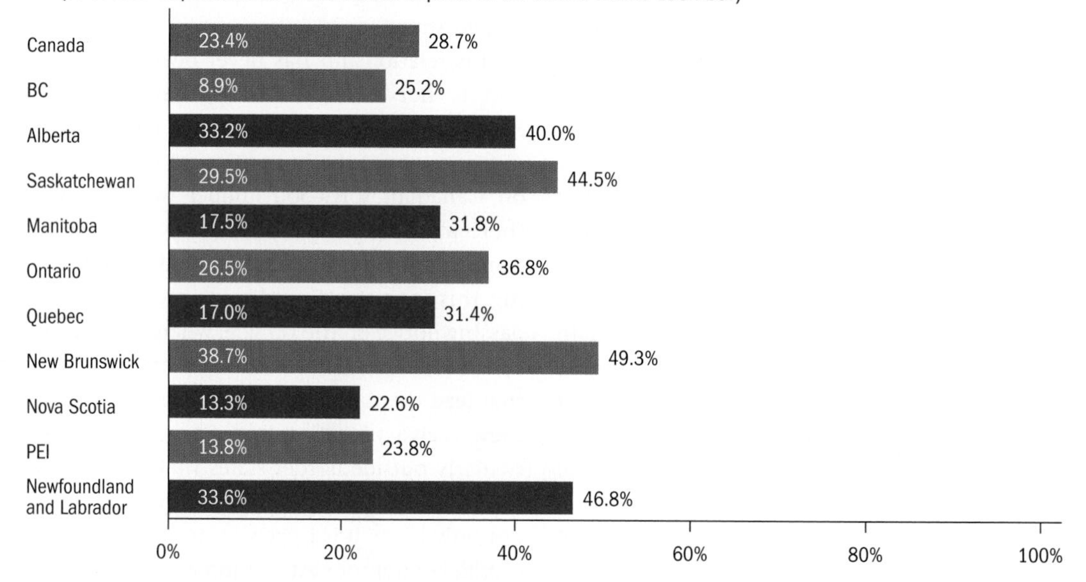

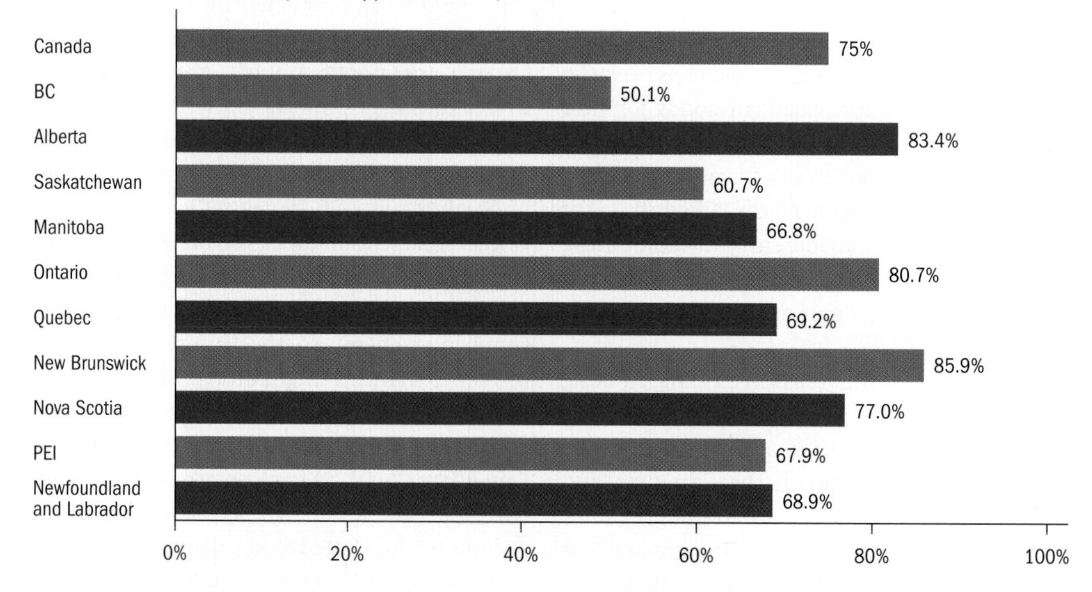

FIGURE 17.1 Dependence of Provincial Economies on Export Trade and on Merchandise Exports to the United States, 2009

Source: Statistics Canada.

of American automotive imports from Canada represents less than 1 per cent of American GDP.

This enormous and unavoidable imbalance in the Canada–US trade relationship was one of the chief arguments put forward in the 1980s by the Canadian advocates of free trade. The federal government's official policy of reducing Canada's reliance on trade and investment with the United

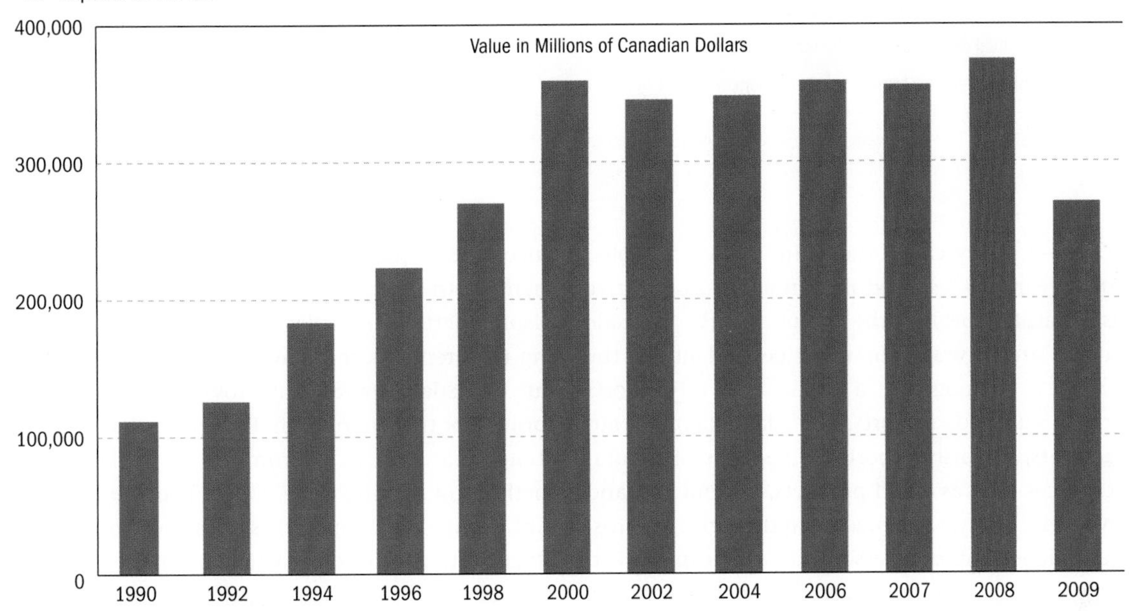

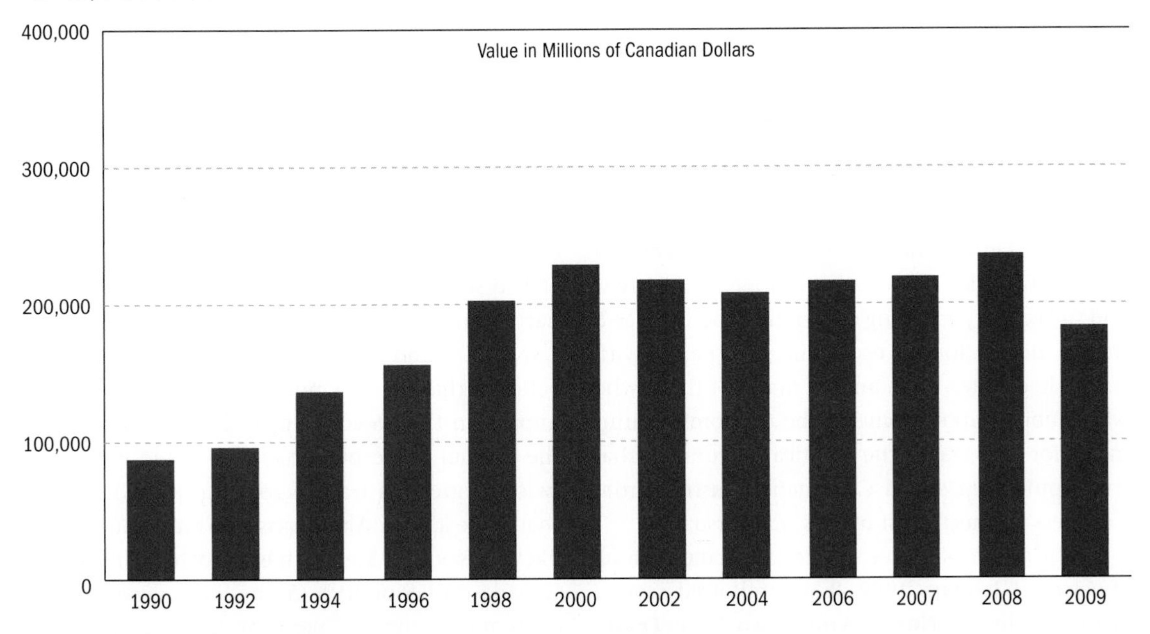

FIGURE 17.2 Total Value of Canadian Trade with the US, 1990–2009

Source: Data from Industry Canada, at: <www.ic.gc.ca/sc_mrkti/tdst/tdo/tdo.php>. Reproduced with the permission of the Minister of Public Works and Government Services, 2011.

TABLE 17.1 An Asymmetrical Economic Relationship, 2009

	Canada	United States
1. Exports to the other country as a share of total GDP	25%	2%
2. Investment from the other country as a share of total stock of foreign investment	53% (1st)	10% (4th)
3. Share of total exports going to the other country	75%	19%
4. Share of total imports coming from the other country	51%	14%

Sources: CIA Fact Book: <www.cia.gov/cia/publications/factbooks/geos/us/html>; <www.cia.gov/cia/publications/factbook/geos/ca.html>.

States—a policy called the Third Option, adopted in the early 1970s—had proven about as effective as a statute repealing the law of gravity. A decade later, Canada was even more dependent on the American economy as a destination for exports and a source of imports. Canada's major manufacturers, but also important exporters of natural resources such as wood products, oil and gas, and hydroelectricity, recognized that their growth prospects depended on access to the American market. The Canadian Manufacturers' Association (since renamed Canadian Manufacturers & Exporters), which began life a century earlier calling for protectionist tariffs, became a convert to and a politically weighty advocate of a Canada–US free trade agreement. A growing wave of protectionist sentiment in the American Congress during the 1980s seemed to lend urgency to Canadian free traders' case, helped by the pro-free trade recommendations of the 1981–5 Royal Commission on the Economic Union and Development Prospects for Canada. Canada's best economic hope, big business and the country's leading economic experts agreed, was in tighter formal economic integration with the United States. Even among many of those who were dubious about some of the economic claims made for free trade, the political argument that this would help shield Canadian industries from Congress's protectionist moods was persuasive.

The Canada–US Free Trade Agreement took effect on 1 January 1989. It was followed several years later by the **North American Free Trade Agreement**, bringing Canada, the United States, and Mexico together into a free trade zone that encompasses most industries and forms of investment. Both agreements created an architecture of dispute settlement rules, agencies, and monitoring requirements that have not taken the politics out of trade disputes, but provide administrative forums for their resolution. Experience has demonstrated that these new forums do not replace other methods of making trade policy. The older forums and channels still matter, as does the World Trade Organization. But on the whole it is fair to say that the rules and the dispute settlement mechanisms created under the FTA and NAFTA make it more difficult for the member governments to pursue trade policies that favour their domestic interests. They may still do so, but they run the risk of eventually having to pay the cost of sanctions if their policies are found to be in violation of these agreements.

The asymmetry in the Canada–US economic relationship is not helped, from Canada's point of view, by the fact that Americans—from policy-makers to average citizens—often have little awareness of the scale of these relations or, perhaps worse, harbour misconceptions about them. A 2001 *Time*/CNN poll found that 64 per cent of those surveyed believed that Mexico, not Canada, had more of an impact on the US economy,[13] despite the fact that the annual value of Canada–US trade was about twice as great as trade across the Rio Grande. In that same survey Americans also were much more likely to say that Mexico has a greater impact than Canada on US politics (50 per cent versus 34 per cent) and culture (65 per cent versus 26 per cent). Cable news programs on American business are full of stories about the US economy's relations with China and other Asian countries, the EU, and OPEC countries, but Canada is seldom on the radar screen. When it comes to Canada's economic importance to the United States, most Americans are quite simply unaware.

Ignorance may sometimes be benign. In this case, however, the fact that neither American policy-makers nor American public opinion demonstrates much in the way of awareness of the size and nature of Canadian–American economic relations may be, on balance, a liability for Canada. The long-standing saga of Canadian softwood lumber exports to the United States, which over a period of more than 20 years involved American measures to protect US producers from Canadian competition, illustrates the problem. Leaving aside the thorny and extremely contentious question of whether Canadian softwood lumber exporters were subsidized by timber licence fees that were so low as to effectively undervalue Canadian timber in comparison to that produced in the American market, it was certainly the case that home builders and homebuyers in the US benefited from less expensive Canadian softwood. Moreover, the overall thrust of American trade policy for the last few decades has been towards trade liberalization, a position that all American presidents since Ronald Reagan have defended with some vigour. None of this made much difference in the face of effective US lumber industry lobbying of Congress and the US Commerce Department to impose duties on Canadian softwood imports. Three years after these duties were imposed in May 2002, it was estimated that the cost to the Canadian lumber industry had reached about $5.5 billion. Under the 2006 Softwood Lumber Agreement the US government agreed to repay about $4.5 billion of these duties.

As Allan Gotlieb, Canada's ambassador to the United States from 1981 to 1989, has observed, part of Canada's problem in its trade relations with the United States is getting the attention of those who matter in Washington.[14] He argues, however, that the answer may not lie in government-financed media blitzes designed to let Americans know how important we are to them. Nor does he put much stock in Canadian efforts to lobby US interests, such as home builders' associations or Chambers of Commerce, in the hope that they will pressure Congress and administrative officials in ways congruent with Canadian trade interests. 'Like it or not,' Gotlieb says, 'in the US political system a foreign country is just another special interest. And not a very special one at that. It lacks the clout of a domestic special interest because it cannot contribute to political campaigns or deliver votes.' What, if anything, can Canadian policy-makers do to change this rather bleak prognosis?

Gotlieb's answer has two parts. 'First and foremost,' he argues, 'influence must be aimed at the highest level of the US political system, the presidency, the top personal advisors to the President and the key cabinet secretaries.' Gotlieb places special importance on the personal relationship between Prime Minister and President, complemented, ideally, by a good rapport between the Canadian Foreign Minister and the US Secretary of State. The personal relationship factor tends to be dismissed as irrelevant or of distinctly minor importance by most political scientists. Gotlieb's own experience in Washington, however, leads him to believe that '[i]f a matter is on the President's personal agenda, there is far better chance of a favourable outcome. If the President is concerned, word goes down to many hundreds of top loyal political appointees.'

Second, Gotlieb argues that tighter formal integration across the Canada–US border would help protect Canadian economic interests from precisely the sort of US domestic political pressures at play in the softwood lumber dispute. 'It is possible', he maintains, 'that a single market or customs union would enhance our interests.' Moreover, Gotlieb notes that Canadian governments may well have more leverage in economic matters than is often believed if they are willing to offer trade-offs on border control, terrorism, and defence issues. To be sure, this is a rather large 'if'. His conclusion extends the logic that led the Canadian government to embrace the free trade option in the 1980s. 'Canada', Gotlieb states, 'should look to a broader and deeper economic and security zone in which the rules of engagement would be less arbitrary, more predictable and provide greater common security.' He advocates a 'grand bargain' with the United States, establishing a North American community of law.[15] This, he believes, is the best hope for overcoming the unavoidable and lopsided asymmetry—both political and economic—in the Canada–US relationship.

Gotlieb's proposal for a 'grand bargain' that would establish a North American community of law—really something along the lines of the institutional and policy integration that exists under the European Union—is a political non-starter

NO CURRENCY, NO BORDER . . . NO COUNTRY.*
*LIBERALS TO DISCUSS UNIFIED CURRENCY AND REMOVAL OF CANADIAN U.S. BORDER!
©99 LARTER CALGARY SUN...

John Larter/© Simon Fraser University

The idea of Canada's deep integration with the US, including both a single border agency and a single currency, has been debated for some time, with proponents on each side of the argument. What would Canadians be giving up if such integration were to occur? What would they gain?

in both Canada and the United States. As one of the most astute observers of Canada–US relations, Gotlieb doubtless realizes as well as anyone the intractability of the political forces that would immediately mobilize against what he proposes. But the purpose of an argument like his, and its supporting analysis, is to nudge the conversation on Canada–US relations in a particular direction. It is particularly important to have an impact on the ideas of opinion leaders and policy-makers who, in turn, may be able to influence the direction of public opinion over time.

Seven years after Gotlieb's call for a dramatic next step in Canada–US integration, the Canadian International Council, led by Research In Motion's CEO, Jim Balsillie, issued a report entitled *Open Canada: A Global Positioning Strategy for a Networked Age*. Its analysis of the Canada–US relationship was broadly similar to Gotlieb's. 'Nothing [we have considered] imperils Canada's vital national interests more than obstacles to a free-flowing Canada–US border', states the report.[16] But instead of the 'Big Bang' approach that Gotlieb proposed, the Council recommends a 'series of little bangs, a steady drumbeat of small gains that build confidence and momentum toward a more ambitious plan at a more propitious date'.[17] The Council rejects what it believes is an ideologically driven and false dichotomy between multilateralism and closer integration with the United States. In words guaranteed to send Canadian nationalists reaching for the nearest defibrillator, the Council observes:

> To insulate ourselves from US political capriciousness or border hardening, we need to become America's indispensable ally. That may sound subservient to some Canadians, but it falls within the best traditions of independent Canadian internationalism. The relative decline of American influence means it has to reach out to trusted allies. Canada does not need to play little brother to the US to stay in the family—just the opposite. Still, progress will require mature bipartisan leadership. Any attempt to exploit this for political gain will scupper a deepening of Canada's national interest.[18]

Not everyone agrees with this analysis. Critics argue that it makes no sense to tie Canada even more tightly to an American economy that they believe to be in decline. Indeed, the Conservative government of Stephen Harper, generally thought to be quite sympathetic to arguments for greater Canada–US integration, has gone further than any previous Canadian government in negotiating a formal trade agreement with the European Union. Such an agreement has been discussed in Canada since the 1970s but always came to nothing because Canadian enthusiasm was not matched by much interest from the European side. What has changed is that EU negotiators now see Canada, with its close and formal trade and investment ties to the United States, as a stepping stone to entry into the American economy.

But is it a question of greater integration with the United States or diversification in trade and investment? In fact, this is a false opposition. One does not preclude the other. Finding a balance between these options is simple prudence (see Box 17.3).

The Canadian Dilemma in Foreign Affairs

As the foregoing discussion suggests, the Canadian dilemma boils down to this: Is it possible for Canada to maintain a margin of foreign policy independence when this country has a population about one-tenth that of the United States and an economy about one-eleventh the size of that of its giant neighbour to the south, especially when Canadian economic prosperity is more dependent on its leading trade and investment partner than is the economy of any other rich democracy? (See Figure 17.3.) In what circumstances does this margin exist? How large is it? And is economic dependence, on balance, a liability or an opportunity?

These questions have occupied centre stage in debates over Canadian foreign policy since the end of World War II and the emergence of the United States as the unchallenged leader of the Western world. Former Canadian Prime Minister and Nobel Peace Prize winner Lester B. Pearson, undeniably

Politics in Focus

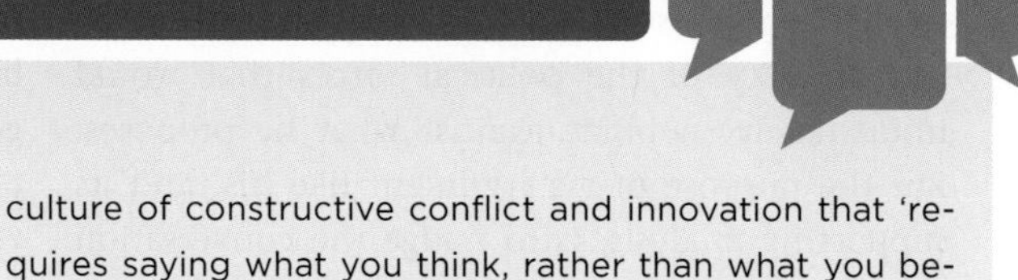

Box 17.3 Striking a Balance

It may be the current conventional wisdom that the US is in decline, but Canadians would be wise not to write off a country that has successfully created and recreated itself over the past century. As we obsess about the rise of China, we should remember that the conventional wisdom in the 1980s was that Japan would have eclipsed the US by now. The capacity of others to stumble and the capacity of the US to soar anew should never be discounted.

In her rallying cry for America in 2009, Anne-Marie Slaughter, at that time the dean of the Woodrow Wilson School of Public and International Affairs at Princeton University and now the director of policy planning for the US State Department, argued eloquently against all those who say that America is in decline. She noted that in 2003, the University of California alone had more patents than either India or China, which she ascribed to a culture of constructive conflict and innovation that 'requires saying what you think, rather than what you believe your boss wants to hear'—a culture for which, she said, the US is ideally suited and China, with its intolerance of dissent, is poorly suited.[19]

Even in decline, according to Slaughter, the US will remain the richest country and greatest power in the world for some time to come. The ultimate narrative of the new multi-polar era will not be written for decades. Will the US decline in the way the British Empire did? Will China's rise burn out in the same manner as the rise of Japan has? Will China and the United States stand above the rest in a functional dual-superpower system? We simply don't know, which is why Canada needs to hedge its bet on the US and make new friends elsewhere, while deepening its historical cross-border relationship.

one of the chief architects of Canadian foreign policy in the post-war era, acknowledged in his memoirs that American dominance and Canada's particular dependence on the United States were among the key hard realities confronting Canadian policy-makers.[20] These realities, Pearson observed, 'brought us anxiety as well as assurance'.

This continues to be the Canadian condition when it comes to the possibilities open to this country in world affairs. The asymmetrical economic relationship between Canada and the United States, overlain by structures of policy integration that operate through the Canada–US Free Trade Agreement and NAFTA—and before these comprehensive trade agreements, through sectoral treaties including the Auto Pact and the Canada–US Defence Production Sharing Agreement—leave Canada with little room to throw its weight around in conflicts with its American neighbour. As discussed above, Canada's economic prosperity continues to be highly dependent on trade with the United States, notwithstanding some decline in the volume of trade during the recent recession. The policy implications of this dependence can hardly be overstated.

For several decades the response of successive Canadian governments—the Progressive Conservative government of Brian Mulroney (1984–93) excluded—has been to search for and support counterweights to American dominance. Chief among these have been the United Nations and multilateral institutions more generally. **Multilateralism** involves the resolution of international differences and conflicts through structures and processes that represent many states and that give all of them a voice, though not necessarily an equal voice, in decision-making. The United Nations has been the most prominent structure for multilateralism in the post–World War II era. There are, however, many other international organizations to which Canada belongs, including the North Atlantic Treaty Organization (NATO), the World Bank, the Organisation for Economic Co-operation and Development (OECD), the World Trade Organization (WTO), the Organization of American States (OAS), the Commonwealth, and la Francophonie.

Some of these multilateral organizations are dominated by the United States and therefore can hardly be said to serve as counterweights to its might. NATO, for example, has almost never blocked the will or modified the military objectives of American administrations, the 2003 refusal of several of its members to guarantee the alliance's support for Turkey in the event of an attack by Iraq being the chief exception to this rule. Influence in the International Monetary Fund's decision-making is weighted, based on the size of member-state contributions, and the United States is its major contributor. Multilateralism does not, therefore, necessarily dilute American influence. It can, in fact, magnify this influence by providing greater political legitimacy to American goals through their association with other countries and structures of multilateral decision-making. On the whole, however, multilateralism clearly holds out the possibility of allowing for the representation of interests and points of view that might dilute the dominance of the United States.

'One of the great foreign policy challenges facing Canada', observes Michael Ignatieff, 'is staying independent in an age of [American] empire.'[21] This is a large part of the explanation for multilateralism's attractiveness in the eyes of many Canadians and those who govern them. Multilateralism, when it is not a convenient cover for the ambitions and interests of a single member state, as the Warsaw Pact clearly was for the former Soviet Union or as the IMF and World Bank are alleged to be by critics of America's global economic power, implies that states are willing to accept some limitations on their national sovereignty. Canada's governing elites and opinion leaders, like their counterparts in Europe, 'have a vision of a multilateral world in which . . . sovereignty is not unconditional, but limited and bound by human rights agreements, or multilateral engagements which limit and constrain the sovereignty of states in the name of collective social goods.'[22] Canadian leadership in the creation of the International Criminal Court and in the negotiations, known as the Ottawa Process, that led to the international treaty banning landmines, and Canada's ratification of the Kyoto Protocol on greenhouse gas emissions and support for the United Nations as the proper and necessary forum for the discussion of issues of war and peace and the authorization of the use of force have reflected this commitment to multilateralism. It would be an overstatement to say that all Canadians accept

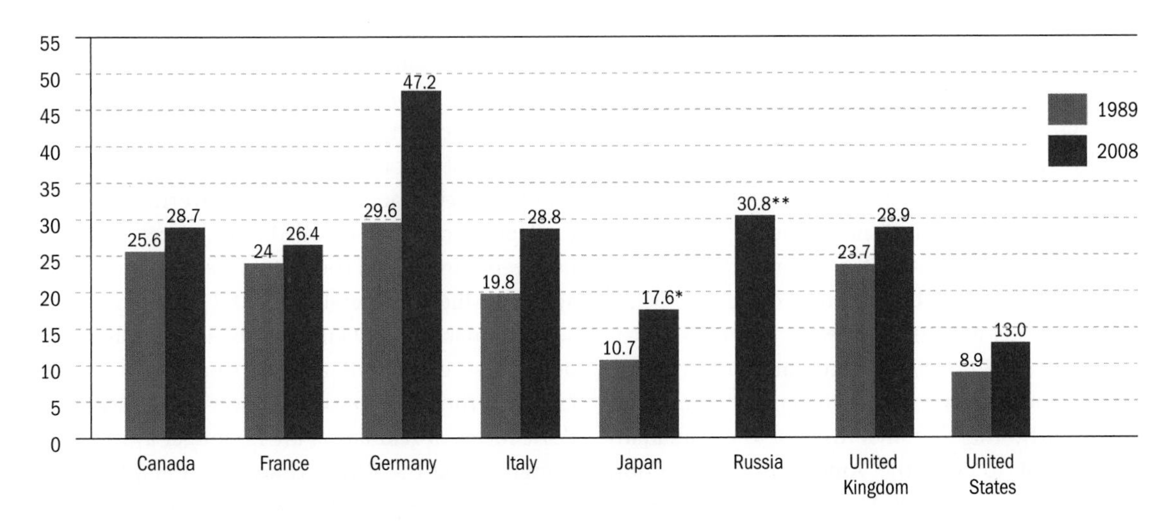

FIGURE 17.3 Trade Dependence for G8 Countries, Exports as a Percentage of GDP, 1989 and 2008

*Figure is for 2007.

**Russia was part of the Soviet Union in 1989.

Sources: Adapted from Canada, Department of Foreign Affairs and International Trade, *State of Trade 2005*, statistical annex, Table 1B; World Bank.

this multilateral vision of the world, but recent history suggests it has broad popular support. The problem for Canada—a problem also experienced by many other allies of the United States, though less acutely—is that multilateralism has not been embraced as enthusiastically by its major trading partner and sometimes produces outcomes that set Canada seriously at odds with the United States.

The election of President Obama in 2008 and the Democratic Party's sweep of Congress that year produced a significant tilt towards multilateralism in American foreign policy. But the Republican Party's comeback in the 2010 mid-term elections, recapturing the House of Representatives and making gains in the Senate, put the brakes on this reorientation. Canadians and their political leaders need always to be mindful of the fact that both multilateralism and a go-it-alone style of foreign policy have strong constituencies and historical roots in the United States. The temporary ascendance of one does not obliterate the other.

One of the ironies of Canadian politics in recent times is that Canada's greater economic integration with the United States, under the free trade architecture of the FTA and NAFTA, may well have created the political space for Canada to pursue a more independent line in matters of foreign policy than was available before free trade. This is exactly opposite to the prediction of Canadian critics of free trade, who argued that the last shreds of Canadian sovereignty and policy autonomy would be vaporized by the tighter economic embrace produced by the FTA and NAFTA. If, however, one looks at the actual record of recent Canadian foreign policy, at least under the Chrétien-led Liberal government, there are several notable instances of Canada being at loggerheads with the United States: over global warming, landmines, an International Criminal Court, continental missile defence, and, most importantly, the formal refusal of the Canadian government to join the American-led 'coalition of the willing' in the 2003 invasion of Iraq. In all of these cases it can be argued that the Canadian refusal to side with the Americans and Canadian criticism of the American position did not have serious and enduring consequences beyond a loss of goodwill in Washington towards Canada. While not wanting to diminish the importance of political goodwill in the Can–Am bilateral relationship, this is certainly a more nebulous consequence than being slapped with trade duties by the US Commerce Department or facing the punitive wrath of Congress.

Of course, the 2006 Canadian federal election brought to office a minority Conservative government intent on improving relations and influence with the US—exemplified by Prime Minister Harper's March 2006 trip to Afghanistan to visit Canadian troops stationed there and by the new government's aim to boost military spending and bolster the image of the Canadian Forces, to the extent of placing posters advertising the Canadian military in the Washington, DC, subway system. The successful negotiation of a resolution to the more than two decades' old softwood lumber dispute in April 2006—an agreement criticized by some in Canada as a giveaway to the United States, but supported by the provincial governments of BC, Ontario, and Quebec and most lumber interests in Canada—was hailed by the Conservative government and its supporters as proof that its new approach to Canada–US relations was paying off. The celebrations were toned down when American claims of unfair lumber subsidies provided by the Ontario and Quebec governments were upheld by the London Court of International Arbitration in January 2011, forcing these governments and the Canadian government to increase their duties on exported softwood by a marginal amount.

Before free trade, Canadian governments had to depend on the so-called 'special relationship' between Canada and the United States as protection against American retaliation if Canadian policy strayed unacceptably far from the line Washington deemed acceptable. It may be that free trade has loosened the leash to some degree, because some of these forms of retaliation are no longer available to Congress and the White House or, if employed, at least can be challenged under the terms of the free trade agreements that now join us at the hip.

There are, however, as there have long been, limits to how far and in what circumstances Canadian foreign policy can depart from that of the United States. In the case of Canada's refusal to support the war on Iraq, this did not damage the security interests and military goals of the United States. The fact that the United Kingdom, Spain, over a dozen other European governments, Japan, Australia, and an assortment of other countries lent their support to this military action made the absence of Canadian support virtually unnoticed in the United States. Indeed, this was only noticed when some American media outlets reported the booing of the American national anthem at a hockey game in Montreal! In the case of the 'war on terrorism', launched after the terrorist attacks of 11 September 2001, the space available for Canada to ignore American preferences has been considerably less. This is because the policy actions taken by the American government involved border security, air travel, and immigration, matters that directly affected Canada. With about $1.5 billion per day in trade crossing the border between the two countries, and given the enormous number of jobs and investments in Canada that depend on the smooth flow of goods and people across this border, the Canadian government has had little choice but to co-ordinate its policies with those of the American government. This co-ordination, however, has stopped short of Canadian acceptance of the idea of a common security perimeter around Canada and the United States, a concept that would require that Canadian immigration policy be brought into line with American policy.

During the Jean Chrétien–Paul Martin years of Liberal government, from 1993 to 2006, the dominant paradigm for Canadian foreign policy became what is known as **soft power**. This is a term first coined by Harvard's Joseph Nye. It involves international influence based on intangible or indirect factors that include culture, values, and a sense of legitimacy ascribed to a nation's international aims. Soft power operates, says Nye, through 'the complex machinery of interdependence, rather than . . . expensive new weapons systems'.[23] Nye identified Canada, the Netherlands, and the Scandinavian countries as examples of countries whose governments have successfully exercised soft power, 'hitting above their weight' as a former Canadian Minister of Foreign Affairs, Lloyd Axworthy, liked to say.

It is easy to see why the doctrine of soft power would be attractive for many Canadians, suggesting as it does that their country can make a difference on the international stage through the values it stands for, its reputation as a good global citizen, and without having to spend much on defence. Canadians see themselves as peacekeepers and internationalists, a self-image that can be maintained without the latest military technology or much in the way of combat-readiness. Indeed, despite significant increases over the last several years, Canada spends less on defence, at about 1.2 per cent of GDP, than most of the countries in NATO.

Some have argued, however, that this self-image is an illusion. Although Canadians never hear this from those who govern them, by 2003 Canada had fallen to thirty-fourth in the world in terms of countries' contributions to UN peacekeeping. Bangladesh and India were first and second, respectively, and the United States was ahead of Canada. Writing at the beginning of 2003, Michael Ignatieff, then a Harvard professor, and leader of the federal Liberal Party from December 2008 to May 2011, has argued that the Canadian belief in multilateralism is laudable, but that international influence cannot be sustained by good intentions alone. It requires, he maintains, three national attributes:

- moral authority as a good global citizen;
- military capacity;
- international assistance capability.

Canada still has a good deal of the first attribute, Ignatieff argues, but far too little of the latter two. Indeed, the decline in our international assistance capability, of which peacekeeping is an important part, he blames on the steep decline in Canada's military capacity. Peacekeeping, he notes, is seldom about simply imposing bodies between two belligerents who have laid down their arms and agreed not to fight. It has become an often dangerous task that requires military capability, as was true in the Balkans in the 1990s and is the case today in Afghanistan. Indeed, the job has morphed into an activity that has been dubbed 'peace-building' and 'peace enforcement', because it often involves attempting to create conditions where more traditional peacekeeping activities can take place and where the belligerents represent different factions within a single nation-state.[24] Patrolling dangerous areas, engaging in combat, helping to build schools and roads, and training local soldiers and police officers may all be part of this broader set of activities when conflicts occur in places like Afghanistan, Darfur province in Sudan, and Rwanda.

Moral authority on the international stage, Ignatieff argues, cannot be totally disconnected from a willingness to bear some of the military and economic burdens of defending the values and interests important to Canadians. The images that Canadians have long had of themselves as 'honest brokers', 'fixers', peacekeepers, and good global citizens certainly are not false. But Ignatieff raises the important question of whether a price eventually must be paid to sustain the reality of this image. 'The disagreeable reality for those who believe in human rights', he argues, 'is that there are some occasions when war is the only real remedy for regimes that live by terror. This does not mean that the choice is morally unproblematic.'[25] In other words, soft power cannot abandon the occasional need for the older weapons- and sanctions-based varieties (see Box 17.4).

Conclusion

The boundary separating Canadian politics from events and influence in the rest of the world has always been porous, and never more so than today. This fundamental truth of life in an inescapably globalized world was brought home to Canadians, and to people throughout the world, by the attacks on the United States of 11 September 2001 and, again, in the early months of 2011 as popular uprisings surged across the Arab states of North Africa and the Persian Gulf. Scenes of protest and rebellion, defeated dictators and regimes fighting back against popular aspirations for democracy, were broadcast from Tunisia, Egypt, Bahrain, and Libya. As in Iran, after the regime stole the election of 2009 from those who opposed the rule of the mullahs, social media—Facebook, Twitter, and video captured and sent from cell phones—were crucial in organizing popular resistance to autocratic rule and equally crucial in getting the story to the outside world. Canadians, whose politicians often seemed more focused on the prospect of a spring 2011 election that seemed devoid of compelling issues, were far more interested in the drama of democratic revolts being played out several thousand kilometres from home and in real time on their video screens.

As Canadians and their government struggled to come to grips with the world after the terrorist attacks on New York City and the Pentagon of 9/11, the bombing of Afghanistan, the American-led invasion of Iraq, and, most recently, the surge towards a new order in much of the Arab world, it became increasingly evident that the choices facing them were about nothing less than the meaning of democracy, what threatened it, and what sort of world order would best protect it. Although many Canadians supported the 'war on terror' launched by the United States after the terrorist attacks, and their government sent troops to Afghanistan and ships to the Persian Gulf in support of removal of the repressive Taliban regime and the Al-Qaeda camps that were allowed to operate in Afghanistan under its protection, Canadian public opinion was deeply divided and more than a little skeptical on the question of attacking Iraq without the authorization of a UN Security Council resolution.

When the American and British governments decided to attack Iraq without the support of most of their traditional allies and in the face of rather overwhelming public opposition in most countries, the Canadian government found itself in a difficult and unenviable position. On the one hand, Canada historically has supported the principles and institutions of multilateralism, particularly the United Nations, and has sought not to appear to be a mere lackey of the US administration. On the other hand, the tug of continentalist realities described in this chapter appears almost unavoidable. The ambiguous position taken by the Chrétien government—unwillingness to give official support to the Anglo-American war effort at the same time as the Prime Minister and some members of his government made cautiously approving noises at various

Politics in Focus

Box 17.4 What Would Lester Pearson Think about Canada's Role in Afghanistan?

In early 2008 former Liberal cabinet minister John Manley issued a report on Canada's mission in Afghanistan in which he argued that it was very much in the spirit of internationalism that former Prime Minister Lester Pearson, the father of modern peacekeeping, advocated for Canada. J.L. Granatstein, one of Canada's foremost military historians, agrees.

Pearson . . . was no pacifist. He wanted Canada to play a strong role, and he understood that this favoured land had to work with its friends to guarantee its security. He supported increasing defence budgets and raising troop numbers, and he understood that Canada had to be prepared to fight in defence of its national interests. To Pearson, strength and alliances were key to advancing our interests.

. . . Pearson won the Nobel Peace Prize for his extraordinary efforts at the UN [towards resolving the 1956 Suez crisis]. After that triumph, Canadians began to believe that peacekeeping was their invention and that Canadians did the UN's work better than any others.

This was a noble ideal. And the idea of conflict resolution became a Canadian value right up there—for a time—with collective security, defence preparation and co-operation with Canada's allies. Peacekeeping appealed to Canadians because it seemed to differentiate us from the Americans; and it appealed to our governments because it was far easier on hard-pressed budgets than purchasing heavy weaponry. The 1990s development of a Canadian 'human security' agenda during the Chrétien years fit seamlessly into this post-Pearsonian mental construct. Over time, the hard-edged values that Mike Pearson stood for so strongly began to fade in the Canadian memory. . . .

John Manley's report [on Afghanistan] had it right. Traditional peacekeeping cannot be practised in Kandahar because there is no peace to keep. But what we do there 'can affect Canada's reputation in the world [and] our influence in international affairs.' Manley remembered the real Pearsonian legacy of resolve and strength. . . .

Source: J.L. Granatstein, 'Mike Pearson's True Heir: Stephen Harper', *National Post*, 2 Feb. 2008, at: <network.nationalpost.com/np/blogs/fullcomment/archive/2008/02/02/j-l-granatstein-on-canada-s-role-abroad-mike-s-pearson-s-true-heir-stephen-harper.aspx>.

points during the war and after the fall of Saddam Hussein's regime—fairly accurately reflected the ambivalence among Canadians. The government's position satisfied neither the NDP or BQ on the left nor the Conservatives on the right, but in the successful Liberal tradition of sticking to the middle of the road it seemed to be one that most Canadians could live with.

But the tough questions will not go away. Events since 9/11 have brought home to Canadians and people throughout the world the remarkable lopsidedness of the world's power structure, dominated by the United States, and have forced them to think hard about what this means for Canada and the world. There can be no doubt about whether the United States has become a new imperium, whose power is perhaps unmatched in the history of the world. The only serious question in this regard is whether this is a good or bad thing. Ranged on one side are those, such as Canadians Michael Ignatieff (at least before he entered Canadian politics in 2006), J.L. Granatstein, Charles Krauthammer, Robert Fulford, and Mark Steyn, who maintain that a world under the Pax Americana is, on the whole, a good thing or at least the lesser of evils in the contemporary world. On the other side are those Canadians, such as Mark Kingwell, Janice Gross Stein, Gwynne Dyer, and Lloyd Axworthy, who argue that decisions involving war and peace should always be made multilaterally and that the UN is the proper forum and sanctioning body for the use of force against any state.

More than virtually any other country, Canada is caught in a vice on this question. American decisions relating to what has come to be called 'homeland security' have affected Canada because of the long border between the two countries and the volume of goods and people crossing that border each day, to the point that as of June 2009 all Canadians travelling to the US were required to carry passports. Although many Canadian politicians and opinion leaders echoed French President Jacques Chirac's post-9/11 pronouncement that the terrorist attacks were an attack on us all, it soon became clear that most Canadians, and most people outside the United States, did not believe this. Polls taken shortly after the September 2001 terrorist attacks showed that 80 per cent of Canadians believed

Politics in Focus

Box 17.5 Alberta's Oil Sands and Canada–US Relations

John Podesta served as President Bill Clinton's chief of staff and was a member of the National Security Council under Clinton. These days he is head of the Center for American Progress, a liberal think-tank whose star has shone brighter since the 2008 election of President Barack Obama. Podesta doesn't speak for the current administration, but he certainly represents the views of many within the Democratic Party. So when he was invited to give the keynote address at 'Greening the Oil Sands', a conference held in Washington in June 2010, at which industry and government heavyweights from both sides of the border were in attendance, people listened. And among those listening most attentively were Canada's ambassador to the United States, Gary Doer, and business executives with a stake in the continuation and growth of Alberta's oil exports to the United States.

Here is some of what Podesta said:

> I'm skeptical about a 'green' vision for tar sands, and I want to level with you about how I see the future of energy policy playing out. . . .
>
> Today, tar sands oil accounts for 4 per cent of America's overall oil use, but will become our top source of imported oil this year, ahead of conventional Canadian imports and those from Saudi Arabia and Kuwait combined. Expert projections find that US imports from tar sands could rise to as much as 36 per cent over just the next two decades.
>
> As we look down this road, there are a few things it's tough not to agree on at the outset. Oil extraction from tar sands is polluting, destructive, expensive, and energy intensive. These things are facts. I think suggesting this process can come close to approximating being 'greened' is largely misleading, or far too optimistic, or perhaps both. It stands alongside clean coal and error-free deepwater drilling as more PR than reality. . . .
>
> Instead of pursuing energy sources that [are environmentally destructive and that contribute to global warming], the United States and Canada should join in partnership to put in place clean energy policies that will help us harness sources of energy that will never run out and can't risk catastrophe. As President Obama said in Ottawa last year, as two of the wealthiest countries, we can and must be leaders. Energy security is now intertwined with climate and economic security—all of which will be improved by reducing our dependence on oil and accelerating our transformation to clean energy.[26]

To repeat, John Podesta does not speak for Barack Obama. But his views do reflect those of many Democratic Party lawmakers and perhaps even those of the President himself. Although the most remarkable and least commented-upon aspect of the Canada–US relationship is how free of serious disagreement most of it is, major conflicts do arise from time to time. The future of Alberta's oil sands in Canada–US relations has the potential to become such a conflict.

that the actions and policies of the US were at least partly responsible for the attacks. It also was clear that Canadians did not feel vulnerable in the way that Americans, whose territory was the target of those attacks, did.[27] The arrest of 18 'homegrown' terrorists in June 2006 and the eventual conviction of 11 of them do not appear to have changed Canadians' thinking on this matter.

This creates a dilemma for Canada. Actions taken in and by the United States, in the name of combatting terrorism and eliminating regimes deemed to pose a threat to American security and to a world order that does not endanger American interests, carry a cost. That cost involves individual liberties, such as personal privacy and equality rights that may be jeopardized by practices like ethnic profiling. The debate over the issue of national security versus preservation of democratic rights and freedoms has been raging in the US since 11 September 2001. But it also concerns Canada. Likewise, the question of whether the UN is capable of dealing with international threats to human rights and peace, or whether the American globo-cop is a sort of *faute de mieux* way of dealing with these problems, is one that Canadians and others—including Americans—will continue to face for the foreseeable future. Questions about what promotes and what threatens democracy do not stop at Canada's borders. This becomes clear when Canadians ask themselves what sort of world, governed in what way, is most likely to guarantee the values and interests they cherish.

The presidency of Barack Obama was greeted by many Canadians, as was true of populations in much of the world, with high expectations. Several of the immediate steps taken by the President, including the promise to close the Guantanamo Bay military prison, end secretive CIA detention facilities in places throughout the world, and stop the practice of 'waterboarding', widely considered to be a form of torture, were applauded by most. And the intention to shift American troops and other military resources from Iraq to Afghanistan was viewed positively by most Canadians and their leaders. The emphasis on diplomacy and multilateralism that Obama's Secretary of State, Hillary Clinton, struck from her first day on the job accorded well with the dominant Canadian tradition in world affairs.

Less clear, however, was what the Obama presidency would mean for Canada–US relations. The announcement that the new President would make Canada his first foreign visit was greeted with enthusiasm by Canadians and marked a return to a practice that had long existed until George W. Bush decided in 2001 to make an official visit to Mexico the first of his presidency. But tone and optics aside, the fundamentals of the Canada–US relationship did not change as a result of the Democratic Party's recapture of the White House and its strengthened control over Congress. There was little reason to think that an Obama administration would take a different line on the issue of Canadian claims to full sovereignty over the waters and seabed of the Arctic. The increased influence of organized labour in American politics as a result of Democratic control of both the White House and Congress created the possibility that protectionist pressures might receive a more sympathetic hearing in Washington. Although Canadian exporters of gas and hydroelectric power had little to fear, businesses and workers in manufacturing industries, already hit hard by softened demands for their products in the American export market, were more vulnerable. Exporters of oil from Alberta's oil sands were also nervous about their future under the new administration and a Congress in which environmental voices appeared to be more numerous and louder than in the past (see Box 17.5). And there was no indication that the stickiness created at the Canada–US border by the Western Hemisphere Travel Initiative, a direct consequence of American concerns about terrorism, would change under the Obama administration. Although most Canadians have found life with Obama to be more agreeable than life with Bush, the substance of the Canada–US relationship has not changed very much.

Listen to the 'Who Owns the Arctic?' podcast, available at www.oupcanada.com/Brooks7e

Appendix: Timeline of Canada in the World

late 1400s–early 1500s	Fishing by Basque, English, Portuguese, French, and Spanish ships on the Grand Banks off the east coast of Newfoundland, and whaling, especially by the Basques, off the Labrador coast and in the Strait of Belle Isle, the first economic exploitation of Canadian resources by Europeans.
Late 1500s	Trade in beaver pelts and other furs begins, providing the basis for the eventual extension of trading routes from Quebec all the way to the north of Saskatchewan and Alberta.
1603–8	Samuel de Champlain makes two visits to Canada, establishing the city of Quebec in 1608 on his second voyage; European colonization of Canada begins.
1759–63	The war between Britain and France spills over into a rivalry in the New World, British troops defeating French forces at Quebec in 1759. The formal transfer of New France to Britain takes place in 1763 under the Treaty of Paris.
Early 1800s	Canada becomes a major supplier of white pine for British ships.
1812–14	The War of 1812 between Britain and the United States produces many battles on Canadian territory and the shared waters of the Great Lakes.
1820s	In an effort to dilute the influence of American-born residents of Canada the colonial authorities encourage immigration from the British Isles. The arrival of tens of thousands of immigrants from Ireland during the Potato Famine of the 1840s marks the significant beginning of ethnic pluralism that went beyond the French and English ethnic communities.
1854	The first Reciprocity Treaty with the United States is signed, abrogated by the US government in 1865.
1867	The creation of Canada as a sovereign state—in most respects, but with some important limitations—is prompted by fears that the United States might have designs on parts of British North America and by Britain's unwillingness to continue to pay for the defence of Canadian territory.
1870–1	The vast territories controlled by the Hudson's Bay Company are transferred by Britain to Canada in 1870 and British Columbia becomes the fifth province in 1871, after which Canada stretches from the Atlantic to the Pacific oceans.
1879	The National Policy is adopted by the Conservative government. It includes a sharp increase in tariffs on manufactured goods, a policy intended to protect fledgling Canadian producers from American competition but which also has the effect of encouraging US-based companies to set up operations in Canada, leading to very high levels of foreign ownership and lower levels of productivity in Canadian industry as a result of foreign-owned corporations that produce only for the small Canadian market.
1909	The International Boundary Waters Treaty between the United States and Canada takes effect, creating the International Joint Commission, with equal representation from both countries (see 2009, below).
1911	The Canadian general election is fought largely on the issue of reciprocity in trade with the United States. The pro-reciprocity government of Wilfrid Laurier is defeated.
1914–18	World War I: Canada is a junior partner in the alliance against Germany, Canadian troops falling under the command of British officers.
1919	Canada becomes a founding member of the League of Nations.
1920	Canada passes from the economic orbit of Great Britain into that of the United States: American investment now officially exceeds the value of British investment.

1921 Canada's Prime Minister, Mackenzie King, sees multilateralism as a way to assert Canada's independence from Great Britain in international affairs.

1931 Under the Statute of Westminster, Canada acquires the authority to negotiate and sign foreign treaties in its own right, a power that Great Britain had exercised on Canada's behalf.

1939–45 Canada participates in World War II, but no longer as a subordinate of Great Britain. Canada emerges from the war as one of the world's leading economies.

1945 Canada becomes a founding member of the United Nations. The UN and multilateralism generally are seen as counterweights to the influence of the United States on Canadian foreign policy.

1947 Canada is a founding member of the General Agreement on Tariffs and Trade (GATT) and the North Atlantic Treaty Organization (NATO).

1950–3 Canada participates in the Korean War under the umbrella of a UN Security Council resolution.

1956 Suez crisis: Canada sides with the United States against the Franco–British invasion of Egypt, and Canadian Foreign Minister Lester Pearson, who brokers a settlement to end the crisis, is awarded the Nobel Peace Prize.

1957 The North American Air Defense Command (NORAD) is created, a partnership of Canada and the United States against the possibility of a Soviet missile attack. Early warning radar stations are established on Canadian territory: the Pinetree Line across southern Canada in 1954, and the Mid-Canada Line, at the 55th parallel, and the Distant Early Warning (DEW) line, along the 70th parallel, in 1957.

1960s Under Lester Pearson, the Canadian government becomes critical of US involvement in the Vietnam War, although Canadian companies continue to profit from the production of defence-related exports used in that war. Under Quebec Premier Daniel Johnson, that province becomes more assertive in its demands for representation and an independent voice abroad. Canadian dependence on the United States becomes a prominent political issue as the level of American ownership in key resource and manufacturing sectors of the Canadian economy reaches unprecedented levels.

1962 The Kennedy administration's request that the Canadian government permit nuclear warheads on missiles located on Canadian territory, which the American administration argued was required by Canada's obligations under NORAD and NATO, is refused by the Diefenbaker government, creating a major rift in Canada–US relations. The Liberal government elected in 1963 complies with the request.

1973 The Liberal government of Pierre Trudeau announces the 'Third Option' policy of diversifying Canadian trade and thus reducing Canada's economic dependence on the United States. By the end of the decade the percentage of total export and import trade tied to the American economy is at an all-time high.

1976 The G7, the annual meeting of the leaders of the world's seven largest capitalist democracies, is created when Canada joins the G6 countries of Britain, France, Italy, Japan, the United States, and West Germany.

1985 The Macdonald Royal Commission on the Economic Union and Development Prospects for Canada, created by the Trudeau government in 1982, makes free trade with the United States its major recommendation. The Conservative government of Brian Mulroney approaches the Reagan administration in 1985 to open free trade talks.

1989 The Canada–US Free Trade Agreement takes effect.

1994	The North American Free Trade Agreement (NAFTA) among Canada, Mexico, and the United States takes effect.
1997	Canada signs the Kyoto Accord, later ratified in 2002. A decade after signing Canada's CO_2 emissions exceed the targets agreed to in the accord by about 25 per cent.
2000	Over 80 per cent of Canada's imports and exports are tied to the United States and about one-third of Canada's GDP depends on trade with the United States.
2001	After the terrorist attacks of 11 September 2001, movement across the Canada–US border becomes a major issue in the bilateral relations between these two countries. As a member of NATO, Canada supports the American-led invasion of Afghanistan to replace the Taliban regime. Eventually, Canada becomes a major contributor of combat forces in Afghanistan.
2003	The Liberal government of Jean Chrétien decides not to join the Anglo-American alliance that invades Iraq to overthrow the Saddam Hussein regime. Massive opposition to the war in Quebec, and within the Liberal Party's Quebec caucus, is an important factor in the government's decision to withhold any significant support.
Early 2000s	Canada's claim to full sovereignty in the waters of the High Arctic is not accepted by other nations with a direct Arctic presence, including the United States, Russia, Denmark, and Norway. As the possibility of a shipping passage through the Arctic increases and the prospects for natural resource exploitation in the High Arctic also become greater, the issue of Arctic sovereignty assumes greater urgency.
2005	Canada, Mexico, and the United States agree to the Security and Prosperity Partnership, an agreement that appears to pave the way towards greater policy co-ordination among the three countries. The first formal summit of the SPP is held in Montebello, Quebec, in 2007.
2008	Canada has roughly 2,500 troops stationed in Afghanistan and plays a major combat role within the NATO mission fighting the resurgent Taliban. Canadian public opinion remains divided on Canada's involvement as the number of Canadians killed in combat and on patrols exceeds 100.
2009	The 100th anniversary of the Boundary Waters Treaty between Canada and the United States, creating the IJC. Despite some high expectations associated with the IJC when it was created, most policy experts agree that the complex and important web of trans-boundary environmental governance between the countries now operates largely through agreements and networks of sub-national governments. Barack Obama assumes the presidency of the United States and Prime Minister Harper's office announces that the President's first official visit outside the US will be to Canada. Canadians have high expectations for the new President and his foreign policies.
2010	In March the Conservative government announces that Canadian troops in Afghanistan will be withdrawn in 2011, in compliance with a motion passed in the House of Commons in 2008. As of July 2010, 151 Canadian troops and four civilians had been killed since the beginning of the NATO mission.

Starting Points for Research

Robert Bothwell and Jean Daudelin, eds, *Canada Among Nations 2008: 100 Years of Canadian Foreign Policy* (Montreal and Kingston: McGill-Queen's University Press, 2008). The *Canada Among Nations* series, produced out of the Norman Paterson School of International Affairs at Carleton University, is published annually and includes analyses from leading scholars of Canadian foreign policy and Canada's role in the world.

Mark Brawley, *The Politics of Globalization: Gaining Perspective, Assessing Consequences* (Peterborough, Ont.: Broadview Press, 2002). Brawley presents a very accessible introduction to the phenomenon of globalization, including an examination of the evidence for the various claims made about its consequences.

Paul Cellucci, *Unquiet Diplomacy* (Toronto: Key Porter, 2007). This memoir of a former US ambassador to Canada provides an interesting perspective on Canada–US relations during years that included 9/11, the invasion of Afghanistan, and the Canadian government's decision not to participate in continental missile defence.

Stephen Clarkson, *Uncle Sam and Us: Globalization, Neoconservatism, and the Canadian State* (Toronto: University of Toronto Press, 2002). Clarkson presents a critical examination of the impact of globalization and neo-conservative ideology on the ability of governments in Canada to respond to non-corporate interests and values.

Tom Keating, *Canada and World Order: The Multilateralist Tradition in Canadian Foreign Policy*, 2nd edn (Toronto: Oxford University Press, 2001). A very good historical survey and thematic interpretation of Canadian foreign policy.

Stephen Randall and John Herd Thompson, *Canada and the United States: Ambivalent Allies*, 3rd edn (Athens: University of Georgia Press, 2002). Quite simply the best history of the Canada–US relationship.

Review Exercises

1. Canada participates in a large number of international organizations. For each of the following organizations explain what it does, the nature of Canada's participation, and the leading issues faced by the organization in recent years.
   - Organization of American States
   - North Atlantic Treaty Organization
   - World Trade Organization
   - International Criminal Court
2. How dependent is your community on international trade? To find out, identify the five or six leading employers in your area. You can do this by contacting your local Chamber of Commerce or the economic development office of city hall. Contact these companies and ask for information about how much of their goods or services they export, to what countries, and how many people they employ.
3. In September of 2008 Prime Minister Stephen Harper announced that the Canadian mission in Afghanistan would end in 2011. 'By 2011, we will have been in Kandahar, which is probably the toughest province in the country, for six years', Harper said. He added, 'At that point, the mission, as we've known it, we intend to end.' Identify the arguments for and against Canadian involvement in Afghanistan and discuss the politics associated with a decision to stay or withdraw.

Glossary

Aboriginal self-government A concept premised on the idea that Native communities should be viewed as possessing at least some of the attributes of sovereign peoples and that, therefore, they have a right to be self-governing. Various models and degrees of self-government have been implemented over the last couple of decades, one of the most ambitious being the territory of Nunavut.

Advocacy advertising The purchase of newspaper/magazine space, signs or billboards, or broadcast time to convey a political message.

Affirmative action Measures intended to increase the representation of a targeted group or groups beyond what it would be without special intervention. These measures may include hiring and promotion practices, school admission policies, selection rules for committees, and so on.

Authority A form of power based on the recognition by the person or persons who obey that the person or organization issuing a command or making a rule has the right to do so and should be obeyed.

Bilingual belt A term coined by Richard Joy in *Languages in Conflict*, it refers to the narrow region running from Moncton, New Brunswick, in the east to Sault Ste Marie, Ontario, in the west, in which is found the vast majority of Canada's francophone population and where the rate of francophone assimilation is lower than elsewhere in Canada.

Bill 101 Quebec's Charte de la langue française, the first piece of legislation passed by Quebec's National Assembly, in 1977, after the Parti Québécois came to power. It made French the sole official language in Quebec for purposes of provincial public administration, restricted access to English-language schools, and imposed French-language requirements on business in Quebec. Despite some setbacks in the courts over the years, Quebec's language policy continues to be based on the principles set forth in Bill 101.

Block funding Under this formula, Ottawa's financial contribution to a provincially administered program or policy field is not geared to the level of provincial spending. The Federal–Provincial Fiscal Arrangements Act of 1977 began this practice of replacing the *shared-cost program* model with block funding. The Canada Health Transfer and Canada Social Transfer are the major block funding transfers from Ottawa to the provinces.

Brokerage politics Style of politics that stresses the ability of parties to accommodate diverse interests, a feat that requires flexibility in policy positions and ideological stance. Brokerage politics is often characterized as non-ideological, a characterization that is somewhat misleading because the claim of brokerage-style parties to be non-ideological simply means that they represent the dominant ideology accepted uncritically by most members of society. The Liberal and Conservative parties have been the main practitioners of brokerage politics on Canada's national stage, the Liberal Party being the more successful of the two over the last century.

Bureaucracie Word coined by the French writer Vincent de Gournay in the mid-1700s, which referred to rule by unelected officials. Today, the term 'bureaucracy' encompasses all of the unelected officials of the public service whose employment is within the central administration of a government and who may wield power on behalf of that government.

Calgary Declaration A statement agreed to in 1997 by all of the provincial premiers except Quebec's Lucien Bouchard. It stopped short of endorsing the recognition of Quebec as a distinct society, instead referring to the 'unique character of Quebec society'.

Canada–US Free Trade Agreement (FTA) A wide-ranging trade agreement between Canada and the United States that has been in effect since January 1989. The FTA reversed the historical pattern of Canadian protectionism that was enshrined in the National Policy of 1878–9 but that had been steadily eroded after World War II. The FTA created an architecture of dispute settlement rules, agencies, and monitoring requirements.

Canadian Bill of Rights Passed by the Canadian Parliament in 1960, it includes many of the same rights and freedoms guaranteed by the Charter. However, the Bill of Rights is a statute and does not have the status of constitutional law.

Canadian content Media content that is demonstrably Canadian according to various criteria related to writers and composers, performers (musicians, actors, etc.), producers, and place of production. Regulations developed and enforced by the Canadian Radio-television and Telecommunications Commission require television and radio broadcasters and cable companies to ensure that a specified share of their programming satisfies the criteria of Canadian content.

Caucus The elected members of a particular political party in the legislature. When Parliament is sitting, each party's caucus usually will meet at least once per week, during which time matters of policy and political strategy may be discussed.

Central agencies Parts of the bureaucracy whose main or only purpose is to support the decision-making activities of cabinet. The five organizations usually considered to have central agency status are the Privy Council Office, the Prime Minister's Office, the Department of Finance, the Treasury Board Secretariat, and the Intergovernmental Affairs Office within the PCO.

Charter groups (old and new) Until a generation ago it was common in Canada to speak of French and British Canadians as Canada's two founding peoples or 'charter groups'. With the 1982 passage of the Charter of Rights and Freedoms and the explosion of Charter-based litigation, the term 'Charter groups' has come to be associated with rights-seeking organizations representing such groups as women, gays and lesbians, disabled persons, and Aboriginal Canadians. Another reason for the eclipse of the older meaning of the term 'charter groups' is that it is thought by many to ignore the original pre-European inhabitants of what would become Canada.

Cité libre The intellectual review founded in the 1950s by such prominent Quebecers as Pierre Trudeau and Gérard Pelletier, which was one of the key centres for opposition to the so-called *unholy alliance* of the Church, anglophone capital, and the Union Nationale under Maurice Duplessis.

'Citizens plus' Alan Cairns's proposal for a new form of citizenship based on what he calls the 'positive recognition of difference'. In addition to being thought of and treated under law as Canadian citizens, Native Canadians would also have a status based on treaty rights and laws and institutions that recognize them as different in some respects (e.g., fishing or hunting rights).

Clarity Act A federal law passed in 2000 that empowers Parliament to review any future referendum question on Quebec independence to determine whether it is unambiguously worded. This, according to a 1998 Supreme Court ruling, is one of the requirements that a question must satisfy if the outcome of a referendum is to be considered constitutional.

Class analysis A perspective on politics that insists on the overriding importance of social classes based on their relationship to the means of producing and distributing wealth.

Coercion A form of power based on the use or threat of force (e.g., fines, imprisonment).

Common law In Anglo-American legal systems such as Canada's, the component of the law based on the decisions of courts. Like statute law, passed by legislatures, common-law rules are enforceable in the courts.

Communitarianism Those belief systems, like socialism, based on the premise that real human freedom and dignity are only possible in the context of communal relations that allow for the public recognition of group identities and that are based on equal respect for these different group identities.

Concurrent powers Legislative powers, including those relating to agriculture, immigration, and public pensions, that under the written Constitution are shared between Ottawa and the provinces.

Conquest, 1759 The military victory of the British forces led by Wolfe over Montcalm in what was New France, but which subsequently became British territory under the Treaty of Paris of 1763. The Conquest has always been a symbol in French Canada, particularly in Quebec, of subjugation to the English community and the loss of communal autonomy.

Conservatism Historically, an ideology based on the importance of tradition that accepted human inequality and the organization of society into hierarchically arranged groups as part of the natural order of things. Today, conservatism in Canada and the United States is associated with the defence of private property rights and free trade, individualism, opposition to the welfare state, and, in the case of social conservatives, emphasis on the traditional family, religion, and what are sometimes referred to as 'traditional values'.

Constituencies Also known as ridings, these are the territories represented by members of Parliament. At present there are 308 constituencies, the populations of which range from a low of about 20,000 to a high of roughly 200,000 constituents.

Constitution The fundamental law of a political system. In Canada it includes written components—chiefly the Constitution Acts—and unwritten conventions that are more or less established, such as the understanding that the calling of an election is the Prime Minister's prerogative.

Constitutional conventions Practices that emerge over time and are generally accepted as binding rules of the political system, such as the convention that the leader of the political party with the most seats in the House of Commons after an election shall be called upon to try to form a government with majority support in the House. Unlike the written Constitution, conventions are not enforceable in the courts.

Constitutional supremacy Section 52(1) of the Constitution Act, 1982 declares that 'The Constitution of Canada is the supreme law of Canada, and any law that is inconsistent with the provisions of the Constitution is, to the extent of the inconsistency, of no force or effect.' This means that the laws of all governments and their agencies must conform to the Constitution. Before the Constitution Act, 1982 came into force, Parliament and provincial legislatures were supreme so long as each acted within its own sphere of legislative competence. This was known as parliamentary supremacy.

Co-operative Commonwealth Federation (CCF) Predecessor to the New Democratic Party, the CCF was created in 1932 as an alliance of three main elements: disgruntled farmers, chiefly from western Canada, central Canadian intellectuals, and labour activists. The party first ran candidates in the 1935 federal election. Its founding policy document, the Regina Manifesto, called for extensive state planning and control of the economy, a steeply progressive income tax, and the creation of a welfare state.

Corporate elite Those who control the dominant corporations and investment firms in an economy. John Porter defined the term in *The Vertical Mosaic* (1965) to include the directors of Canada's dominant corporations, a usage that was followed by Wallace Clement and Milan Korac in their later studies of this elite. All of these researchers concluded that the Canadian corporate elite is a largely self-perpetuating group whose exclusive social backgrounds and activities set them apart from the general population.

Corporatism A political structure characterized by the direct participation of organizations representing business and labour in public policy-making.

Crisis of the state Marxist scholars began in the 1970s to talk about various sorts of crises said to afflict the capitalist state, including the fiscal crisis of the state. The central idea is that during the 1970s and 1980s the rate of capitalist expansion was slowing compared to the decades of the 1950s and 1960s and pressures on state spending were increasing. This led to increased deficit spending but also to pressure on capitalist governments to cut back on their spending and reduce the size of government.

Cross-border regions (CBRs) Distinct groupings of neighbouring and nearby Canadian provinces and American states whose economic, cultural, and institutional linkages create commonalities between the members of these binational groupings and set each such region apart from other regions.

Cultural hegemony According to Marxists and some elements within contemporary feminism, the values and beliefs of the dominant class or of males, respectively, are accepted as normal and inevitable by society as a whole, despite the fact that they are contrary to the true interests of subordinate classes or females.

Democracy A political system based on the formal equality of all citizens, in which there is a realistic possibility that voters can replace the government, and in which certain basic rights and freedoms are protected.

Democratic deficit A term signifying the gap that critics argue exists between the principles and aspirations embodied in Canada's democratic political culture—including accountability, participation, and openness—and the actual practices and institutions of governance.

Dependence The limitations on a country's autonomy that may arise from its economic, cultural, or military ties to another country or countries. During the 1960s and 1970s it was popular on the left of Canadian politics to characterize Canada as a dependent satellite within the orbit of the United States. The ties between these two countries have not weakened since then, but it is now more common to view Canada's dependent condition within the broader framework of economic and cultural globalization.

Distinct society The Meech Lake Accord of 1987 proposed the amendment of the Constitution to recognize Quebec as a distinct society unlike other provincial societies. In both the Meech Lake and Charlottetown (1992) Accords the distinct society clause was explicitly linked to the fact that Quebec is the only province in which a majority of the population is francophone and would have required the Quebec government to protect and promote the French language. In 1995 Parliament passed a resolution recognizing Quebec as a distinct society. It does not, however, have the force of constitutional law.

Election Expenses Act, 1974 Before 1974 party and candidate spending on election campaign activities was essentially unregulated and there were no legal requirements that revenues and expenditures be publicly disclosed. The Election Expenses Act places spending limits on registered political parties and their candidates during election campaigns, allows for the reimbursement for part of the expenses of candidates who receive at least 15 per cent of the vote, and requires the public disclosure of all contributions of $100 or more to parties and candidates.

'End of ideology' A thesis advanced by American sociologist Daniel Bell in the 1960s, which argued that traditional right/left ideological thinking had become irrelevant and outmoded as a consequence of a developing consensus on the desirability of the welfare state, government regulation of business, and political pluralism.

Entitlements What might be called social rights of citizenship, such as public education, pensions, welfare, and various forms of assistance for those in need. It is a concept associated with the welfare state and a redistributive ethic in public life.

Equalization Transfers made by Ottawa to provincial governments whose per capita tax revenues (according to a complex formula negotiated between Ottawa and the provinces) fall below the average of the two most affluent provinces. Equalization is the second largest federal transfer to the provinces, after the Canada Health Transfer and Canada Social Transfer.

Estimates Sometimes referred to as the expenditure budget. Every year towards the end of February the government will table its spending estimates for the forthcoming fiscal year (1 April to 31 March) in the House of Commons.

Executive federalism A term often used to describe the relations between the Prime Minister and premiers and cabinet ministers of the two levels of government. The negotiations between them and the agreements they reach have often been undertaken with minimal, if any, input from their legislatures or the public.

False consciousness A Marxist concept describing the inability of subordinate social classes to see where their real interests lie and their acceptance of cultural values and beliefs that justify their exploitation by the dominant class.

Feminism A framework for interpreting and explaining politics and society that sees gender as the fundamental basis of conflict in society and associates politics, in all its forms, with the systemic domination of males over females.

First Nations A term commonly used in Canada to refer to communities descended from those who inhabited North America before the arrival of Europeans. This term is not generally used in several other countries that have Aboriginal, pre-contact minorities.

Fiscal imbalance A term used to describe two aspects of public intergovernmental finance in Canada. It has been used since the 1930s to refer to the shortfall between the spending requirements of provincial governments and their revenues, while the federal government had revenues sufficient to pay for its program requirements and to transfer revenue to the provinces. This was described as the 'fiscal gap' until fairly recently. The other meaning ascribed to this term involves the gap that exists between what citizens and corporations in the wealthier provinces, particularly Alberta and Ontario, contribute to the federal government in various forms of taxation and what they and their provincial governments receive back in federal program spending and transfers. As of 2008, the fiscal imbalance for Ontario was estimated by that provincial government to be $20 billion.

Formal equality One of two different standards, the other being *substantive equality*, that may be applied by the courts to the Charter's equality guarantees. The formal equality standard requires that all individuals be treated the same under the law, regardless of the fact that the life circumstances of members of different groups may be significantly different and may affect the likelihood of their achieving constitutional guarantees of equality.

Fragment theory American historian Louis Hartz developed this theory, which maintains that the ideological development of New World societies such as Canada, settled by European colonization, was strongly determined by the social characteristics and cultural values of their early immigrants. Such societies were fragments of the Old World because their creation coincided with a particular ideological epoch in the Old World from which the founding immigrants came.

Free-rider problem As the number of members in an organization increases, the likelihood that some individuals will believe that they can reap the benefits of the organization's actions without having to contribute to it also increases.

Gender roles One of the fundamental premises of much of contemporary feminism is that male and female genders are socially constructed. As Simone de Beauvoir put it, 'One is not born, but rather becomes, a woman.' This premise provides the intellectual basis for attacks on many of the traditional roles and expectations associated with males and females. A spirited debate exists between those who argue that gender roles are fundamentally socially constructed and those who maintain that biological differences between the sexes provide the basis for many of the important differences in male and female behaviour, aptitudes, and preferences.

Globalization The increasing interdependence of states, economies, and societies throughout the world, a phenomenon characterized by, among other things, dramatically higher levels of international trade and capital mobility than in the past, the increased mobility and migration of peoples, cultural convergence in terms of consumer tastes between societies, particularly in the developed countries of the world, and the emergence of international institutions for the development and enforcement of economic and human rights standards.

Government The elected individuals and party controlling the state at a particular point in time.

Human rights All the basic rights and freedoms of citizens. Also called 'civil liberties' or 'civil rights', these include political rights, democratic rights, legal rights, economic rights, and equality rights. Other human rights can include language rights, social entitlements, and environmental rights.

Ideology A set of interrelated beliefs about how society is organized and how it ought to function.

Influence A form of power that depends on the ability of a person or group of persons to persuade others that it is reasonable and/or in their self-interest to behave in a particular way (e.g., to vote for a particular candidate or party).

Infotainment A hybrid television form that packages news and public affairs reporting in an entertainment format that typically includes a 'celebrity journalist/host', short analysis that emphasizes action, confrontation, and controversy, and relatively little historical and background information. It is sometimes called 'soft news'.

Institutional groups Interest groups characterized by a high degree of organizational sophistication, the distinguishing features of which include organizational continuity, stable membership, extensive knowledge of sectors of government that affect their members and easy access to public officials in these sectors, concrete and immediate objectives, and overall organizational goals that are more important than any specific objective.

Interculturalism A Quebec variant of *multiculturalism*. As explained by Quebec's Consultation Commission on Accommodation Practices Related to Cultural Differences (the Bouchard-Taylor Commission, 2008), interculturalism involves a policy of reconciliation and mutual adaptation on the part of both the dominant majority and minorities: both sides must be prepared to make cultural concessions. This is rather different from the more pluralistic concept of multiculturalism, which does not assume a majority group as part of the equation or an explicit need for concession.

Intrastate federalism The representation and accommodation of regional interests within national political institutions such as the Senate. In Canada, federalism has operated mainly through intergovernmental relations. Intrastate federalism, while often argued to be a means of overcoming decentralist tendencies in Canada, has not achieved much success.

Inuit Aboriginal people who comprise the vast majority of those living in the Canadian Arctic, including in Nunavut, Nunavik (Arctic Quebec), Nunatsiavut (northern Labrador), and the Inuvialuit Settlement Region in the western Arctic (Northwest Territories). The forebears of the Inuit migrated from northeast Asia to North America thousands of years later than most other Aboriginal peoples migrated to the Americas.

Iron triangle An American term used to describe the closed system of relations between an interest group and the administrative or regulatory agencies and congressional committees with which the group normally deals.

JPMs Acronym for 'jolts-per-minute', a term coined by Canadian media analyst Morris Wolfe to refer to what he calls The First Law of Commercial Television: 'Thou shalt give them enough jolts per minute or thou shalt lose them.'

Judicial independence The principle according to which judges should be free from any and all interference in their decision-making. It is particularly important that they be free from interference by the government to ensure that the courts are seen to be independent and non-partisan. One of the key protections for judicial independence is the fact that once judges are appointed they cannot be removed from office before retirement age, usually 75, except for serious cause (such as criminal behaviour or serious incompetence).

Judicial restraint The practice of judges deferring to the will of elected governments when their laws and actions are challenged as being unconstitutional. Before the Charter was passed in 1982, it was extremely rare for Canadian courts to declare duly passed laws unconstitutional, unless they were *ultra vires*. Section 1 of the Charter, the reasonable limits clause, provides the courts with the opportunity to defer to elected public officials. However, many critics charge that the tradition of judicial restraint has been replaced by American-style judicial activism.

Legitimacy The acceptance by most people that the rules and institutions comprising the state are fair and should be obeyed. It is closely related to the concept of consent in democracies.

Liberalism Historically, an individualistic ideology associated with freedom of religious choice and practice, free enterprise and free trade, and freedom of expression and association in politics. During the latter half of the twentieth century in Canada and the United States, liberalism came to be associated with support for the welfare state, the protection of minority rights, and the regulation of business.

Libertarianism The belief that individuals should be allowed the largest possible margin of freedom in all realms of life, including those that involve moral choices. Although they are often thought of as ideologically conservative, libertarians are more likely to align themselves with people and groups thought of as left-leaning on such issues as abortion, homosexual rights, and banning prayer from public schools.

Lobbying Any form of direct or indirect communication with public officials that is intended to influence public policy. Although often associated in the public mind with unfair privilege and corruption, lobbying is not limited to organizations representing the powerful and is not inherently undemocratic.

Loyalism The value system associated with the Loyalists, those who opposed the American Revolution and who migrated north to the British colonies after the defeat of the British in the American War of Independence. Their ideological beliefs have been the subject of much debate, but there is a consensus that they brought to Canada a loyalty to the British Crown and to that which was deemed 'British' and a rejection of the developing American identity.

Maîtres chez nous The Quebec Liberal Party's 1962 election campaign slogan, meaning 'masters in our own house'. It captured the new spirit of Quebec nationalism that emerged during the period of the Quiet Revolution.

Manufacturing consent Phrase originally used by Walter Lippmann to refer to government's use of propagandistic techniques to cultivate popular acceptance of its rule. It is also the title of a 1988 book by Noam Chomsky and Edward Herman, in which they argue that the privately owned and oligopolistic media system in the United States—and, according to like-minded critics, in Canada as well—fosters popular consent for a social system that operates mainly in the interests of a privileged minority.

Marxism A framework for interpreting and explaining politics and society that sees class divisions as the fundamental basis of conflict in society and associates politics with a pervasive pattern of domination by those who own and control the means of creating and distributing wealth over those who do not.

Materialism Stresses economic security, material well-being, and acquisition; consequently, from a materialist perspective, incomes and employment are of greater concern than human rights or the environment, for example.

Maternal feminism Also called social feminism, this describes the early women's movement from the late 1800s to the early twentieth century. Maternal feminism accepted the assumption that the biological differences between men and women provided the basis for their different social roles, women being by nature more caring about life and the conditions that nurture it. Maternal feminists fought for legal and political reforms that they expected would improve the conditions of women and their families. The temperance movement was clearly allied to maternal feminism, for the simple reason that alcohol was widely seen as one of the chief threats to the security of women and their families.

Merit principle The practice of making hiring and promotion decisions based on such qualifications as relevant experience, academic degrees, professional credentials and certification, and other attributes deemed to be relevant to the competent performance of the job. This policy was first adopted by the federal government with the passage of the Civil Service Amendment Act, 1908.

Métis Originally, the mixed-blood descendants of unions between Indian women and Scots or French-speaking traders and settlers in the Red River region of Manitoba; more recently, the term has been applied to and appropriated by other groups in Canada of mixed Aboriginal and European ancestry.

Ministerial responsibility The obligation of a cabinet minister to explain and defend in the legislature—and, ultimately, to be responsible for—the policies and actions of his or her department.

Minority government A situation where no single political party controls a majority of seats in the House of Commons. In such circumstances the party with the largest number of seats will require the support of at least some members of one or more other parties in order to win votes in the House of Commons and govern. Majority government, when one party controls a majority of the seats in the House, has been more common in Canada, although the elections of 2004, 2006, and 2008 produced minority governments.

Mobility of capital Producers and investors enjoy a wide, but not absolute, freedom to shift their operations or investments between sectors of the economy and from one national economy to another. This mobility of capital is a major reason why governments must be concerned with business confidence and will often be reluctant to take measures that, while politically popular, may offend important business interests.

Multiculturalism A value system based on the premise that ethnic and cultural identities and traditions are important to human happiness and dignity and that public policy ought to recognize, support, and promote the retention of these identities and traditions. In Canada an official policy of multiculturalism has existed since 1971. The Charter of Rights and Freedoms acknowledges the 'multicultural heritage of Canadians' and the Multiculturalism Act,

1988 commits the Canadian government to a policy of promoting multiculturalism. This is done largely through the Department of Canadian Heritage.

Multilateralism An approach to the resolution of problems that relies on collective decision-making through international organizations such as the UN, the International Criminal Court, NATO, and the WTO. It is based on an assumption that member states should be willing to give up some national sovereignty and accept the decisions of multilateral organizations to which they belong.

Nation A group of people who share a sense of being a community based on religion, language, ethnicity, a shared history, or some combination of these. See also Box 1.7.

National Action Committee on the Status of Women An umbrella organization that represented roughly 700 women's organizations across Canada. During the 1980s the NAC was generally viewed by the media and government as the major organizational voice for the women's movement, and most of the group's revenue came from the federal government. The organization fell on hard financial times by the late 1990s and ceased to operate by 2003.

National Energy Program (NEP) Nationalist economic policy introduced in 1981 that limited the price that could be charged in Canada for oil and gas from Canadian sources and provided preferential tax treatment for Canadian-owned companies investing in the petroleum sector. It was viewed by Alberta as a thinly disguised subsidy that their province—Canada's leading petroleum producer—was made to pay to the petroleum-consuming populations and industries of central Canada. The NEP was opposed by multinational petroleum companies and the American government as discriminating against foreign investors.

National Policy (1878–9) The Conservative Party's election platform in 1878, this nation-building strategy began to be implemented in 1879. Its three components included a significant increase in protective tariffs to promote manufacturing in Ontario and Quebec, construction of a transcontinental railroad, and encouragement of western settlement to expand the market for the manufactured products of central Canada and to protect this territory from American encroachment.

National standards Rules established by the federal government that apply to areas of provincial jurisdiction, particularly health care and social assistance. For example, the Canada Health Act, 1984 prohibits extra-billing by doctors and imposes financial penalties on provinces that allow the practice. The enforcement of national standards depends primarily on the fact that Ottawa transfers money to the provinces to pay for certain social programs.

Neo-institutionalism A perspective on policy-making that emphasizes the impact of formal and informal structures and rules on political outcomes. The roots of this perspective lie in economics, organization theory, and a reaction to society-centred approaches to understanding politics and policy.

News management The practice of organizing press conferences, photo opportunities, and other planned events in ways that accommodate the media's need for images and information that are available by newspaper/broadcaster deadlines and in a form likely to be attractive to news editors and to readers or viewers.

North American Free Trade Agreement (NAFTA) A treaty signed by Canada, Mexico, and the United States, under which most duties on goods and services traded between these economies are eliminated and the treatment of each country's investors is, with some limited exceptions, the same as that of domestic investors.

Notwithstanding clause Section 33 of the Charter of Rights and Freedoms, which states that either Parliament or a provincial legislature may expressly declare that a law shall operate even if it contravenes the fundamental freedoms (s. 2), legal rights (ss. 7–14), or equality rights (s. 15) in the Charter. This clause has been invoked rarely, most controversially by the Quebec government in 1989.

***Oakes* test** Established by the Supreme Court of Canada, this is a test that the courts apply in determining whether a law or government action that contravenes a right or freedom guaranteed by the Charter is nevertheless constitutional under the 'reasonable limits' section of the Charter (s. 1). To be considered 'reasonable', a limitation must be based on an important public policy goal and must be proportionate to the importance of this goal.

Operationalize To define a concept in terms of the method or methods used to measure it. For example, democracy might be defined as a political system in which all adults have the legal right to vote and more than one political party competes to form the government. Both of these criteria can be measured.

'Ottawa mandarins' 'Mandarins', the term given to high officials in the ancient Chinese empire, was applied to the coterie of top officials, particularly deputy ministers and the governor of the Bank of Canada, who dominated federal policy-making during the period of the 1940s to the 1960s.

Outsourcing The movement by transnational corporations of jobs and material inputs for production to less developed countries where labour and inputs cost less.

Paid access opportunities Fundraising events, i.e., dinners and cocktail parties, where, for a donation that can range up to several thousand dollars, donors receive the opportunity to meet and exchange views with party leaders or cabinet ministers.

Parliamentary supremacy This means that Parliament's authority is superior to that of all other institutions of government. In concrete terms this means that the courts will not second-guess the right of the legislature to pass any law, on any subject, as long as it does not involve a matter that, under the Constitution, is properly legislated on by another level of government. Parliamentary supremacy was effectively replaced by *constitutional supremacy* as a result of the Constitution Act, 1982.

Party discipline The practice of MPs belonging to the same party voting as a unified bloc in the way directed by their leader. This practice is based on a combination of reasons, the foremost being the understanding that the government is required to resign if it loses an important vote in the House of Commons. The Prime Minister and other party leaders control various levers that can be used to maintain party discipline, including expulsion of a member from party caucus, withholding promotion or other rewards from an MP, or refusing to allow him or her to run as the party's candidate in the next election.

Patronage The awarding of favours, such as contracts, jobs, or public spending in a community, in exchange for political support. This was the central preoccupation of Canadian politics during the first several decades after Confederation. It continues to be an important practice in Canada and other democracies, although when the exchange of support for government largesse is too obvious this is seen by many to border on corruption.

'Peace, order, and good government of Canada' (POGG) The preamble to section 91 of the Constitution Act, 1867 includes this phrase, which has been interpreted by some as a general grant of legislative power to the federal government. Over time, however, court rulings reduced POGG to an emergency power that can only provide the constitutional basis for federal actions in special circumstances. In a 1977 decision, the Supreme Court indicated that it would not be quick to question Parliament's judgement that special circumstances, warranting legislation under the authority of POGG, exist.

'(The) personal is political' The slogan of the modern feminist movement that emerged in the 1960s, 'the personal is political' expresses the feminist view that the roots of gender inequality are found in structured male–female relations throughout society and that therefore the achievement of equality for women requires that attitudes and practices in the home, school, workplace, media, and elsewhere must be changed.

***Persons* case (1929)** In this decision of the Judicial Committee of the Privy Council, the JCPC overturned a Supreme Court of Canada ruling that women were not considered persons for purposes of holding certain public offices.

Pluralism An explanation of politics that sees organized interests as the central fact of political life and explains politics chiefly in terms of the activities of groups.

Plurality electoral system An electoral system in which the candidate with the most votes is elected by a simple plurality; in multi-party states such as

Canada, in most instances those who are elected do not receive a majority of the votes.

Policy community The constellation of state and societal actors active in a particular policy field.

Policy network The nature of relations among the actors in a *policy community*.

Political faction A group of citizens whose goals and behaviour are contrary to those of other groups or to the interests of the community as a whole.

Political identities An identity is a state of mind, a sense of belonging to a community that is defined by its language, ethnic origins, religion, regional location, gender, or some other social or cultural characteristics. Identities become political when those who share them make demands on the state or when the state recognizes a group identity as a reason for treating a group's members in a special way.

Politics The activity by which rival claims are settled by public authorities. See also Box 1.1.

Politics–administration dichotomy Advocated by progressive reformers beginning in the late nineteenth century, this concept involves an ideal of governance whereby only elected politicians should make choices between competing values and interests, choices that would be embodied in the laws. The proper function of non-elected state officials is to implement these choices without regard for their personal views and preferences.

Populism A vision of politics based on the premise that the general population should have as many opportunities as possible to participate directly in political decision-making and that those elected to govern ought to view themselves as delegates of the people and therefore obliged to reflect their preferences. Populists favour recall votes to remove unfaithful public officials, plebiscites and referendums, short terms of office and term limits for public officials, and citizen initiatives to force action on an issue or policy proposal. They oppose party discipline.

Positive state A state that is active in attempting to shape society and influence its direction. It was championed by liberal intellectuals such as John Dewey in the United States (*The Public and Its Problems*, 1927), socialist thinkers in the United Kingdom, most prominently the members of the Fabian Society, and in Canada by Progressive movement intellectuals early in the twentieth century.

Post-materialism Emphasizes human needs for belonging, self-esteem, and personal fulfillment; consequently; high value is placed on quality-of-life issues such as the environment, group equality, and human rights.

Postmodernism A world view that rejects absolute truths of any kind and conceives of state–society relations as contingent and relative but of the state as nonetheless oppressive, whereby oppression may be targeted at groups based on their race, gender, ethnicity, sexual preference, or some other trait that places them outside the dominant group in control of the levers of state power.

Poverty lines Statistics Canada has established what it calls 'low-income cut-offs' (LICOs) that are routinely referred to by journalists, politicians, academics, and others as 'poverty lines'. These cut-offs or poverty lines represent a relative measure of low income, currently defined to mean that more than 56.2 per cent of income (20 percentage points above the national average) is spent on food, clothing, and shelter. In May 2003 Statistics Canada and Human Resources Development Canada introduced a 'market basket measure' for determining poverty that would have the effect of fewer people being considered as living below the poverty line, but Statistics Canada continues to use LICOs as its principal measure of poverty.

Power The ability to influence what happens. It may assume various forms, including *coercion*, *influence* (persuasion), and *authority*.

Prime ministerial government The argument made in recent years by commentators such as Jeffrey Simpson and Donald Savoie that the concentration of power in the hands of the Prime Minister and his advisers has reached unprecedented levels and that both Parliament and cabinet have been relegated to the margins of the policy-making process. While both Simpson and Savoie suggest that the development of prime ministerial government was partly due to the leadership style of Liberal Prime Minister Jean Chrétien, they argue that there are more fundamental and enduring factors that have contributed to this concentration of power.

Privy Council Essentially the cabinet, under the leadership of the Prime Minister. Formally, however, anyone who has ever been a member of cabinet retains the title of privy councillor, but only those who are members of the government of the day exercise the constitutional and legal powers associated with the Privy Council.

Propaganda The promotion of a particular ideology or view on public policy by the public media dissemination of selected information and/or misinformation. Although propaganda is commonly understood to be a tool used by non-democratic governments to mislead and deceive the populace, powerful economic interests and governments in democratic societies are able to use the media system for what are essentially propagandistic purposes.

Proportional representation Under this system, variants of which exist in many European countries, the number of seats that a party receives in the legislature is based roughly on the share of the popular vote cast for that party.

Protest parties Political parties that have arisen out of dissatisfaction with the operation of brokerage politics in Canada and what has been seen, particularly in western Canada, as the inability of the Liberal and Conservative parties to represent certain regional interests. The *Reform Party*, created in 1987, was the most recent of these parties. Others have included the Progressives, Social Credit, the Western Canada Concept, and the early *Co-operative Commonwealth Federation*.

Province-building The phenomenon of powerful provincial governments creating large and competent bureaucracies and using the various constitutional, legal, taxation, and public opinion levers available to them to increase their control over activities and interests within their provincial borders and, in consequence, vis-à-vis Ottawa. Province-building is most often associated with Alberta in the 1970s and Quebec during the 1960s and 1970s, but is observed more generally in several provinces at various points in time.

Public agenda The issues, concepts, and ideas current in a society's politics at any point in time. The capacity to get an issue onto the agenda or framed in a particular way may be an indication of political influence, but the ability to keep an issue from being formulated as a matter on which most people think government should act may also be a sign of a group's influence.

Purchasing power parities (PPPs) A measure of average real purchasing power that takes into account both average nominal incomes and what a standardized currency unit can purchase in a country. Although average nominal incomes are much higher in many countries than in Canada, if PPPs are used to measure standardized purchasing power Canadians are among the most affluent people in the world.

Quality of life (QOL) This concept may refer to the level of satisfaction with life that members of a society experience, their material well-being, their level of health, the state of their environment, the level of equality between groups, or some combination of these. The United Nations annually ranks countries according to its 'human development index', which combines various factors, including literacy, infant mortality, average life expectancy, average income, and average years of formal education. This UN index is accepted by some as a measure of QOL.

Québécois de souche Quebecers, and more specifically francophone Quebecers, whose roots in the province go back many generations. The term is used to distinguish what in English might be called old-stock Quebecers from more recent arrivals whose first language usually is not French and whose cultural heritage is not French Canadian. A similar term is '*Québécois pur laine*' (pure-wool Quebecers). This distinction between old-stock Quebecers and others is objected to by some as being fundamentally discriminatory, but others maintain that the attachment of immigrants to the French language and Quebec's distinctive culture has often been weak.

Quiet Revolution The early 1960s in Quebec when the provincial Liberal government of Jean Lesage reorganized and developed the Quebec state to take control of important institutions such as education and the economy. During the Lesage years (1960–6) the conservative traditional nationalism was swept away by a more aggressive Quebec nationalism that turned to the Quebec state as the chief instrument for the modernization of Quebec society and the advancement of francophone interests.

Rattrapage French for 'catching up', this was one of the key goals of the anti-establishment challenge to the conservative ideology and elites that dominated Quebec during the 1940s and 1950s. *Rattrapage* involved bringing Quebec's society, economy, and government up to the level of development that existed in the rest of Canada, a goal that required a larger and more interventionist provincial government.

Realignment election An election (or series of elections) that produces a durable change in the political parties' bases of support within a region or regions of a country.

Reasonable limits Section 1 of the Charter of Rights and Freedoms states that the rights and freedoms guaranteed by the Charter are subject to 'such reasonable limits prescribed by law as can be demonstrably justified in a free and democratic society'. See also *Oakes test*.

Receptive bilinguals People who are capable of responding to French communication but do not themselves initiate conversations in French, consume French-language media, or seek out opportunities to live in their acquired second language.

Red Toryism The belief system associated with Canadian conservatives who believe that government has a responsibility to act as an agent for the collective good and that this responsibility goes far beyond maintaining law and order. Red Tories have supported the creation of public enterprises to achieve a range of cultural and economic goals and are generally supportive of Canadian nationalism.

Reform Party Founded in 1987 under the slogan 'The West wants in', it became the Canadian Alliance Party in 2000. The Reform Party emerged out of the feelings of alienation that peaked in western Canada during the 1980s, triggered by the Conservative government's 1987 decision to award a major defence contract to Quebec instead of Manitoba and the widespread view that whether the Liberal or Progressive Conservative Party was in power federally, western interests would continue to be sacrificed to those of central Canada.

Regionalism A political identity based on a shared sense of place. It may be linked to a variety of cultural, economic, institutional, and historical factors that tend to distinguish the inhabitants of one region of a country from those of other regions.

'Repertory of stereotypes' A term coined by Walter Lippmann, it refers to the media's tendency to fit current news to a limited number of stereotypes that make news stories more easily understandable for audiences/readers, but that also sacrifice nuance and even distort the news by squeezing it into a familiar package.

Representative bureaucracy The practice of hiring and promotion so that the composition of the bureaucracy reflects in fair proportion the representation of demographic characteristics in society. In Canada, the concept and practice of representative bureaucracy were first applied to increase the share of francophones in the public service. Since the 1980s it has been expanded to include women, Aboriginal people, visible minorities, and disabled persons.

Representative democracy A form of democracy in which citizens delegate law-making authority to elected representatives, holding them responsible for their actions through periodic elections.

Reserves Territories set aside under treaties between the federal government and Indian communities for the members of such communities; the vast majority of those residing on reserves are status Indians.

Responsible government The constitutional principle according to which the Prime Minister and cabinet require the support of a majority of members in the House of Commons in order to govern. If the government can no longer maintain majority support in the House, in other words, if it loses the confidence of the House, it is compelled by constitutional convention to resign.

Revanche des berceaux French for 'revenge of the cradles', a term that referred to the high birth rate that enabled French Canada to maintain its numerical strength vis-à-vis English Canada from Confederation until the 1960s. Since then the birth rate in predominantly francophone Quebec has fallen to one of the lowest provincial rates in Canada. This, combined with non-francophone immigration to Canada and the assimilation of francophones outside Quebec, has contributed to a gradual decline in the francophone share of Canada's population.

Revenue budget A taxation budget presented from time to time in Parliament, announcing changes to the taxation system. Whereas the expenditure budget (*estimates*) is tied to a regular cycle of decision-making, a new revenue budget may be tabled at any time as, in the government's view, conditions require.

Revolutionary origins and counter-revolutionary origins American sociologist Seymour Martin Lipset argues in *Revolution and Counter-Revolution* (1960) that the political histories and ideological development of the United States and Canada have been significantly marked by the American Revolution of 1776. The political values, symbols, and institutions of the United States have been based on the liberal ideas of the Revolution while, historically, those in Canada have been based on a rejection of what the Revolution stood for.

Right, left, and centre Labels that signify a range of ideological beliefs from collectivist (left) at one end of the spectrum to individualistic (right) at the other, with those in the middle ground (centre) embracing elements from both extremes.

Royal Commission on Aboriginal Peoples Commission established by the federal government in 1991 and chaired by Georges Erasmus and René Dussault, its 1996 *Report* included about 440 recommendations for the reform of Aboriginal policy. The fundamental premise of the *Report* was that the original sovereignty of Native peoples and their ownership of the land to which they laid historic claim should be acknowledged and their right to self-government should be embedded in the Constitution.

Royal Commission on Bilingualism and Biculturalism This federal Royal Commission was created in 1963 in response to the new assertive nationalism of the Quiet Revolution. The B&B Commission recommended numerous reforms aimed at protecting the rights of the francophone minority outside Quebec and transforming the federal government into a more bilingual institution. The Official Languages Act of 1969 embodied some of the recommendations made by the B&B Commission, as did the federal policy of *multiculturalism* announced in 1971.

Royal Proclamation of 1763 Dealt with the North American territories that were formally surrendered by France to England under the terms of the Treaty of Paris and included detailed provisions regarding relations between the British and the Native inhabitants of these territories, whereby unsettled lands were reserved for the Indians and could be alienated only by the Crown, as occurred in much of Canada through the treaty process in the last half of the nineteenth century and in the first decades of the twentieth century.

Rule of law A vital principle of democratic government, it means that the actions of governments and their agents must be based on the authority of law and that all persons, the governed and those who govern, are subject to the same laws.

Secularization A trend observable throughout the developed world whereby people place greater value on materialism and less value on the spiritual or eternal dimension of life.

Separation of powers A constitutional principle, supported by s. 24 of the Charter, that guarantees the special role of the judiciary, without interference from the legislature or the executive, to interpret what the law and the Constitution mean when disputes arise.

Sexism Term coined during the 1960s as a label for behaviour that treats males and females unequally for no other reason than the fact of being male or female.

Shared-cost programs Provincially administered programs, such as those in the field of health care, to which Ottawa contributes money earmarked for a particular purpose. During the 1960s and 1970s it was common for Ottawa's contribution to be determined by how much a province spent on such a program. Since the late 1970s successive federal governments have abandoned this model in favour of *block funding*.

Single-member constituency A voting system under which each member of the legislature is elected to represent a particular constituency or riding, receiving this right when he or she receives more votes than any other single candidate in the election held in that constituency. It is not necessary to receive a majority of the votes cast in a constituency, and under Canada's multi-party system most successful candidates do not.

Social capital A concept that refers to norms of interpersonal trust, a sense of civic duty, and a belief that one's political participation matters. Contemporary theorists like Robert Putnam argue that the successful functioning of democracies depends on a high level of social capital among the general population. Social capital reflects the power within society that the individual derives from attachment to social networks, such as work, church groups, community associations, clubs, and the like.

Socialism An ideology based on the principle of equality of condition. Historically, socialists led the fight for a greater state role in managing the economy, better working conditions and rights for workers, and the egalitarian and redistributive policies associated with the welfare state. Modern socialists, or social democrats, often temper their advocacy of an egalitarian society with an acceptance of capitalism and the inequalities that inevitably are generated by a market economy.

Socio-economic mobility The ability of individuals, families, and groups to move from one social or economic position to another. Where socio-economic mobility is high, movement up and down the social ladder is relatively common and the barriers to entry into high-paying occupations, prestigious status groups, or powerful elites are relatively low.

Soft power Term coined by American scholar Joseph Nye to describe forms of international influence based on culture, values, and the perceived legitimacy of a nation's international aims, rather than on armaments, sanctions, and coercion. Soft power is associated with *multilateralism* and support for international structures of governance and problem resolution such as the UN and the International Criminal Court.

Sovereignty-association A term generally understood to mean that a politically sovereign (independent) Quebec would continue to be linked to Canada through some sort of commercial union, free trade agreement, and shared currency. Sovereignty-association was the option proposed to Quebecers in the 1980 referendum.

Split-run publications American magazines, such as *Time* and *Sports Illustrated*, that published a Canadian edition at low cost by importing the American version via satellite, adding some pages of Canadian content, and thereby qualifying for the same advertising rates that apply to Canadian-based magazines.

State The structures through which public authority is exercised, including the legislature, bureaucracy, courts, police, armed forces, and other publicly owned or controlled institutions, such as schools and hospitals. See also Box 1.2.

State capacity A term used in a 2002 UN report on globalization to refer to a state's ability to maintain social safety nets and pursue non-market goals such as protection of the environment and promotion of equality. This report suggested that a 'deficit' in state capacity, resulting from low levels of training and professionalism, inadequate technology, and corruption, impedes the ability of many developing countries to take advantage of economic opportunities presented by globalization.

Substantive equality An approach to the interpretation of equality rights and s. 15 of the Charter premised on the idea that individuals may experience advantages or disadvantages as a result of belonging to a particular group and that their equality rights claims should be judged against the reality of these group-based inequalities in society. This approach rejects the concept of *formal equality* that treating all individuals identically under the law can guarantee equality.

Suffragists Advocates of the right to vote for women. Many of the early suffragists supported female enfranchisement on the grounds that women voters would inject a morally uplifting element into politics. Nellie McClung was Canada's best-known suffragist.

Survivance, la French for 'survival'. *La survivance* captures the conservative character of traditional French-Canadian nationalism, focused as it was on preserving the religious and linguistic heritage of French Canada in the face of assimilationist pressures.

Systemic discrimination Discrimination without conscious individual intent. Systemic discrimination inheres in traditions, customary practices, rules, laws, and institutions that have the effect of placing the members of one or more ascriptive groups at a disadvantage compared to other groups.

'The higher, the fewer' Canadian political scientist Sylvia Bashevkin's characterization of the fact that, although female participation levels in politics are about the same as men's for activities like voting and campaigning, the proportion of women tends to decrease as the political activity becomes more demanding, such as holding office in a political party or being a candidate for public office.

Totalitarianism A system of government that suppresses all dissent in the name of some supreme goal.

Two-nations theory Canada, viewed from this perspective, is fundamentally a partnership between two ethnolinguistic communities or nations, one French-speaking and the other English-speaking. This premise underlies such constitutional proposals as a Quebec right of veto over constitutional reform and recognition of Quebec as a distinct society. Although the two-nations theory continues to enjoy popularity among French-Canadian nationalists and some English-Canadian intellectuals, it appears to have much less public support in English-speaking Canada.

Tyranny of the majority Alexis de Tocqueville used this term in *Democracy in America* (1835) to refer to the danger that majoritarian democracy might oppress the rights of minorities.

Ultra vires From the Latin, meaning 'beyond its strength'; a judicial ruling of ultra vires means that a legislative act is beyond or outside the constitutional power or authority of that legislature; in contrast, an 'intra vires' judicial ruling means that a legislature has acted within its constitutional competence.

Unholy alliance The term that critics sometimes applied to the three pillars of the conservative Quebec establishment during the 1940s and 1950s: the Catholic Church, anglophone capital, and the Union Nationale under the leadership of *le chef*, Maurice Duplessis.

Universal Declaration of Human Rights A declaration passed by the United Nations in 1948 that provides the basis for various international covenants to which Canada is a signatory, such as the International Covenant on Civil and Political Rights and the International Covenant on Economic, Social and Cultural Rights.

Vertical mosaic The title of a 1965 book by Canadian sociologist John Porter in which he argued that Canadian society was characterized by a vertical mosaic of patterned inequality between different ethnic and religious groups. See also *corporate elite*.

Visible minority A term that refers to people who belong to a minority that is non-white in colour or race, but that does not include Aboriginal Canadians. This is the definition that is used in the federal Employment Equity Act and by Statistics Canada and the Census of Canada. The term entered the Canadian political lexicon in the 1980s. It is not commonly used in the United States or France to refer to non-white minorities.

Welfare gap The difference between total welfare income (social assistance benefits, child tax benefits, and federal and provincial sales tax credits) and the low-income cut-offs established by Statistics Canada. See Figure 3.8.

Western alienation A belief held by many in western Canada, but particularly in Alberta and British Columbia, that Ottawa and the mainstream political parties are by and large insensitive to the interests and preferences of western Canadians. The roots of this sentiment go back to the high tariff policies and freight rates of the federal government from the late nineteenth century. Regional parties of protest such as the Progressives after World War I and, more recently, the *Reform Party* have emerged from this sense of regional grievance.

Whistleblowing When a public servant brings attention to government actions or policies that he or she believes endanger public health or safety. Such actions are protected by law, but in deciding to go public with information acquired in the course of his or her job, a public servant must be mindful of his or her duty of loyalty to the government and take care to get the facts right.

White Paper (1969) An ambitious set of reforms to Aboriginal policy proposed by the Liberal government, it would have ended the system of Indian reserves and abolished different status for Indians under law. It was strongly opposed by most Native spokespersons and was soon abandoned.

Women's liberation This term came into widespread use during the 1960s to refer to the struggle for equal rights for women. Feminist intellectuals such as Betty Friedan, Germaine Greer, and Gloria Steinem were among the leaders of the women's liberation movement. The character and demands of the movement were to some degree influenced by the black civil rights movement in the United States, feminist leaders drawing parallels between the systematic oppression and subordination of blacks and what they argued was the rather similar treatment of women.

Notes

PART I Introduction

1 An Introduction to Political Life

1. *Reader's Digest Canada*, June 2009.
2. World Values Survey, 2000.
3. Wislawa Szymborska, 'Children of Our Era', *Miracle Fair: Selected Poems of Wislawa Szymborska* (New York: Norton & Company, 2002), 44.
4. Charles Merriam, *Public and Private Government* (New Haven: Yale University Press, 1944).
5. Jill Vickers, *Reinventing Political Science* (Halifax: Fernwood, 1997), 113–14.
6. The full exchange may be viewed on-line at <archives.cbc.ca/IDC-1-71-101-610/conflict_war/october_crisis/clip6>.
7. Leo Panitch, 'State', in *The Canadian Encyclopedia*, 2nd edn (Edmonton: Hurtig, 1988), vol. 4, 2071.
8. Quoted in Vickers, *Reinventing Political Science*, 42.
9. Noam Chomsky and Edward S. Herman, *Manufacturing Consent: The Political Economy of the Mass Media* (New York: Pantheon Books, 1988).
10. Victor Davis Hanson, talk at Woodrow Wilson Center, 2 June 2005, Washington, DC.
11. C.B. Macpherson, *The Real World of Democracy* (Toronto: CBC Enterprises, 1965).
12. Gabriel A. Almond and Sidney Verba, *The Civic Culture* (Princeton, NJ: Princeton University Press, 1963).
13. Quoted in Henry Steele Commager, *Living Ideas in America* (New York: Harper, 1951), 556.
14. Colin Samson, James Wilson, and Jonathan Mazower, *Canada's Tibet: The Killing of the Innu* (London: Survival, 1999), p. 3. For a more extensive and accessible account, see Colin Samson, *A Way of Life That Does Not Exist: Canada and the Extinguishment of the Innu* (St John's and London: ISER Books and Virgo, 2003).
15. Neil Postman, *Amusing Ourselves to Death* (New York: Viking, 1985), 107.
16. 'The People Get It Right, On the Whole', *The Economist*, 7 Nov. 1998, 24.
17. Eugene Forsey, *How Canadians Govern Themselves*, 6th edn (Ottawa: Library of Parliament, Public Information Office, 2005), 32.
18. Robert B. Reich, *Supercapitalism: The Transformation of Business, Democracy and Everyday Life* (New York: Knopf, 2007), 18.
19. See <www.worldvaluessurvey.org>.
20. Centre for Social Justice, at: <www.socialjustice.org>.

PART II The Societal Context of Politics

2 Political Culture

1. 'In Search of the Canadian Dream', The Atlantic (Dec. 2004).
2. R. Kirk, *The Conservative Mind* (London: Faber & Faber, 1953).
3. Daniel Bell, *The End of Ideology* (New York: Free Press, 1962), 402–3.
4. David Bell and Lorne Tepperman, *The Roots of Disunity* (Toronto: McClelland & Stewart, 1979), 23.
5. Fernand Ouellet, *Histoire économique et sociale du Québec, 1760–1850* (Paris: Fides, 1966).
6. Bell and Tepperman note that the estimated number of anglophones in what are now the Maritimes, Quebec, and Ontario at the time of the American Revolution was about 15,000. Between 30,000 and 60,000 Loyalists immigrated to these British colonies in the years immediately after 1776, and a steady stream of 'late Loyalists', perhaps attracted by British offers of free land, immigrated north to Upper Canada over the next few decades. See *The Roots of Disunity*, 45, 80–1.
7. William Christian and Colin Campbell, *Political Parties and Ideologies in Canada*, 2nd edn (Toronto: McGraw-Hill Ryerson, 1982), 23–5; Gad Horowitz, 'Conservatism, Liberalism and Socialism in Canada: An Interpretation', *Canadian Journal of Economics and Political Science* (1966).
8. Kenneth McRae, 'The Structure of Canadian History', in Louis Hartz, ed., *The Founding of New Societies* (New York: Harcourt, Brace & World, 1964), 235.
9. Bell and Tepperman, *The Roots of Disunity*, 76–7.
10. Horowitz, 'Conservatism, Liberalism and Socialism'.
11. Seymour Martin Lipset, *Continental Divide* (Montreal: C.D. Howe Institute, 1989), 1.
12. Bell and Tepperman, *The Roots of Disunity*, 61–2.
13. Reg Whitaker, 'Images of the State in Canada', in Leo Panitch, ed., *The Canadian State* (Toronto: University of Toronto Press, 1977), 30.
14. Patricia Marchak, *Ideological Perspectives on Canada* (Toronto: McGraw-Hill Ryerson, 1975), 115.
15. Pierre Trudeau, 'Some Obstacles to Democracy in Quebec', in Trudeau, *Federalism and the French Canadians* (Toronto: Macmillan, 1968).

16. In 1951, 80 per cent of Quebec's workforce was in secondary industries (manufacturing and construction) and the service sector, a percentage that was higher than for Canada as a whole (78 per cent).
17. See Kenneth McRoberts, *Quebec: Social Change and Political Crisis*, 3rd edn (Toronto: McClelland & Stewart, 1988), 90–100.
18. W.L. Morton, 'The Dualism of Culture and the Federalism of Power', in Richard Abbott, ed., *A New Concept of Confederation*, Proceedings of the Seventh Seminar of the Canadian Union of Students (Ottawa, 1965), 121.
19. Donald Smiley, *The Canadian Political Nationality* (Toronto: Methuen, 1967).
20. All of these statements are based on the rankings in Charles Lewis Taylor and David A. Jodice, *The World Handbook of Political and Social Indicators*, 3rd edn, vol. 2, *Political Protest and Government Change* (New Haven: Yale University Press, 1983); see also Judith Torrance, *Public Violence in Canada 1867–1982* (Toronto: University of Toronto Press, 1986), 57–66.
21. See the analysis of Oka in Robert Campbell and Leslie Pal, 'Feather and Gun', *The Real Worlds of Canadian Politics*, 2nd edn (Peterborough, Ont.: Broadview Press, 1991), 267–345.
22. McRoberts, *Quebec*, 239.
23. En collaboration, *Québec un pays incertains. Reflexions sur le Québec post-referendaire* (Montréal: Québec/Amérique, 1980), 170–2.
24. Status Indians are those registered under the Indian Act.
25. *Globe and Mail*, 26 Sept. 1990.
26. Lipset, *Continental Divide*, 136.
27. Pierre Berton, *Why We Act Like Canadians* (Toronto: McClelland & Stewart, 1982), 16.
28. Paul M. Sniderman et al., *Liberty, Authority, and Community: Civil Liberties and the Canadian Political Culture* (Berkeley: Survey Research Center, University of California, 1988), Figures 9A–9D.
29. Miles Corak, 'Chasing the Same Dream, Climbing Different Ladders: Economic Mobility in the United States and Canada', Economic Mobility Project of the Pew Charitable Trusts, Jan. 2010, at: <www.economic-mobility.org>.
30. Stephen Brooks, 'A Tale of Two Elections: What the Leaders' Rhetoric in the 2000 Elections Tells Us about Canada–US Differences', in Rick Farmer et al., eds, *The Elections of 2000: Politics, Culture, and Economics in North America* (Akron, Ohio: University of Akron Press, 2006), 136–66.
31. Frank Graves, 'The Shifting Public Outlook on Risk and Security', in Karlyn Bowman and Frank Graves, *Threat Perceptions in the United States and Canada: Assessing the Public's Attitudes toward Risk and Security*, One Issue, Two Voices Series, Issue Four (Washington: Canada Institute, Woodrow Wilson Center, Oct. 2005), 10–15.
32. Robert Kudrle and Theodore Marmor, 'The Development of Welfare States in North America', in Peter Flora and Arnold J. Heidersheimer, eds, *The Development of Welfare States in Europe and America* (New Brunswick, NJ: Transaction Books, 1981), 110.
33. Gerard Boychuk, 'National Health Insurance in Canada and the United States: Race, Territorial Integration and the Roots of Difference', paper presented at the annual meeting of the Canadian Political Science Association, Vancouver, June 2008.
34. Lipset, *Continental Divide*, 156.
35. Lars Osberg and Timothy Smeeding, 'Fair Inequality? An International Comparison of Attitudes toward Pay Differentials', working paper, Russell Sage Foundation, 2005, 31, at: <www.russellsage.org/programs/main/inequality/workingpapers/051025.267178/>.
36. Corak, 'Chasing the Same Dream', 3.
37. Ibid., 14.
38. Canada, Constitution Act, 1982, s. 27.
39. Canada, Constitution Act 1982, s. 15(2).
40. Neil Bissoondath, *Selling Illusions: The Cult of Multiculturalism in Canada* (Toronto: Penguin Books, 1994).
41. Reginald Bibby, *Mosaic Madness: The Poverty and Potential of Life in Canada* (Toronto: Stoddart, 1990).
42. Raymond Breton and Jeffrey Reitz, *The Illusion of Difference* (Toronto: C.D. Howe Institute, 1994), 133.
43. Martin Turcotte, 'Passing on the Ancestral Language', *Canadian Social Trends* no. 80 (Spring 2006): 20–7.
44. Berton, *Why We Act Like Canadians*, 16–17.
45. Charles Taylor, 'Deep Diversity and the Future of Canada', accessed at: <www.uni.ca/taylor.html>.
46. Peter C. Newman, *The Canadian Revolution, 1985–1995* (Toronto: Penguin Books, 1995), 12–13.
47. Neil Nevitte, *The Decline of Deference: Canadian Value Change in Cross-National Perspective* (Peterborough, Ont.: Broadview Press, 1996).
48. Michael Adams, *Fire and Ice: The United States, Canada and the Myth of Converging Values* (Toronto: Penguin, 2003).
49. Philip Resnick, *The European Roots of Canadian Identity* (Peterborough, Ont.: Broadview Press, 2005).
50. Christian Boucher, 'Canada–U.S. Values: Distinct, Inevitably Carbon Copy, or Narcissism of Small Differences?', *Horizons* 7, 1 (2004): 46.

3 The Social and Economic Setting

1. See, for example, Stephen Cohen and John Zysman, *Manufacturing Matters* (New York: Basic Books, 1987).
2. John Porter, *The Vertical Mosaic* (Toronto: University of Toronto Press, 1965), 3–4.

3. National Council of Welfare, *A New Poverty Line: Yes, No or Maybe?* (Ottawa: Minister of Public Works and Government Services Canada, 1999), 1.
4. John A. Price, 'Native People, Economic Conditions', *The Canadian Encyclopedia*, 2nd edn (Edmonton: Hurtig, 1988), vol. 3, 1449.
5. Statistics Canada, *Income in Canada 2006* (Ottawa: Statistics Canada Catalogue no. 75–202–X, 2008), 15.
6. Corak explains that the data and literature available on the relationship between daughters' income rankings and their parents' earnings are still too meagre and incomplete to allow for the same sort of analysis. See Miles Corak, 'Chasing the Same Dream, Climbing Different Ladders: Economic Mobility in the United States and Canada', Economic Mobility Project of the Pew Charitable Trusts, Jan. 2010, at: <www.economic-mobility.org>.
7. Ibid., Figures 2 and 3.
8. Jo Blanden, Paul Gregg, and Stephen Machin, *Intergenerational Mobility in Europe and North America* (London: Sutton Trust, Apr. 2005).
9. Miles Corak, *Intergenerational Earnings Mobility among the Children of Canadian Immigrants* (Bonn: Institute for the Study of Labor, 2006).
10. Statistics Canada, 'Study: Projections of the Diversity of the Canadian Population', *The Daily*, 9 Mar. 2010, at: <www.statcan.gc.ca/daily-quotidien/100309/dq100309a-eng.htm>.
11. Abdurrahman Aydemir, Wen-Hao Chen, and Miles Corak, *Intergenerational Earnings Mobility among the Children of Canadian Immigrants*, Statistics Canada Catalogue no. 11F0019MIE, no. 267 (Ottawa: Minister of Industry, 2005).
12. Porter, *The Vertical Mosaic*; Wallace Clement, *The Canadian Corporate Elite* (Toronto: McClelland & Stewart, 1975).
13. Milan Korac, 'Corporate Concentration and the Canadian Corporate Elite: Change and Continuity', MA thesis (University of Windsor, 1992).
14. World Values Survey, 2000.
15. Jan van Dijk et al., *Criminal Victimisation in International Perspective* (Tilburg, Netherlands: Tilburg University and United Nations Office on Drugs and Crime, 2007), 132, Figure 28.
16. Michael Tjepkema, *Alcohol and Illicit Drug Dependence* (Ottawa: Statistics Canada, 2004).
17. Canadian Association of Food Banks, 'Hunger Count 2007', at: <www.cafb.ca>.
18. Statistics Canada and Department of Foreign Affairs and International Trade, *State of Trade 2004* (Ottawa, 2005).
19. Canada, Royal Commission on Newspapers, *Newspapers and Their Readers* (Ottawa: Supply and Services, 1981), 26, Table 19; Pew Research Center, *What the World Thinks in 2002* (Washington: Pew Research Center for the People and the Press, Dec. 2002), at: <www.people-press.org>. The Pew study found that Canadians, by a 2:1 ratio, relied on television instead of newspapers as their main source of information about national and international affairs.

4 Regionalism and Canadian Politics

1. Cited in *The Economist*, special survey of Canada, 15 Feb. 1986, 16.
2. Institute of Sustainable Energy, Environment and Economy, University of Calgary, 2005 study.
3. Richard Simeon and David Elkins, 'Regional Political Cultures in Canada', *Canadian Journal of Political Science* 7, 3 (Sept. 1974): 397–437.
4. Centre for Research and Information on Canada, *The Charter: Dividing or Uniting Canadians?* (Apr. 2002), 30. At: <www.cric.ca>.
5. Ibid., 31.
6. Michael Ornstein and Michael Stevenson, *Politics and Ideology in Canada* (Montreal and Kingston: McGill-Queen's University Press, 1999), ch. 5.
7. Ibid., 206.
8. Ibid., 201, Table 5–2.
9. Debora VanNijnatten, 'Canada–US Relations and the Emergence of Cross-Border Regions', 4, Briefing Notes, Government of Canada, Policy Research Initiatives, 2006, at: <www.policyresearch.gc.ca>.
10. Stephen Brooks and Barry Rabe, eds, *Transboundary Environmental Governance between Canada and the United States: The Second Century* (Washington: Woodrow Wilson Center, 2009).
11. Roger Gibbins and Sonia Arrison, *Western Visions: Perspectives on the West in Canada* (Peterborough, Ont.: Broadview Press, 1995), 45.
12. W.L. Morton, 'The Bias of Prairie Politics', *Transactions of the Royal Society of Canada* series 3, 49 (June 1955): 66.
13. George Woodcock, *Confederation Betrayed: The Case against Trudeau's Canada* (Vancouver: Harbour Publishing, 1981).
14. Barry Cooper, 'Western Political Consciousness', in Stephen Brooks, ed., *Political Thought in Canada: Contemporary Perspectives* (Toronto: Irwin, 1984), 230.
15. Patrick Boyer, *Direct Democracy in Canada: The History and Future of Referendums* (Toronto: Dundurn Press, 1992).
16. Michael Bliss, 'The Multicultural North American Hotel', *National Post*, 15 Jan. 2003.

PART III The Structures of Governance

5 The Constitution

1. Canada, Constitution Act, 1982, s. 16(1).
2. Pierre Trudeau, *Federalism and the French Canadians* (Toronto: Macmillan, 1968), 187.
3. Constitution Act, 1867, preamble.
4. Constitution Act, 1867, s. 121.
5. Constitution Act, 1867, s. 145 (repealed in 1893).
6. Constitution Act, 1982, s. 36.
7. Supreme Court of Canada, *Reference re Secession of Quebec*, Aug. 1998, at p. 18 of on-line decisions.
8. Supreme Court of Canada, *OPSEU v. A.G. of Ontario*, 1987, 2 S.C.R. 2, S7.
9. *Reference re Secession of Quebec*, 19.
10. Ibid., 20.
11. Ibid., 21.
12. Ibid., 22.
13. Supreme Court of Canada, *R. v. Oakes*, 1986, 1 S.C.R. 103, 136.
14. *Reference re Secession of Quebec*, 22.
15. Ibid., 23.
16. Ibid.
17. Ibid., 25.
18. Constitution Act, 1982, s. 6(3)(6).
19. Constitution Act, 1982, s. 6(4).
20. Supreme Court of Canada, *Morgentaler, Smoling and Scott v. The Queen* (1988), 37 C.C.C. (3rd) 449.
21. Constitution Act, 1982, s. 15(1).
22. Constitution Act, 1982, s. 15(2).
23. Constitution Act, 1867, ss. 96–100.
24. *The Queen v. Beauregard* (1986), 2 S.C.R. 56.
25. This was the basis of a 1986 court action brought against the Quebec government by several Provincial Court judges and the Chief Justice of the Quebec Superior Court.
26. Philip Resnick, *Parliament vs. People* (Vancouver: New Star Books, 1984), 19.
27. Ibid., 25.
28. Ibid., 38.
29. Section 91(1). Repealed by the Constitution Act, 1982.
30. Section 92(1). Repealed by the Constitution Act, 1982.
31. Supreme Court of Canada, *Re Constitution of Canada* (1981), 125 D.L.R. (3rd) 1.
32. *Re Attorney General of Quebec and Attorney General of Canada* (1982), 140 D.L.R. (3rd) 385.
33. Cited in Paul Gerin-Lajoie, *Constitutional Amendment in Canada* (Toronto: University of Toronto Press, 1950), 241.
34. Cited ibid., 234.
35. *Reference re Secession of Quebec*, 26.
36. Ibid., 19.
37. Ibid., 27.
38. Ibid., 35.
39. Ibid., 4.

6 Rights and Freedoms

1. *Schenck v. United States*, 249 U.S. 47 (1919).
2. These are the words used in the 'anti-hate' section of Canada's Criminal Code.
3. University of Calgary, *Charter Database*.
4. Michael Mandel, *The Charter of Rights and the Legalization of Politics in Canada* (Toronto: Wall and Thompson, 1989), 4.
5. Alan Borovoy, *When Freedoms Collide: The Case for Our Civil Liberties* (Toronto: Lester & Orpen Dennys, 1988), 24.
6. Walter S. Tarnopolsky, 'Human Rights', in *The Canadian Encyclopedia*, 2nd edn (Edmonton: Hurtig, 1988), vol. 2, 1024.
7. United States Constitution, 14th amendment, 1868.
8. *Hunter et al. v. Southam Inc.* (1984), 11 D.L.R. (4th) 641.
9. *RJR-MacDonald Inc. v. Canada* (1995), 3 S.C.R. (4th).
10. *R. v. Big M Drug Mart* (1985), 18 D.L.R. (4th) 321.
11. *Public Service Alliance of Canada et al. v. The Queen in Right of Canada et al.* (1987), 38 D.L.R. (4th) 249 (Supreme Court of Canada).
12. Mandel, *The Charter of Rights*, 218.
13. *Borowski v. Attorney General for Canada* (1987), 39 D.L.R. (4th) 731; *R. v. Morgentaler, Smoling and Scott* (1985), 48 C.R. (3d) 1 (Ontario Court of Appeal).
14. Carol Smart, *Feminism and the Power of Law* (London: Routledge, 1989), 160.
15. Ibid., 161.
16. Borovoy, *When Freedoms Collide*, ch. 10.
17. R. MacGregor Dawson, *Constitutional Issues in Canada, 1900–1931* (London: Oxford University Press, 1933).
18. R. MacGregor Dawson, *The Government of Canada* (Toronto: University of Toronto Press, 1947).
19. J.A. Corry and J.E. Hodgetts, *Democratic Government and Politics* (Toronto: University of Toronto Press, 1946).
20. *Reference re Alberta Statutes* (1938), S.C.R. 100 (Supreme Court of Canada).
21. *Saumur v. Quebec and Attorney General of Quebec* (1953), 2 S.C.R. 299 (Supreme Court of Canada).
22. *Switzman v. Elbing and Attorney General of Quebec* (1957), S.C.R. 285 (Supreme Court of Canada).
23. *Attorney General of Canada and Dupond v. Montreal* (1978), 2 S.C.R. 770 (Supreme Court of Canada).

24. Quoted in Peter H. Russell, *Leading Constitutional Decisions*, 4th edn (Ottawa: Carleton Library Series, 1987), 390.
25. Norman Ward, *The Government of Canada* (Toronto: University of Toronto Press, 1987), 84.
26. Corry and Hodgetts, *Democratic Government and Politics*, 462.
27. *Robertson and Rosetanni v. The Queen* (1963), quoted in Russell, *Leading Constitutional Decisions*, 399.
28. Quoted in Walter S. Tarnopolsky, *The Canadian Bill of Rights*, 2nd edn (Toronto: McClelland & Stewart, 1975), 132.
29. *R. v. Drybones* (1970), S.C.R. 282.
30. *Attorney General of Canada v. Lavell* (1974), S.C.R. 1349.
31. *Hogan v. The Queen* (1975), 2 S.C.R. 574.
32. *City of Winnipeg v. Barrett* (1892), A.C. 445.
33. *Ottawa Roman Catholic Separate School Trustees v. Mackell* (1917), A.C. 62; *Protestant School Board of Greater Montreal v. Minister of Education of Quebec* (1978), 83 D.L.R. (3d) 645.
34. *Attorney General of Quebec v. Blaikie* (1979), 2 S.C.R. 1016 (Supreme Court of Canada).
35. *Attorney General of Manitoba v. Forest* (1979), 101 D.L.R. (3d) 385 (Supreme Court of Canada).
36. James B. Kelly, *Governing with the Charter* (Vancouver: University of British Columbia Press, 2005).
37. Patrick Monahan, 'Constitutional Cases 2007: An Overview', *Supreme Court Law Review* (2008) 42 S.C.L.R. (2d), 4.
38. Supreme Court of Canada, at: <www.scc-csc.gc.ca/statistics/ecourt.htm>.
39. *R. v. Oakes* (1986), 26 D.L.R. (4th) 20 (Supreme Court of Canada).
40. *Ford v. Attorney General of Quebec* (1988).
41. Quoted in F.L. Morton, Rainer Knopff, and Peter Russell, *Federalism and the Charter* (Ottawa: Carleton University Press, 1989), 578.
42. Ibid., 579.
43. Quoted in 'Tobacco Ad Ban Struck Down', *Globe and Mail*, 22 Sept. 1995, A1, A11.
44. Roy Romanow et al., *Canada . . . Notwithstanding: The Making of the Constitution 1976–1982* (Toronto: Carswell, 1984), 211.
45. Borovoy, *When Freedoms Collide*, 211–12.
46. *Alliance des Professeurs de Montreal et al. v. Attorney General of Quebec* (1983), 9 C.C.C. (3d) 268.
47. F.L. Morton, 'The Political Impact of the Canadian Charter of Rights and Freedoms', *Canadian Journal of Political Science* 20, 1 (Mar. 1987): 47.
48. Morton, Knopff, and Russell, *Federalism and the Charter*, 446.
49. Ibid., 389.
50. *Singh v. Minister of Employment and Immigration* (1985), 17 D.L.R. (4th) 469.
51. Morton, Knopff, and Russell, *Federalism and the Charter*, 446.
52. *Reference re Section 94(2) of the Motor Vehicle Act (B.C.)*, [1985] S.C.R. 486.
53. *Hunter et al. v. Southam Inc.*, [1984] 2 S.C.R. 145.
54. *Canada v. Khadr*, 2010 S.C.C. 3.
55. *Attorney General of Quebec v. Quebec Protestant School Boards* (1984), 10 D.L.R. (4th) 321 (Supreme Court of Canada).
56. *Reference re Public Service Employee Relations Act, Labour Relations Act and Police Officers Collective Bargaining Act* (1987), 38 D.L.R. (4th) 161.
57. *Operation Dismantle Inc. et al. v. The Queen* (1985), 18 D.L.R. (4th) 481 (Supreme Court of Canada).
58. *Retail, Wholesale & Department Store Union, Local 580 et al. v. Dolphin Delivery Ltd.* (1986), 33 D.L.R. (4th) 174.
59. Quoted in Mandel, *Charter of Rights*, 204.
60. *Reference re Public Service Employees Relations Act (Alberta)*, quoted in Morton, Knopff, and Russell, *Federalism and the Charter*, 496.
61. Quoted in Michael Mandel, *The Charter of Rights and the Legalization of Politics in Canada*, 2nd edn (Toronto: Thompson Educational Publishing, 1994), 193.
62. *Dunmore et al. v. Attorney General for Ontario and Fleming Chicks* (2001), S.C.C. 94.
63. *Morgentaler, Smoling and Scott v. The Queen* (1988), 37 C.C.C. (3d) 449.
64. *R. v. Keegstra*, [1990] 3 S.C.R. 697.
65. *Harper v. Canada*, [2004] 1 S.C.R. 827.
66. *WIC Radio Ltd. v. Simpson* (2008), S.C.C. 40.
67. *R. v. Keegstra*, [1990] 3 S.C.R. 697.
68. Peter Hogg, *Constitutional Law of Canada*, 2nd edn (Toronto: Carswell, 1988), 786.
69. *Reference Re An Act to Amend the Education Act (Ontario)* (1987), 40 D.L.R. (4th) 18 (Supreme Court of Canada).
70. Before the law was passed, provincial support to Roman Catholic schools ended after Grade 10.
71. *Law v. Minister of Human Resources Development*, [1999] 1 S.C.R. 497.
72. See, for example, the majority and dissenting judgements in the right to strike case, *Re Public Service Employees Relations Act* (1987), and in the Ontario Roman Catholic high school funding case, *Reference re An Act to Amend the Education Act* (1987).
73. See <www.scc-csc.gc.ca/AboutCourt/judges/speeches/index_e.asp>.

7 Federalism

1. William S. Livingston, *Federalism and Constitutional Change* (Oxford: Clarendon Press, 1956), 2.
2. Ibid., 4.
3. Based on the ranking system used in Charles Lewis Taylor and Michael C. Hudson, *World Handbook of*

Social and Political Indicators, 3rd edn (New Haven: Yale University Press, 1985), 271–3, Table 4.15.

4. Pierre Elliott Trudeau, 'Federalism, Nationalism and Reason', in Trudeau, *Federalism and the French Canadians* (Toronto: Macmillan, 1968), 195.
5. The term is a translation of 'rois-nègres', coined by André Laurendeau, in 'A Search for Balance', *Canadian Forum* (Apr. 1963): 3–4.
6. Donald Smiley, *The Canadian Political Identity* (Toronto: Methuen, 1967), 30–1.
7. Profiles of Canada 2005, at: <www.cric.ca>.
8. Peter Waite, *The Life and Times of Confederation 1864–1867* (Toronto: University of Toronto Press, 1962), 96.
9. The diversity of expectations was reflected in newspaper accounts of the Confederation agreement. See ibid., 111.
10. There are some exceptions. In *Citizens Insurance Co. v. Parsons; Queen Insurance Co. v. Parsons* (1881), the Judicial Committee of the Privy Council ruled that Ottawa's trade and commerce power did not take pre-eminence over enumerated provincial powers. Why? In the words of Sir Montague Smith, the founders 'could not have intended that the powers exclusively assigned to the provincial legislature should be absorbed in those given to the dominion parliament.' Reproduced in Peter H. Russell, ed., *Leading Constitutional Decisions*, 4th edn (Ottawa: Carleton University Press, 1987), 35.
11. Ibid., 527, *Re Constitution of Canada* (1981).
12. *Amicus curiae* concerning Certain Questions Relating to the Secession of Quebec, 31 Jan. 1998.
13. See the discussion in Keith G. Banting, *The Welfare State and Canadian Federalism*, 2nd edn (Montreal and Kingston: McGill-Queen's University Press, 1987), 52–4.
14. *Attorney General of Ontario v. Attorney General of Canada* (Local Prohibition case), 1896, in Russell, ed., *Leading Constitutional Decisions*, 59.
15. *Re Board of Commerce Act and Combines and Fair Prices Act*, 1919, 1922, ibid., 75.
16. *Co-operative Committee on Japanese Canadians v. A. G. Canada* (1947), A.C. 87; *Reference re Validity of Wartime Leasehold Regulations*, [1950] S.C.R. 124.
17. *Attorney General of Canada v. Attorney General of Ontario* (Employment and Social Insurance Act Reference), 1937.
18. See Peter Russell, 'The Anti-Inflation Case: The Anatomy of a Constitutional Decision', *Canadian Public Administration* 10, 4 (Winter 1977).
19. Constitution Act, 1867, s. 91(2).
20. Constitution Act, 1867, s. 92(13).
21. Russell, ed., *Leading Constitutional Decisions*, 39.
22. *The King v. Eastern Terminal Elevator Co.*, [1925] S.C.R. 434; *A.G. of British Columbia v. A.G. of Canada* (Natural Products Marketing Reference) (1937), A.C. 377; *Canadian Federation of Agriculture v. A.G. of Quebec* (Margarine Reference) (1951), A.C. 179.
23. *Ontario Farm Products Marketing Reference*, [1957] S.C.R. 198; *R. v. Klassen* (1959), 20 D.L.R. (2nd) 406 (Manitoba Court of Appeal); *Caloil v. A.G. of Canada*, [1971] S.C.R. 543.
24. *Caloil*, 551.
25. Russell, ed., *Leading Constitutional Decisions*, 194.
26. Ibid., 199.
27. Peter Hogg, *Constitutional Law of Canada*, student edn (Toronto: Carswell, 1998), 479–82.
28. *General Motors of Canada Ltd. v. City National Leasing*, [1989] 1 S.C.R. 641.
29. Trudeau, 'Federalism, Nationalism and Reason', 198.
30. Henri Bourassa, 'The French Language and the Future of Our Race', in Ramsay Cook, ed., *French Canadian Nationalism* (Toronto: Macmillan, 1969), 141.
31. Kenneth McRoberts, *Quebec: Social Change and Political Crisis*, 3rd edn (Toronto: McClelland & Stewart, 1988), 214.
32. See Richard Simeon, *Federal–Provincial Diplomacy* (Toronto: University of Toronto Press, 1972), 115–22.
33. Quoted in George Woodcock, *Confederation Betrayed!* (Vancouver: Harbour Publishing, 1981), 8.
34. This argument is developed by Barry Cooper in 'Western Political Consciousness', in Stephen Brooks, ed., *Political Thought in Canada* (Toronto: Irwin, 1984), 213–38.
35. James Bickerton, *Nova Scotia, Ottawa, and the Politics of Regional Development* (Toronto: University of Toronto Press, 1990).
36. G.V. LaForest, *Disallowance and Reservation of Provincial Legislation* (Ottawa, 1955).
37. Ottawa ceded control to Manitoba in 1930.
38. Alberta and Saskatchewan also acquired these powers in 1930.
39. Doug Owram, 'Reluctant Hinterland', in Larry Pratt and Garth Stevenson, eds, *Western Separatism* (Edmonton: Hurtig, 1981), 61.
40. Alan Cairns, 'The Governments and Societies of Canadian Federalism', in Cairns, *Constitution, Government, and Society in Canada* (Toronto: McClelland & Stewart, 1988), 153–4.
41. R.A. Young, Philippe Faucher, and Andre Blais, 'The Concept of Province-Building: A Critique', *Canadian Journal of Political Science* 17, 4 (Dec. 1984): 785.
42. Two of the major works using this concept are John Richards and Larry Pratt, *Prairie Capitalism* (Toronto: McClelland & Stewart, 1979), and McRoberts, *Quebec*.
43. Privy Council Office, 'First Ministers' Conferences, 1906–2004', Office of Intergovernmental Affairs, at: <www.pco-bcp.gc.ca/aia/index.asp?lang=eng&page=relations>, updated.
44. Donald Smiley, 'An Outsider's Observations of Federal–Provincial Relations', in R.D. Olling and W.M. Westmacott, eds, *Perspectives on Canadian Federalism* (Scarborough, Ont.: Prentice-Hall Canada, 1988).

45. Constitution Act, 1867, s. 118.
46. Ibid., s. 111.
47. Paul Boothe and Derek Hermourtz, 'Paying for ACCESS: Province by Province', paper delivered before the Political Economy Research Group, University of Western Ontario, 24 Oct. 1997, Figure 3b.
48. Department of Finance Canada, *Budget 1995: Key Actions and Impacts*, unpaginated.
49. Ibid.
50. Ibid.
51. France St-Hilaire, 'Fiscal Gaps and Imbalances: The New Fundamentals of Canadian Federalism', paper presented at Queen's University, Institute of Intergovernmental Relations, 12–14 May 2005, 11.

8 The Machinery of Government

1. 'The Executive Government and Authority of and over Canada is hereby declared to continue and be vested in the Queen.' Constitution Act, 1867, s. 9.
2. In the provinces, the Crown's authority is exercised through the lieutenant-governors, who are appointed by the Governor General to serve five-year terms.
3. James R. Mallory, *The Structure of Canadian Government*, rev. edn (Toronto: Gage, 1984), 42–3.
4. Eugene Forsey, *How Canadians Govern Themselves*, 7th edn (Ottawa: Public Works and Government Services, 2010), at: <www2.parl.gc.ca/sites/lop/aboutparliament/forsey/can_am_gov_print-e.asp>.
5. Constitution Act, 1867, s. 54.
6. Donald Savoie, *Governing from the Centre: The Concentration of Power in Canadian Politics* (Toronto: University of Toronto Press, 1999), ch. 4.
7. Colin Campbell and George Szablowski, *The Super-Bureaucrats: Structure and Behaviour in Central Agencies* (Toronto: Macmillan, 1979).
8. See David A. Good, *The Politics of Anticipation: Making Canadian Federal Tax Policy* (Ottawa: School of Public Administration, 1980).
9. Leslie Pal, *Beyond Policy Analysis* (Toronto: Nelson Canada, 1998), 92.
10. Savoie, *Governing from the Centre*, 189.
11. Ibid., 109.
12. Campbell and Szablowski, *The Super-Bureaucrats*, 29.
13. Gordon Robertson, 'The Changing Role of the Privy Council Office', *Canadian Public Administration* 14 (Winter 1971): 506.
14. Savoie, *Governing from the Centre*, 109.
15. Ibid., 121.
16. Ibid., 195.
17. Ibid.
18. Robertson, 'The Changing Role of the Privy Council Office', 506.
19. Savoie, *Governing from the Centre*, 101.
20. Ibid., 103.
21. Colin Campbell, *Governments under Stress* (Toronto: University of Toronto Press, 1983), 90.
22. At <www.pco.gc.ca>.
23. Both Donald Savoie in *Governing from the Centre* and Jeffrey Simpson in *The Friendly Dictatorship* (Toronto: McClelland & Stewart, 2001) make the case for this characterization.
24. Savoie, *Governing from the Centre*, 260.
25. Simpson, *The Friendly Dictatorship*, 248.
26. The total number of Senate seats rose from 104 to 105 with the creation of the new territory of Nunavut on 1 April 1999.
27. Robert J. Jackson and Michael A. Atkinson, *The Canadian Legislative System*, 2nd edn (Toronto: Gage, 1980), 22.
28. Savoie, *Governing from the Centre*, 91.
29. Ibid., 92.
30. David C. Docherty, *Mr. Smith Goes to Ottawa: Life in the House of Commons* (Vancouver: University of British Columbia Press, 1998), 234.
31. Simpson, *The Friendly Dictatorship*, 23.
32. Savoie, *Governing from the Centre*, 91–2.
33. Docherty, *Mr. Smith Goes to Ottawa*, 204.
34. Ibid., 206.
35. C.E.S. Franks, 'From Gomery to the Accountability Act: The Devil Is in the Details', *Policy Options* (June 2006): 46–52.
36. See the Constitution Act, 1867, s. 99(1). This phrase, or reference to 'misbehaviour', is found in the federal and provincial statutes that govern the removal of judges.
37. Ralph Miliband, *The State in Capitalist Society* (London: Quartet Books, 1973), 124.
38. Judges of county courts and all higher courts are appointed by Ottawa. Provincial court judges are appointed by the provinces. See Figure 8.5 in the text.
39. Canada, Department of Justice, *Canada's System of Justice* (Ottawa: Supply and Services, 1988), 7.
40. *Reference re Public Service Employee Relations Act (Alberta)* (1987), 38 D.L.R. (4th) 161.
41. Ibid., 200.
42. Ibid., 232.
43. Ibid., 200.
44. See Tonda MacCharles, 'Top Court Speculation Begins Anew', *Toronto Star*, 19 Jan. 1999.
45. See, for example, Cristin Schmitz, 'Political Patronage a "Huge Problem" in Appointing Judges Says Former Premier', *Ottawa Citizen*, 25 Sept. 2005.
46. James Mallory, *Social Credit and the Federal Power* (Toronto: University of Toronto Press, 1954).
47. Rainer Knopff and Ted Morton, *Charter Politics* (Toronto: Nelson Canada, 1992), 79.

9 The Administrative State

1. Henry David Thoreau, 'A Yankee in Canada' (1850), p. 38, at: <www.thoreau-online.org>.
2. Susanna Moodie, *Roughing It in the Bush* (1852).
3. Royal Commission to Enquire into and Report on the Operation of the Civil Service Act and Kindred Legislation, *1908—Report of the Commissioners*, 13, at: <www.psc-cfp.gc.ca/plcy-pltq/rprt/impart/chapter4-chapitre4-eng.htm>.
4. Max Weber, *The Protestant Ethic and the Spirit of Capitalism* (New York: Charles Scribner, 1958 [1904–5]), 182.
5. *Fraser v. PSSRB*, [1985] 2 S.C.R. 455, para. 41.
6. *Osborne v. Canada (Treasury Board)*, [1991] 2 S.C.R. 69.
7. *Haydon v. Canada (Treasury Board)*, 2004 FC 749. Office of the Commissioner for Federal Judicial Affairs Canada. See: http://reports.fja.gc.ca/eng/2005/2004fc749.html. Reproduced with the permission of the Minister of Public Works and Government Services Canada, 2011.
8. Quoted in Carl Berger, *The Writing of Canadian History*, 2nd edn (Toronto: University of Toronto Press, 1986), 24.
9. John Porter, *The Vertical Mosaic* (Toronto: University of Toronto Press, 1965), 611.
10. Ibid., 435.
11. Doug Owram, *The Government Generation: Canadian Intellectuals and the State, 1900–1945* (Toronto: University of Toronto Press, 1986).
12. All figures in this section are based on F.H. Leacy, ed., *Historical Statistics of Canada*, 2nd edn (Ottawa: Statistics Canada, 1983).
13. This includes teachers, hospital workers, police officers, firefighters, public transit workers, social workers, and others whose salaries derive mainly or entirely from the budget of one or more levels of government.
14. World Values Survey, 2005.
15. Donald Savoie, *Governing from the Centre: The Concentration of Power in Canadian Politics* (Toronto: University of Toronto Press, 1999), 248.
16. Alexander Brady, *Democracy in the Dominions* (Toronto: University of Toronto Press, 1947), 82.
17. Porter, *The Vertical Mosaic*.
18. Precise figures on the ethnic origins of the Canadian population are impossible to come by, because of intermarriage between members of different ethnic groups and because Statistics Canada, in the census, now allows multiple responses to the ethnic origin question as well as the imprecise 'Canadian' ethnic origin as a response.

PART IV Participation in Politics

10 Parties and Elections

1. Eugene A. Forsey, *How Canadians Govern Themselves* (Ottawa: Supply and Services Canada, 1982), 32.
2. Leon Epstein, *Political Parties in Western Democracies* (New Brunswick NJ: Transaction Books, 1980 [1967]), 9.
3. John Meisel, 'Decline of Party in Canada', in Hugh G. Thorburn, ed., *Party Politics of Canada*, 4th edn (Scarborough, Ont.: Prentice-Hall, 1979).
4. This section was co-authored by Professor A. Brian Tanguay, Wilfrid Laurier University.
5. George M. Hougham, 'The Background and Development of National Parties', in Hugh G. Thorburn, ed., *Party Politics in Canada* (Toronto: Prentice-Hall, 1963), 3.
6. Ibid., 13.
7. Escott Reid, 'The Rise of National Parties in Canada', in Hugh G. Thorburn, ed., *Party Politics in Canada*, 5th edn (Scarborough, Ont.: Prentice-Hall, 1985), 12. See also Norman Ward, *The Canadian House of Commons* (Toronto: University of Toronto Press, 1950), 157–62.
8. See, in particular, Martin Shefter, 'Party and Patronage: Germany, England, and Italy', *Politics and Society* 7, 4 (1977): 403–51; Epstein, *Political Parties in Western Democracies*, ch. 5.
9. André Siegfried, *The Race Question in Canada* (Toronto: McClelland & Stewart, Carleton Library Edition, 1966 [English translation first published 1907]), 114.
10. J.A. Corry, *Democratic Government and Politics*, 2nd edn (Toronto: University of Toronto Press, 1951), 22. Variations on this theme can be found in R.M. Dawson and Norman Ward, *The Government of Canada*, 5th edn (Toronto: University of Toronto Press, 1987), 430–3, and Hugh G. Thorburn, 'Interpretations of the Canadian Party System', in Thorburn, ed., *Party Politics in Canada*, 5th edn (Scarborough, Ont.: Prentice-Hall, 1985), 20–40. For a critique of the adequacy of brokerage theory, see Janine Brodie and Jane Jenson, *Crisis, Challenge and Change: Party and Class Revisited* (Ottawa: Carleton University Press, 1988), ch. 1.
11. Robert Alford, *Party and Society* (Westport, Conn.: Greenwood Press, 1963), 250–1. Alford computed his index of class voting by subtracting the percentage of non-manual workers voting for left parties (in Canada, the Liberals and the NDP, according to Alford) from the percentage of manual workers voting for the left parties, on the assumption that a party of the left should receive the bulk of its support from the traditional blue-collar (manual) occupations. See the discussion ibid., chs 4 and 5. Obviously, Alford's index leaves a great deal to be desired and has been subjected to substantial criticism over the years. Many critics of his work are particularly exercised by his classification of the Liberal Party of Canada as a party of the 'left'.
12. Ibid., 251.

13. Brodie and Jenson, *Crisis, Challenge and Change.*
14. Janine Brodie and Jane Jenson, 'Piercing the Smokescreen: Brokerage Parties and Class Politics', in Alain G. Gagnon and A. Brian Tanguay, eds, *Canadian Parties in Transition: Discourse, Organization, and Representation* (Scarborough, Ont.: Nelson, 1989), 28.
15. Ibid., 34.
16. Robert M. Campbell and Leslie A. Pal, *The Real Worlds of Canadian Politics* (Peterborough, Ont.: Broadview Press, 1989), 5.
17. Canadian Institute of Public Opinion, *The Gallup Report*, 'Confidence in Political Parties Declines', 1 Feb. 1989, and 'Government Increasingly Becoming Object of Scorn among Canadians', 20 Feb. 1991.
18. Walter Young, *The Anatomy of a Party: The National CCF, 1932–61* (Toronto: University of Toronto Press, 1969), 298, 300.
19. Canada, Royal Commission on Electoral Reform and Party Financing, *Reforming Electoral Democracy*, vol. 7 (Ottawa: Supply and Services Canada, 1991), 221.
20. William P. Irvine, *Does Canada Need a New Electoral System?* (Kingston, Ont.: Institute of Intergovernmental Relations, Queen's University, 1979), 46–7.
21. Alan Cairns, 'The Electoral System and the Party System in Canada, 1921–1965', *Canadian Journal of Political Science* 1, 1 (Mar. 1968): 55–80.
22. 22. Irvine, Does Canada Need a New Electoral System?, 14.
23. See, e.g., Paul Nesbitt-Larking, cited in Tara Brautigam, 'Conservative Urban Shutout Deepens Divide', at: <www.canada.com>, 24 Jan. 2006; Allan Gregg, cited in David Warren, 'The Urban Angle', *Ottawa Citizen*, 26 Jan. 2006, on-line edition.
24. André Blais et al., 'Where Does Turnout Decline Come From?', *European Journal of Political Research* 43 (2004): 221–2.
25. Ibid., 224.
26. Ibid., 225.
27. Ibid., 227.
28. Statistics Canada, *2003 General Social Survey on Social Engagement: An Overview of Findings*, Catalogue no. 89–598–XIE (Ottawa, 2004).
29. See Khayyam Paltiel, *Political Party Financing in Canada* (Toronto: McGraw-Hill Ryerson, 1970), 19–75.
30. These services are discussed by Reg Whitaker, *The Government Party: Organizing and Financing the Liberal Party of Canada, 1930–1958* (Toronto: University of Toronto Press, 1977), 204–6, 216–63.
31. According to Khayyam Paltiel, 'For the 1972 [national] election half the funds raised in Ontario by the Liberal Party were collected personally by the chairman of the party's Treasury Committee from 90 large corporations.' Paltiel, 'Campaign Financing in Canada and Its Reform', in Howard R. Penniman, ed., *Canada at the Polls: The General Election of 1974* (Washington: American Enterprise Institute, 1975), 182.
32. See A.B. Stevenson, *Canadian Election Reform: Dialogue on Issues and Effects* (Toronto: Ontario Commission on Election Contributions and Expenses, 1982); Whitaker, *The Government Party.*
33. The number of hours per network and the division of time between the parties are determined by the CRTC. In deciding how much time each party receives the CRTC is guided by a formula weighted according to each party's share of the seats and popular vote in the previous election.
34. Khayyam Paltiel, 'Political Marketing, Party Finance, and the Decline of Political Parties', in Gagnon and Tanguay, eds, *Canadian Parties in Transition*, 342.
35. See Larry Sabato, *The Rise of Political Consultants* (New York: Basic Books, 1981), especially ch. 4.
36. Dalton Camp, *Points of Departure* (Toronto: Deneau and Greenberg, 1979), 91.
37. Ibid.

11 Interest Groups

1. V.O. Key, *Politics, Parties, and Pressure Groups*, 4th edn (New York, 1958), 23.
2. James Madison, *The Federalist Papers*, no. 10 (New York: New American Library, 1961).
3. This slogan is attributed to Thomas Sloan, a chairman of GM during the 1920s.
4. *Associations Canada: An Encyclopedic Directory* (Mississauga, Ont.: Canadian Almanac & Directory Publishing Co., 2010).
5. Estimates based on ibid.
6. Robert Wolfe, 'Trade Policy Begins at Home: Information and Consultation in the Trade Policy Process', in Mark Halle and Robert Wolfe, eds, *Process Matters: Sustainable Development and Domestic Trade Transparency* (Winnipeg: International Institute for Sustainable Development, 2009).
7. E.E. Schattschneider, *The Semi-Sovereign People* (New York: Holt, Rinehart and Winston, 1960), 35.
8. Ibid.
9. Ibid.
10. Charles E. Lindblom, *Politics and Markets* (New York: Basic Books, 1977), especially chs 13–16.
11. Bruno S. Frey, *Modern Political Economy* (New York: John Wiley & Sons, 1978), ch. 11.
12. Business's ideological and academic spokespersons adopt an essentially pluralistic position on the matter of interest group influence. William Stanbury's remarks are typical: 'The relationship between business firms and governments in either positive or normative terms

cannot be characterized in a single phrase. It is inevitably plural and diverse. Depending upon the industry, the time, the other issues on the public policy agenda, the individuals involved, and what each "side" is seeking to do vis-à-vis the other, the relationship might be characterized as adversarial, cooperative, symbiotic, supportive, or protective.' Stanbury, *Business–Government Relations in Canada* (Toronto: Methuen, 1986), 9.

13. Michael Bliss, *Northern Enterprise: Five Centuries of Canadian Business* (Toronto: McClelland & Stewart, 1987), 578.
14. David Vogel, *Fluctuating Fortunes: The Political Power of Business in America* (New York: Basic Books, 1989), 193.
15. James Q. Wilson, 'The Politics of Regulation', in Wilson, ed., *The Politics of Regulation* (New York: Basic Books, 1980), 370.
16. Earl Latham, *The Group Basis of Politics* (New York: Octagon Books, 1965), 35.
17. Arthur F. Bentley, *The Process of Government* (Evanston, Ill., 1935), 208.
18. David B. Truman, *The Governmental Process* (New York: Alfred Knopf, 1951); Robert Dahl, *Who Governs?* (New Haven: Yale University Press, 1961); John Kenneth Galbraith, *American Capitalism: The Concept of Countervailing Power* (Boston: Houghton Mifflin, 1952).
19. Theodore Lowi, *The End of Liberalism* (New York: W.W. Norton, 1969), 97.
20. P. Bachrach and M. Baratz, 'Two Faces of Power', *American Political Science Review* 56, 4 (1962): 948.
21. This is true of Nicos Poulantzas, *Political Power and Social Classes* (London: New Left Books, 1973); Fred Block, *Revising State Theory* (Philadelphia: Temple University Press, 1987); Bob Jessop, *The Capitalist State* (New York: New York University Press, 1982). Interest groups are given some passing mention in James O'Connor, *The Fiscal Crisis of the State* (New York: St Martin's Press, 1973); Claus Offe, *Contradictions of the Welfare State* (Cambridge, Mass.: MIT Press, 1984). Among the leading Marxist intellectuals, it is perhaps fair to say that only Ralph Miliband has very much to say on interest groups; see Miliband, *The State in Capitalist Society* (London: Quartet Books, 1973).
22. The term 'political economy' includes three separate streams or meanings today: the Canadian tradition of political economy, which, after Harold Innis's early work, moved squarely to the left; the political economy in the Downs–Buchanan tradition, with a centre of gravity in the United States and a pro-market orientation; and the political economy work among those in international relations, whose focus is globalization and its discontents and whose orientation is more often than not on the left.
23. Miliband, *The State in Capitalist Society*, 131.
24. Wallace Clement, *The Challenge of Class Analysis* (Ottawa: Carleton University Press, 1988), chs 7 and 8.
25. Ibid., 132.
26. Rianne Mahon, *The Politics of Industrial Restructuring: Canadian Textiles* (Toronto: University of Toronto Press, 1984).
27. Jurg Steiner, *European Democracies* (New York: Longman, 1986), 221.
28. William D. Coleman, *Business and Politics: A Study of Collective Action* (Montreal and Kingston: McGill-Queen's University Press, 1988), 224.
29. It occasionally happens, however, that the CCC is capable of taking a firm position on issues that are more divisive in the business community. Its support for the Canada–US Free Trade Agreement was an example of this.
30. Gerhard Lehmbruch, 'Concertation and the Structure of Corporatist Networks', in John Goldthorpe, ed., *Order and Conflict in Contemporary Capitalism* (Oxford: Clarendon, 1984), 65–6.
31. Coleman, *Business and Politics*, ch. 6.
32. These tripartite initiatives are discussed in detail in Pierre Fournier, 'Consensus Building in Canada: Case Studies and Prospects', in Keith Banting, research coordinator, *The State and Economic Interests*, vol. 32 of the research studies for the Royal Commission on the Economic Union and Development Prospects for Canada (Ottawa: Supply and Services, 1986), 291–335.
33. William Coleman is among those who have argued that such structures would benefit Canada economically. See Coleman, *Business and Politics*, ch. 13.
34. William D. Coleman and Grace Skogstad, 'Introduction', in Coleman and Skogstad, eds, *Policy Communities and Public Policy in Canada* (Toronto: Copp Clark Pitman, 1990), 2.
35. Michels's argument was that the specialization of function that accompanies organization inevitably results in domination of the organization by a minority and, therefore, creates the likelihood that the goals pursued by the organization will more closely reflect those of its leadership than its membership. Robert Michels, *Political Parties* (London: Jarrold, 1915).
36. Some of the classics of this literature include Anthony Downs, *An Economic Theory of Democracy* (New York: Harper and Row, 1957); Mancur Olson, *The Logic of Collective Action* (Cambridge, Mass.: Harvard University Press, 1965); James M. Buchanan and Gordon Tullock, *The Calculus of Consent* (Ann Arbor: University of Michigan Press, 1965); Anthony Downs, *Inside Bureaucracy* (Boston: Little, Brown and Company, 1967).
37. Michael Atkinson, 'How Do Institutions Constrain Policy?', paper delivered at the conference 'Governing Canada: Political Institutions and Public Policy', McMaster University, 25 Oct. 1991, 8. A good introduction to this approach and its application to politics is

provided by Queen's University economist Dan Usher in *Political Economy* (London: Blackwell, 2003).

38. Alan Cairns, 'The Governments and Societies of Canadian Federalism', *Canadian Journal of Political Science* 10, 4 (Dec. 1977): 695–725.
39. These works include James G. March and Herbert Simon, *Organizations* (New York: John Wiley, 1958); James G. March, *Decisions and Organizations* (Oxford: Blackwell, 1988); James G. March and Johan P. Olsen, 'The New Institutionalism: Organizational Factors in Political Life', *American Political Science Review* 78 (1984): 734–49; James G. March and Johan P. Olsen, *Rediscovering Institutions: The Organizational Basis of Politics* (New York: Free Press, 1989).
40. Charles Perrow, *Complex Organizations: A Critical Essay*, 3rd edn (New York: Random House, 1986), 260.
41. James Q. Wilson, *Political Organizations* (New York: Basic Books, 1973), 3–4.
42. These definitions are the ones used in Coleman and Skogstad, 'Introduction'. They are not, however, agreed upon by everyone who mines this vein.
43. Coleman and Skogstad, 'Introduction', 25.
44. Ibid., 23.
45. Ibid., 24.
46. J.L. Granatstein, *The Ottawa Men* (Toronto: Oxford University Press, 1982).
47. O. Mary Hill, *Canada's Salesman to the World: The Department of Trade and Commerce, 1892–1939* (Montreal and Kingston: McGill-Queen's University Press, 1977), 172.
48. Leslie A. Pal, *Interests of State* (Montreal and Kingston: McGill-Queen's University Press, 1992), ch. 6.
49. A. Paul Pross, *Group Politics and Public Policy* (Toronto: University of Toronto Press, 1986), 68–9.
50. Ibid., 114–16.
51. Larry Pynn, 'Recession Hits Environmental Organizations as Funding Slides', *Vancouver Sun*, 18 Dec. 2008, at: <www.sierraclub.bc.ca/.../recession-hits-environmental-organizations-as-funding-slides>.
52. Ontario Trillium Foundation, 'Recession Not Over, Not-for-Profits Still Struggling', at: <www.trilliumfoundation.org>.
53. G. Bruce Doern and Brian W. Tomlin, *Fear and Faith: The Free Trade Story* (Toronto: Stoddart, 1991), 219.
54. John W. Kingdon, *Agendas, Alternatives, and Public Policies* (Boston: Little, Brown and Company, 1984), 54–7.
55. Olson, *The Logic of Collective Action*.
56. Wilson, *Political Organizations*, 36–8.
57. Schattschneider, *The Semi-Sovereign People*, 37.
58. Ibid., 38.
59. Good analyses of several Canadian policy communities are found in Coleman and Skogstad, eds, *Policy Communities and Public Policy in Canada*.
60. This literature is brought together in Hugh G. Thorburn, *Interest Groups in the Canadian Federal System*, vol. 69 of the research studies for the Royal Commission on the Economic Union and Development Prospects for Canada (Ottawa: Supply and Services, 1985).
61. Richard J. Schultz, *Federalism, Bureaucracy and Public Policy: The Politics of Highway Transport Regulation* (Montreal and Kingston: McGill-Queen's University Press, 1980), 148.
62. See, for example, M.W. Bucovetsky, 'The Mining Industry and the Great Tax Reform Debate', in A. Paul Pross, ed., *Pressure Group Behaviour in Canadian Politics* (Toronto: McGraw-Hill Ryerson, 1975), 89–114.
63. The long-accepted claim that Canada's federal Constitution has led most associations to adopt a federal form of organization is not supported by the facts—at least not in the case of business associations. A survey by William Coleman finds that about three-quarters of business associations have unitary structures. Coleman's conclusion is that Canada's industrial structure has a far greater impact on how business associations organize themselves than does the Constitution. See Coleman, *Business and Politics*, 260.
64. See Schultz, *Federalism, Bureaucracy and Public Policy*, especially ch. 8.
65. Alan Cairns, 'The Governments and Societies of Canadian Federalism', in Cairns, *Constitution, Government, and Society in Canada* (Toronto: McClelland & Stewart, 1988), 167.
66. Leslie A. Pal, *State, Class, and Bureaucracy* (Montreal and Kingston: McGill-Queen's University Press, 1988).
67. See Ecojustice, at: <www.ecojustice.ca/cases/killer-whale-lawsuit>.
68. CBCM News, 'Anti-Oil Sands Ads Target Alberta Tourism', 14 July 2010, at: <www.cbc.ca/money.story/2010/07/14/con-oilsand-tourism.html>.
69. CBS News, 'BP Spent $93M on Advertising after Gulf Spill', 1 Sept. 2010, at: <www.cbsnews.com/stories/2010/09/01/national/main6827683.shtml>.
70. Quoted in Duncan McDowall, ed., *Advocacy Advertising: Propaganda or Democratic Right?* (Ottawa: Conference Board of Canada, 1982), v.
71. For example, a former federal Minister of Justice defended his government's advertising on proposed constitutional reforms by saying, 'Government is too complex nowadays to rely on policy by press release. Programs must be explained—not by reporters but by people who created them.' Ibid., 7. On the subject of government advertising, see Jonathan Rose, *Making 'Pictures in Our Heads': Government Advertising in Canada* (Westport, Conn.: Greenwood Publishing Group, 2000).
72. Privately funded think-tanks like the C.D. Howe Institute, the Fraser Institute, and the Conference

Board of Canada are another way of promoting group interests, in this case the general interests of business, by producing studies and funding experts whose perspectives and options for public policy are favourable to business interests. Direct-mail campaigns, targeted at selected groups whose opinions and actions may, in turn, affect policy-makers are another technique employed mainly by business groups.

73. A fascinating though somewhat dated account of lobbying in Canada is John Sawatsky, *The Insiders: Government, Business, and the Lobbyists* (Toronto: McClelland & Stewart, 1987).
74. Keith Head and John Ries, 'Do Trade Missions Increase Trade?', *Canadian Journal of Economics* 43, 3 (Aug. 2010): 754–75.

12 The Media

1. Neil Postman, *Amusing Ourselves to Death: Public Discourse in the Age of Show Business* (New York: Penguin, 1985).
2. Henry Commager, ed., *Documents of American History*, 8th edn (New York: Appleton, Century, Crofts, 1968), 104.
3. Walter Lippmann, *Public Opinion* (New York: Harcourt, Brace and Company, 1922), 13.
4. See Bureau of Broadcast Measurement data, at: <www.bbm.ca/en/top_programs.html>.
5. 'ITAC Media Choice & Trust Poll', at: <www.itac.ca>.
6. The Royal Commission on Newspapers expressed this view, although only the case of newspapers owned by the Irving family in New Brunswick was cited explicitly. See also the comments of the former Premier of Saskatchewan, Allan Blakeney, in Diane Francis, *Controlling Interest: Who Owns Canada?* (Toronto: Macmillan, 1986), 316.
7. Edward Herman and Noam Chomsky, *Manufacturing Consent* (New York: Pantheon, 1988), 8.
8. Walter I. Romanow et al., 'Correlates of Newspaper Coverage of the 1979 Canadian Election: Chain Ownership, Competitiveness of Market, and Circulation', study done for the Royal Commission on Newspapers (Ottawa: Supply and Services, 1981).
9. Audit Bureau of Circulations, *Fas-Fax: United States and Canadian Periodicals and Canadian Circulation of U.S. Magazines* (Toronto, 1999).
10. Lippmann, *Public Opinion*, 345.
11. Quoted in Todd Gitlin, *Inside Prime Time* (New York: Pantheon, 1983), 253.
12. Edward Jay Epstein, *News from Nowhere: Television and the News* (New York: Random House, 1973).
13. Friends of Canadian Broadcasting, 'Split Screen', at: <http://friendscb.org/Split_Screen/splt7.html>.
14. See the discussions in Frank Peers, *The Politics of Broadcasting 1920–1951* (Toronto: University of Toronto Press, 1969); and Marc Raboy, *Missed Opportunities: The Story of Canada's Broadcasting Policy* (Montreal and Kingston: McGill-Queen's University Press, 1990).
15. Task Force on Broadcasting, *Report*, 433.
16. Morris Wolfe, *Jolts: The TV Wasteland and the Canadian Oasis* (Toronto: James Lorimer, 1985), 14.
17. Ibid., 16.
18. Ibid., 18.
19. Richard DeGrandpre, *Ritalin Nation: Rapid-fire Culture and the Transformation of Human Consciousness* (New York: W.W. Norton, 1999).
20. Epstein, *News from Nowhere*, 263.
21. Ibid., 262.
22. Ibid.
23. Nicholas Carr, 'Is Google Making Us Stupid? What the Internet Is Doing to Our Brains', *The Atlantic* (July–Aug. 2008). See also Nicholas Carr, *The Shallows: What the Internet Is Doing to Our Brains* (New York: W.W. Norton, 2010).
24. Pew Project for Excellence in Journalism, 2010 report, at: <www.stateofthemedia.org>.
25. Herman and Chomsky, *Manufacturing Consent*, 19.
26. Epstein, *News from Nowhere*, 146.
27. Ibid., 147.
28. Ibid., 199.
29. Stanley Rothman and S. Robert Lichter, 'Personality, Ideology and World View: A Comparison of Media and Business Elites', *British Journal of Political Science* 15, 1 (1984): 36.
30. Ibid., 46.
31. Barry Cooper, *Sins of Omission: Shaping the News at CBC TV* (Toronto: University of Toronto Press, 1994), xi.
32. Ibid., 227.
33. Lydia Miljan and Barry Cooper, *Hidden Agendas: How the Beliefs of Canadian Journalists Influence the News* (Vancouver: University of British Columbia Press, 2003).
34. Blake Andrew, Antonia Maioni, and Stuart Soroka, 'Just When You Thought It Was Out, Policy Is Pulled Back In', *Policy Options* (Mar. 2006): 74–9.
35. Ralph Miliband, *The State in Capitalist Society* (London: Quartet Books, 1973), 211.
36. Leon Epstein, *Political Parties in Western Democracies* (New York: Praeger, 1967), 237.
37. Jay Rosen, *Jay Rosen's PressThink: Ghost of Democracy in the Media Machine*, at: <pressthink.org>.
38. Ibid.
39. Aldous Huxley, *Brave New World Revisited* (New York: Harper & Brothers, 1958), 44.
40. The term is used by Herman and Chomsky in their analysis of the political role of the American media. They, in turn, borrow it from Walter Lippmann, who had in mind, however, government's use of propagandistic techniques to cultivate popular acceptance of their rule.

PART V Contemporary Issues in Canadian Political Life

13 Language Politics

1. Information on mother tongue was first collected with the census of 1931. Before then, the census only asked about ethnic origin. Demographer Jacques Henripin suggests that French ethnic origin was probably a good surrogate measure for language group at the time of Confederation.
2. In fact, Henripin predicted that over 40 per cent of Montrealers would be anglophone by 2001. This prediction was based on census data from 1971. See *L'Immigration et le déséquilibre linguistique* (Ottawa: Main d'oeuvre et immigration, 1974), 31, tableau 4.7.
3. Henripin estimated that at the rate of decline experienced in the early 1970s, Quebec would still be 77 per cent French-speaking by 2001.
4. Richard Joy, *Languages in Conflict* (Toronto: McClelland & Stewart, 1972), 58, Table 25.
5. Ibid., 39, Table 14.
6. Roger Bernard, *Le choc des nombres* (Ottawa: Université d'Ottawa, 1990).
7. Jacques Henripin, 'The 1986 Census: Some Enduring Trends Abate', *Language and Society* 24 (Fall 1988): 8–9.
8. The first experience with immersion education was in 1975 in St Lambert, Quebec.
9. See Peter C. Waite, *Pre-Confederation* (Toronto: Prentice-Hall, 1965), 54–5.
10. Louis Hemon, *Maria Chapdelaine*, trans. Sir Andrew Macphail (Toronto: Oxford University Press, 1921), 212–13.
11. Henri Bourassa, *La langue, guardienne de la foi* (Montreal: Bibliothèque de l'action française, 1918).
12. Henri Bourassa, 'The French Language and the Future of Our Race', in Ramsay Cook, ed., *French Canadian Nationalism* (Toronto: Macmillan, 1969), 133.
13. Marcel Rioux, 'Sur l'evolution des ideologies au Quebec', English translation in Richard Schultz et al., eds, *The Canadian Political Process*, 3rd edn (Toronto: Holt, Rinehart and Winston, 1979), 99–102.
14. Denis Monière, *Ideologies in Quebec* (Toronto: University of Toronto Press, 1981), esp. ch. 2.
15. These voices included such figures as Gonzalve Doutre, Errol Bouchette, and Olivar Asselin, and the activities of the Institut Canadien.
16. F.H. Leacy, ed., *Historical Statistics of Canada* (Ottawa: Supply and Services, 1983), R1–22, R81–97.
17. The numbers were about 390,000 in manufacturing compared to 249,000 in agriculture. The figure for the agricultural labour force counts only males.
18. Quoted by Pierre Trudeau in 'Quebec on the Eve of the Asbestos Strike', in Cook, ed., *French Canadian Nationalism*, 35–6.
19. Victor Barbeau, *Mesure de notre taille* (1936); Barbeau, *Avenir de notre bourgeoisie* (Montréal: Editions de l'action canadienne française, 1939); Jacques Melançon, 'Retard de croissance de l'entreprise canadienne-francaise', *L'actualité économique* (jan.–mars 1956): 503–22.
20. Rioux, 'Sur l'évolution', 105–8.
21. Ibid., 105.
22. René Lévesque, *An Option for Quebec* (Toronto: McClelland & Stewart, 1968), 14.
23. See Melançon, 'Retard de croissance'.
24. Lois du Quebec, 1974, c. 6.
25. Lois du Quebec, 1977, c. 5.
26. See *Attorney General of Quebec v. Blaikie et al.* (1979), 101 D.L.R. (3d) 394 (Supreme Court of Canada).
27. *Ford v. Attorney General of Quebec* (1988), Supreme Court of Canada.
28. See the discussion of these economic initiatives in Kenneth McRoberts, *Quebec: Social Change and Political Crisis*, 3rd edn (Toronto: McClelland & Stewart, 1988), 132–5.
29. Eric Waddell, 'State, Language and Society: The Vicissitudes of French in Quebec and Canada', in Alan Cairns and Cynthia Williams, eds, *The Politics of Gender, Ethnicity and Language in Canada*, vol. 34 of the research studies for the Royal Commission on the Economic Union and Development Prospects for Canada (Toronto: University of Toronto Press, 1985), 97.
30. Raymond Breton, 'The Production and Allocation of Symbolic Resources: An Analysis of the Linguistic and Ethnocultural Fields in Canada', *Canadian Review of Sociology and Anthropology* 21, 2 (1984): 129.
31. Commissioner of Official Languages, *Annual Report 1985* (Ottawa: Supply and Services, 1986), 50.
32. Commissioner of Official Languages, *Annual Report 1998*, at: <ocol-clo.gc.ca/e298_3.htm#anchor304>.
33. Commissioner of Official Languages, *Annual Report 2009–10*, at: <www.ocol-clo.gc.ca/html/ar_ra_2009_10_e.ph>.
34. 'Francophones in the National Capital Region represent over 35 per cent of the Public Service population but, on average, they work more than 60 per cent of their time in English. In bilingual areas of Ontario the corresponding figures are 23 per cent and 66 per cent; roughly one-quarter of all employees are thus working two-thirds of their time in their second language.' *Annual Report 1985*, 54.
35. Commissioner of Official Languages, *Annual Report 1998*, at: <ocol-clo.gc.ca/e298_3.htm#anchor305>.
36. *Attorney General of Manitoba v. Forest* (1979), 101 D.L.R. (3d) 385 (Supreme Court of Canada); *Reference re Language Rights under the Manitoba Act, 1870* (No. 1) (1985), 19 D.L.R. (4th) 1.

37. *Attorney General of Quebec v. Quebec Protestant School Boards* (1984), 10 D.L.R. (4th) 321 (Supreme Court of Canada); *Ford v. Attorney General of Quebec* (1988), Supreme Court of Canada.
38. These figures are from the annual reports of Commissioner of Official Languages.
39. Commissioner of Official Languages, *Annual Report 1985*, 172.
40. Statistics Canada, *Use of English and French at Work*, Catalogue no. 96F0030XIE2001011 (Ottawa: Feb. 2003).
41. Waddell, 'State, Language and Society', 101.
42. Sharon Lapkin, ed., *French as a Second Language Education in Canada: Recent Empirical Studies* (Toronto: University of Toronto Press, 1998); Sheryl Ubelacher, 'Few Chances to Use French Immersion Skills', *Toronto Star*, 4 Dec. 2007.
43. Richard Simeon and David Elkins, 'Regional Political Cultures in Canada', *Canadian Journal of Political Science* 7, 3 (Sept. 1974): 397–437.
44. Peter Russell et al., 'Liberty, Authority, and Community: Civil Liberties and the Canadian Political Culture', paper presented at the annual meeting of the Canadian Political Science Association, Windsor, Ont., 9 June 1988.
45. Michael Ornstein, 'Regionalism and Canadian Political Ideology', in Robert Brym, ed., *Regionalism in Canada* (Toronto: Irwin, 1986), 78.
46. Ibid., 66, Table 2.
47. See <www.uni.ca/curriculum.html>. Also 'Whose History for Whose Future?', Sixth Biennial Conference on the Teaching and Learning of History, Quebec City, 24–6 Oct. 2008.
48. Ontario, Ministry of Education and Training, *The Ontario Curriculum: Social Studies Grades 1 to 6, History and Geography Grades 7 and 8* (Toronto: Queen's Printer for Ontario, 1998), 49–54.
49. Québec, Commission sur l'avenir politique et constitutionnel du Québec, *Rapport* (Québec, 1991), 17.
50. Ibid.
51. Robert Sheppard, 'For a Really Distinct Society, Try Saskatchewan, Not Quebec', *Globe and Mail*, 20 Nov. 1989.
52. 'Survey: 30 Years after the 1980 Referendum, Quebeckers Believe That Issue Is Outmoded', 18 May 2010, at: <www.ideefederal.ca>.
53. CRIC Quebec Youth Survey.

14 Diversity and Multiculturalism

1. John Porter, *The Vertical Mosaic* (Toronto: University of Toronto Press, 1965).
2. Statistics Canada, 'Study: Projections of the Diversity of the Canadian Population', *The Daily*, 9 Mar. 2010, at: <www.statcan.gc.ca/daily-quotidien/100309/dq100309a-eng.htm>.
3. *Multani v. Commission scolaire Marguerite-Bourgeoys*, [2006] 1 S.C.R. 256.
4. CBC News, 'Sikhs with Kirpan Not Allowed in Que. Legislature', 18 Jan. 2011, at: <www.cbc.ca/canada/montreal/story/2011/01/18/sikhs-denied-entry-nat-ass-quebec.html>.
5. Leslie A. Pal, *Interests of State: The Politics of Language, Multiculturalism, and Feminism in Canada* (Montreal and Kingston: McGill-Queen's University Press, 1993).
6. Ibid., 281.
7. R. Brian Howe and David Johnson, *Restraining Equality: Human Rights Commissions in Canada* (Toronto: University of Toronto Press, 2000), 35.
8. Paul Sniderman and Louk Hagendoorn, *When Ways of Life Collide: Multiculturalism and Its Discontents* (Princeton, NJ: Princeton University Press, 2007), 15.
9. Peter Skerry, 'Beyond Sushiology: Does Diversity Work?', *Brookings Review* 20 (Winter 2002): 20–3.
10. James Banks, Professor of Diversity Studies at the University of Washington, for the National Council for Social Studies, at: <www.socialstudies.org/positions/multicultural>.
11. NPR/Kaiser/Kennedy School Poll, 'Immigration', 2004.
12. See <municipalite.herouxville.qc.ca/Standards.pdf>.
13. CBC News, 'Minority Report "Misses the Point" PQ Says', 23 May 2008, at: <www.cbc.ca>.
14. Alexander Panetta, 'PQ: Multiculturalism Is Not a Quebec Value', 19 Jan. 2011, at: <ipolitics.ca/2011/01/19/pq-multiculturalism-not-a-quebec-value/>.
15. Statistics Canada, *Longitudinal Survey of Immigrants to Canada: Progress and Challenges of New Immigrants in the Workforce* (Ottawa, 2003), at: <www.statcan.gc.ca/pub/89-615-x/2005001/4079178-eng.htm>. For detailed comparative analyses of contemporary immigration to Canada and the United States, see Carlos Teixeira, Wei Li, and Audrey Kobayashi, eds, *Immigrants in Canadian and American Cities* (Toronto: Oxford University Press, 2011).
16. See Canadian Information Centre for International Credentials, at: <www.cicic.ca/en/index.aspx>.

15 Women and Politics

1. Nellie McClung, 'Hardy Perennials', in McClung, *In Times Like These* (Toronto: University of Toronto Press, 1972), 43–58.
2. Simone de Beauvoir, *The Second Sex*, trans. H.M. Parshley (London: Jonathan Cape, 1970), 273.
3. E.E. Maccoby and C.N. Jacklin, *The Psychology of Sex Differences* (Stanford, Calif.: Stanford University Press, 1974).
4. Ibid.
5. Margaret Mead, *Sex and Temperament in Three Primitive Societies* (New York: Dell, 1969 [1935]), 260.
6. Margaret Mead, *Male and Female* (New York: William Morrow, 1950), 191–2.

7. John Stuart Mill, *On the Subjugation of Women* (1869), at: <www.fordham.edu/halsall/mod/jsmill-women.html>.
8. Ibid.
9. Friedrich Engels, *The Origin of Family, Private Property and the State* (1884), at: <www.marxists.org/archive/marx/works/1884/origin-family/index.htm#intro>.
10. *2008 Catalyst Census of Women Corporate Officers and Top Earners of the FP500 in Canada* (Toronto: Catalyst Canada Inc., Dec. 2008).
11. Sylvia Bashevkin, *Toeing the Lines* (Toronto: University of Toronto Press, 1985).
12. See the literature review in Pat Armstrong and Hugh Armstrong, *The Double Ghetto: Canadian Women and Their Segregated Work*, 3rd edn (Toronto: McClelland & Stewart, 1994), 182–9.
13. Statistics Canada, 'The Changing Profile of Canada's Labour Force', Catalogue no. 96F0030XIE2001009, 11 Feb. 2003.
14. See Anthony Thomson, *The Making of Social Theory: Order, Reason, and Desire*, 2nd edn (Toronto: Oxford University Press, 2010), 54–5.
15. Sheila Rowbotham, *Hidden from History* (London: Pluto Press, 1974), 47.
16. Terry Copp, *Anatomy of Poverty* (Toronto: McClelland & Stewart, 1974), 43.
17. The statement was made by Montreal's Chief Inspector of Factories in the late 1800s. Quoted ibid., 49.
18. Nellie McClung, 'Hardy Perennials', in McClung, *In Times Like These* (Toronto: University of Toronto Press, 1972), 56.
19. See the discussion in Penny Kome, *Women of Influence* (Toronto: Doubleday Canada, 1985), ch. 2.
20. Quoted ibid., 32.
21. This was the title of a retrospective article that Macphail wrote in 1949, after having served five terms as an MP for Ontario's South Grey constituency.
22. Quoted in Bashevkin, *Toeing the Lines*, 16.
23. McClung, 'Hardy Perennials', 48.
24. See, for example, Bashevkin, *Toeing the Lines*, 20–3.
25. Catherine L. Cleverdon, *The Woman Suffrage Movement in Canada* (Toronto: University of Toronto Press, 1974), 98, 114, 204.
26. The terms 'hard-core' and 'soft-core' feminism were first used by William O'Neill in *Everyone Was Brave: A History of Feminism in America* (New York: Quadrangle, 1971).
27. Deborah Gorhan, 'Flora MacDonald Denison: Canadian Feminist', in Linda Kealey, ed., *A Not Unreasonable Claim: Women and Reform in Canada* (Toronto: Women's Press, 1979), 47–70.
28. Joan Sangster, 'The Role of Women in the Early CCF', in Linda Kealey and Joan Sangster, eds, *Beyond the Vote: Canadian Women and Politics* (Toronto: University of Toronto Press, 1989), 127.
29. Beauvoir, *The Second Sex*, ch. 2; Germaine Greer, *The Female Eunuch* (Nylesbury, UK: Hazel Watson and Viney, 1970); Betty Friedan, *The Feminine Mystique* (New York: Norton, 1963), ch. 5; Kate Millet, *Sexual Politics* (Garden City, NY: Doubleday, 1970).
30. A. Richard Allen, 'Social Gospel', in *The Canadian Encyclopedia*, 2nd edn (Edmonton: Hurtig, 1988), vol. 3, 2026.
31. See Richard Allen, *The Social Passion* (Toronto: University of Toronto Press, 1971).
32. Nellie McClung, 'Women and the Church', in McClung, *In Times Like These*, 67–79.
33. Friedan, *The Feminine Mystique*.
34. Ibid., 32.
35. Armstrong and Armstrong, *The Double Ghetto*, 42–3.
36. The ratio of males to females in universities was 5:1 in 1920, 3.1:1 in 1960, and 1.8:1 in 1970. Today, more females than males are enrolled in university undergraduate programs.
37. Anne Firor Scott, *Making the Invisible Woman Visible* (Urbana: University of Illinois Press, 1984).
38. See Kealey and Sangster, eds, *Beyond the Vote*.
39. Ibid.
40. Judy Rebick, 'Fighting Racism', *Feminist Action* 6, 2 (June 1992).
41. Barbara Frum, 'Why There Are So Few Women in Ottawa', *Chatelaine* 44 (Oct. 1971): 33, 110.
42. Bashevkin, *Toeing the Lines*, 110–19.
43. See the summaries of landmark judgements in National Action Committee on the Status of Women, *Women and Legal Action* (Oct. 1984), 8–27.
44. This was true in *Murdoch* (1973), *Canard* (1975), and *Bliss* (1979).
45. Michael Mandel, *The Charter of Rights and the Legalization of Politics in Canada* (Toronto: Wall and Thompson, 1995), 389–99.
46. *Re Casagrande and Hinton Roman Catholic Separate School District* (1987), 38 D.L.R. (4th) 382.
47. Canadian Advisory Council on the Status of Women, *Canadian Charter and Equality Rights for Women: One Step Forward or Two Steps Back?* (Sept. 1989), 19.
48. *Hunter v. Southam?* (1984); *R. v. Big M Drug Mart* (1985).
49. *Edwards Books and Art Ltd. et al. v. The Queen* (1986), 30 C.C.C. (3d) 385.
50. Quoted in F.L. Morton, Rainer Knopff, and Peter Russell, *Federalism and the Charter* (Ottawa: Carleton University Press, 1989), 483.
51. *Alberta Labour Reference* (1987).
52. *Law Society of British Columbia v. Andrews and Kinersley*, [1989] 1 S.C.R. 143.
53. Christopher P. Manfredi, *Judicial Power and the Charter: Canada and the Paradox of Liberal Constitutionalism*, 2nd edn (Toronto: Oxford University Press, 2001), 123–4.

54. See the abridged text of the ruling in Morton et al., *Federalism and the Charter*, 582–603.
55. Canadian Advisory Council on the Status of Women, *Every Voice Counts: A Guide to Personal and Political Action* (Ottawa, 1989), 39–58.
56. Penney Kome, *The Taking of Twenty-Eight: Women Challenge the Constitution* (Toronto: Women's Press, 1983).
57. Kome, *Women of Influence*, 93.
58. Pal, *Interests of State*, ch. 10.
59. Sylvia Bashevkin, 'Free Trade and Canadian Feminism: The Case of the National Action Committee on the Status of Women', *Canadian Public Policy* 15, 4 (Dec. 1989): 363–75.
60. Janine Brodie, 'We Are All Equal Now: Contemporary Gender Politics in Canada', *Feminist Theory* 9, 2 (2008): 145–64.
61. Daniel Indiviglio, 'Why Working Mothers Fall Behind', *The Atlantic* (on-line edition), 4 Aug. 2010.
62. Moya Greene, 'Remarks for the HSBC Women of Influence Luncheon Series', Metro Toronto Convention Centre, 28 Sept. 2007.

16 Aboriginal Politics

1. The RCAP estimated the difference at 49 per cent for 1992–3. In a study for Infometrica's *Monthly Economic Review* 15, 7 (28 Nov. 1996), a former policy co-ordinator for the RCAP put the difference at 57 per cent for that same year.
2. *Regina v. Howson* (1894), 1 Terr. L.R. 492 (S.C.N.W.T.), 494.
3. Peter A. Cumming and Neil H. Mickenberg, eds, *Native Rights in Canada* (Toronto: General Publishing, 1972), 9.
4. *Reference Re: Whether Eskimos are Indians*, C.L.R. (1939), 104.
5. Olive Patricia Dickason, with David T. McNab, *Canada's First Nations: A History of Founding Peoples from Earliest Times*, 4th edn (Toronto: Oxford University Press, 2009), 517, n. 27.
6. Harvey McCue, 'Indian Reserve', *The Canadian Encyclopedia*, 2nd edn (Edmonton: Hurtig, 1988), vol. 2, 1056.
7. For a valuable discussion of Aboriginal languages in contemporary Canada, see James S. Frideres, *First Nations in the Twenty-First Century* (Toronto: Oxford University Press, 2011), ch. 6.
8. G.F.G. Stanley, 'The First Indian "Reserves" in Canada', *Revue d'histoire de l'Amérique française* (1950): 168,209–10.
9. Francis Parkman, *The Jesuits in North America in the Seventeenth Century* (Toronto: George N. Morang, 1907 [1867]), 131.
10. Quoted in Royal Commission on Aboriginal Peoples, *Report*, vol. 2, *Restructuring the Relationship* (Ottawa, 1996), 531–2.
11. Harold Cardinal, *The Unjust Society* (Edmonton: Hurtig, 1969), 1.
12. Indian leader James Gosnell, quoted in Michael Asch, *Home and Native Land: Aboriginal Rights and the Canadian Constitution* (Vancouver: University of British Columbia Press, 1993), 29.
13. Quoted in Melvin H. Smith, *Our Home or Native Land?* (Toronto: Stoddart, 1995), 143.
14. Georges Erasmus and Joe Sanders, 'Canadian History: An Aboriginal Perspective', in Diane Engelstad and John Bird, eds, *Nation to Nation: Aboriginal Sovereignty and the Future of Canada* (Concord, Ont.: House of Anansi Press, 1992), 6.
15. Ibid., 8.
16. Quoted in Cumming and Mickenberg, eds, *Native Rights in Canada*, 17.
17. Ibid., 18.
18. See excerpts from this ruling in David De Brou and Bill Waiser, eds, *Documenting Canada: A History of Modern Canada in Documents* (Saskatoon: Fifth House Publishers, 1992), 158.
19. Quoted ibid., 572.
20. Ibid.
21. Ibid., 665.
22. Ibid., 666.
23. Cumming and Mickenberg, eds, *Native Rights in Canada*, 55.
24. Erasmus and Sanders, 'Canadian History', 3.
25. Ibid., 4.
26. Cumming and Mickenberg, eds, *Native Rights in Canada*, 58.
27. Quoted ibid., 61–2.
28. *Nowegijick v. The Queen*, [1983] 1 S.C.R. 29.
29. Cumming and Mickenberg, eds, *Native Rights in Canada*, 53.
30. *R. v. Marshall*, [1999] 3 S.C.R. 456.
31. *R. v. Marshall* (2005), S.C.C. 30063.
32. Sally Weaver, 'The Joint Cabinet/National Indian Brotherhood Committee: A Unique Experiment in Pressure Group Politics', *Canadian Public Administration* 25 (Summer 1982): 211–39.
33. J. Hugh Faulkner, 'Pressuring the Executive', *Canadian Public Administration* 25 (Summer 1982): 248.
34. Ninth annual presidential address to the National Indian Brotherhood, Fredericton, New Brunswick, Sept. 1978.
35. Rick Ponting and Roger Gibbins, *Out of Irrelevance: A Socio-Political Introduction to Indian Affairs in Canada* (Toronto: Butterworths, 1980), 124.
36. Gary Granzberg et al., 'New Magic for Old: TV in Cree Culture', *Journal of Communication* 27, 4 (1977): 155–77; Gary Granzberg, 'Television as Storyteller: The Algonkian Indians of Central Canada', *Journal of Communication* 32, 1 (1982): 43–52.
37. Inuit Tapiriit Kanatami, at: <www.itk.ca/media/press-archive-20040607.php>.

38. Cairns, *Citizens Plus*, 111.
39. Thomas Flanagan, *First Nations? Second Thoughts* (Montreal and Kingston: McGill-Queen's University Press, 2000), 116.
40. Ibid., 103.
41. Naomi Lakritz, 'Why Race-based Justice Is Always Wrong', *Calgary Herald*, 14 Apr. 2010.
42. Ibid., 106.
43. Ibid.

17 Canada in the World

1. Mark Kingwell, 'What Distinguishes Us from the Americans', *National Post*, 5 Mar. 2003, A16.
2. John Ralston Saul, *Reflections on a Siamese Twin: Canada at the End of the Twentieth Century* (Toronto: Penguin, 1997), 171.
3. Published as Michael Ignatieff, 'Canada in the Age of Terror—Multilateralism Meets a Moment of Truth', *Policy Options* (Feb. 2003), at: <www.irpp.org>.
4. The Pew Research Center for the People and the Press, 'What the World Thinks in 2002', part of the Pew Global Attitudes Project, at: <www.people-press.org>.
5. See Transparency International, at <www.transparency.org>.
6. Jeffrey Sachs, 'Nature, Nurture and Growth', *The Economist*, 14 June 1997, 19–22.
7. Robert Reich, *The Work of Nations: Preparing Ourselves for 21st Century Capitalism* (New York: Alfred A. Knopf, 1991).
8. Francis Fukayama, 'Economic Globalization and Culture', at: <www.ml.com/woml/forum/global.htm>.
9. United Nations, Department of Economic and Social Affairs, *World Public Sector Report: Globalization and the State* (New York: UN, 2001).
10. Ibid., ch. 3.
11. Barry Lynn, 'Unmade in America: The True Cost of a Global Assembly Line', *Harper's* (June 2002): 37.
12. Ibid., 41.
13. *Time*, 11 June 2001, 30.

14. Allan Gotlieb, 'Getting Attention', *National Post*, 17 May 2002, A17.
15. Allan Gotlieb, 'A Grand Bargain with the U.S.', *National Post*, 5 Mar. 2003, A16.
16. Canadian International Council, *Open Canada: A Global Positioning Strategy for a Networked Age?* (Toronto: CIC, 2010), 18, at: <www.onlinecic.org/opencanada>.
17. Ibid., 21.
18. Ibid., 20.
19. Anne-Marie Slaughter, 'America's Edge: Power in the Networked Century', *Foreign Affairs* (Jan.–Feb. 2009): 94–113.
20. For an interesting revisionist view of the Pearson legacy in foreign affairs, which takes to task those on the right (see Box 17.4) and those on the left for using Lester Pearson in support of their ideological stances, see Mark Neufeld, '"Happy Is the Land That Needs No Hero": The Pearsonian Tradition and the Canadian Intervention in Afghanistan', in J. Marshall Beier and Lana Wylie, eds, *Canadian Foreign Policy in Critical Perspective* (Toronto: Oxford University Press, 2010), 126–38.
21. Ignatieff, 'Canada in the Age of Terror'.
22. Ibid.
23. Joseph Nye, 'The Misleading Metaphor of Decline', *The Atlantic* (Mar. 1990): 86–94.
24. Nik Hynek and David Bosold, eds, *Canada's Foreign and Security Policy: Soft and Hard Strategies of a Middle Power* (Toronto: Oxford University Press, 2010), xviii.
25. Michael Ignatieff, 'The Burden', *New York Times Magazine*, 5 Jan. 2003, at: <www.nytimes.com/2003/01/05/magazine/05EMPIRE.html>.
26. Excerpts from John Podesta, keynote address at Canada 2020 conference, 'Greening the Oil Sands: Debunking the Myths and Confronting the Realities', Washington, DC, 23 June 2010.
27. Canada Institute, Woodrow Wilson International Center for Scholars, 'Threat Perceptions in the United States and Canada', number 4 in the *One Issue, Two Voices* series (Nov. 2005), at: <www.wilsoncenter.org>.

Index

Note: Page numbers in *italics* refer to figures.